# OPEN-CHANNEL HYDRAULICS

# McGRAW-HILL CIVIL ENGINEERING SERIES

### HARMER E. DAVIS, *Consulting Editor*

---

BABBITT · Engineering in Public Health

BENJAMIN · Statically Indeterminate Structures

CHOW · Open-channel Hydraulics

DAVIS, TROXELL, AND WISKOCIL · The Testing and Inspection of Engineering Materials

DUNHAM · Foundations of Structures

DUNHAM · The Theory and Practice of Reinforced Concrete

DUNHAM AND YOUNG · Contracts, Specifications, and Law for Engineers

GAYLORD AND GAYLORD · Structural Design

HALLERT · Photogrammetry

HENNES AND EKSE · Fundamentals of Transportation Engineering

KRYNINE AND JUDD · Principles of Engineering Geology and Geotechnics

LINSLEY AND FRANZINI · Elements of Hydraulic Engineering

LINSLEY, KOHLER, AND PAULHUS · Applied Hydrology

LINSLEY, KOHLER, AND PAULHUS · Hydrology for Engineers

LUEDER · Aerial Photographic Interpretation

MATSON, SMITH, AND HURD · Traffic Engineering

MEAD, MEAD, AND AKERMAN · Contracts, Specifications, and Engineering Relations

NORRIS, HANSEN, HOLLEY, BIGGS, NAMYET, AND MINAMI · Structural Design for Dynamic Loads

PEURIFOY · Construction Planning, Equipment, and Methods

PEURIFOY · Estimating Construction Costs

TROXELL AND DAVIS · Composition and Properties of Concrete

TSCHEBOTARIOFF · Soil Mechanics, Foundations, and Earth Structures

URQUHART, O'ROURKE, AND WINTER · Design of Concrete Structures

WANG AND ECKEL · Elementary Theory of Structures

# OPEN-CHANNEL HYDRAULICS

**VEN TE CHOW, Ph.D.**

*Professor of Hydraulic Engineering*
*University of Illinois*

McGRAW-HILL BOOK COMPANY, INC.

New York    Toronto    London

KŌGAKUSHA COMPANY, LTD.

Tokyo

# OPEN-CHANNEL HYDRAULICS

*INTERNATIONAL STUDENT EDITION*

TOSHO PRINTING CO., LTD., TOKYO, JAPAN

To
Humanity and Human Welfare

# PREFACE

In recent years water-resources projects and hydraulic engineering works have been developing rapidly throughout the world. The knowledge of open-channel hydraulics, which is essential to the design of many hydraulic structures, has thus advanced by leaps and bounds. To the students and engineers in the field of hydraulic engineering, such valuable new knowledge should be made available in suitable book form. It is therefore not surprising that some new books have already appeared. However, most of them are presented in limited scope and all are written in foreign languages.[1] In the English language, the two well-known books, respectively by Bakhmeteff and by Woodward and Posey, were published nearly two decades ago.[2]

This book gives broad coverage of recent developments; it should meet the present need. It is designed as a textbook for both undergraduate and graduate students and also as a compendium for practicing engineers. Emphasis is given to the qualities of "teachability" and "practicability," and attempts were made in presenting the material to bridge the gap which is generally recognized to exist between the theory and the practice. In order to achieve these objectives, the use of advanced mathematics is deliberately avoided as much as possible, and the explanation of hydraulic

[1] Such as: Étienne Crausse, "Hydraulique des canaux découverts en régime permanent" ("Hydraulics of Open Channels with Steady Flow"), Éditions Eyrolles, Paris, 1951; R. Silber, "Étude et tracé des écoulements permanents en canaux et rivières" ("Study and Sketch of Steady Flows in Canals and Rivers"), Dunod, Paris, 1954; Martin Schmidt, "Gerinnehydraulik" ("Open-channel Hydraulics"), VEB Verlag Technik-Bauverlag GMBH, Berlin and Wiesbaden, 1957; N. N. Pavlovskiĭ, "Otkrytye rusla i sopriazhenie biefov sooruzheniĭ" (Open channels and adjustment of water levels), in the "Sobranie sochineniĭ" ("Collected Works"), vol. 1, pp. 309–543, Academy of Sciences of U.S.S.R., Moscow and Leningrad, 1955; and the new edition of M. D. Chertousov, "Gidravlika" ("Hydraulics"), Gosenergoizdat, Moscow and Leningrad, 1957.

[2] Boris A. Bakhmeteff, "Hydraulics of Open Channels," McGraw-Hill Book Company, Inc., New York, 1932; and Sherman M. Woodward and Chesley J. Posey, "Hydraulics of Steady Flow in Open Channels," John Wiley and Sons, Inc., New York, 1941.

theories is greatly simplified as far as practicable. Illustrative examples are given to show the application of the theories, and practical problems are provided for exercises. Furthermore, short historical accounts are given in footnotes in order to stimulate the reader's interest, and ample references are supplied for his independent studies. Some references, however, may not be readily available to the reader, but they are listed for academic and historical interest.

In essence, the book is the outgrowth of the author's 20 years' experience as a student, teacher, engineer, researcher, and consultant in the field of hydraulic engineering. The manuscript of the book was drafted for the first time in the academic year of 1951–1952 for use in teaching the students of civil, agricultural, and mechanical engineering and of theoretical and applied mechanics at the University of Illinois. Since then several revisions have been made. In the beginning, the material was prepared solely for graduate students. Owing to the general demand for a book on the design of hydraulic structures for undergraduate studies, the manuscript was expanded to include more fundamental principles and design procedures. At the same time, most of the advanced mathematics and theories were either omitted or replaced by more practical approaches using mathematical operations of a level not higher than calculus.

From 1951 to 1955, the author made several special visits to many major engineering agencies and firms in the United States to discuss problems with their engineers. As a result, a vast fund of information on hydraulic design practices was collected and incorporated into the manuscript. Thereafter, the author also visited many hydraulic institutions and laboratories in other countries and exchanged knowledge with their staff members. In 1956 he visited England, France, Belgium, the Netherlands, Germany, Italy, and Switzerland. In 1958 he visited Austria, Turkey, India, and Japan, and again England, France, and Belgium. The information obtained from these countries and from other countries through publications and correspondence was eventually added to the final draft of the manuscript as supplements to the American practice.

The text is organized into five parts—namely, Basic Principles, Uniform Flow, Gradually Varied Flow, Rapidly Varied Flow, and Unsteady Flow. The first three parts cover the material which would ordinarily be treated in a one-semester course on open-channel hydraulics. For a one-semester course on the design of hydraulic structures, Chaps. 7 and 11 and Part IV should supply most of the material for the teaching purpose. Part V on unsteady flow may be used either for advanced studies or as supplemental material to the one-semester course, depending largely on the discretion of the instructor with reference to the time available and the interest shown by the students.

In Part I on basic principles, the type of flow in open channels is classified according to the variation in the parameters of flow with respect to space and time. For simplicity, the depth of flow is used as the flow parameter in the classification. The state of flow is classified according to the range of the invariants of flow with respect to viscosity and gravity. The flow invariants used are the Reynolds number and the Froude number. Since the effect of surface tension of water is insignificant in most engineering problems, the Weber number as a flow invariant is not introduced. In fact, the state of flow can be further classified for its stability in accordance with the Vedernikov number or other suitable criteria. However, such a criterion has not been well established in engineering practice, and therefore it is taken up only briefly later in Chap. 8.

Four coefficients for velocity and pressure distributions are introduced. In particular, the energy coefficient is presented throughout the book. This coefficient is usually ignored in most books on hydraulics. In practical applications, the effect of the energy coefficient on computations and hence on designs is quite significant and therefore should not be overlooked, even though the value of the coefficient may not always be determined accurately.

The energy and momentum principles constitute the basis of interpretation for most hydraulic phenomena. A thorough treatment of the two principles is given in Chap. 3. Since the book is intended for the use of practicing engineers, the treatment of a problem is in most cases based on a one- or two-dimensional flow.

In Part II on uniform flow, several uniform-flow formulas are introduced. Despite many new proposals for a formula having a theoretical background, the Manning formula still holds its indisputable top position in the field of practical applications. This formula is therefore used extensively in the book. In certain specific problems, however, the Chézy formula is used occasionally.

The design for uniform flow covers nonerodible, erodible, and grassed channels. The erodible channels in general may be classified under three types: channels which scour but do not silt, channels which silt but do not scour, and channels which scour and silt simultaneously. In channels of the second and third types, it is necessary for the water to carry sediments. As will be stated later, the sediment transportation is considered as a subject in the domain of river hydraulics. Therefore, only the channels of the first type, which carry relatively clear water in stable condition, are treated in this book.

In Part III on gradually varied flow, several methods for the computation of flow profiles are discussed. A new method of direct integration is introduced which requires the use of a varied-flow function table first

developed by Professor Boris A. Bakhmeteff in 1912.[1]  The table given in
Appendix D of this book is an extension of the table to nearly three times
its original size.  This extended table and a table for negative slopes were
prepared during 1952 to 1954 by the author for teaching purposes at the
University of Illinois.[2]  For the computation of flow profiles in circular
conduits, a varied-flow function table is also provided in Appendix E.

The method of singular point is a powerful tool for the analysis of flow
profiles.  Since this method requires the use of advanced mathematics,
it is described only briefly in Chap. 9 for the purpose of stimulating further interest in the theoretical study of flow problems.

In Part IV on rapidly varied flow, the treatment of the problems is
largely supported by experimental data, because this type of flow is so
complicated that a mere theoretical analysis in most cases will not yield
sufficient information for the purpose of practical design.  The use of the
flow-net method and the method of characteristics is mentioned but no
details are given, because the former is so popular that it can be found
in most hydraulics books, while the latter requires the knowledge of
advanced mathematics beyond the scope of this work.

In Part V on unsteady flow, the treatment is general but practical.  It
should be recognized that this type of flow is a highly specialized subject.[3]
The knowledge of advanced mathematics would be required if a comprehensive treatment were given.

It should be noted that the subject matter of this book dwells mainly
on the flow of water in channels where water contains little foreign material.  Consequently, problems related to sediment transportation and
air entrainment are not fully discussed.  In recent years, sediment transportation in channels has become a broad subject that is generally covered
in the study of river hydraulics, which is often treated independently.[4]

[1] Boris A. Bakhmeteff, "O Neravnomernom Dvizhenii Zhidkosti v Otkrytom
Rusle" ("Varied Flow in Open Channels"), St. Petersburg, Russia, 1912.

[2] Ven Te Chow, Integrating the equation of gradually varied flow, paper no. 838,
*Proceedings, American Society of Civil Engineers*, vol. 81, pp. 1–32, November, 1955.
Closing discussion by the author in *Journal of Hydraulics Division*, vol. 83, no. HY1,
paper no. 1177, pp. 9–22, February, 1957.

[3] Special references are: J. J. Stoker, "Water Waves," vol. IV of "Pure and Applied
Mathematics," Interscience Publishers, New York, 1957; V. A. Arkhangelskiĭ,
"Raschety Neustanovivshegosia Dvizheniia v Otkrytykh Vodotokakh" ("Calcu-
lation of Unsteady Flow in Open Channels"), Academy of Sciences, U.S.S.R., 1947;
and S. A. Khristianovich, "Neustanovivsheiesia dvizhenie v kanalakh i rekakh"
("Unsteady Motion in Channels and Rivers"), in "Nekotoryie Voprosy Mekhaniki
Sploshnoĭ Sredy" ("Several Questions on the Mechanics of Continuous Media"),
Academy of Sciences, U.S.S.R., 1938, pp. 13–154.

[4] Special references on the subject of river hydraulics are: Serge Leliavsky, "An
Introduction to Fluvial Hydraulics," Constable and Co., Ltd., London, 1955; and
T. Blench, "Regime Behaviour of Canals and Rivers," Butterworth & Co. (Publishers)
Ltd., London, 1957.

Similarly, the transient flow in channels subject to the influence of the tides is a special topic in the rapidly developed fields of tidal hydraulics and coastal engineering and is therefore beyond the scope of this book.

In a science which has reached so advanced a state of development, a large portion of the work is necessarily one of coordination of existing contributions. Throughout the text, the author has attempted to make specific acknowledgment regarding the source of material employed, and any failure to do so is an unintentional oversight.

In the preparation of this book, engineers and administrators in many engineering agencies have enthusiastically furnished information and extended cooperation. The author is especially indebted to those in the U.S. Bureau of Reclamation, U.S. Geological Survey, U.S. Soil Conservation Service, U.S. Agricultural Research Service, U.S. Army Engineer Waterways Experiment Station, Offices of the Chief Engineer and District Engineers of the U.S. Army Corps of Engineers, U.S. Weather Bureau, U.S. Bureau of Public Roads, and the Tennessee Valley Authority. Also, many friends and colleagues have kindly supplied information and generously offered suggestions. In particular, the author wishes to thank Dr. Hunter Rouse, Professor of Fluid Mechanics and Director of Iowa Institute of Hydraulic Research, State University of Iowa; Dr. Arthur T. Ippen, Professor of Hydraulics and Director of Hydrodynamics Laboratory, Massachusetts Institute of Technology; Dr. Giulio De Marchi, Professor of Hydraulics and Director of Hydraulic Laboratory, Institute of Hydraulics and Hydraulic Construction, Polytechnic Institute of Milan, Italy; Dr. Roman R. Chugaev, Professor and Head of Hydraulic Construction, Scientific Research Institute of Hydraulic Engineering, Polytechnic Institute of Leningrad, U.S.S.R.; Monsieur Pierre Danel, President of SOGRÉAH (Société Grenobloise d'Etudes et d'Applications Hydrauliques), France, and President of the International Association of Hydraulic Research; Dr. Charles Jaeger, Special Lecturer at the Imperial College of Science and Technology, University of London, and Consulting Engineer of The English Electric Company, Ltd., England; Professor L. J. Tison, Director of Hydraulic Institute, University of Ghent, Belgium; Dr. Tojiro Ishihara, Professor of Hydraulics and Dean of Faculty of Engineering, Kyoto University, Japan; and Dr. Otto Kirschmer, Professor of Hydraulics and Hydraulic Structures, Technical Institute of Darmstadt, Germany.

Special acknowledgments are due Dr. Nathan M. Newmark, Professor and Head of the Department of Civil Engineering, University of Illinois, for his encouragement and unfailing support of this project; Dr. James M. Robertson, Professor of Theoretical and Applied Mechanics, University of Illinois, for his review of and comments on Chapter 8 on theoretical concepts; and Dr. Steponas Kolupaila, Professor of Civil Engineering,

University of Notre Dame, for his reading of the entire manuscript and his valuable suggestions.   Dr. Kolupaila also helped in interpreting and collecting information from the hydraulic literature written in Russian, Polish, Lithuanian, and several other languages which are unfamiliar to the author.   The author also wishes to express his warm gratitude to those who have constantly shown a keen interest in his work, as this interest lent a strong impetus toward the completion of this volume.

*Ven Te Chow*

# CONTENTS

Preface . . . . . . . . . . . . . . . . . . . . . . . . vii

## PART I.  BASIC PRINCIPLES

**Chapter 1.  Open-channel Flow and Its Classifications** . . . . . . . . . 3

  1-1. Description . . . . . . . . . . . . . . . . . . . . 3
  1-2. Types of Flow . . . . . . . . . . . . . . . . . . . 4
  1-3. State of Flow . . . . . . . . . . . . . . . . . . . 7
  1-4. Regimes of Flow . . . . . . . . . . . . . . . . . . 14

**Chapter 2.  Open Channels and Their Properties** . . . . . . . . . . 19

  2-1. Kinds of Open Channel . . . . . . . . . . . . . . . 19
  2-2. Channel Geometry . . . . . . . . . . . . . . . . . 20
  2-3. Geometric Elements of Channel Section . . . . . . . . . 22
  2-4. Velocity Distribution in a Channel Section . . . . . . . . 24
  2-5. Wide Open Channel . . . . . . . . . . . . . . . . . 26
  2-6. Measurement of Velocity . . . . . . . . . . . . . . . 27
  2-7. Velocity-distribution Coefficients . . . . . . . . . . . . 27
  2-8. Determination of Velocity-distribution Coefficients . . . . . 28
  2-9. Pressure Distribution in a Channel Section . . . . . . . . 30
  2-10. Effect of Slope on Pressure Distribution . . . . . . . . . 32

**Chapter 3.  Energy and Momentum Principles** . . . . . . . . . . . 39

  3-1. Energy in Open-channel Flow . . . . . . . . . . . . . 39
  3-2. Specific Energy . . . . . . . . . . . . . . . . . . . 41
  3-3. Criterion for a Critical State of Flow . . . . . . . . . . 42
  3-4. Interpretation of Local Phenomena . . . . . . . . . . . 43
  3-5. Energy in Nonprismatic Channels . . . . . . . . . . . 46
  3-6. Momentum in Open-channel Flow . . . . . . . . . . . 49
  3-7. Specific Force . . . . . . . . . . . . . . . . . . . 53
  3-8. Momentum Principle Applied to Nonprismatic Channels . . . 56

**Chapter 4.  Critical Flow: Its Computation and Applications** . . . . . . 63

  4-1. Critical Flow . . . . . . . . . . . . . . . . . . . . 63
  4-2. The Section Factor for Critical-flow Computation . . . . . 64
  4-3. The Hydraulic Exponent for Critical-flow Computation . . . 66
  4-4. Computation of Critical Flow . . . . . . . . . . . . . 69
  4-5. Control of Flow . . . . . . . . . . . . . . . . . . . 70
  4-6. Flow Measurement . . . . . . . . . . . . . . . . . . 74

# PART II. UNIFORM FLOW

**Chapter 5. Development of Uniform Flow and Its Formulas** . . . . . 89

5-1. Qualifications for Uniform Flow . . . . . . . . . . . . 89
5-2. Establishment of Uniform Flow . . . . . . . . . . . . 89
5-3. Expressing the Velocity of a Uniform Flow . . . . . . . . . 91
5-4. The Chézy Formula . . . . . . . . . . . . . . . . 93
5-5. Determination of Chézy's Resistance Factor . . . . . . . . 94
5-6. The Manning Formula. . . . . . . . . . . . . . . . 98
5-7. Determination of Manning's Roughness Coefficient . . . . . . 101
5-8. Factors Affecting Manning's Roughness Coefficient . . . . . . 101
5-9. The Table of Manning's Roughness Coefficient . . . . . . . 108
5-10. Illustrations of Channels with Various Roughnesses . . . . . . 114

**Chapter 6. Computation of Uniform Flow** . . . . . . . . . . . 128

6-1. The Conveyance of a Channel Section . . . . . . . . . . 128
6-2. The Section Factor for Uniform-flow Computation . . . . . . 128
6-3. The Hydraulic Exponent for Uniform-flow Computation . . . . . 131
6-4. Flow Characteristics in a Closed Conduit with Open-channel Flow . . 134
6-5. Flow in a Channel Section with Composite Roughness . . . . . 136
6-6. Determination of the Normal Depth and Velocity . . . . . . . 140
6-7. Determination of the Normal and Critical Slopes . . . . . . . 142
6-8. Problems of Uniform-flow Computation . . . . . . . . . . 144
6-9. Computation of Flood Discharge . . . . . . . . . . . . 146
6-10. Uniform Surface Flow . . . . . . . . . . . . . . . . 148

**Chapter 7. Design of Channels for Uniform Flow** . . . . . . . . 157

A. NONERODIBLE CHANNELS

7-1. The Nonerodible Channel . . . . . . . . . . . . . . . 157
7-2. Nonerodible Material and Lining . . . . . . . . . . . . 157
7-3. The Minimum Permissible Velocity . . . . . . . . . . . 158
7-4. Channel Slopes . . . . . . . . . . . . . . . . . . 158
7-5. Freeboard . . . . . . . . . . . . . . . . . . . . 159
7-6. The Best Hydraulic Section . . . . . . . . . . . . . . 160
7-7. Determination of Section Dimensions . . . . . . . . . . . 162

B. ERODIBLE CHANNELS WHICH SCOUR BUT DO NOT SILT

7-8. Methods of Approach . . . . . . . . . . . . . . . . 164
7-9. The Maximum Permissible Velocity . . . . . . . . . . . . 165
7-10. Method of Permissible Velocity . . . . . . . . . . . . . 167
7-11. The Tractive Force . . . . . . . . . . . . . . . . . 168
7-12. Tractive-force Ratio . . . . . . . . . . . . . . . . . 170
7-13. Permissible Tractive Force . . . . . . . . . . . . . . . 172
7-14. Method of Tractive Force . . . . . . . . . . . . . . . 175
7-15. The Stable Hydraulic Section . . . . . . . . . . . . . . 176

C. GRASSED CHANNELS

7-16. The Grassed Channel . . . . . . . . . . . . . . . . 179
7-17. The Retardance Coefficient . . . . . . . . . . . . . . 179
7-18. The Permissible Velocity . . . . . . . . . . . . . . . 184

7-19. Selection of Grass . . . . . . . . . . . . . . . . . . 184
7-20. Procedure of Design . . . . . . . . . . . . . . . . 184

**Chapter 8. Theoretical Concepts of Boundary Layer, Surface Roughness, Velocity Distribution, and Instability of Uniform Flow.** . . . . . . . 192

8-1. The Boundary Layer . . . . . . . . . . . . . . . . . 192
8-2. Concept of Surface Roughness . . . . . . . . . . . . 194
8-3. Computation of Boundary Layer. . . . . . . . . . . . 198
8-4. Velocity Distribution in Turbulent Flow . . . . . . . . 200
8-5. Theoretical Uniform-flow Equations . . . . . . . . . . 202
8-6. Theoretical Interpretation of Manning's Roughness Coefficient . . . 205
8-7. Methods for Determining Manning's Roughness Coefficient . . . . 206
8-8. Instability of Uniform Flow . . . . . . . . . . . . . . 210

PART III.  GRADUALLY VARIED FLOW

**Chapter 9. Theory and Analysis.** . . . . . . . . . . . . . . 217

9-1. Basic Assumptions . . . . . . . . . . . . . . . . . 217
9-2. Dynamic Equation of Gradually Varied Flow . . . . . . . . 218
9-3. Characteristics of Flow Profiles . . . . . . . . . . . . 222
9-4. Classification of Flow Profiles. . . . . . . . . . . . . 227
9-5. Analysis of Flow Profile . . . . . . . . . . . . . . . 232
9-6. Method of Singular Point . . . . . . . . . . . . . . . 237
9-7. The Transitional Depth . . . . . . . . . . . . . . . 242

**Chapter 10. Methods of Computation** . . . . . . . . . . . . 249

10-1. The Graphical-integration Method . . . . . . . . . . . 249
10-2. Method of Direct Integration. . . . . . . . . . . . . 252
10-3. The Direct Step Method . . . . . . . . . . . . . . . 262
10-4. The Standard Step Method . . . . . . . . . . . . . . 265
10-5. Computation of a Family of Flow Profiles . . . . . . . . 268
10-6. The Standard Step Method for Natural Channels . . . . . . 274
10-7. The Stage-fall-discharge Method for Natural Channels . . . . . 280
10-8. The Ezra Method for Natural Channels. . . . . . . . . . 284

**Chapter 11. Practical Problems .** . . . . . . . . . . . . . 297

11-1. Delivery of a Canal for Subcritical Flow . . . . . . . . 297
11-2. Delivery of a Canal for Supercritical Flow . . . . . . . . 302
11-3. Problems Related to Canal Design . . . . . . . . . . . 303
11-4. Computation of Flow Profile in Nonprismatic Channels . . . . 306
11-5. Design of Transitions . . . . . . . . . . . . . . . . 307
11-6. Transitions between Canal and Flume or Tunnel . . . . . . 310
11-7. Transitions between Canal and Inverted Siphon . . . . . . 317
11-8. Backwater Effect of a Dam . . . . . . . . . . . . . 319
11-9. Flow Passing Islands . . . . . . . . . . . . . . . . 320
11-10. River Confluence . . . . . . . . . . . . . . . . . 321

**Chapter 12. Spatially Varied Flow** . . . . . . . . . . . . . 327

12-1. Basic Principles and Assumptions . . . . . . . . . . . 327
12-2. Dynamic Equation for Spatially Varied Flow . . . . . . . 329

12-3. Analysis of Flow Profile . . . . . . . . . . . . . . . . 333
12-4. Method of Numerical Integration . . . . . . . . . . . 341
12-5. The Isoclinal Method . . . . . . . . . . . . . . . . 346
12-6. Spatially Varied Surface Flow . . . . . . . . . . . . 347

### PART IV. RAPIDLY VARIED FLOW

## Chapter 13. Introduction . . . . . . . . . . . . . . . . . 357

13-1. Characteristics of the Flow . . . . . . . . . . . . . . 357
13-2. Approach to the Problem . . . . . . . . . . . . . . . 357

## Chapter 14. Flow over Spillways . . . . . . . . . . . . . 360

14-1. The Sharp-crested Weir . . . . . . . . . . . . . . . 360
14-2. Aeration of the Nappe . . . . . . . . . . . . . . . . 362
14-3. Crest Shape of Overflow Spillways . . . . . . . . . . 363
14-4. Discharge of the Overflow Spillway . . . . . . . . . . 365
14-5. Rating of Overflow Spillways . . . . . . . . . . . . . 368
14-6. Upper Nappe Profile of Flow over Spillways . . . . . . 370
14-7. Effect of Piers in Gated Spillways . . . . . . . . . . 370
14-8. Pressure on Overflow Spillways . . . . . . . . . . . 374
14-9. Drum Gates . . . . . . . . . . . . . . . . . . . . . 380
14-10. Flow at the Toe of Overflow Spillways . . . . . . . . 382
14-11. The Ski-jump Spillway . . . . . . . . . . . . . . . 384
14-12. Submerged Overflow Spillways . . . . . . . . . . . 385

## Chapter 15. Hydraulic Jump and Its Use as Energy Dissipator . . . . 393

15-1. The Hydraulic Jump . . . . . . . . . . . . . . . . 393
15-2. Jump in Horizontal Rectangular Channels . . . . . . . 395
15-3. Types of Jump . . . . . . . . . . . . . . . . . . . 395
15-4. Basic Characteristics of the Jump . . . . . . . . . . 396
15-5. Length of Jump . . . . . . . . . . . . . . . . . . . 398
15-6. The Surface Profile . . . . . . . . . . . . . . . . . 399
15-7. Location of Jump . . . . . . . . . . . . . . . . . . 399
15-8. Jump as Energy Dissipator . . . . . . . . . . . . . 404
15-9. Control of Jump by Sills . . . . . . . . . . . . . . . 408
15-10. Control of Jump by Abrupt Drop . . . . . . . . . . . 412
15-11. Stilling Basins of Generalized Design . . . . . . . . . 414
15-12. The SAF Stilling Basin . . . . . . . . . . . . . . . 415
15-13. USBR Stilling Basin II . . . . . . . . . . . . . . . 417
15-14. USBR Stilling Basin IV . . . . . . . . . . . . . . . 422
15-15. The Straight Drop Spillway . . . . . . . . . . . . . 423
15-16. Jump in Sloping Channels . . . . . . . . . . . . . . 425
15-17. The Oblique Jump . . . . . . . . . . . . . . . . . 429

## Chapter 16. Flow in Channels of Nonlinear Alignment . . . . . . 439

16-1. Nature of the Flow . . . . . . . . . . . . . . . . . 439
16-2. Spiral Flow . . . . . . . . . . . . . . . . . . . . . 439
16-3. Energy Loss . . . . . . . . . . . . . . . . . . . . 441
16-4. Superelevation . . . . . . . . . . . . . . . . . . . 444
16-5. Cross Waves . . . . . . . . . . . . . . . . . . . . 448
16-6. Design Considerations for Subcritical Flow . . . . . . 455
16-7. Design Considerations for Supercritical Flow . . . . . . 456

**Chapter 17. Flow through Nonprismatic Channel Sections** . . . . . . 461

17-1. Sudden Transitions . . . . . . . . . . . . . . . 461
17-2. Subcritical Flow through Sudden Transitions . . . . . . . 464
17-3. Contractions in Supercritical Flow . . . . . . . . . . 468
17-4. Expansions in Supercritical Flow . . . . . . . . . . . 470
17-5. Constrictions . . . . . . . . . . . . . . . . . 475
17-6. Subcritical Flow through Constrictions . . . . . . . . . 476
17-7. Backwater Effect due to Constriction . . . . . . . . . 490
17-8. Flow through Culverts . . . . . . . . . . . . . . 493
17-9. Obstructions . . . . . . . . . . . . . . . . . 499
17-10. Flow between Bridge Piers . . . . . . . . . . . . 501
17-11. Flow through Pile Trestles . . . . . . . . . . . . 506
17-12. Flow through Trash Racks . . . . . . . . . . . . . 506
17-13. Underflow Gates . . . . . . . . . . . . . . . 507
17-14. Channel Junctions . . . . . . . . . . . . . . . 512

## PART V. UNSTEADY FLOW

**Chapter 18. Gradually Varied Unsteady Flow** . . . . . . . . 525

18-1. Continuity of Unsteady Flow . . . . . . . . . . . 525
18-2. Dynamic Equation for Unsteady Flow . . . . . . . . . 526
18-3. Monoclinal Rising Wave . . . . . . . . . . . . . 528
18-4. Dynamic Equation for Uniformly Progressive Flow . . . . . 531
18-5. Wave Profile of Uniformly Progressive Flow . . . . . . . 533
18-6. Wave Propagation . . . . . . . . . . . . . . . 537
18-7. Solution of the Unsteady-flow Equations . . . . . . . . 540
18-8. Spatially Varied Unsteady Surface Flow . . . . . . . . 543

**Chapter 19. Rapidly Varied Unsteady Flow** . . . . . . . . . 554

19-1. Uniformly Progressive Flow . . . . . . . . . . . . 554
19-2. The Moving Hydraulic Jump . . . . . . . . . . . . 557
19-3. Positive Surges . . . . . . . . . . . . . . . . 559
19-4. Negative Surges . . . . . . . . . . . . . . . . 566
19-5. Surge in Power Canals . . . . . . . . . . . . . . 568
19-6. Surge in Navigation Canals . . . . . . . . . . . . 572
19-7. Surge through Channel Transitions . . . . . . . . . . 575
19-8. Surge at Channel Junctions . . . . . . . . . . . . 578
19-9. Pulsating Flow . . . . . . . . . . . . . . . . 580

**Chapter 20. Flood Routing** . . . . . . . . . . . . . . 586

20-1. Routing of Flood . . . . . . . . . . . . . . . 586
20-2. Method of Characteristics . . . . . . . . . . . . . 587
20-3. Method of Diffusion Analogy . . . . . . . . . . . . 601
20-4. Principle of Hydrologic Routing . . . . . . . . . . . 604
20-5. Methods of Hydrologic Routing . . . . . . . . . . . 607
20-6. A Simple Hydrologic Method of Routing . . . . . . . . 609

Appendix A.  Geometric Elements for Circular Channel Sections  .  .  .  .  625

Appendix B.  Geometric Elements for Trapezoidal, Triangular, and Parabolic Channel Sections  .  .  .  .  .  .  .  .  .  .  .  .  .  .  .  .  .  .  629

Appendix C.  Nomographic Solution of the Manning Formula  .  .  .  .  .  .  640

Appendix D.  Table of the Varied-flow Functions

$$F(u,N) = \int_0^u \frac{du}{1-u^N} \quad \text{and} \quad F(u,N)_{-s_0} = \int_0^u \frac{du}{1+u^N} \quad . \quad . \quad 641$$

Appendix E.  Table of the Varied-flow Functions for Circular Sections  .  .  657

Name Index  .  .  .  .  .  .  .  .  .  .  .  .  .  .  .  .  .  .  .  .  663

Subject Index  .  .  .  .  .  .  .  .  .  .  .  .  .  .  .  .  .  .  669

PART I

# BASIC PRINCIPLES

# CHAPTER 1

# OPEN-CHANNEL FLOW AND ITS CLASSIFICATIONS

**1-1. Description.** The flow of water in a conduit may be either *open-channel flow* or *pipe flow.* The two kinds of flow are similar in many ways but differ in one important respect. Open-channel flow must have a *free surface,* whereas pipe flow has none, since the water must fill the whole conduit. A free surface is subject to atmospheric pressure. Pipe flow, being confined in a closed conduit, exerts no direct atmospheric pressure but hydraulic pressure only.

The two kinds of flow are compared in Fig. 1-1. Shown on the left side is pipe flow. Two piezometer tubes are installed on the pipe at sections 1 and 2. The water levels in the tubes are maintained by the pressure in the pipe at elevations represented by the so-called *hydraulic grade line.* The pressure exerted by the water in each section of the pipe is indicated in the corresponding tube by the height $y$ of the water column above the center line of the pipe. The total energy in the flow of the section with reference to a datum line is the sum of the elevation $z$ of the pipe-center line, the piezometric height $y$, and the velocity head $V^2/2g$, where $V$ is the mean velocity of flow.[1] The energy is represented in the figure by what is called the *energy grade line* or simply the *energy line.* The loss of energy that results when water flows from section 1 to section 2 is represented by $h_f$. A similar diagram for open-channel flow is shown on the right side of Fig. 1-1. For simplicity, it is assumed that the flow is parallel and has a uniform velocity distribution and that the slope of the channel is small. In this case, the water surface is the hydraulic grade line, and the depth of the water corresponds to the piezometric height.[2]

Despite the similarity between the two kinds of flow, it is much more difficult to solve problems of flow in open channels than in pressure pipes. Flow conditions in open channels are complicated by the fact that the

---

[1] It is here assumed that the velocity is uniformly distributed across the conduit section; otherwise a correction would have to be made, such as is described in Art. 2-7 for open channels.

[2] If the flow were curvilinear or if the slope of the channel were large, the piezometric height would be appreciably different from the depth of flow (Arts. 2-9 and 2-10). As a result, the hydraulic grade line would not coincide exactly with the water surface.

position of the free surface is likely to change with respect to time and
space and also by the fact that the depth of flow, the discharge, and the
slopes of the channel bottom and of the free surface are interdependent.
Reliable experimental data on flow in open channels are usually difficult to
obtain.    Furthermore, the physical condition of open channels varies
much more widely than that of pipes.    In pipes the cross section of flow
is fixed, since it is completely defined by the geometry of the conduit.
The cross section of a pipe is generally round, but that of an open channel
may be of any shape—from the circular to the irregular forms of natural
streams.    In pipes, the interior surface ordinarily ranges in roughness

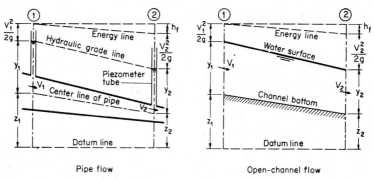

Pipe flow                         Open-channel flow

Fig. 1-1. Comparison between pipe flow and open-channel flow.

from that of new smooth brass or wooden-stave pipes, on the one hand,
to that of old corroded iron or steel pipes, on the other.    In open channels
the surface varies from that of the polished metal used in testing flumes
to that of rough irregular river beds.    Moreover, the roughness in an
open channel varies with the position of the free surface.    Therefore, the
selection of friction coefficients is attended by greater uncertainty for
open channels than for pipes.    In general, the treatment of open-channel
flow is somewhat more empirical than that of pipe flow.    The empirical
method is the best available at present and, if cautiously applied, can
yield results of practical value.

The flow in a closed conduit is not necessarily pipe flow.    It must be
classified as open-channel flow if it has a free surface.    The storm sewer,
for example, which is a closed conduit, is generally designed for open-
channel flow because the flow in the sewer is expected to maintain a free
surface most of the time.

**1-2. Types of Flow.**    Open-channel flow can be classified into many
types and described in various ways.    The following classification is made
according to the change in flow depth with respect to time and space.

*Steady Flow and Unsteady Flow: Time as the Criterion.* Flow in an open channel is said to be *steady* if the depth of flow does not change or if it can be assumed to be constant during the time interval under consideration. The flow is *unsteady* if the depth changes with time. In most open-channel problems it is necessary to study flow behavior only under steady conditions. If, however, the change in flow condition with respect to time is of major concern, the flow should be treated as unsteady. In floods and surges, for instance, which are typical examples of unsteady flow, the stage of flow changes instantaneously as the waves pass by, and the time element becomes vitally important in the design of control structures.

For any flow, the discharge $Q$ at a channel section is expressed by

$$Q = VA \tag{1-1}$$

where $V$ is the mean velocity and $A$ is the flow cross-sectional area normal to the direction of the flow, since the mean velocity is defined as the discharge divided by the cross-sectional area.

In most problems of steady flow the discharge is constant throughout the reach of the channel under consideration; in other words, the flow is *continuous.* Thus, using Eq. (1-1),

$$Q = V_1A_1 = V_2A_2 = \cdots \tag{1-2}$$

where the subscripts designate different channel sections. This is the *continuity equation* for a continuous steady flow.

Equation (1-2) is obviously invalid, however, where the discharge of a steady flow is *nonuniform* along the channel, that is, where water runs in or out along the course of flow. This type of flow, known as *spatially varied or discontinuous flow,* is found in roadside gutters, side-channel spillways, the washwater troughs in filters, the effluent channels around sewage-treatment tanks, and the main drainage channels and feeding channels in irrigation systems.

The law of continuity of unsteady flow requires consideration of the time effect. Hence, the continuity equation for continuous unsteady flow should include the time element as a variable (Art. 18-1).

*Uniform Flow and Varied Flow: Space as the Criterion.* Open-channel flow is said to be *uniform* if the depth of flow is the same at every section of the channel. A uniform flow may be steady or unsteady, depending on whether or not the depth changes with time.

*Steady uniform flow* is the fundamental type of flow treated in open-channel hydraulics. The depth of the flow does not change during the time interval under consideration. The establishment of *unsteady uniform flow* would require that the water surface fluctuate from time to time while remaining parallel to the channel bottom. Obviously, this is a practically impossible condition. The term "uniform flow" is, therefore, used hereafter to refer only to steady uniform flow.

Flow is *varied* if the depth of flow changes along the length of the channel. Varied flow may be either steady or unsteady. Since unsteady uniform flow is rare, the term "unsteady flow" is used hereafter to designate *unsteady varied flow* exclusively.

Varied flow may be further classified as either *rapidly* or *gradually varied*. The flow is rapidly varied if the depth changes abruptly over a comparatively short distance; otherwise, it is gradually varied. A rapidly varied flow is also known as a *local phenomenon;* examples are the hydraulic jump and the hydraulic drop.

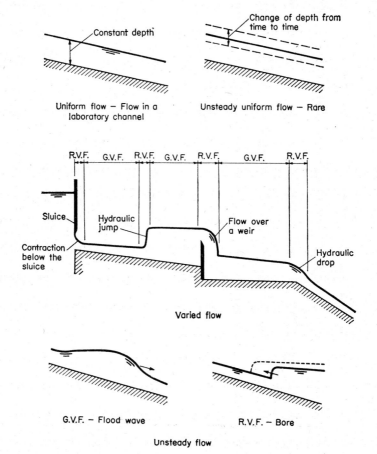

FIG. 1-2. Various types of open-channel flow. G.V.F. = gradually varied flow; R.V.F. = rapidly varied flow.

For clarity, the classification of open-channel flow is summarized as follows:

A. Steady flow
    1. Uniform flow
    2. Varied flow
        a. Gradually varied flow
        b. Rapidly varied flow
B. Unsteady flow
    1. Unsteady uniform flow (rare)
    2. Unsteady flow (i.e., unsteady varied flow)
        a. Gradually varied unsteady flow
        b. Rapidly varied unsteady flow

Various types of flow are sketched in Fig. 1-2. For illustrative purposes, these diagrams, as well as other similar sketches of open channels in this book, have been drawn to a greatly exaggerated vertical scale, since ordinary channels have small bottom slopes.

**1-3. State of Flow.** The state or behavior of open-channel flow is governed basically by the effects of viscosity and gravity relative to the inertial forces of the flow. The surface tension of water may affect the behavior of flow under certain circumstances, but it does not play a significant role in most open-channel problems encountered in engineering.

*Effect of Viscosity.* Depending on the effect of viscosity relative to inertia, the flow may be laminar, turbulent, or transitional.

The flow is *laminar* if the viscous forces are so strong relative to the inertial forces that viscosity plays a significant part in determining flow behavior. In laminar flow, the water particles appear to move in definite smooth paths, or streamlines, and infinitesimally thin layers of fluid seem to slide over adjacent layers.

The flow is *turbulent* if the viscous forces are weak relative to the inertial forces. In turbulent flow, the water particles move in irregular paths which are neither smooth nor fixed but which in the aggregate still represent the forward motion of the entire stream.

Between the laminar and turbulent states there is a mixed, or *transitional*, state.

The effect of viscosity relative to inertia can be represented by the *Reynolds number*, defined as

$$\mathbf{R} = \frac{VL}{\nu} \tag{1-3}$$

where $V$ is the velocity of flow in fps; $L$ is a characteristic length in ft, here considered equal to the hydraulic radius $R$ of a conduit; and $\nu$ (nu) is the kinematic viscosity of water in ft$^2$/sec. The kinematic viscosity in ft²/sec is equal to the dynamic viscosity $\mu$ (mu) in slug/ft-sec divided by the mass density $\rho$ (rho) in slug/ft³. For water at 68°F (20°C), $\mu = 2.09 \times 10^{-5}$ and $\rho = 1.937$; hence, $\nu = 1.08 \times 10^{-5}$.

An open-channel flow is laminar if the Reynolds number **R** is small and turbulent if **R** is large. Numerous experiments have shown that the flow in a pipe changes from laminar to turbulent in the range of **R** between the critical value 2,000 and a value that may be as high as 50,000.* In these experiments the diameter of the pipe was taken as the characteristic length in defining the Reynolds number. When the hydraulic radius is taken as the characteristic length, the corresponding range is from 500 to 12,500,* since the diameter of a pipe is four times its hydraulic radius.

The laminar, turbulent, and transitional states of open-channel flow can be expressed by a diagram that shows a relation between the Reynolds number and the friction factor of the Darcy-Weisbach formula. Such a diagram, generally known as the *Stanton diagram* [1], has been developed for flow in pipes. The *Darcy-Weisbach formula*,[1] also developed primarily for flow in pipes, is

$$h_f = f \frac{L}{d_0} \frac{V^2}{2g} \tag{1-4}$$

where $h_f$ is the frictional loss in ft for flow in the pipe, $f$ is the friction factor, $L$ is the length of the pipe in ft, $d_0$ is the diameter of the pipe in ft, $V$ is the velocity of flow in fps, and $g$ is the acceleration due to gravity in ft/sec². 

Since $d_0 = 4R$ and the energy gradient $S = h_f/L$, the above equation may be rewritten for the friction factor

$$f = \frac{8gRS}{V^2} \tag{1-5}$$

This equation may also be applied to uniform and nearly uniform flows in open channels.

The $f$-**R** relationship for smooth pipes can be expressed by the *Blasius equation* [5]

$$f = \frac{0.223}{\mathbf{R}^{0.25}} \tag{1-6}\dagger$$

---

* It should be noted that there is actually no definite upper limit.

[1] As a result of Darcy's study [2] on flow in pipes, his name is commonly associated with that of Weisbach [3] in designating this equation which Weisbach first formulated. Actually, d'Aubuisson [4] presented, prior to Darcy, a formula that can be reduced to the form of Eq. (1-4).

† In this equation, the hydraulic radius is used as the characteristic length in defining the Reynolds number. If the diameter of pipe were used as the characteristic length, the numerical constant of the numerator in this equation would be 0.316.

which is believed to be valid only where the value of **R** is between 750 and 25,000. For higher values of **R**, von Kármán [6] developed a general expression, which was later modified by Prandtl [7] to agree more closely with the data obtained by Nikuradse [8]. The resulting *Prandtl-von Kármán* equation is

$$\frac{1}{\sqrt{f}} = 2 \log (\mathbf{R} \sqrt{f}) + 0.4 \qquad (1\text{-}7)$$

Equations (1-6) and (1-7) will be used in the following discussion as a basis for comparing flow conditions in open channels. It may be noted that corresponding equations for flow in open channels have been derived by Keulegan [9] and appear to be very similar to the pipe-flow equations given above. It must be remembered, however, that, owing to the free surface and to the interdependence of the hydraulic radius, discharge, and slope, the *f*-**R** relationship in open-channel flow does not follow *exactly* the simple concepts that hold for pipe flow. Some specific features of the *f*-**R** relationship in open-channel flow are described below.

Experimental data available for the determination of the *f*-**R** relationship in open-channel flow can be found in various publications on hydraulics.[1] Figure 1-3, which plots the relationship for flow in *smooth channels*, is based on data developed at the University of Illinois[2] [21] and the University of Minnesota [20]. In this plot the following features may be noted:

1. The plot shows clearly how the state of flow changes from laminar to turbulent as the Reynolds number increases. The discontinuity of the plot and the spread of data characterize the transitional region, as they do in the Stanton diagram for flow in pipes. The transitional range, however, is not so well defined as it is for pipe flow. The lower critical Reynolds number depends to some extent on channel shape. The value varies from 500 to 600, being generally larger than the value for pipe flow. For practical purposes, the transitional range of **R** for open-channel flow may be assumed to be 500 to 2,000. It should be noted, however, that the upper value is arbitrary, since there is no definite upper limit for all flow conditions.

2. The data in the laminar region can be defined by a general equation

$$f = \frac{K}{\mathbf{R}} \qquad (1\text{-}8)$$

From Eqs. (1-3) and (1-5) it can be shown that

$$K = \frac{8g R^2 S}{\nu V} \qquad (1\text{-}9)$$

[1] See [10] to [23].
[2] The data for the rectangular channel were furnished through the courtesy of Professor W. M. Lansford and processed for the present purpose by the author.

Since $V$ and $R$ have specific values for any given channel shape, $K$ is a purely numerical factor dependent only on channel shape.   For laminar flow in smooth channels, the value of $K$ can be determined theoretically [20].   The plot in Fig. 1-3 indicates that $K$ is approximately 24 for the rectangular channels and 14 for the triangular channel under consideration.

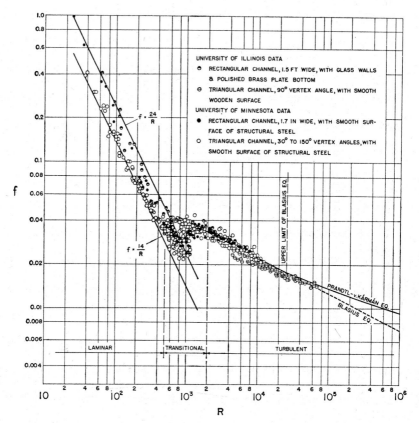

FIG. 1-3. The $f$-**R** relationship for flow in smooth channels.

3. The data in the turbulent region correspond closely to the Blasius-Prandtl-von Kármán curve.   This indicates that the law for turbulent flow in smooth pipes may be approximately representative of all smooth channels.   The plot also shows that the shape of the channel does not have an important influence on friction in turbulent flow, as it does in laminar flow.

The data for laminar flow obtained at the University of Minnesota [20] and the data for turbulent flow collected individually by Kirschmer

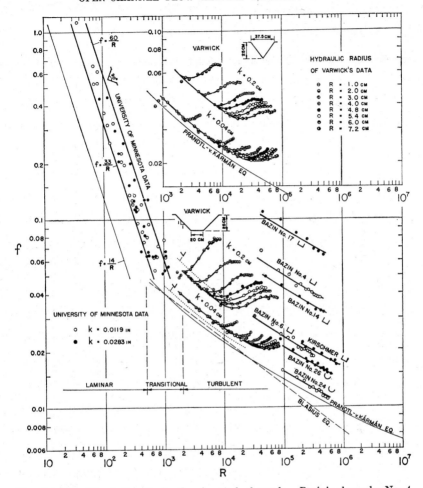

Fig. 1-4. The $f$-$R$ relationship for flow in rough channels.  Bazin's channels: No. 4, gravel embedded in cement; No. 6, unpolished wood; No. 14, unpolished wood roughened by transverse wooden strips 27 mm long, 10 mm high, and 10 mm in spacing; No. 17, same as No. 14 except with a spacing of 50 mm; No. 24, cement lining; and No. 26, unpolished wood.  Kirschmer's channel: smooth concrete.

[15,16], Eisner [22], and Koženy [23] are shown in the diagram for flow in *rough channels* (Fig. 1-4).  In some of the data channel roughness is represented by $k$, which is a size measure of the roughness particles forming the channel surface.  The diagram illustrates the following features:

1. In the laminar region the data can be defined by Eq. (1-8).  In this region, the value of $K$ is generally higher than it is for smooth channels

and ranges between 60 and 33, indicating the pronounced influence of the channel roughness on the friction factor.

2. In the turbulent region the channel shape has a pronounced effect on the friction factor. It is believed that, when the degree of roughness is constant, the friction factor decreases roughly in the order of rectangular, triangular, trapezoidal, and circular channels. At the suggestion of Prandtl, Kirschmer [15,16] explained that the effect of channel shape may be due to the development of secondary flow, which is apparently more pronounced in rectangular channels than in, say, triangular channels. The secondary flow is the movement of water particles on a cross section normal to the longitudinal direction of the channel. A high secondary flow involves high energy loss and thus accounts for high channel resistance.

3. In the turbulent region most plots appear parallel to the Prandtl-von Kármán curve. This curve serves as an approximate limiting position toward which a plot moves as the over-all resistance becomes less. According to a concept advanced by Morris [24] (Art. 8-2), the rise of the plots above the smooth-conduit curve may be explained as a result of additional energy loss generated by the roughness elements. When the Reynolds number is very high, some plots become essentially horizontal, reaching a state of so-called *complete turbulence*. At this state the value of $f$ is independent of Reynolds number and depends solely on roughness, hydraulic radius, and channel shape.

4. The plot of Varwick's data [16] for a given roughness, hydraulic radius, and channel shape starts off from a curve parallel to the Prandtl-von Kármán curve, then rises as the Reynolds number increases, and finally becomes horizontal as a state of complete turbulence is reached. The rise of the plot is a peculiar phenomenon which demands explanation,[1] and, since this finding has not been verified by other data, more experimental studies seem necessary to substantiate it.

It should be noted that the above descriptions are limited to low-velocity, or subcritical, flow (which will be defined later in this article) and to flow on which surface tension does not have a significant influence.

In most open channels laminar flow occurs very rarely. The fact that the surface of a stream appears smooth and glassy to an observer is by no means an indication that the flow is laminar; most probably, it indicates that the surface velocity is lower than that required for capillary waves to form. Laminar open-channel flow is known to exist, however, usually where thin sheets of water flow over the ground or where it is created deliberately in model testing channels.

---

[1] According to the concept of Morris [24], this phenomenon probably represents a transition of the flow to another type of flow having higher energy loss. As the Reynolds number increases, the flow may be changing from quasi-smooth flow to wake-interference flow, and then to isolated-roughness flow (Art. 8-2).

As the flow in most channels is turbulent, a model employed to simulate a prototype channel should be designed so that the Reynolds number of flow of the model channel is in the turbulent range.

*Effect of Gravity.* The effect of gravity upon the state of flow is represented by a ratio of inertial forces to gravity forces. This ratio is given by the *Froude number*,[1] defined as

$$\mathbf{F} = \frac{V}{\sqrt{gL}} \tag{1-10}$$

where $V$ is the mean velocity of flow in fps, $g$ is the acceleration of gravity in ft/sec², and $L$ is a characteristic length in ft. In open-channel flow the characteristic length is made equal to the *hydraulic depth D*, which is defined as the cross-sectional area of the water normal to the direction of flow in the channel divided by the width of the free surface. For rectangular channels this is equal to the depth of the flow section.

When $\mathbf{F}$ is equal to unity, Eq. (1-10) gives

$$V = \sqrt{gD} \tag{1-11}$$

and the flow is said to be in a *critical* state. If $\mathbf{F}$ is less than unity, or $V < \sqrt{gD}$, the flow is *subcritical*. In this state the role played by gravity forces is more pronounced; so the flow has a low velocity and is often described as tranquil and streaming. If $\mathbf{F}$ is greater than unity, or $V > \sqrt{gD}$, the flow is *supercritical*. In this state the inertial forces become dominant; so the flow has a high velocity and is usually described as rapid, shooting, and torrential.

In the mechanics of water waves, the critical velocity $\sqrt{gD}$ is identified as the *celerity* of the small gravity waves that occur in shallow water in channels as a result of any momentary change in the local depth of the water (Art. 18-6). Such a change may be developed by disturbances or obstacles in the channel that cause a displacement of water above and below the mean surface level and thus create waves that exert a weight or gravity force. It should be noted that a gravity wave can be propagated upstream in water of subcritical flow but not in water of supercritical flow, since the celerity is greater than the velocity of flow in the former case and less in the latter. Therefore, the possibility or impossibility of propagating a gravity wave upstream can be used as a criterion for distinguishing between subcritical and supercritical flow.

Since the flow in most channels is controlled by the gravity effect, a model used to simulate a prototype channel for testing purposes must be

---

[1] Other dimensionless ratios used for the same purpose include (1) the *kinetic-flow factor* $\lambda = V^2/gL = \mathbf{F}^2$, first used by Rehbock [25] and then by Bakhmeteff [26]; (2) the *Boussinesq number* $\mathbf{B} = V/\sqrt{2gR}$, first used by Engel [27]; and (3) the *kineticity* or *velocity-head ratio* $k = V^2/2gL$, proposed by Stevens [28] and Posey [29], respectively.

designed for this effect; that is, the Froude number of the flow in the model channel must be made equal to that of the flow in the prototype channel.

**1-4. Regimes of Flow.** A combined effect of viscosity and gravity may produce any one of four *regimes of flow* in an open channel, namely, (1) *subcritical-laminar*, when **F** is less than unity and **R** is in the laminar range; (2) *supercritical-laminar*, when **F** is greater than unity and **R** is in the laminar range; (3) *supercritical-turbulent*, when **F** is greater than unity

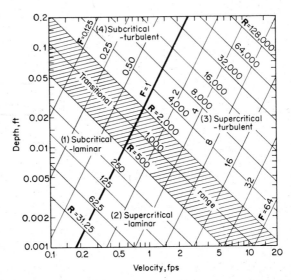

Fig. 1-5. Depth-velocity relationships for four regimes of open-channel flow. (*After Robertson and Rouse* [30].)

and **R** is in the turbulent range; and (4) *subcritical-turbulent*, when **F** is less than unity and **R** is in the turbulent range. The depth-velocity relationships for the four flow regimes in a wide open channel can be shown by a logarithmic plot (Fig. 1-5) [30]. The heavy line for **F** = 1 and the shaded band for the laminar-turbulent transitional range intersect on the graph and divide the whole area into four portions, each of which represents a flow regime. The first two regimes, subcritical-laminar and supercritical-laminar, are not commonly encountered in applied open-channel hydraulics, since the flow is generally turbulent in the channels considered in engineering problems. However, these regimes occur frequently where there is very thin depth—this is known as *sheet flow*—and they become significant in such problems as the testing of hydraulic models, the study of overland flow, and erosion control for such flow.

Photographs of the four regimes of flow are shown in Fig. 1-6. In each

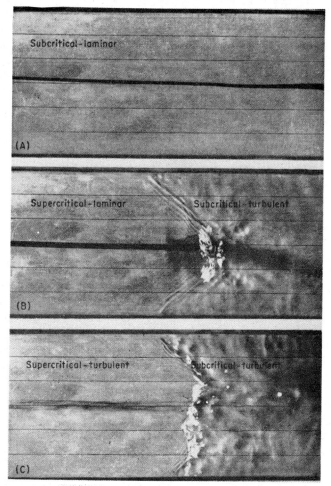

Fig. 1-6. Photographs showing four flow regimes in a laboratory channel.   (*Courtesy of H. Rouse.*)

photograph the direction of flow is from left to right.    All flows are uniform except those on the right side of the middle and bottom views. The top view represents uniform subcritical-laminar flow.    The flow is subcritical, since the Froude number was adjusted to slightly below the critical value; and the streak of undiffused dye indicates that it is laminar. The middle view shows a uniform supercritical-laminar flow changing to varied subcritical-turbulent.    The bottom view shows a uniform supercritical-turbulent flow changing to varied subcritical-turbulent.    In both cases, the diffusion of dye is the evidence of turbulence.

It is believed that gravity action may have a definitive effect upon the flow resistance in channels at the turbulent-flow range. The experimental data studied by Jegorow [31] and Iwagaki [32] for smooth rectangular channels and by Hom-ma [33] for rough channels have shown that, in the supercritical-turbulent regime of flow, the friction factor is likely to increase with increasing Froude number. Generally, the effect of gravity is practically negligible where the Froude number is small, say, less than 3. A further investigation by Iwagaki [34] indicates that, with increasing Froude number, the friction factor of turbulent flow in both smooth and rough open channels becomes larger than that in pipes. It is possible that the presence of the free surface in open-channel flow makes the channel rougher than the pipe. When more data and evidence become available, the Froude number, representing the gravity effect, may have to be considered as an additional factor in defining the $f$-R relationship for supercritical-turbulent flow.

## PROBLEMS

**1-1.** With reference to Fig. 1-1, show that the theoretical discharge of the open-channel flow may be expressed by

$$Q = A_2 \sqrt{\frac{2g(\Delta y - h_f)}{1 - (A_2/A_1)^2}} \qquad (1\text{-}12)$$

where $A_1$ and $A_2$ are the cross-sectional areas of the flow at sections 1 and 2, respectively, and $\Delta y$ is the drop in water surface between the sections.

**1-2.** Verify Eq. (1-10).

**1-3.** Verify by computation the depth-velocity relationships shown in Fig. 1-5 for the four flow regimes in a wide rectangular open channel. The temperature of the water is taken as 68°F.

**1-4.** A model channel is used to simulate a prototype channel 100 ft wide, carrying a discharge of 500 cfs at a depth of 4 ft. The model is designed for gravity effect, and a turbulent-flow condition is assured. Determine the minimum size of the model and the scale ratio, assuming the upper limit of the transitional-flow region to be **R** = 2,000. The scale ratio is the ratio of the linear dimension of the model to that of the prototype.

## REFERENCES

1. T. E. Stanton and J. R. Pannell: Similarity of motion in relation to surface friction of fluids, *Philosophical Transactions, Royal Society of London*, vol. 214A, pp. 199–224, 1914.
2. H. Darcy: Sur des recherches expérimentales relatives au mouvement des eaux dans les tuyaux (Experimental researches on the flow of water in pipes), *Comptes rendus des séances de l'Académie des Sciences*, vol. 38, pp. 1109–1121, June 26, 1854.
3. Julius Weisbach: "Lehrbuch der Ingenieur- und Maschinenmechanik" ("Textbook of Engineering Mechanics"), Brunswick, Germany, 1845.
4. J. F. d'Aubuisson de Voisins: "Traité d'hydraulique" ("Treatise on Hydraulics"), Levrant, Paris, 2d ed., 1840; translated into English by Joseph Bennett, Little, Brown & Company, Boston, 1852, pp. 202–211.

5. H. Blasius: Das Ähnlichkeitsgesetz bei Reibungsvorgängen in Flüssigkeiten (The law of similitude for frictions in fluids), *Forschungsheft des Vereins deutscher Ingenieure, No.* 131, Berlin, 1913.

6. Theodor von Kármán: Mechanische Ähnlichkeit und Turbulenz (Mechanical similitude and turbulence), *Proceedings of the 3d International Congress for Applied Mechanics, Stockholm*, vol. I, pp. 85–93, 1930.

7. L. Prandtl: The mechanics of viscous fluids, in W. F. Durand (editor-in-chief): "Aerodynamic Theory," Springer-Verlag, Berlin, 1935, vol. III, div. G, p. 142.

8. J. Nikuradse: Gesetzmässigkeiten der turbulenten Strömung in glatten Rohren (Laws of turbulent flow in smooth pipes), *Forschungsheft des Vereins deutscher Ingenieure, No.* 356, Berlin, 1932.

9. Garbis H. Keulegan: Laws of turbulent flow in open channels, paper RP1151, *Journal of Research, U.S. National Bureau of Standards*, vol. 21, pp. 707–741, December, 1938.

10. J. Allen: Streamline and turbulent flow in open channels, *The London, Edinburgh and Dublin Philosophical Magazine and Journal of Science*, ser. 7, vol. 17, pp. 1081–1112, June, 1934.

11. H. Bazin: Recherches expérimentales sur l'écoulement de l'eau dans les canaux découverts (Experimental researches on the flow of water in open channels), *Mémoires présentés par divers savants à l'Académie des Sciences*, Paris, vol. 19, 1865.

12. Studies of river bed materials and their movement, with special reference to the lower Mississippi River, *U.S. Waterways Experiment Station, Technical Paper* 17, January, 1935.

13. S. P. Raju: Versuche über den Strömungswiderstand gekrümmter offener Kanäle (Study of flow resistance in curved open channels), *Mitteilungen des hydraulischen Instituts der technischen Hochschule München*, no. 6, pp. 45–60, Munich, 1933. English translation by Clarence E. Bardsley: Resistance to flow in curved open channels, *Proceedings, American Society of Civil Engineers*, vol. 63, pt. 2, p. 49 after p. 1834, November, 1937.

14. Lorenz G. Straub: Studies of the transition-region between laminar and turbulent flow in open channels, *Transactions, American Geophysical Union*, vol. 20, pt. IV, pp. 649–653, 1939.

15. Otto Kirschmer: Reibungsverluste in Röhren und Kanälen (Frictional losses in pipes and channels), *Die Wasserwirtschaft*, Stuttgart, vol. 39, no. 7, pp. 137–142, April; no. 8, pp. 168–174, May, 1949.

16. Otto Kirschmer: Pertes de charge dans les conduites forcées et les canaux découverts (Energy losses in pressure conduits and open channels), *Revue générale de l'hydraulique*, Paris, vol. 15, no. 51, pp. 115–138, May–June, 1949.

17. Yuichi Iwagaki: Discussion on Laminar to turbulent flow in a wide open channel, by W. M. Owen, *Transactions, American Society of Civil Engineers*, vol. 119, pp. 1165–1166, 1954.

18. Horace William King: "Handbook of Hydraulics," revised by Ernest F. Brater, McGraw-Hill Book Company, Inc., New York, 4th ed., 1954, p. 7-35.

19. F. Bettes: Non-uniform flow in channels, *Civil Engineering and Public Works Review*, London, vol. 52, no. 609, pp. 323–324, March; no. 610, pp. 434–436, April, 1957.

20. Lorenz G. Straub, Edward Silberman, and Herbert C. Nelson: Open-channel flow at small Reynolds numbers, *Transactions, American Society of Civil Engineers*, vol. 123, pp. 685–706, 1958.

21. Wallace M. Lansford and James M. Robertson: Discussion of Open-channel flow at small Reynolds numbers, by Lorenz G. Straub, Edward Silberman, and Her-

bert C. Nelson, *Transactions, American Society of Civil Engineers*, vol. 123, pp. 707–712, 1958.

22. Franz Eisner: Offene Gerinne (Open channel), sec. 4 of vol. IV, "Hydro- und Aerodynamik," in W. Wien and F. Harms (editors-in-chief): "Handbuch der Experimentalphysik," Akademische Verlagsgesellschaft mbH, Leipzig, 1932, p. 298.

23. Josef Koženy: "Hydraulik" ("Hydraulics"), Springer-Verlag, Vienna, 1953, p. 574.

24. Henry M. Morris, Jr.: Flow in rough conduits, *Transactions, American Society of Civil Engineers*, vol. 120, pp. 373–398, 1955. Discussions on pp. 399–410.

25. Th. Rehbock: Zur Frage des Brückenstaues (On the problem of bridge constrictions), *Zentralblatt der Bauverwaltung*, Berlin, vol. 39, no. 37, pp. 197–200, 1919.

26. Boris A. Bakhmeteff: "Hydraulics of Open Channels," McGraw-Hill Book Company, Inc., New York, 1932, p. 64.

27. F. V. A. E. Engel: Non-uniform flow of water: Problems and phenomena in open channels with side contractions, *The Engineer*, vol. 155, pp. 392–394, 429–430, 456–457, 1933.

28. J. C. Stevens: Discussion on The hydraulic jump in sloping channels, by C. E. Kindsvater, *Transactions, American Society of Civil Engineers*, vol. 109, pp. 1125–1135, 1944.

29. C. J. Posey: Discussion on The hydraulic jump in sloping channels, by C. E. Kindsvater, *Transactions, American Society of Civil Engineers*, vol. 109, pp. 1135–1138, 1944.

30. J. M. Robertson and Hunter Rouse: On the four regimes of open-channel flow, *Civil Engineering*, vol. 11, no. 3, pp. 169–171, March, 1941.

31. S. A. Jegorow: Turbulente Überwellenströmung (Schiessen) in offenen Gerinnen mit glatten Wänden (Turbulent supercritical flow in open channel with smooth walls), *Wasserkraft und Wasserwirtschaft*, Munich, vol. 35, no. 3, pp. 55–59, 1940.

32. Yuichi Iwagaki: On the laws of resistance to turbulent flow in open smooth channels, *Memoirs of the Faculty of Engineering, Kyoto University*, Japan, vol. 15, no. 1, pp. 27–40, January, 1953.

33. Masashi Hom-ma: Fluid resistance in water flow of high Froude number, *Proceedings of the 2d Japan National Congress for Applied Mechanics*, pp. 251–254, 1952.

34. Yuichi Iwagaki: On the laws of resistance to turbulent flow in open rough channels, *Proceedings of the 4th Japan National Congress for Applied Mechanics*, pp. 229–233, 1954.

# CHAPTER 2

# OPEN CHANNELS AND THEIR PROPERTIES

**2-1. Kinds of Open Channel.** An open channel is a conduit in which water flows with a free surface. Classified according to its origin a channel may be either *natural* or *artificial*.

Natural channels include all watercourses that exist naturally on the earth, varying in size from tiny hillside rivulets, through brooks, streams, small and large rivers, to tidal estuaries. Underground streams carrying water with a free surface are also considered natural open channels.

The hydraulic properties of natural channels are generally very irregular. In some cases empirical assumptions reasonably consistent with actual observations and experience may be made such that the conditions of flow in these channels become amenable to the analytical treatment of theoretical hydraulics. A comprehensive study of the behavior of flow in natural channels requires knowledge of other fields, such as hydrology, geomorphology, sediment transportation, etc. It constitutes, in fact, a subject of its own, known as *river hydraulics*.

Artificial channels are those constructed or developed by human effort: navigation channels, power canals, irrigation canals and flumes, drainage ditches, trough spillways, floodways, log chutes, roadside gutters, etc., as well as model channels that are built in the laboratory for testing purposes. The hydraulic properties of such channels can be either controlled to the extent desired or designed to meet given requirements. The application of hydraulic theories to artificial channels will, therefore, produce results fairly close to actual conditions and, hence, are reasonably accurate for practical design purposes.

Under various circumstances in engineering practice the artificial open channel is given different names, such as "canal," "flume," "chute," "drop," "culvert," "open-flow tunnel," etc. These names, however, are used rather loosely and can be defined only in a very general way. The *canal* is usually a long and mild-sloped channel built in the ground, which may be unlined or lined with stone masonry, concrete, cement, wood, or bituminous materials. The *flume* is a channel of wood, metal, concrete, or masonry, usually supported on or above the surface of the ground to carry water across a depression. The *chute* is a channel having steep slopes. The *drop* is similar to a chute, but the change in elevation is effected in a short distance. The *culvert* flowing partly full is a covered channel of comparatively short length installed to drain water through highway and railroad embankments. The *open-flow tunnel* is a comparatively long covered channel used to carry water through a hill or any obstruction on the ground.

**2-2. Channel Geometry.** A channel built with unvarying cross section and constant bottom slope is called a *prismatic channel.* Otherwise, the channel is *nonprismatic;* an example is a trough spillway having variable width and curved alignment. Unless specifically indicated, the channels described in this book are prismatic.

The term *channel section* used in this book refers to the cross section of a channel taken normal to the direction of the flow. A *vertical channel section*, however, is the vertical section passing through the lowest or bottom point of the channel section. For horizontal channels, therefore, the channel section is always a vertical channel section.

Natural channel sections are in general very irregular, usually varying from an approximate parabola to an approximate trapezoid. For streams subject to frequent floods, the channel may consist of a main channel section carrying normal discharges and one or more side channel sections for accommodating overflows.

Artificial channels are usually designed with sections of regular geometric shapes. Table 2-1 lists seven geometric shapes that are in common use. The trapezoid is the commonest shape for channels with unlined earth banks, for it provides side slopes for stability. The rectangle and triangle are special cases of the trapezoid. Since the rectangle has vertical sides, it is commonly used for channels built of stable materials, such as lined masonry, rocks, metal, or timber. The triangular section is used only for small ditches, roadside gutters, and laboratory works. The circle is the popular section for sewers and culverts of small and medium sizes. The parabola[1] is used as an approximation of sections of small and medium-size natural channels. The round-cornered rectangle is a modification of the rectangle. The round-bottom triangle is an approximation of the parabola; it is a form usually created by excavation with shovels.

Closed geometric sections other than the circle are frequently used in sewerage, particularly for sewers large enough for a man to enter. These sections are given various names according to their form; they may be

---

[1] The side slope $z:1$ of a parabolic section at the intersection of the sides with the free surface can be computed easily by the simple formula $z = T/4y$.

Russian engineers [1] also use semielliptical and parabolic sections of higher order: $y = ax^p$ with $p = 3$ or 4. The constant $a$ is computed from the side slope assumed at the free surface.

TABLE 2-1. GEOMETRIC ELEMENTS OF CHANNEL SECTIONS

| Section | Area $A$ | Wetted perimeter $P$ | Hydraulic radius $R$ | Top width $T$ | Hydraulic depth $D$ | Section factor $Z$ |
|---|---|---|---|---|---|---|
| Rectangle | $by$ | $b + 2y$ | $\dfrac{by}{b+2y}$ | $b$ | $y$ | $by^{1.5}$ |
| Trapezoid | $(b+zy)y$ | $b + 2y\sqrt{1+z^2}$ | $\dfrac{(b+zy)y}{b+2y\sqrt{1+z^2}}$ | $b + 2zy$ | $\dfrac{(b+zy)y}{b+2zy}$ | $\dfrac{[(b+zy)y]^{1.5}}{\sqrt{b+2zy}}$ |
| Triangle | $zy^2$ | $2y\sqrt{1+z^2}$ | $\dfrac{zy}{2\sqrt{1+z^2}}$ | $2zy$ | $\tfrac{1}{2}y$ | $\dfrac{\sqrt{2}}{2}zy^{2.5}$ |
| Circle | $\tfrac{1}{8}(\theta - \sin\theta)d_0^2$ | $\tfrac{1}{2}\theta d_0$ | $\tfrac{1}{4}\left(1 - \dfrac{\sin\theta}{\theta}\right)d_0$ | $(\sin\tfrac{1}{2}\theta)d_0$ or $2\sqrt{y(d_0 - y)}$ | $\tfrac{1}{8}\left(\dfrac{\theta - \sin\theta}{\sin\tfrac{1}{2}\theta}\right)d_0$ | $\dfrac{\sqrt{2}}{32}\dfrac{(\theta - \sin\theta)^{1.5}}{(\sin\tfrac{1}{2}\theta)^{0.5}}d_0^{2.5}$ |
| Parabola | $\tfrac{2}{3}Ty$ | $T + \dfrac{8}{3}\dfrac{y^2}{T}$ * | $\dfrac{2T^2y}{3T^2+8y^2}$ * | $\dfrac{3}{2}\dfrac{A}{y}$ | $\tfrac{2}{3}y$ | $\tfrac{2}{9}\sqrt{6}\,Ty^{1.5}$ |
| Round-cornered rectangle ($y>r$) | $\left(\dfrac{\pi}{2} - 2\right)r^2 + (b+2r)y$ | $(\pi - 2)r + b + 2y$ | $\dfrac{(\pi/2 - 2)r^2 + (b+2r)y}{(\pi - 2)r + b + 2y}$ | $b + 2r$ | $\dfrac{(\pi/2 - 2)r^2}{b+2r} + y$ | $\dfrac{[(\pi/2 - 2)r^2 + (b+2r)y]^{1.5}}{\sqrt{b+2r}}$ |
| Round-bottomed triangle | $\dfrac{T^2}{4z} - \dfrac{r^2}{z}(1 - z\cot^{-1}z)$ | $\dfrac{T}{z}\sqrt{1+z^2} - \dfrac{2r}{z}(1 - z\cot^{-1}z)$ | $\dfrac{A}{P}$ | $2[z(y - r) + r\sqrt{1+z^2}]$ | $\dfrac{A}{T}$ | $A\sqrt{\dfrac{A}{T}}$ |

* Satisfactory approximation for the interval $0 < x \leq 1$, where $x = 4y/T$. When $x > 1$, use the exact expression $P = (T/2)[\sqrt{1+x^2} + 1/x \ln (x + \sqrt{1+x^2})]$.

egg-shaped, ovoid, semielliptical, $U$-shaped, catenary, horseshoe, basket-handle, etc. The complete rectangle and square are also common for large sewers. Dimensions and properties of sewer sections may be found in textbooks on sewerage.[1]

A special geometric section known as *hydrostatic catenary* or *lintearia* [4,5] is the shape of the cross section of a trough, formed of flexible sheets assumed to be weightless, filled with water up to the top of the section, and firmly supported at the upper edges of the sides but with no effects of fixation. The hydrostatic catenary has been used for the design of the sections of some elevated irrigation flumes. These flumes are constructed of metal plates so thin that their weight is negligible, and are firmly attached to beams at the upper edges.

**2-3. Geometric Elements of Channel Section.** *Geometric elements* are properties of a channel section that can be defined entirely by the geometry of the section and the depth of flow. These elements are very important and are used extensively in flow computations.

For simple regular channel sections, the geometric elements can be expressed mathematically in terms of the depth of flow and other dimensions of the section. For complicated sections and sections of natural streams, however, no simple formula can be written to express these elements, but curves representing the relation between these elements and the depth of flow can be prepared for use in hydraulic computations.

The definitions of several geometric elements of basic importance are given below. Other geometric elements used in this book will be defined where they first appear.

The *depth of flow y* is the vertical distance of the lowest point of a channel section from the free surface. This term is often used interchangeably with the *depth of flow section d*. Strictly speaking, the depth of flow section is the depth of flow normal to the direction of flow, or the height of the channel section containing the water. For a channel with a longitudinal slope angle $\theta$, it can be seen that the depth of flow is equal to the depth of flow section divided by cos $\theta$. In the case of steep channels, therefore, the two terms should be used discriminately.

The *stage* is the elevation or vertical distance of the free surface above a datum. If the lowest point of the channel section is chosen as the datum, the stage is identical with the depth of flow.

The *top width T* is the width of channel section at the free surface.

The *water area A* is the cross-sectional area of the flow normal to the direction of flow.

The *wetted perimeter P* is the length of the line of intersection of the channel wetted surface with a cross-sectional plane normal to the direction of flow.

---

[1] Many typical sewer sections are described in [2] and [3].

The *hydraulic radius R* is the ratio of the water area to its wetted perimeter, or

$$R = \frac{A}{P} \tag{2-1}$$

The *hydraulic depth D* is the ratio of the water area to the top width, or

$$D = \frac{A}{T} \tag{2-2}$$

The *section factor for critical-flow computation Z* is the product of the water area and the square root of the hydraulic depth, or

$$Z = A \sqrt{D} = A \sqrt{\frac{A}{T}} \tag{2-3}$$

The *section factor for uniform-flow computation $AR^{2/3}$* is the product of the water area and the two-thirds power of the hydraulic radius.

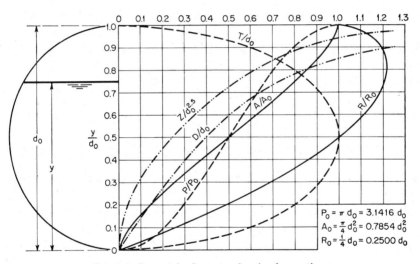

FIG. 2-1. Geometric elements of a circular section.

Table 2-1 furnishes a list of formulas for six basic geometric elements of seven commonly used channel sections. For a circular section, the curves in Fig. 2-1 represent the ratios of the geometric elements of the section to the corresponding elements when the section is flowing full. These curves are prepared from a table given in Appendix A. For certain trapezoidal, triangular, and parabolic sections commonly found in practical uses, the diagrams given in Appendix B provide a convenient means of determining the geometric elements.

**Example 2-1.** Compute the hydraulic radius, hydraulic depth, and section factor $Z$ of the trapezoidal channel section in Fig. 2-2. The depth of flow is 6 ft.

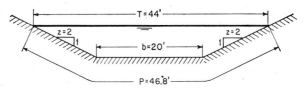

FIG. 2-2. A channel cross section.

*Solution.* By formulas given in Table 2-1, the following are computed: $P = 20 + 2 \times 6 \sqrt{5} = 46.8$ ft; $A = 0.5(20 + 44) \times 6 = 192.0$ ft²; $R = 192/46.8 = 4.10$ ft; $D = {}^{192}\!/_{44} = 4.37$ ft; and $Z = 192 \sqrt{4.37} = 401$ ft².⁵.

**2-4. Velocity Distribution in a Channel Section.** Owing to the presence of a free surface and to the friction along the channel wall, the velocities in a channel are not uniformly distributed in the channel section. The measured maximum velocity in ordinary channels usually appears to occur below the free surface at a distance of 0.05 to 0.25 of the depth;

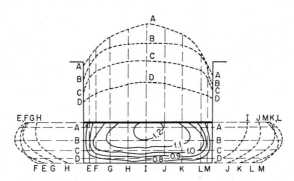

FIG. 2-3. Velocity distribution in a rectangular channel.

the closer to the banks, the deeper is the maximum. Figure 2-3 illustrates the general pattern of velocity distribution over various vertical and horizontal sections of a rectangular channel section and the curves of equal velocity in the cross section. The general patterns for velocity distribution in several channel sections of other shapes are illustrated in Fig. 2-4.

The velocity distribution in a channel section depends also on other factors, such as the unusual shape of the section, the roughness of the

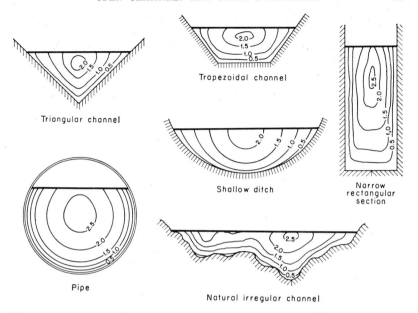

Triangular channel

Trapezoidal channel

Shallow ditch

Narrow rectangular section

Pipe

Natural irregular channel

FIG. 2-4. Typical curves of equal velocity in various channel sections.

channel, and the presence of bends.  In a broad, rapid, and shallow stream or in a very smooth channel, the maximum velocity may often be found at the free surface.  The roughness of the channel will cause the curvature of the vertical-velocity-distribution curve to increase (Fig. 2-5).   On a bend the velocity increases greatly at the convex side, owing to the centrifugal action of the flow.  Contrary to the usual belief, a surface wind has very little effect on velocity distribution.

As revealed by careful laboratory investigations, the flow in a straight prismatic channel is in fact three-dimensional, manifesting a spiral motion, although the velocity component in the transverse channel section is usually small and insignificant compared with the longitudinal velocity components.  Shukry [6] found that, in short labora-

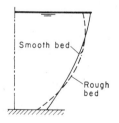

FIG. 2-5. Effect of roughness on velocity distribution in an open channel.

tory flumes, a small disturbance at the entrance, which is usually unavoidable, is sufficient to cause the zone of highest water level to shift to one side, thus giving rise to a single spiral motion (Fig. 2-6).  In a long and uniform reach remote from the entrance, a double spiral motion will occur to permit equalization of shear stresses on both sides of the channel [7,8].

The pattern will include one spiral on each side of the center line, where the water level is the highest. In practical considerations, it is quite safe to ignore the spiral motion in straight prismatic channels. Spiral flow in curved channels, however, is an important phenomenon to be considered in design and will be discussed later (Art. 16-2).

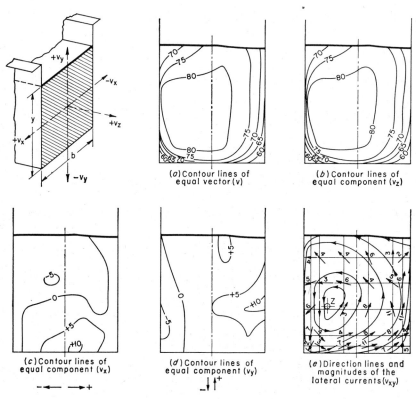

Fig. 2-6. Distribution of the velocity components, facing downstream at the mid-section of a straight flume. Velocities are in cm/sec ($= 0.0328$ fps); $y/b = 1.0$; $R = 73,500$; and $Q = 70$ liters/sec ($= 2.47$ cfs). (*After A. Shukry* [6].)

**2-5. Wide Open Channel.** Observations in very wide open channels have shown that the velocity distribution in the central region of the section is essentially the same as it would be in a rectangular channel of infinite width. In other words, under this condition, the sides of the channel have practically no influence on the velocity distribution in the central region, and the flow in the central region can therefore be regarded as two-dimensional in hydraulic analyses. Careful experiments indicate, further, that this central region exists in rectangular channels only when the width is greater than 5 to 10 times the depth of flow, depending on the condition of surface roughness. Thus, a *wide open channel* can safely be defined as a rectangular channel whose width is greater than 10 times the depth of flow. For either experimental or analytical purposes, the flow in the central region of a wide open channel may be considered to be the same as the flow in a rectangular channel of infinite width.

**2-6. Measurement of Velocity.** According to the stream-gaging procedure of the U.S. Geological Survey,[1] the channel cross section is divided into vertical strips by a number of successive verticals, and mean velocities in verticals are determined by measuring the velocity at 0.6 of the depth in each vertical, or, where more reliable results are required, by taking the average of the velocities at 0.2 and 0.8 of the depth. When the stream is covered with ice, the mean velocity is no longer close to 0.6 of the water depth, but the average at 0.2 and 0.8 of the water depth still gives reliable results. The average of the mean velocities in any two adjacent verticals multiplied by the area between the verticals gives the discharge through this vertical strip of the cross section. The sum of discharges through all strips is the total discharge. The mean velocity of the whole section is, therefore, equal to the total discharge divided by the whole area.

It should be noted that the above methods are simple and approximate. For precise measurements more elaborate methods must be used, which are beyond the scope of this book.

**2-7. Velocity-distribution Coefficients.** As a result of nonuniform distribution of velocities over a channel section, the velocity head of an open-channel flow is generally greater than the value computed according to the expression $V^2/2g$, where $V$ is the mean velocity. When the energy principle is used in computation, the true velocity head may be expressed as $\alpha V^2/2g$, where $\alpha$ is known as the *energy coefficient* or *Coriolis coefficient*, in honor of G. Coriolis [12] who first proposed it. Experimental data indicate that the value of $\alpha$ varies from about 1.03 to 1.36 for fairly straight prismatic channels. The value is generally higher for small channels and lower for large streams of considerable depth.

The nonuniform distribution of velocities also affects the computation of momentum in open-channel flow. From the principle of mechanics, the momentum of the fluid passing through a channel section per unit time is expressed by $\beta w Q V/g$, where $\beta$ is known as the *momentum coefficient* or *Boussinesq coefficient*, after J. Boussinesq [13] who first proposed it; $w$ is the unit weight of water; $Q$ is the discharge; and $V$ is the mean velocity. It is generally found that the value of $\beta$ for fairly straight prismatic channels varies approximately from 1.01 to 1.12.

The two velocity-distribution coefficients are always slightly larger than the limiting value of unity, at which the velocity distribution is

[1] For details see [9] to [11].

strictly uniform across the channel section. For channels of regular cross section and fairly straight alignment, the effect of nonuniform velocity distribution on the computed velocity head and momentum is small, especially in comparison with other uncertainties involved in the computation. Therefore, the coefficients are often assumed to be unity. In channels of complex cross section, the coefficients for energy and momentum can easily be as great as 1.6 and 1.2, respectively, and can vary quite rapidly from section to section in case of irregular alignment. Upstream from weirs, in the vicinity of obstructions, or near pronounced irregularities in alignment, values of $\alpha$ greater than 2.0 have been observed.[1] Precise studies or analyses of flow in such channels will require measurement of the actual velocity and accurate determination of the coefficients. In regard to the effect of channel slope, the coefficients are usually higher in steep channels than in flat channels.

For practical purposes, Kolupaila [16] proposed the values shown below for the velocity-distribution coefficients. Actual values of the coefficients for a number of channels may be found in [17] and [18].

| Channels | Value of $\alpha$ | | | Value of $\beta$ | | |
|---|---|---|---|---|---|---|
| | Min | Av | Max | Min | Av | Max |
| Regular channels, flumes, spillways..... | 1.10 | 1.15 | 1.20 | 1.03 | 1.05 | 1.07 |
| Natural streams and torrents.......... | 1.15 | 1.30 | 1.50 | 1.05 | 1.10 | 1.17 |
| Rivers under ice cover................ | 1.20 | 1.50 | 2.00 | 1.07 | 1.17 | 1.33 |
| River valleys, overflooded............ | 1.50 | 1.75 | 2.00 | 1.17 | 1.25 | 1.33 |

**2-8. Determination of Velocity-distribution Coefficients.** Let $\Delta A$ be an elementary area in the whole water area $A$, and $w$ the unit weight of water; then the weight of water passing $\Delta A$ per unit time with a velocity $v$ is $wv \, \Delta A$. The kinetic energy of water passing $\Delta A$ per unit time is $wv^3 \, \Delta A/2g$. This is equivalent to the product of the weight $wv \, \Delta A$ and the velocity head $v^2/2g$. The total kinetic energy for the whole water area is equal to $\Sigma wv^3 \, \Delta A/2g$.

Now, taking the whole area as $A$, the mean velocity as $V$, and the

---

[1] A value of $\alpha = 2.08$ was computed by Lindquist [14] using data from weir measurements made by Ernest W. Schoder and Kenneth B. Turner.

In the case of closed conduits, much larger values of $\alpha$ have been observed [15]. A value of $\alpha = 3.87$, observed at the outlet section of a draft tube in the Rublevo power plant, is probably the largest known value obtained from actual measurements; the real value there must have been still larger—10.2% more, if the effect of a 15° curvature of the streamlines is taken into account. The largest known value from laboratory measurements is believed to be $\alpha = 7.4$, which was derived by V. S. Kviatkovskii in 1940 in the VIGM (All-Union Institute for Hydraulic Machinery, U.S.S.R.) for the spiral flow under a model turbine wheel.

corrected velocity head for the whole area as $\alpha V^2/2g$, the total kinetic energy is $\alpha w V^3 A/2g$. Equating this quantity with $\Sigma w v^3 \, \Delta A/2g$ and reducing,

$$\alpha = \frac{\int v^3 \, dA}{V^3 A} \approx \frac{\Sigma v^3 \, \Delta A}{V^3 A} \qquad (2\text{-}4)$$

The momentum of water passing $\Delta A$ per unit time is the product of the mass $wv \, \Delta A/g$ and the velocity $v$, or $w v^2 \, \Delta A/g$. The total momentum is $\Sigma w v^2 \, \Delta A/g$. Equating this quantity with the corrected momentum for the whole area, or $\beta w A V^2/g$, and reducing,

$$\beta = \frac{\int v^2 \, dA}{V^2 A} \approx \frac{\Sigma v^2 \, \Delta A}{V^2 A} \qquad (2\text{-}5)$$

O'Brien and Johnson [19] used a graphical solution of the above formulas as follows:

From the measured velocity-distribution curves, the area within each curve of equal velocity is planimetered. Taking the velocity indicated by each equal-velocity curve as $v$, a curve of $v^3$ against the corresponding planimetered area is constructed. It is evident that the area beneath this $v^3$ curve is the integral $\Sigma v^3 \, \Delta A$, which can be obtained by planimetering again. Similarly, integrals $\Sigma v^2 \, \Delta A$ and $\Sigma v \, \Delta A$ can also be obtained. The integral $\Sigma v \, \Delta A$ divided by $A$ gives $V$. With these quantities determined, the above equations can be solved for the coefficients $\alpha$ and $\beta$.

For approximate values, the energy and momentum coefficients can be computed by the following formulas:[1]

$$\alpha = 1 + 3\epsilon^2 - 2\epsilon^3 \qquad (2\text{-}6)$$
$$\beta = 1 + \epsilon^2 \qquad (2\text{-}7)$$

where $\epsilon = v_M/V - 1$, $v_M$ being the maximum velocity and $V$ being the mean velocity.

Computation of the velocity-distribution coefficients for irregular natural channels will be discussed later (Art. 6-5). In most practical problems dealing with regular channels it is not necessary to consider the variation of velocity throughout the cross section, since use of the average velocity will give the accuracy required. The expressions $V^2/2g$ and $wQV/g$ are used extensively in this book with the understanding either that these items have been corrected for the effect of the non-uniform velocity distribution, or that a value of unity is assumed.[2]

[1] These formulas are obtained by assuming a logarithmic distribution of velocity (Art. 8-5, Prob. 8-9). Assuming a linear velocity distribution, Rehbock [20] obtained $\alpha = 1 + \epsilon^2$ and $\beta = 1 + \epsilon^2/3$.

[2] For discussions on this subject, the reader may look into [21] and [22]. However, he should use judgment in reading these references because they contain erroneous

**2-9. Pressure Distribution in a Channel Section.** The pressure at any point on the cross section of the flow in a channel of small slope can be measured by the height of the water column in a piezometer tube installed at the point (Fig. 2-7). Ignoring minor disturbances due to turbulence, etc., it is apparent that this water column should rise from the point of measurement up to the hydraulic grade line or the water surface. Therefore, the pressure at any point on the section is directly proportional to the depth of the point below the free surface and equal to the hydrostatic pressure corresponding to this depth. In other words, the distribution of pressure over the cross section of the channel is the same as the distribution of hydrostatic pressure; that is, the distribution is linear and can be represented by a straight line $AB$ (Fig. 2-7a). This is known as the *hydrostatic law of pressure distribution.*

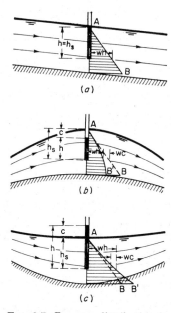

Fig. 2-7. Pressure distribution in straight and curved channels of small or horizontal slope at the section under consideration. $h$ = piezometric head; $h_s$ = hydrostatic head; and $c$ = pressure-head correction for curvature. (a) Parallel flow; (b) convex flow; (c) concave flow.

Strictly speaking, the application of the hydrostatic law to the pressure distribution in the cross section of a flowing channel is valid only if the flow filaments have no acceleration components in the plane of cross section. This type of flow is theoretically known as *parallel flow,*[1] that is, such that the streamlines have neither substantial curvature nor divergence. Consequently, there are no appreciable acceleration components normal to the direction of flow that would disturb the hydrostatic-pressure distribution in the cross section of a parallel flow.

---

statements. Some authors have proposed the use of the momentum coefficient to replace the energy coefficient even in computations based on the energy principle. This is not correct. Whether the energy coefficient or the momentum coefficient is to be used depends on whether the energy or the momentum principle is involved. The two coefficients are derived independently from basically different principles (Art. 3-6). Neither of them is wrong and neither can be replaced by the other; both should be used in the correct sense.

[1] Specific qualifications for parallel flow were clearly stated for the first time by Bélanger [23].

In actual problems uniform flow is practically parallel flow.   Gradually varied flow may also be regarded as parallel flow, since the change in depth of flow is so mild that the streamlines have neither appreciable curvature nor divergence; that is, the curvature and divergence are so small that the effect of the acceleration components in the cross-sectional plane is negligible.   *For practical purposes, therefore, the hydrostatic law of pressure distribution is applicable to gradually varied flow as well as to uniform flow.*

If the curvature of streamlines is substantial, the flow is theoretically known as *curvilinear flow*.   The effect of the curvature is to produce appreciable acceleration components or centrifugal forces normal to the direction of flow.   Thus, the pressure distribution over the section deviates from the hydrostatic if curvilinear flow occurs in the vertical plane.   Such curvilinear flow may be either convex or concave (Fig. 2-7b and c).   In both cases the nonlinear pressure distribution is represented by $AB'$ instead of the straight distribution $AB$ that would occur if the flow were parallel. It is assumed that all streamlines are horizontal at the section under consideration.   In concave flow the centrifugal forces are pointing downward to reinforce the gravity action; so the resulting pressure is greater than the otherwise hydrostatic pressure of a parallel flow.   In convex flow the centrifugal forces are acting upward against the gravity action; consequently, the resulting pressure is less than the otherwise hydrostatic pressure of a parallel flow.   Similarly, when divergence of streamlines is great enough to develop appreciable acceleration components normal to the flow, the hydrostatic pressure distribution will be disturbed accordingly.

Let the deviation from an otherwise hydrostatic pressure $h_s$ in a curvilinear flow be designated by $c$ (Fig. 2-7b and c).   Then the true pressure or the piezometric height $h = h_s + c$.

If the channel has a curved longitudinal profile, the approximate centrifugal pressure may be computed, by Newton's law of acceleration, as the product of the mass of water having height $d$ and a cross section of 1 sq ft, that is, $wd/g$, and the centrifugal acceleration $v^2/r$; or

$$P = \frac{wd}{g} \frac{v^2}{r} \qquad (2\text{-}8)$$

where $w$ is the unit weight of water, $g$ is the gravitational acceleration, $v$ is the velocity of flow, and $r$ is the radius of curvature.   The pressure-head correction is, therefore,

$$c = \frac{d}{g} \frac{v^2}{r} \qquad (2\text{-}9)$$

For computing the value of $c$ at the channel bottom, $r$ is the radius of curvature of the bottom, $d$ is the depth of flow, and for practical purposes

$v$ may be assumed equal to the average velocity of the flow. Apparently, $c$ is positive for concave flow, negative for convex flow, and zero for parallel flow.

In parallel flow the pressure is hydrostatic, and the pressure head may be represented by the depth of flow $y$. For simplicity, the pressure head of a curvilinear flow may be represented by $\alpha'y$, where $\alpha'$ is a correction coefficient for the curvature effect. The correction coefficient is referred to as a *pressure-distribution coefficient*. Since this coefficient is applied to a pressure head, it may be specifically called a *pressure coefficient*. It can be shown that the pressure coefficient is expressed by

$$\alpha' = \frac{1}{Qy} \int_0^A hv \, dA = 1 + \frac{1}{Qy} \int_0^A cv \, dA \qquad (2\text{-}10)$$

where $Q$ is the total discharge and $y$ is the depth of flow. It can easily be seen that $\alpha'$ is greater than 1.0 for concave flow, less than 1.0 for convex flow, and equal to 1.0 for parallel flow.

For complicated curved profiles, the total pressure distribution can be determined approximately by the flow-net method or more exactly by model testing.

In rapidly varied flow the change in depth of flow is so rapid and abrupt that the streamlines possess substantial curvature and divergence. Consequently, *the hydrostatic law of pressure distribution does not hold strictly for rapidly varied flow.*

It should be noted at the outset that throughout this book flow is treated in general as either parallel or gradually varied. Therefore, the effect of the curvature of streamlines will not be considered (that is, it will be assumed that $\alpha' = 1$) unless the flow is specifically described as either curvilinear or rapidly varied.

**2-10. Effect of Slope on Pressure Distribution.** With reference to a straight sloping channel of unit width and slope angle $\theta$ (Fig. 2-8), the weight of the shaded water element of length $dL$ is equal to $wy \cos \theta \, dL$. The pressure due to this weight is $wy \cos^2 \theta \, dL$. The unit pressure is, therefore, equal to $wy \cos^2 \theta$, and the head[1] is

$$h = y \cos^2 \theta \qquad (2\text{-}11)$$
or
$$h = d \cos \theta \qquad (2\text{-}12)$$

where $d = y \cos \theta$, the depth measured perpendicularly from the water surface. It should be noted from geometry (Fig. 9-1) that Eq. (2-11) does not apply strictly to varied flow, particularly when $\theta$ is very large, whereas Eq. (2-12) still applies. Equation (2-11) states that the pres-

[1] M. Hasumi has measured the distribution of pressure along the sloping faces of weirs [24]. The data obtained from these experiments have verified Eqs. (2-11) and (2-12) very satisfactorily [25].

sure head at any vertical depth is equal to this depth multiplied by a correction factor $\cos^2 \theta$. Apparently, if the angle $\theta$ is small, this factor will not differ appreciably from unity. In fact, the correction tends to decrease the pressure head by an amount less than 1% until $\theta$ is nearly 6°, a slope of about 1 in 10. Since the slope of ordinary channels is far less than 1 in 10, the correction for slope effect can usually be safely ignored. However, when the channel slope is large and its effect becomes appreciable, the correction should be made if accurate computation is

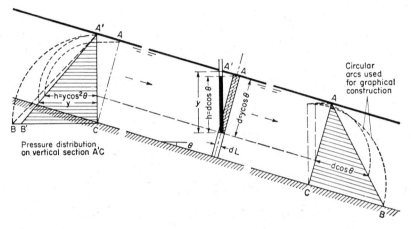

FIG. 2-8. Pressure distribution in parallel flow in channels of large slope.

desired. A channel of this type, say, with a slope greater than 1 in 10, is hereafter called a *channel of large slope*. Unless specifically mentioned, all channels described hereafter are considered to be *channels of small slope*, where the slope effect is negligible.

If a channel of large slope has a longitudinal vertical profile of appreciable curvature, the pressure head should be corrected for the effect of the curvature of streamlines (Fig. 2-9). In simple notation, the pressure head may be expressed as $\alpha' y \cos^2 \theta$, where $\alpha'$ is the pressure coefficient.

In channels of large slope the velocity of flow is usually high, and higher than the critical velocity. When this velocity reaches a certain magnitude, the flowing water will entrain air, producing a swell in its volume and an increase in depth.[1] For this reason the pressure computed by Eq. (2-11) or (2-12) has been shown in several cases to be higher than the

[1] Air becomes entrained in water generally at velocities of about 20 fps and higher. Besides velocity, however, other factors such as entrance condition, channel roughness, distance traveled, channel cross section, volume of discharge, etc., all have some bearing on air entrainment.

actual measured pressure obtained by model testing. If the average density of the air-water mixture is known, it should be used to replace the density of pure water in the computation when air entrainment is expected. The actual density of the mixture varies from the bottom to the surface of the flow. For practical purposes, however, the density may be assumed constant; this assumption of uniform air distribution in

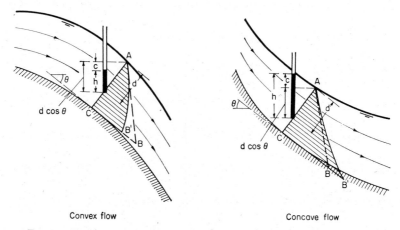

Convex flow    Concave flow

Fig. 2-9. Pressure distribution in curvilinear flow in channels of large slope.

the cross section will simplify computation, with the errors on the safe side.

## PROBLEMS

**2-1.** Verify the formulas for geometric elements of the seven channel sections given in Table 2-1.

**2-2.** Verify the curves shown in Fig. 2-1.

**2-3.** Construct curves similar to those shown in Fig. 2-1, for a square channel section.

**2-4.** Construct curves similar to those shown in Fig. 2-1 for an equilateral triangle with one side as the channel bottom.

**2-5.** From the data given below on the cross section[1] of a natural stream (a) con-

---

[1] It is common practice to show the cross section of a stream in a direction looking downstream and to prepare the longitudinal profile of a channel so that the water flows from left to right, unless this arrangement would fail to show the feature to be illustrated by the cross section and profile. This practice is generally followed by most engineering offices. However, for geographical reasons or in order to depict clearly the location and profile of a stream, the profile may be shown with water flowing from right to left and the cross section may be shown looking upstream. This happens in many drawings prepared by the Tennessee Valley Authority, because the Tennessee River and most of its tributaries flow from east to west, and so are shown with the direction of flow from right to left on a conventional map.

struct curves showing the relationships between the depth $y$ and the section elements $A$, $R$, $D$, and $Z$; and (b) determine from the curves the geometric elements for $y = 4$.

| Distance from a reference point near left bank, ft | Stage, ft | Distance from a reference point near left bank, ft | Stage, ft |
|---|---|---|---|
| Left bank:  −5 | 5.6 | 7 | −0.1 |
| −4 | 4.6 | 9 | −0.1 |
| −2 | 4.0 | 11 | −0.4 |
| 0 | 1.9 | 13 | −0.1 |
| 1 | 0.8 | 15 | 0.7 |
| 2 | 0.2 | 17 | 2.6 |
| 3 | 0.3 | 19 | 3.2 |
| 5 | 0.2 | Right bank:  20 | 4.1 |

**2-6.** The hydrostatic catenary may be plotted for any given depth $y$ and slope angle $\theta_0$ at its ends by the following two approximate equations:

$$x_1 = \frac{y}{2k} [(1 - \tfrac{3}{4}k^2 - \tfrac{15}{64}k^4)\phi + (\tfrac{3}{8}k^2 + \tfrac{5}{32}k^4) \sin 2\phi - \tfrac{5}{256}k^4 \sin 4\phi] \qquad (2\text{-}13)$$

$$y_1 = y \cos \phi \qquad (2\text{-}14)$$

where $x_1$ and $y_1$, respectively, are the ordinate and abscissa measured from the midpoint of the free surface; $k = \sin (\theta_0/2)$; $\phi = \sin^{-1} \{[\sin (\phi/2)]/k\}$; and $\theta$ is the slope angle at the point $(x_1, y_1)$, varying from 0 at the bottom of the curve to $\theta_0$ at the ends. The above equations will define the cross section when the flow is at its full depth. The slope angle at the ends of a hydrostatic catenary of best hydraulic efficiency is found mathematically to be $\theta_0 = 35°37'7''$. (a) Plot this section with a depth $y = 10$ ft, and (b) determine the values of $A$, $R$, $D$, and $Z$ at the full depth.

**2-7.** Estimate the values of momentum coefficient $\beta$ for the given values of energy coefficient $\alpha = 1.00$, 1.50, and 2.00.

**2-8.** Compute the energy and momentum coefficients of the cross section shown in Fig. 2-3 (a) by Eqs. (2-4) and (2-5), and (b) by Eqs. (2-6) and (2-7). The cross section and the curves of equal velocity can be transferred to a piece of drawing paper and enlarged for desired accuracy.

**2-9.** In designing side walls of steep chutes and overflow spillways, prove that the overturning moment due to the pressure of the flowing water is equal to $\tfrac{1}{6}wy^3 \cos^4 \theta$, where $w$ is the unit weight of water, $y$ is the vertical depth of the flowing water, and $\theta$ is the slope angle of the channel.

**2-10.** Prove Eq. (2-10).

**2-11.** A high-head overflow spillway (Fig. 2-10) has a 60-ft-radius flip bucket at its downstream end. The bucket is not submerged, but acts to change the direction of the flow from the slope of the spillway face to the horizontal and to discharge the flow into the air between vertical training walls 80 ft apart. At a discharge of 56,100 cfs, the water surface at the vertical section $OB$ is at El. 8.52. Verify the curve that represents the computed hydraulic pressure acting on the training wall at section $OB$. The computation is based on Eq. (2-9) and on the following assumptions: (1) the velocity is uniformly distributed across the section; (2) the value used for $r$, for pressure values near the wall base, is equal to the radius of the bucket but, for other pressure values, is equal to the radius of the concentric flow lines; and (3) the flow is entrained with air, and the density of the air-water mixture can be estimated by the

Douma formula,[1] that is,

$$u = 10 \sqrt{\frac{0.2V^2}{gR} - 1} \tag{2-15}$$

where $u$ is the percentage of entrained air by volume, $V$ is the velocity of flow, and $R$ is the hydraulic radius.

**2-12.** Compute the wall pressure on the section $OA$ (Fig. 2-10) of the spillway described in Prob. 2-11. It is assumed that the depth of flow section is the same as that at section $OB$.

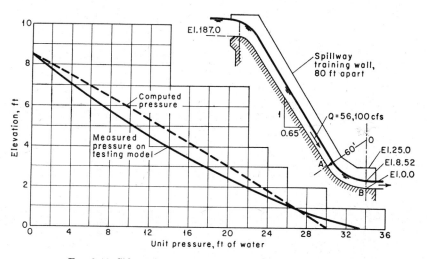

Fig. 2-10. Side-wall pressures on the flip bucket of a spillway.

**2-13.** Compute the wall pressure on the section $OA$ (Fig. 2-10) of the spillway described in Prob. 2-11 if the bucket is submerged with a tailwater level at El. 75.0. It is assumed that the pressure resulting from the centrifugal force of the submerged jet need not be considered because the submergence will result in a severe reduction in velocity.

**REFERENCES**

1. S. F. Averianov: O gidravlicheskom raschete rusel krivolineĭnoĭ formy poperechnogo secheniia (Hydraulic design of channels with curvilinear form of the cross section), *Izvestiia Akademii Nauk S.S.S.R., Otdelenie Tekhnicheskikh Nauk,* Moscow, no. 1, pp. 54–58, 1956.
2. Leonard Metcalf and H. P. Eddy: "American Sewerage Practice," McGraw-Hill Book Company, Inc., New York, 3d ed., 1935, vol. I.
3. Harold E. Babbitt: "Sewerage and Sewage Treatment," John Wiley & Sons, Inc., New York, 7th ed., 1952, pp. 60–66.
4. H. M. Gibb: Curves for solving the hydrostatic catenary, *Engineering News,* vol. 73, no. 14, pp. 668–670, Apr. 8, 1915.

[1] This formula [26] is based on data obtained from actual concrete and wooden chutes, involving errors of $\pm 10\%$.

5. George Higgins: "Water Channels," Crosby, Lockwood & Son Ltd., London, 1927, pp. 15–36.

6. Ahmed Shukry: Flow around bends in an open flume, *Transactions, American Society of Civil Engineers*, vol. 115, pp. 751–779, 1950.

7. A. H. Gibson: "Hydraulics and Its Applications," Constable & Co., Ltd., London, 4th ed., 1934, p. 332.

8. J. R. Freeman: "Hydraulic Laboratory Practice," American Society of Mechanical Engineers, New York, 1929, p. 70.

9. Don M. Corbett and others: Stream-gaging procedure, *U.S. Geological Survey, Water Supply Paper* 888, 1943.

10. N. C. Grover and A. W. Harrington: "Stream Flow," John Wiley & Sons, Inc., New York, 1943.

11. Standards for methods and records of hydrologic measurements, *United Nations Economic Commission for Asia and the Far East, Flood Control Series, No.* 6, Bangkok, 1954, pp. 26–30.

12. G. Coriolis: Sur l'établissement de la formule qui donne la figure des remous, et sur la correction qu'on doit y introduire pour tenir compte des différences de vitesse dans les divers points d'une même section d'un courant (On the backwater-curve equation and the corrections to be introduced to account for the difference of the velocities at different points on the same cross section), *Mémoire No.* 268, *Annales des ponts et chaussées*, vol. 11, ser. 1, pp. 314–335, 1836.

13. J. Boussinesq: Essai sur la théorie des eaux courantes (On the theory of flowing waters), *Mémoires présentés par divers savants à l'Académie des Sciences*, Paris, 1877.

14. Erik G. W. Lindquist: Discussion on Precise weir measurements, by Ernest W. Schoder and Kenneth B. Turner, *Transactions, American Society of Civil Engineers*, vol. 93, pp. 1163–1176, 1929.

15. N. M. Shchapov: "Gidrometriia Gidrotekhnicheskikh Sooruzhenii i Gidromashin" ("Hydrometry of Hydraulic Structures and Machinery"), Gosenergoizdat, Moscow, 1957, p. 88.

16. Steponas Kolupaila: Methods of determination of the kinetic energy factor, *The Port Engineer*, Calcutta, India, vol. 5, no. 1, pp. 12–18, January, 1956.

17. M. P. O'Brien and G. H. Hickox: "Applied Fluid Mechanics," McGraw-Hill Book Company, Inc., New York, 1st ed., 1937, p. 272.

18. Horace William King: "Handbook of Hydraulics," 4th ed., revised by Ernest F. Brater, McGraw-Hill Book Company, Inc., New York, 1954, p. 7-12.

19. Morrough P. O'Brien and Joe W. Johnson: Velocity-head correction for hydraulic flow, *Engineering News-Record*, vol. 113, no. 7, pp. 214–216, Aug. 16, 1934.

20. Th. Rehbock: Die Bestimmung der Lage der Energielinie bei fliessenden Gewässern mit Hilfe des Geschwindigkeitshöhen-Ausgleichwertes (The determination of the position of the energy line in flowing water with the aid of velocity-head adjustment), *Der Bauingenieur*, Berlin, vol. 3, no. 15, pp. 453–455, Aug. 15, 1922.

21. Boris A. Bakhmeteff: Coriolis and the energy principle in hydraulics, in "Theodore von Kármán Anniversary Volume," California Institute of Technology, Pasadena, 1941, pp. 59–65.

22. W. S. Eisenlohr: Coefficients for velocity distribution in open-channel flow, *Transactions, American Society of Civil Engineers*, vol. 110, pp. 633–644, 1945. Discussions, pp. 645–668.

23. J. B. Bélanger: "Essai sur la solution numérique de quelques problèmes relatifs au mouvement permanent des eaux courantes" ("Essay on the Numerical Solution of Some Problems Relative to Steady Flow of Water"), Carilian-Goeury, Paris, 1828, pp. 10–24.

24. R. Ehrenberger: Versuche über die Verteilung der Drücke an Wehrrücken infolge des abstürzenden Wassers (Experiments on the distribution of pressures along the face of weirs resulting from the impact of the falling water), *Die Wasserwirtschaft,* Vienna, vol. 22, no. 5, pp. 65–72, 1929.

25. Harald Lauffer: Druck, Energie und Fliesszustand in Gerinnen mit grossem Gefälle (Pressure, energy, and flow type in channels with high gradients), *Wasserkraft und Wasserwirtschaft,* Munich, vol. 30, no. 7, pp. 78–82, 1935.

26. J. H. Douma: Discussion on Open channel flow at high velocities, by L. Standish Hall, in Entrainment of air in flowing water: a symposium, *Transactions, American Society of Civil Engineers,* vol. 108, pp. 1462–1473, 1943.

# CHAPTER 3

# ENERGY AND MOMENTUM PRINCIPLES

**3-1. Energy in Open-channel Flow.** It is known in elementary hydraulics that the total energy in foot-pounds per pound of water in any streamline passing through a channel section may be expressed as the total head in feet of water, which is equal to the sum of the elevation

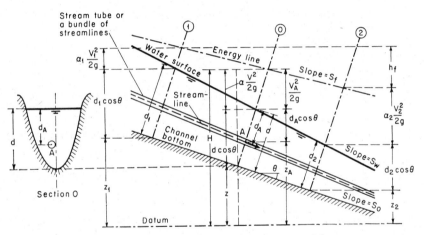

Fig. 3-1. Energy in gradually varied open-channel flow.

above a datum, the pressure head, and the velocity head. For example, with respect to the datum plane, the total head $H$ at a section $O$ containing point $A$ on a streamline of flow in a channel of large slope (Fig. 3-1) may be written

$$H = z_A + d_A \cos \theta + \frac{V_A{}^2}{2g} \qquad (3\text{-}1)$$

where $z_A$ is the elevation of point $A$ above the datum plane, $d_A$ is the depth of point $A$ below the water surface measured along the channel section, $\theta$ is the slope angle of the channel bottom, and $V_A{}^2/2g$ is the velocity head of the flow in the streamline passing through $A$.

In general, every streamline passing through a channel section will have a different velocity head, owing to the nonuniform velocity distribution in actual flow. Only in an ideal parallel flow of uniform velocity distribution can the velocity head be truly identical for all points on the cross section. In the case of gradually varied flow, however, it may be assumed, for practical purposes, that the velocity heads for all points on the channel section are equal, and the energy coefficient may be used to correct for the over-all effect of the nonuniform velocity distribution. Thus, the total energy at the channel section is

$$H = z + d \cos \theta + \alpha \frac{V^2}{2g} \tag{3-2}$$

For channels of small slope, $\theta \approx 0$. Thus, the total energy at the channel section is

$$H = z + d + \alpha \frac{V^2}{2g} \tag{3-3}$$

Consider now a prismatic channel of large slope (Fig. 3-1). The line representing the elevation of the total head of flow is the energy line. The slope of the line is known as the *energy gradient*, denoted by $S_f$. The slope of the water surface is denoted by $S_w$ and the slope of the channel bottom[1] by $S_0 = \sin \theta$. In uniform flow, $S_f = S_w = S_0 = \sin \theta$.

According to the principle of conservation of energy, the total energy head at the upstream section 1 should be equal to the total energy head at the downstream section 2 plus the loss of energy $h_f$ between the two sections; or

$$z_1 + d_1 \cos \theta + \alpha_1 \frac{V_1^2}{2g} = z_2 + d_2 \cos \theta + \alpha_2 \frac{V_2^2}{2g} + h_f \tag{3-4}$$

This equation applies to parallel or gradually varied flow. For a channel of small slope, it becomes

$$z_1 + y_1 + \alpha_1 \frac{V_1^2}{2g} = z_2 + y_2 + \alpha_2 \frac{V_2^2}{2g} + h_f \tag{3-5}$$

Either of these two equations is known as the *energy equation*. When $\alpha_1 = \alpha_2 = 1$ and $h_f = 0$, Eq. (3-5) becomes

$$z_1 + y_1 + \frac{V_1^2}{2g} = z_2 + y_2 + \frac{V_2^2}{2g} = \text{const} \tag{3-6}$$

This is the well-known *Bernoulli energy equation*.[2]

---

[1] The slope is generally defined as $\tan \theta$. For the present purpose, however, it is defined as $\sin \theta$.

[2] It is believed that this equation is ascribed to the Swiss mathematician Daniel Bernoulli only by inference, to give recognition to his pioneer achievement in hydrodynamics, in particular the introduction of the concept of "head." Actually, this equation was first formulated by Leonhard Euler and later popularized by Julius Weisbach [1].

**3-2. Specific Energy.** *Specific energy*[1] in a channel section is defined as the energy per pound of water at any section of a channel measured with respect to the channel bottom. Thus, according to Eq. (3-2) with $z = 0$, the specific energy becomes

$$E = d \cos \theta + \alpha \frac{V^2}{2g} \tag{3-7}$$

or, for a channel of small slope and $\alpha = 1$,

$$E = y + \frac{V^2}{2g} \tag{3-8}$$

which indicates that the specific energy is equal to the sum of the depth of water and the velocity head. For simplicity, the following discussion will be based on Eq. (3-8) for a channel of small slope. Since $V = Q/A$, Eq. (3-8) may be written $E = y + Q^2/2gA^2$. It can be seen that, for a given channel section and discharge $Q$, the specific energy in a channel section is a function of the depth of flow only.

When the depth of flow is plotted against the specific energy for a given channel section and discharge, a *specific-energy curve* (Fig. 3-2) is obtained. This curve has two limbs $AC$ and $BC$. The limb $AC$ approaches the horizontal axis asymptotically toward the right. The limb $BC$ approaches the line $OD$ as it extends upward and to the right. Line $OD$ is a line that passes through the origin and has an angle of inclination equal to 45°. For a channel of large slope, the angle of inclination of the line $OD$ will be different from 45°. (Why?) At any point $P$ on this curve, the ordinate represents the depth, and the abscissa represents the specific energy, which is equal to the sum of the pressure head $y$ and the velocity head $V^2/2g$.

The curve shows that, for a given specific energy, there are two possible depths, for instance, the *low stage* $y_1$ and the *high stage* $y_2$. The low stage is called the *alternate depth* of the high stage, and vice versa. At point $C$, the specific energy is a minimum. It will be proved later that this condition of minimum specific energy corresponds to the critical state of flow. Thus, at the critical state the two alternate depths apparently become one, which is known as the *critical depth* $y_c$. When the depth of flow is greater than the critical depth, the velocity of flow is less than the critical velocity for the given discharge, and, hence, the flow is subcritical. When the depth of flow is less than the critical depth, the flow is supercritical. Hence, $y_1$ is the depth of a supercritical flow, and $y_2$ is the depth of a subcritical flow.

If the discharge changes, the specific energy will be changed accordingly. The two curves $A'B'$ and $A''B''$ (Fig. 3-2) represent positions of

[1] The concept of specific energy was first introduced by Bakhmeteff [2] in 1912.

the specific-energy curve when the discharge is less and greater, respectively, than the discharge used for the construction of the curve $AB$.

**3-3. Criterion for a Critical State of Flow.** The critical state of flow has been defined (Art. 1-3) as the condition for which the Froude number is equal to unity. A more common definition is that it is the state of flow at which the specific energy is a minimum for a given discharge.[1] A

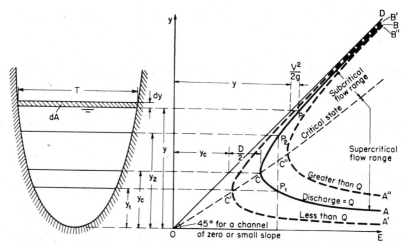

FIG. 3-2. Specific-energy curve.

theoretical criterion for critical flow may be developed from this definition as follows:

Since $V = Q/A$, Eq. (3-8), the equation for specific energy in a channel of small slope with $\alpha = 1$, may be written

$$E = y + \frac{Q^2}{2gA^2} \tag{3-9}$$

Differentiating with respect to $y$ and noting that $Q$ is a constant,

$$\frac{dE}{dy} = 1 - \frac{Q^2}{gA^3}\frac{dA}{dy} = 1 - \frac{V^2}{gA}\frac{dA}{dy}$$

The differential water area $dA$ near the free surface (Fig. 3-2) is equal to $T\,dy$. Now $dA/dy = T$, and the hydraulic depth $D = A/T$; so the above equation becomes

$$\frac{dE}{dy} = 1 - \frac{V^2 T}{gA} = 1 - \frac{V^2}{gD}$$

---

[1] The concept of critical depth based on the theorem of minimum energy was first introduced by Böss [3].

At the critical state of flow the specific energy is a minimum, or $dE/dy = 0$. The above equation, therefore, gives

$$\frac{V^2}{2g} = \frac{D}{2} \qquad (3\text{-}10)$$

This is the criterion for critical flow, which states that *at the critical state of flow, the velocity head is equal to half the hydraulic depth.* The above equation may also be written $V/\sqrt{gD} = 1$, which means $\mathbf{F} = 1$; this is the definition of critical flow given previously (Art. 1-3).

If the above criterion is to be used in any problem, the following conditions must be satisfied: (1) flow parallel or gradually varied, (2) channel of small slope, and (3) energy coefficient assumed to be unity. If the energy coefficient is not assumed to be unity, the critical-flow criterion is

$$\alpha \frac{V^2}{2g} = \frac{D}{2} \qquad (3\text{-}11)$$

For a channel of large slope angle $\theta$ and energy coefficient $\alpha$, the criterion for critical flow can easily be proved to be

$$\alpha \frac{V^2}{2g} = \frac{D \cos \theta}{2} \qquad (3\text{-}12)$$

where $D$ is the hydraulic depth of the water area normal to the channel bottom. In this case, the Froude number may be defined as

$$\mathbf{F} = \frac{V}{\sqrt{gD \cos \theta / \alpha}} \qquad (3\text{-}13)$$

It should be noted that the coefficient $\alpha$ of a channel section actually varies with depth. In the above derivation, however, the coefficient is assumed to be constant; therefore, the resulting equation is not absolutely exact.

**3-4. Interpretation of Local Phenomena.** Change of the state of flow from subcritical to supercritical or vice versa occurs frequently in open channels. Such change is manifested in a corresponding change in the depth of flow from a high stage to a low stage or vice versa. If the change takes place rapidly over a relatively short distance, the flow is rapidly varied, and is known as a *local phenomenon.* The hydraulic drop and hydraulic jump are the two types of local phenomena, and may be described as follows:

*Hydraulic Drop.* A rapid change in the depth of flow from a high stage to a low stage will result in a steep depression in the water surface. Such a phenomenon is generally caused by an abrupt change in the channel slope or cross section and is known as a *hydraulic drop* (Fig. 1-2). At the transitory region of the hydraulic drop a reverse curve usually appears, connecting the water surfaces before and after the drop. The point of inflection on the reverse curve marks the approximate position of the critical depth at which the specific energy is a minimum and the flow passes from a subcritical state to a supercritical state.

The *free overfall* (Fig. 3-3) is a special case of the hydraulic drop. It occurs where the bottom of a flat channel is discontinued. As the free overfall enters the air in the form of a nappe, there will be no reverse curve in the water surface until it strikes some object at a lower elevation. It is the law of nature that, if no energy were added from the outside, the

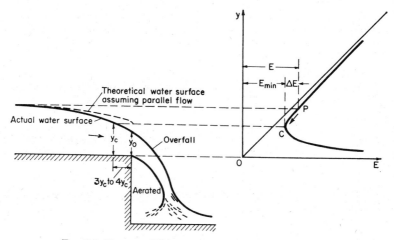

FIG. 3-3. Free overfall interpreted by specific-energy curve.

water surface would seek its lowest possible position corresponding to the least possible content of energy dissipation. If the specific energy at an upstream section is $E$, as shown on the specific-energy curve, it will continue to be dissipated on the way downstream and will finally reach a minimum energy content $E_{min}$. The specific-energy curve shows that the section of minimum energy or the critical section should occur at the brink. The brink depth cannot be less than the critical depth because further decrease in depth would require an increase in specific energy, which is impossible unless compensating external energy is supplied. The theoretical water-surface curve of an overfall is shown with a dashed line in Fig. 3-3.

It should be remembered that the determination of critical depth by Eq. (3-10) or (3-11) is based on the assumption of parallel flow and is applicable only approximately to gradually varied flow. The flow at the brink is actually curvilinear, for the curvature of flow is pronounced; hence, the method is invalid for determining the critical depth as the

depth at the brink.   The actual situation is that the brink section is the
*true* section of minimum energy, but it is not the critical section as computed by the principle based on the parallel-flow assumption.   Rouse [4]
found that for small slopes the computed critical depth is about 1.4 times
the brink depth, or $y_c = 1.4y_0$, and that it is located about $3y_c$ to $4y_c$
behind the brink in the channel.   The actual water surface of the overfall is shown by the full line (Fig. 3-3).

It should be noted that, if the change in the depth of flow from a high
stage to a low stage is gradual, the flow becomes a gradually varied flow

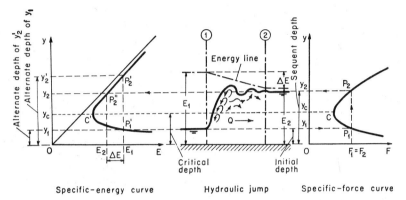

Specific-energy curve          Hydraulic jump          Specific-force curve

Fig. 3-4. Hydraulic jump interpreted by specific-energy and specific-force curves.

having a prolonged reversed curve of water surface; this phenomenon may
be called a *gradual hydraulic drop* and is no longer a local phenomenon.

*Hydraulic Jump.*   When the rapid change in the depth of flow is from
a low stage to a high stage, the result is usually an abrupt rise of water
surface (Fig. 3-4, in which the vertical scale is exaggerated).   This local
phenomenon is known as the *hydraulic jump*.   It occurs frequently in a
canal below a regulating sluice, at the foot of a spillway, or at the place
where a steep channel slope suddenly turns flat.

If the jump is low, that is, if the change in depth is small, the water will
not rise obviously and abruptly but will pass from the low to the high
stage through a series of undulations gradually diminishing in size.
Such a low jump is called an *undular jump.*

When the jump is high, that is, when the change in depth is great, the
jump is called a *direct jump.*   The direct jump involves a relatively large
amount of energy loss through dissipation in the turbulent body of water
in the jump.   Consequently, the energy content in the flow after the
jump is appreciably less than that before the jump.

It may be noted that the depth before the jump is always less than the depth after the jump.    The depth before the jump is called the *initial depth* $y_1$ and that after the jump is called the *sequent depth* $y_2$.    The initial and sequent depths $y_1$ and $y_2$ are shown on the specific-energy curve (Fig. 3-4).    They should be distinguished from the alternate depths $y_1$ and $y_2'$, which are the two possible depths for the same specific energy. The initial and sequent depths are actual depths before and after a jump in which an energy loss $\Delta E$ is involved.    In other words, the specific energy $E_1$ at the initial depth $y_1$ is greater than the specific energy $E_2$ at the sequent depth $y_2$ by an amount equal to the energy loss $\Delta E$.    If there were no energy losses, the initial and sequent depths would become identical with the alternate depths in a prismatic channel.

**3-5. Energy in Nonprismatic Channels.**    In preceding discussions the channel has been assumed prismatic so that one specific-energy curve could be applied to all sections of the channel.    For nonprismatic channels, however, the channel section varies along the length of the channel and, hence, the specific-energy curve differs from section to section.    This complication can be seen in a three-dimensional plot of the energy curves along the given reach of a nonprismatic channel.

For demonstrative purposes, a nonprismatic channel with variable slope is taken as an example, in which a gradually varied flow is carried from a subcritical state to a supercritical state (Fig. 3-5).    The vertical profile of the channel along its center line is plotted on the $Hx$ plane with the $x$ axis chosen as the datum.    For a variable-slope channel, it is more convenient to plot the total energy head $H = z + y + V^2/2g$, instead of the specific energy, against the depth of flow on the $Hy$ plane.    For simplicity, the pressure correction due to the slope angle and curvature of flow is ignored in this discussion.    An energy line is then plotted on the $Hx$ plane below a line parallel to the $x$ axis and passing through the initial total head at the $H$ axis.    The exact position of the energy line depends on the energy losses along the channel.    Four channel sections are then selected, and four energy curves for these sections are plotted in the $Hy$ planes, as shown.    The initial section 0 is an upstream section in the subcritical-flow region.    The two depths corresponding to a given total energy $H_0$ can be obtained from the energy curve.    Since this section is in the subcritical-flow region, the high stage $y_0$ should be the actual depth of flow, whereas the low stage is the alternate depth.    Similarly, the alternate depths in other sections can be obtained.    In the downstream sections 1 and 2, the low stages $y_1$ and $y_2$ are the actual depths of flow since they are in the supercritical-flow region.    The critical depth at each section can also be obtained from the energy curve at the point of minimum energy.    At section $C$ the critical flow occurs, and the depth $y_c$ is the critical depth.    On the $Hx$ plane, various lines can finally be plotted, showing the channel bottom, water surface, critical-depth line, and alternate-depth line. At the critical section, it is noted that the three lines, namely, the water surface, the critical-depth line, and the alternate-depth line, intersect at a single point. It is seen that, in passing through the critical section, the water surface enters the supercritical-flow region smoothly.

The three-dimensional plot of energy curves is complicated. The description given here is used only for helping the reader to visualize the problem. In actual applications, the energy curves may be constructed

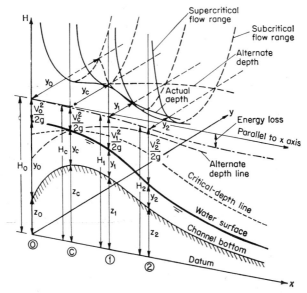

FIG. 3-5. Energy in a nonprismatic channel of variable-slope, carrying gradually varied flow from subcritical to supercritical state.

separately on a number of two-dimensional $Hy$ planes for the chosen sections. The data obtained from these curves are then used to plot the water surface, critical-depth line, and alternate-depth line on a two-dimensional $Hx$ plane. For simple channels, the energy curves are not necessary because the critical depth and alternate depths can easily be computed directly.

**Example 3-1.** A rectangular channel 10 ft wide is narrowed down to 8 ft by a contraction 50 ft long, built of straight walls and a horizontal floor. If the discharge is 100 cfs and the depth of flow is 5 ft on the upstream side of the transition section, determine the flow-surface profile in the contraction (*a*) allowing no gradual hydraulic drop in the contraction, and (*b*) allowing a gradual hydraulic drop having its point of inflection at the mid-section of the contraction. The frictional loss through the contraction is negligible.

*Solution.* From the given data, the total energy in the approaching flow measured above the channel bottom is $E = 5 + [100/(5 \times 10)]^2/2g = 5.062$ ft. This energy is kept constant throughout the contraction, since energy losses are negligible. A horizontal energy line showing the elevation of the total head is, therefore, drawn on the channel profile (Fig. 3-6).

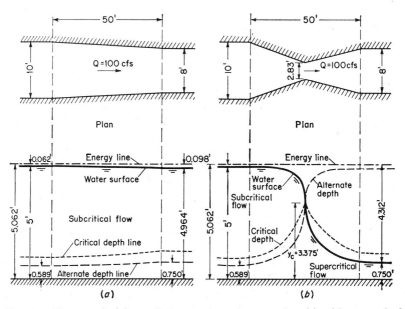

FIG. 3-6. Energy principle applied to a channel contraction (*a*) without gradual hydraulic drop; (*b*) with gradual hydraulic drop.

The alternate depths for the given total energy can be computed by Eq. (3-9) as follows:

$$5.062 = y + \frac{100^2}{2g(by)^2}$$

or

$$y^3 - 5.062y^2 + \frac{155.25}{b^2} = 0$$

This is a cubic equation in which *b* is the width of the channel. At the entrance section, where $b = 10$ ft, its solution gives two positive roots: a low stage $y_1 = 0.589$ ft, which is the alternate depth; and a high stage $y_2 = 5.00$ ft, which is the depth of flow. At the exit section where $b = 8$ ft, this equation gives a low stage $y_1 = 0.750$ ft and a high stage $y_2 = 4.964$ ft.

When no gradual hydraulic drop is allowed in the contraction (Fig. 3-6*a*), the depth of flow at the exit section should be kept at the high stage, as shown. The high stages for other intermediate sections are then computed by the above equation, which gives the flow-surface profile. Similarly, the low stages are computed by the above procedure and indicated by the alternate-depth line.

When a gradual hydraulic drop is desired in the contraction (Fig. 3-6*b*), the depth of flow at the exit section should be at the low stage. Since the point of inflection of the drop or a critical section is maintained at the mid-section of the contraction, the critical depth at this section is equal to the total head divided by 1.5 (Prob. 3-3), or 5.062/1.5 = 3.375 ft. By Eq. (3-10), the critical velocity is equal to $V_c = \sqrt{3.375g} =$ 10.45 fps. Hence, the width of this critical section should be $100/(10.45 \times 3.38) =$ 2.83 ft.

With the size of the mid-section determined, the side walls of the contraction can be drawn in with straight lines. The low and high stages at each section are then computed by the equation previously given. As the flow upstream from the critical section is subcritical, its water surface should follow the high stage. Downstream from the critical section, the flow is supercritical and its surface profile follows the low-stage line.

The critical-depth line is shown to separate the high from the low stage or the subcritical from the supercritical region of flow. On the basis of Eq. (3-10), the critical depth can be computed from the equation

$$\frac{(100/by_c)^2}{2g} = \frac{y_c}{2}$$

or

$$y_c = \sqrt[3]{\frac{10,000}{gb^2}}$$

where $b$ is the width of the channel, which can be measured from the plan.

It should be noted that the vertical scale of the channel profile is greatly exaggerated. Furthermore, the outline of the gradual hydraulic drop is only theoretical, based on the theory of parallel flow. In reality, the flow near the drop is more or less curvilinear, and the actual profile would deviate from the theoretical one.

This example also serves to demonstrate a method of designing a channel transition (Arts. 11-5 to 11-7). The designer may fit any type of contraction walls he desires to suit a given flow profile, or vice versa.

**3-6. Momentum in Open-channel Flow.** As stated earlier (Art. 2-7), the momentum of the flow passing a channel section per unit time is expressed by $\beta wQV/g$, where $\beta$ is the momentum coefficient, $w$ is the unit weight of water in lb/ft$^3$, $Q$ is the discharge in cfs, and $V$ is the mean velocity in fps.

According to Newton's second law of motion, the change of momentum per unit of time in the body of water in a flowing channel is equal to the resultant of all the external forces that are acting on the body. Applying this principle to a channel of large slope (Fig. 3-7), the following expression for the momentum change per unit time in the body of water enclosed between sections 1 and 2 may be written:

$$\frac{Qw}{g}(\beta_2 V_2 - \beta_1 V_1) = P_1 - P_2 + W \sin \theta - F_f \qquad (3-14)$$

where $Q$, $w$, and $V$ are as previously defined, with subscripts referring to sections 1 and 2; $P_1$ and $P_2$ are the resultants of pressures acting on the two sections; $W$ is the weight of water enclosed between the sections; and $F_f$ is the total external force of friction and resistance acting along the surface of contact between the water and the channel. The above equation is known as the *momentum equation*.[1]

[1] The application of the momentum principle was first suggested by Bélanger [5].

For a parallel or gradually varied flow, the values of $P_1$ and $P_2$ in the momentum equation may be computed by assuming a hydrostatic distribution of pressure. For a curvilinear or rapidly varied flow, however, the pressure distribution is no longer hydrostatic; hence the values of $P_1$ and $P_2$ cannot be so computed but must be corrected for the curvature effect of the streamlines of the flow. For simplicity, $P_1$ and $P_2$ may be replaced, respectively, by $\beta_1'P_1$ and $\beta_2'P_2$, where $\beta_1'$ and $\beta_2'$ are the correction coefficients at the two sections. The coefficients are referred

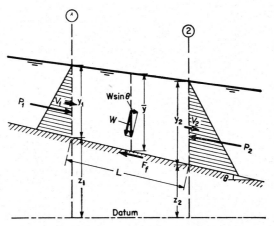

Fig. 3-7. Application of the momentum principle.

to as *pressure-distribution coefficients*. Since $P_1$ and $P_2$ are forces, the coefficients may be specifically called *force coefficients*. It can be shown that the force coefficient is expressed by

$$\beta' = \frac{1}{A\bar{z}} \int_0^A h \, dA = 1 + \frac{1}{A\bar{z}} \int_0^A c \, dA \qquad (3\text{-}15)$$

where $\bar{z}$ is the depth of the centroid of the water area $A$ below the free surface, $h$ is the pressure head on the elementary area $dA$, and $c$ is the pressure-head correction [Eq. (2-9)]. It can easily be seen that $\beta'$ is greater than 1.0 for concave flow, less than 1.0 for convex flow, and equal to 1.0 for parallel flow.

It can be shown that the momentum equation is similar to the energy equation when applied to certain flow problems. In this case, a gradually varied flow is considered; accordingly, the pressure distribution in the sections may be assumed hydrostatic, and $\beta' = 1$. Also, the slope of the channel is assumed relatively small.[1] Thus, in the short reach of a

[1] If the slope angle $\theta$ is large, then $P_1 = \frac{1}{2}wd_1^2 \cos \theta$ and $P_2 = \frac{1}{2}wd_2^2 \cos \theta$, where $d_1$ and $d_2$ are the depths of flow section and $\cos \theta$ is a correction factor (Art. 2-10).

rectangular channel of small slope and width $b$ (Fig. 3-7),

$$P_1 = \tfrac{1}{2}wby_1{}^2$$

and
$$P_2 = \tfrac{1}{2}wby_2{}^2$$

Assume
$$F_f = wh_f'b\bar{y}$$

where $h_f'$ is the friction head and $\bar{y}$ is the average depth, or $(y_1 + y_2)/2$. The discharge through the reach may be taken as the product of the average velocity and the average area, or

$$Q = \tfrac{1}{2}(V_1 + V_2)b\bar{y}$$

Also, it is evident (Fig. 3-7) that the weight of the body of water is

$$W = wb\bar{y}L$$

and
$$\sin\theta = \frac{z_1 - z_2}{L}$$

Substituting all the above expressions for the corresponding items in Eq. (3-14) and simplifying,

$$z_1 + y_1 + \beta_1\frac{V_1{}^2}{2g} = z_2 + y_2 + \beta_2\frac{V_2{}^2}{2g} + h_f' \qquad (3\text{-}16)$$

This equation appears to be practically the same as the energy equation (3-5).

Theoretically speaking, however, the two equations not only use different velocity-distribution coefficients, although these are nearly equal, but also involve different meanings of the frictional losses. In the energy equation, the item $h_f$ measures the *internal* energy dissipated in the whole mass of the water in the reach, whereas the item $h_f'$ in the momentum equation measures the losses due to *external* forces exerted on the water by the walls of the channel. Ignoring the small difference between the coefficients $\alpha$ and $\beta$, it seems that, in gradually varied flow, the internal-energy losses are practically identical with the losses due to external forces. In uniform flow, the rate with which surface forces are doing work is equal to the rate of energy dissipation. In that case, therefore, a distinction between $h_f$ and $h_f'$ does not exist except in definition.

The similarity between the applications of the energy and momentum principles may be confusing. A clear understanding of the basic differences in their constitution is important, despite the fact that in many instances the two principles will produce practically identical results. The inherent distinction between the two principles lies in the fact that energy is a scalar quantity whereas momentum is a vector quantity; also, the energy equation contains a term for internal losses, whereas the momentum equation contains a term for external resistance.

Generally speaking, the energy principle offers a simpler and clearer explanation than does the momentum principle. But the momentum principle has certain advantages in application to problems involving high internal-energy changes, such as the problem of the hydraulic jump. If the energy equation is applied to such problems, the unknown internal-energy loss represented by $h_f$ is indeterminate, and the omission of this term would result in considerable errors. If instead the momentum equation is applied to these problems, since it deals only with external forces, the effects of the internal forces will be entirely out of consideration and need not be evaluated. The term for frictional losses due to external forces, on the other hand, is unimportant in such problems and can safely be omitted, because the phenomenon takes place in a short reach of the channel and the effect due to external forces is negligible compared with the internal losses. Further discussions on the solution of the hydraulic-jump problem by both principles will be given later (Example 3-3).

An example showing the application of the momentum principle to the problem of a broad-crested weir is given below.

**Example 3-2.** Derive the discharge per unit width of a broad-crested weir across a rectangular channel.

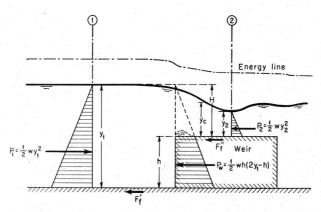

FIG. 3-8. Momentum principle applied to flow over a broad-crested weir.

*Solution.* The assumptions to be made in this solution (Fig. 3-8) are (1) the frictional forces $F_f'$ and $F_f''$ are negligible; (2) the depth $y_2$ is the minimum depth on the weir; (3) at the channel sections under consideration there is parallel flow; and (4) the water pressure $P_w$ on the weir surface is equal to the total hydrostatic pressure measured below the upstream water surface, or

$$P_w = \tfrac{1}{2}wh[y_1 + (y_1 - h)] = \tfrac{1}{2}wh(2y_1 - h)$$

The accuracy of the last assumption has been checked experimentally [6]. If the momentum equation (3-14) is applied to the body of water between the upstream approach section 1 and the downstream section 2 at the minimum depth on the top of the weir, the following equation may be written:

$$\frac{qw}{g}\left(\frac{q}{y_2} - \frac{q}{y_1}\right) = \frac{1}{2}wy_1^2 - \frac{1}{2}wy_2^2 - \frac{1}{2}wh(2y_1 - h)$$

where $q$ is the discharge per unit width of the weir.

Experiments by Doeringsfeld and Barker [6] have shown that, on the average, $y_1 - h = 2y_2$. In that case the above equation can be simplified and solved for $q$,

$$q = 0.433 \sqrt{2g}\left(\frac{y_1}{y_1 + h}\right)^{1/2} H^{3/2} \tag{3-17}$$

Considering the limit of $h$ from zero to infinity, this equation varies from $q = 3.47H^{3/2}$ to $q = 2.46H^{3/2}$. It is interesting to note that the practical range of the coefficient to $H^{3/2}$ obtained by actual observations[1] is from 3.05 to 2.67. In applying the momentum principle to this problem, it can be seen that knowledge of the internal-energy losses due to separation of flow at the entrance and to other causes is not needed in the analysis.

**3-7. Specific Force.** In applying the momentum principle to a short horizontal reach of a prismatic channel, the external force of friction and the weight effect of water can be ignored. Thus, with $\theta = 0$ and $F_f = 0$ and assuming also $\beta_1 = \beta_2 = 1$, Eq. (3-14) becomes

$$\frac{Qw}{g}(V_2 - V_1) = P_1 - P_2$$

The hydrostatic forces $P_1$ and $P_2$ may be expressed as

$$P_1 = w\bar{z}_1A_1 \qquad \text{and} \qquad P_2 = w\bar{z}_2A_2$$

where $\bar{z}_1$ and $\bar{z}_2$ are the distances of the centroids of the respective water areas $A_1$ and $A_2$ below the surface of flow. Also, $V_1 = Q/A_1$ and $V_2 = Q/A_2$. Then, the above momentum equation may be written

$$\frac{Q^2}{gA_1} + \bar{z}_1A_1 = \frac{Q^2}{gA_2} + \bar{z}_2A_2 \tag{3-18}$$

[1] The value of the coefficient actually depends on many factors: mainly, the rounding of the upstream corner, the length and slope of the weir crest, and the height of the weir. Many experiments on *broad-crested weirs* have been performed. From several of the well-known experiments King [7] has interpolated the data and prepared tables for the coefficient under various conditions. A comprehensive analysis including more recent data and a presentation of the results for practical applications were made by Tracy [8]. The well-known experiments on broad-crested weirs are (1) *Bazin tests* performed in Dijon, France, in 1886 [9]; (2) *U.S.D.W.B. Cornell tests* performed at Cornell University in 1899 by the U.S. Deep Waterways Board under the direction of G. W. Rafter, and *U.S.G.S. Cornell tests* performed by the U.S. Geological Survey under the direction of Robert E. Horton in 1903 [10]; (3) *Michigan tests* performed at the University of Michigan during 1928–1929 [11]; and (4) *Minnesota* and *Washington tests* performed, respectively, at the university of Minnesota and Washington State University [6]. For some formulas and coefficients of discharge developed in the U.S.S.R., see [12]. For an analytical treatment of the problem, see [13].

The two sides of Eq. (3-18) are analogous and, hence, may be expressed for any channel section by a general function

$$F = \frac{Q^2}{gA} + \bar{z}A \qquad (3\text{-}19)$$

This function consists of two terms. The first term is the momentum of the flow passing through the channel section per unit time per unit weight of water, and the second is the force per unit weight of water. Since both terms are essentially force per unit weight of water, their sum may be called the *specific force*.[1] Accordingly, Eq. (3-18) may be expressed

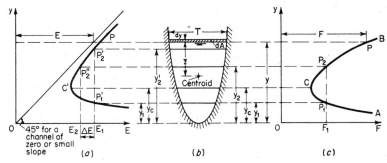

Fig. 3-9. Specific-force curve supplemented with specific-energy curve. (a) Specific-energy curve; (b) channel section; (c) specific-force curve.

as $F_1 = F_2$. This means that the specific forces of sections 1 and 2 are equal, provided that the external forces and the weight effect of water in the reach between the two sections can be ignored.

By plotting the depth against the specific force for a given channel section and discharge, a *specific-force curve* is obtained (Fig. 3-9). This curve has two limbs $AC$ and $BC$. The limb $AC$ approaches the horizontal axis asymptotically toward the right. The limb $BC$ rises upward and extends indefinitely to the right. For a given value of the specific force, the curve has two possible depths $y_1$ and $y_2$. As will be shown later, the two depths constitute the initial and sequent depths of a hydraulic jump. At point $C$ on the curve the two depths become one, and the specific force is a minimum. The following argument shows that the depth at the minimum value of the specific force is equal to the critical depth.[2]

---

[1] This has been variously called the "force plus momentum," the "momentum flux," the "total force," or, briefly, the "force" of a stream (see pp. 81 and 82 of [14]). The function represented by Eq. (3-19) was formulated by Bresse [15] for the study of the hydraulic jump to be described in Example 3-3.

[2] The concept of critical depth based on the theorem of momentum is believed to have been developed by Boussinesq [16].

For a minimum value of the specific force, the first derivative of $F$ with respect to $y$ should be zero, or, from Eq. (3-19),

$$\frac{dF}{dy} = -\frac{Q^2}{gA^2}\frac{dA}{dy} + \frac{d(\bar{z}A)}{dy} = 0$$

For a change $dy$ in the depth, the corresponding change $d(\bar{z}A)$ in the static moment of the water area about the free surface is equal to $[A(\bar{z} + dy) + T(dy)^2/2] - \bar{z}A$ (Fig. 3-9). Ignoring the differential of higher degree, that is, assuming $(dy)^2 = 0$, the change in static moment becomes $d(\bar{z}A) = A\,dy$. Then the preceding equation may be written

$$\frac{dF}{dy} = -\frac{Q^2}{gA^2}\frac{dA}{dy} + A = 0$$

Since $dA/dy = T$, $Q/A = V$, and $A/T = D$, the above equation may be reduced to

$$\frac{V^2}{2g} = \frac{D}{2} \tag{3-10}$$

This is the criterion for the critical state of flow, derived earlier (Art. 3-3). Therefore, it is proved that the depth at the minimum value of the specific force is the critical depth.[1] It may also be stated that *at the critical state of flow the specific force is a minimum for the given discharge.*

Now, compare the specific-force curve with the specific-energy curve (Fig. 3-9). For a given specific energy $E_1$, the specific-energy curve indicates two possible depths, namely, a low stage $y_1$ in the supercritical flow region and a high stage $y_2'$ in the subcritical flow region.[2] For a given value of $F_1$, the specific-force curve also indicates two possible depths, namely, an initial depth $y_1$ in the supercritical region and a sequent depth $y_2$ in the subcritical flow region. It is assumed that the low stage and the initial depth are both equal to $y_1$. Thus, the two curves indicate jointly that the sequent depth $y_2$ is always less than the high stage $y_2'$. Furthermore, the specific-energy curve shows that the energy content $E_2$ for the depth $y_2$ is less than the energy content $E_1$ for the depth $y_2'$. Therefore, in order to maintain a constant value of $F_1$, the depth of flow may be changed from $y_1$ to $y_2$ at the price of losing a certain amount of energy, which is equal to $E_1 - E_2 = \Delta E$. One example of this is the

[1] It should be noted that the above proof is based on the assumptions of parallel flow and uniform velocity distribution. However, the concept of critical depth is a general concept that is valid for all flows, whether derived from energy or from momentum considerations. This validity has been proved by Jaeger [14,17,18], and the proof is known as the *Jaeger theorem* [19].

[2] In order to make a clear distinction between the sequent depth and the high stage of the alternate depths, the sequent depth is designated by $y_2$ and the high stage by $y_2'$. In some other places in this book, however, both are designated by $y_2$.

hydraulic jump on a horizontal floor, in which the specific forces before and after the jump are equal and the loss of energy is a consequence of the phenomenon. This will be explained further in the following example. It may be noted at this point, however, that the depths $y_1$ and $y_2'$ shown by the specific-energy curve are the alternate depths; whereas the depths $y_1$ and $y_2$ shown by the specific-force curve are, respectively, the initial depth and the sequent depth of a hydraulic jump.

**Example 3-3.** Derive a relationship between the initial depth and the sequent depth of a hydraulic jump on a horizontal floor in a rectangular channel.

*Solution.* The external forces of friction and the weight effect of water in the hydraulic jump on a horizontal floor are negligible, because the jump takes place in a relatively short distance and the slope angle of the horizontal floor is zero. The specific forces of sections 1 and 2 (Fig. 3-4), respectively, before and after the jump, can therefore be considered equal; that is,

$$\frac{Q^2}{gA_1} + \bar{z}_1 A_1 = \frac{Q^2}{gA_2} + \bar{z}_2 A_2 \tag{3-18}$$

For a rectangular channel of width $b$, $Q = V_1 A_1 = V_2 A_2$, $A_1 = b y_1$, $A_2 = b y_2$, $\bar{z}_1 = y_1/2$, and $\bar{z}_2 = y_2/2$. Substituting these relations and $\mathbf{F}_1 = V_1/\sqrt{g y_1}$ in the above equation and simplifying,

$$\left(\frac{y_2}{y_1}\right)^3 - (2\mathbf{F}_1{}^2 + 1)\left(\frac{y_2}{y_1}\right) + 2\mathbf{F}_1{}^2 = 0 \tag{3-20}$$

Factoring,

$$\left[\left(\frac{y_2}{y_1}\right)^2 + \frac{y_2}{y_1} - 2\mathbf{F}_1{}^2\right]\left(\frac{y_2}{y_1} - 1\right) = 0$$

Then, let

$$\left(\frac{y_2}{y_1}\right)^2 + \frac{y_2}{y_1} - 2\mathbf{F}_1{}^2 = 0$$

The solution of this quadratic equation is

$$\frac{y_2}{y_1} = \frac{1}{2}(\sqrt{1 + 8\mathbf{F}_1{}^2} - 1) \tag{3-21}$$

For a given Froude number $\mathbf{F}_1$ of the approaching flow, the ratio of the sequent depth to the initial depth is given by the above equation.

It should be understood that the momentum principle is used in this solution because the hydraulic jump involves a high amount of internal-energy losses which cannot be evaluated in the energy equation.

The joint use of the specific-energy curve and the specific-force curve helps to determine graphically the energy loss involved in the hydraulic jump for a given approaching flow. For the given approaching depth $y_1$, points $P_1$ and $P_1'$ are located on the specific-force curve and the specific-energy curve, respectively (Fig. 3-4). The point $P_1'$ gives the initial energy content $E_1$. Draw a vertical line, passing through the point $P_1$ and intercepting the upper limb of the specific-force curve at point $P_2$, which gives the sequent depth $y_2$. Then, draw a horizontal line passing through the point $P_2$ and intercepting the specific-energy curve at point $P_2''$, which gives the energy content $E_2$ after the jump. The energy loss in the jump is then equal to $E_1 - E_2$, represented by $\Delta E$.

**3-8. Momentum Principle Applied to Nonprismatic Channels.** The specific force, like the specific energy, varies with the shape of the channel section. In applying the momentum principle to nonprismatic channels, therefore, a three-dimensional plot similar to that shown for the application of the energy principle (Fig. 3-5) can be constructed. For practical purposes, however, this is rarely necessary.

Where there is no intervention of external forces or where these forces are either negligible or given, the momentum principle can be applied to its best advantage to problems, such as the hydraulic jump, that deal with high internal-energy losses that cannot be evaluated if the energy principle alone is used. The following example shows how the momentum principle is applied to the design of a channel transition in which a hydraulic jump is involved.

**Example 3-4.** A rectangular channel 8 ft wide, carrying 100 cfs at a depth of 0.5 ft, is connected by a straight-wall transition to a channel 10 ft wide, flowing at a depth

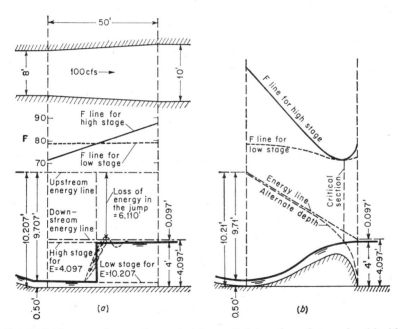

Fig. 3-10. Energy and momentum principles applied to a channel expansion (a) with hydraulic jump; (b) without hydraulic jump.

of 4 ft (Fig. 3-10). Determine the flow profile in the transition if the frictional loss through the transition is negligible. If a hydraulic jump occurs in the transition, how can it be eliminated?

*Solution.* From the given data, the total energy with respect to the channel bottom in the approaching flow is $E = 0.5 + [100/(0.5 \times 8)]^2/2g = 10.207$ ft, and in the downstream, $E = 4.0 + [100/(4 \times 10)]^2/2g = 4.097$ ft. It is apparent that this energy difference of 6.110 ft must be dissipated through the transition by some means, since the frictional loss is negligible. Furthermore, the Froude numbers 6.24 and 0.22 of the approaching and downstream flows are, respectively, greater and less than unity, indicating a change of the flow from supercritical to subcritical. Therefore, a hydraulic jump can be expected to occur to dissipate the energy difference and to effect a change in the flow state. Whether this jump will occur within the transition or in the upstream or the downstream channel is, however, to be disclosed by further analysis.

TABLE 3-1. COMPUTATION FOR A CHANNEL EXPANSION DESCRIBED IN
EXAMPLE 3-4

| Section width $b$, ft | Low stage $y_1$, ft for $E = 10.207$ | $F_1$ | High stage $y_2$, ft for $E = 4.097$ | $F_2$ |
|---|---|---|---|---|
| 8.00 | 0.500 | 78.6 | 3.940 | 71.9 |
| 8.50 | 0.470 | 78.7 | 3.960 | 75.9 |
| 9.00 | 0.443 | 78.8 | 3.979 | 79.9 |
| 9.50 | 0.419 | 78.8 | 3.987 | 83.6 |
| 10.00 | 0.398 | 78.8 | 4.000 | 87.8 |

Take five sections of the transition with their widths shown in Table 3-1. For the total approaching energy of 10.207 ft, the low stage $y_1$ for each section can be computed by means of Eq. (3-8) or (3-9), or

$$\frac{(100/by_1)^2}{2g} + y_1 = 10.207$$

where $b$ is the width of the section. Similarly, the high stage $y_2$ for a total energy of 4.097 can be computed from

$$\frac{(100/by_2)^2}{2g} + y_2 = 4.097$$

The low- and high-stage lines are then constructed along with the energy lines (Fig. 3-10a). After these stage and energy lines are determined, the specific forces $F_1$ and $F_2$ for low and high stages, respectively, at each section are computed and plotted to any convenient scale and datum. The hydraulic jump must occur where the specific forces for the low and high stages are equal, or at the intersection of the $F$ lines. At this section the water surface at low stage will jump to the high stage, as indicated by a vertical line (Fig. 3-10a). Actually, however, the jump will take place over a short distance, as shown by the dotted line. The energy loss in the jump is represented by the vertical intercept between the upstream and downstream energy lines, which is equal to 6.110 ft, covering the energy difference between the flows in the connecting channels. By varying the shape of the cross sections of the connecting channels the location of the intersection of the $F$ lines, or the position of the jump, can be altered. Changing the depth of flow in the downstream channel will also change the position of the jump. Generally, an increase in the downstream depth will move the jump upstream, and a decrease in the depth will move the jump downstream.

The hydraulic jump can be eliminated if the energy loss can be dissipated gradually and smoothly. This can be done by introducing proper roughness in the transition, for instance, by bolting cross timbers to the bottom of the transition. It can be assumed in this example that the energy difference of 6.110 ft is dissipated uniformly in the transition by artificial roughness. Thus, the energy line in the transition is simply a straight line joining the total heads of the two end sections (Fig. 3-10b). For design purposes, it is convenient first to assume the flow profile and then to proportion the dimensions of the transition so that the jump can be eliminated. In proportioning the transition, the jump is eliminated either by varying the width or by raising the bottom of the transition. In this example, it is assumed that the bottom is to be raised, or "humped" (Fig. 3-10b). The subsequent procedure of the computation is to (1) assume the flow profile; (2) compute the velocity head, which is equal to the difference between the total head and the water-surface elevation, at a number of selected sections; (3) compute the velocity and then the water area and depth of flow for each section; (4) determine the elevation of the bottom of the transition, which is equal to the elevation of the water surface minus the depth of flow; (5) compute the alternate depth, since the bottom of the transition is fixed; and (6) compute $F_1$ and $F_2$ lines for the low and high stages, and plot them on a convenient scale. It can be seen that the two $F$ lines intersect and become tangent to each other at a critical section, where the flow changes from low to high stage, that is, from supercritical to subcritical state. If the critical-depth line is plotted, it will intersect the alternate-depth line and the water surface simultaneously at the critical section. Based on the critical-depth line, a line of minimum specific energy can also be constructed. This line should be tangent to the total-energy line at the critical section.

## PROBLEMS

**3-1.** With reference to a channel of small slope and a section shown in Fig. 2-2, (a) construct a family of specific-energy curves for $Q = 0$, 50, 100, 200, 300, and 400 cfs, (b) draw the locus of the critical-depth point on these curves, (c) plot a curve of the critical depth against the discharge, and (d) plot a family of curves of alternate depths, $y_1$ vs. $y_2$, for the given discharges.

**3-2.** Construct the specific-energy curve for a 36-in. pipe carrying an open-channel flow of 20 cfs (a) on a flat slope, and (b) on a 30° slope.

**3-3.** Show that at the critical state of flow the specific-energy head in a rectangular channel is equal to 1.5 times the depth of flow, assuming zero slope and $\alpha = 1$.

**3-4.** Derive the equations for the locus of the critical-depth point on the specific-energy curve and for the curve of critical depth vs. discharge, as obtained in Prob. 3-1.

**3-5.** Prove Eq. (3-12).

**3-6.** Prove Eq. (3-13).

**3-7.** Prove that at the critical state of flow the discharge is a maximum for a given specific energy.[1]

**3-8.** Show that the relation between the alternate depths $y_1$ and $y_2$ in a rectangular channel can be expressed by

$$\frac{2y_1{}^2y_2{}^2}{y_1 + y_2} = y_c{}^3 \tag{3-22}$$

where $y_c$ is the critical depth. Using values of $y_1/y_c$ as ordinates and of $y_2/y_c$ as abscissas, construct a dimensionless graph for the above equation and study its characteristics.

[1] The concept of critical depth based on the theorem of maximum discharge was first introduced by Bélanger [20].

**3-9.** Solve the problem given in Example 3-1 (*a*) if there is a total energy loss of 0.60 ft uniformly distributed throughout the length of the contraction, and (*b*) if a gradual hydraulic drop is desired with its point of inflection at a distance 20 ft upstream from the exit section.

**3-10.** Applying the momentum principle and the continuity equation to the analysis of a submerged hydraulic jump which occurs at the sluice outlet in a rectangular channel (Fig. 3-11), prove that

$$\frac{y_s}{y_2} = \sqrt{1 + 2\mathbf{F}_2{}^2 \left(1 - \frac{y_2}{y_1}\right)} \tag{3-23}$$

where $y_s$ is the submerged depth; $y_1$ is the height of sluice-gate opening; $y_2$ is the tailwater depth; and $\mathbf{F}_2{}^2 = q^2/gy_2{}^3$, $q$ being the discharge per unit width of the channel. Neglect the channel-bed friction $F_f$.

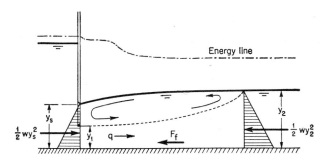

Fig. 3-11. A submerged hydraulic jump at sluice outlet.

**3-11.** Prove that the energy loss in a horizontal hydraulic jump is

$$\Delta E = \frac{(y_2 - y_1)^3}{4y_1y_2} \tag{3-24}*$$

**3-12.** If a hydraulic jump is formed on the horizontal floor at the toe of the spillway described in Prob. 2-11, determine the sequent depth and the energy loss involved in the jump.

**3-13.** With reference to a channel of small slope and a section shown in Fig. 2-2, (*a*) construct a family of specific-force curves for $Q = 0, 50, 100, 200, 300$, and 400 cfs, and (*b*) plot a family of curves of initial depth against sequent depth for the given discharges.

**3-14.** Construct the specific-force curve for a 36-in. pipe carrying an open-channel flow of 20 cfs on a small slope.

**3-15.** Prove Eq. (3-15).

**3-16.** Using the momentum principle, show that the Froude number of a parallel or gradually varied flow in a channel of slope angle $\theta$ may be defined by

$$\mathbf{F} = \frac{V}{\sqrt{gD \cos \theta/\beta}} \tag{3-25}$$

* This formula was shown by Bresse early in 1860 [15]. At the same time Bresse introduced the concept of critical depth, as a depth at which the subcritical flow changes to supercritical, or vice versa.

where $V$ is the mean velocity, $D$ is the hydraulic depth of the section, and $\beta$ is the momentum coefficient for nonuniform velocity distribution.

**3-17.** For eliminating the hydraulic jump in Example 3-4, the flow profile is assumed to be composed of two reversed circular curves tangent to each other at the middle section of the transition and also to the water surfaces in the connecting channels at the two ends of the transition. Verify the computation (shown in scale on Fig. 3-10$b$).

**3-18.** A frictional loss of 1.0 ft is assumed to be uniformly distributed along the length of the transition in Example 3-4. Determine the flow profile in the transition.

## REFERENCES

1. Hunter Rouse and Simon Ince: "History of Hydraulics," Iowa Institute of Hydraulic Research, Iowa City, Iowa, 1957.
2. Boris A. Bakhmeteff: "O Neravnomernom Dvizhenii Zhidkosti v Otkrytom Rusle" ("Varied Flow in Open Channel"), St. Petersburg, Russia, 1912.
3. Paul Böss: "Berechnung der Wasserspiegellage beim Wechsel des Fliesszustandes" ("Computation of Water Surface with Change of the Flow Type"), Springer-Verlag, Berlin, 1919, pp. 20 and 52.
4. Hunter Rouse: Discharge characteristics of the free overfall, *Civil Engineering*, vol. 6, no. 7, pp. 257–260, April, **1936.**
5. J. B. Bélanger: "Résumé de leçons" ("Summary of Lectures"), Paris, 1838.
6. H. A. Doeringsfeld and C. L. Barker: Pressure-momentum theory applied to the broad-crested weir, *Transactions, American Society of Civil Engineers*, vol. 106, pp. 934–946, 1941.
7. Horace William King: "Handbook of Hydraulics," 4th ed., revised by Ernest F. Brater, McGraw-Hill Book Company, Inc., New York, 1954, pp. 5-1 to 5-16.
8. H. J. Tracy: Discharge characteristics of broad-crested weirs, *U.S. Geological Survey, Circular 397*, 1957.
9. H. Bazin: Experiences nouvelles sur l'écoulement en déversoir (Recent experiments on the flow of water over weirs), *Mémoires et Documents, Annales des ponts et chaussées*, 2e semestre, pp. 393–448, October, 1888. English translation by Arthur Marichal and John C. Trautwine, Jr., *Proceedings, Engineers' Club of Philadelphia*, vol. 7, no. 5, pp. 259–310, 1890; vol. 9, no. 3, pp. 231–244, and no. 4, pp. 287–319, 1892; and vol. 10, no. 2, pp. 121–164, 1893.
10. R. E. Horton: Weir experiments, coefficients, and formulas, *U.S. Geological Survey, Water Supply and Irrigation Paper 150*, 1906; revised as *Paper 200*, 1907.
11. James G. Woodburn: Tests of broad-crested weirs, *Transactions, American Society of Civil Engineers*, vol. 96, pp. 387–416, 1932.
12. M. A. Mostkow: "Handbuch der Hydraulik" ("Handbook of Hydraulics"), VEB Verlag Technik, Berlin, 1956, pp. 188–195.
13. L. J. Tison: Le déversoir à seuil épais (The broad-crested weir), *La Houille blanche*, Grenoble, 5th yr., no. 4, pp. 426–439, July-August, 1950.
14. Charles Jaeger: "Engineering Fluid Mechanics," translated from the German by P. O. Wolf, Blackie & Son, Ltd., London and Glasgow, pp. 98–112, 1956.
15. J. A. Ch. Bresse: "Cours de mécanique appliquée," 2e partie, Hydraulique ("Course in Applied Mechanics," pt. 2, Hydraulics), Mallet-Bachelier, Paris, 1860.
16. J. V. Boussinesq: Essai sur la théorie des eaux courantes (Essay on the theory of water flow), *Mémoires présentés par divers savants à l'Académie des Sciences*, Paris, vol. 23, ser. 2, no. 1, pp. 1–680, 1877.

17. Charles Jaeger: Contribution à l'étude des courants liquides à surface libre (Contribution to the study of free-surface liquid flows), *Revue générale de l'hydraulique*, Paris, vol. 9, no. 33, pp. 111–120; no. 34, pp. 139–153, 1943.

18. Charles Jaeger: De l'impulsion totale et de ses rapports avec l'énergie totale d'un courant liquide à surface libre (The total impulse and its relations with the total energy of a free-surface liquid flow), *Revue générale de l'hydraulique*, Paris, vol. 13, no. 37, pp. 12–19; no. 38, pp. 86–87; no. 39, pp. 143–151; no. 40, pp. 191–197; no. 41, pp. 257–261, 1947.

19. Étienne Crausse: "Hydraulique des canaux découverts en régime permanent" ("Hydraulics of Open Channels with Steady Flow"), Éditions Eyrolles, Paris, 1951, pp. 111–112.

20. J. B. Bélanger: Notes sur le cours d'hydraulique (Notes on the course in hydraulics), *Mémoire, École Nationale des Ponts et Chaussées*, Paris, 1849–1850, pp. 32–33.

CHAPTER 4

# CRITICAL FLOW: ITS COMPUTATION
# AND APPLICATIONS

**4-1. Critical Flow.** As described in the previous chapter, the critical state of flow through a channel section is characterized by several important conditions.[1] Recapitulating, they are (1) the specific energy is a minimum for a given discharge; (2) the discharge is a maximum for a given specific energy (Prob. 3-7); (3) the specific force is a minimum for a given discharge; (4) the velocity head is equal to half the hydraulic depth in a channel of small slope; (5) the Froude number is equal to unity; and (6) the velocity of flow in a channel of small slope with uniform velocity distribution is equal to the celerity of small gravity waves in shallow water caused by local disturbances.

Discussions on critical state of flow have referred mainly to a particular section of a channel, known as the *critical section*. If the critical state of flow exists throughout the entire length of the channel or over a reach of the channel, the flow in the channel is a *critical flow*. Since, as indicated by the critical-flow criterion Eq. (3-10), the depth of critical flow depends on the geometric elements $A$ and $D$ of the channel section when the discharge is constant, the critical depth in a prismatic channel of uniform slope will be the same in all sections, and critical flow in a prismatic channel should, therefore, be uniform flow. At this condition, the slope of the channel that sustains a given discharge at a uniform and critical depth is called the *critical slope* $S_c$. A slope of the channel less than the critical slope will cause a slower flow of subcritical state for the given discharge, as will be shown later, and, hence, is called a *mild* or *subcritical slope*. A slope greater than the critical slope will result in a faster flow of supercritical state, and is called a *steep* or *supercritical slope*.

A flow at or near the critical state is unstable. This is because a minor change in specific energy at or close to critical state will cause a major change in depth. This fact can also be recognized in the specific-energy curve (Fig. 3-2). As the curve is almost vertical near the critical depth, a slight change in energy would change the depth to a much smaller or much greater alternate depth corresponding to the specific energy after

[1] For a historical account of the theory of critical flow, see [1].

63

the change. It can be observed also that, when the flow is near the critical state, the water surface appears unstable and wavy. Such phenomena are generally caused by the minor changes in energy due to variations in channel roughness, cross section, slope, or deposits of sediment or debris. In the design of a channel, if the depth is found at or near the critical depth for a great length of the channel, the shape or slope of the channel should be altered, if practicable, in order to secure greater stability.

The criterion for a critical state of flow (Art. 3-3) is the basis for the computation of critical flow, which will be explained in subsequent articles. Two major applications of critical-flow theory are flow control and flow measurement, which will also be discussed in this chapter.

**4-2. The Section Factor for Critical-flow Computation.** Substituting $V = Q/A$ in Eq. (3-10) and simplifying,

$$Z = \frac{Q}{\sqrt{g}} \qquad (4\text{-}1)$$

When the energy coefficient is not assumed to be unity,

$$Z = \frac{Q}{\sqrt{g/\alpha}} \qquad (4\text{-}2)$$

In the above equations, $Z = A \sqrt{D}$, which is the *section factor for critical-flow computation* [Eq. (2-3)]. Equation (4-2) states that the section factor $Z$ for a channel section at the critical state of flow is equal to the discharge divided by the square root of $g/\alpha$. Since the section factor $Z$ is a function of the depth, the equation indicates that there is *only one* possible critical depth for maintaining the given discharge in a channel and similarly that, when the depth is fixed, there can be *only one* discharge that maintains a critical flow and makes the depth critical in the given channel section.

Equation (4-1) or (4-2) is a very useful tool for the computation and analysis of critical flow in an open channel. When the discharge is given, the equation gives the critical section factor $Z_c$ and, hence, the critical depth $y_c$. On the other hand, when the depth and, hence, the section factor are given, the critical disharge can be computed by Eq. (4-1) in the following form:

$$Q = Z \sqrt{g} \qquad (4\text{-}3)$$

or by Eq. (4-2) in the following form:

$$Q = Z \sqrt{\frac{g}{\alpha}} \qquad (4\text{-}4)$$

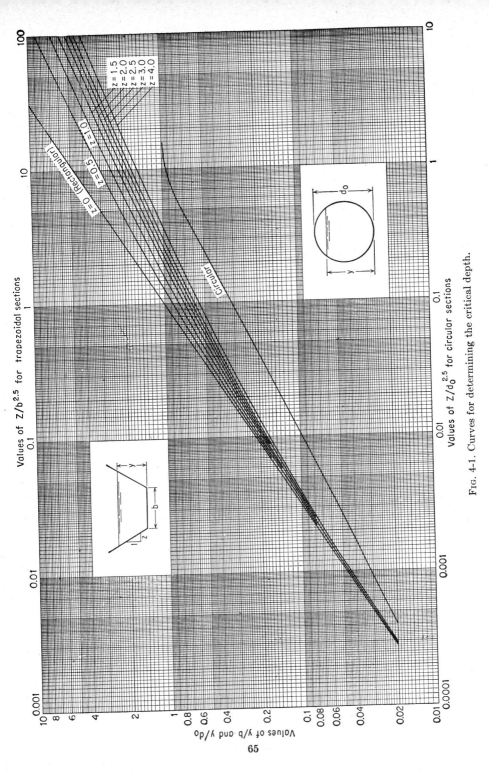

Values of $Z/b^{2.5}$ for trapezoidal sections

Values of $Z/d_0^{2.5}$ for circular sections

$z = 1.5$
$z = 2.0$
$z = 2.5$
$z = 3.0$
$z = 4.0$

$z = 1.0$
$z = 0.5$
$z = 0$ (Rectangular)

Circular

Values of $y/b$ and $y/d_0$

Fig. 4-1. Curves for determining the critical depth.

A subscript $c$ is sometimes used to specify the condition of critical flow. Formulas for the section factor $Z$ of seven common channel sections are given in Table 2-1. The $Z$ values for a circular section can be found either from the curve in Fig. 2-1 or from the table in Appendix A.

In order to simplify the computation of critical flow, dimensionless curves showing the relation between the depth and section factor $Z$ (Fig. 4-1) have been prepared for rectangular, trapezoidal, and circular channels. These self-explanatory curves will help to determine the depth $y$ for a given section factor $Z$, and vice versa.

**Example 4-1.** Derive an equation showing critical discharge through a rectangular channel section in terms of the channel width and the total head.

*Solution.* For the rectangular section, Table 2-1 gives the section factor $Z = by^{1.5}$. At the critical state of flow, the depth $y = H/1.5$ (see Prob. 3-3). Substituting these expressions in Eq. (4-3), using $g = 32.16$, and simplifying, we find that the critical discharge is

$$Q_c = 3.087bH^{1.5} \tag{4-5}$$

**4-3. The Hydraulic Exponent for Critical-flow Computation.** Since the section factor $Z$ is a function of the depth of flow $y$, it may be assumed that

$$Z^2 = Cy^M \tag{4-6}$$

where $C$ is a coefficient and $M$ is a parameter called the *hydraulic exponent for critical-flow computation.*

Taking logarithms on both sides of Eq. (4-6) and then differentiating with respect to $y$,

$$\frac{d(\ln Z)}{dy} = \frac{M}{2y} \tag{4-7}$$

Now, taking logarithms on both sides of Eq. (2-3), or $Z = A\sqrt{A/T}$, and then differentiating with respect to $y$,

$$\frac{d(\ln Z)}{dy} = \frac{3}{2}\frac{T}{A} - \frac{1}{2T}\frac{dT}{dy} \tag{4-8}$$

Equating the right sides of Eqs. (4-7) and (4-8) and solving for $M$,

$$M = \frac{y}{A}\left(3T - \frac{A}{T}\frac{dT}{dy}\right) \tag{4-9}$$

This is a general equation for the hydraulic exponent $M$, which is a function of the channel section and the depth of flow. For a trapezoidal section, the expressions for $A$ and $T$ obtained from Table 2-1 are substituted in Eq. (4-9); the resulting equation [2] is simplified and becomes

$$M = \frac{3[1 + 2z(y/b)]^2 - 2z(y/b)[1 + z(y/b)]}{[1 + 2z(y/b)][1 + z(y/b)]} \tag{4-10}*$$

* This equation was also developed independently by Chugaev [3]. In this equation, $M$ can be regarded as a function of $z(y/b)$; accordingly, a single curve of $M$ versus

This equation indicates that the value of $M$ for the trapezoidal section is a function of $z$ and $y/b$. For values of $z = 0, 0.5, 1.0, 1.5, 2.0, 2.5, 3.0$, and $4.0$, a family of curves for $M$ versus $y/b$ are constructed (Fig. 4-2). These curves indicate that the value of $M$ varies in a range from 3.0 to 5.0.

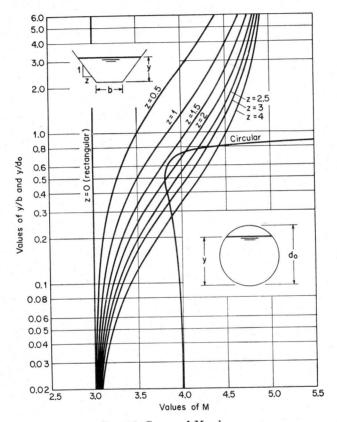

Fɪɢ. 4-2. Curves of $M$ values.

A curve for a circular section with $M$ plotted against $y/d_0$, where $d_0$ is the diameter, is also shown (Fig. 4-2). This curve was developed by a similar procedure but constructed from a much more complicated formula. The curve shows that the value of $M$ varies within a rather narrow range for values of $y/d_0$ less than 0.7 or so, but increases rapidly as the value of $y/d_0$ becomes greater than 0.7. The significance of this

---

$z(y/b)$ may be constructed. It is obvious that this curve would be identical with the curve for $z = 1$ in Fig. 4-2. For convenience in application, however, a family of curves of $M$ versus $y/b$ are shown, using $z$ as a parameter.

characteristic is that, when the depth of flow in a circular section approaches the top of the circle, the section factor and with it the critical discharge, as shown by Eq. (4-3), become indefinitely large. In other words, it is practically impossible to maintain a critical flow in a circular conduit at a depth approaching the top of the section. In fact, the wavy surface of the critical flow will touch the top of the conduit before it actually comes so near as to approach the top. A similar characteristic and phenomenon occur also in other types of closed conduit with gradually closing crown, when the water surface approaches the crown of the conduit.

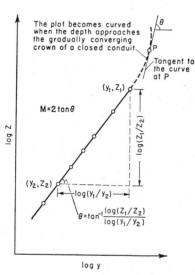

FIG. 4-3. Graphical determination of the M value.

For channel sections of other than trapezoidal or circular shape, exact values of $M$ can be computed directly by Eq. (4-9), provided that the derivative $dT/dy$ can be evaluated. Approximate values of $M$ for any channel section, however, may be obtained from the following equation

$$M = 2 \frac{\log (Z_1/Z_2)}{\log (y_1/y_2)} \quad (4\text{-}11)$$

where $Z_1$ and $Z_2$ are section factors for any two depths $y_1$ and $y_2$ of the given section. This equation can easily be derived from Eq. (4-6).

In applying Eq. (4-11), a graphical method is recommended instead of direct computation. This involves a logarithmic plotting of $Z$ as ordinate against the depth as abscissa (Fig. 4-3). For most channels, except for closed conduits with depth approaching a gradually closing crown and some channels of peculiar shapes, the plot takes a more or less straight-line form. The hydraulic exponent is equal to twice the slope of the plotted straight line. For a depth approaching the gradually closing crown of a closed conduit, the plot becomes a curve, and the hydraulic exponent of a given depth is equal to twice the slope of the tangent to the curve at that depth.

The hydraulic exponent $M$ is described here only as a characteristic value of a channel section under the condition of critical flow. The application of this exponent will be further described in the computation of gradually varied flow (Art. 10-2).

**4-4. Computation of Critical Flow.** Computation of critical flow involves the determination of critical depth and velocity when the discharge and the channel section are known. Three methods illustrated by simple examples will be given below. On the other hand, if the critical depth and channel section are known, the critical discharge can be determined by the method described in Art. 4-2.

*A. Algebraic Method.* For a simple geometric channel section, the critical flow can be determined by an algebraic computation using the basic equations. The method has already been used (Example 3-1), but the following example is given for further illustration:

**Example 4-2.** Compute the critical depth and velocity of the trapezoidal channel (Fig. 2-2) carrying a discharge of 400 cfs.

*Solution.* The hydraulic depth and water area of the trapezoidal section are expressed in terms of the depth $y$ as

$$D = \frac{y(10 + y)}{10 + 2y} \quad \text{and} \quad A = y(20 + 2y)$$

The velocity is

$$V = \frac{Q}{A} = \frac{400}{y(20 + 2y)}$$

Substituting the above expressions for $D$ and $V$ in Eq. (3-10) and simplifying,

$$2{,}484(5 + y) = [y(10 + y)]^3$$

Solving this equation for $y$ by a trial-and-error procedure, $y_c = 2.15$ ft. This is the critical depth. The corresponding area is $A_c = 52.2$ ft$^2$, and the critical velocity is $V_c = 400/52.2 = 7.66$ fps.

*B. Graphical Method.* For a complicated or natural channel section, a graphical procedure for critical-flow computation is generally employed. By this procedure a curve of $y$ versus $Z$ is constructed. The value of $Q/\sqrt{g}$ is then computed. Using Eq. (4-1), the critical depth may be obtained directly from the curve, where $Z = Q/\sqrt{g}$.

**Example 4-3.** A 36-in. concrete circular culvert carries a discharge of 20 cfs. Determine the critical depth.

*Solution.* Construct a curve of $y$ vs. $Z$ (Fig. 4-4). Then compute $Z = Q/\sqrt{g} = 20/\sqrt{g} = 3.53$. From the curve the critical depth for this value of $Z$ is found to be $y_c = 1.44$ ft.

The dimensionless curve (Fig. 2-1) or the table in Appendix A for the geometric elements of a circular section might also be used to solve this problem. Since $d_0 = 3.0$ ft and $d_0{}^{2.5} = 15.6$, $Z/d_0{}^{2.5} = 3.53/15.6 = 0.226$. From the dimensionless curve or from the table, $y/d_0 = 0.48$, and so $y_c = 0.48 \times 3 = 1.44$ ft.

*C. Method of Design Chart.* The design chart for determining the critical depth (Fig. 4-1) can be used with great expediency.

In Example 4-2, $Z = 400/\sqrt{g} = 70.5$ [Eq. (4-1)]. The value of $Z/b^{2.5}$ is 0.0394. For this value, the chart gives $y/b = 0.108$ or $y_c = 2.16$ ft.

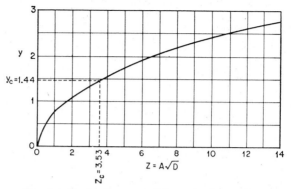

FIG. 4-4. Curve of $y$ versus $Z$ for a circular section.

In Example 4-3, $Z/d_0^{2.5} = 0.226$. For this value the chart gives $y/d = 0.48$ or $y_c = 1.44$ ft.

**4-5. Control of Flow.** The control of flow in an open channel is defined loosely in many ways. As used here the term means the establishment of a definitive flow condition in the channel or, more specifically, a definitive relationship between the stage and the discharge of the flow. When the control of flow is achieved at a certain section of the channel, this section is a *control section*. It will be shown later that the control section controls the flow in such a way that it restricts the transmission of the effect of changes in flow condition either in an upstream direction or in a downstream direction depending on the state of flow in the channel. Since the control section holds a definitive stage-discharge relationship, it is always a suitable site for a gaging station and for developing the *discharge rating curve*, a curve representing the depth-discharge relationship at the gaging station.

At the critical state of flow a definitive stage-discharge relationship can be established and represented by Eq. (4-1). This equation shows that the stage-discharge relationship is theoretically independent of the channel roughness and other uncontrolled circumstances. Therefore, a critical-flow section is a control section.

The location of the control section in a prismatic channel is generally governed by the state of flow, which in turn is determined by the slope of the channel. Take for an example a long straight prismatic channel in which a pool is created by a dam across the channel and the water flows over the dam through an overflow spillway (Fig. 4-5). Three flow conditions in the channel are shown, representing the subcritical, critical, and supercritical flows, respectively. The slopes of the channel in the three cases are, correspondingly, *mild* or subcritical, critical, and *steep* or supercritical.

If the channel has a critical slope (middle sketch in Fig. 4-5), then the flow is initially uniform and critical throughout the channel. In the presence of the dam, however, the flow through the pool will be subcritical and the pool surface will approach the horizontal. At the downstream end a so-called *drawdown curve* will be developed, extending upstream

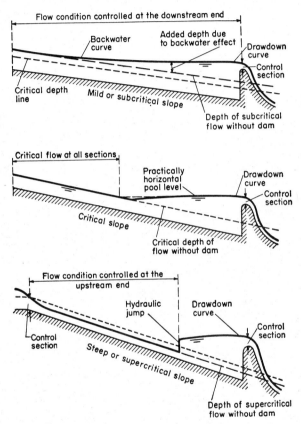

Fig. 4-5. Flow conditions in a long prismatic channel.

from a section near the spillway crest and becoming asymptotic to the pool level.

If the channel has a subcritical slope (top sketch in Fig. 4-5), the flow is initially subcritical. In the presence of the dam, the pool surface will be further raised for a long distance upstream from the pool in a so-called *backwater curve*. The additional depth of water is required to build up enough head to give the increased velocity necessary to pass water over the spillway. This effect of backing up the water behind the dam is

known as the *backwater effect*. At the downstream end the backwater
curve is connected with a smooth drawdown curve which leads the water
over the spillway.

If the channel has a supercritical slope (bottom sketch in Fig. 4-5), the
flow is initially supercritical. In the presence of the dam, the backwater

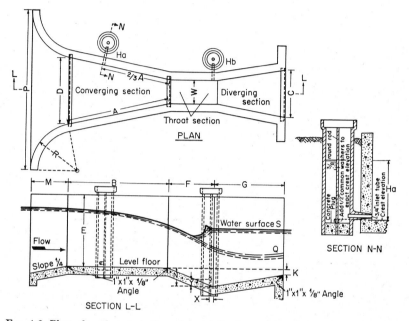

Fig. 4-6. Plan, elevation, and dimensions of the Parshall flume. (*U.S. Soil Conservation Service* [26].)    Plan and elevation of a concrete Parshall measuring flume showing lettered dimensions as follows:

$W$ = size of flume in in. or ft; $A$ = length of side wall of converging section; $\frac{2}{3}A$ = distance back from end of crest to gage point; $B$ = axial length of converging section; $C$ = width of downstream end of flume; $D$ = width of upstream end of flume; $E$ = depth of flume; $F$ = length of throat; $G$ = length of diverging section; $K$ = difference in elevation between lower end of flume and crest; $M$ = length of approach floor; $N$ = depth of depression in throat below crest; $P$ = width between ends of curved wing walls; $R$ = radius of curved wing wall; $X$ = horizontal distance to $H_b$ gage point from low point in throat; $Y$ = vertical distance to $H_b$ gage point from low point in throat. See the table on the next page for actual dimensions for various sizes of flume.

effect originating from the pool will not extend far upstream. Instead,
the flow in the upstream channel will continue in the downstream direction at a supercritical state until the flow-surface profile is actually below
the pool level;[1] then it will rise abruptly to the pool elevation in a hydrau-

[1] It should be noted that the pool level in this case is not horizontal but curved.
The curved water surface has an S1 profile, which will be described later (Art. 9-4).

Dimensions and Capacities of the Parshall Measuring Flume, for Various Throat Widths, *W*

[Letters refer to dimensions shown in Fig. 4-6]

| *W* | | *A* | | ⅔*A* | | *B* | | *C* | | *D* | | *E* | | *F* | | *G* | | *K* | *N* | *R* | | *M* | | *P* | | *X* | *Y* | Free-flow capacity | |
|---|---|---|---|---|---|---|---|---|---|---|---|---|---|---|---|---|---|---|---|---|---|---|---|---|---|---|---|---|---|
| | | | | | | | | | | | | | | | | | | | | | | | | | | | | Min | Max |
| Ft | In. | Ft | In. | Ft | In. | Ft | In. | Ft | In. | Ft | In. | Ft | In. | Ft | In. | Ft | In. | In. | In. | Ft | In. | Ft | In. | Ft | In. | In. | In. | Cfs | Cfs |
| 0 | 3 | 1 | 6⅜ | 1 | ¼ | 1 | 6 | 0 | 7 | 0 | 10³⁄₁₆ | 2 | 0 | 0 | 6 | 1 | 0 | 1 | 2¼ | 1 | 4 | 1 | 0 | 2 | 6¼ | 1 | 1½ | 0.03 | 1.9 |
| 0 | 6 | 2 | ⁷⁄₁₆ | 1 | 4⁵⁄₁₆ | 2 | 0 | 1 | 3½ | 1 | 3⅝ | 2 | 0 | 1 | 0 | 2 | 0 | 3 | 4½ | 1 | 4 | 1 | 0 | 2 | 11½ | 2 | 3 | .05 | 3.9 |
| 0 | 9 | 2 | 10⅝ | 1 | 11⅛ | 2 | 10 | 1 | 3 | 1 | 10⅝ | 2 | 6 | 1 | 0 | 1 | 6 | 3 | 4½ | 1 | 4 | 1 | 0 | 3 | 6½ | 2 | 3 | .09 | 8.9 |
| 1 | 0 | 4 | 6 | 3 | 0 | 4 | 4⅞ | 2 | 0 | 2 | 9¼ | 3 | 0 | 2 | 0 | 3 | 0 | 3 | 9 | 1 | 8 | 1 | 3 | 4 | 10¾ | 2 | 3 | .11 | 16.1 |
| 1 | 6 | 4 | 9 | 3 | 2 | 4 | 7⅞ | 2 | 6 | 3 | 4⅜ | 3 | 0 | 2 | 0 | 3 | 0 | 3 | 9 | 1 | 8 | 1 | 3 | 5 | 6 | 2 | 3 | .15 | 24.6 |
| 2 | 0 | 5 | 0 | 3 | 4 | 4 | 10⅞ | 3 | 0 | 3 | 11½ | 3 | 0 | 2 | 0 | 3 | 0 | 3 | 9 | 1 | 8 | 1 | 3 | 6 | 1 | 2 | 3 | .42 | 33.1 |
| 3 | 0 | 5 | 6 | 3 | 8 | 5 | 4¾ | 4 | 0 | 5 | 1⅞ | 3 | 0 | 2 | 0 | 3 | 0 | 3 | 9 | 1 | 8 | 1 | 3 | 7 | 3½ | 2 | 3 | .61 | 50.4 |
| 4 | 0 | 6 | 0 | 4 | 0 | 5 | 10⅝ | 5 | 0 | 6 | 4¼ | 3 | 0 | 2 | 0 | 3 | 0 | 3 | 9 | 2 | 0 | 1 | 6 | 8 | 10¾ | 2 | 3 | 1.3 | 67.9 |
| 5 | 0 | 6 | 6 | 4 | 4 | 6 | 4½ | 6 | 0 | 7 | 6⅝ | 3 | 0 | 2 | 0 | 3 | 0 | 3 | 9 | 2 | 0 | 1 | 6 | 10 | 1¼ | 2 | 3 | 1.6 | 85.6 |
| 6 | 0 | 7 | 0 | 4 | 8 | 6 | 10⅜ | 7 | 0 | 8 | 9 | 3 | 0 | 2 | 0 | 3 | 0 | 3 | 9 | 2 | 0 | 1 | 6 | 11 | 3½ | 2 | 3 | 2.6 | 103.5 |
| 7 | 0 | 7 | 6 | 5 | 0 | 7 | 4¼ | 8 | 0 | 9 | 11⅜ | 3 | 0 | 2 | 0 | 3 | 0 | 3 | 9 | 2 | 0 | 1 | 6 | 12 | 6 | 2 | 3 | 3.0 | 121.4 |
| 8 | 0 | 8 | 0 | 5 | 4 | 7 | 10⅛ | 9 | 0 | 11 | 1¾ | 3 | 0 | 2 | 0 | 3 | 0 | 3 | 9 | 2 | 0 | 1 | 6 | 13 | 8¼ | 2 | 3 | 3.5 | 139.5 |

lic jump. The backwater effect will not extend upstream through the hydraulic jump. The flow upstream from the jump is governed entirely by the upstream conditions.

The above example explains the important fact that on subcritical slopes the effect of change in water-surface elevation downstream is transmitted upstream by a backwater curve, whereas on supercritical slopes the effect cannot be transmitted far upstream. The flow condition in a subcritical channel is affected by downstream conditions; but, in a supercritical channel, the flow condition is dependent entirely upon the condition upstream or at the place where water enters the channel. Accordingly, the control of flow is said to be at the downstream end for channels with subcritical slope and at the upstream end for channels with supercritical slope.

When the channel is on a subcritical slope a control section at the downstream end may be a critical section, such as that created on the top of an overflow spillway. On a supercritical slope, the control section at the upstream end may also be a critical section, as shown in the figure. A sluice gate or an orifice or other control structure may also be used to create a control section. It should be noted that whether the channel slope is critical, subcritical, or supercritical will depend not only on the measure of the actual slope but also on the discharge or the depth of flow.

**4-6. Flow Measurement.** It was mentioned in the preceding article that, at a critical control section, the relationship between the depth and the discharge is definitive, independent of the channel roughness and other uncontrollable circumstances. Such a definitive stage-discharge relationship offers a theoretical basis for the measurement of discharge in open channels.

Based on the principle of critical flow, various devices for flow measurement have been developed. In such devices the critical depth is usually created either by the construction of a low hump on the channel bottom, such as a weir, or by a contraction in the cross section, such as a *critical-flow flume*. The use of a weir is a simple method, but it causes relatively high head loss. If water contains suspended particles, some will be deposited in the upstream pool formed by the weir, resulting in a gradual change in the discharge coefficient. These difficulties, however, can be overcome at least partially by the use of a critical-flow flume.

The critical-flow flume, also known as the *Venturi flume*, has been designed in various forms.[1] It is usually operated with an unsubmerged

---

[1] The critical-flow flumes mentioned in the text are those developed and studied in the United States. Outstanding designs of critical-flow flumes were also developed and tested by Jameson [4,5], Engel [6,7], and Linford [8] in England; by Crump [9] and Inglis [10] in India; by De Marchi [11,12], Contessini [11], Nebbia [13–15], and Citrini [16,17] in Italy; by Khafagi [18] in Switzerland; and by Balloffet [19] in Argentina.

or free-flow condition having the critical depth at a contracted section and a hydraulic jump in the exit section. Under certain conditions of flow, however, the jump may be submerged.

One of the most extensively used critical-flow flumes is the *Parshall flume*[1] (Fig. 4-6) which was developed in 1920 by R. L. Parshall. The depth-discharge relationships of Parshall flumes of various sizes, as calibrated empirically, are represented by the following equations:

| Throat width | Equation | |
|---|---|---|
| 3" | $Q = 0.992 H_a{}^{1.547}$ | (4-12) |
| 6" | $Q = 2.06 H_a{}^{1.58}$ | (4-13) |
| 9" | $Q = 3.07 H_a{}^{1.53}$ | (4-14) |
| 12" to 8' | $Q = 4WH_a{}^{1.522W^{0.026}}$ | (4-15) |
| 10' to 50' | $Q = (3.6875W + 2.5)H_a{}^{1.6}$ | (4-16) |

In the above equations $Q$ is the free discharge in cfs, $W$ is the width of throat in ft, and $H_a$ is the gage reading in ft. When the ratio of gage reading $H_b$ (Fig. 4-6) to $H_a$ exceeds the limits of 0.6 for 3-, 6-, and 9-in. flumes, 0.7 for 1- to 8-ft flumes, and 0.8 for 10- to 50-ft flumes, the flow becomes submerged. The effect of submergence is to reduce the discharge. In this case the discharge computed by the above equations must be corrected by a negative quantity. The diagrams in Fig. 4-7 give the corrections for submergence for Parshall flumes of various sizes. The correction for the 1-ft flume is made applicable to the larger flumes by multiplying the correction for the 1-ft flume by the factor given below for the particular size of the flume in use.

| Size of flume $W$, ft | Correction factor |
|---|---|
| 1 | 1.0 |
| 1.5 | 1.4 |
| 2 | 1.8 |
| 3 | 2.4 |
| 4 | 3.1 |
| 6 | 4.3 |
| 8 | 5.4 |

Similarly, the correction for the 10-ft flume is made applicable to the

---

[1] Experiments on this type of measuring device, then called the *Venturi flume*, were began by V. M. Cone at the hydraulic laboratory of the Colorado Agricultural Experiment Station, Fort Collins, Colo. The initial studies were reported in [20] and [21]. The name "Parshall measuring flume" was adopted for the device by the Executive Committee of the Irrigation Division, American Society of Civil Engineers, during its December meeting of 1929. Further developments on the Parshall flume are described by R. L. Parshall in [22] to [26].

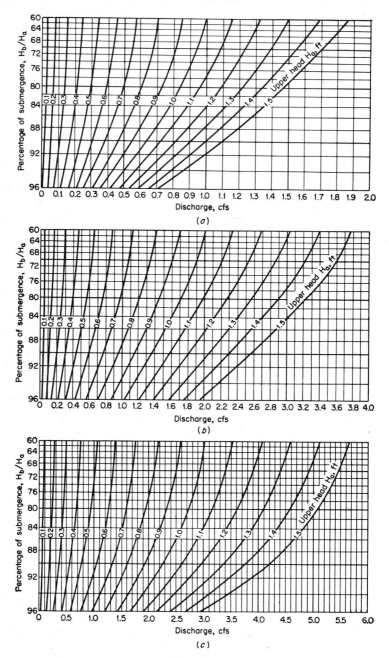

Fig. 4-7

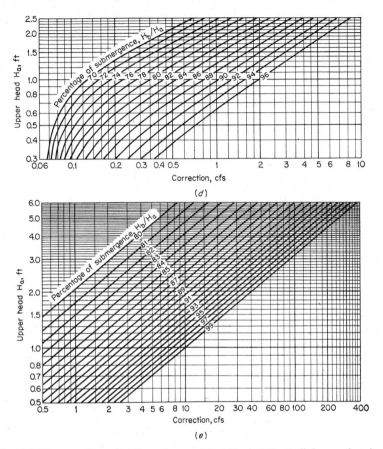

FIG. 4-7. Diagrams for computing submerged flow through Parshall flumes of various sizes. (*Colorado Agricultural Experiment Station* [25] *and U.S. Soil Conservation Service* [26].) (*a*) Diagram showing the rate of submerged flow, in cubic feet per second, through a 3-in. Parshall measuring flume. (*b*) Diagram showing the rate of submerged flow, in cubic feet per second, through a 6-in. Parshall measuring flume. (*c*) Diagram showing the rate of submerged flow, in cubic feet per second, through a 9-in. Parshall measuring flume. (*d*) Diagram for computing the rate of submerged flow, in cubic feet per second, through a 1-ft Parshall measuring flume. (*e*) Diagram for determining the correction in cubic feet per second per 10 ft of crest for submerged-flow discharge.

larger flumes by multiplying the correction for the 10-ft flume by the factor given below for the particular flume in use.

| Size of flume $W$, ft | Correction factor |
|:---:|:---:|
| 10 | 1.0 |
| 12 | 1.2 |
| 15 | 1.5 |
| 20 | 2.0 |
| 25 | 2.5 |
| 30 | 3.0 |
| 40 | 4.0 |
| 50 | 5.0 |

It is desirable to set the crest of the Parshall flume so that free flow will occur. If conditions do not permit free-flow operation, the percentage of submergence $H_b/H_a$ should be kept, whenever possible, below the practical limit of about 95%, since the flume will not measure dependably if the submergence is greater. The size and elevation of the crest depend upon the discharge to be measured and upon the size of the flume and, consequently, upon the loss of head through the flume. The loss of head can be determined from the diagrams in Fig. 4-8. A practical example (Example 4-5) will be given to show the determination of the size and elevation of the flume crest.

Because of the contraction at the throat, the velocity of water flowing through the flume is higher than that of the flow in the channel. For this reason any sand or silt in suspension or rolled along the bottom can be carried through, leaving the flume free of deposit. When a heavy burden of erosion debris is present in the stream, however, the Parshall flume will become invalid like the weir, because deposition of the debris will produce undependable results. For use under such circumstances, a modified Parshall flume known as the San Dimas flume [27,28] has been developed, which has the advantage of a self-cleaning mechanism for heavily debris-laden flows in the stream.

For measuring open-channel flow in closed conduits, such as sewers and covered irrigation canals, critical-flow flumes of special designs have been proposed. Palmer and Bowlus [29–31] have developed several of these flumes, including one which is simply a flat slab on the bottom and has no side contractions, one with a rectangular cross section, and several with trapezoidal-shaped throats. Stevens [32] recommended a critical-flow flume in which he used a blister-shaped hump control on the bed of the conduit to produce a critical flow over it. The frictional losses in this design are believed to be very small.

Like many measuring devices, the critical-flow flume has certain disadvantages. The flume cannot be used directly with or combined with a head gate. It is more expensive to build and requires more accurate

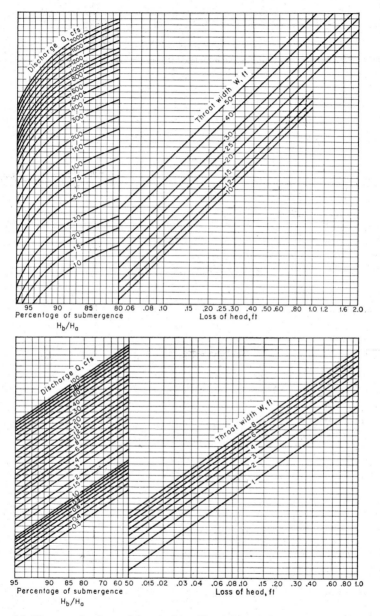

FIG. 4-8. Diagrams for determining the loss of head through Parshall flumes of various sizes. (*Colorado Agricultural Experiment Station* [25] *and U.S. Soil Conservation Service* [26].)

workmanship in its construction than other commonly used devices, such as weirs or submerged orifices. Technical information on other kinds of open-channel measuring devices and methods can easily be found in many textbooks and handbooks on hydraulics (such as [33] to [35]).

Many culverts along modern highways can be used as or converted to critical-flow flumes for measuring runoff from the adjoining agricultural lands. This idea was first suggested by Mavis [36] and others and was later studied at the Oklahoma Agricultural Experiment Station [37,38] by carrying out extensive experimental tests on rectangular highway culverts. The results of this experimental study indicate that the culvert can be used as a flow-rate measuring device if it flows part full and has free outlet fall. A weir sill should be installed, however, to improve the accuracy of the measurement in the low-flow range. In this investigation, a standard Villemonte-type weir sill[1] was developed and its location on the culvert floor determined. Head-discharge relationships were also determined for various flow ranges.

**Example 4-4.** Using the theory of critical flow, derive an equation for the discharge over a broad-crested weir.

*Solution.* Consider the section on the weir crest where critical flow occurs. At this section, $y_c = 2(V_c^2/2g) = H_c/1.5$ or $V_c = \sqrt{gH_c/1.5}$, where $H_c$ is the specific-energy head at the section. The discharge per foot width of the weir is, therefore, equal to

$$q = V_c y_c = \tfrac{2}{3} H_c \sqrt{\tfrac{2}{3} g H_c} = 3.09 H_c^{1.5} \qquad (4\text{-}17)$$

This is a theoretical discharge equation in which $H_c$ is uncertain since the critical section is usually difficult to locate. For practical purposes, however, the equation is generally written $q = CH^{1.5}$, where $H$ is the elevation of the upstream water surface above the weir crest. This is the form described earlier (Example 3-2).

If an aerated free overfall exists at the downstream end of the weir, the above equation can be expressed in terms of the brink depth $y_0$, which can easily be measured. Since $y_c = 1.4 y_0$ (Art. 3-4), the equation required is

$$q = 9.39 y_0^{1.5} \qquad (4\text{-}18)$$

Experiments have shown that, when the head on the broad-crested weir is greater than about 1.5 times the length of the crest, the nappe of the free overfall becomes detached and the weir is in effect a sharp-crested weir.

**Example 4-5.** Design a Parshall flume for handling 20 cfs of flow in a channel of moderate slope when the water depth in the channel is 2.5 ft.*

*Solution.* The discharge given can be measured by flumes of several sizes, but the best selection is the flume of most practical and economical size.

Assume $W = 4$ ft and $H_b/H_a = 0.7$. For $Q = 20$ cfs, Eq. (4-15) gives $H_a = 1.15$ ft. Hence, $H_b = 0.81$ ft.

At 70% submergence, the water surface in the throat, at $H_b$ gage, is essentially level with the surface of the tailwater. Under this condition of flow, shown in Fig. 4-9,

---

[1] The Villemonte weir sill consists of two triangular, tapered converging sills placed on the culvert floor with an opening left between them [39].

* This example is adopted from [26].

the tailwater depth $D = 2.5$ ft, and the elevation of the crest above the channel bottom is $X = 2.5 - 0.81 = 1.69$ ft.

From Fig. 4-8, the head loss corresponding to $H_b/H_a = 0.7$, $Q = 20$ cfs, and $W = 4$ ft is 0.43 ft. Therefore, the depth of water upstream from the flume will be $2.50 + 0.43 = 2.93$ ft.

Similarly, try 2- and 3-ft flumes. It is found that the respective crest elevations are 1.53 and 1.23 ft and that the respective upstream water depths are 2.98 and 3.12 ft.

In deciding the most practical size of flume to use, it will be necessary to examine the freeboard of the channel and the effect of rise of the water surface upon the flow through the headgate. If these conditions are satisfactory, the 2-ft flume will be the

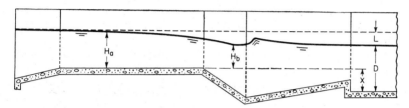

FIG. 4-9. Section of a Parshall flume illustrating the determination of the proper crest elevation [26].

most economical because of its small dimensions. However, when the width of the channel is considered, the final selection may be in favor of the 3- or 4-ft flume because moderate or long wing walls may be required for a small structure. Usually, the throat width of the flume will be from one-third to one-half of the channel width.

## PROBLEMS

**4-1.** Prove the following critical-discharge equations for the triangular, trapezoidal, and circular sections:

| Channel Section | Equation | |
|---|---|---|
| Triangular | $Q_c = 2.295z H_c^{2.5}$ | (4-19) |
| Trapezoidal | $Q_c = \dfrac{5.671[(b + zy)y]^{1.5}}{(b + 2zy)^{0.5}}$ | (4-20) |
| Circular | $Q_c = \dfrac{0.251(\theta - \sin \theta)^{1.5}}{(\sin \frac{1}{2}\theta)^{0.5}} d_0^{2.5}$ | (4-21) |
| Parabolic | $Q_c = 2.005T H_c^{1.5}$ | (4-22) |

In the above equations, $\alpha = 1$ and $H_c$ is the specific-energy head; other notation follows that of Table 2-1.

**4-2.** Compute the hydraulic exponent $M$ of the trapezoidal channel section (Fig. 2-2) having a flow depth of 6 ft, using (a) Eq. (4-10), (b) Fig. 4-2, and (c) the graphical method based on Eq. (4-11).

**4-3.** Compute the hydraulic exponent $M$ of a 36-in. circular conduit having a flow depth of 24 in. above the invert, using (a) Fig. 4-2 and (b) the graphical method based on Eq. (4-11).

**4-4.** Prove that the critical depth and velocity for a rectangular channel are expressed by

$$y_c = \sqrt[3]{\frac{\alpha Q^2}{gb^2}} \tag{4-23}$$

and
$$V_c = \sqrt{\frac{gy_c}{\alpha}} = \sqrt[3]{\frac{Qg}{\alpha b}} \tag{4-24}$$

where $Q$ is the discharge, $b$ is the channel width, and $\alpha$ is the energy coefficient.

**4-5.** A rectangular channel, 20 ft wide, carries a discharge of 200 cfs. Compute the critical depth and velocity.

**4-6.** Solve Example 4-2 by various methods if the discharge is 300 cfs.

**4-7.** Solve Example 4-3 by various methods if the discharge is 15 cfs.

**4-8.** An approximate but practical formula for the critical depth of a circular section of diameter $d_0$, derived by Braine [40] from an equation equivalent to Eq. (4-21), is

$$y_c = 0.325 \left(\frac{Q}{d_0}\right)^{2/3} + 0.083 d_0 \tag{4-25}$$

which is accurate only when $0.3 < y_c/d_0 < 0.9$. Solve Example 4-3 and Prob. 4-7 by this formula.

**4-9.** Referring to the natural channel given in Prob. 2-5, construct a curve of critical depth against discharge, ranging from 0 to 400 cfs.

**4-10.** Prove that the section of a channel in which the flow is critical at any stage takes the form expressed by

$$x^2 y^3 = \frac{Q^2}{32g} \tag{4-26}$$

where $x$ is half the top width and $y$ is the distance of the water surface below the energy line. Draw a sketch of the section and describe its properties. Is this channel possible? If not, how could it be made possible? Is this channel practicable and the flow stable?

**4-11.** Verify the computations for the 2- and 3-ft Parshall flumes tried in Example 4-5.

**4-12.** Determine the discharge through the 4-ft Parshall flume described in Example 4-5 if the percentage of submergence is 80%.

**4-13.** Determine the discharge measured by a 10-ft Parshall flume if the gage reading $H_a$ is 3.41 ft at a free-flow condition.

**4-14.** Design a Parshall flume to measure 10 cfs of flow in a channel having a depth of flow equal to 1.5 ft.

**4-15.** A uniform flow of 300 cfs occurs at a depth of 5 ft in a long rectangular channel 10 ft wide. Compute the minimum height of a flat-top hump that can be built on the floor of the channel in order to produce a critical depth. What will result if the hump is lower or higher than the computed minimum height?

**4-16.** If the critical depth in the above problem is produced by a contraction of the channel, what will be the maximum contracted width?

**4-17.** A low dam 5 ft high having a broad horizontal crest is built in a rectangular channel 20 ft wide. Assuming that a depth of 2.5 ft measured on the crest is the critical depth, compute the discharge and the depth of flow upstream from the dam.

**4-18.** On the basis of the theory of critical flow, Stevens [32] has derived the rating curves for the blister-shaped critical-flow flume that he proposed for use in circular conduits (Fig. 4-10). In the derivation, it is assumed (1) that there is no energy loss from $y_1$ to $y_c$, (2) that the approaching velocity in the pipe is equal to the discharge

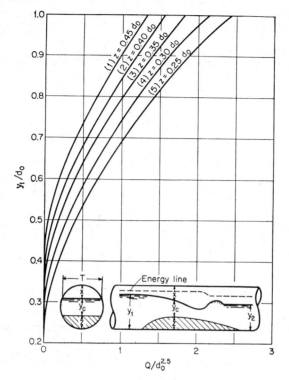

Fig. 4-10. Rating curves of a critical-flow flume proposed for a closed conduit. (*After J. C. Stevens* [32].)  $d_0$ = diameter of the conduit.

divided by the water area corresponding to the energy head instead of the actual area corresponding to $y_1$, and (3) that the critical-flow section is at the maximum height of the control "hump." The second assumption eliminates a trial procedure in determining the velocity head of the approaching flow and, furthermore, tends to compensate for the error involved in the first assumption. Verify any one of the rating curves.

## REFERENCES

1. Charles Jaeger: "Engineering Fluid Mechanics," translated from the German by P. O. Wolf, Blackie & Son, Ltd., London and Glasgow, 1956, pp. 93–119.

2. Ven Te Chow: Integrating the equations of gradually varied flow, paper 833, *Proceedings, American Society of Civil Engineers*, vol. 81, pp. 1–32, November, 1955.

3. R. R. Chugaev: Nekotorye voprosy neravonomernogo dvizheniia vody v otkrytykh prizmaticheskikh ruslakh (About some questions concerning nonuniform flow of water in open prismatic channels), *Izvestiia Vsesoiuznogo Nauchno-Issledovatel'skogo Instituta Gidrotekhniki (Transactions, All-Union Scientific Research Institute of Hydraulic Engineering)*, Leningrad, vol. 1, pp. 157–289, 1931.

4. A. H. Jameson: The Venturi flume and the effect of contractions in open channels, *Transactions, Institution of Water Engineers,* vol. 30, pp. 19–24, June 30, 1925.

5. A. H. Jameson: The development of the Venturi flume, *Water and Water Engineering,* London, vol. 32, no. 375, pp. 105–107, Mar. 20, 1930.

6. F. V. A. E. Engel: Non-uniform flow of water: Problems and phenomena in open channels with side contractions, *The Engineer,* vol. 155, pp. 392–394, Apr. 21; pp. 429–430, Apr. 28; pp. 456–457, May 5, 1933.

7. F. V. A. E. Engel: The Venturi flume, *The Engineer,* vol. 158, pp. 104–107, Aug. 3; pp. 131–133, Aug. 10, 1934.

8. A. Linford: Venturi flume flow meter, *Civil Engineering and Public Works Review,* London, vol. 36, no. 424, pp. 582–587, October, 1941. An abstract is given in *Journal, American Water Works Association,* vol. 34, pp. 1473–1475, September, 1942.

9. E. S. Crump: Moduling of irrigation channels, *Punjab Irrigation Branch Publications, Paper Nos.* 26 and 30A, Lahore, India, 1922 and 1933.

10. C. C. Inglis, Notes on standing wave flumes and flume meter baffle falls, *Public Works Department, Government of Bombay, Technical Papers, No.* 15, India, 1928.

11. Giulio De Marchi (author, pts. I and III) and Francesco Contessini (author, pt. II): Dispositivi per la misura della portata dei canali con minime perdite di quota: Nuove ricerche sperimentali sui misuratori a risalto idraulico (Canali Venturi); Parte I, Esame del processo idraulico; Parte II, Descrizione delle esperienze; Parte III, Risultati delle esperienze [Devices for measuring discharge in canals with minimum loss of level: New experimental researches on standing wave flumes (Venturi flumes); pt. I, Analysis of the hydraulic process; pt. II, Description of the experiments; and pt. III, Results of the experiments], *L'Energia elettrica, Milano,* vol. 13, no. 1, pp. 6–15, January, 1936; vol. 13, no. 5, pp. 236–244, May, 1936; vol. 14, no. 3, pp. 189–214, March, 1937. Reprinted as *Istituto di Idraulica e Costruzioni Idrauliche, Milano, Memorie e studi Nos.* 17, 25, and 26, 1936–1937.

12. Giulio De Marchi: Nouvelles recherches expérimentales sur le jaugeur à ressaut hydraulique, canal Venturi (New experimental researches on standing-wave flume, Venturi flume), Ministry of Agriculture, Paris, France, 1937. This is an abstract of pt. I of [11].

13. Guido Nebbia: Venturimetri per canali a sezioni di forma generica (Venturi meter for canals with cross sections of general forms), *Acqua e gas,* vol. 25, no. 11, pp. 270–291, November, 1936.

14. Guido Nebbia: Venturimetri per canali a sezioni di tipo monomio (Venturi meter for canals with cross sections of monomial type), *Acqua e gas,* vol. 25, no. 12, pp. 326–333, December, 1936.

15. Guido Nebbia: Venturimetri per canali a sezione di forma generica: Primi risultati sperimentali (Venturi meter for canals with cross sections of general forms: Preliminary experimental results), *Acqua e gas,* vol. 27, no. 5, pp. 155–181, May, 1938; vol. 27, no. 6, pp. 199–214, June, 1938.

16. Duilio Citrini: Misuratori a risalto (Standing-wave flumes), *L'Energia elettrica, Milano,* vol. 16, no. 10, pp. 758–763, October, 1939; reprinted as *Istituto di Idraulica e Costruzioni Idrauliche, Milano, Memorie e studi No.* 35, 1939.

17. Duilio Citrini: Modellatori a risalto: Guida al progetto (Standing-wave meters: Directions for design), Centro studi per le applicazioni dell'ingegneria all'agricoltura, *Sindacato ingegneri di Milano, Separate Paper No.* 5, Milan, 1941; reprinted as *Istituto di Idraulica e Costruzione Idrauliche, Milano, Memorie e studi No.* 44, 1941.

18. Anwar Khafagi: Der Venturikanal: Theorie und Anwendung (The Venturi flume: theory and application), *Eidgenössische technische Hochschule Zürich, Mitteilungen der Versuchsanstalt für Wasserbau und Erdbau, No.* 1, Zürich, 1942.

19. Armando Balloffet: Critical flow meters (Venturi flumes), paper 743, *Proceedings, American Society of Civil Engineers*, vol. 81, pp. 1–31, July, 1955.
20. V. M. Cone: The Venturi flume, *Journal of Agricultural Research*, vol. 9, no. 4, pp. 115–129, Apr. 23, 1917.
21. Ralph L. Parshall and Carl Rohwer: The Venturi flume, *Colorado Agricultural Experiment Station, Bulletin No.* 265, February, 1921.
22. R. L. Parshall: The improved Venturi flume, *Transactions, American Society of Civil Engineers*, vol. 89, pp. 841–851, 1926.
23. R. L. Parshall: The Parshall measuring flume, *Colorado Agricultural Experiment Station Bulletin No.* 423, March, 1936.
24  R. L. Parshall: Measuring water in irrigation channels, *U.S. Department of Agriculture, Farmer's Bulletin No.* 1683, January, 1932; revised, October, 1941.
25. R. L. Parshall: Parshall flumes of large size, *Colorado Agricultural Experiment Station, Bulletin No.* 386, May, 1932; revised as *Bulletin No.* 426A, March, 1953.
26. R. L. Parshall: Measuring water in irrigation channels with Parshall flumes and small weirs, *U.S. Soil Conservation Service, Circular* 843, May, 1950. This circular supersedes [24].
27. H. G. Wilm, John S. Cotton, and H. C. Storey: Measurement of debris-laden stream flow with critical-depth flumes, *Transactions, American Society of Civil Engineers*, vol. 103, pp. 1237–1253, 1938.
28. K. J. Bermel: Hydraulic influence of modifications to the San Dimas critical-depth measuring flume, *Transactions, American Geophysical Union*, vol. 31, no. 5, pp. 763–768, October, 1950.
29. Harold K. Palmer and Fred D. Bowlus: Adaptation of Venturi flumes to flow measurements in conduits, *Transactions, American Society of Civil Engineers*, vol. 101, pp. 1195–1216, 1936.
30. John H. Ludwig and Russel G. Ludwig: Design of Palmer-Bowlus flumes, *Sewage and Industrial Wastes*, vol. 23, no. 9, pp. 1096–1107, September, 1951.
31. Edwin A. Wells, Jr., and Harold B. Gotaas: Design of Venturi flumes in circular conduits, *Transactions, American Society of Civil Engineers*, vol. 123, pp. 749–771, 1958.
32. J. C. Stevens: Discussion on Adaptation of Venturi flumes to flow measurements in conduits, by Harold K. Palmer and Fred D. Bowlus, *Transactions, American Society of Civil Engineers*, vol. 101, pp. 1229–1231, 1936.
33. Herbert Addison: "Hydraulic Measurements," John Wiley & Sons, Inc., New York, 1941.
34. "Water Measurement Manual," U.S. Bureau of Reclamation, May, 1953, pp. 43–58.
35. Horace William King: "Handbook of Hydraulics," 4th ed., revised by Ernest F. Brater, McGraw-Hill Book Company, Inc., New York, 1954.
36. F. T. Mavis: Reducing unknowns in small culvert design, *Engineering News-Record*, vol. 137, no. 2, pp. 51–52, July 11, 1946.
37. W. O. Ree and F. R. Crow: Measuring runoff rates with rectangular highway culverts, *Oklahoma Agricultural Experiment Station, Technical Bulletin T-51*, November, 1954.
38. W. O. Ree and F. R. Crow: Culverts as water runoff measuring devices, *Agricultural Engineering*, vol. 35, no. 1, pp. 28–31 and 39, January, 1954.
39. James R. Villemonte: New type gaging station for small streams, *Engineering News-Record*, vol. 131, no. 21, pp. 748–750, Nov. 18, 1953.
40. C. D. C. Braine: Draw-down and other factors relating to the design of storm-water outflows on sewers, *Journal, Institution of Civil Engineers, London*, vol. 28, no. 6, pp. 136–163, April, 1947.

PART II

# UNIFORM FLOW

# CHAPTER 5

# DEVELOPMENT OF UNIFORM FLOW
# AND ITS FORMULAS

**5-1. Qualifications for Uniform Flow.** The uniform flow to be considered has the following main features: (1) the depth, water area, velocity, and discharge at every section of the channel reach are constant; and (2) the energy line, water surface, and channel bottom are all parallel; that is, their slopes are all equal, or $S_f = S_w = S_0 = S$. For practical purposes, the requirement of constant velocity may be liberally interpreted as the requirement that the flow possess a constant mean velocity. Strictly speaking, however, this should mean that the flow possesses a constant velocity at every point on the channel section within the uniform-flow reach. In other words, the velocity distribution across the channel section is unaltered in the reach. Such a stable pattern of velocity distribution can be attained when the so-called "boundary layer" is fully developed (Art. 8-1).

Uniform flow is considered to be steady only, since unsteady uniform flow is practically nonexistent. In natural streams, even steady uniform flow is rare, for rivers and streams in natural states scarcely ever experience a strict uniform-flow condition. Despite this deviation from the truth, the uniform-flow condition is frequently assumed in the computation of flow in natural streams. The results obtained from this assumption are understood to be approximate and general, but they offer a relatively simple and satisfactory solution to many practical problems.

As turbulent uniform flow is most commonly encountered in engineering problems, it will be discussed extensively in the following chapters. Laminar uniform flow has limited engineering applications, and will be described only in Art. 6-10.

It should be noted that uniform flow cannot occur at very high velocities, usually described as *ultrarapid*. This is because, when uniform flow reaches a certain high velocity, it becomes very unstable. At higher velocities the flow will eventually entrain air and become unsteady. The criterion for instability of uniform flow will be discussed in Art. 8-8.

**5-2. Establishment of Uniform Flow.** When flow occurs in an open channel, resistance is encountered by the water as it flows downstream.

This resistance is generally counteracted by the components of gravity forces acting on the body of the water in the direction of motion (Fig. 5-2). A uniform flow will be developed if the resistance is balanced by the gravity forces. The magnitude of the resistance, when other physical factors of the channel are kept unchanged, depends on the velocity of flow.

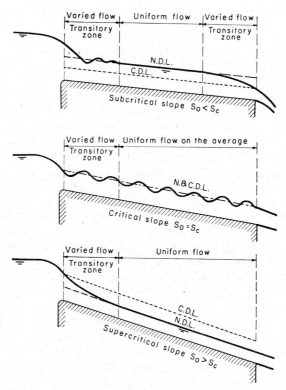

Fig. 5-1. Establishment of uniform flow in a long channel.

If the water enters the channel slowly, the velocity and hence the resistance are small, and the resistance is outbalanced by the gravity forces, resulting in an accelerating flow in the upstream reach. The velocity and the resistance will gradually increase until a balance between resistance and gravity forces is reached. At this moment and afterward the flow becomes uniform. The upstream reach that is required for the establishment of uniform flow is known as the *transitory zone*. In this zone the flow is accelerating and varied. If the channel is shorter than the transitory length required by the given conditions, uniform flow cannot be attained. Toward the downstream end of the channel the resistance may again be exceeded by gravity forces, and the flow may become varied again.

For purposes of explanation, a long channel is shown with three different slopes: subcritical, critical, and supercritical (Fig. 5-1). At the subcritical slope (top sketch in Fig. 5-1) the water surface in the transitory zone appears undulatory. The flow is uniform in the middle reach of the channel but varied at the two ends.[1] At the critical slope (middle sketch in Fig. 5-1) the water surface of the critical flow is unstable. Possible undulations may occur in the middle reach, but on the average the depth is constant and the flow may be considered uniform. At the supercritical slope (bottom sketch in Fig. 5-1) the transitory water surface passes from the subcritical stage to the supercritical stage through a gradual hydraulic drop. Beyond the transitory zone the flow is approaching uniformity. The depth of a uniform flow is called the *normal depth*. In all figures the long dashed line represents the normal-depth line, abbreviated as N.D.L., and the short dashed or dotted line represents the critical-depth line, or C.D.L.

The length of the transitory zone depends on the discharge and on the physical conditions of the channel, such as entrance condition, shape, slope, and roughness. From a hydrodynamic standpoint (see Art. 8-1), the length of the transitory zone should not be less than the length required for the full development of the boundary layer under the given conditions.

**5-3. Expressing the Velocity of a Uniform Flow.** For hydraulic computations the mean velocity of a turbulent uniform flow in open channels is usually expressed approximately by a so-called *uniform-flow formula*. Most practical uniform-flow formulas can be expressed in the following general form:

$$V = CR^xS^y \tag{5-1}$$

where $V$ is the mean velocity in fps; $R$ is the hydraulic radius in ft; $S$ is the energy slope,[2] $x$ and $y$ are exponents; and $C$ is a factor of flow resistance, varying with the mean velocity, hydraulic radius, channel roughness, viscosity, and many other factors.

For practical purposes, the flow in a natural channel may be assumed uniform under normal conditions, that is, if there are no flood flows or markedly varied flows caused by channel irregularities. In applying

[1] Theoretically speaking, the varied depth at each end approaches the uniform depth in the middle asymptotically and gradually. For practical purposes, however, the depth may be considered constant if the variation in depth is within a certain margin, say, 1% of the average uniform-flow depth.

[2] In uniform flow, $S = S_f = S_w = S_0$. When the uniform-flow formula is applied to the computation of energy slope in a gradually varied flow, the energy slope will be denoted specifically by $S_f$ instead of $S$.

the uniform-flow formula to a natural stream, it is understood that the result is very approximate since the flow condition is subject to more uncertain factors than would be involved in a regular artificial channel. As pointed out by Schneckenberg [1], a good uniform-flow formula for an alluvial channel with sediment transport and turbulent flow should take equal account of all the following variables:

$A$    the water area

$V$    the mean velocity

$V_{ms}$   the maximum surface velocity

$P$    the wetted perimeter

$R$    the hydraulic radius

$y$    the maximum depth of water area

$S_w$   the slope of the water surface

$n$    a coefficient representing the channel roughness, known as the *coefficient of roughness*[1]

$Q_s$   the suspended sediment charge

$Q_b$   the bed load

$\mu$    the dynamic viscosity of the water

$T$    the temperature of the water

There have been developed and published a large number of practical uniform-flow formulas,[2] but none of these formulas meets the qualifications of a good formula as defined above. The best known and most widely used formulas are the Chézy and Manning formulas, which will be described in the following articles and used extensively in this book. Theoretical uniform-flow formulas have also been derived on the basis of a theoretical velocity distribution across the channel section, which will be discussed later (Art. 8-5).

A different approach to the determination of the velocity in a natural channel has been attempted by Toebes [6]. In this approach a multiple-correlation analysis is applied to the following significant factors affecting the velocity in a given alluvial channel: water area, maximum surface velocity, wetted perimeter, maximum depth, slope of water surface, coefficient of roughness, and temperature of water. By this method it is possible to evaluate the independent individual influence of each variable on the magnitude of the velocity. When such an evaluation is made, the velocity under any given condition of the variables is simply equal to the algebraic summation of the individual contributions as affected by each variable. However, this method applies only to the streams in the geographical region for which the analysis is made; hence, its application cannot be generalized.

---

[1] In British literature the term "rugosity coefficient" is used.

[2] A number of well-known uniform-flow formulas are given and discussed in [2] to [5].

**5-4. The Chézy Formula.** As early as 1769 the French engineer Antoine Chézy was developing probably the first uniform-flow formula, the famous *Chézy formula*[1] which is usually expressed as follows:

$$V = C \sqrt{RS} \tag{5-2}$$

where $V$ is the mean velocity in fps, $R$ is the hydraulic radius in ft, $S$ is the slope of the energy line, and $C$ is a factor of flow resistance, called *Chézy's C*.

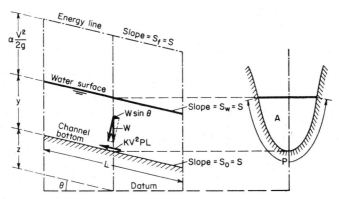

FIG. 5-2. Derivation of the Chézy formula for uniform flow in open channel.

The Chézy formula can be derived mathematically from two assumptions. The first assumption was made by Chézy. It states that the force resisting the flow per unit area of the stream bed is proportional to the square of the velocity; that is, this force is equal to $KV^2$ where $K$ is a constant of proportionality. The surface of contact of the flow with the stream bed is equal to the product of the wetted perimeter and the length of the channel reach, or $PL$ (Fig. 5-2). The total force resisting the flow[2] is then equal to $KV^2PL$.

---

[1] The source of this famous formula is not mentioned in most hydraulics textbooks. In fact, this knowledge has long been sought for. In 1876, the German engineer Gotthilf Heinrich Ludwig Hagen mentioned in his work [7] that Gaspard de Prony had stated that Chézy set up this formula in 1775, on the occasion of a report that Chézy made on the Canal de l'Yvette in conjunction with Jean-Rodolphe Perronet. "But," says Hagen, "I have sought in vain for further information on the subject." Then, in 1897, the American engineer Clemens Herschel through the assistance of a friend in Paris traced the original Canal de l'Yvette report to its hiding place, then translated the portion relating to the formula, and published it in [8]. Chézy's report revealed that the formula was developed and verified by experiments made on an earthen canal, the Courpalet Canal, and on the Seine River in late 1769.

[2] This channel resisting force may also be explained by the principles of fluid dynamics. The open channel can be conceived as a flat plate warped into a cylinder

The second assumption is the basic principle of uniform flow, which is believed to have been claimed first by Brahms [9] in 1754. It states that, in uniform flow, the effective component of the gravity force causing the flow must be equal to the total force of resistance. The effective gravity-force component (Fig. 5-2) is parallel to the channel bottom and equal to $wAL \sin \theta = wALS$, where $w$ is the unit weight of water, $A$ is the water area, $\theta$ is the slope angle, and $S$ is the channel slope.[1]   Thence, $wALS = KV^2PL$. Let $A/P = R$ and let $\sqrt{w/K}$ be replaced by a factor $C$; then the previous equation is reduced to the Chézy formula, or $V = \sqrt{(w/K)(A/P)S} = C\sqrt{RS}$.

Many attempts have been made to determine the value of Chézy's $C$. Three important formulas developed for this purpose will be given in the next article

**5-5. Determination of Chézy's Resistance Factor.**   Three important formulas for the determination of Chézy's $C$ are given as follows:

*A. The G. K. Formula.*   In 1869, two Swiss engineers, Ganguillet and Kutter [10], published a formula expressing the value of $C$ in terms of the slope $S$, hydraulic radius $R$, and the coefficient of roughness $n$. In English units, the formula is

$$C = \frac{41.65 + \dfrac{0.00281}{S} + \dfrac{1.811}{n}}{1 + \left(41.65 + \dfrac{0.00281}{S}\right)\dfrac{n}{\sqrt{R}}} \tag{5-3}$$

The coefficient $n$ in this formula is specifically known as *Kutter's n*.   The value of $n$ will be discussed in Arts. 5-7 and 5-8.

The G. K. formula was derived elaborately from flow-measurement data in channels of various types, including Bazin's gagings and the gagings of many European rivers and of the Mississippi River.[2]   Although

---

but unclosed on one side which corresponds to the free surface of the open-channel flow.   A fluid flowing in the unclosed cylinder will create a drag or resisting force on the inside surface.   This force is equal to the drag created by the flow of fluid along a flat plate whose two surfaces offer resistance to the flow.   The latter is equal to $C_d\rho V^2PL/2$, where $C_d$ is the coefficient of drag and $\rho$ is the mass density of the fluid. Thus, the factor $C_d\rho/2$ is equivalent to the constant of proportionality $K$.

[1] The slope under consideration is defined as the sine of the angle of inclination, or $S = \sin \theta$.

[2] The Mississippi River gagings were made by Humphreys and Abbot on the lower Mississippi River between 1850 and 1860, and the data thus obtained were published in a report submitted to the U.S. Army Corps of Topographical Engineers in 1861 [11]. The term containing $S$ was introduced into the G. K. formula simply in order to make the formula agree with the Humphreys and Abbot data.   This seems somewhat ridiculous now, because these data are known to have been quite inaccurate (see pp. 133–136 of [2]).   Some authors have suggested that the slope term $0.00281/S$ of

the formula appears cumbersome, it usually produces satisfactory results. It has been so widely used that many tables and charts are available for its application; so the use of the formula itself is seldom found necessary in engineering offices. Figure 5-3 gives a popular chart for the solution of the G. K. formula.

B. *The Bazin Formula.* In 1897, the French hydraulician H. Bazin[1] proposed a formula according to which Chézy's $C$ is considered a function of $R$ but not of $S$. Expressed in English units, this formula is

$$C = \frac{157.6}{1 + m/\sqrt{R}} \tag{5-4}$$

where $m$ is a coefficient of roughness whose values proposed by Bazin are given in Table 5-1.

TABLE 5-1. PROPOSED VALUES OF BAZIN'S $m$

| Description of channel | Bazin's $m$ |
|---|---|
| Very smooth cement of planed wood............... | 0.11 |
| Unplaned wood, concrete, or brick................. | 0.21 |
| Ashlar, rubble masonry, or poor brickwork........... | 0.83 |
| Earth channels in perfect condition................ | 1.54 |
| Earth channels in ordinary condition............... | 2.36 |
| Earth channels in rough condition................. | 3.17 |

The Bazin formula was developed primarily from data collected from small experimental channels; hence, its general application is found to be less satisfactory than the G. K. formula.

The Miami Conservancy District [2] has made a study comparing the variations in Chézy's $C$, Bazin's $m$, and Kutter's $n$ for Bazin's experimental data and several natural streams. The results based on this study are shown in Table 5-2. The values of the average variation indicate that Bazin's formula is not as good as Kutter's even for his own measurements.

C. *The Powell Formula.* In 1950, Powell [14] suggested a logarithmic formula for the roughness of artificial channels. This formula, an implicit function of $C$, is

$$C = -42 \log\left(\frac{C}{4\mathbf{R}} + \frac{\epsilon}{R}\right) \tag{5-5}$$

the G. K. formula be omitted in order to simplify the appearance of the formula and even to make the general results more satisfactory.

[1] From 1855 and 1862 an extensive series of experiments on open-channel flow were first begun by H. Darcy and then completed by Bazin. The results were published by Bazin in 1865 [12]. On the basis of the accumulated data, Bazin finally proposed the formula in 1897 [13].

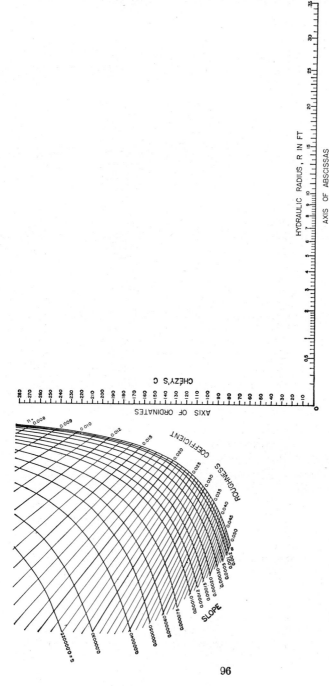

Fig. 5-3. Graphical solution of the G.K. formula.

To find $C$ when $R$, $S$, and $n$ are given: A straight line uniting $R$ on the axis of abscissas with the point where the slope curve $S$ intersects the line $n$ will indicate upon the axis of ordinates the value of $C$.

To find $R$ when $C$, $S$, and $n$ are given: A straight line from the point where the slope curve $S$ intersects the line $n$ to the point $C$ on the axis of ordinates will, when extended to the axis of abscissas, indicate thereon the value of $R$.

To find $S$ when $C$, $R$, and $n$ are given: A straight line from $R$ on the axis of abscissas to $C$ on the axis of ordinates will, when extended to the given line $n$, indicate upon it the value of $S$.

To find $n$ when $C$, $R$, and $S$ are given: A straight line from $R$ on the axis of abscissas to $C$ on the axis of ordinates will, when prolonged to the slope curve $S$, indicate upon it the value of $n$.

where $R$ is the hydraulic radius in ft; $\mathbf{R}$ is the Reynolds number; and $\epsilon$ is a measure of the channel roughness, having the tentative values shown in Table 5-3.

For rough channels, the flow is generally so turbulent that $\mathbf{R}$ becomes very large compared with $C$; thus, Eq. (5-5) approximates the form

TABLE 5-2. COMPARISON OF VARIATIONS IN CHÉZY'S $C$, BAZIN'S $m$, AND KUTTER'S $n$

| Measurements | Average values | | | Average variations, % | | |
|---|---|---|---|---|---|---|
| | $C$ | $m$ | $n$ | $C$ | $m$ | $n$ |
| Bazin's Series  6 | | 0.185 | 0.0127 | | 5.2 | 1.1 |
| 7 | | 0.156 | 0.0120 | | 3.4 | 1.0 |
| 8 | | 0.142 | 0.0116 | | 3.8 | 2.5 |
| 9 | | 0.199 | 0.0130 | | 10.6 | 1.2 |
| 10 | | 0.144 | 0.0117 | | 3.4 | 1.4 |
| 11 | | 0.129 | 0.0113 | | 3.7 | 3.8 |
| 12 | | 0.324 | 0.0151 | | 1.6 | 1.0 |
| 13 | | 0.311 | 0.0148 | | 2.7 | 1.2 |
| 14 | | 0.321 | 0.0150 | | 4.4 | 1.8 |
| 15 | | 0.715 | 0.0209 | | 4.2 | 1.2 |
| 16 | | 0.711 | 0.0212 | | 5.7 | 1.6 |
| 17 | | 0.721 | 0.0215 | | 6.7 | 2.2 |
| 32 | | 0.424 | 0.0168 | | 1.8 | 0.4 |
| 33 | | 0.444 | 0.0171 | | 3.1 | 1.2 |
| 44 | | 0.658 | 0.0195 | | 18.6 | 8.8 |
| 46 | | 0.704 | 0.0205 | | 11.1 | 5.7 |
| Miami River at Tadmor, Ohio, 1915–1916 | 67.4* | 1.98 | 0.0316 | 4.08 | 10.9 | 4.9 |
| Bogue Phalia River, Miss., 1914 | 63.3* | 4.09 | 0.0704 | 24.20 | 35.7 | 22.2 |
| Arkansas Drainage Canals, Ark., 1915 | 65.9* | 2.12 | 0.0324 | 3.18 | 4.8 | 1.6 |
| Mississippi River, Carrolton, La., 1912 | | 1.33 | 0.0320 | 1.30 | 5.4 | 3.0 |
| Mississippi River, Carrolton, La., 1913 | | 1.46 | 0.0334 | 2.80 | 12.8 | 2.8 |
| Irrawaddy River, Burma | | 1.35 | 0.0332 | 4.10 | 23.0 | 6.2 |
| Volga River at Samara, Russia | | 1.58 | 0.0311 | 1.87 | 13.0 | 4.1 |
| Volga River at Zhiguly, Russia | | 1.76 | 0.0363 | 18.80 | 36.5 | 5.0 |
| Average variation | | | | 7.54 | 9.67 | 3.58 |

\* Values averaged by the author.

$C = 42 \log (R/\epsilon)$. For smooth channels, the surface roughness may be so slight that $\epsilon$ becomes negligible compared with $R$; then the formula approaches the form $C = 42 \log (4R/C)$. Since Chézy's $C$ is expressed implicitly in the Powell formula, the solution of the formula for $C$ requires a trial-and-error procedure.

The Powell formula was developed from limited laboratory experiments on smooth and rough channels and from the theoretical velocity distribution studied by Keulegan (Art. 8-4).   The practical application of this formula is limited, since further investigation is needed for determination of the proper values of. $\epsilon$.

TABLE 5-3.   TENTATIVE VALUES OF POWELL'S $\epsilon$

| Description of channel | Powell's $\epsilon$ | |
| --- | --- | --- |
| | New | Old |
| Neat cement surface.................... | 0.0002 | 0.0004 |
| Unplaned-plank flumes.................. | 0.0010 | 0.0017 |
| Concrete-lined channels................ | 0.004 | 0.006 |
| Earth, straight and uniform............. | 0.04 | |
| Dredged earth channels................ | 0.10 | |

**Example 5-1.** Compute the velocity and discharge in the trapezoidal channel described in Example 2-1, having a bottom width of 20 ft, side slopes 2:1, and a depth of water 6 ft.   Given: Kutter's $n = 0.015$, and $S = 0.005$.
*Solution.*   From Example 2-1, $A = 192.0$ ft$^2$ and $R = 4.10$ ft.   Using the G. K. formula, the value of Chézy's $C$ is

$$C = \frac{41.65 + \dfrac{0.00281}{0.005} + \dfrac{1.811}{0.015}}{1 + \left(41.65 + \dfrac{0.00281}{0.005}\right)\dfrac{0.015}{\sqrt{4.10}}} = 124.2$$

Then, by the Chézy formula,

$$V = 124.2 \sqrt{4.10 \times 0.005} = 17.8 \text{ fps}$$

Therefore,

$$Q = 192.0 \times 17.8 = 3,420 \text{ cfs}$$

**5-6. The Manning Formula.**   In 1889 the Irish engineer· Robert Manning[1] presented a formula, which was later modified to its present

---

[1] Manning first presented the formula in a paper read on December 4, 1889, at a meeting of the Institution of Civil Engineers of Ireland.   The paper was later published in the Transactions of the Institution [15].   The formula was first given in a complicated form and then simplified to $V = CR^{2/3}S^{1/2}$, where $V$ is the mean velocity, $C$ is a factor of flow resistance, $R$ is the hydraulic radius, and $S$ is the slope.   This was further modified by others and expressed in metric units as $V = (1/n)R^{2/3}S^{1/2}$.   Later, it was converted back again to English units, resulting in $V = (1.486/n)R^{2/3}S^{1/2}$.   In this conversion, as in the conversion of the Ganguillet and Kutter formula, the numerical value of $n$ is kept unaffected.   Consequently, the same value of $n$ is widely used in both systems of units.

In the view of modern fluid mechanics, which pays much attention to dimensions, the dimensions of $n$ become a matter of consideration.   Directly from the Manning formula, the dimensions of $n$ are seen to be $TL^{-1/3}$.   Since it is unreasonable to suppose that the roughness coefficient would contain the dimension $T$, some authors assume that the numerator contains $\sqrt{g}$, thus yielding the dimensions of $L^{1/6}$ for $n$. Also, for physical reasons, it will be seen that $n = [\phi(R/k)]k^{1/6}$ [Eq. (8-26)], where $k$ is well-known form

$$V = \frac{1.49}{n} R^{2/3} S^{1/2} \tag{5-6}$$

where $V$ is the mean velocity in fps, $R$ is the hydraulic radius in ft, $S$ is the slope of energy line, and $n$ is the coefficient of roughness, specifically known as *Manning's n*. This formula was developed from seven different formulas, based on Bazin's experimental data, and further verified by 170 observations.[1]   Owing to its simplicity of form and to the satis-

---

a linear measure of roughness and $\phi(R/k)$ is a function of $R/k$.   If $\phi(R/k)$ is considered dimensionless, $n$ will have the same dimensions as those of $k^{1/6}$, that is, $L^{1/6}$.

On the other hand, of course, it is equally possible to assume that the numerator of $1.486/n$ can absorb the dimensions of $L^{1/3}T^{-1}$, or that $\phi(R/k)$ involves a dimensional factor, thus leaving no dimensions for $n$.   Some authors, therefore, preferring the simpler choice, consider $n$ a dimensionless coefficient.

It is interesting to note that the conversion of the units for the Manning formula is independent of the dimensions of $n$, as long as the same value of $n$ is used in both systems of units.   If $n$ is assumed dimensionless, then the formula in English units gives the numerical constant $3.2808^{1/3} = 1.486$ since 1 meter $= 3.2808$ ft.   Now, if $n$ is assumed to have the dimensions of $L^{1/6}$, its numerical value in English units must be different from its value in metric units, unless a numerical correction factor is introduced for compensation.   Let $n$ be the value in metric units and $n'$ the value in English units.   Then, $n' = (3.2808^{1/6})n = 1.2190n$.   When the formula is converted from metric to English units, the resulting form takes the numerical constant $3.2808^{1/3+1/6} = 3.2808^{1/2} = 1.811$, since $n$ has the dimensions of $L^{1/6}$.   Thus, the resulting equation should be written $V = 1.811R^{2/3}S^{1/2}/n'$.   Since the same value of $n$ is used in both systems, the practical form of the formula in the English system is $V = 1.811R^{2/3}S^{1/2}/1.2190n = 1.486R^{2/3}S^{1/2}/n$, which is identical with the formula derived on the assumption that $n$ has no dimensions.

In a search of early literature on hydraulics, the author has failed to find any significant discussion regarding the dimensions of $n$.   It seems that this was not a problem of concern to the forefathers of hydraulics.   It is most likely, however, that $n$ was unconsciously taken as dimensionless in the conversion of the Manning formula, because such a conversion, as shown above, is more direct and simpler.

Now, considering the approximations involved in the derivation of the formula and the uncertainty in the value of $n$, it seems unjustifiable to carry the numerical constant to more than three significant figures.   For practical purposes, a value of 1.49 is believed to be sufficiently accurate [16].

Manning mentioned that the simplified form of the formula had been suggested independently by G. H. L. Hagen prior to Manning's own work, according to a statement by Major Cunningham [17].   Hagen's formula was believed to have appeared first in 1876 [7].   It is also known that Philippe-Gaspard Gauckler [18] had an early proposal of the simplified form of Manning's formula in 1868 and that Strickler [19] presented independently the same form of the formula in 1923.

[1] For the derivation of the exponent of $R$, use was made of Bazin's experimental data on artificial channels [12].   For different shapes and roughnesses, the average value of the exponent was found to vary from 0.6499 to 0.8395.   Considering these variations, Manning adopted an approximate value of $2/3$ for the exponent.   On the

factory results it lends to practical applications, the Manning formula has become the most widely used of all uniform-flow formulas for open-channel flow computations.[1] A nomographic solution of the formula is given in Appendix C.

Within the normal ranges of slope and hydraulic radius, the values of Manning's $n$ and Kutter's $n$ are generally found to be numerically very close. For practical purposes, the two values may be considered identical when the slope is equal to or greater than 0.0001 and the hydraulic radius is between 1.0 and 30 ft. Typical values good for both Kutter's $n$ and Manning's $n$ are shown in Table 5-6 and illustrated in Fig. 5-5.

Comparing the Chézy formula with the Manning formula, it can be seen that

$$C = \frac{1.49}{n} R^{\frac{1}{6}} \qquad (5\text{-}7)$$

This equation provides an important relationship[2] between Chézy's $C$ and Manning's $n$.

The exponent of the hydraulic radius in the Manning formula is actually not a constant but varies in a range depending mainly on the channel shape and roughness (see a previous footnote). For this reason, some hydraulicians prefer to use the formula with a variable exponent. For example, the uniform-flow formula widely used in the U.S.S.R. is of this type; this is the *Pavlovskii formula* [21], proposed in 1925.* This formula in *metric* units is

$$C = \frac{1}{n} R^{y} \qquad (5\text{-}8)$$

where $\qquad y = 2.5 \sqrt{n} - 0.13 - 0.75 \sqrt{R}(\sqrt{n} - 0.10) \qquad (5\text{-}9)$

and where $C$ is the resistance factor in the Chézy formula expressed in *metric* units. The exponent $y$ depends on the roughness coefficient and hydraulic radius. The formula is valid for $R$ between 0.1 and 3.0 m and

---

basis of other later studies, some authors suggested a value of $\frac{3}{4}$ [20], and others suggested a variable depending on $R$ and $n$ [21].

[1] The Manning formula was suggested for international use by Lindquist [3] at the Scandinavia Sectional Meeting of the World Power Conference in 1933 in Stockholm. The final recommendation for such use was made by the Executive Committee at the 3d World Power Conference in 1936 in Washington, D.C.

[2] On account of this relationship, the Manning formula is sometimes considered a variation of the Chézy formula with Chézy's $C$ defined by Eq. (5-7).

* The Pavlovskiĭ formula was published in several editions of Pavlovskiĭ's "Handbook of Hydraulics" [21]. An article about this formula entitled *Formula dlia koeffitsienta Chézy (Formula for a Chézy coefficient)* is given in pp. 140–149 of the 1937 edition of the book. A footnote in this article reads: "The formula was proposed in 1925."

for $n$ between 0.011 and 0.040. For practical purposes, the following approximate forms of Eq. (5-9) are generally suggested for use:

$$y = 1.5 \sqrt{n} \quad \text{for } R < 1.0 \text{ m} \tag{5-10}$$
$$y = 1.3 \sqrt{n} \quad \text{for } R > 1.0 \text{ m} \tag{5-11}$$

**5-7. Determination of Manning's Roughness Coefficient.**   In applying the Manning formula or the G. K. formula, the greatest difficulty lies in the determination of the roughness coefficient $n$; for there is no exact method of selecting the $n$ value.   At the present stage of knowledge, to select a value of $n$ actually means to estimate the resistance to flow in a given channel, which is really a matter of intangibles.   To veteran engineers, this means the exercise of sound engineering judgment and experience; for beginners, it can be no more than a guess, and different individuals will obtain different results.

In order to give guidance in the proper determination of the roughness coefficient, four general approaches will be discussed; namely, (1) to understand the factors that affect the value of $n$ and thus to acquire a basic knowledge of the problem and narrow the wide range of guesswork, (2) to consult a table of typical $n$ values for channels of various types, (3) to examine and become acquainted with the appearance of some typical channels whose roughness coefficients are known, and (4) to determine the value of $n$ by an analytical procedure based on the theoretical velocity distribution in the channel cross section and on the data of either velocity or roughness measurement.   The first three approaches will be given in the next three articles, and the fourth approach will be taken up in Art. 8-7.

**5-8. Factors Affecting Manning's Roughness Coefficient.**   It is not uncommon for engineers to think of a channel as having a single value of $n$ for all occasions.   In reality, the value of $n$ is highly variable and depends on a number of factors.   In selecting a proper value of $n$ for various design conditions, a basic knowledge of these factors should be found very useful.   The factors that exert the greatest influence upon the coefficient of roughness in both artificial and natural channels are therefore described below.   It should be noted that these factors are to a certain extent interdependent; hence discussion about one factor may be repeated in connection with another.

*A. Surface Roughness.*   The surface roughness is represented by the size and shape of the grains of the material forming the wetted perimeter and producing a retarding effect on the flow.   This is often considered the only factor in selecting a roughness coefficient, but it is actually just one of several major factors.   Generally speaking, fine grains result in a relatively low value of $n$ and coarse grains, in a high value of $n$.

In alluvial streams where the material is fine in grain, such as sand, clay, loam, or silt, the retarding effect is much less than where the material is coarse, such as gravels or boulders.   When the material is fine, the value of $n$ is low and relatively unaffected by change in flow stage.   When the material consists of gravels and boulders, the value of $n$ is generally high, particularly at low or high stage.   Larger boulders usually collect at the bottom of the stream, making the channel bottom rougher than the banks and increasing the value of $n$ at low stages.   At high stages, a portion of the energy of flow is used in rolling the boulders downstream, thus increasing the value of $n$.   A theoretical discussion of surface roughness will be given in Art. 8-2.

*B. Vegetation.*   Vegetation may be regarded as a kind of surface roughness, but it also markedly reduces the capacity of the channel and retards the flow.   This effect depends mainly on height, density, distribution, and type of vegetation, and it is very important in designing small drainage channels.

At the University of Illinois an investigation has been made to determine the effect of vegetation on the coefficient of roughness [22].   On one of the drainage ditches in central Illinois under investigation, an average $n$ value of 0.033 was measured in March, 1925, when the channel was in good condition.   In April, 1926, there were bushy willows and dry weeds on the side slopes, and $n$ was found to be 0.055.   This increase in $n$ represents the result of one year's growth of vegetation.   During the summers of 1925 and 1926 there was a thick growth of cattails on the bottom of the channel.   The $n$ value at medium summer stages was about 0.115, and at a nearly bankfull stage it was 0.099.   The cattails in the channel were washed out by the high water in September, 1926; the average value of $n$ found after this occurrence was 0.072.   The conclusions drawn from this investigation were, in part, as follows:

1. The minimum value of $n$ that should be used for designing drainage ditches in central Illinois is 0.040.   This value is obtainable at high stages during the summer months in the most carefully maintained channels, where the bottom of the channel is clear of vegetation and the side slopes are covered with grass or low weeds, but no bushes.   This low value of $n$ should not be used unless the channel is to be cleared annually of all weeds and bushes.

2. A value of $n = 0.050$ should be used if the channel is to be cleared in alternate years only.   Large weeds and bushy willows from 3 to 4 ft high on the side slopes will produce this value of $n$.

3. In channels that are not cleared for a number of years, the growth may become so abundant that values of $n > 0.100$ may be found.

4. Trees from 6 to 8 in. in diameter growing on the side slopes do not impede the flow so much as do small bushy growths, provided overhanging branches are cut off.

The U.S. Soil Conservation Service has made studies on flow of water in small shallow channels protected by vegetative linings (Chap. 7, Sec. C). It was found that $n$ values for these channels varied with the shape and cross section of the channel, the slope of the channel bed, and the depth of flow. Comparing two channels, all other factors being equal, the lesser average depth gives the higher $n$ value, owing to a larger proportion of affected vegetation. Thus, a triangular channel has a higher $n$ value than a trapezoidal channel, and a wide channel has a lower $n$ value than a narrow channel. A flow of sufficient depth tends to bend over and submerge the vegetation and to produce low $n$ values. A steep slope causes greater velocity, greater flattening of the vegetation, and low $n$ values.

The effect of vegetation on flood plains will be discussed later in item $H$.

C. *Channel Irregularity.* Channel irregularity comprises irregularities in wetted perimeter and variations in cross section, size, and shape along the channel length. In natural channels, such irregularities are usually introduced by the presence of sand bars, sand waves, ridges and depressions, and holes and humps on the channel bed. These irregularities definitely introduce roughness in addition to that caused by surface roughness and other factors. Generally speaking, a gradual and uniform change in cross section, size, and shape will not appreciably affect the value of $n$, but abrupt changes or alternation of small and large sections necessitates the use of a large value of $n$. In this case, the increase in $n$ may be 0.005 or more. Changes that cause sinuous flow from side to side of the channel will produce the same effect.

D. *Channel Alignment.* Smooth curvature with large radius will give a relatively low value of $n$, whereas sharp curvature with severe meandering will increase $n$. On the basis of flume tests, Scobey [23] suggested that the value of $n$ be increased 0.001 for each 20 degrees of curvature in 100 ft of channel. Although it is doubtful whether curvature ever increases $n$ more than 0.002 or 0.003, its effect should not be ignored, for curvature may induce the accumulation of drift and thus indirectly increase the value of $n$. Generally speaking, the increase of roughness in unlined channels carrying water at low velocities is negligible. An increase of 0.002 in $n$ value would constitute an adequate allowance for curve losses in most flumes containing pronounced curvatures, whether built of concrete or other materials. The meandering of natural streams, however, may increase the $n$ value as high as 30%.

E. *Silting and Scouring.* Generally speaking, silting may change a very irregular channel into a comparatively uniform one and decrease $n$, whereas scouring may do the reverse and increase $n$. However, the dominant effect of silting will depend on the nature of the material deposited. Uneven deposits such as sand bars and sand waves are channel irregularities and will increase the roughness. The amount and uniformity of scouring will depend on the material forming the wetted perimeter. Thus, a sandy or gravelly bed will be eroded more uniformly than a clay bed. The deposition of silt eroded from the uplands will tend to even out the irregularities in a channel dredged through clay. The energy used in eroding and carrying the material in suspension or rolling it along the bed will also increase the $n$ value. The effect of scouring is not significant as long as the erosion on channel bed caused by high velocities is progressing evenly and uniformly.

*F. Obstruction.* The presence of log jams, bridge piers, and the like tends to increase $n$. The amount of increase depends on the nature of the obstructions, their size, shape, number, and distribution.

*G. Size and Shape of Channel.* There is no definite evidence about the size and shape of a channel as an important factor affecting the value of $n$. An increase in hydraulic radius may either increase or decrease $n$, depending on the condition of the channel (Fig. 5-4).

*H. Stage and Discharge.* The $n$ value in most streams decreases with increase in stage and in discharge. When the water is shallow, the irregularities of the channel bottom are exposed and their effects become pronounced. However, the $n$ value may be large at high stages if the banks are rough and grassy.

When the discharge is too high, the stream may overflow its banks and a portion of the flow will be along the flood plain. The $n$ value of the flood plains is generally larger than that of the channel proper, and its magnitude depends on the surface condition or vegetation. If the bed and banks of a channel are equally smooth and regular and the bottom slope is uniform, the value of $n$ may remain almost the same at all stages; so a constant $n$ is usually assumed in the flow computation. This happens mostly in artificial channels. On flood plains the value of $n$ usually varies with the stage of submergence of the vegetation at low stages. This can be seen, for example, from Table 5-4, which shows the $n$ values for various flood stages according to the type of cover and depth

TABLE 5-4. VALUES OF $n$ FOR VARIOUS STAGES IN THE NISHNABOTNA RIVER, IOWA, FOR THE AVERAGE GROWING SEASON

| Depth of water, ft | Channel section | Flood-plain cover | | | | |
|---|---|---|---|---|---|---|
| | | Corn | Pasture | Meadow | Small grains | Brush and waste |
| Under 1 | 0.03 | 0.06 | 0.05 | 0.10 | 0.10 | 0.12 |
| 1 to 2 | 0.03 | 0.06 | 0.05 | 0.08 | 0.09 | 0.11 |
| 2 to 3 | 0.03 | 0.07 | 0.04 | 0.07 | 0.08 | 0.10 |
| 3 to 4 | 0.03 | 0.07 | 0.04 | 0.06 | 0.07 | 0.09 |
| Over 4 | 0.03 | 0.06 | 0.04 | 0.05 | 0.06 | 0.08 |

of inundation, as observed in the Nishnabotna River, Iowa, for the average growing season [24].   It should be noted, however, that vegetation has a marked effect only up to a certain stage and that the roughness coefficient can be considered to remain constant for practical purposes in determining overbank flood discharges.

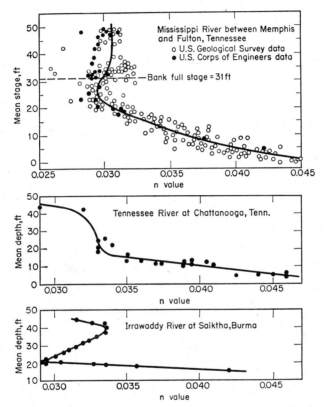

FIG. 5-4. Variations of the $n$ value with the mean stage or depth.

Curves of $n$ value versus stage (Fig. 5-4) in streams have been given by Lane [25], showing how value of $n$ varies with stage in three large river channels.   For the roughness of large canals, a study in connection with the design of the Panama Canal was made by Meyers and Schultz [26].[1]   The two most important conclusions reached from this study were (1) that the $n$ value for a river channel is least when the stage is at or somewhat above normal bankfull stage, and tends to increase for both

---

[1] A table of $n$ values for eleven large channels at the most efficient depths and the curves showing the variations of $n$ value with hydraulic radius in eight river channels are also given in this reference.

higher and lower stages; and (2) that the bankfull $n$ values do not vary greatly for rivers and canals in different kinds of material and in widely separated locations.

For circular conduits, Camp [27,28] was able to show that the $n$ value for a conduit flowing partially full is greater than that for a full conduit. Using measurements on clean sewer pipe and drain tile, both clay and concrete, from 4 to 12 in. in size, he found an increase of about 24% in the $n$ value at the half-depth (Fig. 6-5).[1] The $n$ value for the pipe flowing full was found to vary from 0.0095 to 0.011. Taking an average value of 0.0103, the $n$ value at half-depth should be about 0.013. This is identical with the usual design value, which is based largely on measured values in sewers flowing partially full.

*I. Seasonal Change.* Owing to the seasonal growth of aquatic plants, grass, weeds, willow, and trees in the channel or on the banks, the value of $n$ may increase in the growing season and diminish in the dormant season. This seasonal change may cause changes in other factors.

*J. Suspended Material and Bed Load.* The suspended material and the bed load, whether moving or not moving, would consume energy and cause head loss or increase the apparent channel roughness.

All the above factors should be studied and evaluated with respect to conditions regarding type of channel, state of flow, degree of maintenance, and other related considerations. They provide a basis for determining the proper value of $n$ for a given problem. As a general guide to judgment, it may be accepted that conditions tending to induce turbulence and cause retardance will increase $n$ value and that those tending to reduce turbulence and retardance will decrease $n$ value.

Recognizing several primary factors affecting the roughness coefficient, Cowan [32] developed a procedure for estimating the value of $n$. By this procedure, the value of $n$ may be computed by

$$n = (n_0 + n_1 + n_2 + n_3 + n_4)m_5 \qquad (5\text{-}12)$$

where $n_0$ is a basic $n$ value for a straight, uniform, smooth channel in the natural materials involved, $n_1$ is a value added to $n_0$ to correct for the effect of surface irregularities, $n_2$ is a value for variations in shape and size of the channel cross section, $n_3$ is a value for obstructions, $n_4$ is a value for vegetation and flow conditions, and $m_5$ is a correction factor for meandering of channel. Proper values of $n_0$ to $n_4$ and $m_5$ may be selected from Table 5-5 according to the given conditions.

---

[1] The $n/n_0$ curve was based on measurements by Wilcox [29] on 8-in. clay and concrete sewer pipes and by Yarnell and Woodward [30] on open-butt-joint concrete and clay drain tiles 4 to 12 in. in size. For depths less than about $0.15d_0$, the curve was verified by the data of Johnson [31] for large sewers.

In selecting the value of $n_1$, the degree of irregularity is considered *smooth* for surfaces comparable to the best attainable for the materials involved; *minor* for good dredged channels, slightly eroded or scoured side slopes of canals or drainage channels; *moderate* for fair to poor dredged channels, moderately sloughed or eroded side slopes of canals or drainage channels; and *severe* for badly sloughed banks of natural streams, badly eroded or sloughed sides of canals or drainage channels, and unshaped, jagged, and irregular surfaces of channels excavated in rock.

In selecting the value of $n_2$, the character of variations in size and shape of cross section is considered *gradual* when the change in size or shape occurs gradually, *alternating occasionally* when large and small sections alternate occasionally or when shape changes cause occasional shifting of main flow from side to side, and *alternating frequently* when large and small sections alternate frequently or when shape changes cause frequent shifting of main flow from side to side.

The selection of the value of $n_3$ is based on the presence and character-istics of obstructions such as debris deposits, stumps, exposed roots, boulders, and fallen and lodged logs. One should recall that conditions considered in other steps must not be reevaluated or double-counted in this selection. In judging the relative effect of obstructions, consider the following: the extent to which the obstructions occupy or reduce the average water area, the character of obstructions (sharp-edged or angular objects induce greater turbulence than curved, smooth-surfaced objects), and the position and spacing of obstructions transversely and longitudi-nally in the reach under consideration.

In selecting the value of $n_4$, the degree of effect of vegetation is considered

(1) *Low* for conditions comparable to the following: (*a*) dense growths of flexible turf grasses or weeds, of which Bermuda and blue grasses are examples, where the average depth of flow is 2 to 3 times the height of vegetation, and (*b*) supple seedling tree switches, such as willow, cotton-wood, or salt cedar where the average depth of flow is 3 to 4 times the height of the vegetation.

(2) *Medium* for conditions comparable to the following: (*a*) turf grasses where the average depth of flow is 1 to 2 times the height of vegetation, (*b*) stemmy grasses, weeds, or tree seedlings with moderate cover where the average depth of flow is 2 to 3 times the height of vegetation, and (*c*) brushy growths, moderately dense, similar to willows 1 to 2 years old, dormant season, along side slopes of a channel with no significant vegetation along the channel bottom, where the hydraulic radius is greater than 2 ft.

(3) *High* for conditions comparable to the following: (*a*) turf grasses where the average depth of flow is about equal to the height of vegetation,

(b) dormant season—willow or cottonwood trees 8 to 10 years old, inter-grown with some weeds and brush, none of the vegetation in foliage, where the hydraulic radius is greater than 2 ft, and (c) growing season—bushy willows about 1 year old intergrown with some weeds in full foliage along side slopes, no significant vegetation along channel bottom, where hydraulic radius is greater than 2 ft.

(4) *Very high* for conditions comparable to the following: (a) turf grasses where the average depth of flow is less than one-half the height of vegetation, (b) growing season—bushy willows about 1 year old, inter-grown with weeds in full foliage along side slopes, or dense growth of cattails along channel bottom, with any value of hydraulic radius up to 10 or 15 ft, and (c) growing season—trees intergrown with weeds and brush, all in full foliage, with any value of hydraulic radius up to 10 or 15 ft.

In selecting the value of $m_5$, the degree of meandering depends on the ratio of the meander length to the straight length of the channel reach. The meandering is considered *minor* for ratios of 1.0 to 1.2, *appreciable* for ratios of 1.2 to 1.5, and *severe* for ratios of 1.5 and greater.

In applying the above method for determining the $n$ value, several things should be noted. The method does not consider the effect of suspended and bed loads. The values given in Table 5-5 were developed from a study of some 40 to 50 cases of small and moderate channels. Therefore, the method is questionable when applied to large channels whose hydraulic radii exceed, say, 15 ft. The method applies only to unlined natural streams, floodways, and drainage channels and shows a minimum value of 0.02 for the $n$ value of such channels. The minimum value of $n$ in general, however, may be as low as 0.012 in lined channels and as 0.008 in artificial laboratory flumes.

**5-9. The Table of Manning's Roughness Coefficient.** Table 5-6 gives a list of $n$ values for channels of various kinds.[1] For each kind of channel the minimum, normal, and maximum values of $n$ are shown. The normal values for artificial channels given in the table are recommended only for channels with good maintenance. The boldface figures are values generally recommended in design. For the case in which poor mainte-nance is expected in the future, values should be increased according to the situation expected. Table 5-6 will be found very useful as a guide to the quick selection of the $n$ value to be used in a given problem. A popular table of this type was prepared by Horton [34] from an examina-tion of the best available experiments at his time.[2] Table 5-6 is compiled

---

[1] The minimum value for Lucite was observed in the Hydraulic Engineering Labora-tory at the University of Illinois [33]. Such a low $n$ value may perhaps be obtained also for smooth brass and glass, but no observations have yet been reported.

[2] A table showing $n$ values and other elements from 269 observations made on many existing artificial channels is also given by King [35].

TABLE 5-5. VALUES FOR THE COMPUTATION OF THE ROUGHNESS COEFFICIENT
BY EQ. (5-12)

| Channel conditions | | | Values |
|---|---|---|---|
| Material involved | Earth | $n_0$ | 0.020 |
| | Rock cut | | 0.025 |
| | Fine gravel | | 0.024 |
| | Coarse gravel | | 0.028 |
| Degree of irregularity | Smooth | $n_1$ | 0.000 |
| | Minor | | 0.005 |
| | Moderate | | 0.010 |
| | Severe | | 0.020 |
| Variations of channel cross section | Gradual | $n_2$ | 0.000 |
| | Alternating occasionally | | 0.005 |
| | Alternating frequently | | 0.010–0.015 |
| Relative effect of obstructions | Negligible | $n_3$ | 0.000 |
| | Minor | | 0.010–0.015 |
| | Appreciable | | 0.020–0.030 |
| | Severe | | 0.040–0.060 |
| Vegetation | Low | $n_4$ | 0.005–0.010 |
| | Medium | | 0.010–0.025 |
| | High | | 0.025–0.050 |
| | Very high | | 0.050–0.100 |
| Degree of meandering | Minor | $m_5$ | 1.000 |
| | Appreciable | | 1.150 |
| | Severe | | 1.300 |

TABLE 5-6. VALUES OF THE ROUGHNESS COEFFICIENT $n$
(**Boldface** figures are values generally recommended in design)

| Type of channel and description | Minimum | Normal | Maximum |
|---|---|---|---|
| A. CLOSED CONDUITS FLOWING PARTLY FULL | | | |
| A-1. Metal | | | |
|     *a.* Brass, smooth | 0.009 | **0.010** | 0.013 |
|     *b.* Steel | | | |
|       1. Lockbar and welded | 0.010 | 0.012 | 0.014 |
|       2. Riveted and spiral | 0.013 | 0.016 | 0.017 |
|     *c.* Cast iron | | | |
|       1. Coated | 0.010 | 0.013 | 0.014 |
|       2. Uncoated | 0.011 | 0.014 | 0.016 |
|     *d.* Wrought iron | | | |
|       1. Black | 0.012 | **0.014** | 0.015 |
|       2. Galvanized | 0.013 | **0.016** | 0.017 |
|     *e.* Corrugated metal | | | |
|       1. Subdrain | 0.017 | **0.019** | 0.021 |
|       2. Storm drain | 0.021 | **0.024** | 0.030 |
| A-2. Nonmetal | | | |
|     *a.* Lucite | 0.008 | 0.009 | 0.010 |
|     *b.* Glass | 0.009 | **0.010** | 0.013 |
|     *c.* Cement | | | |
|       1. Neat, surface | 0.010 | 0.011 | 0.013 |
|       2. Mortar | 0.011 | 0.013 | 0.015 |
|     *d.* Concrete | | | |
|       1. Culvert, straight and free of debris | 0.010 | 0.011 | 0.013 |
|       2. Culvert with bends, connections, and some debris | 0.011 | **0.013** | 0.014 |
|       3. Finished | 0.011 | 0.012 | 0.014 |
|       4. Sewer with manholes, inlet, etc., straight | 0.013 | 0.015 | 0.017 |
|       5. Unfinished, steel form | 0.012 | 0.013 | 0.014 |
|       6. Unfinished, smooth wood form | 0.012 | **0.014** | 0.016 |
|       7. Unfinished, rough wood form | 0.015 | **0.017** | 0.020 |
|     *e.* Wood | | | |
|       1. Stave | 0.010 | 0.012 | 0.014 |
|       2. Laminated, treated | 0.015 | 0.017 | 0.020 |
|     *f.* Clay | | | |
|       1. Common drainage tile | 0.011 | **0.013** | 0.017 |
|       2. Vitrified sewer | 0.011 | 0.014 | 0.017 |
|       3. Vitrified sewer with manholes, inlet, etc. | 0.013 | 0.015 | 0.017 |
|       4. Vitrified subdrain with open joint | 0.014 | **0.016** | **0.018** |
|     *g.* Brickwork | | | |
|       1. Glazed | 0.011 | 0.013 | 0.015 |
|       2. Lined with cement mortar | 0.012 | 0.015 | 0.017 |
|     *h.* Sanitary sewers coated with sewage slimes, with bends and connections | 0.012 | 0.013 | 0.016 |
|     *i.* Paved invert, sewer, smooth bottom | 0.016 | 0.019 | 0.020 |
|     *j.* Rubble masonry, cemented | 0.018 | 0.025 | 0.030 |

TABLE 5-6. VALUES OF THE ROUGHNESS COEFFICIENT n (continued)

| Type of channel and description | Minimum | Normal | Maximum |
|---|---|---|---|
| B. LINED OR BUILT-UP CHANNELS | | | |
| B-1. Metal | | | |
| a. Smooth steel surface | | | |
| 1. Unpainted | 0.011 | **0.012** | 0.014 |
| 2. Painted | 0.012 | 0.013 | 0.017 |
| b. Corrugated | 0.021 | 0.025 | 0.030 |
| B-2. Nonmetal | | | |
| a. Cement | | | |
| 1. Neat, surface | 0.010 | 0.011 | 0.013 |
| 2. Mortar | 0.011 | 0.013 | 0.015 |
| b. Wood | | | |
| 1. Planed, untreated | 0.010 | 0.012 | 0.014 |
| 2. Planed, creosoted | 0.011 | 0.012 | 0.015 |
| 3. Unplaned | 0.011 | 0.013 | 0.015 |
| 4. Plank with battens | 0.012 | 0.015 | 0.018 |
| 5. Lined with roofing paper | 0.010 | 0.014 | 0.017 |
| c. Concrete | | | |
| 1. Trowel finish | 0.011 | **0.013** | 0.015 |
| 2. Float finish | 0.013 | 0.015 | 0.016 |
| 3. Finished, with gravel on bottom | 0.015 | 0.017 | 0.020 |
| 4. Unfinished | 0.014 | 0.017 | 0.020 |
| 5. Gunite, good section | 0.016 | 0.019 | 0.023 |
| 6. Gunite, wavy section | 0.018 | 0.022 | 0.025 |
| 7. On good excavated rock | 0.017 | 0.020 | |
| 8. On irregular excavated rock | 0.022 | 0.027 | |
| d. Concrete bottom float finished with sides of | | | |
| 1. Dressed stone in mortar | 0.015 | 0.017 | 0.020 |
| 2. Random stone in mortar | 0.017 | 0.020 | 0.024 |
| 3. Cement rubble masonry, plastered | 0.016 | 0.020 | 0.024 |
| 4. Cement rubble masonry | 0.020 | 0.025 | 0.030 |
| 5. Dry rubble or riprap | 0.020 | 0.030 | 0.035 |
| e. Gravel bottom with sides of | | | |
| 1. Formed concrete | 0.017 | 0.020 | 0.025 |
| 2. Random stone in mortar | 0.020 | 0.023 | 0.026 |
| 3. Dry rubble or riprap | 0.023 | 0.033 | 0.036 |
| f. Brick | | | |
| 1. Glazed | 0.011 | **0.013** | 0.015 |
| 2. In cement mortar | 0.012 | **0.015** | 0.018 |
| g. Masonry | | | |
| 1. Cemented rubble | 0.017 | 0.025 | 0.030 |
| 2. Dry rubble | 0.023 | 0.032 | 0.035 |
| h. Dressed ashlar | 0.013 | 0.015 | 0.017 |
| i. Asphalt | | | |
| 1. Smooth | 0.013 | 0.013 | |
| 2. Rough | 0.016 | 0.016 | |
| j. Vegetal lining | 0.030 | . . . . . | 0.500 |

TABLE 5-6. VALUES OF THE ROUGHNESS COEFFICIENT $n$ (*continued*)

| Type of channel and description | Minimum | Normal | Maximum |
|---|---|---|---|
| C. EXCAVATED OR DREDGED | | | |
| a. Earth, straight and uniform | | | |
| 1. Clean, recently completed | 0.016 | 0.018 | 0.020 |
| 2. Clean, after weathering | 0.018 | **0.022** | 0.025 |
| 3. Gravel, uniform section, clean | 0.022 | 0.025 | 0.030 |
| 4. With short grass, few weeds | 0.022 | 0.027 | 0.033 |
| b. Earth, winding and sluggish | | | |
| 1. No vegetation | 0.023 | 0.025 | 0.030 |
| 2. Grass, some weeds | 0.025 | 0.030 | 0.033 |
| 3. Dense weeds or aquatic plants in deep channels | 0.030 | 0.035 | 0.040 |
| 4. Earth bottom and rubble sides | 0.028 | 0.030 | 0.035 |
| 5. Stony bottom and weedy banks | 0.025 | 0.035 | 0.040 |
| 6. Cobble bottom and clean sides | 0.030 | 0.040 | 0.050 |
| c. Dragline-excavated or dredged | | | |
| 1. No vegetation | 0.025 | 0.028 | 0.033 |
| 2. Light brush on banks | 0.035 | 0.050 | 0.060 |
| d. Rock cuts | | | |
| 1. Smooth and uniform | 0.025 | 0.035 | 0.040 |
| 2. Jagged and irregular | 0.035 | 0.040 | 0.050 |
| e. Channels not maintained, weeds and brush uncut | | | |
| 1. Dense weeds, high as flow depth | 0.050 | 0.080 | 0.120 |
| 2. Clean bottom, brush on sides | 0.040 | 0.050 | 0.080 |
| 3. Same, highest stage of flow | 0.045 | 0.070 | 0.110 |
| 4. Dense brush, high stage | 0.080 | 0.100 | 0.140 |
| D. NATURAL STREAMS | | | |
| D-1. Minor streams (top width at flood stage <100 ft) | | | |
| a. Streams on plain | | | |
| 1. Clean, straight, full stage, no rifts or deep pools | 0.025 | **0.030** | 0.033 |
| 2. Same as above, but more stones and weeds | 0.030 | 0.035 | 0.040 |
| 3. Clean, winding, some pools and shoals | 0.033 | 0.040 | 0.045 |
| 4. Same as above, but some weeds and stones | 0.035 | 0.045 | 0.050 |
| 5. Same as above, lower stages, more ineffective slopes and sections | 0.040 | 0.048 | 0.055 |
| 6. Same as 4, but more stones | 0.045 | 0.050 | 0.060 |
| 7. Sluggish reaches, weedy, deep pools | 0.050 | 0.070 | 0.080 |
| 8. Very weedy reaches, deep pools, or floodways with heavy stand of timber and underbrush | 0.075 | 0.100 | 0.150 |

TABLE 5-6. VALUES OF THE ROUGHNESS COEFFICIENT n (continued)

| Type of channel and description | Minimum | Normal | Maximum |
|---|---|---|---|
| b. Mountain streams, no vegetation in channel, banks usually steep, trees and brush along banks submerged at high stages | | | |
|     1. Bottom: gravels, cobbles, and few boulders | 0.030 | 0.040 | 0.050 |
|     2. Bottom: cobbles with large boulders | 0.040 | 0.050 | 0.070 |
| D-2. Flood plains | | | |
|   a. Pasture, no brush | | | |
|     1. Short grass | 0.025 | 0.030 | 0.035 |
|     2. High grass | 0.030 | 0.035 | 0.050 |
|   b. Cultivated areas | | | |
|     1. No crop | 0.020 | 0.030 | 0.040 |
|     2. Mature row crops | 0.025 | 0.035 | 0.045 |
|     3. Mature field crops | 0.030 | 0.040 | 0.050 |
|   c. Brush | | | |
|     1. Scattered brush, heavy weeds | 0.035 | 0.050 | 0.070 |
|     2. Light brush and trees, in winter | 0.035 | 0.050 | 0.060 |
|     3. Light brush and trees, in summer | 0.040 | 0.060 | 0.080 |
|     4. Medium to dense brush, in winter | 0.045 | 0.070 | 0.110 |
|     5. Medium to dense brush, in summer | 0.070 | 0.100 | 0.160 |
|   d. Trees | | | |
|     1. Dense willows, summer, straight | 0.110 | 0.150 | 0.200 |
|     2. Cleared land with tree stumps, no sprouts | 0.030 | 0.040 | 0.050 |
|     3. Same as above, but with heavy growth of sprouts | 0.050 | 0.060 | 0.080 |
|     4. Heavy stand of timber, a few down trees, little undergrowth, flood stage below branches | 0.080 | 0.100 | 0.120 |
|     5. Same as above, but with flood stage reaching branches | 0.100 | 0.120 | 0.160 |
| D-3. Major streams (top width at flood stage >100 ft). The n value is less than that for minor streams of similar description, because banks offer less effective resistance. | | | |
|   a. Regular section with no boulders or brush | 0.025 | ..... | 0.060 |
|   b. Irregular and rough section | 0.035 | ..... | 0.100 |

from up-to-date information collected from various sources ([34,36,38], and unpublished data); hence it is much broader in scope than the Horton table.

**5-10. Illustrations of Channels with Various Roughnesses.** Photographs of a number of typical channels, accompanied by brief descriptions of the channel conditions and the corresponding $n$ values, are shown in Fig. 5-5. These photographs are collected from different sources and arranged in order of increasing magnitude of the $n$ values. They provide a general idea of the appearance of the channels having different $n$ values and so should facilitate selection of the $n$ value for a given channel condition. The $n$ value given for each channel represents approximately the coefficient of roughness when the photograph was taken.

The above type of visual aid is also employed by the U.S. Geological Survey. The Survey has made several determinations of channel roughness in streams, mostly in the northwestern United States. These include measurements of cross-sectional area, width, depth, mean velocity, slope, and computation of the roughness coefficient. The reaches were photographed in stereoscopic color, and the photographs have been circulating among the district offices of the Survey as a guide in evaluating $n$.

FIG. 5-5. Typical channels showing different $n$ values. (*These photographs are reproduced from [37] and [38] with the permission of the U.S. Department of Agriculture. The original pictures used for reproduction purposes were supplied through the courtesy of Mr. F. C. Scobey for photographs 1 to 14 and photograph 19, and through the courtesy of Mr. C. E. Ramser for the others.*)

Fig. 5-5 (1–3)

1. $n = 0.012$.  Canal lined with concrete slabs having smooth neat cement joints and very smooth surface, hand-troweled and with cement wash on concrete base.

2. $n = 0.014$.  Concrete canal poured behind screeding and smoothing platform.

3. $n = 0.016$.  Small concrete-lined ditch, straight and uniform, bottom slightly dished, the sides and bottom covered with a rough deposit, which increases the $n$ value.

FIG. 5-5 (4–6)

4. $n = 0.018$. Shot-concrete lining without smooth treatment. Surface covered with fine algae and bottom with drifting sand dunes.

5. $n = 0.018$. Earth channel excavated in a clay loam, with deposit of clean sand in the middle and slick silty mud near the sides.

6. $n = 0.020$. Concrete lining made in a rough lava-rock cut, clean-scoured, very rough, and deeply pitted.

(7)

(8)

(9)

Fig. 5-5 (7–9)

7. $n = 0.020$.　Irrigation canal, straight, in hard-packed smooth sand.
8. $n = 0.022$.　Cement-plaster lining applied directly to the trimmed surface of the earth channel.　With weeds in broken places and loose sand on bottom.
9. $n = 0.024$.　Canal excavated in silty clay loam.　Slick and hard bed.

(10)

(11)

(12)

FIG. 5-5 (10–12)

10. $n = 0.024$.  Ditch lined on both sides and bottom with dry-laid unchinked rubble.  Bottom quite irregular, with scattered loose cobbles.

11. $n = 0.026$.  Canal excavated on hillside, with upper bank mostly of willow roots and lower bank with well-made concrete wall.  Bottom covered with coarse gravel.

12. $n = 0.028$.  Cobble-bottom channel, where there is insufficient silt in the water or too high a velocity, preventing formation of a graded smooth bed.

(13)

(14)

(15)

Fig. 5-5 (13–15)

13. $n = 0.029$.   Earth canal excavated in alluvial silt soil, with deposits of sand on bottom and growth of grass.

14. $n = 0.030$.   Canal with large-cobblestone bed.

15. $n = 0.035$.   Natural channel, somewhat irregular side slopes; fairly even, clean and regular bottom; in light gray silty clay to light tan silt loam; very little variation in cross section.

Fig. 5-5 (16–18)

16. $n = 0.040$. Rock channel excavated by explosives.

17. $n = 0.040$. Ditch in clay and sandy loam; irregular side slopes, bottom, and cross section; grass on slopes.

18. $n = 0.045$. Dredge channel, irregular side slopes and bottom, in black, waxy clay at top to yellow clay at bottom, sides covered with small saplings and brush, slight and gradual variations in cross section.

(19)

(20)

(21)

Fig. 5-5 (19–21)

19. $n = 0.050$. Dredge channel with very irregular side slopes and bottom, in dark-colored waxy clay, with growth of weeds and grass. Slight variation in shape of cross section for variation in size.

20. $n = 0.060$. Ditch in heavy silty clay; irregular side slopes and bottom; practically entire section filled with large-size growth of trees, principally willows and cottonwoods. Quite uniform cross section.

21. $n = 0.080$. Dredge channel in black slippery clay and gray silty clay loam, irregular wide slopes and bottom, covered with dense growth of bushy willows, some in bottom; remainder of both slopes covered with weeds and a scattering growth of willows and poplars, no foliage; some silting on bottom.

(22)

(23)

(24)

FIG. 5-5 (22–24)

22. $n = 0.110$. Same as (21), but with much foliage and covered for about 40 ft with growth resembling smart weed.

23. $n = 0.125$. Natural channel floodway in median fine sand to fine clay, none side slopes; fairly even and regular bottom with occasional flat bottom sloughs; variation in depth; practically virgin timber, very little undergrowth except occasional dense patches of bushed and small trees, some logs and dead fallen trees.

24. $n = 0.150$. Natural river in sandy clay soil. Very crooked course, irregular side slopes and uneven bottom. Many roots, trees and bushes, large logs and other drift on bottom; trees continually falling into channel due to bank caving.

## PROBLEMS

**5-1.** Explain why a uniform flow cannot occur (*a*) in a frictionless channel, and (*b*) in a horizontal channel.

**5-2.** When Chézy's $C$ determined by the G. K. formula becomes independent of the slope $S$, show that the value of $R = 3.28$. Find the corresponding relation between $C$ and Kutter's $n$.

**5-3.** For the conditions given in Example 5-1, compute the values of Bazin's $m$ and Powell's $\epsilon$.

**5-4.** Compute the velocity and discharge of flow in a new earth canal having the same shape, size, slope, and depth of flow as the channel given in Example 5-1. Use (*a*) the G. K. formula, assuming Kutter's $n = 0.022$; (*b*) the Bazin formula, selecting a proper value of $m$; and (*c*) the Powell formula, selecting a proper value of $\epsilon$.

**5-5.** Taking Manning's $n$ as the given value of Kutter's $n$, solve Example 5-1 by the Manning formula.

**5-6.** If the coefficient of roughness $n$ is unknown for the channel in Example 5-1, but a discharge of 2,000 cfs is observed under the given conditions, compute the values of Kutter's $n$ and Manning's $n$.

**5-7.** From the Manning formula (using a constant of 1.486 instead of 1.49 for theoretical accuracy) and the Chézy formula, determine the relation between Chézy's $C$ and Manning's $n$ for the condition described in Prob. 5-2. This will show that the G. K. formula and the Manning formula are theoretically identical at the condition when Chézy's $C$ is independent of the slope $S$.

**5-8.** Prove that the friction factor $f$ in the Darcy-Weisbach formula, Eq. (1-4), is related to Manning's $n$ by $f = 116n^2/R^{1/3}$.

**5-9.** Run 12-4 of Bazin's tests [12] was made on a rectangular plank flume 6.44 ft wide, with wooden strips 1 cm thick and 2.7 cm wide nailed crosswise on the bottom and sides at a spacing of 3.7 cm center to center of strips. This flume gave a mean velocity of 3.33 fps at a flow depth of 1.02 ft and a slope of 0.0015. The temperature reading was 8.5°C. Determine Manning's $n$, and compute (*a*) Chézy's $C$, (*b*) Kutter's $n$, (*c*) Bazin's $m$, and (*d*) Powell's $\epsilon$.

**5-10.** Run 15-4 of Bazin's tests was the same as run 12-4, described in the preceding problem, except that the spacing of strips was increased to 7.7 cm. Using the same discharge as that of run 12-4, the depth of flow was found to be 1.33 ft. Determine Manning's $n$, and compute (*a*) Chézy's $C$, (*b*) Kutter's $n$, (*c*) Bazin's $m$, and (*d*) Powell's $\epsilon$. Compare the values of $\epsilon$ obtained from runs 12-4 and 15-4 with the height of the strips, and explain the effect of roughness in both cases.

**5-11.** Using the Manning formula, construct a discharge-rating curve[1] for the natural channel section given in Prob. 2-5. The slope is 0.0016, and $n = 0.035$. Extend the sides of the channel by straight lines at high stages if necessary.

**5-12.** The actual rating curve of the channel section in Prob. 2-5 is described below. Construct a curve showing the variation in Manning's $n$ with respect to the stage above the datum.

---

[1] It should be noted that the synthetic rating curve thus obtained is very approximate, particularly for a natural channel, because the $n$ value is actually not a constant but a function of the depth (see Art. 5-8).

| Stage, ft | Discharge, cfs | Stage, ft | Discharge, cfs |
|-----------|----------------|-----------|----------------|
| 0.3 | 1.0 | 1.50 | 50.0 |
| 0.4 | 2.3 | 1.75 | 62.0 |
| 0.5 | 4.6 | 2.00 | 75.0 |
| 0.6 | 7.8 | 2.25 | 88.0 |
| 0.7 | 11.0 | 2.50 | 102.0 |
| 0.8 | 15.0 | 3.00 | 132.0 |
| 0.9 | 20.0 | 3.50 | 164.0 |
| 1.0 | 25.0 | 4.00 | 199.0 |
| 1.25 | 38.0 | | |

**5-13.** By the Cowan method, estimate the $n$ value for a slightly curved reach in channel 21 of Fig. 5-5.

## REFERENCES

1. E. C. Schnackenberg: Slope discharge formulae for alluvial streams and rivers, *Proceedings, New Zealand Institution of Engineers*, vol. 37, pp. 340–409, Wellington, 1951. Discussions, pp. 410–449.
2. Ivan E. Houk: Calculation of flow in open channels, *Miami Conservancy District, Technical Report, Pt. IV*, Dayton, Ohio, 1918.
3. Erik Lindquist: On velocity formulas for open channels and pipes, *Transactions of the World Power Conference, Sectional Meeting, Scandinavia, Stockholm*, vol. 1, pp. 177–234, 1933.
4. Philipp Forchheimer, "Hydraulik" ("Hydraulics"), Teubner Verlagsgesellschaft, Leipzig and Berlin, pp. 139–163, 1930.
5. Zivko Vladislavljevitch: Aperçu critique sur les formules pour la prédétermination de la vitesse moyenne de l'écoulement uniforme (Critical survey of the formulae for predetermination of mean velocity of uniform flow), *Transactions of the 1st Congress, International Commission on Irrigation and Drainage, New Delhi*, vol. 2, rept. 12, question 2, pp. 405–428, 1951.
6. Cornelis Toebes: Streamflow: Poly-dimensional treatment of variable factors affecting the velocity in alluvial streams and rivers, *Proceedings, Institution of Civil Engineers, London*, vol. 4, no. 3, pt. III, pp. 900–938, December, 1955.
7. G. H. L. Hagen: "Untersuchungen über die gleichförmige Bewegung des Wassers" ("Researches on Uniform Flow of Water"), Berlin, 1876.
8. Clemens Herschel: On the origin of the Chézy formula, *Journal, Association of Engineering Societies*, vol. 18, pp. 363–368. Discussion, pp. 368–369, January–June, 1897.
9. A. Brahms: "Anfangsgründe der Deich- und Wasserbaukunst" ("Elements of Dam and Hydraulic Engineering"), Aurich, Germany, 1754 and 1757, vol. I, p. 105.
10. E. Ganguillet and W. R. Kutter: Versuch zur Aufstellung einer neuen allegemeinen Formel für die gleichförmige Bewegung des Wassers in Canälen und Flüssen (An investigation to establish a new general formula for uniform flow of water in canals and rivers), *Zeitschrift des Oesterreichischen Ingenieur- und Architekten Vereines*, vol. 21, no. 1, pp. 6–25; no. 2–3, pp. 46–59, Vienna, 1869. Published as a book in Bern, Switzerland, 1877; translated into English by Rudolph Hering and John C.

Trautwine, Jr., as "A general Formula for the Uniform Flow of Water in Rivers and Other Channels," John Wiley & Sons, Inc., New York, 1st ed., 1888; 2d ed., 1891 and 1901.

11. Captain A. A. Humphreys and Lieut. H. L. Abbot, U.S. Army Corps of Topographical Engineers: "Report upon the physics and hydraulics of the Mississippi River; upon the protection of the alluvial region against overflow; and upon the deepening of the mouths; based upon surveys and investigations . . . ," J. B. Lippincott Company, Philadelphia, 1861; reprinted in Washington, D.C., in 1867, and as U.S. Army Corps of Engineers, Professional Paper No. 13, 1876.

12. H. Darcy and H. Bazin: "Recherches hydrauliques," 1re partie, Recherches expérimentales sur l'écoulement de l'eau dans les canaux découverts; 2e partie, Recherches expérimentales relatives aux remous et à la propagation des ondes ("Hydraulic Researches," pt. 1, Experimental research on flow of water in open channels; pt. 2, Experimental research on backwater and the propagation of waves), Académie des Sciences, Paris, 1865.

13. H. Bazin: Étude d'une nouvelle formule pour calculer le débit des canaux découverts (A new formula for the calculation of discharge in open channels), Mémoire No. 41, Annales des ponts et chaussées, vol. 14, ser. 7, 4me trimestre, pp. 20–70, 1897.

14. Ralph W. Powell: Resistance to flow in rough channels, Transactions, American Geophysical Union, vol. 31, no. 4, pp. 575–582, August, 1950.

15. Robert Manning: On the flow of water in open channels and pipes, Transactions, Institution of Civil Engineers of Ireland, vol. 20, pp. 161–207, Dublin, 1891; supplement, vol. 24, pp. 179–207, 1895.

16. Ven Te Chow: A note on the Manning formula, Transactions, American Geophysical Union, vol. 36, no. 4, p. 688, August, 1955.

17. Allen J. C. Cunningham: Recent hydraulic experiments, Proceedings, Institution of Civil Engineers, London, vol. 71, pp. 1–36, 1883.

18. Ph. Gauckler: Du mouvement de l'eau dans les conduites (The flow of water in conduits), Annales des ponts et chaussées, vol. 15, ser. 4, pp. 229–281, 1868.

19. A. Strickler: Beiträge zur Frage der Geschwindigkeitsformel und der Rauhigkeitszahlen für Ströme, Kanäle und geschlossene Leitungen (Some contributions to the problem of velocity formula and roughness coefficient for rivers, canals, and closed conduits), Mitteilungen des eidgenössischen Amtes für Wasserwirtschaft, Bern, Switzerland, no. 16, 1923.

20. Thomas Blench: A new theory of turbulent flow in liquids of small viscosity, Journal, Institution of Civil Engineers, London, vol. 11, no. 6, pp. 611–612, April, 1939.

21. N. N. Pavlovskiĭ: "Gidravlicheskiĭ Spravochnik" ("Handbook of Hydraulics"). This book has many editions: (1) "Gidravlicheskiĭ Spravochnik," Put, Leningrad, 1924, 192 pp.; (2) "Uchebnyĭ Gidravlicheskiĭ Spravochnik" (for schools), Kubuch, Leningrad, 1929, 100 pp.; 2d ed, 1931, 168 pp.; (3) "Gidravlicheskiĭ Spravochnik," Onti, Leningrad and Moscow, 1937, 890 pp; and (4) "Kratkiĭ Gidravlicheskiĭ Spravochnik," (concise version), Gosstroĭizdat, Leningrad and Moscow, 1940, 314 pp.

22. George W. Pickels: Run-off investigations in central Illinois, University of Illinois, Engineering Experiment Station, Bulletin 232, vol. 29, no. 3, September, 1931.

23. Frederick C. Scobey: The flow of water in flumes, U.S. Department of Agriculture, Technical Bulletin No. 393, December, 1933.

24. Methodology for crop and pasture inundation damage appraisal: "Training manual for hydrologists on watershed protection and flood prevention work plan

parties," preliminary draft, U.S. Soil Conservation Service, Milwaukee, Wis., 1954.
25. E. W. Lane: Discussion on Slope discharge formulae for alluvial streams and rivers, by E. C. Schnackenberg, *Proceedings, New Zealand Institution of Engineers,* vol. 37, pp. 435–438, Wellington, 1951.
26. J. S. Meyers and E. A. Schultz: Panama Canal: The sea-level project, in A symposium: Tidal currents, *Transactions, American Society of Civil Engineers,* vol. 114, pp. 668–671, 1949.
27. Thomas R. Camp: Design of sewers to facilitate flow, *Sewage Works Journal,* vol. 18, pp. 1–16, January–December, 1946.
28. Thomas R. Camp: Discussion on Determination of Kutter's n for sewers partly filled, by C. Frank Johnson, *Transactions, American Society of Civil Engineers,* vol. 109, pp. 240–243, 1944.
29. E. R. Wilcox: A comparative test of the flow of water in 8-inch concrete and vitrified clay sewer pipes, *University of Washington, Engineering Experiment Station, Bulletin 27,* Mar. 1, 1924.
30. D. L. Yarnell and S. M. Woodward: The flow of water in drain tile, *U.S. Department of Agriculture, Bulletin No. 854,* 1920.
31. C. Frank Johnson: Determination of Kutter's n for sewers partly filled, *Transactions, American Society of Civil Engineers,* vol. 109, pp. 223–239, 1944.
32. Woody L. Cowan: Estimating hydraulic roughness coefficients, *Agricultural Engineering,* vol. 37, no. 7, pp. 473–475, July, 1956.
33. Donald Schnepper and Ven Te Chow: Full scale toe-of-slope gutter model, unpublished report of an investigation conducted by the Department of Civil Engineering, University of Illinois, in cooperation with the Division of Highways, State of Illinois, and the Bureau of Public Roads, U.S. Department of Commerce, May, 1954 (available at the University of Illinois library).
34. Robert E. Horton: Some better Kutter's formula coefficients, *Engineering News,* vol. 75, no. 8, pp. 373–374, Feb. 24, 1916. Discussions by Fred C. Scobey and Robert E. Horton, vol. 75, no. 18, pp. 862–863, May 4, 1916.
35. Horace William King, "Handbook of Hydraulics," 4th ed., revised by Ernest F. Brater, McGraw-Hill Book Company, Inc., New York, 1954, pp. 7-102 to 7-111.
36. "Engineering Handbook: Hydraulics," U.S. Department of Agriculture, Soil Conservation Service, 1955, sec. 5.
37. F. C. Scobey: Flow of water in irrigation and similar canals, *U.S. Department of Agriculture, Technical Bulletin No. 652,* February, 1939.
38. C. E. Ramser: Flow of water in drainage channels, *U.S. Department of Agriculture, Technical Bulletin No. 129,* November, 1929.

# CHAPTER 6

# COMPUTATION OF UNIFORM FLOW

**6-1. The Conveyance of a Channel Section.** The discharge of uniform flow in a channel may be expressed as the product of the velocity, represented by Eq. (5-1), and the water area, or

$$Q = VA = CAR^x S^y = KS^y \tag{6-1}$$

where

$$K = CAR^x \tag{6-2}$$

The term $K$ is known as the *conveyance* of the channel section; it is a measure of the carrying capacity of the channel section, since it is directly proportional to $Q$.

When either the Chézy formula or the Manning formula is used as the uniform-flow formula, i.e., when $y = \frac{1}{2}$, the discharge by Eq. (6-1) becomes

$$Q = K\sqrt{S} \tag{6-3}$$

and the conveyance is

$$K = \frac{Q}{\sqrt{S}} \tag{6-4}$$

This equation can be used to compute the conveyance when the discharge and slope of the channel are given.

When the Chézy formula is used, Eq. (6-2) becomes

$$K = CAR^{\frac{1}{2}} \tag{6-5}$$

where $C$ is Chézy's resistance factor. Similarly, when the Manning formula is used,

$$K = \frac{1.49}{n} AR^{\frac{2}{3}} \tag{6-6}$$

The above two equations are used to compute the conveyance when the geometry of the water area and the resistance factor or roughness coefficient are given. Since the Manning formula is used extensively, most of the following discussions and computations will be based on Eq. (6-6).

**6-2. The Section Factor for Uniform-flow Computation.** The expression $AR^{\frac{2}{3}}$ is called the *section factor for uniform-flow computation;* it is an important element in the computation of uniform flow. From Eq.

(6-6), this factor may be expressed as

$$A R^{\frac{2}{3}} = \frac{nK}{1.49} \qquad (6\text{-}7)$$

and, from Eq. (6-4),
$$A R^{\frac{2}{3}} = \frac{nQ}{1.49 \sqrt{S}} \qquad (6\text{-}8)$$

Primarily, Eq. (6-8) applies to a channel section when the flow is uniform. The right side of the equation contains the values of $n$, $Q$, and $S$; but the left side depends only on the geometry of the water area. Therefore, it shows that, for a given condition of $n$, $Q$, and $S$, there is *only one* possible depth for maintaining a uniform flow, provided that the value of $A R^{\frac{2}{3}}$ always increases with increase in depth, which is true in most cases. This depth is the *normal depth*. When $n$ and $S$ are known at a channel section, it can be seen from Eq. (6-8) that there can be *only one* discharge for maintaining a uniform flow through the section, provided that $A R^{\frac{2}{3}}$ always increases with increase of depth.[1] This discharge is the *normal discharge*.

Equation (6-8) is a very useful tool for the computation and analysis of uniform flow. When the discharge, slope, and roughness are known, this equation gives the section factor $A_n R_n^{\frac{2}{3}}$ and hence the normal depth $y_n$. On the other hand, when $n$, $S$, and the depth, hence the section factor, are given, the normal discharge $Q_n$ can be computed from this equation in the following form:

$$Q = \frac{1.49}{n} A R^{\frac{2}{3}} \sqrt{S} \qquad (6\text{-}9)$$

This is essentially the product of the water area and the velocity defined by the Manning formula. The subscript $n$ is sometimes used to specify the condition of uniform flow.

In order to simplify the computation, dimensionless curves showing the relation between depth and section factor $A R^{\frac{2}{3}}$ (Fig. 6-1) have been prepared for rectangular, trapezoidal, and circular channel sections. These self-explanatory curves will help to determine the depth for a given section factor $A R^{\frac{2}{3}}$, and vice versa. The $A R^{\frac{2}{3}}$ values for a circular section can also be found from the table in Appendix A.

---

[1] This is true for channels in which the value of $A R^{\frac{2}{3}}$ always increases with increase of depth, since Eq. (6-8) will give one value of $A R^{\frac{2}{3}}$, which in turn gives only one depth. In the case of a closed conduit having a gradually closing top, the value of $A R^{\frac{2}{3}}$ will first increase with depth and then decrease with depth when the full depth is approached, because a maximum value of $A R^{\frac{2}{3}}$ usually occurs in such a conduit at a depth slightly less than the full depth. Consequently, it is possible to have two depths for the same value of $A R^{\frac{2}{3}}$, one greater and the other less than the depth for the maximum value of $A R^{\frac{2}{3}}$. For further discussion on this subject see Art. 6-4.

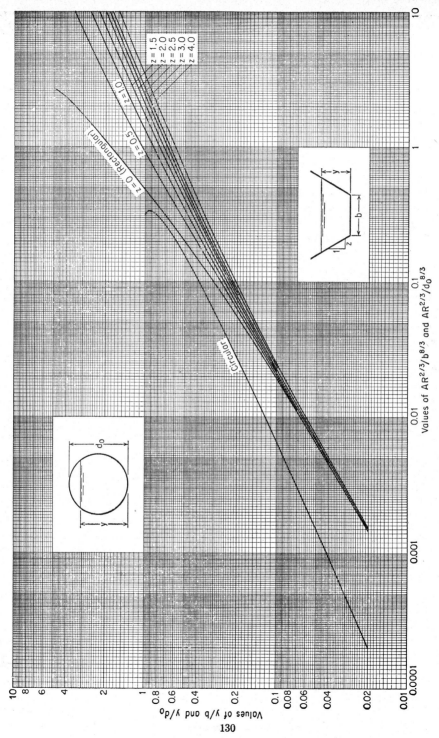

Fig. 6-1. Curves for determining the normal depth.

Values of $AR^{2/3}/b^{8/3}$ and $AR^{2/3}/d_0^{8/3}$

Values of $y/b$ and $y/d_0$

$z = 1.5$
$z = 2.0$
$z = 2.5$
$z = 3.0$
$z = 4.0$

$z = 1.0$

$z = 0.5$

$z = 0$ (Rectangular)

Circular

**6-3. The Hydraulic Exponent for Uniform-flow Computation.** Since the conveyance $K$ is a function of the depth of flow $y$, it may be assumed that

$$K^2 = Cy^N \tag{6-10}$$

where $C$ is a coefficient and $N$ is a parameter called the *hydraulic exponent for uniform-flow computation.*

Taking logarithms on both sides of Eq. (6-10) and then differentiating with respect to $y$,

$$\frac{d(\ln K)}{dy} = \frac{N}{2y} \tag{6-11}$$

Now, taking logarithms on both sides of Eq. (6-6), $K = 1.49AR^{2/3}/n$, and then differentiating this equation with respect to $y$ under the assumption that $n$ is independent of $y$,

$$\frac{d(\ln K)}{dy} = \frac{1}{A}\frac{dA}{dy} + \frac{2}{3}\frac{1}{R}\frac{dR}{dy} \tag{6-12}$$

Since $dA/dy = T$ and $R = A/P$, the above equation becomes

$$\frac{d(\ln K)}{dy} = \frac{1}{3A}\left(5T - 2R\frac{dP}{dy}\right) \tag{6-13}$$

Equating the right sides of Eqs. (6-11) and (6-13) and solving for $N$,

$$N = \frac{2y}{3A}\left(5T - 2R\frac{dP}{dy}\right) \tag{6-14}$$

This is the general equation for the hydraulic exponent $N$. For a trapezoidal channel section having a bottom width $b$ and side slopes 1 on $z$, the expressions for $A$, $T$, $P$, and $R$ may be obtained from Table 2-1. Substituting them in Eq. (6-14) and simplifying, the resulting equation[1] is

$$N = \frac{10}{3}\frac{1 + 2z(y/b)}{1 + z(y/b)} - \frac{8}{3}\frac{\sqrt{1 + z^2}\,(y/b)}{1 + 2\sqrt{1 + z^2}\,(y/b)} \tag{6-15}$$

This equation indicates that the value of $N$ for the trapezoidal section is a function of $z$ and $y/b$. For values of $z = 0$, 0.5, 1.0, 1.5, 2.0, 2.5, 3.0, and 4.0, a family of curves for $N$ versus $y/b$ can be constructed (Fig. 6-2).[2] These curves indicate that the value of $N$ varies within a range of 2.0 to 5.3.

The curve for a circular section with $N$ plotted against $y/d_0$, where $d_0$ is the diameter, is also shown in Fig. 6-2. This curve shows that the

---

[1] This equation [1] was also developed independently by Chugaev [2] through the use of the Chézy formula.

[2] Similar curves to those in **Fig.** 6-2 for trapezoidal channels were constructed by Kirpich [3] and also prepared independently by Pavlovskiĭ [4] and Rakhmanoff [5].

value of $N$ decreases rapidly as the depth of flow approaches the top of the channel. Further mathematical analysis has revealed that the value of $N$ will be equal to zero at $y/d_0 = 0.938$ and will then become negative at greater depths. The significance of this fact will be discussed later in this article and the next.

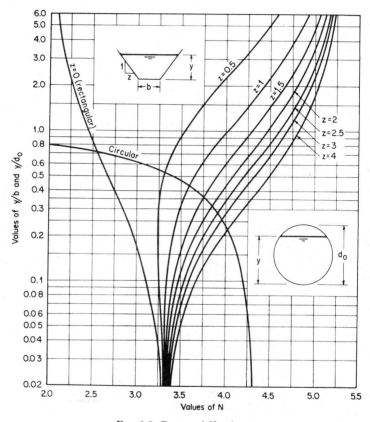

FIG. 6-2. Curves of $N$ values.

For channel sections other than the rectangular, trapezoidal, and circular shapes, exact values of $N$ may be computed directly by Eq. (6-14), provided that the derivative $dP/dy$ can be evaluated. For most channels, except for channels with abrupt changes in cross-sectional form and for closed conduits with gradually closing top, a logarithmic plot of $K$ as ordinate against the depth as abscissa (Fig. 6-3) will appear approximately as a straight line. This can also be seen from the dimensionless curves for $AR^{2/3}$ in Fig. 6-1, which are plotted similarly except that the ordinate and abscissa are interchanged. If a constant $n$ value is assumed, Eq. (6-6) indicates that $K \propto A R^{\frac{2}{3}}$; hence, these curves for $A R^{\frac{2}{3}}$ should show the same characteristics as if the curves were plotted for $K$. From Eq. (6-10), it can be seen that the hydraulic exponent for the straight-line range of the plot is equal to twice the slope of the plotted straight line. Thus, if any two points with coordinates $(K_1, y_1)$ and $(K_2, y_2)$ are taken from the straight line, the approximate value of $N$ may be computed by the following equation:

$$N = 2 \frac{\log (K_1/K_2)}{\log (y_1/y_2)} \quad (6\text{-}16)$$

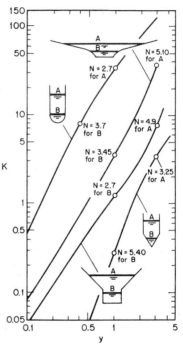

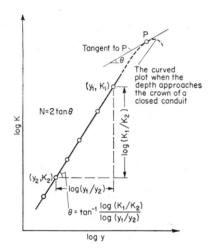

FIG. 6-3. Graphical determination of $N$ by logarithmic plotting.

FIG. 6-4. Typical channel sections having appreciable variation in $N$ value with respect to depth. (*After R. R. Chugaev* [2].)

When the cross section of a channel changes abruptly with respect to depth, the hydraulic exponent will change accordingly. Several typical sections are shown in Fig. 6-4. In such cases the logarithmic plot of $N$ against $y$ may appear as a broken line or an evident curve. For the nearly straight portions of the broken line or curve, the hydraulic exponents may be assumed constant.

When the depth of flow approaches the gradually closing crown of a closed conduit, the logarithmic plot will appear as a curve. The hydraulic exponent in the range of the curved plot is equal to twice the slope of the tangent to the curve at the given depth (Fig. 6-3). For practical purposes, the curve may be divided into a number of short segments, and each segment may be considered a straight line having a constant slope or hydraulic exponent.

Now take the circular section as an example. The dimensionless logarithmic plot of $AR^{2/3}$ against depth is shown in Fig. 6-1. Assuming a constant value of $n$, this curve will show the same characteristics as if the depth were plotted against $K$. As the depth increases, the curve deviates gradually from a straight line and finally reaches a pronounced curvature at $y/d_0 = 0.938$, where the value of $AR^{2/3}/d_0^{8/3}$ is a maximum. Since the $n$ value is assumed constant, this ratio $y/d_0 = 0.938$ also corresponds to the maximum value of the conveyance $K$. The slope of the tangent to the curve at this depth, according to the graph in which the ordinate and abscissa are interchanged, is horizontal, and thus the hydraulic exponent $N$ is equal to zero. For depths with ratio greater than $y/d_0 = 0.938$, the curve shows a decrease in the value of $AR^{2/3}/d_0^{8/3}$ and, hence, a decrease in the conveyance $K$ if $n$ is assumed constant. The slope of the tangent to the curve and with it the hydraulic exponent will thus become negative.

**6-4. Flow Characteristics in a Closed Conduit with Open-channel Flow.** Taking the circular section as an example, the dimensionless curves for $AR^{2/3}/A_0R_0^{2/3}$ and $R^{2/3}/R_0^{2/3}$ are shown by the full lines in Fig. 6-5. The subscript zero indicates the full-flow condition. If the $n$ value is assumed constant or independent of the depth variation, these two curves will represent the variation of the ratios of the discharge and velocity to their corresponding full-flow values (i.e., $Q/Q_0$ and $V/V_0$). Both the discharge and velocity curves show maximum values, which occur at about $0.938d_0$ and $0.81d_0$ respectively. Mathematically, the depth for the maximum discharge, or $0.938d_0$, can be obtained simply by equating to zero the first derivative of $AR^{2/3}$ with respect to $y$, since the discharge computed by the Manning formula is proportional to $AR^{2/3}$ for constant $n$ and $S$. Similarly, as the velocity by the Manning formula is proportional to $R^{2/3}$, the depth for the maximum velocity, or $0.81d_0$, can be obtained by equating the first derivative of $R^{2/3}$ to zero. Furthermore, the dimensionless curve of $Q/Q_0$ shows that, when the depth is greater than about $0.82d_0$, it is possible to have two different depths for the same discharge, one above and one below the value of $0.938d_0$. Similarly, the curve of $V/V_0$ shows that, when the depth is greater than the half-depth, it is possible to have two different depths for the same velocity, one above and one below the value of $0.81d_0$.

The above discussion is based on the assumption that the roughness coefficient remains constant as the depth changes. Actually, the value of $n$ for average clean sewer pipes and drain tiles, both clay and concrete, for example, has been shown to increase by as much as 28% from $1.00d_0$ to $0.25d_0$, where it appears to be a maximum (see Fig. 6-5 and the discussion in Art. 5-8 regarding the stage as a factor affecting $n$ value). This effect causes the actual maximum discharge and velocity to occur at depths of about $0.97d_0$ and $0.94d_0$, respectively. The corresponding curves of $Q/Q_0$ and $V/V_0$ are shown by the dashed lines in Fig. 6-5. According to the assumption of constant $n$ value, the velocity would be the same for a half-full pipe as for a full pipe; whereas, if the $n$ value is

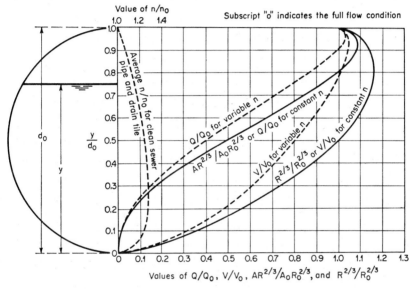

FIG. 6-5. Flow characteristics of a circular section. (*After T. R. Camp,* [27] *of Chap. 5.*)

taken to vary with the depth, as shown, the velocity at the half-depth is only 0.8 the full velocity.

The discussion for the circular conduit applies also to any closed conduit with a gradually closing top. The exact depths for maximum discharge and velocity, however, will depend on the shape and roughness variation of the specific conduit section. Since the maximum discharge and velocity of a closed conduit of gradually closing top do not occur at the full depth, this means that the conduit will not flow full at the maximum capacity as long as it maintains an open-channel flow on a uniform grade free from obstructions. For practical purposes, however, it may sometimes be assumed that the maximum discharge of a circular conduit or similar closed conduit with gradually closing top does occur at the full depth, because the depth for maximum discharge is so close to the top that there is always a possibility of slight backwater to increase this depth closer to and eventually equal to the full depth.

**6-5. Flow in a Channel Section with Composite Roughness.**  In simple channels, the roughness along the wetted perimeter may be distinctly different from part to part of the perimeter, but the mean velocity can still be computed by a uniform-flow formula without actually subdividing the section.  For example, a rectangular channel built with a wooden bottom and glass walls must have different $n$ values for the bottom and the walls.  In applying the Manning formula to such channels, it is sometimes necessary to compute an *equivalent n value* for the entire perimeter and use this equivalent value for the computation of the flow in the whole section.

For the determination of the equivalent roughness, the water area is divided imaginatively into $N$ parts of which the wetted perimeters $P_1$, $P_2$, . . . , $P_N$ and the coefficients of roughness $n_1$, $n_2$, . . . , $n_N$ are known. Horton [6] and Einstein [7,8] assumed that each part of the area has the same mean velocity, which at the same time is equal to the mean velocity of the whole section; that is, $V_1 = V_2 = \cdots = V_N = V$.  On the basis of this assumption, the equivalent coefficient of roughness may be obtained by the following equation:

$$ n = \left[ \frac{\sum\limits_{1}^{N} (P_N n_N^{1.5})}{P} \right]^{2/3} = \frac{(P_1 n_1^{1.5} + P_2 n_2^{1.5} + \cdots + P_N n_N^{1.5})^{2/3}}{P^{2/3}} \quad (6\text{-}17) $$

There are many other assumptions for the determination of an equivalent roughness.  Pavlovskiĭ [9] and also Mühlhofer [10] and Einstein and Banks [11] assumed that the total force resisting the flow (that is, $KV^2PL$; see Art. 5-4) is equal to the sum of the forces resisting the flow developed in the subdivided areas.  By this assumption, the equivalent roughness coefficient is

$$ n = \frac{\left[ \sum\limits_{1}^{N} (P_N n_N^{2}) \right]^{1/2}}{P^{1/2}} = \frac{(P_1 n_1^{2} + P_2 n_2^{2} + \cdots + P_N n_N^{2})^{1/2}}{P^{1/2}} \quad (6\text{-}18) $$

Lotter [12] assumed that the total discharge of the flow is equal to the sum of the discharges of the subdivided areas.  Thus, the equivalent roughness coefficient is

$$ n = \frac{P R^{5/3}}{\sum\limits_{1}^{N} \left( \dfrac{P_N R_N^{5/3}}{n_N} \right)} = \frac{P R^{5/3}}{\dfrac{P_1 R_1^{5/3}}{n_1} + \dfrac{P_2 R_2^{5/3}}{n_2} + \cdots + \dfrac{P_N R_N^{5/3}}{n_N}} \quad (6\text{-}19) $$

where $R_1, R_2, \ldots, R_N$ are hydraulic radii of the subdivided areas.   For simple channel sections, it may be assumed that

$$R_1 = R_2 = \cdots = R_N = R$$

*Roughness of Ice-covered Channels.*   When a channel is covered with ice, the wetted perimeter of the flow is greatly increased.   The bottom surface of the ice cover may be either as smooth as a finished concrete surface or as rough as the natural channel bed when drifting ice blocks exist.   Table 6-1 gives the $n$ values for dredged channels covered with ice, as proposed by Lotter [13].

TABLE 6-1. $n$ VALUES FOR ICE-COVERED DREDGED CHANNELS

| Ice condition | Velocity of flow, fps | $n$ Value |
|---|---|---|
| Smooth ice: | | |
| Without drifting ice blocks | 1.3–2.0 | 0.010–0.012 |
| | >2.0 | 0.014–0.017 |
| With drifting ice blocks | 1.3–2.0 | 0.016–0.018 |
| | >2.0 | 0.017–0.020 |
| Rough ice with drifting ice blocks | . . . . . . . | 0.023–0.025 |

Let $n$ and $n_1$ be the roughness coefficients for channels with and without ice cover, respectively.   By means of Eqs. (6-17) to (6-19) it is possible to compute the roughness coefficient $n_2$ of the ice cover.   However, the coefficient thus computed may sometimes be a negative value, which is, of course, unrealistic.

In order to develop a realistic approach to the problem, Pavlovskiĭ [14] assumed that the total force resisting the flow is equal to the sum of the resisting forces due to the channel bed and the ice cover.   Thus, from Art. 5-4,

$$KV^2LP = K_1V^2LP_1 + K_2V^2LP_2 \tag{6-20}$$

where the subscript 1 refers to the channel bed and 2 to the ice cover. Since Chézy's $C = \sqrt{w/K}$ or $K = w/C^2$, the above equation becomes

$$\frac{P}{C^2} = \frac{P_1}{C_1{}^2} + \frac{P_2}{C_2{}^2} \tag{6-21}$$

Let the wetted perimeter $P_2 = aP_1$ or $P = P_1 + P_2 = (1 + a)P_1$; then

$$\frac{1+a}{C^2} = \frac{1}{C_1{}^2} + \frac{a}{C_2{}^2} \tag{6-22}$$

Since, by Eq. (5-7), $C = 1.49R^{1/6}/n$,

$$\frac{(1+a)n^2}{R^{1/3}} = \frac{n_1{}^2}{R_1{}^{1/3}} + \frac{an_2{}^2}{R_2{}^{1/3}} \tag{6-23}$$

It is further assumed that the total hydraulic radius $R$ is made up of two parts: the hydraulic radius $R_1$ due to the channel bed and the hydraulic radius $R_2$ due to the ice cover; that is, that $R = R_1 + R_2$. Now, let $\epsilon_1 = R_1/R_2$ and $\epsilon_2 = n_1/n_2$. Then Eq. (6-23) is reduced to

$$(1 + a)n^2 = n_2{}^2 \left(1 + \frac{1}{\epsilon_1}\right)^{\frac{1}{3}} (\epsilon_2{}^2 + a\epsilon_1{}^{\frac{1}{3}}) \qquad (6\text{-}24)$$

For the condition of maximum discharge, Pavlovskiĭ postulated that the relation among $R_1$, $R_2$, and $n$ is such that $dn/d\epsilon_1 = 0$. Thus, from Eq. (6-24), $\epsilon_2{}^2 = a\epsilon_1{}^{\frac{1}{3}}$, and

$$n = \frac{n_2}{\sqrt{1 + a}} (a^{\frac{3}{4}} + \epsilon_2{}^{\frac{3}{2}})^{\frac{2}{3}} \qquad (6\text{-}25)*$$

For wide channels, it may be assumed that $P_1 = P_2$, that is, that $a = 1$. Thus, $\epsilon_2{}^2 = \epsilon_1{}^{\frac{1}{3}}$, and

$$n = \frac{n_2}{\sqrt{2}} (1 + \epsilon_2{}^{\frac{3}{2}})^{\frac{2}{3}} \qquad (6\text{-}27)$$

The roughness coefficient for the ice cover is, therefore,

$$n_2 = (1.68n^{\frac{3}{2}} - n_1{}^{\frac{3}{2}})^{\frac{2}{3}} \qquad (6\text{-}28)$$

Now let the discharges with and without ice cover be $Q$ and $Q_1$, respectively. Then, using the Manning formula and assuming $R = R_1/2$, where $R$ and $R_1$ are the hydraulic radii with and without ice cover, respectively, the discharge of an ice-covered channel is

$$Q = 0.63 \frac{n_1}{n} Q_1 \qquad (6\text{-}29)$$

*Channels of Compound Section.* The cross section of a channel may be composed of several distinct subsections with each subsection different in roughness from the others. For example, an alluvial channel subject to seasonal floods generally consists of a main channel and two side channels (Fig. 6-6). The side channels are usually found to be rougher than the main channel; so the mean velocity in the main channel is greater than the mean velocities in the side channels. In such a case, the Manning formula may be applied separately to each subsection in determining the mean velocity of the subsection. Then, the discharges in the subsections can be computed. The total discharge is, therefore, equal to the sum of these discharges. The mean velocity for the whole

---

* Pavlovskiĭ [14] used the relation $C = R^{\frac{1}{4}}/n$ instead of Eq. (5-7), obtaining

$$n = \frac{n_2}{\sqrt{1 + a}} (a^{\frac{2}{3}} + \epsilon_2{}^{\frac{4}{3}})^{\frac{3}{4}} \qquad (6\text{-}26)$$

It was Belokon [15] who used Eq. (5-7).

channel section is equal to the total discharge divided by the total water area.

Owing to the differences that exist among the velocities of the subsections, the velocity-distribution coefficients of the whole section are different from those of the subsections. The values of these coefficients may be computed as follows:

Let $v_1, v_2, \ldots, v_N$ be the mean velocities in the subsections; let $\alpha_1, \alpha_2, \ldots, \alpha_N$ and $\beta_1, \beta_2, \ldots, \beta_N$ be the velocity-distribution coefficients for the corresponding subsections; let $\Delta A_1, \Delta A_2, \ldots, \Delta A_N$ be

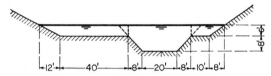

FIG. 6-6. A channel consisting of one main section and two side sections.

the water areas of the corresponding subsections; let $K_1, K_2, \ldots, K_N$ be the conveyances of the corresponding subsections; let $V$ be the mean velocity of the total section; and let $A$ be the total water area. From the continuity equation and Eq. (6-3), the following can be written:

$$v_1 = \frac{K_1}{\Delta A_1} S^{1/2} \qquad v_2 = \frac{K_2}{\Delta A_2} S^{1/2} \qquad \cdots \qquad v_N = \frac{K_N}{\Delta A_N} S^{1/2}$$

$$Q = VA = v_1 \Delta A_1 + v_2 \Delta A_2 + \cdots + v_N \Delta A_N$$

$$= (K_1 + K_2 + \cdots + K_N)S^{1/2} = \left(\sum_1^N K_N\right) S^{1/2}$$

and

$$V = \frac{\left(\sum_1^N K_N\right) S^{1/2}}{A}$$

Incorporating the above expressions with Eqs. (2-4) and (2-5) and simplifying, the velocity-distribution coefficients of the entire section are

$$\alpha = \frac{\sum\limits_1^N (\alpha_N K_N{}^3 / \Delta A_N{}^2)}{\left(\sum\limits_1^N K_N\right)^3 \Big/ A^2} \tag{6-30}$$

and

$$\beta = \frac{\sum\limits_1^N (\beta_N K_N{}^2 / \Delta A_N)}{\left(\sum\limits_1^N K_N\right)^2 \Big/ A} \tag{6-31}$$

**Example 6-1.** Compute the velocity-distribution coefficients at a peak flow in a natural stream channel consisting of a main section and an overflow side section. The data obtained at the peak flow stage are:

| Subsection | $A$, ft² | $P$, ft | $n$ value | $\alpha$ | $\beta$ |
|---|---|---|---|---|---|
| Main section........ | 5,360 | 225 | 0.035 | 1.10 | 1.04 |
| Side section......... | 5,710 | 405 | 0.040 | 1.11 | 1.04 |

*Solution.* The computations are given below.

| Subsection | $\Delta A$ | $P$ | $R$ | $R^{2/3}$ | $n$ | $K$ | $\beta K^2/\Delta A$ | $\alpha K^3/\Delta A^2$ |
|---|---|---|---|---|---|---|---|---|
| Main section. | 5,360 | 225 | 23.8 | 8.29 | 0.035 | $1.892 \times 10^6$ | $6.94 \times 10^8$ | $25.93 \times 10^{10}$ |
| Side section... | 5,710 | 405 | 14.1 | 5.85 | 0.040 | $1.244 \times 10^6$ | $2.82 \times 10^8$ | $6.56 \times 10^{10}$ |
| Total...... | 11,070 | ..... | ..... | ..... | ..... | $3.136 \times 10^6$ | $9.76 \times 10^8$ | $32.49 \times 10^{10}$ |

By Eqs. (6-30) and (6-31), the coefficients are

$$\alpha = \frac{32.49 \times 10^{10}}{(3.136 \times 10^6)^3/11,070^2} = 1.29$$

and

$$\beta = \frac{9.76 \times 10^8}{(3.136 \times 10^6)^2/11,070} = 1.10$$

**6-6. Determination of the Normal Depth and Velocity.** The normal depth and velocity may be computed by a uniform-flow formula. In the following computations, the Manning formula is used with three different methods of solution.[1]

*A. Algebraic Method.* For geometrically simple channel sections, the uniform-flow condition may be determined by an algebraic solution, as illustrated by the following example:

**Example 6-2.** A trapezoidal channel (Fig. 2-2), with $b = 20$ ft, $z = 2$, $S_0 = 0.0016$, and $n = 0.025$, carries a discharge of 400 cfs. Compute the normal depth and velocity.

*Solution 1: The Analytical Approach.* The hydraulic radius and water area of the given section are expressed in terms of the depth $y$ as

$$R = \frac{y(10 + y)}{10 + y\sqrt{5}} \quad \text{and} \quad A = y(20 + 2y)$$

The velocity is

$$V = \frac{Q}{A} = \frac{400}{y(20 + 2y)}$$

Substituting the given quantities and the above expressions in the Manning formula

[1] Besides the methods described here, there are other methods for the computation of uniform flow, such as the use of hydraulic tables. Popular tables for this purpose can be found in [16] to [20].

and simplifying,

$$\frac{200}{y(10 + y)} = \frac{1.49}{0.025}\left[\frac{y(10 + y)}{10 + y\sqrt{5}}\right]^{2/3} 0.0016^{1/2}$$

or

$$7{,}680 + 1{,}720y = [y(10 + y)]^{2.5}$$

Solving this equation for $y$ by trial and error, $y_n = 3.36$ ft. This is the normal depth. The corresponding area is $A_n = 89.8$ ft$^2$ and the normal velocity is $V_n = 400/89.8 = 4.46$ fps. From Example 4-2, it is known that the critical depth for the same discharge in the channel is 2.15 ft. Since the normal depth is greater than the critical depth, the flow is subcritical.

*Solution 2: The Trial-and-error Approach.* Some engineers prefer to solve this type of problem by trial and error. Using the given data, the right side of Eq. (6-8) is $nQ/1.49\sqrt{S} = 167.7$. Then, assume a value of $y$ and compute the section factor $AR^{2/3}$. Make several such trials until the computed value of $AR^{2/3}$ is very closely equal to 167.7; then the assumed $y$ for the closest trial is the normal depth. This trial-and-error computation is shown as follows:

| $y$ | $A$ | $R$ | $R^{2/3}$ | $AR^{2/3}$ | Remarks |
|------|------|------|-------|-------|---------|
| 3.00 | 78.0 | 2.34 | 1.762 | 137.4 | $y$ too small |
| 3.50 | 94.5 | 2.65 | 1.915 | 181.0 | $y$ too large |
| 3.30 | 87.7 | 2.53 | 1.852 | 162.6 | |
| 3.35 | 89.5 | 2.56 | 1.870 | 167.2 | |
| 3.36 | 89.8 | 2.56 | 1.870 | 168.0 | The closest |

The normal depth is, therefore, $y_n = 3.36$ ft.

*B. Graphical Method.* For channels of complicated cross section and variable flow conditions, a graphical solution of the problem is found to be convenient. By this procedure, a curve of $y$ against the section factor $AR^{2/3}$ is first constructed and the value of $nQ/1.49\sqrt{S}$ is computed. According to Eq. (6-8), it is evident that the normal depth may be found from the $y$-$AR^{2/3}$ curve where the coordinate of $AR^{2/3}$ equals the computed value of $nQ/1.49\sqrt{S}$. When the discharge changes, new values of $nQ/1.49\sqrt{S}$ are then computed and the corresponding new normal depths can be found from the same curve.

**Example 6-3.** Determine the normal depth of flow in a 36-in. culvert (Example 4-3) laid on a slope of 0.0016, having $n = 0.015$, and carrying a discharge of 20 cfs.

*Solution.* Construct a curve of $y$ vs. $AR^{2/3}$ for the given culvert (Fig. 6-7). Compute $nQ/1.49\sqrt{S} = 0.015 \times 20/1.49\sqrt{0.0016} = 5.04$. From the $y$-$AR^{2/3}$ curve, find the depth corresponding to the value of 5.04 for $AR^{2/3}$. This depth is the required normal depth, or $y_n = 2.16$ ft. Since this depth is greater than the critical depth determined in Example 4-3 under the same condition, the flow is subcritical.

The table in Appendix A for the geometric elements of a circular section may also be used for the solution of this problem. Since $d_0 = 3.0$ ft and $d_0^{8/3} = 18.75$, $AR^{2/3}/d_0^{8/3} = 5.04/18.75 = 0.269$. From the table, $y/d_0 = 0.72$, or $y = 0.72 \times 3 = 2.16$ ft.

*C. Method of Design Chart.* The design chart for determining the normal depth (Fig. 6-1) can be used with great expediency.

In Example 6-2, $AR^{2/3} = 167.7$. The value of $AR^{2/3}/b^{8/3}$ is 0.0569. For this value, the chart gives $y/b = 0.168$, or $y_n = 3.36$ ft.

In Example 6-3, $AR^{2/3}/d_0^{8/3} = 0.269$. For this value, the chart gives $y/d_0 = 0.72$, or $y = 0.72 \times 3 = 2.16$ ft.

**6-7. Determination of the Normal and Critical Slopes.** When the discharge and roughness are given, the Manning formula can be used to determine the slope of a prismatic channel in which the flow is uniform at a given normal depth $y_n$. The slope thus determined is sometimes called specifically the *normal slope $S_n$*.

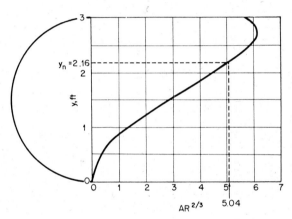

Fig. 6-7. A curve of $y$ vs. $AR^{2/3}$ for a circular section.

By varying the slope of the channel to a certain value, it is possible to change the normal depth and make the uniform flow occur in a critical state for the given discharge and roughness. The slope thus obtained is the *critical slope $S_c$*, and the corresponding normal depth is equal to the critical depth. The smallest critical slope for a channel of given shape and roughness is called the *limit slope $S_L$*.

Furthermore, by adjusting the slope and the discharge, a critical uniform flow may be obtained at the given normal depth. The slope thus obtained is known as the *critical slope at the given normal depth $S_{cn}$*.

The following examples will illustrate the above discussion.

**Example 6-4.** A trapezoidal channel has a bottom width of 20 ft, side slopes of 2:1, and $n = 0.025$.

a. Determine the normal slope at a normal depth of 3.36 ft when the discharge is 400 cfs.

b. Determine the critical slope and the corresponding normal depth when the discharge is 400 cfs.

c. Determine the critical slope at the normal depth of 3.36 ft, and compute the corresponding discharge.

*Solution.*  (a) From the given data it is found that $R = 2.56$ ft and $V = 4.46$ fps. Substituting these values in the Manning formula and solving for $S_n$,

$$4.46 = \frac{1.49}{0.025} 2.56^{2/3} S_n^{1/2}$$

or

$$S_n = 0.0016$$

This is the slope that will maintain a uniform flow in the given channel at a depth of 3.36 ft and a discharge of 400 cfs (see Example 6-2).

b. From the given data the critical depth is found to be 2.15 ft (see Example 4-2). The corresponding values of $R$ and $V$ are $R = 1.97$ ft and $V = 7.66$ fps. Substituting the known values in the Manning formula and solving for $S_c$,

$$7.66 = \frac{1.49}{0.025} 1.97^{2/3} S_c^{1/2}$$

or

$$S_c = 0.0067$$

This is the slope that will maintain a uniform and critical flow in the given channel for a discharge of 400 cfs.  The depth of flow is 2.15 ft.

c. For the given normal depth of 3.36 ft, it is found that $R = 2.56$ ft, $A = 89.8$ ft$^2$, $D = 2.68$ ft, and, by Eq. (1-11), the critical velocity $V_c = \sqrt{2.68g} = 9.3$ fps.  Substituting the known values in the Manning formula and solving for $S_{cn}$,

$$9.3 = \frac{1.49}{0.025} 2.56^{2/3} S_{cn}^{1/2}$$

or

$$S_{cn} = 0.0070$$

This is the slope that will maintain a uniform and critical flow in the given channel at the given normal depth of 3.36 ft.  The corresponding discharge is equal to 9.3 × 89.8 = 835 cfs.

**Example 6-5.**  Determine the limit slope of a rectangular channel (Fig. 6-8) with $b = 10$ ft and $n = 0.015$.

*Solution.*  Since the limit slope is the smallest critical slope, its value may be determined graphically from a curve of the critical slope plotted against discharge.

For the determination of a critical slope, the following two conditions should be satisfied:

1. The first condition, from Eq. (6-3), is

$$Q = K \sqrt{S_c} \tag{6-32}$$

or, when the Manning formula is used,

$$Q = \frac{1.49}{n} A R^{2/3} \sqrt{S_c} \tag{6-33}$$

or, for the rectangular channel,

$$Q = \frac{1.49}{n} 10y \left(\frac{10y}{10 + 2y}\right)^{2/3} \sqrt{S_c} \tag{6-34}$$

2. The second condition, from Eq. (4-3), is

$$Q = Z_c \sqrt{g} \tag{6-35}$$

or, for the rectangular channel,

$$Q = 10 \sqrt{g}\, y^{1.5} \tag{6-36}$$

By using Eqs. (6-34) and (6-36) and eliminating $y$, the relation between $Q$ and $S_c$ can be established. This relation is expressed, however, as an implicit function, and a direct solution is mathematically complicated. A practical solution of the problem is to assume different values of $y$, substitute $y$ in Eq. (6-36) and solve for $Q$, and then substitute $y$ and $Q$ in Eq. (6-34) and solve for $S_c$. Following this procedure, the relation between $Q$ and $S_c$ was computed and plotted as shown in Fig. 6-8. The plotted

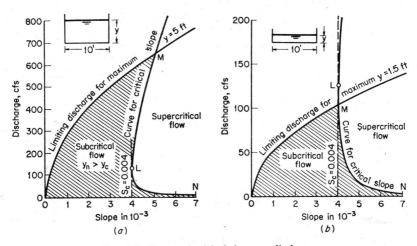

Fig. 6-8. Curves of critical slope vs. discharge.

curve $MLN$ indicates a minimum value of $S_c = 0.004$ at $L$, which is the required limit slope.

Assuming that the maximum expected depth of flow in the channel is 5 ft, a discharge curve $OM$ (Fig. 6-8a) can be constructed according to Eq. (6-9). It becomes evident that, within the shaded area between the curves $OM$ and $MLN$, all expected flows will be subcritical. On the right side of the curves, the flows will be supercritical. Since the point $L$ is below the curve $OM$, the limit slope is possible in the expected range of flow.

Similarly, the maximum expected depth of flow is assumed to be 1.5 ft, and the curves are shown in Fig. 6-8b. In this case, the point $L$ is above the curve $OM$; therefore, the limit slope cannot be expected to occur in the realm under consideration.

**6-8. Problems of Uniform-flow Computation.** The computation of uniform flow may be performed by the use of two equations: the continuity equation and a uniform-flow formula. When the Manning formula is used as the uniform-flow formula, the computation will involve the following six variables:

1. The normal discharge $Q$
2. The mean velocity of flow $V$
3. The normal depth $y$
4. The coefficient of roughness $n$
5. The channel slope $S$
6. The geometric elements that depend on the shape of the channel section, such as $A$, $R$, etc.

When any four of the above six variables are given, the remaining two unknowns can be determined by the two equations.  The following are some types of problems of uniform-flow computation:

$A$. To compute the normal discharge.  In practical applications, this computation is required for the determination of the capacity of a given channel or for the construction of a synthetic rating curve of the channel.

$B$. To determine the velocity of flow.  This computation has many applications.  For example, it is often required for the study of scouring and silting effects in a given channel.

$C$. To compute the normal depth.  This computation is required for the determination of the stage of flow in a given channel.

$D$. To determine the channel roughness.  This computation is used to ascertain the roughness coefficient in a given channel; the coefficient thus determined may be used in other similar channels.

$E$. To compute the channel slope.  This computation is required for adjusting the slope of a given channel.

$F$. To determine the dimensions of the channel section.  This computation is required mainly for design purposes.

Table 6-2 lists the known and unknown variables involved in each of the six types of problems mentioned above.  The known variables are indicated by a check mark ($\checkmark$) and the unknowns required in the problem by a question mark (?).  The unknown variables that can be determined from the known variables are indicated by a dash (—).  The last

TABLE 6-2. SOME TYPES OF PROBLEMS OF UNIFORM-FLOW COMPUTATION

| Type of problem | Discharge $Q$ | Velocity $V$ | Depth $y$ | Roughness $n$ | Slope $S$ | Geometric elements | Example |
|---|---|---|---|---|---|---|---|
| $A$ | ? | — | $\checkmark$ | $\checkmark$ | $\checkmark$ | $\checkmark$ | Prob. 5-5, (Ex. 5-1) |
| $B$ | — | ? | $\checkmark$ | $\checkmark$ | $\checkmark$ | $\checkmark$ | Prob. 5-5, (Ex. 5-1) |
| $C$ | $\checkmark$ | — | ? | $\checkmark$ | $\checkmark$ | $\checkmark$ | Example 6-2 |
| $D$ | $\checkmark$ | — | $\checkmark$ | ? | $\checkmark$ | $\checkmark$ | Prob. 5-6 |
| $E$ | $\checkmark$ | — | $\checkmark$ | $\checkmark$ | ? | $\checkmark$ | Example 6-4a |
| $F$ | $\checkmark$ | — | $\checkmark$ | $\checkmark$ | $\checkmark$ | ? | Example 7-2 |

column of the table shows the example given in this book for each type of problem. The examples shown in parentheses are solved by the use of the Chézy formula. It should be noted, however, that Table 6-2 does not include all types of problems. By varying combinations of various known and unknown variables, more types of problems can be formed. In design problems, the use of the best hydraulic section and of empirical rules is generally introduced (Art. 7-7) and thus new types of problems are created.

**6-9. Computation of Flood Discharge.** In uniform-flow computation it is understood, theoretically, that the energy slope $S_f$ in the uniform-flow formula is equal to the slope of the longitudinal water-surface profile and also to the slope of the channel bottom (Art. 5-1). In natural streams, however, these three slopes are only approximately equal. Owing to irregular channel conditions, the energy line, water surface, and channel bottom cannot be strictly parallel to one another. If the change in velocity within the channel reach is not appreciable, the energy slope may be taken roughly equal to the bottom or the surface slope. On the other hand, if the velocity varies appreciably from one end of the reach to the other, the energy slope should be taken as the difference between the total heads at the ends of the reach divided by the length of the reach. Since the total head includes the velocity head, which is unknown, a solution by successive approximation is necessary in the discharge computation.

During flood stages, the velocity varies greatly, and the velocity head should be included in the total head for defining the energy slope. Furthermore, flood flow is in fact varied and unsteady, and use of a uniform-flow formula for discharge computation is acceptable only when the changes in flood stage and discharge are relatively gradual.

The direct use of a uniform-flow formula for the determination of flood discharges is known as the *slope-area method*. The flood discharge may also be determined by another well-known method called the *contracted-opening method*, in which the principle of energy is applied directly to a contracted opening in the stream. Both methods[1] require information about the highwater marks that are detectable in the flooded reach. Good locations for collecting such information may be found not only on main streams but also on smaller tributaries, but they must be either comparatively regular valley channels free from bends and thus well suited to the slope-area method or else contracted openings with sufficient constriction to produce definite increase in head and velocity and thus suited to the contracted-opening method.

The following is a description of the slope-area method.[2] The con-

---

[1] For a comprehensive description of the methods, see [21].

[2] It should be noted that the slope-area method actually deals with gradually varied

tracted-opening method is related to rapidly varied flow and, therefore, will be described later, in Art. 17-6.

*The Slope-area Method.* The following information is necessary for the slope-area method: the determination of the energy slope in the channel reach; the measurement of the average cross-sectional area and the length of the reach; and the estimation of the roughness coefficient applicable to the channel reach, so that frictional losses can be calculated. When this information is obtained, the discharge can be computed by a uniform-flow formula, such as Manning's. The procedure of computation is as follows:

1. From the known values of $A$, $R$, and $n$, compute the conveyances $K_u$ and $K_d$, respectively, of the upstream and downstream sections of the reach.

2. Compute the average conveyance $K$ of the reach as the geometric mean of $K_u$ and $K_d$, or

$$K = \sqrt{K_u K_d} \tag{6-37}$$

3. Assuming zero velocity head, the energy slope is equal to the fall $F$ of water surface in the reach divided by the length $L$ of the reach, or

$$S = \frac{F}{L} \tag{6-38}$$

The corresponding discharge may, therefore, be computed by Eq. (6-3), or

$$Q = K \sqrt{S} \tag{6-3}$$

which gives the first approximation of the discharge.

4. Assuming the discharge equal to the first approximation, compute the velocity heads at the upstream and downstream sections, or $\alpha_u V_u{}^2/2g$ and $\alpha_d V_d{}^2/2g$. The energy slope is, therefore, equal to

$$S = \frac{h_f}{L} \tag{6-39}$$

where
$$h_f = F + k(\alpha_u V_u{}^2/2g - \alpha_d V_d{}^2/2g) \tag{6-40}$$

and $k$ is a factor. When the reach is contracting ($V_u < V_d$), $k = 1.0$. When the reach is expanding ($V_u > V_d$), $k = 0.5$. The 50% decrease in the value of $k$ for an expanding reach is customarily assumed for the recovery of the velocity head due to the expansion of the flow. The corresponding discharge is then computed by Eq. (6-3) using the revised

---

flow, but it is believed that at this stage of reading the reader should be able to follow the procedure described here. This method shows how the uniform-flow formula can be applied to gradually varied flow and thus paves the way for a more comprehensive treatment on the subject of gradually varied flow in Part III.

slope obtained by Eq. (6-39). This gives the second approximation of the discharge.

5. Repeat step 4 for the third and fourth approximations, and so on until the assumed and computed discharges agree.

6. Average the discharges computed for several reaches, weighting them equally or as circumstances indicate.

**Example 6-6.** Compute the flood discharge through a river reach of 500 ft having known values of the water areas, conveyances, and energy coefficients of the upstream and downstream end sections. The fall of water surface in the reach was found to be 0.50 ft.

*Solution.* The water areas, conveyances, and energy coefficients for the two end sections of the reach are:

$$
\begin{aligned}
A_u &= 11{,}070 & K_u &= 3.034 \times 10^6 & \alpha_u &= 1.134 \\
A_d &= 10{,}990 & K_d &= 3.103 \times 10^6 & \alpha_d &= 1.177
\end{aligned}
$$

The average $K = \sqrt{3.034 \times 10^6 \times 3.103 \times 10^6} = 3.070 \times 10^6$.

For the first approximation, assume $h_f = 0.50$ ft. Then $S = 0.50/500 = 0.0010$, $\sqrt{S} = 0.0316$, and $Q = K\sqrt{S} = 3.070 \times 10^6 \times 0.0316 = 97{,}000$ cfs.

For the second approximation, assume $Q = 97{,}000$ cfs. Then the velocity heads at the two end sections are:

$$
\alpha_u \frac{V_u^2}{2g} = 1.134 \frac{(97{,}000/11{,}070)^2}{2g} = 1.354
$$

$$
\alpha_d \frac{V_d^2}{2g} = 1.177 \frac{(97{,}000/10{,}990)^2}{2g} = \underline{\quad 1.424 \quad} \\
-0.070
$$

Since $V_u$ is less than $V_d$, the flow is contracting, and $k = 1.0$. Hence, $h_f = 0.500 - 0.070 = 0.430$, $S = 0.430/500 = 0.00086$, $\sqrt{S} = 0.0293$, and $Q = 3.070 \times 10^6 \times 0.0293 = 90{,}000$ cfs.

Similarly, other approximations are made, as shown in Table 6-3. The estimated discharge is found to be 91,000 cfs.

TABLE 6-3. COMPUTATION OF FLOOD DISCHARGE BY THE SLOPE-AREA METHOD FOR EXAMPLE 6-6

| Approximation | Assumed $Q$ | $F$ | $\alpha_u \dfrac{V_u^2}{2g}$ | $\alpha_d \dfrac{V_d^2}{2g}$ | $h_f$ | $S$ | $\sqrt{S}$ | Computed $Q$ |
|---|---|---|---|---|---|---|---|---|
| 1st | ...... | 0.500 | ..... | ..... | 0.500 | 0.001000 | 0.0316 | 97,000 |
| 2d | 97,000 | 0.500 | 1.354 | 1.424 | 0.430 | 0.000860 | 0.0293 | 90,000 |
| 3d | 90,000 | 0.500 | 1.165 | 1.225 | 0.440 | 0.000880 | 0.0297 | 91,200 |
| 4th | 91,200 | 0.500 | 1.195 | 1.258 | 0.437 | 0.000874 | 0.0296 | 91,000 |
| 5th | 91,000 | 0.500 | 1.190 | 1.253 | 0.437 | 0.000874 | 0.0296 | 91,000 |

**6-10. Uniform Surface Flow.** When water flows across a broad surface, so-called *surface flow* is produced. The depth of the flow may be so thin in comparison with the width of flow that the flow becomes a wide-open-channel flow, known specifically as *sheet flow*. In a drainage basin surface flow occurs mostly as a result of natural runoff, and is called *overland flow.*

Uniform flow may be turbulent or laminar, depending upon such factors as discharge, slope, viscosity, and degree of surface roughness. If velocities and depths of flow are relatively small, the viscosity becomes a dominating factor and the flow is laminar. In this case the Newton's law of viscosity applies. This law expresses the relation between the

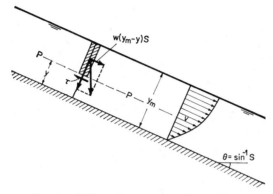

Fig. 6-9. Uniform laminar open-channel flow.

dynamic viscosity $\mu$ and the shear stress $\tau$ at a distance $y$ from the boundary surface (Fig. 6-9), as follows:

$$\tau = \mu \frac{dv}{dy} \tag{6-41}$$

For uniform laminar flow, the component of the gravitational force parallel to the flow in any laminar layer is balanced by the frictional force. In other words, the shear stress $\tau$ per unit area of the flow along the laminar layer $PP$ (Fig. 6-9) is equal to the effective component of the gravitational force, that is, $\tau = w(y_m - y)S$. Since the unit weight $w = \rho g$ and $\mu/\rho = \nu$ (Art. 1-3), $\tau = g\mu(y_m - y)S/\nu$. Thus, from Eq. (6-41),

$$dv = \frac{gS}{\nu}(y_m - y)\,dy$$

Integrating and noting that $v = 0$ when $y = 0$,

$$v = \frac{gS}{\nu}\left(yy_m - \frac{y^2}{2}\right) \tag{6-42}$$

This is a quadratic equation indicating that the velocity of uniform laminar flow in a wide open channel has a parabolic distribution. Integrate Eq. (6-42) from $y = 0$ to $y = y_m$ and divide the result by $y_m$; the average velocity is

$$V = \frac{1}{y_m} \int_0^{y_m} v \, dy = \frac{gSy_m^2}{3\nu} \tag{6-43}$$

and the discharge per unit width is

$$q = C_L y_m^3 \tag{6-44}$$

where $C_L = gS/3\nu$, a coefficient involving slope and viscosity.

Uniform surface flow becomes turbulent if the surface is rough and if the depth of flow is sufficiently large to produce persisting eddies. In this case the surface roughness is a dominating factor, and the velocity can readily be expressed by the Manning formula. Thus, the discharge per unit width is

$$q = C_T y_m^{5/3} \tag{6-45}$$

where $y_m$ is the average depth of flow and where $C_T = 1.49S^{0.5}/n$, a coefficient involving slope and roughness.

The change of state of sheet flow from laminar to turbulent has been studied by many hydraulicians. The transitional region was found variously at $\mathbf{R} = 310$ by Jeffreys [22], from $\mathbf{R} = 300$ to 330 by Hopf [23], and from $\mathbf{R} = 548$ to 773 by Horton [24]. However, Horton believed that the Reynolds criterion is not satisfactory for sheet flow over relatively rough surfaces. He reasoned that, at the transition point, the velocities for laminar and turbulent flow are nearly equal, because this condition of equal velocities represents the minimum amount of energy capable of maintaining turbulent flow. Thus, the flow cannot be turbulent if the velocity is less than

$$V = \frac{\nu}{4.83n^2 y_m^{2/3}} \tag{6-46}$$

where $y_m$ is the average depth of flow.

As the natural ground surface is rarely even and uniform in slope, overland flow is apt to change from laminar to turbulent, and vice versa, within a short distance. Consequently, the flow is mixed between the laminar and turbulent. For very rough surfaces or areas densely covered with vegetation, the flow in general is highly turbulent. Experiments have indicated that the discharge of overland flow per unit width of flow varies with the average depth of flow as follows:

$$q = Cy_m^x \tag{6-47}$$

where $C$ is a coefficient and where the exponent $x$ varies between 1.0 for highly turbulent flow and 3.0 for mixed flow.

## PROBLEMS

**6-1.** Determine the normal discharges in channels having the following sections for $y = 6$ ft, $n = 0.015$, and $S = 0.0020$:

a. A rectangular section 20 ft wide
b. A triangular section with a bottom angle equal to 60°
c. A trapezoidal section with a bottom width of 20 ft and side slopes of 1 on 2
d. A circular section 15 ft in diameter
e. A parabolic section having a width of 16 ft at the depth of 4 ft

**6-2.** Prove the following equation for the discharge in a triangular highway gutter (Fig. 6-10) having one side vertical, one side sloped at 1 on $z$, Manning's $n$, depth of

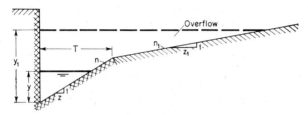

Fig. 6-10. A highway gutter section.

flow $y$, and longitudinal slope $S$:

$$Q = \frac{0.47}{n} f(z) y^{8/3} S^{1/2} \qquad (6\text{-}48)$$

where

$$f(z) = \frac{z^{5/3}}{[1 + \sqrt{1 + z^2}]^{2/3}}$$

**6-3.** Compute the discharge in the triangular highway gutter described in the preceding problem when $z = 24$, $n = 0.017$, $y = 0.22$ ft, and $S = 0.03$.

**6-4.** Using the Manning formula, determine the hydraulic exponent $N$ for the following channel sections: (a) a very narrow rectangle, (b) a very wide rectangle, (c) a very wide parabola for which the wetted perimeter is practically equal to the top width, and (d) an equilateral triangle with a vertex at the bottom.

**6-5.** Using the Chézy formula,[1] show that the general equation for the hydraulic exponent $N$ is

$$N = \frac{y}{A}\left(3T - R\frac{dP}{dy}\right) \qquad (6\text{-}49)$$

**6-6.** Solve Prob. 6-4 if the determination of the hydraulic exponent is based on the Chézy formula. Compare the results with those obtained in Prob. 6-4.

[1] The G. K. formula shows that Chézy's $C$ is a function of the hydraulic radius and hence of the depth $y$. Thus, the Chézy formula has not been found very convenient for determination of the $N$ value. For canals in earth and gravelly soil, the $N$ value is generally found to have an increase of 0.30 to 0.50 due to the variation in Chézy's $C$ with respect to the depth. This increase, however, brings the $N$ value closer to that based on the Manning formula.

**6-7.** Compute the hydraulic exponent $N$ of the trapezoidal channel section (Fig. 2-2) having a normal depth of 6 ft, using (a) Eq. (6-15), (b) Fig. 6-2, and (c) the graphical method based on Eq. (6-16).

**6-8.** Compute the hydraulic exponent $N$ of a 36-in. circular conduit having a normal depth of 24 in. above the invert, using (a) Fig. 6-2 and (b) the graphical method based on Eq. (6-16).

**6-9.** Using the Manning formula, show that the depths for a maximum discharge and velocity in a circular conduit are, respectively, $0.938d_0$ and $0.81d_0$.

**6-10.** On the basis of the Chézy formula, determine the respective depths for maximum discharge and maximum velocity in a circular conduit.

**6-11.** At what depths will the maximum discharge and velocity occur in a square conduit laid flat on one side?

**6-12.** Prepare the curves of discharge and velocity variations with respect to the depth in a square conduit laid on one side.

**6-13.** A channel is assumed to have a constant hydraulic radius $R$ for any depth of flow. Prove that the cross section of this channel can be defined by

$$y = R[\ln (x + \sqrt{x^2 - R^2}) - \ln R] \qquad (6\text{-}50)$$

where $x = R$ when $y = 0$. Draw the sketch of this section and discuss its properties. (HINT: From the given condition, $R = A/P = dA/dP = x \, dy/\sqrt{dx^2 + dy^2}$. Solve this differential equation, and evaluate the integration constant by the condition that $x = R$ when $y = 0$. Mathematically, the section is formed by two catenaries as sides. For practical purposes, an artificial bottom should be provided since the theoretical section is bottomless. A uniform-flow formula, such as the Manning formula, indicates that the hydraulic radius is the sole shape parameter for the velocity. The adequacy of this indication can be verified experimentally by testing a channel built of the section of constant hydraulic radius. If the indication is true, then, once this channel is designed for a safe velocity, it should be nonscouring and nonsilting over a wide range of stages. In earthen canals, however, the large variation in water surface during the change of stage would erode the sides very easily.)

**6-14.** Verify Eqs. (6-17) to (6-19).

**6-15.** A rectangular testing channel is 2 ft wide and laid on a slope of 0.1035%. When the channel bed and walls were made smooth by neat cement, the measured normal depth of flow was 1.36 ft for a discharge of 8.9 cfs. The same channel was then roughened by cemented sand grains, and thus the measured normal depth became 1.31 ft for a discharge of 5.2 cfs.

*a.* Determine the discharge for a normal depth of 1.31 ft if the bed were roughened and the walls were kept smooth.

*b.* Determine the discharge for a normal depth of 1.31 ft if the walls were roughened and the bed were smooth.

*c.* The discharges for the conditions described in *a* and *b* were actually measured and found to be 6.60 and 6.20 cfs, respectively. Determine the corresponding $n$ values, and compare these values with those computed by Eqs. (6-17) to (6-19).

**6-16.** A channel consists of a main section and two side sections (Fig. 6-6). Compute the total discharge, assuming that the main section and the two side sections are separated (a) by vertical division lines and (b) by extended sides of the main channel. Given: $n = 0.025$ for the main channel, $n = 0.030$ for the side channels, and $S = 0.001$.

**6-17.** The hydrographic survey of a stream indicates that the hydraulic properties of the stream are relatively uniform for a length of over 2 miles. The data obtained by the survey are:

*a.* The cross section of the stream at a typical upstream station in the uniform reach is given by the following coordinates:

| Station | Elev. m.s.l. | | Station | Elev. m.s.l. |
|---|---|---|---|---|
| Left bank: 0 + 00 | 590.0 | | 6 + 00 | 543.7 |
| 1 + 00 | 580.7 | | 8 + 00 | 540.0 |
| 1 + 50 | 578.2 | | 10 + 00 | 572.2 |
| 3 + 00 | 582.0 | | 11 + 00 | 573.2 |
| 4 + 00 | 581.0 | | 12 + 00 | 568.5 |
| 5 + 00 | 580.0 | | 14 + 00 | 590.0 |

*b.* The value of $n$ for the main channel is estimated as 0.035, for the side channels as 0.050.

*c.* The natural slope of the stream is about 1 ft/mile.

Construct a synthetic rating curve. It is suggested that the water areas of the main channel and the side channels be separated by the extended sides of the main channel.

**6-18.** Compute the discharge in an overflowed highway gutter (Fig. 6-10) having a depth of flow of 3 in. and a longitudinal slope of 0.03. The gutter is made of concrete with $n = 0.017$ and has a triangular section with a vertical curb side, a sloped side of $z = 12$, and a top width of $T = 2$ ft. The overflowed soil-aggregate pavement has a cross slope of $z_1 = 24$ and $n_1 = 0.020$.

**6-19.** For an equal amount of discharge, an ice-covered channel should have greater depth of flow than an uncovered channel, for two reasons: (1) the wetted perimeter is greater in an ice-covered channel and thus results in greater resistance or less velocity, and (2) the thickness of the ice cover is greater than a depth of water of equal weight, since the specific gravity of ice is about 0.917. Show that the increase in depth due to resistance in an ice-covered wide open channel may be expressed by

$$\Delta y = \left[ 1.32 \left( \frac{n_1}{n} \right)^{3\!\!\!/_{\!5}} - 1 \right] y \tag{6-51}$$

where $n_1$ is the roughness coefficient of the channel with ice cover, $n$ is the roughness coefficient of the channel without ice cover, and $y$ is the depth of flow in the channel carrying the same discharge but without ice cover.

**6-20.** Compute the conveyance and velocity-distribution coefficients of a channel section 500 ft downstream from the section described in Example 6-1. The survey data at the section for the same flood are:

| Subsection | $A$, ft² | $P$, ft | $n$ | $\alpha$ | $\beta$ |
|---|---|---|---|---|---|
| Main section........ | 5,320 | 205 | 0.035 | 1.12 | 1.05 |
| Side section......... | 5,670 | 408 | 0.040 | 1.10 | 1.04 |

**6-21.** Solve Example 6-2 by the G. K. Formula.

**6-22.** A rectangular channel with 20 ft width, $S = 0.006$, and $n = 0.015$, carries a discharge of 200 cfs. Compute the normal depth and velocity.

**6-23.** Using the Manning formula, determine the normal depths in channels having the following sections when $Q = 100$ cfs, $n = 0.015$, and $S = 0.0020$:

*a.* A rectangular section 20 ft wide
*b.* A triangular section with the bottom angle equal to 60°
*c.* A trapezoidal section with a bottom width of 20 ft and side slopes of 1 on 2
*d.* A circular section 15 ft in diameter
*e.* A parabolic section having a width of 16 ft at the depth of 4 ft

**6-24.** Solve Example 6-2 by the graphical method.

**6-25.** A rectangular channel 20 ft wide has a roughness coefficient $n = 0.015$.

*a.* Determine the normal slope at a normal depth of 1.23 ft when the discharge is 200 cfs.

*b.* Determine the critical slope and the corresponding normal depth when the discharge is 200 cfs.

*c.* Determine the critical slope at the normal depth of 1.23 ft, and compute the corresponding discharge.

**6-26.** Show that the critical slope at a given normal depth $y_n$ may be expressed by

$$S_{cn} = \frac{14.5n^2 D_n}{R_n^{4/3}} \tag{6-52}$$

and that this slope for a wide channel is

$$S_{cn} = \frac{14.5n^2}{y^{1/3}} \tag{6-53}$$

**6-27.** Determine the limit slope of the channel described in Example 6-4.

**6-28.** Construct the critical-slope curves of the channel described in Example 6-5 for bottom widths $b = 1$ ft, 4 ft, 20 ft, and $\infty$.

**6-29.** Determine the critical-slope curves of the channel described in Example 6-4 for side slopes $z = 0$, 0.2, 0.5, 1, 2, 5, and $\infty$.

**6-30.** A channel reach 1,000 ft long has a fall of 0.35 ft in water surface during a flood. Compute the flood discharge through this reach, using the following data:

| Subsection | $A$, ft² | $P$, ft | $n$ | $\alpha$ | $\beta$ |
|---|---|---|---|---|---|
| Upstream: | | | | | |
| Main channel............ | 4,250 | 210 | 0.038 | 1.10 | 1.04 |
| Side channel............ | 25,620 | 2,050 | 0.038 | 1.20 | 1.08 |
| Downstream: | | | | | |
| Main channel............ | 5,760 | 320 | 0.042 | 1.10 | 1.04 |
| Side channel............ | 25,610 | 1,905 | 0.038 | 1.18 | 1.06 |

**6-31.** Prove Eq. (6-46).

**6-32.** Using Eqs. (1-5) and (6-43), determine the value of $K$ in Eq. (1-8).

**6-33.** Compute the discharges per unit width of a sheet flow on a surface with $n = 0.01$ and $S = 0.036$ when the depth of flow is (*a*) 0.01 ft and (*b*) 0.004 ft. The temperature of water is 68°F.

**6-34.** Compare Horton's criteria for sheet flow in Prob. 6-33 with those shown by the chart of Fig. 1-3.

**6-35.** Show that the velocity-distribution coefficients for laminar uniform flow in wide open channels are $\alpha = 1.54$ and $\beta = 1.20$.

**6-36.** Using the Blasius equation (1-6) for turbulent flow in open channels, show that the corresponding exponent in Eq. (6-47) is $x = 1\frac{2}{7}$.

## REFERENCES

1. Ven Te Chow: Integrating the equation of gradually varied flow, paper 838, *Proceedings, American Society of Civil Engineers*, vol. 81, pp. 1–32, November, 1955.

2. R. R. Chugaev: Nekotorye voprosy neravnomernogo dvizheniia vody v otkrytykh prizmaticheskikh ruslakh (About some questions concerning nonuniform flow of water in open channels), *Izvestiia Vsesoiuznogo Nauchno-Issledovatel'skogo Instituta Gidrotekhniki (Transactions, All-Union Scientific Research Institute of Hydraulic Engineering)*, Leningrad, vol. 1, pp. 157–227, 1931.

3. Phillip Z. Kirpich: Dimensionless constants for hydraulic elements of open-channel cross-sections, *Civil Engineering*, vol. 18, no. 10, p. 47, October, 1948.

4. N. N. Pavlovskiĭ: "Gidravlicheskiĭ Spravochnik" ("Handbook of Hydraulics"), Onti, Leningrad and Moscow, 1937, p. 515.

5. A. N. Rakhmanoff: O postroenii krivykh svobodnoĭ poverkhnosti v prizmaticheskikh i tsilindricheskikh ruslakh pri ustanovivshemsia dvizhenii (On the construction of curves of free surfaces in prismatic and cylindrical channels with established flow), *Izvestiia Vsesoiuznogo Nauchno-Issledovatel'skogo Instituta Gidrotekhnini (Transactions, All-Union Scientific Research Institute of Hydraulic Engineering)*, Leningrad, vol. 3, pp. 75–114, 1931.

6. Robert E. Horton: Separate roughness coefficients for channel bottom and sides, *Engineering News-Record*, vol. 111, no. 22, pp. 652–653, Nov. 30, 1933.

7. H. A. Einstein: Der hydraulische oder Profil-Radius (The hydraulic or cross section radius), *Schweizerische Bauzeitung*, Zürich, vol. 103, no. 8, pp. 89–91, Feb. 24, 1934.

8. Ahmed M. Yassin: Mean roughness coefficient in open channels with different roughness of bed and side walls, *Eidgenössische technische Hochschule Zürich, Mitteilungen aus der Versuchsanstalt für Wasserbau und Erdbau, No. 27*, Verlag Leemann, Zürich, 1954.

9. N. N. Pavlovskiĭ: K voprosu o raschetnoĭ formule dlia ravnomernogo dvizheniia v vodotokahk s neodnorodnymi stenkami (On a design formula for uniform movement in channels with nonhomogeneous walls), *Izvestiia Vsesoiuznogo Nauchno-Issledovatel'skogo Instituta Gidrotekhniki (Transactions, All-Union Scientific Research Institute of Hydraulic Engineering)*, Leningrad, vol. 3, pp. 157–164, 1931.

10. L. Mühlhofer: Rauhigkeitsuntersuchungen in einem Stollen mit betonierter Sohle und unverkleideten Wänden (Roughness investigations in a shaft with concrete bottom and unlined walls), *Wasserkraft und Wasserwirtschaft*, Munich, vol. 28, no. 8, pp. 85–88, 1933.

11. H. A. Einstein and R. B. Banks: Fluid resistance of composite roughness, *Transactions, American Geophysical Union*, vol. 31, no. 4, pp. 603–610, August, 1950.

12. G. K. Lotter: Soobrazheniia k gidravlicheskomu raschetu rusel s razlichnoĭ sherokhovatostiiu stenok (Considerations on hydraulic design of channels with different roughness of walls), *Izvestiia Vsesoiuznogo Nauchno-Issledovatel'skogo Instituta Gidrotekhniki (Transactions, All-Union Scientific Research Institute of Hydraulic Engineering)*, Leningrad, vol. 9, pp. 238–241, 1933.

13. G. K. Lotter: Vliianie uslovii ledoobrazovaniia i tolshchiny l'da na raschet derivatsionnykh kanalov (Influence of conditions of ice formation and thickness on the design of derivation canals), *Izvestiia Vsesoiuznogo Nauchno-Issledovatel'skogo Instituta Gidrotekhniki (Transactions, All-Union Scientific Research Institute of Hydraulic Engineering)*, Leningrad, vol. 7, pp. 55–80, 1932.

14. G. K. Lotter: Metod akademika N. N. Pavlovskogo dlia opredeleniia koeffitsienta

sherokhovatosti rusel, pokrytykh l'dom (Method by Academy Member N. N. Pavlovskiĭ for determination of roughness coefficients of ice-covered channels), *Izvestiia Vsesoiuznogo Nauchno-Issledovatel'skogo Instituta Gidrotekhniki (Transactions, All-Union Scientific Research Institute of Hydraulic Engineering)*, Leningrad, no. 29, 1941.

15. P. N. Belokon: "Inzhenernaia gidravlika potoka pod ledianym pokrovom" ("Engineering Hydraulics of a Current under Ice Cover"), Gosenergoizdat, Moscow and Leningrad, 1940.

16. Horace William King, "Manning Formula Tables," vol. II, "Flow in Open Channels," McGraw-Hill Book Company, Inc., New York, 1939.

17. "Hydraulic and Excavation Tables," U.S. Bureau of Reclamation, 10th ed., 1950.

18. "Hydraulic Tables," U.S. Corps of Engineers, U.S. Government Printing Office, Washington, D.C., 2d ed., 1944.

19. Horace William King: "Handbook of Hydraulics," 4th ed., revised by Ernest F. Brater, McGraw-Hill Book Company, Inc., New York, 1954, sec. 7, table 90.

20. P. A. Arghyropoulos: "Calcul de l'écoulement en conduites sous pression ou à surface libre, d'après la formule de Manning-Strickler" ("Computation of Flow in Conduits under Pressure or with Free Surface, Using Manning-Strickler Formula"), Dunod, Paris, 1958.

21. Ivan E. Houk: Calculation of flow in open channels, *Miami Conservancy District, Technical Report, Pt. IV*, Dayton, Ohio, 1918.

22. H. Jeffreys: Flow of water in an inclined channel of rectangular section, *London, Edinburgh and Dublin Philosophical Magazine and Journal of Science*, vol. 49, no. 293, pp. 793–807, May, 1925.

23. L. Hopf: Turbulenz bei einem Flusse (Turbulence in a flow), *Annalen der Physik*, Halle and Leipzig, vol. 32, sec. 4, pp. 777–808, April-July, 1925.

24. Robert E. Horton, H. R. Leach, and R. Van Vliet: Laminar sheet flow, *Transactions, American Geophysical Union*, vol. 15, pt. 2, pp. 393–404, 1934.

CHAPTER 7

# DESIGN OF CHANNELS FOR UNIFORM FLOW

Channels to be discussed in this chapter include nonerodible channels erodible channels, and grassed channels. For erodible channels, the discussion will be limited mostly to those which scour but do not silt (see Preface).

## A. NONERODIBLE CHANNELS

**7-1. The Nonerodible Channel.** Most lined channels and built-up channels can withstand erosion satisfactorily and are therefore considered *nonerodible*. Unlined channels are generally erodible, except those excavated in firm foundations, such as rock bed. In designing nonerodible channels, such factors as the maximum permissible velocity (Art. 7-9) and the permissible tractive force (Art. 7-13) are not the criteria to be considered. The designer simply computes the dimensions of the channel by a uniform-flow formula and then decides the final dimensions on the basis of hydraulic efficiency, or empirical rule of best section, practicability, and economy [1,2]. The factors to be considered in the design are: the kind of material forming the channel body, which determines the roughness coefficient; the minimum permissible velocity, to avoid deposition if the water carries silt or debris; the channel bottom slope and side slopes; the freeboard; and the most efficient section, either hydraulically or empirically determined.

**7-2. Nonerodible Material and Lining.**[1] The nonerodible materials used to form the lining of a channel and the body of a built-up channel include concrete, stone masonry, steel, cast iron, timber, glass, plastic, etc. The selection of the material depends mainly on the availability and cost of the material, the method of construction, and the purpose for which the channel is to be used.

The purpose of lining a channel is in most cases to prevent erosion, but occasionally it may be to check seepage losses. In lined channels, the *maximum permissible velocity*, i.e., the maximum that will not cause erosion, can be ignored, provided that the water does not carry sand, gravel, or stones. If there are to be very high velocities over a lining, however, it should be remembered that there is a tendency for the rapidly

---

[1] For detailed information on channel lining, see [3].

157

moving water to pick up lining blocks and push them out of position. Accordingly, the lining should be designed against such possibilities.

**7-3. The Minimum Permissible Velocity.** The *minimum permissible velocity*, or the *nonsilting velocity*, is the lowest velocity that will not start sedimentation and induce the growth of aquatic plant and moss. This velocity is very uncertain and its exact value cannot be easily determined. For water carrying no silt load or for desilted flow, this factor has little significance except for its effect on plant growth. Generally speaking, a mean velocity of 2 to 3 fps may be used safely when the percentage of silt present in the channel is small, and a mean velocity of not less than 2.5 fps will prevent a growth of vegetation that would seriously decrease the carrying capacity of the channel.

**7-4. Channel Slopes.** The longitudinal bottom slope of a channel is generally governed by the topography and the energy head required for the flow of water. In many cases, the slope may depend also on the purpose of the channel. For example, channels used for water-distribution purposes, such as those used in irrigation, water supply, hydraulic mining, and hydropower projects, require a high level at the point of delivery; therefore, a small slope is desirable in order to keep the loss in elevation to a minimum.

The side slopes of a channel depend mainly on the kind of material. Table 7-1 gives a general idea of the slopes suitable for use with various

TABLE 7-1. SUITABLE SIDE SLOPES FOR CHANNELS BUILT IN VARIOUS KINDS OF MATERIALS

| Material | Side slope |
|---|---|
| Rock | Nearly vertical |
| Muck and peat soils | $\frac{1}{4}$:1 |
| Stiff clay or earth with concrete lining | $\frac{1}{2}$:1 to 1:1 |
| Earth with stone lining, or earth for large channels | 1:1 |
| Firm clay or earth for small ditches | $1\frac{1}{2}$:1 |
| Loose sandy earth | 2:1 |
| Sandy loam or porous clay | 3:1 |

kinds of material. For erodible material, however, a more accurate determination of the slopes should be checked against the criterion of maximum permissible velocity (Art. 7-10) or by the principle of tractive force (Art. 7-14). Other factors to be considered in determining slopes are method of construction, condition of seepage loss, climatic change, channel size, etc. Generally speaking, side slopes should be made as steep as practicable and should be designed for high hydraulic efficiency and stability. For lined canals, the U.S. Bureau of Reclamation [4] has been considering standardizing on a 1.5:1 slope for the usual sizes of canals. One advantage of this slope is that it is sufficiently flat to allow the practicable use of just about any type of lining or lining treatment now or in the future anticipated by the Bureau.

**7-5. Freeboard.** The *freeboard* of a channel is the vertical distance from the top of the channel to the water surface at the design condition. This distance should be sufficient to prevent waves or fluctuations in water surface from overflowing the sides. This factor becomes important particularly in the design of elevated flumes, for the flume substructure may be endangered by any overflow.

There is no universally accepted rule for the determination of freeboard, since wave action or water-surface fluctuation in a channel may be created by many uncontrollable causes. Pronounced waves and fluctuation of water surface are generally expected in channels where the velocity is so high and the slope so steep that the flow becomes very unstable, or on curves where high velocity and large deflection angle may cause appreciable superelevated water surface on the convex side of a curve, or in channels where the velocity of flow approaches the critical state at which the water may flow at alternate depths and thus jump from the low stage to the high stage at the least obstruction. Other natural causes such as wind movement and tidal action may also induce high waves and require special consideration in design.

Freeboards varying from less than 5% to greater than 30% of the depth of flow are commonly used in design. For smooth, interior, semicircular metal flumes on tangents, carrying water at velocities not greater than 80% of the critical velocity with a maximum of 8 fps, experience has indicated that a freeboard of 6% of the flume diameter should be used. For flumes on curves with high velocity or deflections, wave action will be produced; so freeboard must be increased to prevent water from slopping over.

Freeboard in an unlined canal or lateral will normally be governed by considerations of canal size and location, storm-water inflow, and water-table fluctuations caused by checks, wind action, soil characteristics, percolation gradients, operating road requirements, and availability of excavated material. According to the U.S. Bureau of Reclamation [4], the approximate range of freeboard frequently used extends from 1 ft for small laterals with shallow depths to 4 ft in canals of 3,000 cfs or more capacity with relatively large water depths. The Bureau recommends that preliminary estimates of the freeboard required under ordinary conditions be made according to the following formula:

$$F = \sqrt{Cy} \qquad (7\text{-}1)$$

where $F$ is the freeboard in ft, $y$ is the depth of water in the canal in ft, and $C$ is a coefficient varying from 1.5 for a canal capacity of 20 cfs to 2.5 for a canal capacity of 3,000 cfs or more. This approximation is based upon average Bureau practice; it will not, however, serve for all conditions.

For lined canals or laterals, the height of lining above the water surface will depend upon a number of factors: size of canal, velocity of water, curvature of alignment, condition of storm- and drain-water inflow, fluctuations in water level due to operation of flow-regulating structures, and wind action. In a somewhat similar manner, the height of bank above the water surface will vary with size and location of canal, type of soil, amount of intercepted storm or drain water, etc. As a guide for lined-canal design, the U.S. Bureau of Reclamation [3] has prepared curves (Fig. 7-1) for average freeboard and bank heights in relation to capacities.

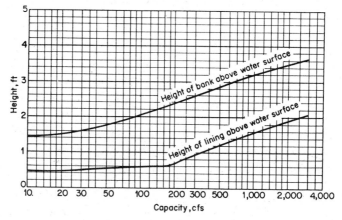

Fig. 7-1. Recommended freeboard and height of bank of lined channels. (*U.S. Bureau of Reclamation.*)

**7-6. The Best Hydraulic Section.** It is known that the conveyance of a channel section increases with increase in the hydraulic radius or with decrease in the wetted perimeter. From a hydraulic viewpoint, therefore, the channel section having the least wetted perimeter for a given area has the maximum conveyance; such a section is known as the *best hydraulic section.* The semicircle has the least perimeter among all sections with the same area; hence it is the most hydraulically efficient of all sections.

The geometric elements of six best hydraulic sections are listed in Table 7-2, but these sections may not always be practical owing to difficulties in construction and in use of material. In general, a channel section should be designed for the best hydraulic efficiency but should be modified for practicability. From a practical point of view, it should be noted that a best hydraulic section is the section that gives the minimum area for a given discharge but not necessarily the minimum excavation. The section of minimum excavation occurs only if the water surface is at the level of the bank tops. Where the water surface is below the bank tops, as frequently occurs, channels narrower than those of the best hydraulic section will give minimum excavation. If the water surface overtops the banks and these are even with the ground level, wider channels will provide minimum excavation.

TABLE 7-2. BEST HYDRAULIC SECTIONS

| Cross section | Area $A$ | Wetted perimeter $P$ | Hydraulic radius $R$ | Top width $T$ | Hydraulic depth $D$ | Section factor $Z$ |
|---|---|---|---|---|---|---|
| Trapezoid, half of a hexagon | $\sqrt{3}\,y^2$ | $2\sqrt{3}\,y$ | $\tfrac{1}{2}y$ | $\tfrac{4}{3}\sqrt{3}\,y$ | $\tfrac{3}{4}y$ | $\tfrac{3}{2}y^{2.5}$ |
| Rectangle, half of a square | $2y^2$ | $4y$ | $\tfrac{1}{2}y$ | $2y$ | $y$ | $2y^{2.5}$ |
| Triangle, half of a square | $y^2$ | $2\sqrt{2}\,y$ | $\tfrac{1}{4}\sqrt{2}\,y$ | $2y$ | $\tfrac{1}{2}y$ | $\dfrac{\sqrt{2}}{2}y^{2.5}$ |
| Semicircle | $\dfrac{\pi}{2}y^2$ | $\pi y$ | $\tfrac{1}{2}y$ | $2y$ | $\dfrac{\pi}{4}y$ | $\dfrac{\pi}{4}y^{2.5}$ |
| Parabola, $T = 2\sqrt{2}\,y$ | $\tfrac{4}{3}\sqrt{2}\,y^2$ | $\tfrac{8}{3}\sqrt{2}\,y$ | $\tfrac{1}{2}y$ | $2\sqrt{2}\,y$ | $\tfrac{2}{3}y$ | $\tfrac{8}{9}\sqrt{3}\,y^{2.5}$ |
| Hydrostatic catenary | $1.39586y^2$ | $2.9836y$ | $0.46784y$ | $1.917532y$ | $0.72795y$ | $1.19093y^{2.5}$ |

The principle of the best hydraulic section applies only to the design of nonerodible channels. For erodible channels, the principle of tractive force must be used to determine an efficient section (Art. 7-15).

**Example 7-1.** Show that the best hydraulic trapezoidal section is one-half of a hexagon.

*Solution.* Table 2-1 gives the water area and wetted perimeter of a trapezoid as

$$A = (b + zy)y \quad \text{and} \quad P = b + 2\sqrt{1 + z^2}\,y$$

where $y$ is the depth, $b$ is the bottom width, and $z:1$ is the side slope.

First, consider $A$ and $z$ to be constant. Differentiating the above two equations with respect to $y$ and solving simultaneously for $dP/dy$,

$$\frac{dP}{dy} = 2(\sqrt{1 + z^2} - z) - \frac{b}{y}$$

For a minimum wetted perimeter, $dP/dy = 0$, or

$$b = 2y(\sqrt{1 + z^2} - z)$$

Substituting this equation for $b$ in the previous two equations for $A$ and $P$ and solving simultaneously for $P$,

$$P = 2 \sqrt{A(2 \sqrt{1 + z^2} - z)}$$

Now, find the value of $z$ that makes $P$ the least. Differentiating $P$ with respect to $z$, equating $dP/dz$ to zero, and solving for $z$,

$$z = \frac{\sqrt{3}}{3} = \tan 30°$$

This means that the section is a half hexagon.

**7-7. Determination of Section Dimensions.** The determination of section dimensions for nonerodible channels includes the following steps:

1. Collect all necessary information, estimate $n$, and select $S$.
2. Compute the section factor $AR^{2/3}$ by Eq. (6-8), or

$$AR^{2/3} = \frac{nQ}{1.49 \sqrt{S}} \qquad (6\text{-}8)$$

3. Substitute in Eq. (6-8) the expressions for $A$ and $R$ obtained from Table 2-1, and solve for the depth. If there are other unknowns, such as $b$ and $z$ of a trapezoidal section, then assume the values for these unknowns and solve Eq. (6-8) for the depth. By assuming several values of the unknowns, a number of combinations of section dimensions can be obtained. The final dimensions are decided on the basis of hydraulic efficiency and practicability. For lined canals, the trapezoidal section is commonly adopted, and the U.S. Bureau of Reclamation [3] has developed experience curves (Fig. 7-2) showing the average relation of bottom widths and water depths to canal capacities. These curves can be used as a guide in selecting proper section dimensions.

The determination of the depth for the computed value of $AR^{2/3}$ can be simplified by use of the design chart (Fig. 6-1). Some engineers prefer a solution by trial and error, similar to Solution 2 for Example 6-2 of Art. 6-6.

4. If the best hydraulic section is required directly, substitute in Eq. (6-8) the expressions for $A$ and $R$ obtained from Table 7-2 and solve for the depth. This best hydraulic section may be modified for practicability.

5. For the design of irrigation channels, the channel section is sometimes proportioned by empirical rules such as the simple rule given by the early U.S. Reclamation Service [5] for the full supply depth of water in feet.

$$y = 0.5 \sqrt{A} \qquad (7\text{-}2)$$

where $A$ is the water area in ft². For a trapezoidal section it can be shown that this rule may also be expressed by a simple formula

$$x = 4 - z \qquad (7\text{-}3)$$

where $x$ is the width-depth ratio $b/y$ and $z$ is the horizontal projection of the side slope corresponding to 1 ft vertical.  Similarly, engineers in India [6] have used an empirical formula $y = \sqrt{A/3} = 0.577 \sqrt{A}$, which is equivalent to $x = 3 - z$ for trapezoidal sections; and Philippine engineers [7] use Eq. (7-3) with $z = 1.5$, or $x = 2.5$, for earth canals.

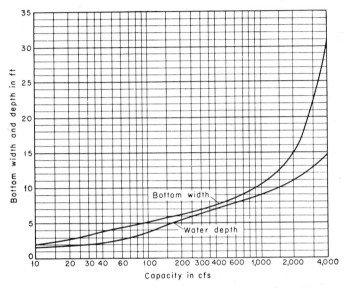

FIG. 7-2. Experience curves showing bottom width and depth of lined channels. (*U.S. Bureau of Reclamation.*)

6. Check the minimum permissible velocity if the water carries silt.
7. Add a proper freeboard to the depth of the channel section.

**Example 7-2.** A trapezoidal channel carrying 400 cfs is built with nonerodible bed having a slope of 0.0016 and $n = 0.025$.  Proportion the section dimensions.

*Solution.*  By Eq. (6-8),

$$AR^{\frac{2}{3}} = \frac{0.025 \times 400}{1.49 \sqrt{0.0016}} = 167.7$$

Substituting $A = (b + zy)y$ and $R = (b + zy)y/(b + 2 \sqrt{1 + z^2}\, y)$ in the above expression,

$$\frac{[(b + zy)y]^{\frac{5}{3}}}{(b + 2 \sqrt{1 + z^2}\, y)^{\frac{2}{3}}} = 167.7$$

Assuming $b = 20$ ft and $z = 2$ and simplifying,

$$7,680 + 1,720y = [y(10 + y)]^{2.5}$$
$$y = 3.36 \text{ ft}$$

It should be noted that this solution is exactly the same as the computation of the normal depth given in Solution 1 of Example 6-2. Accordingly, the solutions by trial and error and by the graphical method described in Example 6-2 can also be applied to the present problem.

Similarly, assume other suitable values of $b$ and $z$, and compute the corresponding depths. The final decision on dimensions will depend on practical considerations. If the values of $b$ and $z$ are decided at the beginning of the computation, the depth will be computed only once.

Suppose that $b = 20$ ft, $z = 2$, and $y = 3.36$ ft are the final values. Assign a free-board of 2 ft; the total depth of the channel is, therefore, 5.36 ft and the top width of the channel (not the width of the water surface) is 41.4 ft. The water area is 89.8 ft², and the velocity is 4.46 fps, which is greater than the minimum permissible velocity for inducing silt, if any.

When the best hydraulic section is required, substitute $A = \sqrt{3}\,y^2$ and $R = 0.5y$, obtained from Table 7-2, in $AR^{\frac{2}{3}} = 167.7$ and simplify; the depth is found to be $y = 6.6$ ft. Add 3 ft freeboard; the total depth is 9.6 ft. The corresponding bottom width is 7.6 ft, the top width of the channel is 18.7 ft, the water area is 75.2 ft², and the velocity is 5.32 fps. Since the best hydraulic trapezoidal section is the half hexagon, the side slopes are 1 on $\sqrt{3}/3$.

## B. ERODIBLE CHANNELS WHICH SCOUR BUT DO NOT SILT

**7-8. Methods of Approach.** The behavior of flow in an erodible channel is influenced by so many physical factors and by field conditions so complex and uncertain that precise design of such channels at the present stage of knowledge is beyond the realm of theory.[1] The uniform-flow formula, which is suitable for the design of stable nonerodible channels, provides an insufficient condition for the design of erodible channels. This is because the stability of erodible channels, which governs the design, is dependent mainly on the properties of the material forming the channel body, rather than only on the hydraulics of the flow in the channel. Only after a stable section of the erodible channel is obtained can the uniform-flow formula be used for computing the velocity of flow and discharge.

Two methods of approach to the proper design of erodible channels are described here: the *method of permissible velocity* and the *method of tractive force*. The method of permissible velocity has been used extensively for the design of earth canals in the United States to ensure freedom from scour. The method of tractive force has sometimes been used in Europe; it is now under comprehensive investigation by the U.S. Bureau

[1] It has been noticed that certain channels are erodible whereas others very similar in channel geometry, hydraulics, and soil physical properties are not. As a further step in investigation, the chemical properties of the material forming the channel body should be explored. It may be that an ion exchange between water and soil or hydration of the material is providing a binder in some places and thus affecting the erosion. For a general discussion of the complexity of this problem, see [8] and [9].

of Reclamation and is tentatively recommended for design of erodible channels. It should be noted that either method at the present stage will serve only as a guide and will not supplant experience and sound engineering judgment. '

**7-9. The Maximum Permissible Velocity.** The *maximum permissible velocity*, or the *nonerodible velocity*, is the greatest mean velocity that will not cause erosion of the channel body. This velocity is very uncertain and variable, and can be estimated only with experience and judgment. In general, old and well-seasoned channels will stand much higher veloci-

TABLE 7-3. MAXIMUM PERMISSIBLE VELOCITIES RECOMMENDED BY FORTIER
AND SCOBEY AND THE CORRESPONDING UNIT-TRACTIVE-FORCE VALUES
CONVERTED BY THE U.S. BUREAU OF RECLAMATION*
(For straight channels of small slope, after aging)

| Material | $n$ | Clear water | | Water transporting colloidal silts | |
|---|---|---|---|---|---|
| | | $V$, fps | $\tau_0$, lb/ft² | $V$, fps | $\tau_0$, lb/ft² |
| Fine sand, colloidal.................... | 0.020 | 1.50 | 0.027 | 2.50 | 0.075 |
| Sandy loam, noncolloidal................ | 0.020 | 1.75 | 0.037 | 2.50 | 0.075 |
| Silt loam, noncolloidal................. | 0.020 | 2.00 | 0.048 | 3.00 | 0.11 |
| Alluvial silts, noncolloidal............. | 0.020 | 2.00 | 0.048 | 3.50 | 0.15 |
| Ordinary firm loam..................... | 0.020 | 2.50 | 0.075 | 3.50 | 0.15 |
| Volcanic ash.......................... | 0.020 | 2.50 | 0.075 | 3.50 | 0.15 |
| Stiff clay, very colloidal................ | 0.025 | 3.75 | 0.26 | 5.00 | 0.46 |
| Alluvial silts, colloidal................. | 0.025 | 3.75 | 0.26 | 5.00 | 0.46 |
| Shales and hardpans................... | 0.025 | 6.00 | 0.67 | 6.00 | 0.67 |
| Fine gravel........................... | 0.020 | 2.50 | 0.075 | 5.00 | 0.32 |
| Graded loam to cobbles when noncolloidal.. | 0.030 | 3.75 | 0.38 | 5.00 | 0.66 |
| Graded silts to cobbles when colloidal...... | 0.030 | 4.00 | 0.43 | 5.50 | 0.80 |
| Coarse gravel, noncolloidal.............. | 0.025 | 4.00 | 0.30 | 6.00 | 0.67 |
| Cobbles and shingles................... | 0.035 | 5.00 | 0.91 | 5.50 | 1.10 |

* The Fortier and Scobey values were recommended for use in 1926 by the Special Committee on Irrigation Research of the American Society of Civil Engineers.

ties than new ones, because the old channel bed is usually better stabilized, particularly with the deposition of colloidal matter. When other conditions are the same, a deeper channel will convey water at a higher mean velocity without erosion than a shallower one. This is probably because the scouring is caused primarily by the bottom velocities and, for the same mean velocity, the bottom velocities are greater in the shallower channel.

Attempts[1] were made early to define a mean velocity that would cause neither silting nor scouring. From the present-day viewpoint, however, it is doubtful whether such a velocity actually exists. In 1915,

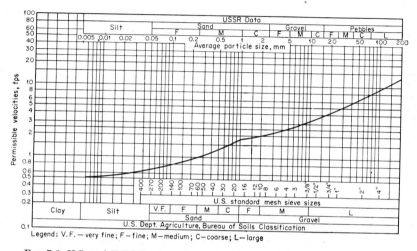

FIG. 7-3. U.S. and U.S.S.R. data on permissible velocities for noncohesive soils.

Etcheverry [26] published probably the first table of maximum mean velocities that are safe against erosion. In 1925, Fortier and Scobey [27] published the well-known table of "Permissible Canal Velocities" shown in Table 7-3. The values in this table are for well-seasoned channels of small slopes and for depths of flow less than 3 ft. The table also shows

[1] The first famous formula for this nonsilting and noneroding velocity for silt-laden water was published in 1895 by Kennedy [10]. From a study of the discharge and depth of 22 canals of the Upper Bari Doab irrigation system in Punjab, India, the Kennedy formula was developed as

$$V_0 = Cy^x \qquad (7-4)$$

where $V_0$ is the nonsilting and noneroding mean velocity in fps; $y$ is the depth of flow in ft; $C = 0.84$, depending primarily on the firmness of the material forming the channel body; and $x = 0.64$, an exponent which varies only slightly. Based on later studies by other engineers, the values of $C$ generally recommended are 0.56 for extremely fine soils such as those found in Egypt; 0.84 for fine light sand soils such as those found in the Punjab, India; 0.92 for coarse light sandy soils; 1.01 for sandy loamy silts; and 1.09 for coarse silt or hard-soil debris. For clear water, a value of $x = 0.5$ has been suggested.

For the design of canals carrying sediment-laden water, the Kennedy formula is now practically obsolete and is being replaced by methods based on Lacey's regime theory [11–16], Einstein's bed-load function [17], and Maddock-Leopold's principle of channel geometry [18]. There are voluminous writings on these methods. Comprehensive bibliographies can be found in [19] to [25].

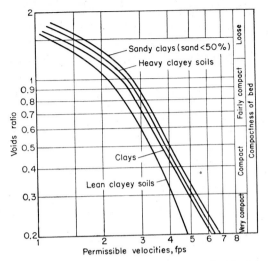

Fig. 7-4. Curves showing U.S.S.R. data on permissible velocities for cohesive soils.

suitable $n$ values for various materials and the converted values for the corresponding permissible tractive force, which will be discussed later (Art. 7-13). In 1936, a Russian magazine [28] published values of maximum permissible velocities (Figs. 7-3 and 7-4) above which scour would be produced in noncohesive material of a wide range of particle sizes and various kinds of cohesive soil. It also gave the variation of these velocities with channel depth (Fig. 7-5).

The maximum permissible velocities mentioned above are with reference to straight channels. For sinuous channels, the velocities should be lowered in order to reduce scour. Percentages of reduction suggested by Lane [29] are 5% for slightly sinuous canals, 13% for moderately sinuous canals, and 22% for very sinuous canals. These percentage values, however, are very approximate, since no accurate data are available at the present time.

**7-10. Method of Permissible Velocity.** Using the maximum permissible velocity as a criterion, the design procedure for a channel section, assumed to be trapezoidal, consists of the following steps:

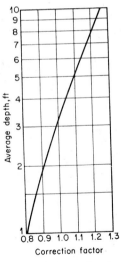

Fig. 7-5. Curves showing U.S.S.R. corrections of permissible velocity for depth for both cohesive and noncohesive materials.

1. For the given kind of material forming the channel body, estimate the roughness coefficient $n$ (Art. 5-7), side slope $z$ (Table 7-1), and the maximum permissible velocity $V$ (Table 7-3 and Figs. 7-3 to 7-5).

2. Compute the hydraulic radius $R$ by the Manning formula.

3. Compute the water area required by the given discharge and permissible velocity, or $A = Q/V$.

4. Compute the wetted perimeter, or $P = A/R$.

5. Using the expressions for $A$ and $P$ from Table 2-1, solve simultaneously for $b$ and $y$. The solution may be expedited by using the charts given in Appendix B.

6. Add a proper freeboard, and modify the section for practicability.

**Example 7-3.** Compute the bottom width and the depth of flow of a trapezoidal channel laid on a slope of 0.0016 and carrying a design discharge of 400 cfs. The channel is to be excavated in earth containing noncolloidal coarse gravels and pebbles.

*Solution.* For the given conditions, the following are estimated: $n = 0.025$, $z = 2$, and maximum permissible velocity = 4.5 fps.

Using the Manning formula, solve for $R$.

$$4.5 = \frac{1.49}{0.025} R^{2/3} \sqrt{0.0016}$$

or

$$R = 2.60 \text{ ft}$$

Then $A = 400/4.5 = 88.8$ ft², and $P = A/R = 88.8/2.60 = 34.2$ ft. Now

$$A = (b + zy)y = (b + 2y)y = 88.8 \text{ ft}^2$$

and

$$P = b + 2\sqrt{1 + z^2}\, y = (b + 2\sqrt{5}\, y) = 34.2 \text{ ft}$$

Solving the above two equations simultaneously, $b = 18.7$ ft and $y = 3.46$ ft.

**7-11. The Tractive Force.** When water flows in a channel, a force is developed that acts in the direction of flow on the channel bed. This force, which is simply the pull of water on the wetted area, is known as the *tractive force*.[1] In a uniform flow the tractive force is apparently equal to the effective component of the gravity force acting on the body of water, parallel to the channel bottom and equal to $wALS$, where $w$ is the unit weight of water, $A$ is the wetted area, $L$ is the length of the channel reach, and $S$ is the slope (Art. 5-4). Thus, the average value of the tractive force per unit wetted area, or the so-called *unit tractive force* $\tau_0$, is equal to $wALS/PL = wRS$, where $P$ is the wetted perimeter and $R$ is the hydraulic radius; that is

$$\tau_0 = wRS \qquad (7\text{-}5)$$

In a wide open channel, the hydraulic radius is equal to the depth of flow $y$; hence $\tau_0 = wyS$.

[1] This is also known as the *shear force* or the *drag force*. The idea of tractive force is generally believed to have been first introduced into hydraulic literature by du Boys in 1879 [p. 149 of 30]. However, the principle of balancing this force with the channel resistance in a uniform flow was stated by Brahms early in 1754 (see Art. 5-4).

It should be noted that the unit tractive force in channels, except for wide open channels, is not uniformly distributed along the wetted perimeter. Many attempts have been made to determine the distribution of the tractive force in a channel. Leighly [31] attempted to determine this distribution in many trapezoidal and several rectangular and triangular channels from the published data on the velocity distribution in the

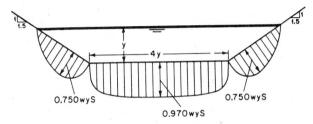

Fig. 7-6. Distribution of tractive force in a trapezoidal channel section.

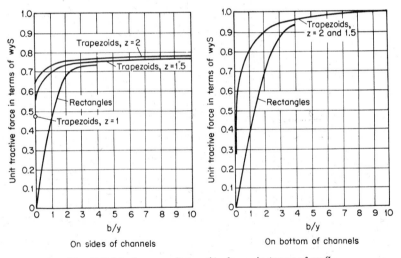

On sides of channels      On bottom of channels

Fig. 7-7. Maximum unit tractive forces in terms of $wyS$.

channels. Unfortunately, owing to deficiency of data, the results of his study were not very conclusive. In the U.S. Bureau of Reclamation, Olsen and Florey [32] and other engineers have used the membrane analogy and analytical and finite-difference methods for determining the distribution of tractive force in trapezoidal, rectangular, and triangular channels. A typical distribution of tractive force in a trapezoidal channel resulting from the membrane-analogy study is shown in Fig. 7-6. The pattern of distribution varies with the shape of the section but is practically unaffected by the size of the section.    Based on such studies, curves (Fig. 7-7) showing the maximum unit tractive forces on the sides and bottom of various channel sections have been prepared for use in canal design.    Generally speaking, for trapezoidal channels of the shapes ordinarily used in canals, the maximum tractive force on the bottom is close to the value $wyS$, and on the sides close to $0.76\ wyS$.

**7-12. Tractive-force Ratio.**    On a soil particle resting on the sloping side of a channel section (Fig. 7-8) in which water is flowing, two forces are acting: the tractive force $a\tau_s$ and the gravity-force component $W_s \sin \phi$,

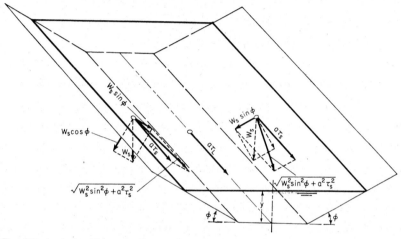

Fig. 7-8. Analysis of forces acting on a particle resting on the surface of a channel bed.

which tends to cause the particle to roll down the side slope.[1]    The symbols used are $a$ = effective area of the particle, $\tau_s$ = unit tractive force on the side of the channel, $W_s$ = submerged weight of the particle, and $\phi$ = angle of the side slope.    The resultant of these two forces, which are at right angles to each other, is

$$\sqrt{W_s{}^2 \sin^2 \phi + a^2 \tau_s{}^2}$$

When this force is large enough, the particle will move.

By the principle of frictional motion in mechanics, it may be assumed that, when motion is impending, the resistance to motion of the particle

[1] The concept of the three-dimensional analysis of the gravity and tractive forces acting on a particle resting on a slope at the state of impending motion was first given by Forchheimer [33].    A complete analysis of a channel section using this concept was first developed by Chia-Hwa Fan [34].    The analysis was also developed independently by the U.S. Bureau of Reclamation under the direction of E. W. Lane [29,35].

is equal to the force tending to cause the motion. The resistance to motion of the particle is equal to the normal force $W_s \cos \phi$ multiplied by the coefficient of friction, or $\tan \theta$, where $\theta$ is the angle of repose. Hence,

$$W_s \cos \phi \tan \theta = \sqrt{W_s^2 \sin^2 \phi + a^2 \tau_s^2} \qquad (7\text{-}6)$$

Solving for the unit tractive force $\tau_s$ that causes impending motion on a sloping surface,

$$\tau_s = \frac{W_s}{a} \cos \phi \tan \theta \sqrt{1 - \frac{\tan^2 \phi}{\tan^2 \theta}} \qquad (7\text{-}7)$$

Similarly, when motion of a particle on the level surface is impending owing to the tractive force $a\tau_L$, the following is obtained from Eq. (7-6) with $\phi = 0$:

$$W_s \tan \theta = a\tau_L \qquad (7\text{-}8)$$

Solving for the unit tractive force $\tau_L$ that causes impending motion on a level surface,

$$\tau_L = \frac{W_s}{a} \tan \theta \qquad (7\text{-}9)$$

The ratio of $\tau_s$ to $\tau_L$ is called the *tractive-force ratio;* this is an important ratio for design purposes. From Eqs. (7-7) and (7-9), the ratio is

$$K = \frac{\tau_s}{\tau_L} = \cos \phi \sqrt{1 - \frac{\tan^2 \phi}{\tan^2 \theta}} \qquad (7\text{-}10)$$

Simplifying,[1]

$$K = \sqrt{1 - \frac{\sin^2 \phi}{\sin^2 \theta}} \qquad (7\text{-}11)$$

It can be seen that this ratio is a function only of the inclination of the sloping side $\phi$ and of the angle of repose of the material $\theta$. For cohesive and fine noncohesive materials, the cohesive forces, even with comparatively clear water, become so great in proportion to the gravity-force component causing the particle to roll down that the gravity force can safely be neglected. Therefore, the angle of repose need be considered only for coarse noncohesive materials. According to the U.S. Bureau of Reclamation's investigation, it was found in general that the angle of repose increases with both size and angularity of the material. For use in design, curves (Fig. 7-9) were prepared by the Bureau, showing values of the angle of repose for noncohesive material above 0.2 in. in diameter for various degrees of roughness. The diameter referred to is the diameter of a particle than which 25% (by weight) of the material is larger.

[1] Equation (7-10) was presented by the U.S. Bureau of Reclamation [35,36] and Eq. (7-11) by Fan [34]. The two equations are mathematically identical.

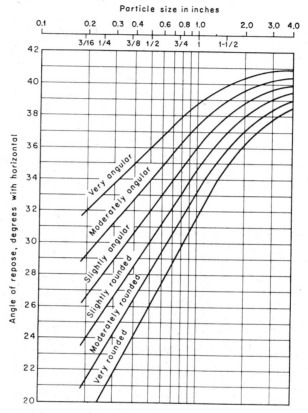

Fig. 7-9. Angles of repose of noncohesive material.   (*U.S. Bureau of Reclamation.*)

**7-13. Permissible Tractive Force.**   The *permissible tractive force* is the maximum unit tractive force that will not cause serious erosion of the material forming the channel bed on a level surface.   This unit tractive force can be determined by laboratory experiments, and the value thus obtained is known as the *critical tractive force*.   However, experience has shown that actual canals in coarse noncohesive material can stand substantially higher values than the critical tractive forces measured in the laboratory.   This is probably because the water and soil in actual canals contain slight amounts of colloidal and organic matter which provide a binding power and also because slight movement of soil particles can be tolerated in practical designs without endangering channel stability. Since the permissible tractive force is the design criterion for field conditions, the permissible value may be taken less than the critical value.

The determination of permissible tractive force is now based upon particle size for noncohesive material and upon compactness or voids ratio for cohesive material.   Other soil properties such as the plasticity index[1] or the chemical action may probably also be taken as indexes for defining permissible tractive force more precisely.   However, sufficient data and information on these indexes are lacking.   The U.S. Bureau of Reclamation has made a comprehensive study of the problem, using data for coarse noncohesive material obtained from the San Luis Valley

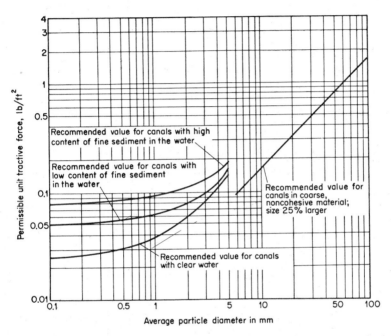

FIG. 7-10.  Recommended permissible unit tractive forces for canals in noncohesive material.   (*U.S. Bureau of Reclamation.*)

canals [37], values converted from permissible velocities, given by Etcheverry and by Fortier and Scobey, the U.S.S.R. values, etc. (Art. 7-9). As a result, values of permissible tractive force recommended for canal design were developed as follows:

[1] The plasticity index is the difference in per cent of moisture between plastic limit and liquid limit in Atterberg soil tests.   This index has been investigated by the U.S. Bureau of Reclamation as a soil characteristic that can be used to indicate resistance to scour for cohesive materials.   For canal design, a plasticity index of 7 may be taken tentatively as the critical value, with scour occurring for moderate tractive forces below this value.   However, scours are still observed in many cases where the index is above 7.   Research shows that determination of the plasticity index in conjunction with consolidated-shear tests may possibly be necessary.

For *coarse* noncohesive material, with sufficient factor of safety, the Bureau recommends tentatively a value of permissible tractive force in pounds per square foot equal to 0.4 times the diameter in inches of a particle than which 25% (by weight) of the material is larger. This recommendation is shown by the straight line in the design chart (Fig. 7-10).

For *fine* noncohesive material, the size specified is the median size, or size smaller than 50% of the weight. Three design curves (Fig. 7-10)

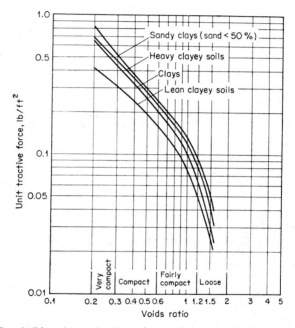

FIG. 7-11. Permissible unit tractive forces for canals in cohesive material as converted from the U.S.S.R. data on permissible velocities.

are tentatively recommended (1) for canals with high content of fine sediment in the water, (2) for canals with low content of fine sediment in the water, and (3) for canals with clear water.

For cohesive materials, the data based on conversion of permissible velocities to unit tractive forces and given in Table 7-3 and Fig. 7-11 are recommended as design references.

The permissible tractive forces mentioned above refer to straight channels. For sinuous channels, the values should be lowered in order to reduce scour. Approximate percentages of reduction, suggested by Lane [29], are 10% for slightly sinuous canals, 25% for moderately sinuous canals, and 40% for very sinuous canals.

**7-14. Method of Tractive Force.** The first step in the design of erodible channels by the method of tractive force consists in selecting an approximate channel section by experience or from design tables,[1] collecting samples of the material forming the channel bed, and determining the required properties of the samples. With these data, the designer investigates the section by applying tractive-force analysis to ascertain probable stability by reaches and to determine the minimum section that appears stable. For channels in noncohesive materials the rolling-down effect should be considered in addition to the effect of the distribution of tractive forces; for channels in cohesive material the rolling-down effect is negligible, and the effect of the distribution of tractive force alone is a criterion sufficient for design. The final proportioning of the channel section, however, will depend on other nonhydraulic practical considerations. The analysis for tractive force is best described by the following example:

**Example 7-4.** Design a trapezoidal channel laid on a slope of 0.0016 and carrying a discharge of 400 cfs. The channel is to be excavated in earth containing noncolloidal coarse gravels and pebbles, 25 % of which is 1.25 in. or over in diameter. Manning's $n = 0.025$.

*Solution.* For trapezoidal channels, the maximum unit tractive force on the sloping sides is usually less than that on the bottom (Fig. 7-7); hence, the side force is the controlling value in the analysis. The design of the channel should therefore include (a) the proportioning of the section dimensions for the maximum unit tractive force on the sides and (b) checking the proportioned dimensions for the maximum unit tractive force on the bottom.

*a. Proportioning the Section Dimensions.* Assuming side slopes of 2:1, or $z = 2$, and a base-depth ratio $b/y = 5$, the maximum unit tractive force on the sloping sides (Fig. 7-7) is $0.775wyS = 0.775 \times 62.4 \times 0.0016y = 0.078y$ lb/ft².

Considering a very rounded material 1.25 in. in diameter, the angle of repose (Fig. 7-9) is $\theta = 33.5°$. With $\theta = 33.5°$ and $z = 2$, or $\phi = 26.5°$, the tractive-force ratio by Eq. (7-11) is $K = 0.587$. For a size of 1.25 in., the permissible tractive force on a level bottom is $\tau_L = 0.4 \times 1.25 = 0.5$ lb/ft² (same from Fig. 7-10), and the permissible tractive force on the sides is $\tau_s = 0.587 \times 0.5 = 0.294$ lb/ft².

For a state of impending motion of the particles on side slopes, $0.078y = 0.294$, or $y = 3.77$ ft. Accordingly, the bottom width is $b = 3.77 \times 5 = 18.85$ ft. For this trapezoidal section, $A = 99.5$ ft² and $R = 2.79$ ft. With $n = 0.025$ and $S = 0.0016$, the discharge by the Manning formula is 470 cfs. Further computation will show that, for $z = 2$ and $b/y = 4.1$, the section dimensions are $y = 3.82$ ft and $b = 15.66$ ft and that the discharge is 414 cfs, which is close to the design discharge.

Alternative section dimensions may be obtained by assuming other values of $z$ or side slopes.

*b. Checking the Proportioned Dimensions.* With $z = 2$ and $b/y = 4.1$, the maximum unit tractive force on the channel bottom (Fig. 7-7) is $0.97wyS = 0.97 \times 62.4 \times 3.82 \times 0.0016 = 0.370$ lb/ft², less than 0.5 lb/ft², which is the permissible tractive force on the level bottom.

---

[1] Typical average earth sections of irrigation canals and laterals, constructed or proposed by the U.S. Bureau of Reclamation and selected for the flows required on the basis of economy and stability, are given in Fig. 5, paragraph 1.12C, of [4].

**7-15. The Stable Hydraulic Section.** The section of an erodible channel in which no erosion will occur at a minimum water area for a given discharge is called the *stable hydraulic section*. Empirical profiles, such as the ellipse and the parabola, have been suggested as stable hydraulic sections by many hydraulicians. The U.S. Bureau of Reclamation [38] has employed the principle of tractive force to develop a theoretically stable section for erodible channels carrying clear water in *noncohesive* materials.

In designing trapezoidal sections, as described in the preceding article, the tractive force is made equal to the permissible value over only a part of the perimeter of the section, where the forces are close to maximum; on most of the perimeter forces are less than the permissible value. In other words, the impending instability occurs only over a small part of the perimeter. In developing a stable hydraulic section for maximum efficiency, it is necessary to satisfy the condition that impending motion shall prevail everywhere on the channel bed. For material with a given angle of repose and for a given discharge, this optimal section will provide not only the channel of minimum water area, but also the channel of minimum top width, maximum mean velocity, and minimum excavation. In the mathematical derivation of this section by the Bureau, the following assumptions are made:

1. The soil particle is held against the channel bed by the component of the submerged weight of the particle acting normal to the bed.

2. At and above the water surface the side slope is at the angle of repose of the material under the action of gravity.

3. At the center of the channel the side slope is zero and the tractive force alone is sufficient to hold the particles at the point of incipient instability.

4. At points between the center and edge of the channel the particles are kept in a state of incipient motion by the resultant of the gravity component of the particle's submerged weight acting on the side slope and the tractive force of the flowing water.

5. The tractive force acting on an area of the channel bed is equal to the weight component of the water directly above the area acting in the direction of flow. This weight component is equal to the weight times the longitudinal slope of the channel.

If assumption 5 is to hold there can be no lateral transfer of tractive force between adjacent currents moving at different velocities in the section—a situation, however, that never actually occurs. Fortunately, the mathematical analysis made by the Bureau[1] has shown that the actual

---

[1] Taking the effect of lateral tractive force into account, an alternative assumption was made by the Bureau, which states that the tractive force acting on a particle is proportional to the square of the mean velocity in the channel at the point where the

transfer of tractive force has little effect on the results and can safely be ignored.

According to assumption 5, the tractive force acting on any elementary area $AB$ on the sloping side (Fig. 7-12a) per unit length of the channel is equal to $wyS\,dx$, where $w$ is the unit weight of water, $y$ is the depth of water above $AB$, and $S$ is the longitudinal slope. Since the area $AB$ is $\sqrt{(dx)^2 + (dy)^2}$, the unit tractive force is equal to

$$\frac{wyS\,dx}{\sqrt{(dx)^2 + (dy)^2}} = wyS\cos\phi$$

where $\phi$ is the slope angle of the tangent at $AB$.

The other assumptions stated above have been used previously to develop the equation for the tractive-force ratio $K$ (Art. 7-12). The unit tractive force on the level bottom at the channel center is $\tau_L = wy_0 S$, where $y_0$ is the depth of flow at the center. The corresponding unit tractive force on the sloping area $AB$ is, therefore, equal to $wy_0 SK$.

In order to achieve impending motion over the entire periphery of the channel bed, the two forces mentioned in the above paragraphs should be equal; that is,

$$wyS\cos\phi = wy_0 SK$$

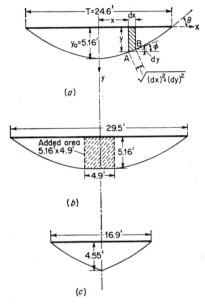

Fig. 7-12. Analysis and design of stable hydraulic section. (a) Theoretical section for given soil properties and channel slope, providing $Q = 220$ cfs; (b) modified section for $Q'' = 400$ cfs; (c) modified section for $Q' = 100$ cfs.

Substituting Eq. (7-10) for $K$ and $\tan^{-1}(dy/dx)$ for $\phi$ in the above equation and simplifying,

$$\left(\frac{dy}{dx}\right)^2 + \left(\frac{y}{y_0}\right)^2 \tan^2\theta = \tan^2\theta$$

At the center of the channel, $y = y_0$ and $x = 0$. With this condition

particle is located. This assumption gives a solution that agrees very closely with the solution based on assumption 5. Therefore, neglect of the transfer of tractive force in the analysis will give equally satisfactory results, and with considerably less work.

the solution of the above differential equation is

$$y = y_0 \cos\left(\frac{\tan \theta}{y_0} x\right) \qquad (7\text{-}12)$$

This equation shows that the shape of a stable hydraulic section under the specified assumptions is a simple cosine curve. From the results of the Bureau's mathematical analysis, the following properties of this stable section can be stated:

$$y_0 = \frac{\tau_0}{0.97wS} \qquad (7\text{-}13)$$

$$V = \frac{1.35 - 1.19 \tan \theta}{n} y_0^{\frac{2}{3}} S^{\frac{1}{2}} \qquad (7\text{-}14)$$

$$A = \frac{2.04 y_0^2}{\tan \theta} \qquad (7\text{-}15)$$

where $\tau_0$ is the permissible tractive force in lb/ft², $V$ is the mean velocity in the section in fps, $A$ is the water area in ft², $\theta$ is the angle of repose for the material or the slope angle of the section at the water edge of the channel, $T$ is the top width, and the rest of the symbols are as previously defined.

The discharge of the theoretical section is equal to $Q = VA$. If the channel is to carry a discharge less than $Q$, it is necessary to remove a vertical portion of the section at the channel center. Suppose the discharge to be carried is $Q'$, which is less than $Q$, and the top widths of the designed section and the removed area are $T$ and $T'$, respectively. The value of $T'$ may be computed by

$$T' = 0.96\left(1 - \sqrt{\frac{Q'}{Q}}\right) T \qquad (7\text{-}16)$$

On the other hand, if the channel is to carry more than the theoretical section will carry, it is necessary to add a rectangular section at the center. Suppose the discharge to be carried is $Q''$, which is greater than $Q$, and the top width of the added rectangular area is $T'''$. The value of $T'''$ may be computed by

$$T'' = \frac{n(Q'' - Q)}{1.49 y_0^{\frac{5}{3}} S^{\frac{1}{2}}} \qquad (7\text{-}17)$$

**Example 7-5.** Determine the profile of the stable hydraulic section to replace the trapezoidal section of the channel described in Example 7-4.

*Solution.* For the given conditions, $\tau_0 = 0.5$ lb/ft², $S = 0.0016$, $\theta = 33.5°$, and $n = 0.025$. By Eq. (7-13), the center depth is $y_0 = 0.5/(0.97 \times 62.4 \times 0.0016) = 5.16$ ft. From Eq. (7-12), the shape of the theoretical section is

$$y = 5.16 \cos 0.128x$$

which is plotted as shown in Fig. 7-12a. It should be noted that the angle of the cosine function is expressed in radians; it may be converted to degrees by multiplying it by $180/\pi$ or 57.3. The top width may be computed by Eq. (7-12) with $y = 0$, or $\cos 0.128x = 0$. Thus, $0.128x = \pi/2$ and $x = 12.3$ ft. The top width is $T = 2x = 24.6$ ft.

By Eq. (7-14), the mean velocity is $V = (1.35 - 1.19 \tan 33.5°) 5.16^{2/3} \times 0.0016^{1/2}/0.025 = 2.69$ fps. By Eq. (7-15), the water area is $A = 2.04 \times 5.16^2/\tan 33.5° = 82.2$ ft². Hence the discharge is 220 cfs. Since the design discharge is 400 cfs, it is necessary to add a rectangular area at the middle (Fig. 7-12b). The width of the rectangle may be computed by Eq. (7-17) as

$$T'' = \frac{0.025(400 - 220)}{1.49 \times 5.16^{5/3} \times 0.0016^{1/2}} = 4.9 \text{ ft}$$

Therefore the top width is $24.6 + 4.9 = 29.5$ ft.

If the channel is designed to carry 100 cfs, it is necessary to remove a vertical area from the middle (Fig. 7-12c). The top width of the removed area may be computed by Eq. (7-16).

$$T' = 0.96(1 - \sqrt{100/220}) \times 24.6 = 7.7 \text{ ft}$$

Therefore the top width is $24.6 - 7.7 = 16.9$ ft.

## C. GRASSED CHANNELS

**7-16. The Grassed Channel.** Presence of grass or vegetation in channels will result in considerable turbulence, which means loss of energy and retardance of flow. For earth channels used for carrying water on farm lands, however, a lining of grass is often found to be advantageous and desirable. The grass will stabilize the body of the channel, consolidate the soil mass of the bed, and check the erosion on the channel surface and the movement of soil particles along the channel bottom. The U.S. Soil Conservation Service [39–41] has conducted a series of experiments on channels lined with various kinds of grass (Fig. 7-13). The results thus obtained under different testing conditions and the procedure suggested for the design of grassed channels will be described in the following articles.

**7-17. The Retardance Coefficient.** The Manning coefficient of roughness for grassed channels is specifically known as the *retardance coefficient*. According to the investigation by the Soil Conservation Service, it was found that Manning's $n$ for just one kind of grass varied over a wide range depending on the depth of flow and the shape and slope of the channel. Thus, the selection of a design value for $n$ would be nearly impossible. Fortunately, it was discovered that the retardance coefficient $n$ holds a certain relationship with the product of the mean velocity of flow $V$ and the hydraulic radius $R$. This relationship is characteristic of the vegetation and practically independent of channel slope and shape. As a result, therefore, a number of experimental curves for $n$ versus $VR$ (Fig. 7-14) were developed for five different degrees of retardance: very high, high, moderate, low, and very low. For very low retardance

Fig. 7-13. Centipede grassed channel. (*Courtesy of W. O. Ree, U.S. Agricultural Research Service.*) (A) Before experiment; (B) after test at a flow equal to 15 cfs for 40 min; (C) during test at a flow equal to 30 cfs; (D) at completion of the whole experiment.

only the average curve is shown, together with the curves for low retardance. The classification of degree of retardance is based on the kind of vegetation and the condition of growth, as described in Table 7-4. The term "stand" used in the table refers to the density of grass, or the count of vegetation, which is sometimes expressed as the number of stems per square foot. The $n$-$VR$ curves thus developed may also be applied to other kinds of grass, provided that their characteristics and degree of retardance can be identified. For this purpose, Table 7-5 is provided as a guide in the selection of the vegetal retardance for different conditions of stand and average length of the grass.

TABLE 7-4. CLASSIFICATION OF DEGREE OF RETARDANCE FOR VARIOUS KINDS
OF GRASS*

| Retardance | Cover | Condition |
|---|---|---|
| A Very high | Weeping love grass............<br>Yellow bluestem ischaemum.... | Excellent stand, tall (av 30 in.)<br>Excellent stand, tall (av 36 in.) |
| B High | Kudzu......................<br>Bermuda grass................<br>Native grass mixture (little blue-<br>stem, blue grama, and other<br>long and short Midwest<br>grasses)...................<br>Weeping love grass............<br>Lespedeza sericea.............<br><br>Alfalfa......................<br>Weeping love grass............<br>Kudzu......................<br>Blue grama.................. | Very dense growth, uncut<br>Good stand, tall (av 12 in.)<br><br><br><br>Good stand, unmowed<br>Good stand, tall (av 24 in.)<br>Good stand, not woody, tall<br>(av. 19 in.)<br>Good stand, uncut (av 11 in.)<br>Good stand, mowed (av 13 in.)<br>Dense growth, uncut<br>Good stand, uncut (av 13 in.) |
| C Moderate | Crab grass...................<br>Bermuda grass...............<br>Common lespedeza...........<br>Grass-legume mixture—summer<br>(orchard grass, redtop, Italian<br>rye grass, and common les-<br>pedeza)...................<br>Centipede grass..............<br>Kentucky bluegrass........... | Fair stand, uncut (10 to 48 in.)<br>Good stand, mowed (av 6 in.)<br>Good stand, uncut (av 11 in.)<br><br><br><br>Good stand, uncut (6 to 8 in.)<br>Very dense cover (av 6 in.)<br>Good stand, headed (6 to 12 in.) |
| D Low | Bermuda grass...............<br>Common lespedeza...........<br><br>Buffalo grass.................<br>Grass-legume mixture—fall, spring<br>(orchard grass, redtop, Italian<br>rye grass, and common les-<br>pedeza)...................<br>Lespedeza sericea............. | Good stand, cut to 2.5 in. height<br>Excellent stand, uncut (av 4.5<br>in.)<br>Good stand, uncut (3 to 6 in.)<br><br><br><br>Good stand, uncut (4 to 5 in.)<br>After cutting to 2 in. height,<br>very good stand before cutting |
| E Very low | Bermuda grass...............<br>Bermuda grass............... | Good stand, cut to 1.5 in. height<br>Burned stubble |

* U.S. Soil Conservation Service [41].

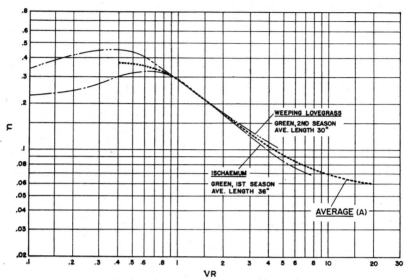

(a) Curves for A or very high vegetal retardance.

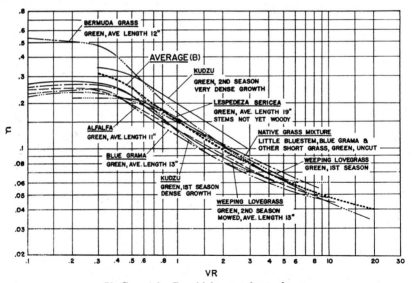

(b) Curves for B or high vegetal retardance.

FIG. 7-14. Experimental n-VR curves. (U.S. Soil Conservation Service.)

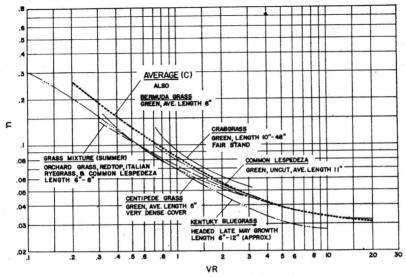

(c) Curves for C or moderate vegetal retardance.

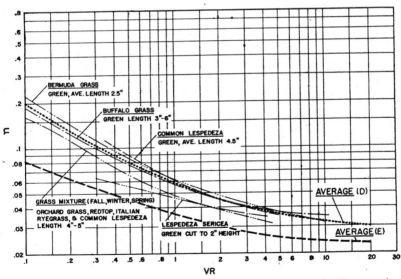

(d) Curves for D or low vegetal retardance, and an average curve for E or very low vegetal retardance.

FIG. 7-14 (Continued).

TABLE 7-5. GUIDE IN SELECTION OF VEGETAL RETARDANCE*

| Stand | Average length of grass, in. | Degree of retardance |
|-------|------------------------------|----------------------|
| Good | >30 | A  Very high |
| | 11–24 | B  High |
| | 6–10 | C  Moderate |
| | 2–6 | D  Low |
| | <2 | E  Very low |
| Fair | >30 | B  High |
| | 11–24 | C  Moderate |
| | 6–10 | D  Low |
| | 2–6 | D  Low |
| | <2 | E  Very low |

* U.S. Soil Conservation Service [41].

**7-18. The Permissible Velocity.**   The permissible velocity of flow in a grassed channel is the velocity that will prevent severe erosion in the channel for a reasonable length of time.   Permissible velocities for different vegetal covers, channel slopes, and soil conditions, recommended on the basis of investigation by the Soil Conservation Service, are shown in Table 7-6.

**7-19. Selection of Grass.**   The selection of grass for the channel lining depends mainly on the climate and soil in which the plant will grow and survive under the given conditions.   From the hydraulic viewpoint, stability and other factors should also be considered.   In general, a higher discharge requires a stronger or better lining.   On steep slopes, bunch grasses, such as alfalfa, lespedeza, and kudzu, will develop channeling of the flow and, hence, are unsatisfactory for lining.   For slopes greater than 5%, only fine and uniformly distributed sod-forming grasses, such as Bermuda grass, Kentucky bluegrass, and smooth brome, are recommended for lining where the main flow occurs.   Because of the objectionable spreading nature of sod-forming grasses, the top portion of the sides and the berm may be planted with grasses that do not spread easily, such as weeping love grass.   For fast establishment of the lining, Bermuda grass and weeping love grass are recommended.   Sometimes annuals are used as temporary protection until permanent covers by native grasses are established.   Silt deposition in channels may be controlled by lining with bunch grasses, which will develop channeled flow, increase velocity, and thus reduce silting.

**7-20. Procedure of Design.**   After the kind of grass for channel lining is selected, the degree of retardance can be determined from the condition of the stem length and the density of growth.   During the period of establishment, the grass will grow and the channel will be stabilized under a condition of low degree of retardance. The channel will not reach its maximum capacity until the grass cover is fully developed and well established. Therefore, it is suggested that the hydraulic design of a grassed channel consist of two stages. The first stage (*A*) is to design the channel for stability, that is, to determine the channel dimensions under the condition of a *lower* degree of retardance. The second stage

TABLE 7-6. PERMISSIBLE VELOCITIES FOR CHANNELS LINED WITH GRASS*

| Cover | Slope range, % | Permissible velocity, fps | |
|---|---|---|---|
| | | Erosion-resistant soils | Easily eroded soils |
| Bermuda grass | 0–5 | 8 | 6 |
| | 5–10 | 7 | 5 |
| | >10 | 6 | 4 |
| Buffalo grass, Kentucky bluegrass, smooth brome, blue grama | 0–5 | 7 | 5 |
| | 5–10 | 6 | 4 |
| | >10 | 5 | 3 |
| Grass mixture | 0–5 | 5 | 4 |
| | 5–10 | 4 | 3 |
| | Do not use on slopes steeper than 10% | | |
| Lespedeza sericea, weeping love grass, ischaemum (yellow bluestem), kudzu, alfalfa, crabgrass | 0–5 | 3.5 | 2.5 |
| | Do not use on slopes steeper than 5%, except for side slopes in a combination channel | | |
| Annuals—used on mild slopes or as temporary protection until permanent covers are established, common lespedeza, Sudan grass | 0–5 | 3.5 | 2.5 |
| | Use on slopes steeper than 5% is not recommended | | |

REMARKS. The values apply to average, uniform stands of each type of cover. Use velocities exceeding 5 fps only where good covers and proper maintenance can be obtained.

* U.S. Soil Conservation Service [41].

(*B*) is to review the design for maximum capacity, that is, to determine the increase in depth of flow necessary to maintain a maximum capacity under the condition of a *higher* degree of retardance. For instance, if common lespedeza is selected as the grass for lining, the common lespedeza of low vegetal retardance (green, average length 4.5 in.) is used for the first stage in design. Then, in the second stage, the common lespedeza of moderate vegetal retardance (green, uncut, average length 11 in.) should be used. Finally, a proper freeboard is added to the computed depth of the channel, which will further increase the maximum design capacity. The design procedure[1] is described as follows:

A. *Design for Stability.* Given the discharge, channel slope, and kind of grass, the first stage of design may proceed in the following steps:

1. Assume a value of $n$, and determine the corresponding values of $VR$ from the $n$-$VR$ curve (Fig. 7-14).

2. Select the permissible velocity from Table 7-6, and compute the value of $R$.

3. Using the Manning formula, compute the value of

$$VR = \frac{1.49 R^{\frac{2}{3}} S^{\frac{1}{2}}}{n}$$

and check this value against the value of $VR$ obtained in step 1.

4. Make other trials until the computed value of $VR$ is equal to the $VR$ value obtained from the $n$-$VR$ curve.

5. Compute the water area, or $A = Q/V$.

6. Since the correct values of $A$ and $R$ have been obtained, the section dimensions may be determined by the procedure described in Art. 7-7.

The sections generally used for grassed channels are the trapezoid, parabola, and triangle, named in order of increasing depth required in excavation. Owing to the normal action of channel deposition and erosion, trapezoidal and triangular sections, if selected but not well maintained, will generally become parabolic after a long period of service.

**Example 7-6.** Determine the section of a channel lined with grass mixture, laid on erosion-resistant soil at a slope of 0.04, and carrying a discharge of 50 cfs.

*Solution.* In designing for stability, the grass mixture that offers a low vegetal retardance, i.e., that of the dormant season, is considered. Therefore, the corresponding $n$-$VR$ curve should be used in the computation.

From Table 7-6, the permissible velocity for design is taken as 5 fps. Using the $n$-$VR$ curve (Fig 7-14) for grass mixture for fall, winter, and spring, the trial computations involved in the design procedure are as follows:

| Trial no. | $n$ | $VR$ | $R$ | $\dfrac{1.49 R^{\frac{2}{3}} S^{\frac{1}{2}}}{n}$ |
|---|---|---|---|---|
| 1 | 0.04 | 1.80 | 0.36 | 1.36 |
| 2 | 0.05 | 0.90 | 0.18 | 0.34 |
| 3 | 0.035 | 3.50 | 0.70 | 4.72 |
| 4 | 0.0375 | 2.50 | 0.50 | 2.50 |

The correct values for the determination of sections are $R = 0.50$ ft and $A = \frac{50}{5} = 10$ ft². Several channel sections meeting these requirements are proposed as follows (using charts in Appendix B):

[1] For an example of the practical design of a grassed channel, see [42].

| Section | Side slope z:1 | Bottom width b, ft | Depth y, ft | Top width T, ft |
|---|---|---|---|---|
| Trapezoid......... | 3:1 | 17.0 | 0.53 | 20.18 |
| Trapezoid......... | 6:1 | 12.5 | 0.62 | 19.94 |
| Triangle.......... | 10:1 | 0 | 1.00 | 20.00 |
| Parabola.......... | .... | .... | 0.73 | 20.00 |

*B. Design for Maximum Capacity.* The second stage in design is to determine the additional depth necessary to sustain the maximum capacity of a fully developed lining. The procedure is as follows:

1. Assume the depth $y$, and compute the water area $A$ and the hydraulic radius $R$.

2. Compute the velocity $V$ by $V = Q/A$ and the value of $VR$.

3. From the $n$-$VR$ curve of a higher degree of retardance for the selected lining, determine the value of $n$.

4. Compute the velocity by the Manning formula, and check this value of $V$ against the value obtained in step 2.

5. Make trial computations until the computed $V$ in step 4 is equal to the computed $V$ in step 2. It should be noted that this velocity is always less than the permissible velocity assumed in the first stage of design, that is, in design for stability, since the cross section has been enlarged in the second stage of the design.

6. Add proper freeboard to the computed depth.

**Example 7-7.** Modify the selected sections in Example 7-6 for maximum capacity.

*Solution.* For determining the proper depth for maximum capacity of the proposed sections, the grass mixture of the growing season, which offers a moderate vegetal retardance, is considered in the computation. The $n$-$VR$ curve (Fig. 7-14) for grass mixture in summer is therefore used. Other known data are $Q = 50$ cfs and $S = 0.04$.

For the trapezoidal section with 3:1 side slope and $b = 17.0$ ft, the trial computations are given below:

| Trial no. | $y$ | $A$ | $R$ | $V$ | $VR$ | $n$ | $V = \dfrac{1.49R^{2/3}S^{1/2}}{n}$ |
|---|---|---|---|---|---|---|---|
| 1 | 0.70 | 13.4 | 0.63 | 3.73 | 2.35 | 0.051 | 4.22 |
| 2 | 0.60 | 11.3 | 0.54 | 4.42 | 2.39 | 0.050 | 3.96 |
| 3 | 0.65 | 12.3 | 0.58 | 4.07 | 2.36 | 0.051 | 4.07 |

The correct depth is 0.65 ft. Adding a freeboard of 0.2 ft, the total depth is 0.85 ft.

For the trapezoidal section with a side slope of 6:1 and $b = 12.5$ ft, the computation results in a total depth of 0.94 ft. Similarly, the total depth of the triangular section with a side slope of 10:1 is found to be 1.33 ft.

For the parabolic section of $y = 0.73$ ft and $T = 20$ ft, the trial computations are as follows:

| Trial no. | $y$ | $T$ | $A$ | $R$ | $V$ | $VR$ | $n$ | $\dfrac{1.49R^{2/3}S^{1/2}}{n}$ |
|---|---|---|---|---|---|---|---|---|
| 1 | 0.80 | 21.0 | 11.2 | 0.52 | 4.46 | 2.32 | 0.051 | 3.78 |
| 2 | 0.90 | 22.2 | 13.3 | 0.60 | 3.76 | 2.25 | 0.051 | 4.16 |
| 3 | 0.85 | 21.6 | 12.2 | 0.57 | 4.10 | 2.34 | 0.051 | 4.03 |
| 4 | 0.86 | 21.7 | 12.4 | 0.58 | 4.03 | 2.34 | 0.051 | 4.07 |

It should be noted that the computation for the parabolic section is simplified by the use of the equation for $R$ in Table 2-1 and by the fact that the depth is proportional to the square of the top width; that is, $T = 20\sqrt{y/0.73}$. Allowing a freeboard of 0.20 ft, the total depth is 1.06 ft and the top width is 24.1 ft.

The final choice of the channel section and its dimensions will depend on practicability and on the circumstances under which the problem is proposed.

### PROBLEMS

**7-1.** Show that the most efficient rectangular or triangular section is one-half of a square.

**7-2.** Explain (a) that any section formed by a polygon which can be inscribed by a semicircle with the center in the water surface will have its hydraulic radius equal to one-half the radius of the inscribed circle, and (b) that such section will have the best hydraulic efficiency.

**7-3.** Determine the best hydraulic section of the channel in Example 7-2 if the section is (a) rectangular, (b) triangular, (c) circular, (d) parabolic, and (e) in the form of a hydraulic catenary.

**7-4.** Solve Example 7-2 by the empirical rule of Eqs. (7-2) and (7-3).

**7-5.** Design a nonerodible channel carrying 200 cfs with $n = 0.020$ and $S = 0.0020$. Use your own judgment and assumptions.

**7-6.** Based on the practice of the U.S. Bureau of Reclamation, determine (a) the freeboard of the channel designed in Example 7-2 when the channel is unlined, and (b) the heights of the lining and bank if the channel is lined.

**7-7.** Solve Example 7-3 if the material forming the channel body is fine silt having an average particle size of 0.006 mm. Estimate the permissible velocity with the aid of (a) Fortier and Scobey's table, (b) U.S.S.R. data, and (c) the Kennedy formula modified for clear water.

**7-8.** Solve Example 7-3 if the material forming the channel body is fairly compact heavy clayey soil with a voids ratio of 1.0.

**7-9.** Solve Example 7-3 if the channel has a parabolic section.

**7-10.** Design the section of a canal to carry a discharge of 200 cfs through a land of erodible soils with $n = 0.020$ and $S = 0.0020$. Assume other necessary data and use your own judgment.

**7-11.** The All-American Canal is designed to divert 15,155 cfs of desilted water from the Colorado River to irrigate the Imperial Valley in southern California. This canal is 80 miles long. The typical maximum section has a bottom width of 160 ft, width at water surface of 232 ft, water depth of 20.6 ft, minimum freeboard of 6 ft, and bank width of 27 to 30 ft. The terminal capacity is 2,600 cfs. The canal was excavated mostly in alluvial soil, ranging from light sandy or silty loams to adobe and having an average particle size of 0.0025 in. Review the hydraulic design of the channel section.

**7-12.** Review the stability of the section dimensions obtained in Example 7-3 by the method of tractive force, assuming that 25% of the material forming the channel bed is 1.25 in. or over in diameter.

**7-13.** Solve Example 7-4 for the following conditions, respectively:

(*a*) If the side slopes are assumed as 1 on 1.5.

(*b*) If the material forming the channel bed contains fine noncohesive particles, 50% of which are larger than 1 mm in diameter. The water is clear.

(*c*) If the material forming the channel bed is cohesive compact clay, having a voids ratio equal to 0.5.

(*d*) If the channel is moderately sinuous.

**7-14.** The conversion from the maximum permissible velocity to permissible tractive force (Table 7-3) is based on a flow depth of 3 ft and an average channel section having a bottom width of 10 ft and side slopes of 1.5:1. For alluvial noncolloidal silts and clear-water flow, the maximum permissible velocity recommended by Fortier and Scobey is 2.00 fps and the $n$ value is taken as 0.020. Compute the corresponding permissible tractive force.

**7-15.** Compute the maximum tractive force per unit area on the section of the All-American Canal described in Prob. 7-11.

**7-16.** Determine the cross section and discharge of the stable hydraulic section of a channel excavated in a noncohesive material having $\tau_0 = 0.1$ lb/ft², $S = 0.0004$, $\theta = 31°$, and $n = 0.020$.

**7-17.** Determine the modified profile for the channel section obtained in the preceding problem if the channel is to carry (*a*) 75 cfs and (*b*) 300 cfs.

**7-18.** Design a waterway lined with Bermuda grass on erosion-resistant soil and carrying a discharge of 200 cfs. The average slope of the channel is 3%. Use the curve for moderate vegetal retardance.

**7-19.** Determine the total depth for maximum capacity of the channel section proposed for the preceding problem. Allow a freeboard equal to 20% of the computed depth.

## REFERENCES

1. Victor L. Streeter: Economical canal cross sections, *Transactions, American Society of Civil Engineers*, vol. 110, pp. 421–430, 1945.
2. Ivan E. Houk: "Irrigation Engineering," vol. 2, "Projects, Conduits, and Structures," John Wiley & Sons, Inc., New York, 1956.
3. "Linings for Irrigation Canals," U.S. Bureau of Reclamation, July, 1952.
4. Canals and related structures, *U.S. Bureau of Reclamation, Design and Construction Manual, Design Supplement No. 3*, Apr. 17, 1952, vol. X, pt. 2, chap. 1, paragraphs 1.15, 1.8, and 1.18.
5. B. A. Etcheverry: "Irrigation Practice and Engineering," vol. II, "Conveyance of Water," McGraw-Hill Book Company, Inc., New York, 1st ed., 1915, p. 122.
6. Guilford L. Molesworth: "Pocket-book of Engineering Formulae (Useful Formulae and Memoranda) for Civil and Mechanical Engineers," E. & F. N. Spon, London, 7th ed., 1871, p. 176.
7. Isidro D. Cariño: A graphical solution for flow in earth channels, paper 1360, *Proceedings, American Society of Civil Engineers, Journal, Irrigation and Drainage Division*, vol. 83, no. IR2, pp. 1–9, September, 1957.

8. Pete W. Terrell and Whitney M. Borland: Design of stable canals and channels in erodible material, *Transactions, American Society of Civil Engineers*, vol. 123, pp. 101–115, 1958.

9. E. W. Lane: Stable channels in erodible material, *Transactions, American Society of Civil Engineers*, vol. 102, pp. 123–142, 1937; and discussions.

10. Robert G. Kennedy: The prevention of silting in irrigation canals, *Proceedings, Institution of Civil Engineers, London*, vol. 119, pp. 281–290, 1895.

11. Edward S. Lindley: Regime channels, *Minutes of Proceedings, Punjab Engineering Congress, Lahore, India*, vol. 7, pp. 63–74, 1919.

12. Gerald Lacey: Stable channels in alluvium, *Proceedings, Institution of Civil Engineers, London*, vol. 229, pp. 259–384, 1930.

13. Gerald Lacey: Regime flow in incoherent alluvium, *Central Board of Irrigation, Publication No.* 20, Simla, India, 1940.

14. Gerald Lacey: A general theory of flow in alluvium, *Journal, Institution of Civil Engineers, London*, vol. 27, pp. 16–47, 1946.

15. Thomas Blench: "Hydraulics of Sediment-bearing Canals and Rivers," Evans Industries, Ltd., Vancouver, B.C., Canada, 1951.

16. Thomas Blench: Regime theory for self-formed sediment bearing channels, *Transactions, American Society of Civil Engineers*, vol. 117, pp. 383–400, 1952.

17. H. A. Einstein: The bed-load function for sediment transportation in open channel flows, *U.S. Department of Agriculture, Technical Bulletin No.* 1026, 1950.

18. L. B. Leopold and Thomas Maddock, Jr.: The hydraulic geometry of stream channels and some physiographic implications, *U.S. Geological Survey, Professional Paper* 252, 1953.

19. E. W. Lane: Stable channels in erodible material, *Transactions, American Society of Civil Engineers*, vol. 102, pp. 123–142, 1937.

20. Serge Leliavsky: "An Introduction to Fluvial Hydraulics," Constable & Co., Ltd., London, 1955.

21. Institution Research Committee: Recent developments in hydraulics, *Proceedings, Institution of Civil Engineers, London*, pt. III, vol. 4, pp. 990–1049, December, 1955.

22. Ning Chien: The present status of research on sediment transport, *Transactions, American Society of Civil Engineers*, vol. 121, pp. 833–868, 1956.

23. Ning Chien: Graphic design of alluvial channels, *Transactions, American Society of Civil Engineers*, vol. 121, pp. 1267–1280, 1956.

24. Ning Chien: A concept of the regime theory, *Transactions, American Society of Civil Engineers*, vol. 122, pp. 785–793, 1957.

25. Enos J. Carlson and Carl R. Miller: Research needs in sediment hydraulics, paper 953, *Proceedings, American Society of Civil Engineers, Journal, Hydraulics Division*, vol. 82, no. HY2, pp. 1–33, April, 1956.

26. B. A. Etcheverry: "Irrigation Practice and Engineering," vol. II, McGraw-Hill Book Company, Inc., New York, 1915.

27. S. Fortier and F. C. Scobey: Permissible canal velocities, *Transactions, American Society of Civil Engineers*, vol. 89, pp. 940–956, 1926.

28. The maximum permissible mean velocity in open channels, *Gidrotekhnicheskoie Stroitel'stvo, (Hydrotechnical Construction)*, Moscow, no. 5, pp. 5–7, May, 1936.

29. Emory W. Lane: Design of stable channels, *Transactions, American Society of Civil Engineers*, vol. 120, pp. 1234–1260, 1955.

30. P. du Boys: Études du régime du Rhône et l'action exercée par les eaux sur un lit à fond de graviers indéfiniment affouillable (The Rhone and streams with movable beds), *Annales des ponts et chaussées*, ser. 5, vol. 18, pp. 141–195, 1879.

31. J. B. Leighly: Toward a theory of the morphologic significance of turbulence in the flow of water in stream, *University of California, Publications in Geography*, vol. 6, no. 1, pp. 1–22, Berkeley, 1932.
32. O. J. Olsen and Q. L. Florey (compilers): Sedimentation studies in open channels: Boundary shear and velocity distribution by membrane analogy, analytical and finite-difference methods, reviewed by D. McHenry and R. E. Glover, *U.S. Bureau of Reclamation, Laboratory Report, No. Sp-34*, Aug. 5, 1952.
33. Philipp Forchheimer: "Hydraulik" ("Hydraulics"), Teubner Verlagsgesellschaft, Leipzig and Berlin, 1st ed., 1924, p. 495; 3d ed., 1930, p. 551.
34. Chia-Hwa Fan: A study of stable channel cross section (in Chinese), *Hydraulic Engineering, Chinese Society of Hydraulic Engineers*, vol. 15, no. 1, pp. 71–79, Nanking, 1947.
35. E. W. Lane: Progress report on results of studies on design of stable channels, *U.S. Bureau of Reclamation, Hydraulic Laboratory Report, No. Hyd-352*, June, 1952.
36. A. C. Carter: Critical tractive forces on channel side slopes, *U.S. Bureau of Reclamation, Hydraulic Laboratory Report No. Hyd-366* (supersedes *Hyd-295*) Feb. 18, 1953.
37. E. W. Lane and E. J. Carlson: Some factors affecting the stability of canals constructed in coarse granular materials, *Proceedings of the Minnesota International Hydraulics Convention, Sept. 1–4, 1953, Joint Meeting of International Association for Hydraulic Research and Hydraulics Division, American Society of Civil Engineers*, pp. 37–48, August, 1953.
38. R. E. Glover and Q. L. Florey: Stable channel profiles, *U.S. Bureau of Reclamation, Hydraulic Laboratory Report No. Hyd-325*, Sept. 27, 1951. The work was started by R. G. Conard and reviewed by E. W. Lane.
39. W. O. Ree: Hydraulic characteristics of vegetation for vegetated waterways, *Agricultural Engineering*, vol. 30, no. 4, pp. 184–187 and 189, April, 1949.
40. W. O. Ree and V. J. Palmer: Flow of water in channels protected by vegetative lining, *U.S. Soil Conservation Service, Technical Bulletin No. 967*, February, 1949.
41. Stillwater Outdoor Hydraulic Laboratory: Handbook of channel design for soil and water conservation, *U.S. Soil Conservation Service, SCS-TP-61*, March, 1947; revised, June, 1954.
42. V. B. Fredenhagen and E. H. Doll: Grassed waterways, *Agricultural Engineering*, vol. 35, no. 6, pp. 417–419, June, 1954.

# CHAPTER 8

# THEORETICAL CONCEPTS OF BOUNDARY LAYER, SURFACE ROUGHNESS, VELOCITY DISTRIBUTION, AND INSTABILITY OF UNIFORM FLOW

This chapter presents assorted theoretical concepts which have been developed in the mechanics of open-channel flow. These concepts, though not to be thoroughly discussed, may shed some light upon the solution of many practical problems.

**8-1. The Boundary Layer.** When water enters a channel, the velocity distribution across the channel section, owing to the presence of boundary

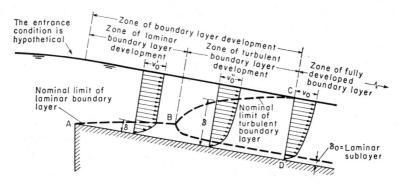

FIG. 8-1. Development of the boundary layer in an open channel with an ideal entrance condition.

roughness, will vary with the distance over which the water travels in the channel (Fig. 8-1).[1] If the flow is uniform and stable and if the channel is prismatic and of constant roughness, the velocity distribution will eventually reach a definite pattern. For simplicity of discussion the following are assumed: (1) the flow entering the channel is laminar and of uniform velocity distribution; (2) no restriction exists at the entrance that will cause abrupt disturbance of the water surface and the velocity distri-

[1] For the sake of simplicity, the two-dimensional profile of a wide open channel with exaggerated vertical scale is shown.

bution; (3) the depth of flow is indefinitely large, so the depth of flow can be considered constant as the water enters the channel.    In the channel, the effect on the velocity distribution due to boundary roughness is indicated by the line $ABC$.    Outside the surface represented by $ABC$, the velocity distribution is practically uniform.    Near the channel surface and within the region $ABC$, velocity varies according to distance from the channel surface.    The region inside $ABC$, though not distinctive, is known as the *boundary layer*[1] and its thickness is designated by $\delta$.

Since the boundary layer is not distinctive, its thickness has been defined arbitrarily in various ways. A common definition is that the thickness $\delta$ is the magnitude of the normal distance from the boundary surface at which the velocity $v_1$ is equal to 99% of the limiting velocity $v_0$, which the velocity-distribution curve in the boundary layer approaches asymptotically (Fig. 8-2).

The effect of the boundary layer on the flow is equivalent to a fictitious upward displacement of the channel bottom to a virtual position by an amount equal to the so-called *displacement thickness* $\delta^*$ (Fig. 8-2), which is defined as

$$\delta^* = \int_0^\delta \left(1 - \frac{v}{v_1}\right) dy \quad (8\text{-}1)$$

where $v$ is the velocity at any dis-

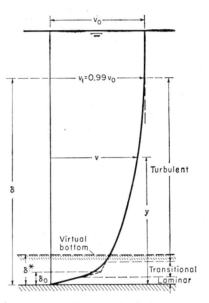

FIG. 8-2. Distribution of velocity over a smooth channel surface (not in scale).

tance $y$ from the channel surface and $v_1$ is the velocity at the edge of the boundary layer.    The value of the displacement thickness generally varies from one-eighth to one-tenth of the thickness of the boundary layer, depending on the magnitude of the Reynolds number.

At the beginning of the flow in the channel (Fig. 8-1) the flow is entirely laminar and a *laminar boundary layer* is developed along the channel surface, as shown by the curve $AB$.    The velocity distribution in the layer is approximately parabolic.    As the water travels farther along in the channel, the flow in the boundary layer will eventually change to turbulent.    The point where the change takes place is indicated by $B$.

Downstream from $B$ a *turbulent boundary layer* is developed, as shown

[1] For a comprehensive treatment of this subject see [1] to [4].

by $BC$.   The velocity distribution in this layer can be shown analytically to be approximately logarithmic (Art. 8-4).

If the channel surface is relatively smooth, the velocity close to the channel surface is low; thus, a very thin stable film of flow known as the *laminar sublayer* will be developed on the surface.   Within the laminar sublayer the flow is kept laminar.[1]   The top surface of the laminar sublayer corresponds to the transitional zone of flow from laminar to turbulent (Art. 1-3) and, hence, cannot be precisely defined.

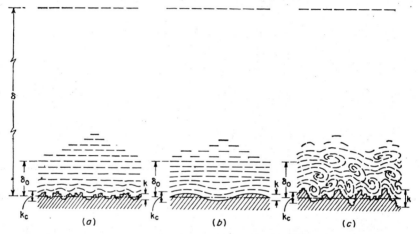

Fig. 8-3. Nature of surface roughness.   (a) Smooth; (b) wavy; (c) rough.

If the conditions for uniform flow exist throughout the channel, the turbulent boundary layer will be fully developed at section $CD$; thereafter the velocity distribution will have a definite pattern.   In a laboratory channel, the laminar boundary layer $AB$ can be eliminated easily by placing a roughness element at the entrance.   Thus, the turbulent boundary layer will be developed at the very beginning of the channel, and the total length of the zone for the full development of boundary layer can be shortened.   Since the flow in ordinary channels is usually turbulent, the following articles will deal only with the turbulent boundary layer.

**8-2. Concept of Surface Roughness.**   The concept of the existence of a laminar sublayer in the turbulent boundary layer offers a picturesque explanation of the behavior of surface roughness.   When the surface profile of a channel is enlarged (Fig. 8-3), it can be seen that the surface is composed of irregular peaks and valleys.   The *effective* height of the

---

[1] A refined concept of the laminar sublayer will consider that there exists in the sublayer a small amount of eddy which decreases very rapidly to zero at the boundary surface.

irregularities forming the roughness elements is called the *roughness height*[1] $k$.   The ratio $k/R$ of the roughness height to the hydraulic radius is known as the *relative roughness*.

If the roughness height is less than a certain fraction of the thickness of the laminar sublayer, the surface irregularities will be so small that all roughness elements will be entirely submerged in the laminar sublayer (Fig. 8-3a).[2]   Under this condition the roughness has no effect upon the flow outside the laminar sublayer, and the surface is said to be *hydraulically smooth*.   A hydraulically smooth surface is said to be *wavy* if the average surface profile follows a curve (Fig. 8-3b).

In connection with flow in pipes or on flat plates at zero incidence, Schlichting (see p. 454 of [1]) gives the following condition for a surface to be hydraulically smooth:

$$\frac{V_f k}{\nu} < 5 \qquad \text{or} \qquad k < \frac{5\nu}{V_f} \tag{8-2}$$

where $V_f = \sqrt{gRS}$, a term known as the *friction velocity* (Art. 8-4).

Using the Chézy formula, it can be shown from the above condition that, for a surface to be hydraulically smooth, the roughness height must be less than a *critical roughness* expressed by

$$k_c = \frac{5C}{\sqrt{g}} \frac{\nu}{V} \tag{8-3}$$

where $C$ is Chézy's $C$, $\nu$ is the kinematic viscosity, and $V$ is the mean velocity.   The above condition is given for roughness obtained with sand having values of $C$ greater than 100, probably.   For the average condition, Schlichting gives $k_c = 100\nu/V$, which corresponds to $C = 113.5$. As an approximation, Eq. (8-3) may be applied to channels.

If the roughness height is greater than the critical value defined by Eq. (8-3) (Fig. 8-3c), the roughness elements will have sufficient magnitude and angularity to extend their effects beyond the laminar sublayer and thus to disturb the flow in the channel.   The surface is therefore said to be *rough*.   In rough channels, the velocity distribution will depend on the form and size of the roughness projections, and a stable laminar sublayer can no longer be formed.

[1] It should be noted that the roughness height is merely a measure of the linear dimension of the roughness elements but is not necessarily equal to the actual, or even an average, height.   For example, two roughness elements may have different linear dimensions, but, owing to the difference in shape and orientation, they may produce identical roughness effect and, thus, their roughnesses will be designated by the same roughness height.

[2] The position from which the roughness height should be measured is a disputable matter.   It is assumed here that $k$ is measured from a datum that lies at a distance of $0.5k$ below the average bottom of the channel.

The average roughness height for a given surface can be determined by experiment. Table 8-1 gives values of $k$ for several kinds of material, averaged from many experimental data.

The concept of roughness in conduits was further advanced by Morris [5]. Morris assumed that the loss of energy in turbulent flow over a rough surface is due largely to the formation of wakes behind each roughness element. The intensity of such vorticity sources in the direction of flow will determine, to a large extent, the character of the turbulence and energy-dissipation phenomena in the flow. Therefore, the longi-

TABLE 8-1. APPROXIMATE VALUES OF ROUGHNESS HEIGHT $k$

| Material | $k$, ft |
|---|---|
| Brass, copper, lead, glass | 0.0001–0.0030 |
| Wrought iron, steel | 0.0002–0.0080 |
| Asphalted cast iron | 0.0004–0.0070 |
| Galvanized iron | 0.0005–0.0150 |
| Cast iron | 0.0008–0.0180 |
| Wood stave | 0.0006–0.0030 |
| Cement | 0.0013–0.0040 |
| Concrete | 0.0015–0.0100 |
| Drain tile | 0.0020–0.0100 |
| Riveted steel | 0.0030–0.0300 |
| Natural river bed | 0.1000–3.0000 |

tudinal spacing $\lambda$ of the roughness elements is the roughness dimension of paramount importance in rough-conduit flow. Under this concept, flow over rough surfaces can be classified into three basic types (Fig. 8-4): *isolated-roughness flow*, *wake-interference flow*, and *quasi-smooth* (or *skimming*) *flow*.

*Isolated-roughness flow* prevails when the roughness elements are so far apart that the wake and vortex at each element are completely developed and dissipated before the next element is reached. The apparent roughness would therefore result from the form drag on the roughness elements, represented primarily by the height of projection $k$ of the element, in addition to the friction drag on the wall surface between elements, which depends on the spacing of the elements. In such a flow, the ratio $k/\lambda$ may be taken as a significant correlating parameter influencing the apparent friction factor in the flow.

*Wake-interference flow* results when the roughness elements are placed so close together that the wake and vortex at each element will interfere with those developed at the following element, resulting in intense and complex vorticity and turbulence mixing. In such a flow, the height of the element is relatively unimportant, but the spacing is obviously of major importance. Also, the average depth $y$ of flow above the crests of the elements will control in part the vertical extent of the surface region of abnormal turbulence.[1]    In such a flow, therefore, the ratio $y/\lambda$ will be an important correlating parameter.

*Quasi-smooth flow* occurs when the roughness elements are so close together that the flow essentially skims the crests of the elements.    The grooves between the elements will be filled with dead water containing

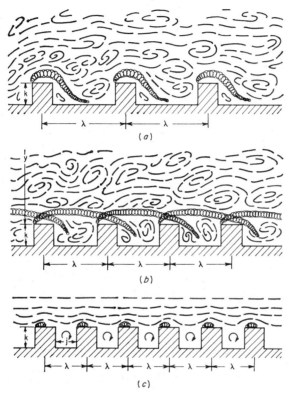

FIG. 8-4. Sketches showing concept of three basic types of rough-surface flow: (*a*) isolated-roughness flow; (*b*) wake-interference flow; (*c*) quasi-smooth flow.

stable eddies, creating a pseudo wall.    Large roughness projections are absent from this pseudo wall, and the surface acts hydraulically smooth. In such a flow, the ratio $k/\lambda$ (or $j/\lambda$, where $j$ is the groove width) will again be a significant parameter.    Quasi-smooth flow has a higher friction factor than flow over a true smooth surface, because the eddies in the grooves consume a certain amount of energy.

The above concept appears to be substantiated adequately by experi-

[1] Morris used the pipe radius instead of the depth in defining the parameter because he was concerned primarily with pipes instead of channels.

mental data from many different sources. The concept can also be extended to surfaces of variable roughness by using average values of the roughness dimensions that vary or by combining the friction factors for each flow type to give an over-all apparent friction factor of the flow.

**8-3. Computation of Boundary Layer.** For the development of a turbulent boundary layer in wide channels, an approximate but practical method of computation has been proposed by Bauer [6]. This method was developed primarily for flow in channels of large slope, but it has been found applicable also to channels of small slope, provided the flow is

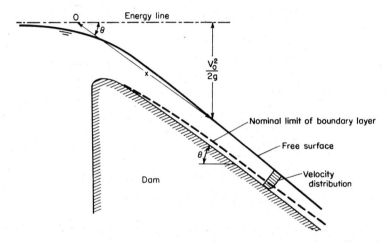

Fig. 8-5. Growth of boundary layer over the surface of an overflow spillway.

either accelerating or uniform, and, if accelerating, then not so rapidly and highly as to cause boundary-layer separations.

The study of boundary-layer development by Bauer was made on concrete overflow spillways (Fig. 8-5). In this case the transition from the laminar to the turbulent boundary layer usually occurs far upstream from the zone under consideration; hence the laminar boundary layer can be ignored, for it is an insignificant part of the problem. From the results of Bauer's investigation, the following equation may be written:

$$\frac{\delta}{x} = \frac{0.024}{(x/k)^{0.13}} \tag{8-4}$$

where $\delta$ is the thickness of the turbulent boundary layer at distance $x$ from 0 in the direction of flow (Fig. 8-5) and where $k$ is the roughness height. Bauer has shown the application of this method by the following example. It should be noted that the flow on the spillway surface to be described in this example is varied and that a simplified method of computing the varied-flow surface is used.  In the case of the boundary-layer development of a uniform flow, the application of Bauer's method is just the same except that the water surface requires no computation, for it is simply parallel to the channel bottom.

**Example 8-1.**  A concrete overflow spillway of indefinite length has a surface slope angle $\theta = 53°8'$ (Fig. 8-5) and a roughness such that $k = 0.005$ ft.  When the discharge is 360 cfs per foot of spillway width, compute the length for boundary-layer development, the profile of the boundary layer, and the water surface.

*Solution.*  The computation is shown in Table 8-2; the headings are explained as follows:

Col. 1.  Arbitrarily assigned length of $x$ in ft, measured from 0
Col. 2.  Values of $x/k$, where $k = 0.005$ ft
Col. 3.  Values of $\delta/x$, computed by Eq. (8-4)
Col. 4.  Values of $\delta$ in ft, obtained by multiplying $x$ by $\delta/x$
Col. 5.  Velocity head $v_0{}^2/2g$ in ft, equal to $x \sin \theta = 0.80x$
Col. 6.  Velocity in fps corresponding to the velocity head in the preceding column
Col. 7.  Potential thickness of flow in ft, equal to the discharge 360 cfs/ft divided by the velocity $v_0$
Col. 8.  Actual thickness of the flow in ft, equal to the potential thickness plus the displacement thickness, which is assumed to be 10% of the thickness $\delta$ of the boundary layer

TABLE 8-2. BOUNDARY-LAYER COMPUTATION
$k = 0.005$ ft      $\theta = 53°8'$      $q = 360$ cfs/ft

| $x$ | $x/k$ | $\delta/x$ | $\delta$ | $v_0{}^2/2g$ | $v_0$ | $q/v_0$ | $y$ |
|-----|-------|------------|----------|--------------|-------|---------|-----|
| (1) | (2) | (3) | (4) | (5) | (6) | (7) | (8) |
| 50 | $1 \times 10^4$ | 0.0073 | 0.36 | 40 | 50.8 | 7.09 | 7.13 |
| 100 | $2 \times 10^4$ | 0.0066 | 0.66 | 80 | 71.8 | 5.00 | 5.07 |
| 200 | $4 \times 10^4$ | 0.0060 | 1.20 | 160 | 101.5 | 3.53 | 3.65 |
| 400 | $8 \times 10^4$ | 0.0055 | 2.20 | 320 | 143.5 | 2.50 | 2.72 |
| 600 | $1.2 \times 10^5$ | 0.0052 | 3.12 | 480 | 175.8 | 2.04 | 2.35 |

The computed water surface and the boundary layer are plotted on logarithmic paper (Fig. 8-6).  The point of intersection of the two profiles indicates the location of the section where the boundary layer reaches its maximum, or where it is fully developed.  The length of the development is shown to be approximately 460 ft.

It should be noted that the simplified method of computing the water-surface profile of a varied flow is justified in this problem because the flow is relatively thin and the slope is very steep.  As the frictional loss in this case is negligibly small, the potential energy of water is practically entirely converted into the kinetic energy expressed by the velocity head.  For the computation of surface profiles of varied flow in general, various methods will be described in Part III.

To illustrate the effect of change in roughness upon the growth of a boundary layer, the computation has been repeated using the same data but with a roughness twice as large.  The line marked with "$y = \delta$, $k = 0.01$ ft" (Fig. 8-6) is the result of this computation.  The change in water surface is practically negligible.  It can be seen that the difference between the values of the development length for the two cases is

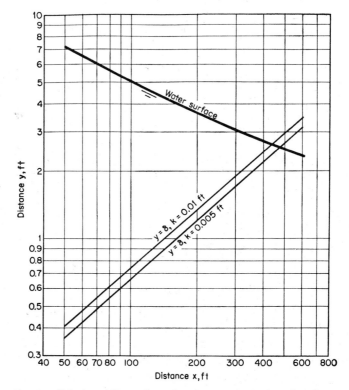

FIG. 8-6. Solution of Example 8-1 for the growth of a boundary layer.

about 30 ft, or a variation of less than 10%. This shows that an increase in roughness has a tendency to speed up the boundary-layer growth or to reduce the development length.

**8-4. Velocity Distribution in Turbulent Flow.** The velocity distribution in a uniform channel flow will become stable when the turbulent boundary layer is fully developed. In the turbulent boundary layer, the distribution can be shown to be approximately logarithmic.

The shearing stress at any point in a turbulent flow moving over a solid surface has been given by Prandtl [7] as

$$\tau = \rho l^2 \left(\frac{dv}{dy}\right)^2 \tag{8-5}$$

where $\rho$ = mass density = $w/g$, where $w$ is the unit weight of the fluid and $g$ is the gravitational acceleration

$l$ = a characteristic length known as the *mixing length*

$dv/dy$ = velocity gradient at a normal distance $y$ from the solid surface

For the region near the solid surface, Prandtl introduced two assumptions: (1) that the mixing length is proportional to $y$, and (2) that the shearing stress is constant. Since the shearing stress at the channel surface is equal to the unit tractive force (Art. 7-11), the second assumption gives $\tau = \tau_0$. From these two assumptions, Eq. (8-5) may be written

$$dv = \frac{1}{\kappa} \sqrt{\frac{\tau_0}{\rho}} \frac{dy}{y} \tag{8-6}$$

where $\kappa$ is a constant for the proportionality between $l$ and $y$. The value of $\kappa$ has been determined by many experiments [8] to be about 0.40. Integrating Eq. (8-6),

$$v = 2.5 \sqrt{\frac{\tau_0}{\rho}} \ln \frac{y}{y_0} \tag{8-7}$$

where $y_0$ is a constant of integration.

From Eq. (7-5) and $w = \rho g$, it can be shown that

$$\sqrt{\frac{\tau_0}{\rho}} = \sqrt{gRS} = V_f \tag{8-8}$$

The quantity represented by $V_f$ has the dimensions of a velocity. Since it varies with the boundary friction $\tau_0$, it is known as the *friction velocity* or *shear velocity*. Thus, Eq. (8-7) may be written

$$v = 2.5 V_f \ln \frac{y}{y_0} \tag{8-9}$$

This equation indicates that the velocity in the turbulent region is a logarithmic function of the distance $y$. It is commonly known as the *Prandtl–von Kármán universal-velocity-distribution law.*[1]

This law has been verified by several experiments [10]. The results indicate a striking similarity between observed and computed distributions and, therefore, offer reasonable justification for use of this logarithmic law in practical problems.

When the surface is smooth, the constant $y_0$ in Eq. (8-9) has been found to depend solely on the friction velocity and the kinematic viscosity; that is,

$$y_0 = \frac{m\nu}{V_f} \tag{8-10}$$

where $m$ is a constant equal to about $\frac{1}{9}$ for smooth surfaces.[2]     For wavy

---

[1] Von Kármán [9] also proved this law by a similarity hypothesis which assumes a linear shearing-stress distribution, the mixing length being proportional to $(dv/dy)/(d^2v/dy^2)$.

[2] This value is derived from Nikuradse's experimental data on smooth pipes [11].

surfaces, the value of $m$ will depend on the shape of the wave profiles. Substituting Eq. (8-10) for $y_0$ in Eq. (8-9) and simplifying,

$$v = 5.75 V_f \log \frac{9yV_f}{\nu} \qquad \text{for smooth surfaces} \qquad (8\text{-}11)$$

This equation gives the velocity distribution in turbulent flow over smooth surfaces.

When the surface is rough, the constant $y_0$ is found to depend on the roughness height; that is,

$$y_0 = mk \qquad (8\text{-}12)$$

where the constant[1] $m$ is equal to approximately $\frac{1}{30}$. Substituting Eq. (8-12) for $y_0$ in Eq. (8-9) and simplifying,

$$v = 5.75 V_f \log \frac{30y}{k} \qquad \text{for rough surfaces} \qquad (8\text{-}13)$$

This equation gives the velocity distribution in turbulent flow over rough surfaces. It should be noted that the roughness height $k$ in this equation is the mean diameter of the sand grains used by Nikuradse; it is known specifically as the *Nikuradse sand roughness.*

It is to be noted that the constants used in the above velocity-distribution equations for smooth and rough surfaces were derived from data on pipes. It is assumed, however, that it is permissible to apply the universal-velocity-distribution law to other cases of turbulent flow, using the constants determined from tests on circular pipes.

**8-5. Theoretical Uniform-flow Equations.** Using the Prandtl–von Kármán universal-velocity-distribution law, Keulegan [13][2] has derived equations for mean velocity of turbulent flow in open channels. For the sake of clarity and simplicity, Keulegan's derivation will be modified below.

By the continuity equation, the total discharge through an ordinary channel section (Fig. 8-7) may be written

$$Q = VA = \int_{\delta_0=0}^{y=h} v \, dA = \int_0^h vB \, dy \qquad (8\text{-}14)$$

where $h$ is the depth of water, $A$ is the water area, $B$ is the length of the curve of equal velocity, and $y$ is the vertical depth measured from the boundary to the curve of equal velocity. Since the laminar sublayer is relatively very thin, $\delta_0$ can be assumed to be zero. It is further assumed that the maximum velocity is at the free surface and that the length $B$ is

---

[1] This value is derived from Nikuradse's experimental data on rough pipes [12]. In Nikuradse's experiments, sand grains were cemented to the inner walls of pipes to simulate roughness. Such roughness is known as *artificial roughness.*

[2] Other references on this subject are [14] to [21].

proportional to its vertical distance $y$ from the boundary; that is,

$$B = P - \gamma y \tag{8-15}$$

where $P$ is the wetted perimeter and $\gamma$ is a function depending on the shape of the section. Thus, the water area is equal to

$$A = \int_0^h B \, dy = Ph - \frac{\gamma}{2} h^2 \tag{8-16}$$

Substituting in Eq. (8-14) the value of $v$ from Eq. (8-9), that of $B$ from Eq. (8-15), and that for $A$ from Eq. (8-16) and then integrating and

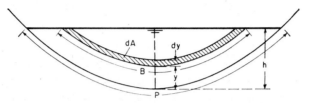

FIG. 8-7. Channel section to illustrate notation.

simplifying, the following equation is obtained:

$$V = 2.5 V_f \ln \left[ \frac{R}{y_0} \frac{h}{R} \exp \left( -1 - \frac{\gamma h^2}{4A} \right) \right]$$

$$\text{or} \quad V = V_f \left\{ 5.75 \log \left[ \frac{h}{mR} \exp \left( -1 - \frac{\gamma h^2}{4A} \right) \right] + 5.75 \log \frac{mR}{y_0} \right\} \tag{8-17}$$

In the above equation the quantity represented by the first term on the right-hand side is a function of the shape of the channel section. However, the variation of this quantity with different shapes of the section is relatively small. For the sake of simplicity, the quantity may be represented by an over-all constant* $A_0$. This constant will include not only the shape function but also other uncertain factors, such as the effect of free surface and the effect of nonuniform distribution of the tractive force at the boundary. Accordingly, Eq. (8-17) may be written

$$V = V_f \left( A_0 + 5.75 \log \frac{mR}{y_0} \right) \tag{8-18}$$

This is the general theoretical equation for the mean velocity of uniform flow in open channels.

For smooth channels, $y_0$ may be represented by Eq. (8-10). Also,

* It is entirely feasible to simplify the derivation by assuming this constant at the very beginning. However, the procedure given here is aimed to give a logical demonstration of the basic principles involved.

from Keulegan's study of Nikuradse's data [11], $A_0$ is found to be 3.25. The theoretical uniform-flow equation for smooth channels is, therefore,

$$V = V_f \left( 3.25 + 5.75 \log \frac{RV_f}{\nu} \right) \qquad \text{for smooth channels} \qquad \text{(8-19)}$$

Using Bazin's data [22] for wavy surfaces, Keulegan obtained a value of $A_0 = 1.3$ for small wood channels and $-3.0$ for large wood channels.

For rough channels, $y_0$ may be expressed by Eq. (8-12). From Keulegan's study of Bazin's data [22], the value of $A_0$ was found to have a wide range, varying from 3.23 to 16.92. Thus, a mean value of 6.25 for $A_0$ may be used. The theoretical uniform-flow equation for rough channels is, therefore,

$$V = V_f \left( 6.25 + 5.75 \log \frac{R}{k} \right) \qquad \text{for rough channels} \qquad \text{(8-20)}$$

From the Chézy formula $V = C \sqrt{RS}$ and from the definition of friction velocity $V_f = \sqrt{gRS}$, it can be shown that

$$\frac{V}{V_f} = \frac{C}{\sqrt{g}} \qquad \text{(8-21)}$$

Substituting this equation and the Reynolds number $\mathbf{R} = RV/\nu$ in Eqs. (8-19) and (8-20), the following expressions for Chézy's $C$ are obtained:

$$C = 32.6 \log \frac{20.8\mathbf{R}}{C} \qquad \text{for smooth channels} \qquad \text{(8-22)}$$

$$C = 32.6 \log \frac{12.2R}{k} \qquad \text{for rough channels} \qquad \text{(8-23)}$$

After Keulegan's analytical study on laws of turbulent flow in channels, Powell [16–18] experimented with small rectangular sills used as artificial roughness and arrived at Eq. (5-5) for Chézy's $C$. Similarly, Robinson and Albertson [19] used baffle plates as artificial roughness and developed another empirical formula of $C$ for rough channels. Moore, Rand, and Hama [3] also conducted similar studies, using transverse-bar roughness of various sizes.

A further study was made by Iwagaki [21] on experimental data obtained from many sources. The results of the study have disclosed that resistance to turbulent flow in open channels becomes obviously larger than that in pipes with increase in the Froude number. Iwagaki reasoned that this is due to the increased instability of the free surface at high Froude numbers. Using the data presented by Iwagaki, therefore, it is possible to introduce the effect of free-surface instability into Keulegan's equations by assuming that the constants in the equations are functions of the Froude number.   Let Eqs. (8-19) and (8-20) be expressed as follows:

$$V = V_f \left( A_s + 5.75 \log \frac{RV_f}{\nu} \right) \qquad \text{for smooth channels} \qquad (8\text{-}24)$$

$$V = V_f \left( A_r + 5.75 \log \frac{R}{k} \right) \qquad \text{for rough channels} \qquad (8\text{-}25)$$

In the above equations, $A_s$ and $A_r$ are functions of the Froude number. These constants may also include the effects of other minor factors.   The

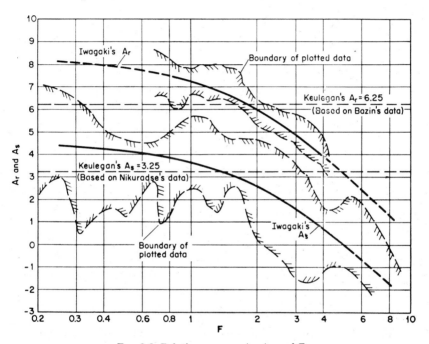

FIG. 8-8. Relations among $A_r$, $A_s$, and **F**.

plotted data are found to be much scattered (as shown in Fig. 8-8 by the shaded boundaries) probably owing to these effects.   When the channel slope becomes too large, the flow will be unstable (Art. 8-8).   In such cases, the laws of turbulent flow described in this article are no longer valid.

**8-6. Theoretical Interpretation of Manning's Roughness Coefficient.** It should be interesting to study Manning's $n$ by relating it to the theoretical channel roughness for rough channels, as developed in the preceding article.   Eliminating $C$ from Eqs. (5-7) and (8-23), Manning's $n$

may be expressed as follows:

$$n = \phi\left(\frac{R}{k}\right) k^{1/6} \qquad (8\text{-}26)$$

where

$$\phi\left(\frac{R}{k}\right) = \frac{(R/k)^{1/6}}{21.9 \log (12.2R/k)} \qquad (8\text{-}27)$$

The plot of this equation (Fig. 8-9) indicates that, for a wide range of $R/k$, the variation in $\phi(R/k)$ is small. As an approximation, $\phi(R/k)$ may be assumed constant and equal to an average value. On the basis of actual observations made in Switzerland, Strickler [23] arrived at a formula which, when compared with Eq. (8-26), gives an average value[1] of $\phi(R/k) = 0.0342$. The roughness height used by Strickler is the

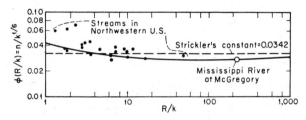

Fig. 8-9. Function $\phi(R/k)$

median sieve size of the material. Data [24] collected from several streams in the northwestern United States and from the Mississippi River are also shown in Fig. 8-9 for purposes of comparison.

If $\phi(R/k)$ is assumed constant, Eq. (8-26) will lead to the interesting conclusion that Manning's $n$ varies with the one-sixth power of the roughness height. In other words, a thousandfold change in the linear measure of the roughness height results in about a threefold change in $n$. Thus, the roughness height as a measure of channel roughness is more sensitive than Manning's $n$. Consequently, the effect of errors involved in estimating the roughness height for the determination of Manning's $n$ by Eq. (8-26) is comparatively small.

Bakhmeteff and Feodoroff [25] have made a comparison of the Manning formula with the Prandtl–von Kármán formula [in a form corresponding to Eq. (8-26)], the G. K. formula, and the Bazin formula. Their results indicated that the Manning formula in the form of Eq. (5-7) is the best suited to all formulas under consideration.

**8-7. Methods for Determining Manning's Roughness Coefficient.** Based on the theoretical velocity distribution in rough channels, two approaches for determining Manning's $n$ have been developed.

[1] This constant has been converted to ft-lb-sec units. The value of $k$ is expressed in ft.

A. *Method of Velocity Measurement.* With reference to the logarithmic law of velocity distribution expressed in Eq. (8-13), it can be seen that the velocity distribution depends on the roughness height, which may be related to Manning's $n$ by Eq. (8-26). In other words, the roughness in terms of Manning's $n$ can be taken as a dominating factor that affects the velocity distribution. If the distribution is known, the value of Manning's $n$ can, therefore, be determined. This concept has been used by Boyer [24] and others [25–28] in estimating the value of $n$ from the vertical velocity distribution in a stream.

Let $v_{0.2}$ be the velocity at two-tenths the depth, that is, at a distance $0.8y$ from the bottom of a wide rough channel, where $y$ is the depth of flow. By Eq. (8-13), the velocity may be expressed as

$$v_{0.2} = 5.75V_f \log \frac{24y}{k}$$

Similarly, let $v_{0.8}$ be the velocity at eight-tenths the depth; then

$$v_{0.8} = 5.75V_f \log \frac{6y}{k}$$

Eliminating $V_f$ from the above two equations,

$$\log \frac{y}{k} = \frac{0.778x - 1.381}{1 - x} \tag{8-28}$$

where $x = v_{0.2}/v_{0.8}$. Substituting Eq. (8-28) in Eq. (8-20), with $R = y$, and simplifying,

$$\frac{V}{V_f} = \frac{1.78(x + 0.95)}{x - 1} \tag{8-29}$$

From Eqs. (5-7) and (8-21), with $R = y$,

$$\frac{V}{V_f} = \frac{y^{1/6}}{3.81n} \tag{8-30}$$

Equating the right-hand sides of Eqs. (8-29) and (8-30) and solving for $n$,

$$n = \frac{(x - 1)y^{1/6}}{6.78(x + 0.95)} \tag{8-31}$$

This equation gives the value for $n$ for a wide rough channel with logarithmic velocity distribution. When this equation is applied to actual streams, the value of $y$ may be taken as the mean depth. A plot of this equation ($n/y^{1/6}$ vs. $x$) has been made to compare with a similar curve developed by Boyer [24] and also with actual observations taken from several streams in the northwestern United States and the Mississippi River. The comparison leads to the belief that a general relationship exists between Manning's $n$ and the velocity distribution. However, more data are necessary to verify this theory more convincingly and to delineate the relationship so that it can be used extensively for practical purposes.

The simple measurement of stream flow is usually made by taking velocity measurements in several verticals at 0.2 and 0.8 depths (Art. 2-6). These measurements, which are averaged to give the mean velocity in the vertical, can be used to estimate Manning's $n$ by means of Eq. (8-31). If this method can be shown to be satisfactory for practical applications, it will provide an easy way of determining roughness in streams where velocity observations have been made.

B. *Method of Roughness Measurement.* In this method it is assumed that Eq. (8-27) for the function $\phi(R/k)$ is acceptable. Thus, the value of Manning's $n$ can be computed by Eq. (8-26) when the roughness height is known.

This method can be extended to streams containing moving sediment beds. According to Einstein and Barbarossa [29], the hydraulic radius $R$ for such streams may be assumed to consist of two parts: the hydraulic radius $R'$ due to surface roughness and the hydraulic radius $R - R'$ due to roughness caused by moving sediment beds. For surface roughness, the roughness height is represented by $k_{65}$ in feet, which is the grain size just coarser than 65% of the material, as obtained from an average curve of mechanical analysis. This curve is to be prepared from the material sampled from the wetted perimeter within the chosen reach of the stream. The roughness height for moving sediments is represented by the size $k_{35}$ in feet, which is the size just coarser than 35% of the sediment grain. This size is taken from a mechanical-analysis curve obtained from sediment samples collected within the reach of the stream. Following this concept, Doland and Chow [30] have shown that the function $\phi(R/k)$ for the combined effect of the surface roughness and moving sediments is

$$\phi\left(\frac{R}{k}\right) = \frac{0.0342}{(R'/R)^{\frac{2}{3}}} \qquad (8\text{-}32)$$

where the value of $R'/R$ depends on the hydraulic radius $R$, the slope $S$, and the grain sizes $k_{65}$ and $k_{35}$. By computing values of $(R/k_{65})^{\frac{1}{4}}$ and $k_{35}/RS$, the value of $R'/R$ can be obtained from the semiempirical curves of Fig. 8-10. These curves are based on data taken from seven typical rivers in the United States.[1] When $\phi(R/k)$ is computed by Eq. (8-32), the value of $n$ can be determined by Eq. (8-26), with $k = k_{65}$. When

[1] Missouri River at Pierre and Ft. Randall, S.D., and Omaha, Nebr.; Elkhorn River at Waterloo, Nebr.; Big Sioux River at Akron, Iowa; Niobrara River at Butte, Nebr.; Platte River at Ashland, Nebr.; Salinas River at San Lucas and Paso Robles, Calif.; and Nacimiento River at Junction, Calif.

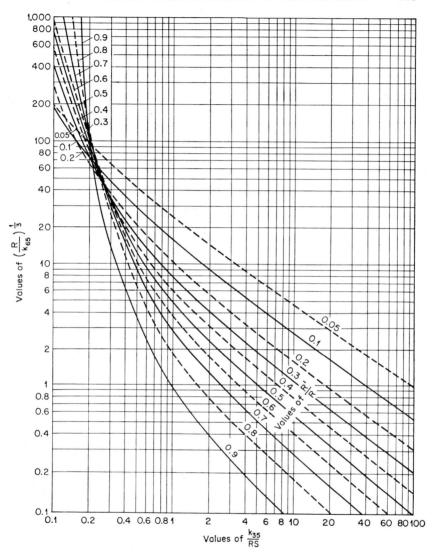

FIG. 8-10. Relationship between $(R/k_{65})^{1/6}$ and $k_{35}/RS$.

there is little moving sediment in the stream, or $R - R' = 0$, it can be seen that Eq. (8-32) is reduced to Strickler's constant (Art. 8-6).

The method described above does not consider kinds of roughness other than surface roughness and the roughness due to moving-sediment beds. Therefore, it is applicable only to problems in which the bushy-bank friction is negligible and in which the active channel, even though split by sand bars and possibly by islands, is free of debris and vegetation.

**8-8. Instability of Uniform Flow.** Uniform flow will become unstable when the velocity of flow is very high or the channel slope is very steep. When this happens, the instability of the free surface is characterized by the formation of a series of roll waves. This phenomenon was first reported by Cornish [31] in 1910 when he observed it in open channels in the Alps. The roll wave is a phenomenon of unsteady flow and its nature will be described in Art. 19-9.

Many attempts [32–45] have been made to develop a criterion for instability of uniform flow. In 1945, Vedernikov [35], employing certain approximations of Saint-Venant, developed a criterion which may be called the *Vedernikov number* **V**. Later, Craya [41] and Iwasa [43] studied the initiation of continuous time growth or decay of an infinitesimal disturbance wave on fluid surface, and developed similar criteria.

The Vedernikov number may be expressed as

$$\mathbf{V} = \frac{x\gamma V}{V_w - V} \tag{8-33}$$

where $x$ = exponent of the hydraulic radius in the general uniform-flow formula Eq. (5-1). Thus, $x = 2$ for laminar flow (Art. 6-10), $x = 0.5$ for turbulent flow if the Chézy formula is used, and $x = \frac{2}{3}$ for turbulent flow if the Manning formula is used.

$V$ = mean velocity

$V_w$ = absolute velocity of disturbance waves in channel

$\gamma$ = a shape factor of channel section, defined by

$$\gamma = 1 - R\frac{dP}{dA} \tag{8-34}$$

where $R$ is the hydraulic radius, $P$ is the wetted perimeter, and $A$ is the water area. Thus, $\gamma = 1$ for very wide channels, and $\gamma = 0$ for very narrow channels.

It will be shown that $V_w - V$ is equal to the celerity $c$ of the waves (Art. 18-6), or to the critical velocity $V_c$. Since the Froude number $\mathbf{F} = V/V_c$, Eq. (8-33) may be reduced to

$$\mathbf{V} = x\gamma\mathbf{F} \tag{8-35}$$

When the Vedernikov number **V** is less than unity, any wave in the channel will be depressed and the flow can be stable. But when **V** is equal to or greater than unity, waves will amplify so that stable flow will become impossible, unsteady flow will prevail, and roll waves will form.

In computing **V** for a turbulent flow, it should be noted that a suitable uniform-flow formula for flow in channels of large slope should be used in providing the value of $x$. For lack of such a formula, the Manning or Chézy formula is used as an approximation only. Since the channel slope is usually large when instability of flow develops, the Froude number in Eq. (8-35) should be computed by Eq. (3-13), which considers the slope effect.

## PROBLEMS

**8-1.** Show that Eq. (8-1) is derived from the condition that the presence of the boundary layer raises the bottom of the channel to a virtual distance equal to the displacement thickness.

**8-2.** A laboratory rectangular channel 1.5 ft wide carries a uniform flow of 0.34 cfs at a depth of 0.15 ft and a slope of 0.0009. The roughness height of the channel surface is 0.0025 ft. Plot the profile of the turbulent boundary layer, and estimate the length of channel required for a full development of the boundary layer which begins to be turbulent at the entrance.

**8-3.** Determine whether the channel described in the preceding problem is hydraulically smooth or rough.

**8-4.** A trapezoidal channel (Fig. 2-2) with $b = 20$ ft, $z = 2$, and $S = 0.001$ carries a uniform flow at a depth of 6 ft. Compute the average unit tractive force and the friction velocity developed in the channel. What are the maximum friction velocities on the sides and bottom of the channel?

**8-5.** Show that

$$\frac{V}{V_f} = \sqrt{\frac{8}{f}} = \frac{R^{1/6}}{3.8n} \tag{8-36}$$

where $f$ is Darcy's friction factor and $n$ is Manning's roughness coefficient.

**8-6.** Using Eq. (8-13) for expressing the theoretical velocity distribution in wide rough channels, (a) show that the average of the velocity of 0.2 depth and the velocity at 0.8 depth gives the velocity at 0.6 depth, and (b) compute the position of the mean velocity below the free surface, and compare the result with that determined by the rule of the U.S. Geological Survey (Art. 2-6).

**8-7.** A wide channel carries a uniform flow at a depth of 5 in. on a slope of 0.0001. The channel surface is rough, having a value of $k = 0.25$ in. Compute and construct a curve showing the theoretical velocity distribution in the channel section. What are the mean velocity and its position?

**8-8.** Determine the values of $k$ in Probs. 5-9 and 5-10.

**8-9.** Using Eq. (8-13), show that the theoretical velocity-distribution coefficients in wide rough channels can be expressed as

$$\alpha = 1 + 3\epsilon^2 - 2\epsilon^3 \tag{2-6}$$
$$\beta = 1 + \epsilon^2 \tag{2-7}$$

where $\epsilon = 2.5V_f/V$. Also show that $\epsilon = 14.2/C = 0.883\sqrt{f} = 9.5n/R^{1/6} = (v_M/V) - 1$ where $C$ is Chézy's resistance factor, $f$ is Darcy's friction factor, $n$ is Manning's roughness coefficient, $R$ is the hydraulic radius, $v_M$ is the maximum velocity, and $V$ is the mean velocity.

**8-10.** Plot a curve showing the relationship between $\alpha$ and $\beta$ defined by Eqs. (2-6) and (2-7), respectively.

**8-11.** Compute the velocity-distribution coefficients of the flow in the channel described in Prob. 8-7.

**8-12.** A wide stream carries approximately uniform flow at a depth of 12 ft. The velocities at 0.2 and 0.8 depths are found to be 1.85 and 1.32 fps, respectively. Estimate (a) the roughness coefficient $n$, (b) the mean velocity, (c) the slope of the channel, and (d) the discharge per unit width of the channel.

**8-13.** In a wide stream having moving sediment bed, the following data are available: $S = 0.003$, $k_{65} = 0.50$ mm, and $k_{35} = 0.40$ mm. The hydraulic radius and water area are found to be $R = 0.85y - 1.8$ and $A = 273y - 797$, where $R$ and $y$ are in ft and $A$ is in ft². Construct the discharge-rating curve of the stream.

**8-14.** Show that the Vedernikov number in wide channels is $V = 2F$ for laminar flow, $V = 0.67F$ for turbulent flow if the Manning formula is used, and $V = 0.5F$ for turbulent flow if the Chézy formula is used.

**8-15.** Using the Vedernikov criterion, explain the general effects of the following factors upon flow instability: (a) the value of $x$ in the uniform-flow formula, (b) the shape of the channel cross section, (c) the viscosity of the fluid, (d) the energy coefficient, and (e) the channel slope.

## REFERENCES

1. Hermann Schlichting: "Boundary Layer Theory," translated from the German by J. Kestin, McGraw-Hill Book Company, Inc., New York, Pergamon Press Ltd., London, and Verlag G. Braun, Karlsruhe, 1955.
2. J. W. Delleur: The boundary layer development in open channels, paper 1138, *Proceedings, American Society of Civil Engineers, Journal, Engineering Mechanics Division*, vol. 83, no. EM1, pp. 1–24, January, 1957.
3. Francis R. Hama: Boundary-layer characteristics for smooth and rough surfaces, *Transactions, Society of Naval Architects and Marine Engineers*, vol. 62, pp. 333–351, 1954.
4. Yoshiaki Iwasa: Boundary layer growth of open channel flows on a smooth bed and its contribution to practical application to channel design, *Memoirs of the Faculty of Engineering, Kyoto University*, Japan, vol. XIX, no. III, pp. 229–254, July, 1957.
5. Henry M. Morris, Jr.: A new concept of flow in rough conduits, *Transactions, American Society of Civil Engineers*, vol. 120, pp. 373–398, 1955. Discussions by Victor L. Streeter, Walter Rand, Harry H. Ambrose, and Henry M. Morris, Jr., pp. 399–410.
6. William J. Bauer: Turbulent boundary layer on steep slopes, *Transactions, American Society of Civil Engineers*, vol. 119, pp. 1212–1233, 1954.
7. Ludwig Prandtl: Über die ausgebildete Turbulenz (On fully developed turbulence), *Proceedings of the 2d International Congress of Applied Mechanics, Zürich*, pp. 62–74, 1926.
8. Boris A. Bakhmeteff: "The Mechanics of Turbulent Flow," Princeton University Press, Princeton, N.J., 1936, p. 66.
9. Theodor von Kármán: Mechanische Äehnlichkeit und Turbulenz (Mechanical similarity and turbulence), *Proceedings of the 3d International Congress of Applied Mechanics, Stockholm*, vol. 1, pp. 85–92, 1930.
10. Vito A. Vanoni: Velocity distribution in open channels, *Civil Engineering*, vol. 11, no. 6, pp. 356–357, June, 1941.
11. J. Nikuradse: Gesetzmässigkeiten der turbulenten Strömung in glatten Rohren (Laws of turbulent flow in smooth pipes), *Verein deutscher Ingenieure, Forschungsheft No. 356*, Berlin, 1932.
12. J. Nikuradse: Strömungsgesetze in rauhen Röhren (Laws of flow in rough pipes), *Verein deutscher Ingenieure, Forschungsheft No. 361*, Berlin, 1933.

13. Garbis H. Keulegan: Laws of turbulent flow in open channels, *Research Paper RP 1151, Journal of Research, U.S. National Bureau of Standards*, vol. 21, pp. 707–741, December, 1938.

14. Erik Lindquist: On velocity formulas for open channels and pipes, *Transactions of the World Power Conference, Sectional Meeting, Scandinavia*, Stockholm, vol. 1, pp. 177–234, 1933.

15. A. E. Bretting: A set of practical hydraulic formulae based on recent experimental research; comparison with older formulae, *Appendix 24, 2d Meeting, International Association of Hydraulic Structures Research*, Stockholm, *Apr.* 7–9, 1948, 20 pp.

16. Ralph W. Powell: Flow in a channel of definite roughness, *Transactions, American Society of Civil Engineers*, vol. 111, pp. 531–566, 1946.

17. Ralph W. Powell: Resistance to flow in smooth channels, *Transactions, American Geophysical Union*, vol. 30, no. 6, pp. 875–878, December, 1949.

18. Ralph L. Powell: Resistance to flow in rough channels, *Transactions, American Geophysical Union*, vol. 31, no. 4, pp. 575–582, August, 1950.

19. A. R. Robinson and M. L. Albertson: Artificial roughness standard for open channels, *Transactions, American Geophysical Union*, vol. 33, no. 6, pp. 881–888, December, 1952.

20. Yuichi Iwagaki: On the laws of resistance to turbulent flow in open smooth channels, *Memoirs of the Faculty of Engineering, Kyoto University*, Japan, vol. 15, no. 1, pp. 27–40, January, 1953.

21. Yuichi Iwagaki: On the law of resistance to turbulent flow in open rough channels, *Proceedings of the 4th Japan National Congress for Applied Mechanics*, pp. 229–233, 1954.

22. H. Darcy and H. Bazin: Recherches hydrauliques: I, Recherches expérimentales sur l'écoulement de l'eau dans les canaux découverts (Hydraulic research: I, Experimental research on the flow of water in open channels), *Mémoires présentés par divers savants à l'Académie des Sciences*, vol. 19, no. 1, Dunod, Paris, 1865.

23. A. Strickler: Beiträge zur Frage der Geschwindigkeitsformel und der Rauhigkeitszahlen für Ströme, Kanäle und geschlossene Leitungen (Some contributions to the problem of the velocity formula and roughness factors for rivers, canals, and closed conduits), *Mitteilungen des eidgenössischen Amtes für Wasserwirtschaft*, Bern, Switzerland, no. 16, 1923.

24. M. C. Boyer: Estimating the Manning coefficient from an average bed roughness in open channels, *Transactions, American Geophysical Union*, vol. 35, no. 6, pp. 957–961, December, 1954.

25. Boris A. Bakhmeteff and Nicholas V. Feodoroff: Discussion on open channel flow, *Transactions, American Society of Civil Engineers*, vol. 108, pp. 492–502, 1943.

26. M. P. O'Brien: The vertical distribution of velocity in wide rivers, *Transactions, American Geophysical Union*, vol. 18, pt. 2, pp. 467–470, 1937.

27. F. C. Scobey: The flow of water in irrigation channels, *U.S. Department of Agriculture, Professional Paper, Bulletin No.* 194, 1915.

28. W. E. Langbein: Determination of Manning's *n* from vertical-velocity curve, *Transactions, American Geophysical Union*, pt. II, pp. 618–620, July, 1940.

29. Hans A. Einstein and H. L. Barbarossa: River channel roughness, *Transactions, American Society of Civil Engineers*, vol. 117, pp. 1121–1132, 1952.

30. James J. Doland and Ven Te Chow: Discussion of River channel roughness, by Hans A. Einstein and H. L. Barbarossa, *Transactions, American Society of Civil Engineers*, vol. 117, pp. 1134–1139, 1952.

31. Vaughan Cornish: "Waves of the Sea and Other Water Waves," The Open Court Publishing Company, La Salle, Ill., and T. Fisher Unwin, London, 1910.

32. Harold Jeffreys: The flow of water in an inclined channel of rectangular section, *London, Edinburgh and Dublin Philosophical Magazine and Journal of Science*, ser. 6, vol. 49, pp. 793–807, May, 1925.

33. G. H. Keulegan and G. W. Patterson: A criterion for instability of flow in steep channels, *Transactions, American Geophysical Union*, vol. 21, pt. II, pp. 594–596, July, 1940.

34. Harold A. Thomas: The propagation of waves in steep prismatic conduits, *Proceedings of Hydraulics Conference, University of Iowa Studies in Engineering, Bulletin 20*, pp. 214–229, 1940.

35. V. V. Vedernikov: Conditions at the front of a translation wave distributing a steady motion of a real fluid, *Comptes rendus (Doklady) de l'Académie des Sciences de l'U.R.S.S.*, vol. 48, no. 4, pp. 239–242, 1945.

36. V. V. Vedernikov: Characteristic features of a liquid flow in an open channel, *Comptes rendus (Doklady) de l'Académie des Sciences de l'U.R.S.S.*, vol. 52, pp. 207–210, 1946.

37. Ralph W. Powell: Vedernikov's criterion for ultra-rapid flow, *Transactions, American Geophysical Union*, vol. 29, no. 6, pp. 882–886, December, 1948. Discussions by V. V. Vedernikov and Ralph W. Powell, vol. 32, no. 4, pp. 603–607, August, 1951.

38. Robert F. Dressler: Mathematical solutions of the problems of roll waves in inclined open channels, *Communications on Pure and Applied Mathematics*, vol. 2, no. 2–3, pp. 149–194, 1949.

39. Robert F. Dressler: Stability of uniform flow and roll-wave formation, *Proceedings of the Gravity Waves Symposium, U.S. National Bureau of Standards, Circular 521*, 1952, pp. 237–241.

40. Francis F. Escoffier: A graphical method for investigating the stability of flow in open channels or in closed conduits flowing partly full, *Transactions, American Geophysical Union*, vol. 31, no. 4, pp. 583–586, 1950.

41. A. Craya: The criterion for the possibility of roll wave formation, *Proceedings of the Gravity Waves Symposium, U.S. National Bureau of Standards, Circular 521*, 1952, pp. 294–332.

42. Tojiro Ishihara, Yuichi Iwagaki, and Yasuo Ishihara: On the rollwave-trains appearing in the water flow on a steep slope surface, *Memoirs of the Faculty of Engineering, Kyoto University*, Japan, vol. XIV, no. 2, pp. 83–91, March, 1952.

43. Yoshiaki Iwasa: The criterion for instability of steady uniform flows in open channels, *Memoirs of the Faculty of Engineering, Kyoto University*, Japan, vol. XVI, no. 6, pp. 264–275, March, 1954.

44. Chia-Shun Yih: Stability of parallel laminar flow with a free surface, *Proceedings of the 2d U.S. National Congress of Applied Mechanics*, American Society of Mechanical Engineers, 1954, pp. 623–628.

45. C. C. Lin: "The Theory of Hydrodynamic Stability," Cambridge University Press, Cambridge, England, 1955.

PART III

# GRADUALLY VARIED FLOW

# CHAPTER 9

# THEORY AND ANALYSIS

**9-1. Basic Assumptions.** The gradually varied flow to be discussed in Part III of this book is the steady flow whose depth varies gradually along the length of the channel (Art. 1-2). This definition signifies two conditions: (1) that the flow is steady; that is, that the hydraulic characteristics of flow remain constant for the time interval under consideration; and (2) that the streamlines are practically parallel; that is, that hydrostatic distribution of pressure prevails over the channel section.

The development of the theory of gradually varied flow dates back to the eighteenth century. Many early hydraulicians[1] have contributed to this development. The theories thus developed practically all hinge on the following basic assumption:

*A. The head loss at a section is the same as for a uniform flow having the velocity and hydraulic radius of the section.*

According to this assumption, *the uniform-flow formula may be used to evaluate the energy slope of a gradually varied flow at a given channel section, and the corresponding coefficient of roughness developed primarily for uniform flow is applicable to the varied flow.* This assumption has never been precisely confirmed by either experiment[2] or theory, but errors arising from it are believed to be small compared with those ordinarily incurred in the use of a uniform-flow formula and in the selection of the roughness coefficient. Over years of use this assumption has proved to be a reliable basis for design. The assumption is undoubtedly more correct for varied flow where the velocity increases than where the velocity decreases, because in a flow of increasing velocity the head loss is caused almost entirely by frictional effects, whereas in a flow of decreasing velocity there may be large-scale eddy losses.

[1] Bélanger [1] is believed to be the outstanding contributor. Also among early contributors are Bernoulli, Bresse, Poncelet, Saint-Venant, Boussinesq, and others [2] to [5].

[2] Using the experimental data from the Sunderland Technical College and King's College in England and from the University of Illinois, Bettes [6] has derived an $f$-$\mathbf{R}$ relationship (Art. 1-3) for gradually varied flow in smooth open channels, which was found to agree very closely with the relationship for uniform flow obtained by Allen [7]. Also, the computation of backwater curves based on this assumption has been verified satisfactorily by many experiments. These experimental verifications, though not very rigorous, indicate the validity of the assumption for practical purposes.

In addition to the above basic assumption, the following assumptions will also be used where further simplification is necessary in subsequent discussions:

*B.* The slope of the channel is small; so that:

1. The depth of flow is the same whether the vertical or normal (to the channel bottom) direction is used.

2. The pressure-correction factor cos $\theta$ [applied to the depth of the flow section, Eq. (2-12)] is equal to unity.

3. No air entrainment occurs. In case of notable air entrainment, the computation may be carried out assuming no entrainment and then corrected approximately, at the end, using Eq. (2-15).

*C.* The channel is prismatic; that is, the channel has constant alignment and shape.

*D.* The velocity distribution in the channel section is fixed. Thus, the velocity-distribution coefficients are constant.

*E.* The conveyance $K$ (Art. 6-3) and section factor $Z$ (Art. 4-3) are exponential functions of the depth of flow.

*F.* The roughness coefficient is independent of the depth of flow and constant throughout the channel reach under consideration.

**9-2. Dynamic Equation of Gradually Varied Flow.** Consider the profile of gradually varied flow in the elementary length $dx$ of an open channel (Fig. 9-1). The total head above the datum at the upstream section 1 is

$$H = z + d \cos \theta + \alpha \frac{V^2}{2g} \qquad (3\text{-}2)$$

where $H$ is the total head in ft; $z$ is the vertical distance of the channel bottom above the datum in ft; $d$ is the depth of flow section in ft; $\theta$ is the bottom-slope angle; $\alpha$ is the energy coefficient; and $V$ is the mean velocity of flow through the section in fps.

It is assumed that $\theta$ and $\alpha$ are constant throughout the channel reach under consideration. Taking the bottom of the channel as the $x$ axis and differentiating Eq. (3-2) with respect to the length $x$ of the water-surface profile, which is measured along the $x$ axis, the following equation is obtained:

$$\frac{dH}{dx} = \frac{dz}{dx} + \cos \theta \frac{dd}{dx} + \alpha \frac{d}{dx}\left(\frac{V^2}{2g}\right) \qquad (9\text{-}1)$$

It should be noted that the slope is defined as the sine of the slope angle and that it is assumed *positive* if it *descends* in the direction of flow and *negative* if it *ascends*. Hence,[1] in Fig. 9-1, the energy slope $S_f = -dH/dx$,

---

[1] It should be noted that the frictional loss $dH$ is always a negative quantity in the direction of flow (unless outside energy is added to the course of the flow) and that the change in the bottom elevation $dz$ is a negative quantity when the slope descends.

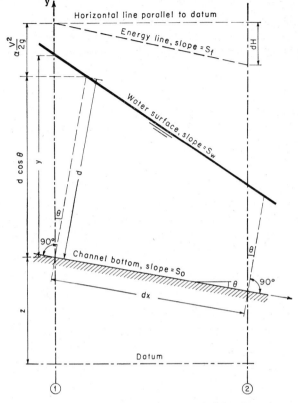

Fig. 9-1. Derivation of the gradually-varied-flow equation.

and the slope of the channel bottom $S_0 = \sin \theta = -dz/dx$. Substituting these slopes in Eq. (9-1) and solving for $dd/dx$,

$$\frac{dd}{dx} = \frac{S_0 - S_f}{\cos \theta + \alpha \, d(V^2/2g)/dd} \tag{9-2}$$

This is the general differential equation for gradually varied flow, referred to hereafter as the *dynamic equation of gradually varied flow,* or simply as the *gradually-varied-flow equation.* It represents the slope of the water surface *with respect to the bottom of the channel.* The depth $d$ is measured from the bottom of the channel, and the channel bottom is taken as the $x$ axis. Thus, the slope of the water surface is equal to the bottom slope $S_0$ if $dd/dx = 0$, less than $S_0$ if $dd/dx$ is positive, and greater than $S_0$ if $dd/dx$ is negative. In other words, the water surface is parallel to the channel bottom when $dd/dx = 0$, rising when $dd/dx$ is positive, and lowering when $dd/dx$ is negative.

In the above equation, the slope angle $\theta$ has been assumed constant or independent of $x$. Otherwise, a term $-d \sin \theta (d\theta/dd)$, where $\theta$ is a function of $x$, would have been added to the denominator. For small $\theta$, $\cos \theta \approx 1$, $d \approx y$, and $dd/dx \approx dy/dx$. Thus Eq. (9-2) becomes

$$\frac{dy}{dx} = \frac{S_0 - S_f}{1 + \alpha\, d(V^2/2g)/dy} \tag{9-3}$$

In most problems, the channel slope is small; accordingly, Eq. (9-3) will be used in subsequent discussions.

The term $\alpha\, d(V^2/2g)/dy$ in the varied-flow equation represents the change in velocity head. The coefficient $\alpha$ has been assumed to be constant from section to section of the channel reach under consideration. Otherwise, the change in velocity head would have been expressed as $d(\alpha V^2/2g)/dy$, where $\alpha$ is a function of $x$. Since $V = Q/A$, $Q$ is constant, and $dA/dy = T$, the velocity-head term may be developed as follows:

$$\alpha \frac{d}{dy}\left(\frac{V^2}{2g}\right) = \frac{\alpha Q^2}{2g}\frac{dA^{-2}}{dy} = -\frac{\alpha Q^2}{gA^3}\frac{dA}{dy} = -\frac{\alpha Q^2 T}{gA^3} \tag{9-4}$$

Since $Z = \sqrt{A^3/T}$, the above may be written

$$\alpha \frac{d}{dy}\left(\frac{V^2}{2g}\right) = -\frac{\alpha Q^2}{gZ^2} \tag{9-5}$$

Suppose that a critical flow of discharge equal to $Q$ occurs at the section; Eq. (4.4) gives

$$Q = Z_c \sqrt{\frac{g}{\alpha}} \tag{9-6}$$

where $Z_c$ is the section factor for critical-flow computation for discharge $Q$ at depth $y_c$. The symbol $Z_c$ used herein should be carefully distinguished from the $Z$ in Eq. (9-5). The symbol $Z$ simply represents the numerical value of $\sqrt{A^3/T}$, which is computed for the discharge $Q$ at a depth equal to $y$ of the gradually varied flow. The value of $Z_c$ is the section factor, which is computed for $Q$ at the depth $y_c$ as if the flow were considered critical. Now, substituting Eq. (9-6) for $Q$ in Eq. (9-5) and simplifying,

$$\alpha \frac{d}{dy}\left(\frac{V^2}{2g}\right) = -\frac{Z_c^2}{Z^2} \tag{9-7}$$

The term $S_f$ in Eq. (9-3) represents the energy slope. According to the first assumption in Art. 9-1, this slope at a channel section of the gradually varied flow is equal to the energy slope of the uniform flow that has the velocity and hydraulic radius of the section. When the Manning formula is used, the energy slope is

$$S_f = \frac{n^2 V^2}{2.22 R^{4/3}}$$  (9-8)

When the Chézy formula is used,

$$S_f = \frac{V^2}{C^2 R}$$  (9-9)

In a general form, expressed in terms of the conveyance $K$, the energy slope, from Eq. (6-4), may be written

$$S_f = \frac{Q^2}{K^2}$$  (9-10)

Suppose that a uniform flow of a discharge equal to $Q$ occurs in the section. The energy slope would be equal to the bottom slope, and Eq. (9-10) may be written

$$S_0 = \frac{Q^2}{K_n^2}$$  (9-11)

where $K_n$ is the conveyance for uniform flow at a depth $y_n$. This $K_n$ should be distinguished from $K$ in Eq. (9-10). The notation $K$ represents simply the numerical value of the conveyance at a depth $y$ of the gradually varied flow. The value $K_n$ is the conveyance computed for $Q$ at the depth $y_n$ as if the flow were considered uniform.

Dividing Eq. (9-10) by Eq. (9-11),

$$\frac{S_f}{S_0} = \frac{K_n^2}{K^2}$$  (9-12)

Substituting Eqs. (9-7) and (9-12) in Eq. (9-3),

$$\frac{dy}{dx} = S_0 \frac{1 - (K_n/K)^2}{1 - (Z_c/Z)^2}$$  (9-13)

This is another form of the gradually-varied-flow equation.

There are other popular forms of the gradually-varied-flow equation that can readily be derived, such as

$$\frac{dy}{dx} = S_0 \frac{1 - (K_n/K)^2}{1 - r(K_n/K)^2}$$  (9-14)

where $r = S_0/S_{cn}$, or the ratio of the channel slope to the critical slope at the normal depth of discharge $Q$ (Art. 6-7);

$$\frac{dy}{dx} = S_0 \frac{1 - (Q/Q_n)^2}{1 - (Q/Q_c)^2}$$  (9-15)

where $Q$ is the given discharge of the gradually varied flow at the actual depth $y$; $Q_n$ is the normal discharge at a depth equal to $y$; and $Q_c$ is the critical discharge at a depth equal to $y$; and

$$\frac{dy}{dx} = \frac{S_0 - Q^2/C^2A^2R}{1 - \alpha Q^2/gA^2D} \tag{9-16}$$

where $D$ is the hydraulic depth, $C$ is Chézy's resistance factor, and the rest of the notation is as defined in this article.

For wide rectangular channels,

1. When the Manning formula is used,

$$\frac{dy}{dx} = S_0 \frac{1 - (y_n/y)^{10/3}}{1 - (y_c/y)^3} \tag{9-17}$$

2. When the Chézy formula is used,

$$\frac{dy}{dx} = S_0 \frac{1 - (y_n/y)^3}{1 - (y_c/y)^3} \tag{9-18}$$

**9-3. Characteristics of Flow Profiles.** The dynamic equation of gradually varied flow developed in Art. 9-2 expresses the longitudinal surface slope of the flow with respect to the channel bottom. It can therefore be used to describe the characteristics of various *flow profiles* or profiles of the water surface of the flow. For simplicity, the channel is considered *prismatic*, and Eq. (9-13) is used for discussion. The values of $K$ and $Z$ in this equation are assumed to increase or decrease continuously with the depth $y$. This is true for all open-channel sections except for conduits with a gradually closing top. In such conduits, the value of $K$, after reaching its maximum value, will decrease as the depth of flow approaches the top of the conduit (Art. 6-3).

The flow profile represents the *surface curve* of the flow. It will represent a backwater curve[1] (Art. 4-5) if the depth of flow increases in the direction of flow and a drawdown curve (Art. 4-5) if the depth decreases in the direction of flow. Following the description in the preceding article, it can be seen that the flow profile is a backwater curve if $dy/dx$ is positive and a drawdown curve if $dy/dx$ is negative.

For a backwater curve, $dy/dx$ is positive; thus, Eq. (9-13) gives two possible cases:

1. $1 - (K_n/K)^2 > 0$ and $1 - (Z_c/Z)^2 > 0$
2. $1 - (K_n/K)^2 < 0$ and $1 - (Z_c/Z)^2 < 0$

---

[1] The term "backwater curve" is used primarily to indicate the longitudinal surface curve of the water backed up above a dam or into a tributary by flood in the main stream. Many authors have extended its meaning to include all types of flow profiles.

Since the values of $K$ and $Z$ increase or decrease continuously with the depth $y$, the first case indicates $y > y_n$ and $y > y_c$. As $y > y_c$, the flow must be subcritical. If $y > y_n > y_c$, the subcritical flow must occur in a *mild channel* (i.e., a channel of subcritical slope). On the other hand, if $y > y_c > y_n$, the subcritical flow must occur in a *steep channel* (i.e., a channel of supercritical slope). Similarly, the second case indicates $y < y_n$ and $y < y_c$. The corresponding flow must be supercritical; and it occurs in a mild channel if $y_n > y_c > y$ and in a steep channel if $y_c > y_n > y$.

For a drawdown curve, $dy/dx$ is negative and Eq. (9-13) gives two possible cases:

1. $1 - (K_n/K)^2 > 0$ and $1 - (Z_c/Z)^2 < 0$
2. $1 - (K_n/K)^2 < 0$ and $1 - (Z_c/Z)^2 > 0$

The first case indicates that $y_c > y > y_n$ and, thus, that the flow is supercritical in a steep channel. Similarly, the second case indicates that $y_n > y > y_c$, or that the flow is subcritical in a mild channel.

When the water surface is parallel to the bottom of the channel, $dy/dx = 0$, and Eq. (9-13) gives $1 - (K_n/K)^2 = 0$, or $y = y_n$, which indicates a uniform flow. The flow is a uniform critical flow if $y = y_n = y_c$, a uniform subcritical flow if $y = y_n > y_c$, and a uniform supercritical flow if $y_c > y_n = y$.

For purposes of discussion, channel slope may be classified as *sustaining* and *nonsustaining*. A sustaining slope is a channel slope that falls in the direction of flow. Hence, a sustaining slope is always positive and may also be called a *positive slope*. A sustaining or positive slope may be critical, mild (subcritical), or steep (supercritical). A nonsustaining slope may be either *horizontal* or *adverse*. A horizontal slope is a *zero slope*. An adverse slope is a *negative slope* that rises in the direction of flow.

In a channel of horizontal slope, or $S_0 = 0$, Eq. (9-11) gives $K_n = \infty$ or $y_n = \infty$. Since $K_n \sqrt{S_0} = Q$, Eq. (9-13) for horizontal channels may be written

$$\frac{dy}{dx} = \frac{-(Q/K)^2}{1 - (Z_c/Z)^2} \qquad (9\text{-}19)$$

Considering $y_n = \infty$, this equation indicates two possible conditions:

1. $y_n > y > y_c$
2. $y_n > y_c > y$

The first case represents a subcritical flow with a drawdown curve, since $dy/dx$ is shown as negative. The second case represents a supercritical flow with a backwater curve, since $dy/dx$ is shown as positive.

In a channel of adverse slope, or $S_0 < 0$, Eq. (9-11) indicates that, for negative values of $S_0$, $K_n$ must be imaginary or $K_n{}^2$ must be negative [8]. Consequently, Eq. (9-13) gives two possible cases:

1. A subcritical flow in which $y > y_c$
2. A supercritical flow in which $y < y_c$

In the first case, $dy/dx$ is negative, and the flow profile is a drawdown curve. In the second case, $dy/dx$ is positive, and the flow profile is a backwater curve. Since $K_n$ is imaginary, the value of $y_n$ cannot be easily expressed.[1] In fact, a finite positive value of $y_n$ is physically impossible because a uniform flow can never occur in an adverse channel. (Why?)

The above discussions are summarized in Table 9-1 and in Figs. 9-2 and 9-4. Some special features of the theoretical flow profiles are as follows:

*A. Discontinuity in Flow Profile.* When $y = y_c$, Eq. (9-13) indicates that $dy/dx = \infty$, that is, that the flow profile will be vertical in crossing the critical-depth line. If the depth of flow is changed suddenly from a low stage to a high stage in crossing the critical-depth line, a hydraulic jump will occur, representing a discontinuity in the flow profile. If the depth changes from a high to low stage, then a hydraulic drop will occur. It should be noted that, at or near the critical-depth line, the flow profile is bent to produce such great curvature that the parallel-flow assumption for the definition of gradually varied flow will introduce large errors. In fact, the flow may become so curvilinear or rapidly varied that the theory and equations developed in the preceding article become inapplicable. Therefore, Eq. (9-13) cannot be used to describe or compute accurately the flow profile near the critical depth.

*B. Behavior of Flow Profile at Specific Depths.* For the subsequent discussion, it is important to recognize the theoretical behavior of the flow profile at several specific depths. When $y = \infty$, Eq. (9-13) shows that $dy/dx = S_0$, that is, that the flow surface is horizontal. When $y = y_n$, Eq. (9-13) shows that $dy/dx = 0$, that is, that the flow surface is parallel to the bottom of the channel; this signifies uniform flow. When $y = y_c$, a hydraulic jump or drop in flow profile may occur, as noted. When $y = y_n = y_c$, the flow is uniform and critical.

*C. Points of Inflection on Flow Profile.* When $y = 0$, Eq. (9-13) seems to produce an indeterminate form $\infty/\infty$ for $dy/dx$. However,

---

[1] Some authors regard $y_n$ as negative [9]. Then the Chézy formula may be used for explanation. By the Chézy formula, $K = CAR^{1/2}$ and $K^2 = C^2A^2R$. Thus, for a negative value of $K^2$, $R$ and hence $y_n$ must be negative. The value $y_n$ has also been assumed to be positive [10]. In this case, the Chézy $C$ is taken as an imaginary value in order to keep values of $A$ and $R$ invariably positive.

TABLE 9-1. TYPES OF FLOW PROFILES IN PRISMATIC CHANNELS

| Channel slope | Designation | | | Relation of $y$ to $y_n$ and $y_c$ | | | General type of curve | Type of flow |
|---|---|---|---|---|---|---|---|---|
| | Zone 1 | Zone 2 | Zone 3 | Zone 1 | Zone 2 | Zone 3 | | |
| Horizontal $S_0 = 0$ | None | | | $y >$ | $y_n >$ | $y_c$ | None | None |
| | | $H2$ | | | $y_n > y > y_c$ | | Drawdown | Subcritical |
| | | | $H3$ | $y_n >$ | | $y_c > y$ | Backwater | Supercritical |
| Mild $0 < S_0 < S_c$ | $M1$ | | | $y > y_n$ | | $> y_c$ | Backwater | Subcritical |
| | | $M2$ | | | $y_n > y > y_c$ | | Drawdown | Subcritical |
| | | | $M3$ | $y_n >$ | | $y_c > y$ | Backwater | Supercritical |
| Critical $S_0 = S_c > 0$ | $C1$ | | | $y > y_c$ | $=$ | $y_n$ | Backwater | Subcritical |
| | | $C2$ | | | $y_c = \; y = y_n$ | | Parallel to channel bottom | Uniform-critical |
| | | | $C3$ | $y_c$ | $=$ | $y_n > y$ | Backwater | Supercritical |
| Steep $S_0 > S_c > 0$ | $S1$ | | | $y > y_c$ | $>$ | $y_n$ | Backwater | Subcritical |
| | | $S2$ | | | $y_c \; > y > y_n$ | | Drawdown | Supercritical |
| | | | $S3$ | $y_c$ | $>$ | $y_n > y$ | Backwater | Supercritical |
| Adverse $S_0 < 0$ | None | | | $y > (y_n)*$ | $>$ | $y_c$ | None | None |
| | | $A2$ | | | $(y_n)* > y > y_c$ | | Drawdown | Subcritical |
| | | | $A3$ | $(y_n)*$ | $>$ | $y_c > y$ | Backwater | Supercritical |

\* $y_n$ in parentheses is assumed a positive value.

it can be shown that the theoretical behavior of the flow profile at or near $y = 0$ depends on the type of uniform-flow formula used in the computation. For a wide rectangular channel, Eq. (9-17) represents the slope of flow profile if the Manning formula is used. By this equation, it can be shown that $dy/dx$ becomes infinite when $y = 0$. This means that the curve is vertical at the channel bottom. If the Chézy formula is used, it can be shown that $dy/dx = S_0(y_n/y_c)^3$ for $y = 0$. This means that the curve will make a certain angle with the bottom. It is apparent that there should be a point of inflection on the flow profile when $y < y_c < y_n$. Mathematical investigations by Gunder [11] and Mouret [12] have revealed that this point of inflection is at a depth very close to the channel

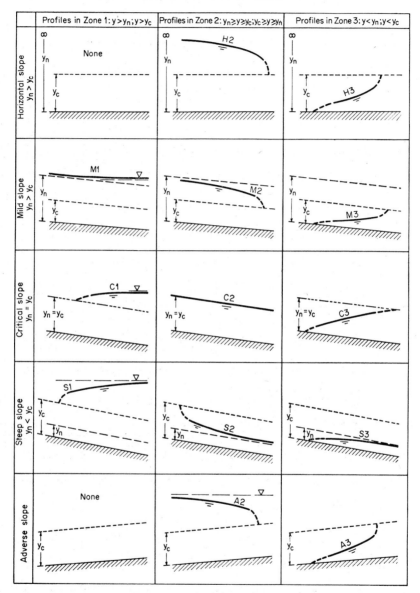

FIG. 9-2. Classification of flow profiles of gradually varied flow.

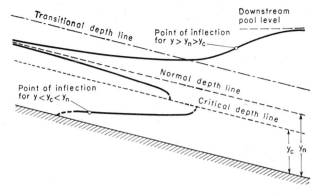

FIG. 9-3. Theoretical points of inflection on flow profiles.

bottom (Fig. 9-3).[1] Similarly, Mouret found that another point of inflection exists on the flow profile when $y > y_n > y_c$ (Fig. 9-3).[2]

**9-4. Classification of Flow Profiles.**[3] For the given discharge and channel conditions the normal-depth and critical-depth lines divide the space in a channel into three zones:

Zone 1. The space above the upper line
Zone 2. The space between the two lines
Zone 3. The space below the lower line

Thus, the flow profiles may be classified into thirteen different types according to the nature of the channel slope and the zone in which the flow surface lies. These types are designated as $H2$, $H3$; $M1$, $M2$, $M3$; $C1$, $C2$, $C3$; $S1$, $S2$, $S3$; and $A2$, $A3$; where the letter is descriptive of the slope: $H$ for horizontal, $M$ for mild (subcritical), $C$ for critical, $S$ for steep (supercritical), and $A$ for adverse slope; and where the numeral represents the zone number. Of the thirteen flow profiles, twelve are for gradually varied flow and one, $C2$, is for uniform flow. It should be noted that a continuous flow profile usually occurs only in one zone. The general characteristics of these profiles are given in Table 9-1, and the shapes are shown in Figs. 9-2 and 9-4. Since the profiles near the critical depth and the channel bottom cannot be accurately defined by the theory of gradu-

[1] It is believed that the question of points of inflection was first discussed by Merten [13].
[2] This point of inflection occurs because the profile must have a horizontal slope in crossing the transitional profile and then bend forward tangent to the downstream pool level (Art. 9-6).
[3] It is believed that a comprehensive description and classification of different flow profiles were first given by Boudin [14].

ally varied flow, they are shown with short dashed or dotted lines. Various flow profiles are discussed below.

*A. M Profiles.*  $S_0 < S_c$ and $y_n > y_c$.

The $M1$ *profile* represents the most well-known backwater curve; it is the most important of all flow profiles from the practical point of view. This profile occurs when the downstream end of a long mild channel is submerged in a reservoir to a greater depth than the normal depth of the flow in the channel. This flow profile lies in zone 1. The upstream end of the curve is tangent to the normal-depth line, since $dy/dx = 0$ as $y = y_n$; and the downstream end is tangent to the horizontal pool surface, since $dy/dx = S_0$ as $y = \infty$. Typical examples of the $M1$ profile are the profile behind a dam in a natural river (Fig. 9-4a) and the profile in a canal joining two reservoirs (Fig. 9-4b).

An $M2$ *profile* occurs when the bottom of the channel at the downstream end is submerged in a reservoir to a depth less than the normal depth. The upstream end of the flow profile is tangent to the normal-depth line, since $dy/dx = 0$ as $y = y_n$. If the amount of submergence at the downstream end is less than the critical depth, the flow profile will terminate abruptly, with its end tangent to a vertical line at a depth equal to the critical depth, since $dy/dx = \infty$ for $y = y_c$. This means the creation of a hydraulic drop. If the depth of submergence at the downstream end is greater than the critical depth, then as much of the profile will form as lies above the water surface in the reservoir. Examples are the profile at the upstream side of a sudden enlargement of a canal cross section (Fig. 9-4c) and the profile in a canal leading to a reservoir, where the pool level is shown both above and below the critical-depth line (Fig. 9-4d).

The $M3$ *profile* starts theoretically from the upstream channel bottom, at either a vertical-angle slope or an acute angle, depending on the type of uniform-flow formula used (Art. 9-3), and terminates with a hydraulic jump at the downstream end. This type of profile usually occurs when a supercritical flow enters a mild channel. The beginning of the profile, although it cannot be defined precisely by the theory, depends on the initial velocity of the issuing water. The higher the velocity, the farther downstream the profile will begin. The theoretical upstream end of the profile will intersect the channel bottom. At this end $y = 0$; thus the velocity would become infinite. Therefore, the theoretical upstream end of an $M3$ profile can never exist physically. Examples of the $M3$ profile are the profile in a stream below a sluice (Fig. 9-4e) and the profile after the change in bottom slope from steep to mild (Fig. 9-4f).

*B. S Profiles.*  $S_0 > S_c$ and $y_n < y_c$.

The $S1$ *profile* begins with a jump at the upstream and becomes tangent to the horizontal pool level at the downstream end. Examples are the

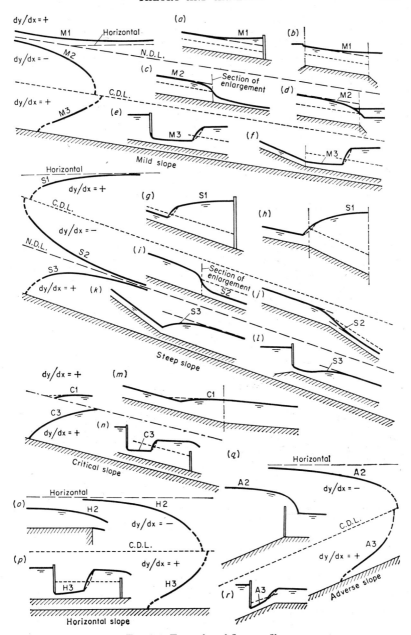

Fig. 9-4. Examples of flow profiles.

profiles of flow behind a dam in a steep channel (Fig. 9-4$g$) and in a steep canal emptying into a pool of high elevation (Fig. 9-4$h$).

The $S2$ *profile* is a drawdown curve. It is usually very short and rather like a transition between a hydraulic drop and uniform flow, since it starts upstream with a vertical slope at the critical depth and is tangent to the normal-depth line at the downstream end. Examples are the profiles formed on the downstream side of an enlargement of channel section (Fig. 9-4$i$) and on the steep-slope side as the channel slope changes from steep to steeper (Fig. 9-4$j$).

The $S3$ *profile* is also of the transitional type, formed between an issuing supercritical flow and the normal-depth line to which the profile is tangent. Examples are the profile on the steep-slope side as the channel slope changes from steep to milder steep (Fig. 9-4$k$), and that below a sluice with the depth of the entering flow less than the normal depth on a steep slope (Fig. 9-4$l$).

C. *C Profiles.* $S_0 = S_c$ and $y_n = y_c$.

These profiles represent the transition conditions between $M$ and $S$ profiles. Assuming a wide rectangular channel, Eq. (9-17) shows that $C1$ and $C3$ *profiles* are curved and that the $C1$ profile is asymptotic to a horizontal line (Fig. 9-4$m$ and $n$). When the Chézy formula is used, Eq. (9-18) will show that the two profiles are horizontal lines. The $C2$ *profile* represents the case of uniform critical flow.

D. *H Profiles.* $S_0 = 0$ and $y_n = \infty$.

These are the limiting cases of $M$ profiles when the channel bottom becomes horizontal. The $H2$ and $H3$ *profiles* correspond to the $M2$ and $M3$ profiles, but no $H1$ profile can actually be established, since $y_n$ is infinite. Examples of $H$ profiles are shown in Fig. 9-4$o$ and $p$.

E. *A Profiles.* $S_0 < 0$.

The $A1$ profile is impossible, since the value of $y_n$ is not real. The $A2$ and $A3$ *profiles* are similar to the $H2$ and $H3$ profiles, respectively. In general, $A$ profiles occur infrequently. Examples are shown in Fig. 9-4$q$ and $r$.

F. *Profiles in Conduits with a Gradually Closing Top.* For any conduit with a gradually closing top, the normal discharge will increase as the depth of flow increases. It will increase first to the value of full discharge $Q_0$ at a depth $y_0'$ less than the full depth $y_0$. Thereafter, the discharge will reach a maximum value $Q_{max}$ at a depth $y_n^*$. Further increase in depth of flow will decrease the discharge eventually to the full discharge at the moment when the flow surface touches the top of the conduit. Figure 9-5$a$ shows the variation of normal discharge in such a conduit. In the case of a circular conduit, the depth $y_0' = 0.82y_0$ and $y_n^* = 0.938y_0$ where $y_0$ is the diameter of the conduit (Art. 6-4). Within the region of $y = y_0'$ and $y = y_0$, there are two possible normal depths for a given discharge, namely, the *lower normal depth* $y_n$ and the *upper* or *conjugate normal depth* $y_n'$.

Following the principle used in the preceding paragraphs, it can be demonstrated that four types of flow profiles are possible for a given slope [15–19]. Figure 9-5b, c, and d shows these profiles for mild and steep slopes. The positions of the depths $y_n$ and $y_n'$ are assumed constant in

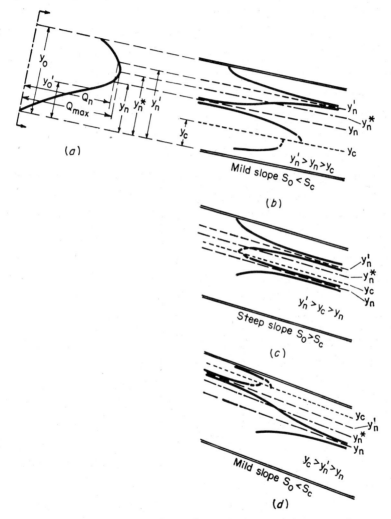

FIG. 9-5. Flow profiles in a closed conduit.

these figures. It should be noted that the critical depth in Fig. 9-5d is greater than the normal depths $y_n'$ and $y_n$, but that its corresponding lower normal depth is less than $y_n'$ and $y_n$. Consequently, the corresponding critical slope should be less than the normal slope, and the channel slope is considered mild.

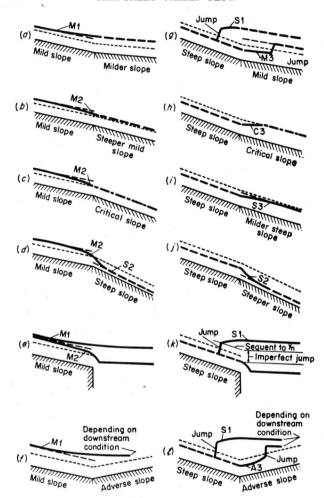

FIG. 9-6. Profiles of gradually varied flow in a long prismatic channel with a break in bottom slope.

**9-5. Analysis of Flow Profile.** Flow-profile analysis is a procedure used to predict the general shape of the flow profile. It enables the engineer to learn beforehand the possible flow profiles that may occur in a given channel layout. This procedure constitutes a very significant part of all problems in channel design for gradually varied flow.

*A. Prismatic Channel with Constant Slope.* The flow profile in a long prismatic channel with a constant slope has been described in Art. 9-4.

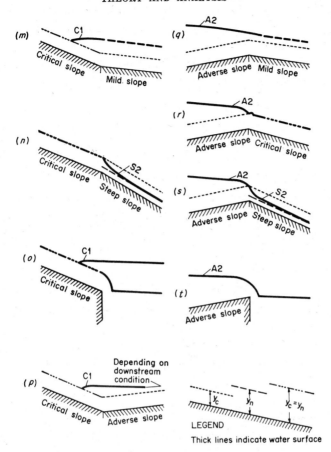

FIG. 9-6 (*Continued*).

Typical examples shown in Fig. 9-4 should be helpful in determining the type of flow profile in a given problem.

*B. Prismatic Channel with a Change in Slope.* This channel is equivalent to a pair of connected prismatic channels of the same cross section but with different slopes. Twenty typical flow profiles in a long prismatic channel with a break in slope are shown in Fig. 9-6. These profiles are self-explanatory. However, some special features should be mentioned:

1. The profile near or at the critical depth cannot be predicted precisely by the theory of gradually varied flow, since the flow is generally rapidly varied.

2. In passing a critical line, the flow profile should, theoretically, have a

vertical slope.   Since the flow is usually rapidly varied when passing the critical line, the actual slope of the profile cannot be predicted precisely by the theory.   For the same reason, the critical depth may not occur exactly above the break of the channel bottom and may be different from the depth shown in the figure.

3. In some cases (Fig. 9-6$g$ and $l$), the hydraulic jump may occur either in the upstream channel or in the downstream channel, depending upon the relative steepness of the two slopes.[1]   In case $g$, for instance, the jump will occur in the downstream channel if the normal depth in this channel is comparatively small.   When the slope of the downstream channel decreases and, accordingly, the normal depth increases, the jump will move upstream, eventually into the upstream channel.   The exact location of the jump will be discussed in Art. 15-7.

4. If the upstream channel has an adverse slope (Fig. 9-6$q$ to $t$), the discharge is fixed not by upstream channel conditions but by the elevation of the upstream pool level, which is the horizontal asymptote of the $A2$ profile.   The procedure of analysis is to assume a discharge and to determine to which case $q$ to $t$ the profile should belong.   Then, compute the flow profile in the upstream direction and determine the pool level. If the computed level does not agree with the given pool level, then repeat the computation with another assumed discharge until the computed level agrees with the given level.

5. Typical profiles (Fig. 9-6) are illustrated for long channels in which a uniform flow can be established far upstream and downstream.

*C. Prismatic Channel with Several Changes in Slope.*   For such channels the general procedure of analysis is as follows:

1. Plot the channel profile with an exaggerated vertical scale.

2. Compute $y_n$ for each reach, and plot the normal-depth line, shown by dashed lines, throughout the entire channel.

3. Compute $y_c$ for each reach, and plot the critical-depth line, shown by dotted lines, throughout the channel.

4. Locate all possible control sections.   At the control section,[2] flow must pass through a control depth which may be the critical depth, the normal depth, or any other known depth.   There are three types of control section:

*a.* UPSTREAM CONTROL SECTION.   This occurs in any steep reach at the upstream end, since the flow in a steep channel has to pass through the critical section at the upstream end and then follow either the $S1$ or $S2$ profile.   The critical depth is, therefore, the control depth (see also Art.

---

[1] Also depending on the relative roughness and shape of the two connecting channels.   In this discussion these factors are assumed constant.

[2] The term "control section" used here has a broad meaning.   It refers to any section at which the depth of flow is known or can be controlled to a required stage.

4-5).   If the downstream water surface is very high, it may raise the flow surface at the upstream control.   When several steep reaches occur in succession, the control section is at the upstream end of the uppermost reach.   Upstream control also occurs in long mild reaches, because the $M1$ or $M2$ curves will approach the normal depth at the upstream end.

   *b.* DOWNSTREAM CONTROL SECTION.   This occurs at the downstream end in any long steep reach, because the flow will approach the normal depth at the downstream end.   If the downstream end of a mild channel terminates at a free overfall, the control section may be assumed at the brink where the depth is critical.[1]

   *c.* ARTIFICIAL CONTROL SECTION.   This occurs at a control structure, such as a weir, dam, or sluice gate, at which the control depth either is known or can be determined.

   5. Starting at the control depth at each control section, trace in each reach a continuous profile.   The position of the profile in each reach can be correctly located with respect to the normal- and critical-depth lines. For this purpose, typical profiles described previously (Art. 9-4) should be found useful.

   6. When flow is supercritical in the upstream portion of a reach but subcritical in the downstream portion, the flow profile has to pass the critical depth somewhere in the reach.   In crossing the critical-depth line, a hydraulic jump is usually created in raising the water surface from a low depth to its sequent depth.   The exact location of the jump will be discussed later (Art. 15-7).

   **Example 9-1.**   The normal and critical depths of the flow in a channel have been computed and are shown in Fig. 9-7.   Sketch the possible flow profiles.
   *Solution.*   First locate the possible control sections, such as those for upstream control U.C., downstream control D.C., and artificial control A.C.   The artificial control in this example is a sluice which backs up water to form an $S1$ profile on the upstream side.   The formation of the hydraulic jumps in the middle and downstream reaches is apparent, but the determination of their exact positions requires further consideration.   In the lowermost reach, for instance, the $M2$ and $M3$ profiles should be computed first.   Then, compute the curve representing the sequent depth of the $M3$ profile.   The intersection of the sequent-depth curve and the $M2$ profile gives the approximate position of the jump.   A more exact value for the position of the jump may be obtained by correcting the position for the length of the jump. Various types of flow profile are sketched in the figure.

   *D. Nonprismatic Channels and Channels with Spatially Varied Flow.* In nonprismatic channels and channels with spatially varied flow, the analysis of flow becomes complicated by the fact that the control section may occur at any section in the channel and its position cannot be determined easily.   Consider three different channel slopes for three types of flow: (1) continuous flow in a prismatic channel (Fig. 9-8a), (2) spatially

---

[1] Actually the computed critical depth is somewhat behind the brink (Art. 3-4).

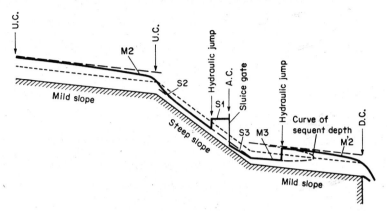

Fig. 9-7. Analysis of flow profile for Example 9-1. U.C. = upstream control; D.C. = downstream control; A.C. = artificial control.

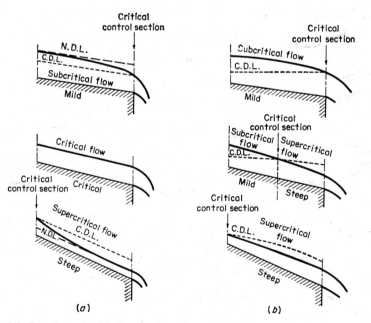

Fig. 9-8. Location of critical control section. (a) Flow in a prismatic channel; (b) flow in a nonprismatic channel or spatially varied flow.

varied flow of increasing discharge in a prismatic channel (Fig. 9-8b), and (3) continuous flow in a nonprismatic channel having a constant slope but varying cross section (Fig. 9-8b). All channels have a free overfall.

In the first type of flow, the flow changes from subcritical to supercritical as the channel slope varies from mild to steep. Accordingly, the critical control section will be transferred from the downstream end to the upstream end. It should be noted that the transfer of the critical control section occurs almost instantaneously. At the instant of transition,[1] the critical flow takes place throughout the entire length of the channel (middle view of Fig. 9-8a), and any section in the reach is, therefore, a critical section.

In the second and third types of flow, the transition of the state of flow will take place gradually from section to section as the critical control section moves upstream. At any moment during the time of transition (middle view of Fig. 9-8b), the flow downstream from the control section is supercritical, and the flow upstream is subcritical. The determination of the control section will be described in the next article.

**9-6. Method of Singular Point.** The preceding analysis of flow profiles was given primarily for prismatic channels. For a comprehensive treatment of flow profiles, in either prismatic or nonprismatic channels with constant or variable slope, use has been made of advanced mathematical approaches.[2] One approach is the use of the theory of the singular point. This theory was developed by Poincaré [22] but was first applied to flow studies in channels of variable slope by Massé [23]. The method based on this theory has been further discussed and extended by Jaeger [24], De Marchi [25], Hom-ma [26,27], Escoffier [28], Iwasa [29], and others.

For simplicity of discussion, channels with small slopes will be considered. Let the numerator and denominator of Eq. (9-15) be represented by two functions, or

$$\frac{dy}{dx} = S_0 \frac{1 - (Q/Q_n)^2}{1 - (Q/Q_c)^2} = \frac{F_1(x,y)}{F_2(x,y)} \qquad \text{or} \qquad \frac{F_1}{F_2} \qquad (9\text{-}20)$$

Then, set each of these functions equal to zero, or

$$F_1 = S_0 \left[ 1 - \left(\frac{Q}{Q_n}\right)^2 \right] = 0 \qquad (9\text{-}21)$$

and

$$F_2 = 1 - \left(\frac{Q}{Q_c}\right)^2 = 0 \qquad (9\text{-}22)$$

The solution of Eq. (9-21) $F_1 = 0$ will give $Q = Q_n$ or $y = y_n$. Hence,

---

[1] At this moment, the normal depth coincides with the critical depth, becoming a so-called transitional depth (Art. 9-6).

[2] See another method of analysis by Merten [20,21].

$F_1 = 0$ represents the normal-depth line in a prismatic channel. In nonprismatic channels, $F_1 = 0$ results in a fictitious normal-flow[1] profile. It is fictitious because uniform flow in nonprismatic channels is unrealistic.

Similarly, Eq. (9-22), $F_2 = 0$, represents the critical-flow profile. Since $Q_c$ is independent of the channel slope, the concept of the critical-flow profile is valid in channels of variable slope.

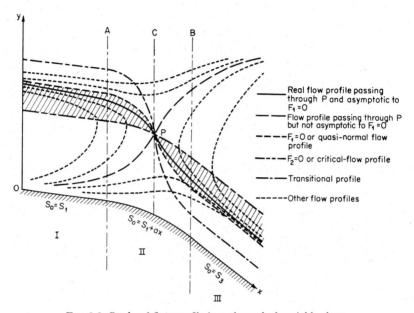

FIG. 9-9. Study of flow profile in a channel of variable slope.

In prismatic channels, $F_1 = 0$ and $F_2 = 0$ represent two parallel lines. In nonprismatic channels, however, the two profiles may intersect, say at point $P$ (Fig. 9-9). At point $P$, Eq. (9-20) gives $dy/dx = \%$, an indeterminate form. Such a point is known in mathematics as a *singular point.*

When $Q_n = Q_c$, $y_n = y_c$, which is a depth known as the *transitional depth.*[2] The curve representing this depth is called the *transitional profile.* A flow passing through this profile at the singular point will change its state from subcritical to supercritical or vice versa. In fact, the transitional profile must pass through the singular point, since at this point $Q_n = Q_c = Q$ or $y_n = y_c = y$. At other places where $Q_n = Q_c = Q$,

---

[1] Called by Massé [23] *quasi-normal flow.*

[2] Also known as the *characteristic depth,* which was first applied to uniform channels by Mouret [12] and later was discussed by Lazard [30].

Eq. (9-20) gives $dy/dx = S_0$; that is, a flow profile must be horizontal in crossing the transitional profile. Since the transitional profile is defined by the condition that $Q_n = Q_c$, its position is fixed by the channel characteristics but, unlike the normal and critical profiles, it is independent of change in discharge.

At this stage of the discussion, the reader must try to see clearly the differences between the transitional, normal, and critical profiles.

At the singular point, $y = y_c$; that is, the flow profile passes through the critical depth. Hence, there exists a critical section.

The slope of the water surface at the singular point is equal to the limiting value of the indeterminate form $dy/dx = \%$ if this form is convergent. By the differential calculus, this limiting value can be evaluated by

$$\frac{dy}{dx}\Big|_{\lim x \to x_c} = \left(\frac{dy}{dx}\right)_c = \left(\frac{dF_1}{dF_2}\right)_c = \left(\frac{dF_1/dx}{dF_2/dx}\right)_c \qquad (9\text{-}23)$$

The above discussion can be illustrated by a simple example. Consider a wide rectangular channel (Fig. 9-9) in which the flow changes from subcritical to supercritical according to the change in slope from a subcritical $S_1$ in reach I to a supercritical $S_3$ in reach III. The slope in the intermediate reach II is variable and may be expressed by $S_0 = S_1 + ax$, in which $a$ is a coefficient. Somewhere in reach II, at which $S_0 = S_c$, a critical section exists. This section can be determined by the simultaneous solution of $F_1 = 0$ and $F_2 = 0$. Graphically, this section lies at the intersection of the curves $F_1 = 0$ and $F_2 = 0$. The critical depth can be shown to be

$$y_c = \frac{g^3 n^6}{11 a^3 S_c^3} \qquad (9\text{-}24)$$

Considering a unit width of the channel, the critical depth is constant throughout the length of the channel; hence, the profile $F_2 = 0$ is equidistant from the channel bottom. In reach I the flow is subcritical; hence, the profile $F_1 = 0$ should be above $F_2 = 0$. In reach III the flow is supercritical, and the profile $F_1 = 0$ should be below $F_2 = 0$. The flow profile under consideration is shown by the heavy full curve in the shaded area between $F_1 = 0$ and $F_2 = 0$ in Fig. 9-9.

Since the transitional profile is defined by $Q_n = Q_c$, its equation can be shown to be

$$y = \frac{g^3 n^6}{11 a^3 (S_1 + ax)^3} \qquad (9\text{-}25)$$

At the critical section, where $S_1 + ax = S_c$, the above equation becomes Eq. (9-24).

To determine the slope of the water surface at the singular point in the present example by Eq. (9-23), the following equation can be obtained (using Manning's formula):

$$\left(\frac{dy}{dx}\right)_c^2 - \frac{10S_0}{9}\left(\frac{dy}{dx}\right)_c - \frac{y_c}{3}\left(\frac{dS_0}{dx}\right)_c = 0 \qquad (9\text{-}26)$$

This equation has two roots opposite in sign. The negative root will define a flow profile passing through the singular point $P$, with depth decreasing in the direction of flow. Since the flow in the present problem changes from subcritical to supercritical, this flow profile is evidently the profile of the flow under consideration. At $x = \pm\infty$, this profile is asymptotic to the profile of the quasi-normal flow, or $F_1 = 0$. The other root of Eq. (9-26) will define a flow profile also passing through $P$ but not asymptotic to $F_1 = 0$. Other profiles, which do not pass through $P$, will intersect the transitional profile with a horizontal slope, pass through $F_1 = 0$ with a hydraulic jump, and become asymptotic to the two profiles that pass through $P$.

The flow profile passing through $P$ but not asymptotic to $F_1 = 0$ is not the profile of the flow under consideration. However, such a flow profile may become real under some other circumstances. In Fig. 9-10,

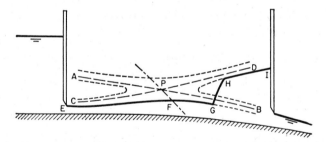

Fig. 9-10. Illustration of flow profiles defined by a singular point.

for example,[1] $P$ represents a singular point; $APB$ is the profile passing through $P$ and asymptotic to $F_1 = 0$; $CPD$ is the profile passing through $P$ but not asymptotic to $F_1 = 0$; and $EFG$ and $HI$ are other profiles not passing through $P$. The upstream gate has been adjusted to give the supercritical profile $EFG$ and the downstream gate to give the subcritical profile $HI$. The transition from one to the other takes place by means of the hydraulic jump $GH$. The upstream gate is now raised slowly to cause the profile $EF$ to approach $CP$ as a limit. As this is done, the pool is adjusted to keep the discharge constant. Simultaneously, the downstream gate is lowered to cause the profile $HI$ to approach $PD$ as a limit.

[1] This example was suggested by Mr. F. F. Escoffier of the U.S. Army Corps of Engineers. For simplicity, the curve for $F_1 = 0$ is not shown in Fig. 9-10.

As these operations are carried out, the jump $GH$ is forced upstream until its height is finally reduced to zero. In this way the profile $CPD$ is realized. Such a profile, however, is unstable, because a very slight increase in level in the profile $PD$ will entail a change from the profile $CP$ to the profile $AP$ and the space between the two will be filled with water.

A general solution of the condition $dy/dx = F_1/F_2 = \%$ for any kind of channel can be achieved mathematically by the method of singular point [31]. The result will produce four types of flow profile that can be developed theoretically around the singular point.[1] The four types are known as the *saddle*, *nodal*, *spiral*, and *vortex* types, as shown in Fig. 9-11,

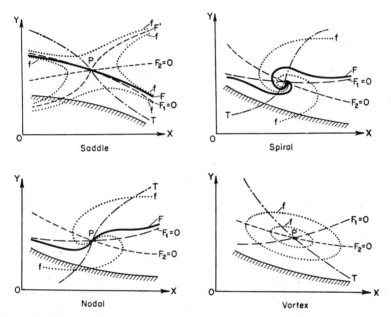

FIG. 9-11. Flow profiles around a singular point. $P$ = singular point; $F$ = flow profile passing through $P$ and asymptotic to $F_1 = 0$; $F'$ = flow profile passing through $P$ but not asymptotic to $F_1 = 0$; $f$ = other flow profiles; $F_1$ = quasi-normal flow profile; $F_2$ = critical-flow profile; and $T$ = transitional profile.

where the profiles are plotted with the ordinate $Y$ representing the distance above a horizontal datum and the abscissa $X$ representing the distance along the datum.

The possible flow profiles presented in the example of Fig. 9-9 are of the saddle type. In this case, the flow profile that passes through $P$ and is asymptotic to $F_1 = 0$ indicates a continuous flow changing

[1] For further discussion, see [23] and [28].

from subcritical to supercritical in a channel with slightly convex bed $(S_1 < S_c < S_3)$.

In the nodal type, the flow profile that passes through $P$ and is asymptotic to $F_1 = 0$ indicates a continuous flow changing from supercritical to subcritical in a channel with slightly concave bed $(S_1 > S_c > S_3)$.

In the spiral type, the flow profile that passes through $P$ and is asymptotic to $F_1 = 0$ indicates a discontinuous flow[1] changing from supercritical to subcritical in a channel with slightly concave bed $(S_1 > S_c > S_3)$.

In the vortex type, the flow profile that passes through the singular point is the point itself and has no hydraulic significance. A general solution for the transitional profile in all four types has been given by Escoffier [28].

**9-7. The Transitional Depth.** A little more may be said about the transitional depth,[2] which has been defined as the depth at which $Q_n = Q_c$, $y_n = y_c$, and the slope of the flow profile is horizontal, or $dy/dx = S_0$. Equate the right side of Eq. (9-13) to $S_0$ and simplify the equation; then

$$\frac{K_n}{K} = \frac{Z_c}{Z} \qquad (9\text{-}27)$$

Let $K_n = Q/\sqrt{S_0}$, $K = 1.49 A R^{\frac{2}{3}}/n$, $Z_c = Q/\sqrt{g}$, and $Z = A\sqrt{D}$. Then, the above equation becomes

$$2.22 R^{\frac{4}{3}} S_0 = n^2 g D \qquad (9\text{-}28)$$

This is a theoretical condition for the establishment of the transitional depth. It indicates that the transitional depth depends only on the channel geometry, roughness, and slope. This equation contains no discharge; therefore, the transitional depth is independent of the actual discharge.

It is logical to say that there is a certain discharge $Q_t$ that occurs at the transitional depth $y_t$. This discharge may be called the *transitional discharge*. According to the definition of the transitional depth, the transitional discharge should be a normal discharge and also a critical discharge. Referring to the critical-slope curve discussed in Example 6-5 (Figs. 6-8 and 9-12), the transitional discharge can be represented by a point on the curve. It is evident from the curve that, for a given slope $S_0$, which is greater than the limit slope $S_L$, there are two possible critical discharges, say, $Q_a$ and $Q_b$, both of which are transitional discharges. The actual discharge is designated by $Q$ and the corresponding critical slope by $S_c$.

---

[1] Here the upstream normal flow changes to the downstream normal flow at an abrupt transition formed by a hydraulic jump.

[2] See [12], [19], [28] to [30], and [32].

For purposes of discussion, take the case of the backwater behind a dam as an example.   When $S_0 < S_L$ (Fig. 9-12a), it is apparent that the flow is always subcritical and that the corresponding backwater profile is of the $M1$ type.   When $S_0 > S_L$, the condition depends as follows on the relation of $S_0$ to $S_L$.

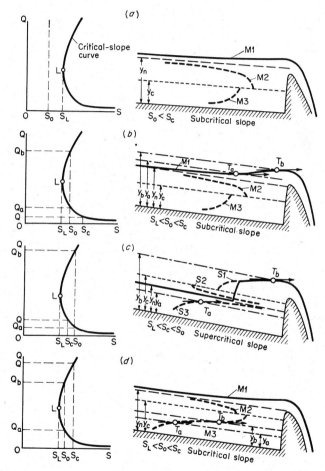

Fig. 9-12. Flow profiles explained by a critical-slope curve.

A. When the slope is close to the limit slope.   In this case, the condition will depend further on the magnitude of the actual discharge $Q$ with respect to the smaller and larger transitional discharges $Q_a$ and $Q_b$, respectively.

If $Q < Q_a$ (Fig. 9-12$b$), then $S_0 < S_c$ and $y_c < y_n < y_a < y_b$. Since $S_0 < S_c$, the flow is subcritical, and the profile should be of the $M1$ type. However, the profile will contain two points $T_a$ and $T_b$ at which the slope is horizontal. Between these two points a point of inflection apparently exists. The depths at the two points are transitional depths $y_a$ and $y_b$.

If $Q_a < Q < Q_b$ (Fig. 9-12$c$), then $S_0 > S_c$ and $y_a < y_n < y_c < y_b$. Since $S_0 > S_c$, the flow profiles are of the $S$ type. However, there will be a point $T_b$ where the slope is horizontal on the $S1$ profile and a point $T_a$ where the slope is horizontal on the $S3$ profile.

If $Q_a < Q_b < Q$ (Fig. 9-12$d$), then $S_0 < S_c$ and $y_a < y_b < y_c < y_n$. The transitional depths will intersect only the $M3$ profile, and the backwater profile will be of the ordinary $M1$ type.

B. *When the slope is far away from the limit slope.* In this case, $Q_a$ and $y_a$ are relatively very small, and their existence is practically insignificant. If $Q > Q_b$, the flow will be subcritical and the profile will be of the $M1$ type. If $Q < Q_b$, the flow will be supercritical and the profile will be of the $S1$ type.

C. *When the slope is very large.* In this case, the large transitional discharge $Q_b$ is considered to exceed the maximum expected discharge (see Fig. 6-8). Thus, the flow is supercritical and the profile is of the $S1$ type. The highest point of the $S1$ profile is very close to the downstream end.

The above discussion was developed for the case in which the point $L$ of the limit slope is below the curve of maximum expected discharge (Fig. 6-8$a$) and in which the channel sections are rectangular or trapezoidal or similar to such forms. If the point $L$ is above the curve of maximum expected discharge (Fig. 6-8$b$), the larger transitional depth of the flow will be greater than the maximum expected depth, or $y_b > y_m$, and the larger transitional discharge will be greater than the maximum expected discharge, or $Q_b > Q_m$. The foregoing discussion, however, remains valid as long as the actual discharge $Q$ does not exceed $Q_m$. If $Q$ exceeds $Q_m$, the discussion has no practical meaning. Similarly, the flow profiles remain the same, but the useful part of the profiles will be where the depths are less than $y_m$.

## PROBLEMS

**9-1.** Show that the water-surface slope $S_w$ of a gradually varied flow is equal to the sum of the energy slope $S$ and the slope due to velocity change $d(\alpha V^2/2g)/dx$.

**9-2.** Show that the gradually-varied-flow equation is reduced to a uniform-flow formula if $dy/dx = 0$.

**9-3.** Prove Eq. (9-14).

**9-4.** Prove Eq. (9-15).

**9-5.** Prove Eq. (9-16).

**9-6.** Prove Eqs. (9-17) and (9-18).

**9-7.** Sketch the possible flow profiles in the channels shown in Fig. 9-13.

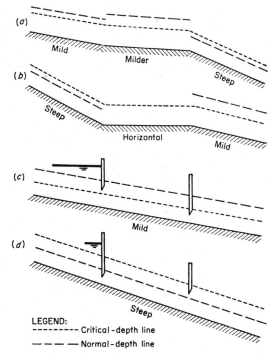

Fig. 9-13. Channels for Prob. 9-7. The vertical scale is exaggerated.

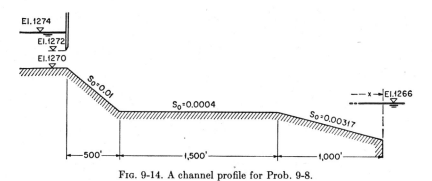

Fig. 9-14. A channel profile for Prob. 9-8.

**9-8.** A rectangular channel (Fig. 9-14), 20 ft wide, consists of three reaches of different slopes. The channel has a roughness coefficient $n = 0.015$ and carries a discharge of 500 cfs. Determine:

*a.* the normal and critical depths in each reach

    *b.* the possible flow profiles

    *c.* the distance $x$ from the outlet of the channel to the point where the backwater curve terminates. The backwater curve is assumed to be a horizontal line.

**9-9.** Prove Eqs. (9-24) to (9-26).

**9-10.** A change in slope from 0.0016 to 0.0064 occurs in a wide rectangular channel (Fig. 9-9). The length of the transition is 10 ft, and the slope in the transition reach is $S_0 = 0.0016 + 0.00048x$, where $x$ is the distance measured from the beginning of the change. The channel carries a discharge of 100 cfs per unit width. Assume that $\alpha = 1$ and $n = 0.02$.

    *a.* Determine the control section.

    *b.* Compute the slope of the flow profile at the control section.

    *c.* Construct the transitional, normal, and critical profiles.

    *d.* Construct the real and some other possible flow profiles.

**9-11.** Show that the gradually-varied-flow equation for flow in a rectangular channel of variable width $b$ may be expressed as

$$\frac{dy}{dx} = \frac{S_0 - S_f + (\alpha Q^2 y / gA^3)(db/dx)}{1 - \alpha Q^2 b / gA^3} \tag{9-29}$$

All notation has been previously defined.

## REFERENCES

1. J. B. Bélanger: "Essai sur la solution numérique de quelques problèmes relatifs au mouvement permanent des eaux courantes" ("Essay on the Numerical Solution of Some Problems Relative to the Steady Flow of Water"), Carilian-Goeury, Paris, 1828.
2. J. A. Ch. Bresse: "Cours de mecanique appliquée," 2e partie, Hydraulique ("Course in Applied Mechanics," pt. 2, Hydraulics), Mallet-Bachelier, Paris, 1860.
3. Boris A. Bakhmeteff: "Hydraulics of Open Channels," appendix I, Historical and bibliographical notes, McGraw-Hill Book Company, Inc., New York, 1932, pp. 299–301.
4. Charles Jaeger: Steady flow in open channels: The problem of Boussinesq, *Journal, Institution of Civil Engineers, London*, vol. 29–30, pp. 338–348, November, 1947–October, 1948.
5. Charles Jaeger: "Engineering Fluid Mechanics," translated from the German by P. O. Wolf, Blackie & Son, Ltd., Glasgow, 1956, pp. 93–97.
6. F. Bettes: Non-uniform flow in channels, *Civil Engineering and Public Works Review*, London, vol. 52, no. 609, pp. 323–324, March, 1957; no. 610, pp. 434–436, April, 1957.
7. J. Allen: Streamline and turbulent flow in open channels, *The London, Edinburgh and Dublin Philosophical Magazine and Journal of Science*, ser. 7, vol. 17, pp. 1081–1112, June, 1934.
8. Hunter Rouse and Merit P. White: Discussion on Varied flow in open channels of adverse slope, by Arthur E. Matzke, *Transactions, American Society of Civil Engineers*, vol. 102, pp. 671–676, 1937.
9. Sherman M. Woodward and Chesley J. Posey: "Hydraulics of Steady Flow in Open Channels," John Wiley & Sons, Inc., New York, 1941, p. 70.
10. Ivan M. Nelidov: Discussion on Surface curves for steady nonuniform flow, by Robert B. Jansen, *Transactions, American Society of Civil Engineers*, vol. 117, pp. 1098–1102, 1952.

11. Dwight F. Gunder: Profile curves for open-channel flow, *Transactions, American Society of Civil Engineers*, vol. 108, pp. 481–488, 1943.

12. G. Mouret: "Hydraulique: Cours de mécanique appliquée" ("Hydraulics: Course in Applied Mechanics"), L'École Nationale des Ponts et Chaussées, Paris, 1922–1923, pp. 447–458; revised as "Hydraulique générale" ("General Hydraulics"), cours de l'École Nationale des Ponts et Chaussées, Paris, 1927–1928.

13. A. Merten: Recherches sur la forme des axes hydrauliques dans un lit prismatique (Studies on the form of flow profiles in a prismatic channel), *Annales de l' Association des Ingénieurs sortis des Écoles Spéciales de Gand*, Ghent, Belgium, vol. 5, ser. 3, 1906.

14. M. Boudin: De l'axe hydraulique des cours d'eau contenus dans un lit prismatique et des dispositifs réalisant, en pratique, ses formes diverses (The flow profiles of water in a prismatic channel and actual dispositions in various forms), *Annales des travaux publiques de Belgique*, Brussels, vol. 20, pp. 397–555, 1861–1862.

15. Pierre Koch: Justification de l'étude rationnelle du remous dans les aqueducs de forme circulaire, ovoide ou analogue (Justification of the rational study of backwater in circular conduits of ovoid or similar shape), *Annales des ponts et chaussées*, pp. 153–202, September–October, 1933.

16. L. Gherardelli: Sull'equazione del moto permanente in alvei prismatici (On the equation for steady flow in prismatic channels), *L'Energia elettrica, Milano*, vol 28, no. 4, pp. 185–189, April, 1951.

17. Gianni Formica: Nota sui profili di rigurgito delle correnti permanenti gradualmente variate defluenti in gallerie cilindriche (Note on backwater curves of gradually varied steady flow in cylindrical closed conduits), *L'Energia elettrica, Milano*, vol. 29, no. 8, pp. 480–491, August, 1952; reprinted as *Istituto di Idraulica e Costruzioni Idrauliche, Milano, Memorie e studi No. 97*, 14 pp.

18. R. Silber: Sur la forme des courbes des remous en galerie couverte (On backwater curves in closed conduit), extrait des *Comptes rendus des séances de l'Académie des Sciences*, vol. 236, pp. 2377–2379, June 22, 1953.

19. R. Silber: "Étude et tracé des écoulements permanents en canaux et rivières" ("Study and Outline of Steady Flow in Open Channels"), Dunod, Paris, 1954.

20. A. Merten: Théorèmes fondamentaux d'hydraulique fluviale (Fundamental theorems of fluvial hydraulics), *Annales de l'Association des Ingénieurs sortis des Écoles Spéciales de Gand*, Ghent, Belgium, ser. 5, vol. 5, no. 2, pp. 206–210, 1912.

21. L. J. Tison: "Cours d'hydraulique" ("Hydraulics"), Université de Gand, Ghent, Belgium, 1953, pt. II, pp. 170–182.

22. H. Poincaré: Mémoire sur les courbes definies par une equation differentielle (Memoir on the curves defined by a differential equation), *Journal de mathématiques pures et appliquées*, Paris, vol. 7, pp. 375–422, 1881.

23. Pierre Massé: Ressaut et ligne d'eau dans les cours d'eau à pente variable (Hydraulic jump and flow profile in channels of variable slope), *Revue générale de l'hydraulique*, Paris, vol. 4, no. 19, pp. 7–11, January, and no. 20, pp. 61–64, April, 1938.

24. Charles Jaeger: Erweiterung der Boussinesqschen Theorie des Abflüsses in offenen Gerinnen und der Abflüsse über abgerundete Wehre (Extension of the Boussinesq theory of flow in open channels and over a round-crested weir), *Wasserkraft und Wasserwirtschaft*, Munich, vol. 35, no. 4, pp. 83–86, Apr. 15, 1940.

25. Giulio De Marchi: Sul cambiamento di regime di una correnti lineare a pelo libero in un alvea di sezione costante (On the transition between supercritical and subcritical conditions in free-surface gradually varied flow in a cylindrical channel), *L'Energia elettrica, Milano*, vol. 27, no. 3, pp. 125–132, March, 1950; reprinted as *Istituto di Idraulica e Costruzioni Idrauliche, Milano, Memorie e studi No. 82*, 1950.

26. Masashi Hom-ma: "General Hydraulics" (in Japanese), vol. 1 of "Applied Hydraulics," edited by Masashi Hom-ma and Tojiro Ishihara, Maruzen, Tokyo, 1958, pp. 108–111.

27. Masahi Hom-ma and Sukeyuki Shima: On the flow in a gradually diverged open channel, *The Japan Science Review, Series* I, Tokyo, vol. 2, no. 3, pp. 253–260, 1952.

28. Francis F. Escoffier: Transition profiles in nonuniform channels, *Transactions, American Society of Civil Engineers*, vol. 123, pp. 43–56, 1958.

29. Yoshiaki Iwasa, Hydraulic significance of transitional behaviours of flows in channel transitions and controls, *Memoirs of the Faculty of Engineering, Kyoto University*, Japan, vol. XX, no. 4, pp. 237–276, October, 1958.

30. Achille Lazard: Contribution à l'étude théorique du mouvement graduellement varié en hydraulique (Contribution to the theoretical study of gradually varied flow in hydraulics), *Annales des ponts et chaussées*, vol. 117, no. 2, pp. 185–219, March-April, 1947.

31. Theodore von Kármán and Maurice A. Biot: "Mathematical Methods in Engineering," McGraw-Hill Book Company, Inc., New York, 1940, pp. 150–158.

32. E. Crausse: "Hydraulique des canaux découverts en régime permanent" ("Hydraulics of Open Channels with Steady Flow Regime"), Éditions Eyrolles, Paris, 1951.

# CHAPTER 10

# METHODS OF COMPUTATION

The computation of gradually-varied-flow profiles involves basically the solution of the dynamic equation of gradually varied flow. The main objective of the computation is to determine the shape of the flow profile. Broadly classified, there are three methods of computation; namely, the graphical-integration method, the direct-integration method, and the step method. The development and procedure of several typical methods will be described in this chapter.

**10-1. The Graphical-integration Method.** This method is to integrate the dynamic equation of gradually varied flow by a graphical procedure. Consider two channel sections (Fig. 10-1a) at distances $x_1$ and $x_2$, respectively, from a chosen origin and with corresponding depths of flow $y_1$ and $y_2$. The distance along the channel floor is

$$x = x_2 - x_1 = \int_{x_1}^{x_2} dx = \int_{y_1}^{y_2} \frac{dx}{dy}\, dy$$
$$(10\text{-}1)$$

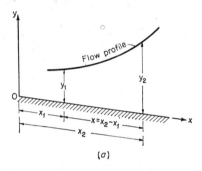

(a)

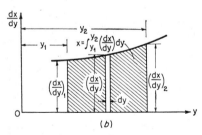

(b)

Fig. 10-1. Principle of the graphical-integration method.

Assume several values of $y$, and compute the corresponding values of $dx/dy$, which is the reciprocal of the right-side member of a gradually-varied-flow equation, say Eq. (9-13). A curve of $y$ against $dx/dy$ is then constructed (Fig. 10-1b). According to Eq. (10-1), it is apparent that the value of $x$ is equal to the shaded area formed by the curve, the $y$ axis, and the ordinates of $dx/dy$ corresponding to $y_1$ and $y_2$. This area can be measured and the value of $x$ determined.

This method has broad application. It applies to flow in prismatic as well as nonprismatic channels of any shape and slope. The procedure is straightforward and easy to follow. It may, however, become very laborious when applied to actual problems. A relatively simple example will be given as an illustration.

**Example 10-1.** A trapezoidal channel having $b = 20$ ft, $z = 2$, $S_0 = 0.0016$, and $n = 0.025$ carries a discharge of 400 cfs. Compute the backwater profile created by a dam which backs up the water to a depth of 5 ft immediately behind the dam. The upstream end of the profile is assumed at a depth equal to 1% greater than the normal depth. The energy coefficient $\alpha = 1.10$.

*Solution.* Following the solutions of Examples 4-2 and 6-2, the critical and normal depths are found to be $y_c = 2.22$ ft and $y_n = 3.36$ ft, respectively. Since $y_n$ is greater than $y_c$ and the flow starts with a depth greater than $y_n$, the flow profile is of the $M1$ type. The section factor $Z_c = 400/\sqrt{g/\alpha} = 74.0$ and the conveyance $K_n = 400/\sqrt{0.0016} = 10,000$.

For simplicity, the channel bottom at the site of the dam is chosen as the origin and the $x$ value in the upstream direction is taken as positive. The computation of $dx/dy$ by means of Eq. (9-13) is given in Table 10-1 for various values of $y$ varying from 5 ft

TABLE 10-1. COMPUTATION OF THE FLOW PROFILE FOR EXAMPLE 10-1 BY
GRAPHICAL INTEGRATION

$Q = 400$ cfs    $n = 0.025$    $S_0 = 0.0016$    $y_c = 2.22$ ft    $y_n = 3.36$ ft    $\alpha = 1.10$

| $y$ | $T$ | $A$ | $R$ | $R^{2/3}$ | $K$ | $Z$ | $dx/dy$ | $\Delta A$ | $x$ |
|------|-------|--------|------|-------|--------|-------|--------|------|-------|
| 5.00 | 40.00 | 150.00 | 3.54 | 2.323 | 20,800 | 290.2 | 760 | | |
| 4.80 | 39.20 | 142.08 | 3.43 | 2.274 | 19,230 | 270.4 | 792 | 155 | 155 |
| 4.60 | 38.40 | 134.32 | 3.31 | 2.221 | 17,770 | 251.5 | 836 | 163 | 318 |
| 4.40 | 37.60 | 126.72 | 3.19 | 2.167 | 16,360 | 232.3 | 913 | 175 | 493 |
| 4.20 | 36.80 | 119.28 | 3.08 | 2.117 | 15,050 | 214.5 | 1,000 | 191 | 684 |
| 4.00 | 36.00 | 112.00 | 2.96 | 2.062 | 13,750 | 197.5 | 1,140 | 214 | 898 |
| 3.80 | 35.20 | 104.88 | 2.84 | 2.006 | 12,550 | 181.0 | 1,430 | 257 | 1,155 |
| 3.70 | 34.80 | 101.38 | 2.77 | 1.972 | 11,910 | 173.0 | 1,750 | 159 | 1,314 |
| 3.60 | 34.40 | 97.92 | 2.71 | 1.944 | 11,350 | 165.0 | 2,260 | 201 | 1,515 |
| 3.55 | 34.20 | 96.21 | 2.68 | 1.929 | 11,060 | 161.1 | 2,770 | 126 | 1,641 |
| 3.50 | 34.00 | 94.50 | 2.65 | 1.916 | 10,800 | 157.3 | 3,480 | 156 | 1,797 |
| 3.47 | 33.88 | 93.48 | 2.63 | 1.904 | 10,600 | 155.2 | 4,520 | 120 | 1,917 |
| 3.44 | 33.76 | 92.45 | 2.61 | 1.894 | 10,440 | 153.0 | 5,990 | 158 | 2,075 |
| 3.42 | 33.68 | 91.80 | 2.60 | 1.890 | 10,340 | 151.7 | 7,930 | 139 | 2,214 |
| 3.40 | 33.60 | 91.12 | 2.59 | 1.886 | 10,230 | 150.0 | 10,760 | 187 | 2,401 |
| 3.36 | 33.44 | 89.78 | 2.56 | 1.872 | 10,000 | 147.0 | | | |

to 1% greater than $y_n$ or 3.40 ft. For instance, when $y = 5.00$ ft, the values in other columns of the table are

$T = 40.00$ ft
$A = 150.00$ ft$^2$
$R = 3.54$ ft
$R^{2/3} = 2.323$

$$K = \frac{1.49AR^{\frac{2}{3}}}{n} = \frac{1.49 \times 150.00 \times 2.323}{0.025} = 20{,}800$$

$$Z = \sqrt{\frac{A^3}{T}} = \sqrt{\frac{150.00^3}{40.00}} = 290.2$$

$$\frac{dx}{dy} = \frac{1}{S_0}\frac{1 - (Z_c/Z)^2}{1 - (K_n/K)^2} = \frac{1}{0.0016}\frac{1 - (74.0/290.2)^2}{1 - (10{,}000/20{,}800)^2} = 760$$

Values of $y$ are then plotted against the corresponding values of $dx/dy$ (Fig. 10-2). The increments in area $\Delta A$ are planimetered and listed in the table. According to Eq. (10-1), the cumulative values of $\Delta A$ should give the length $x$ of the flow profile. Finally, the backwater profile is obtained by plotting $y$ against $x$ (Fig. 10-3).

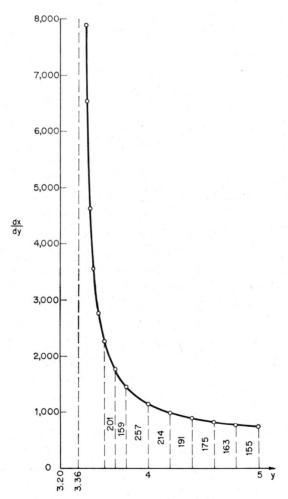

FIG. 10-2. A curve of $y$ vs. $dx/dy$.

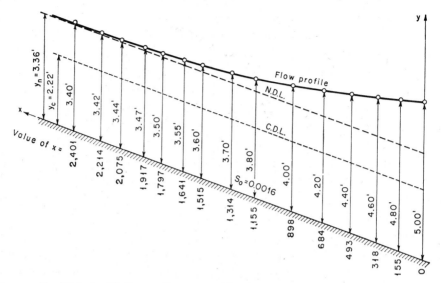

FIG. 10-3. An $M1$ flow profile computed by the graphical-integration method.

It should be noted that, when the depth approaches the normal depth, the incremental area varies so greatly with the change in $y$ value that it becomes difficult to planimeter. In such a case, the area may be computed by assuming it is a trapezoid. For instance, the incremental area between $y = 3.42$ and $3.40$ is $\Delta A = (7,930 + 10,760)(3.42 - 3.40)/2 = 187$.

**10-2. Method of Direct Integration.** The differential equation of gradually varied flow cannot be expressed explicitly in terms of $y$ for all types of channel cross section; hence, a direct and exact integration of the equation is practically impossible. Many attempts have been made either to solve the equation for a few special cases or to introduce assumptions that make the equation amenable to mathematical integration. Table 10-2 gives a list of many existing methods of direct integration, arranged chronologically. Although the list is incomplete, it provides a general idea of the development of the direct-integration method. Note that most of the early methods were developed for channels of a specific cross section but that later solutions, since Bakhmeteff, were designed for channels of all shapes. Most early methods use Chézy's formula, whereas later methods use Manning's formula.

In the Bakhmeteff method [8] the channel length under consideration is divided into short reaches. The change in the critical slope within the small range of the varying depth in each reach is assumed constant,[1] and

[1] In the Bakhmeteff method, Eq. (9-14) is used. The coefficient $r$ in this equation is assumed constant in the reach. Thus, it can be shown that the ratio of the change

TABLE 10-2. EXISTING METHODS OF INTEGRATING THE
GRADUALLY-VARIED-FLOW EQUATION

| Year of publication | Investigator | Type of channel | Effect of change in kinetic energy | Velocity formula | Assumptions for hydraulic exponents | Reference |
|---|---|---|---|---|---|---|
| 1848 | Dupuit | Broad rectangle | Ignored | Chézy | $N = 3, M = 3$ | [1] |
| 1860 | Bresse | Broad rectangle | Considered | Chézy | $N = 3, M = 3$ | [2] |
| 1875 | Grashof | Broad rectangle | Considered | Chézy | $N = 3, M = 3$ | [3] |
| 1880 | Rühlmann | Broad rectangle | Ignored | Chézy | $N = 3, M = 3$ | [4] |
| 1898 | Tolkmitt | Broad parabola | Considered | Chézy | $N = 4, M = 4$ | [5] |
| 1900 | Masoni | Common rectangle | Considered | Chézy | $N = 3, M = 3$ | [6] |
| 1912 (1932) | Bakhmeteff | All shapes | Considered by steps | Chézy | $K^2 \propto y^N$ | [7,8] |
| 1914 | Schaffernak-Ehrenberger | Broad rectangle | Ignored | $Cy^{0.75}S^{0.5}$ $23.78y^{0.775}S^{0.458}$ $22.11y^{0.55}S^{0.43}$ | $N = 3.5, M = 3$ $N = 3.552, M = 3$ $N = 3.16, M = 3$ | [9] |
| 1921 | Baticle | Approximate trapezoid | Ignored | Chézy | $K^2 = z^5 = A^2R$, where $z$ is a variable and $dy/dz = $ const | [10] |
| 1928 | Koženy | Broad rectangle | Considered | $Cy^{0.7}S^{0.5}$ | $N = 3.4, M = 3$ | [11] |
| 1930 | Schoklisch | Broad rectangle | Ignored | $CR^m S^p$ | $N = 2 + 2m, M = 3$ | [12] |
| 1938 | Mononobe | All shapes | Considered | $CR^m S^{0.5}$ | $P \propto y^{\text{const}}, A^2 \propto y^{\text{const}}$ | [13] |
| 1947 | Lee | All shapes | Considered | Manning | $K^2 \propto y^N, A^2 \propto y^{\text{const}}$ | [14,15] |
| 1950 | Von Seggern | All shapes | Considered | Manning | $K^2 \propto y^N, Z^2 \propto y^M$ | [16] |
| 1954 | Keifer-Chu | Circular, but the method may be extended to other shapes | Considered | Manning | None | [17] |

the integration is carried out by short-range steps and with the aid of a varied-flow function.

In an attempt to improve Bakhmeteff's method, Mononobe [13] introduced two assumptions for hydraulic exponents. By these assumptions the effects of velocity change and friction head are taken into account integrally without the necessity of dividing the channel length into short reaches. Thus, the Mononobe method affords a more direct and accurate computation procedure whereby results can be obtained without recourse

in kinetic energy to the friction slope, or $r$ in Eq. (9-14), is assumed constant in each reach. Since an increase or decrease in depth will change both these factors in the same direction, their ratio is relatively stable and can be assumed constant for practical purposes.

to successive steps.  In applying this method to practical problems, it has been found that the first assumption (see Table 10-2) is not very satisfactory in many cases.  Another drawback of this method perhaps lies in the difficulty of using the accompanying charts, which are not sufficiently accurate for practical purposes.

Later, Lee [14] and Von Seggern [16] suggested new assumptions which result in more satisfactory solutions.  Von Seggern introduced a new varied-flow function in addition to the function used by Bakhmeteff; hence, an additional table for the new function is necessary in his method.  In Lee's method, however, no new function is required.

The method [18] described here is the outcome of a study of many existing methods.  By this method, the hydraulic exponents are expressed in terms of the depth of flow.  From Eqs. (6-10) and (4-6), $K_n{}^2 = C_1 y_n{}^N$, $K^2 = C_1 y^N$, $Z_c{}^2 = C_2 y_c{}^M$, and $Z^2 = C_2 y^M$, where $C_1$ and $C_2$ are coefficients.  If these expressions are substituted in Eq. (9-13), the gradually-varied-flow equation becomes

$$\frac{dy}{dx} = S_0 \frac{1 - (y_n/y)^N}{1 - (y_c/y)^M} \qquad (10\text{-}2)$$

Let $u = y/y_n$; the above equation may be expressed for $dx$ as

$$dx = \frac{y_n}{S_0}\left[ 1 - \frac{1}{1 - u^N} + \left(\frac{y_c}{y_n}\right)^M \frac{u^{N-M}}{1 - u^N}\right] du \qquad (10\text{-}3)$$

This equation can be integrated for the length $x$ of the flow profile.  Since the change in depth of a gradually varied flow is generally small, the hydraulic exponents may be assumed constant within the range of the limits of integration.  In a case where the hydraulic exponents are noticeably dependent on $y$ within the limits of a given reach, the reach should be subdivided for integration; then the hydraulic exponents in each subdivided reach may be assumed constant.  Integrating Eq. (10-3),

$$x = \frac{y_n}{S_0}\left[ u - \int_0^u \frac{du}{1 - u^N} + \left(\frac{y_c}{y_n}\right)^M \int_0^u \frac{u^{N-M}}{1 - u^N} du\right] + \text{const} \qquad (10\text{-}4)$$

The first integral on the right side of the above equation is designated by $F(u,N)$, or

$$F(u,N) = \int_0^u \frac{du}{1 - u^N} \qquad (10\text{-}5)$$

which is known as the *varied-flow function*.

The second integral in Eq. (10-4) may also be expressed in the form of the varied-flow function.  Let $v = u^{N/J}$ and $J = N/(N - M + 1)$; this integral can be transformed into

$$\int_0^u \frac{u^{N-M}}{1 - u^N} du = \frac{J}{N} \int_0^v \frac{dv}{1 - v^J} = \frac{J}{N} F(v,J) \qquad (10\text{-}6)$$

where 
$$F(v,J) = \int_0^v \frac{dv}{1 - v^J} \tag{10-7}$$

This is a varied-flow function like $F(u,N)$, except that the variables $u$ and $N$ are replaced by $v$ and $J$, respectively.[1]

Using the notation for varied-flow functions, Eq. (10-4) may be written

$$x = \frac{y_n}{S_0}\left[u - F(u,N) + \left(\frac{y_c}{y_n}\right)^M \frac{J}{N} F(v,J)\right] + \text{const} \tag{10-8}$$

or 
$$x = A[u - F(u,N) + BF(v,J)] + \text{const} \tag{10-9}$$

where

$$A = \frac{y_n}{S_0}, \quad B = \left(\frac{y_c}{y_n}\right)^M \frac{J}{N}, \quad u = \frac{y}{y_n}, \quad v = u^{N/J}, \quad J = \frac{N}{N - M + 1}$$

and where $F(u,N)$ and $F(v,J)$ are varied-flow functions.

By Eq. (10-9), the length of flow profile between two consecutive sections 1 and 2 is equal to

$$
\begin{aligned}
L &= x_2 - x_1 \\
&= A\{(u_2 - u_1) - [F(u_2,N) - F(u_1,N)] + B[F(v_2,J) - F(v_1,J)]\}
\end{aligned}
\tag{10-10}
$$

where the subscripts 1 and 2 refer to sections 1 and 2, respectively.

Equation (10-10) contains varied-flow functions, and its solution can be simplified by the use of the *varied-flow-function table*, which is given in Appendix D.[2] This table gives values of $F(u,N)$ for $N$ ranging from 2.2 to 9.8. Replacing values of $u$ and $N$ by corresponding values of $v$ and $J$, this table also gives values of $F(v,J)$.

---

[1] This transformation was also performed independently by Levi [19].

[2] The preparation of such a table was undertaken and performed for the first time during 1914-1915 by the Research Board of the then Russian Reclamation Service under the direction of Boris A. Bakhmeteff, then Professor of General and Advanced Hydraulics at Polytechnic Institute Emperor Peter the Great, St. Petersburg, Russia. It was said that the work had involved a long and tedious procedure [8]. In the turmoil of the Russian Revolution in 1917, the table so computed became unavailable; so the task of computing was done over again by Professor Kholodovsky and partly by Dr. Pestrečov. The recomputed table was more precise and complete, covering a range of $N$ from 2.8 to 5.4. This table was published in 1932 [8] when Bakhmeteff became Professor of Civil Engineering at Columbia University. In the meantime, in the U.S.S.R. in 1928, the unavailable table, copied in hand-written form, had been published in a second edition of [7] with values of $N$ equal to 2.0, 2.5, 3.0, 3.25, 3.5, 3.75, 4.0, 4.5, 5.0, and 5.5. Methods of computing the varied-flow-function table are explained in pp. 303–305 of Bakhmeteff's book [8]. An error in printing should be noted in that book; that is, a negative sign should be placed in front of the entire right-side member of the equation printed near the bottom of p. 305. Table D-1 given in Appendix D is an extension of Bakhmeteff's table to almost triple its original size. It was prepared by the author in 1952–1954 for teaching purposes at the University of Illinois, and was published in 1955 [18].

In computing a flow profile, first the flow in the channel is analyzed (Art. 9-5), and the channel is divided into a number of reaches. Then, the length of each reach is computed by Eq. (10-10) from known or assumed depths at the ends of the reach. The procedure of computation is as follows:

1. Compute the normal depth $y_n$ and critical depth $y_c$ from the given data $Q$ and $S_0$ (see Arts. 6-6 and 4-4).

2. Determine the hydraulic exponents $N$ and $M$ for an estimated average depth of flow in the reach under consideration (see Arts. 6-3 and 4-3). It is assumed that the channel section under consideration has approximately constant hydraulic exponents.

3. Compute $J$ by $J = N/(N - M + 1)$.

4. Compute values of $u = y/y_n$ and $v = u^{N/J}$ at two end sections of the reach.

5. From the varied-flow-function table in Appendix D, find values of $F(u,N)$ and $F(v,J)$.

6. Compute the length of the reach by Eq. (10-10).

The above procedure is illustrated by the following examples:

**Example 10-2.** With reference to the channel described in Example 10-1, compute the length of the backwater profile extending from the dam site to an upstream section where the depth of flow is 1% greater than the normal depth.

*Solution.* The given data are $Q = 400$ cfs, $b = 20$ ft, $z = 2$, $S_0 = 0.0016$, $\alpha = 1.10$, and $n = 0.025$.

1. Following Example 6-2, $y_n = 3.36$ ft. Following Example 4-2 with $\alpha = 1.10$, $y_c = 2.22$ ft.

2. The depth at the downstream end of the backwater profile is $y_2 = 5$ ft. At the upstream end, the depth is $y_1 = 1.01 \times 3.36 = 3.40$ ft. The average depth may be taken as 4.20 ft and $y/b = 0.21$. From Figs. 6-2 and 4-2, the corresponding hydraulic exponents are found to be $N = 3.65$ and $M = 3.43$.

3. The value of $J = 3.65/(3.65 - 3.43 + 1) = 2.99$.

4. For each section, values of $u$ and $v$ are computed, as given in the second and third columns of the following table:

| $y$ | $u$ | $v$ | $F(u,N)$ | $F(v,J)$ |
|---|---|---|---|---|
| 5.00 | 1.488 | 1.625 | 0.148 | 0.213 |
| 3.40 | 1.012 | 1.015 | 1.025 | 1.293 |
| Dif.... | 0.476 | ... | −0.877 | −1.080 |

5. The varied-flow functions $F(u,N)$ and $F(v,J)$ are obtained from the table in Appendix D and given in the fourth and fifth columns of the above table.

6. In Eq. (10-9), $A = y_n/S_0 = 2,100$ and $B = (y_c/y_n)^M J/N = 0.197$. The length of the backwater profile is, therefore,

$$L = 2,100[0.476 - (-0.877) + 0.197 \times (-1.080)] = 2,395 \text{ ft}$$

**Example 10-3.** Water flows from under a sluice into a trapezoidal channel having $b = 20$ ft, $z = 2$, $S_0 = 0.0036$, $\alpha = 1.10$, and $n = 0.025$. The sluice gate is regulated

TABLE 10-3. COMPUTATION OF THE FLOW PROFILE FOR EXAMPLE 10-3 BY THE DIRECT-INTEGRATION METHOD

$Q = 400$ cfs    $n = 0.025$    $S_0 = 0.0036$    $\alpha = 1.10$    $y_c = 2.22$ ft    $y_n = 2.67$ ft

| $y$ | $u$ | $v$ | $F(u,N)$ | $F(v,J)$ | $x$ | $L$ |
|------|-------|-------|---------|---------|-----|-----|
| 2.22 | 0.831 | 0.792 | 0.979 | 0.962 | 206 | 0 |
| 2.14 | 0.800 | 0.755 | 0.917 | 0.888 | 204 | 2 |
| 1.87 | 0.700 | 0.638 | 0.756 | 0.699 | 188 | 18 |
| 1.60 | 0.600 | 0.525 | 0.627 | 0.552 | 161 | 45 |
| 1.33 | 0.500 | 0.420 | 0.511 | 0.431 | 134 | 72 |
| 1.07 | 0.400 | 0.315 | 0.404 | 0.319 | 102 | 104 |
| 0.80 | 0.300 | 0.219 | 0.301 | 0.219 | 71 | 135 |
| 0.53 | 0.200 | 0.132 | 0.200 | 0.132 | 43 | 163 |
| 0.27 | 0.100 | 0.055 | 0.100 | 0.055 | 18 | 188 |
| 0.00 | 0.000 | 0.000 | 0.000 | 0.000 | 0 | 206 |

to discharge 400 cfs with a depth equal to 0.55 ft at the vena contracta. Compute the flow profile. If a hydraulic jump occurs at the downstream end, starting with a depth of 1.6 ft, determine the distance from the vena contracta to the foot of the jump.

*Solution.* From the given data, $y_n = 2.67$ ft and $y_c = 2.22$ ft. Since $y_n > y_c$, the channel slope is mild. As the depth of flow issuing from the sluice gate is less than the critical depth, the flow profile is of the $M3$ type.

Considering an average depth of 1.61 ft, the hydraulic exponents are $N = 3.43$ and $M = 3.17$. Thus, $J = 2.72$, $N/J = 1.26$, and $(y_c/y_n)^M J/N = 0.442$.

Table 10-3 shows the computation of the flow profile. For convenience in inter-

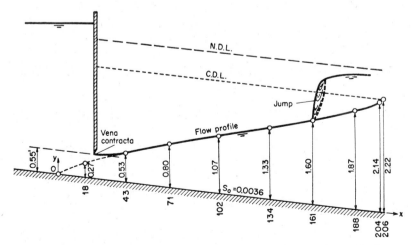

FIG. 10-4. An $M3$ flow profile computed by the direct-integration method.

polating values of $F(u,N)$ from the varied-flow-function table, values of $u$ are assigned at regular intervals. Values of $x$ are thereby computed·by Eq. (10-8), in which the constant is assumed equal to zero. The last column gives the length of the profile measured from the section under consideration to the downstream end, where the profile terminates theoretically at the critical depth.

The computed flow profile is plotted as shown in Fig. 10-4. The actual profile between the sluice-gate opening and the computed profile is uncertain and, hence, is fitted in by eye. The distance from the gate opening to the section of the vena contracta is known as the *contraction distance*. For a sharp-edged sluice gate, this distance has been assumed equal to approximately the height of the gate opening (Art. 15-7). If a hydraulic jump starts off at a depth of 1.6 ft, the distance from the jump to the vena contracta would be about 130 ft, as shown.

**Example 10-4.** Determine the profile of flow in a wide rectangular channel, using the Chézy formula.

*Solution.* For a wide rectangular channel, Fig. 4-2 gives $M = 3$ and Eq. (6-49) gives $N = 3$. Thus, $J = 3$, $v_{.} = u$, and Eq. (10-8) becomes

$$x = \frac{y_n}{S_0}\left[ u - \left(1 - \frac{y_c^3}{y_n^3}\right)F(u,3) \right] + \text{const} \tag{10-11}$$

where $F(u,3)$ can be found from the varied-flow-function table in Appendix D. Mathematically, $F(u,3)$ is integrable, or

$$F(u,3) = \int_0^u \frac{du}{1 - u^3} = \frac{1}{6}\ln\frac{u^2 + u + 1}{(u - 1)^2} - \frac{1}{\sqrt{3}}\cot^{-1}\frac{2u + 1}{\sqrt{3}} \tag{10-12}$$

This integration was first performed by Bresse [2]. A determination of the flow profile by this solution is, therefore, widely known as the *Bresse method*.

The critical and normal depths in a wide rectangular channel may be expressed, respectively, by

$$y_c = \sqrt[3]{\frac{q^2}{g}} \tag{10-13}$$

and

$$y_n = \sqrt[3]{\frac{q^2}{C^2 S_0}} \tag{10-14}$$

where $q$ is the discharge per unit width of the channel. Thus,

$$\frac{y_c^3}{y_n^3} = \frac{C^2 S_0}{g} \tag{10-15}$$

Substituting this expression for $y_c^3/y_n^3$, Eq. (10-11) may also be written

$$x = \frac{y_n}{S_0}\left[ u - \left(1 - \frac{C^2 S_0}{g}\right)F(u,3) \right] + \text{const} \tag{10-16}$$

or

$$x = A[u - BF(u,3)] + \text{const} \tag{10-17}$$

where $A = y_n/S_o$ and $B = 1 - C^2 S_0/g$.

The length of flow profile between two consecutive sections of depths $y_1$ and $y_2$ is

$$L = A\{(u_2 - u_1) - B[F(u_2,3) - F(u_1,3)]\} \tag{10-18}$$

**Example 10-5.** Solve Example 10-2 by the Bresse method.

*Solution.* The Bresse method is derived primarily for an infinitely wide rectangular channel. When this method is applied to channels of other cross-sectional shapes, the solution is therefore very approximate.

As the depth of flow varies from 5.00 to 3.40 ft, an average value of $y = 4.20$ ft may be assumed for the evaluation of Chézy's $C$. For a wide rectangular channel, Eq. (5-7) gives $C = 75.6$. Since $y_n = 3.36$ ft and $S_0 = 0.0016$, $A = 2,100$ and $B = 0.715$, Eq. (10-17) gives

$$x = 2,100[u - 0.715F(u,3)] + \text{const} \tag{10-19}$$

Assuming a constant of zero in Eq. (10-19), the computation of $x$ is as follows:

| $y$ | $u$ | $F(u,3)$ | $x$ |
|---|---|---|---|
| 5.00 | 1.488 | 0.260 | 2,720 |
| 3.40 | 1.012 | 1.360 | 80 |

The length of the backwater curve is, therefore, equal to $2,720 - 80 = 2,640$ ft, about 10% larger than the values determined by the previous methods.

*Channels of Nonsustaining Slopes.* When the above procedure is applied to channels of adverse slopes, the slope of the channel bottom may be taken as negative. Thus, Eq. (9-3) becomes

$$\frac{dy}{dx} = \frac{-S_0 - S}{1 + \alpha\, d(V^2/2g)/dy} \tag{10-20}$$

The corresponding equation for the flow profile can be shown to be

$$x = -\frac{y_n}{S_0}\left[ u - \int_0^u \frac{du}{1 + u^N} - \left(\frac{y_c}{y_n}\right)^M \int_0^u \frac{u^{N-M}}{1 + u^N}\,du \right] + \text{const} \tag{10-21}$$

where the varied-flow functions for adverse slopes are

$$F(u,N)_{-S_0} = \int_0^u \frac{du}{1 + u^N} \tag{10-22}$$

and

$$F(v,J)_{-S_0} = \int_0^u \frac{u^{N-M}}{1 + u^N}\,du = \frac{J}{N}\int_0^v \frac{dv}{1 + v^J} \tag{10-23}$$

where $v = u^{N/J}$ and $J = N/(N - M + 1)$. For evaluating these functions a table [18][1] has been prepared which is Table D-2 in Appendix D. Accordingly, the length of flow profile between two sections 1 and 2 may be expressed by Eq. (10-10), where $A = -y_n/S_0$, $B = -(y_c/y_n)^M J/N$, and the varied-flow functions are replaced by those for adverse slopes.

**Example 10-6.** Derive an expression for the flow profile in a horizontal channel. *Solution.* For horizontal channels, $S_0 = 0$, and the differential equation is

$$\frac{dy}{dx} = \frac{-(Q/K)^2}{1 - (Z_c/Z)^2} \tag{9-19}$$

Since the critical slope $S_c$ is defined as the slope that will produce a discharge $Q$ at a

[1] Tables of varied-flow functions for adverse slopes with limited range of the hydraulic exponent $N$ have also been prepared by Matzke [20] and others [21].

normal depth equal to the critical depth $y_c$ (Art. 6-7), the discharge may be expressed as

$$Q = K_c \sqrt{S_c} \tag{10-24}$$

Substituting Eq. (10-24) in Eq. (9-19) and letting $(K_c/K)^2 = (y_c/y)^N$, $(Z_c/Z)^2 = (y_c/y)^M$, and $p = y/y_c$,

$$\frac{dy}{dx} = S_c \frac{p^{M-N}}{1 - p^M} \tag{10-25}$$

Integrating and solving for $x$,

$$x = \frac{y_c}{S_c} \left( \frac{p^{N-M+1}}{N - M + 1} - \frac{p^{N+1}}{N + 1} \right) + \text{const} \tag{10-26}$$

This equation can be used for the computation of the length of flow profile in a horizontal channel.

*Channels with Variable Hydraulic Exponents.* It should be noted that the assumption of constant hydraulic exponents in the foregoing discus-

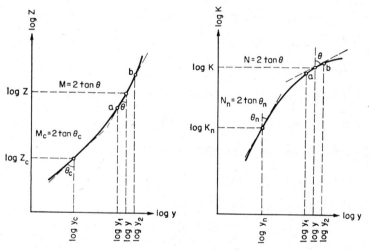

FIG. 10-5. Logarithmic plots of depth against $Z$ and $M$, respectively, for variable hydraulic exponents.

sion is satisfactory in most rectangular and trapezoidal channels. As described in Arts. 4-3 and 6-3, the hydraulic exponents may vary appreciably with respect to the depth of flow when the channel section has abrupt changes in cross-sectional geometry or is topped with a gradually closing crown. In such cases, the channel length should be divided into a number of reaches in each of which the hydraulic exponents appear to be constant.

Referring to Fig. 10-5, it is assumed that the hydraulic exponents in the range of depth from $y_1$ to $y_2$ of a reach are practically constant. Let $N_n$ be the $N$ value at the normal depth $y_n$; let $N$ be the average $N$ value for the range of $y_1$ to $y_2$; let $M_c$ be the $M$ value at the critical depth $y_c$; and let $M$ be the average $M$ value for the range $y_1$ to $y_2$. Thus, Eq. (9-13) may be written

$$\frac{dy}{dx} = S_0 \frac{1 - y_n^{N_n}/y^N}{1 - y_c^{M_c}/y^M} \tag{10-27}$$

Let $u = y/y_n^{N_n/N}$ and, hence, $dy = y_n^{N_n/N}\, du$. Then, Eq. (10-27) may be reduced to

$$dx = \frac{y_n^{N_n/N}}{S_0}\left[1 - \frac{1}{1 - u^N} + \left(\frac{y_c^{M_c/M}}{y_n^{N_n/N}}\right)^M \frac{u^{N-M}}{1 - u^N}\right] du \tag{10-28}$$

Following a procedure of integration and transformation similar to that applied to the solution of Eq. (10-3),

$$x = \frac{y_n^{N_n/N}}{S_0}\left[u - F(u,N) + \left(\frac{y_c^{M_c/M}}{y_n^{N_n/N}}\right)^M \frac{J}{N} F(v,J)\right] + \text{const} \tag{10-29}$$

where $u = y/y_n^{N_n/N}$, $v = u^{N/J}$, $J = N/(N - M + 1)$, and $F(u,N)$ and $F(v,J)$ are varied-flow functions. If the hydraulic exponents are constant, or $N_n = N$ and $M_c = M$, Eq. (10-29) obviously becomes Eq. (10-8).

The length of the flow profile between two consecutive sections of depths $y_1$ and $y_2$ can be computed by Eq. (10-10), except where $A = y_n^{N_n/N}/S_0$ and $B = (y_c^{M_c/M}/y_n^{N_n/N})^M J/N$.

*Channels with Gradually Closing Crown.* For channels with gradually closing crown, the hydraulic exponents are variable near the crown, and the method proposed above may be used. For more accurate results, however, the integration of the dynamic equation may be performed by a procedure of numerical integration. Such a procedure has been applied to circular conduits by Keifer and Chu [17].

Let $Q_0$ be the discharge of a circular conduit, flowing full at a depth equal to the diameter $d_0$ of the conduit and having the energy gradient equal to the bottom slope $S_0$, and let $K_0$ be the corresponding conveyance. Thus,

$$Q_0 = K_0\sqrt{S_0} \tag{10-30}$$

For a uniform flow in the circular conduit with a discharge equal to $Q$ of the actual flow, Eq. (9-11) gives

$$Q = K_n\sqrt{S_0} \tag{10-31}$$

From the above two equations the following may be developed:

$$\left(\frac{K_n}{K}\right)^2 = \left(\frac{K_n}{K_0}\right)^2\left(\frac{K_0}{K}\right)^2 = \left(\frac{Q}{Q_0}\right)^2\left(\frac{K_0}{K}\right)^2 = \left(\frac{Q}{Q_0}\right)^2 f_1\left(\frac{y}{d_0}\right) \tag{10-32}$$

where $(K_0/K)^2$ is evidently a function of $y/d_0$ and, hence, can be represented by $f_1(y/d_0)$.

From Eqs. (9-4) and (9-7), the following may be written:

$$\left(\frac{Z_c}{Z}\right)^2 = \frac{\alpha Q^2 T}{g A^3} = \frac{\alpha Q^2}{d_0^5} \frac{T/d_0}{g(A/d_0^2)^3} = \frac{\alpha Q^2}{d_0^5} f_2\left(\frac{y}{d_0}\right) \quad (10\text{-}33)$$

where $(T/d_0)/g(A/d_0^2)^3$ is apparently a function of $y/d_0$ and, hence, can be represented by $f_2(y/d_0)$.

Substituting Eqs. (10-32) and (10-33) in Eq. (9-13) and simplifying,

$$dx = \frac{d_0}{S_0}\left[\frac{1 - (\alpha Q^2/d_0^5)f_2(y/d_0)}{1 - (Q/Q_0)^2 f_1(y/d_0)}\right] d\left(\frac{y}{d_0}\right) \quad (10\text{-}34)$$

Integrating,

$$x = \frac{d_0}{S_0}\left[\int_0^{y/d_0} \frac{d(y/d_0)}{1 - (Q/Q_0)^2 f_1(y/d_0)}\right.$$
$$\left. - \frac{\alpha Q^2}{d_0^5} \int_0^{y/d_0} \frac{f_2(y/d_0)\, d(y/d_0)}{1 - (Q/Q_0)^2 f_1(y/d_0)}\right] + \text{const} \quad (10\text{-}35)$$

or

$$x = -\frac{d_0}{S_0}\left(X - \frac{\alpha Q^2}{d_0^5} Y\right) + \text{const} \quad (10\text{-}36)$$

where

$$X = F_1\left(\frac{y}{d_0}, \frac{Q}{Q_0}\right) = \int_0^{y/d_0} \frac{-d(y/d_0)}{1 - (Q/Q_0)^2 f_1(y/d_0)} \quad (10\text{-}37)$$

and

$$Y = F_2\left(\frac{y}{d_0}, \frac{Q}{Q_0}\right) = \int_0^{y/d_0} \frac{-f_2(y/d_0)\, d(y/d_0)}{1 - (Q/Q_0)^2 f_1(y/d_0)} \quad (10\text{-}38)$$

These are the varied-flow functions for circular conduits, depending on $y/d_0$ and $Q/Q_0$. They can be evaluated by a procedure of numerical integration, say Simpson's rule. A table of these functions for positive slopes,[1] prepared by Keifer and Chu, is given in Appendix E.

The length of flow profile between two consecutive sections of depth $y_1$ and $y_2$, respectively, in a circular conduit may be expressed as

$$L = A[(X_2 - X_1) - B(Y_2 - Y_1)] \quad (10\text{-}39)$$

where $A = -d_0/S_0$ and $B = \alpha Q^2/d_0^5$.

**10-3. The Direct Step Method.** In general, a step method is characterized by dividing the channel into short reaches and carrying the computation step by step from one end of the reach to the other. There is a great variety of step methods. Some methods appear superior to others in certain respects, but no one method has been found to be the best in all

---

[1] If $S_0 = 0$, then $Q_0 = 0$, $Q/Q_0 = \infty$, and the varied-flow functions become meaningless. If $S_0$ is negative, Eq. (10-30) shows that $Q_0^2$ is negative. Since the actual discharge $Q$ must be positive, $(Q/Q_0)^2$ becomes negative. Thus, the integration procedure must be done for negative values of $(Q/Q_0)^2$ in the two varied-flow functions.

applications. The direct step method[1] is a simple step method applicable to prismatic channels.

Figure 10-6 illustrates a short channel reach of length $\Delta x$. Equating the total heads at the two end sections 1 and 2, the following may be written:

$$S_0 \Delta x + y_1 + \alpha_1 \frac{V_1^2}{2g}$$

$$= y_2 + \alpha_2 \frac{V_2^2}{2g} + S_f \Delta x \qquad (10\text{-}40)$$

Solving for $\Delta x$,

$$\Delta x = \frac{E_2 - E_1}{S_0 - S_f} = \frac{\Delta E}{S_0 - S_f} \qquad (10\text{-}41)$$

where $E$ is the specific energy or, assuming $\alpha_1 = \alpha_2 = \alpha$,

$$E = y + \alpha \frac{V^2}{2g} \qquad (10\text{-}42)$$

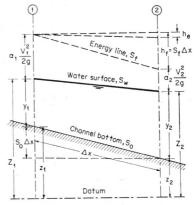

FIG. 10-6. A channel reach for the derivation of step methods.

In the above equations, $y$ is the depth of flow, $V$ is the mean velocity, $\alpha$ is the energy coefficient, $S_0$ is the bottom slope, and $S_f$ is the friction slope. The average value of $S_f$ is denoted by $\bar{S}_f$. When the Manning formula is used, the friction slope is expressed by

$$S_f = \frac{n^2 V^2}{2.22 R^{4/3}} \qquad (9\text{-}8)$$

The direct step method is based on Eq. (10-41), as may be illustrated by the following example:

**Example 10-7.** Compute the flow profile required in Example 10-1 by the direct step method.

*Solution.* With the data given in Example 10-1, the step computations are carried out as shown in Table 10-4. The values in each column of the table are explained as follows:

Col. 1. Depth of flow in ft, arbitrarily assigned from 5.00 to 3.40 ft

Col. 2. Water area in ft² corresponding to the depth $y$ in col. 1

Col. 3. Hydraulic radius in ft corresponding to $y$ in col. 1

Col. 4. Four-thirds power of the hydraulic radius

Col. 5. Mean velocity in fps obtained by dividing 400 cfs by the water area in col. 2

Col. 6. Velocity head in ft

Col. 7. Specific energy in ft obtained by adding the velocity head in col. 6 to the depth of flow in col. 1

[1] First suggested by the Polish engineer Charnomskiĭ [22] in 1914 and then by Husted [23] in 1924.

TABLE 10-4. COMPUTATION OF THE FLOW PROFILE BY THE DIRECT STEP METHOD FOR EXAMPLE 10-7

$Q = 400$ cfs    $n = 0.025$    $S_0 = 0.0016$    $\alpha = 1.10$    $y_c = 2.22$ ft    $y_n = 3.36$ ft

| $y$ (1) | $A$ (2) | $R$ (3) | $R^{4/3}$ (4) | $V$ (5) | $\alpha V^2/2g$ (6) | $E$ (7) | $\Delta E$ (8) | $S_f$ (9) | $\bar{S}_f$ (10) | $S_0 - \bar{S}_f$ (11) | $\Delta x$ (12) | $x$ (13) |
|---|---|---|---|---|---|---|---|---|---|---|---|---|
| 5.00 | 150.00 | 3.54 | 5.40 | 2.667 | 0.1217 | 5.1217 | ...... | 0.000370 | | | | |
| 4.80 | 142.08 | 3.43 | 5.17 | 2.819 | 0.1356 | 4.9356 | 0.1861 | 0.000433 | 0.000402 | 0.001198 | 155 | 155 |
| 4.60 | 134.32 | 3.31 | 4.94 | 2.979 | 0.1517 | 4.7517 | 0.1839 | 0.000507 | 0.000470 | 0.001130 | 163 | 318 |
| 4.40 | 126.72 | 3.19 | 4.70 | 3.156 | 0.1706 | 4.5706 | 0.1811 | 0.000598 | 0.000553 | 0.001047 | 173 | 491 |
| 4.20 | 119.28 | 3.08 | 4.50 | 3.354 | 0.1925 | 4.3925 | 0.1781 | 0.000705 | 0.000652 | 0.000948 | 188 | 679 |
| 4.00 | 112.00 | 2.96 | 4.25 | 3.572 | 0.2184 | 4.2184 | 0.1741 | 0.000850 | 0.000778 | 0.000822 | 212 | 891 |
| 3.80 | 104.88 | 2.84 | 4.02 | 3.814 | 0.2490 | 4.0490 | 0.1694 | 0.001020 | 0.000935 | 0.000665 | 255 | 1,146 |
| 3.70 | 101.38 | 2.77 | 3.88 | 3.948 | 0.2664 | 3.9664 | 0.0826 | 0.001132 | 0.001076 | 0.000524 | 158 | 1,304 |
| 3.60 | 97.92 | 2.71 | 3.78 | 4.085 | 0.2856 | 3.8856 | 0.0808 | 0.001244 | 0.001188 | 0.000412 | 196 | 1,500 |
| 3.55 | 96.21 | 2.68 | 3.72 | 4.158 | 0.2958 | 3.8458 | 0.0398 | 0.001310 | 0.001277 | 0.000323 | 123 | 1,623 |
| 3.50 | 94.50 | 2.65 | 3.66 | 4.233 | 0.3067 | 3.8067 | 0.0391 | 0.001382 | 0.001346 | 0.000254 | 154 | 1,777 |
| 3.47 | 93.48 | 2.63 | 3.63 | 4.278 | 0.3131 | 3.7831 | 0.0236 | 0.001427 | 0.001405 | 0.000195 | 121 | 1,898 |
| 3.44 | 92.45 | 2.61 | 3.59 | 4.326 | 0.3202 | 3.7602 | 0.0229 | 0.001471 | 0.001449 | 0.000151 | 152 | 2,050 |
| 3.42 | 91.80 | 2.60 | 3.57 | 4.357 | 0.3246 | 3.7446 | 0.0156 | 0.001500 | 0.001486 | 0.000114 | 137 | 2,187 |
| 3.40 | 91.12 | 2.59 | 3.55 | 4.388 | 0.3292 | 3.7292 | 0.0154 | 0.001535 | 0.001518 | 0.000082 | 188 | 2,375 |

264

Col. 8. Change of specific energy in ft, equal to the difference between the $E$ value in col. 7 and that of the previous step

Col. 9. Friction slope computed by Eq. (9-8) with $n = 0.025$ and with $V$ as given in col. 5 and $R^{4/3}$ in col. 4

Col. 10. Average friction slope between the steps, equal to the arithmetic mean of the friction slope just computed in col. 9 and that of the previous step

Col. 11. Difference between the bottom slope 0.0016 and the average friction slope

Col. 12. Length of the reach in ft between the consecutive steps, computed by Eq. (10-41) or by dividing the value of $\Delta E$ in col. 8 by the value in col. 11

Col. 13. Distance from the section under consideration to the dam site. This is equal to the cumulative sum of the values in col. 12 computed for previous steps.

The flow profile thus computed is practically identical with that obtained by graphical integration (Fig. 10-3).

**Example 10-8.** A 72-in. reinforced-concrete pipe culvert, 250 ft long, is laid on a slope of 0.02 with a free outlet. Compute the flow profile if the culvert discharges 252 cfs, $n = 0.012$, and $\alpha = 1.0$.

*Solution.* From the data, $y_c = 4.35$ ft and $y_n = 2.60$ ft. Since $y_c > y_n$, the channel slope is steep. As shown in Fig. 10-7, the control section is at the entrance; water will enter the culvert at the critical depth and thereafter flow at a depth less than $y_c$ but greater than $y_n$. The flow profile is of the $S2$ type.

Table 10-5 shows the computation of the flow profile, which is self-explanatory. The computed profile is plotted as shown in Fig. 10-7. Plotted also in the figure is the energy line indicating the variation of energy along the culvert. The computation has been carried to exceed the length of the culvert, so that the depth of flow at the outlet can be interpolated. This depth is found to be 2.81 ft, and the corresponding outlet velocity is 19.4 fps. It should be noted that, if the pipe were flowing full at the outlet, the outlet velocity would be only 10 fps.

Note that, in either the direct step method or the standard step method which will be described in the next article, the step computation should be carried upstream if the flow is subcritical and downstream if the flow is supercritical. Step computations carried in the wrong direction tend inevitably to make the result diverge from the correct flow profile.

**10-4. The Standard Step Method.** This method is applicable also to nonprismatic channels. In nonprismatic channels, the hydraulic elements are no longer independent of the distance along the channel. In natural channels, it is generally necessary to conduct a field survey to collect the data required at all sections considered in the computation. The computation is carried on by steps from station to station where the hydraulic characteristics have been determined. In such cases the distance between stations is given, and the procedure is to determine the depth of flow at the stations. Such a procedure is usually carried out by trial and error.

In explaining this method it is convenient to refer the position of the water surface to a horizontal datum. In Fig. 10-6, the water-surface elevations above the datum at the two end sections are

$$Z_1 = S_0 \, \Delta x + y_1 + z_2 \tag{10-43}$$

Table 10-5. Computation of the Flow Profile for Example 10-8 by the Direct Step Method

$Q = 252$ cfs  $n = 0.012$  $S_0 = 0.02$  $\alpha = 1.0$  $y_c = 4.35$ ft  $y_n = 2.60$ ft

| $y/D$ | $y$ | $A$ | $R$ | $R^{4/3}$ | $V$ | $\alpha V^2/2g$ | $E$ | $\Delta E$ | $S_f$ | $\bar{S}_f$ | $S_0 - \bar{S}_f$ | $\Delta x$ | $x$ |
|---|---|---|---|---|---|---|---|---|---|---|---|---|---|
| 0.725 | 4.35 | 21.95 | 1.794 | 2.180 | 11.48 | 2.048 | 6.398 | | 0.00392 | | | | |
| 0.70 | 4.20 | 21.13 | 1.777 | 2.154 | 11.93 | 2.211 | 6.411 | 0.013 | 0.00429 | 0.00411 | 0.01589 | 0.8 | 0.8 |
| 0.65 | 3.90 | 19.45 | 1.728 | 2.073 | 12.96 | 2.609 | 6.509 | 0.098 | 0.00525 | 0.00477 | 0.01523 | 6.4 | 7.2 |
| 0.60 | 3.60 | 17.71 | 1.666 | 1.976 | 14.23 | 3.145 | 6.745 | 0.236 | 0.00666 | 0.00596 | 0.01404 | 16.8 | 24.0 |
| 0.55 | 3.30 | 15.93 | 1.590 | 1.855 | 15.85 | 3.901 | 7.201 | 0.456 | 0.00880 | 0.00773 | 0.01227 | 37.2 | 61.2 |
| 0.50 | 3.00 | 14.13 | 1.500 | 1.717 | 17.85 | 4.947 | 7.947 | 0.746 | 0.01202 | 0.01041 | 0.00959 | 77.8 | 139.0 |
| 0.48 | 2.88 | 13.42 | 1.460 | 1.656 | 18.76 | 5.465 | 8.345 | 0.398 | 0.01378 | 0.01290 | 0.00710 | 56.1 | 195.1 |
| 0.47 | 2.82 | 13.06 | 1.440 | 1.626 | 19.30 | 5.785 | 8.605 | 0.260 | 0.01486 | 0.01432 | 0.00568 | 45.8 | 240.9 |
| 0.46 | 2.76 | 12.70 | 1.420 | 1.596 | 19.85 | 6.119 | 8.879 | 0.274 | 0.01600 | 0.01543 | 0.00457 | 60.0 | 300.9 |

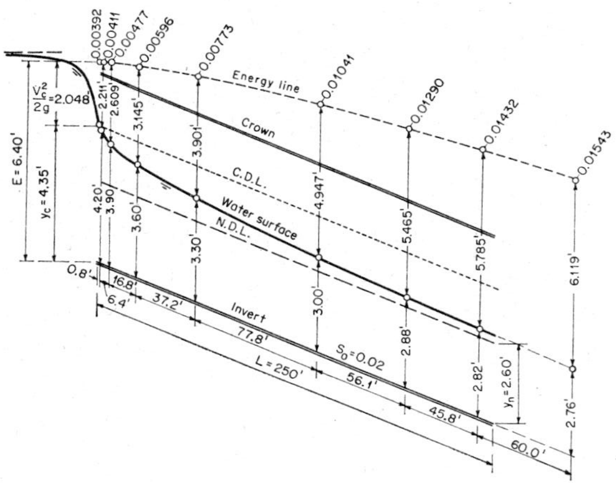

Fig. 10-7. An S2 flow profile computed by the direct step method.

and
$$Z_2 = y_2 + z_2 \tag{10-44}$$

The friction loss is
$$h_f = S_f \, \Delta x = \tfrac{1}{2}(S_1 + S_2) \, \Delta x \tag{10-45}$$

where the friction slope $S_f$ is taken as the average of the slopes at the two end sections, or as $\bar{S}_f$.

Substituting the above expressions in Eq. (10-40), the following may be written:
$$Z_1 + \alpha_1 \frac{V_1{}^2}{2g} = Z_2 + \alpha_2 \frac{V_2{}^2}{2g} + h_f + h_e \tag{10-46}$$

where $h_e$ is added for the eddy loss, which may be appreciable in non-prismatic channels. No rational method of evaluating eddy loss is available. The eddy loss depends mainly on the velocity head change and may be expressed as a part of it, or $k(\Delta \alpha V^2/2g)$ where $k$ is a coefficient. For gradually converging and diverging reaches, $k = 0$ to 0.1 and 0.2, respectively. For abrupt expansions and contractions, $k$ is about 0.5. For prismatic and regular channels, the eddy loss is practically zero, or $k = 0$. For convenience of computation, $h_e$ may sometimes be considered part of the friction loss and Manning's $n$ may be properly increased in computing $h_f$. Then, $h_e$ is zero in the computation.

The total heads at two end sections are
$$H_1 = Z_1 + \alpha_1 \frac{V_1{}^2}{2g} \tag{10-47}$$
and
$$H_2 = Z_2 + \alpha_2 \frac{V_2{}^2}{2g} \tag{10-48}$$

Therefore, Eq. (10-46) becomes
$$H_1 = H_2 + h_f + h_e \tag{10-49}$$

This is the basic equation that defines the procedure of the standard step method.

The standard step method is best suited to computations for natural channels. A prismatic channel, however, will be used in the following example in order to simplify the illustration and to allow comparison with results obtained by the other methods that have been described. For application to natural channels, an example will be shown later (Art. 10-6).

**Example 10-9.** Compute the flow profile required in Example 10-1 by the standard step method. Assume that stations along the channel are fixed at the distances determined in the solution of Example 10-7. The elevation at the dam site is 600 m.s.l.

*Solution.* The step computations are arranged in tabular form, as shown in Table 10-6. Values in each column of the table are explained as follows:

Col. 1. Section identified by station number such as "station 1 + 55." The location of the stations is fixed at the distances determined in Example 10-7 in order to compare the procedure with that of the direct step method.

Col. 2. Water-surface elevation at the station. A trial value is first entered in this column; this will be verified or rejected on the basis of the computations made in the remaining columns of the table. For the first step, this elevation must be given or assumed. Since the elevation of the dam site is 600 m.s.l. and the height of the dam is 5 ft, the first entry is 605.00 m.s.l. When the trial value in the second step has been verified, it becomes the basis for the verification of the trial value in the next step, and so on.

Col. 3. Depth of flow in ft, corresponding to the water-surface elevation in col. 2. For instance, the depth of flow at station 1 + 55 is equal to water-surface elevation minus elevation at the dam site minus (distance from the dam site times bed slope), or $605.048 - 600.000 - 155 \times 0.0016 = 4.80$ ft.

Col. 4. Water area corresponding to $y$ in col. 3

Col. 5. Mean velocity equal to the given discharge 400 cfs divided by the water area in col. 4

Col. 6. Velocity head in ft, corresponding to the velocity in col. 5

Col. 7. Total head computed by Eq. (10-47), equal to the sum of $Z$ in col. 2 and the velocity head in col. 6

Col. 8. Hydraulic radius in ft, corresponding to $y$ in col. 3

Col. 9. Four-thirds power of the hydraulic radius

Col. 10. Friction slope computed by Eq. (9-8), with $n = 0.025$, $V$ from col. 5, and $R^{4/3}$ from col. 9

Col. 11. Average friction slope through the reach between the sections in each step, approximately equal to the arithmetic mean of the friction slope just computed in col. 10 and that of the previous step

Col. 12. Length of the reach between the sections, equal to the difference in station numbers between the stations

Col. 13. Friction loss in the reach, equal to the product of the values in cols. 11 and 12.

Col. 14. Eddy loss in the reach, equal to zero

Col. 15. Elevation of the total head in ft. This is computed by Eq. (10-49), that is, by adding the values of $h_f$ and $h_e$ in cols. 13 and 14 to the elevation at the lower end of the reach, which is found in col. 15 of the previous reach. If the value so obtained does not agree closely with that entered in col. 7, a new trial value of the water-surface elevation is assumed, and so on, until agreement is obtained. The value that leads to agreement is the correct water-surface elevation. The computation may then proceed to the next step. The computed flow profile is practically identical with that obtained by the graphical-integration method shown in Fig. 10-3.

## 10-5. Computation of a Family of Flow Profiles.

In previous articles methods were described for determining a single flow profile. Frequently, several flow profiles, or a family of flow profiles, are desired for various conditions of stage and discharge. An example of this type of problem is the determination of the economical height of a dam, where the initial elevation is indeterminate and, hence, a number of flow profiles may have to be computed for the same discharge with different assumed

TABLE 10-6. COMPUTATION OF THE FLOW PROFILE FOR EXAMPLE 10-9 BY THE STANDARD STEP METHOD

$Q = 400$ cfs    $n = 0.025$    $S_0 = 0.0016$    $\alpha = 1.10$    $h_e = 0$    $y_c = 2.22$ ft    $y_n = 3.36$ ft

| Station | $Z$ | $y$ | $A$ | $V$ | $\alpha V^2/2g$ | $H$ | $R$ | $R^{2/3}$ | $S_f$ | $\bar{S}_f$ | $\Delta x$ | $h_f$ | $h_e$ | $H$ |
|---|---|---|---|---|---|---|---|---|---|---|---|---|---|---|
| (1) | (2) | (3) | (4) | (5) | (6) | (7) | (8) | (9) | (10) | (11) | (12) | (13) | (14) | (15) |
| 0 + 00 | 605.000 | 5.00 | 150.00 | 2.667 | 0.1217 | 605.122 | 3.54 | 5.40 | 0.000370 | ...... | ... | ...... | ... | 605.122 |
| 1 + 55 | 605.048 | 4.80 | 142.08 | 2.819 | 0.1356 | 605.184 | 3.43 | 5.17 | 0.000433 | 0.000402 | 155 | 0.062 | 0 | 605.184 |
| 3 + 18 | 605.109 | 4.60 | 134.32 | 2.979 | 0.1517 | 605.261 | 3.31 | 4.92 | 0.000507 | 0.000470 | 163 | 0.077 | 0 | 605.261 |
| 4 + 91 | 605.186 | 4.40 | 126.72 | 3.156 | 0.1706 | 605.357 | 3.19 | 4.70 | 0.000598 | 0.000553 | 173 | 0.096 | 0 | 605.357 |
| 6 + 79 | 605.286 | 4.20 | 119.28 | 3.354 | 0.1925 | 605.479 | 3.08 | 4.50 | 0.000705 | 0.000652 | 188 | 0.122 | 0 | 605.479 |
| 8 + 91 | 605.426 | 4.00 | 112.00 | 3.572 | 0.2184 | 605.644 | 2.96 | 4.25 | 0.000850 | 0.000778 | 212 | 0.165 | 0 | 605.644 |
| 11 + 46 | 605.633 | 3.80 | 104.88 | 3.814 | 0.2490 | 605.882 | 2.84 | 4.02 | 0.001020 | 0.000935 | 255 | 0.238 | 0 | 605.882 |
| 13 + 04 | 605.786 | 3.70 | 101.38 | 3.948 | 0.2664 | 606.052 | 2.77 | 3.88 | 0.001132 | 0.001076 | 158 | 0.170 | 0 | 606.052 |
| 15 + 00 | 605.999 | 3.60 | 97.92 | 4.085 | 0.2856 | 606.285 | 2.71 | 3.78 | 0.001244 | 0.001188 | 196 | 0.233 | 0 | 606.285 |
| 16 + 23 | 606.146 | 3.55 | 96.21 | 4.158 | 0.2958 | 606.442 | 2.68 | 3.72 | 0.001310 | 0.001277 | 123 | 0.157 | 0 | 606.442 |
| 17 + 77 | 606.343 | 3.50 | 94.50 | 4.233 | 0.3067 | 606.650 | 2.65 | 3.66 | 0.001382 | 0.001346 | 154 | 0.208 | 0 | 606.650 |
| 18 + 98 | 606.507 | 3.47 | 93.48 | 4.278 | 0.3131 | 606.820 | 2.63 | 3.63 | 0.001427 | 0.001405 | 121 | 0.170 | 0 | 606.820 |
| 20 + 50 | 606.720 | 3.44 | 92.45 | 4.326 | 0.3202 | 607.040 | 2.61 | 3.59 | 0.001471 | 0.001449 | 152 | 0.220 | 0 | 607.040 |
| 21 + 87 | 606.919 | 3.42 | 91.80 | 4.357 | 0.3246 | 607.244 | 2.60 | 3.57 | 0.001500 | 0.001486 | 137 | 0.204 | 0 | 607.244 |
| 23 + 75 | 607.201 | 3.40 | 91.12 | 4.388 | 0.3292 | 607.530 | 2.59 | 3.55 | 0.001535 | 0.001518 | 188 | 0.286 | 0 | 607.530 |

initial elevations. Another example is the tracing of flow profiles in a tributary stream for different stages and discharges in the main river, or in a river with a tidal estuary for different tidal elevations, or in a canal connecting two reservoirs for changing reservoir elevations and variable discharges. The following are some time-saving methods which may help in the computation of a family of flow profiles.

*A. Curves of Geometric Elements.* When a number of flow profiles are desired for different stage and discharge conditions, it is best to construct curves showing the geometric and hydraulic elements (Figs. 10-8 and

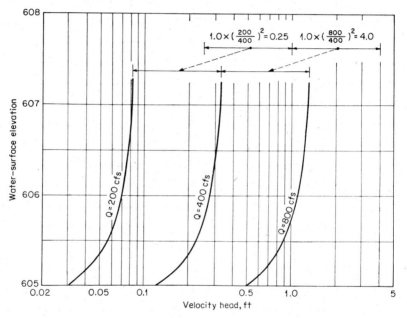

FIG. 10-8. Plot of velocity head against water-surface elevation.

10-9) required in the computation. Considerable time can be saved in the computation by interpolating values from these curves, provided the curves are not extended needlessly beyond the expected range of the water-surface elevation.

When the discharge of flow in a channel varies, the velocity head and friction slope will change, and the water-surface elevation will be affected. Thus, for general use in the computation, the velocity head in logarithmic scale can be plotted against the water-surface elevation (Fig. 10-8), and the friction slope in logarithmic scale can be plotted against the water-surface elevation (Fig. 10-9). From consideration of the Manning formula and the continuity of flow, it can be shown that the velocity head and the friction slope vary with the square of the discharge. Therefore, after the curves for one value of $Q$, say 400 cfs, in Figs. 10-8 and 10-9 have been computed, curves for other discharges, say 200 and 800 cfs, may be obtained either by shifting the curves horizontally (Fig. 10-8) or by shifting the abscissas (Fig. 10-9). The distance by which either the curve or the abscissa should be shifted is determined by the square of the ratio of the new to the original discharge.

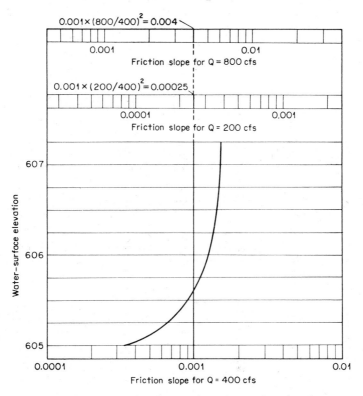

FIG. 10-9. Plot of friction slope against water-surface elevation.

B. *The Leach Diagram.* When a large number of flow profiles is required for the same discharge but different stages, a diagram developed by Leach [24] may be used to advantage. Such a diagram (Fig. 10-10) may be prepared after a few flow profiles within an expected range have been computed by any method. In the diagram, each curve represents the relationship between the water-surface elevations at the beginning and end sections of a reach. For instance, when the elevation at section 1 is plotted against the elevation at section 2 for the first reach 1-2, then the curve for reach 1-2 as shown in the figure is obtained. For simplifying the identification of the curves, elevations at sections of odd number are represented by abscissas and those at sections of even number by ordinates. With the diagram thus prepared, the flow profile for any assumed initial elevation can be determined. Taking the initial elevation as 605.00 and following the dotted line in the direction of the arrows, the corresponding water-surface elevations at subsequent sections can be obtained easily. The diagram is constructed for a discharge of 400 cfs. For any other discharge under investigation a different diagram must be prepared.

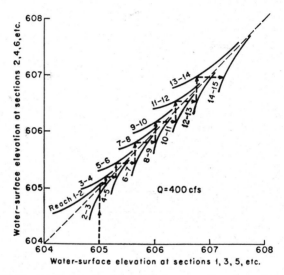

Fig. 10-10. The Leach diagram for flow-profile computation when a large number of flow profiles are required for the same discharge.

C. *The Ezra Method.* The Leach diagram is recommended if flow profiles for the same discharge are required for various initial stages. When flow profiles for various discharges are desired for different initial stages, a method developed by Ezra [25] may be used. Similar methods have also been developed by others [26–28].

Substituting Eq. (10-45) in Eq. (10-46), the following equation may be written:

$$Z_1 + F(Z_1) = Z_2 + F(Z_2) + h_e \qquad (10\text{-}50)$$

where

$$F(Z_1) = \alpha_1 \frac{V_1{}^2}{2g} - \tfrac{1}{2} S_1 \, \Delta x \qquad (10\text{-}51)$$

and

$$F(Z_2) = \alpha_2 \frac{V_2{}^2}{2g} + \tfrac{1}{2} S_2 \, \Delta x \qquad (10\text{-}52)$$

By Eq. (9-8),
$$S_1 = \frac{n^2 V_1^2}{2.22 R_1^{4/3}}$$
(10-53)

and
$$S_2 = \frac{n^2 V_2^2}{2.22 R_2^{4/3}}$$
(10-54)

or, by Eq. (9-10),
$$S_1 = \left(\frac{Q}{K_1}\right)^2$$
(10-55)

and
$$S_2 = \left(\frac{Q}{K_2}\right)^2$$
(10-56)

It can be seen that functions $F(Z_1)$ and $F(Z_2)$ are proportional directly to the squares of the velocities or of the discharge $Q$. For any other discharge $Q_x$, the corresponding values of these functions can be obtained by multiplying the functions by a factor $(Q_x/Q)^2$.

The Ezra method gives a graphical solution of Eq. (10-50). There are two major parts of this solution:

1. COMPUTATION AND CONSTRUCTION OF $Z + F(Z)$ CURVES. For each chosen section in a channel under consideration, several values of water-surface elevation are selected, and necessary geometric elements $A$ and $R$ for each of these water-surface elevations are determined and tabulated. This procedure is the same as in the standard step method.

For given values of $Q$ and $n$, values of $\alpha V^2/2g$ and $S_f$ are determined at each section for each of the selected elevations. In artificial prismatic channels, the friction slope $S_f$ may be computed by Eqs. (10-53) and (10-54). In irregular channels, the value of $K$ is determined first and the value of $S_f$ is then computed by Eqs. (10-55) and (10-56). This will be shown in Example 10-12.

For each section, the corresponding values of $F(Z)$ are then computed by Eqs. (10-51) and (10-52). It should be noted that two values, $F(Z_1)$ and $F(Z_2)$, should be computed for each section. In computing $F(Z_1)$ of the section, the value of $\Delta x$ is the value $\Delta x_d$ measured downstream from that section. In computing $F(Z_2)$, the value of $\Delta x$ is the value $\Delta x_u$ measured upstream from that section. In the computation, this rule ensures that values of $\Delta x$ will be common to sections at both ends of any reach, since it will be shown that the same value of $\Delta x$ is used on both sides of Eq. (10-50). In other words, at each section $Z_1 = Z_2 = Z$.

Now, for each section with $Z = Z_1 = Z_2$, values of $Z_1 + F(Z_1)$ and $Z_2 + F(Z_2)$ are computed, and curves of $Z_1 + F(Z_1)$ and $Z_2 + F(Z_2)$ are plotted against $Z$ for each section (Fig. 10-14).

2. DETERMINATION OF WATER-SURFACE ELEVATIONS. The effect of eddy losses may be included in the value of the roughness coefficient $n$, as described in Art. 10-4; thus, the term $h_e$ in Eq. (10-50) is zero. The resulting value of $Z_2 + F(Z_2)$ for a downstream section is therefore equal to $Z_1 + F(Z_1)$ for the next upstream section of the same reach, and vice versa.

For subcritical flow, the flow profile is determined in an upstream direction. Starting with a given initial water-surface elevation at a downstream section, the value of $Z_2 + F(Z_2)$ can be obtained from the appropriate $Z_2 + F(Z_2)$ curve. Entering the curve of $Z_1 + F(Z_1)$ for the next upstream section with this value, the corresponding water-surface elevation is determined directly. This procedure is repeated from section to section, tracing the desired flow profile.

For supercritical flow, the flow profile is traced in a downstream direction. Starting with the value of $Z_1 + F(Z_1)$ at the initial section and taking this value to the $Z_2 + F(Z_2)$ curve for the next downstream section, the corresponding water-surface elevation is determined.

If eddy losses are not included in the roughness, the term $h_e$ may be expressed as $k(\alpha V^2/2g)$, where $k$ is a coefficient described in Art. 10-4. Accordingly, the procedure of computation should be modified. First of all, it is necessary to plot curves of $k(\alpha V^2/2g)$ against the elevation $Z$ for each section.

For subcritical flow, water-surface elevations for two consecutive sections are determined in an upstream direction by the procedure described previously for $h_e = 0$. Values of $k(\alpha V^2/2g)$ may, therefore, be obtained from the plotted $k(\alpha V^2/2g)$ curves for these elevations. The difference $k\alpha(V_1^2/2g - V_2^2/2g)$, or $h_e'$ in the reach, is then added to the value of $Z_2 + F(Z_2)$ for the lower one of the two sections. The resulting value is taken to the $Z_1 + F(Z_1)$ curve for the higher of the two sections, and the corresponding corrected water-surface elevation is determined.

For supercritical flow, the procedure is similar. However, the flow profile should be traced in a downstream direction, and the correction for eddy losses should be deducted from the value of $Z_1 + F(Z_1)$ before this value is taken to the $Z_2 + F(Z_2)$ curve.

The application of the Ezra method will be illustrated by examples in Art. 10-8.

**10-6. The Standard Step Method for Natural Channels.** For flow in most natural channels at a normal stage, the flow profile in short reaches is very close to that of a uniform flow, but slightly modified by local channel irregularities. For apparently gradually varied flow, an approximate solution may be obtained by either the direct-integration method or the direct step method, assuming a prismatic channel having the average geometric and hydraulic characteristics of the natural channel. For a practical and precise solution, however, the standard step method is recommended.

The standard step method has many obvious advantages in application to natural channels. When the velocity head is small, the step method can be carried even in the wrong direction without resulting in serious errors, although it is always advisable to carry the computation upstream if the flow is subcritical and downstream if it is supercritical. The water-surface elevation of the initial section, where a flow-profile computation should start, may not be known in a natural stream; use of the step computation in this connection offers a special advantage. If the step computation is started at an assumed elevation that is incorrect for the given discharge, the resulting flow profile will become more nearly correct after every step, provided the computation is carried in the right direction. Therefore, if no elevation is known within or near the reach under consideration, an arbitrary elevation may be assumed at a distant section far enough away, above or below as the case may be, from the initial section. By the time the step computation has been carried to the initial section, the elevations will be correct. A check may be made by performing the same computation with another assumed elevation at the distant section. The computed elevation at the initial section is the correct elevation if the second computed value agrees with the first value. The two values usually agree if the distance from the distant section to the initial section is sufficient.

In computing a flow profile, the following information is generally required:

1. The discharge for which the flow profile is desired.

2. The water-surface elevation at the control section. If this is not available, the computation may start from an assumed elevation at a section far enough away from the initial section through which the profile is desired.

3. The geometric elements at various channel sections along the reach for all depths of flow within the range expected. These data may be obtained by a hydrographic survey or from a contour map of the channel bottom. A convenient method of recording these data is shown in Table 10-7. In the table, the cross sections are identified by number and river mileage in conformity with the map in Fig. 10-11. Other data include the reach length between sections, channel width, wetted perimeter, and water area. The column for remarks is provided to indicate the limiting features of the cross section, such as the side slopes, making it possible to estimate the water area and wetted perimeter within a moderate range of water-surface elevation.

If flow profiles for different discharges are contemplated, it will be convenient to construct curves of the geometric elements (Fig. 10-12) and to interpolate their values at different elevations.

4. The channel roughness and eddy losses at various sections. In flow-profile computation, it has been found that the smaller the value of Manning's $n$, the longer will be the profile, and vice versa. Hence, a smallest possible $n$ value should be selected in the computation if knowledge of the longest possible flow profile is required. This knowledge is

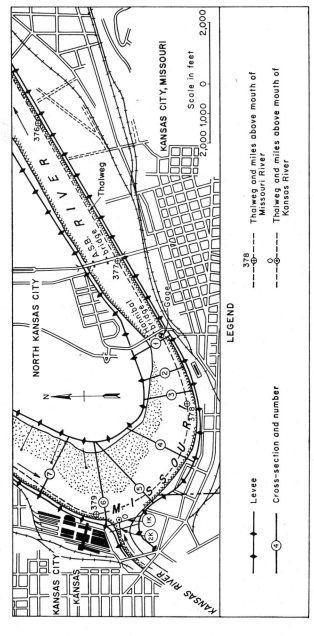

Fig. 10-11. Index map for Missouri and Kansas Rivers at Kansas City, Mo. (*U.S. Army Corps of Engineers.*)

TABLE 10-7. TABULATION OF DATA FOR MISSOURI AND KANSAS RIVERS AT KANSAS CITY, MO.*

| Sec no.† (1) | River mile (2) | Reach, ft (3) | W.S. El., ft m.s l. (4) | Water area (5) | From sta. (6) | To sta. (7) | Width, ft (8) | Wetted perimeter, ft (9) | Area, ft² (10) | Remarks (11) |
|---|---|---|---|---|---|---|---|---|---|---|
| | | | | | Missouri River | | | | | |
| 1 | 377.58 | ..... | 745.1 | Left over-bank | 0 + 35 | 5 + 05 | 470 | 470 | 2,650 | Levee 1 on 3 |
| | | | | Channel | 5 + 05 | 13 + 90 | 885 | 900 | 31,900 | Bank 1 on 1 |
| | | 1,060 | | | | | | | | |
| 2 | 377.78 | ..... | 745.3 | Left over-bank | 0 + 62 | 2 + 40 | 178 | 181 | 1,190 | Levee 1 on 4 |
| | | | | Channel | 2 + 40 | 14 + 97 | 1,260 | 1,290 | 32,500 | Bank 1 on 5 |
| | | 845 | | | | | | | | |
| 3 | 377.94 | ..... | 745.5 | Left over-bank | 0 + 61 | 1 + 50 | 89 | 92 | 580 | Levee 1 on 4 |
| | | | | Channel | 1 + 50 | 16 + 72 | 1,520 | 1,550 | 38,300 | Bank 1 on 4 |
| | | 2,060 | | | | | | | | |
| 4 | 378.33 | ..... | 745.9 | Channel | 2 + 91 | 23 + 72 | 2,080 | 2,110 | 48,500 | Levee 1 on 4 Bank 1 on 4½ |
| | | 1,690 | | | | | | | | |
| 5 | 378.65 | ..... | 746.2 | Left over-bank | 4 + 62 | 11 + 80 | 720 | 720 | 3,020 | Levee 1 on 4 |
| | | | | Channel | 11 + 80 | 32 + 24 | 2,040 | 2,080 | 47,300 | Bank 1 on 1 |
| | | 1,580 | | | | | | | | |
| 6 | 378.95 | ..... | 746.2 | Left over-bank | 4 + 62 | 11 + 80 | 720 | 720 | 3,020 | Levee 1 on 4 |
| | | | | Channel | 11 + 80 | 32 + 24 | 2,040 | 2,080 | 47,300 | Bank 1 on 1 |
| | | 2,430 | | | | | | | | |
| 7 | 379.41 | ..... | 746.9 | Left dike | 0 + 61 | 9 + 40 | 880 | 880 | 8,270 | Levee 1 on 4 |
| | | | | Channel | 9 + 40 | 22 + 35 | 1,300 | 1,320 | 34,700 | Levee 1 on 3 |
| | | | | | Kansas River | | | | | |
| 1K | 0.00 | 1,430‡ | 757.0 | Channel | ......, | ....... | 840 | 860 | 29,400 | Levee 1 on 3 both sides |
| | | 298 | | | | | | | | |
| 2K | 0.056 | ..... | 757.0 | Channel | ...... | ....... | 840 | 860 | 29,400 | Levee 1 on 3 both sides |
| | | | | | Missouri River | | | | | |
| 10 | 383.54 | ..... | 750.3 | Left over-bank | 32 + 80 | 44 + 50 | 1,170 | 1,180 | 12,900 | Levee 1 on 3 |
| | | | | Channel | 44 + 50 | 57 + 40 | 1,290 | 1,310 | 34,600 | |
| | | | - | Dike | 57 + 40 | 62 + 29 | 490 | 490 | 5,700 | Levee 1 on 4 |
| | | 2,430 | | | | | | | | |
| Fairfax Bridge | 384.00 | ..... | 750.3 | Left over-bank | ...... | ....... | 560 | 640 | 5,010 | 1 levee surface, 3 pier surfaces |
| | | | | Channel | ...... | ....... | 1,400 | 1,580 | 36,600 | 7 pier surfaces |
| | | | | Right over-bank | ...... | ....... | 125 | 130 | 1,100 | Bank 1 on 4 |
| | | 8,290 | | | | | | | | |
| 11 | 385.57 | ..... | 751.6 | Left over-bank | 59 + 60 | 81 + 10 | 2,159 | 2,150 | 13,900 | Levee 1 on 3 |
| | | | | Channel | 81 + 10 | 89 + 32 | 820 | 840 | 22,300 | Bank 1 on 1 |

* U.S. Army Corps of Engineers [29].
† See Fig. 10-11 for location of cross sections.
‡ Distance upstream from section 5.

important in certain engineering problems, such as the determination of the backwater effect due to a dam.

On the other hand, when knowledge of a shortest possible flow profile is required, a largest possible $n$ value should be used, for example, in the problem of improving a channel for navigation. Since the navigable depth should be greater than a certain minimum value, the shortest possible profile will indicate the lowest depth of flow at a given channel section. The eddy losses may be estimated separately and included in the computation. Sometimes, however, it is convenient to raise the value of $n$ and thus cover the effect of the losses.

**Example 10-10.** Compute the flow profile in the Missouri River near Kansas City, Mo., for a design discharge of 431,000 cfs. The plan indicating the locations of the cross sections is shown in Fig. 10-11. The geometric elements of these cross sections are shown in Table 10-7 for given water-surface elevations. For other elevations, the geometric elements are to be estimated from such data.[1]

*Solution.* The computations are tabulated as shown in Table 10-8. The column headings in the table are explained below:

Col. 1. Section number in conformity with the plan of Fig. 10-11

Col. 2. Subsections, for which M.C. designates the main channel section and L.O. designates the left overbank section

Col. 3. River mileage above the mouth of Missouri River

Col. 4. Water-surface elevation. The initial elevation of 752.25 at section 1 was estimated from the rating curve of the Kansas City gaging station on the Hannibal Bridge at Missouri River mile 377.58.

Col. 5. Water area. For instance, section 1 is subdivided into left-overbank and main-channel areas. At elevation 752.25, the area is determined for each subdivided area from Table 10-7 or from a curve prepared as shown in Fig. 10-12.

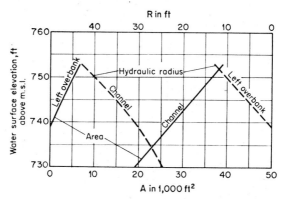

FIG. 10-12. $A$ and $R$ vs. water-surface elevation for channel section No. 1 of Missouri River at Kansas City, Mo. (*U.S. Army Corps of Engineers.*)

[1] The plan and data used in this example were obtained from [29]. Some numerical values, however, have been modified to suit the present purpose.

TABLE 10-8. COMPUTATION OF THE FLOW PROFILE FOR EXAMPLE 10-10 BY THE STANDARD-STEP METHOD
(Missouri and Kansas Rivers at Kansas City, Mo.)

| Sec. no. | Sub-sec. | River mile | $Z$ | $A$ | $P$ | $R$ | $R^{2/3}$ | $n$ | $K$ | $\frac{K^3}{A^2}$ | $\alpha$ | $V$ | $\alpha\frac{V^2}{2g}$ | $H$ | $S_f$ | $\bar{S}_f$ | $\Delta x$ | $h_f$ | $h_e$ | $H$ |
|---|---|---|---|---|---|---|---|---|---|---|---|---|---|---|---|---|---|---|---|---|
| (1) | (2) | (3) | (4) | (5) | (6) | (7) | (8) | (9) | (10) | (11) | (12) | (13) | (14) | (15) | (16) | (17) | (18) | (19) | (20) | (21) |
| 1 | M.C. | 377.58 | 752.25 | 38,600 | 910 | 42.4 | 12.2 | 0.025 | 280.5 × 10⁵ | 148.3 × 10¹¹ | | | | | | | | | | |
| | L.O. | | | 6,060 | 497 | 12.2 | 5.3 | 0.050 | 9.6 × 10⁵ | 0.2 × 10¹¹ | | | | | | | | | | | 754.01 |
| | | | | 44,660 | | | | | 290.1 × 10⁵ | 148.5 × 10¹¹ | 1.213 | 9.65 | 1.76 | 754.01 | 0.000220 | | | | 0 | |
| 2 | M.C. | 377.78 | 752.69 | 41,600 | 1,310 | 31.8 | 10.1 | 0.025 | 250.5 × 10⁵ | 91.0 × 10¹¹ | | | | | | | | | | |
| | L.O. | | | 2,580 | 210 | 12.3 | 5.4 | 0.050 | 4.2 × 10⁵ | 0.1 × 10¹¹ | | | | | | | | | | | 754.28 |
| | | | | 44,180 | | | | | 254.7 × 10⁵ | 91.1 × 10¹¹ | 1.078 | 9.76 | 1.59 | 754.28 | 0.000287 | 0.000254 | 1,060 | 0.27 | 0 | |
| 3 | M.C. | 377.94 | 753.37 | 50,300 | 1,570 | 32.0 | 10.1 | 0.025 | 303.0 × 10⁵ | 109.0 × 10¹¹ | | | | | | | | | | |
| | L.O. | | | 1,400 | 123 | 11.4 | 5.1 | 0.050 | 2.1 × 10⁵ | 0.0 × 10¹¹ | | | | | | | | | | | 754.49 |
| | | | | 51,700 | | | | | 305.1 × 10⁵ | 109.0 × 10¹¹ | 1.035 | 8.34 | 1.12 | 754.49 | 0.000200 | 0.000244 | 845 | 0.21 | 0 | |
| 4 | M.C. | 378.33 | 754.15 | 65,400 | 2,170 | 30.2 | 9.7 | 0.025 | 387.0 × 10⁵ | 109.9 × 10¹¹ | 1.000 | 6.59 | 0.68 | 754.83 | 0.000130 | 0.000165 | 2,060 | 0.34 | 0 | 754.83 |
| 5 | M.C. | 378.65 | 754.41 | 64,200 | 2,100 | 30.6 | 9.8 | 0.025 | 375.0 × 10⁵ | 128.0 × 10¹¹ | | | | | | | | | | |
| | L.O. | | | 9,040 | 754 | 12.0 | 5.2 | 0.050 | 14.0 × 10⁵ | 0.3 × 10¹¹ | | | | | | | | | | | 755.04 |
| | | | | 73,240 | | | | | 389.0 × 10⁵ | 128.3 × 10¹¹ | 1.167 | 5.88 | 0.63 | 755.04 | 0.000123 | 0.000127 | 1,690 | 0.21 | 0 | |

350,000 cfs from Upper Missouri River    81,000 cfs from Kansas River

Balance section

Mouth of Kansas River, $Q$ = 81,000 cfs

| Sec. no. | Sub-sec. | River mile | $Z$ | $A$ | $P$ | $R$ | $R^{2/3}$ | $n$ | $K$ | $\frac{K^3}{A^2}$ | $\alpha$ | $V$ | $\alpha\frac{V^2}{2g}$ | $H$ | $S_f$ | $\bar{S}_f$ | $\Delta x$ | $h_f$ | $h_e$ | $H$ |
|---|---|---|---|---|---|---|---|---|---|---|---|---|---|---|---|---|---|---|---|---|
| 1K | M.C. | | 755.06 | 27,700 | 844 | 32.8 | 10.3 | 0.025 | 170.3 × 10⁵ | 64.5 × 10¹¹ | 1.000 | 2.93 | 0.13 | 755.19 | 0.000023 | 0.000073 | 1,430 | 0.10 | 0.05 | 755.19 |

Missouri River, $Q$ = 350,000 cfs

| 6 | M.C. | 378.95 | 754.80 | 64,900 | 2,100 | 30.9 | 9.8 | 0.025 | 379.0 × 10⁵ | 129.3 × 10¹¹ | | | | | | | | | | |
|---|---|---|---|---|---|---|---|---|---|---|---|---|---|---|---|---|---|---|---|---|
| | L.O. | | | 9,300 | 755 | 12.4 | 5.4 | 0.050 | 14.9 × 10⁵ | 0.3 × 10¹¹ | | | | | | | | | | 755.20 |
| | | | | 74,200 | | | | | 393.9 × 10⁵ | 129.6 × 10¹¹ | 1.168 | 4.72 | 0.40 | 755.20 | 0.000078 | 0.000101 | 1,580 | 0.16 | 0 | |

Proceeding up the Missouri River

| 7 | M.C. | 379.41 | 754.78 | 45,100 | 1,330 | 34.0 | 10.5 | 0.025 | 282.2 × 10⁵ | 110.6 × 10¹¹ | | | | | | | | | | |
|---|---|---|---|---|---|---|---|---|---|---|---|---|---|---|---|---|---|---|---|---|
| | L.O. | | | 15,400 | 914 | 16.9 | 6.6 | 0.040 | 37.9 × 10⁵ | 2.3 × 10¹¹ | | | | | | | | | | 755.44 |
| | | | | 60,500 | | | | | 320.1 × 10⁵ | 112.9 × 10¹¹ | 1.261 | 5.79 | 0.66 | 755.44 | 0.000120 | 0.000099 | 2,430 | 0.24 | 0 | |

Col. 6. Wetted perimeter. For elevation 752.25 at section 1, the wetted perimeter is determined from Table 10-7 or from Fig. 10-12.

Col. 7. Hydraulic radius, obtained by dividing the area in col. 5 by the wetted perimeter in col. 6.

Col. 8. Two-thirds power of the hydraulic radius in col. 7.

Col. 9. The value of Manning's $n$. It is assumed that the general losses due to contraction, expansion, and bend are included in the friction losses computed from the selected $n$ values.

Col. 10. The conveyance $K = 1.49 A R^{2/3}/n$

Col. 11. The value of $K^3/A^2$

Col. 12. Energy coefficient for nonuniform velocity distribution. From col. 5 to col. 12, the procedure of computation is the same as that described in Art. 6-5. The coefficients for the subdivided channel sections are assumed equal to unity.

Col. 13. Mean velocity, which is equal to the section discharge of 431,000 cfs divided by the water area in col. 5. Above section 5, the discharge is divided between the Missouri River (350,000 cfs) and the Kansas River (81,000 cfs). The velocities should be computed for the divided discharges accordingly. The division of discharge is based on a hydrologic study of the drainage basins of the two rivers.

Col. 14. Velocity head

Col. 15. Total head, which is equal to the sum of the elevation in col. 4 and the velocity head in col. 14

Col. 16. Friction slope, which is equal to $(Q/K)^2$. The $K$ value is the total value for the section under consideration. Thus, for section 1, $S_f = [431,000/(290.1 \times 10^5)]^2 = 0.000220$.

Col. 17. Average friction slope through the reach between the two sections, that is, the arithmetic mean of the friction slope just computed in col. 16 and that for the previous step

Col. 18. Length of the reach between the sections, that is, the difference in river miles between the sections as converted into ft

Col. 19. Friction loss in the reach, that is, the product of the slope in col. 17 and the reach length in col. 18

Col. 20. Eddy loss in the reach. The general losses are included in the friction loss computed in col. 19. However, at the entrance of the Kansas River to the Missouri River, an additional eddy loss at the confluence is expected. This is estimated at 10% of the increase in velocity head, or $0.10 \times (0.63 - 0.13) = 0.05$ ft.

Col. 21. Total head, which is obtained by adding the sum of the losses $h_f$ in col. 19 and $h_e$ in col. 20 to the total head in the same column for the previous section. If the value so obtained does not agree closely with that entered in col. 15, the water-surface elevation in col. 4 should be assumed again until a fair agreement is reached.

For the computation of water-surface elevations at sections 1K, 2K, 6, and 7, see Art. 11-10.

## 10-7. The Stage-fall-discharge Method for Natural Channels.

When flow profiles of a stream in its natural state, without backwater effect, are available for a number of discharges, the stage-fall-discharge method may be used; this method has the advantages of simplicity and economy [29]. Similar methods have been also developed by others [30–34].[1]

[1] Reference [30] describes the so-called *Grimm method*. It requires a trial computation which, however, can be avoided by using nomographs, as suggested by Steinberg [31].

The friction slope $S_f$ in a short reach of length $L$ may be expressed as

$$S_f = \frac{F + h_{v2} - h_{v1}}{L} \qquad (10\text{-}57)$$

where $F$ is the fall in water surface and $h_{v2} - h_{v1}$ is the change in velocity head. If $h_{v2} - h_{v1}$ is zero or negligible, then $S_f = F/L$, and the normal discharge of a uniform flow by the Manning formula is

$$Q = \frac{1.49}{n} A R^{\frac{2}{3}} \left(\frac{F}{L}\right)^{\frac{1}{2}} \qquad (10\text{-}58)$$

For a gradually varied flow with backwater effect having a discharge $Q_x$ and a corresponding $F_x$ in the same reach, it may be assumed that a form similar to Eq. (10-58) may be written, i.e., that

$$Q_x = \frac{1.49}{n} A R^{\frac{2}{3}} \left(\frac{F_x}{L}\right)^{\frac{1}{2}} \qquad (10\text{-}59)$$

where the velocity-head changes due to backwater effect are also neglected. From Eqs. (10-58) and (10-59),

$$F_x = \left(\frac{Q_x}{Q/\sqrt{F}}\right)^2 \qquad (10\text{-}60)$$

where $Q/\sqrt{F}$ is called the *discharge for 1-ft fall*.[1] This equation can be used in the flow-profile computation if the stage-fall-discharge relationship for uniform flow in the reach is known.

The stage-fall-discharge relationship for a selected reach may be determined from records of observed stages and discharges (Table 10-9). The stages or water-surface elevations at the beginning section of the reach are plotted as ordinates, and corresponding values of $Q/\sqrt{F}$ are plotted as abscissas, resulting in a *stage-versus-$Q/\sqrt{F}$ curve* (Fig. 10-13). When any water-surface elevation at the beginning section of the reach is given, the corresponding value of $Q/\sqrt{F}$ can be read from the curve, and the fall for a discharge $Q_x$ be computed by Eq. (10-60). The computed fall, when added to the water-surface elevation at the beginning section of the reach, gives the water-surface elevation at the end section of the reach, which is also the water-surface elevation at the beginning section of the next reach. The procedure is repeated for each reach until the complete required flow profile is obtained.

The stage-versus-$Q/\sqrt{F}$ curve is generally constructed as an average curve for varying river conditions, such as rising and falling of stage,

[1] In a similar method developed by Rakhmanoff [34] a term $F/Q^2$ is used in lieu of $Q/\sqrt{F}$. This term has the nature of a resistance factor and therefore is given a name of *resistance modulus* by Pavlovskiĭ [21, p. 115].

fluctuating stream bed, and effects of wind, aquatic growth, ice, and over-bank flow. Owing to these varying conditions, the plotted points are often scattered; and a smooth line, giving consideration to the varying conditions, should be drawn through the points, representing the average condition of the channel. Where sufficient measurements are available, data of doubtful accuracy should be rejected. In general, the more recent measurements should be given greater weight, as reflecting recent channel changes. Other factors that should be considered in constructing the curve are the relative accuracy of individual discharge measurements; the flow condition during the measurements, whether rising, falling, or stationary; conditions affecting the stage-fall-discharge relationship, such as the changes in channel roughness, levee breaks, and shifts of channel controls; and the existence of substantial local inflow between the stations.

The stage-versus-$Q/\sqrt{F}$ curve may be extrapolated above or below the range of the observed data by extending the curve at its ends in accordance with the general trend of the curvature. However, any abrupt change in hydraulic elements of the channel section will produce a corresponding change in the curvature of the curve. In this case, a correction for the change, if known, should be made in extrapolating the curve.

This method is used most advantageously when a number of discharges corresponding to known stages, or vice versa, are desired in a stream. By making proper allowance for variable conditions, satisfactory results can be obtained for reaches of large rivers 50 to 100 miles from the measuring station. The data required by the method are often less expensive than those required by the standard step method. However, this advantage is usually offset by the inaccuracy of the results, because the effect of the change in velocity head is ignored in the present method. For this reason, the stage-fall discharge method is more satisfactory for problems in which the velocity is well below critical and decreases in the downstream direction.

**Example 10-11.** Compute the water-surface elevation at section 1 of the Missouri River problem in Example 10-10 by the stage-fall-discharge method. The reach from section 1 to section 5 is taken as the first reach. The water-surface elevations are available from stage records for gages located at sections 1 and 5. The discharges have been observed at the A.S.B. Bridge located about 3,000 ft downstream from section 1. These data are tabulated in Table 10-9.[1]

*Solution.* The data and computations for the stage versus discharge for a 1-ft-fall curve are given in Table 10-9, which contains the following headings:

Col. 1. Recorded water-surface elevations at section 1

Col. 2. Recorded water-surface elevations at section 5

Col. 3. Fall in ft, which is equal to the difference between elevations entered in cols. 2 and 1

---

[1] This example is taken from [29] with modifications.

Col. 4.   Observed discharges at the A.S.B. Bridge, in cfs

Col. 5.   Discharge per 1-ft fall, or $Q/\sqrt{F}$, where $Q$ is the discharge in col. 4 and $F$ is the fall in col. 3

Using water-surface elevations at section 1 as listed in col. 1 of the table and the corresponding values of $Q/\sqrt{F}$ in col. 5, construct a stage-versus-$Q/\sqrt{F}$ curve (Fig. 10-13).

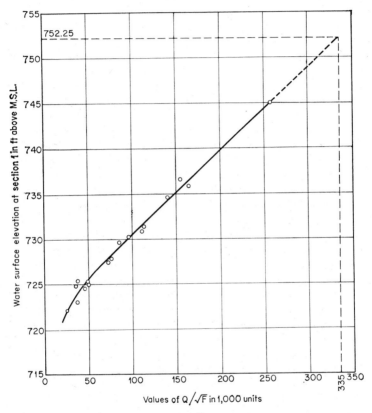

Fig. 10-13. The stage-vs.-$Q/\sqrt{F}$ curve for Example 10-11.

For a water-surface elevation of 752.25, a value of $Q/\sqrt{F} = 335{,}000$ is obtained by extrapolation. By Eq. (10-60), the fall between sections 1 and 5 is equal to $(431{,}000/335{,}000)^2 = 1.65$ ft. Adding this value to the elevation at section 1, the required water-surface elevation at section 5 is 753.90. This is about half a foot lower than the elevation computed by the standard step method; the difference results primarily from the neglect of velocity-head changes in the present method.

The computation may be continued for subsequent reaches. A tabulation, as shown in Table 10-10, is suggested for the computation if a complete flow profile is required.

If desired, the water-surface elevations at the intermediate sections 2 to 4 may be obtained by breaking up the reach 1–5 into four short reaches.   The profile elevations at the intermediate sections may be obtained by interpolation.   The stage-versus-$Q/\sqrt{F}$ curves can be drawn for each section, and the computation can be carried out for the subdivided reaches.

TABLE 10-9. DATA AND COMPUTATIONS FOR STAGE-vs.-$Q/\sqrt{F}$ CURVE USED
IN EXAMPLE 10-11
(Missouri River at Kansas City, Mo., sections 1 to 5)

| Water-surface elevation, m.s.l. | | Fall, ft | Discharge, cfs | $\dfrac{Q}{\sqrt{F}}$ |
|---|---|---|---|---|
| Section 1 | Section 5 | | | |
| (1) | (2) | (3) | (4) | (5) |
| 724.8 | 725.7 | 0.9 | 33,600 | 35,400 |
| 725.3 | 726.2 | 0.9 | 36,100 | 38,000 |
| 729.6 | 730.2 | 0.6 | 66,100 | 85,300 |
| 727.4 | 728.3 | 0.9 | 69,500 | 73,200 |
| 727.8 | 728.8 | 1.0 | 76,000 | 76,000 |
| 730.2 | 731.2 | 1.0 | 97,200 | 97,200 |
| 730.8 | 731.7 | 0.9 | 105,000 | 111,000 |
| 731.3 | 732.3 | 1.0 | 113,000 | 113,000 |
| 734.6 | 735.6 | 1.0 | 141,000 | 141,000 |
| 735.8 | 736.7 | 0.9 | 157,000 | 165,000 |
| 736.6 | 737.7 | 1.1 | 164,000 | 156,000 |
| 745.0 | 746.6 | 1.6 | 326,000 | 258,000 |
| 722.2 | 723.1 | 0.8 | 22,900 | 25,600 |
| 724.6 | 725.6 | 1.0 | 45,400 | 45,400 |
| 725.0 | 726.0 | 1.0 | 49,900 | 49,900 |
| 725.3 | 726.4 | 1.1 | 52,300 | 49,800 |

TABLE 10-10. COMPUTATION OF THE FLOW PROFILE FOR EXAMPLE 10-11 BY
THE STAGE-FALL-DISCHARGE METHOD
(Missouri River at Kansas City, Mo.; sections 1 to 5, $Q_x = 431{,}000$ cfs)

| Sec. no. | River mile | Length of reach | Water-surface elevation | $Q/\sqrt{F}$ | $F_x = \dfrac{Q_x{}^2}{(Q/\sqrt{F})^2}$ |
|---|---|---|---|---|---|
| 1 | 377.58 | . . . . . | 752.25 | 335,000 | 1.65 |
| | | | 1.65 | | |
| 5 | 378.65 | 5,655 | 753.90 | . . . . . . . | . . . . . |
| . . . | . . . . . . | . . . . . | To be continued if desired | | |

**10-8. The Ezra Method for Natural Channels.**   If flow profiles for a number of discharges or stages are desired, the stage-fall-discharge method can be used most advantageously for a simple and economical but approximate solution.   However, if a precise computation, including the effects of velocity-head changes and eddy losses, is required, the Ezra method described in Art. 10-5 should provide more satisfactory results.

**Example 10-12.** Determine the water-surface elevations at sections 1 to 5 of the Missouri River at Kansas City, Mo., as described in Example 10-10. The data required for the computation by the Ezra method are given in Table 10-7. The discharge is 431,000 cfs. The initial water-surface elevation at section 1 is 752.25. It is assumed that eddy losses are included in the friction losses.

*Solution.* The first step is to compute value of $Z + F(Z)$ from the given data. The computation is tabulated in Table 10-11 with the following column headings:

Col. 1. Channel-section number

Col. 2. River mileage

Col. 3. Length of reach in ft. The upper value $\Delta x_d$ is the length of the downstream reach from the selected section, and the lower value $\Delta x_u$ is the length of the upstream reach.

Col. 4. Water-surface elevations. Three elevations are given for each section. Generally, at least three elevations are selected for each section to provide at least three points for plotting each $Z + F(Z)$ curve.

Cols. 5 to 14. These columns correspond exactly to those in Table 10-8 for the standard step method. The values in the top row for each elevation are for the main channel, and those in the bottom row are for the left-overbank section.

Col. 15. Friction slope, which is equal to $(Q/K)^2$, where $Q = 431,000$ cfs and $K$ is from col. 10

Col. 16. Value of $-S_1 \Delta x_d/2$, where $S_1$ is the value from col. 15 and $\Delta x_d$ is the upper value in col. 3

Col. 17. Value of $S_2 \Delta x_u/2$, where $S_2$ is the value from col. 15 and $\Delta x_u$ is the lower value in col. 3

Col. 18. Value of $F(Z_1)$, which is equal to the sum of the value in col. 14 and the value in col. 16

Col. 19. Value of $F(Z_2)$, which is equal to the sum of the value in col. 14 and the value in col. 17

Col. 20. Sum of the values of $Z$ in col. 4 and $F(Z_1)$ in col. 18

Col. 21. Sum of the values of $Z$ in col. 4 and $F(Z_2)$ in col. 19

The second step is to plot curves of $Z + F(Z)$ against $Z$ for each cross section, using values from cols. 4, 20, and 21 of Table 10-11. The resulting curves are shown in Fig. 10-14.

The third step is to determine the water-surface elevations from the $Z + F(Z)$ curves. At section 1, for an initial water-surface elevation of 752.25, the value of $Z_2 + F(Z_2)$ is found from the appropriate curve (Fig. 10-14) to be 754.14. Taking this value to the $Z_1 + F(Z_1)$ curve for the next upstream section 2, the corresponding water-surface elevation is found to be 752.72. Continuing the procedure for other sections, the values are traced in the direction shown by the dashed line in Fig. 10-14. The results of the water-surface-elevation determination are tabulated in Table 10-12. They are in very close agreement with those obtained by the standard step method.

**Example 10-13.** Solve the problem in Example 10-12 for a discharge of 500,000 cfs. The corresponding initial water-surface elevation at section 1 was estimated from the rating curve to be 752.30.

*Solution.* The values of $F(Z_1)$ and $F(Z_2)$ for $Q = 500,000$ cfs may be obtained by multiplying the corresponding values in Table 10-11 by $(500,000/431,000)^2 = 1.34$. The values thus obtained are tabulated in cols. 3 and 4 of Table 10-13, respectively, and the values of $Z_1 + F(Z_1)$ and $Z_2 + F(Z_2)$ in cols. 5 and 6, respectively.

## TABLE 10-11. COMPUTATION OF $Z_1 + F(Z_1)$ AND $Z_2 + F(Z_2)$ FOR EXAMPLE 10-12

(Missouri River at Kansas City, Mo.; $Q = 431,000$ cfs)

| Sec. no. | River mile | $\Delta x_d$ $\Delta x_u$ | $Z$ | $A$ | $P$ | $R$ | $R^{2/3}$ | $n$ | $K$ | $\frac{K^3}{A^2}$ | $\alpha$ | $V$ | $\alpha\frac{V^2}{2g}$ | $S_f$ | $-\frac{1}{2}S_f\Delta x_d$ | $\frac{1}{2}S_f\Delta x_u$ | $F(Z_1)$ | $F(Z_2)$ | $Z_1 + F(Z_1)$ | $Z_2 + F(Z_2)$ |
|---|---|---|---|---|---|---|---|---|---|---|---|---|---|---|---|---|---|---|---|---|
| (1) | (2) | (3) | (4) | (5) | (6) | (7) | (8) | (9) | (10) | (11) | (12) | (13) | (14) | (15) | (16) | (17) | (18) | (19) | (20) | (21) |
| 1 | 377.58 | ..... | 752.0 | 38,100 | 910 | 41.9 | 12.06 | 0.025 | 274 × 10⁵ | 142 × 10¹¹ | | | | | | | | | | |
| | | 1,060 | ..... | 6,000 | 496 | 12.1 | 5.27 | 0.050 | 9 × 10⁵ | 0 | 1.22 | 9.77 | 1.81 | 0.000232 | ..... | 0.12 | ..... | 1.93 | ..... | 753.93 |
| | | | | 44,100 | | | | | 283 × 10⁵ | 142 × 10¹¹ | | | | | | | | | | |
| | | | 753.0 | 39,000 | 911 | 42.8 | 12.24 | 0.025 | 284 × 10⁵ | 150 × 10¹¹ | | | | | | | | | | |
| | | | | 6,500 | 499 | 13.0 | 5.53 | 0.050 | 11 × 10⁵ | 0 | 1.21 | 9.48 | 1.69 | 0.000213 | ..... | 0.11 | ..... | 1.80 | ..... | 754.80 |
| | | | | 45,500 | | | | | 295 × 10⁵ | 150 × 10¹¹ | | | | | | | | | | |
| | | | 754.0 | 39,900 | 912 | 43.7 | 12.41 | 0.025 | 295 × 10⁵ | 162 × 10¹¹ | | | | | | | | | | |
| | | | | 7,000 | 502 | 13.9 | 5.78 | 0.050 | 12 × 10⁵ | 0 | 1.23 | 9.19 | 1.61 | 0.000197 | ..... | 0.10 | ..... | 1.71 | ..... | 755.71 |
| | | | | 46,900 | | | | | 307 × 10⁵ | 162 × 10¹¹ | | | | | | | | | | |
| 2 | 377.78 | 1,060 | 752.0 | 41,000 | 1,320 | 31.0 | 9.87 | 0.025 | 241 × 10⁵ | 83 × 10¹¹ | | | | | | | | | | |
| | | 845 | | 2,500 | 209 | 12.0 | 5.24 | 0.050 | 4 × 10⁵ | 0 | 1.07 | 9.91 | 1.63 | 0.000311 | -0.17 | 0.13 | 1.46 | 1.76 | 753.46 | 753.76 |
| | | | | 43,500 | | | | | 245 × 10⁵ | 83 × 10¹¹ | | | | | | | | | | |
| | | | 753.0 | 42,300 | 1,325 | 32.0 | 10.08 | 0.025 | 254 × 10⁵ | 92 × 10¹¹ | | | | | | | | | | |
| | | | | 2,700 | 213 | 12.5 | 5.39 | 0.050 | 4 × 10⁵ | 0 | 1.08 | 9.58 | 1.54 | 0.000280 | -0.15 | 0.12 | 1.39 | 1.66 | 754.39 | 754.66 |
| | | | | 45,000 | | | | | 258 × 10⁵ | 92 × 10¹¹ | | | | | | | | | | |
| | | | 754.0 | 43,600 | 1,330 | 32.8 | 10.25 | 0.025 | 267 × 10⁵ | 100 × 10¹¹ | | | | | | | | | | |
| | | | | 2,900 | 217 | 13.4 | 5.64 | 0.050 | 5 × 10⁵ | 0 | 1.08 | 9.27 | 1.44 | 0.000252 | -0.13 | 0.11 | 1.31 | 1.55 | 755.31 | 755.55 |
| | | | | 46,500 | | | | | 272 × 10⁵ | 100 × 10¹¹ | | | | | | | | | | |

TABLE 10-11. COMPUTATION OF $Z_1 + F(Z_1)$ AND $Z_2 + F(Z_2)$ FOR EXAMPLE 10-12 (continued)

| Sec. no. | River mile | $\Delta z_d$ $\Delta z_u$ | $Z$ | $A$ | $P$ | $R$ | $R^{2/3}$ | $n$ | $K$ | $\dfrac{K^2}{A^3}$ | $\alpha$ | $V$ | $\alpha\dfrac{V^2}{2g}$ | $S_f$ | $-\tfrac{1}{2}S_f \Delta z_d$ | $\tfrac{1}{2}S_f \Delta z_u$ | $F(Z_1)$ | $F(Z_2)$ | $Z_1 + F(Z_1)$ | $Z_2 + F(Z_2)$ |
|---|---|---|---|---|---|---|---|---|---|---|---|---|---|---|---|---|---|---|---|---|
| (1) | (2) | (3) | (4) | (5) | (6) | (7) | (8) | (9) | (10) | (11) | (12) | (13) | (14) | (15) | (16) | (17) | (18) | (19) | (20) | (21) |
| 3 | 377.94 | 845 | 752.0 | 48,300 | 1,577 | 30.6 | 9.78 | 0.025 | 281 × 10⁵ | 95 × 10¹¹ | | | | | | | | | | |
| | | 2,060 | | 1,200 | 120 | 10.0 | 4.64 | 0.050 | 2 × 10⁵ | 0 | 1.03 | 8.70 | 1.21 | 0.000232 | −0.10 | 0.24 | 1.11 | 1.45 | 753.11 | 753.45 |
| | | | | 49,500 | | | | | 283 × 10⁵ | 95 × 10¹¹ | | | | | | | | | | |
| | | | 753.0 | 49,900 | 1,581 | 31.5 | 9.97 | 0.025 | 297 × 10⁵ | 105 × 10¹¹ | | | | | | | | | | |
| | | | | 1,300 | 124 | 10.5 | 4.80 | 0.050 | 2 × 10⁵ | 0 | 1.03 | 8.42 | 1.13 | 0.000208 | −0.09 | 0.21 | 1.04 | 1.34 | 754.04 | 754.34 |
| | | | | 51,200 | | | | | 299 × 10⁵ | 105 × 10¹¹ | | | | | | | | | | |
| | | | 754.0 | 51,400 | 1,585 | 32.5 | 10.18 | 0.025 | 312 × 10⁵ | 115 × 10¹¹ | | | | | | | | | | |
| | | | | 1,400 | 128 | 11.0 | 4.95 | 0.050 | 2 × 10⁵ | 0 | 1.04 | 8.17 | 1.08 | 0.000189 | −0.08 | 0.19 | 1.00 | 1.27 | 755.00 | 755.27 |
| | | | | 52,800 | | | | | 314 × 10⁵ | 115 × 10¹¹ | | | | | | | | | | |
| 4 | 378.33 | 2,060 | 752.0 | 61,400 | 2,163 | 28.4 | 9.31 | 0.025 | 344 × 10⁵ | ...... | 1.00 | 7.02 | 0.77 | 0.000157 | −0.16 | 0.13 | 0.61 | 0.90 | 752.61 | 752.90 |
| | | 1,690 | 753.0 | 63,500 | 2,172 | 29.2 | 9.48 | 0.025 | 360 × 10⁵ | ...... | 1.00 | 6.78 | 0.71 | 0.000144 | −0.15 | 0.12 | 0.56 | 0.83 | 753.56 | 753.83 |
| | | | 754.0 | 65,700 | 2,181 | 30.1 | 9.68 | 0.025 | 380 × 10⁵ | ...... | 1.00 | 6.57 | 0.67 | 0.000128 | −0.13 | 0.11 | 0.54 | 0.78 | 754.54 | 754.78 |
| 5 | 378.65 | 1,690 | 752.0 | 59,100 | 2,084 | 28.5 | 9.33 | 0.025 | 330 × 10⁵ | 103 × 10¹¹ | | | | | | | | | | |
| | | | | 7,200 | 745 | 9.8 | 4.58 | 0.050 | 10 × 10⁵ | 0 | 1.15 | 6.50 | 0.76 | 0.000160 | −0.14 | ... | 0.62 | ..... | 752.62 | |
| | | | | 66,300 | | | | | 340 × 10⁵ | 103 × 10¹¹ | | | | | | | | | | |
| | | | 753.0 | 61,200 | 2,085 | 29.3 | 9.50 | 0.025 | 347 × 10⁵ | 112 × 10¹¹ | | | | | | | | | | |
| | | | | 7,900 | 749 | 10.6 | 4.83 | 0.050 | 11 × 10⁵ | 0 | 1.17 | 6.23 | 0.70 | 0.000145 | −0.12 | ... | 0.58 | ..... | 753.58 | |
| | | | | 69,100 | | | | | 358 × 10⁵ | 112 × 10¹¹ | | | | | | | | | | |
| | | | 754.0 | 63,300 | 2,087 | 30.3 | 9.72 | 0.025 | 367 × 10⁵ | 123 × 10¹¹ | | | | | | | | | | |
| | | | | 8,700 | 753 | 11.6 | 5.12 | 0.050 | 12 × 10⁵ | 0 | 1.17 | 5.99 | 0.65 | 0.000129 | −0.11 | ... | 0.54 | ..... | 754.54 | |
| | | | | 72,000 | | | | | 379 × 10⁵ | 123 × 10¹¹ | | | | | | | | | | |

TABLE 10-12. COMPUTATION OF THE FLOW PROFILE FOR EXAMPLE 10-12 BY
THE EZRA METHOD
(Missouri River at Kansas City, Mo., $Q$ = 431,000 cfs)

| Sec. no. | River mile | $Z_1 + F(Z_1)$ | $Z_2 + F(Z_2)$ | Water-surface elevation $Z$, ft |
|---|---|---|---|---|
| 1 | 377.58 | ...... | 754.14 | 752.25 |
| 2 | 377.78 | 754.14 | 754.41 | 752.72 |
| 3 | 377.94 | 754.41 | 754.68 | 753.38 |
| 4 | 378.33 | 754.68 | 754.93 | 754.15 |
| 5 | 378.65 | 754.93 | ...... | 754.43 |

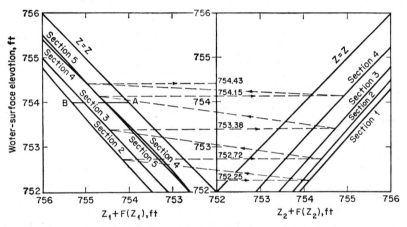

FIG. 10-14. Curves of $Z + F(Z)$ for Example 10-12.

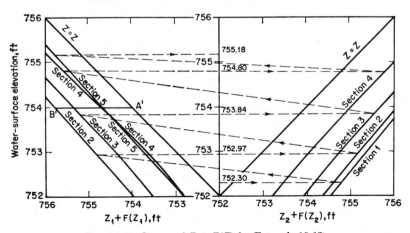

FIG. 10-15. Curves of $Z + F(Z)$ for Example 10-13.

TABLE 10-13. COMPUTATION OF $Z + F(Z)$ FOR EXAMPLE 10-13
(Missouri River at Kansas City, Mo., $Q = 500,000$ cfs)

| Sec. no. | $Z$ | $F(Z_1)$ | $F(Z_2)$ | $Z_1 + F(Z_1)$ | $Z_2 + F(Z_2)$ |
|---|---|---|---|---|---|
| (1) | (2) | (3) | (4) | (5) | (6) |
| 1 | 752 | .... | 2.59 | ...... | 754.59 |
|   | 753 | .... | 2.41 | ...... | 755.41 |
|   | 754 | .... | 2.29 | ...... | 756.29 |
| 2 | 752 | 1.96 | 2.36 | 753.96 | 754.36 |
|   | 753 | 1.86 | 2.22 | 754.86 | 755.22 |
|   | 754 | 1.78 | 2.08 | 755.78 | 756.08 |
| 3 | 752 | 1.49 | 1.94 | 753.49 | 753.94 |
|   | 753 | 1.40 | 1.80 | 754.40 | 754.80 |
|   | 754 | 1.34 | 1.70 | 755.34 | 755.70 |
| 4 | 752 | 0.82 | 1.21 | 752.82 | 753.21 |
|   | 753 | 0.75 | 1.11 | 753.75 | 754.11 |
|   | 754 | 0.73 | 1.05 | 754.73 | 755.05 |
| 5 | 752 | 0.83 | .... | 752.83 | ...... |
|   | 753 | 0.78 | .... | 753.78 | ...... |
|   | 754 | 0.73 | .... | 754.73 | ...... |

The $Z + F(Z)$ curves are then plotted (Fig. 10-15). These can also be obtained by a simple graphical method. In Fig. 10-14, straight lines $Z = Z$ may be drawn along with the $Z + F(Z)$ curves. For example, referring to the curve for section 2, the intercept $AB$ between the line $Z = Z$ and the curve for $Z + F(Z)$ is equal to $F(Z)$ for $Q = 431,000$ cfs at the water-surface elevation of 754.00. This intercept $AB$ multiplied by 1.34 gives the corresponding intercept $A'B'$ in Fig. 10-15 for the same elevation but different discharge. In this manner, the point $B'$ and, hence, the $Z + F(Z)$ curves for $Q = 500,000$ cfs can be plotted. From these curves, the required water-surface elevations are determined, as shown in Table 10-14.

TABLE 10-14. COMPUTATION OF THE FLOW PROFILE FOR EXAMPLE 10-13 BY
THE EZRA METHOD, EDDY LOSSES BEING INCLUDED IN THE
FRICTION LOSSES
(Missouri River at Kansas City, Mo., $Q = 500,000$ cfs)

| Sec. no. | River mileage | $Z_1 + F(Z_1)$ | $Z_2 + F(Z_2)$ | Water-surface elevation $Z$, ft |
|---|---|---|---|---|
| 1 | 377.58 |        | 754.83 | 752.30 |
| 2 | 377.78 | 754.83 | 755.20 | 752.97 |
| 3 | 377.94 | 755.20 | 755.56 | 753.84 |
| 4 | 378.33 | 755.56 | 755.83 | 754.80 |
| 5 | 378.65 | 755.83 |        | 755.18 |

**Example 10-14.** Solve the problem in Example 10-12 by treating the eddy losses separately. It is assumed that the values of the roughness coefficient $n$ do not include the effect of eddy losses and that the latter is to be computed as 50% of the change in velocity head when the velocity head is decreasing downstream or as 10% of the increase in velocity head when it is increasing downstream.

*Solution.* Curves of $Z + F(Z)$ constructed for Example 10-12 (Fig. 10-14) are also applicable to this solution. The computation for the determination of the water-surface elevation is tabulated in Table 10-15, in which the numbers in parentheses

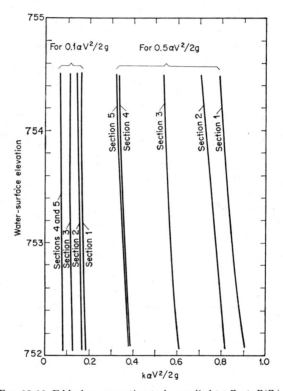

Fig. 10-16. Eddy-loss correction to be applied to $Z_2 + F(Z_2)$.

indicate the order of the computation steps. The curves of $0.5\alpha V^2/2g$ and $0.1\alpha V^2/2g$ are then plotted (Fig. 10-16). These curves are used to correct for eddy losses, as explained previously (Art. 10-5).

Starting at section 1 with a water-surface elevation of 752.25 (see step 1 in Table 10-15), the value of $Z_2 + F(Z_2)$ is found from the $Z_2 + F(Z_2)$ curve for section 1 as 754.14 (see step 2). The corresponding values of $0.5\alpha V^2/2g$ and $0.1\alpha V^2/2g$ are found from Fig. 10-16 to be 0.89 (see step 3) and 0.18 (see step 4), respectively. Taking the value of 754.14 to the $Z_1 + F(Z_1)$ curve for the next upstream section 2 (see step 6), the corresponding water-surface elevation is 752.72 (see step 7), and the value of $0.5\alpha V^2/2g$ is 0.78 (see step 9) and that of $0.1\alpha V^2/2g$ is 0.16 (see step 10). Since the

TABLE 10-15. COMPUTATION OF THE FLOW PROFILE FOR EXAMPLE 10-14 BY THE EZRA METHOD, TREATING EDDY LOSSES SEPARATELY

(Missouri River at Kansas City, Mo., $Q$ = 431,000 cfs)

| Sec. no. | River mile | $Z_1 + F(Z_1)$ | Corrected $Z_1 + F(Z_1)$ | $Z_2 + F(Z_2)$ | $0.5\alpha \frac{V^2}{2g}$ | $0.1\alpha \frac{V^2}{2g}$ | $h_e$ | $Z_2 + F(Z_2) + h_e$ | Trial $Z$ value | Corrected $Z$ value |
|---|---|---|---|---|---|---|---|---|---|---|
| 1 | 377.58 | ......... | ......... | (2) 754.14 | (3) 0.89 | (4) 0.18 | ......... | (12) 754.16 | (1)* 752.25 | (5) 752.25 |
| 2 | 377.78 | (6) 754.14 | (13) 754.16 | (8) 754.42 | (9) 0.78 | (10) 0.16 | (11) 0.02 | (21) 754.47 | (7) 752.72 | (14) 752.74 |
| 3 | 377.94 | (15) 754.42 | (22) 754.47 | (17) 754.71 | (18) 0.56 | (19) 0.11 | (20) 0.05 | (30) 754.75 | (16) 753.40 | (23) 753.45 |
| 4 | 378.33 | (24) 754.71 | (31) 754.75 | (26) 754.93 | (27) 0.34 | (28) 0.07 | (29) 0.04 | (38) 754.94 | (25) 754.18 | (32) 754.22 |
| 5 | 378.65 | (33) 754.93 | (39) 754.94 | ......... | (35) 0.32 | (36) 0.06 | (37) 0.01 | ......... | (34) 754.43 | (40) 754.44 |

* The numbers in parentheses indicate the order of the computation steps.

velocity is increasing downstream (or decreasing upstream), the eddy loss is 0.18 − 0.16 = 0.02 (see step 11). In order to include the effect of this eddy loss, add 0.02 to 754.14 (see step 2) which was previously found to be the value of $Z_2 + F(Z_2)$ at section 1. The resulting value is 754.16 (see step 13). Referring to the $Z_1 + F(Z_1)$ curve for section 2 with this value, the water-surface elevation is found to be 752.74 (see step 14).

Repeating the above procedure and correcting for the eddy losses accordingly, the water-surface elevations at all sections over the reach are obtained.

## PROBLEMS

**10-1.** Show that the flow profile in a wide horizontal channel may be expressed as

$$x = \frac{\alpha C^2}{g}\left(y - \frac{y^4}{4y_c^3}\right) + \text{const} \tag{10-61}$$

where $C$ is Chézy's resistance factor.

**10-2.** Show that the condition for the existence of a point of inflection on the flow profile may be expressed as

$$Mu^N - N\left(\frac{y_n}{y_c}\right)^M u^M + N - M = 0 \tag{10-62}$$

**10-3.** Complete the computation of the flow profile in Example 10-2.

**10-4.** Complete the computation of the flow profile in Example 10-5, and compare the result with that of Prob. 10-3.

**10-5.** Show that the flow profile in a frictionless rectangular channel may be expressed as

$$x = \frac{y}{2S_0}\left[2 - 3\frac{y_c}{y} + \left(\frac{y_c}{y}\right)^3\right] + \text{const} \tag{10-63}$$

**10-6.** Solve Example 10-1 by assuming $\alpha = 1.0$, and examine the effect of the value of $\alpha$ on the shape of the flow profile. Use:

a. The graphical-integration method
b. The direct-integration method
c. The direct step method
d. The standard step method

**10-7.** Compute the flow profile in the channel described in Example 10-1 if $S_0 = 0.0169$. Assume that the profile starts at the dam site at a depth of 5 ft and terminates upstream at a critical depth. Use:

a. The graphical-integration method
b. The direct-integration method
c. The direct step method
d. The standard step method

**10-8.** A free fall instead of the dam controls the depth at the downstream end of the channel described in Example 10-1. Compute the flow profile from the control to an upstream section where the depth of flow is 1% less than the normal depth, using:

a. The graphical-integration method
b. The direct-integration method

*c.* The direct step method
*d.* The standard step method

**10-9.** If the slope of a channel having the section properties described in Example 10-1 has a break in grade changing from 0.0016 on the upstream side to 0.0169 on the downstream side, compute the flow profile on the downstream side from the break to a section where the depth is 1% greater than the normal depth. Use:

    *a.* The graphical-integration method
    *b.* The direct-integration method
    *c.* The direct step method
    *d.* The standard step method

**10-10.** If the slope of a channel having the section properties described in Example 10-1 has a break in grade changing from 0.0169 on the upstream side to 0.0016 on the downstream side, compute the flow profile on the downstream side from the break to a critical section. The flow in the upstream channel is assumed uniform. Use:

    *a.* The graphical-integration method
    *b.* The direct-integration method
    *c.* The direct step method
    *d.* The standard step method

**10-11.** Solve Example 10-3 if $S_0 = 0.0016$, using:

    *a.* The graphical-integration method
    *b.* The direct-integration method
    *c.* The direct step method
    *d.* The standard step method

**10-12.** Solve Example 10-3 if $S_0 = 0.0169$, using:

    *a.* The graphical-integration method
    *b.* The direct-integration method
    *c.* The direct step method
    *d.* The standard step method

**10-13.** Solve Example 10-3 if $S_0 = 0$, using:

    *a.* The graphical-integration method
    *b.* The direct-integration method
    *c.* The direct step method
    *d.* The standard step method

**10-14.** If the channel described in Prob. 10-8 is horizontal, compute the flow profile from the control section to an upstream section where the depth of flow is 10 ft. Use:

    *a.* The graphical-integration method
    *b.* The direct-integration method
    *c.* The direct step method
    *d.* The standard step method

**10-15.** Solve Prob. 10-14 if $S_0 = -0.0016$.
**10-16.** Solve Example 10-8 if $\alpha = 1.10$.
**10-17.** Solve Example 10-8 by the method of numerical integration, using the varied-flow-function table (Appendix D).

**10-18.** A prismatic trapezoidal earth spillway with 3:1 side slopes is discharging 1,500 cfs. The bottom of the spillway is horizontal and is 200 ft long and 75 ft wide in the reach between a downstream critical control section and the upstream reservoir. Manning's $n$ is estimated to be 0.035. Using any method given in this chapter, determine:

    *a.* The flow profile between the reservoir and the control section
    *b.* The friction loss through this spillway measured in ft
    *c.* The elevation of the pool level in the reservoir

**10-19.** A prismatic trapezoidal earth spillway with 3:1 side slopes and a bottom width of 75 ft is discharging 1,500 cfs. The spillway has a horizontal bottom upstream from a critical control section for a distance of 90 ft and an adverse slope of 10:1 for an upstream distance of 100 ft from the reservoir. Manning's $n$ is 0.035. Using any method given in this chapter, determine:

    *a.* The flow profile in the spillway
    *b.* The energy line in the spillway

**10-20.** Solve the problem in Example 10-10 by the standard step method, for a design discharge of 500,000 cfs.

**10-21.** Carry out the computation in Example 10-11 by breaking up reach 1-5 into four short reaches at the intermediate sections.

**10-22.** Solve the problem in Example 10-11 by the stage-fall-discharge method for a design discharge of 500,000 cfs.

**10-23.** Solve Example 10-1 by the stage-fall-discharge method.

**10-24.** Solve Example 10-1 by the Ezra method.

**10-25.** Solve Example 10-1 by the Ezra method if $Q = 500$ cfs.

## REFERENCES

1. A. J. E. J. Dupuit: "Études théoriques et pratiques sur le mouvement des eaux" ("Theoretical and Practical Studies on Flow of Water"), Paris, 2d ed., 1863.
2. J. A. Ch. Bresse: "Cours de mécanique appliquée," 2e partie, Hydraulique, ("Course in Applied Mechanics," pt. 2, Hydraulics), Mallet-Bachelier, Paris, 1860.
3. F. Grashof, "Theoretische Maschinenlehre" ("Theoretical Course on Machines"), Leipzig, 1875, vol. 1.
4. M. Rühlmann: "Hydromechanik" ("Hydromechanics"), Leipzig, 1st ed., 1857; Hahnsche Buchhandlung, Hanover, 2d ed., 1880.
5. G. Tolkmitt: "Grundlagen der Wasserbaukunst" ("Fundamentals of Hydraulic Engineering"), Ernst & Sohn, Berlin, 1898.
6. U. Masoni: "Corso di Idraulica Teorica e Pratica" ("Course of Theoretical and Practical Hydraulics"), 2d ed., Naples, 1900.
7. Boris A. Bakhmeteff: "O Neravnomernom Dvizhenii Zhidkosti v Otkrytom Rusle" ("Varied Flow in Open Channels"), St. Petersburg, Russia, 1912.
8. Boris A. Bakhmeteff: "Hydraulics of Open Channels," McGraw-Hill Book Company, Inc., New York, 1932.
9. Philipp Forchheimer: "Hydraulik" ("Hydraulics"), 1st ed., Teubner Verlagsgesellschaft, Leipzig and Berlin, 1914.
10. E. Baticle: Nouvelle méthode pour la détermination des courbes de remous (New method for the determination of backwater curves), *Le Génie civil*, vol. 79, no. 23, Dec. 3, pp. 488–492, 1921; no 24, Dec. 10, pp. 515–516, 1921.

11. Josef Koženy: Berechnung der Senkungskurve in regelmässigen breiten Gerinnen (Computation of surface curve in uniform broad channels), *Wasserkraft und Wasserwirtschaft*, Munich, vol. 23, no. 16, pp. 232–234, Aug. 15, 1928.

12. Armin Schoklitsch: "Wasserbau" ("Hydraulic Structures"), translated from the German by Samuel Shulits, American Society of Mechanical Engineers, New York, 1934, vol. 1, p. 105.

13. Nagaho Mononobe: Back-water and drop-down curves for uniform channels, *Transactions, American Society of Civil Engineers*, vol. 103, pp. 950–989, 1938.

14. Ming Lee: Steady gradually varied flow in uniform channels on mild slopes, Ph.D. thesis, University of Illinois, Urbana, 1947.

15. Ming Lee, Harold E. Babbitt, and E. Robert Baumann: Gradually varied flow in uniform channels on mild slopes, *University of Illinois, Engineering Experiment Station, Bulletin Series No. 404*, vol. 50, no. 28, November, 1952.

16. M. E. Von Seggern: Integrating the equation of nonuniform flow, *Transactions, American Society of Civil Engineers*, vol. 115, pp. 71–88, 1950.

17. Clint J. Keifer and Henry Hsien Chu: Backwater functions by numerical integration, *Transactions, American Society of Civil Engineers*, vol. 120, pp. 429–442, 1955.

18. Ven Te Chow: Integrating the equation of gradually varied flow, paper 838, *Proceedings, American Society of Civil Engineers*, vol. 81, pp. 1–32, November, 1955. Discussions by Clint J. Keifer and Henry Hsien Chu, Robert Y. D. Chun, Masashi Hom-ma, Allan Newman, and Steponas Kolupaila, paper 955, *Journal, Hydraulics Division*, vol. 82, no. HY2, pp. 51–60, April, 1956; corrections on p. 60. Discussions by R. Silvester and Alfred S. Harrison, paper 1010, vol. 82, no. HY3, pp. 13–21, June, 1956. Closing discussion by the author, paper 1177, vol. 83, no. HY1, pp. 9–22, February, 1957.

19. I. I. Levi: Gidravlicheskie pokazateli rusla i ikh prilozhenie k teorii neravnomernogo dvizheniia zhidkosti v otkrytykh kanalakh i ruslakh (The hydraulic exponents of channels and their application to the theory of nonuniform flow in open channel), *Vestnik Irrigatsii (Herald of Irrigation)*, Tashkent, U.S.S.R., no. 2, pp. 35–49, 1925.

20. Arthur E. Matzke: Varied flow in open channels of adverse slope, *Transactions, American Society of Civil Engineers*, vol. 102, pp. 651–660, 1937.

21. M. D. Chertousov: "Gidravlika: Spetsialnyĭ Kurs" ("Hydraulics: Special Course"), Gosenergoizdat, Moscow, 1957.

22. V. J. Charnomskiĭ: Zadachi na ustanovivsheiesia neravnomernoie techenie vody v otkrytykh ruslakh s priamolineinym i trapetsoidalnym poperechnym secheniem (Problems on steady nonuniform flow of water in open channels with straightlined trapezoidal cross section), *Trudy Varshavskago Politekhnicheskago Instituta*, Warsaw, 1914.

23. Alva G. Husted: New method of computing backwater and drop-down curves, *Engineering News-Record*, vol. 92, no. 17, pp. 719–722, Apr. 24, 1924.

24. H. R. Leach: New methods for the solution of backwater problems, *Engineering News-Record*, vol. 82, no. 16, pp. 768–770, April, 1919.

25. Arthur A. Ezra: A direct step method for computing water-surface profiles, *Transactions, American Society of Civil Engineers*, vol. 119, pp. 453–462, 1954.

26. Francis F. Escoffier: Graphic calculation of backwater eliminates solution by trial, *Engineering News-Record*, vol. 136, no. 26, p. 71, June 27, 1946.

27. N. Raytchine and P. Chatelain: Détermination graphique de la ligne d'eau et calcul des remous (Graphical determination of backwater curves), *La Houille blanche*, Grenoble, 5th yr., no. 3, pp. 373–379, May-June, 1950.

28. Josef Frank: Graphische Berechnung von Wasserspiegel-Linien (Graphical calcu-

lation of water flow profiles), *Schweizerische Bauzeitung*, Zürich, vol. 102, no. 6, pp. 65–71, Aug. 5, 1933.

29. Hydrologic and hydraulic analysis: Computation of backwater curves in river channels, *U.S. Army Corps of Engineers, Engineering Manual for Civil Works Construction*, pt. CXIV, chap. 9, May, 1952.

30. C. I. Grimm: Backwater slopes above dams, *Engineering News-Record*, vol. 100, no. 23, p. 902, June 7, 1928.

31. I. H. Steinberg: The nomograph as an aid in computing backwater curves, *Civil Engineering*, vol. 9, no. 6, pp. 365–366, June, 1939.

32. Sherman M. Woodward and Chester J. Posey: "Hydraulics of Steady Flow in Open Channels," John Wiley & Sons, Inc., New York, 1941; pp. 103–107.

33. L. E. Jones: The $Q/\sqrt{F}$ technique in open channel hydraulics, *Proceedings of the 2d Midwestern Conference of Fluid Mechanics, The Ohio State University, Engineering Experiment Station, Bulletin* 149, pp. 81–87, September, 1952.

34. A. N. Rakhmanoff: O postroenii krivykh svobodnoĭ poverkhnosti dlia estestvennykh vodotokov pri ustanovivshemsia dvizhenii (On the construction of curves of free surface for natural streams at steady flow), *Izvestiia Nauchno-Melioratsionnogo Instituta (Transactions, Scientific Institute of Reclamation)*, no. 21, 1930.

35. J. Chabert: "Calcul des courbes de remous" ("Calculations of Backwater Curves"), Éditions Eyrolles, Paris, 1955. This reference gives several methods of flow-profile computation, including some which are not discussed in this book.

CHAPTER 11

# PRACTICAL PROBLEMS

**11-1. Delivery of a Canal for Subcritical Flow.** When a canal connects two reservoirs having varying levels, the discharge of the canal under various conditions of reservoir level is called the *delivery* of the canal; this problem was discussed by Bakhmeteff [1]. Bakhmeteff has treated this subject for prismatic canals with subcritical flow under three general cases. The cases are classified according to the condition of three variables, namely, the depth of flow $y_1$ at the upstream end of the canal, the depth of flow $y_2$ at the downstream end, and the discharge $Q$ of the canal.

*A. Case of Constant $y_1$.* This is the case in which the water level at the upstream end of the canal does not change (Fig. 11-1). The depth $y_1$ is

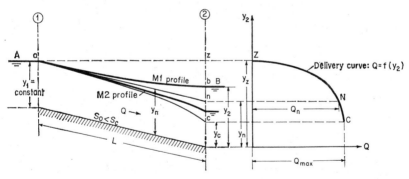

Fig. 11-1. Delivery of a canal with subcritical flow and constant $y_1$.

assumed to remain constant, owing to a constant pool level $A$; while $y_2$, determined by level $B$, fluctuates. Also shown in Fig. 11-1 are the flow profiles for various conditions of $y_2$ and the corresponding discharges $Q$. The relationship between $y_2$ and $Q$ is shown by a so-called *delivery curve* $Q = f(y_2)$. Several flow conditions may be described as follows:

1. UNIFORM FLOW. When $y_2 = y_1 = y_n$, the flow is uniform, with its surface represented by a straight line $an$ parallel to the channel bottom. The corresponding normal discharge $Q_n$ is indicated on the delivery curve.

297

The value of this discharge is $Q_n = K_n \sqrt{S_0}$, where $K_n$ is the conveyance of the cross section with the depth $y_2$ equal to $y_1$ and where $S_0$ is the bottom slope.

2. FLOW OF MAXIMUM DISCHARGE. When $y_2$ is equal to the critical depth $y_c$ of section 2, the discharge will reach its maximum possible value, since $y_2$ cannot be less than $y_c$ and the head is at its maximum. If the downstream pool level $B$ falls below the depth $y_c$, a free overfall at that depth will occur. This discharge, as indicated on the delivery curve, is equal to the critical discharge at section 2, or $Q_c = Z_c \sqrt{g}$, where $Z_c$ is the section factor of cross section 2.

For the determination of the maximum discharge, a trial computation is required. The procedure is first to take a series of discharges, beginning from $Q_n$ and going upward. Then, making $y_2 = y_c$ in each case, determine the corresponding $y_1$. The discharge that makes $y_1$ equal to the given depth at the upstream end is the $Q_{\max}$ required.

3. FLOW OF $M1$ PROFILE. When $y_2 > y_n$, the flow profile is of the $M1$ type. The upper limit of this curve is a horizontal level, indicated by $az$; at this condition the discharge is zero, since the head, or difference between the pool levels, is zero. For $y_2 > y_z$, the flow will reverse its direction. The lower limit of the $M1$ profile is, apparently, the uniform-flow surface $an$. For any intermediate flow between these two limits, the depth $y_2$ and the corresponding discharge can be determined by a trial flow-profile computation. The procedure is first to assume a discharge less than $Q_n$ and then to compute the corresponding depth $y_2$. Consequently, the delivery curve can be plotted.

4. FLOW OF $M2$ PROFILE. When $y_2 < y_n$, the flow profile belongs to the $M2$ type. The lower limit is, evidently, the critical flow surface $ac$. The $y_2$-$Q$ relationship can be determined by the procedure described above for the $M1$ profile.

From the delivery curve, it becomes evident that the portion $NC$ of the curve is very steep, so that $Q_{\max}$ exceeds $Q_n$ by only a very small amount. It will be seen that this is true in most practical cases except for very short or very flat canals. Referring to Fig. 11-2, it is assumed that the end point $d$ of the limiting $M2$ curve is located at a depth $0.99y_n$. If the length $L$ of the canal is greater than the length $L'$ of the limiting $M2$ profile, then no change in $y_2$ between $y_c$ and $y_n$ will affect the condition upstream from the point $d$; that is, the discharge will remain the same. As long as $L > L'$, the maximum discharge $Q_{\max}$ will be practically equal to $Q_n$, that is, the portion $NC$ of the corresponding delivery curve will be practically vertical. The flow-profile equation indicates that the length of the flow profile is inversely proportional to the bottom slope; the smaller the slope, the longer the profile, and vice versa. For this reason, reducing the slope will have an effect similar to that of making the canal

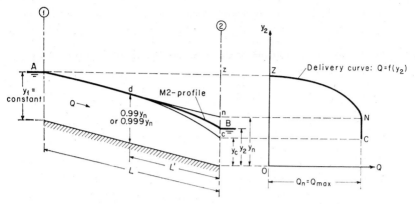

Fig. 11-2. Delivery of a canal, the length of which exceeds the length of the falling $M2$ profile.

shorter. Therefore, for practical purposes, it may be assumed that *the maximum possible discharge in a long canal or a canal of not-too-small slope is equal to the normal discharge.*

*B. Case of Constant* $y_2$. This is the case in which the water level at the downstream end of the canal, or the depth $y_2$, is constant, while $y_1$ fluctuates. The corresponding delivery curve $Q = f(y_1)$ is shown in Fig. 11-3.

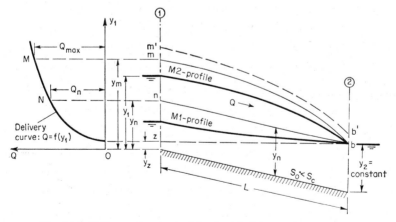

Fig. 11-3. Delivery of a canal with subcritical flow and constant $y_2$.

1. UNIFORM FLOW. When $y_1 = y_2 = y_n$, the flow is uniform, the flow profile $nb$ is parallel to the channel bottom, and the discharge $Q_n$ corresponds to point $N$ on the delivery curve. The value of $Q_n$ is equal to

$K_n \sqrt{S_0}$, where $K_n$ is the conveyance of cross section 1 with depth $y_1 = y_2$ and where $S_0$ is the bottom slope.

2. *Flow of Maximum Discharge.* When $y_1$ reaches a depth $y_m$ that corresponds to a critical discharge at section 2, the discharge becomes maximal. Any depth $y_1 > y_m$ is out of consideration, because it would simply raise the flow profile $mb$ to the position shown by the dashed line $m'b'$ and, consequently, require an increase in the downstream depth $y_2$. The value of $Q_{\max}$ is equal to the critical discharge at section 2, or $Z_c \sqrt{g}$, where $Z_c$ is the section factor at section 2 for a depth equal to $y_2$.

3. FLOW OF $M1$ PROFILE. For any depth $y_1 < y_n$, the flow profile belongs to the $M1$ type, and the discharge is less than $Q_n$. The lowest possible limit for $y_1$ is $y_z$; at this condition the flow profile is horizontal and the discharge is zero.

4. FLOW OF $M2$ PROFILE. For any depth $y_1$ varying between $y_m$ and $y_n$, the flow profile belongs to the $M2$ type, and the discharge is less than $Q_{\max}$ but greater than $Q_n$.

*C. Case of Constant Q.* This is the case in which the delivery of the canal is constant, while the pool levels at the two extremities of the canal fluctuate.

1. UNIFORM FLOW. Referring to Fig. 11-4, various possible flow profiles are sketched. When $y_1 = y_2 = y_n$, the flow is uniform, and the surface is a straight line $ab$ parallel to the channel bottom. This normal depth $y_n$ can be determined by the Manning formula for a given constant discharge $Q$.

2. FLOW OF $M1$ PROFILE. For positions above $ab$, the flow profile belongs to the $M1$ type. The upper limit of the $M1$ profile is a horizontal line; at this position $y_2$ approaches $y_1 + S_0L$ as a limit. As this condition is approached, the difference between pool levels and hence the head, or velocity of flow, decrease. However, the water area increases as the depths increase; whereas the discharge, as a product of the area and the velocity, can still be kept constant and equal to a given value.

3. FLOW OF $M2$ PROFILE. For positions below $ab$, the flow profile is of the $M2$ type. The lowest possible position of the $M2$ profile is $a'b'$; at this position $y_2$ is equal to the critical depth corresponding to the given discharge $Q$.

*The Q-constant Curve.* The relationship between the depths $y_1$ and $y_2$ for constant $Q$ can be plotted (Fig. 11-4). The resulting curve $CNP$ is known as the *Q-constant curve.* Several auxiliary curves have also been constructed to make clearer certain characteristic features of the $Q$-constant curve.

The *N line* is a straight line drawn from the origin of the coordinates and inclined at an angle of 45° with the coordinate axes. This line is the locus of the normal depth for all discharges. For any point on this line,

$y_1 = y_2 = y_n$. The $Q$-constant curve intersects this line at the point $N$ where $y_1 = y_2 = y_n$, which is the normal depth for the given discharge $Q$.

The $C$ *curve* is the curve on which $y_2$ is equal to the critical depth $y_c$ of cross section 2 for a given discharge and on which $y_1$ is the corresponding depth at section 1. It is apparent that $y_2$ cannot be less than $y_c$ of section 2 for the given discharge $Q$. Hence, the $Q$-constant curve terminates at the point $C$ on this curve that makes $y_2 = y_c$ at section 2 for the discharge $Q$.

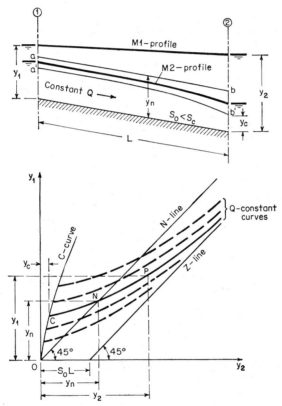

Fig. 11-4. Delivery of a canal with subcritical flow and constant $Q$.

The $Z$ *line* is a straight line drawn parallel to the $N$ line from a point on the $y_2$ axis at a distance $S_0L$ from the origin 0. This line represents the condition $y_2 = y_1 + S_0L$, or the upper limit of the $M1$ profile. Hence, the $Q$-constant curve approaches this line asymptotically from the left when both $y_1$ and $y_2$ become very large.

The coordinates $y_1$ and $y_2$ of any point $P$ on the $Q$-constant curve for a given discharge $Q$ can be determined by a flow-profile computation. Generally, when points $C$ and $N$ and one or two other points are located, the $Q$-constant curve can be drawn in smoothly.

By plotting a series of $Q$-constant curves for various discharges, such as the dashed lines, a general chart can be obtained, representing all possible flow conditions in the given canal.

**11-2. Delivery of a Canal for Supercritical Flow.** When the slope of the canal is steep, that is, greater than the critical slope, the flow in the channel becomes supercritical (Fig. 11-5). In practical applications, steep canals are usually short, such as the raft and log chutes that are used as spillways. If the canal is too steep, so that an ultrarapid flow develops, then the flow is no longer steady. A study of unsteady flow in canals is beyond the scope of this chapter.

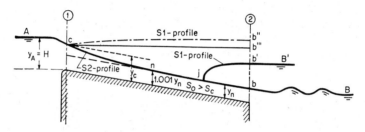

Fig. 11-5. Delivery of a canal with supercritical flow.

*A. Discharge.* As the control section in a channel of supercritical flow is at the upstream end, the delivery of the canal is fully governed by the critical discharge at section 1, which is simply equal to the discharge through a weir.

*B. Flow Profile.* The type of flow profile developed in a steep canal depends on the tailwater situation.

1. When the tailwater level $B$ is less than the outlet depth at section 2, the flow in the canal is unaffected by the tailwater. The flow profile passes through the critical depth near point $c$ from a convex to a concave shape and approaches the normal depth by means of a smooth drawdown curve of the $S2$ type. As a rule, the drawdown curve $cn$ is comparatively short, and $y_n$ is the lowest possible stage in the canal. In designing such canals, the normal depth is made equal to the depth required for passing floating craft or for allowable scouring effect.

2. When the tailwater level $B$ is greater than the outlet depth, the tailwater will raise the water level in the downstream portion of the canal to form an $S1$ profile between $j$ and $b'$, producing a hydraulic jump at the end $j$ of the profile. However, the flow upstream from the jump will not be affected by the tailwater.

3. As the tailwater level rises further, the jump will move upstream, maintaining its height and form in the uniform-flow zone $nb$, until it reaches point $n$. From there on, the jump will move upstream on the $cn$ curve, gradually diminishing in height. The height of the jump becomes zero when it reaches the critical depth at $c$. In the meantime, the flow profile reaches its theoretical limit $cb''$ of the $S1$ profile. Beyond this limit the incoming flow will be directly affected by the tailwater, and the entrance acts as a submerged weir. In practical calculations, the horizontal line $cb'''$ may be taken as the practical limit of the tailwater stage. This will avoid the computation of $b'''b''$ and will also provide a margin of safety.

**11-3. Problems Related to Canal Design.** Knowledge about the delivery of a canal, as described in the preceding articles, has useful

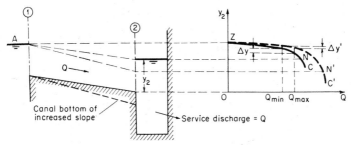

Fig. 11-6. Canal design for variable service discharge.

applications in the hydraulic design of canals. Several important problems related to such applications are described below.

*A. Change in Depth Due to Changing Delivery.* In designing a canal, it is often necessary for the engineer to anticipate the fluctuation in depth of flow due to any possible change in delivery. This fluctuation in depth can be estimated easily from the delivery curve of the canal for the given range of fluctuation in discharge.

In most cases, except where the canal is very short or where the bottom of the canal is unusually flat, the canal can be designed for a uniform-flow condition, because the maximum discharge will be practically equal to the normal discharge. The procedure of canal design for uniform flow has been discussed in Chap. 7. The relationship between the depth and discharge can be obtained easily on the basis of any uniform-flow formula, such as the Manning formula.

When a canal is designed to deliver water from a reservoir of constant pool level to a service channel at the downstream end, the discharge in the canal should meet the variable demand, when and as required by the service channel (Fig. 11-6). This, with a subcritical flow, falls into the case of constant $y_1$, $A$ in Art. 11-1, in which the upstream depth is kept constant while the downstream depth fluctuates. The delivery curves in Fig. 11-6 will explain how the fluctuation in the downstream end depth, caused by the variation in the service discharge demand, can be reduced. The method is simply to increase the bottom slope of the canal. This increases the normal discharge, and the delivery curve will change in position from $ZNC$ to $ZN'C'$. It is apparent that, for the same range of $Q_{max}$ to $Q_{min}$, the fluctuation in depth $\Delta y'$ is reduced and becomes less than $\Delta y$.

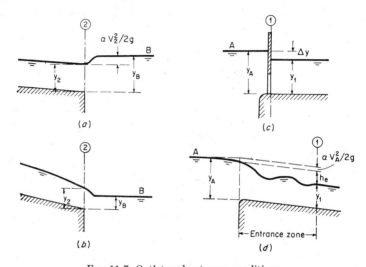

Fig. 11-7. Outlet and entrance conditions.

**B. Outlet and Entrance Conditions.** In the preceding articles, the delivery of the canal was related to the depths $y_1$ and $y_2$ at the ends of the canal; but the conditions that accompany the inflow or outflow of the water were not considered.

1. OUTLET. When the canal empties into a reservoir, an amount of kinetic energy equal to $\alpha V_2^2/2g$, carried with the flowing water, is expected to be restored as a potential energy. Thus, the pool level should be higher by this amount than the depth at the outlet of the canal (Fig. 11-7a). This energy, however, is usually dissipated entirely in eddies and whirls. In practical computations it may be ignored, and $y_2$ may be taken equal to $y_B$. If the outflow is accompanied by a hydraulic drop (Fig. 11-7b) and if $y_B < y_2$, the depth $y_2$ is equal to the critical depth $y_c$ of section 2, irrespective of the pool-level position $B$.

2. REGULATED ENTRANCE. When the entrance is regulated by a sluice or some other device (Fig. 11-7c), the depth $y_1$ is independent of the

upstream-pool-level position $A$. The difference $\Delta y$ between $y_A$ and $y_1$ may be set by judgment or may depend on the design of the entrance.

3. FREE ENTRANCE. When water enters a mild-slope canal freely (Fig. 11-7$d$), the depth $y_1$ is related to the static pool level $A$ by the law of energy. The relation between the depths $y_1$ and $y_A$ can be expressed by

$$y_A = y_1 + h_e + \alpha \frac{V_A{}^2}{2g} \tag{11-1}$$

where $\alpha V_A{}^2/2g$ is the velocity head of the approaching flow, which is usually a small quantity and can be ignored. Hence,

$$y_A = y_1 + h_e \tag{11-2}$$

For subcritical flow, the term $h_e$ is the head loss due to friction and may be expressed in terms of the velocity head at section 1, that is,

$$h_e = C_e \frac{V_1{}^2}{2g} \tag{11-3}$$

where $C_e$ is a coefficient which has an average value of 1.25 for a well-rounded entrance.[1]  Solving for $V_1$ from the above equation,

$$V_1 = \frac{1}{\sqrt{C_e}} \sqrt{2gh_e} \tag{11-4}$$

The delivery of the canal is equal to

$$Q = V_1 A_1 = \frac{1}{\sqrt{C_e}} A_1 \sqrt{2gh_e} = \frac{1}{\sqrt{C_e}} A_1 \sqrt{2g(y_A - y_1)} \tag{11-5}$$

In most practical problems, the depth $y_A$, instead of $y_1$, is given. For example, in the case of the constant upstream depth, $A$ in Art. 11-1, the depth $y_A$ would be given as constant. For any given condition of $y_A$, the relation between $Q$ and $y_1$ can be established by Eq. (11-5). A curve representing this relation can therefore be constructed. By means of this so-called *inflow-discharge-rating curve*, the relations among $y_A$, $y_1$, and $Q$ can be determined.

For supercritical flow, the flow at section 1 is critical. The problem is simplified by the fact that the relation between $y_1$ and $y_A$ is practically fixed, irrespective of the entrance friction loss.

*C. Elimination of Hydraulic Jump in a Steep Canal.* As pointed out in Art. 11-2, when the tailwater-pool level is higher than the critical depth in a steep canal, a hydraulic jump will develop in the canal (Fig. 11-5). Such a hydraulic jump is objectionable and dangerous, particularly when

---

[1] Data on the losses in entrance structures may be found in some hydraulics textbooks, handbooks, or other literature [2].

the canal is a raft chute or some other structure intended to transport a floating raft from the upstream reservoir to a downstream pool. Bakhmeteff [1] suggested that the design of a *neutralizing reach* (Fig. 11-8) might be a solution. In this reach the bottom slope of the channel is made equal to the critical slope. According to a corresponding case of $C1$ profile in Fig. 9-2, the tailwater levels will be approximately horizontal lines[1] which intersect the surface of flow in the canal without causing any disturbance. At the point of intersection, theoretically, there is a jump of zero height.

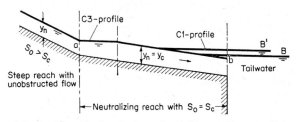

FIG. 11-8. Elimination of hydraulic jump by Bakhmeteff's neutralizing reach.

**11-4. Computation of Flow Profile in Nonprismatic Channels.** The theory and analysis of gradually varied flow in nonprismatic channels has been discussed previously (Art. 9-5). The integration of the differential equation for the flow profile of such a flow is mathematically complicated. If the control section is uncertain in a given problem, its position may be determined by the method of singular point. For the computation of the flow profile, the step method is recommended. The computation should proceed upstream from the control section if the flow is subcritical and downstream from the control section if it is supercritical. The procedure of computation is practically the same as that applied to a prismatic channel, as will be seen in the following example:

**Example 11-1.** A spillway channel, as shown in Fig. 11-9, has been designed tentatively for La Tuna Canyon Debris Basin at Los Angeles County, Calif.[2] According

---

[1] When the Chézy formula is applied, the lines are theoretically horizontal.

[2] The data for this example are taken from [3]. For additional information, the following is extracted from this reference: The spillway was designed to pass the maximum probable flood 19,000 cfs with the maximum water surface 5 ft below the top of the dam. The wide inlet sill would provide maximum sill elevation for retention of debris with minimum height of dam. The invert slope was designed such that control, or critical depth for 19,000 cfs, would occur at the relatively narrow base width of 65 ft at station 11 + 22. Establishing control at this narrow width would minimize the formation of large waves produced by the rapidly converging walls. For a design flood of 6,200 cfs, waves would have no adverse effect, because a relatively large freeboard would be available. The spillway transition was developed to carry 19,000 cfs with 2.5 ft of freeboard to station 13 + 95. This station was considered to be a

to this design, the channel starts with a 140-ft-wide rectangular concrete section. The 140-ft base width extends from station 10 + 00 to the sill at station 10 + 45. From station 10 + 45 to station 11 + 45 the walls converge on circular curves to a base width of 60 ft. From station 11 + 45 to station 15 + 82.50 the walls converge in a straight-line transition to a base width of 25 ft. The channel below the transition consists of a rectangular concrete section with a constant width of 25 ft. Compute the flow profile in the spillway channel for a design discharge of 6,200 cfs. The control for this discharge was designed to occur at the inlet sill station 10 + 45. Use $\alpha = 1$ and $n = 0.014$ in the computation.

*Solution.* In this problem the flow is supercritical, for the control section is placed at the upstream station 10 + 45. The critical depth at this section is equal to $y_c = \sqrt[3]{(6,200/140)^2/32.2} = 3.93$ ft. The critical depths at other stations may also be computed. If the computed depth happens to be greater than the corresponding critical depth, the flow will be subcritical.

The computation of the flow profile is given in Table 11-1, with the following headings:

Col. 1. Station number

Col. 2. Length of reach in ft, which is equal to the difference between the two station numbers at the two ends of the reach

Col. 3. Width of the channel in ft

Cols. 4 to 16. Same as the steps from cols. 1 to 12 in Table 10-4, except that an extra column for $S_0$ (col. 14) is provided since $S_0$ is not constant throughout the whole channel length under consideration.

The computation is arranged in a form similar to that used for the direct step method, but it is performed by trial and error. This procedure is introduced because an additional variable for the channel width is involved. In this computation, the depth of flow $y$ is assumed and entered in col. 4 at each step. The assumed depth is considered correct when the resulting value of $\Delta x$ entered in col. 16 agrees with the length of reach in col. 2. It should be noted that the depth of flow computed in this example has been carried to more decimal places than would be necessary for practical purposes.

The flow profile thus computed should be corrected for air entrainment for high-velocity flow occurring at the downstream end of the channel.[1] When a high-velocity supercritical flow occurs in a nonprismatic channel, it is likely that standing waves would appear as a result of the lateral-boundary changes (Arts. 17-3 and 17-4).

**11-5. Design of Transitions.** The *transition* in a channel is a structure designed to change the shape or cross-sectional area of the flow. Under normal design and installation conditions, practically all canals and flumes require some type of transition structure to and from the waterways. The function of such a structure is to avoid excessive energy losses, to

---

safe distance downstream from the dam for the release of spillway flows. Downstream of station 13 + 95, the transition and the channel were designed to carry the design flood of 6,200 cfs with a minimum freeboard of 1.5 ft. The channel alignment below the transition would provide for transition spirals, and the channel invert would be banked through all curved reaches to maintain uniform depth of flow.

[1] A procedure for computing the flow profile in steep chutes with a correction for air entrainment has been proposed by L. S. Hall [4]. For a simple correction, the Douma formula, Eq. (2-15), may be used.

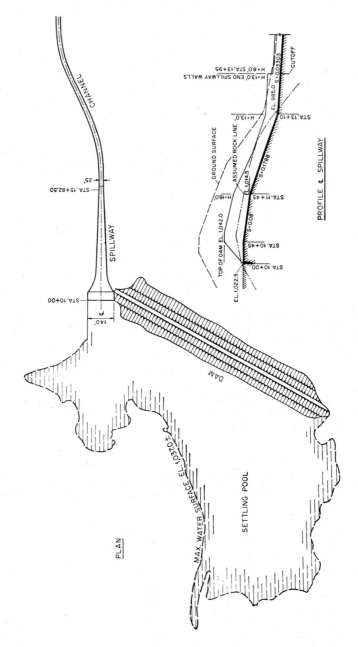

PLAN

CHANNEL

SPILLWAY

STA. 15+82.50

25'

STA. 10+00

140'

DAM

MAX. WATER SURFACE EL. 1,037.0±

SETTLING POOL

PROFILE ⅊ SPILLWAY

CUTOFF

H=8.0', STA. 13+95

H=13.0', END SPILLWAY WALLS

S=0.0303

EL. 985.0

STA. 13+10

H=13.0'

GROUND SURFACE

ASSUMED ROCK LINE

H=18.0'

EL. 1,014.5

STA. 11+45

S=0.0788

TOP OF DAM EL. 1,042.0

S=0.08

STA. 10+45

STA. 10+00

EL. 1,022.5

FIG. 11-9. Tentative design of the spillway for a debris basin.

308

TABLE 11-1. COMPUTATION OF THE FLOW PROFILE IN A NONPRISMATIC CHANNEL FOR EXAMPLE 11-1
(La Tuna Canyon spillway, Los Angeles County, Calif., $Q$ = 6,200 cfs)

| Station | $\Delta x$ | $b$ | $y$ | $A$ | $R$ | $R^{2/3}$ | $V$ | $\alpha V^2/2g$ | $E$ | $\Delta E$ | $S_f$ | $\bar{S}_f$ | $S_0$ | $S_0 - \bar{S}_f$ | $\Delta x$ |
|---|---|---|---|---|---|---|---|---|---|---|---|---|---|---|---|
| (1) | (2) | (3) | (4) | (5) | (6) | (7) | (8) | (9) | (10) | (11) | (12) | (13) | (14) | (15) | (16) |
| 10 + 45 | | 140.0 | 3.93 | 550.0 | 3.72 | 5.78 | 11.27 | 1.97 | 5.90 | | 0.0019 | | | | |
| 10 + 51 | 6.0 | 130.0 | 3.54 | 460.0 | 3.36 | 5.04 | 13.48 | 2.82 | 6.36 | 0.46 | 0.0032 | 0.0026 | 0.0800 | 0.0774 | 5.9 |
| 10 + 58 | 7.0 | 120.0 | 3.48 | 417.5 | 3.29 | 4.90 | 14.85 | 3.42 | 6.90 | 0.54 | 0.0042 | 0.0036 | 0.0800 | 0.0764 | 7.1 |
| 10 + 65 | 7.0 | 110.0 | 3.58 | 393.9 | 3.36 | 5.04 | 15.75 | 3.85 | 7.43 | 0.53 | 0.0043 | 0.0042 | 0.0800 | 0.0758 | 7.0 |
| 10 + 73 | 8.0 | 100.0 | 3.71 | 371.0 | 3.45 | 5.22 | 16.71 | 4.33 | 8.04 | 0.61 | 0.0046 | 0.0045 | 0.0800 | 0.0755 | 8.1 |
| 10 + 83 | 10.0 | 90.0 | 3.87 | 348.2 | 3.56 | 5.44 | 17.80 | 4.92 | 8.79 | 0.75 | 0.0052 | 0.0049 | 0.0800 | 0.0751 | 10.0 |
| 10 + 95 | 12.0 | 80.0 | 4.08 | 326.2 | 3.70 | 5.72 | 19.00 | 5.60 | 9.68 | 0.89 | 0.0056 | 0.0054 | 0.0800 | 0.0746 | 11.9 |
| 11 + 10 | 15.0 | 70.0 | 4.35 | 304.5 | 3.87 | 6.08 | 20.35 | 6.44 | 10.79 | 1.11 | 0.0060 | 0.0058 | 0.0800 | 0.0742 | 15.0 |
| 11 + 22 | 12.0 | 65.0 | 4.41 | 286.7 | 3.88 | 6.10 | 21.62 | 7.26 | 11.67 | 0.88 | 0.0068 | 0.0064 | 0.0800 | 0.0736 | 12.0 |
| 11 + 45 | 23.0 | 60.0 | 4.28 | 256.8 | 3.75 | 5.83 | 24.14 | 9.05 | 13.33 | 1.66 | 0.0088 | 0.0078 | 0.0800 | 0.0722 | 23.0 |
| 12 + 07.5 | 62.5 | 55.0 | 3.123 | 171.8 | 2.81 | 3.97 | 36.09 | 20.21 | 23.33 | 10.00 | 0.0290 | 0.0189 | 0.1788 | 0.1599 | 62.5 |
| 12 + 70 | 62.5 | 50.0 | 2.855 | 142.8 | 2.57 | 3.52 | 43.41 | 29.27 | 32.13 | 8.80 | 0.0473 | 0.0381 | 0.1788 | 0.1407 | 62.5 |
| 13 + 10 | 40.0 | 46.8 | 2.817 | 131.8 | 2.51 | 3.41 | 47.04 | 34.38 | 37.20 | 5.07 | 0.0572 | 0.0522 | 0.1788 | 0.1266 | 40.0 |
| 13 + 32.5 | 22.5 | 45.0 | 2.958 | 133.1 | 2.61 | 3.60 | 46.61 | 33.74 | 36.70 | −0.50 | 0.0532 | 0.0552 | 0.0330 | −0.0222 | 22.5 |
| 13 + 95 | 62.5 | 40.0 | 3.399 | 135.9 | 2.91 | 4.16 | 45.62 | 32.32 | 35.72 | −0.98 | 0.0442 | 0.0487 | 0.0330 | −0.0157 | 62.4 |
| 14 + 57.5 | 62.5 | 35.0 | 3.948 | 138.2 | 3.22 | 4.75 | 44.89 | 31.28 | 35.23 | −0.49 | 0.0374 | 0.0408 | 0.0330 | −0.0078 | 62.8 |
| 15 + 20 | 62.5 | 30.0 | 4.650 | 139.5 | 3.55 | 5.42 | 44.45 | 30.69 | 35.34 | 0.11 | 0.0322 | 0.0348 | 0.0330 | 0.0018 | 61.2 |
| 15 + 82.5 | 62.5 | 25.0 | 5.652 | 141.3 | 3.89 | 6.11 | 43.87 | 29.88 | 35.53 | 0.19 | 0.0278 | 0.0300 | 0.0330 | 0.0030 | 63.3 |

eliminate cross waves and other turbulence, and to provide safety for the structure and waterway.   When the transition is designed to keep stream-lines smooth and nearly parallel and to minimize standing waves, the theory of gradually varied flow may be used in the design.   The essence of such a design has been discussed earlier (Arts. 3-5 and 3-8) in connec-tion with the application of the energy and momentum principles.   In this article, emphasis is on design practice.

The form of transition may vary from straight-line headwalls normal to the flow of water to very elaborate streamlined warped structures. Straight-line headwalls are usually found satisfactory for small structures or where head is not valuable.   For the sake of economy, the U.S. Department of Agriculture [5] has tested a cylinder-quadrant transition as a substitute for the expensive warped structure.   The cylinder-quadrant transition is essentially a pair of circular wings or vertical walls, tangent to the flume sides and curving through a quarter turn to meet the sides of the canal.   For the same reason, the trend of practice in the U.S. Bureau of Reclamation [6] has been toward simplification, with the top edges of walls and the intersections between warped walls and floors designed in straight lines.   Further simplification of an elaborate form is permitted, however, only when a close control of water areas and velocities is unnecessary and when excessive wave action or turbulence would not be developed.

The common types of transition are inlet and outlet transitions between canal and flume, inlet and outlet transitions between canal and tunnel, and inlet and outlet transitions between canal and inverted siphon.   It should be noted that appreciable change in depth of flow generally occurs in all types of transition.   If the change in depth or width is very rapid the flow may become rapidly varied, and standing waves may occur.

**11-6. Transitions between Canal and Flume or Tunnel.**   On the basis of the performance of existing structures, the following features have been found important in design.   For more complete information, the reader should refer to [2], [6], and [7].

*A. Proportioning.*   For a well-designed transition the following rules for proportioning should be considered:

1. The optimum maximum angle between the channel axis and a line connecting the channel sides between entrance and exit sections is 12.5°.

2. Sharp angles either in the water surface or in the structure that will induce extreme standing waves and turbulence should be avoided.

*B. Losses.*   The energy loss in a transition consists of the *friction loss* and the *conversion loss*.   The friction loss may be estimated by means of any uniform-flow formula, such as the Manning formula.   This loss usually has very little effect on the transition flow profile and may be ignored in preliminary design.   The conversion loss is generally expressed in terms of the change in velocity head between the entrance and exit sections of the structure.

For inlet structures, the entrance velocity is less than the exit velocity; hence, the water surface must always drop at least a full difference between the velocity heads, plus a small conversion loss known as the *inlet loss.* The drop $\Delta y'$ in water surface for inlet structures may therefore be expressed as

$$\Delta y' = \Delta h_v + c_i \Delta h_v = (1 + c_i) \Delta h_v \qquad (11\text{-}6)$$

where $\Delta h_v$ is the difference in velocity head and $c_i$ is a coefficient of inlet loss.

For outlet structures, the velocity is reduced, at least in part, in order to lift the water surface. This rise in water surface, known as the *recovery of velocity head,* is usually accompanied by a conversion loss known as the *outlet loss.* The rise $\Delta y'$ in water surface for outlet structures may be expressed as

$$\Delta y' = \Delta h_v - c_o \Delta h_v = (1 - c_o) \Delta h_v \qquad (11\text{-}7)$$

where $c_o$ is a coefficient of outlet loss.

The average safe design values of $c_i$ and $c_o$ that are recommended are as follows:

| Type of Transition | $c_i$ | $c_o$ |
|---|---|---|
| Warped type | 0.10 | 0.20 |
| Cylinder-quadrant type | 0.15 | 0.25 |
| Simplified straight-line type | 0.20 | 0.30 |
| Straight-line type | 0.30 | 0.50 |
| Square-ended type | 0.30+ | 0.75 |

*C. Freeboard.* Approximate rules for freeboard estimation for lined and unlined canals (Art. 7-5) may be used. For depth of flow over 12 ft, the freeboard in transition should be given special consideration.

Figures 11-10 and 11-11 show, respectively, typical designs for an inlet transition from canal to flume and for an outlet transition from flume to canal. The design of the inlet transition will be described in Example 11-2. The design of the outlet transition may follow the same general steps. However, the expanding flow in the outlet transition often presents special hydraulic behavior that should not be overlooked. In an expanding flow, the distribution of velocity in the cross section can be extremely uneven; so the velocity-distribution coefficients may become appreciably greater than 1.0, and their values should be calculated or properly assumed in the design. Furthermore, uneven distribution of velocity may cause asymmetry of flow and thus develop scour at places of highly concentrated velocities. Caution in this respect, therefore, should be taken when the transition is designed in erodible channels.

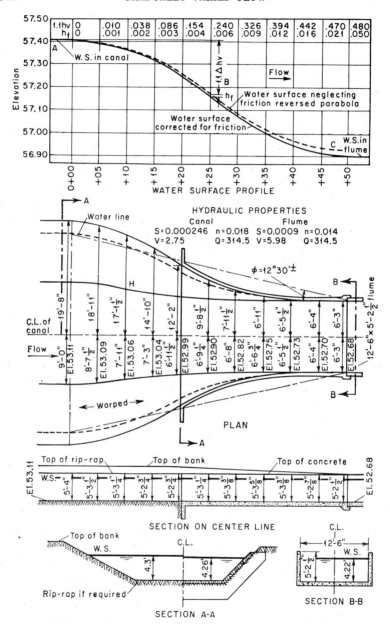

FIG. 11-10. Typical design of an inlet transition.   (*After J. Hinds* [2].)

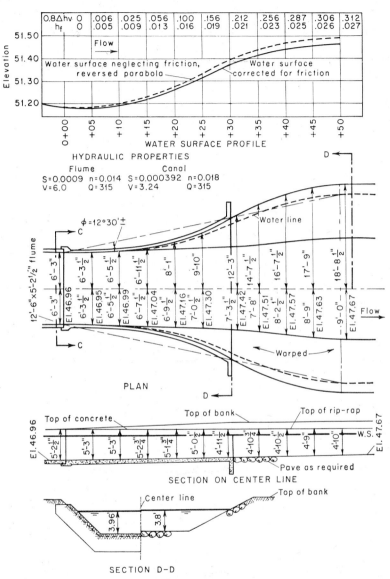

Fig. 11-11. Typical design of an outlet transition. (*After J. Hinds* [2].)

*D. Elimination of Hydraulic Jump.* Existence of hydraulic jump in a transition may become objectionable if it hinders the flow and consumes useful energy. When the transition leads from a supercritical flow to a subcritical flow, the hydraulic jump may be avoided by carefully proportioning the transition dimensions (Example 3-4).

In an example illustrated by Hinds [7], a transition from a segmental canal to a circular tunnel was designed for flow from one subcritical flow stage to another (Fig. 11-12). In the design, liberal allowance was made

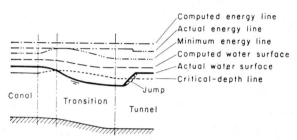

FIG. 11-12. A faulty transition design.    *(After J. Hinds [7].)*

for transitions and friction losses, and a safe coefficient of roughness was used to determine the depth of flow in the tunnel. After construction, however, the transition losses were found to be practically negligible; so the actual normal depth of the flow entering the tunnel entrance was considerably less than the assumed value. As a result, an objectionable hydraulic jump was observed inside the tunnel. Actually, the transition should have been proportioned to avoid the jump on the basis of negligible transition losses. Since the structure had already been constructed, the hydraulic jump was finally eliminated by bolting cross timbers to the channel bottom, thus increasing the friction and bringing the normal depth up to above the critical depth.

**Example 11-2.*** It is required to design an inlet structure connecting an earth canal having a bottom width of 18 ft and side slopes of 2:1, to a rectangular concrete flume 12 ft 6 in. wide. The hydraulic properties of the canal and the flume are given (Fig. 11-10). The design discharge is 314.5 cfs.

*Solution.* The design procedure involves the following steps:

1. *Determination of the Length of the Transition.* The length of the transition is determined so that a straight line joining the flow line at the two ends of the transition will make an angle of about 12.5° with the axis of the structure. This length in the design is found to be 50 ft.

2. *Determination of the Flow Profile Neglecting Friction.* For the type of structure under contemplation, the inlet loss may be safely assumed to be 10% of the change in velocity head, or 0.1 $\Delta h_v$. The total drop in water surface is, therefore, equal to 1.1 $\Delta h_v$ plus the drop necessary to overcome channel friction. The change in velocity

* This example is taken from [2].

head from $V = 2.75$ fps to $5.98$ fps is equal to $\Delta h_v = 0.553 - 0.117 = 0.436$ ft. Neglecting the channel friction for the time being, the total drop in water surface is, therefore, $1.10 \times 0.436 = 0.480$ ft.

For a smooth and continuous flow, the theoretical flow profile may be assumed as two equal parabolas, tangent to each other at point $B$ and horizontal, respectively, at $A$ and $C$. Strictly speaking, the parabolas should be tangent to the water surfaces in the canal and the flume, but a small deviation of these water surfaces from the horizontal is not important in the present example.

A number of sections are then selected along the transition, where the flow profile will be computed and the structural dimensions determined.

3. *Computation of the Flow Profile Including Friction.* The computation is shown in Table 11-2 with the following headings:

Col. 1. Number for stations equally spaced every 5 ft and measured in the direction of flow.

Col. 2. Drop in water surface. The total drop in water surface from $A$ to $C$, neglecting friction, is $0.480$ ft. The drop from $A$ to the mid-point $B$ of the antisymmetrical reversed parabola is made equal to half the drop, or $0.240$ ft.

Col. 3. Change in velocity head. Assuming that the conversion loss is distributed over the entire length of the transition in proportion to the change in velocity head, values of $\Delta h_v$ are obtained by dividing values of $\Delta y'$ in col. 1 by 1.10.

Col. 4. Total velocity head, equal to the cumulative value of $\Delta h_v$ entering the preceding column

Col. 5. Velocity in fps corresponding to the velocity head in the preceding column

Col. 6. Water area in ft² , equal to the discharge $314.5$ cfs divided by the velocity in the preceding column

Col. 7. Half the top width in ft, obtained from the cross sections of the sketched plan (Fig. 11-10). The plan may be chosen either arbitrarily or by trial until satisfactory results are obtained. The choice of a proper shape for the plan is a matter of judgment.

Col. 8. Half the bottom width in ft, obtained from the sketched plan

Col. 9. The depth of flow in ft, equal to $A/(0.5T + 0.5b)$

Col. 10. Hydraulic radius in ft

Col. 11. The friction slope, computed by Eq. (9-8) with $n = 0.014$ for all sections in the transition

Col. 12. The friction head, equal to the distance between stations, or 5 ft, multiplied by the average of the friction slope of the section and that of the preceding section

Col. 13. Cumulative friction head in ft

Col. 14. The water-surface elevation, including the effect of the channel friction, equal to $57.41 - \Delta y' - \Sigma h_f$. The flow profile thus obtained should be free from objectionable irregularities; if not, the plan may be altered. It should be noted, however, that a slight change in the elevation of water surface at a given point may cause an appreciable change in the dimensions of the structure.

Col. 15. The elevation of the channel bottom, equal to $Z - y$

4. *Determination of Structural Dimensions.* After the arbitrarily sketched plan for the transition is found to be satisfactory, the structural dimensions may be determined as given under the following headings of Table 11-2:

Col. 16. The side slope $z = (0.5T - 0.5b)/y$

Col. 17. The elevation of the top of lining. The recommended height of lining above the water surface for a discharge of 314.5 cfs is about 1 ft (Fig. 7-1). Draw a straight line above the computed water surface at an average distance of approximately 1 ft. From this line the elevation $Z_L$ is obtained.

TABLE 11-2. COMPUTATION FOR THE DESIGN OF A FLUME INLET FOR EXAMPLE 11-2*

In flume, V = 5.98, hᵥ = 0.553    Elevation of water surface at Sta. 0 + 00 = 57.41

In canal, V = 2.75, hᵥ = 0.117    Entrance loss = 0.1 Δhᵥ

Δhᵥ = 0.436    Water surface is assumed as two reverse parabolas tangent at Sta. 0 + 25

| Sta. | $\Delta y'$ | $\Delta h_v$ | $h_v$ | $V$ | $A$ | $0.5T$ | $0.5b$ | $y$ | $R$ | $S_f$ | $\Delta h_f$ | $\Sigma \Delta h_f$ | $Z$ | $Z_0$ | $z$ | $Z_L$ | $H_L$ | $0.5W$ (comp.) | $0.5W$ (used) |
|---|---|---|---|---|---|---|---|---|---|---|---|---|---|---|---|---|---|---|---|
| (1) | (2) | (3) | (4) | (5) | (6) | (7) | (8) | (9) | (10) | (11) | (12) | (13) | (14) | (15) | (16) | (17) | (18) | (19) | (20) |
| 0 + 00 | 0.000 | 0.000 | 0.117 | 2.75 | 114.40 | 17.600 | 9.000 | 4.300 | 3.06 | 0.00015 | ...... | ...... | 57.410 | 53.110 | 2.000 | 58.440 | 5.330 | 19.660 | 19'8" |
| 0 + 05 | 0.010 | 0.009 | 0.126 | 2.85 | 110.50 | 17.000 | 8.625 | 4.309 | 3.07 | 0.00016 | 0.0008 | 0.0008 | 57.399 | 53.090 | 1.945 | 58.385 | 5.295 | 18.935 | 18'11" |
| 0 + 10 | 0.038 | 0.035 | 0.152 | 3.13 | 100.60 | 15.427 | 7.917 | 4.310 | 3.04 | 0.00020 | 0.0009 | 0.0017 | 57.370 | 53.060 | 1.744 | 58.330 | 5.270 | 17.127 | 17'1½" |
| 0 + 15 | 0.086 | 0.079 | 0.196 | 3.55 | 88.75 | 13.460 | 7.250 | 4.280 | 3.00 | 0.00026 | 0.0012 | 0.0029 | 57.321 | 53.041 | 1.447 | 58.275 | 5.234 | 14.825 | 14'10" |
| 0 + 20 | 0.154 | 0.140 | 0.257 | 4.07 | 77.40 | 11.228 | 6.958 | 4.260 | 2.98 | 0.00034 | 0.0015 | 0.0044 | 57.252 | 52.992 | 1.000 | 58.220 | 5.228 | 12.186 | 12'2" |
| 0 + 25 | 0.240 | 0.218 | 0.335 | 4.64 | 67.88 | 9.139 | 6.771 | 4.264 | 2.92 | 0.00045 | 0.0020 | 0.0064 | 57.164 | 52.900 | 0.554 | 58.165 | 5.265 | 9.691 | 9'8½" |
| 0 + 30 | 0.326 | 0.296 | 0.413 | 5.15 | 61.20 | 7.717 | 6.667 | 4.252 | 2.75 | 0.00061 | 0.0027 | 0.0091 | 57.075 | 53.823 | 0.247 | 58.110 | 5.287 | 7.971 | 7'11½" |
| 0 + 35 | 0.394 | 0.357 | 0.474 | 5.52 | 57.10 | 6.847 | 6.563 | 4.253 | 2.64 | 0.00074 | 0.0034 | 0.0125 | 57.003 | 53.750 | 0.067 | 58.053 | 5.305 | 6.917 | 6'11" |
| 0 + 40 | 0.442 | 0.401 | 0.518 | 5.77 | 54.60 | 6.458 | 6.458 | 4.225 | 2.56 | 0.00084 | 0.0040 | 0.0165 | 56.951 | 52.726 | ...... | 58.000 | 5.274 | 6.458 | 6'5½" |
| 0 + 45 | 0.470 | 0.427 | 0.544 | 5.91 | 53.30 | 6.315 | 6.315 | 4.220 | 2.53 | 0.00090 | 0.0044 | 0.0209 | 56.919 | 52.699 | ...... | 59.945 | 5.246 | 6.315 | 6'4" |
| 0 + 50 | 0.480 | 0.436 | 0.553 | 5.97 | 52.70 | 6.250 | 6.250 | 4.220 | 2.52 | 0.00092 | 0.0046 | 0.0255 | 56.904 | 52.684 | ...... | 57.890 | 5.205 | 6.250 | 6'3" |

*Slide-rule computation.

Col. 18. Height of lining in ft, equal to $Z_L - Z_0$
Col. 19. Computed value of half the width at the top of the lining, equal to $0.5W = zH_L + 0.5b$
Col. 20. $0.5W$ to nearest 0.5 in.

## 11-7. Transitions between Canal and Inverted Siphon.

Figure 11-13 shows a typical design of siphon inlet and outlet transitions between canals and an inverted siphon. The method of design is similar to that for the transitions between canal and flume. However, the following special features of design are recommended by the U.S. Bureau of Reclamation [6]:

1. In the design of an inlet transition, it is generally desirable to have the top of the siphon opening set slightly below the approaching normal water surface. This practice will minimize possible reduction in siphon capacity caused by the introduction of air into the siphon. The depth of submergence of the top of the siphon opening is known as the *water seal*. The recommended value of the water seal is between a minimum of $1.1 \Delta h_v$ and a maximum of 18 in. or $1.5 \Delta h_v$, whichever is greater. It should be noted that use of the minimum value in a well-designed transition theoretically allows the flow barely to touch the top of the siphon opening; whereas use of larger values up to the maximum provides a seal of water above the top of the opening. An adequate amount of seal depends upon the slope and size of the siphon barrel. Generally, a large and steep barrel requires a large seal. In the design illustrated (Fig. 11-13) a seal of 18 in. is used.

It should also be noted that the seal may make it impracticable to construct the lower end of the transition strictly in accordance with the hydraulic computation. When this is the case, the computed bottom elevation a short distance upstream from the inlet headwall may be altered arbitrarily to meet the practical requirement. In the design illustrated, computations have been carried to the end of the transition; beyond this the conduit floor is simply extended smoothly to connect with the floor of the siphon barrel.

For long siphons, under certain conditions, the inlet may not necessarily be sealed. Consequently, a hydraulic jump may occur in the siphon barrel, and the resulting operating condition will be unfavorable.

2. After the seal is determined for the inlet structure, the velocity at the headwall is computed, and the total drop in water surface, neglecting friction losses, is taken as $1.1 \Delta h_v$. A smooth flow profile is then assumed, tangent to the water surface in the canal at the beginning of the transition and passing through the point at the headwall set by the above computation. There are no data available for determining the best form of the flow profile. In the illustrated design, a simple parabola is assumed.

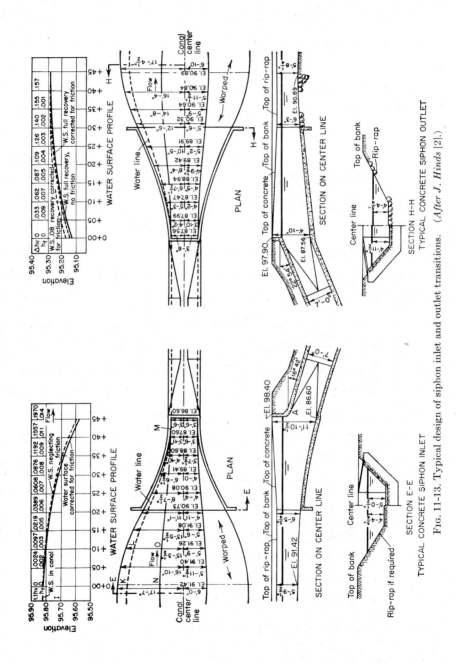

Fig. 11-13. Typical design of siphon inlet and outlet transitions. (*After J. Hinds* [2].)

318

3. In the design of the outlet structure, the theoretical rise in water surface from the headwall to the end of the transition, neglecting recovery losses, should be equal to the total change in velocity head $\Delta h_v$. The flow profile in the illustrated design is made as a simple parabola.

4. In the design of the outlet structure, the bottom slope need not be tangent to the slope of the closed conduit at the headwall as it was in the case of the inlet, unless the siphon velocity is high and the transition slope is steep.

**11-8. Backwater Effect of a Dam.** It is often necessary to investigate the probable damage caused by backwater due to an obstacle in a stream, say a dam. To study this problem, a so-called *backwater envelope curve* is usually found to be useful. This curve represents the locus of the upstream *end point* of the backwater curve ($M1$ profile). Theoretically speaking, the backwater curve extends indefinitely in the upstream direction; hence, it has no upstream end point. For practical purposes, however, the end point may be selected at the place where the rise in water surface begins to cause damage. This can be assumed at a place where the depth of flow is equal to a certain fraction of the normal depth, depending on the nature of the problem, say about 1% higher than the normal depth, or $y = 1.01y_n$. When a freeboard is allowed, the end point is at a place where the depth is equal to the normal depth plus the freeboard.

It is apparent that the backwater envelope curve starts at a point where the static pool level in the reservoir at zero inflow intersects the channel floor. As the inflow to the reservoir increases, the end point of the backwater curve may move either upstream or downstream, depending upon many factors, such as condition of the channel, shape of the cross section, presence of flood plains, effect of tributaries, and possible change in reservoir level. When the reservoir level is kept constant and when the channel is prismatic and has a simple cross section, it is most likely that the end point will move in a downstream direction as the discharge is increased. Increase in channel roughness usually results in downstream movement of the end point, since its effect is to reduce the length of the flow profile. The presence of flood plains has a similar effect. In field studies, however, an approximate point of tangency of the normal-depth line to the backwater curve is often taken as the end point. This point is determined simply by eye observation from the drawing of flow profiles. The end point defined in this way generally shows an upstream movement when discharge increases. Prior to a study of the backwater effect, therefore, the upstream limit of the backwater effect should be properly defined in order to meet the particular need of the given problem.[1]

[1] See [8] and [9] for further discussion.

**11-9. Flow Passing Islands.**    When flow in a stream is divided by a long island (Fig. 11-14$a$), the division of flow between the two channels may be determined roughly with the aid of flow-profile computations.

In the case illustrated it is considered that the flow throughout all channels is subcritical.    The procedure is to assume first a set of discharges $Q_1$ and $Q_2$ for the divided flows such that the sum of the discharges is equal to the total discharge $Q$.    Then, compute flow profiles in the two channels past each side of the island to a point $A$ where the flow is divided.    Since the flow is subcritical, the computation should

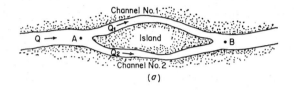

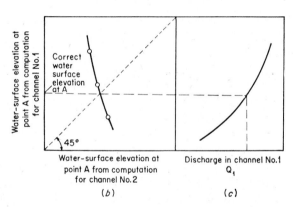

Fig. 11-14. Solution for flow passing an island.

proceed upstream from the downstream point $B$ where the divided flows unite again.    The initial water-surface elevation at point $B$ may be determined from the rating curve at this station for a total discharge $Q$. The computed water-surface elevation at point $A$ for channel 1 is then plotted against the same for channel 2.    A curve may, therefore, be drawn (Fig. 11-14$b$) for several assumed sets of discharges $Q_1$ and $Q_2$ of different proportions.    Since the flow is divided at point $A$, the two computed water-surface elevations at this point for the channels should be equal if the assumed division of flow is correct.    Thus, the elevation at point $A$ corresponding to this correct division of flow may be obtained from the plotted curve at which the curve is intersected by a dashed line bisecting the coordinate axes. The dashed line represents the condition that the two computed elevations are equal. In the meantime, the computed elevation at point $A$ for channel 1 is plotted against the discharge $Q_1$ (Fig. 11-14c). From this curve the correct discharge $Q_1$ may be obtained for the correct elevation. The corresponding discharge in channel 2 is, therefore, equal to $Q_2 = Q - Q_1$.

If the divided flows are supercritical, the control point will be at $A$; hence, division of flow will depend on the entrance condition of the divided channels. During the normal-flow condition, it may be assumed that all flows are uniform, and division of flow may be roughly determined from the following relations: $Q_1 = K_1 \sqrt{S_1}$, $Q_2 = K_2 \sqrt{S_2}$, and $Q = Q_1 + Q_2$.

**11-10. River Confluence.** When the flow-profile computation is carried upstream through the confluence of a river and its tributary, it is necessary to determine the water-surface elevations immediately upstream from the confluence. The procedure for solving this problem is illustrated in Example 10-10 for the confluence of the Missouri and Kansas Rivers. In this example, a discharge of 81,000 cfs from the Kansas River is combined with 350,000 cfs from the Missouri River to give a total discharge of 431,000 cfs immediately below the confluence. Cross sections 1K and 6 are located immediately upstream from the confluence of the two streams (Fig. 10-11). In Table 10-8, the hydraulic elements, velocity heads, and total heads are computed separately at the two sections. The velocity head at cross section 5 is computed for a total discharge of 431,000 cfs. This value is divided between the cross sections 6 and 1K corresponding to the discharges of 350,000 cfs and 81,000 cfs, respectively. The friction slope at each cross section is computed for the discharge of 81,000 cfs at cross section 1K and for 350,000 cfs at cross section 6. The friction head loss $h_f$ is then computed, using the average of the friction slopes from cross sections 5 to 1K in the Kansas River and from cross sections 5 to 6 in the Missouri River.

At the confluence, eddy loss is usually high. In Example 10-10, this is estimated as 10% of the increase in velocity head from cross section 1K to 5, or $0.10 (0.63 - 0.13) = 0.05$ ft. The total energy in cross section 5 is, therefore, equal to $h_f + h_e + H = 0.10 + 0.05 + 755.04 = 755.19$. Subtracting the velocity head from this value gives $755.19 - 0.13 = 755.06$, which should be equal to the assumed water-surface elevation at cross section 1K.

The above method should be applied to subcritical flow of relatively low velocities not exceeding about 10 fps. At high velocities, the eddy losses are high, and the error involved in the estimation may become quite appreciable.

The problem of river confluence may be further illustrated by an example given by Stoker [10], using the junction of the Ohio and Mississippi Rivers (Fig. 11-15). The initial conditions of the uniform flows in the Upper Mississippi, the Ohio, and the Lower Mississippi Rivers are, respectively, as follows: the normal depths, $y_{n1}$, $y_{n2}$, and $y_{n3}$; the channel slopes, $S_{01}$, $S_{02}$, and $S_{03}$; and the roughness coefficients, $n_1$, $n_2$, and $n_3$. From these data the normal discharges $Q_{n1}$, $Q_{n2}$, and $Q_{n3}$ can be computed. Now, a flood wave is assumed to initiate in the Ohio River at a place $L$

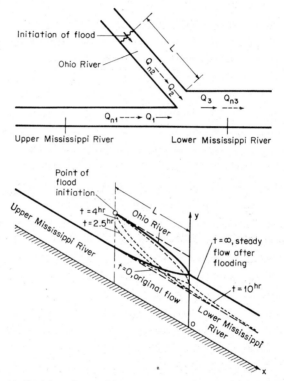

FIG. 11-15. A junction problem of the Ohio and Mississippi Rivers.

miles upstream from the junction and to be such that the Ohio River rises rapidly at that point from the initial normal depth $y_{n2}$ to a final maximum depth $y_2$. The point of flood initiation is shown at $x = -L$ on the coordinate axes, where $x$ is the distance measured from the junction along the channel. The wave of the flood thus originated will move down the Ohio River to the junction and create new waves, which travel both upstream and downstream in the Mississippi River, and also a reflected wave which travels back up the Ohio. After a certain time, a steady-flow condition is expected to develop; at this time the depth at the place of flood initiation becomes $y_2$, but the depth far upstream in the Mississippi River remains $y_{n1}$. As a general rule, the backwater effect in a long stream resulting from even fairly large discharges of its tributaries does not persist very far upstream. Therefore, the backwater curve in the Upper Mississippi River should be relatively short. At the final steady-flow condition, steady backwater curves will be formed in the Ohio and Upper Mississippi Rivers. Downstream in the Mississippi River, the depth will change from $y_{n3}$ to $y_3$, but the flow may be assumed to remain uniform.

The flow involved in the above-mentioned problem is considered to be subcritical, which is the usual case and can be verified easily by a computation of the Froude numbers. At the final steady-flow condition, the following conditions are evident: (1) the discharge in the Upper Mississippi River remains the same, or $Q_1 = Q_{n1}$; (2) the depths of the three channels at the junction are all equal to $y_j$ at $x = 0$; and (3) the sum of the discharges from the Ohio and Upper Mississippi Rivers is equal to the discharge in the Lower Mississippi River, or $Q_1 + Q_2 = Q_3$. By assuming a value of $y_j$, $Q_3$ may be computed and then

$$Q_2 = Q_3 - Q_1 = Q_3 - Q_{n1}$$

Since $y_j$, $Q_2$, and $y_2$ are now known, the length $L$ of the backwater curve can be computed. If the computed $L$ agrees with the given $L$, the assumed $y_j$ is the correct value. Otherwise, new values of $y_j$ should be assumed until a correct value is obtained. This is a trial-and-error solution. A solution may also be obtained by assuming $Q_2$ at the beginning and checking finally for either $y_j$ or $L$.

### PROBLEMS

**11-1.** A rectangular channel 5 ft wide and 500 ft long connects two reservoirs of varying surface levels (Fig. 11-16). Assuming a frictionless channel, construct the $Q$-constant curves of $y_1 = f(y_2)$ for $Q = 10, 50, 100, 150,$ and $200$ cfs. The loss at the channel entrance is negligible.

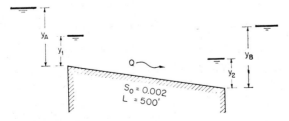

FIG. 11-16. Profile of a canal for Prob. 11-1.

**11-2.** Construct the $Q$-constant curves of $y_A = f(y_B)$ for Prob. 11-1. The entrance discharge may be computed by $Q = 3bH^{1.5}$ where $b$ is the channel width and $H$ is the total head.

**11-3.** A trapezoidal channel connecting two reservoirs 2 miles apart has $b = 50$ ft, $z = 2$, $\alpha = 1$, $n = 0.025$, and $S_0 = 0.004$. The upstream depth $y_1$ is maintained constant and equal to 6 ft (Fig. 11-1). Construct the delivery curve $Q = f(y_2)$.

**11-4.** Construct the delivery curve $Q = f(y_1)$ for Prob. 11-3 if the downstream depth $y_2$ is maintained constant and equal to 6 ft (Fig. 11-3).

**11-5.** Assuming a variable $y_1$ in Prob. 11-3, construct a curve of $y_1$ against $Q_{max}$ for a range of discharge varying from 0 to 2,000 cfs.

**11-6.** Assuming variable depths $y_1$ and $y_2$ in Prob. 11-3, construct the $Q$-constant curves for discharges having the normal depth equal to 2, 4, 6, and 8 ft, respectively.

**11-7.** Solve Prob. 11-3 if the reservoirs are 2,500 ft apart.

**11-8.** Solve Prob. 11-4 if the reservoirs are 2,500 ft apart.

**11-9.** Solve Prob. 11-5 if the reservoirs are 2,500 ft apart.

**11-10.** Solve Prob. 11-6 if the reservoirs are 2,500 ft apart.

**11-11.** Construct the delivery curve $Q = f(y_B)$ for Prob. 11-3 if the upstream reservoir depth $y_A$ is maintained constant and equal to 6 ft. The free entrance is well-rounded, or $C_e = 1.25$.

**11-12.** Construct the delivery curve $Q = f(y_A)$ for Prob. 11-4 if the downstream reservoir depth $y_B$ is maintained constant and equal to 6 ft. $C_e = 1.25$.

**11-13.** A rectangular raft chute 20 ft wide, as described by Bakhmeteff [1], is to be built between levels $A$ and $B$ (Fig. 11-17). The design conditions are:

1. The tailwater fluctuates by 8 ft.
2. The depth in the steep reach is kept to a minimum navigable depth of 2.5 ft.
3. The average velocity should not exceed 14.7 fps.
4. The discharge should be kept below 750 cfs.
5. The roughness coefficient $n = 0.03$.
6. The entrance discharge is computed by a weir formula $Q = 0.4 \sqrt{2g}\, by_A{}^{1.5}$.

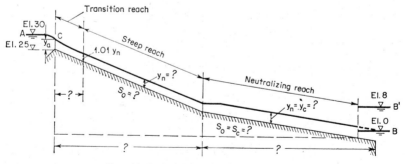

Fig. 11-17. A raft chute for Prob. 11-13.

Determine the following items by the Manning formula and by any method of flow-profile computation as described in this book:

*a.* Slope of the steep reach
*b.* The entrance depth $y_a$
*c.* Length of the flow profile in the transition reach

    *d.* Slope of the neutralizing reach
    *e.* Length of the neutralizing reach
    *f.* Length of the steep reach

**11-14.** Correct the flow profile computed in Example 11-1 for air entrainment, using Eq. (2-15).

**11-15.** Solve Example 11-1 for $Q = 19,000$ cfs.

**11-16.** A trapezoidal earth spillway with 3:1 side slopes is 190 ft long from the reservoir at Sta. 0 + 00 to the downstream critical control section at Sta. 1 + 90. The bottom of the spillway at Sta. 0 + 00 is 95 ft wide and converges uniformly to a width of 75 ft at Sta. 1 + 00. The bottom width of 75 ft is constant from Sta. 1 + 00 to Sta. 1 + 90. The bottom slope of the spillway between Sta. 0 + 00 and Sta. 1 + 00 is adverse, and is $-3\%$ between Sta. 0 + 00 and Sta. 0 + 80 and $-20\%$ between Sta. 0 + 80 and Sta. 1 + 00. The bottom of the spillway is horizontal between Sta. 1 + 00 and Sta. 1 + 90. Manning's $n = 0.035$. Determine:

    *a.* The flow profiles for discharges of 600, 800, 1,000, 1,200, 1,500, and 1,800 cfs in the spillway

    *b.* Curve showing discharge vs. elevation of pool level in the reservoir

    *c.* Friction loss in spillway between the reservoir and the control section for a discharge of 1,500 cfs

**11-17.** Review the design of an outlet transition from flume to canal (Fig. 11-11). The flume and canal are the same as those described in Example 11-2.

**11-18.** Review the design of the siphon inlet and outlet transitions (Fig. 11-13). Given the hydraulic properties: $A = 91.52$ ft², $R = 2.89$ ft, $S_0 = 0.0003$, and $n = 0.0225$ for the canals; and $A = 38.48$ ft², $R = 1.75$ ft, $S_0 = 0.0012$, and $n = 0.014$ for the circular siphon barrel.

**11-19.** Compute and construct a backwater envelope curve for the backwater caused by a 5-ft dam in the channel described in Example 10-1,

    *a.* Assuming the end point at a depth equal to $1.01y_n$.
    *b.* Assuming the end point at a depth equal to $y_n$ plus a freeboard of 6 in.

**11-20.** A discharge of 1,000 cfs is divided between two rectangular channels excavated in rock. The channels are later joined again (Fig. 11-14). Channel 1 is 10 ft wide and 200 ft long. Channel 2 is 15 ft wide and 150 ft long. The bottom of channel 2 is on the average about 2 ft lower than that of channel 1. Assuming $n = 0.035$ and a total drop of water surface between the dividing and joining points of the channels equal to 6 in., compute the divided uniform flows.

**11-21.** With reference to the problem shown in Fig. 11-15, the following data are assumed: $y_{n1} = y_{n2} = y_{n3} = 20$ ft, $S_{01} = S_{02} = 0.5$ ft/mile, $S_{03} = 0.49$ ft/mile, $n_1 = n_2 = n_3 = 0.03$, the widths of the Ohio and Upper Mississippi Rivers = 1,000 ft, the width of the Lower Mississippi River = 2,000 ft, $y_2 = 40$ ft, and $L = 50$ miles. All rivers are assumed to have rectangular channels. Determine the junction depth and the flow profiles in the rivers after the flood flow approaches a steady condition.

## REFERENCES

**1.** Boris A. Bakhmeteff: "Hydraulics of Open Channels," McGraw-Hill Book Company, Inc., New York, 1932, pp. 143–215.

2. Julian Hinds: The hydraulic design of flume and siphon transitions, *Transactions, American Society of Civil Engineers*, vol. 92, pp. 1423–1459, 1928.
3. "Civil Works: Flood Control in the Los Angeles Area," The Engineer School, Fort Belvoir, Virginia, 1950, E206.09 (4-50) ML, pp. 22–28 and plate 10.
4. L. Standish Hall: Open channel flow at high velocities, in Entrainment of air in flowing water: a symposium, *Transactions, American Society of Civil Engineers*, vol. 108, pp. 1394–1447, 1943.
5. Fred C. Scobey: The flow of water in flumes, *U.S. Department of Agriculture, Technical Bulletin No.* 393, December, 1933.
6. Hydraulic design data, appendix I of Canals and related structures, *U.S. Bureau of Reclamation, Design and Construction Manual, Design Supplement No.* 3, 1952, vol. X, pt. 2, paragraph I-13.
7. Julian Hinds: The hydraulic jump and critical depth in the design of hydraulic structures, *Engineering News-Record*, vol. 85, no. 22, pp. 1034–1040, Nov. 25, 1920.
8. Wallace M. Lansford and William D. Mitchell: An investigation of the backwater profile for steady flow in prismatic channels, *University of Illinois, Engineering Experiment Station, Bulletin Series No.* 381, vol. 46, no. 51, March, 1949.
9. William D. Mitchell: Stage-fall-discharge relations for steady flow in prismatic channels, *U.S. Geological Survey, Water Supply Paper* 1164, 1954.
10. J. J. Stoker: "Water Waves," vol. IV of "Pure and Applied Mathematics," Interscience Publishers, Inc., New York, 1957, pp. 456–461.

CHAPTER 12

# SPATIALLY VARIED FLOW

**12-1. Basic Principles and Assumptions.** Spatially (gradually) varied flow, as previously defined (Art. 1-2), has a nonuniform discharge resulting from the addition or diminution of water along the course of flow. The added or diminished water will cause disturbance in the energy or momentum content of the flow. As a result, the hydraulic behavior of a spatially varied flow is more complicated than that of a flow of constant discharge. Furthermore, the hydraulic behavior of spatially varied flow with increasing discharge is different in certain respects from that of similar flow with decreasing discharge. Therefore, the two types of spatially varied flow will be discussed separately.

*A. Flow with Increasing Discharge.* In this type of spatially varied flow, an appreciable portion of the energy loss is due to the turbulent mixing of the added water and the water flowing in the channel. In most cases, this mixing is of relatively high magnitude and uncertainty. Because of the resulting high and uncertain losses, the momentum equation will be found more convenient than the energy equation in solving this problem. From a practical viewpoint, the high energy loss seems to make channels designed for such spatially varied flow hydraulically inefficient, but physical circumstances sometimes make the use of such structures desirable.

A substantially correct form of the fundamental differential equation for spatially varied flow with increasing discharge was probably first established by Hinds [1] for the design of lateral spillway channels. A more complete equation, however, was developed by Favre [2,3], including a friction term and a component of inflow velocity in the direction of the axis of the channel. The methods developed by Hinds and Favre are applicable to any channel, prismatic and nonprismatic, but the procedure requires a step computation with successive approximations. For prismatic rectangular channels with uniform inflow throughout the channel length, the differential equation of the flow has been integrated by Camp [4] and Li [5]. Li also treated prismatic channels of sloping walls. Theoretical and experimental studies of the flow were also made by De Marchi [6], Citrini [7], Forchheimer [8], Schoklitsch [9], and others. In practical applications, the theory has covered a variety of problems,

327

from the study of flow in roof gutters [10] to the design of wash-water troughs in water-treatment plants [11,12] and of side-channel spillways on dams (Fig. 12-1).

B. *Flow with Decreasing Discharge.* Fundamentally, this type of spatially varied flow may be treated as a flow diversion where the diverted water does not affect the energy head. This concept has been

Fig. 12-1. The side-channel spillway on the Arizona side of Hoover Dam, looking upstream. (*U.S. Bureau of Reclamation.*)

verified by both theory and experiment. Therefore, the use of the energy equation will be found more convenient in solving this problem.

The theory of spatially varied flow with decreasing discharge was probably employed first in the design of lateral spillways or side-spillway weirs. This type of structure is usually a long notch installed along the side of a channel for the purpose of diverting or spilling excess flow. Laboratory tests on such structures were first made by Engels [13] and by Coleman and Smith [14].[1] Forchheimer [15] has approached the

---

[1] Engels's experiments indicated a rising and those by Coleman and Smith, on the contrary, a dropping flow profile along the spillway crest. This confusion was later explained by De Marchi [16] as resulting from the fact that flow was subcritical in Engels's but supercritical in Coleman and Smith's experiments.

problem analytically by assuming the energy line to be parallel to the spillway crest and to the channel bottom and also by assuming the flow profile along the spillway crest to be linear. Theoretically, De Marchi [16,17] proved that the energy head along the spillway crest is essentially constant and that the flow profile is curved, rising in subcritical flow and dropping in supercritical flow. This theoretical investigation was further verified experimentally by Gentilini [18]. Theoretical and practical studies of the flow were also performed and advanced by Favre [2,19], Nimmo [20], Noseda [21–23], Schmidt [24–26], Mostkow [27,28], Ackers [29], Allen [30], Collinge [31], Frazer [32], and many others.

In the derivation of the spatially-varied-flow equation in the next article, the following assumptions will be made:

1. The flow is unidirectional. Actually, there are strong cross currents present in the form of spiral flow, particularly in lateral spillway channels. The effects of these currents and of the accompanying turbulence cannot be easily evaluated, but will be included in computations if the momentum principle is used. The lateral unevenness of the water surface, as a result of cross currents, can be ignored.

2. The velocity distribution across the channel section is constant and uniform; that is, the velocity distribution coefficients are taken as unity. However, proper values of the coefficients may be introduced, if necessary.

3. The pressure in the flow is hydrostatic; that is, the flow is parallel. The flow at the outlet, however, may be curvilinear and deviate greatly from the parallel-flow assumption if a hydraulic drop occurs. In such cases, proper values of the pressure-distribution coefficients may be introduced, if necessary.

4. The slope of the channel is relatively small; so its effects on the pressure head and on the force on channel sections are negligible. If the slope is appreciable, corrections for these effects may be applied.

5. The Manning formula is used to evaluate the friction loss due to the shear developed along the channel wall.

6. The effect of air entrainment is neglected. A correction, however, may be applied to the computed result when necessary.

**12-2. Dynamic Equation for Spatially Varied Flow.** The discussion is given separately for flow with increasing discharge and flow with decreasing discharge.

*A. Flow with Increasing Discharge.* Referring to the lateral spillway channel in Fig. 12-2, the momentum passing section 1 per unit time is

$$\frac{w}{g} QV$$

where $w$ is the unit weight of water, $Q$ is the discharge, and $V$ is the velocity.   Similarly, the momentum passing section 2 per unit time is

$$\frac{w}{g}(Q + dQ)(V + dV)$$

where $dQ$ is the added discharge between sections 1 and 2.   The momentum change of the body of water between sections 1 and 2 is, therefore, equal to

$$\frac{w}{g}(Q + dQ)(V + dV) - \frac{w}{g}QV = \frac{w}{g}[Q\,dV + (V + dV)\,dQ]$$

Let $W$ be the weight of the body of water between the sections.   The component of $W$ in the direction of flow is

$$W \sin \theta = wS_0(A + \tfrac{1}{2}\,dA)\,dx = wS_0A\,dx$$

where slope $S_0$ is equal to $\sin \theta$ and the term containing the product of differentials is dropped.

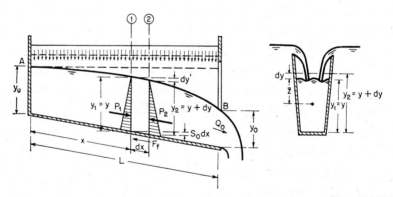

FIG. 12-2. Analysis of spatially varied flow.

The friction head between the two sections is equal to the friction slope $S_f$ multiplied by the length $dx$, or

$$h_f = S_f\,dx$$

where the friction slope may be represented by the Manning formula as

$$S_f = \frac{V^2n^2}{2.22R^{\frac{4}{3}}} = \frac{Q^2n^2}{2.22A^2R^{\frac{4}{3}}}$$

The frictional force along the channel wall is equivalent to the pressure due to friction head multiplied by the average area (see Art. 5-4), or

$$F_f = w(A + \tfrac{1}{2}\,dA)S_f\,dx = wAS_f\,dx$$

where the product of the differentials is dropped.

The total pressure on section 1 in the direction of flow is equal to the unit hydrostatic pressure at the centroid of the water area $A$ multiplied by the area, which is equivalent to the moment of $A$ about the free surface multiplied by $w$, or

$$P_1 = w\bar{z}A$$

where $\bar{z}$ is the depth of the centroid of $A$ below the surface of flow. Similarly, the total pressure on section 2 is

$$P_2 = w(\bar{z} + dy)A + \frac{w}{2}\,dA\,dy$$

where $dy$ is the difference between the depths of the two sections 1 and 2. Neglecting the term containing differentials of higher order,

$$P_2 = w(\bar{z} + dy)A$$

The resultant hydrostatic pressure acting on the body of water between sections 1 and 2 is

$$P_1 - P_2 = -wA\,dy$$

Equating the momentum change of the water body to all the external forces acting on the body,

$$\frac{w}{g}[Q\,dV + (V + dV)\,dQ] = P_1 - P_2 + W\sin\theta - F_f \qquad (12\text{-}1)$$

Neglecting $dV\,dQ$ and substituting in the above equation all expressions for external forces expressed previously,

$$dy = -\frac{1}{g}\left(V\,dV + \frac{V}{A}\,dQ\right) + (S_0 - S_f)\,dx \qquad (12\text{-}2)$$

Since $V = Q/A$ and $V + dV = (Q + dQ)/(A + dA)$, the above equation becomes

$$dy = -\frac{V}{g}\left(\frac{2A\,dQ - Q\,dA + dA\,dQ}{A^2 + A\,dA}\right) + (S_0 - S_f)\,dx \qquad (12\text{-}3)$$

Neglecting $dA$ in the denominator and $dA\,dQ$ in the numerator, and simplifying,

$$\frac{dy}{dx} = \frac{S_0 - S_f - 2Qq_*/gA^2}{1 - Q^2/gA^2D} \qquad (12\text{-}4)$$

where $q_* = dQ/dx$, or the discharge per unit length of the channel, and $D$ is the hydraulic depth. If nonuniform velocity distribution in the channel section is considered, an energy coefficient can be introduced in the equation, or

$$\frac{dy}{dx} = \frac{S_0 - S_f - 2\alpha Qq_*/gA^2}{1 - \alpha Q^2/gA^2D} \qquad (12\text{-}5)$$

This is the *dynamic equation for spatially varied flow with increasing discharge.* Theoretically speaking, a momentum coefficient should be used in the equation. However, the energy coefficient is used because the friction slope $S_f$ is evaluated by a formula for energy loss, such as the Manning formula.[1] When $q_* = 0$, this equation becomes the dynamic equation for gradually varied flow of constant discharge.

B. *Flow with Decreasing Discharge.* For the analysis of this type of spatially varied flow, the energy principle is directly applicable. Let $z$ be the distance of the bottom of the channel section above a horizontal datum (not shown in Fig. 12-2); the total energy at a channel section is

$$H = z + y + \frac{\alpha Q^2}{2gA^2} \tag{12-6}$$

Differentiating this equation with respect to $x$,

$$\frac{dH}{dx} = \frac{dz}{dx} + \frac{dy}{dx} + \frac{\alpha}{2g}\left(\frac{2Q\,dQ}{A^2\,dx} - \frac{2Q^2}{A^3}\frac{dA}{dx}\right) \tag{12-7}$$

Noting that $dH/dx = -S_f$, $dz/dx = -S_0$, $dQ/dx = q_*$, and

$$\frac{dA}{dx} = \left(\frac{dA}{dy}\right)\left(\frac{dy}{dx}\right) = \frac{T\,dy}{dx}$$

the above equation may be reduced to

$$\frac{dy}{dx} = \frac{S_0 - S_f - \alpha Q q_*/gA^2}{1 - \alpha Q^2/gA^2D} \tag{12-8}$$

which is the *dynamic equation for spatially varied flow with decreasing discharge.* It should be noted that this equation differs from Eq. (12-5) only in the coefficient of the third term of the numerator.

Now it is interesting to know [33] that the momentum principle can also be used for the derivation of Eq. (12-8). In a spatially varied flow, with decreasing discharge, no momentum is added to the water. Following a procedure similar to the derivation of Eq. (12-5), the term containing $dQ$ may be dropped from Eq. (12-1); the resulting equation will be identical with Eq. (12-8).

Likewise, the energy principle can also be used for the derivation of Eq. (12-5). In applying this principle to spatially varied flow with increasing discharge, the energy due to the added discharge $dQ$ per elementary length $dx$ should be added to the total energy along the course of the flow during the time interval $dt$. This kinetic energy per pound of water is equal to

$$\frac{\text{mass} \times \text{velocity}^2}{g \times \text{unit weight of water} \times \text{volume}} = \frac{(w\,dQ\,dt)(\alpha V^2)}{gw(A\,dx)} = \frac{\alpha V\,dQ}{gA}$$

---

[1] This is merely a practical interpretation, which has no theoretical basis.

Adding this term to the right side of Eq. (12-6) and differentiating, the resulting equation will be identical with Eq. (12-5).

**12-3. Analysis of Flow Profile.** In discussing the analysis of the flow profile, a simple example will be given first.

**Example 12-1.** A horizontal rectangular lateral-spillway channel has a free-overfall outlet. The inflow is uniformly distributed along the channel with a rate of $q_*$ per unit length of the channel. Derive the equation of the flow profile, ignoring the friction loss.

*Solution.* In this problem the rate of inflow is $q_* = Q_o/L$, where $Q_o$ is the discharge at the outlet and $L$ is the channel length. Thus, $dQ = q_*\,dx$ and $Q = q_*x$. Let $b$ be the channel width; then $A = by$ and $V = Q/A = q_*x/by$. Also, $S_0 = S_f = 0$. Substituting these expressions in Eq. (12-4) and simplifying,

$$\frac{dx^2}{dy} - \frac{x^2}{y} = -\frac{gb^2y^2}{q_*{}^2} \tag{12-9}$$

This is a linear differential equation of the first order. The general solution of this equation is

$$x^2 = -\frac{gb^2y^3}{2q_*{}^2} + cy \tag{12-10}$$

where $c$ is an integration constant which may be determined by the boundary conditions of the flow profile.

At the outlet, $x = L$ and $y = y_o$. Thus, Eq. (12-10) gives

$$c = \frac{1}{y_o}\left(L^2 + \frac{gb^2y_o{}^3}{2q_*{}^2}\right) \tag{12-11}$$

and Eq. (12-10) becomes

$$\left(\frac{x}{L}\right)^2 = \left(1 + \frac{1}{2F_o{}^2}\right)\frac{y}{y_o} - \frac{1}{2F_o{}^2}\left(\frac{y}{y_o}\right)^3 \tag{12-12}$$

where

$$F_o{}^2 = \frac{q_*{}^2L^2}{gb^2y_o{}^3} \tag{12-13}$$

It is apparent that $F_o$ is in the form of a Froude number of the flow at the outlet. When free overfall occurs at the outlet, the flow is critical; therefore, $F_o = 1$. The equation of the flow profile becomes

$$\left(\frac{x}{L}\right)^2 = \tfrac{3}{2}\frac{y}{y_o} - \tfrac{1}{2}\left(\frac{y}{y_o}\right)^3 \tag{12-14}$$

where depth $y_o$ is the critical depth at the outlet for $Q_o$.

When the outlet is submerged, the depth $y_o$ is determined by the downstream surface elevation, and $F_o$ can be computed from the knowledge of $y_o$ and $Q_o$. For each value of $x/L$, Eq. (12-14) will give two real positive solutions. However, only values of $y/y_o \geqq 1$ are true solutions, because the energy in flow must decrease as the flow proceeds downstream and $y$ cannot be less than $y_o$.

The above example illustrates spatially varied flow in horizontal channels of rectangular cross section. Similar analyses can be made for channels with parallel side walls having irregular bottoms and for channels with sloping side walls. For channels with sloping bed, however, a general explicit equation of the flow profile such as Eq. (12-12) cannot be obtained. If no hydraulic jump occurs in the channel, the flow profile can be computed directly by the method of numerical integration[1] (Art. 12-4), starting from a known control depth of flow.

Li [5] has performed an analysis of spatially varied flow in channels of sloping bed by means of numerical integration. The results of this analysis can be summarized in a general diagram (Fig. 12-3). For channels with parallel side walls, the diagram is shown in Fig. 12-4.

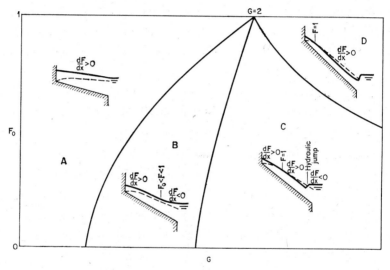

FIG. 12-3. Types of spatially varied flow as determined by $F_o$ and $G$. The diagram is shown for a channel of an arbitrary section. For rectangular channels, the line dividing regions $B$ and $C$ is $G = 1 + F_o$; for triangular channels, it is $G = 2$. The dashed line in each channel is the critical-depth line.

This diagram indicates the relationship between the Froude number $F_o$ and the value of $G = S_0 L / y_o$. It consists of four regions, representing four conditions of flow.

*Region A.* This region represents the condition where flow is sub-critical throughout the channel and where the value of $F$ increases as the flow proceeds downstream; that is, $dF/dx > 0$. The symbol $F$ represents the Froude number of flow at a section a distance $x$ from the upstream end of the channel. The value of $F$ can be computed from Eq. (12-13) by replacing $F_o$ with $F$ and $L$ with $x$. Since the flow is subcritical, the depth of flow at any section is greater than the critical depth, as shown

---

[1] The profile can also be computed by a graphical method developed by Camp [4], which requires trial adjustments.

by the dashed line. In region $A$, $\mathbf{F}_o = 1$, and the flow condition is governed by the upstream depth $y_u$. In other words, the water surface recedes in the downstream direction, and only the value of $y_u$ is of interest in determining the channel dimensions. Values of $y_u/y_o$ for region $A$ have been computed by numerical integration and have been plotted as solid lines (Fig. 12-4). The computation was made on the condition that $y_u/y_o \geq 1$ at $x/L = 1$.

It can be proved that, when $d\mathbf{F}/dx > 0$, $G < \frac{2}{3}(1 + 2\mathbf{F}_o^2)$. This is represented by the line dividing regions $A$ and $B$ in the diagram (Fig. 12-3).

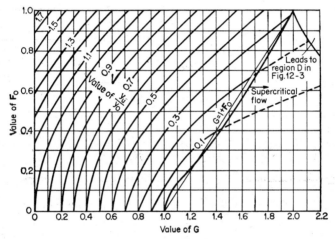

Fig. 12-4. Solutions for channels with sloping bed and parallel side walls. (*After W. H. Li* [5].)

*Region B.* This region represents the condition where the flow is subcritical throughout the channel but where the value of $\mathbf{F}$ will first increase as the flow proceeds downstream, reaching a maximum value less than unity, and then decrease. It has been found that the line dividing regions $B$ and $C$ can be represented approximately by $G = 1 + \mathbf{F}_o$. This line indicates all the cases in which the maximum value of $\mathbf{F}$ reaches unity.

*Region C.* This region represents the condition at which there is supercritical flow in the downstream portion of the channel and a hydraulic jump in the channel. It has been found that supercritical flow occurs when $G$ is greater than approximately $1 + \mathbf{F}_o$. The hydraulic jump will form only if the outlet is sufficiently submerged. As the jump occurs, the control section will be shifted into the channel, and the elevation of the water surface at the outlet will not affect the entire flow profile.

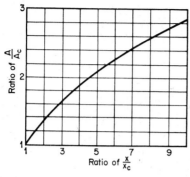

FIG. 12-5. Dimensionless flow profile in supercritical reaches in a spatially-varied-flow channel of sloping bed and parallel walls. (*After W. H. Li* [5].)

The flow profile upstream from the jump cannot be determined from the value of $y_o$, but it can be determined from the critical depth $y_c$ and the position of the critical section $x_c$. A dimensionless flow profile in the supercritical reach (Fig. 12-5, in which $A_c$ and $A$ are water areas, respectively, of the critical section and the section a distance $x$ from the upstream end of the channel) has been computed by numerical integration. This curve can be used to compute the flow profile below the critical section and above the hydraulic jump.

The position of a critical section in the lateral-spillway channel can be determined by the method of singular point (Art. 9-6).

*Region D.* This region represents the flow condition at which there is supercritical flow throughout the downstream portion of the channel but where the depth of submergence at the outlet is not great enough to create a hydraulic jump in the channel. Thus, the value of $\mathbf{F}_o$ is not determined by the depth of submergence. The dividing line between regions $C$ and $D$ (Figs. 12-3 and 12-4) was obtained by numerical integration on the condition of a minimum depth of submergence required to produce a hydraulic jump at the outlet. This minimum depth is equal to the depth necessary to set the downstream pool level at a sequent depth. A depth of submergence greater than this minimum depth will force the jump to move upstream into the channel, and the condition of flow will be represented by region $C$.

When the slope of the channel is extremely steep or when the value of $G$ is very large, the flow will become unsteady. The limiting value of $G$ that will keep the flow in a steady condition has not been determined.

In the above analysis, the effect of friction has been neglected. This has been verified as justifiable for the design of wash-water troughs and side-channel spillways. For effluent channels around sewage-treatment tanks, however, the effect of friction may increase the upstream depth $y_u$ as much as 10%.*

* Li [5] has computed curves representing the increase of $y_u$ as a result of friction in horizontal channels.

For an advanced theoretical analysis of spatially varied flow, the method of singular point (Art. 9-6) may be used.

**Example 12-2.** Analyze the flow in a rectangular channel of small slope with a bottom rack (Fig. 12-6) and derive the equation of the flow profile.[1]

*Solution.* The flow in a channel with bottom rack is a case of spatially varied flow with decreasing discharge. The rack is usually made of parallel bars or perforated screen. There are various applications of such a device. For example, the channel may be an "intake" to withdraw water from, say, a mountain torrent, or a "skimmer" to reduce the volume of water required to transport, say, fish.

Assuming $\alpha = 1$ and $\theta \approx 0$, the specific energy at any section of the channel (Fig. 12-6) is

$$E = y + \frac{V^2}{2g} = y + \frac{Q^2}{2gb^2y^2} \quad (12\text{-}15)$$

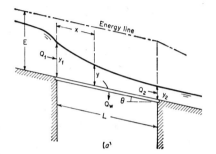

For a spatially varied flow with decreasing discharge, the specific energy can be considered constant along the channel.[2] Thus, $dE/dx = 0$; or, from Eq. (12-15),

$$\frac{dy}{dx} = \frac{Qy(-dQ/dx)}{gb^2y^3 - Q^2} \quad (12\text{-}16)$$

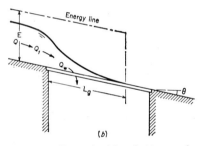

where $-dQ/dx$ is obviously the discharge withdrawn through a length $dx$ of the rack. Equation (12-16) is the general dynamic equation for the flow under consideration.

The discharge through the rack depends upon the effective head on the rack. When the direction of flow through the rack openings is nearly vertical ($A$, below), the energy loss in the process is

Fig. 12-6. Channel with a bottom rack. (*a*) Partial withdrawal; (*b*) complete withdrawal.

negligible and, thus, the effective head on the rack is practically equal to the specific energy $E$. Mostkow [28] found that this is true of racks such as those composed of parallel bars. On the other hand, when the direction of flow through the rack openings makes an appreciable angle with the vertical ($B$), the flow will impinge on the sides of the openings, resulting in a loss of energy and a change in direction of the flow from inclined eventually to vertical. From experiments, Mostkow found that this is true of racks such as those composed of a perforated screen and that the corresponding energy loss is approximately equal to the velocity

---

[1] There have been many investigations on this problem. The actual flow phenomenon is rather complicated, particularly when the slope of the rack is taken into consideration. For details, see [21] to [23], [26] to [28], and [34] to [38].

[2] This assumption was found to agree with the experiments [21].

head of the flow over the rack. It may, therefore, be assumed that the effective head on the rack is equal to the static head, or the depth of flow over the rack.

　　A. *For Vertical Flow through the Rack.* In this case the discharge through a length $dx$ of the rack may be expressed by

$$- \frac{dQ}{dx} = \epsilon cb \sqrt{2gE} \tag{12-17}$$

where $\epsilon$ is the ratio of the opening area to the total area of the rack surface and $c$ is the coefficient of discharge through the openings.

　　From Eq. (12-15), the discharge is

$$Q = by \sqrt{2g(E - y)} \tag{12-18}$$

　　Substituting Eq. (12-17) for $-dQ/dx$ and Eq. (12-18) for $Q$ in Eq. (12-16) and simplifying,

$$\frac{dy}{dx} = \frac{2\epsilon c \sqrt{E(E - y)}}{3y - 2E} \tag{12-19}$$

Integration of this equation gives the equation of the flow profile as

$$x = \frac{-E}{\epsilon c} \frac{y}{E} \sqrt{1 - \frac{y}{E}} + C \tag{12-20}$$

For $y = y_1$ and $x = 0$, the integration constant is determined from Eq. (12-20) as $C = (E/\epsilon c)(y_1/E) \sqrt{1 - y_1/E}$. Thus,[1]

$$x = \frac{E}{\epsilon c} \left( \frac{y_1}{E} \sqrt{1 - \frac{y_1}{E}} - \frac{y}{E} \sqrt{1 - \frac{y}{E}} \right) \tag{12-21}$$

　　When $y = 0$, Eq. (12-21) gives the length of the rack required for a complete withdrawal of the main flow through the rack, or

$$L_\varrho = \frac{E}{\epsilon c} \left( \frac{y_1}{E} \sqrt{1 - \frac{y_1}{E}} \right) \tag{12-22}$$

　　By Eq. (12-18), the above equation may be reduced to

$$L_\varrho = \frac{Q_1}{\epsilon cb \sqrt{2gE}} \tag{12-23}$$

where $Q_1$ is the discharge through the entrance to the reach of the rack and is also equal to the withdrawal discharge $Q_w$ through the rack.

　　B. *For Inclined Flow through the Rack.* In this case the discharge through a length $dx$ of the rack may be expressed by

$$- \frac{dQ}{dx} = \epsilon cb \sqrt{2gy} \tag{12-24}$$

---

[1] This equation may also be derived by means of Eqs. (12-17) and (12-18). By Eq. (12-17), the discharge through the rack of length $x$ is $Q_w = \epsilon cbx \sqrt{2gE}$. By Eq. (12-18), $Q_w = Q_1 - Q = by_1 \sqrt{2g(E - y_1)} - by \sqrt{2g(E - y)}$. Equating these two expressions for $Q_w$, Eq. (12-21) is obtained.

Substituting Eq. (12-24) for $-dQ/dx$ and Eq. (12-18) for $Q$ in Eq. (12-16) and simplifying,

$$\frac{dy}{dx} = \frac{2\epsilon c \sqrt{y(E-y)}}{3y - 2E} \tag{12-25}$$

Integration of this equation gives the equation of the flow profile as[1]

$$x = \frac{E}{\epsilon c}\left[\frac{1}{4}\sin^{-1}\left(1 - \frac{2y}{E}\right) - \frac{3}{2}\sqrt{\frac{y}{E}\left(1 - \frac{y}{E}\right)}\right] + C_1 \tag{12-26}$$

or

$$x = \frac{E}{\epsilon c}\left[\frac{1}{2}\cos^{-1}\sqrt{\frac{y}{E}} - \frac{3}{2}\sqrt{\frac{y}{E}\left(1 - \frac{y}{E}\right)}\right] + C_2 \tag{12-27}$$

The integration constants in the above equation may be evaluated by the condition that $y = y_1$ and $x = 0$. Then, when $y = 0$, Eq. (12-26) will give the length of the rack required for a complete withdrawal of the main flow through the rack, or

$$L_g = \frac{E}{\epsilon c}\left[\frac{3}{2}\sqrt{\frac{y_1}{E}\left(1 - \frac{y_1}{E}\right)} - \frac{1}{4}\sin^{-1}\left(1 - \frac{2y_1}{E}\right) + \frac{\pi}{8}\right] \tag{12-28}$$

In both cases $A$ and $B$ described above, the entrance to the reach of the rack may be regarded as a broad-crested weir. Thus, $Q_1 = c'bE^{1.5}$, where $c'$ may have an average value of 2.80. Also, Eq. (12-18) gives $Q_1 = by_1\sqrt{2g(E-y_1)}$ and $Q_2 = by_2\sqrt{2g(E-y_2)}$. Thus, the discharge of a partial withdrawal from the main flow through the rack is $Q_w = Q_1 - Q_2$, or

$$Q_w = c'b\left(1 - \frac{y_2\sqrt{E-y_2}}{y_1\sqrt{E-y_1}}\right)E^{1.5} \tag{12-29}$$

For a complete withdrawal of the main flow through the rack, it is evident that $Q_w = Q_1 = c'bE^{1.5}$, from which $E = (Q_1/c'b)^{2/3}$. Thus, $E$ may be computed if the incoming discharge $Q_1$, $b$, and $c'$ are given.

The value $c$ of the coefficient of discharge through the rack openings actually varies considerably along the rack. For example, typical values determined experimentally were found to vary from 0.435, for a grade of 1 on 5, to 0.497, for a horizontal slope of the racks of parallel bars; and from 0.750, for a grade of 1 on 5, to 0.800, for a horizontal slope of the racks of perforated screens [27]. In general, the value is higher for racks of perforated screens than for racks of parallel bars. The value is higher for horizontal racks than for inclined racks. The local value increases as the flow depth on the rack increases if the bars are parallel to the direction of the main flow, but decreases with the depth if the bars are in transverse direction.

The analysis of this problem may be further extended by considering the effects of the streamline curvature, the nonuniform velocity distribution, and the bottom slope, and by classifying various types of the flow profiles thus created. In general, there are five types of flow profiles, which are similar to those to be described in the next example.

It may be interesting to note that, when a critical state of flow exists on the upstream side of the rack, the critical depth will occur at a section somewhere upstream from

---

[1] Equation (12-26) is given by Mostkow [27] and Eq. (12-27) by Noseda [21]. The two equations are mathematically identical. The relationship between the integration constants is $C_1 = C_2 + \pi E/8\epsilon c$.

the entrance section. This phenomenon is, therefore, similar to that of a free over-fall (Art. 3-4). The ratio $y_1/y_c$, of the entrance depth to the critical depth, decreases with increase in the value of $\epsilon$ and of the rack slope. Typical average ratios vary from 0.70 to 0.90, which correspond approximately to the values of $y_1/E$ from 0.47 to 0.60.

**Example 12-3.** Analyze the flow through a side weir in a prismatic horizontal rectangular channel.[1]

*Solution.* The flow through a side weir is a case of spatially varied flow with decreasing discharge (Fig. 12-7). According to Frazer [32], the following five types of flow profile can be produced:

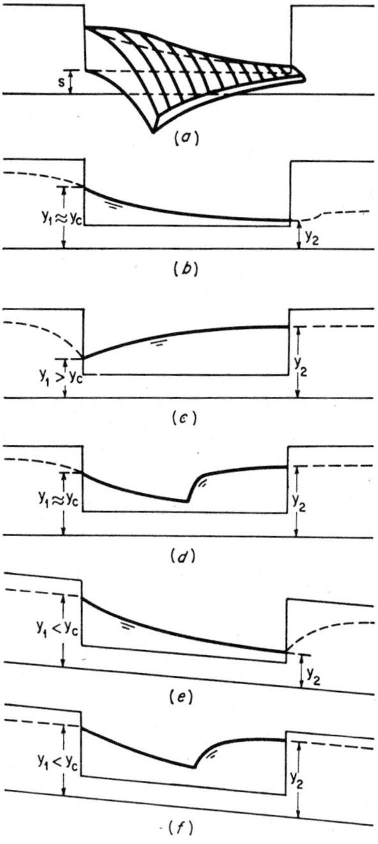

*Type a.* Critical conditions at or near the entrance with supercritical flow in the weir section, the depth of flow decreasing along the weir (Fig. 12-7b)

*Type b.* Depth of flow greater than critical at the entrance with subcritical flow in the weir section, the depth of flow increasing along the weir section (Fig. 12-7c)

*Type c.* Type a flow at the beginning of the weir section with a hydraulic jump occurring in the weir section, and type b flow after the jump at a lower specific-energy level owing to jump losses (Fig. 12-7d)

*Type d.* Depth of flow less than critical at the entrance with supercritical flow in the weir section, the depth of flow decreasing along the weir section (Fig. 12-7e)

*Type e.* Type d flow at the entrance section with a hydraulic jump occurring in the weir section and type b flow after the jump at a lower specific-energy level owing to jump losses (Fig. 12-7f)

The last two types of flow are possible if the approach flow is supercritical. In a conventional analysis, it is assumed that the velocity through the side weir is in general at right angles to the weir. This assumption is more satisfactory for subcritical flow than for supercritical flow. In supercritical flow the velocity will be high and the angle that the over-

FIG. 12-7. Various flow profiles along a side weir.

flow makes with the weir will be small. Consequently, types $d$ and $e$ cannot easily be analyzed successfully. Furthermore, the discharge in types $d$ and $e$ flow is controlled upstream, where additional consideration in the analysis is required.

In the present problem the specific energy along the side weir may be assumed

[1] For detailed studies of the side weir, see [24] to [27] and [29] to [32].

constant, or $S_f = S_0$. Since the channel is horizontal, $S_0 = 0$. Thus, assuming $\alpha = 1$, Eq. (12-8) gives an equation identical with Eq. (12-16), or

$$\frac{dy}{dx} = \frac{Qy(-dQ/dx)}{gb^2y^3 - Q^2} \tag{12-16}$$

The discharge over any given length of the weir can be computed by a weir formula, or

$$\frac{dQ_w}{dx} = -\frac{dQ}{dx} = c\sqrt{2g}\,(y - s)^{1.5} \tag{12-30}$$

where $c$ is the discharge coefficient and $s$ is the height of the weir sill above the bottom of the channel. The sill of the weir is parallel to the bottom of the channel. Equation (12-18) also is applicable to the present problem. Thus, the discharge at any section is

$$Q = by\sqrt{2g(E - y)} \tag{12-18}$$

where $b$ is the width of the channel and $E$ is the specific energy.

With Eqs. (12-30) and (12-18), Eq. (12-16) becomes

$$\frac{dy}{dx} = \frac{2c}{b}\frac{\sqrt{(E - y)(y - s)^3}}{3y - 2E} \tag{12-31}$$

Integrating Eq. (12-31) and solving for $x$,

$$x = \frac{b}{c}F\left(\frac{y}{E}\right) + \text{const} \tag{12-32}$$

where

$$F\left(\frac{y}{E}\right) = \frac{2E - 3s}{E - s}\sqrt{\frac{E - y}{y - s}} - 3\sin^{-1}\sqrt{\frac{E - y}{y - s}} \tag{12-33}$$

$F(y/E)$ is a varied-flow function which was first solved by De Marchi [16].

**12-4. Method of Numerical Integration.** This method will be applied first to a flow with increasing discharge and then to a flow with decreasing discharge.

*A. Flow with Increasing Discharge.* Considering the differentials as finite increments, Eq. (12-1) may be written

$$\frac{w}{g}[Q\,\Delta V + (V + \Delta V)\,\Delta Q] = -w\int_0^{\Delta y} A\,dy + wS_0\int_0^{\Delta x} A\,dx$$
$$- wS_f\int_0^{\Delta x} A\,dx$$
$$= -w\bar{A}\,\Delta y + wS_0\bar{A}\,\Delta x - wS_f\bar{A}\,\Delta x \tag{12-34}$$

where $\bar{A}$ is the average area. Since the discharge varies with the finite increment of the channel length, the average area may be taken as $\bar{A} = (Q_1 + Q_2)/(V_1 + V_2)$. Also taking $Q = Q_1$ and $V + \Delta V = V_2$ and simplifying,

$$\Delta y = -\frac{Q_1(V_1 + V_2)}{g(Q_1 + Q_2)}\left(\Delta V + \frac{V_2}{Q_1}\Delta Q\right) + S_0\,\Delta x - S_f\,\Delta x \tag{12-35}$$

The drop in water-surface elevation between sections 1 and 2 (Fig. 12-2) may be expressed by

$$dy' = -dy + S_0\,dx \qquad (12\text{-}36)$$

Converting the differentials to finite increments,

$$\Delta y' = -\Delta y + S_0\,\Delta x \qquad (12\text{-}37)$$

Substituting Eq. (12-35) for $\Delta y$ in Eq. (12-37) and introducing an energy coefficient $\alpha$ for nonuniform velocity distribution,[1] the drop in water surface is

$$\Delta y' = \frac{\alpha Q_1(V_1 + V_2)}{g(Q_1 + Q_2)}\left(\Delta V + \frac{V_2}{Q_1}\Delta Q\right) + S_f\,\Delta x \qquad (12\text{-}38)$$

This equation can be used to compute the flow profile of a spatially varied flow with increasing discharge. On the right-hand side of the equation, the first term represents the effect of impact loss and the second term represents the effect of friction. It is interesting to note that, if $\Delta Q$ and $S_f$ are zero, or $Q_1 = Q_2$, then this equation will be reduced to $\Delta y' = \alpha(V_2{}^2 - V_1{}^2)/2g$, which is the energy equation for flow of constant discharge, neglecting friction. The procedure of numerical integration is illustrated by the following example.

**Example 12-4.**[*] A trapezoidal lateral spillway channel 400 ft long is designed to carry a varying discharge of 40 cfs/ft. The cross section has a bottom width of 10 ft and side slopes of $\frac{1}{2}$:1. The longitudinal slope of the channel is 0.1505, starting at an upstream bottom elevation of 73.70. Assuming $n = 0.015$ and $\alpha = 1$, compute the flow profile for the design discharge.

*Solution.* The first step is to determine the control section from which the flow profile computation can start. The control section may be determined by the method of singular point (Art. 9-6). In this example, however, a method developed by Hinds [1] is employed. The computation is shown in Tables 12-1 and 12-2.

Table 12-1 shows the computation of critical velocities and discharges corresponding to a number of arbitrarily assigned depths, shown in col. 1. The critical velocities in col. 5 correspond to the critical velocity heads in col. 4. The hydraulic radii are also computed and recorded in this table for use in computing friction losses.

Table 12-2 shows the computation of the drop in water surface necessary to maintain a flow at the critical depth throughout the full length of the channel. The column headings are explained as follows:

Col. 1. Distance of the station along the channel, in ft
Col. 2. Increment of the distance
Col. 3. The inflow discharge, equal to $x$ times 40 cfs/ft
Col. 4. Sum of the discharges $Q_1$ of the previous station and $Q_2$ of the station under consideration

---

[1] The use of an energy coefficient instead of a momentum coefficient has the same reason given in Art. 12-2.

[*] This example is taken from [1].

TABLE 12-1. COMPUTATION OF CRITICAL DEPTHS FOR EXAMPLE 12-4

| $y$ | $A$ | $T$ | $A/2T$ | $V_c$ | $Q_c$ | $R_c$ |
|-----|-----|-----|--------|-------|-------|-------|
| (1) | (2) | (3) | (4) | (5) | (6) | (7) |
| 2 | 22 | 12 | 0.92 | 7.68 | 169 | 1.52 |
| 4 | 48 | 14 | 1.71 | 10.49 | 504 | 2.52 |
| 6 | 78 | 16 | 2.44 | 12.52 | 978 | 3.33 |
| 8 | 112 | 18 | 3.11 | 14.15 | 1,585 | 4.01 |
| 10 | 150 | 20 | 3.75 | 15.53 | 2,330 | 4.63 |
| 12 | 192 | 22 | 4.36 | 16.75 | 3,216 | 5.22 |
| 14 | 238 | 24 | 4.96 | 17.86 | 4,252 | 5.76 |
| 16 | 288 | 26 | 5.54 | 18.88 | 5,440 | 6.29 |
| 18 | 342 | 28 | 6.11 | 19.82 | 6,780 | 6.82 |
| 20 | 400 | 30 | 6.67 | 20.71 | 8,284 | 7.31 |
| 22 | 462 | 32 | 7.22 | 21.55 | 9,960 | 7.81 |
| 24 | 528 | 34 | 7.76 | 22.34 | 11,800 | 8.29 |
| 26 | 598 | 36 | 8.31 | 23.12 | 13,820 | 8.77 |
| 28 | 672 | 38 | 8.84 | 23.84 | 16,020 | 9.26 |

TABLE 12-2. COMPUTATION FOR THE DETERMINATION OF THE CONTROL SECTION FOR EXAMPLE 12-4

| $x$ | $\Delta x$ | $Q$ | $Q_1 + Q_2$ | $y_c$ | $V_c$ | $V_1 + V_2$ | $\Delta Q$ | $\Delta V$ | $y_m'$ | $R_c$ | $h_f$ | $\Delta y'$ | $\Sigma \Delta y'$ |
|-----|------------|-----|-------------|-------|-------|-------------|------------|------------|--------|-------|-------|-------------|--------------------|
| (1) | (2) | (3) | (4) | (5) | (6) | (7) | (8) | (9) | (10) | (11) | (12) | (13) | (14) |
| 0 + 00 | | | | | | | | | | | | | |
| 0 + 10 | 10 | 400 | 400 | 3.4 | 10.0 | 10.0 | 400 | 10.0 | .... | 2.25 | 0.03 | | |
| 0 + 25 | 15 | 1,000 | 1,400 | 6.2 | 12.5 | 22.5 | 600 | 2.5 | 4.25 | 3.41 | 0.05 | 4.30 | 4.30 |
| 0 + 50 | 25 | 2,000 | 3,000 | 9.2 | 14.9 | 27.4 | 1,000 | 2.4 | 4.91 | 4.40 | 0.08 | 4.99 | 9.29 |
| 1 + 00 | 50 | 4,000 | 6,000 | 13.5 | 17.6 | 32.5 | 2,000 | 2.7 | 6.77 | 5.63 | 0.16 | 6.93 | 16.22 |
| 1 + 50 | 50 | 6,000 | 10,000 | 16.9 | 19.3 | 36.9 | 2,000 | 1.7 | 5.21 | 6.53 | 0.16 | 5.37 | 21.59 |
| 2 + 00 | 50 | 8,000 | 14,000 | 19.7 | 20.6 | 39.9 | 2,000 | 1.3 | 4.33 | 7.23 | 0.15 | 4.48 | 26.07 |
| 2 + 50 | 50 | 10,000 | 18,000 | 22.1 | 21.6 | 42.2 | 2,000 | 1.0 | 3.74 | 7.83 | 0.16 | 3.90 | 29.97 |
| 3 + 00 | 50 | 12,000 | 22,000 | 24.2 | 22.4 | 44.0 | 2,000 | 0.8 | 3.30 | 8.34 | 0.16 | 3.46 | 33.43 |
| 3 + 50 | 50 | 14,000 | 26,000 | 26.2 | 23.2 | 45.6 | 2,000 | 0.8 | 3.04 | 8.82 | 0.15 | 3.19 | 36.62 |
| 4 + 00 | 50 | 16,000 | 30,000 | 28.0 | 23.8 | 47.0 | 2,000 | 0.6 | 2.73 | 9.26 | 0.15 | 2.88 | 39.50 |

Col. 5. Critical depth in ft, interpolated from Table 12-1 corresponding to the discharge in col. 3

Col. 6. Critical velocity in fps, interpolated from Table 12-1 corresponding to the discharge in col. 3

Col. 7. Sum of the velocities in the previous station and in the station under consideration

Col. 8. Increment of discharge $\Delta Q = Q_2 - Q_1$

Col. 9. Increment of velocity $\Delta V = V_2 - V_1$

Col. 10. Drop in water surface due to impact loss, or

$$\Delta y_m' = \frac{Q_1(V_1 + V_2)}{g(Q_1 + Q_2)}\left(\Delta V + \frac{V_2}{Q_1}\Delta Q\right) \tag{12-39}$$

Col. 11.   Critical hydraulic radius in ft, interpolated from Table 12-1 corresponding to the discharge in col. 3

Col. 12.   Friction loss, based on Eq. (9-8) with $n = 0.015$, $V$ from col. 6, and $R$ from col. (11).   Since this is a minor item compared with the impact loss, it may be ignored if desired.

Col. 13.   The total drop in water surface $\Delta y' = \Delta y_m' + h_f$

Col. 14.   Cumulative drop in water surface

The cumulative drop in water surface is plotted as the heavy dashed line in Fig. 12-8, starting from an arbitrary elevation 120 ft from some station at $x = 10$ ft.   The critical depths from col. 5 of Table 12-2 are then plotted from the dashed line as shown by the dotted line.   It is apparent that this dotted line represents the bottom of a

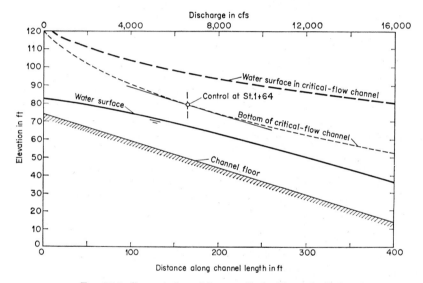

Fig. 12-8.  Computation of flow profile for Example 12-4.

fictitious channel in which the flow at the given discharge condition is critical at every section throughout the full length of the channel.   The dashed line is the corresponding water surface.   A tangent parallel to the bottom of the actual channel can be drawn to the dotted bottom line of the fictitious critical-flow channel.   The point of tangency, at which the two bottoms have the same slope, gives the location of the critical section, which is found at Sta. 1 + 64.   It is evident that the slope required to maintain critical flow to the left of this section is greater than the actual slope and that to the right it is less, which is the condition necessary for the formation of a control.   If more than one point of tangency is possible, the one giving the lowest position of the tangent will be likely to control.   It is also possible to have two or more control sections with hydraulic jumps between.

Having located the control section, the flow-profile computation can be carried out as shown in Table 12-3.   The computation proceeds upstream from the control section for the subcritical flow in the upper part of the channel and downstream for the

TABLE 12-3. COMPUTATION OF THE FLOW PROFILE FOR EXAMPLE 12-4

**Subcritical flow, computation by steps in the upstream direction**

| $x$ (1) | $\Delta x$ (2) | $Z_0$ (3) | $\Delta y'$ (4) | $Z$ (5) | $y$ (6) | $A$ (7) | $Q$ (8) | $V$ (9) | $Q_1+Q_2$ (10) | $V_1+V_2$ (11) | $\Delta Q$ (12) | $\Delta V$ (13) | $\Delta y_m'$ (14) | $R$ (15) | $h_f$ (16) | $\Delta y'$ (17) |
|---|---|---|---|---|---|---|---|---|---|---|---|---|---|---|---|---|
| 1 + 64 |    | 49.10 | .... | 66.80 | 17.70 | 333.6 | 6,560 | 19.70 | 10,560 |       | 2,560 |      |      |      |      |      |
| 1 + 00 | 64 | 58.70 | 7.90 | 74.70 | 16.00 | 288.0 | 4,000 | 13.89 |        | 33.59 |       | 5.81 | 7.29 | 6.28 | 0.11 | 7.40 |
|        |    |       | 7.10 | 73.90 | 15.20 | 267.5 | ...... | 14.95 | ...... | 34.65 | ..... | 4.75 | 7.09 | 6.10 | 0.13 | 7.22 |
|        |    |       | 7.27 | 74.07 | 15.37 | 271.8 |       | 14.72 | ...... | 34.42 | ..... | 4.98 | 7.13 | 6.13 | 0.12 | 7.25 |
| 0 + 50 | 50 | 66.20 | 5.08 | 79.15 | 12.95 | 213.5 | 2,000 | 9.37 | 6,000 | 24.09 | 2,000 | 5.35 | 5.01 | 5.49 | 0.05 | 5.06 |
| 0 + 25 | 25 | 69.95 | 2.06 | 81.21 | 11.26 | 176.0 | 1,000 | 5.68 | 3,000 | 15.05 | 1,000 | 3.69 | 2.04 | 5.00 | 0.01 | 2.05 |
| 0 + 10 | 15 | 72.20 | 0.87 | 82.08 | 9.88 | 147.6 | 400 | 2.71 | 1,400 | 8.39 | 600 | 2.97 | 0.86 | 4.60 | 0.01 | 0.87 |
| 0 + 00 | 10 | 73.70 | 0.23 | 82.31 | 8.61 |       |       |      |       |       |       |      |      |      |      |      |

($\Delta y'$ assumed $= 2V^2/2g$ at $x = 10$)

**Supercritical flow, computation by steps in the downstream direction**

| $x$ (1) | $\Delta x$ (2) | $Z_0$ (3) | $\Delta y'$ (4) | $Z$ (5) | $y$ (6) | $A$ (7) | $Q$ (8) | $V$ (9) | $Q_1+Q_2$ (10) | $V_1+V_2$ (11) | $\Delta Q$ (12) | $\Delta V$ (13) | $\Delta y_m'$ (14) | $R$ (15) | $h_f$ (16) | $\Delta y'$ (17) |
|---|---|---|---|---|---|---|---|---|---|---|---|---|---|---|---|---|
| 1 + 64 |    | 49.10 | .... | 66.80 | 17.70 | 333.6 | 6,560 | 19.70 |        |       |       |      |      |      |      |      |
| 2 + 00 | 36 | 43.70 | 4.45 | 62.35 | 18.65 | 360.4 | 8,000 | 22.20 | 14,560 | 41.90 | 1,440 | 2.50 | 4.34 | 6.97 | 0.14 | 4.48 |
| 2 + 50 | 50 | 36.20 | 6.22 | 56.13 | 19.93 | 397.9 | 10,000 | 25.13 | 18,000 | 47.33 | 2,000 | 2.93 | 6.03 | 7.29 | 0.23 | 6.26 |
| 3 + 00 | 50 | 28.70 | 6.39 | 49.74 | 21.04 | 431.7 | 12,000 | 27.79 | 22,000 | 52.92 | 2,000 | 2.66 | 6.16 | 7.57 | 0.26 | 6.42 |
| 3 + 50 | 50 | 21.20 | 6.48 | 43.26 | 22.06 | 463.9 | 14,000 | 30.18 | 26,000 | 57.97 | 2,000 | 2.39 | 6.18 | 7.82 | 0.31 | 6.49 |
| 4 + 00 | 50 | 13.50 | 6.92 | 36.34 | 22.84 | 489.2 | 16,000 | 32.71 | 30,000 | 62.89 | 2,000 | 2.53 | 6.58 | 8.02 | 0.36 | 6.94 |

345

supercritical flow in the lower part of the channel. The procedure of computation is the same as that explained for Table 12-2, except that the water-surface drop $\Delta y'$ in col. 4 is finally obtained when it agrees with the computed $\Delta y'$ in col. 17. This is shown for the computation at Sta. 1 + 00. In cols. 3 and 5 are elevations of the channel bottom and the water surface, respectively. The value of $\Delta y'$ between $x = 10$ and $x = 0$ cannot be computed, but it is arbitrarily assumed to be twice the velocity head at $x = 10$ ft. The final flow profile is constructed as shown in Fig. 12-8. The accuracy of the computation will depend on the length and number of subdivisions assumed.

*B. Flow with Decreasing Discharge.* For spatially varied flow with decreasing discharge, an equation for numerical integration similar to Eq. (12-38) can be obtained. Referring to Fig. 12-2, the velocity and discharge at section 1 are assumed as $V$ and $Q$ and at section 2 as $V - \Delta V$ and $Q - \Delta Q$. The momentum lost because of diminished discharge may be taken as $w \Delta Q (V - \Delta V/2)/g$. Adding this lost momentum to the momentum at section 2 and following the procedure described for the flow with increasing discharge, the equation for numerical integration can be shown to be

$$\Delta y' = \frac{\alpha Q_1(V_1 + V_2) \Delta V}{g(Q_1 + Q_2)} \left(1 - \frac{\Delta Q}{2Q_1}\right) + S_f \Delta x \qquad (12\text{-}40)$$

Owing to the variable velocity distribution in the channel cross section, the value of the energy coefficient may be very high. According to Schmidt [25], values up to 1.30 have been observed at the beginning of the spillway, and even higher values were found at the end of the spillway crest. By experimental study, Schmidt was able to develop an adjustment procedure to correct for the effect of the nonuniform velocity distribution.

The value of $\Delta Q$ in Eq. (12-40) is the discharge over the spillway per $\Delta x$ of the crest length. Many formulas have been proposed for its determination. For practical purposes, the formula for the regular weir of similar crest shape may be used if the corresponding discharge coefficient is reduced by 5%.

**12-5. The Isoclinal Method.** For a simple but approximate computation of a flow profile, a graphical method suggested by Werner [39] may be used. By this method the spatially-varied-flow equation in any form is plotted with $y$ against $x$ for different values of $dy/dx$ as parameters, resulting in a number of isoclinal curves (Fig. 12-9). Starting from the depth at the control section $C$, a line is drawn with a slope ( = 0.03) equal to the average value of $dy/dx$ ( = 0.05) indicated by the isoclinal curve passing through the control depth and $dy/dx$ ( = 0.01) of the next isoclinal curve, which the line intersects at $P$. Starting at $P$, repeat the procedure to determine $P'$, and determine similarly other points of intersection. The flow profile is the curve joining all the points of intersection. Actually, this method can be applied equally well to any type of varied-flow equation for flow in prismatic as well as nonprismatic channels.

**12-6. Spatially Varied Surface Flow.** An important type of surface flow encountered frequently in engineering problems deals with runoff from a plane surface as the result of rainfall. Apparently, this is a problem in spatially varied flow with increasing discharge and can be treated as such; it may, however, be very complicated, becoming a three-dimensional problem if the surface is curved in space, as in the case of a road pavement that has a cambered transverse profile and a longitudinal slope. The theory of spatially varied flow was first used in surface flow by Keulegan [40], and the equation thus derived was applied

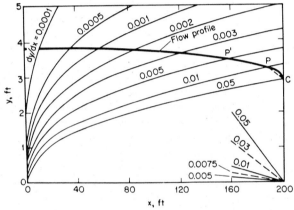

FIG. 12-9. Computation of flow profile by the isoclinal method.

to experimental data by Izzard [41]. For flow on a road surface, a comprehensive analysis was performed by Iwagaki [42].

For practical purposes, an approximate equation for discharge of surface flow is generally assumed, such as

$$q = ky^m \qquad (12\text{-}41)$$

where $q$ is the discharge per unit width of the flow, $y$ is the depth of flow at the point of outflow, and $k$ and $m$ are constants. At equilibrium condition, the discharge $q$ at a point $x$ distance below the drainage divide is

$$q = xq_* \qquad (12\text{-}42)$$

where $q_*$ is the constant inflow due to rainfall excess, or supply rate, per unit area. The rainfall excess is equal to rainfall minus infiltration and other losses that will not become surface runoff. Combining the above two equations and simplifying,

$$y = \left(\frac{xq_*}{k}\right)^{1/m} \tag{12-43}$$

This is the equation for the flow profile, which is generally applicable when $x$ is not too large. The value of $k$ has to be determined experimentally since it depends on the surface characteristics, slope, type of flow, and viscosity (in the case of laminar flow). The value $m$ depends on the type of flow; it is approximately $\frac{5}{3}$ for turbulent and 3 for laminar.

For turbulent flow, the differential equation for the surface flow, from Eq. (12-4), may be written

$$\frac{dy}{dx} = \frac{S_0 - S - 2(y/x)\mathbf{F}^2}{1 - \mathbf{F}^2} \tag{12-44}$$

where $\mathbf{F}^2 = V^2/gy$. If the raindrop momentum is ignored, it can be shown that the coefficient 2 in the numerator will become 1 [cf. Eq. (12-8)]. For analytical studies, the profile of the surface flow can be computed by the method of numerical integration. The control section of the flow profile can be determined by the method of singular point or by a criterion developed by Keulegan [43].

For laminar flow on a road surface, Iwagaki [42] has performed an elaborate mathematical analysis, in which the continuity and momentum equations are applied to a three-dimensional element of the flow. By considering a general case in which the velocity and depth of the flow do not change in the longitudinal direction of the road surface, he was able to derive a differential equation as follows:

$$\frac{dy}{dx} = \frac{F_1}{F_2} \tag{12-45}$$

where
$$F_1 = \frac{gy^3 n S_0}{\nu^2}\left(\frac{x}{L}\right)^{n-1} - \frac{12q_*^2 xy}{5\nu^2} - \frac{3q_* x}{\nu}$$

and
$$F_2 = \frac{gy^3}{\nu^2} - \frac{6q_*^2 x}{5\nu^2}$$

The notation is given in Fig. 12-10. The transverse profile of the road surface is represented by $y = -H(x'/L)^n$. Equation (12-45) was then applied to a numerical example, and flow profiles were computed by the isoclinal method. From this investigation, the following conclusions were obtained:

1. The flow profile is independent of the longitudinal slope of the road surface.

2. In case of natural runoff, the flow profile is approximately represented by the curve $dy/dx = 0$ except for the part near the crown of the road.

3. The depth is theoretically constant when the transverse profile of the road is a parabola with its vertex at the crown, that is, when $n = 2$. When the road surface is formed by straight lines connecting the crown and the edges, that is, when $n = 1$, the depth becomes smaller near the crown and greater toward the sides.

4. The effect of the longitudinal slope on mean velocity and friction velocity is to increase the mean velocity and the friction velocity of the flow. This effect is greater near the crown of the road for larger $n$ and greater near the sides for smaller $n$.

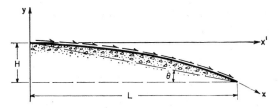

Fig. 12-10. Cross section of road for surface-flow analysis.

5. The effect of the longitudinal slope is practically negligible when this slope is very small, say, less than 0.002 under the normal condition of $H/L = 0.02$.

6. In order to minimize erosion due to raindrops on unpaved road surface, the longitudinal slope should be kept as small as possible. To maintain a uniform grade of erosion, a cross section with $n = 1$ is preferable.

## PROBLEMS

**12-1.** A rectangular wash-water trough 20 ft long and 1.32 ft wide carries a discharge at a slope of 0.065 to a free-fall outlet. If the measured upstream depth is 0.34 ft, compute the discharge by means of the chart in Fig. 12-4.

**12-2.** An approximate formula for calculating the discharge capacity of rapid sand-filter wash-water troughs has been developed by Miller [11] by assuming a parabolic flow profile at a maximum discharge. The formula is

$$Q = 1.91b(y_u + L \tan \theta) \qquad (12-46)$$

where $b$ is the width of the rectangular channel in ft, $y_u$ is the upstream depth in ft, $L$ is the channel length in ft, and $\theta$ is the angle that the channel bottom makes with the horizontal. Using this formula, compute the discharge required in Prob. 12-1.

**12-3.** A rectangular wash-water trough 30 ft long is required to carry a discharge of 8 cfs, having a free fall at the outlet. Design the trough for the least amount of material required for the construction (neglecting the end wall and making the total wall and bottom wall of the channel a minimum). Assume:

a. A horizontal channel
b. That the channel has a slope

**12-4.** Compute the flow profile in Prob. 12-1.  Assume

a.  A horizontal channel
b.  A channel with slope equal to 0.065

**12-5.** Derive the equation of the flow profile in Example 12-2 if $\alpha$ is not equal to unity.

**12-6.** A horizontal bottom rack made of perforated screen is designed to divert water from a channel.  Determine the length of the rack required to withdraw the total main flow of 26 cfs from the channel.  Given: $\epsilon = 0.5$, $c = 0.8$, $c' = 2.80$, $b = 3$ ft, and $y_1/E = 0.60$.

**12-7.** Solve the preceding problem if the rack is made of parallel bars.

**12-8.** A side weir is used to divert the excess of a storm flow of 75 cfs from a 48-in.-diameter sewer.  The sewer has a grade of 1 in 400, a full-flow capacity of 78 cfs, and an unrestricted outlet.  The dry-weather flow is 5 cfs.  Determine (a) the height of the weir sill, and (b) the length of the weir, assuming $\alpha = 1$.  It is also assumed that the top width of the water area is constant and equal to the diameter of the sewer; so the equations derived for rectangular channels can be applied.

**12-9.** Solve the preceding problem if $\alpha = 1.20$.

**12-10.** By converting increments to differentials, show that Eq. (12-35) is identical with Eq. (12-4).

**12-11.** Determine the control section in Example 12-4 by the method of singular point.

**12-12.** Demonstrate analytically that Hinds's method for the determination of control section is identical with the method of singular point.

**12-13.** Compute the flow profile in the channel described in Example 12-4 carrying a varying discharge of 50 cfs per foot of channel length.

**12-14.** Compute the flow profile in Example 12-4 by the isoclinal method.

**12-15.** Verify Eq. (12-40).

**12-16.** Show that the flow in a rectangular prismatic channel with a lateral spillway may be expressed by

$$Q = b \sqrt{(Hy^2 - y^3)\frac{2g}{\alpha}} \qquad (12\text{-}47)$$

where $b$ is the channel width, $y$ is the depth, $H$ is the constant energy head in the spillway section measured above the channel bottom, and $\alpha$ is the energy coefficient.

**12-17.** Artificial rainfall of a constant intensity equal to 3.6 in./hr is applied on a concrete pavement having a slope of 0.01 and a roughness coefficient $n = 0.025$.  Compute the flow profile, ignoring the raindrop momentum.  Assume that:

a.  The lower end of the pavement is a free-fall outlet.
b.  There is a dam $\frac{1}{4}$ in. high at a distance of 5 ft from the lower end of the pavement.

## REFERENCES

1. Julian Hinds: Side channel spillways: Hydraulic theory, economic factors, and experimental determination of losses, *Transactions, American Society of Civil Engineers*, vol. 89, pp. 881–927, 1926.
2. H. Favre: "Contribution à l'étude des courants liquides" ("Contribution to the Study of Flow of Liquid"), Dunod, Paris, 1933.
3. E. Meyer-Peter and Henry Favre: Analysis of Boulder Dam spillways made by Swiss laboratory, *Engineering News-Record*, vol. 113, no. 17, pp. 520–522, Oct. 25, 1934.

4. Thomas R. Camp: Lateral spillway channels, *Transactions, American Society of Civil Engineers*, vol. 105, pp. 606–617, 1940.

5. Wen-Hsiung Li: Open channels with nonuniform discharge, *Transactions, American Society of Civil Engineers*, vol. 120, pp. 255–274, 1955.

6. G. De Marchi: Canali con portata progressivamente crescente (Channels with increasing discharge), *L'Energia elettrica, Milano*, vol. 18, no. 6, pp. 351–360, July, 1941; reprinted as *Istituto di Idraulica e Costruzioni Idrauliche, Milano, Memorie e studi No.* 45, 1941.

7. Duilio Citrini: Canali rettangolari con portata e larghezza gradualmente variabili (Rectangular channels with gradually varying discharge and width), *L'Energia elettrica, Milano*, vol. 19, no. 5, pp. 254–262, May, and no. 6, pp. 297–301, June, 1942; reprinted as *Istituto di Idraulica e Costruzioni Idrauliche, Milano, Memorie e studi No.* 52, 1942.

8. Philipp Forchheimer: "Grundriss der Hydraulik" ("Outline of Hydraulics"), Teubner Verlagsgesellschaft, Leipzig and Berlin, 1920, pp. 93–95.

9. Armin Schoklitsch "Handbuch des Wasserbaues" ("Handbook of Hydraulic Engineering"), Springer-Verlag, Vienna, 1950, vol. 1, pp. 136–142.

10. K. Hilding Beij: Flow in roof gutters, *Journal of Research, U.S. National Bureau of Standards*, vol. 12, no. 2, pp. 193–213, February, 1934.

11. C. N. Miller: An approximate formula for calculating the design capacity of rapid sand filter wash water troughs, appendix B in J. W. Ellms: "Water Purification," McGraw-Hill Book Company, Inc., New York, 1928.

12. M. F. Stein: The design of wash water troughs for rapid sand filters, *Journal, American Water Works Association*, vol. 13, pp. 411–415. Discussion by Clifford N. Miller, pp. 415–417, 1925.

13. Hubert Engels: Mitteilungen aus dem Dresdener Flussbau-Laboratorium (Report of the Dresden Hydraulic Laboratory), *Zeitschrift des Vereins deutscher Ingenieure*, Berlin, vol. 62, no. 24, pp. 362–365, June 15; no. 25, pp. 387–390, June 22; no. 26, pp. 412–416, June 29, 1918; and vol. 64, no. 5, pp. 101–106, Jan. 31, 1920; also *Forschungsarbeiten auf dem Gebiete des Ingenieurwesens*, Berlin, nos. 200 and 201, 55 pp., 1917.

14. G. S. Coleman and Dempster Smith: The discharging capacity of side weirs, *Institution of Civil Engineers, London, Selected Engineering Papers, No.* 6, 1923.

15. Philipp Forchheimer, "Hydraulik" ("Hydraulics"), Teubner Verlagsgesellschaft, Leipzig and Berlin, 3d ed., 1930, pp. 406–409.

16. G. De Marchi: Saggio di teoria del funzionamento degli stramazzi laterali (Essay of the performance of lateral weirs), *L'Energia elettrica, Milano*, vol. 11, no. 11, pp. 849–860, November, 1934; reprinted as *Istituto di Idraulica e Costruzioni Idrauliche, Milano, Memorie e studi No.* 11, 1934.

17. G. De Marchi: Profili longitudinali della superficie libera delle correnti permanenti lineari con portata progressivamente crescente o progressivamente decrescente entro canali di sezione costante (Longitudinal flow profiles of linear steady flow with increasing discharges or decreasing discharges in prismatic channels), *Ricerca scientifica e ricostruzione*, Rome, nos. 2 and 3, pp. 202–216, February-March, 1947. Also published as Des formes de la surface libre de courants permanents avec débit progressivement croissant ou progressivement décroissant dans un canal de section constante, *Revue générale de l'hydraulique*, Paris, vol. 13, no. 38, pp. 81–85, 1947.

18. B. Gentilini: Ricerche sperimentali sugli sfioratori longitudinali (Experimental researches on side weirs), *L'Energia elettrica, Milano*, vol. 15, no. 9, pp. 583–595, September, 1938; reprinted as *Istituto di Idraulica e Costruzioni Idrauliche, Milano, Memorie e studi No.* 65, 1938.

19. H. Favre: Sur les lois régissant le mouvement des fluides dans les conduites en charge avec adduction latérale (On the laws governing the flow in conduits with lateral discharge), *Revue universelle des mines*, Liége, vol. 13, ser. 8, no. 12, pp. 502–512, December, 1937.

20. W. H. R. Nimmo: Side spillways for regulating diversion canals, *Transactions, American Society of Civil Engineers*, vol. 92, pp. 1561–1584, 1928.

21. Giorgio Noseda: Operation and design of bottom intake racks, *Proceedings of the 6th General Meeting, International Association of Hydraulic Research, The Hague 1955*, vol. 3, pp. C17-1 to C17-11, 1955; reprinted as *Istituto di Idraulica e Costruzioni Idrauliche, Milano, Memorie e studi No. 130*, 1956.

22. Giorgio Noseda: Correnti permanenti con portata progressivamente decrescente, defluenti su griglie di fondo (Steady flow with gradually decreasing discharges on bottom intake racks), *L'Energia elettrica, Milano*, vol. 33, no. 1, pp. 41–51, January, 1956; reprinted as *Istituto di Idraulica e Costruzioni Idrauliche, Milano, Memorie e studi No. 132*, 1956.

23. Giorgio Noseda: Correnti permanenti con portata progressivamente decrescente, defluenti su griglie di fondo: Ricerca sperimentale (Steady flow with gradually decreasing discharge on bottom intake racks: Experimental results), *L'Energia elettrica, Milano*, vol. 33, no. 6, pp. 565–588, June, 1956; reprinted as *Istituto di Idraulica e Costruzioni Idrauliche, Milano, Memorie e studi No. 134*, 1956.

24. Martin Schmidt: Zur Frage des Abflusses über Streichwehre (Discharge over side weirs), *Technische Universität Berlin-Charlottenburg, Institut für Wasserbau, Mitteilung 41*, 1954.

25. Martin Schmidt: Die Berechnung von Streichwehren (Computation of side weirs), *Die Wasserwirtschaft*, Stuttgart, vol. 45, no. 4, pp. 96–100, January, 1955.

26. Martin Schmidt: "Gerinnehydraulik" ("Open-channel Hydraulics"), VEB Verlag Technik, Berlin, and Bauverlag GMBH, Wiesbaden, 1957, pp. 188–196.

27. M. A. Mostkow: "Handbuch der Hydraulik" ("Handbook of Hydraulics"), VEB Verlag Technik, Berlin, 1956, pp. 204–208 and 213–221.

28. Michel A. Mostkow: Sur le calcul des grilles de prise d'eau (Theoretical study of bottom type water intake), *La Houille blanche*, Grenoble, 12th yr., no. 4, pp. 570–580, September, 1957.

29. Peter Ackers: A theoretical consideration of side weirs as storm-water overflows, *Proceedings, Institution of Civil Engineers*, London, vol. 6, pp. 250–269, February, 1957.

30. John William Allen: The discharge of water over side weirs in circular pipes, *Proceedings, Institution of Civil Engineers*, London, vol. 6, pp. 270–287, February, 1957.

31. Vincent Knight Collinge: The discharge capacity of side weirs, *Proceedings, Institution of Civil Engineers*, London, vol. 6, pp. 288–304, February, 1957.

32. William Frazer: The behaviour of side weirs in prismatic rectangular channels, *Proceedings, Institution of Civil Engineers*, London, vol. 6, pp. 305–328, February, 1957.

33. Ven Te Chow: Discussion of Flood protection of canals by lateral spillways by Harald Tults, paper 1077, *Proceedings, American Society of Civil Engineers, Journal, Hydraulics Division*, vol. 83, no. HY2, pp. 47–49, April, 1957.

34. F. Garot: De Watervang met liggend rooster (Channel with bottom grid), *De Ingenieur in Nederlandsch-Indië*, no. 7, 1939.

35. M. Bouvard: Débit d'une grille par en dessous (Discharge passing through a bottom grid), *La Houille blanche*, Grenoble, 8th yr., no. 2, pp. 290–291, May, 1953.

36. J. Kuntzmann and M. Bouvard: Étude théorique des grilles de prises d'eau du type "en dessous" (Theoretical study of bottom-type water-intake grids), *La Houille blanche*, Grenoble, 9th yr., no. 5, pp. 569–574, September-October, 1954.

37. J. Orth, E. Chardonnet, and G. Meynardi: Étude des grilles pour prises d'eau du type "en dessous" (Study of bottom-type water-intake grids), *La Houille blanche*, Grenoble, 9th yr., no. 3, pp. 343–351, June, 1954.

38. Josef Frank: Hydraulische Untersuchungen für das Tiroler Wehr (Hydraulic analysis for the Tirol weir), *Der Bauingenieur*, Berlin, vol. 31, no. 3, pp. 96–101, 1956.

39. P. Wilh. Werner: Wasserspiegelberechung von Kanälen bei gleichmässiger Bewegung und veränderlicher Wassermenge (Computation of water surface in channels with steady flow and variable discharge), *Die Bautechnik*, Berlin, vol. 19, no. 23, pp. 251–252, May 30, 1941.

40. G. H. Keulegan: Spatially variable discharge over a sloping plane, *Transactions, American Geophysical Union*, pt. VI, pp. 956–959, 1944.

41. C. F. Izzard: The surface-profile of overland flow, *Transactions, American Geophysical Union*, pt. VI, pp. 959–968, 1944.

42. Yuichi Iwagaki: Theory of flow on road surface, *Memoirs of the Faculty of Engineering, Kyoto University*, Japan, vol. 13, no. 3, pp. 139–147, July, 1951.

43. Garbis H. Keulegan: Determination of critical depth in spatially variable flow, *Proceedings of the 2d Midwestern Conference of Fluid Mechanics, The Ohio State University, Engineering Experiment Station, Bulletin* 149, September, 1952, pp. 67–80.

PART IV

# RAPIDLY VARIED FLOW

# CHAPTER 13

# INTRODUCTION

**13-1. Characteristics of the Flow.** Rapidly varied flow has very pronounced curvature of the streamlines. The change in curvature may become so abrupt that the flow profile is virtually broken, resulting in a state of high turbulence; this is rapidly varied flow of discontinuous profile, of which the hydraulic jump is an example.

In view of the contrast with gradually varied flow, the following characteristic features of rapidly varied flow should be noted:

1. The curvature of the flow is so pronounced that the pressure distribution cannot be assumed to be hydrostatic.

2. The rapid variation in flow regime often takes place in a relatively short reach. Accordingly, the boundary friction, which would play a primary role in a gradually varied flow, is comparatively small and in most cases insignificant.

3. When rapidly varied flow occurs in a sudden-transition structure, the physical characteristics of the flow are basically fixed by the boundary geometry of the structure as well as by the state of the flow.

4. When rapid changes in water area occur in rapidly varied flow, the velocity-distribution coefficients $\alpha$ and $\beta$ are usually far greater than unity and cannot be accurately determined.

5. The separation zones, eddies, and rollers that may occur in rapidly varied flow tend to complicate the flow pattern and to distort the actual velocity distribution in the stream. In such cases, the flow is actually confined by one or more separation zones rather than by solid boundaries.

**13-2. Approach to the Problem.** The theory that assumes a parallel flow with hydrostatic pressure distribution is known in classic hydraulics as the *Bresse theory*;[1] such a theory is used for uniform flow and gradually varied flow. This theory, of course, does not apply to rapidly varied flow, even with continuous flow profile. For rapidly varied flow of continuous flow profile, classic hydraulics has shown that a mathematical equation of the flow can be established on the basis of an inviscid- (i.e., frictionless or nonviscous) and potential-flow condition [1–4]. A direct

---

[1] This is so called because of the early contribution by Bresse to the solution of the dynamic equation for gradually varied flow (see Example 10-4).

solution of the mathematical equation will require further knowledge of the curvature of the flow. In the classic *theory of Boussinesq* [5], the curvature is assumed to increase linearly from the channel bed to the curved flow surface, and the problem is solved by the momentum principle. In the *theory of Fawer* [6], the curvature is assumed to vary exponentially with the distance from the channel bed to the free surface, and the problem is solved by the energy principle. Modern approaches to the solution of an inviscid potential flow often resort to a graphical method or to a numerical method of approximation. A popular graphical method is flow-net analysis [7,8], which was first suggested by Prášil [9] and later generalized by Barillon [10]. There are many numerical methods; of these the method of relaxation [11] is frequently used.

The above-mentioned theories and methods of analysis for rapidly varied flow with continuous profile can be found in many hydraulics textbooks and in the references listed here. Despite such developments, a satisfactory general solution of this type of problem has not yet been obtained. Practical hydraulicians, therefore, have long ago come to regard the various phenomena of rapidly varied flow as a number of isolated cases, each requiring its own specific empirical treatment. In the following chapters, typical problems of rapidly varied flow are treated more or less in this way. In most cases, the experimental results are to be used empirically. The physical aspects of the flow will be interpreted qualitatively, whenever possible, according to the principles of energy, momentum, and geometry, and sometimes by dimensional analysis.

## REFERENCES

1. Charles Jaeger: "Engineering Fluid Mechanics," translated from the German by P. O. Wolf, Blackie & Son, Ltd., London and Glasgow, 1956, pp. 120–130.
2. Philipp Forchheimer: "Hydraulik" ("Hydraulics"), Teubner Verlagsgesellschaft, Leipzig and Berlin, 3d ed., 1930. Section 82, pp. 230–237, is on Boussinesq's backwater curve with uniform bottom slope, taking the curvature of the flow filaments into consideration; sec. 83, pp. 237–242, is on Boussinesq's backwater curve with varying bottom slope, surface with undulating bottom.
3. François Serre: Contribution à l'étude des écoulements permanents et variables dans les canaux (Contribution to the study of permanent and nonpermanent flows in channels), *La Houille blanche*, Grenoble, 8th yr., no. 3, pp. 374–388, June-July, 1953; no. 6, pp. 830–872, December, 1953. Differential equations for steady flow, taking into account the effects of stream curvature, are developed and applied to the determination of flow profiles.
4. Josef Koženy: "Hydraulik" ("Hydraulics"), Springer-Verlag, Vienna, 1953, pp. 46–47 and p. 229.
5. J. Boussinesq: Essai sur la théorie des eaux courantes (Essay on the theory of water flow), *Mémoires présentés par divers savants à l'Académie des Sciences*, Paris, vol. 23, pp. 1–680, 1877; vol. 24, no. 2, 1878.
6. C. Fawer: Étude de quelques écoulements permanents à filets courbes (Study of

some permanent flows with curved filaments), thesis, Université de Lausanne, Lausanne, Switzerland, 1937.

7. H. Alden Foster: Construction of the flow net for hydraulic design, *Transactions, American Society of Civil Engineers*, vol. 110, pp. 1237–1252, 1945.

8. E. W. Lane, F. B. Campbell, and W. H. Price: The flow net and the electric analogy, *Civil Engineering*, pp. 510–514, October, 1934.

9. Franz Prášil: Über Flüssigkeitsbewegungen in Rotationshohlräumen (On fluid motion in rotational vacuums), *Schweizerische Bauzeitung*, Zürich, vol. 41, no. 18, pp. 207–209; no. 21, 233–237; no. 22, 249–251; no. 25, 282–283; and no. 26, 293–295, May-June, 1903. Also, "Technische Hydrodynamik" ("Technical Hydrodynamics"), Springer-Verlag, Berlin, 1913, p. 61; 2d ed., 1926, pp. 201–236.

10. E. G. Barillon: Note sur les rayons de courbure intervenant dans la construction des réseaux hydrodynamiques (Note on the radii of curvature involved in the construction of hydrodynamic networks), *Revue générale de l'hydraulique*, Paris, vol. 2, no. 8, pp. 411–415, 1936.

11. John S. McNown, En-Yun Hsu, and Chia-Shun Yih: Applications of the relaxation technique in fluid mechanics, *Transactions, American Society of Civil Engineers*, vol. 120, pp. 650–669, 1955.

CHAPTER 14

# FLOW OVER SPILLWAYS

**14-1. The Sharp-crested Weir.** The sharp-crested weir is not only a measuring device for open-channel flow but also the simplest form of overflow spillway. The characteristics of flow over a weir were recognized early in hydraulics as the basis of design for the round-crested overflow spillway; that is, the profile of the spillway was determined in conformity with the shape of the lower surface of the flow nappe over a sharp-crested weir.

The shape of the flow nappe over a sharp-crested weir can be interpreted by the principle of the projectile (Fig. 14-1). According to this

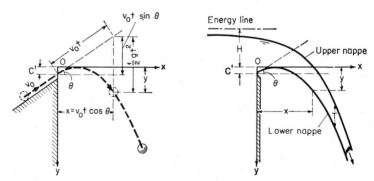

FIG. 14-1. Derivation of nappe profiles over sharp-crested weir by the principle of projectile.

principle, it is assumed that the horizontal velocity component of the flow is constant and that the only force acting on the nappe is gravity. In time $t$, a particle of water in the lower surface of the nappe will travel a horizontal distance $x$ from the face of the weir, equal to

$$x = v_0 t \cos \theta \qquad (14\text{-}1)$$

where $v_0$ is the velocity at the point where $x = 0$, and $\theta$ is the angle of inclination of the velocity $v_0$ with the horizontal. In the same time $t$, the particle will travel a vertical distance $y$ equal to

$$y = -v_0 t \sin \theta + \tfrac{1}{2} g t^2 + C' \qquad (14\text{-}2)$$

360

where $C'$ is the value of $y$ at $x = 0$; apparently, $C'$ is equal to the vertical distance between the highest point of the nappe and the elevation of the crest. Eliminating $t$ from the above two equations, dividing each term by the total head $H$ above the crest, and expressing the resulting general equation for the lower surface of the nappe in dimensionless terms,

$$\frac{y}{H} = A \left(\frac{x}{H}\right)^2 + B \frac{x}{H} + C \tag{14-3}$$

where $A = gH/2v_0{}^2 \cos^2 \theta$, $B = -\tan \theta$, and $C = C'/H$. Since the horizontal velocity component is constant, the vertical thickness of the nappe $T$ may be assumed constant. Adding a term $D = T/H$ to the above equation, the general equation for the upper surface of the nappe is

$$\frac{y}{H} = A \left(\frac{x}{H}\right)^2 + B \frac{x}{H} + C + D \tag{14-4}$$

The above nappe equations are quadratic; hence, the nappe surfaces are theoretically parabolic.

Numerous tests on nappe over a vertical sharp-crested weir have been made. On the basis of data of the U.S. Bureau of Reclamation [1], of Hinds, Creager, and Justin [2,3], and of Ippen [4], Blaisdell [5] has developed the following equations for the constants in the general nappe equations:

$$A = -0.425 + 0.25 \frac{h_v}{H} \tag{14-5}$$

$$B = 0.411 - 1.603 \frac{h_v}{H} - \sqrt{1.568 \left(\frac{h_v}{H}\right)^2 - 0.892 \frac{h_v}{H} + 0.127} \tag{14-6}$$

$$C = 0.150 - 0.45 \frac{h_v}{H} \tag{14-7}$$

$$D = 0.57 - 0.02(10m)^2 \exp(10m) \tag{14-8}$$

where $m = h_v/H - 0.208$, and $h_v$ is the velocity head of the approach flow. For high weirs, the velocity of approach is relatively small and can be ignored. Thus, the constants become $A = -0.425$, $B = 0.055$, $C = 0.150$, and $D = 0.559$. Experimental data have indicated that these equations are not valid when $x/H$ is less than about 0.5 and that, for $h_v/H > 0.2$, additional data for verification are needed. For $x/H < 0.5$, the pressure within the nappe in the vicinity of the weir crest is actually above atmospheric because of the convergence of the streamlines. Consequently, forces other than gravity are acting on the nappe, which makes the principle of the projectile invalid.

It should be noted that the above theory and equations apply only if the approach flow is subcritical. For supercritical flow, or $\mathbf{F} > 1$, the nappe profile becomes essentially a function of the Froude number rather than a function of the boundary geometry as described above [4, p. 533].

Many experimental formulas for the discharge over sharp-crested weir have been developed.[1] Most such formulas can be expressed in the general form.[2]

$$Q = CLH^{1.5} \tag{14-9}$$

where $C$ is the discharge coefficient, $L$ is the effective length of the weir crest, and $H$ is the measured head above the crest, *excluding* the velocity head. The effective length of the weir may be computed by

$$L = L' - 0.1NH \tag{14-10}$$

where $L'$ is the measured length of the crest and $N$ is the number of contractions. For two end contractions, $N = 2$. For one end contraction, $N = 1$. When no contractions are present at the two ends, $N = 0$.

According to a well-known weir formula of Rehbock [10], the coefficient $C$ in Eq. (14-9) is approximately

$$C = 3.27 + 0.40 \frac{H}{h} \tag{14-11}$$

where $h$ is the height of weir. Measurements by Rouse [4, p. 532] indicate that this equation holds up to $H/h = 5$ but can be extended to $H/h = 10$ with fair approximation. For $H/h$ greater than about 15, the weir becomes a sill, and the discharge is controlled by a critical section immediately upstream from the sill. The critical depth of the section is approximately equal to $H + h$. By the critical depth–discharge relationship, it can be shown that the coefficient $C$ is

$$C = 5.68 \left(1 + \frac{H}{h}\right)^{1.5} \tag{14-12}$$

The transition between weir and sill (between $H/h = 10$ and 15), however, has not yet been clearly defined.

Experiments have shown that the coefficient $C$ in Eq. (14-9) remains approximately constant for sharp-crested weirs under varying heads if the nappe is aerated.

**14-2. Aeration of the Nappe.** In the preceding article the overfalling nappe is considered aerated; that is, the upper and lower nappe surfaces are subject to full atmospheric pressure. Insufficient aeration below the

[1] For a general description of sharp-crested-weir experiments and formulas, see [6]. For further studies of the discharge characteristics of sharp-crested weirs, see [7] and [8].

[2] The derivation of a theoretical weir-discharge formula can be found in many hydraulics textbooks. The first mathematical analysis on discharge of weirs was performed by Boussinesq [9].

nappe, however, usually occurs in overflow spillways and measuring weirs. This means a reduction of pressure beneath the nappe due to the removal of air by the overfalling jet. This reduction of pressure will cause undesirable effects, such as (1) increase in pressure difference on the spillway or weir itself, (2) change in the shape of the nappe for which the spillway crest is generally designed, (3) increase in discharge, sometimes accompanied by fluctuation or pulsation of the nappe, which may be very objectionable if the weir or spillway is used for measuring purposes, and (4) unstable performance of the hydraulic model.

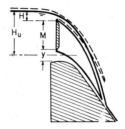

On the basis of experimental studies on spillways with gates (Fig. 14-2), Hickox [11] developed the following equation giving the quantity of air required for aeration in cubic feet per second per foot of length of weir:

FIG. 14-2. Experimental setup for studying aeration below the nappe. Dashed lines indicate the condition of full aeration. (*After G. H. Hickox* [11].)

$$q_a = \frac{5.68(CH)^{3.64}}{p^{1.14}} \qquad (14\text{-}13)$$

where $H$ is the measured head in ft over the top of the gate; $p$ is the reduction of pressure in feet of water to be maintained beneath the nappe; and $C$ is a coefficient depending on the ratio of the discharge beneath the gate to the discharge over the top of the gate. The ratio is represented by a dimensionless value

$$\sigma = \frac{y \sqrt{H_u}}{H^{1.5}} \qquad (14\text{-}14)$$

where $y$ is the height of the opening below the gate in ft and $H_u$ is the head on the center of the gate in ft. For ungated weir or spillway, $\sigma = 0$. The values of $C$ are as follows:

| $\sigma$ | 0 | 0.5 | 1.0 | 1.5 | 2.0 | 2.5+ |
|---|---|---|---|---|---|---|
| $C$ | 0.077 | 0.135 | 0.175 | 0.202 | 0.220 | 0.225 |

Intermediate values can be interpolated from a curve constructed with the above values.

**14-3. Crest Shape of Overflow Spillways.** Early crest shapes were usually based on a simple parabola designed to fit the trajectory of the falling nappe, as already described in Art. 14-1. From 1886 to 1888 Bazin [12] made the first comprehensive laboratory investigation of nappe shapes. The use of Bazin's data in design will produce a crest shape that coincides with the lower surface of an aerated nappe over a sharp-crested weir. Theoretically, the adoption of such a profile, generally known as the *Bazin profile*, should cause no negative pressures on the crest. Under actual conditions, however, there exists friction due to roughness on the surface of the spillway. Hence, negative pressures on such a profile cannot be avoided. The presence of negative pressures will lead to danger of cavitation damage. In selecting a suitable profile, avoidance of negative pressures should be considered an objective, along with such other factors as maximum hydraulic efficiency, practicability, stability, and economy. Consequently, the Bazin profile has been variously modified, and many other profiles for design purposes have been proposed.[1]

From 1932 to 1948, extensive experiments on the shape of the nappe over a sharp-crested weir were conducted by the U.S. Bureau of Reclamation.[2] On the basis of experimental data including Bazin's, the Bureau has developed coordinates of nappe surfaces for vertical and various slope-faced weirs. This information is indeed invaluable for accurate analysis and precise design of spillway overflow sections. For practical purposes, however, this information can be used more simply without essential loss of accuracy, through modifications that will be described below:

On the basis of the Bureau of Reclamation data, the U.S. Army Corps of Engineers has developed several standard shapes at its Waterways Experiment Station. Such shapes (Fig. 14-3), designated as the WES standard spillway shapes,[3] can be represented by the following equation:

$$X^n = KH_d^{n-1}Y \qquad (14\text{-}15)$$

where $X$ and $Y$ are coordinates of the crest profile with the origin at the highest point of the crest, $H_d$ is the design head *excluding* the velocity head of the approach flow, and $K$ and $n$ are parameters depending on the slope of the upstream face. The values of $K$ and $n$ are given as follows:

| Slope of upstream face | K | n |
|---|---|---|
| Vertical | 2.000 | 1.850 |
| 3 on 1 | 1.936 | 1.836 |
| 3 on 2 | 1.939 | 1.810 |
| 3 on 3 | 1.873 | 1.776 |

[1] Examples of other well-known profiles are (1) the *Creager profile* [13] developed from a mathematical extension of Bazin's data, (2) the *modified Creager profile* [2] based on the U.S. Bureau of Reclamation data from Denver tests [1], (3) the *Lane-Davis profile* [14] based on the U.S. Bureau of Reclamation data from Fort Collins tests [1] and the data of Bazin [12] and Scimemi [15], (4) the *Scimemi profile* [15], (5) the *Smetana profile* [16], (6) the *De Marchi profile* [17], and (7) the *Escande profile* [18]. For a good discussion of various well-known profiles, see [19].

[2] See [1]. The main project was started in 1936, and the tests were conducted in the Bureau's Hydraulic Laboratory in Denver, Colo. Earlier experiments conducted by the Bureau were performed in 1932 at the Colorado Agricultural Experiment Station, Fort Collins, Colo. The former are usually referred to as the *Denver tests*, the latter as the *Fort Collins tests*.

[3] From [20], Hydraulic Design Charts: 111-1, WES 4-1-52; and 111-7 to 111-9, WES 2-54. The development of the WES standard shapes is described in [21].

For intermediate slopes, approximate values of $K$ and $n$ may be obtained by plotting the above values against the corresponding slopes and interpolating from the plot the required values for any given slope within the plotted range.

The upstream face of the spillway crest may sometimes be designed to set back, as shown by the dashed lines in Fig. 14-3. The shape of the crest

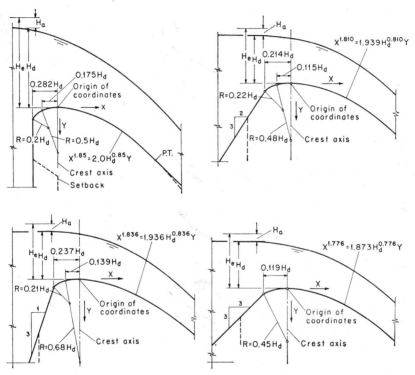

FIG. 14-3. The WES-standard spillway shapes. (*U.S. Army Engineers Waterways Experiment Station.*)

will not be affected materially by such details, provided the modification begins with at least one-half the total head $H_e$ vertically below the origin of coordinates. This is because the vertical velocities are small below this depth and the corresponding effect on nappe profile is negligible.

**14-4. Discharge of the Overflow Spillway.** The discharge over a spillway can be computed by an equation in the form of Eq. (14-9). For spillways designed for the WES shapes, the equation is

$$Q = CLH_e^{1.5} \tag{14-16}$$

where $H_e$ is the total energy head on the crest in ft, *including* the velocity head in the approach channel.   Model tests of the spillways have shown that the effect of the approach velocity is negligible when the height $h$ of the spillway is greater than $1.33H_d$, where $H_d$ is the design head *excluding* the approach velocity head.   Under this condition and with the design

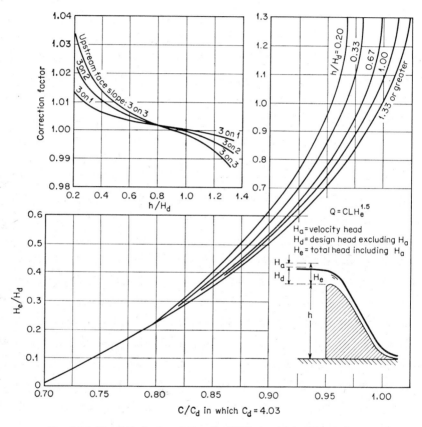

FIG. 14-4. Head-discharge relation for WES-standard spillway shapes.

head (that is, $h/H_d$ greater than 1.33 and $H_e = H_d$, for the approach velocity head is negligible) the coefficient of discharge $C$ has been found to be $C_d = 4.03$.

In low spillways with $h/H_d < 1.33$, the approach velocity will have appreciable effect upon the discharge or the discharge coefficient and, consequently, upon the nappe profile.   A dimensionless plot (Fig. 14-4) based on the data of the Waterways Experiment Station [20] can be used to show the effect of the approach velocity on the relationship between $H_e/H_d$ and $C/C_d$ for spillways designed for WES shapes having vertical upstream face. For spillways having sloping upstream face, the value of $C$ can be corrected approximately for the effect of the upstream-face slope by multiplying $C$ by a correction factor obtained from the attached chart in Fig. 14-4. This correction was developed from the Bureau of Reclamation data [1].

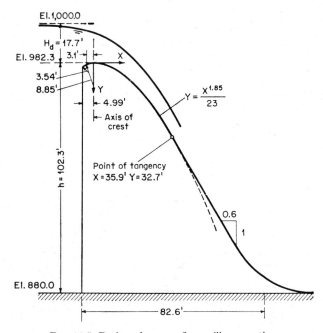

Fig. 14-5. Design of an overflow-spillway section.

**Example 14-1.** Determine the crest elevation and the shape of an overflow-spillway section having a vertical upstream face and a crest length of 250 ft. The design discharge is 75,000 cfs. The upstream water surface at design discharge is at El. 1,000.0 and the average channel floor is at El. 880.0 (Fig. 14-5).

*Solution.* Assuming a high overflow spillway, the effect of approach velocity is negligible, and $C_d = 4.03$. By the discharge equation, $H_e^{1.5} = Q/CL = 75,000/(4.03 \times 250) = 74.4$ and $H_e = 17.8$ ft.

The approach velocity is $V_a = 75,000/(250 \times 120) = 2.5$ fps, and the corresponding velocity head is $H_a = 2.5^2/2g = 0.1$ ft. Thus, the design head is $H_d = 17.8 - 0.1 = 17.7$ ft, and the height of the dam is $h = 120 - 17.7 = 102.3$ ft. This height is greater than $1.33H_d$, and, hence, the effect of approach velocity is negligible.

The crest elevation is at $1000.0 - 17.7 = 982.3$.

By Eq. (14-15), the crest shape is expressed by $Y = X^{1.85}/23$. Coordinates of the shape computed by this equation are plotted as shown in Fig. 14-5. The crest shape upstream from the origin of the coordinates is constructed according to the dimensions recommended in the chart of Fig. 14-3. The design of the straight portion of the spillway surface below the crest section depends on the stability requirement and on the features of the stilling basin at the toe of the spillway. A slope of 0.6:1 is assumed for the straight portion of the downstream spillway surface.

**14-5. Rating of Overflow Spillways.** The profile of an overflow spillway can be designed for one head only. This head is the *design head*, which generally produces a lower nappe of flow that agrees closely with the spillway profile. The spillway, however, must also operate under other heads, either lower or higher than the design head. For lower heads, the pressure on the crest will be above atmospheric but still less than hydrostatic. For higher heads, on the other hand, the pressure will be lower than atmospheric, and it may become so low that separation in flow will occur. Model experiments indicate, however, that the design head may be safely exceeded by at least 50%; beyond this, harmful cavitation may develop [4, p. 535].

For spillways designed for WES shapes, the curves given in Fig. 14-4 can be used to determine the coefficient of discharge for heads other than the design head. Thus, a rating curve of the spillway can be computed.

For spillways designed for other shapes, Bradley [22] has developed a universal curve (Fig. 14-6) showing the relationship between $H_e/H_D$ and $C/C_D$. The term $H_D$ is the design head *including* the approach velocity head, and $C_D$ is the corresponding coefficient of discharge. The term $H_e$ is the total head other than the design head, and $C$ is the corresponding discharge coefficient. This curve is well supported by tests of some 50 overflow spillway crests of various shapes and operating conditions. It can be used to compute approximately the rating curves of most overflow spillways.

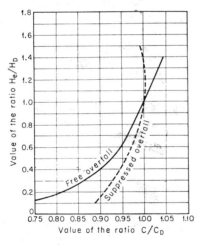

FIG. 14-6. Coefficient of discharge of overflow spillways for other than the design head. (*After J. N. Bradley* [22].)

The dashed curve in Fig. 14-6, supported by data from 29 existing spillways, applies to spillways with overfall suppressed. This is the type of spillway the flow over which is affected by downstream channel conditions; it occurs when the downstream slope is flat and the approach depth is shallow. The spillway in such a case is usually so low that the design head is greater than about twice the height of the spillway above the upstream bed. Such spillways are often found in earth dams.

In using the Bradley curve, it is necessary to know the coefficient of discharge for the design head. If this coefficient is unknown, but the spillway shape is given, a method[1] suggested by Buehler [23] may be used. By this method, based on an equation derived by Brudenell [24], the coefficient of discharge is computed by the equation

$$C = 3.97 \left(\frac{H_e}{H_D}\right)^{0.12}$$ (14-17)

where $H_e$ is an operating head and $H_D$ is the theoretical design head, *including* the approach velocity head, for a standard profile having a

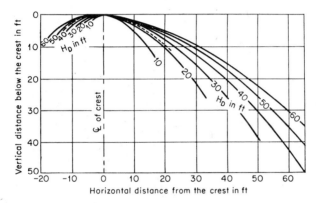

Fig. 14-7. Standard spillway shapes for different values of $H_D$. (*After B. Buehler* [23].)

vertical upstream face. It should be noted that $H_D$ is the theoretical design head of the standard profile for which the Brudenell equation was developed; therefore, it may not be equal to the actual design head used by Bradley or defined for other profiles.

The value of $H_D$ may be obtained from a chart (Fig. 14-7) showing the standard profiles. The profile of the given spillway as designed or built is first drawn on a piece of transparent paper on the same scale as the standard profiles. This paper is laid over the chart; then the value of $H_D$ associated with the standard profile that gives the best fit is selected. For a given profile, the $H_D$ values that give the best fit may be different on the upstream and downstream sides. The higher of the two indicated values of $H_D$ should be used. For example, the profile of a spillway is shown by the dashed line on the chart. The higher value of $H_D$ is approximately 45 ft, on the upstream side of the crest.

[1] A method for the same purpose is also proposed by Bradley [22]; this method fits the given profile to existing profiles of known discharge coefficient.

Using the chart and Eq. (14-17), the rating curve of a spillway of given profile can be computed.

According to comparisons with actual model tests, both the Bradley and Buehler methods have been shown to give highly accurate discharges at all but very low heads. At low heads of 5 ft or so, the computed discharge may be as low as 8% below the actual value. For practical purposes, however, both methods are sufficiently accurate.

**14-6. Upper Nappe Profile of Flow over Spillways.** The shape of upper nappe profile of flow over a spillway crest is significant in the design of spillway abutment walls and for the selection of pivot elevation of tainter gates. The WES shapes for high overflow spillways with vertical upstream face have been investigated, using model tests,[1] by the U.S. Army Engineers Waterways Experiment Station. Figure 14-8 shows the shapes and coordinates $X$ and $Y$ of the upper nappe profile obtained from such tests for negligible approach velocity, for conditions with and without piers, and for three different head ratios. The term $H_d$ is the design head *excluding* the velocity head, and $H$ is the operating head other than the design head, also *excluding* the velocity head. Profiles for intermediate head ratios may be interpolated. Owing to the contraction effect of piers, a pronounced hump between $X/H_d = -0.6$ and $0$ occurs on the upper nappe profile along piers when the discharge is high. Upper nappe profiles for three gate bays adjacent to abutments are given in Fig. 14-9, showing the abutment effects on the nappe profiles.

It should be noted that the upper nappe surface is exposed to the atmosphere and, hence, subject to alteration due to wind and air currents and the absorption of surrounding air. As a result, the flow is aerated and the surface becomes wavy and unstable. The upper-nappe-shape coordinates given in Figs. 14-8 and 14-9 represent only the ideal cases, where air plays little or no part. The upper nappe surface for sloping upstream face should have a lower elevation than that for vertical upstream face. Hence, the given coordinates may also be used safely for spillways with sloping upstream face for which the actual data are not yet available.

**14-7. Effect of Piers in Gated Spillways.** Piers are needed to form the sides of the gates in gated spillways. The effect of the piers is to contract the flow and, hence, to alter the effective crest length of the spillways. The effective length of one bay of a gated spillway may be expressed as

$$L = L_0 - KNH_e \qquad (14-18)$$

where $L_0$ is the clear span of the gate bay between piers; $K$ is the pier contraction coefficient; $N$ is the number of side contractions, equal to 2 for

[1] These tests are designated as "General Spillway Tests—CW 801." The information given here is from [20], Hydraulic Design Charts 111-11 to 111-15 WES 9-54.

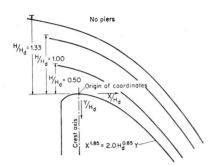

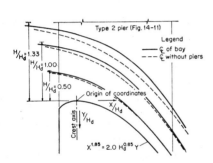

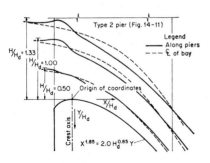

COORDINATES FOR UPPER NAPPE WITH NO PIERS*

| $H/H_d = 0.50$ | | $H/H_d = 1.00$ | | $H/H_d = 1.33$ | |
|---|---|---|---|---|---|
| $X/H_d$ | $Y/H_d$ | $X/H_d$ | $Y/H_d$ | $X/H_d$ | $Y/H_d$ |
| −1.0 | −0.490 | −1.0 | −0.933 | −1.0 | −1.210 |
| −0.8 | −0.484 | −0.8 | −0.915 | −0.8 | −1.185 |
| −0.6 | −0.475 | −0.6 | −0.893 | −0.6 | −1.151 |
| −0.4 | −0.460 | −0.4 | −0.865 | −0.4 | −1.110 |
| −0.2 | −0.425 | −0.2 | −0.821 | −0.2 | −1.060 |
| 0.0 | −0.371 | 0.0 | −0.755 | 0.0 | −1.000 |
| 0.2 | −0.300 | 0.2 | −0.681 | 0.2 | −0.019 |
| 0.4 | −0.200 | 0.4 | −0.586 | 0.4 | −0.821 |
| 0.6 | −0.075 | 0.6 | −0.465 | 0.6 | −0.705 |
| 0.8 | 0.075 | 0.8 | −0.320 | 0.8 | −0.569 |
| 1.0 | 0.258 | 1.0 | −0.145 | 1.0 | −0.411 |
| 1.2 | 0.470 | 1.2 | 0.055 | 1.2 | −0.220 |
| 1.4 | 0.705 | 1.4 | 0.294 | 1.4 | −0.002 |
| 1.6 | 0.972 | 1.6 | 0.563 | 1.6 | 0.243 |
| 1.8 | 1.269 | 1.8 | 0.857 | 1.8 | 0.531 |

\* Based on CW 801 tests for negligible velocity of approach.

COORDINATES FOR UPPER NAPPE AT CENTER LINE OF BAY WITH TYPE 2 PIERS*

| $H/H_d = 0.50$ | | $H/H_d = 1.00$ | | $H/H_d = 1.33$ | |
|---|---|---|---|---|---|
| $X/H_d$ | $Y/H_d$ | $X/H_d$ | $Y/H_d$ | $X/H_d$ | $Y/H_d$ |
| −1.0 | −0.482 | −1.0 | −0.941 | −1.0 | −1.230 |
| −0.8 | −0.480 | −0.8 | −0.932 | −0.8 | −1.215 |
| −0.6 | −0.472 | −0.6 | −0.913 | −0.6 | −1.194 |
| −0.4 | −0.457 | −0.4 | −0.890 | −0.4 | −1.165 |
| −0.2 | −0.431 | −0.2 | −0.855 | −0.2 | −1.122 |
| 0.0 | −0.384 | 0.0 | −0.805 | 0.0 | −1.071 |
| 0.2 | −0.313 | 0.2 | −0.735 | 0.2 | −1.015 |
| 0.4 | −0.220 | 0.4 | −0.647 | 0.4 | −0.944 |
| 0.6 | −0.088 | 0.6 | −0.539 | 0.6 | −0.847 |
| 0.8 | 0.075 | 0.8 | −0.389 | 0.8 | −0.725 |
| 1.0 | 0.257 | 1.0 | −0.202 | 1.0 | −0.564 |
| 1.2 | 0.462 | 1.2 | 0.015 | 1.2 | −0.356 |
| 1.4 | 0.705 | 1.4 | 0.266 | 1.4 | −0.102 |
| 1.6 | 0.977 | 1.6 | 0.521 | 1.6 | 0.172 |
| 1.8 | 1.278 | 1.8 | 0.860 | 1.8 | 0.465 |

\* Based on CW 801 tests for negligible velocity of approach.

COORDINATES FOR UPPER NAPPE ALONG PIERS*

| $H/H_d = 0.50$ | | $H/H_d = 1.00$ | | $H/H_d = 1.33$ | |
|---|---|---|---|---|---|
| $X/H_d$ | $Y/H_d$ | $X/H_d$ | $Y/H_d$ | $X/H_d$ | $Y/H_d$ |
| −1.0 | −0.495 | −1.0 | −0.950 | −1.0 | −1.253 |
| −0.8 | −0.492 | −0.8 | −0.940 | −0.8 | −1.221 |
| −0.6 | −0.490 | −0.6 | −0.929 | −0.6 | −1 209 |
| −0.4 | −0.482 | −0.4 | −0.933 | −0.4 | −1.218 |
| −0.2 | −0.440 | −0.2 | −0.925 | −0.2 | −1.244 |
| 0.0 | −0.383 | 0.0 | −0.779 | 0.0 | −1.103 |
| 0.2 | −0.265 | 0.2 | −0.651 | 0.2 | −0.950 |
| 0.4 | −0.185 | 0.4 | −0.545 | 0.4 | −0.821 |
| 0.6 | −0.076 | 0.6 | −0.425 | 0.6 | −0.689 |
| 0.8 | 0.060 | 0.8 | −0.285 | 0.8 | −0.549 |
| 1.0 | 0.240 | 1.0 | −0.121 | 1.0 | −0.389 |
| 1.2 | 0.445 | 1.2 | 0.067 | 1.2 | −0.215 |
| 1.4 | 0.675 | 1.4 | 0.236 | 1.4 | 0.011 |
| 1.6 | 0.925 | 1.6 | 0.521 | 1.6 | 0.208 |
| 1.8 | 1.177 | 1.8 | 0.779 | 1.8 | 0.438 |

\* Based on CW 801 tests for negligible velocity of approach.

FIG. 14-8. Upper nappe profiles of flow over WES spillways with and without piers. (*U.S. Army Engineers Waterways Experiment Station.*)

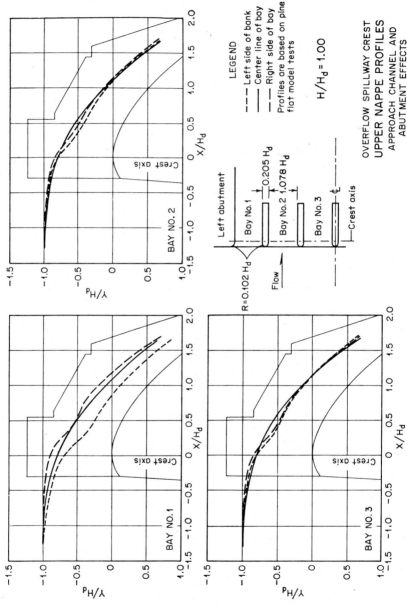

FIG. 14-9. Upper nappe profiles of flow over WES spillways showing approach channel and abutment effects. (*U.S. Army Engineers Waterways Experiment Station.*)

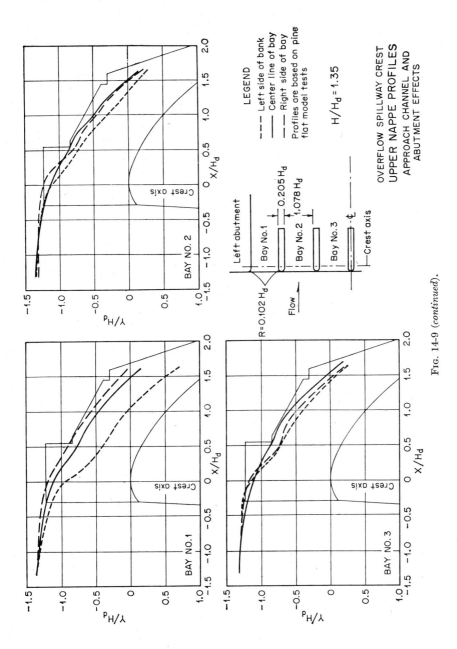

LEGEND

--- Left side of bank
—·— Center line of bay
—— Right side of bay
Profiles are based on pine
flat model tests

$H/H_d = 1.35$

OVERFLOW SPILLWAY CREST
UPPER NAPPE PROFILES
APPROACH CHANNEL AND
ABUTMENT EFFECTS

FIG. 14-9 (continued).

each gate bay; and $H_e$ is the total head on the crest *including* the velocity head. In computing the discharge through gated spillways, the effective length determined by the above equation should be used. The discharge coefficient, however, is assumed the same in both gated and ungated spillways.

The pier contraction coefficient varies mainly with the shape and position of the pier nose, the head condition, the approach depth of flow, and the operation of the adjacent gates. The approximate $K$ value given by Creager and Justin [3, p. 120] ranges from 0.1 for thick, blunt noses to 0.04 for thin or pointed noses and is 0.035 for round noses. These values apply to piers having a thickness equal to about one-third the head on the crest when all gates are open. When one gate is open and the adjacent gates are closed, these values become roughly 2.5 times larger.

The U.S. Army Engineers Waterways Experiment Station has conducted tests (General Spillway Test CW 801 [20]) on different forms of pier nose for spillways of the WES shape. On the basis of these tests, a round-nose pier is recommended for general use with high heads. The $K$ value for the round-nose pier plotted against the ratio of $H_e/H_d$ with variable distances upstream from the crest is shown in Fig. 14-10. The effect of other nose shapes on the contraction coefficient is shown in Fig. 14-11. The height of the test spillways was $6.67H_d$, which had negligible velocity of approach. Under the testing conditions, these data are applicable to high spillways and to the condition that the adjacent gates are open. For low spillways with appreciable approach velocity, the pier contraction coefficient for the round-nose pier with various approach depths is shown in Fig. 14-12. In the absence of adequate data, pier contraction coefficients for other nose shapes for low spillways may be obtained by proportioning from the data for high spillways (i.e., from Fig. 14-11).

**14-8. Pressure on Overflow Spillways.** If the spillway profile is designed exactly in the shape of the lower nappe of a free overflow, the pressure on the spillway crest under the design head should be theoretically nil. For practical reasons, however, such an ideal profile is generally modified so that low pressures will develop under the design head. As the spillway must be operated under heads other than the design head, the pressure will increase under the lower heads and decrease under the higher heads. Assuming a two-dimensional irrotational flow, the pressure on the spillway crest may be accurately determined analytically by a numerical method, graphically by flow-net analysis, or instrumentally by an electronic analogy.[1] More exact determination of the pressure, however, will depend upon model tests.

---

[1] See references given in Art. 13-2. A practical procedure for the relaxation method applied to the problem under consideration is given in [25].

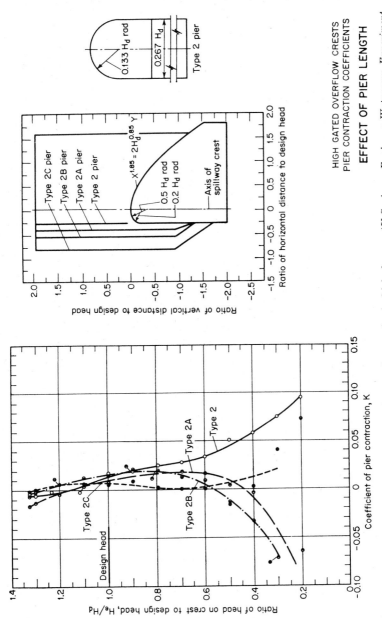

HIGH GATED OVERFLOW CRESTS
PIER CONTRACTION COEFFICIENTS
EFFECT OF PIER LENGTH

FIG. 14-10. Coefficient of contraction for the round-nose pier in high dams. (*U.S. Army Engineers Waterways Experiment Station* [20], *Hydraulic Design Chart* 111-6, *WES* 4-1-53.)

375

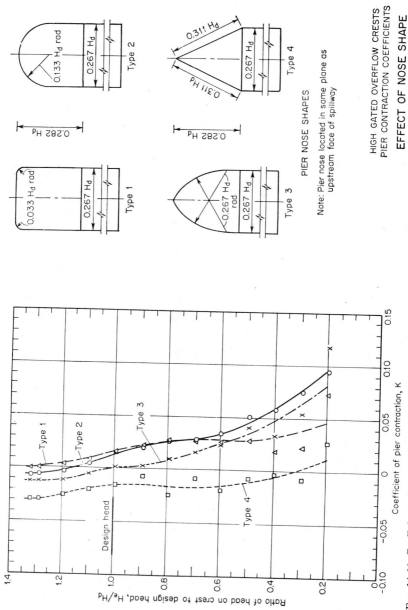

Fig. 14-11. Coefficient of contraction for piers of various nose shapes in high dams with the nose located in the same vertical plane as the upstream face of the WES spillway. (*U.S. Army Engineers Waterways Experiment Station* [20], *Hydraulic Design Chart* 111-5, *WES 4-1-53.*)

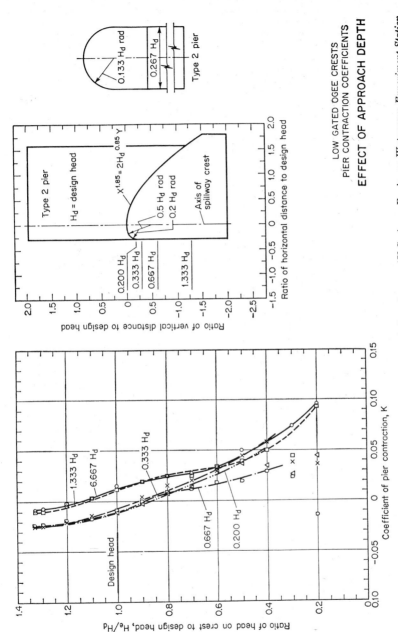

LOW GATED OGEE CRESTS
PIER CONTRACTION COEFFICIENTS
EFFECT OF APPROACH DEPTH

Fig. 14-12. Coefficient of contraction for the round-nose pier in low dams. *(U.S. Army Engineers Waterways Experiment Station* [20], *Hydraulic Design Chart 122-2, WES 4-1-53.)*

The pressure distributions on a spillway crest with and without piers under three different head ratios, based on CW 801 tests of WES shapes [20], are shown in dimensionless plots (Fig. 14-13). Pressures for intermediate head ratios can be obtained by interpolation.

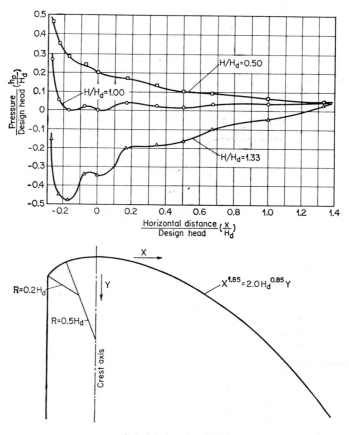

Fig. 14-13. Crest pressures on WES high overflow spillways. (a) No piers. (U.S. Army Engineers Waterways Experiment Station [20], Hydraulic Design Chart 111-16, WES 9-54.)

Because of the conversion of static to kinetic energy as the water flows over the spillway, the hydrostatic pressure on the upstream face of the spillway crest is actually reduced. This reduction in pressure is not appreciable, but, where the moment arm is long, as in high dams, the effect on stability may be worth considering. The usual method of analysis by assuming straight-line pressure distribution near the crest

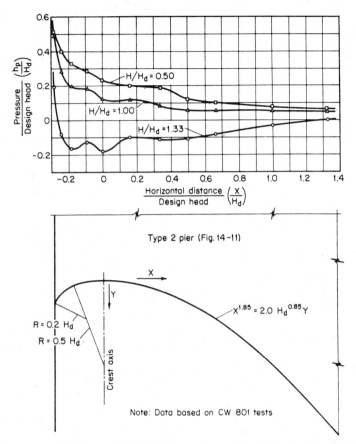

FIG. 14-13. Crest pressures on WES high overflow spillways (*continued*). (*b*) Along center line of pier bay. (*U.S. Army Engineers Waterways Experiment Station* [20], *Hydraulic Design Chart* 111-16/1, *WES* 3-55.)

will result in overdesign of the spillway, particularly for high dams. Such overdesign is an accepted procedure, providing an additional factor of safety.[1]

The pressure reduction on the upstream face of a vertical weir has been determined both theoretically and experimentally by Harris [26]. On the basis of CW 801 tests for ungated WES-shape crests of vertical upstream face and of U.S. Bureau of Reclamation tests of pressure on a

---

[1] Actually, the effect on structural stability due to this pressure reduction is compensated to a large extent by the moment of the horizontal component of the nappe pressure on the crest surface.

sharp-crested weir under the design head, the resultant of the reduced pressure is found to be approximately $12.9H_d{}^2$ lb per unit length of the spillway, acting horizontally at a distance of $0.161H_d$ ft below the top of the crest.

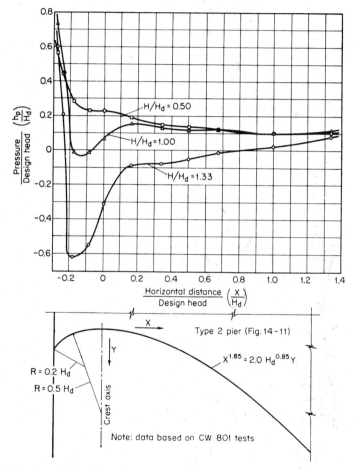

FIG. 14-13. Crest pressures on WES high overflow spillways (*continued*). (*c*) Along piers. (*U.S. Army Engineers Waterways Experiment Station* [20], *Hydraulic Design Chart* 111-16/2, *WES* 3-55.)

**14-9. Drum Gates.** The drum gate is a hinged gate which floats in a chamber and is buoyed into position by regulating the water level in the chamber. Primarily, it is used to control the surface elevation of the water upstream. As a measuring device, the drum gate resembles a weir

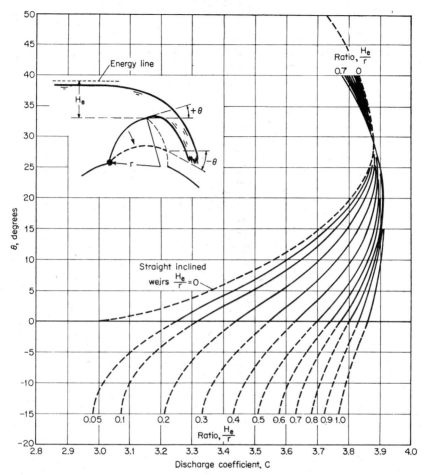

FIG. 14-14. Curves for determination of the discharge coefficient of drum gates. (*After J. N. Bradley* [27].)

with a curved upstream face over the major portion of its travel. The angle $\theta$ (Fig. 14-14) is formed between the horizontal and a line drawn tangent to the downstream lip of the gate. This angle is considered positive when it is measured above the horizontal and negative when measured below the horizontal. For positive values of $\theta$, the gate acts as a sharp-crested weir, the control point is the downstream lip of the gate, and the head is measured above this point. For negative values of $\theta$, the gate acts as a curved-crested weir, the control point is the highest point of the gate surface, and the head is measured above this point.

Since the drum gate acts as a weir, the discharge through the gate may be expressed as

$$Q = CLH_e^{1.5} \tag{14-16}$$

where $C$ is the coefficient of discharge, $L$ is the length of the gate, and $H_e$ is the total head.    Laboratory investigations have shown that the flow over this type of gate can be completely defined by $H_e$, $\theta$, $C$, the radius $r$ of the gate, and the depth of approach.    The depth of approach, however, has very little influence on the flow behavior when the approach depth, measured below the highest point of the gate, is equal to or greater than twice the head on the gate.    This condition is well satisfied by most drum-gate installations, especially when the gate is in a raised position.    Therefore, the coefficient $C$ may be considered to be a function of $H_e$, $\theta$, and $r$.

Bradley [27] has made a comprehensive study of the drum gate, using data obtained from 40 hydraulic models of existing drum-gate structures of various sizes and scales.    The results of this study are shown by a family of curves (Fig. 14-14) where $C$ is plotted against $\theta$ with the ratio $H_e/r$ as a parameter.    When $H_e/r = 0$, the gate becomes a straight inclined weir, and the corresponding dashed line in the family of curves is based on Bazin's data [12].    The curves extend downward to $\theta = -15°$. The discharge coefficients in the region between $\theta = -15°$ and the gate completely down can be obtained by graphical interpolation of the rating curves of the gate.    The computation of the rating curve when the gate is completely down is the same as that for a spillway with an ungated crest (Art. 14-5).

**14-10. Flow at the Toe of Overflow Spillways.**    The theoretical velocity of flow at the toe of an overflow spillway (Fig. 14-15) may be computed by

$$V_1 = \sqrt{2g(Z + H_a - y_1)} \tag{14-19}$$

where $Z$ is the fall, or vertical distance in ft from the upstream reservoir level to the floor at the toe; $H_a$ is the upstream approach velocity head; and $y_1$ is the depth of flow at the toe.    Owing to the energy loss involved in the flow over the spillway, the actual velocity is always less than the theoretical value.    The magnitude of the actual velocity depends mainly on the head on the spillway crest, the fall, the slope of the spillway surface, and the spillway-surface roughness.[1]    By reasoning and experiments it is shown that the deviation of the actual velocity from its theoretical value becomes larger when the head is smaller and the fall is greater.

On the basis of experience, theoretical analysis, and a limited amount of experimental information obtained from prototype tests on Shasta and Grand Coulee dams, the U.S. Bureau of Reclamation [29] has studied the

---

[1] See [28] for further information.

relationship between the actual velocity and a theoretical value.[1] From
the results of this study, a chart (Fig. 14-15) was prepared to show the
actual velocity at the toe of spillways under various heads, falls, slopes
from 1 on 0.6 to 1 on 0.8, and the condition of average surface roughness.
It is felt that this chart is sufficiently accurate for preliminary-design

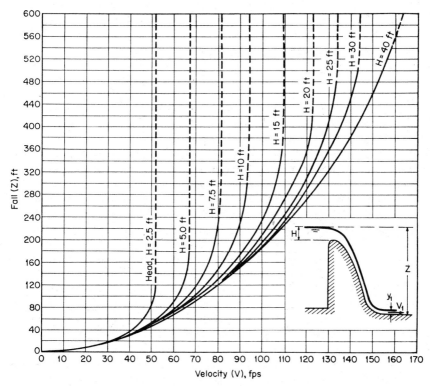

FIG. 14-15. Curves for determination of velocity at the toe of spillways with slopes
1 on 0.6 to 0.8.

purposes, although it can be refined by additional experimental information which may become available in the future.

Experiments by Bauer [30] indicate that friction losses in accelerating
the flow down the face of a spillway may be considerably less than the
normal friction loss in flow with well-developed turbulence. Therefore,
the friction loss is not significant on steep slopes, but it would become
important if the slope were small. For this reason, the chart in Fig.

[1] The theoretical velocity defined by the Bureau is $V_1 = \sqrt{2g(Z - 0.5H)}$.

14-15 is not applicable to slopes flatter than 1 on 0.6.    For flatter slopes, the problem may be analyzed by the method described in Art. 11-4.

At the end of the sloping spillway surface, the flow changes its direction rather abruptly and thereby produces appreciable centrifugal pressures. In order to create a smooth transition of the flow and to prevent the impact of the falling water from scouring the foundation, the surface at the spillway toe is usually designed as a curved bucket [31].    To be thoroughly effective the bucket should be tangent to the foundation or nearly so.    The radius $R$ of the bucket, measured in feet, may be estimated approximately by the following empirical formula:

$$R = 10^{(V+6.4H+16)/(3.6H+64)}$$    (14-20)

where $V$ is the velocity in fps of the flow at the toe and $H$ is the head in ft, *excluding* approach velocity head, on the spillway crest.    The design bucket pressure and the maximum side-wall pressure should be equal to the centrifugal pressure plus the hydrostatic pressure corresponding to the tailwater depth.    The centrifugal pressure may be computed by Eq. (2-8) for known radius of the bucket and velocity of the flow at the toe.    Determination of the bucket pressure, however, can be made more accurately by flow-net analysis or by the relaxation method, or, still more precisely, by model tests.    The results of such determination have indicated that the effect of the bucket curve on pressure actually extends even beyond the ends of the curve.

The flow leaving the toe of a high overflow spillway is a high-velocity jet, containing a large amount of energy capable of causing heavy scouring.    Unless the downstream approach is resistant to such scouring, measures to avoid the danger of scouring should be taken in the design. Popular methods are design of a ski-jump spillway, utilization of submerged tailwater as a brake, and use of a hydraulic jump as an energy dissipator.

**14-11. The Ski-jump Spillway.**    In this type of spillway the toe is designed in the form of a large specially shaped lip or bucket which throws the whole jet of flow into the air.    Part of the energy in the jet is dissipated in the air, but in any case the jet falls back into the river channel at a safe distance from the dam.    This design was first proposed by Coyne [32,33].    Figure 14-16 shows a typical ski-jump spillway    In this design, the spillway-bottom slab is also the roof of the power house which is built against the downstream side of the dam.    The slab is heavily reinforced in order to take the tremendous loads due largely to the centrifugal pressure of the jet acting on the spillway toe.[1]

[1] See [34] to [36] for further information.    Well-known ski-jump spillways are installed in Castelo do Bode Dam in Portugal; and the Marèges, Bort, l'Agle, Saint-Étienne-Cantalès, and Chastang Dams in France.    Each of the last three dams has two ski-jump spillways.    The jets from the two spillways may meet and collide in the air, thus dissipating a large amount of energy.

**14-12. Submerged Overflow Spillways.** Spillways and weirs are said to be submerged when the tailwater is higher than the crest. As submerged flow is usually unstable, having considerable surface disturbance immediately downstream, such a spillway or weir is unsatisfactory for

FIG. 14-16. The ski-jump spillways of l'Aigle Dam. (*Courtesy of P. Danel, Ets. NEYRPIC.*)

accurate flow measurements. Studies on submerged round-crested weirs are useful, however, for they will furnish information needed in the design of low overflow dams which may be occasionally subject to submergence.

Extensive studies on submerged round-crested weirs have been performed by the U.S. Bureau of Reclamation [1,37].[1] In these studies, the flow is classified into four distinct types according to the flow condition

[1] Other well-known studies are reported in [38] to [40].

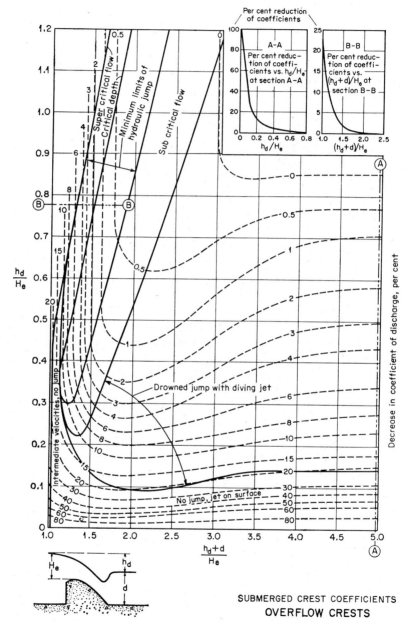

SUBMERGED CREST COEFFICIENTS
OVERFLOW CRESTS

Fig. 14-17. Decrease in discharge coefficient for submerged overflow spillways. (*U.S. Army Engineers Waterways Experiment Station.*)

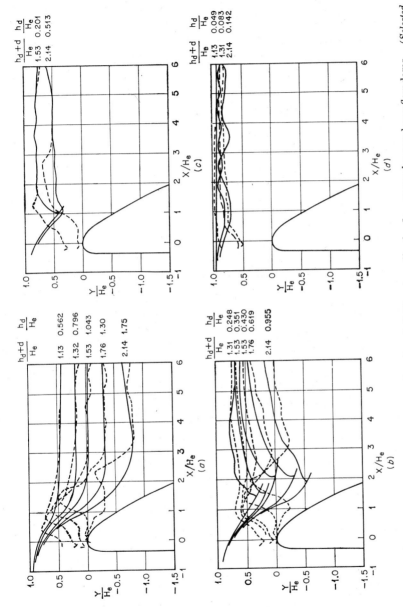

Fig. 14-18. Typical pressure (dashed lines) and surface (solid lines) profiles for flow over submerged overflow dams. (*Selected from U.S. Bureau of Reclamation data* [1].) (*a*) Supercritical flow; (*b*) flow involving hydraulic jump; (*c*) flow with a drowned hydraulic jump; (*d*) flow approaching complete submergence.

prevalent on the downstream apron: (1) supercritical flow, (2) subcritical flow involving hydraulic jump, (3) flow accompanied by a drowned jump with diving jet, and (4) flow approaching complete submergence.

Submergence of spillway or weir will reduce the coefficient of discharge of the corresponding unsubmerged flow. The Bureau of Reclamation's test results on this reduction, expressed in percentage of the discharge coefficient for unsubmerged flow (Fig. 14-4), have been presented in a chart for the four types of flow mentioned above. This chart in a slightly modified form (Fig. 14-17) was further checked against other data[1] by the U.S. Army Engineers Waterways Experiment Station.[2] It was found that the chart is also applicable to the determination of coefficients for WES shapes under submerged conditions.

In the chart (Fig. 14-17) $h_d$ is the drop from the upper pool to the tailwater elevation, $H_e$ is the total head above the crest, and $d$ is the tailwater depth. The general pattern of the curves shows that, for low ratios $(h_d + d)/H_e$, the flow is of type 1, or supercritical, and that the reduction in coefficient is affected essentially by this ratio and is practically independent of $h_d/H_e$. The cross section $BB$ in the upper right-hand corner of the chart shows the variation of $(h_d + d)/H_e$ at $h_d/H_e = 0.78$. For large values of $(h_d + d)/H_e$, on the other hand, the reduction in coefficient is affected essentially by the ratio $h_d/H_e$. Under this condition, for values of $h_d/H_e$ less than 0.10, the flow is of type 4, the jet is on the surface, and no jump occurs. For values of $h_d/H_e$ greater than 0.10, the flow is of type 3, or accompanied by a drowned jump with diving jet. The cross section $AA$ shows the variations of $h_d/H_e$ at $(h_d + d)/H_e$ near 5.0. Subcritical flow, or flow of type 2, occurs in the region indicated on the chart. Other regions for transitional flow conditions are also shown.

The typical pressure and surface profiles for submerged spillway flow are shown for different values of $(h_d + d)/H_e$ and $h_d/H_e$ for four types of flow (Fig. 14-18). These were selected from the data of the Bureau of Reclamation. They are useful in the design of spillways for stability.

## PROBLEMS

**14-1.** A vertical sharp-crested weir, 20 ft high and 60 ft long, is built as an overflow spillway without end contractions. When the head is 20 ft above the crest of the weir and the nappe is completely aerated, compute (a) the nappe profiles, and (b) the hydrostatic load acting on the weir.

**14-2.** During tests on the aeration of the spillway described in the preceding problem, negative pressures under the nappe of 9.7 ft of water were observed. Compute the increase in the total load on the weir. How much air, measured in cubic feet per

---

[1] Data given in [41] to [44].

[2] From [20], Hydraulic Design Chart 111-4, WES 4-1-53.

second, will be required for aeration beneath the nappe to a pressure reduction of 2 ft? Compute the load on the weir after this aeration.

**14-3.** If the channel floor is at El. 975.0 instead of El. 880.0, and other data remain the same, determine the spillway section required in Example 14-1. A trial-and-error procedure is required for the determination of the value of $C$.

**14-4.** If the upstream face has a slope of 3 on 2 instead of vertical and other data remain the same, determine the spillway section required in Example 14-1.

**14-5.** Determine the rating curve of the spillway developed in Example 14-1.

**14-6.** An overflow spillway of unknown profile designed for a total head of 14.5 ft has a crest length of 64 ft and a coefficient of discharge equal to 3.48. Determine the rating curve by the Bradley curve.

**14-7.** If the spillway in the preceding problem has a profile shown by the dashed line in Fig. 14-7, determine the rating curve.

**14-8.** Compute the upper nappe profile of the flow over the spillway designed in Example 14-1, assuming no piers.

**14-9.** Determine the wall heights for the overflow-dam section designed in Example 14-1, assuming six bays formed by WES round-nose piers and a maximum operating head 35% higher than the design head.

**14-10.** Determine the discharge over the spillway section designed in Example 14-1 if the spillway has six bays formed by WES round-nose piers.

**14-11.** Determine the pressure on the crest of the spillway designed in Example 14-1, for operating head equal to 0.50, 1.00, and 1.33 times the design head; assume (a) no piers and (b) six bays formed by WES round-nose piers.

**14-12.** A drum gate (Fig. 14-19) 50 ft long and 20 ft in radius is installed on top of a high overflow spillway. Determine the rating curve of the gate, i.e., discharge vs.

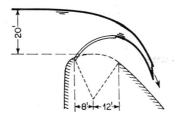

Fig. 14-19. The drum gate for Prob. 14-12.

elevation of the highest point of the gate surface. The position of the highest point of the gate surface and the value of $\theta$ may be determined graphically.

**14-13.** Estimate the depth and velocity of flow and also the radius of the bucket at the toe of the spillway designed in Example 14-1.

**14-14.** Determine the discharge of the spillway designed in Prob. 14-3 if the tailwater elevation is at El. 990. Would a hydraulic jump be possible at the toe of the spillway?

## REFERENCES

1. Studies of crests for overfall dams, *Boulder Canyon Project Final Reports*, pt. VI, *U.S. Bureau of Reclamation, Hydraulic Investigations, Bulletin* 3, 1948.
2. Julian Hinds, William P. Creager, and Joel D. Justin: "Engineering for Dams," John Wiley & Sons, Inc., New York, 1945, vol. 2, pp. 358–361.

3. William P. Creager and Joel D. Justin: "Hydroelectric Handbook," 2d ed., John Wiley & Sons, Inc., New York, 1950, pp. 362–363.
4. A. T. Ippen: Channel transitions and controls, chap. VIII in Hunter Rouse (editor): "Engineering Hydraulics," John Wiley & Sons, Inc., New York, 1950, pp. 496–588.
5. Fred W. Blaisdell: Equation of the free-falling nappe, *Proceedings, American Society of Civil Engineers*, vol. 80, separate no. 482, 16 pp., August, 1954.
6. Horace William King, "Handbook of Hydraulics," revised by Ernest F. Brater, 4th ed., McGraw-Hill Book Company, Inc., 1954, sec. 4, pp. 1–67.
7. Carl E. Kindsvater and Rolland W. Carter: Discharge characteristics of rectangular thin-plate weirs, paper 1453, *Proceedings, American Society of Civil Engineers, Journal, Hydraulics Division*, vol. 83, no. HY6, pt. 1, pp. 1–36, December, 1957.
8. P. K. Kandaswamy and Hunter Rouse: Characteristics of flow over terminal weirs and sills, paper 1345, *Proceedings, American Society of Civil Engineers, Journal, Hydraulics Division*, vol. 83, no. HY4, pp. 1–13, August, 1957.
9. J. V. Boussinesq: "Théorie approchée de l'écoulement de l'eau sur un déversoir en mince paroi et sans contraction latérale" ("Theoretical Approach to the Flow over a Knife-edge Weir without Side Contraction"), Paris, 1907.
10. Th. Rehbock: Discussion on Precise weir measurements, by Ernest W. Schoder and Kenneth B. Turner, *Transactions, American Society of Civil Engineers*, vol. 93, pp. 1143–1162, 1929.
11. G. H. Hickox: Aeration of spillways, *Transactions, American Society of Civil Engineers*, vol. 109, pp. 537–556, 1944.
12. H. E. Bazin: Expériences nouvelles sur l'écoulement en déversoir (Recent experiments on the flow of water over weirs), *Mémoires et documents, Annales des ponts et chaussées*, ser. 6, vol. 16, 2d half-yr., pp. 393–448, 1888; ser. 6, vol. 19, 1st half-yr., pp. 9–82, 1890; ser. 7, vol. 2, 2d half-yr., pp. 445–520, 1891; ser. 7, vol. 7, 1st half-yr., pp. 249–357, 1894; ser. 7, vol. 12, 2d half-yr., pp. 645–731, 1896; and ser. 7, vol. 15, 2d quarter-yr., pp. 151–264, 1898. English translation of the first part by Arthur Marichal and John C. Trautwine, Jr., *Proceedings, Engineers' Club of Philadelphia*, vol. 7, no. 5, pp. 259–310, 1890; vol. 9, no. 3, pp. 231–244, 1892; and vol. 10, no. 2, pp. 121–164, 1893. Bazin's data were reprinted almost entirely by G. W. Rafter in Report on special water-supply investigation, *Congressional Documents* 4146 and 4147, Washington, D.C., pp. 571–950, 1900; and Hydrology of the State of New York, *New York State Museum, Bulletin* 85, Albany, N.Y., 1905.
13. William P. Creager: "Engineering for Masonry Dams," John Wiley & Sons, Inc., New York, 1929, p. 106.
14. Calvin Victor Davis (editor-in-chief): "Handbook of Applied Hydraulics," 2d ed., McGraw-Hill Book Company, Inc., New York, 1952, pp. 259–263; Sec. 7, Spillways and Streambed Protection Works, by Emory W. Lane and Calvin V. Davis, pp. 253–289.
15. Ettore Scimemi: Sulla forma delle vene tracimanti (The form of flow over weirs), *L'Energia elettrica, Milano*, vol. 7, no. 4, pp. 293–305, April, 1930.
16. J. Smetana: Étude de la surface d'écoulement des grands barrages (Study of flow profile of large dams), *Revue générale de l'hydraulique*, Paris, vol. 14, no. 46, pp. 185–194, July, 1948; vol. 15, no. 49, pp. 19–32, January, 1949.
17. Giulio De Marchi: Ricerche sperimentali sulle dighe tracimanti (Experimental study on overflow dams), *Annali dei lavori pubblici*, Rome, vol. 7, 1928.
18. L. Escande: "Barrages" ("Dams"), Hermann & Cie., Paris, 1937.
19. Anton Grzywienski: Anti-vacuum profiles for spillways of large dams, *Transac-*

*tions of the 4th Congress on Large Dams*, vol. 2, pp. 105–124, International Commission on Large Dams of the World Power Conference, New Delhi, India, January, 1951.

20. "Corps of Engineers Hydraulic Design Criteria," prepared for Office of the Chief of Engineers, U.S. Army Corps of Engineers, Waterways Experiment Station, Vicksburg, Miss., 1952; revised in subsequent years.

21. John C. Harrold: Discussion on Equation of the free-falling nappe, by Fred W. Blaisdell, *Proceedings, American Society of Civil Engineers*, vol. 80, separate no. 624, pp. 16–19, August, 1955.

22. J. N. Bradley: Discharge coefficients for irregular overfall spillways, *U.S. Bureau of Reclamation, Engineering Monograph No. 9*, March, 1952.

23. Bob Buehler: Discussion on Rating curves for flow over drum gates, by Joseph N. Bradley, *Transactions, American Society of Civil Engineers*, vol. 119, pp. 421–428, 1954.

24. Ross N. Brudenell: Flow over rounded crests, *Engineering News-Record*, vol. 115, no. 3, p. 95, July 18, 1935.

25. M. K. Ganguli and S. K. Roy: On the standardization of the relaxation treatment of systematic pressure computations for overflow spillway discharges, *Irrigation and Power, The Journal of the Central Board of Irrigation and Power*, vol. 9, no. 2, pp. 187–209, New Delhi, India, April, 1952.

26. Charles W. Harris: An analysis of the weir coefficient for suppressed weirs, *University of Washington, Engineering Experiment Station, Bulletin 22*, 1923.

27. Joseph N. Bradley: Rating curves for flow over drum gates, *Transactions, American Society of Civil Engineers*, vol. 119, pp. 403–420, 1954.

28. Robert B. Jansen: Flow characteristics on the ogee spillway, paper 1452, *Proceedings, American Society of Civil Engineers, Journal, Hydraulics Division*, vol. 83, no. HY6, pt. 1, pp. 1–11, December, 1957.

29. Research study on stilling basins, energy dissipators, and associated appurtenances, *U.S. Bureau of Reclamation, Hydraulic Report, No. Hyd-399*, June 1, 1955, pp. 41–43.

30. William J. Bauer: Turbulent boundary layer on steep slopes, *Transactions, American Society of Civil Engineers*, vol. 119, pp. 1212–1233, 1954.

31. J. H. Douma: Discussion on Design of side walls in chutes and spillways, by D. B. Gumensky, *Transactions, American Society of Civil Engineers*, vol. 119, pp. 364–368, 1954.

32. A. Coyne: Latest development of dams and hydro-electric power stations in France, paper read before a joint meeting of the Institution of Civil Engineers and the British Section of the Société des Ingénieurs Civils de France, London, Nov. 25, 1947. Editorial review entitled Development of dams in France, *Engineering*, vol. 164, no. 4274, pp. 613–614, Dec. 26, 1947.

33. A. Coyne: Barrages-usines de l'Aigle et de Saint-Étienne-Cantalès (Dams and hydroplants of Aigle and Saint-Étienne-Cantalès), *Travaux*, Paris, vol. 34, no. 185, pp. 194–215, March, 1950.

34. R. Maitre and S. Obolensky: Étude de quelques caractéristiques de l'écoulement dans la partie aval des évacuateurs de surface (Study of some flow characteristics in the downstream part of spillways), *La Houille blanche*, Grenoble, 9th year, no. 4, pp. 481–511, July-August, 1954.

35. F. Auroy: Les évacuateurs de crues du barrage de Chastang (The spillways of Chastang Dam), *Transactions of the 4th Congress on Large Dams*, vol. II, pp. 661–686, International Commission on Large Dams of the World Power Conference, New Delhi, January, 1951.

36. E. A. Elevatorski: Trajectory bucket-type energy dissipators, paper 1553, *Pro-*

*ceedings, American Society of Civil Engineers, Journal, Power Division*, vol. 84, no. PO1, pp. 1–17, February, 1958.

37. J. N. Bradley: Studies of flow characteristics, discharge and pressure relative to submerged dams, *U.S. Bureau of Reclamation, Hydraulic Laboratory Report* 182, 1945.

38. Report of the Board of Engineers on Deep Waterways, U.S. Board of Engineers, pt. 1, p. 291, 1900.

39. R. E. Horton: Weir experiments, coefficients and formulas, *U.S. Geological Survey, Water Supply and Irrigation Paper* 200, 1907.

40. Glen Nelson Cox: The submerged weir as a measuring device, *University of Wisconsin, Engineering Experiment Station, Bulletin* 67, pp. 48–75, 1928.

41. H. J. Koloseus: Discharge characteristics of submerged spillways, Master's thesis, Colorado Agricultural and Mechanical College, Fort Collins, December, 1951.

42. M. Bar Shany: Pressure distribution on downstream face of a submerged weir, Master's thesis, State University of Iowa, Iowa City, June, 1950.

43. Spillway and lock approach, Jim Woodruff Dam, Apalachicola River, Florida: Model investigation, *U.S. Army Engineers Waterways Experiment Station, Technical Memorandum* 2-340, May, 1952.

44. Morgantown spillway, Special tests, unpublished report, U.S. Army Engineers Waterways Experiment Station, Vicksburg, Miss., 1949.

# CHAPTER 15

# HYDRAULIC JUMP AND ITS USE AS
# ENERGY DISSIPATOR

**15-1. The Hydraulic Jump.** The hydraulic jump was first investigated experimentally by Bidone [1,2], an Italian, in 1818.[1] This led Bélanger [3] (1828) to distinguish between mild (subcritical) and steep (supercritical) slopes, since he had observed that in steep channels hydraulic jump is frequently produced by a barrier in originally uniform flow. Thereafter, abundant studies were made and the results were quoted by many writers. Outstanding contributors to our present knowledge about the hydraulic jump are Bresse (1860) [4], Darcy and Bazin (1865) [5], Ferriday and Merriman (1894) [6], Gibson (1913) [7], Kennison (1916) [8], Woodward and Riegel-Beebe (1917) [9], Koch and Carstanjen (1926) [10], Lindquist (1927) [11], Safranez (1927) [12], Einwachter (1933) [13,14], Smetana (1934) [15,16], Bakhmeteff and Matzke (1936) [17], Escande (1938) [18], Citrini (1939) [19], Nebbia (1940) [20], Kindsvater (1944) [21], Blaisdell (1948) [22], Forster and Skrinde (1950) [23], Rouse, Siao, and Nagaratnam (1958) [24], and many others.[2]

The theory of jump developed in early days is for horizontal or slightly inclined channels in which the weight of water in the jump has little effect upon the jump behavior and hence is ignored in the analysis. The results thus obtained, however, can be applied to most channels encountered in engineering problems. For channels of large slope, the weight effect of water in the jump may become so pronounced that it must be included in the analysis.

Practical applications of the hydraulic jump are many; it is used (1) to dissipate energy in water flowing over dams, weirs, and other hydraulic structures and thus prevent scouring downstream from the structures (Art. 15-8); (2) to recover head or raise the water level on the downstream side of a measuring flume and thus maintain high water level in the

[1] The experiment was made in Paris in 1818 and reported the following year in [1]. The hydraulic jump is also known as a *standing wave*. In French, it is called *le ressaut hydraulique*. In German, it is *der Wassersprung*. In honor of Bidone, the hydraulic jump in Italian is named *il salto di Bidone* (the jump of Bidone).

[2] For a comprehensive review of the studies on hydraulic jump, see [25]. For a mathematical treatment of the subject, see [26].

channel for irrigation or other water-distribution purposes; (3) to increase weight on an apron and thus reduce uplift pressure under a masonry structure by raising the water depth on the apron; (4) to increase the discharge of a sluice by holding back tailwater, since the effective head will be reduced if the tailwater is allowed to drown the jump;[1] (5) to indicate

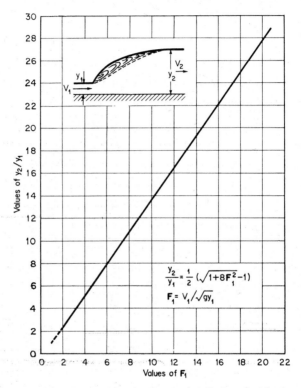

FIG. 15-1. Relation between $F_1$ and $y_2/y_1$ for a hydraulic jump in a horizontal rectangular channel.

special flow conditions, such as the existence of supercritical flow or the presence of a control section so that a gaging station may be located; (6) to mix chemicals used for water purification, and so forth [28]; (7) to aerate water for city water supplies; and (8) to remove air pockets from water-supply lines and thus prevent air locking [29].

[1] This principle has been applied by Saugey [27] to an interesting device known as *fall increaser*. The device is intended to increase the effective head in a water-power plant during periods of flood by holding back tailwater from the outlet of the draft tube by a hydraulic jump.

**15-2. Jump in Horizontal Rectangular Channels.**[1] For supercritical flow in a horizontal rectangular channel, the energy of flow is dissipated through frictional resistance along the channel, resulting in a decrease in velocity and an increase in depth in the direction of flow. A hydraulic jump will form in the channel if the Froude number $F_1$ of the flow, the flow depth $y_1$, and a downstream depth $y_2$ satisfy the equation

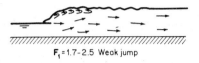

$F_1 = 1-1.7$ Undular jump

$$\frac{y_2}{y_1} = \frac{1}{2}(\sqrt{1 + 8F_1^2} - 1) \qquad (3\text{-}21)$$

This equation may be represented by the curve in Fig. 15-1. This curve has been verified satisfactorily with many experimental data and will be found very useful in the analysis and design for hydraulic jumps.

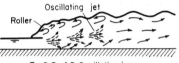

$F_1 = 1.7-2.5$ Weak jump

**15-3. Types of Jump.** Hydraulic jumps on horizontal floor are of several distinct types. According to the studies of the U.S. Bureau of Reclamation [34,35], these types can be conveniently classified according to the Froude number $F_1$ of the incoming flow (Fig. 15-2), as follows:

$F_1 = 2.5-4.5$ Oscillating jump

For $F_1 = 1$, the flow is critical, and hence no jump can form.

For $F_1 = 1$ to 1.7, the water surface shows undulations, and the jump is called an *undular jump*.

For $F_1 = 1.7$ to 2.5, a series of small rollers develop on the surface of the jump, but the downstream water surface remains smooth. The velocity throughout is fairly uniform, and the

$F_1 = 4.5-9.0$ Steady jump

$F_1 > 9.0$ Strong jump

FIG. 15-2. Various types of hydraulic jump.

energy loss is low. This jump may be called a *weak jump*.

For $F_1 = 2.5$ to 4.5, there is an oscillating jet entering the jump bottom to surface and back again with no periodicity. Each oscillation produces

[1] For hydraulic jumps in trapezoidal channels, see [30] and [31]. For jumps in closed conduits, see [29] and [32]. For a general treatment of nonrectangular channels, see [33].

a large wave of irregular period which, very commonly in canals, can travel for miles doing unlimited damage to earth banks and ripraps. This jump may be called an *oscillating jump*.

For $F_1 = 4.5$ to 9.0, the downstream extremity of the surface roller and the point at which the high-velocity jet tends to leave the flow occur at practically the same vertical section. The action and position of this jump are least sensitive to variation in tailwater depth. The jump is well-balanced and the performance is at its best. The energy dissipation ranges from 45 to 70%. This jump may be called a *steady jump*.

For $F_1 = 9.0$ and larger, the high-velocity jet grabs intermittent slugs of water rolling down the front face of the jump, generating waves downstream, and a rough surface can prevail. The jump action is rough but effective since the energy dissipation may reach 85%. This jump may be called a *strong jump*.

It should be noted that the ranges of the Froude number given above for the various types of jump are not clear-cut but overlap to a certain extent depending on local conditions.

**15-4. Basic Characteristics of the Jump.** Several basic characteristics of the hydraulic jump in horizontal rectangular channels are to be discussed below:

*Energy Loss.* The loss of energy in the jump is equal to the difference in specific energies before and after the jump. It can be shown that the loss is

$$\Delta E = E_1 - E_2 = \frac{(y_2 - y_1)^3}{4y_1y_2} \tag{3-24}$$

The ratio $\Delta E/E_1$ is known as the *relative loss*.

*Efficiency.* The ratio of the specific energy after the jump to that before the jump is defined as the *efficiency of the jump*. It can be shown that the efficiency is

$$\frac{E_2}{E_1} = \frac{(8F_1^2 + 1)^{3/2} - 4F_1^2 + 1}{8F_1^2(2 + F_1^2)} \tag{15-1}$$

This equation indicates that the efficiency of a jump is a dimensionless function, depending only on the Froude number of the approaching flow. The relative loss is equal to $1 - E_2/E_1$; this also is a dimensionless function of $F_1$.

*Height of Jump.* The difference between the depths after and before the jump is the *height of the jump*, or $h_j = y_2 - y_1$. Expressing each term as a ratio with respect to the initial specific energy,

$$\frac{h_j}{E_1} = \frac{y_2}{E_1} - \frac{y_1}{E_1}$$

where $h_j/E_1$ is the *relative height*, $y_1/E_1$ is the *relative initial depth*, and

$y_2/E_1$ is the *relative sequent depth*. All these ratios can be shown to be dimensionless functions of $\mathbf{F}_1$. For example,

$$\frac{h_j}{E_1} = \frac{\sqrt{1 + 8\mathbf{F}_1^2} - 3}{\mathbf{F}_1^2 + 2} \tag{15-2}$$

Since the relative loss, efficiency, relative height, and relative initial and sequent depths of a hydraulic jump in a horizontal rectangular channel are functions of $\mathbf{F}_1$, they can be plotted against $\mathbf{F}_1$, resulting in a

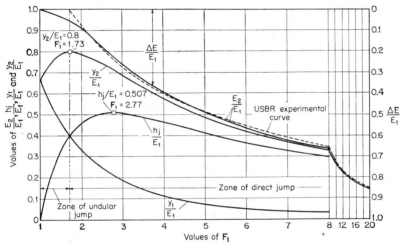

Fig. 15-3. Characteristic curves of hydraulic jumps in horizontal rectangular channels.

set of characteristic curves (Fig. 15-3). With reference to these curves, the following interesting features may be noted:

1. The maximum relative height $h_j/E_1$ is 0.507, which occurs at $\mathbf{F}_1 = 2.77$.

2. The maximum relative depth $y_2/E_1$ is 0.8, which occurs at $y_1/E_1 = 0.4$ and $\mathbf{F}_1 = 1.73$. Experiments have shown that the transition from an undular jump to a direct jump takes place approximately at this point $\mathbf{F}_1 = 1.73$.

3. When $\mathbf{F}_1 = 1$, the flow is critical and $y_1 = y_2 = \frac{2}{3}E_1$.

4. When $\mathbf{F}_1$ increases, the changes in all characteristic ratios become gradual.

The characteristic curves will provide the designer with a general idea about the range of conditions under which the structure is to be operated. For instance, in the design of a sluice gate involving a jump below the gate, such curves will show clearly the formation of the jump for different gate openings under a given head. The above discussion applies to horizontal rectangular channels. For horizontal nonrectangular channels, similar curves may also be prepared.

The theoretical curves for $y_2/E_1$ and $h_j/E_1$ have been verified experimentally by Bakhmeteff and Matzke [17], who found that these curves give values of $y_2/E_1$ and $h_j/E_1$ about 3 to 4% greater than the experimental values.[1] The characteristic curves were also checked with U.S.

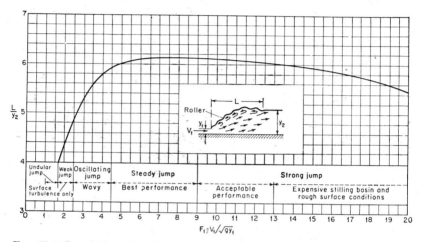

FIG. 15-4. Length in terms of sequent depth $y_2$ of jumps in horizontal channels. (*Based on data and recommendations of U.S. Bureau of Reclamation* [34].)

Bureau of Reclamation data [34,35] obtained from six test flumes. Perfect agreement was found between the $y_1/E_1$ curve and the data. The agreement between the $E_2/E_1$ or $\Delta E/E_1$ curve and the data was fairly good except for $\mathbf{F}_1 < 2$. The experimental curve for $\Delta E/E_1$ recommended by the Bureau is shown by the dashed line (Fig. 15-3). The agreement between the $y_2/E_1$ and $h_j/E_1$ curves and the data was good for high $\mathbf{F}_1$ values, but the scattered data failed to define the curves accurately for $\mathbf{F}_1 < 3$.

**15-5. Length of Jump.** The *length of a jump* may be defined as the distance measured from the front face of the jump to a point on the surface immediately downstream from the roller. This length cannot be determined easily by theory, but it has been investigated experimentally by many hydraulicians.[2]

---

[1] It is possible that at least part of this discrepancy is due to the scale effect of the testing model (see next article).

[2] Among them Safranez at the Technical University of Berlin [36,37], Wóycicki at the Federal Institute of Technology in Zürich, Switzerland [38], Aravin in Russia [39], Bakhmeteff and Matzke at Columbia University [17], Moore at the California Institute of Technology [40], and the engineers of the U.S. Bureau of Reclamation [34,35].

The experimental data on length of jump can be plotted conveniently with the Froude number $F_1$ against a dimensionless ratio $L/(y_2 - y_1)$, $L/y_1$, or $L/y_2$. The plot of $F_1$ vs. $L/y_1$ is probably the best, for the resulting curve can be best defined by the data. For practical purposes, however, the plot of $F_1$ vs. $L/y_2$ is desirable, because the resulting curve shows regularity or a fairly flat portion for the range of well-established jumps. A curve of $F_1$ vs. $L/y_2$ (Fig. 15-4) based on the experimental data of six test flumes has been prepared by the Bureau of Reclamation. In comparing this curve with the well-known Bakhmeteff-Matzke curve [17], pronounced disagreement was found. Investigation of the matter has led to the belief that this disagreement is due to the scale effect involved in Bakhmeteff and Matzke's experimental data. This scale effect means that the prototype action was not faithfully reproduced in the model. The curve shown in Fig. 15-4 was developed primarily for jumps occurring in rectangular channels. In the absence of adequate data, this curve may also be applied approximately to jumps formed in trapezoidal channels.

**15-6. The Surface Profile.** Knowledge of the surface profile of a jump is desirable in designing the freeboard for the retaining walls of the stilling basin where the jump takes place. It is important also for determining the pressure for use in structural design, because experiments have shown that the vertical pressure on the horizontal floor under a hydraulic jump is practically the same as would be indicated by the water-surface profile.

On the basis of their experimental data, Bakhmeteff and Matzke [17] have found that the surface profile of a hydraulic jump can be represented by dimensionless curves for various $F_1$ values, as shown in Fig. 15-5. Moore [40] has developed similar curves for jumps below a free overfall. The profiles shown by Moore rise more rapidly at the beginning than do Bakhmeteff and Matzke's profiles. It is believed that this is because the nonhydrostatic-pressure distribution in the jump was not registered properly by the piezometric measurements for Bakhmeteff and Matzke's data. Furthermore, Moore's length of jump was about 20% longer than that shown by the Bakhmeteff-Matzke curves. Since the jump in the latter case was formed downstream from a regulating sluice, lack of agreement may be caused by a difference in the velocity profile of the shooting flow entering the jump.

**15-7. Location of Jump.** Hydraulic jump occurs in a supercritical flow when the depth changes abruptly to its sequent depth. Theoretically speaking, the jump will occur in a horizontal rectangular channel if the initial and sequent depths and the approaching Froude number satisfy Eq. (3-21). This theoretical condition is generally used to locate the position of a jump. For a closer estimate of the jump position, however, the length of the jump should be considered. The following will illustrate the location of a hydraulic jump in three typical cases (Fig. 15-6):

*Case A* shows the jump below a regulating sluice in a mild channel. The profiles $AB$ and $CD$ can easily be identified as of $M3$ and $M2$ type, respectively. The methods of computing these profiles are discussed in Chap. 10. The curve $A'B$ is a plot of the depth sequent to $AB$. By

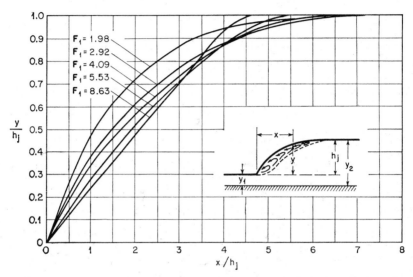

Fig. 15-5. Dimensionless surface profiles of hydraulic jumps in horizontal channels. (*Based on Bakhmeteff-Matzke data* [17].)

the position of $F'$, the length of the jump can be estimated. By trial and error, a horizontal intercept between the curves $A'B$ and $CD$ can be found equal to the length of jump. For instance, the horizontal distance $EF$ is equal to the length of the jump corresponding to the depth $y_2$ at $F$. It becomes apparent that the jump will form between $G$ and $F$, since the depth at $F$ is sequent to the depth at $G$ and the distance $EF$ measures the length of the jump. It may be noted that, if the length of the jump were not taken into account in the analysis, the jump would have been considered to form at the upstream point $F'$, resulting in an error represented by $F'F$. In case A, it can be seen that, by increasing the downstream water depth or raising the curve $CD$, the jump can be moved upstream. The downstream depth may be raised to such a height that the jump will eventually be drowned out in front of the sluice. Decreasing the downstream depth or lowering $CD$ will move the jump downstream.

The above discussion applies also to the location of a jump formed at the foot of a weir or overflow spillway.

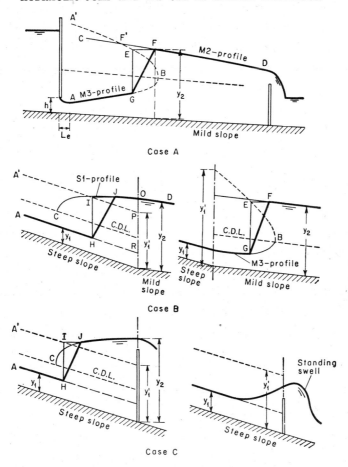

FIG. 15-6. Location of a hydraulic jump.

When there is a hydraulic jump below a sluice, the issuing flow from the sluice will form a jet that possesses a vena contracta. The distance $L_e$ from the vena contracta to the sluice opening is usually short. Regarding this distance, there is a generally adopted rule which states that the vena contracta is located approximately at a distance $h$ from the sluice opening.[1]

---

[1] This rule was first used by Agroskin [41]. It is based on the assumptions that flow from a sluice corresponds to one-half the flow from a circular orifice and that the vena contracta in the flow from a circular orifice is located approximately at a distance of half an orifice diameter from the orifice. The rule of half orifice diameter was originated by Weisbach [42].

*Case B* shows the jump in a channel having a break in the bottom slope that changes from steep to mild. For simplicity, it is assumed that the flow is uniform in the channel except in the reach between the jump and the break. The jump may occur in either the steep channel or the mild channel, depending on whether the downstream depth $y_2$ is greater or less than the depth $y_1'$ sequent to the upstream depth $y_1$. If the depth $y_2$ is greater than $y_1'$, the jump will occur in the steep region. Then the surface curve $OC$ is of $S1$ type. The line $A'P$ indicates the depth sequent to the line $AR$. Now, determine a horizontal intercept $IJ$ between $A'P$ and $CO$ that is equal to the length of a jump. It is apparent that a jump $HJ$ will begin at the section containing $I$. If the depth $y_2$ is lowered approximately to less than $y_1'$, the jump will start to move into the mild channel. In this case, the jump can be located as described in case A.

*Case C* shows the jump behind an overflow barrier. Theoretically, a jump will form if the depth at the barrier is greater than the depth $y_1'$ sequent to the approaching supercritical depth $y_1$. The location of the jump is the same as that for case B if the jump occurs in the steep region. Increasing the height of the barrier will move the jump upstream. Decreasing the height will move the jump downstream. When the depth at the barrier is less than the sequent depth $y_1'$, the barrier will be crossed by a *standing swell* in the form of a single undular surface rise which will not be followed by further undulations.

**Example 15-1.** Locate the hydraulic jump in Example 10-3 if the flow downstream from the jump is uniform.

*Solution.* From the given data, the specific-energy curve $E = y + \alpha V^2/2g$ and the specific-force curve $F = \beta Q^2/gA + \bar{z}A$ of the channel may be constructed as shown in Fig. 15-7. In computing the specific-force curve, the value of $\beta$ may be estimated as 1.04 for $\alpha = 1.10$ [using Eqs. (2-6) and (2-7)].

Below the sluice, the $M3$ profile has been computed in Example 10-3, as shown by $AGB$ in Fig. 15-8. Using the curves in Fig. 15-7 and following the method described in Art. 3-7, the curve of sequent depth $A'F'B$ corresponding to the curve of initial depth $AGB$ can be determined.[1] The curve $A'F'B$ and the downstream flow profile $CFD$ (equal to the normal-depth line in this example) intersect at $F'$. The initial depth of flow at $F'$ is then found from the $M3$ profile to be 1.70 ft. The corresponding $F = 1.52$ and. from Fig. 15-4, $L/y_2 = 3.6$. The length of the jump is therefore equal to $L = 3.6 \times 2.67 = 9.6$ ft. At this point there is an approximation involved, because the length of jump should be based on $F$ at $E$ (instead of $F'$), which, however, is as yet unknown.

In this example $y_2$ is equal to the normal depth of flow in the channel since the flow downstream is uniform. If the flow downstream is not uniform but gradually varied, then the depth at the intersection $F'$ of the downstream profile with the curve $A'F'B$ should be taken as $y_2$. This is also an approximation, because the actual depth $y_2$ should be at $F$, the position of which is as yet unknown.

---

[1] Owing to the difference between $\alpha$ and $\beta$, the computed critical depths indicated by the specific-energy and specific-force curves are not precisely identical. However, the discrepancy is so small that it can be ignored.

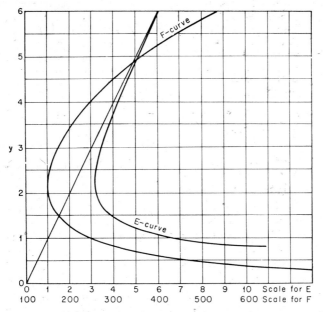

FIG. 15-7. The $E$ curve and $F$ curve for the determination of jump location.

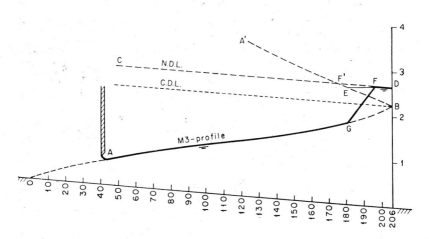

FIG. 15-8. Location of a hydraulic jump.

After the length of jump is determined, a horizontal intercept $EF$ equal to 9.6 ft is found between the curve $A'F'B$ and $CF'D$. The hydraulic jump will, therefore, occur between $G$ and $F$. As shown in Fig. 15-8, the jump appears to start at a distance of about 140 ft from the vena contracta. Since the location of the jump is determined, the approximations mentioned above can be checked, and more exact determination can be made by repeating the procedure if desired. Such verification seems unnecessary, however, on account of the approximations involved in the theory and other aspects of the problem.

**15-8. Jump as Energy Dissipator.** From a practical viewpoint, hydraulic jump is a useful means of dissipating excess energy in supercritical flow. Its merit is in preventing possible erosion below overflow spillways, chutes, and sluices, for it quickly reduces the velocity of the flow on a paved apron to a point where the flow becomes incapable of scouring the downstream channel bed.

The hydraulic jump used for energy dissipation is usually confined partly or entirely to a channel reach that is known as the *stilling basin*. The bottom of the basin is paved to resist scouring. In practice, the stilling basin is seldom designed to confine the entire length of a free hydraulic jump on the paved apron, because such a basin would be too expensive. Consequently, accessories to control the jump are usually installed in the basin. The main purpose of such control is to shorten the range within which the jump will take place and thus to reduce the size and cost of the stilling basin. The control has additional advantages, for it improves the dissipation function of the basin, stabilizes the jump action, and in some cases increases the factor of safety. In designing a stilling basin using hydraulic jump as energy dissipator, the following practical features should be considered.[1]

*A. Jump Position.* There are three alternative patterns (Fig. 15-9) that allow a hydraulic jump to form downstream from the source (such source as an overflow spillway, a chute, or a sluice):

Case 1 represents the pattern in which the tailwater depth $y_2'$ is equal to the depth $y_2$ sequent to $y_1$. In this case, the values of $\mathbf{F}_1$, $y_1$, and $y_2'$ ($= y_2$) will satisfy Eq. (3-21), and the jump will occur on a solid apron immediately ahead of the depth $y_1$. For scour-protection purposes, this is an ideal case. One big objection to this pattern, however, is that a little difference between the actual and assumed values of the relevant hydraulic coefficients may cause the jump to move downstream from its estimated position. Consequently, some device to control the position of the jump is always necessary.

Case 2 represents the pattern in which the tailwater depth $y_2'$ is less

---

[1] For simplicity, the length of the hydraulic jump will not be considered in the present discussion. See [25], [34], [35], [43], and "Hydraulic Energy Dissipators," by E. A. Elevatorski, McGraw-Hill Book Company, Inc., New York, 1959, for further information on the design of stilling basins.

than $y_2$.  This means that the tailwater depth in case 1 is decreased.
As a result, the jump will recede downstream to a point where Eq. (3-21)
is again satisfied.  This case must, if possible, be avoided in design,
because the jump, repelled from the scour-resisting apron, will take place
either on the loose rubble bed or, still worse, in entirely unprotected

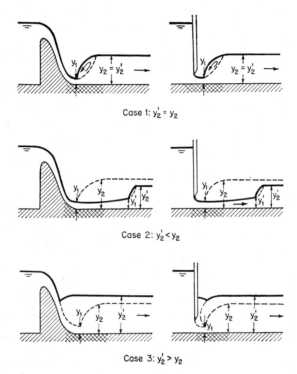

Case 1: $y_2' = y_2$

Case 2: $y_2' < y_2$

Case 3: $y_2' > y_2$

FIG. 15-9. Effect of tailwater depth on the formation of a hydraulic jump below a weir
or sluice.

channel, resulting in severe erosion.   The remedy for the design is to use
a certain control in the channel bottom, which will increase the tailwater
depth and thus ensure a jump within the protected apron.

Case 3 represents the pattern in which the tailwater depth $y_2'$ is greater
than $y_2$.  This means that the tailwater depth in case 1 is increased.  As
a result, the jump will be forced upstream and may finally be drowned out
at the source, becoming a submerged jump.   This is possibly the safest
case in design, because the position of the submerged jump can be most
readily fixed.   Unfortunately, the design is not efficient, for little energy
will be dissipated.

B. *Tailwater Conditions.* In the above discussion it is assumed that the tailwater has a certain fixed position, whether its depth $y_2'$ is equal to, less than, or greater than the sequent depth $y_2$. In most practical problems, however, the tailwater fluctuates, owing to changes in discharge of flow in the channel. In such cases, a tailwater rating curve is usually available to show the relation between the tailwater stage $y_2'$ and the discharge $Q$. In a similar way, a jump rating curve may be constructed

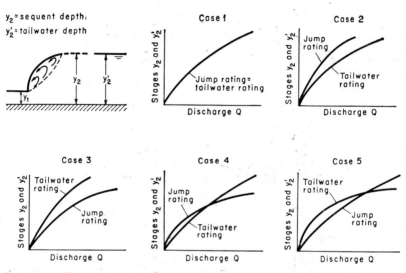

FIG. 15-10. Classification of tailwater conditions for the design of scour-protection works.

to show the relation between the sequent depth $y_2$ and the discharge $Q$. Because of the difference in the relative positions of the two rating curves, Leliavsky [43] has suggested that the design may be considered according to five different classes of conditions (shown respectively by five cases in Fig. 15-10):

Class 1 represents all ideal conditions in which the two rating curves always coincide. This means that case 1 in Fig. 15-9 exists at all times and that a jump will form at the desired place on a protective apron at all discharges. Conditions of this class are rarely encountered naturally.

Class 2 represents the conditions in which the jump rating curve is always at a higher stage than the tailwater rating curve. This means that case 2 in Fig. 15-9 exists at all times (i.e., the tailwater depth is lower than the jump sequent depth) and that the jump will form at a certain place far downstream. An effective method of ensuring that the jump will occur on the protected apron is to use sills to create a stilling basin (Art. 15-9).

Class 3 represents the conditions in which the jump rating curve is always at a lower stage than the tailwater rating curve. This means that case 3 in Fig. 15-9 occurs at all times (i.e., the tailwater is higher than the sequent depth) and that the jump will move upstream and will probably be drowned out at the source. Consequently, little energy will be dissipated. An effective method to ensure a jump is to build a sloping apron above the channel-bed level (Art. 15-16). The slope of the apron can be such that proper conditions for a jump will be developed on the apron at all discharges. Another method is to provide a drop in the channel floor and thus to lower the tailwater depth (Art. 15-10).

Class 4 represents the conditions in which the jump rating curve is at a higher stage than the tailwater rating curve at low discharges but at a lower stage at high discharges. An effective method to ensure a jump is to provide a stilling basin for forming a jump at low discharges and to combine with the basin a sloping apron for developing a satisfactory jump at high discharges.

Class 5 represents the conditions in which the jump rating curve is at a lower stage than the tailwater rating curve at low discharges but at a higher stage at high discharges. An effective method to ensure a jump is to increase the tailwater depth sufficiently high by providing a stilling pool, thus forming a jump at high discharges.

*C. Jump Types.* In view of the various types of hydraulic jump described in Art. 15-3, the U.S. Bureau of Reclamation [34,35] gives the following practical considerations:

1. All types of jump are encountered in the design of stilling basins.

2. The weak jump requires no baffles or special consideration. The only requirement necessary is to provide the proper length of a pool, which is relatively short. This can be determined from Fig. 15-4.

3. The oscillating jump, frequently encountered in the design of canal structures, diversion dams, and even outlet works, is difficult to handle. If possible, jumps in the 2.5-to-4.5 Froude-number range should be avoided. In many cases use of this jump cannot be avoided but, in other cases, altering of dimensions may bring the jump into the desirable range. Baffle blocks or appurtenances are of little value. Waves are the main source of difficulty; hence specially designed wave suppressors may be used to cope with them.

4. No particular difficulty is encountered in steady jumps. Arrangements of baffles and sills to be discussed later will be found valuable as a means of shortening the length of the stilling basin.

5. As the Froude number increases, the jump becomes more sensitive to tailwater depth. For Froude numbers as low as 8, a tailwater depth

greater than the sequent depth is advisable to make certain that the jump will stay on the apron.

6. When the Froude number is greater than 10, a stilling basin using the jump as a dissipator may no longer be the most economical dissipation device. In this case, the difference between the initial and sequent depths is great, and, generally speaking, a very deep basin with high retaining wall is required. The cost of the stilling basin may not be commensurate with the results obtained. A bucket type of dissipator[1] may give comparable results at lower cost.

**15-9. Control of Jump by Sills.** The hydraulic jump can be controlled or effected by sills of various designs, such as sharp-crested weir, broad-crested weir, and abrupt rise and drop in channel floor. The function of the sill is to ensure the formation of a jump and to control its position under all probable operating conditions.

Interesting experiments [46] have shown that the forces acting on the sill in a jump decrease rapidly to a minimum as the downstream end of the jump is moved upstream to a position approximately over the sill. The force then increases slowly to a constant value as the jump is moved farther upstream. This change in force on the sill is probably due to a change in the velocity distribution from one end of the jump to the other, since nonuniform distribution of velocity is a characteristic of such rapidly varied flow. As a result, the momentum in the nonuniform-distribution section is greatly increased. Theoretically speaking, the control of hydraulic jump by sills can be analyzed by the momentum theory. Because of lack of accurate knowledge of the velocity distribution, however, the theoretical analysis cannot predict the quantitative result very closely. For useful design information one has to rely upon experimental studies.

Dimensional analysis shows that the relations between the Froude number $F_1$ or $F$ of the approaching flow, the height $h$ of the sill, the approaching depth $y_1$, the depth $y_2$ upstream from the sill, the distance $X$ from the toe of the jump to the sill, and the downstream depth $y_3$ may be expressed as

$$\frac{h}{y_1} = \phi\left(F, \frac{X}{y_2}, \frac{y_3}{y_1}\right) \qquad (15\text{-}3)$$

This function can be determined quantitatively by model studies. The

---

[1] This is an upturned bucket provided at the toe of a spillway to deflect the overflow up through the tailwater. If the tailwater is high enough to submerge the bucket, a roller will form downstream from the bucket and tend to move bed materials toward the dam, thus preventing serious scour at the toe of the dam. On the other hand, if the tailwater is low, the overflow will be thrown up and out so that it will strike a solid-rock channel, if any, at a safe distance below the dam. See [44], [45], and Arts. 14-10 and 14-11.

exact position of the jump, as controlled by the sill, however, cannot be determined analytically. In the model study, this position can be represented by the ratio between $X$ and $y_2$. The ratio is taken as constant in each test, having a magnitude sufficient to ensure a complete jump. In the design, the length of a stilling basin should be made at least equal to $X$. For economic reasons, however, the length of the basin

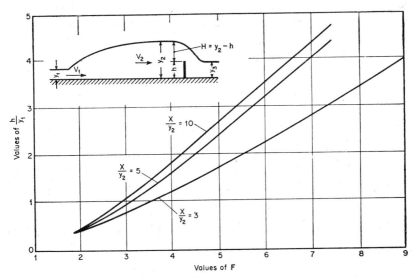

Fig. 15-11. Experimental relations among $\mathbf{F}$, $h/y_1$, and $X/y_2$ for a sharp-crested weir. (*After Forster and Skrinde* [23].)

may be designed for less than $X$, provided that the high bottom velocities at the end of the basin have reached a value considered safe for the downstream channel condition.

*A. Control by Sharp-crested Weir.* On the basis of experimental data and theoretical analysis, Forster and Skrinde [23] have developed a diagram (Fig. 15-11) showing the relations among (1) Froude number $\mathbf{F}$ of the approaching flow, (2) the ratio between the weir height $h$ and the approaching depth $y_1$, and (3) the ratio between the distance $X$ from the toe of the jump to the weir and the depth $y_2$ upstream from the weir. This diagram permits an analysis of the effect of a given weir for known approach and tailwater conditions, provided that the normal tailwater depth $y_3$ does not affect the discharge over the weir crest;[1] that is, provided $y_3 < y_2 - 0.75h$. Ordinarily, unsubmerged conditions prevail over

[1] This condition was first observed by Bazin (see reference [12] of Chap. 14) and later demonstrated theoretically by Bakhmeteff [27].

a wide range of discharge. Thus, $y_3/y_1$ in Eq. (15-3) can be dropped. If submergence occurs, the jump is forced upstream with possible drowning as a result.

In the diagram, any point is represented by a pair of coordinates $(\mathbf{F}, h/y_1)$. If the point lies within the curves, hydraulic jump will occur, with its relative position indicated by the corresponding interpolated value of $X/y_2$. Points lying above and to the left of an interpolated curve represent the conditions under which the weir is too high, so that the jump will be forced upstream and possibly drowned at the source. Points lying to the right of the curve represent the conditions under which the weir is too low, so that the jump will be forced downstream and possibly washed out. When the weir is as low as this, it may be crossed only by a single undular surface rise, forming a standing swell (Fig. 15-6).

For design purposes, it is proposed that the curve $X/y_2 = 5$ in the diagram be used. Laboratory experience has shown that the highest required weir does not necessarily occur under conditions of maximum discharge [20]. Consequently, the highest required weir should have the largest required value of $h$ within the expected range of discharge as determined from the diagram.

*B. Control by Broad-crested Weir.* For a broad-crested weir, if the downstream depth is lower than the critical depth on top of the weir, that is, if $y_3 < (2y_2 + h)/3$, the tailwater will not affect appreciably the relation between the head water elevation and the discharge. Thus, the discharge over a unit width of the weir can be written[1]

$$q = 0.433 \sqrt{2g} \left( \frac{y_2}{y_2 + h} \right)^{\frac{1}{2}} H^{\frac{3}{2}} \qquad (15\text{-}4)$$

Since $q = V_1 y_1$, $H = y_2 - h$, and $\mathbf{F} = V_1/\sqrt{gy_1}$, the above equation can be reduced to

$$2.667\mathbf{F}^2 \left( 1 + \frac{h/y_1}{y_2/y_1} \right) = (y_2/y_1 - h/y_1)^3 \qquad (15\text{-}5)$$

When a hydraulic jump is effected by the weir, $y_2/y_1$ can be related to $\mathbf{F}$ through Eq. (3-21). Then, Eq. (15-5) becomes

$$\frac{21.33\mathbf{F}^2}{\sqrt{1 - 8\mathbf{F}^2} - 1} = \frac{(\sqrt{1 + 8\mathbf{F}^2} - 1 - 2h/y_1)^3}{(\sqrt{1 + 8\mathbf{F}^2} - 1 + 2h/y_1)} \qquad (15\text{-}6)$$

This equation gives the relation between $h/y_1$ and $\mathbf{F}$ and can be plotted as the curve shown in Fig. 15-12. Forster and Skrinde [23] have found that this curve coincides with the experimental data for an abrupt rise with $y_3 = y_c$ for $X = 5(h + y_3)$. Despite the lack of further experi-

---

[1] This is Eq. (3-17) except that $y_1$ is replaced by $y_2$.

mental data, this curve may be used as a guide in proportioning a stilling basin using broad-crested weir as jump control, provided $y_3 < (2y_2 + h)/3$.

A broad-crested weir has certain advantages in comparison with some other types of control. It has greater structural stability than a sharp-crested weir and usually requires lower cost of excavation than an abrupt rise.

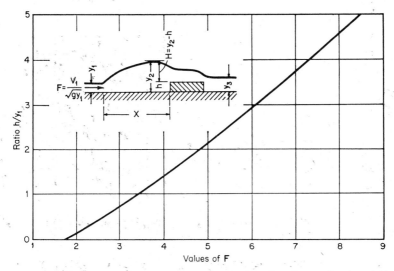

Fig. 15-12. Analytical relations between $F$ and $h/y_1$ for a broad-crested weir. (*After Forster and Skrinde* [23].)

C. *Control by Abrupt Rise.* From the experimental data, Forster and Skrinde [23] have developed a diagram (Fig. 15-13) showing the relations among $F$, $y_3/y_1$, and $h/y_1$ of an abrupt rise for $X = 5(h + y_3)$. The consistency of the relations was verified by a theoretical analysis, using the momentum theory, similar to that made for a broad-crested weir (Example 3-2). This diagram permits the prediction of the performance of a given abrupt rise when $V_1$, $y_1$, $y_2$, $y_3$, and $h$ are known.

In the diagram, a point $(F, y_3/y_1)$ lying above the line $y_3 = y_2$ represents the condition of $y_3 > y_2$ in which the abrupt rise would serve only to increase the drowning effect. For a point lying within the experimental range between the lines for $y_3 = y_2$ and $y_3 = y_c$, the position of the point relative to the corresponding $h/y_1$ curve indicates the effect of the abrupt rise on the flow pattern. Thus, if the point lies on the corresponding $h/y_1$ curve, a jump will form with $X = 5(h + y_3)$. If the point lies on the left and above the curve, the rise is too high, and the jump will be forced upstream and may finally be drowned. If the point is at the right of the curve, the rise is too low, and the jump will be forced downstream toward the abrupt rise and may finally be washed out.

If a point $(\mathbf{F}, y_3/y_1)$ lies in the diagram below the line $y_3 = y_c$, then the normal downstream flow is supercritical. A jump is followed by a critical section created over the crest of the abrupt rise, so that the rise acts as a weir, and the design diagram (Fig. 15-11) for the sharp-crested weir may be used.

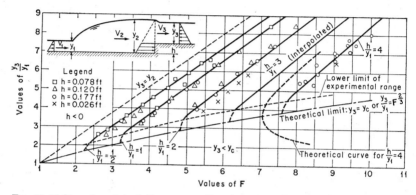

FIG. 15-13. Experimental relations among $\mathbf{F}$, $y_3/y_1$, and $h/y_1$ for an abrupt rise. (*After Forster and Skrinde* [23].)

For design purposes, the diagram (Fig. 15-13) can be used to determine the necessary length and depth of stilling basin when $V_1$, $y_1$, and $y_3$ are known. It is proposed that a point $(\mathbf{F}, y_3/y_1)$ be first defined for conditions at or near maximum discharge and that the corresponding value of $h/y_1$ be determined by interpolation. By repeating this procedure for other discharges within the expected range of discharge, a largest required value of $h$ can be obtained. This value should be used for the highest required rise. A minimum height of rise necessary to prevent the jump from being washed out can also be thus determined.

**15-10. Control of Jump by Abrupt Drop.** The control of hydraulic jump by sills is useful if the downstream depth is smaller than the sequent depth for a normal jump. If the downstream depth is larger than the sequent depth for a normal jump, a drop in the channel floor must be used in order to ensure a jump. This condition occurs generally at the end of the expansion of a supercritical flow.

For a given approaching Froude number, the downstream depth of a drop may fall in any of the five regions as shown in Fig. 15-14a. The lower limit of region 1 is the depth at which the jump will begin to travel upstream. The upper limit of region 5 is the depth at which the jump

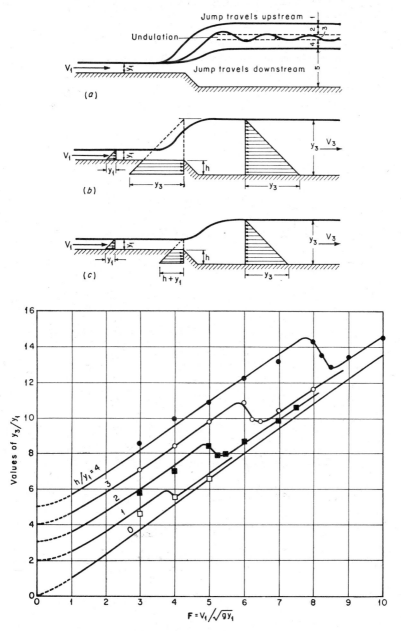

Fig. 15-14. Experimental and analytical relations among $\mathbf{F}$, $y_3/y_1$, and $h/y_1$ for an abrupt drop. (*After E. Y. Hsu* [47].)

will begin to travel downstream. Evidently, the drop does not control the jump in these two regions. The jump is stable and the drop is effective for its desired purpose only in regions 2 and 4. The intermediate region 3 represents an undular state of flow without a breaking front.

By applying the continuity and momentum equations in an analysis similar to that made for the broad-crested weir (Example 3-2), Hsu [47] has shown that, for region 2,

$$\mathbf{F}^2 = \tfrac{1}{2} \frac{y_3/y_1}{1 - y_3/y_1} \left[ 1 - \left( \frac{y_3}{y_1} - \frac{h}{y_1} \right)^2 \right] \qquad (15\text{-}7)$$

and, for region 4,

$$\mathbf{F}^2 = \tfrac{1}{2} \frac{y_3/y_1}{1 - y_3/y_1} \left[ \left( \frac{h}{y_1} + 1 \right)^2 - \left( \frac{y_3}{y_1} \right)^2 \right] \qquad (15\text{-}8)$$

These equations have been verified by experiments.[1] The relations among $\mathbf{F}$, $y_3/y_1$, and $h/y_1$ are shown in Fig. 15-14.

In Fig. 15-14, each curve for a given $h/y_1$ has two relatively straight limbs connected by a short straight portion near the middle. The left-side limb represents the condition corresponding to region 2 and the right-side limb represents the condition corresponding to region 4. This diagram may be used for design purposes to determine the relative height of drop required to stabilize a jump for any given combination of discharge, upstream depth, and downstream depth.

**15-11. Stilling Basins of Generalized Design.** In important works or works that involve a large number of stilling basins, generalized designs for the basins are often necessary for economy and to meet specific requirements. These designs can be developed through years of experience and observations on existing structures, or by model investigations, or from both. The basins thus designed are usually provided with special appurtenances, including chute blocks, sills, and baffle piers.

The chute blocks are used to form a serrated device at the entrance to the stilling basin. Their function is to furrow the incoming jet and lift a portion of it from the floor, producing a shorter length of jump than would be possible without them. These blocks also tend to stabilize the jump and thus to improve its performance.

The sill, either dentated[2] or solid, is usually provided at the end of the stilling basin. Its function is to reduce further the length of the jump and to control scour. For large basins that are designed for high incom-

---

[1] A simplified analysis and further experiments were also made later by Moore and Morgan [48].

[2] The dentated sill or serrated baffle is also known as the *Rehbock sill*, because it was first patented by Prof. Theodor Rehbock after it was developed from experiments made during 1924 to 1927 at the Technical University of Karlsruhe, Germany.

ing velocities, the sill is usually dentated to perform the additional function of diffusing the residual portion of the high-velocity jet that may reach the end of the basin.

Baffle piers are blocks placed in intermediate positions across the basin floor. Their function is to dissipate energy mostly by impact action. The baffle piers are very useful in small structures with low incoming velocities. They are unsuitable, however, where high velocities make cavitation possible. In certain circumstances, they must be designed to withstand impact from ice or floating debris.

There are many generalized designs of stilling basin that use a hydraulic jump as the means of energy dissipation.[1] Three typical designs will be described in the subsequent articles:

1. The SAF basin. This is recommended for use on small structures such as small spillways, outlet works, and small canal structures where $F_1 = 1.7$ to 17. The reduction in basin length achieved through the use of appurtenances designed for the basin is about 80% (70 to 90%).

2. The USBR basin II. This is recommended for use on large structures such as large spillways, large canal structures, etc., for $F_1 > 4.5$. The jump-and-basin length is reduced about 33% with the use of appurtenances.

3. The USBR basin IV. This is recommended for use with jumps of $F_1 = 2.5$ to 4.5, which usually occur on canal structures and diversion dams. This design reduces excessive waves created in imperfect jumps.

It should be noted that these designs are only typical examples and that caution should be used in applying them to stilling basins under entirely different design conditions.

The principle of the stilling basin applies also to the design of a *canal drop* (or *canal fall*), which is a structure built to secure the lowering of the water surface of a canal and the safe destruction of the energy so liberated. The canal drop is sometimes designed with a contracted width like the Parshall flume. Such a drop is known as a *flumed drop*, which can economically be built together with a crossing bridge and used as a meter or a regulator as well [50,60–63].

**15-12. The SAF Stilling Basin.** This basin (Fig. 15-15; SAF denotes "Saint Anthony Falls") was developed at the St. Anthony Falls Hydraulic Laboratory, University of Minnesota, for use on small drainage structures such as those built by the U.S. Soil Conservation Service. The design rules summarized by the investigator Blaisdell [22,64] are as follows:

1. The length $L_B$ of the stilling basin for Froude numbers between $F_1 = 1.7$ and $F_1 = 17$ is determined by $L_B = 4.5y_2/F_1^{0.76}$.

---

[1] For more information see [9], [25], [34], [35], [43], and [49] to [58]. For designs developed by the U.S. Army Corps of Engineers, see [59].

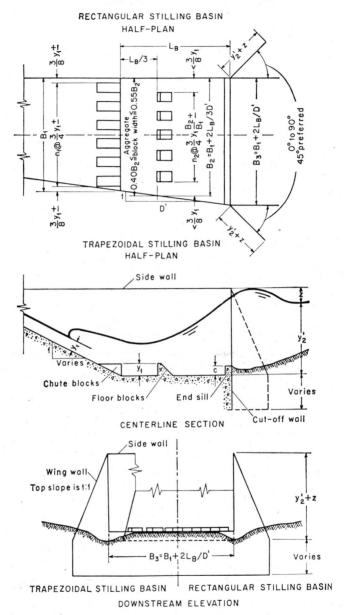

FIG. 15-15. Proportions of the SAF basin.    (*U.S. Soil Conservation Service* [64].)

2. The height of the chute blocks and floor blocks is $y_1$, and the width and spacing are approximately $0.75y_1$.

3. The distance from the upstream end of the stilling basin to the floor blocks is $L_B/3$.

4. No floor block should be placed closer to the side wall than $3y_1/8$.

5. The floor blocks should be placed downstream from the openings between the chute blocks.

6. The floor blocks should occupy between 40 and 55% of the stilling-basin width.

7. The widths and spacings of the floor blocks for diverging stilling basins should be increased in proportion to the increase in stilling-basin width at the floor-block location.

8. The height of end sill is given by $c = 0.07y_2$, where $y_2$ is the theoretical sequent depth corresponding to $y_1$.

9. The depth of tailwater above the stilling-basin floor is given by $y_2' = (1.10 - F_1{}^2/120)y_2$, for $F_1 = 1.7$ to 5.5; by $y_2' = 0.85y_2$, for $F_1 = 5.5$ to 11; and by $y_2' = (1.00 - F_1{}^2/800)y_2$, for $F_1 = 11$ to 17.

10. The height of the side wall above the maximum tailwater depth to be expected during the life of the structure is given by $z = y_2/3$.

11. Wing walls should be equal in height to the stilling-basin side walls. The top of the wing wall should have a slope of 1 on 1.

12. The wing wall should be placed at an angle of 45° to the outlet center line.

13. The stilling-basin side walls may be parallel (as in a rectangular stilling basin) or they may diverge as an extension of the transition side walls (as in a trapezoidal stilling basin).

14. A cutoff wall of nominal depth should be used at the end of the stilling basin.

15. The effect of entrained air should be neglected in the design of the stilling basin.

**15-13. USBR Stilling Basin II.** From intensive studies of many existing structures and laboratory investigations, various types of generalized design of stilling basin have been developed by the U.S. Bureau of Reclamation [34,35]. USBR basin I is the basin created by a jump occurring on a flat floor with no appurtenances. This can be designed easily by following the principles described in the early articles of this chapter. However, such a basin is usually not very practical because of its expensive length and its lack of control. USBR basin III is designed for a purpose similar to that of the SAF basin, but it has a higher factor of safety, which is necessary for Bureau use. The performance of this basin indicates that the jump-and-basin length can be reduced about 60% with the appurtenances, as compared with 80% for the SAF basin. Therefore, the SAF basin is shorter and more economical but, in conse-

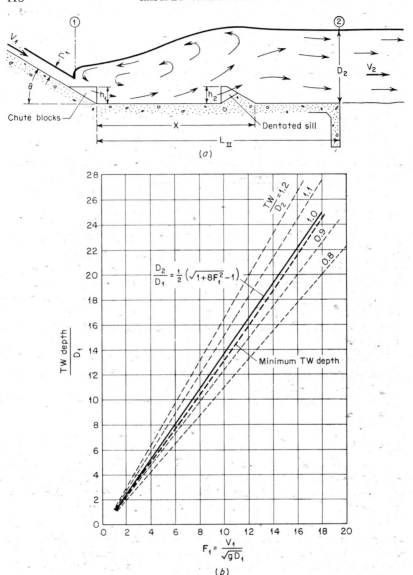

FIG. 15-16. Design curves and proportions of USBR basin II. (*U.S. Bureau of Reclamation* [34].) (*a*) Definition of symbols; (*b*) minimum tailwater depths; (*c*) length of hydraulic jump; (*d*) approximate water surface and pressure profiles (conjugate depth = sequent depth); (*e*) recommended proportions.

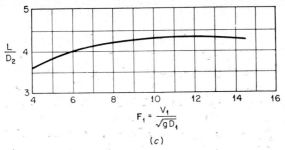

$$F_1 = \frac{V_1}{\sqrt{g D_1}}$$

(c)

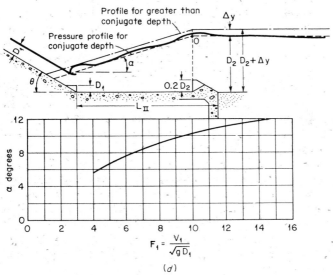

$$F_1 = \frac{V_1}{\sqrt{g D_1}}$$

(d)

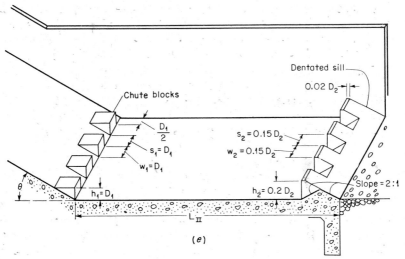

(e)

FIG. 15-16 (Continued).

quence, has a lower safety factor. USBR basin V is used where structural economies dictate the use of a sloping apron, usually on high-dam spillways. The principle of design for hydraulic jumps on sloping apron will be described in Art. 15-16. USBR basins II and IV will be described in this and the next articles, respectively.

USBR basin II was developed for stilling basins in common use for high-dam and earth-dam spillways and for large canal structures. The basin contains chute blocks at the upstream end and a dentated sill near the downstream end. No baffle piers are used because the relatively high velocities entering the jump might cause cavitation on piers. The detailed design and the data for computations are shown in Fig. 15-16. The rules recommended for the design are as follows:

1. Set apron elevation to utilize full sequent tailwater depth, plus an added factor of safety if needed. The dashed lines in Fig. 15-16b are guides drawn for various ratios of actual tailwater depth to sequent depth. Studies of existing designs indicate that most of the basins were designed for sequent tailwater depth or less. However, there is a limit, which is governed by the curve labeled "Minimum TW depth." This curve indicates the point at which the front of the jump moves away from the chute blocks. In other words, any additional lowering of the tailwater depth would cause the jump to leave the basin; that is, would produce a "sweep-out." For design purposes, the basin should not be designed for less than sequent depth. For additional safety, in fact, the Bureau recommends that a minimum safety margin of 5% of $D_2$ be added to the sequent depth.

2. Basin II may be effective down to a Froude number of 4, but the lower values should not be taken for granted. For lower values, designs considering wave suppression are recommended.

3. The length of basin can be obtained from the length-of-jump curve in Fig. 15-16c.

4. The height of chute blocks is equal to the depth $D_1$ of flow entering the basin. The width and spacing should be approximately equal to $D_1$; however, this may be varied to eliminate the need for fractional blocks. A space equal to $0.5D_1$ is preferable along each wall to reduce spray and maintain desirable pressures.

5. The height of the dentated sill is equal to $0.2D_2$, and the maximum width and spacing recommended is approximately $0.15D_2$. In this design a block is recommended adjacent to each side wall (Fig. 15-16e). The slope of the continuous portion of the end sill is 2:1. In the case of narrow basins, which would involve only a few dentates according to the above rule, it is advisable to reduce the width and the spacing, provided this is done proportionally. Reducing the width and spacing actually

improves the performance in narrow basins; thus, the minimum width and spacing of the dentates is governed only by structural considerations.

6. It is not necessary to stagger the chute blocks and the sill dentates. In fact this practice is usually inadvisable from a construction standpoint.

7. The verification tests on basin II indicated no perceptible change in the stilling-basin action with respect to the slope of the chute preceding the basin. The slope of chute varied from 0.6:1 to 2:1 in these tests. Actually, the slope of the chute does have an effect on the hydraulic jump in some cases.[1] It is recommended that the sharp intersection between chute and basin apron be replaced with a curve of reasonable radius ($R \geqq 4D_1$) when the slope of the chute is 1:1 or greater. Chute blocks can be incorporated on the curved face as readily as on the plane surfaces. On steep chutes the length of top surface on the chute blocks should be made sufficiently long to deflect the jet.

The above rules will result in a safe, conservative stilling basin for spillways with fall up to 200 ft and for flows up to 500 cfs per foot of basin width, provided the jet entering the basin is reasonably uniform both in velocity and in depth. For greater falls, larger unit discharges, or possible asymmetry, a model study of the specific design is recommended.

8. The approximate water-surface and pressure profiles of a jump in the basin are shown in Fig. 15-16d.

**Example 15-2.** Proportion a USBR stilling basin II for the overflow spillway designed in Example 14-1. The tailwater elevation is at El. 920.0.

*Solution.* Entering Fig. 14-15 with a head of 17.7 ft over the crest and a total fall of 120 ft, the velocity of flow at the toe of the spillway is 79 fps. Thus, the depth of flow is 75,000/(250 × 79) = 3.8 ft, and the Froude number is $79/\sqrt{3.8g} = 7.13$.

Entering Fig. 15-16b with $\mathbf{F}_1 = 7.13$, the solid line gives the ratio of TW depth to $D_1$ as 9.7. As TW depth and sequent tailwater depth $D_2$ are identical in this case, $D_2 = 9.7 \times 3.8 = 36.9$ ft. The minimum tailwater line for basin II on Fig. 15-16b shows that a margin of safety of about 4% can be expected for the above Froude number. The elevation of the basin floor is placed at El. 883.1. Thus, the total fall will be 116.9 ft, but this will not change the flow velocity appreciably.

Should it be desired to provide a margin of safety of 8%, the following procedure may be followed. Consulting Fig. 15-16b, the line for minimum TW depth for basin II gives TW depth/$D_1$ = 9.2 for $\mathbf{F}_1 = 7.13$. The tailwater depth at which sweep-out is incipient is $TW_{so} = 9.2 \times 3.8 = 35.0$ ft. Adding 8% to this figure, the stilling basin should be positioned again for a tailwater depth of 35.0 × 1.08 = 37.8 ft or $1.024D_2$. The basin floor will be placed at El. 882.2.

[1] The slope of the chute has little effect on the jump as long as the velocity distribution and depth of flow are reasonably uniform on entering the jump. If the chute is long and flat, the velocity may be concentrated in one part of the flow section, resulting in an asymmetrical jump with strong side eddies. The operation of such a jump is expensive and should be avoided in all stilling basins. Also, when the angle of divergence of the chute is too large for water to follow properly, the jump will become rough and uncertain of its position.

The length of basin can be obtained by entering the curve in Fig. 15-16c with $F_1 = 7.13$. Thus, $L/D_2 = 4.16$, or $L = L_{II} = 4.16 \times 36.9 = 154$ ft.

The heighⱨ, width, and spacing of the chute blocks as recommended are $D_1$; thus the dimension can be 3 ft 10 in. The height of the dentated sill is $0.2D_2$, or 7 ft 5 in., and the width and spacing of the dentates can be $0.15D_2$, or 5 ft 6 in.

**15-14. USBR Stilling Basin IV.** When $F_1 = 2.5$ to $4.5$, an oscillating jump will be produced in the stilling basin, generating a wave that is difficult to dampen (Art. 15-3). USBR basin IV (Fig. 15-17) is designed to combat this problem bⱼ eliminating the wave at its source.[1] This is

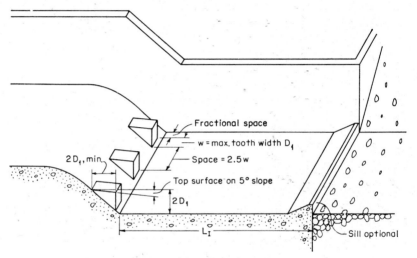

Fɪɢ. 15-17. Proportions of USBR basin IV. (*U.S. Bureau of Reclamation* [34].)

achieved by intensifying the roller, which appears in the upper portion of the jump (Fig. 15-2), with directional jets deflected from large chute blocks. The number of chute blocks shown in Fig. 15-17 is the minimum required to serve the purpose. For better hydraulic performance, it is desirable to construct the blocks narrower than indicated, preferably $0.75D_1$, and to set the tailwater depth 5 to 10% greater than the sequent depth of the jump. The length of the basin is made equal to the length of the jump in a horizontal stilling basin without appurtenances and, thus, can be determined from the curve in Fig. 15-4 (i.e., also equal to the length of USBR basin I or $L_I$). Basin IV is applicable to rectangular cross sections only.

---

[1] The Bureau has also developed alternative designs to substitute for basin IV, such as the drop energy dissipator (Art. 15-15), wave suppressors, and the impact-type energy dissipator [34,35].

**15-15. The Straight Drop Spillway.**   The aerated free-falling nappe in a straight drop spillway (Fig. 15-18) will reverse its curvature and turn smoothly into supercritical flow on the apron.   Consequently, a hydraulic jump may be formed downstream.   Based on his own experimental data

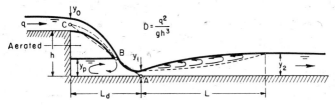

FIG. 15-18. Flow geometry of a straight drop spillway.

and those of Moore [40] and Bakhmeteff and Feodoroff [65], Rand [66] found that the flow geometry at straight drop spillways can be described by functions of the *drop number*, which is defined as

$$D = \frac{q^2}{gh^3} \tag{15-9}$$

where $q$ is the discharge per unit width of the crest of overfall, $g$ is the acceleration of gravity, and $h$ is the height of the drop.   The functions are

$$\frac{L_d}{h} = 4.30 D^{0.27} \tag{15-10}$$

$$\frac{y_p}{h} = 1.00 D^{0.22} \tag{15-11}$$

$$\frac{y_1}{h} = 0.54 D^{0.425} \tag{15-12}$$

$$\frac{y_2}{h} = 1.66 D^{0.27} \tag{15-13}$$

where $L_d$ is the drop length, that is, the distance from the drop wall to the position of the depth $y_1$; $y_p$ is the pool depth under the nappe; $y_1$ is the depth at the toe of the nappe or the beginning of the hydraulic jump; and $y_2$ is the tailwater depth sequent to $y_1$.   The position of the depth $y_1$ can be approximately determined by the straight line $ABC$ which joins the point $A$ on the apron at the position of $y_1$, the point $B$ on the axis of the nappe at the height of pool depth, and the point $C$ on the axis of the nappe at the crest of the fall.   The fact that these three points lie on a straight line was also verified by experiment.

For a given height $h$ and discharge $q$ per unit width of the fall crest, the sequent depth $y_2$ and the drop length $L_d$ can be computed by Eqs. (15-10) and (15-13).   On the one hand, if the tailwater depth is less than

$y_2$, the hydraulic jump will recede downstream. On the other hand, if the tailwater depth is greater than $y_2$, the jump will be submerged. As the tailwater level rises, the spillway crest may be finally submerged. The spillway will still be effective if the submergence does not reach the control depth on the spillway crest. The upper surface of the submerged nappe may be assumed as a straight line tangent to the upper surface of the free nappe at the point where the nappe plunges into the tailwater. The upper surface of the free nappe may be represented by the general equation given in Art. 14-1.

In the above discussion it is assumed that the length of the spillway crest is the same as the width of the approach channel. If the crest length is less than the width of the approach channel, the contraction at the ends of the spillway notch will be so great that the ends of the nappe may land beyond the stilling-basin sidewalls and the concentration of high velocities at the center of the outlet may cause additional scour in the downstream channel. It is, therefore, important to design the approach end properly by shaping the approach channel to reduce the effect of end contractions.

The straight drop spillway is commonly installed in small drainage structures by the U.S. Soil Conservation Service. The simplest form of such a structure, known as the *box inlet drop spillway*, is simply a rectangular box open at the top and at the downstream end [67–69]. Storm runoff is directed to the box by dikes and headwalls, enters over the upstream end and two sides, and leaves through the open downstream end leading to a channel outlet. A generalized design has also been developed by the Service as a result of tests and analyses at the St. Anthony Falls Hydraulic Laboratory [70,71].

By placing a gridiron or grate on top of the straight drop spillway, the overfalling jet can be separated into a number of long thin sheets of water which fall nearly vertically into the channel below. Thus the energy in the jet can be dissipated without resort to the use of hydraulic jump, and hence wave action can be reduced if $F_1 = 2.5$ to $4.5$. This scheme has been adopted by the U.S. Bureau of Reclamation [34,35] for developing a so-called *drop energy dissipator* as a substitute design for USBR basin IV (Art. 15-14). In this design, the grate may be composed of a series of beams, such as steel rails, channel irons, or timbers, which form slots parallel to the direction of flow. The width of the slots is equal to two-thirds the width of the beams. If the rails are tilted downward at an angle of 3° or more, the grate is self-cleaning. On the other hand, if the grate is tilted upward, it can check the upstream water level but may pose a cleaning problem. The length of the grate slots can be computed by

$$L_G = \frac{4.1Q}{WN\sqrt{2gy_1}} \qquad (15\text{-}14)$$

where $Q$ is the total discharge in cfs, $W$ is the width of a space in ft, $N$ is the number of spaces, $g$ is the gravitational acceleration, and $y_1$ is the depth of flow in the canal upstream.

**15-16. Jump in Sloping Channels.**    In the analysis of hydraulic jumps in sloping channels or channels having appreciable slope, it is essential to consider the weight of water in the jump; in horizontal channels the effect of this weight is negligible.    Thus, the momentum formulas for jumps on horizontal floor cannot be applied straightforwardly to jumps on sloping floor.    As will be shown in this article, however, the momentum principle can be used to derive an equation analogous to Eq. (3-21), which will contain an empirical function that has to be determined experimentally.

Early studies on hydraulic jumps in sloping channels were made by Riegal and Beebe [9] and by Ellms [72,73].    Later investigations were made by Bakhmeteff and Matzke [74] and also by Yarnell[1] and Kindsvater [75].

Hydraulic jump in sloping channels may occur in various forms, as shown in Fig. 15-19.    Case 1 is a typical form, but it is not common in practical problems.    Cases 2 to 4, known as *drowned-out jumps*, are common forms and usually appear simply as jets of water plunging into a downstream pool below the steep slope.    For practical purposes, it is believed that the solutions for the typical form of case 1 and for the drowned-out jumps are mutually applicable.    Case 5 shows the jump on an adverse slope.    This is a rare type of jump, and no adequate experimental data are available at the present moment.

For the analysis of the jump of case 1, a rectangular channel of unit width is assumed.    Considering all effective forces parallel to the channel bottom, the momentum equation may be written

$$\frac{Qw}{g}(\beta_2 V_2 - \beta_1 V_1) = P_1 - P_2 + W \sin\theta - F_f \qquad (3\text{-}14)$$

where $Q = V_1 d_1$, $V_2 = V_1 d_1/d_2$, $P_1 = 0.5wd_1{}^2 \cos\theta$, $P_2 = 0.5wd_2{}^2 \cos\theta$, $F_f$ is negligible, and $\beta_1$ and $\beta_2$ may be taken as unity.    If the surface profile of the jump is a straight line, the weight of water in the jump can be computed.    The discrepancy between the straight-line and actual profiles and the effect of slope may be corrected by a factor $K$.    Thus,

$$W = \tfrac{1}{2}KwL(d_1 + d_2) \qquad (15\text{-}15)$$

Substituting Eq. (15-15) in Eq. (3-14), letting $\mathbf{F}_1 = V_1/\sqrt{gd_1}$, and

---

[1] The work started in 1936 by David L. Yarnell at the Iowa Institute of Hydraulic Research, Iowa City, Iowa, was interrupted by his death in 1937.    The Yarnell data were lent to the Tennessee Valley Authority in 1939 for an extensive investigation by Kindsvater.

simplifying,

$$\left(\frac{d_2}{d_1}\right)^3 - (2G^2 + 1)\frac{d_2}{d_1} + 2G^2 = 0 \tag{15-16}$$

where

$$G = \frac{F_1}{\sqrt{\cos\theta - \dfrac{KL\sin\theta}{d_2 - d_1}}} \tag{15-17}$$

There is a general belief [76] that $K$ and $L/(d_2 - d_1)$ vary primarily with $F_1$ and, hence, that $G$ is a function of $F_1$ and $\theta$, or $G = f(F_1,\theta)$.

If Eq. (15-16) is compared with Eq. (3-20) for level-floor jump, a similarity between the two equations is evident. Following the solution for Eq. (3-20), the solution of Eq. (15-16) is apparently

$$\frac{d_2}{d_1} = \tfrac{1}{2}(\sqrt{1 + 8G^2} - 1) \tag{15-18}$$

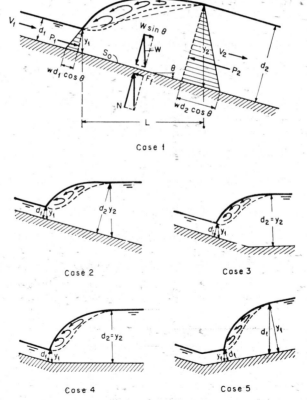

Case 1

Case 2

Case 3

Case 4

Case 5

Fig. 15-19. Hydraulic jumps in sloping channels.

Since $d_1 = y_1 \cos \theta$ and $d_2 = y_2 \cos \theta$, Eq. (15-18) may also be written

$$\frac{y_2}{y_1} = \tfrac{1}{2}(\sqrt{1 + 8G^2} - 1) \qquad (15\text{-}19)$$

The above two equations are analogous to Eq. (3-21). Since $G = f(\mathbf{F}_1, \theta)$, these equations indicate that $d_2/d_1$ and $y_2/y_1$ are functions of $\mathbf{F}_1$ and $\theta$.

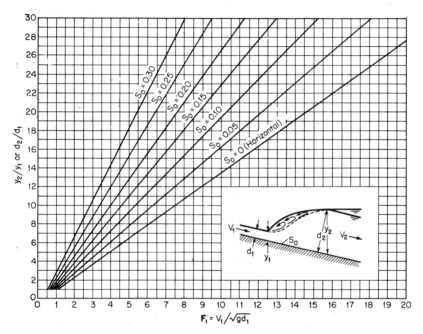

FIG. 15-20. Experimental relations between $\mathbf{F}_1$ and $y_2/y_1$ or $d_2/d_1$ for jumps in sloping channels.

The depth ratio $y_2/y_1$ or $d_2/d_1$ can be shown as a function of $\mathbf{F}_1$ and $S_0$ (i.e. $\sin \theta$) by the chart in Fig. 15-20, which is based on the experimental data of Hickox [77], Kindsvater [75], Bakhmeteff and Matzke [74], and the U.S. Bureau of Reclamation [34,35]. Similarly, the relative length of jump $L/y_2$ may also be shown as a function of $\mathbf{F}_1$ and $S_0$ and represented by curves based on the experimental data of the Bureau of Reclamation (Fig. 15-21). The dashed lines indicate the parts where the curves are not well defined by the available data. The diagrams in Figs. 15-20 and 15-21 are based on limited experimental data with considerable interpolation; nevertheless they provide useful information for practical purposes.

The following rules for designing a stilling basin with sloping apron

(USBR basin V) are extracted from recommendations made by the U.S. Bureau of Reclamation [34,35]:

1. Determine an apron arrangement that will give the greatest economy for the maximum discharge condition. This is the governing factor and the only justification for using a sloping apron.

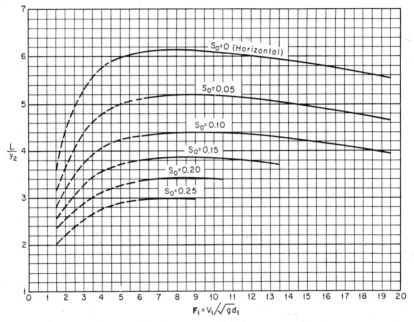

FIG. 15-21. Length in terms of sequent depth of jumps in sloping channels. (*U.S. Bureau of Reclamation* [34].)

2. Position the apron so that the front of the jump will form at the upstream end of the slope for the maximum discharge and tailwater condition.

3. The portion of the jump to be confined on the stilling basin is a decision for the designer, depending on the quality of the material in the river bed and other conditions. The average over-all apron is about 60% of the length of jump for the maximum discharge condition.

4. With the apron designed properly for the maximum discharge condition, the next step is to be certain that the tailwater depth and basin length available for energy dissipation are sufficient for, say, one-quarter, one-half, and three-quarters of capacity.

5. A horizontal apron will perform on par with the sloping apron for high Froude numbers, if proper tailwater is provided.

6. The slope of the chute upstream from a stilling basin has little effect on the jump as long as the distribution of velocity and depth of flow are reasonably uniform on entering the jump.

7. A small solid triangular sill with a sloping upstream surface, placed at the end of the apron, is the only appurtenance needed. This serves to lift the flow as it leaves the apron and thus acts to control scour. Its dimensions are not critical; the most effective height is between 0.05 and 0.10 of the vertical distance of the sequent tailwater elevation above the bottom of the toe of the jump, and the surface slope can be 3:1 to 2:1.

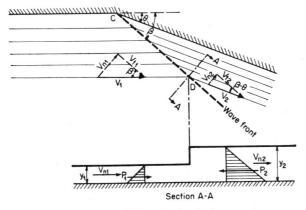

Section A-A

Fig. 15-22. Oblique hydraulic jump.

**15-17. The Oblique Jump.** When a supercritical flow is deflected inward to the course of the flow by a vertical boundary (Fig. 15-22), the depth of flow $y_1$ will increase abruptly to a depth $y_2$ along a wavefront $CD$ which extends out from the point of boundary discontinuity at a *wave angle* $\beta$ that depends in magnitude on the angle of deflection $\theta$ of the boundary. This phenomenon resembles a normal hydraulic jump but with the change in depth occurring along an oblique front; hence it may be called an *oblique hydraulic jump*.[1] When $\theta = 0$, oblique jump becomes the familiar hydraulic jump in which the wavefront is normal to the direction of flow, or $\beta = 90°$.

Referring to the relationship of velocity vectors before the jump in Fig. 15-22, the velocity normal to the wavefront is $V_{n1} = V_1 \sin \beta$ where $V_1$ is the velocity of flow before the jump. The Froude number normal to

[1] For original information see [78] and [79]. The oblique hydraulic jump or oblique standing wave is also known as the *shock wave*, by analogy to the case in supersonic flow of gases. The basic development of this subject was accomplished by Rouse and White [80].

the wavefront before the jump is, therefore,

$$\mathbf{F}_{n1} = \frac{V_{n1}}{\sqrt{gy_1}} = \frac{V_1 \sin \beta}{\sqrt{gy_1}} = \mathbf{F}_1 \sin \beta \qquad (15\text{-}20)$$

Considering a section $A$-$A$ normal to the wavefront, it is seen that a normal hydraulic jump occurs in this section and that Eq. (3-21) can be applied. Substituting Eq. (15-20) for $\mathbf{F}_1$ in Eq. (3-21), the ratio of the sequent to initial depth is

$$\frac{y_2}{y_1} = \frac{1}{2}(\sqrt{1 + 8\mathbf{F}_1^2 \sin^2 \beta} - 1) \qquad (15\text{-}21)$$

This is the equation that represents the condition for an oblique hydraulic jump to take place.

Referring to Fig. 15-22, the tangential velocities before and after the jump are $V_{t1} = V_{n1}/\tan \beta$ and $V_{t2} = V_{n2}/\tan (\beta - \theta)$. Since no momentum change takes place parallel to the wavefront, these two velocities should be equal, or

$$\frac{V_{n1}}{V_{n2}} = \frac{\tan \beta}{\tan (\beta - \theta)} \qquad (15\text{-}22)$$

By the condition of continuity $y_1 V_{n1} = y_2 V_{n2}$, the above equation can be written

$$\frac{y_2}{y_1} = \frac{\tan \beta}{\tan (\beta - \theta)} \qquad (15\text{-}23)$$

Eliminating $y_2/y_1$ from Eqs. (15-21) and (15-23), a relationship involving $\mathbf{F}_1$, $\theta$, and $\beta$ is obtained:

$$\tan \theta = \frac{\tan \beta \, (\sqrt{1 + 8\mathbf{F}_1^2 \sin^2 \beta} - 3)}{2 \tan^2 \beta + \sqrt{1 + 8\mathbf{F}_1^2 \sin^2 \beta} - 1} \qquad (15\text{-}24)$$

This equation should produce the value of $\beta$ if $\mathbf{F}_1$ and $\theta$ are given. However, a direct solution of this equation for $\beta$ in terms of $\mathbf{F}_1$ and $\theta$ is practically impossible. Ippen [78] has prepared a four-quadrant graph (Fig. 15-23) showing all relationships expressed by Eqs. (15-21), (15-23), and (15-24). This graph is self-explanatory and can be used for the solution of an oblique hydraulic jump.

Since the oblique jump is a normal jump across the section $A$-$A$, the energy loss in the oblique jump can be computed by Eq. (3-24). In practical problems involving an oblique jump, $y_2/y_1$ is usually small. Thus, the head loss may often be neglected in design. Like a normal jump, if $y_2/y_1 < 2$ (or $\mathbf{F}_{n1} < 1.7$, according to Art. 15-3), the oblique jump becomes undular. This fact has been confirmed both experimentally and theoretically by Ippen [79].

It should be noted that an oblique jump will rarely occur alone in an

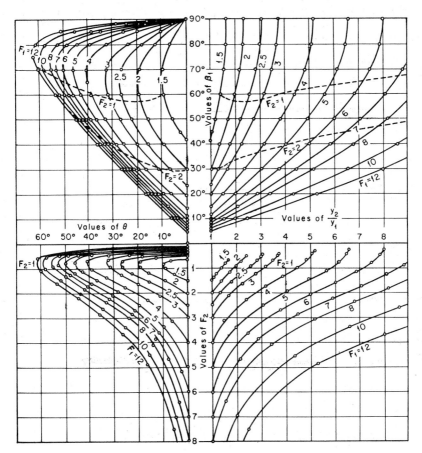

FIG. 15-23. General relations among $F_1$, $\theta$, $\beta$, $y_2/y_1$, and $F_2$ for oblique hydraulic jumps. (*After A. T. Ippen* [78].)

ordinary channel, because multiple oblique jumps due to reflections on opposite walls and intersections with other wavefronts will develop. Further discussion on this subject will be given in the subsequent chapters.

## PROBLEMS

**15-1.** Show that the following equation may be written for a hydraulic jump taking place in a horizontal trapezoidal channel (some of the notation is given in Table 2-1):

$$r^4 + (2.5t + 1)r^3 + (1.5t + 1)(t + 1)r^2 + [0.5t^2 + (t - 3F_1{}^2)(t + 1)]r - 3F_1{}^2(t + 1)^2 = 0 \quad (15\text{-}25)$$

where $r = y_2/y_1$, $t = b/zy_1$, and $F_1 = V_1/\sqrt{gy_1}$.

**15-2.** Show that the equation for a hydraulic jump in a parabolic channel may be written

$$r^4 - (2.5F_1{}^2)r^{1.5} + 2.5F_1{}^2 = 0 \qquad (15\text{-}26)$$

where $r = y_2/y_1$ and $F_1 = V_1/\sqrt{gy_1}$.

**15-3.** Verify Eqs. (15-1) and (15-2).

**15-4.** In Bidone's experiment it was found that, for $V_1 = 5.59$ fps and $y_1 = 0.208$ ft in a rectangular channel, the sequent depth $y_2$ was 0.613 ft. Determine (a) the alternate depth, (b) the theoretical sequent depth, (c) the energy loss in the jump, (d) the relative loss, (e) the efficiency of the jump, (f) the relative height of the jump, (g) the length of the jump, and (h) the type of jump.

**15-5.** In a rectangular channel with $b = 20$ ft, $n = 0.03$, and $S_0 = 0.04$, the depth of uniform flow is 3 ft. A low dam which keeps 7 ft of water immediately behind it is built at the downstream end of the channel. If the backwater surface behind the dam is assumed horizontal, find the possibility of developing a hydraulic jump in the channel. If the jump will occur, determine (a) the discharge over the spillway of the dam, (b) the jump height, (c) the energy loss in the jump, (d) the efficiency of jump, and (e) the distance of the jump from the dam.

**15-6.** Locate the hydraulic jump in Example 15-1 if the channel has a free-overfall outlet 500 ft downstream from the vena contracta.

**15-7.** Water flowing over a low spillway of broad width passes on to a level concrete apron at 12 ft below the spillway crest. The head over the spillway crest is 8 ft, and the tailwater depth is 10 ft. Determine the location of the jump. Use Eq. (14-9) with $C = 3.61$ for computing the discharge and Eq. (14-19) for computing the depth of flow at the spillway toe with a velocity coefficient of 0.9 (i.e., the actual velocity is equal to $0.9V_1$).

**15-8.** A wide rectangular channel with $n = 0.025$ is laid with a change in slope from steep $S_0 = 0.01$ to mild $S_0 = 0.002$. The depth of uniform flow in the mild channel is 5 ft. Determine the location of the hydraulic jump.

**15-9.** Solve the preceding problem if the steep slope is 0.03.

**15-10.** Determine the initial and sequent depths of a hydraulic jump in a horizontal channel 30 ft wide and carrying 300 cfs. The loss of energy in the jump is 5 ft. (HINT: The solution requires a trial-and-error procedure such as: First assume $F_1$; then compute $y_2/y_1$ by Eq. (3-21) and $y_1$ by Eq. (3-24); finally check for $F_1$. A graphical solution using specific-energy and specific-force curves is also suitable.)

**15-11.** The canal fall (Fig. 15-24) carrying 300 cfs is a rectangular channel having a width of 30 ft, slope of 1 on 5, and sufficient length. It is designed to dissipate a head

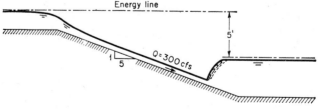

Fig. 15-24. A canal fall.

loss of 5 ft by hydraulic jump. Determine the position of the hydraulic jump, assuming negligible channel friction and ignoring the effect of channel slope on the jump. (HINT: Use the result obtained in the preceding problem.)

**15-12.** A canal fall 40 ft long and carrying 240 cfs is designed to dissipate a head loss of 4 ft.   The channel of the fall has a slope of 1 on 5 and diverges from a width of 8 ft at the upstream end to 24 ft at the downstream end.   Determine the location of the hydraulic jump, assuming a frictionless channel and ignoring the slope effect on the jump.   (HINT: Divide the channel into, say, four reaches, and compute $E_1$ and $E_2$ at each section for $\Delta E = 4$ ft.)

**15-13.** Water flowing under a sluice gate discharges into a rectangular plain stilling basin having the same width as the gate.   After the contraction of the jet the flow has an average velocity of 80 fps and a depth of 6 ft.   Determine (a) the sequent tail-water depth, (b) the length of the basin required to confine the jump, (c) the effectiveness of the basin to dissipate energy (i.e., efficiency of the jump), and (d) the type of jump to be expected.

**15-14.** Design the stilling basin for Example 15-2, using a jump control by (a) sharp-crested weir, (b) broad-crested weir, and (c) abrupt rise.

**15-15.** Design the stilling basin for Example 15-2, using a jump control by abrupt drop.

**15-16.** Proportion an SAF stilling basin for Example 15-2.

**15-17.** Construct the jump rating curve at the toe of the spillway designed in Example 14-1.

**15-18.** Discuss the development of an energy-dissipation structure at the toe of the spillway under consideration in the preceding problem, provided the tailwater rating curve can be represented by (a) $Q = 40y^2$, (b) $Q = 100y^2$, (c) $Q = 2y^3$, and (d) $Q = 900y^{1.2}$.

**15-19.** Design the energy-dissipation structure, if needed, for the different tailwater conditions given in the preceding problem.

FIG. 15-25. A ladder of cascades.

**15-20.** Poggi [81,82] has proposed a ladder of cascades, as shown in Fig. 15-25. Design this structure for the given data.   The profile of the spillway crest is assumed of WES shape.

**15-21.** Derive an equation of the upper surface of the free nappe over a straight drop spillway.   (HINT: See Art. 14-1, and note that $h_v/H = \frac{1}{3}$.)

**15-22.** A straight drop spillway is used in a ditch to effect a drop of 6 ft in the ditch grade.   The ditch is 14 ft wide and carries a uniform flow of 330 cfs.   The spillway has a crest length of 12.5 ft and takes a head of 4 ft for the given discharge.   The normal depth of flow in the downstream ditch is 4 ft, but under flood conditions backwater from a stream may raise the tailwater so that its level is 1.5 ft above the spillway crest.   Proportion the structure assuming any type of stilling basin.   The upstream approach to the spillway is properly designed, and the velocity head on the spillway crest may be ignored.

**15-23.** Solve Prob. 15-13 if the floor slope of the stilling basin is 0.10.

**15-24.** Solve Prob. 15-11 if the sloping effect of the channel is considered.

**15-25.** Design the stilling basin for Example 15-2 on an apron with a slope of 0.15.

**15-26.** In a flow 23.8 fps in velocity and 0.70 ft deep, an oblique hydraulic jump is produced by a deflecting vertical wall making a 15° angle with the direction of the flow. Determine (a) the wave angle, (b) the sequent depth, and (c) the energy loss.

## REFERENCES

1. Giorgio Bidone: Observations sur le hauteur du ressaut hydraulique en 1818 (Observations on the height of the hydraulic jump in 1818), a report presented at the Dec. 12, 1819, meeting of the Royal Academy of Science of Turin and later incorporated as a part of [2], pp. 21–80.
2. Giorgio Bidone: Expériences sur le remous et la propagation des ondes (Experiments on backwater and the propagation of waves), *Memorie della Reale Accademia delle Scienze di Torino*, Turin, vol. 25, pp. 21–112, 1820.
3. J. B. Bélanger: "Essai sur la solution numérique de quelques problèmes relatifs au mouvement permanent des eaux courantes" ("Essay on the Numerical Solution of Some Problems Relative to the Steady Flow of Water"), Carilian-Goeury, Paris, 1828.
4. J. A. Ch. Bresse: "Cours de mécanique appliquée," 2e partie, Hydraulique ("Course in Applied Mechanics," pt. 2, Hydraulics), Mallet-Bachelier, Paris, 1860.
5. H. Darcy and H. Bazin: Recherches expérimentales relatives aux remous et à la propagation des ondes (Experimental research on backwater and wave propagation), in vol. II of "Recherches hydrauliques" ("Hydraulic Researches"), Académie des Sciences, Paris, 1865.
6. Mansfield Merriman: "A Treatise on Hydraulics," John Wiley & Sons, New York, and Chapman and Hall, London, 4th ed., 1894; 10th ed., 1916. Also see R. Ferriday: The hydraulic jump, *Engineering News-Record*, vol. 34, no. 2, p. 28, July 11, 1895.
7. A. H. Gibson: The formation of standing waves in an open stream, paper 4081, *Minutes of Proceedings of the Institution of Civil Engineers, London*, vol. 197, pt. III, pp. 233–242, 1913–14.
8. K. R. Kennison: The hydraulic jump in open channel flow at high velocities, *Transactions, American Society of Civil Engineers*, vol. 80, pp. 338–353, 1916.
9. Sherman M. Woodward: Theory of the hydraulic jump and backwater curves; and Ross M. Riegel and John C. Beebe: The hydraulic jump as a means of dissipating energy, *Miami Conservancy District, Technical Report, pt. III*, Dayton, Ohio, 1917, pp. 63–118.
10. A. Koch and M. Carstanjen: "Von der Bewegung des Wassers und den dabei auftretenden Kräften" ("On Flow of Water and the Associated Forces"), Springer-Verlag, Berlin, 1926.
11. E. G. W. Lindquist: Anordningar för effektiv energieomvandling vid foten av överfallsdammar (Arrangements for effective energy dissipation at the toes of dams), "Anniversary Volume," Royal Technical University, Stockholm, Sweden, 1927.
12. Kurt Safranez: Wechselsprung und die Energievernichtung des Wassers (Hydraulic jump and energy dissipation of water), *Der Bauingenieur*, Berlin, vol. 8, no. 49, pp. 898–905; no. 50, p. 926, 1927.
13. J. Einwachter: Berechnung der in der Wehrbreite gemessenen Längenausdehnung von Deckwalzen (Computation of expansion of rollers with respect to width of weir) *Wasserkraft und Wasserwirtschaft*, Munich, vol. 27, No. 14, pp. 157–159, and no. 21, pp. 245–249, 1932; vol. 28, no. 17, pp. 200–202, 1933.

14. J. Einwachter: Wassersprung- und Deckwalzenlänge (The length of the hydraulic jump and of the surface roller), *Wasserkraft und Wasserwirtschaft*, Munich, vol. 30, no. 8, pp. 85–88, Apr. 17, 1935.

15. J. Smetana: Experimentální studie vodního skoku (Experimental study of hydraulic jump), č. 2–143, 1933; and Experimentální studie vodního skoku vzdutého (Experimental study of drowned hydraulic jump), *Zprávy Veřejné Služby Technické*, Czechoslovakia, 1934.

16. J. Smetana: Modern types of movable dams: Greatest dimensions attained in each type. Principles of design of the fixed and movable parts of these dams and principles to be followed in their working, in order to reduce undermining to a minimum, paper 51, *16th International Congress of Navigation, Brussels*, pt. III, 1935.

17. Boris A. Bakhmeteff and Arthur E. Matzke: The hydraulic jump in terms of dynamic similarity, *Transactions, American Society of Civil Engineers*, vol. 101, pp. 630–647, 1936.

18. L. Escande: Étude théorique et expérimentale de l'écoulement par vanne de fond (Theoretical and experimental study of flow through sluice gates), *Revue générale de l'hydraulique*, Paris, vol. 4, no. 19, pp. 25–29, no. 20, pp. 72–79, and no. 21, pp. 120–128, 1938; vol. 5, no. 25, pp. 21–34, no. 26, pp. 65–77, and no. 28, pp. 131–139, 1939.

19. D. Citrini: Il salto di Bidone (The hydraulic jump), *L'Energia elettrica, Milano*, vol. 16, no. 6, pp. 441–465, June, and no. 7, pp. 517–527, July, 1939. Contains a résumé of work done up to 1939.

20. Guido Nebbia: Sui dissipatori a salto di Bidone: Ricerca sperimentale (On dissipation by hydraulic jump: Experimental researches), *L'Energia elettrica, Milano*, vol. 17, no. 6, pp. 325–356, June, 1940.

21. Carl E. Kindsvater: The hydraulic jump in sloping channels, *Transactions, American Society of Civil Engineers*, vol. 109, pp. 1107–1120, 1944.

22. Fred W. Blaisdell: Development and hydraulic design, Saint Anthony Falls stilling basin, *Transactions, American Society of Civil Engineers*, vol. 113, pp. 483–520, 1948.

23. John W. Forster and Raymond A. Skrinde: Control of the hydraulic jump by sills, *Transactions, American Society of Civil Engineers*, vol. 115, pp. 973–987, 1950.

24. Hunter Rouse, T. T. Siao, and S. Nagaratnam: Turbulence characteristics of the hydraulic jump, paper 1528, *Proceedings, American Society of Civil Engineers, Journal, Hydraulics Division*, vol. 84, no. HY1, pt. 1, pp. 1–30, February, 1958.

25. The standing wave or hydraulic jump, *Government of India Central Board of Irrigation and Power, Publication 7*, Simla, India, 2d ed., Aug. 15, 1950.

26. J. O. De Mello Flôres: Le ressaut (The hydraulic jump), *La Houille blanche*, Grenoble, 9th yr., no. 6, pp. 811–822, December, 1954.

27. Boris A. Bakhmeteff: "Hydraulics of Open Channels," McGraw-Hill Book Company, Inc., New York, 1932.

28. A. G. Levy and J. W. Ellms: The hydraulic jump as a mixing device, *Journal, American Waterworks Association*, no. 1, pp. 1–23, January, 1927.

29. A. A. Kalinske and James M. Robertson: Closed conduit flow, in Entrainment of air in flowing water: A symposium, *Transactions, American Society of Civil Engineers*, vol. 108, pp. 1435–1447, 1943.

30. G. H. Hickox: Graphical solution for hydraulic jump, *Civil Engineering*, vol. 4, no. 5, p. 270, May, 1934.

31. C. J. Posey and P. S. Hsing: Hydraulic jump in trapezoidal channels, *Engineering News-Record*, vol. 121, no. 25, pp. 797–798, Dec. 22, 1938.

32. E. W. Lane and C. E. Kindsvater: Hydraulic jump in enclosed conduits, *Engineering News-Record*, vol. 121, no. 26, pp. 815–817, Dec. 29, 1938.

33. J. C. Stevens: The hydraulic jump in standard conduits, *Civil Engineering*, vol. 3, no. 10, pp. 565–567, October, 1933.

34. Research studies on stilling basins, energy dissipators, and associated appurtenances, *U.S. Bureau of Reclamation, Hydraulic Laboratory Report No. Hyd-399*, June 1, 1955.

35. J. N. Bradley and A. J. Peterka: The Hydraulic design of stilling basins: Hydraulic jumps on a horizontal apron (Basin I), paper 1401; High dams, earth dams, and large canal structures (Basin II), paper 1402; Short stilling basins for canal structures, small outlet works, and small spillways (Basin III), paper 1403; Stilling basin and wave suppressors for canal structures, outlet works, and diversion dams (Basin IV), paper 1404; Stilling basin with sloping apron (Basin V), paper 1405; Small basins for pipe or open channel outlets—no tailwater required (Basin VI), paper 1406, *Proceedings, American Society of Civil Engineers, Journal, Hydraulics Division*, vol. 83, no. HY5, pp. 1-24, 1-14, 1-22, 1-20, 1-32, and 1-17, October, 1957.

36. Kurt Safranez: Untersuchungen über den Wechselsprung (Researches relating to the hydraulic jump), *Der Bauingenieur*, Berlin, vol. 10, no. 37, pp. 649–651, 1929. A brief summary is given in Donald P. Barnes: Length of hydraulic jump investigated at Berlin, *Civil Engineering*, vol. 4, no. 5, pp. 262–263, May, 1934.

37. Kurt Safranez: Länge des Wassersprunges (Length of hydraulic jump), *Wasserkraft und Wasserwirschaft*, Munich, vol. 28, no. 24, pp. 277–282, 1933.

38. K. Wóycicki: Wassersprung: Deckwalze und Ausfluss unter einer Schütze (The hydraulic jump: Its top roll and discharge through a sluice gate), Warsaw, 1931.

39. V. I. Aravin: Opredelenie dliny gidravlicheskogo pryzhka (The determination of the length of the hydraulic jump), *Izvestiia Vsesoiuznogo Nauchno-Issledovatelskogo Instituta Gidrotekhniki (Transactions, All-Union Scientific Research Institute of Hydraulic Engineering)*, Leningrad, vol. 15, pp. 48–57, 1935.

40. W. L. Moore: Energy loss at the base of a free overfall, *Transactions, American Society of Civil Engineers*, vol. 108, pp. 1343–1360, 1943.

41. I. I. Agroskin, G. T. Dmitriev, and F. I. Pikalov: "Gidravlika" ("Hydraulics"), Gosenergoizdat, Moscow and Leningrad, 1954, p. 337.

42. Julius Weisbach: "Die Experimentalhydraulik" ("Experimental Hydraulics"), Freiberg, 1855, p. 52.

43. Serge Leliavsky: "Irrigation and Hydraulic Design," Chapman & Hall, Ltd., London, 1955, vol. 1.

44. J. B. Tiffany: Laboratory research applied to the hydraulic design of large dams, *U.S. Waterways Experiment Station, Bulletin* 32, 1948.

45. M. B. McPherson and M. H. Karr: A study of bucket-type energy dissipator characteristics, *Proceedings, American Society of Civil Engineers, Journal, Hydraulics Division*, paper 1266, vol. 83, no. HY3, pp. 1–12, June, 1957, and corrections, paper 1348, no. HY4, pp. 57–64, August, 1957.

46. Ralph M. Weaver: Discussion on Control of the hydraulic jump by sills, by John W. Forster and Raymond A. Skrinde, *Transactions, American Society of Civil Engineers*, vol. 115, pp. 1003–1006, 1950.

47. En-Yun Hsu: Discussion on Control of the hydraulic jump by sills, by John W. Forster and Raymond A. Skrinde, *Transactions, American Society of Civil Engineers*, vol. 115, pp. 988–991, 1950.

48. Walter L. Moore and Carl W. Morgan: The hydraulic jump at an abrupt drop, paper 1449, *Proceedings, American Society of Civil Engineers, Journal, Hydraulics Division*, vol. 83, no. HY6, pt. 1, pp. 1–21, December, 1957.

49. William P. Creager, Joel D. Justin, and Julian Hinds: "Engineering for Dams," John Wiley & Sons, Inc., New York, 1945, vol. 1, pp. 73–89.

50. Calvin Victor Davis (editor-in-chief): "Handbook of Applied Hydraulics," 2d ed., McGraw-Hill Book Company, Inc., New York, 1952, pp. 281–288 and 813–846.

51. Civil and structural design, vol. 1 in "Design of TVA Projects," *Tennessee Valley Authority, Technical Report* 24, 1952, pp. 41–60.

52. Armin Schoklitsch: "Hydraulic Structures," translated from the German by Samuel Shulits, American Society of Mechanical Engineers, New York, 1937, vol. 2, pp. 913–926.

53. Armin Schoklitsch: "Handbuch des Wasserbaues" ("Handbook of Hydraulic Engineering"), Springer-Verlag, Vienna, 1952, vol. 2, pp. 816–825.

54. C. Maxwell Stanley: Study of stilling-basin design, *Transactions, American Society of Civil Engineers*, vol. 99, pp. 490–523, 1934.

55. Jacob E. Warnock: Spillways and energy dissipators, *Proceedings of Hydraulics Conference, University of Iowa, Studies in Engineering, Bulletin* 20, 1940, pp. 142–159.

56. John R. Freeman (editor): "Hydraulic Laboratory Practice," American Society of Mechanical Engineers, New York, 1929.

57. Ahmed Shukry: The efficacy of floor sills under drowned hydraulic jumps, paper 1260, *Proceedings, American Society of Civil Engineers, Journal, Hydraulics Division*, vol. 83, no. HY3, pp. 1–18, June, 1957.

58. L. Escande: L'Étude sur modèle réduit des ouvrages de rupture de charge (The study of energy dissipators with the aid of a small-scale model), *Le Génie civil*, vol. 115, no. 25, pp. 429–433, Dec. 16, 1939.

59. R. H. Berryhill: Stilling basin experiences of the Corps of Engineers, paper 1264, *Proceedings, American Society of Civil Engineers, Journal, Hydraulics Division*, vol. 83, no. HY3, pp. 1–36, June, 1957.

60. B. S. Talwani and S. T. Ghotankar: Design of canal falls, *Irrigation and Power, Journal of the Central Board of Irrigation and Power*, Simla, India, vol. 9, no. 2, pp. 269–293, April, 1952.

61. K. R. Sharma: "Irrigation Engineering," Rama Krishna, Lahore, Punjab, India, 1944, pp. 245–285.

62. A. M. R. Montagu and others: Irrigation canal falls, *Central Board of Irrigation, Publication* 10, Simla, India, 1935.

63. Ivan E. Houk: "Irrigation Engineering," John Wiley & Sons, Inc., New York, 1956, vol. 2.

64. Fred W. Blaisdell: The SAF stilling basin, *U.S. Soil Conservation Service, Report SCS-TP-79*, May, 1949.

65. Boris A. Bakhmeteff and N. V. Feodoroff: Discussion on Energy loss at the base of free overfall, by Walter L. Moore, *Transactions, American Society of Civil Engineers*, vol. 108, pp. 1364–1373, 1943.

66. Walter Rand: Flow geometry at straight drop spillways, paper 791, *Proceedings, American Society of Civil Engineers*, vol. 81, pp. 1–13, September, 1955.

67. Charles A. Donnelly: Design of an outlet for box inlet drop spillways, *U.S. Soil Conservation Service, Report SCS-TP-63*, November, 1947.

68. Fred W. Blaisdell and Charles A. Donnelly: Capacity of box inlet drop spillways under free and submerged flow conditions, *University of Minnesota, St. Anthony Falls Hydraulic Laboratory, Technical Paper* 7, January, 1951.

69. Fred W. Blaisdell and Charles A. Donnelly: Hydraulic design of the box inlet drop spillway, *University of Minnesota, St. Anthony Falls Hydraulic Laboratory, Technical Paper* 8, January, 1951; also *U.S. Soil Conservation Service, Report SCS-TP-106*, July, 1951.

70. Charles A. Donnelly and Fred W. Blaisdell: Straight drop spillway stilling basin,

*University of Minnesota, St. Anthony Falls Hydraulic Laboratory, Technical Paper* 15, *Ser. B*, November, 1954.

71. Fred W. Blaisdell and Charles A. Donnelly: The box inlet drop spillway and its outlet, *Transactions, American Society of Civil Engineers*, vol. 121, pp. 955–986, 1956.

72. R. W. Ellms: Computation of tail-water depth of the hydraulic jump in sloping flumes, paper Hyd. 50-5, *Transactions, American Society of Mechanical Engineers*, vol. 50, no. 36, pp. 1–6, September–December, 1928.

73. R. W. Ellms: Hydraulic jump in sloping and horizontal flumes, paper Hyd. 54-6, *Transactions, American Society of Mechanical Engineers*, vol. 54, no. 22, pp. 113–119, Nov. 30, 1932.

74. B. A. Bakhmeteff and A. E. Matzke: The hydraulic jump in sloped channels, paper Hyd. 60-1, *Transactions, American Society of Mechanical Engineers*, vol. 60, no. 2, pp. 111–118, February, 1938.

75. Carl E. Kindsvater: The hydraulic jump in sloping channels, *Transactions, American Society of Civil Engineers*, vol. 109, pp. 1107–1120, 1944.

76. J. C. Stevens: Discussion on The hydraulic jump in sloping channels, by Carl E. Kindsvater, *Transactions, American Society of Civil Engineers*, vol. 109, pp. 1125–1135, 1944.

77. G. H. Hickox: Discussion on The hydraulic jump in sloping channels, by Carl E. Kindsvater, *Transactions, American Society of Civil Engineers*, vol. 109, pp. 1141–1146, 1944.

78. Arthur T. Ippen: Mechanics of supercritical flow, 1st paper of High-velocity flow in open channels: A symposium, *Transactions, American Society of Civil Engineers*, vol. 116, pp. 268–295, 1951.

79. Arthur T. Ippen and Donald R. F. Harleman: Verification of theory for oblique standing waves, *Transactions, American Society of Civil Engineers*, vol. 121, pp. 678–694, 1956.

80. Hunter Rouse: "Fluid Mechanics for Hydraulic Engineers," McGraw-Hill Book Company, Inc., New York, 1938.

81. Bruno Poggi: Sopra gli scaricatori a scala di stramazzi (On the flow in a ladder of cascades), *L'Energia elettrica, Milano*, vol. 26, no. 10, pp. 600–604, October, 1949.

82. Bruno Poggi: Lo scaricatori a scala di stramazzi (Flow in a ladder of cascades), *L'Energia elettrica, Milano*, vol. 33, no. 1, pp. 33–40, January, 1956. This paper describes the laboratory tests.

# CHAPTER 16

# FLOW IN CHANNELS OF NONLINEAR ALIGNMENT

**16-1. Nature of the Flow.** The presence of curves or bends in alignment is unavoidable in the design of open channels. Difficulties in design often arise because of the complexity of the flow around a curved path. The streamlines of the flow are not only curvilinear but also interwoven, resulting in spiral currents and cross waves. Furthermore, the centrifugal force acting on the flow around a bend produces a unique feature known as *superelevation*, that is, a rise in the water surface at the outer bank with an accompanying lowering at the inner bank. Also, the velocity distribution in the channel sections in the bend is very irregular and the coefficients $\alpha$ and $\beta$ are usually far greater than unity.

In channels of nonlinear alignment, flows behave differently according to the state of the flow. Generally speaking, subcritical flow shows smooth water surface and slight superelevation, whereas supercritical flow exhibits characteristic cross-wave-disturbance patterns on the surface and thus exaggerates the superelevation.

In the study of subcritical flow, the spiral currents are of primary interest. These currents are essentially a friction phenomenon; hence their analysis requires use of the Reynolds number as a parameter.

In the study of supercritical flow, the formation of cross waves is of major concern. These waves represent the gravity effect of the free surface upon the flow; hence their analysis will rely on the use of Froude number as a basic parameter.

**16-2. Spiral Flow.** *Spiral flow* refers to movement of water particles along a helical path in the general direction of the flow. Thus, in addition to the major velocity component normal to the channel cross section, there are transverse velocity components on the cross section. These transverse components will create so-called *secondary flow* in the plane of the cross section.

Spiral flow in curved channels was first observed by Thomson [1] in 1876. Since then many studies have been made [2–7]. It is believed that this phenomenon is due mainly to (1) friction on the channel walls, which causes higher filamental velocities near the center of the channel than near the walls; (2) centrifugal force, which deflects the particles of water from straight-line motion; and (3) a vertical velocity distribution

which exists in the approach channel and thus initiates spiral motion in
the flow. The centrifugal force is responsible also for the superelevation in the flow surface.

It is generally known that, looking downstream, a channel curve to
the right causes a counterclockwise spiral, whereas a channel curve to
the left causes a clockwise spiral. If the curve is followed by a long
tangent, the spiral flow developed in the curve will persist for some distance downstream.

The actual pattern of a spiral flow is complicated and three-dimensional. In order to record the actual flow pattern, it.is desirable to use a
specially designed instrument that can measure directly the velocity
components in different coordinate planes, such as the pitot sphere[1] used
by Shukry [2].

Spiral flow exists in straight channels (Art. 2-4) as well as in curved
channels. In a curved channel, however, the spiral flow induced by the
centrifugal force is very pronounced and irregular along the bend. The
complicated pattern of flow is caused by the interference of the spiral flow
originated in the straight approach channel with that generated in the
curve. The strongest lateral currents usually appear close to the outer
wall at the mid-section of the curve, where they have a general direction
toward the outside of the curve. Their direction and position change
gradually through the second half of the curve until the exit is reached,
where they approach the inside wall with upward inclination.

In order to delineate the magnitude and effect of the spiral flow in different curves under varying conditions of flow, Shukry [2] has used a term
known as the *strength of a spiral flow*. This term is defined as the percentage ratio of the mean kinetic energy of the lateral motion to the total
kinetic energy of flow at a given cross section. It is to be noted that the
kinetic energy of flow depends on the square of the velocity. Referring
to the channel cross section represented by the $xy$ plane in Fig. 2-6, the
strength of the spiral flow at this section is

$$S_{xy} = \frac{V_{xy}{}^2}{V^2} \times 100 \tag{16-1}$$

where $V_{xy}$ is the mean-velocity vector projected on the $xy$ plane and $V$ is
the mean velocity in the section. Thus, for a flow with all streamlines
parallel to the axis of the channel, $S_{xy} = 0$.

[1] The pitot sphere designed by Shukry has·five brass tubes encased in a casing stem.
Each tube has a small brass tapping at the top end to permit a rubber-tubing connection with a pressure manometer. At the bottom end the tube is bent inside a sphere
and then terminates at a certain hole in the shell of the sphere, which thus contains
five holes. The openings of the holes are strategically located on the surface of the
sphere so that, by rotating the sphere and with calibration, the direction and magnitude of a velocity vector of flow can be determined.

From the experimental results obtained by Shukry for subcritical flow around a bend in a rectangular steel flume, the following are noted:

1. $S_{xy}$ is comparatively high at low $R$ of the approach flow, but decreases considerably by increasing $R$.

2. $S_{xy}$ decreases gradually with the increase of the radius-width ratio $r_c/b$ and attains practically its minimum magnitude (i.e., the curve effect approaches the least amount) at $r_c/b = 3.0$.

3. $S_{xy}$ decreases as the depth-width ratio $y/b$ increases.

4. $S_{xy}$ increases as the deviation angle $\theta$ of the curve becomes large. For the range of $\theta/180°$ from 0.0 (straight channel) to 0.5, the increase in $S_{xy}$ is nearly twice that for the range from 0.5 to 1.0.

5. The kinetic energy of the lateral currents in a curve is relatively small compared with the energy in the longitudinal currents and, consequently, plays only a minor part in the energy loss due to bend resistance.

Spiral flow occurs in natural rivers as well as in artificial channels [5]. However, it may not exist at all in a curved channel if the strength of the spiral motion is so weak that its effect is practically eliminated by the channel friction. This is the case in many natural rivers where the ratio of depth to width is small (hence, $S_{xy}$ is small) and where the forces tending to produce spiral flow are overcome by the complicated forces resulting from bed and bank roughnesses [6,7].

**16-3. Energy Loss.** According to Müller [8], the energy line and flow profile in a uniform curved channel may be shown as in Fig. 16-1. Case 1 illustrates the *subcritical* flow in a curve between two tangent channels. Without the curve, flow would occur at the normal depth $y_n$ corresponding to the particular discharge. With the curve, the energy line at the beginning $A$ of the curve is raised by an amount $h_f$. A major part of this energy is dissipated over the length of the curve. The remaining part is carried over a distance $L'$ in the downstream channel $BB'$, which is required for the flow to revert to normal. The slope of the energy line between $A$ and $B'$ is greater than the bottom slope $S_0$, and the energy line meets the energy line for the normal flow at $B'$. In order to raise the energy line at the point $A$ above the normal line, water must be backed up in the channel upstream from $A$. From the specific-energy curve of the flow in the channel, it can be shown that a rise of $h_f$ in the energy line requires a corresponding rise in water surface by an amount $\Delta y$ which is greater than $h_f$. This rise in water surface indicates that the presence of a bend in a channel of subcritical flow has a backwater effect similar to that of a weir or dam. For the computation of the backwater profile, the starting point may be set at $A$ with a depth equal to $y_n + \Delta y$. The backwater profile is of the $M1$ type, which extends upstream from $A$ and is asymptotic to the normal-depth line.

Case 2 illustrates *supercritical* flow in the curved channel. It can be seen that the energy line is dropped by $h_f$ at $B'$, corresponding to the amount of energy dissipated in the curve and the downstream channel $BB'$.   The water surface is raised from the normal depth, starting at $A$, increasing to $\Delta y$ at $B'$, and then returning to normal afterwards.   If the

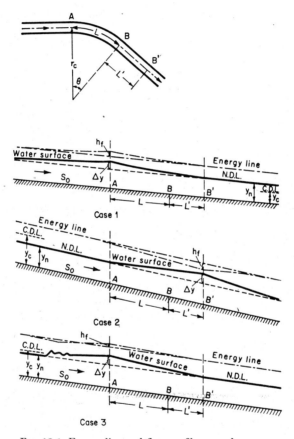

Fig. 16-1. Energy line and flow profile around a curve.

water surface rises above the critical-depth line, a hydraulic jump will be produced.

Case 3 illustrates *supercritical* flow when the normal depth is only slightly below the critical depth.   The wavy surface in the upstream channel is due to the fact that the water surface is raised above the critical depth, so that an undular jump is produced.

The total energy loss due to curve resistance can be expressed in terms

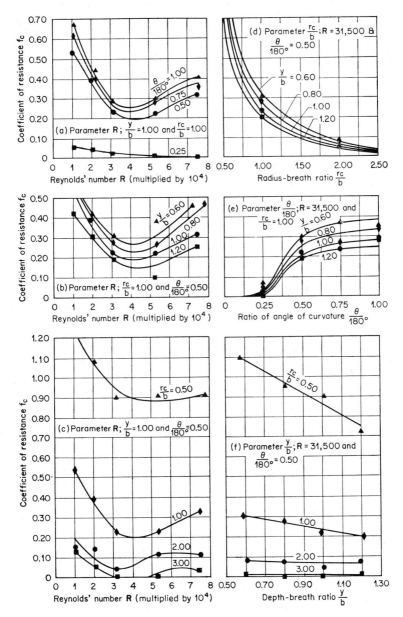

FIG. 16-2. Experimental parametric functions of the coefficient of curve resistance. (*After A. Shukry* [2].)

of the velocity head:

$$h_f = f_c \frac{V^2}{2g} \tag{16-2}$$

where $V$ is the mean velocity in the section and $f_c$ is the coefficient of curve resistance. The coefficient $f_c$ varies considerably with each of the parameters $R$ of the approach flow, $r_c/b$, $y/b$, and $\theta/180°$. Families of curves for these parameters based on the experiments made by Shukry [2] (see [9] and [10] for other studies) are shown in Fig. 16-2. The curves can be used to determine approximately the value of $f_c$ in smooth curved channels. For any given case, $f_c$ is obtained by first fixing its value with respect to two variables and then adjusting with respect to the third and fourth variables.

**Example 16-1.** Given $R = 55,500$, $r_c/b = 1.30$, $y/b = 0.8$, and $\theta/180° = 0.556$. Determine $f_c$.

*Solution.* First, keeping $y/b = 1.00$ and $\theta/180° = 0.50$, it is found that, for $R = 55,500$ and $r_c/b = 1.30, f_c = 0.200$ (Fig. 16-2c). Then, keeping $r_c/b = 1.00$ and $\theta/180° = 0.50$, it is found that, for $R = 55,500$ and $y/b = 1.00$, $f_c = 0.230$ and that, for $R = 55,500$ and $y/b = 0.80$, $f_c = 0.275$ (Fig. 16-2b). Adjusting the condition of $y/b = 1.00$ to that of $y/b = 0.80$, the corrected coefficient $= 0.200 \times 0.275/0.230 = 0.239$. Now, keeping $y/b = 1.00$ and $r_c/b = 1.00$, it is found that, for $R = 55,500$ and $\theta/180° = 0.556$, $f_c = 0.245$ (Fig. 16-2a). Similarly, adjusting the condition of $\theta/180° = 0.50$ to that of $\theta/180° = 0.556$, the finally corrected coefficient $= 0.239 \times 0.245/0.230 = 0.255$, say, 0.26.

The above procedure of interpolation is shown in Table 16-1.

TABLE 16-1. DETERMINATION OF THE COEFFICIENT OF CURVE RESISTANCE
BY INTERPOLATION

| Step | $y/b$ | $\theta/180°$ | $R$ | $r_c/b$ | $f_c$ | Remarks |
|------|------|------|------|------|------|---------|
| (1) | 1.00 | 0.50 | 55,500 | 1.30 | 0.200 | By Fig. 16-2c |
| (2) | 1.00 | 0.50 | 55,500 | 1.00 | 0.230 | By Fig. 16-2b |
| (3) | 0.80 | 0.50 | 55,500 | 1.00 | 0.275 | By Fig. 16-2b |
| (4) | 0.80 | 0.50 | 55,500 | 1.30 | 0.239 | By interpolation: (1)[(3)/(2)] |
| (5) | 1.00 | 0.556 | 55,500 | 1.00 | 0.245 | By Fig. 16-2a |
| (6) | 0.80 | 0.556 | 55,500 | 1.30 | 0.255 | By interpolation: (4)[(5)/(2)] |

**16-4. Superelevation.** Studies on the superelevation in water surface around a curved channel are many [11–14]. From the experimental results obtained by Shukry (Fig. 16-3), it can be seen that the path of the thread of maximum velocity in a curved channel deviates from its normal course at a section upstream from the bend. At point $d$, the path almost touches the inside wall of the channel and the water surface attains its minimum level. Beyond point $d$, the path gradually moves outward until it crosses the center line of the flume at the section that passes

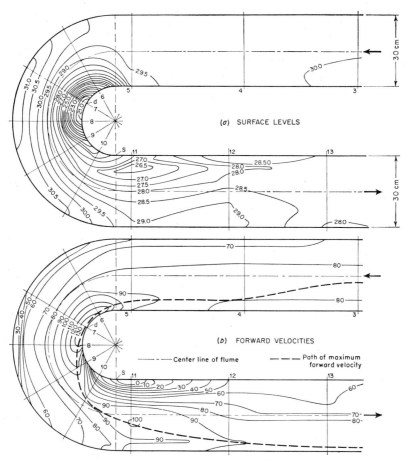

Fig. 16-3. Contour lines of equal surface levels and forward velocities in flow around a 180° bend. (*After A. Shukry* [2].) Surface levels measured in cm ( = 0.3937 in.) and velocities in cm/sec ( = 0.03281 fps). $r_c/b = 1.00$; $y_A/b = 1.00$; and, with $V_A = 77.8$ cm/sec ( = 2.55 fps), $\mathbf{R}_A = 73,500$, where subscript $A$ refers to conditions at the inlet-approach section of the bend.

through the separation point $s$. For different bends under various conditions of flow, the point of maximum surface depression $d$ and the point of separation $s$ were located, as given in Table 16-2. The positions of the two points are given in terms of the ratios of their angles $\theta_d$ and $\theta_s$, measured from the inlet of the bend, to the total angle $\theta$ of the bend. These positions were found to be only slightly affected by varying the parameter $y/b$. Hence, for practical purposes, Table 16-2, which gives position values for $y/b = 1.00$, can also be applied to other values of $y/b$.

In using the table for interpolation, the procedure is similar to that for $f_c$ values (Example 16-1).

TABLE 16-2. LOCATIONS OF POINTS OF MAXIMUM SURFACE DEPRESSION (POINT $d$ IN FIG. 16-3) AND POINTS OF SEPARATION (POINT $s$ IN FIG. 16-3) FOR VARYING PARAMETERS, EXCEPT THAT $y/b = 1.00$*

| Parameter | R = 10,500 | | R = 21,000 | | R = 31,500 | | R = 52,500 | | R = 73,500 | |
|---|---|---|---|---|---|---|---|---|---|---|
| | $\theta_d/\theta$ | $\theta_s/\theta$ | $\theta_d/\theta$ | $\theta_s/\theta$ | $\theta_d/\theta$ | $\theta_s/\theta$ | $\theta_d/\theta$ | $\theta_s/\theta$ | $\theta_d/\theta$ | $\theta_s/\theta$ |
| $r_c/b$ | (A) $\theta/180° = 0.50$, a constant | | | | | | | | | |
| 0.500 | 1.000 | 1.000 | 1.000 | 1.000 | 1.000 | 1.000 | 1.000 | 1.000 | 1.000 | 1.000 |
| 1.00 | 0.111 | 0.250 | 0.189 | 0.500 | 0.250 | 0.611 | 0.306 | 0.889 | 0.667 | 1.000 |
| 2.00 | 0.033 | † | 0.067 | † | 0.100 | † | 0.133 | † | 0.333 | † |
| 3.00 | 0.000 | † | 0.000 | † | 0.044 | † | 0.056 | † | 0.167 | † |
| $\theta/180°$ | (B) $r_c/b = 1.00$, a constant | | | | | | | | | |
| 0.25 | 0.111 | 0.222 | 0.333 | 0.667 | 0.333 | 0.667 | 0.400 | 0.710 | 0.556 | 0.889 |
| 0.50 | 0.111 | 0.250 | 0.189 | 0.500 | 0.250 | 0.611 | 0.306 | 0.889 | 0.667 | 1.000 |
| 0.75 | 0.148 | 0.333 | 0.185 | 0.445 | 0.296 | 0.556 | 0.371 | 0.926 | 0.445 | 1.000 |
| 1.00 | 0.056 | 0.778 | 0.111 | 0.778 | 0.167 | 0.805 | 0.278 | 0.833 | 0.333 | 1.000 |

\* After A. Shukry [2].
† No separation.

The forward-velocity distribution and the water-surface profile at the section of maximum surface depression may be estimated by the assumption of a theoretical free-vortex distribution of velocity. This assumption holds as long as the flow is *subcritical*.

By the law of free-vortex motion,[1] the following expression can be written:

$$v_z = \frac{C}{r} \tag{16-3}$$

where $v_z$ is the forward filamental velocity in the curve at a radial distance $r$ from the center of curvature, and $C$ is the so-called *circulation constant* in a free-vortex motion.

Let $E$ be the specific energy at any section and $y$ the depth of flow at a distance $r$ from the center of curvature; then

$$y = E - \frac{v_z^2}{2g} \tag{16-4}$$

[1] For an elaborate mathematical analysis by the law of free-vortex motion see [12].

The average forward velocity is

$$V_z = \frac{\int_{r_i}^{r_o} (C/r)\, dr}{r_o - r_i} = \frac{C}{r_o - r_i} \ln \frac{r_o}{r_i} \qquad (16\text{-}5)$$

and the average depth of flow is

$$y_m = \frac{\int_{r_i}^{r_o} y\, dr}{r_o - r_i} = \frac{\int_{r_i}^{r_o} (E - C^2/2gr^2)\, dr}{r_o - r_i}$$

$$= E - \frac{C^2}{2gr_o r_i} \qquad (16\text{-}6)$$

In the above equations $r_o$ and $r_i$ are, respectively, the outer and inner radii of the curve. Now, the discharge is

$$Q = V_z y_m (r_o - r_i) = C \left( E - \frac{C^2}{2gr_o r_i} \right) \ln \frac{r_o}{r_i} \qquad (16\text{-}7)$$

If $Q$, $r_o$, $r_i$, and $E$ are given, the constant $C$ can be determined from Eq. (16-7). The velocity and depth at any radius $r$ are then obtained by Eqs. (16-3) and (16-4). Thus, the superelevation $\Delta h$ of the water surface can be shown to be

$$\Delta h = \frac{C^2}{2gr_o^2 r_i^2} (r_o^2 - r_i^2) \qquad (16\text{-}8)$$

For the practical application of the above equations, the position of point $d$ is first determined with the aid of Table 16-2. The specific energy can be computed at any section $A$ in the approach channel by

$$E_A = y_A + \alpha_A \frac{V_A^2}{2g} \qquad (16\text{-}9)$$

where $\alpha_A$ is the energy coefficient and $V_A$ is the mean forward velocity. The specific energy at the radial section passing through point $d$ is

$$E = E_A - LS_f - 0.4h_f \qquad (16\text{-}10)$$

where $L$ is the channel length between section $A$ and the section containing point $d$; $S_f$ is the friction slope, which may be either determined experimentally or computed by the Manning formula; and $h_f$ is the energy loss due to curve resistance, which may be determined as shown in Example 16-1. The coefficient 0.4 was found to be practically constant for any curve.

The above method was found to be reasonably accurate as long as the angle of the curve was greater than 90°. For smaller angles, Shukry assumed that $C$ varies linearly with $\theta$ from $rV_{zs}$ at $\theta = 0$ to its full value at $\theta = 90°$. Therefore, for any angle $\theta$ less than 90°, the circulation constant can be multiplied by a correction factor equal to

$$\frac{\theta}{90°} + \left(1 - \frac{\theta}{90°}\right)\left(\frac{rV_{zs}}{C}\right)$$

where $V_{zs}$ is the mean forward velocity in a straight channel.

Superelevation in curved channels may also be determined by less accurate but simpler formulas which are based on the application of Newton's second law of motion to the centrifugal action in the curve. Assuming that all filamental velocities in the bend are equal to the mean velocity $V_z$ and that all streamlines have a radius of curvature $r_c$, the transverse water surface can be shown to be a straight line, and a simple formula for superelevation can be obtained:

$$\Delta h = \frac{V_z^2 b}{g r_c} \tag{16-11}$$

where $b$ is the width of the channel.

Applying Newton's second law to each streamline and then integrating the whole channel section, Grashof [13] was able to show that the transverse surface profile is a logarithmic curve and that the superelevation is

$$\Delta h = 2.30 \frac{V_z^2}{g} \log \frac{r_o}{r_i} \tag{16-12}$$

Woodward [14,15] assumed that the velocity is zero at the banks and has a maximum value $V_{max}$ at the center, varying in between according to a parabolic curve. Using Newton's second law, he obtained the following formula for superelevation:

$$\Delta h = \frac{V_{max}^2}{g}\left[2\tfrac{2}{3}\frac{r_c}{b} - 16\frac{r_c^3}{b^3} + \left(\frac{4r_c^2}{b^2} - 1\right)^2 \ln\frac{2r_c + b}{2r_c - b}\right] \tag{16-13}$$

Of the above three simple superelevation formulas, it has been found that Eq. (16-13) gives the best results, but none of them is more accurate than the free-vortex formula Eq. (16-8).

**16-5. Cross Waves.** Cross waves[1] are usually found in supercritical flow in channels of nonlinear alignment and channels with nonprismatic

---

[1] Cross waves in supercritical flow of water are analogous to the shock waves in supersonic flow of gases. This analogy was first noticed by Prandtl [16], Riabouchinsky [17], and von Kármán [18] and then investigated experimentally by Preiswerk [19] and others. These scientists, however, were interested primarily in applications of this principle to supersonic flow of gases. Later, comprehensive studies of the subject in hydraulic applications were made by Knapp, Ippen, and others [20–26]. To facilitate the analysis of shock wave in gases, Busemann [27] developed a graphical method known as the *method of characteristics*, which was later applied to hydraulic problems by Preiswerk, Ippen, and Knapp. For detailed descriptions of this method, the reader should refer to [23], [24], and [27].

section (Chap. 17). These waves, forming a disturbance pattern that can persist for a considerable distance downstream, are caused by the turning effect of the curved walls, which does not act equally on all streamlines in the channel section. In a curved channel, the outer wall, which turns inward to the flow, will produce an oblique hydraulic jump and a corresponding positive disturbance line or positive wavefront[1] (Art. 15-17). The inner wall, which turns away from the flow, will develop a so-called *oblique expansion wave* and a negative disturbance line or negative wavefront[1] (Example 16-2). The disturbance lines thus produced by both outer and inner walls will be reflected back and forth between walls and will interfere with each other, resulting in a disturbance pattern of cross waves.

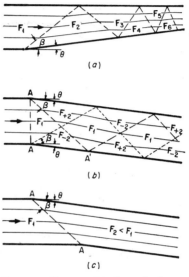

Similarly, in any channel of nonlinear alignment, cross waves may be formed in various patterns, such as those shown in Fig. 16-4. It may be noted that the cross waves in Fig. 16-4b can be canceled, as shown in Fig. 16-4c, by making the line $AA$ coincident with the first positive wavefront $AA'$. For large deflec-

Fig. 16-4. Rectangular channels of non-prismatic alignment.

tion angles of channel walls, the positive wavefront may be determined by the method developed in Art. 15-17 and the negative wavefront by the method to be described later in Example 16-2. For small deflection angles, such as the infinitesimal increment of the deflection angle in curved channels, the cross waves may be determined by the method described below.

In studying the development of these methods it should be noted that, for small deflection angles and for large deflection angles that create negative wavefronts, the specific energy across the wavefront can be assumed constant since little energy dissipation is actually involved. For large deflection angles that create positive wavefronts, however, the

---

[1] The disturbance line or wave angle created by an oblique hydraulic jump is considered positive in order to distinguish it from the negative disturbance line or wavefront due to an oblique expansion wave. The negative disturbance line actually only marks the beginning of a disturbance region; it is not a distinctly defined line like the positive one.

specific energy cannot be assumed constant because the wavefront is built up to a substantial height and so the oblique hydraulic jump across the front will consume an appreciable amount of energy.

Considering the supercritical flow in a curved channel of constant width $b$ and radius $r_c$ (Fig. 16-5), the first small disturbance caused by the

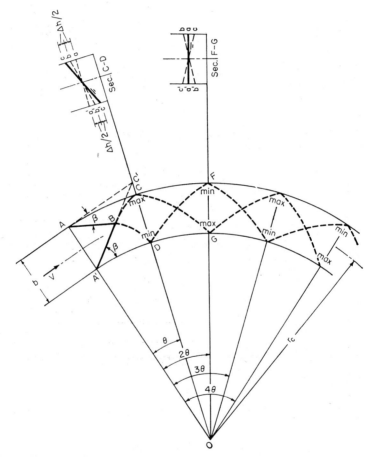

Fig. 16-5. Cross-wave pattern for supercritical flow in a curved channel.

curvature of the outer wall starts at the beginning point $A$ and is propagated along the line $AB$, which makes an initial wave angle $\beta$ with the tangent extended beyond point $A$. In the meantime, the initial disturbance produced by the inner wall is propagated along the line $A'B$. The two propagation fronts meet at point $B$. Upstream from the boundary line $ABA'$, the flow is unaffected by the curve and thus continues to move in its original direction, that is, parallel to the upstream tangent. Beyond point $B$, the two wavefronts $AB$ and $A'B$ affect each other and are no longer propagated in straight lines but in the curved paths $BD$ and $BC$, respectively. The outer concave wall $AC$ tends to deflect the flow, which would otherwise follow the tangential direction. Consequently, the water surface is raised higher and higher around the outer wall up to a maximum at $C$. After $C$ the effect of the inner wall, which is to lower the water surface, begins to operate. Thus, the water surface along the outer wall starts to drop. On the inner convex side, the flow tends to depart from the wall, and the water surface is depressed lower and lower around $A'D$ until the point $D$ is reached. After $D$ the effect of the outer wall comes into play and the surface begins to rise again. The reflection of disturbance waves from the outer and inner walls will not come to equilibrium or stop when they meet near the center of the channel. They will continue to be reflected back and forth across the channel, causing the surface profiles along the walls to have a series of maxima and minima of surface elevation, approximately at angles $\theta$, $3\theta$, $5\theta$, . . . , from the beginning of the curve. The angle $\theta$ marks half the wavelength of the disturbance pattern. For practical purposes, it may be assumed that the points of maximum and minimum for each phase angle $\theta$ occur on the same radial line, such as $OC$ for the first maximum and minimum.[1] By geometry (Fig. 16-5), the central angle to the first maximum can be shown to be

$$\theta = \tan^{-1} \frac{2b}{(2r_c + b) \tan \beta} \tag{16-14}$$

where the wave angle $\beta$ is approximately $\sin^{-1}(\sqrt{gy}/V)$, as will be shown below by Eq. (16-15).

In order to simplify the computation of the water-surface elevation[2] the following major assumptions are to be made: (1) two-dimensional flow, (2) constant velocity across the cross section, (3) horizontal channel, (4) frictionless flow, and (5) vertical channel walls. Assumptions 3 and 4 do not exclude the application of the results to sloping channels if the slope compensates for the friction.

For the curved outer wall, the changes in the angle of deflection and in the depth are gradual and small and, thus, can be represented by $d\theta$ and

[1] Actually the locations of the first maximum and minimum do not occur exactly on the radial line $OC$ but slightly on the left side and right side of $OC$, respectively (Fig. 16-5). However, the error involved in the assumption is negligible. This assumption applies also to the locations of the subsequent maxima and minima.

[2] A detailed study of the complete surface contours is possible by means of the method of characteristics [23].

$dy$, respectively. Assuming $y_1 = y_2 = y$ for an oblique hydraulic jump of infinitesimal height $dy$, Eq. (15-21) becomes[1]

$$\mathbf{F}_1 = \mathbf{F} = \frac{1}{\sin \beta} = \frac{V}{\sqrt{gy}} \tag{16-15}$$

Substituting $y$ for $y_1$ and $y + dy$ for $y_2$, Eq. (15-23) may be reduced to

$$dy = \frac{y \sec^2 \beta \tan \theta}{\tan \beta - \tan \theta} \tag{16-16}$$

For a small angle, $\tan \theta$ may be replaced by $d\theta$, and $\tan \theta$ in the denominator is negligible compared with $\tan \beta$. Thus, Eq. (16-16) becomes

$$dy = \frac{y}{\sin \beta \cos \beta} d\theta \tag{16-17}$$

By combining Eqs. (16-15) and (16-17), the following is obtained:

$$dy = \frac{V^2}{g} \tan \beta \, d\theta \tag{16-18}$$

According to assumption 4 above, the specific energy may be considered constant. Since $E = y + V^2/2g$, $V = \sqrt{2g(E - y)}$. Substituting this expression for $V$ in Eqs. (16-15) and (16-18) and then eliminating $\beta$ by Eq. (16-15), the following is obtained:

$$\frac{dy}{d\theta} = \frac{2(E - y) \sqrt{y}}{\sqrt{2E - 3y}} \tag{16-19}$$

The exact solution of Eq. (16-19) for $\theta$ gives

$$\theta = \sqrt{3} \tan^{-1} \sqrt{\frac{3y}{2E - 3y}} - \tan^{-1} \frac{1}{\sqrt{3}} \sqrt{\frac{3y}{2E - 3y}} + \text{const} \tag{16-20}*$$

Since $2E = y(2 + \mathbf{F}^2)$ (why?), Eq. (16-20) may be written

$$\theta = \sqrt{3} \tan^{-1} \frac{\sqrt{3}}{\sqrt{\mathbf{F}^2 - 1}} - \tan^{-1} \frac{1}{\sqrt{\mathbf{F}^2 - 1}} + \text{const} \tag{16-21}$$

This equation can be used to calculate the change in depth along the walls at the beginning of the curve. The integration constant can be determined by the condition that, for $\theta = 0$, the depth $y$ is the initial

---

[1] This equation is believed to be true only for supercritical flow in wide rectangular channels. For broad applications, Engelund and Munch-Petersen [28] have developed a generalized equation, which has been found in good agreement with experimental data covering considerable variation of the Froude number (even for $\mathbf{F}$ equal to or slightly less than unity) and of the depth-width ratio of the channel.

* The mathematical derivation of the equation of this form was first made by von Kármán [18].

depth $y_1$.  Equation (16-21) is, however, involved and inconvenient for practical usage, even with the aid of a graphical chart such as that developed by Ippen [23].  According to Knapp and Ippen [21–24], adequate results may be obtained by the much simpler equation

$$y = \frac{V^2}{g} \sin^2\left(\beta + \frac{\theta}{2}\right) \qquad (16\text{-}22)$$

This equation was developed as a result of actual flow measurements.[1] In using Eqs. (16-21) and (16-22), the angle $\theta$ is positive for depths along the outer wall and negative for depths along the inner wall.  The depth at the first maximum heights of the cross-wave disturbance may be obtained by using the value of $\theta$ computed by Eq. (16-14).

In cross section $CD$ (Fig. 16-5), where the first maximum height of the cross wave occurs at the outer wall, the line $a'a$ represents the theoretical position of the water surface in the channel cross section if the channel were straight, line $b'b$ the theoretical position of the water surface on the curve if the flow were subcritical, and line $c'c$ the actual water surface on the curve when the flow is supercritical.  It is evident that $b$ is higher than $a$ and $b'$ is lower than $a'$ by an amount equal to half the superelevation, or $\Delta h/2$.  By Eq. (16-11), this amount is $V^2 b/2r_c g$.  According to the experimental investigations made by Ippen and Knapp [21,23], $c$ is higher than $a$ by an amount equal to about $\Delta h$, or higher than $b$ by about $\Delta h/2$.  The position $c'$ is lower than $b'$ by about $\Delta h/2$.  Similar conditions exist in other cross sections where maximum height of water surface occurs at the outer wall.

In cross section $FG$, where the minimum cross-wave height occurs at the outer wall, the actual water surface is identical with $a'a$ because the effect of the disturbance cross wave is practically offset by the superelevation.  Similarly, in other cross sections where the wave height is minimum at the outer wall, the water surface assumes a position as if the flow were in a straight channel.

The distance $AC$ along the wall represents a half wavelength, which sustains a central angle $\theta$.  This length may be approximated by $AC'$

---

[1] On the basis of assumption 4 and, hence, of the conservation of energy, the velocity in any streamline must change as the depth changes, since $E = y + V^2/2g$ must be constant.  The flow around the outer wall, being the deepest, should be the slowest. Actual measurements, however, indicate on the contrary that the velocity around the outer wall remains constant or even increases slightly, whereas along the inner wall the velocity decreases.  It is believed that this disparity is due to varying effects of the channel friction, which actually render assumption 4 invalid.  Consequently, it is reasoned that a constant velocity may be assumed.  Equation (16-22) was, therefore, derived from the assumption of constant velocity, which replaces assumption 4. Since the author cannot discern here the rigor of the original mathematical derivation, he would rather consider Eq. (16-22) to be empirical.

or $b/\tan \beta$ by assuming that the angle $AC'A' = \beta$. Thus, the wavelength is $2b/\tan \beta$.

From the above discussion, it may be concluded that the disturbance wave pattern, which oscillates about the plane represented by $b'b$, has a wavelength of $2b/\tan \beta$ and an amplitude of $V^2b/2r_cg$. This finding can be used to estimate roughly the supercritical-flow profile in simple curved channels.

For disturbance continuing into the downstream tangent channel, the primary wavelength is still $2b/\tan \beta$. As the curvature suddenly changes to straight alignment, a new disturbance pattern, starting with a maximum height on the outer wall at the point of tangency, has a wavelength and magnitude equal to that of the original disturbance pattern developed in the curve. The resulting disturbance pattern in the tangent is the sum of the original and new patterns. The new disturbance pattern may, therefore, be eliminated by adopting curve lengths of $2\theta$, $4\theta$, . . . , which will have a minimum wave height at the outer wall at the end of the curve, just enough to cancel out the newly created maximum wave height.

**Example 16-2.** Describe the characteristics of an oblique expansion wave in channels of nonlinear alignment.

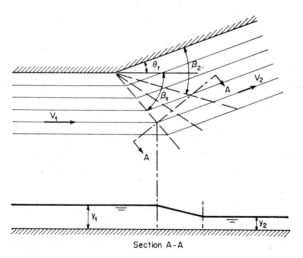

Section A-A

Fig. 16-6. Oblique expansion wave.

*Solution.* The oblique expansion wave occurs when the channel wall is turned outward from the flow at an angle $\theta_t$ (Fig. 16-6). The depth of flow decreases in the fan-shaped region of the wave disturbance delineated by wave angles $\beta_1$ and $\beta_2$, measured with reference to the initial and final flow directions, respectively. By Eq. (16-15),

$$\beta_1 = \sin^{-1}\frac{1}{F_1} \quad \text{and} \quad \beta_2 = \sin^{-1}\frac{1}{F_2} \quad (16\text{-}23)$$

where $F_1$ and $F_2$ are, respectively, the initial and final Froude numbers of the flow. The relation among $F_1$, $F_2$, and the total deflection angle $\theta_t$ can be represented by Eq. (16-21). In that equation, $\theta = 0$ when $F = F_1$ and $\theta = \theta_t$ when $F = F_2$. Thus, if $F_1$ and $\theta_t$ are given, $F_2$ can be determined. The angular range in which the depth change takes place may be determined by Eq. (16-23). Since the depth change does not involve appreciable energy dissipation, the depths before and after the change can be related by assuming a constant specific energy. Thus, the ratio of the final to the initial depth can be shown to be

$$\frac{y_2}{y_1} = \frac{F_1{}^2 + 2}{F_2{}^2 + 2} \tag{16-24}$$

In the disturbance region, the decrease in depth may be considered to continue through a series of infinitesimal steps or wavelets. The wave angle of each succeeding wavelet depends upon the local value of the continuously changing Froude number. Each wavelet may be successively represented by a line of constant depth. The first wavelet is represented by the negative disturbance line. It may be noted that, in contrast to the negative disturbance line, a positive disturbance line represents a more or less sudden increase in depth because it signifies a hydraulic jump. The negative disturbance line marks the beginning of a disturbance region developed by an oblique expansion wave, whereas the positive disturbance line represents the entire disturbance caused by an oblique hydraulic jump.

**16-6. Design Considerations for Subcritical Flow.** In general, curves are undesirable in open channels, because they will increase frictional loss and lead to danger of serious local erosion due to spiral flow. Reduction of spiral flow is the major concern in the design of curved channels for subcritical flow. For a proper proportioning of the curve, a ratio of $r_c/b = 3$ is recommended, because it will give the least radius at which the effect due to spiral flow is minimized (Art. 16-2).

In erodible channels, the action of spiral flow will develop a configuration in the bed. The size of the configuration is minimal if $r_c/b$ is 3.0 or larger. When bank protection is necessary, it is needed most on the outer bank at the downstream end of the curve and to a lesser degree on the inner bank at the beginning of the curve. This is suggested in accordance with the behavior of spiral flow.

In an alluvial bend it seems that the configuration of the channel cross section is defined more or less in accordance with certain natural laws. This subject has been investigated by many scientists and engineers of river hydraulics since Boussinesq [29]. According to the studies by Ripley [30], the configuration at an alluvial river bend (Fig. 16-7) may be represented by the following empirical equation:

$$y = 6.35D \left( \sqrt{0.437 - \frac{x^2}{T^2}} - 0.433 \right) \left( 1 + \frac{xK}{r_o} \right) \tag{16-25}$$

where $y$ is the ordinate or depth in ft, $x$ is the abscissa in ft, $D$ is the hydraulic depth in ft, $T$ is the top width in ft, $r_o$ is the radius of curvature on the concave side of the channel in ft, and $K$ is a coefficient equal to

17.52. The origin of the coordinates for this equation is on the water surface at a point equidistant from the banks. In using this equation the following remarks should be noted:

1. For $r_o$ less than 40 times the square root of the water area, no further deepening of the channel seems to result from the increased curvature; hence, in such cases, the value of $r_o$ used in the equation should be $40 \sqrt{A}$. Consequently, bends are constructive and stable when $r_o$ is greater than $40 \sqrt{A}$, whereas sharper bends are destructive, tending to shift the channel.

2. For $r_o$ greater than about $110 \sqrt{A}$, the equation becomes invalid.

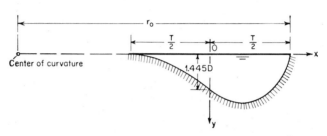

FIG. 16-7. Empirical channel cross section at river bend.

3. The equation may be applied to curved channels not occupying the entire width of the waterway or to those at the river entrance created by a single curved jetty. In such cases, $K = 26.28$ and the value of $y$ thus computed should be increased 14%.

4. On a crossover bar when the channel is neither on a curve nor in a straight reach, the maximum depth is about 14.5% less than the computed value.

5. The equation generally gives a width of channel at hydraulic depth about 20% greater than the actual width.

6. The equation is very approximate; nevertheless, in the absence of a better method for determining shape of cross section at a river bend or at a bend in a dredged canal, it will give satisfactory answers to many practical problems.

**16-7. Design Considerations for Supercritical Flow.** The major issue in the design of curved channels for supercritical flow is to eliminate or reduce the superelevation and cross-wave disturbance pattern. Knapp [24] has suggested the following methods to achieve this objective:

*A. Banking.* By banking is meant use of a bottom cross slope that will supply a lateral force to counteract the centrifugal action of the flow. The required cross slope $S_t$ can be computed by equating the gravity component along the cross slope to the centrifugal force determined by the radius $r$ of the curve and the velocity $V$; that is,

$$S_t = \frac{V^2}{gr} \qquad (16\text{-}26)$$

In order to avoid abrupt changes in flow condition, banking should be introduced gradually from zero to its full amount, starting at both ends of the curve. It should be noted that the slope thus computed is good only for the velocity given. When the velocity changes, the computed banking will be less effective under new flow conditions. Hence, banking is most suitable in channels which ordinarily operate at or near

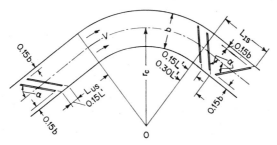

Fig. 16-8. Plan of sill installation in a curved channel. (*After R. T. Knapp* [24].)

the designed flow condition. Factors against banking include costly excavation and possible silting or erosion along the inner wall during low flows.

*B. Multiple Curved Vanes.* The superelevation and disturbance pattern can be reduced by concentric vanes which divide the channel width into a series of narrow curved channels. This method is not generally practical, and it becomes impossible in channels carrying debris of sizes larger than the subdivided width.

*C. Easement Curves.* The disturbance in a simple curved channel may be reduced by employing a compound curve. The best design is a simple curve of radius $r_c$ preceded and followed by a section of another simple curve, whose length is $b/\tan \beta$ and whose radius is $2r_c$. The resulting compound curve will offer a very desirable solution for most curved channels of supercritical flow. Other types of easement curve, such as a spiral transition curve, will increase appreciably the cost of design and construction with only slight improvement in flow characteristics.

*D. Diagonal Sills.* Diagonal sills installed on the bottom of the channel near the ends of the curve will produce an effect corresponding to that of an easement curve. An effective layout of the sills, shown in Fig. 16-8, has been developed experimentally. The optimum sill angle

$\alpha$ is 30°.    The distance $L_{US}$ may be estimated by

$$L_{US} = \frac{Kb}{\tan \beta} \qquad (16\text{-}27)$$

where $K$ is a coefficient.    For normal cases, the value of $K$ lies between 0.9 and 1.15.    In accordance with the figure the length $L_{IS}$ is

$$L_{IS} = 0.30L' + \frac{b}{\tan \alpha} \qquad (16\text{-}28)$$

where $L' = b/\tan \beta$, that is the half wavelength of a channel disturbance.

This method can be used as a remedial measure in existing channels which have been designed as simple circular curves or other unsatisfactory forms.    The major disadvantages of this method are high maintenance cost, pronounced disturbance at low flows, and possible cavitation at extreme high-velocity flows.    The pronounced disturbance at low flows may cause uneasiness and distrust in an unexperienced observer as he may not be easily convinced that the disturbance will be greatly reduced at high design flows.

## PROBLEMS

**16-1.** A 120° bend with $b = 10$ in. and $r_c = 15$ in. is designed to connect two straight channels of the same width, carrying 1.3 cfs at a normal depth of 7 in.    Determine the bend loss.

**16-2.** Determine the specific energy at the section containing maximum surface depression in the bend given in the preceding problem.    Assume $\alpha = 1.0$ and $n = 0.01$.

**16-3.** Compute the water-surface profile in the cross section containing maximum surface depression, as described in the preceding problem, using the law of free vortex. What is the superelevation?

**16-4.** Determine the superelevation in the preceding problem by (a) Eq. (16-11), (b) Eq. (16-12), and (c) Eq. (16-13).

**16-5.** Verify Eq. (16-14).

**16-6.** Determine the approximate flow profile in the curved channel given in Prob. 16-1 if the approach channel carries a supercritical flow at a depth of 0.5 in.

**16-7.** Design the curved channel for a rectangular flume to turn an angle of 50° with a radius of 250 ft.    The flume is 12 ft wide and built of smooth concrete.    The design discharge is 350 cfs at a slope of 1%.

**16-8.** Using Eq. (16-25), compute the channel cross section at a bend in the Mississippi River, where $A = 148,010$ ft², $T = 2,340$ ft, and $r_o = 18,300$ ft.    Compare the result with the actual cross section, which is as follows:

| x | y | x | y | x | y |
|---|---|---|---|---|---|
| 1,170 | 0.00 | 200 | 97.00 | −600 | 44.00 |
| 1,000 | 36.00 | 0 | 74.00 | −800 | 38.00 |
| 800 | 88.00 | −200 | 65.00 | −1,000 | 24.00 |
| 600 | 108.00 | −400 | 55.00 | −1,170 | 0.00 |
| 400 | 111.00 | | | | |

## REFERENCES

1. James Thomson: On the origin and winding of rivers in alluvial plains, with remarks on the flow around bends in pipes, *Proceedings, Royal Society of London*, vol. 25, pp. 5–8, Mar. 4, 1876.

2. Ahmed Shukry: Flow around bends in an open flume, *Transactions, American Society of Civil Engineers*, vol. 115, pp. 751–779, 1950.

3. A. Hinderks: Nebenströmungen in gekrümmten Kanälen (Secondary flow in curved canals), *Zeitschrift des Vereins deutscher Ingenieure*, Berlin, vol. 71, no. 51, pp. 1779–1783, Dec. 17, 1927.

4. Bruno Poggi: Correnti veloci nei canali in curva (Swift flow in curved channels), *L'Energia elettrica, Milano*, vol. 33, no. 5, pp. 465–480, May, 1956.

5. F. L. Blue, Jr., J. K. Herbert, and R. L. Lancefield: Flow around a river bend investigated, *Civil Engineering*, vol. 4, no. 5, pp. 258–260, May, 1934.

6. Herbert D. Vogel and Paul W. Thompson: Flow in river bends, *Civil Engineering*, vol. 3, no. 5, pp. 266–268, May, 1933.

7. Herbert D. Vogel and Paul W. Thompson: Existence of helicoidal flow, *Civil Engineering*, vol. 4, no. 7, pp. 370–371, July, 1934.

8. Robert Müller: Theoretische Grundlagen der Fluss- und Wildbachverbauungen (Theoretical principles for regulation of rivers and torrents), *Eidgenössische Technische Hochschule, Zürich, Mitteilungen der Versuchsanstalt für Wasserbau und Erdbau*, No. 4, 1943.

9. Sanjiva Puttu Raju: Versuche über den Strömungswiderstand gekrümmter offener Kanäle (Study on the flow resistance in curved open channels), *Mitteilungen des Hydraulischen Instituts der Technischen Hochschule München*, no. 6, pp. 45–60, Munich, 1933. English translation by Clarence E. Bardsley, Resistance to flow in curved open channels, *Proceedings, American Society of Civil Engineers*, vol. 63, pt. 2, p. 49 after p. 1834, November, 1937.

10. C. H. Yen and J. W. Howe: Effects of channel shape on losses in a canal bend, *Civil Engineering*, vol. 12, no. 1, pp. 28–29, January, 1942.

11. H. Wittman and P. Böss: "Wasser und Geschiebebewegung in gekrümmten Fluss-strecken" ("Water and Bed-load Movement in Curved River Reaches"), Springer-Verlag, Berlin, 1938.

12. C. E. Mockmore: Flow around bends in stable channels, *Transactions, American Society of Civil Engineers*, vol. 109, pp. 593–618, 1944.

13. Armin Schoklitsch: "Hydraulic Structures," translated from the German by Samuel Shulits, American Society of Mechanical Engineers, New York, 1937, vol. I, p. 151.

14. Sherman M. Woodward: Hydraulics of the Miami flood control project, *Miami Conservancy District, Technical Report, Pt. VII*, Dayton, Ohio, 1920.

15. Sherman M. Woodward and Charles J. Posey, "Hydraulics of Steady Flow in Open Channels," John Wiley & Sons, Inc., New York, 1941, p. 112.

16. L. Prandtl: Abriss der Strömungslehre ("Outline of the Theory of Flow"), Vieweg-Verlag, Brunswick, Germany, 1931.

17. D. Riabouchinsky: Sur l'analogie hydraulique des mouvements d'un fluide compressible (On hydraulic analogy of flows of a compressible fluid), *Comptes rendus de l'Académie des Sciences*, vol. 195, pp. 998–999, 1932; vol. 199, pp. 632–634, 1934.

18. Theodor von Kármán: Eine praktische Anwendung der Analogie zwischen Überschallströmung in Gasen und überkritischer Strömung in offenen Gerinnen (A practical application of analogy between supersonic flow in gases and supercritical flow in open channels), *Zeitschrift für angewandte Mathematik und Mechanik*, Berlin, vol. 18, pp. 49–56, February, 1938.

19. Ernst Preiswerk: Anwendung gasdynamischer Methoden auf Wasserströmungen mit freier Oberfläche (Application of the methods of gas dynamics to water flow with free surface), *Eidgenössische technische Hochschule Zürich, Mitteilungen aus dem Institut für Aerodynamik, No. 7, 1938.* English translation by S. Reiss as *National Advisory Committee for Aeronautics, Technical Memoranda Nos.* 934 and 935, March, 1940.

20. Arthur T. Ippen and Robert T. Knapp: A study of high velocity flow in curved channels of rectangular cross section, *Transactions, American Geophysical Union,* vol. 17, pp. 516–521, 1936.

21. Robert T. Knapp and Arthur T. Ippen: Curvilinear flow of liquids with free surfaces at velocities above that of wave propagation, *Proceedings of the 5th International Congress of Applied Mechanics, Cambridge, Mass.,* John Wiley & Sons, Inc., New York, pp. 531–536, 1938.

22. Arthur T. Ippen: Gas-wave analogies in open-channel flow, *Proceedings of the 2d Hydraulics Conference, June 1–4, 1942, State University of Iowa, Studies in Engineering, Bulletin 27,* no. 400, pp. 248–265, 1943.

23. Arthur T. Ippen: Mechanics of supercritical flow, 1st paper in High-velocity flow in open channels: A symposium, *Transactions, American Society of Civil Engineers,* vol. 116, pp. 268–295, 1951.

24. Robert T. Knapp: Design of channel curves for supercritical flow, 2d paper in High-velocity flow in open channels: A symposium, *Transactions, American Society of Civil Engineers,* vol. 116, pp. 296–325, 1951.

25. Arthur T. Ippen and John H. Dawson: Design of channel contractions, 3d paper in High-velocity flow in open channels: A symposium, *Transactions, American Society of Civil Engineers,* vol. 116, pp. 326–346, 1951.

26. Hunter Rouse, B. V. Bhoota, and En-Yun Hsu: Design of channel expansions, 4th paper in High-velocity flow in open channels: A symposium, *Transactions, American Society of Civil Engineers,* vol. 116, pp. 347–363, 1951.

27. A. Busemann: "Gasdynamik" ("Gasdynamics"), vol. IV, pt. 1 of "Handbuch der Experimentalphysik," Akademische Verlagsgesellschaft mbH, Leipzig, 1931, pp. 423–440.

28. Frank Engelund and Johs. Munch-Petersen: Steady flow in contracted and expanded rectangular channels, *La Houille blanche,* Grenoble, 8th yr., no. 4, pp. 464–474, August-September, 1953.

29. J. Boussinesq: Essai sur la théorie des eaux courantes (Essay on the theory of water flow), *Mémoires présentés par divers savants à l'Académie des Sciences,* Paris, vol. 23, ser. 2, no. 1, supplement 24, pp. 1–680, 1877.

30. H. C. Ripley: Relation of depth to curvature of channels, *Transactions, American Society of Civil Engineers,* vol. 90, pp. 207–238, 1927. Discussions on pp. 239–265.

# CHAPTER 17

# FLOW THROUGH NONPRISMATIC CHANNEL SECTIONS

Rapidly varied flow through nonprismatic sections[1] is found frequently in various open-channel structures. In previous chapters, many examples have been discussed, such as the broad-crested weir (Example 3-2), submerged sluice gate (Prob. 3-10), critical-flow flumes (Art. 4-6), channel outlet and entrance (Art. 11-3), sharp-crested weir (Art. 14-1), overflow spillways (Chap. 14), drum gates (Art. 14-9), stilling basins with various controls (Arts. 15-9 to 15-15), etc. In this chapter, several significant cases which require independent consideration will be discussed.

The problem under consideration often involves an appreciable amount of turbulence loss. In many cases, a practical solution of the problem can be achieved through the use of the continuity, energy, and momentum equations. This has been described in Arts. 3-6 to 3-8; and a typical example is demonstrated in Example 3-2. Such a method, however, does not evaluate theoretically the effects due to uncertain factors. For a more exact solution that takes all factors into account, it is necessary to resort to model studies or actual observations on existing structures. Then the theory can be used to set up an empirical equation or chart in which the coefficients are to be determined by experiments or from actual data.

**17-1. Sudden Transitions.** Transitions with the change of cross-sectional dimensions occurring in a relatively short distance will induce rapidly varied flow. Such transitions (Fig. 17-1) include sudden contractions and expansions vertically, horizontally, or both.

Take the horizontal contraction (Fig. 17-2) as an example.[2] Applying the momentum equation to sections 1-1, 2-2, and 3-3,

$$\frac{Qw}{g}(\beta_3 V_3 - \beta_1 V_1) = P_1 - P_2 - P_3 - F_f$$
$$= \frac{1}{2}wb_1y_1{}^2 - \frac{1}{2}w(b_1 - b_3)y_2{}^2 - \frac{1}{2}wb_3y_3{}^2 - F_f \quad (17\text{-}1)$$

By the continuity equation, $Q = V_1b_1y_1 = V_3b_3y_3$. For convenience

---

[1] Gradually varied flow through nonprismatic channel sections has been covered in Arts. 3-5, 3-8, and 11-4 to 11-7.

[2] The following discussion is based on a treatment given by Jaeger [1–3].

in the theoretical discussion, it may be assumed that $F_f = 0$, $\beta_1 = \beta_3 = 1$, and $y_2 = y_3$. Under these conditions, Eq. (17-1) may be reduced to

$$\mathbf{F}_1{}^2 = \frac{(y_3/y_1)[(y_3/y_1)^2 - 1]}{2[(y_3/y_1) - 1/(b_3/b_1)]} \tag{17-2}$$

where $\mathbf{F}_1{}^2 = V_1{}^2/gy_1$. This equation can be plotted as shown in Fig. 17-3, using $b_3/b_1$ as a parameter. The family of curves thus plotted are

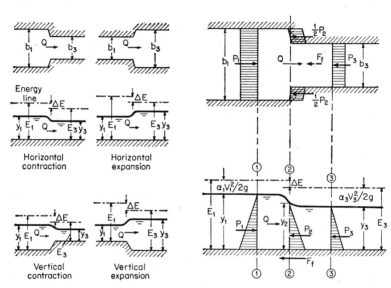

FIG. 17-1. Sudden transitions.

FIG. 17-2. Analysis of a horizontal contraction.

similar hyperbolas of a higher order, having the following characteristics:

1. The curves are considered only for positive values of $\mathbf{F}_1$ and $y_3/y_1$.

2. All hyperbolas pass through the points ($\mathbf{F}_1 = 0$, $y_3/y_1 = 0$) and ($\mathbf{F}_1 = 0$, $y_3/y_1 = 1$) and are asymptotic to the vertical line $y_3/y_1 = b_1/b_3$.

3. The special case of $b_3/b_1 = 1$, indicating the hydraulic jump in a prismatic channel, is represented by the curve

$$\mathbf{F}_1{}^2 = 0.5 \left(\frac{y_3}{y_1}\right) \left[\left(\frac{y_3}{y_1}\right) + 1\right]$$

(Why?)

4. The upstream flow is supercritical in the region above the horizontal line $\mathbf{F}_1{}^2 = 1$ or $\mathbf{F}_1 = 1$ and subcritical below this line. The downstream flow is subcritical in the region below the curve $\mathbf{F}_1{}^2 = (y_3/y_1)^3(b_3/b_1)^2$ and supercritical above it. (Why?) Consequently, four regions in the figure, representing four regimes, are created:

Region 1.   Flow is supercritical throughout the transition.
Region 2.   Flow through the transition passes from supercritical to subcritical.
Region 3.   Flow is subcritical throughout the transition.
Region 4.   Flow through the transition passes from subcritical to supercritical.

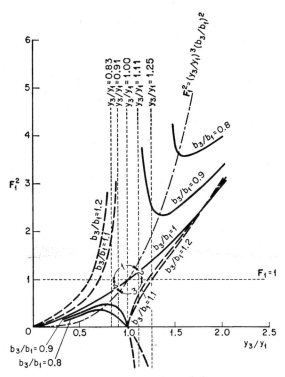

FIG. 17-3. Plot of $F_1{}^2$ against $y_3/y_1$, using $b_3/b_1$ as a parameter for the analysis of sudden horizontal contractions (shown by the full curves) and expansions (shown by the dashed curves).

5. Theoretically speaking, certain parts of the curves represent flows that cannot actually occur, because they necessitate an increase of energy, or a negative energy loss, which is contradictory to the fact that the flow always loses energy in passing through a transition. The difference between the energies before and after the transition is

$$\Delta E = y_1 + \frac{V_1{}^2}{2g} - y_3 - \frac{V_3{}^2}{2g} \tag{17-3}$$

or

$$\frac{\Delta E}{y_1} = 1 + \frac{F_1{}^2}{2} - \left[\frac{y_3}{y_1} + \frac{F_1{}^2}{2(y_3/y_1)^2(b_3/b_1)^2}\right] \tag{17-4}$$

By applying this equation to a certain part of the curves, the flow can be found to be impossible if the computed value of $\Delta E$ is negative. It should be noted, however, that this discussion is intended to present a theoretical analysis of the phenomenon and to develop a classification of the flow through sudden transitions. In real problems, the theoretically impossible flow may become actually possible because the assumptions made in the above derivation may not be true under actual circumstances.[1]

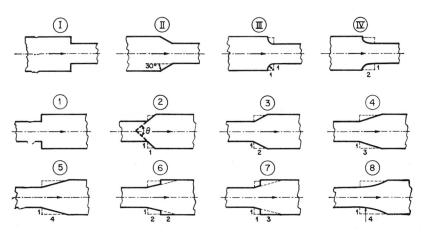

FIG. 17-4. Various designs of sudden transitions for experiments. (*After G. Formica* [4].) Channel width = 355 mm for wider sections and 205 mm for narrower sections. For contractions, channel slope = 0.00023 at wider sections and 0.00096 at narrower sections; for expansions, 0.00104 at narrower sections and 0.00073 at wider sections.

By a similar analysis, the following equation can be written for a horizontal expansion (assuming $y_2 = y_1$):

$$F_1{}^2 = \frac{(b_3/b_1)(y_3/y_1)[1 - (y_3/y_1)^2]}{2[1/(b_3/b_1) - (y_3/y_1)]} \qquad (17\text{-}5)$$

This equation is represented by the dashed curves in Fig. 17-3. Similar analyses may also be made for vertical contractions and expansions.

Experimental investigations on flow through sudden transitions will be discussed in the next three articles.

**17-2. Subcritical Flow through Sudden Transitions.** For subcritical flow passing through sudden transitions, experiments on various designs

---

[1] Under actual circumstances, $\beta_1$ and $\beta_2$ are not exactly equal to 1.0, and $y_2$ could be $y_1 > y_2 > y_3$. Thus, the negative energy loss would become positive, and the theoretically impossible flow would become actually possible. The loss $\Delta E$ is a very small amount and can readily be changed from negative to positive by a slight change in the items in Eq. (17-4).

were made by Formica [4], as shown in Fig. 17-4.   The typical measured flow profiles and energy lines for designs I (contraction) and 1 (expansion) are shown in Fig. 17-5.   The energy lines represent the specific energy $y + \alpha V^2/2g$.   Near the section where the transition takes place, the

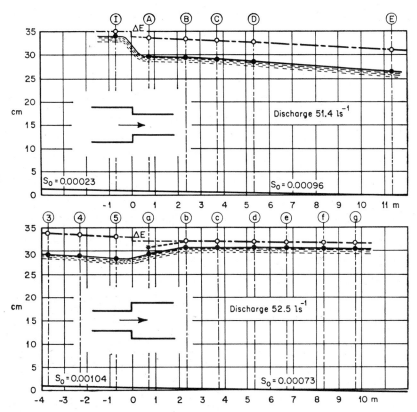

Fig. 17-5. Typical measured flow profiles and energy lines through sudden transitions. (*After G. Formica* [4].) In the figure, 1 ls$^{-1}$ = 0.03532 cfs, 1 m = 3.281 ft, and 1 cm = 0.3937 in.

velocity head cannot be measured easily because of the turbulent condition of flow; hence, the energy lines are simply extended.   The vertical intercept between the extended upstream and downstream lines at the transitional section represents the energy loss $\Delta E$.   The asterisk shown for the sudden expansion indicates the position of the energy line assuming $\alpha = 1$.

Figure 17-6 shows the computed values of the energy coefficient $\alpha$ at different sections of the channel for various designs of transitions.   The values are apparently very close to unity immediately after the sudden contractions but are generally higher than unity after the sudden expansions. This indicates that the flow in a sudden expansion is irregularly diffused.

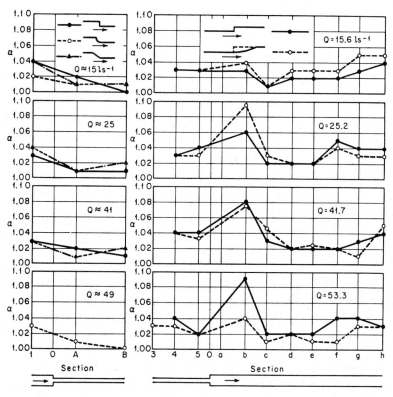

FIG. 17-6. Variation of the energy coefficient near sudden transitions. (*After G. Formica* [4].)   $1 \text{ ls}^{-1} = 0.03532 \text{ cfs.}$

The head losses for various designs of transitions at different discharges are shown in Fig. 17-7. It can be seen that in general the sudden contractions have higher losses than the sudden expansions. In a sudden contraction the flow is first contracted and then expanded. A process of conversion from potential to kinetic energy is followed immediately by a process of reconversion from kinetic to potential energy. As a result, much less energy than in a sudden expansion is recovered. However, the energy loss in a sudden contraction of design I can be greatly reduced by modifying the sharp-edged corners of the entrance of the reduced

channel, as in designs II to IV.   The differences among these three
designs are evidently insignificant.

Again, the energy loss in a sudden expansion can be reduced by gradually enlarging the channel section or decreasing the angle of divergence

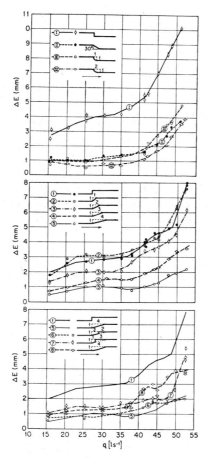

FIG. 17-7. Head losses in sudden transitions.   (*After G. Formica* [4].)   $1 \, \text{ls}^{-1} = 0.03532$
cfs and 1 mm = 0.03937 in.

($\theta$ in Fig. 17-4), but this advantage may be nullified by such modifications
as those in designs 6 to 8.   The length of the gradual enlargement of the
expansion has a limit beyond which the gain in efficiency becomes
insignificant.

In closed conduits [5], the energy loss in a sudden contraction may be expressed by

$$E = K \frac{V_3{}^2}{2g} \tag{17-6}$$

and in a sudden expansion by

$$E = \epsilon \frac{(V_1 - V_3)^2}{2g} \tag{17-7}$$

where $K$ and $\epsilon$ are coefficients, and $V_1$ and $V_3$ are the upstream and downstream velocities, respectively. By applying these equations to open

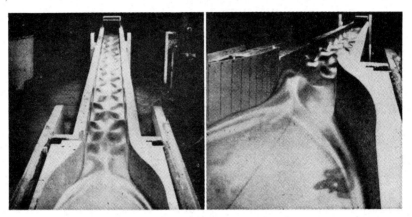

FIG. 17-8. Cross waves in a curved transition. (*Courtesy of A. T. Ippen.*)

channels, Formica obtained the following average values of $\epsilon$ for sudden expansions:

| Type of design | 1 | 2 | 3 | 4 | 5 | 6 | 7 | 8 |
|---|---|---|---|---|---|---|---|---|
| $\epsilon$ | 0.82 | 0.87 | 0.68 | 0.41 | 0.27 | 0.29 | 0.45 | 0.44 |

According to the experimental data obtained by Formica, the values of $K$ for sudden contractions seem to vary in a wide range, generally increasing with the discharge. The approximate median value of $K$ for design I is 0.10 and, for designs II to IV, 0.06.

**17-3. Contractions in Supercritical Flow.** When supercritical flow is introduced through a contraction with symmetrical converging walls, cross waves similar to those developed in a curved channel (Art. 16-5) will appear. The cross waves in a contraction, however, are symmetrical with respect to the center line of the channel (Fig. 17-8). The analytical study of the problem can be performed by the principles of the mechanics of supercritical flow described in the preceding chapter.

From an experimental and analytical investigation, Ippen and Dawson

[6] have found that straight contractions are always better than curved contractions of equal length of contraction from the standpoint of maximum height. Accordingly, they have proposed a procedure of design for straight contractions, which will be described below. For the design

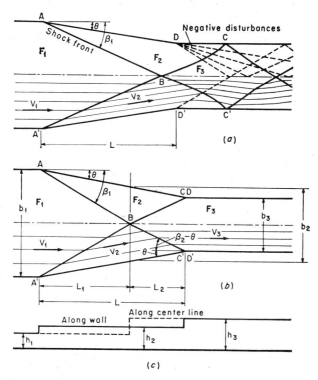

FIG. 17-9. Designs of straight-wall contractions. (*After Ippen and Dawson* [6].) (*a*) General disturbance patterns; (*b*) minimum downstream disturbance; (*c*) schematic profile.

of curved contractions, the cross-wave pattern may be determined experimentally by model test or analytically by the method of characteristics (see first footnote to Art. 16-5).

In supercritical flow through a straight contraction (Fig. 17-9*a*), symmetrical shock waves are developed at points $A$ and $A'$ at the entrance. These waves extend across the channel at wave angles $\beta_1$, intersect at $B$ on the center line of the channel, and, finally, after some modification, reach the opposite walls at $C$ and $C'$. In the regions $ABC$ and $A'BC'$, the flow proceeds through a new field characterized by the Froude number $F_2$. Note that, at the end of the contraction, negative disturbances are created at points $D$ and $D'$. These disturbances will result in more complicated disturbances downstream. In a good contraction design, it is possible to minimize the downstream disturbances. This can be done by directing the shock waves to the opposite walls at $D$ and $D'$, thus canceling off theoretically the newly created negative disturbances. As a result, the flow will be calm in the downstream channel. This is the situation shown in Fig. 17-9b. From the geometry of this situation, the length of the contraction can be shown to be

$$L = \frac{b_1 - b_3}{2 \tan \theta} \qquad (17\text{-}8)$$

By continuity of the flow, $b_1 y_1 V_1 = b_3 y_3 V_3 = Q$, or

$$\frac{b_1}{b_3} = \left(\frac{y_3}{y_1}\right)^{3/2} \left(\frac{\mathbf{F}_3}{\mathbf{F}_1}\right) \qquad (17\text{-}9)$$

The above equations and either Fig. 15-23 or Eq. (15-24) can be used to design a straight contraction with minimum downstream disturbances. Generally speaking, high values of $\mathbf{F}_1$ and low values of $y_3/y_1$ will give a long contraction. To reduce the length of the contraction, the advisable value of $y_3/y_1$ seems to be between 2 and 3, provided that $\mathbf{F}_3$ stays well above the critical value.

**Example 17-1.** Design a straight contraction connecting two rectangular channels 12 ft and 6 ft wide. The discharge through the contraction is 200 cfs. The depth of the approach flow is 0.70 ft.

*Solution.* Since $Q = 200$ cfs and $A = 12 \times 0.70 = 8.4$ ft$^2$, the velocity of the approach flow is $V_1 = 200/8.4 = 23.8$ fps. The Froude number $\mathbf{F}_1 = 5.01$.

Assume $y_3/y_1 = 2$ and take $b_1 = 12$, $b_3 = 6$, and $\mathbf{F}_1 = 5.01$; Eq. (17-9) gives $\mathbf{F}_3 = 3.54$. This value should not be less than 1.0 or even too close to 1.

Now, assume a value of $\theta$, say, 15°, and take $\mathbf{F}_1 = 5.01$; the diagram in Fig. 15-23 gives $y_2/y_1 = 2.60$ and $\mathbf{F}_2 = 2.8$.

A second determination using the same $\theta = 15°$ and replacing $\mathbf{F}_1$ by $\mathbf{F}_2 = 2.8$ produces values of $y_3/y_2 = 1.80$ and $\mathbf{F}_3 = 1.77$ from Fig. 15-23 (corresponding to $y_2/y_1$ and $\mathbf{F}_2$, respectively, in the diagram). However, these values do not necessarily represent the actual flow condition in the required design, since the flow condition downstream may be complicated by the negative disturbances originating from the points $D$ and $D'$.

Multiply $y_2/y_1$ by $y_3/y_2$; the first trial value of $y_3/y_1$ is equal to $2.60 \times 1.80 = 4.68$. Since this does not agree with the assumed value (that is, 2.00), the procedure should be repeated with a new value of $\theta$ until agreement is reached between the assumed $y_3/y_1$ and the value obtained by the trial.

After several trials, the correct angle $\theta$ is found to be 5°. With $\theta = 5°$ and $\mathbf{F}_1 = 5.01$, the diagram in Fig. 15-23 gives $y_2/y_1 = 1.50$ and $y_3/y_2 = 1.35$. The value of $y_3/y_1 = 1.50 \times 1.35 = 2.03$, which is close to the assumed value.

By Eq. (17-8), the length of the contraction is found to be 34.3 ft.

**17-4. Expansions in Supercritical Flow.** Channel expansion in supercritical flow occurs frequently at places where flow emerges at high velocity from a closed conduit, sluice gate, spillway, or steep chute. If such an expansion is made to diverge too rapidly, the major part of the flow will fail to follow the boundaries. Studies by Hom-ma and Shima [7] indicate that separation of flow like that shown in Fig. 17-10 may occur. The separation surfaces shown by the dashed lines act as solid boundaries within which the flow has the characteristics similar to those in a channel of decreasing width. If the divergence of the expansion is

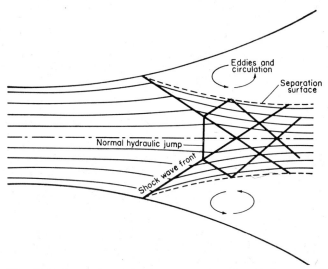

FIG. 17-10. Separation of flow in an expansion of rapid divergence.

too gradual, waste of structural material will result. Furthermore, if local disturbances of great wave height are produced by improper boundary geometry, either at the expansion or farther downstream, the walls may fail to confine the flow. Satisfactory design for the expansion is, therefore, of practical importance.

The best way to study a particular channel expansion is by cut-and-try investigation through model tests. Using an analytical approach, streamlines and water-surface contours for any expansion can be constructed directly by the method of characteristics (see first footnote, Art. 16-5), provided that (1) the channel walls are vertical and the floor is horizontal, (2) the energy loss due to boundary resistance is negligible, and (3) the pressure is hydrostatically distributed. Owing to these limitations, the analytical method can give only approximate results.

From both experimental and analytical studies, Rouse, Bhoota, and Hsu [8] have obtained the following results, which may be found useful in the preliminary design of channel expansions in supercritical flow:

1. The generalization of experimental data for channel expansions may be expressed by the following relationship:

$$\frac{y}{y_1} = f\left(\frac{x}{b_1 \mathbf{F}_1}, \frac{z}{b_1}\right) \tag{17-10}$$

where $y$ is the depth of flow, $y_1$ is the depth of the approach flow, $\mathbf{F}_1$ is the Froude number of the approach flow, $b_1$ is the channel width, $x$ is the

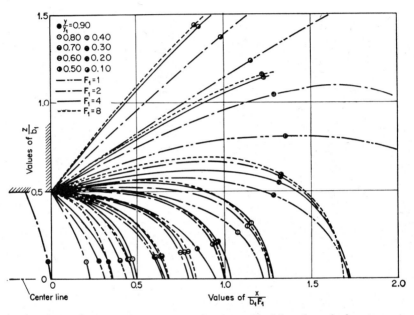

Fig. 17-11. Generalized surface contours for supercritical flow through abrupt expansion. (*After Rouse, Bhoota, and Hsu* [8].)

longitudinal coordinate measured from the outlet section, and $z$ is the lateral coordinate measured from the center line of the channel.

2. For abrupt expansions, a dimensionless diagram (Fig. 17-11) was developed. This diagram, generalizing the experimental data in the functional relationship of Eq. (17-10), may be used for the preliminary analysis of an abrupt expansion.

3. From the experiments, the most satisfactory boundary form for an efficient expansion was found to be

$$\frac{z}{b_1} = \frac{1}{2}\left(\frac{x}{b_1 \mathbf{F}_1}\right)^{3/2} + \frac{1}{2} \tag{17-11}$$

For expansions designed for this form, the surface contours for a mean value of $b_1/y_1$ and for various values of $\mathbf{F}_1$ are shown in Fig. 17-12.   This form of expansion boundary corresponds approximately to the shape of the streamlines that confine about 90% of the flow.   Note that the beginning of this expansion is sufficiently gradual to reduce the effect of nonhydrostatic pressure distribution to a minimum, so that the factor $b_1/y_1$ is no longer an essential variable.   In this form, the general increase

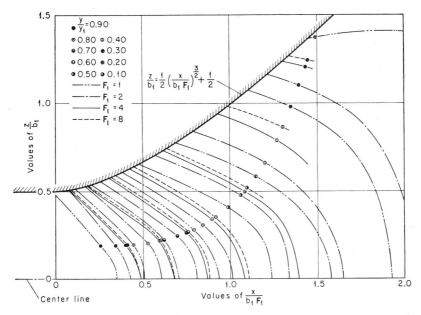

FIG. 17-12.   Generalized surface contours for supercritical flow through gradual expansion.   (*After Rouse, Bhoota, and Hsu* [8].)

in the boundary angle is sufficient to eliminate the formation of cross waves, yet not so great as to cause an undue change in depth across any normal section.

The boundary represented by Eq. (17-11), however, will diverge indefinitely.   For practical purposes, the divergent walls of the expansion will usually be followed by parallel walls with either an abrupt or a gradual transition.   As a result, positive disturbances downstream may be produced.   When practical circumstances permit, such disturbances can be eliminated by a hydraulic jump at or near the end of the expansion.   To avoid dangerous asymmetry of the flow at the end of the expansion, the jump may be stabilized by a drop on the channel floor (Art. 15-10).

4. The disturbance in the downstream channel may also be eliminated if the transition mentioned above is designed with a well-proportioned reversal of the wall curvature.   In such a design, the positive and negative disturbances developed by the reversal of the curvature may offset each other so that the flow is restored to complete uniformity at the end of the transition.   Figure 17-13 shows the boundary curves of such a design, derived by the method of characteristics.   Although these

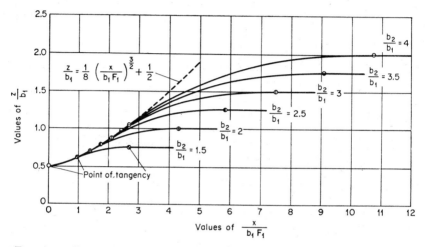

Fig. 17-13. Generalized boundary curves for channel expansion determined by the method of characteristics. (*After Rouse, Bhoota, and Hsu* [8].) $b_2$ = downstream channel width.

curves merely represent generalized conditions, they may be used as guides in preliminary design in order to give as little angularity of the final flow as is consistent with the practical requirements of transition length.

The U.S. Soil Conservation Service [9] has also made tests on supercritical flow through expansions in conjunction with the SAF stilling basin (Art. 15-12).   The tests were made on transitions with straight flaring side walls and 1% channel slope.   The major findings of the tests are:

1. A length of approach channel preceding the transition equal to $5y_1$ is satisfactory, where $y_1$ is the approach depth of flow.

2. The maximum permissible side-wall divergence is 1 in $3F_1$ if cross waves of excessive height are to be avoided.

3. The use of the expansion ahead of a SAF stilling basin is economical.

4. Design charts providing information on relative depth contours and flow conditions within the transition were developed.

**17-5. Constrictions.** A constriction in an open channel constitutes a reach of sudden reduction in the channel cross section. The effect of a constriction on the flow depends mainly on the boundary geometry, the discharge, and the state of flow. The phenomenon is usually so complicated that the resulting flow pattern is not readily subject to any analytical solution. A practical solution is possible, however, through systematic experimental investigation.

The flow through a constriction may be subcritical or supercritical. When the flow is subcritical, the constriction will induce a pronounced backwater effect that extends a long distance upstream (Fig. 17-14a and b). When the flow is supercritical, the constriction will disturb only the water surface that is adjacent to the upstream side of the constriction and will not extend the effect farther upstream (Fig. 17-14c). If the upstream water surface is dammed up to a depth greater than the critical depth, the surface will form an $S1$ profile, extending upstream only for a short distance and then ending with a hydraulic jump (Fig. 17-14d).

A critical control section may or may not exist at the constriction, depending on the magnitude of the energy $E_n$ of the normal flow in com-

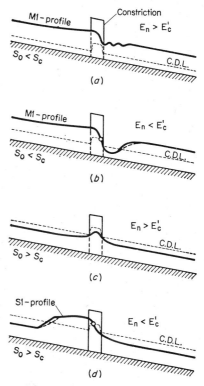

FIG. 17-14. Constriction in uniform-flow channel (a, b) in subcritical flow; (c, d) in supercritical flow.

parison with the energy $E_c'$ of the critical flow at the constriction. For a short constriction, this situation is shown in Fig. 17-14. In the case of a long constriction, the constriction itself constitutes a channel. The control section, when it exists, may be at either the upstream or the downstream end of the constriction, depending on whether the slope of the constricted channel is steep or mild. The entrance and outlet of the constriction then act as a contraction and an expansion, respectively. The critical-flow flume (Art. 4-6) presents a unique case of channel constriction. The flow through the flume may be either free from or drowned by the tailwater. A critical section exists at or near the neck of the flume only when the flow is free.

Investigations on the subject of flow through constrictions are many, but most of them have dealt with subcritical flow. The *contracted-opening method*,[1] a method for determining flood discharges which has been very popular with American engineers since 1918 or earlier, is based on the application of the energy and continuity equations to the flow through a constriction in the waterway. The first laboratory investigation in the United States is believed to have been made by Lane [11]. This investigation dealt with simple constrictions of flows having Froude numbers slightly higher than those usually found in natural channels. In recent years, a new development in the study of constrictions in subcritical flow has been achieved by comprehensive fundamental research carried out at the U.S. Geological Survey by Kindsvater, Carter, and Tracy [12–15]. The method they developed produces more exact results for various given conditions and so will undoubtedly replace the conventional contracted-opening method in engineering practice. The following two articles will cover the essentials of this new development.

**17-6. Subcritical Flow through Constrictions.** When an area constriction is introduced to an otherwise uniform, friction-controlled flow in a prismatic channel of mild slope (Fig. 17-15),[2] a backwater of $M$1-type profile is first developed upstream from the constriction. The upstream end point of the backwater curve is assumed to be at section 0. Near the constriction at section 1 the central body of water begins to accelerate, deceleration occurs along the outer boundaries, and separation zones are created in the corners adjacent to the constriction. An adequate approximation for the location of section 1 may be taken at a point one opening width $b$ from the center of the opening. Between sections 0 and 1, the flow is gradually varied.

At the constriction, the flow is rapidly varied, characterized by marked acceleration in directions both normal and parallel to the streamlines. The longitudinal water surface drops rapidly in this region. Within the constriction, the live stream contracts to a width somewhat less than the nominal width of the opening, and the spaces between the live stream and the constriction boundaries are separation zones occupied by eddying

---

[1] Houk [10] credited S. M. Woodward with the development of this method for use by the Miami Conservancy District. The other equally important method reported by Houk is the slope-area method (Art. 6-9).

[2] In Fig. 17-15, it is shown that the flow through the constriction is subcritical, as in Fig. 17-14$a$. This is the case usually encountered in practical problems. If the water surface drops below the critical-depth line at the constriction, supercritical flow will occur, as shown in Fig. 17-14$b$. To reestablish subcritical flow downstream, a hydraulic jump will be developed near the downstream side of the constriction. The method described here, however, is not applicable to this case.

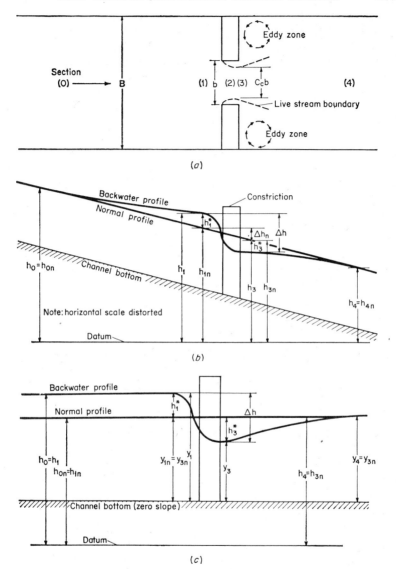

FIG. 17-15. Definition sketch of flow through constriction. (*After Tracy and Carter* [14].) (*a*) Plan; (*b*) elevation; (*c*) elevation, adapted to assumption of zero friction loss.

water.  As the water passes through the contraction, the contracted stream reaches a minimum width at section 2, which corresponds to the vena contracta in an orifice flow.  After the vena contracta, the live stream begins to expand until it reaches downstream section 4, where the uniform-flow regime is reestablished in the full-width channel.  Between sections 3 and 4, the flow is gradually varied.  Over the whole reach from sections 0 to 4 encompassed by the backwater effect of the constriction, the total energy loss is the same as that for uniform flow.

For a simple analysis of the flow characteristics, the following conditions may be assumed:

1. The channel floor is horizontal or nearly so.

2. Laboratory observations have shown that the level of the water at the vena contracta can be closely approximated by the level at section 3, which is at the downstream face of the constriction.  Hence, the depth $y_2$ can be taken as $y_3$.

3. A coefficient of discharge is introduced in the analysis to include the over-all effect of contraction, eddy loss, nonuniform distribution of velocity, and nonhydrostatic distribution of pressure.  The related notation to be used in the analysis is defined as follows:

$h_e$ = eddy loss due to turbulence engendered in the upstream separation zones.  It is assumed that this loss can be expressed in terms of the velocity head at section 3, or

$$h_e = k_e(V_3{}^2/2g)$$

where $k_e$ is a coefficient.

$\alpha_1$ and $\alpha_3$ = energy coefficients at sections 1 and 3, respectively.

$\alpha_1'$ and $\alpha_3'$ = pressure coefficients at sections 1 and 3, respectively.  It is assumed that the deviation from hydrostatic distribution of pressure can be expressed in terms of the velocity head at section 3.  Thus,

$$\alpha_3'y_3 = k_p(V_3{}^2/2g) + y_3$$

where $k_p$ is a coefficient responsible for the nonhydrostatic pressure distribution.

$C_c$ = coefficient of contraction at section 3.

Applying the energy equation to sections 1 and 3 (Fig. 17-15c), the following can be written:

$$\alpha_1 \frac{V_1{}^2}{2g} + \alpha_1'y_1 = \alpha_3 \frac{V_3{}^2}{2g} + \alpha_3'y_3 + h_e + h_f \qquad (17\text{-}12)$$

where $h_f$ is the frictional loss.  Then, assuming $\alpha_1' = 1$, $\alpha_3'y_s = k_p(V_3{}^2/2g) + y_3$, and $h_e = k_e(V_3{}^2/2g)$,

$$\alpha_1 \frac{V_1{}^2}{2g} + y_1 = (\alpha_3 + k_p + k_e) \frac{V_3{}^2}{2g} + y_3 + h_f \qquad (17\text{-}13)$$

The discharge through section 3 is

$$Q = C_c A_3 V_3 \tag{17-14}$$

where $A_3$ is the water area at section 3.   Solving Eqs. (17-13) and (17-14) for the discharge,

$$Q = C A_3 \sqrt{2g \left( \Delta h - h_f + \alpha_1 \frac{V_1^2}{2g} \right)} \tag{17-15}$$

where $\Delta h = y_1 - y_3$ and where $C$ is an over-all coefficient of discharge, equal to

$$C = \frac{C_c}{\sqrt{\alpha_3 + k_e + k_p}} \tag{17-16}$$

This is a theoretical expression.   For practical uses, the value of $C$ may be expressed by a dimensionless function and evaluated experimentally.

By a dimensional analysis of the essential geometric and hydraulic factors that govern the flow, it can be shown that $C$ is expressible as a function of the factors, or

$$C = f[m, \mathbf{F}_3, r/b, W/b, \theta, \phi, (y_a + y_b)/2b, x/b, E, e, t/(y_3 + \Delta h), j, L/b] \tag{17-17}$$

The hydraulic factors contained in this function represent the following various physical effects:

1. The effect of channel contraction is represented by the *contraction ratio m*.   This ratio is equal to $1 - K_b/K_B$, in which $K_B$ is the conveyance of the uncontracted approach section 1 at normal discharge and $K_b$ is the conveyance of the contracted section 3 which has the same normal depth and roughness characteristics as the approach section.   For a rectangular approach section of width $B$ and a rectangular contracted section of width $b$, this ratio is $m = 1 - b/B$.   A *conveyance ratio σ* may be defined as $1 - m$.   Thus $\sigma = 1$ or $m = 0$ when there is no constriction.

2. The effect of Froude number is represented by the Froude number at section 3, or $\mathbf{F}_3 = Q/(A_3 \sqrt{gy_3})$.   It is necessary to assume a discharge for the initial computation of the value $\mathbf{F}_3$.   The final value of $\mathbf{F}_3$ can be determined by successive approximations.   If the value of $\mathbf{F}_3$ is greater than 0.8, nearly critical or supercritical velocities may occur in section 3; then the method described here is inapplicable.

3. The effect of entrance rounding of the abutment is represented by $r/b$, where $r$ is the radius of rounding of the entrance corner of abutments for vertical-faced constrictions.

4. The effect of chamfers of the abutment is represented by $W/b$ and $\theta$, where $W$ is the length of wing wall measured in a direction normal to section 3 and where $\theta$ is the acute angle between a wing wall and the plane of constriction.

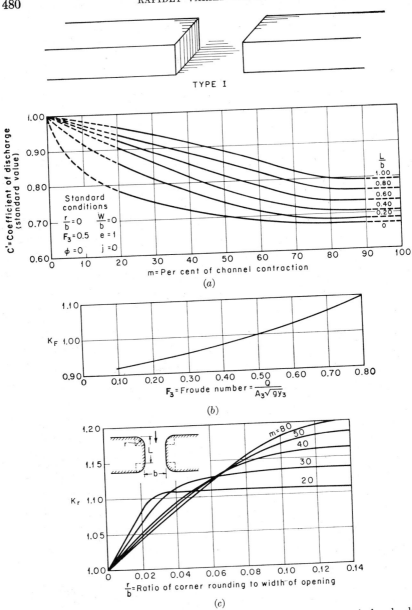

FIG. 17-16. Discharge coefficient for constriction of type I opening, vertical embankments ($E = 0$) and vertical abutments. (*U.S. Geological Survey* [12].) (*a*) Base curve for coefficient of discharge; (*b*) variation of discharge coefficient with Froude number; (*c*) variation of discharge coefficient with entrance rounding.

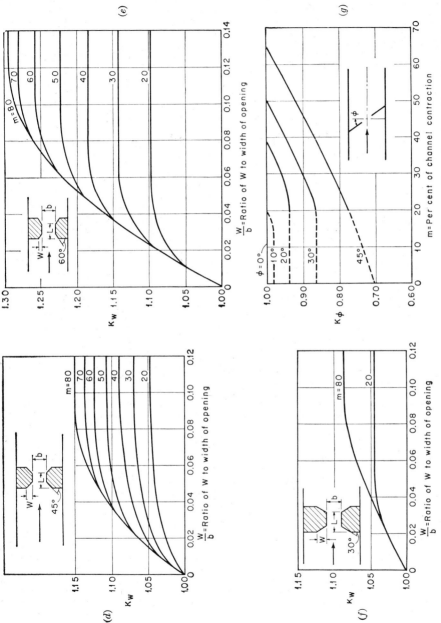

FIG. 17-16 (*Continued*). (*d*) Variation of discharge coefficient with length of 45° wing walls or chamfers; (*e*) variation of discharge coefficient with length of 60° wing walls; (*f*) variation of discharge coefficient with length of 30° wing walls; (*g*) variation of discharge coefficient with angularity.

5. The effect of angularity of constriction is represented by $\phi$, the acute angle between the plane of the constriction and a line normal to the thread of the stream.

6. The effect of side depths at abutments is represented by $(y_a + y_b)/2b$, where $y_a$ and $y_b$ are water depths at the toe of each abutment.

7. The effect of side slope of the abutment is represented by $x/b$ and $E$. The value of $x$ is the horizontal distance from the point of intersection of the abutment and embankment slopes to a point on the upstream embankment that has the same elevation as the water surface at section 1. The value $E$, representing the embankment slope, is a ratio of horizontal to vertical distance.

8. The effect of eccentricity of constriction is represented by $e$, which is equal to the ratio $K_a/K_b$. The conveyance of the whole approach section may be subdivided into the conveyance of the corresponding contracted section and two conveyances of the side sections. The two conveyances of the side sections are designated by $K_a$ and $K_b$ and the conveyance of the corresponding contracted section by $K_c$. Thus, the total conveyance $K_B = K_a + K_b + K_c$. And the ratio $K_a/K_b$ is a measure of the eccentricity of the constriction.

9. The effect of submergence of any possible bridge across the constriction is represented by $t/(y_3 + \Delta h)$, where $t$ is the vertical distance between water level at section 1 and the lowest horizontal member of a partially submerged bridge, and $\Delta h = h_1 - h_3$ (Fig. 17-23b).

10. The effect of bridge piles and piers is represented by $j$ and $L/b$. The value $j$ is equal to $A_j/A_3$, where $A_j$ is the vertical transverse area of the submerged piers or piles at the contraction and $A_3$ is the water area of section 3. The value $L$ is the length of the abutment in the direction of the thread of the stream, variously defined for different types of openings.

For purposes of practical application, the value of $C$ may be expressed as

$$C = C'K_F K_r K_W K_\phi K_y K_x K_e K_t K_j \qquad (17\text{-}18)$$

where $C'$ is the standard value of the coefficient of discharge corresponding to a standard condition of all effects mentioned above; and where the $K$'s are coefficients that can be used to adjust the value of $C'$ to a given nonstandard condition of the Froude number, entrance rounding, chamfer, angularity, side depths, side slope, bridge submergence, and bridge piles and piers, respectively. From the laboratory investigation by the U.S. Geological Survey [12], a set of curves were developed for the determination of these coefficients for four different types of constriction (Figs. 17-16 to 17-23).

When a waterway is contracted by bridge piers or piles alone, it may be assumed that $C' = 1$, and $C$ is adjusted by $K_j$ only. To determine

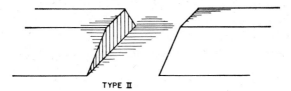

TYPE II

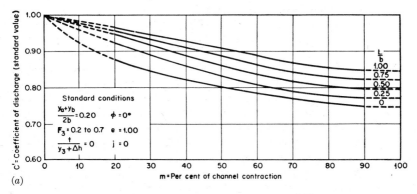

Standard conditions

$\dfrac{y_a + y_b}{2b} = 0.20$    $\phi = 0°$

$F_3 = 0.2$ to $0.7$   $e = 1.00$

$\dfrac{t}{y_3 + \Delta h} = 0$   $j = 0$

(a)   m = Per cent of channel contraction

$\dfrac{y_a + y_b}{2b} = 0.20$ and above

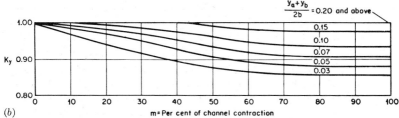

(b)   m = Per cent of channel contraction

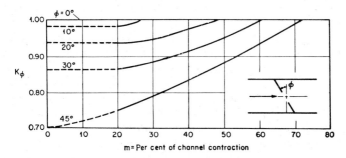

(c)   m = Per cent of channel contraction

Fig. 17-17. Discharge coefficient for constriction of type II opening, embankments with 1:1 slope ($E = 1$) and vertical abutments. (*U.S. Geological Survey* [12].) (*a*) Base curve for coefficient of discharge; (*b*) variation of discharge coefficient with ($y_a + y_b$)/2b ratio; (*c*) variation of discharge coefficient with angularity.

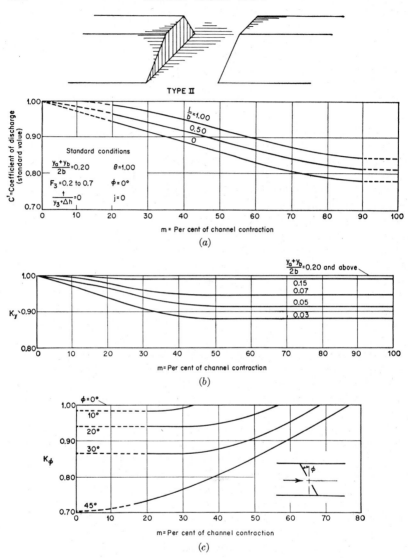

FIG. 17-18. Discharge coefficient for constriction of type II opening, embankments with 2:1 slope ($E = 2$) and vertical abutments. (*U.S. Geological Survey* [12].) (*a*) Base curve for coefficient of discharge; (*b*) variation of discharge coefficient with $(y_a + y_b)/2b$ ratio; (*c*) variation of discharge coefficient with angularity.

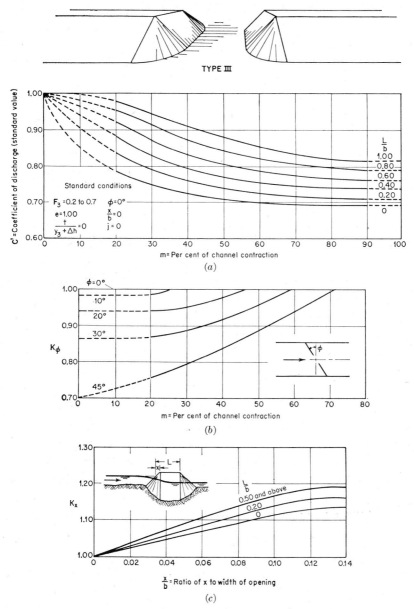

FIG. 17-19. Discharge coefficient for constriction of type III opening, embankments and abutments with 1:1 slope ($E = 1$). (*U.S. Geological Survey* [12].) (*a*) Base curve for coefficient of discharge; (*b*) variation of discharge coefficient with angularity; (*c*) variation of discharge coefficient with $x/b$ ratio.

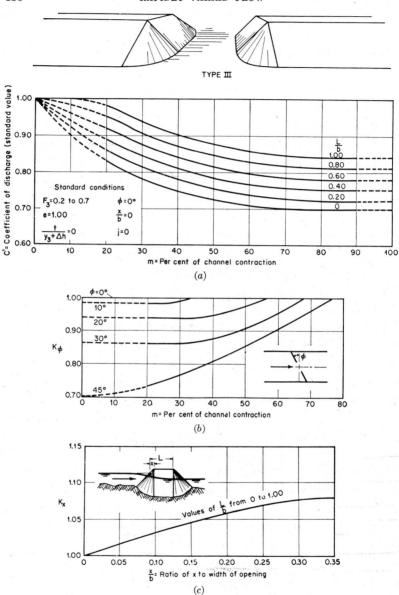

TYPE III

(a)

(b)

(c)

FIG. 17-20. Discharge coefficient for constriction of type III opening, embankments and abutments with 2:1 slope ($E = 2$). (*U.S. Geological Survey* [12].) (*a*) Base curve for coefficient of discharge; (*b*) variation of discharge coefficient with angularity; (*c*) variation of discharge coefficient with $x/b$ ratio.

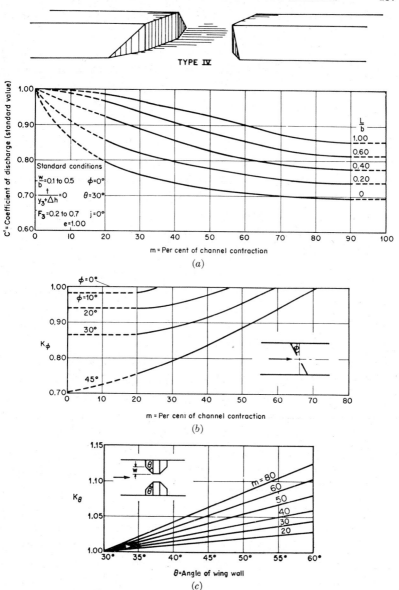

FIG. 17-21. Discharge coefficient for constriction of type IV opening, embankments with 1:1 slope ($E = 1$) and vertical abutments with wing walls. (*U.S. Geological Survey* [12].) (*a*) Base curve for coefficient of discharge; (*b*) variation of discharge coefficient with angularity; (*c*) variation of discharge coefficient with wing-wall angle.

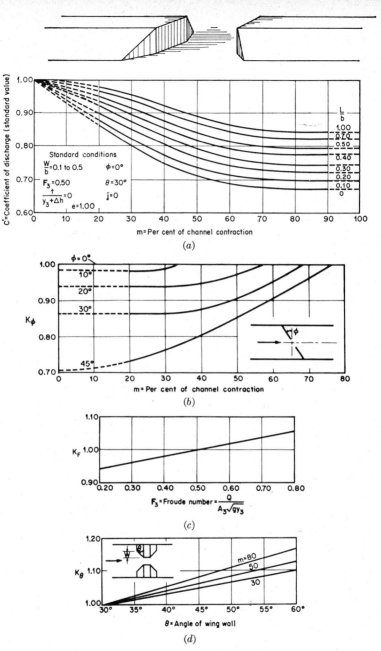

Fig. 17-22. Discharge coefficient for constriction of type IV opening, embankments with 2:1 slope ($E = 2$) and vertical abutments with wing walls. (*U.S. Geological Survey* [12].) (*a*) Base curve for coefficient of discharge; (*b*) variation of discharge coefficient with angularity; (*c*) variation of discharge coefficient with Froude number; (*d*) variation of discharge coefficient with wing-wall angle.

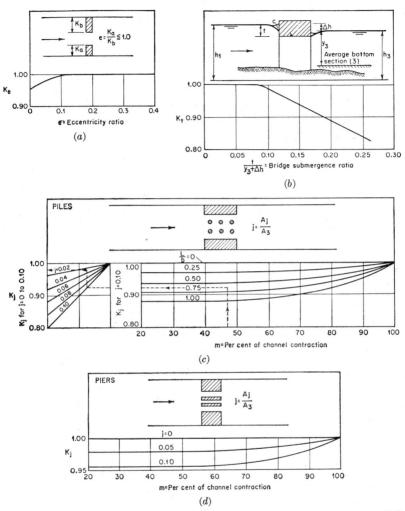

Fig. 17-23. $K_e$, $K_t$, and $K_j$ curves for constrictions of types I to IV openings. (*U.S. Geological Survey* [12].) (*a*) Variation of discharge coefficient with eccentricity; (*b*) variation of discharge coefficient with degree of submergence of bridge; (*c*) variation of discharge coefficient with area of bridge piles; (*d*) variation of discharge coefficient with area of bridge piers.

$K_j$ from the diagram (Fig. 17-23*c*), enter the horizontal scale at the proper value of $m$, then move vertically to the value of $L/b$, horizontally to the line marked $j = 0.10$, vertically to the value of $j$, and horizontally to the value of $K_j$. If $j$ happens to be greater than 0.10, an approximate computation may be made by taking $C = C'$ for the given $m$ and omitting $K_j$.

It is possible that certain combinations of the empirical coefficients applied to $C'$ may appear to yield a value of $C$ greater than 1.0. In such cases, however, a value of $C = 1.0$ should be used.

The friction-loss term $h_f$ in the discharge equation, Eq. (17-15), represents the total loss of head due to friction between sections 1 and 3. This loss is equal to the sum of the loss in the approach reach of length $L_a$ from section 1 to the upstream side of the contracted opening and the loss in the contracted reach of length $L$. The total head-friction loss may be computed by

$$h_f = L_a \left( \frac{Q}{\sqrt{K_1 K_3}} \right)^2 + L \left( \frac{Q}{K_3} \right)^2 \tag{17-19}$$

where $K_1$ and $K_3$ are the total conveyances of sections 1 and 3, respectively. Substitute in Eq. (17-15) the above expression for $h_f$, and $Q/A_1$ for $V_1$; the discharge may be expressed as

$$Q = 8.02 C A_3 \sqrt{\frac{\Delta h}{1 - \alpha_1 C^2 (A_3/A_1)^2 + 2g C^2 (A_3/K_3)^2 (L + L_a K_3/K_1)}} \tag{17-20}$$

This equation can be used for computing the required discharge.

**Example 17-2.** Compute the flood discharge through a highway bridge opening in a practically straight and uniform reach of a river. An approach section 300 ft upstream from the bridge has the characteristics described in Example 6-1. At the contracted section, the bridge spans over the main channel and the side channel is entirely blocked up by the highway embankment. The constriction thus created is 30 ft long and 180 ft wide and has a type I opening (Fig. 17-16). The average water surface at the contracted section was found to be 5 ft below that at the approach section. It is assumed that both the main and side channel sections are approximately rectangular. Thus, the dimensions are 180 ft wide by 29.8 ft deep for the main channel and 390.4 ft wide by 14.6 ft deep for the side channel.

*Solution.* From the data in Example 6-1, the contraction ratio $m = 1.24 \times 10^6/(3.14 \times 10^6) = 0.40$. With this value of $m$ and $L/b = {}^{30}\!/_{180} = 0.17$, the chart in Fig. 17-16a gives $C' = 0.76$ for a constriction with type I opening. The adjustment coefficient for the eccentricity of the opening is $K_e = 0.96$, and other coefficients are equal to 1.0, assuming $\mathbf{F}_3 = 0.5$. Hence, $C = 0.76 \times 0.96 = 0.73$.

For the contracted section, $A_3 = 180 \times 24.8 = 4,460 \text{ ft}^2$, $P_3 = 180 + 2 \times 24.8 = 229.6 \text{ ft}$, $R_3 = 19.5 \text{ ft}$, $n = 0.035$, and thus $K_3 = 1.38 \times 10^6$.

Other required data are $\alpha_1 = 1.29$, $A_1 = 11,070 \text{ ft}^2$, $K_1 = 3.14 \times 10^6$, $\Delta h = 5 \text{ ft}$, $L = 30 \text{ ft}$, and $L_a = 300 \text{ ft}$. By Eq. (17-20), $Q = 60,000 \text{ cfs}$.

The above computation is based on the standard condition that $\mathbf{F}_3 = 0.5$. Now, $\mathbf{F}_3 = 0.475$, so it is necessary to repeat the computation for adjustment of $\mathbf{F}_3$. By successive approximations, the final $Q$ is found to be 59,500 cfs. In the case of type II and III openings, $C$ is not a significant function of $\mathbf{F}_3$; hence, no successive approximations are necessary for the determination of $Q$.

**17-7. Backwater Effect due to Constriction.** In Fig. 17-15 the increase $h_1^*$ (designated hereafter also by $h^*$) in water surface from the normal stage to the backwater stage at section 1 is known as the *backwater of the constriction*. The distance $\Delta h$ is the difference in water-surface elevation between sections 1 and 3. From Eq. (17-15) the value of $\Delta h$ can be shown to be

$$\Delta h = \frac{V_3{}^2}{2gC^2} - \alpha_1 \frac{V_1{}^2}{2g} + h_f \qquad (17\text{-}21)$$

The ratio $h^*/\Delta h$ is called the *backwater ratio*, which is known to be a function of the channel roughness, percentage of channel contraction,

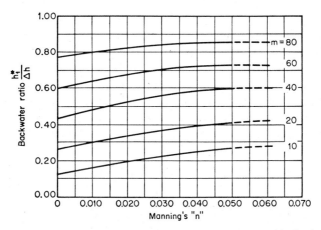

Fig. 17-24. The effect of channel roughness on the backwater ratio for basic-type constrictions. (*After Tracy and Carter* [14].)

and constriction geometry. By means of the continuity, energy, and momentum principles, it is possible to obtain an approximate solution for the backwater ratio on the assumption that normal boundary friction losses are zero. A more practical solution of the problem, however, may be reached by laboratory investigation.

Tracy and Carter [14] have made a laboratory investigation at the Georgia Institute of Technology and the University of Illinois on the backwater effect due to vertical-faced constrictions with square-edged abutments. The experimental data can be plotted as shown in Fig. 17-24 to indicate the relationship among backwater ratio, Manning's $n$, and contraction ratio $m$. It can be seen that the channel roughness is relatively unimportant as a factor in determining the backwater ratio. In fact, the limit of change in the backwater ratio due to roughness is practically reached at an $n$ of about 0.050. The laboratory investigation also reveals that the influence of cross-sectional shape on backwater ratio is included in the contraction ratio.

The backwater ratio in Fig. 17-24 is for constriction of basic type, that is, for a vertical-faced constriction with square abutments. The backwater ratio for other types of constriction may be obtained by multiplying the backwater ratio by an adjustment factor $k_a$. This factor has been found to be a function of the contraction ratio $m$ and the ratio $C/C_{\text{basic}}$. $C_{\text{basic}}$ and $C$ are, respectively, the discharge coefficients for the

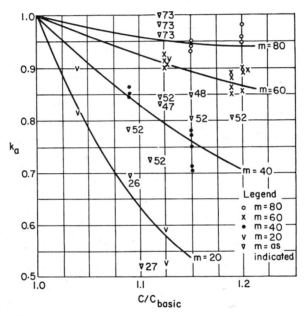

Fig. 17-25. The effect of constriction geometry on the backwater ratio. (*After Tracy and Carter* [14].)

basic type and for other types of constriction that can be determined by the method described in the preceding article. The value of $C_{\text{basic}}$ can be obtained directly from Fig. 17-16a and b. Based on experimental data, the relationship among $k_a$, $m$, and $C/C_{\text{basic}}$ is shown in Fig. 17-25.

**Example 17-3.** A stream discharging 50,000 cfs at flood stage flows through a symmetrical constriction having a type I opening which reduces the normal width of the waterway from 400 to 350 ft. If the average normal depth of flow in the uncontracted section is 20 ft, what will be the height of the backwater caused by the constriction? The opening of the constriction is 30 ft long. The coefficient of roughness of the channel is $n = 0.035$ and $\alpha_1 = 1.10$.

*Solution.* The contraction ratio $m = \frac{50}{400} = 0.125$. With $n = 0.035$, the chart in Fig. 17-24 gives $h_1^*/\Delta h = 0.26$. With $L/b = \frac{30}{350} = 0.086$ and $\mathbf{F}_1 = 0.5$, the chart in Fig. 17-16a gives $C' = C = 0.85$.

Taking an approach section 350 ft upstream from the constriction, the friction slope between this section and the contracted section may be estimated by the Manning equation $S_f = Q^2n^2/2.22A^2R^{4/3}$. Now $Q = 50,000$ cfs, $n = 0.035$, $A = 400 \times 20 = 8,000$ ft$^2$, and $R = 18.2$ ft; hence, $S_f = 0.000448$. The frictional loss $h_f = 0.000448 \times 350 = 0.16$.

Assuming $h_1^* = 0.20$, $\Delta h = 0.20/0.26 = 0.77$. With $A_3 = 350 \times 19.43 = 6,800$ ft$^2$ and $C = 0.87$, $V_3^2/2gC^2 = 1.11$. By Eq. (17-21), $\Delta h = 1.11 - 0.59 + 0.16 = 0.68$. This value is less than the trial value 0.77. The computation is to be repeated until agreement is reached. Before this is done, however, the value of $C$ should be adjusted for $\mathbf{F}_3$. Now $\mathbf{F}_3 = 50,000/(6,800 \times \sqrt{32.2 \times 19.43}) = 0.29$. Using Fig. 17-16b, $C = 0.87 \times 0.955 = 0.83$. Thus, $V_3^2/2gC^2 = 1.22$ and $\Delta h = 0.79$. This is close enough to 0.77; hence, a repeated computation for successive approximation is not required.

**17-8. Flow through Culverts.** A culvert is a unique type of constriction, and its entrance is a special kind of contraction. The culvert acts as an open channel as long as the flow is partly full. The characteristics of the flow are very complicated because the flow is controlled by many variables, including the inlet geometry, slope, size, roughness, approach and tailwater conditions, etc. Hence, an adequate determination of the flow through a culvert should be made by laboratory or field investigations.

Yarnell, Nagler, and Woodward [16] were notable pioneers who made more than 3,000 tests on flow through different pipe and box culverts. Later on, round smooth pipe culverts were tested by Mavis [17], corrugated and concrete pipe culverts by Straub and Morris [18–20] and by Straub, Anderson, and Bowers [21,22], and standard box culverts by Shoemaker and Clayton [23]. In addition, a comprehensive experimental investigation of the hydraulic behavior of commonly used pipe culverts has been conducted at the U.S. Bureau of Standards, as reported by French [24–26].

A culvert will flow full when the outlet is submerged or when the outlet is not submerged but the headwater is high and the barrel is long. According to laboratory investigations, the entrance of an ordinary culvert will not be submerged if the headwater is less than a certain critical value, designated by $H^*$, while the outlet is not submerged. The value of $H^*$ varies from 1.2 to 1.5 times the height of the culvert, depending on the entrance geometry, barrel characteristics, and approach condition. For a preliminary analysis, the upper limit $H^* = 1.5d$ may be used, where $d$ is the culvert height, because computations have shown that, where submergence was uncertain, greater accuracy could be obtained by assuming that the entrance was not submerged.

Laboratory investigations also indicate that a culvert, usually with a square edge at the top of the entrance, will not flow full even if the entrance is below headwater level when the outlet is not submerged. Under these conditions, the flow entering the culvert will contract to a depth less than the height of the culvert barrel in a manner very similar to the contraction of flow in the form of a jet under a sluice gate. This high-velocity jet will continue through the barrel length, but its velocity will be reduced slowly as head is gradually lost by friction. If the culvert is not sufficiently long to allow the expanding depth of flow below the contraction to rise and fill the barrel, the culvert will never flow full.

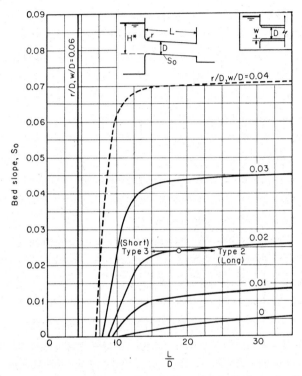

Fig. 17-26. Criteria for hydraulically short and long box and pipe culverts with concrete barrels and square, rounded, or beveled flush entrances from a vertical headwall, either with or without wing walls. (*U.S. Geological Survey* [27].)

Such a culvert is considered *hydraulically short*. Otherwise, the culvert is *hydraulically long*, for it will flow full like a pipe.

Whether a culvert is hydraulically short or long cannot be determined by the length of the barrel alone. It depends on other characteristics, such as slope, size, entrance geometry, headwater, entrance and outlet conditions, etc. A culvert may become hydraulically short, that is, it may flow partly full, even when the headwater is greater than its critical value. For this situation, Carter [27] has prepared charts (Figs. 17-26 and 17-27) which may be used to distinguish roughly between a hydrau-

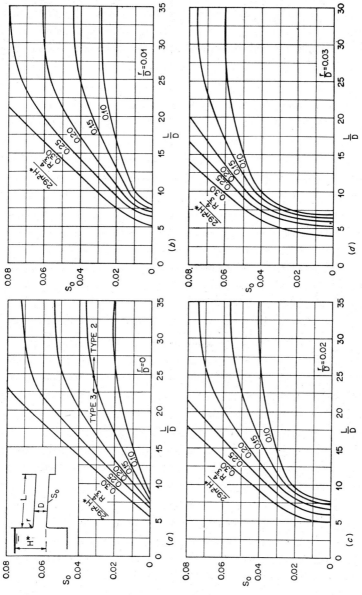

Fig. 17-27. Criteria for hydraulically short and long culverts with rough barrels of corrugated pipes. (*U.S. Geological Survey* [27].)

lically short and a hydraulically long culvert.   Under suitable conditions, a hydraulically short culvert with submerged entrance may prime itself automatically and thus flow full.   According to the laboratory investigations by Li and Patterson [28], this self-priming action is due to a rise of the water up to the top of the culvert caused in most cases by a hydraulic jump, the backwater effect of the outlet, or a standing surface wave developed inside the barrel.

For practical purposes, culvert flow may be classified into six types, as shown in Fig. 17-28.   The identification of each type may be explained according to the following outline:

A. Outlet submerged....................................Type 1
B. Outlet unsubmerged
   1. Headwater greater than the critical value
      *a*. Culvert hydraulically long........................Type 2
      *b*. Culvert hydraulically short.......................Type 3
   2. Headwater less than the critical value
      *a*. Tailwater higher than the critical depth............Type 4
      *b*. Tailwater lower than the critical depth
         i. Slope subcritical.............................Type 5
         ii. Slope supercritical...........................Type 6

If the outlet is submerged, the culvert will flow full like a pipe, and the flow will be of type 1.   If the outlet is not submerged, the headwater may be either greater or less than the critical value.   When the headwater is greater than the critical value, the culvert may be either hydraulically short or long; these can be differentiated by means of the charts in Figs. 17-26 and 17-27.   The flow is of type 2 if the culvert is hydraulically long and of type 3 if it is hydraulically short.   When the headwater is less than the critical value, the tailwater may be either higher or lower than the critical depth of the flow at the culvert outlet.   For higher tailwater, the flow is of type 4.   For lower tailwater, the flow is of type 5 if the culvert slope is subcritical and of type 6 if the slope is supercritical.

In the above classification, there is an exception in that type 1 flow can occur with tailwater slightly higher than the critical depth or with tailwater higher than the top of the outlet if the bed slope is very steep. The first two types of flow are pipe flow, and the other types are open-channel flow.   For type 3 flow, the culvert acts like an orifice.   The coefficient of discharge varies approximately from 0.45 to 0.75.   For type 4, 5, and 6 flows, the entrance is not sealed by water and it acts like a weir.   The discharge coefficient varies approximately from 0.75 to 0.95, depending on the entrance geometry and headwater condition. As shown in Fig. 17-28, type 4 flow is subcritical throughout the barrel length.   Type 5 flow is subcritical and, hence, the control section is at

*Type*                                                    *Profile*

(1) Outlet submerged
    $H > d$
    $y_t > d$
    Full flow

(2) Outlet unsubmerged
    $H > H^*$
    $y_t < d$
    Full flow

(3) Outlet unsubmerged
    $H > H^*$
    $y_t < d$
    Partly full

(4) Outlet unsubmerged
    $H < H^*$
    $y_t > y_c$
    Subcritical flow

(5) Outlet unsubmerged
    $H < H^*$
    $y_t < y_c$
    Subcritical flow
    Control at outlet

(6) Outlet unsubmerged
    $H < H^*$
    $y_t < y_c$
    Supercritical flow
    Control at entrance

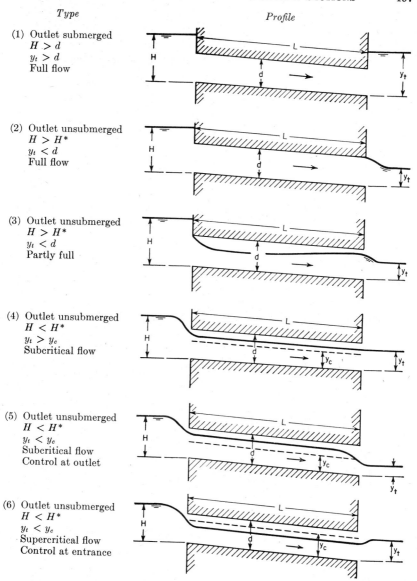

Fig. 17-28. Types of culvert flow.

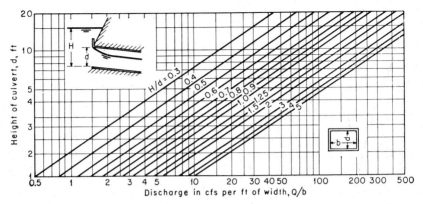

FIG. 17-29. Chart for estimating headwater on box culverts with square-edged entrances, flowing partly full. (*Based on data of U.S. Bureau of Public Roads* [29].)

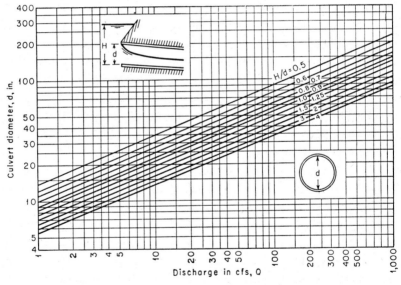

FIG. 17-30. Chart for estimating headwater on circular culverts with square-edged entrances, flowing partly full. (*Based on data of F. T. Mavis* [17].)

the outlet. Type 6 flow is supercritical and, hence, the control section is at the entrance.

Analysis of these flows may follow the procedure described in Arts. 11-1 to 11-3. The U.S. Geological Survey [27] has developed a detailed procedure that may be used for the hydraulic computation of a culvert design    For practical purposes, an approximate solution of the problem may be obtained by means of the charts in Figs. 17-29 and 17-30 for box[1] culverts and circular culverts, respectively. Both charts supply information only for culverts having square-edged entrances. For culverts having rounded entrances under average conditions, the value of $H/d$ may be roughly estimated by the following expressions, in which $H/d$ refers to the ratio of headwater to barrel height for culvert with square-edged entrance:

| Type | $H/d < 1.0$ | $1.0 < H/d < 1.5$ | $H/d > 1.5$ |
|---|---|---|---|
| Circular........ | $0.87H/d$ | $0.87H/d$ | $1.09 + 0.10H/d$ |
| Box.......... | $1.00H/d$ | $0.36 + 0.64H/d$ | $0.62 + 0.46H/d$ |

**17-9. Obstructions.** An obstruction in open-channel flow presents a phenomenon very similar to that of a constriction, since both have the effect of contracting the cross-sectional area of the flow. However, the constriction reduces the cross section to a single opening, whereas the obstruction creates at least two openings. The degree of contraction offered by a constriction is usually higher than that by an obstruction.

The types of obstruction commonly encountered in engineering problems include bridge piers, pile trestles, trash racks, piers and abutments on top of overflow spillways, etc. Investigations of these problems are numerous in hydraulic literature.[2]

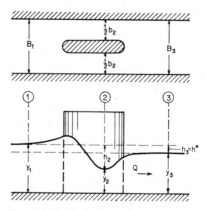

Fig. 17-31. Definition sketch showing flow through an obstruction.

The flow through an obstruction may be subcritical or supercritical. The energy equation for the reach between the contracted section 2 and section 3 below the contraction (Fig. 17-31) is

$$\epsilon\left(y_2 + \frac{V_2{}^2}{2g}\right) = y_3 + \frac{V_3{}^2}{2g} \tag{17-22}$$

or

$$\epsilon y_2(2 + \mathbf{F}_2{}^2) = y_3(2 + \mathbf{F}_3{}^2) \tag{17-23}$$

[1] The data for box culverts were prepared by analogy from experience with circular pipes and are believed to be conservative; that is, they will give head as high as is likely to occur under adverse conditions.

[2] For important references on the subject of flow through bridge piers and pile trestles, see [30] to [52]. On trash racks, see [53] to [61]. On piers and abutments on top of spillways, see Art. 14-7, [43], and [62] to [65].

where $\mathbf{F}_2 = V_2/\sqrt{gy_2}$, $\mathbf{F}_3 = V_3/\sqrt{gy_3}$, and $\epsilon$ represents the percentage of energy recovery, since energy loss will occur between the sections. By the continuity of flow,

$$V_2 b_2 y_2 = V_3 B_3 y_3 \qquad (17\text{-}24)$$

or

$$\mathbf{F}_2{}^2 \sigma^2 y_2{}^3 = \mathbf{F}_3{}^2 y_3{}^3 \qquad (17\text{-}25)$$

where $\sigma = b_2/B_3$. Eliminating $y_2$ and $y_3$ from Eqs. (17-23) and (17-25),

$$\sigma^2 = \frac{\epsilon^3 \mathbf{F}_3{}^2 (2 + \mathbf{F}_2{}^2)^3}{\mathbf{F}_2{}^2 (2 + \mathbf{F}_3{}^2)^3} \qquad (17\text{-}26)$$

When the flow at section 2 is critical, $\mathbf{F}_2 = 1$. The value of $\mathbf{F}_3$ that

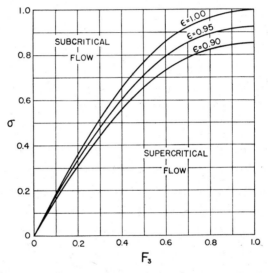

Fig. 17-32. Criterion for subcritical and supercritical flows through an obstruction.

satisfies this condition is called the limiting value and is designated by $\mathbf{F}_{3L}$. Thus, for $\mathbf{F}_2 = 1$, the above equation becomes

$$\sigma^2 = \frac{27 \epsilon^3 \mathbf{F}_{3L}{}^2}{(2 + \mathbf{F}_{3L}{}^2)^3} \qquad (17\text{-}27)$$

For a given $\sigma$, therefore, the flow through the obstruction is critical if $\mathbf{F}_3 = \mathbf{F}_{3L}$. Examination of Eq. (17-26) indicates that the flow through the obstruction is subcritical if $\mathbf{F}_3 < \mathbf{F}_{3L}$ and supercritical if $\mathbf{F}_3 > \mathbf{F}_{3L}$. Equation (17-27) is plotted as shown in Fig. 17-32 for $\epsilon = 1$ (no energy loss), $\epsilon = 0.95$ (5% energy loss), and $\epsilon = 0.9$ (10% energy loss). Accordingly, the flow is subcritical if the value of $\mathbf{F}_3$ falls on the left side of the plotted curve of an assumed energy loss and supercritical if $\mathbf{F}_3$ falls on the right side of the curve.

**17-10. Flow between Bridge Piers.** For flow between bridge piers, Yarnell [42] has made an extensive study of the related literature and conducted a large number of tests on different kinds of pier commonly used in American practice. He found that the bridge-pier formulas most commonly used in the United States were d'Aubuisson's [30], Nagler's [33], Weisbach's [31], and Rehbock's [35–37]. The Weisbach formula was considered theoretically unsound[1] because of the discordant results obtained by Yarnell. In connection with the use of the Rehbock formula, the flow passing through the obstruction is classified as least, moderate, and complete turbulent. Yarnell indicated that this classification might be useful but that classification as subcritical and supercritical is more logical. Least and complete turbulent flow were found to correspond to subcritical and supercritical flow, respectively, and moderate turbulent flow was found to be in the neighborhood of or equal to critical flow. For least and moderate turbulent flow, the Nagler formula seemed to fit Yarnell's experimental data better than the d'Aubuisson formula. For complete turbulent flow, the d'Aubuisson formula seemed to fit the data better. In general, however, neither formula applies too well at high velocities.

The Nagler formula is

$$Q = K_N b_2 \sqrt{2g} \left( y_3 - \theta \frac{V_3{}^2}{2g} \right) \sqrt{h_3 + \beta \frac{V_1{}^2}{2g}} \qquad (17\text{-}28)$$

where $K_N$ is a coefficient depending on the degree of channel contraction and on the characteristics of the obstruction, $\theta$ is an adjustment factor intended to reduce the depth $y_3$ to $y_2$, and $\beta$ is a coefficient which corrects for the velocity of approach. The notation used in the formula is shown in Fig. 17-31. The backwater is represented by $h_3$ or $h^*$. The value of $\theta$ varies, approaching zero as the contraction effect approaches zero and becoming high when the flow is shooting and turbulent, but it can ordinarily be taken as 0.3. The value of $\beta$ varies with the conveyance ratio, as shown in Fig. 17-33.

In deriving the d'Aubuisson formula, the energy equation is applied to the approach channel section 1 and to the contracted section 2 (Fig.

---

[1] The Weisbach formula is based upon the assumption that the flow entering the contracted section may be calculated as the sum of two portions, the lower part flowing through a submerged orifice and the upper part flowing over a weir. Apparently, this assumption is arbitrary and has no theoretical basis. Houk [10] and Bubendey [32] also have called it unwarranted and contrary to established hydraulic theory.

17-31) or, using the notation in the figure,

$$\alpha_1 \frac{V_1^2}{2g} + y_1 = \alpha_2 \frac{V_2^2}{2g} + y_2 + h_f \qquad (17\text{-}29)$$

where $y_1 = y_2 + h_2$, the velocity-distribution coefficients $\alpha_1$ and $\alpha_2$ are assumed equal to 1.0, and the friction loss $h_f$ is assumed zero.  Taking

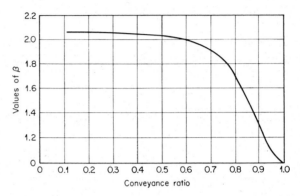

Fig. 17-33. Values of $\beta$ in the Nagler bridge-pier formula.

$V_2 = Q/K_A b_2 y_2$, where $K_A$ is a coefficient of contraction, and simplifying,

$$Q = K_A b_2 y_2 \sqrt{2gh_2 + V_1^2} \qquad (17\text{-}30)$$

d'Aubuisson made no distinction between the depths $y_2$ and $y_3$, but assumed $y_2 = y_3$.  Accordingly, the d'Aubuisson formula is

$$Q = K_A b_2 y_3 \sqrt{2gh_3 + V_1^2} \qquad (17\text{-}31)$$

where $K_A$ depends mainly on the degree of channel contraction and on the shape and orientation of the obstruction.  The assumption $y_2 = y_3$ implies that the backwater $h^* = h_3 = h_2$ in Fig. 17-31.  Accordingly, the backwater ratio has a value of 1.0.  This is, of course, not always true, although in many cases there is very little difference between $y_2$ and $y_3$.  For this reason, the d'Aubuisson formula is generally recognized to be empirical and approximate.

The following are extracted from the results of Yarnell's investigation on bridge piers of various shapes and sizes:

1. The height of the backwater due to bridge piers varies directly with the depth of the unobstructed channel.

2. The Nagler, d'Aubuisson, and Rehbock formulas give approximately correct results for ordinary velocities when the proper coefficients are used, but they do not hold for extremely high velocities.  From his

experimental data, Yarnell derived the coefficients for these formulas. Based on this information, the following values of $K_N$ and $K_A$ are recommended for practical use:

| Type of pier | Conveyance ratio $\sigma$ | | | | | | | | | |
|---|---|---|---|---|---|---|---|---|---|---|
| | 0.9 | | 0.8 | | 0.7 | | 0.6 | | 0.5 | |
| | $K_N$ | $K_A$ | $K_N$ | $K_A$ | $K_N$ | $K_A$ | $K_N$ | $K_A$ | $K_N$ | $K_A$ |
| Square noses and tails | 0.91 | 0.96 | 0.87 | 1.02 | 0.86 | 1.02 | 0.87 | 1.00 | 0.89 | 0.97 |
| Semicircular noses and tails | 0.94 | 0.99 | 0.92 | 1.13 | 0.95 | 1.20 | 1.03 | 1.26 | 1.11 | 1.31 |
| 90° triangular noses and tails | 0.95 | .... | 0.94 | .... | 0.92 | | | | | |
| Twin-cylinder piers, with or without diaphragms | 0.91 | .... | 0.89 | .... | 0.88 | | | | | |
| Lens-shaped noses and tails | 0.95 | 1.00 | 0.94 | 1.14 | 0.97 | 1.22 | | | | |

3. For flow of low velocity and least turbulence, the more efficient shapes are lens-shaped nose and tail, lens-shaped nose and semicircular tail, semicircular nose and lens-shaped tail, convex nose and tail, and semicircular nose and tail.[1] However, the data are not sufficient to differentiate among these shapes for high degree of contraction.

4. Twin-cylinder piers either with or without connecting diaphragms, piers with 90° triangular noses and tails, and piers with recessed webs are less efficient hydraulically than those just mentioned, and piers with square noses and tails are least efficient.

5. Application of batter to the ends of piers slightly increases their hydraulic efficiency, that is, raises the $K_N$ and $K_A$ values.

6. Increasing the length of a pier from 4 times the width to 13 times the width has comparatively little effect on its hydraulic efficiency. In some cases the efficiency is thus increased and in other cases decreased. The optimum length-width ratio probably varies with velocity and is generally between 4 and 7. On the average, the values of $K_N$ and $K_A$ will increase about 3 to 5% for the increase of the ratio from 4 to 13.

7. Placing the piers at an angle with the current has an insignificant effect on the amount of backwater if the angle is less than 10°. Placing the piers at 20° or more materially increases the amount of backwater; the increase depends upon the quantity of flow, the depth, and the degree of channel contraction. In general, the values of $K_N$ and $K_A$ will decrease about 7% at 20°.

In order to utilize the results of the investigation and to facilitate

[1] The lens-shaped nose or tail is formed by two convex curves tangent to the sides of pier and of radius twice the pier width. The convex nose or tail is formed by two curves tangent to the sides of pier and circumscribed on an equilateral triangle.

hydraulic computation for practical applications, Yarnell has developed empirical formulas and graphical solutions for the bridge-pier problem. The chart in Fig. 17-34, designed by Yarnell but slightly modified for the present purpose, supplies a quick solution for subcritical flow through bridge piers. With the appropriate values of $\sigma$ and $V_3$, the value of $x$ can be obtained from the left part of the chart. Then enter this value and the proper values of $F_3{}^2$ and shape factor $K$ on the right part of the chart, and read the backwater $h^*$. The shapes shown on the chart

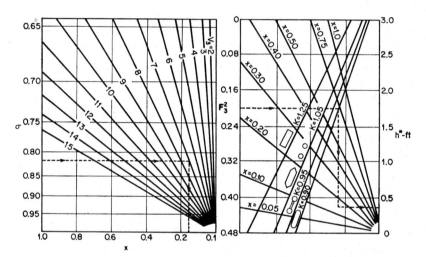

Fig. 17-34. Chart for determining backwater of subcritical flow through bridge piers. (*After D. L. Yarnell* [42].)

are square noses and tails, 90° triangular noses and tails, twin-cylinder piers with and without connecting diaphragm, and semicircular noses and tails. If the backwater is given and it is required to determine the discharge, it will be necessary to assume a value of $V_3$ and to carry out the computation by trial and error until a solution is obtained.

The chart in Fig. 17-35 gives a graphical solution for supercritical flow through bridge piers. With the proper value of $\sigma$, determine the limiting value $\mathbf{F}_{3L}$ from Eq. (17-27) or Fig. 17-32. Then enter $\mathbf{F}_3/\mathbf{F}_{3L}$ on the chart and read $h^*/y_3$ for the given pier shape. This value multiplied by $y_3$ gives the backwater $h^*$. If $y_1$, $y_3$, $b_2$, $B_3$, and the pier shape are known and it is required to determine the discharge, $h^*/y_3$ may be computed from $h^*/y_3 = (y_1 - y_3)/y_3$; $\mathbf{F}_3/\mathbf{F}_{3L}$ may be taken from the chart; $\sigma = b_2/B_3$; and $\mathbf{F}_{3L}$ may be obtained from Fig. 17-27 or Fig. 17-32. The value of $\mathbf{F}_3$ can then be calculated, and from it $V_3$ and then $Q$.

Yarnell's graphical solutions apply to piers with length-width ratio

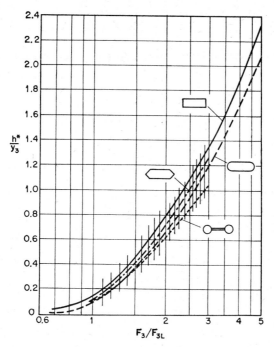

Fig. 17-35. Chart for determining backwater of supercritical flow through bridge piers. (*After D. L. Yarnell* [42].)

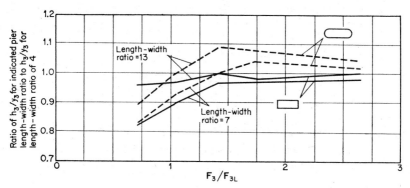

Fig. 17-36. Effect of increase in length of bridge pier. (*Based on data of D. L. Yarnell* [42].)

equal to 4. For ratios of 7 and 13, the effect of increasing length on backwater is shown in Fig. 17-36, which is plotted with Yarnell's data. It seems that the backwater caused by the long piers is greater when the pier ends are semicircular than when they are square. It is probable that an abrupt entrance in the case of square pier ends tends to decrease friction losses for a short distance downstream because of its effect on the velocity distribution, since the velocity along the walls is reduced. The effect of bridge piers present in a constriction has been considered in Art. 17-6 and in Fig. 17-23d.

**17-11. Flow through Pile Trestles.** Yarnell's investigation [41] indicates that the Nagler formula may be suitably applied to subcritical flow passing a pile trestle and the d'Aubuisson formula to supercritical flow passing a pile trestle. The following coefficients are recommended for use in these formulas:

| Type of trestle | $K_N$ | $K_A$ |
|---|---|---|
| Single-track 5-pile trestle bent | | |
| Parallel to current | 0.90 | 0.96 |
| At 10° angle with current | 0.90 | |
| At 20° angle with current | 0.89 | |
| At 30° angle with current | 0.87 | |
| Double-track 10-pile trestle bent | 0.82 | 0.88 |
| Two single-track 5-pile trestle bents | 0.79 | 0.86 |

The amount of channel contraction is to be taken as the average diameter of the piles plus the thickness of the sway bracing, disregarding the angle at which the bent is set with the current.

The effect of trestle piles present in a constriction has been considered in Art. 17-6 and in Fig. 17-23c.

**17-12. Flow through Trash Racks.** For flow through trash racks, the designer is primarily concerned with the amount of head loss due to the resistance of the rack. This may be expressed in terms of the velocity head of the approach flow, or

$$h_f = c \frac{V^2}{2g} \tag{17-32}$$

where $V$ is the velocity of approach ahead of the rack and where $c$ is a coefficient depending on the cross-sectional form, thickness $s$, length $L$ of the rack bar, clear distance $b$ between bars, angle $\delta$ of inclination of the bar from the horizontal, and angle $\alpha$ between the direction of flow and the length of the bar.

On the basis of the experimental data for rack bars of various forms and with $\alpha = 0$, Kirschmer [52,53] has set up the following formula for $c$:

$$c = \beta \left(\frac{s}{b}\right)^{4/3} \sin \delta \tag{17-33}$$

where $\beta$ is a coefficient having the values listed below:

| Form of rack bar | Value of $\beta$ |
|---|---|
| Square nose and tail, $L/s = 5$ | 2.42 |
| Square nose and semicircular tail, $L/s = 5$ | 1.83 |
| Semicircular nose and tail, $L/s = 5$ | 1.67 |
| Round | 1.79 |
| Airfoil | 0.76 |

Spangler [55] has extended the experiment and determined the value of $\beta$ for $\alpha = 30°$, $45°$, and $60°$.

According to Fellenius [54], an empirical formula for $c$ can be given as follows:

$$c = \mu \left(\frac{s}{s + b}\right)^2 \sin^x \delta \qquad (17\text{-}34)$$

where the coefficient $\mu$ and exponent $x$ have the following values:

| Form of rack bar | Value of $\mu$ | Value of $x$ |
|---|---|---|
| Square nose and tail | | |
| With sharp corners, $L/s = 10$ | 7.1 | 1.0 |
| With sharp corners, $L/s = 12$ | 6.2 | 1.0 |
| With slightly rounded corners, $L/s = 8$ to $11$ | 6.1 | 1.0 |
| Semicircular nose and tail, $L/s = 7$ | 5.6 | 1.5 |

In general, $x = 1.0$ for bars having sharp or slightly rounded corners and $x = 1.5$ for bars having rounded corners. For cross-connected and clipped rack bars, the value of $\mu$ should be increased by about 22.5%.

Scimemi [56] and Koženy [50] have provided values of $c$, $\beta$, and $\mu$, and other data for racks installed in several hydropower plants.

**17-13. Underflow Gates.** Certain control gates in canals may be called *underflow gates*[1] from the fact that water passes underneath the structure. Common examples are the sluice gate, Tainter gate (or radial gate), and rolling gate (Fig. 17-37). In designing such gates the hydraulic engineer is most interested in two major features: the head-discharge relationship and the pressure distribution over the gate surfaces for various positions of the gate and forms of the gate lip. The form of the lip will not only affect the velocity and pressure distributions and the energy loss in flow through the gate opening, but may also develop very disturbing vibrations that should be avoided during gate operation. As

---

[1] In contrast to the underflow gate is the *overflow gate* through which the water flows over the structure. The drum gate (Art. 14-9) is an example of an overflow gate. Hydraulically speaking, the overflow gate acts like a weir as much as the underflow gate acts like an orifice. There are also designs for which the water flows above and below the structure at the same time (Fig. 17-37).

the design of the lip varies considerably, independent investigation of the lip for a particular design is usually necessary.[1]

By the energy equation, it can be shown that the discharge through an underflow gate may be expressed as

$$Q = CLh \sqrt{2g\left(y_1 + \alpha \frac{V_1{}^2}{2g}\right)} \tag{17-35}$$

where $C$ is the coefficient of discharge, $L$ is the length of the gate, $h$ is

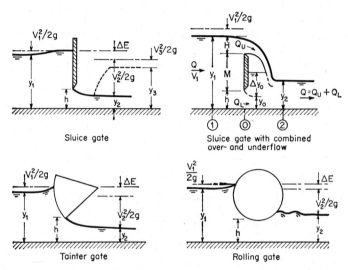

Fig. 17-37. Underflow gates.

the height of the gate opening, $y_1$ is the upstream depth of flow, and $\alpha V_1{}^2/2g$ is the velocity head of the approach flow. The outflow of the gate may be either free or submerged, depending on the tailwater depth. For submerged flow, $y_1$ in the above equation should be replaced by the effective head, or the difference between the upstream and downstream depths.

For the purpose of experimental studies, the velocity-head term in Eq. (17-35) may be omitted, and its effect may be included in the coefficient $C$. Thus,

$$Q = CLh \sqrt{2gy_1} \tag{17-36}$$

where $C$ is a coefficient depending on the geometry of the structure and on the upstream and downstream depths. The form of this equation is the same for both free and submerged flows.

---

[1] For studies on sluice-gate lips of various designs, see [66] and [67].

For the vertical sluice gate,[1] experimentally determined curves representing the value of $C$ have been prepared by Henry [68], as shown in Fig. 17-38.   The dashed line $A$ represents the result obtained by Eq. (17-35) on the basis of the energy principle; the dashed line $B$ is obtained through the use of the momentum principle.   The value of $\mathbf{F}_0$ is the Froude number of the flow through the gate opening.

Similar curves for the Tainter gate (Fig. 17-39) were prepared by Toch [69] on the basis of an experimental study, including the pivot height as a

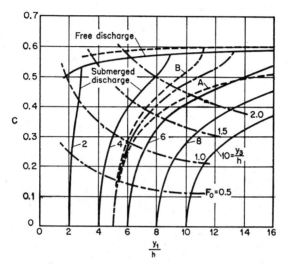

Fig. 17-38. Discharge coefficient for vertical sluice gate.   (*After H. R. Henry* [68].)

variable in addition to other variables that were used by Metzler [70] in an earlier analysis.   The U.S. Army Engineers Waterways Experiment Station [74] has also prepared design charts for use in the design of Tainter gates, particularly for those installed on spillway crests of WES-standard shapes (Art. 14-3).

In the case of a sluice gate with combined overflow and underflow (Fig. 17-37), the overflow discharge $Q_U$ is a function of $H$ only, but the underflow discharge $Q_L$ is a function of $y_0 + \Delta y_0$ as well as $y_1$.   If $\Delta y_0 = 0$ and if the lower (underflow) jet is free, the total discharge $Q = Q_U + Q_L$ is independent of the tailwater depth $y_2$.   If $\Delta y_0$ is greater than zero, the lower jet is drowned.   The problem may be solved by the continuity equation and the momentum equation between cross sections 0 and 2.

[1] For other studies, see [39] and [71].   For a theoretical analysis of the flow through a sharp-edged sluice gate, see [72] and [73].

Under normal conditions, $y_2$ is a function of $Q$. Both $y_0 + \Delta y_0$ and $Q_L$ are unknown but must satisfy an energy equation similar to Eq. (17-35). The use of the momentum equation will automatically include any friction losses. The pair of equations may be solved by trial and error or graphically. The result thus obtained has been found to agree with an experimental finding derived by Escande [2,71].

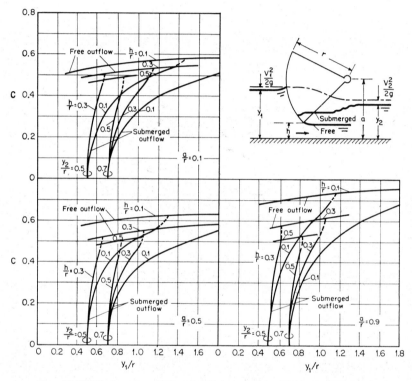

Fig. 17-39. Discharge coefficient for Tainter gate. (*After A. Toch* [69].)

The pressure on the surface of the gate can be determined accurately either from flow-net analysis or by actual measurement on model or prototype. Fig. 17-40a shows the normal pressure on the surface of a Tainter gate (a similar pattern of horizontal-pressure distribution exists on a sluice gate), the horizontal pressure on the gate opening and on the upstream and downstream cross sections, and the vertical pressure on the channel bed. The normal pressure on the gate surface may be represented by its horizontal and vertical components $F_H$ and $F_V$, as shown in Fig. 17-40b. The magnitude and positions of these forces may be

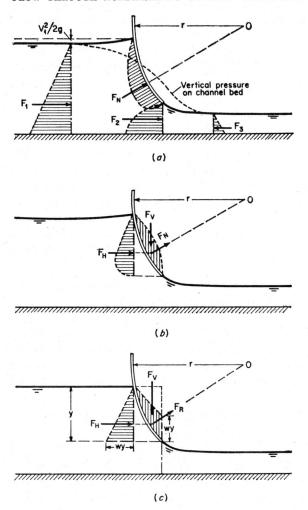

FIG. 17-40. Determination of pressures for Tainter gate.

obtained by graphical determination from the pressure-distribution diagram. A less accurate but simpler method of determining these pressures is to assume that the horizontal pressure on the gate surface is hydrostatically distributed and that the vertical pressure is equal to the weight of the water replaced by the gate structure above its surface (Fig. 17-40c). The horizontal force $F_H$ may also be determined by the momentum relationship. However, this determination will not give the position of the force. Since all water pressures are normal to the gate surface, the resultant of the pressures must pass through the trunnion axis 0.

The outflow from the gate usually constitutes a high-velocity jet, capable of eroding the downstream channel bed.[1] The erosion thus developed may be avoided by means of a stilling basin (Art. 15-11). If no preventive measures are provided, the erosion may result in a deep scour hole, the formation of which will depend on the type of the jet. According to the studies of Escande [71] on flow through a channel drop downstream from a sluice gate,[2] four types of jet are possible: (1) submerged flow with rising jet, (2) submerged flow with diving jet, (3) free flow with rising jet, and (4) free flow with diving jet. Generally speaking, the diving jet will induce less pressure on the vertical surface of the drop than the rising jet and will usually develop a scour hole with its deepest point closer to the drop than the rising jet. In submerged flow, the depth of scour hole depends on the tailwater depth, whereas in free flow the downstream conditions have little or no effect upon the depth of scouring.

**17-14. Channel Junctions.** Flow through a channel junction is a phenomenon that involves numerous variables, such as the number of the adjoining channels, the angles of intersection, the shape and slope of the channels, the directions and discharges of flow, the rounding of the corners at the junction, etc. The problem is so complicated that only a few simple and specific cases have been studied. The conclusions of such studies indicate that generalization of the problem is not possible or even desirable. When the application of hydraulic theory to the problem encounters limitations, a model study will give the best solution for the flow characteristics involved.

For *subcritical flow* passing through the channels at a junction, Taylor [80] has investigated the specific cases shown in Fig. 17-41. The channels are horizontal and of equal width. In the case of *combining flow*, the following assumptions were made: (1) the flow is from channels 1 and 2 into channel 3; (2) channels 1 and 3 lie in a straight line; (3) the flow is parallel to the channel walls, and the velocity is uniformly distributed immediately above and below the junction; (4) ordinary wall friction is negligible in comparison with other forces involved; and (5) the depths in channels 1 and 2 are equal immediately above the junction. With

---

[1] The erosion of channel bed due to jet is a subject beyond the scope of this book. For detailed information see [1] to [3] and [75] to [77].

[2] Other examples of jets below hydraulic structures in channels have been found and studied by Camichel [78]. The erosion due to jet through a bridge opening may cause a deep scour hole generally known as the *blue hole*. An experimental study of such a problem has been reported by Hickenlooper, Guillou, and Chow [79].

these assumptions and by the application of the momentum equation to the junction in the direction of 1 to 3, Taylor was able to obtain the following equation:[1]

$$k_2 = \frac{n_q{}^2(n_y{}^2 - 1)}{4n_y{}^2[2n_q - n_q{}^2(1 + \cos \theta) + n_y - 1]} \tag{17-37}$$

where $k_2 = V_2{}^2/2gy_2$, $n_q = Q_2/Q_3$, $n_y = y_a/y_b$, $V_2$ is the velocity in channel 2, $y_2$ is the depth of flow in channel 2, $y_a$ is the depth above the junction, $y_b$ is the depth below the junction, and $\theta$ is the angle between the merging channels. Taking $n_q$ as a parameter, $k_2$ may be plotted against $n_y$ for any given $\theta$.

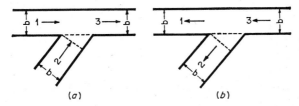

(a)                              (b)

FIG. 17-41. Simple channel junctions (a) combining flow; (b) dividing flow.

Equation (17-37) was verified by experiments on junctions with $\theta = 45°$ and 135°. It was found that the agreement between theory and experiment was good for $\theta = 45°$. There was no agreement, however, for $\theta = 135°$. It is believed that this was because the velocity distribution below the junction was distorted and the flow did not remain parallel to the channel walls. The experimental data showed clearly that assumption 5 above is valid, regardless of the angle of intersection of the channels.

In the case of *dividing flow* the problem cannot easily be analyzed theoretically. The application of the momentum principle is difficult because it involves some unknown quantities, and assumptions which might simplify the determination of these quantities, such as assumption 5 for the combining flow, are not available. Basically, the division of the flow will depend upon the backwater effects of the two branch channels and the dynamic conditions existing at the junction. If the divided flow is to be combined again at a certain point downstream, a solution of the problem described in Art. 11-9 may be applied.

[1] In applying the momentum equation to the problem, the hydrostatic pressure exerted by the flow in channel 2 is counteracted by the pressure on the opposite wall, provided the water surface in the junction is essentially flat. Thus, the only force the flow from channel 2 can contribute to the flow in the straight channel 1-3 is its momentum component in the direction of 1 to 3.

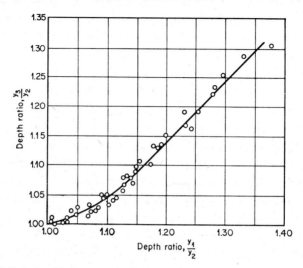

Fig. 17-42. Relationship between depths in a 90° flow division. (*After E. H. Taylor* [80].)

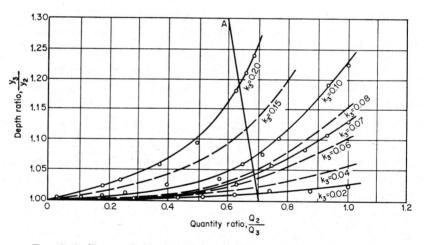

Fig. 17-43. Characteristics of a 90° flow division. (*After E. H. Taylor* [80].)

For the specific junction shown in Fig. 17-41b, Taylor has made an experimental approach to the problem as follows:

For any given value of $\theta$, it is possible to correlate the dimensionless ratios $Q_2/Q_3$, $y_3/y_2$, $y_1/y_2$, and $k_3 = V_3{}^2/2gy_3$, all derived from the experimentally determined data. For $\theta = 90°$, such correlation curves are shown in Figs. 17-42 and 17-43. These curves can be used to determine the division of flow of a given discharge $Q_3$. First assume $Q_1$; then $Q_2 = Q_3 - Q_1$. The corresponding depths $y_1$ and $y_2$ can be obtained from the rating curves of channels 1 and 2. For $y_1/y_2$, the ratio $y_3/y_2$ can be determined from Fig. 17-42. By assuming other values of $Q_1$, the corresponding ratios $y_3/y_2$ can be obtained. Thus, $Q_2/Q_3$ is plotted against $y_3/y_2$, as shown by the curve $A$ in Fig. 17-43. The intersection of this curve with the $k_3$ curves now gives all possible combinations of the variables, among which one value of $k_3$ would correspond to the flow of, say, 500 cfs entering the junction. The next step is to plot the intersected $k_3$ values against the corresponding $y_3$. For the example shown by the line $A$ in Fig. 17-43, $k_3 = 0.10$, $y_3/y_2 = 1.067$, and $Q_2/Q_3 = 0.677$ or $Q_2 = 0.677Q_3$. From the rating curve of channel 2, the $y_2$ corresponding to the $Q_2$ just computed can be found and, hence, $y_3 = 1.067y_2$. The plot of $k_3$ against $y_3$ can be constructed, as shown by the curve $B$ in Fig. 17-44. The proper value of $k_3$ must satisfy not only curve $B$ but also the solid curve showing the relationship $k_3 = V_3^2/2gy_3$. The intersection of the two curves gives the required

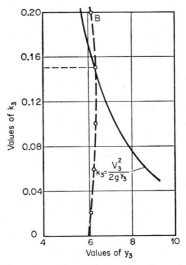

FIG. 17-44. Factor $k_3$ as a function of $y_3$. (*After E. H. Taylor* [80].)

values of $k_3$ and $y_3$. With this $k_3$, the corresponding value of $Q_2/Q_3$ may be determined from Fig. 17-43, and the divided discharges $Q_1$ and $Q_2$ can be determined accordingly.

For *supercritical flow* passing through the channels at a junction, the flow condition is more complicated. Studies of a few cases of combining flow of the general arrangement shown in Fig. 17-41 have been made by the U.S. Soil Conservation Service [81]. In such cases, a hydraulic jump may form in one or both of the inlet channels, depending upon the junction design, the discharges, velocities, and related flow conditions in the adjoining channels. Thus, a large increase in the height of the side walls in the vicinity of the junction may be necessary. When the principle of momentum is applied to such a problem, it is necessary to know the position of the jump or the depth of flow at the upstream edge of the junction in order to compute the momentum contributed by the inlet flows. If the flow passing through the junction is supercritical without the formation of any hydraulic jump upstream, the flow condition will be complicated by the development of cross waves similar to those discussed in Art. 16-5. These waves will propagate for a considerable distance downstream before being damped by the channel friction. Hence, side walls higher than those normally provided are required not only near the junction but also for a considerable distance downstream.

## PROBLEMS

**17-1.** Verify Eq. (17-5), and interpret the dashed curves in Fig. 17-3 that represent this equation.

**17-2.** Using Formica's data for sudden expansions, plot a curve showing the relationship between $\epsilon$ and the angle of divergence $\theta$, and then discuss this relationship.

**17-3.** Compute the wave angles $\beta_1$ and $\beta_2$ of the contraction designed in Example 17-1, and sketch the position of the shock wavefronts.

**17-4.** Design a straight contraction to reduce the width of a rectangular channel from 6 to 3 ft. The channel carries a discharge of 4.33 cfs with an approach velocity of 7.2 fps. Assume $y_3/y_1 = 3.00$.

**17-5.** Compute the wave angles of the design in Prob. 17-4, and sketch the position of the shock wavefronts.

**17-6.** Design the contraction in Example 17-1, assuming $y_3/y_1 = 3.00$.

**17-7.** A channel 6 ft wide carries a discharge of 100 cfs at a velocity of 20 fps. Construct the surface contour of the flow through a square-edged abrupt expansion of the channel.

**17-8.** If the channel described in the preceding problem has a gradual expansion with its boundaries represented by Eq. (17-11), construct the surface contour of the flow in the expansion.

**17-9.** Make a preliminary design of a curved expansion for the channel in Prob. 17-7 with the aid of the dimensionless boundary curves determined by the method of characteristics (Fig. 17-13). Assume $b_2/b_1 = 3$.

**17-10.** Solve Example 17-2 for the following additional conditions: (a) the center line of the bridge and highway embankment makes an angle of 70° with the direction of flow, (b) the entrance is rounded for $r/b = 0.10$, and (c) the bridge has a pier 30 ft long and 10 ft wide at the middle of the waterway opening.

**17-11.** Determine the flood discharge through a bridge constriction having a type III opening with embankment and abutment slope 2:1. The constriction, 30 ft long, reduces the normal width of waterway from 400 ft to 200 ft. The bridge has three piers, each 30 ft long and 6 ft wide. The average depths of water at the approach section 200 ft upstream from the bridge and at the contracted section are 20.5 and 19.2 ft, respectively. The upstream top edge of the embankment is 1 ft above the water-surface elevation at the approach section. The value of $n = 0.035$.

**17-12.** Solve the preceding problem if the bottom of the bridge is 3 ft below the top of the embankment. The bridge deck, however, is not overflowed.

**17-13.** A box culvert $8 \times 8 \times 60$ ft is laid on a slope of $\frac{1}{60}$. It has square-edged entrance and vertical headwalls. The headwater and tailwater elevations are 8.02 ft above the invert of the entrance and 6 ft above the invert of the outlet, respectively. Determine (a) the discharge of the culvert, (b) the type of flow through the culvert, and (c) the normal depth of flow in the barrel. The value of $n = 0.015$.

**17-14.** Solve the preceding problem if the headwater is 13 ft above the invert of the entrance.

**17-15.** Solve Prob. 17-13 if the culvert is circular, having a diameter of 8 ft.

**17-16.** Solve the preceding problem if the headwater is 13 ft above the invert of the entrance and the barrel is rough, having $n = 0.025$.

**17-17.** A highway bridge 350 ft long has six piers with semicircular noses and tails, each 8 ft wide and equally spaced. At the peak of a flood, the backwater was found to be 0.30 ft for the seven openings. The average depth of flow immediately downstream from the opening was 8 ft. Compute the flood discharge, (a) by the Nagler formula, (b) by the d'Aubuisson formula, and (c) by the Yarnell charts.

**17-18.** A bridge has four piers with semicircular noses and tails, each 40 ft long by 10 ft wide. During a flood peak of 45,000 cfs, the total width of the stream was 390 ft, and the average depth at a downstream section was 19.4 ft. Estimate the backwater.

**17-19.** Solve the preceding problem by the USGS method described in Art. 17-7. The channel roughness coefficient is $n = 0.03$. Unavailable data are to be reasonably assumed.

**17-20.** If the bridge in Prob. 17-17 is exposed to a flood discharge of 35,000 cfs, estimate the backwater. The rating curve of the channel gives a normal depth of 8.5 ft for this discharge.

**17-21.** A single-track pile-trestle railroad bridge 840 ft long is supported by bents, each 2 ft wide and spaced 14 ft center to center. At the peak of a flood, the average backwater was found to be 0.15 ft. The average depth of flow immediately downstream from the trestle was 6 ft. Estimate the backwater.

**17-22.** Verify Eq. (17-37).

## REFERENCES

1. Charles Jaeger: Der Mischungsvorgang bei plötzlichem Querschnittsübergang (The mixing process in sudden transitions), *Wasserkraft und Wasserwirtschaft*, Munich, vol. 31, no. 24, pp. 306–309, 1936.
2. Charles Jaeger: "Engineering Fluid Mechanics," translated from the German by P. O. Wolf, Blackie & Son, Ltd., London and Glasgow, 1956, pp. 157–169.
3. Charles Jaeger: De l'impulsion totale et de ses rapports avec l'énergie totale d'un courant liquide à surface libre (The total impulse and its relations with the total energy of a free-surface liquid flow), *Revue générale de l'hydraulique*, Paris, vol. 13, no. 39, pp. 143–151, 1947.
4. Gianni Formica: Esperienze preliminari sulle perdite di carico nei canali, dovute a cambiamenti di sezione (Preliminary test on head losses in channels due to cross-sectional changes), *L'Energia elettrica, Milano*, vol. 32, no. 7, pp. 554–568, July, 1955; reprinted as *Istituto di Idraulica e Costruzioni Idrauliche, Milano, Memorie e studi No. 124*, 1955.
5. R. L. Daugherty and A. C. Ingersoll: "Fluid Mechanics," McGraw-Hill Book Company, Inc., New York, 1954, pp. 190–193.
6. Arthur T. Ippen and John H. Dawson: Design of channel contractions, 3d paper in High-velocity flow in open channels: A symposium, *Transactions, American Society of Civil Engineers*, vol. 116, pp. 326–346, 1951.
7. Masashi Hom-ma and Sukeyuki Shima: On the flow in a gradually diverged open channel, *The Japan Science Review, Series I*, vol. 2, no. 3, pp. 253–260, 1952.
8. Hunter Rouse, B. V. Bhoota, and En-Yun Hsu: Design of channel expansions, 4th paper in High-velocity flow in open channels: A symposium, *Transactions, American Society of Civil Engineers*, vol. 116, pp. 326–346, 1951.
9. Fred W. Blaisdell: Flow through diverging open channel transitions at super-

critical velocities, *U.S. Soil Conservation Service, Progress Rept. SCS-TP-76*, April, 1949.

10. Ivan E. Houk: Calculation of flow in open channels, *Miami Conservancy District, Technical Report, Pt. IV*, Dayton, Ohio, 1918.

11. E. W. Lane: Experiments on the flow of water through contractions in an open channel, *Transactions, American Society of Civil Engineers*, vol. 83, pp. 1149–1208, 1919–1920.

12. Carl E. Kindsvater, Rolland W. Carter, and H. J. Tracy: Computation of peak discharge at contractions, *U.S. Geological Survey, Circular No. 284*, 1953.

13. Carl E. Kindsvater and Rolland W. Carter: Tranquil flow through open-channel constrictions, *Transactions, American Society of Civil Engineers*, vol. 120, pp. 955–980, 1955.

14. Hubert J. Tracy and Rolland W. Carter: Backwater effects of open-channel constrictions, *Transactions, American Society of Civil Engineers*, vol. 120, pp. 993–1006, 1955.

15. Tate Dalrymple: Measuring floods, in Floods, vol. III of *Symposia Darcy, International Association of Scientific Hydrology, Publication No. 42*, 1956, pp. 380–404.

16. David L. Yarnell, Floyd A. Nagler, and Sherman M. Woodward: Flow of water through culverts, *University of Iowa, Studies in Engineering, Bulletin 1*, 1926.

17. F. T. Mavis: The hydraulics of culverts, *The Pennsylvania State College, Engineering Experiment Station, Bulletin 56*, Oct. 1, 1942.

18. Lorenz G. Straub and Henry M. Morris: Hydraulic data comparison of concrete and corrugated metal culvert pipes, *University of Minnesota, St. Anthony Falls Hydraulics Laboratory, Technical Paper 3, Series B*, July, 1950.

19. Lorenz G. Straub and Henry Morris: Hydraulic tests on concrete culvert pipes, *University of Minnesota, St. Anthony Falls Hydraulics Laboratory, Technical Paper No. 4, Series B*, July, 1950.

20. Lorenz G. Straub and Henry Morris: Hydraulic tests on corrugated metal culvert pipes, *University of Minnesota, St. Anthony Falls Hydraulics Laboratory, Technical Paper No. 5, Series B*, July, 1950.

21. Lorenz G. Straub, Alvin G. Anderson, and Charles E. Bowers: Effect of inlet design on capacity of culverts on steep slopes, *University of Minnesota, St. Anthony Falls Hydraulics Laboratory, Project Report No. 37*, August, 1953.

22. Lorenz G. Straub, Alvin G. Anderson, and Charles E. Bowers: Importance of inlet design on culvert capacity, in Culvert hydraulics, *Highway Research Board, Research Report 15-B*, Washington, D.C., 1953, pp. 53–67.

23. Roy H. Shoemaker, Jr., and Leslie A. Clayton: Model studies of tapered inlets for box culverts, in Culvert hydraulics, *Highway Research Board, Research Report 15-B*, Washington, D.C., 1953, pp. 1–45.

24. John L. French: First progress report on hydraulics of short pipes: Hydraulic characteristics of commonly used pipe entrances, *U.S. National Bureau of Standards, Report 4444*, Dec. 28, 1955.

25. John L. French: Second progress report on hydraulics of culverts: Pressure and resistance characteristics of a model pipe culvert, *U.S. National Bureau of Standards, Report 4911*, Oct. 29, 1956.

26. John L. French: Third progress report on hydraulics of culverts: Effect of approach channel characteristics on model pipe culvert operation, *U.S. National Bureau of Standards, Report 5306*, June 3, 1957.

27. R. W. Carter: Computation of peak discharge at culverts, *U.S. Geological Survey, Circular 376*, 1957.

28. Wen-Hsiung Li and Calvin C. Patterson: Free outlets and self-priming action of

culverts, paper 1009, *Proceedings, American Society of Civil Engineers, Journal, Hydraulics Division*, no. HY3, pp. 1–22, June, 1956.

29. Hydraulic chart, No. 1043, *U.S. Bureau of Public Roads, Hydraulic Charts*, March, 1951.

30. J. F. d'Aubuisson de Voisins: "Traité d'hydraulique" ("Treatise on Hydraulics"), 2d ed., Pitois, Levraut & Cie, Paris, 1840.

31. Julius Weisbach: "Die Experimentalhydraulik" ("Experimental Hydraulics"), Freiburg, Germany, 1855.

32. J. F. Bubendey: Stau an Brücken und Durchlässen (Backwater of bridges and culverts), art. 25, chap. 3, pt. 3, vol. 1, in "Handbuch der Ingenieurwissenschaften," 4th ed., W. Engelmann, Leipzig, 1911, pp. 767–773.

33. Floyd A. Nagler: Obstruction of bridge piers to the flow of water, *Transactions, American Society of Civil Engineers*, vol. 82, pp. 334–395, 1918.

34. H. D. Krey: Berechnung des Staues infolge von Querschnittverengungen (Calculation of backwater due to cross-sectional contraction), *Zentralblatt der Bauverwaltung*, Berlin, vol. 39, no. 79, pp. 472–475, Sept. 27, 1919.

35. Th. Rehbock: Zur Frage des Brückenstaues (On the problem of bridge constriction), *Zentralblatt der Bauverwaltung*, Berlin, vol. 39, no. 37, pp. 197–200, 1919.

36. Th. Rehbock: Verfahren zur Bestimmung des Brückenstaues bei rein strömenden Wasserdurchfluss (A method of determining the backwater at bridges for distinctly streaming flow), a volume published to celebrate the dedication of the new building of the Division of Engineering Structures of the Technical Institute of Karlsruhe, Germany, Nov. 26, 1921, pp. 7–13; also in *Der Bauingenieur*, Berlin, vol. 2, no. 22, pp. 603–609, 1921.

37. Th. Rehbock: Brückenstau und Walzenbildung (Backwater and eddies at bridges), *Der Bauingenieur*, Berlin, vol. 2, no. 13, pp. 341–347, 1921.

38. Paul Böss: "Berechnung der Wasserspiegellage beim Wechsel des Fliesszustandes" ("Computation of Water Surface with Changes in Flow Type"), Springer-Verlag, Berlin, 1919, and VDI-Verlag, Berlin, 1927.

39. Alexander Koch and Max Carstanjen: "Von der Bewegung des Wassers und den dabei auftretenden Kräften" ("Movement of Water and Associated Force Phenomena"), Springer-Verlag, Berlin, 1926, pp. 179–185.

40. Giulio De Marchi, "Idraulica" ("Hydraulics"), Ulrico Hoepli, Milan, 1930, vol. 1, pp. 401–404.

41. David L. Yarnell: Pile trestles as channel obstructions, *U.S. Department of Agriculture, Technical Bulletin No.* 429, July, 1934.

42. David L. Yarnell: Bridge piers as channel obstructions, *U.S. Department of Agriculture, Technical Bulletin No.* 442, November, 1934.

43. L. Escande and G. Sabathé: Sur l'emploi des profils aérodynamiques pour les piles de barrages déversoirs, de barrages mobiles et les piles des ponts (Use of aerodynamic profiles for movable dams and bridge piers), *Revue générale de l'hydraulique*, Paris, vol. 2, no. 10, pp. 546–555, 1936.

44. Léopold Escande: Recherches sur l'écoulement de l'eau entre les piles des ponts (Researches on the flow of water through the piers of bridges), pt. A, and Remarque sur le calcul du remous provoqué par un pont (Remark on the calculation of the backwater caused by a bridge), pt. B, *Le Génie civil*, vol. 115, no. 6, pp. 113–117, Aug. 5; no. 7, pp. 138–140, Aug. 12; and no. 13, pp. 259–260, Sept. 13, 1939.

45. Léopold Escande: Expériences sur l'écoulement entre piles de ponts (Experiments on flow through piers of bridges), *Comptes rendus de l'Académie des Sciences*, vol. 209, pp. 14–16, July 3, 1939.

46. Léopold Escande: Sur l'écoulement entre piles de ponts (On the flow through

piers of bridges), *Comptes rendus de l'Académie des Sciences*, vol. 108, pp. 1970–1972, June 19, 1939.

47. Léopold Escande: Recherches sur l'écoulement de l'eau entre piles de ponts (Researches on the flow of water through piers of bridges), *Le Génie civil*, vol. 115, no. 6, pp. 113–117, Aug. 5; and no. 7, pp. 138–140, Aug. 12, 1939.

48. Étienne Crausse: Sur un phénomène d'oscillation du plan d'eau provoqué par l'écoulement autour d'obstacles en form de piles de ponts (On the phenomenon of oscillation of water surface caused by flow around obstacles in the form of bridge piers), *Comptes rendus de l'Académie des Sciences*, vol. 209, pp. 197–199, July 24, 1939.

49. Otto Streck: "Grund- und Wasserbau" ("Foundation and Hydraulic Engineering"), Springer-Verlag, Berlin, 1950, vol. 2, pp. 420–434.

50. Josef Koženy: "Hydraulik" ("Hydraulics"), Springer-Verlag, Vienna, 1953, pp. 546–549.

51. Philipp Forchheimer: "Hydraulik" ("Hydraulics"), 3d ed., Teubner Verlagsgesellschaft, Leipzig and Berlin, 1930, pp. 519–522 on backwater at bridge piers and pp. 522–524 on loss of head at trash racks.

52. Armin Schoklitsch: "Handbuch des Wasserbaues" ("Handbook of Hydraulic Engineering"), Springer-Verlag, Vienna, 1950, vol. 1, pp. 122–124 on backwater at bridge piers and pp. 125–127 on loss of head at trash racks.

53. Otto Kirschmer: Untersuchungen über den Gefällsverlust an Rechen (Studies on the head loss through a rack), *Mitteilungen des hydraulischen Instituts der technischen Hochschule München*, no. 1, pp. 21–41, Munich, 1926.

54. W. Fellenius: Undersökingar betröffande fallförluster i skyddsgrinder vid vattenkraftanlöggninger (Studies of head loss through racks in power plants), *Transactions, Hydraulic Institute of the Royal Technical University of Stockholm*, no. 5, 1927.

55. J. Spangler: Untersuchungen über den Verlust an Rechen bei schräger Zuströmung (Studies on the head loss through a rack inclined to stream flow), *Mitteilungen des hydraulichen Instituts der technischen Hochschule München*, no. 2, pp. 46–60, Munich, 1928.

56. E. Scimemi: Rilievi sperimentali sul funzionamento idraulico dei grandi impianti industriali (Experimental studies on the hydraulic function of large industrial plants, *L'Energia elettrica, Milano*, vol. 10, no. 9, pp. 705–723, September; no. 11, pp. 897–924, November, 1933.

57. Armin Schoklitsch: "Hydraulic Structures," translated from the German by Samuel Shulits, American Society of Mechanical Engineers, New York, 1937, vol. II, pp. 891–892.

58. Léopold Escande: Expression de la perte de charge à la traversée des grilles (Expression of the head loss in water through grills), *Comptes rendus de l'Académie des Sciences*, vol. 218, pp. 179–181, Jan. 31, 1944.

59. Léopold Escande: Étude expérimentale de la perte de charge à la traversée des grilles (Experimental studies of head loss in water through grills), *Comptes rendus de l'Académie des Sciences*, vol. 218, pp. 266–268, Feb. 14, 1944.

60. Léopold Escande: Étude théorique et expérimentale de la perte de charge de l'eau à la traversée d'une grille (Theoretical and experimental study of the head loss in water through a grill), *Le Génie civil*, vol. 122, no. 23, pp. 188–190, Dec. 1; and no. 24, pp. 197–198, Dec. 15, 1945.

61. David H. Kent: Models of hydraulic structures, pt. 1, *Water Power*, London, vol. 7, no. 8, pp. 301–307, August, 1955. Gives head losses through tailrace fish screens.

62. Floyd A. Nagler and Albion Davis: Experiments on discharge over spillways and

models, Keokuk Dam, *Transactions, American Society of Civil Engineers*, vol. 94, pp. 777–820, 1930.

63. Louis G. Puls: Spillway discharge capacity of Wilson Dam, *Transactions, American Society of Civil Engineers*, vol. 95, pp. 316–329, 1931.

64. E. Camichel, L. Escande, and G. Sabathé: Sur la similitude des barrages a contractions latérales (On the similitude of dams with lateral contractions), *Comptes rendus de l'Académie des Sciences*, vol. 194, pp. 807–809, Mar. 7, 1932.

65. E. Camichel, L. Escande, and P. Dupin: Remarques sur certains phénomènes de contractions latérales dans les barrages (Notes on certain phenomena of lateral contractions in dams), *Comptes rendus de l'Académie des Sciences*, vol. 197, pp. 722–725, Oct. 9, 1933.

66. O. Mueller: Schwingungsuntersuchungen an unterströmten Wehren (Vibration studies on underflow weirs), *Mitteilungen der preussischen Versuchsanstalt für Wasserbau und Schiffbau*, no. 13, Berlin, 1933.

67. J. B. Tiffany: Laboratory research applied to the hydraulic design of large dams, *U.S. Army Engineers Waterways Experiment Station*, Bulletin 32, 1948.

68. Harold R. Henry: Discussion of Diffusion of submerged jets, by M. L. Albertson, Y. B. Dai, R. A. Jensen, and Hunter Rouse, *Transactions, American Society of Civil Engineers*, vol. 115, pp. 687–694, 1950.

69. Arthur Toch: Discharge characteristics of Tainter gates, *Transactions, American Society of Civil Engineers*, vol. 120, pp. 290–300, 1955.

70. Hunter Rouse (editor): "Engineering Hydraulics," John Wiley & Sons, Inc., New York, 1950, pp. 540–541.

71. Léopold Escande: Étude théorique et expérimentale de l'écoulement par vanne de fond (Theoretical and experimental study of flow through sluice gates), *Revue générale de l'hydraulique*, Paris, vol. 4, No. 19, pp. 25–29, no. 20, pp. 72–79, and no. 21, pp. 120–128, 1938; vol. 5, no. 25, pp. 21–34, no. 26, pp. 65–77 and 131–139, 1939.

72. Georg Pager: Über den Strömungsvorgang an einer unterströmten scharfkantigen Planschütze (The flow characteristics at an underflow sluice gate), *Zeitschrift für angewandte Mathematik und Mechanik*, Berlin, vol. 17, no. 5, pp. 259–269, October, 1937.

73. T. Brook Benjamin: On the flow in channels when rigid obstacles are placed in the stream, *Journal of Fluid Mechanics*, London, vol. 1, pt. 2, pp. 227–248, July, 1956.

74. U.S. Army Corps of Engineers: Tainter gates on spillway crests—Discharge coefficients, Hydraulic Design Charts 311-1 to 311-5, WES 3-56, in "Corps of Engineers Hydraulic Design Criteria," prepared for the Office of the Chief of Engineers, U.S. Army Engineers Waterways Experiment Station, Vicksburg, Miss., 1952, and revised in subsequent years.

75. Nazir Ahmad: Mechanism of erosion below hydraulic works, *Proceedings of the Minnesota International Hydraulics Convention, Joint meeting of International Association of Hydraulic Research and Hydraulics Division of the American Society of Civil Engineers*, pp. 133–143, August, 1953.

76. Doddiah Doddiah, Maurice L. Albertson, and Robert Thomas: Scour from jets, *Proceedings of the Minnesota International Hydraulics Convention, Joint meeting of International Association of Hydraulic Research and Hydraulics Division of the American Society of Civil Engineers*, pp. 161–169, August, 1953.

77. Armin Schoklitsch: "Stauraumverlandung und Kolkabwehr" ("The Silting of Reservoirs and Scour Prevention"), Springer-Verlag, Vienna, 1935.

78. C. M. Camichel: Contribution à l'étude des veines liquides: Les indéterminations et les solutions multiples dans leurs rapports avec l'hydraulique fluviale (Contribution to the theory of liquid jets: Indeterminacies and multiple solutions in relation

to fluvial hydraulics), *Revue générale de l'hydraulique,* Paris, vol. 1, no. 5, pp. 235–242, and no. 6, pp. 293–299, 1935.

79. Irby J. Hickenlooper, John C. Guillou, and Ven Te Chow: Hydraulic studies of a highway bridge, *University of Illinois, Civil Engineering Studies, Hydraulic Engineering Series No. 4,* June, 1957.

80. Edward H. Taylor: Flow characteristics at rectangular open-channel junctions, *Transactions, American Society of Civil Engineers,* vol. 109, pp. 893–903, 1944.

81. Charles E. Bowers: Studies of open-channel junctions, pt. V of Hydraulic model studies for Whiting Field Naval Air Station, Milton, Florida, *University of Minnesota, St. Anthony Falls Hydraulic Laboratory, Technical Paper No. 6, Series B,* January, 1950.

# PART V

# UNSTEADY FLOW

The unsteady-flow problem most commonly encountered in open channels deals with translatory waves. The *translatory wave* is a gravity wave that propagates in an open channel and results in appreciable displacement of the water particles in a direction parallel to the flow.[1] In actual open-channel flow, the water particles may also oscillate. However, the effect of oscillation is insignificant in the problems to be discussed in this book.

For purposes of analytical discussion, unsteady flow is classified into two types, namely, gradually varied and rapidly varied unsteady flow. In the first type the curvature of the wave profile is mild, and the change in depth is gradual. The vertical component of the acceleration of the water particles is negligible in comparison with the total acceleration, whereas the effect of channel friction is usually appreciable and should be taken into account in an accurate analysis. In the second type the curvature of the wave profile is very large and so the surface of the profile may become virtually discontinuous. The vertical acceleration component, therefore, plays an important part in the phenomenon, whereas the effect of channel friction is practically negligible in comparison with the dynamic effect of the flow. Common examples of gradually varied unsteady flow are flood waves and waves due to slow operation of controlling structures, such as the gates and sluices in ship locks. Examples of rapidly varied unsteady flow are surges of various kinds caused by quick operation of controlling structures.

Gradually varied unsteady flow will be discussed in Chaps. 18 and 20, and rapidly varied unsteady flow in Chap. 19.[2] For extensive information on unsteady flow in open channels, see [5] to [20].

[1] Another basic type of gravity wave is the *oscillatory wave*, in which the water particles oscillate in an orbit about a mean position but do not display appreciable displacement in the direction of wave propagation.

[2] Other kinds of waves and tides in open channels are beyond the scope of the present work. For comprehensive information on water waves, see [1] to [3]. For references on tidal hydraulics, the reader should refer to the extensive bibliographies prepared by the Committee on Tidal Hydraulics, U.S. Army Corps of Engineers [4].

# CHAPTER 18

# GRADUALLY VARIED UNSTEADY FLOW

**18-1. Continuity of Unsteady Flow.** The law of continuity for unsteady flow may be established by considering the conservation of mass in an infinitesimal space between two channel sections (Fig. 18-1). In unsteady flow, the discharge changes with distance at a rate $\partial Q/\partial x$,

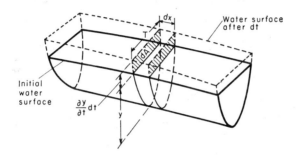

FIG. 18-1. Continuity of unsteady flow.

and the depth changes with time at a rate $\partial y/\partial t$. The change in discharge through space in the time $dt$ is $(\partial Q/\partial x)\, dx\, dt$. The corresponding change in channel storage in space is $T\, dx\, (\partial y/\partial t)\, dt = dx\, (\partial A/\partial t)\, dt$. Since water is incompressible, the net change in discharge plus the change in storage should be zero; that is,

$$\left(\frac{\partial Q}{\partial x}\right) dx\, dt + T\, dx \left(\frac{\partial y}{\partial t}\right) dt = \left(\frac{\partial Q}{\partial x}\right) dx\, dt + dx \left(\frac{\partial A}{\partial t}\right) dt = 0$$

Simplifying,

$$\frac{\partial Q}{\partial x} + T\frac{\partial y}{\partial t} = 0 \tag{18-1}$$

or

$$\frac{\partial Q}{\partial x} + \frac{\partial A}{\partial t} = 0 \tag{18-2}$$

At a given section, $Q = VA$; thus Eq. (18-1) becomes

$$\frac{\partial(VA)}{\partial x} + T\frac{\partial y}{\partial t} = 0 \tag{18-3}$$

525

or
$$A\frac{\partial V}{\partial x} + V\frac{\partial A}{\partial x} + T\frac{\partial y}{\partial t} = 0 \qquad (18\text{-}4)$$

Since the hydraulic depth $D = A/T$ and $\partial A = T\,\partial y$, the above equation may be written

$$D\frac{\partial V}{\partial x} + V\frac{\partial y}{\partial x} + \frac{\partial y}{\partial t} = 0 \qquad (18\text{-}5)$$

The above equations are all forms of the *continuity equation for unsteady flow in open channels*. For a rectangular channel of infinite width, Eq. (18-1) may be written

$$\frac{\partial q}{\partial x} + \frac{\partial y}{\partial t} = 0 \qquad (18\text{-}6)$$

where $q$ is the discharge per unit width. This expression was first introduced by Saint-Venant [21].

When the channel is to feed laterally with a supplementary discharge of $q'$ per unit length, for instance, into an area that is being flooded over a dike, Eq. (18-2) may be written

$$\frac{\partial Q}{\partial x} + \frac{\partial A}{\partial t} + q' = 0 \qquad (18\text{-}7)$$

If the channel consists of a deep main section and an extensive, shallow side section, it may be assumed that, whereas the discharge in the main section is relatively very high, the side section contributes only to storage but not to discharge. Thus, Eq. (18-2) may be written

$$\frac{\partial Q}{\partial x} + \frac{\partial A}{\partial t} + \frac{\partial A'}{\partial t} = 0 \qquad (18\text{-}8)$$

where $A'$ is the water area of the side section. This equation also applies to the case of a channel containing groins; the water circulates between the groins to guide the flow in the main channel but not to contribute discharge.

**18-2. Dynamic Equation for Unsteady Flow.** For simplicity,[1] unsteady flow will be treated like two-dimensional steady flow except that an additional variable for the time element will be used. This time variable takes into account the variation in velocity of flow and accordingly brings to the fore the acceleration, which produces force and causes additional energy losses in the flow.[2]

With reference to Fig. 18-2, the force due to acceleration $\partial V/\partial t$ acting on a unit weight $w$ of water is equal to $(w/g)\,\partial V/\partial t$; that is, force = mass × acceleration. It is assumed that the slope of the channel is

---

[1] For rigorous analyses of unsteady flow, see [5], [6], [9], [11], [15] and [20].

[2] The acceleration is positive for an increasing velocity of flow and negative for a decreasing velocity of flow.

small, that the acceleration is in the direction of $x$, and that its vertical component is negligible. Thus, the work done by this force through a distance $dx$ between the two channel sections shown in the figure is $(w/g)(\partial V/\partial t)\,dx$. This amount of work is equal to the energy loss due to acceleration. Dividing by $w$, the loss in head is expressed by $(1/g)(\partial V/\partial t)\,dx$.

The over-all change in head in the infinitesimal length $dx$ may be treated exactly as in steady flow, except that an additional loss due to

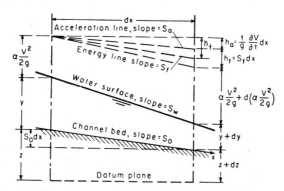

FIG. 18-2. Simplified representation of energy in unsteady flow.

acceleration must be included. The total loss in head will consist of two parts: the loss due to friction $h_f = S_f\,dx$ and the loss due to acceleration $h_a = (1/g)(\partial V/\partial t)\,dx$. The line indicating the loss due to acceleration is shown as the *acceleration line;* its slope is $S_a = (1/g)(\partial V/\partial t)$. By the energy principle, the following may be written:[1]

$$z + y + \frac{\alpha V^2}{2g} = z + dz + y + dy + \frac{\alpha V^2}{2g} + d\left(\frac{\alpha V^2}{2g}\right) + \frac{1}{g}\frac{\partial V}{\partial t}\,dx + S_f\,dx$$

$$(18\text{-}9)$$

Simplifying,

$$d\left(z + y + \frac{\alpha V^2}{2g}\right) = -S_f\,dx - \frac{1}{g}\frac{\partial V}{\partial t}\,dx \qquad (18\text{-}10)$$

The left side of this equation represents the change in total head. The two terms on the right are the head losses due to friction and acceleration, respectively. This equation states that the change in total head

[1] Since there are two independent variables $x$ and $t$, the changes in depth and in velocity head are each composed of two parts; that is, $dy = (\partial y/\partial x)\,dx + (\partial y/\partial t)\,dt$ and $d(\alpha V^2/2g) = [\partial(\alpha V^2/2g)/\partial x]\,dx + [\partial(\alpha V^2/2g)/\partial t]\,dt$. As the channel bottom does not vary with time, $\partial z/\partial x = dz/dx$ and $\partial z/\partial t = 0$. For the sake of simplicity, these mathematical details are omitted from the present analysis.

in gradually varied unsteady flow depends on the effects of friction and acceleration. In gradually varied steady flow, the change in head depends entirely on friction, provided eddy loss is negligible.

Dividing through by $dx$ in Eq. (18-10) and utilizing partial differentials,

$$\frac{\partial(z + y)}{\partial x} + S_f + \frac{\partial}{\partial x}\left(\frac{\alpha V^2}{2g}\right) + \frac{1}{g}\frac{\partial V}{\partial t} = 0 \qquad (18\text{-}11)$$

or

$$\frac{\partial y}{\partial x} + \frac{\alpha V}{g}\frac{\partial V}{\partial x} + \frac{1}{g}\frac{\partial V}{\partial t} + \frac{\partial z}{\partial x} + S_f = 0 \qquad (18\text{-}12)$$

This is the *general dynamic equation for gradually varied unsteady flow.* The friction slope in the equation can be evaluated by the Manning formula, the Chézy formula, or any other suitable uniform-flow formula.

For prismatic channels, i.e., for $-\partial z/\partial x = S_0$, Eq. (18-12) may be written

$$\frac{\partial y}{\partial x} + \frac{\alpha V}{g}\frac{\partial V}{\partial x} + \frac{1}{g}\frac{\partial V}{\partial t} = S_0 - S_f \qquad (18\text{-}13)$$

The continuity and dynamic equations for gradually varied unsteady flow were first published by Saint-Venant [21,22]. The validity of these equations has been verified by many observations and experiments. However, owing to their mathematical complexity, exact integration of the equations is practically impossible. For practical applications, a solution of the equations may be obtained by approximate step methods or by methods based on simplifying assumptions.

**18-3. Monoclinal Rising Wave.** A special case of unsteady flow which is nearly possible in prismatic channels is *uniformly progressive flow.* This type of flow has a stable wave profile that will not change in shape as it moves down the channel. According to this definition, uniformly progressive flow has the following notable features: (1) the successive positions of the wavefront at different times are parallel; (2) the velocity of the wavefront, or *celerity,* is greater than the mean water velocity at any section of the wave; and (3) the wave configuration travels downstream with a constant velocity, but the mean water velocity in the cross section may vary from section to section as the hydraulic radius and surface slope change. Of various forms of wave configuration in uniformly progressive flow, the *monoclinal rising wave* will be taken as a typical case in the following discussion, because such a wave can be approximated to most flood waves in natural channels and because it is subject to simple mathematical treatment.

The monoclinal rising wave (Fig. 18-3) is a translatory wave of stable form, that is, a uniformly progressive wave, that travels down the channel at constant velocity $V_w$ from an upstream region of uniform flow having $y_1$, $V_1$, and $Q_1$ to a downstream region of uniform flow having $y_2$, $V_2$, and

$Q_2$. The depth of the wavefront is gradually varied from the upstream section to the downstream section. During a time interval $t$, the wavefront moves forward a distance equal to $V_w t$. The wave velocity is greater than either of the mean velocities $V_1$ and $V_2$ in the uniform-flow regions. When the wavefront passes over the flow in the channel, it takes in a steady discharge $Q_o = (V_w - V_1)A_1$ at the front. Since the wave configuration is of stable form and constant volume, the front leaves behind an equal steady discharge $Q_o = (V_w - V_2)A_2$ to the

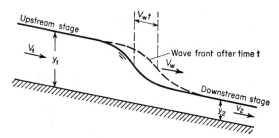

FIG. 18-3. Monoclinal rising wave.

upstream side. The steady discharge $Q_o$ which flows through the wavefront in the upstream direction is called the *overrun*. Equating the values of the steady discharge,

$$Q_o = (V_w - V_1)A_1 = (V_w - V_2)A_2 \qquad (18\text{-}14)$$

Solving for $V_w$,
$$V_w = \frac{V_1 A_1 - V_2 A_2}{A_1 - A_2} \qquad (18\text{-}15)$$

Since in uniform-flow regions $Q_1 = V_1 A_1$ and $Q_2 = V_2 A_2$, Eq. (18-15) may be written

$$V_w = \frac{Q_1 - Q_2}{A_1 - A_2} \qquad (18\text{-}16)$$

The above equations can be used for the computation of the velocity of the monoclinal rising wave. Equation (18-15) shows that, if there is no initial flow, that is, if $V_1 = 0$ and $A_1 = 0$, then $V_w = V_2$. If there is initial flow, then $V_w$ is always greater than either $V_1$ or $V_2$. This is true because the wave must move more rapidly than the water particles if it is to make up the volume of the wave configuration at any time.

In natural channels, the velocity of an assumed monoclinal rising flood wave may be determined by the so-called *Kleitz-Seddon principle*. Equation (18-16) indicates that the velocity of a monoclinal rising wave is a function of the water area and the discharge relationship for the channel. Figure 18-4 shows a curve representing such a relationship. For ordinary channel sections in which the velocity increases as the water area increases, this curve is concave upward. In the figure, $\tan \theta_1 = Q_1/A_1 = V_1$, $\tan \theta_2 = Q_2/A_2 = V_2$, and $\tan \theta_w = (Q_1 - Q_2)/(A_1 - A_2) = V_w = $ the slope of the line $P_1P_2$. Since the curve is concave upward, it can be seen that $V_w$ must be greater than either $V_1$ or $V_2$. For a maximum $V_w$, the slope of the line $P_1P_2$ must be a maximum. This occurs when $Q_1 = Q_2$ or when the point $P_2$ approaches the point $P_1$ and

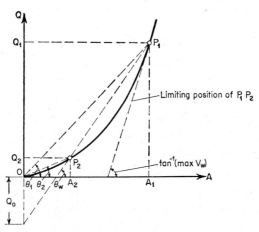

FIG. 18-4. Graphical interpretation of water area, discharge, and velocity relations in monoclinal rising wave.

the slope of the secant $P_1P_2$ approaches the slope of the tangent at point $P_1$ as a limit. Therefore,

$$(V_w)_{max} = \frac{dQ}{dA} \tag{18-17}$$

Since $dA = T\,dy$, the above equation becomes

$$(V_w)_{max} = \frac{1}{T}\frac{dQ}{dy} \tag{18-18}$$

where $dQ/dy$ is the slope of the rating curve of the channel. If the top width of the channel section is known, the maximum velocity can be computed by this equation. Likewise, if the maximum velocity is known, the average width of the channel can be determined. The term $dQ/dy$ at a given stage may be computed from the mean slope of the rating curves at gaging stations in the reach under consideration. The maximum velocity $V_w$ can be determined from the distance and time of the wave travel between the stations.

Equation (18-18) may also be used to determine the ratio between the maximum wave velocity and the water velocity in a prismatic channel. On the basis of the Manning formula, the ratio can be shown to be 1.67, 1.33, and 1.44, for wide rectangular, triangular, and wide parabolic channels, respectively. On the basis of the Chézy formula, the corresponding ratios are 1.50, 1.25, and 1.33.

Equations (18-17) and (18-18) apply only to small rises in flood stage, where the wavefront has such slight slope and rise that the term $dQ/dy$ can appropriately be taken from the rating curve for uniform flow.

The principle of the above method was originally developed mathematically by Kleitz [27], but was discovered from actual observations by Seddon [28] in a study of gage heights on the Mississippi and Missouri Rivers. Wilkinson [29] has described the application of the method to the Clinch and Lower Tennessee Rivers. He concluded that the wave velocity in such natural channels can be well approximated by this method. He found that mid-points of rise or fall stages were best suited for determining the velocity of an observed wave.

**18-4. Dynamic Equation for Uniformly Progressive Flow.** In a time interval $dt$, the wavefront of a uniformly progressive flow (Fig. 18-3) will travel a distance $V_w \, dt$. It can be shown that, as the wave advances, the velocity of flow decreases with distance at a rate $-\partial V/\partial x$. Therefore, the change in velocity in $dt$ is $dV = -V_w \, dt \, (\partial V/\partial x)$. Using partial differentials, $\partial V/\partial t = -V_w(\partial V/\partial x)$.

An equation similar to Eq. (18-14) can be written for the general case of uniformly progressive flow; that is, $Q_o = (V_w - V)A$. Differentiating this equation with respect to $x$, $\partial V/\partial x = (Q_o/AD)(\partial y/\partial x)$.

Substituting the above expressions for $\partial V/\partial t$ and $\partial V/\partial x$, respectively, in Eq. (18-13), assuming $\alpha = 1$, and simplifying, $\partial y/\partial x$ for the flow in a prismatic channel is

$$\frac{\partial y}{\partial x} = \frac{S_0 - S_f}{1 - Q_o^2/gA^2D} \tag{18-19}$$

Since $S_f = Q^2/K^2 = V^2A^2/K^2 = (V_wA - Q_o)^2/K^2$, Eq. (18-19) becomes

$$\frac{\partial y}{\partial x} = \frac{S_0 - (V_wA - Q_o)^2/K^2}{1 - Q_o^2/gA^2D} \tag{18-20}$$

This is the *dynamic equation for uniformly progressive flow in a prismatic channel.* Since the flow is unsteady, the position of the wave profile is changing constantly, but the shape of the profile at any instant remains the same. Equation (18-20), therefore, describes a "snapshot" view of the profile at any instant. For wide rectangular channels, the equation can be further simplified and becomes mathematically integrable. It should be noted that $\partial y/\partial x$ represents the instantaneous surface slope of the wave profile. At a given instant of time, this is the same as the permanent slope $dy/dx$ and hence may also be expressed by the latter.

There is an apparent similarity between Eq. (18-20) and the dynamic equation for steady varied flow [say, Eq. (9-16) with $\alpha = 1$]. This similarity can be explained as follows. Imagine that an observer on the channel bank is running after the uniformly progressive flow of Fig. 18-3, in the same direction and at the same velocity $V_w$ as the wavefront. He will see a picture of a steady flow like that in Fig. 18-5; the water surface will appear stationary to him, and the flow will show a steady discharge $Q_0$ and a velocity $V_w - V$ at every point along the channel. Therefore, if $Q_0$ is regarded as a steady discharge, the steady-varied-flow equation can be applied directly to this uniformly progressive flow except that the discharge used for computing the frictional slope should be set equal to $V_w A - Q_0$. This discharge is responsible for the frictional loss.

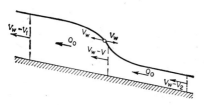

Fig. 18-5. View appearing to the observer who follows the wavefront of a uniformly progressive flow.

The discharge at any section of a uniformly progressive flow is $Q = V_w A - Q_0$. Thus, $Q_0 = V_w A - Q$, and Eq. (18-20) becomes

$$\frac{dy}{dx} = \frac{S_0 - Q^2/K^2}{1 - (V_w A - Q)^2/gA^2D} \tag{18-21}$$

If the velocity is very low, so that the second term of the denominator, which covers the velocity-head effect, can be neglected, the above equation may be written

$$\frac{dy}{dx} = S_0 - \frac{Q^2}{K^2} \tag{18-22}$$

By Eq. (9-11), $K^2 = Q_n{}^2/S_0$. Then, Eq. (18-22) becomes

$$Q = Q_n \sqrt{1 - \frac{1}{S_0}\frac{dy}{dx}} \tag{18-23}$$

Let $j$ represent the rate of rise in the water surface at a given channel section. Then, $j = -V_w\, dy/dx$, or $dy/dx = -j/V_w$. Substituting this expression in Eq. (18-23),

$$Q = Q_n \sqrt{1 + \frac{j}{V_w S_0}} \tag{18-24}$$

This equation can be used to compute approximately the true discharge of an unsteady flow at a given station, provided the velocity is low.

In the equation, the normal discharge $Q_n$ can be determined from the rating curve at the station, and other quantities can be measured in the field. A similar equation has been developed empirically by Jones [30] and is used widely for correcting the normal discharge to obtain the true discharge in a river when the stage is changing. In the Jones formula, however, the wave velocity in Eq. (18-24) is replaced by the surface velocity, which is much easier to determine but lower than the true wave velocity. A more exact equation than Eq. (18-24) may be obtained from Eq. (18-21) by letting $dy/dx = -j/V_w$ and solving for $Q$. However, the derivation and the resulting form of the equation are too complicated for practical purposes.

**18-5. Wave Profile of Uniformly Progressive Flow.** The wave profile of uniformly progressive flow can be easily derived for wide rectangular channels by using the Chézy formula. For the unit width of a wide rectangular channel, $A = R = D = y$. By the Chézy formula, $K^2 = C^2 y^3$. Substituting these expressions in Eq. (18-20), the slope at any point on the wave profile at a given instant of time may be expressed as

$$\frac{dy}{dx} = S_0 \frac{y^3 - (V_w y - Q_o)^2/C^2 S_0}{y^3 - Q_o^2/g} \qquad (18\text{-}25)$$

When $dy/dx = 0$, the above equation gives $y^3 - (V_w y - Q_o)^2/C^2 S_0 = 0$ This is a cubic equation in $y$; the nature of its three roots may be determined by a discriminant $\Delta$.[1] The equation will give three different real roots if $\Delta > 0$; three real roots, two of them alike, if $\Delta = 0$; and one real root and two imaginary roots if $\Delta < 0$. It can be shown that the third case will produce no possible wave profiles and that the second is a special case of the first. For $\Delta > 0$, the cubic equation may be written $(y - y_1)(y - y_2)(y - y_3) = 0$, where the two positive roots $y_1$ and $y_2$ are, respectively, the final and initial normal depths to which the wave profiles are asymptotic. The third root can be found to be $y_3 = Q_o^2/C^2 S_0 y_1 y_2$. Since $y_3$ is not asymptotic to any real branch of the wave profile, it has no physical significance.

When $dy/dx = \infty$, Eq. (18-25) gives $y = \sqrt[3]{Q_o^2/g} = y_c$. This is called the *overrun critical depth*, or the critical depth corresponding to a steady discharge equal to the overrun. Therefore, the wave profile is vertical at the overrun-critical-depth line.

Substituting $y_c^3$ for $Q_o^2/g$ and $(y - y_1)(y - y_2)(y - y_3)$ for the numerator in Eq. (18-25) and solving for $x$,

$$x = \frac{1}{S_0} \int \frac{y^3 - y_c^3}{(y - y_1)(y - y_2)(y - y_3)} \, dy + C_1 \qquad (18\text{-}26)$$

---

[1] The equation can be written in the form $y^3 + c_1 y^2 + c_2 y + c_3 = 0$. Then, $\Delta = 18 c_1 c_2 c_3 - 4 c_1^3 c_3 + c_1^2 c_2^2 - 4 c_2^3 - 27 c_3^2$.

where $C_1$ is an integration constant. With the given values of $V_w$, $Q_o$, $S_0$, and $C$, this equation represents a number of possible wave profiles. For a monoclinal rising wave having an initial stage $y_1$ and a final stage $y_2$, the possible profiles are shown in Fig. 18-6 for $y_c < y_2$ and $y_c > y_2$. Theoretically, in the case $y_c < y_2$, the wavefront extends an infinite distance downstream, since the wave profile is asymptotic to the downstream stage. This may seem unreasonable, because the wave actually starts at a finite time and travels with a finite velocity. The explanation is that the wave profile described above will become stable only after

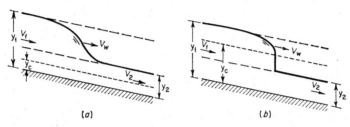

FIG. 18-6. Profiles of uniformly progressive flow (a) when $y_c < y_2$ or $V_w < V_2 + \sqrt{gy_2}$; (b) when $y_c > y_2$ or $V_w > V_2 + \sqrt{gy_2}$.

the wave attains equilibrium. The first traces of the wave are transmitted downstream by dynamic propagation at a velocity $V_2 + \sqrt{gy_2}$, which is much greater than the final wave velocity $V_w$. By this action the downstream end of an actual wave will approach the theoretical asymptotic form very rapidly. If the velocity $V_w$ is greater than $V_2 + \sqrt{gy_2}$, it is evidently impossible for the wavefront to extend an infinite distance downstream. This is the case when $y_c > y_2$. The downstream end of the wave is terminated with an abrupt front which in theory should cross the overrun-critical-depth line vertically. The front is essentially a rapidly varied unsteady flow, known specifically as the *hydraulic bore* (Art. 19-2).

**Example 18-1.** Determine the wave profile of the flood generated by the failure of a dam.[1] The failure causes a sudden release of the impounding water from its reser-

---

[1] This is the so-called *dam-break problem*, which is well-known in hydraulics. In 1892, Ritter [31] offered the first solution of the problem, using the approximate Saint-Venant equation but ignoring the effects of the frictional and turbulence resistance to the unsteady flow. Consequently, this unrealistic classical solution was not supported by the experimental findings and more practical analyses had to be sought. In 1914, Forchheimer [5, pp. 267–271] presented a summary of most of the previous work on this problem, including attempts to include the resistance effects.
    Toward the end of World War II, Ré [32] was instructed by the Allied Command to study the problem in anticipation of possible destruction of the large dams on the

voir into a dry wide rectangular channel.   Use the Manning formula for expressing the velocity of uniform flow.

*Solution.*   In this case the wavefront moves in a steeply inclined wall of water whose profile is apparently unchanging as long as the channel conditions remain fixed and the source of supply is constant.   Therefore, this can be considered a special case of uniformly progressive flow, known specifically as the *roll wave*, in which $A_2 = 0$, $V_2 = 0$, $Q_o = 0$, and $V_w = V_1 = C \sqrt{y_1 S_0}$.   Substituting the values of $Q_0$ and of $V_w$ and $K = CA \sqrt{y}$ in Eq. (18-20),

$$\frac{dy}{dx} = S_0 \left(1 - \frac{y_1}{y}\right) \tag{18-27}$$

Let $y_1 = y_n$, which is the normal depth at the crest of the wave, where the flow is practically uniform.   Solve Eq. (18-27) for $dx$; then

$$dx = \frac{1}{S_0}\left(1 - \frac{1}{1 - y/y_n}\right) dy \tag{18-28}$$

Choose the tip of the wavefront, where $x = 0$ and $y = 0$, as the origin, and integrate the above equation; the length of the wave profile from the wavefront to the section of depth $y$ is

$$x = \frac{1}{S_0}\int_0^y \left(1 - \frac{1}{1 - y/y_n}\right) dy \tag{18-29}$$

Integrating,

$$x = \frac{y_n}{S_0}[z + \ln(1 - z)] \tag{18-30}$$

---

Rhine River at the German-Swiss frontier.   By a finite-difference graphical calculation of the characteristic equations (Art. 20-2) developed by Craya [33], Ré was able to compute the flow to be expected from the destruction of a dam for one specific value of slope and of Chézy's resistance factor.   Ré's solution included the presence of some water initially below the dam, causing the formation of a bore in his problem.

In 1952, Lévin [34] described a solution of the problem by a graphical method.   In the same year, Dressler [35] presented a solution in which the resistance effect was evaluated by the Chézy formula.   This solution gives good agreement with observed data except in the region near the tip of the wavefront.   Accordingly, it is believed that the Chézy formula may not be adequate for application to highly unsteady flow or to the condition of turbulence in the tip region.   In 1953, Dressler and Whitham [36] improved the solution by a more rigorous analysis of the flow at the tip region.   Dressler [36] also developed a method of analyzing the flow during the very small time interval after motion begins.

Experimental data of the dam-breaking problem are few, notably the early experiments made by Schoklitsh [37] and Eguiazaroff [38] and the later ones by the U.S. National Bureau of Standards [36].

A problem similar to that of dam breaking deals with the flow due to sudden lifting of a sluice gate.   A theoretical analysis of the wave profiles thus developed was made by Pohle [39] in 1950, assuming a velocity potential flow in Lagrangian coordinates.   Experiments on this problem also were made at the National Bureau of Standards.   A comparison of the theories and experiments on both problems was presented by Dressler [36] in 1954.   A comprehensive treatment of the dam-breaking problem along lines worked out by Pohle was given by Stoker [5, pp. 513–522] in 1957.

where $z = y/y_n$. This equation represents the required profile of the roll wave due to failure of the dam.[1] If the upstream supply of flow is limited, the profile of the wave propagating upstream will be described in Example 19-5.

**Example 18-2.** Determine the profile of the monoclinal rising wave in a wide rectangular channel. The wave is assumed to move with a constant velocity with the maximum stage unchanged over a long period of time.

*Solution.* For a unit width of the wide rectangular channel, $A_1 = y_1$ and $A_2 = y_2$. Using the Chézy formula, $V_1 = C \sqrt{y_1 S_0}$ and $V_2 = C \sqrt{y_2 S_0}$. Substituting these expressions in Eq. (18-15) and simplifying,

$$V_w = V_2 G \tag{18-31}$$

where
$$G = \frac{1 - (y_1/y_2)^{3/2}}{1 - y_1/y_2} \tag{18-32}$$

By Eq. (18-15), replacing $A_1$ and $V_1$ by $A$ and $V$, respectively, for any given section

$$V_w = \frac{A_2 V_2 - A V}{A_2 - A} \tag{18-33}$$

Eliminating $V_w$ from Eqs. (18-31) and (18-33) and solving for $V$,

$$V = \left( G - \frac{G - 1}{z} \right) V_2 \tag{18-34}$$

where $z = y/y_2$. The wave profile under consideration is long and flat; hence, the mean velocity $V$ will change very slowly with respect to both time $t$ and distance $x$. Thus, $\partial V/\partial x = 0$ and $\partial V/\partial t = 0$. From Eq. (18-13), using differentials,

$$\frac{dy}{dx} = S_0 - S_f \tag{18-35}$$

Since $V = C \sqrt{y S_f}$ and $V_2 = C \sqrt{y_2 S_0}$, Eq. (18-34) gives

$$S_f = \frac{V^2}{C^2 y} = \frac{S_0}{z} \left( G - \frac{G - 1}{z} \right)^2 \tag{18-36}$$

Substituting this equation for $S_f$ in Eq. (18-35),

$$\frac{dy}{dx} = S_0 - \frac{S_0}{z} \left( G - \frac{G - 1}{z} \right)^2 \tag{18-37}$$

or
$$dx = \frac{y_2}{S_0} \left\{ 1 + \frac{(Gz - G + 1)^2}{(z - 1)[z^2 - (G^2 - 1)z + (G - 1)^2]} \right\} dz \tag{18-38}$$

By integration,

$$x = \frac{y_2}{S_0} \left\{ z + \frac{1}{3 - 2G} \ln (1 - z) - \frac{(G - 1)^2(2G + 1)}{2(3 - 2G)} \ln [z^2 - (G^2 - 1)z + (G - 1)^2] \right.$$
$$\left. - \frac{(G - 1)^2[(2G + 1)(G + 1) - 4]}{2(3 - 2G) \sqrt{(G + 1)^2 - 4}} \ln \frac{2z - (G^2 - 1) - (G - 1) \sqrt{(G + 1)^2 - 4}}{2z - (G^2 - 1) + (G - 1) \sqrt{(G + 1)^2 - 4}} \right\}$$
$$+ C_1 \tag{18-39*}$$

where $z = y/y_2$, $y_2$ is the depth at high stage, $y$ is the depth at any section along the wave profile, $G$ is defined by Eq. (18-32), $y_1$ is the depth at low stage, and $C_1$ is a constant that can be determined from the condition that $x = 0$ when $y = (y_1 + y_2)/2$,

---

[1] For a refined solution of this problem, see [36].

* Derivation of this equation was originally given by Moots [40].

**Example 18-3.** Determine the wave velocity and profile of a uniformly progressive flow in a wide open channel if $y_1 = 25$ ft, $y_2 = 10$ ft, Chézy's $C = 100$, and $S_0 = 0.0004$.

*Solution.* By the Chézy formula and Eq. (18-15), $V_w = 12.45$ fps. By Eq. (18-14), $Q_0 = 61.25$ cfs per unit width. Since the discriminant $\Delta$ is positive, the numerator of Eq. (18-25) has three real roots, which are $y_1 = 25$, $y_2 = 10$, and $y_3 = 61.25^2/(100^2 \times 0.0004 \times 25 \times 10) = 3.76$. The overrun critical depth $y_c = \sqrt[3]{61.25^2/32.2} = 4.89$ ft. Since $y_c < y_2$, no hydraulic bore will be formed. Substituting all known values in Eq. (18-26),

$$x = \frac{1}{0.0004} \int \frac{y^3 - 116.7}{(y - 25)(y - 10)(y - 3.76)}\, dy + C_1 \qquad (18\text{-}40)$$

Expressed in partial fractions,

$$x = \frac{1}{0.0004} \int \left(1 - \frac{48.68}{25 - y} - \frac{9.437}{y - 10} - \frac{0.4794}{y - 3.76}\right) dy + C_1 \qquad (18\text{-}41)$$

By integration,

$$x = \frac{1}{0.0004}\left[y + \ln \frac{(25 - y)^{48.68}}{(y - 10)^{9.437}(y - 3.76)^{0.4794}}\right] + C_1 \qquad (18\text{-}42)$$

Taking the origin at $x = 0$, $y = 24$, Eq. (18-42) gives $C_1 = 5,840$. The wave profile by this equation is plotted as shown in Fig. 18-6a.

**18-6. Wave Propagation.** Before further discussions of unsteady flow, it seems pertinent to discuss the propagation of gravity waves in channels. For this purpose, a single form of gravity wave, known as the *solitary wave*, will be described.

The solitary wave was first observed and investigated experimentally by Russell [41].[1] It has a simple form (Fig. 18-7), consisting wholly of an elevation without any associated trough or depression whatever. The wave lies entirely above the normal water surface and moves smoothly and quietly without turbulence at any place along its profile. In a frictionless channel the wave can travel an infinite distance without change of shape or velocity, but in an actual channel the height of the wave is gradually reduced by the effects of friction. Such a wave can be produced in a laboratory by a sudden horizontal displacement of the gate in the channel (Fig. 18-7) or by other means. In nature, such waves have been generated by earthquakes and have been observed to travel across oceans.

Consider a solitary wave, traveling to the right in a rectangular channel, with celerity $c$ (Fig. 18-7a). An observer on the shore running along with the wave crest at a velocity equal to the celerity will see a

[1] It was first discovered by Russell in 1834. The mathematical analysis of the solitary wave was originally worked out independently by Boussinesq [42] and Rayleigh [43]. A complete account of the analysis can be found in Lamb [3, pp. 423–426].

picture of steady flow (Fig. 18-7b) in which the wave appears to stand still while the flow moves at a velocity equal to c in magnitude. Neglecting friction and assuming a small slope and $\alpha = 1$ at all sections, the energy equation between the normal section of the flow and the section

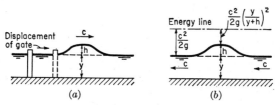

FIG. 18-7. Generation of a solitary wave. (a) Unsteady flow; (b) the flow that appears steady to an observer following the wave crest.

at the wave crest may be written

$$y + \frac{c^2}{2g} = y + h + \frac{c^2}{2g}\left(\frac{y}{y + h}\right)^2 \qquad (18\text{-}43)$$

Solving for $c$,

$$c = \sqrt{\frac{2g(y + h)^2}{2y + h}} \qquad (18\text{-}44)$$

where $h$ is the wave height above the normal water surface. For waves of moderate height, Eq. (18-44) may be approximated by

$$c = \sqrt{gy\left(1 + \frac{3h}{2y}\right)} \approx \sqrt{gy}\left(1 + \frac{3h}{4y}\right) \qquad (18\text{-}45)$$

This equation is commonly known as the *Saint-Venant celerity equation* in honor of its originator [44]. For waves of small height, $h$ is negligible. Thus,

$$c = \sqrt{gy} \qquad (18\text{-}46)$$

This is the equation for the propagation of small waves in rectangular channels. It is commonly known as the *Lagrange celerity equation* after Lagrange [45], who first derived it.

Similarly, it can be shown that the celerity of small waves in non-rectangular channels is

$$c = \sqrt{gD} \qquad (18\text{-}47)$$

where $D$ is the hydraulic depth and is equal to $A/T$.

In the above analysis, neither the centrifugal-force effect of the wave curvature nor the vertical component of the acceleration of the water particles is considered. According to field observations made by Russell [41] and experiments made by Bazin [46], a more suitable equation for the celerity of a solitary wave in a rectangular channel is

$$c = \sqrt{g(y + h)} \qquad (18\text{-}48)$$

According to a complete analysis described by Lamb [3, pp. 423–426], a more accurate equation for gravity waves in general, but still assuming small heights, is

$$c = \sqrt{\frac{g\lambda}{2\pi} \tanh \frac{2\pi y}{\lambda}} \qquad (18\text{-}49)$$

where $\lambda$ is the wavelength from crest to crest. This equation is generally known as the *Airy celerity equation* in honor of its originator [47]. In

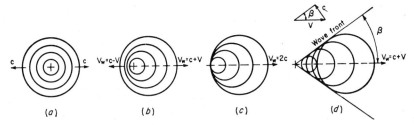

Fig. 18-8. Wave patterns created by disturbances. (*a*) Still water, $V = 0$; (*b*) subcritical flow, $V < c$; (*c*) critical flow, $V = c$; (*d*) supercritical flow, $V > c$.

deep water, where $y$ is large compared with $\lambda$, the above equation becomes $c = \sqrt{g\lambda/2\pi}$. For small wave heights, $\lambda$ is large compared with $h$ and $\tanh (2\pi y/\lambda)$ may be replaced by $2\pi y/\lambda$. Thus, Eq. (18-49) becomes Eq. (18-46).

The equation for celerity, either Eq. (18-46) or (18-47), may be used for studying the propagation of gravity waves. If a pebble is dropped into still water, the wave pattern can be represented by the concentric circles shown in Fig. 18-8a. The waves travel away from the source of the disturbance in all directions with a velocity or celerity equal to $c$.

If the water is flowing, the wave pattern produced by a disturbance will be displaced in the direction of flow. When the velocity $V$ of the water is less than the celerity, the wave pattern is as shown in Fig. 18-8b. Since the velocity of flow is less than the celerity, it is possible for the wave to travel upstream at a velocity equal to

$$V_w = c - V \qquad (18\text{-}50)$$

The wave traveling downstream is in the direction of flow. Its velocity is increased to

$$V_w = c + V \qquad (18\text{-}51)$$

Note that the celerity represented by Eq. (18-47) is identical with the critical velocity of the flow [Eq. (1-10)]. The flow under consideration is, therefore, subcritical.

When the velocity of the water is equal to the celerity, the wavefronts in the upstream direction are stationary, or $V_w = 0$, and those in the downstream direction have a velocity equal to $V_w = 2c$. This wave pattern is shown in Fig. 18-8c. The flow is, apparently, critical.

When the velocity of the water is greater than the celerity, the waves will travel downstream only. This wave pattern is shown in Fig. 18-8d. The flow is, apparently, supercritical. The lines tangent to the wavefronts lie at an angle to the original direction of flow. The angle $\beta$ is the wave angle, and its magnitude is given by Eq. (16-15), or

$$\sin \beta = \frac{c}{V} = \frac{\sqrt{gD}}{V} = \frac{1}{\mathbf{F}} \qquad (18\text{-}52)$$

where $\mathbf{F}$ is the Froude number.

The celerity $c$ must be clearly distinguished from the absolute wave velocity $V_w$. The celerity is the velocity of a wave relative to the velocity of flow. When the wave is propagated through still water, the celerity is identical with the absolute velocity. In open channels, the absolute wave velocity is the velocity of the wave relative to a certain fixed section of the channel. Mathematically, a general equation may be written, expressing the absolute wave velocity as the vectorial sum of the celerity and the undisturbed velocity $V$ of the water through which the wave is propagated; this is

$$\mathbf{V}_w = \mathbf{V} + \mathbf{c} \qquad (18\text{-}53)$$

These vectors are, as a general rule, parallel to the channel axis; so Eq. 18-53 may be reduced to a simple algebraic sum

$$V_w = V \pm c \qquad (18\text{-}54)$$

where the velocities are considered positive in the downstream direction and negative in the upstream direction. The initial flow of water in the channel is assumed to be in the downstream direction.

In discussing the direction of progression of waves in channels, three principal cases may be recognized: (1) *positively progressive flow* if the disturbance progresses downstream, (2) *negatively progressive flow* if the disturbance progresses upstream, and (3) *mixed progressive flow* if the disturbance or disturbances progress both upstream and downstream and will meet and combine.

**18-7. Solution of the Unsteady-flow Equations.** Owing to complexity of flow conditions, the general unsteady-flow equations defy exact mathematical solution. For demonstrative purposes, two approximate methods suggested by Thomas [15] will be discussed briefly. They are the *method of finite increments* (called the *complete method* by Thomas) and the *method of trial and error.*

By the method of finite increments, a rectangular channel is divided into reaches of finite length $\Delta x$. The time interval under consideration

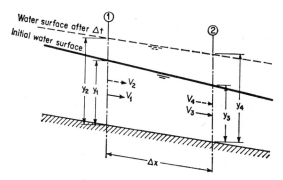

FIG. 18-9. Definition sketch for the method of finite increments. The subscript 1 is for upstream section at initial state; 2 is for upstream section after $\Delta t$; 3 is for downstream section at initial state; and 4 is for downstream section after $\Delta t$.

is $\Delta t$. For a given reach, various elements are designated in Fig. 18-9. The following notation is used to adapt the unsteady-flow equations to the use of finite increments:

$$A = \frac{A_1 + A_2 + A_3 + A_4}{4} = \frac{\Sigma A}{4}$$

$$T = \frac{T_1 + T_2 + T_3 + T_4}{4} = \frac{\Sigma T}{4}$$

$$R = \frac{R_1 + R_2 + R_3 + R_4}{4} = \frac{\Sigma R}{4}$$

$$V = \frac{V_1 + V_2 + V_3 + \dot{V}_4}{4} = \frac{\Sigma V}{4}$$

Expressing the partial differentials by finite increments,

$$\frac{\partial y}{\partial x} = \frac{1}{2}\left(\frac{y_3 - y_1}{\Delta x} + \frac{y_4 - y_2}{\Delta x}\right) = -\frac{y_1 + y_2 - y_3 - y_4}{2\,\Delta x}$$

$$\frac{\partial V}{\partial x} = \frac{1}{2}\left(\frac{V_3 - V_1}{\Delta x} + \frac{V_4 - V_2}{\Delta x}\right) = -\frac{V_1 + V_2 - V_3 - V_4}{2\,\Delta x}$$

$$\frac{\partial Q}{\partial x} = \frac{\partial(AV)}{\partial x} = \frac{1}{2}\left(\frac{A_3 V_3 - A_1 V_1}{\Delta x} + \frac{A_4 V_4 - A_2 V_2}{\Delta x}\right)$$

$$= -\frac{A_1 V_1 + A_2 V_2 - A_3 V_3 - A_4 V_4}{2\,\Delta x}$$

$$\frac{\partial y}{\partial t} = \frac{1}{2}\left(\frac{y_2 - y_1}{\Delta t} + \frac{y_4 - y_3}{\Delta t}\right) = -\frac{y_1 - y_2 + y_3 - y_4}{2\,\Delta t}$$

$$\frac{\partial V}{\partial t} = \frac{1}{2}\left(\frac{V_2 - V_1}{\Delta t} + \frac{V_4 - V_3}{\Delta t}\right) = -\frac{V_1 - V_2 + V_3 - V_4}{2\,\Delta t}$$

Substituting these expressions in Eq. (18-1) and solving for $V_4$,

$$V_4 = \frac{\Delta x\,\Sigma T(y_1 - y_2 + y_3 - y_4)/4\,\Delta t + A_1 V_1 + A_2 V_2 - A_3 V_3}{A_4} \qquad (18\text{-}55)$$

Substituting $S_f = V^2/C^2 R$ and the above expressions in Eq. (18-13) and simplifying,

$$S_0 = \frac{(\Sigma V)^2}{4C^2\,\Sigma R} - \frac{y_1 + y_2 - y_3 - y_4}{2\,\Delta x} - \frac{\alpha\Sigma V(V_1 + V_2 - V_3 - V_4)}{8g\,\Delta x}$$
$$- \frac{V_1 - V_2 + V_3 - V_4}{2g\,\Delta t} \qquad (18\text{-}56)$$

In a given problem, the quantities $y_1$, $A_1$, $V_1$, $y_2$, $A_2$, $V_2$, $y_3$, $A_3$, and $V_3$ are known from the initial conditions and from the computations on previous reaches. The unknown quantities $y_4$ and $V_4$ can be obtained by solving Eqs. (18-55) and (18-56) simultaneously. Repeating the computation for subsequent reaches, the complete profile and velocity variation of the flow can be determined. It is clear, however, that the solution by the method of finite increments is extraordinarily laborious.

In the trial-and-error method, the wave profile through the given reach is first sketched arbitrarily and then revised if the sketched profile fails to satisfy all necessary conditions. The procedure for the computation of a positively progressive flow is as follows:

1. For a given reach, draw the wave profile at the initial instant and sketch the wave profile at the final instant by extending the known wave profile from the upstream reach. The extended profile is shown by the dashed line in Fig. 18-9.

2. Measure the depths $y_1$, $y_2$, $y_3$, and $y_4$ and the surface slopes $S_1$, $S_2$, $S_3$, and $S_4$ at the sections and instants under consideration.

3. Compute the water areas $A_1$, $A_2$, $A_3$, and $A_4$, the hydraulic radii $R_1$, $R_2$, $R_3$, and $R_4$, the velocities $V_1$, $V_2$, $V_3$, and $V_4$, and the discharges $Q_1$, $Q_2$, $Q_3$, and $Q_4$.

4. Substitute the above quantities into the continuity equation. Using finite increments, Eq. (18-2) gives

$$(Q_1 + Q_2 - Q_3 - Q_4)\,\Delta t = (-A_1 + A_2 - A_3 + A_4)\,\Delta x \qquad (18\text{-}57)$$

If this equation is not satisfied by the given values, revise the sketched profile and repeat the work until a satisfactory check in this equation is obtained.

5. Continue the procedure from reach to reach, proceeding downstream.

It should be noted that the above procedure does not include the velocity-head and acceleration-head terms. If these terms were to be included, the procedure would become so tedious as to be almost prohibitive for practical purposes.

One of the most important problems in gradually varied unsteady flow is the routing of a flood wave through a channel. Many practical solutions of this problem have been developed. Because of its unique nature, the problem with its practical solutions will be discussed separately in Chap. 20.

**18-8. Spatially Varied Unsteady Surface Flow.** The general differential equation for spatially varied unsteady flow can be obtained by introducing a term for acceleration effect into the equation for spatially varied steady flow. According to Art. 18-2, such a term is $(1/g)(\partial V/\partial t)\, dx$. Including this term in Eq. (12-2) and using partial differentials,

$$\partial y = -\frac{1}{g}\left(V\,\partial V + \frac{V}{A}\,\partial Q\right) + (S_0 - S_f)\,\partial x - \frac{1}{g}\frac{\partial V}{\partial t}\,\partial x \quad (18\text{-}58)$$

or

$$S_0 - S_f = \frac{\partial y}{\partial x} + \frac{1}{g}\left(V\frac{\partial V}{\partial x} + \frac{V}{A}\frac{\partial Q}{\partial x} + \frac{\partial V}{\partial t}\right) \quad (18\text{-}59)$$

This is the required equation. However, a solution of this equation is extremely difficult even by finite-increment approximations.

One important practical problem dealing with spatially varied unsteady surface flow is the determination of the unsteady runoff of the overland flow resulting from rainfall.[1] The discharge of the runoff changes with the time since the rainfall began; therefore, the flow is unsteady. If the rate of rainfall is kept constant, a time of equilibrium will eventually be reached. At this time, the discharge is equal to the rate of rainfall and the runoff becomes steady. When rainfall ceases, the runoff recedes and the discharge tapers off accordingly. In the recession period the runoff becomes unsteady again. For practical purposes two empirical methods have been developed, one for turbulent flow and the other for laminar flow. The empirical relations used in these methods were obtained from experiments covering a wide range of variation in conditions. Hence, they give only an approximate answer to the problem.

*A. Laminar Flow.* The variation of the runoff discharge with time is usually represented by a *hydrograph*, which is a curve obtained by plotting the discharge against the time.[2] From analyses of the hydrographs resulting from simulated rainfall of constant rate, Izzard [52] found that the form of the rising hydrograph can be represented by a single dimen-

---

[1] For advanced studies of this problem, the reader should refer to the works of Iwagaki [48–51].

[2] A hydrograph may also be a curve of the stage or velocity of the flow plotted against the time (Art. 20-2).

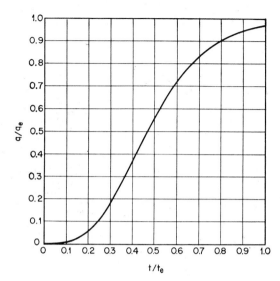

Fɪɢ. 18-10. Dimensionless hydrograph of overland flow. (*After C. F. Izzard* [52].)

sionless curve, as shown in Fig. 18-10. The notation involved is:

$q$ = discharge of surface flow, in cfs per ft of width, at time $t$ since the rainfall began

$q_e$ = discharge of surface flow, in cfs per ft of width, at equilibrium

At the equilibrium condition, the rate of supply of the rainfall is equal to the outflow discharge. If $i$ is the rainfall intensity in in./hr and $L$ is the length of surface flow in ft, then

$$q_e = \frac{iL}{43,200} \qquad (18\text{-}60)$$

It should be noted that the equilibrium condition is reached asymptotically.

$t$ = time in min since the rainfall began

$t_e$ = time of equilibrium, in min

Since the equilibrium condition is approached asymptotically, the time $t_e$ must be determined arbitrarily. In Fig. 18-10, $t_e$ must be determined arbitrarily. In Fig. 18-10, $t_e$ is defined as the time when $q$ reaches $0.97q_e$; that is, $q/q_e = 0.97$. It was found empirically that the volume of water, represented by $D_e$ in ft³, in the surface flow on a strip of unit width at equilibrium (the area above the curve) is substantially equal to the volume of water that has been discharged in the time required to reach equilibrium (the area below the curve). Therefore, the equilibrium time $t_e$ is expressed by

$$t_e = \frac{2D_e}{60q_e} \tag{18-61}$$

$D$ = detention in ft³, that is, the volume of water in surface flow on a strip of unit width at the time $t$ since the rainfall began
$D_e$ = detention in ft³ at equilibrium

It was found empirically that this could be expressed in general by

$$D_e = KLq_e^{\frac{1}{3}} \tag{18-62}$$

Actually, the exponent was found to vary from about 0.2 for very smooth pavement to nearly 0.4 for turf. The value of $K$ depends on the rainfall intensity $i$, the slope of surface $S$, and a roughness factor $c$; that is,

$$K = \frac{0.0007i + c}{S^{\frac{1}{3}}} \tag{18-63}$$

This equation was developed for slope not steeper than about 0.04. The roughness factor $c$ was evaluated as follows:

| Type of surface | Value of c |
|---|---|
| Very smooth asphalt pavement | 0.0070 |
| Tar and sand pavement | 0.0075 |
| Crushed-slate roofing paper | 0.0082 |
| Concrete pavement, normal condition | 0.0120 |
| Tar-and-gravel pavement | 0.0170 |
| Closely clipped sod | 0.0460 |
| Dense bluegrass turf | 0.0600 |

When rainfall ceases, the runoff decreases. The time $t_r$ from the beginning of the recession hydrograph to the point where $q/q_e = r$ is

$$t_r = \frac{D_0 F(r)}{60q_e} \tag{18-64}$$

where $D_0$ is the detention corresponding to $D_e$ after the cease of rainfall, which is the detention when $i = 0$; and where

$$F(r) = 0.5(r^{-\frac{2}{3}} - 1) \tag{18-65}$$

Equation (18-64) is derived mathematically from the finding that detention on the recession curve is proportional to the one-third power of the discharge, i.e.,

$$\frac{D}{D_0} = \left(\frac{q}{q_e}\right)^{\frac{1}{3}} = r^{\frac{1}{3}}$$

Using the dimensionless hydrograph and the above equations, it is possible to construct a hydrograph for surface runoff due to a rainfall of given intensity and duration. It is understood that the experiments conducted for deriving the dimensionless hydrograph and the above empirical equations were made under the condition that the flow was laminar at all times. Therefore, the method is most suitable for laminar flow and, according to Izzard, should be limited to cases where the product of the rainfall intensity in inches per hour and the length of surface flow in feet is less than 500.

**B. Turbulent Flow.** With reference to the type of flow ranging from fully turbulent to laminar, Horton [53] has developed the following equation for the discharge of a spatially varied unsteady surface flow due to a uniform rate of rainfall excess or supply rate:

$$q = \sigma \tanh^m \left[ \frac{m+1}{m} (\sigma K)^{1/m} \frac{t}{60} \right] \tag{18-66}$$

where $q$ = discharge at the lower end of an elementary strip, in cfs/acre or in./hr

$\sigma$ = rate of rainfall excess or supply rate, in in./hr. The rainfall excess is the net amount of rainfall that becomes direct runoff, since a portion of the total rainfall is lost by evaporation, infiltration, etc.

$m$ = an exponent depending on the state of flow; $m = 3.00$ for laminar flow and $\frac{5}{3}$ for fully turbulent flow.

$t$ = time from the beginning of supply, in min

$K$ = a constant depending on characteristics of the drainage surface; it is expressed by

$$K = \frac{1,020 \sqrt{S}}{IcL} \tag{18-67}$$

where $S$ is the surface slope in the direction of flow; $I$ is the factor of turbulence, that is, $0.75(3.0 - m)$; $c$ is the roughness factor; and $L$ is the length of the elementary strip of turfed, bare, or paved surface, in ft.

According to Horton, Eq. (18-66) is strictly rational for 75% turbulent flow, or $m = 2.00$. The equation has been used in drainage design of airfields [54]. For average airfield surfaces, 75% turbulence may be assumed, and the Horton equation may be written

$$q = \sigma \tanh^2 \left[ 0.922t \left( \frac{\sigma}{cL} \right)^{0.50} S^{0.25} \right] \tag{18-68}$$

In connection with the use of this equation, the following values of $c$

are recommended:

| Type of surface | Value of c |
|---|---|
| Smooth pavement | 0.02 |
| Bare, packed soil, free of stone | 0.10 |
| Poor grass cover, or moderately rough bare surface | 0.20 |
| Average grass cover | 0.40 |
| Dense grass cover | 0.80 |

The Horton equation is most suitable for turbulent flow with high discharge. The use of this equation will produce a hydrograph for the

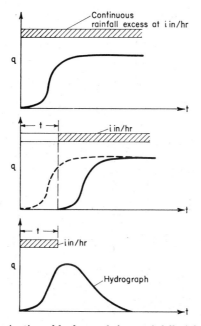

Fig. 18-11. Derivation of hydrograph for a rainfall of finite duration.

overland flow due to a uniform rate of rainfall lasting indefinitely. However, the hydrograph for rainfall of finite duration $t$ can be easily derived. In Fig. 18-11, the top figure shows the hydrograph for rainfall of infinite duration, and the middle figure shows an offset hydrograph for which the same rainfall starts at a time of $t$ later. The difference between these two hydrographs will, evidently, produce the bottom figure, which is the hydrograph for rainfall of duration $t$.

**Example 18-4.** A smooth asphalt highway pavement is 72 ft long and has a slope of 0.005. Determine the hydrograph at the downstream end of the pavement when a rainfall of 1.89 in./hr is applied for 10 min.

TABLE 18-1. COMPUTATION OF THE HYDROGRAPH OF AN OVERLAND FLOW

| $t$ | $t/t_e$ | $q/q_e = r$ | $F(r)$ | $t_r$ | $q$ |
|------|---------|-------------|--------|-------|--------|
| 1.00 | 0.183 | 0.05 | .... | .... | 0.0002 |
| 2.00 | 0.367 | 0.30 | .... | .... | 0.0010 |
| 2.50 | 0.458 | 0.48 | .... | .... | 0.0015 |
| 3.00 | 0.550 | 0.65 | .... | .... | 0.0021 |
| 4.00 | 0.733 | 0.85 | .... | .... | 0.0027 |
| 5.00 | 0.917 | 0.94 | .... | .... | 0.0030 |
| 5.45 | 1.000 | 0.97 | .... | .... | 0.0031 |
| 6.00 | ..... | 1.00 | .... | .... | 0.0032 |
| 7.00 | ..... | 1.00 | .... | .... | 0.0032 |
| 8.00 | ..... | 1.00 | .... | .... | 0.0032 |
| 9.00 | ..... | 1.00 | .... | .... | 0.0032 |
| 10.00 | ..... | 1.00 | .... | .... | 0.0032 |
| 10.43 | ..... | 1.00 | .... | .... | 0.0032 |
| 10.91 | ..... | 0.60 | 0.21 | 0.48 | 0.0019 |
| 11.40 | ..... | 0.40 | 0.42 | 0.97 | 0.0013 |
| 11.86 | ..... | 0.30 | 0.62 | 1.43 | 0.0009 |
| 12.64 | ..... | 0.20 | 0.96 | 2.21 | 0.0006 |
| 14.57 | ..... | 0.10 | 1.80 | 4.14 | 0.0003 |

*Solution.* The given data are $L = 72$ ft, $S = 0.005$, $i = 1.89$ in./hr, and the total $t = 10$ min. Since $1.89 \times 72 < 500$, the Izzard method applies. For smooth asphalt pavement, $c = 0.007$.

By the equations of the Izzard method, the constants are computed as $q_e = 0.00315$, $K = 0.0487$, $D_e = 0.515$, and $t_e = 5.45$. The computation of the rising curve of the hydrograph is shown in Table 18-1 and in Fig. 18-12. The value of $q/q_e$ for the corresponding value of $t/t_e$ is obtained from the dimensionless hydrograph (Fig. 18-10). At $t = t_e = 5.45$ min, the discharge $q = 0.97q_e = 0.0031$ cfs per unit width of the pavement. Henceforth, the discharge is assumed to reach the full value of $q_e$ up to $t = 10$ min.

When the rainfall ceases at 10 min, it will be noted that there is a momentary

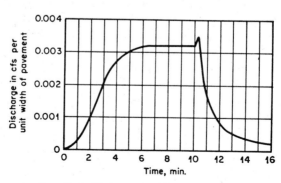

FIG. 18-12. Hydrograph of an overland flow.

increase in discharge, after which the curve drops rapidly. This increase in discharge is due to the fact that during rainfall the amount of detention on the pavement is greater than the amount required to cause the same discharge after rainfall has ceased. For $i = 0$, Eq. (18-63) gives $K = 0.041$ and Eq. (18-62) gives $D_0 = 0.434$ ft³. The excess detention is, therefore, $0.515 - 0.434 = 0.081$ ft³, discharging at a rate equal to or greater than $q_e = 0.00315$ cfs. The length of time required to discharge the excess is, therefore, $0.081/0.00315 = 26$ sec or 0.43 min. Accordingly, the beginning point of the actual recession curve is $10 + 0.43 = 10.43$ min; at this time $q = 0.00316$ cfs and the detention is 0.434 ft³. The recession time of the hydrograph (Fig. 18-12) can easily be computed by Eq. (18-64).

## PROBLEMS

**18-1.** Assuming that the flow condition does not change with time, derive from Eqs. (18-1) and (18-13) the continuity and dynamic equations for gradually varied steady flow in prismatic channels.

**18-2.** Show that the overrun of a monoclinal rising wave may be expressed as

$$Q_o = \frac{A_2 Q_1 - A_1 Q_2}{A_1 - A_2} \tag{18-69}$$

**18-3.** Show that the overrun and velocity of a monoclinal rising wave in a wide rectangular channel of unit width may be expressed, respectively, as

$$Q_o = \frac{y_1 y_2 C \sqrt{S_0}}{\sqrt{y_1} + \sqrt{y_2}} \tag{18-70}$$

and
$$V_w = \frac{1 - (y_1/y_2)^{3/2}}{1 - y_1/y_2} V_2 \tag{18-71}$$

where $C$ is the Chézy resistance factor.

**18-4.** On the 333-mile reach of the Missouri River below Kansas City, Seddon found that an average rating curve and velocity in miles per day can be expressed as $Q_o = 0.15(1.17y + 19)^4$ and $V_w = 70 + 3.27y$, respectively. Show that the average top width of the channel in this reach can be expressed as $T = 5.62(y + 16.3)^3/ (y + 21.4)$, and construct the average shape of the channel section.

**18-5.** On the basis of the Manning formula, determine the ratio of the maximum wave velocity to the water velocity of a monoclinal rising wave in (a) a wide rectangular channel, (b) a triangular channel, and (c) a wide parabolic channel.

**18-6.** Solve the above problem on the basis of the Chézy formula.

**18-7.** Using the Manning formula, derive an expression for the wave profile of the flood due to failure of a dam.

**18-8.** Given $S_0 = 0.0004$ and $y_n = 25$ ft, plot the profile of the roll wave derived in Example 18-1.

**18-9.** Solve the above problem, using the result of Prob. 18-7 for the wave profile, and compare the result with that obtained above.

**18-10.** Plot the wave profile derived in Example 18-2, when $y_1 = 10$ ft, $y_2 = 25$ ft, and $S_0 = 0.0004$.

**18-11.** Solve Example 18-3 for $y_2 = 0$, 2, 5, and 15 ft, and show that the surface slope of the wave configuration decreases with the decrease of the initial stage $y_2$.

**18-12.** Solve Example 18-3 if $S_0 = 0.004$.

**18-13.** Solve Example 18-3 if $S_0 = 0.06$.

**18-14.** The initial and final depths of a monoclinal flood wave are 10 ft and 25 ft, respectively. Given $C = 100$ and $S_0 = 0.0004$, determine the percentage increases in the true discharge over the normal discharge at depths of 15 and 20 ft.

**18-15.** Compute the Reynolds number of the peak discharge from the pavement described in Example 18-4, and show that the flow is laminar. The discharge immediately after the rainfall ceases is assumed to increase momentarily about 10%.

**18-16.** Solve Example 18-4 if the rainfall is 3.78 in./hr.

**18-17.** Solve Example 18-4 if the rainfall is 1.89 in./hr for the first 2 min and then increases to 3.78 in./hr for the remaining 8 min. In solving this problem, it is necessary to convert the first 2 min to a time, say $t_0$, such that rainfall at 3.78 in./hr lasting $t_0$ min would have built up the same absolute volume of detention as was built up in 2 min at 1.89 in./hr. The computation of the hydrograph after 2 min deals simply with a constant rainfall intensity of 3.78 in./hr lasting $t_0 + 8$ min.

**18-18.** In an airfield, a strip of turfed area is 510 ft long and has a slope of 0.9%. Construct the hydrograph of the overland flow on the area due to a rainfall excess of 4.36 in./hr lasting 10 min. For turfed area, assume $c = 0.32$ in the Horton equation.

## REFERENCES

1. J. J. Stoker: "Water Waves," vol. IV of "Pure and Applied Mathematics," Interscience Publishers, Inc., New York, 1957.
2. G. H. Keulegan: Wave motion, chap. XI of "Engineering Hydraulics," edited by Hunter Rouse, John Wiley & Sons, Inc., New York, 1950, pp. 711–768.
3. Sir Horace Lamb: "Hydrodynamics," 6th ed., Dover Publications, New York, 1932. For tidal waves, see chap. VIII, pp. 250–362; for surface waves, see chap. IX, pp. 363–475.
4. U.S. Army Corps of Engineers: Bibliography on tidal hydraulics, *Committee on Tidal Hydraulics, Report No. 2*, February, 1954; *Supplement No. 1*, June, 1955; *Supplement No. 2*, May, 1957; and *Supplement No. 3*, May, 1959.
5. Philipp Forchheimer: "Hydraulik" ("Hydraulics"), 3d ed., Teubner Verlagsgesellschaft, Leipzig and Berlin, 1930.
6. Charles Jaeger: "Engineering Fluid Mechanics," translated from the German by P. O. Wolf, Blackie & Son, Ltd., London and Glasgow, 1956.
7. Takeo Kinosita: Hydrodynamical study on the flood flow, in Floods, vol. III of *Symposia Darcy, International Association of Scientific Hydrology, Publication No. 42*, 1956, pp. 56-63.
8. N. J. Dahl: On non-permanent flow in open canals, *Proceedings of the 6th General Meeting, International Association for Hydraulic Research, The Hague 1955*, vol. 4, pp. D19-1 to D19-16, 1955.
9. François Serre: Contribution à l'étude des écoulements permanents et variables dans les canaux (Contribution to the study of permanent and nonpermanent flows in channels), *La Houille blanche*, Grenoble, 8th yr., no. 3, pp. 374–388, June-July; and no. 6, pp. 830–872, December, 1953.
10. J. C. Schönfeld: Distortion of long waves. Equilibrium and stability, *Assemblée générale de Bruxelles*, 1951, *International Association of Scientific Hydrology, Publication No. 35*, 1951, vol. 4, pp. 140–157.
11. Bruce R. Gilcrest: Flood routing, chap. X in "Engineering Hydraulics," edited by Hunter Rouse, John Wiley & Sons, Inc., New York, 1950, pp. 635–710.
12. Giulio Supino: Sur l'amortissement des intumescences dans les canaux (On the damping of translatory waves in channels), *Revue générale de l'hydraulique*, Paris, vol. 16, no. 57, pp. 144–147, 1950.

13. D. N. Dietz: A new method for calculating the conduct of translation waves in prismatic canals, *Physica*, vol. 8, no. 2, pp. 177–195, February, 1941.

14. Giulio Supino: Sur la propagation des ondes dans les canaux (On the propagation of waves in channels), *Revue générale de l'hydraulique*, Paris, vol. 5, no. 29, pp. 260–262, 1939.

15. Harold A. Thomas: The hydraulics of flood movements in rivers, *Carnegie Institute of Technology, Engineering Bulletin*, 1934; reprinted in 1936 and 1937.

16. L. Cagniard: Hydrodynamique fluviale: Régimes variables (Fluvial hydrodynamics: Variable regimes), *Revue générale de l'hydraulique*, Paris, vol. 3, no. 15, pp. 128–136, May–June, 1937.

17. René Massé: Des intumescences dans les torrents (Translatory waves in torrents), *Revue générale de l'hydraulique*, Paris, vol. 3, no. 18, pp. 305–306, 1937.

18. Ph. Deymié: Propagation d'une intumescence allongée (Propagation of a gradually varied translatory wave), *Revue générale de l'hydraulique*, Paris, vol. 1-2, no. 3, pp. 138–142, 1935–1936.

19. Pierre Massé: L'amortissement des intumescences (The damping of translatory waves), *Revue générale de l'hydraulique*, Paris, vol. 1-2, no. 6, pp. 300–308, 1935–1936.

20. Josef Frank: "Nichtstationäre Vorgänge in den Zuleitungs- und Ableitungskanälen von Wasserkraftwerken" ("Unsteady Flow in Headraces and Tailraces of Hydropower Plants"), Springer-Verlag, Berlin, 1957.

21. A. J. C. Barré de Saint-Venant: "Études théoriques et pratiques sur le mouvement des eaux courantes" ("Theoretical and Practical Studies of Stream Flow"), Paris, 1848.

22. A. J. C. Barré de Saint-Venant: Théorie du mouvement non permanent des eaux, avec application aux crues des rivières et à l'introduction des marées dans leur lits (Theory of the nonpermanent movement of waters with application to the floods of rivers and to the introduction of the tides within their beds), *Comptes rendus des séances de l'Académie des Sciences*, vol. 73, pp. 147–154 and 237–240, 1871.

23. H. Reineke: Die Berechnung der Tidewelle im Tideflusse (Computation of tidal wave in a tidal river), *Besondere Mitteilungen, Jahrbuch für die Gewässerkunde Norddeutschlands*, Berlin, vol. 3, no. 4, 1921.

24. J. Frank and J. Schüller: "Schwingungen in den Zuleitungs- und Ableitungskanälen von Wasserkraftanlagen" ("Oscillations in Headraces and Tailraces of Hydropower Plants"), Springer-Verlag, Berlin, 1938.

25. H. Favre: "Étude théorique et expérimentale des ondes de translation dans les canaux découverts" ("Theoretical and Experimental Study of Translatory Waves in Open Channels"), Dunod, Paris, 1935.

26. Carlo Drioli: Esperienze sul moto perturbato nei canali industriali (Experiment on surges in industrial canals), *L'Energia elettrica, Milano*, vol. 14, no. 4, pp. 285–305, and appendice, pp. 306–311, April, 1937.

27. M. Kleitz: Note sur la théorie du mouvement non permanent des liquides et sur application à la propagation des crues des rivières (Note on the theory of unsteady flow of liquids and on application to flood propagation in rivers), *Annales des ponts et chaussées*, ser. 5, vol. 16, 2e semestre, pp. 133–196, 1877.

28. James A. Seddon: River hydraulics, *Transactions, American Society of Civil Engineers*, vol. 43, pp. 179–229, 1900.

29. J. H. Wilkinson: Translatory waves in natural channels, *Transactions, American Society of Civil Engineers*, vol. 110, pp. 1203–1225, 1945.

30. Benjamin E. Jones: A method for correcting river discharge for a changing stage, *U.S. Geological Survey, Water Supply Paper 375 (e)*, 1916, pp. 117–130.

31. A. Ritter: Die Fortpflanzung der Wasserwellen (Propagation of waves), *Zeitschrift des Vereines deutscher Ingenieure*, vol. 36, no. 33, pp. 947–954, Aug. 13, 1892.

32. R. Ré: Étude du lâcher instantané d'une retenue d'eau dans un canal par la méthode graphique (Study of the instantaneous release of water in a reservoir to a canal by the graphical method), *La Houille blanche*, Grenoble, 1st yr., no. 3, pp. 181–187, May, 1946.

33. A. Craya: Calcul graphique des régimes variables dans les canaux (Graphical calculation of variable flow regimes in open channels), *La Houille blanche*, Grenoble, 1st yr., no. 1, pp. 19–38, November, 1945; no. 2, pp. 117–130, March, 1946.

34. Léon Lévin: Mouvement non permanent sur les cours d'eau à la suite de rupture de barrage (Unsteady flow in channels following the rupture of dam), *Revue générale de l'hydraulique*, Paris, vol. 18, no. 72, pp. 297–315, November-December, 1952.

35. Robert F. Dressler: Hydraulic resistance effect upon the dam-break functions, paper 2356, *Journal of Research, U.S. National Bureau of Standards*, vol. 49, no. 3, pp. 217–225, September, 1952.

36. Robert F. Dressler: Comparison of theories and experiments for the hydraulic dam-break wave, *Assemblée générale de Rome, 1954, International Association of Scientific Hydrology, Publication No. 38*, vol. 3, pp. 319–328, 1954.

37. A. Schoklitsch: Über Dambruchwellen (On waves produced by broken dams), *Stitzungsberichte, Mathematisch-naturwissenschaftliche Klasse, Akademie der Wissenschaften in Wien*, vol. 126, pt. IIa, pp. 1489–1514, Vienna, 1917.

38. I. B. Eguiazaroff: Regulation of the water level in the reaches of canalized rivers and regulation of the flow below the last lock dam according to whether the water power is or is not used, Report no. 8, in Inland Navigation, 2d question, sec. 1, *16th International Congress of Navigation, Brussels*, 1935.

39. Frederick V. Pohle: Motion of wave due to breaking of a dam and related problems, paper No. 8 in Symposium on gravity waves, *U.S. National Bureau of Standards, Circular 521*, 1952, pp. 47–53.

40. Elmer E. Moots: A study in flood waves, *University of Iowa, Studies in Engineering, Bulletin 14*, 1938.

41. J. Scott Russell: Report on waves, *Report of the British Association for the Advancement of Science*, 1844, pp. 311–390.

42. J. V. Boussinesq: Sur le mouvement permanent varié de l'eau dans les tuyaux de conduite et dans les canaux découverts (On the steady varied flow of water in conduits and open channels), *Comptes rendus des séances de l'Académie des Sciences*, vol. 73, pp. 101–105, 1871.

43. Lord Rayleigh: On waves, *The London, Edinburgh and Dublin Philosophical Magazine and Journal of Science*, ser. 5, vol. 1, pp. 257–279, April, 1876.

44. A. J. C. Barré de Saint-Venant: Démonstration élémentaire de la formule de propagation d'une onde ou d'une intumescence dans un canal prismatique; et remarques sur les propagations du son et de la lumière, sur les ressauts, ainsi que sur la distinction des rivières et des torrents (Elementary demonstration of the propagation formula for a wave or a translatory wave in a prismatic channel; and remarks on the propagation of sound and light, on hydraulic jumps, and also on the distinction between rivers and torrents), *Comptes rendus des séances de l'Académie des Sciences*, vol. 71, pp. 186–195, July 18, 1870.

45. Joseph L. de Lagrange: "Mécanique analytique" ("Analytical Mechanics"), Paris, 1788, pt. 2, sec. II, art. 2, p. 192.

46. H. Bazin: Expériences sur la propagation des ondes le long d'un cours d'eau torrentueux, et confirmation par ces expériences des formules données par M.

Boussinesq, dans sa théorie du mouvement graduellement varié des fluides (Experiments on wave propagation in torrential flow and their confirmation of the Boussinesq equations for gradually varied flow), *Comptes rendus des séances de l'Académie des Sciences*, vol. 100, pp. 1492–1494, June 15, 1885.

47. Sir George Biddle Airy: Tides and waves, "Encyclopaedia Metropolitana," London, 1845, pp. 241–396.

48. Yuichi Iwagaki: Theory of flow on road surface, *Memoirs of the Faculty of Engineering, Kyoto University*, Japan, vol. 13, no. 3, pp. 139–147, July, 1951.

49. Y. Iwagaki and T. Sueishi: Approximate method for calculation of unsteady flow in open channels with lateral flow, *Proceedings, 4th Japan National Congress for Applied Mechanics*, pp. 235–240, March, 1954.

50. Yuichi Iwagaki and Tomitaro Sueishi: On the unsteady flow in open channels with uniform lateral inflow (in Japanese), *Proceedings, Japan Society of Civil Engineers*, Tokyo, vol. 39, no. 11, pp. 575–583, November, 1954.

51. Yuichi Iwagaki and Takuma Takasao: On the effects of rainfall and drainage basin characteristics on runoff relation (in Japanese), *Proceedings, 5th Anniversary of the Establishment of the Disaster Prevention Research Institute*, Kyoto University, Kyoto, Japan, pp. 191–200, November, 1956.

52. Carl F. Izzard: Hydraulics of runoff from developed surfaces, *Proceedings of the 26th Annual Meeting of the Highway Research Board*, vol. 26, pp. 129–146, December, 1946.

53. Robert E. Horton: The interpretation and application of runoff plot experiments with reference to soil erosion problems, *Proceedings, Soil Science Society of America*, vol. 3, pp. 340–349, 1938.

54. Gail A. Hathaway: Design of drainage facilities, in Military airfields: A symposium, *Transactions, American Society of Civil Engineers*, vol. 110, pp. 697–733 1945.

# CHAPTER 19

# RAPIDLY VARIED UNSTEADY FLOW

**19-1. Uniformly Progressive Flow.** If the front of a monoclinal rising wave has an abrupt change in curvature or a sudden change in depth, the flow in the front is rapidly varied. This effect may be produced, for example, by a sudden increase in gate opening at the channel entrance, as shown in Fig. 19-1. The velocity of the mass of water

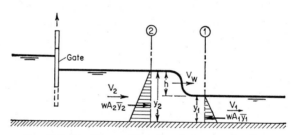

FIG. 19-1. Rapidly varied uniformly progressive flow.

between the gate and the wavefront is increased from $V_1$ to $V_2$, and the momentum is increased accordingly. By Newton's second law of motion, the unbalanced force required to change the momentum per unit time is the product of the mass and the change in velocity per unit time, or

$$F = \frac{1}{g}(V_w - V_2)A_2 w(V_2 - V_1) \tag{19-1}$$

where $w$ is the unit weight of water. The unbalanced force is equal to the difference between the hydrostatic pressures on the areas $A_2$ and $A_1$ at sections 2 and 1, respectively; that is,

$$F = wA_2\bar{y}_2 - wA_1\bar{y}_1 \tag{19-2}$$

where $\bar{y}_2$ and $\bar{y}_1$ are the centroidal depths of the areas. Equating the above values of $F$ and simplifying,

$$(V_w - V_2)(V_2 - V_1) = \left(\bar{y}_2 - \frac{A_1}{A_2}\bar{y}_1\right)g \tag{19-3}$$

Solving Eq. (18-15) for $V_2$,

$$V_2 = \frac{V_1 A_1 + V_w A_2 - V_w A_1}{A_2} \qquad (19\text{-}4)$$

Substituting the above expression for $V_2$ in Eq. (19-3) and reducing,

$$(V_w - V_1)^2 = \frac{(A_2 \bar{y}_2 - A_1 \bar{y}_1)g}{A_1(1 - A_1/A_2)} \qquad (19\text{-}5)$$

or

$$V_w - V_1 = \sqrt{\frac{(A_2 \bar{y}_2 - A_1 \bar{y}_1)g}{A_1(1 - A_1/A_2)}} \qquad (19\text{-}6)$$

or

$$V_w = \sqrt{\frac{(A_2 \bar{y}_2 - A_1 \bar{y}_1)g}{A_1(1 - A_1/A_2)}} + V_1 \qquad (19\text{-}7)$$

This is a general equation expressing the absolute wave velocity of the flow as shown in Fig. 19-1. Mathematically speaking, the sign in front of the square-root term in the above equations may also be negative. However, since the wave is moving downstream in the direction of the initial flow, its velocity must be greater than the velocity of the initial flow. In other words, $V_w - V_1$ should be positive. Therefore, only the plus sign is considered practical.

If the initial velocity $V_1 = 0$, that is, if the wave travels in still water, then the square-root term in the above equations is equal to the absolute velocity of the wave. In any case, this term, being equal to $V_w - V_1$, represents the velocity of the wave with respect to the velocity of the initial flow. It is, therefore, the celerity; that is,

$$c = \sqrt{\frac{(A_2 \bar{y}_2 - A_1 \bar{y}_1)g}{A_1(1 - A_1/A_2)}} \qquad (19\text{-}8)$$

For rectangular channels, $\bar{y}_1 = y_1/2$, $\bar{y}_2 = y_2/2$, $A_1 = by_1$, and $A_2 = by_2$. Thus, Eq. (19-8) becomes

$$c = \sqrt{\frac{gy_2}{2y_1}(y_1 + y_2)} \qquad (19\text{-}9)$$

It can be shown that, for waves of moderate height, Eq. (19-9) becomes Eq. (18-45). For very small waves, Eq. (19-9) becomes Eq. (18-46). For very small waves in nonrectangular channels, Eq. (19-8) becomes Eq. (18-47).

In all cases, Eq. (19-7) may be written

$$V_w = c + V_1 \qquad (19\text{-}10)$$

which is identical with Eq. (18-51).

Theoretically, there are four types of rapidly varied unsteady flow

(Fig. 19-2): type A, having an advancing wavefront moving downstream; type B, having an advancing wavefront moving upstream; type C, having a retreating wavefront moving downstream; and type D, having a retreating wavefront moving upstream. Type A has just been described. For type B, it can be shown that

$$V_w = c - V_1 \qquad (19\text{-}11)$$

which is identical with Eq. (18-50). It can also be shown that Eq. (19-10) applies to type C and Eq. (19-11) to type D. It is theoretically

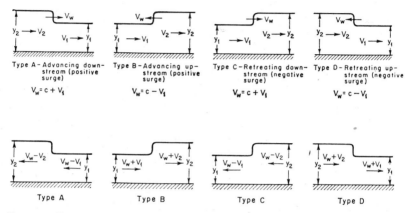

Type A—Advancing downstream (positive surge)
$V_w = c + V_1$

Type B—Advancing upstream (positive surge)
$V_w = c - V_1$

Type C—Retreating downstream (negative surge)
$V_w = c + V_1$

Type D—Retreating upstream (negative surge)
$V_w = c - V_1$

Type A      Type B      Type C      Type D

Fig. 19-2. Four types of rapidly varied uniformly progressive flow. (*Top*) Unsteady flows; (*bottom*) the corresponding flows that appear steady to an observer following the wavefront.

possible for the velocities $V_1$ and $V_2$ to be opposite in direction. In that case, a velocity is considered negative if its direction is opposite to that shown in Fig. 19-2.

The absolute velocity $V_w$ of the wave may also be expressed by Eq. (18-15). Since this equation is derived on the basis of the principle of continuity, it applies to both gradually and rapidly varied monoclinal rising waves.

It should be noted that the wave profile is stable for an advancing front and unstable for a retreating front. The wavefront can be assumed to be made up of a large number of very small waves placed one on top of the other. Since the wave on top has greater depth than the one below it, it has greater velocity, according to Eq. (18-46), and moves faster. In the case of the advancing front, the top waves will, therefore, overtake the bottom waves in the forward direction. The tendency is for the waves to combine and to form eventually a single large wavefront which is steep and stable. In the case of the retreating front, the top waves will retreat faster than the bottom ones. The result is that the wavefront becomes sloping and eventually flattens out.

Owing to the presence of channel friction, however, the wave profile of an advancing front actually changes. This effect may not be noticeable in relatively short artificial channels of small friction effect, but it is significant in long reaches of natural channels, where friction is considerable.

**19-2. The Moving Hydraulic Jump.** When a rapidly varied unsteady flow involves a change in stage from subcritical to supercritical, a so-called *moving hydraulic jump* will result. An observer on the bank running along with the wave crest at the same velocity as the wave will see a stationary hydraulic jump. This is illustrated by the figures at the bottom in Fig. 19-2 for four types of flow. All equations derived in the preceding article apply also to these flows. However, another method of deriving the equation may be described below.

For a stationary hydraulic jump, Eq. (3-21) can be reduced to

$$V_1 = \sqrt{\frac{gy_2}{2y_1}(y_1 + y_2)} \qquad (19\text{-}12)$$

The right side of the equation is equal to the celerity expressed by Eq. (19-9). Applying this equation to the steady hydraulic jump of type A in Fig. 19-2, as seen by the observer, $V_1$ should be replaced by $V_w - V_1$; that is,

$$V_w - V_1 = \sqrt{\frac{gy_2}{2y_1}(y_1 + y_2)} = c \qquad (19\text{-}13)$$

or

$$V_w = \sqrt{\frac{gy_2}{2y_1}(y_1 + y_2)} + V_1 = c + V_1 \qquad (19\text{-}14)$$

This is identical with Eq. (19-10). Applying the same procedure to type B flow,

$$V_w = \sqrt{\frac{gy_2}{2y_1}(y_1 + y_2)} - V_1 = c - V_1 \qquad (19\text{-}15)$$

This equation is identical with Eq. (19-11).

It can be seen that type C and type D flows are not actually possible, because a stable jump cannot be formed if the flow is from high stage to low stage. For this reason, neither type C nor type D can have a stable steep front like that of a hydraulic jump.

The term "moving hydraulic jump" is usually used synonymously with "surge" and "hydraulic bore." However, "surge" more often refers to a moving hydraulic jump due to abrupt decrease or increase in flow, such as that caused by the sudden closing or opening of a gate.

"Hydraulic bore" usually refers to a moving hydraulic jump due to tidal effects; it possesses a sharp and steep advancing front.[1]

When the moving hydraulic jump is specifically noted as a surge, it is further classified into two kinds, namely, the positive surge and the negative surge.[2] The positive surge elevates the water surface, advancing either upstream or downstream with a stable front (Fig. 19-2, types A and B). The negative surge depresses the water surface, retreating

FIG. 19-3. Hangchow bore at Haining on the Chien Tang River, China. The wavefront was about 16 ft high, traveling at high velocity. Seven min after it could first be distinguished on the horizon the wave had passed. The water reached a final height of about 28 ft within 30 min. The width of the river at the place of observation was about 1 mile. (*Courtesy of Mead and Hunt, Inc.*)

either upstream or downstream with an unstable front (Fig. 19-2, types C and D).

For the types of moving hydraulic jump illustrated in Fig. 19-2, typical examples can be quoted. For type A, examples are the famous Johnstown flood of 1889, caused by the failure of an earth dam at the South Fork Reservoir in Pennsylvania [6–8]; the Heppner flood, due to a cloudburst storm on Willow Creek, Oregon, in 1903 [9]; and the flood due to the failure of St. Francis Dam near Los Angeles, Calif., in 1928 [10]. In the Johnstown case, the flood was led by a bore which was initially 125 to 150 ft high at the dam and which was reduced to 30 to 40 ft as it rushed down the 15 miles of the narrow, winding valley to Johnstown

---

[1] For a theoretical and experimental investigation of the bore, see [1] and [2].

[2] See [3] to [5] for analytical and experimental studies.

at a speed of 50 mph or more. The discharge was estimated at about 200,000 cfs.

Type B usually occurs in tidal rivers. Typical examples are the Hang-chow bore at Haining on the Chien Tang River, China (Fig. 19-3); the bore on the Severn River near Gloucester, England; and the bores on rivers connecting the Bay of Fundy, Nova Scotia. In power canals serving hydraulic turbines, type B flow, known as *rejection surge*, will occur as a result of sudden decrease in power output.

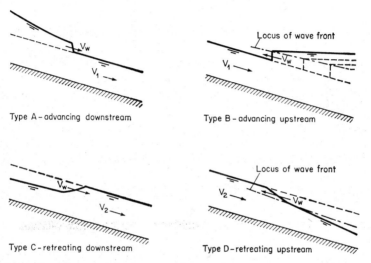

FIG. 19-4. Rapidly varied flow in inclined channels. (*After M. D. Chertousov* [11].)

Type C generally results from a sudden decrease in supply of flow upstream, such as that caused by the closing of a head gate in a canal or at the tailrace of a hydro plant.

Type D, known as *demand surge*, occurs in power canals serving hydraulic turbines if the demand at the lower end of the canal is suddenly increased.

In Fig. 19-2, the initial and final stages of a passing surge are assumed to be uniform. Such surges occur frequently in channels of small slope. In inclined channels, the four types of surge will occur as shown in Fig. 19-4 [11].

**19-3. Positive Surges.** Positive surges have an advancing front with the profile of a moving hydraulic jump. When the height of the surge is small, the surge appears undular like an undular jump. When the height is increasing, the undulation will eventually disappear and the surge will have a sharp and steep front.

Consider the positive surge of type A (Fig. 19-2); the absolute wave velocity can be expressed by Eq. (18-15). For a rectangular channel, the velocity is

$$V_w = \frac{V_1 y_1 - V_2 y_2}{y_1 - y_2} \tag{19-16}$$

Eliminating $V_w$ from Eqs. (19-14) and (19-16) and simplifying,

$$(V_1 - V_2)^2 = (y_1 - y_2)^2 \frac{(y_1 + y_2)g}{2y_1 y_2} \tag{19-17}$$

This equation represents the relationship among the initial and final velocities and depths of the surge. Similarly, it can be shown that Eq. (19-17) applies also to surge of type B (Fig. 19-2). Note that, if Eq. (19-17) is used to determine $y_1$ or $y_2$, it must be solved by trial and error.

Multiplying Eq. (19-17) by the square of Eq. (19-9) and simplifying, it can be shown that

$$V_1 - V_2 = \pm \frac{h}{c} \left( \frac{y_1 + y_2}{2y_1} \right) g \tag{19-18}$$

where $h = y_2 - y_1$, or the height of surge, and where $c$ is the celerity. On the right side of the equation, the positive sign applies to type B surge and the negative sign to type A surge.

When the height of surge is small compared with the depth of flow, $y_1 \approx y_2$. Thus, Eq. (19-18) may be written

$$V_1 - V_2 = \pm \frac{hg}{c} \tag{19-19}$$

In order to avoid the confusion of the sign convention, the use of Eqs. (19-18) and (19-19) may be simplified by ignoring the negative sign on their right sides and remembering that $h$ and $c$ are always assumed to be positive quantities. Accordingly, $V_1 - V_2$ should always be positive. If $V_2 < V_1$, then $V_1 - V_2$ must be replaced by $V_2 - V_1$. If $V_1$ and $V_2$ are in opposite directions, then their sum $V_1 + V_2$ must be used instead of their difference.

Several typical cases of the analysis of positive surges are given as follows:

*A. Surge due to Sudden Stoppage of Flow.* If water flowing in a channel with a velocity $V$ is checked instantaneously, a surge of type B will be produced. In this case, $V_1 = V$ and $V_2 = 0$; so Eq. (19-17) gives

$$V = (y_2 - y_1) \sqrt{\frac{(y_1 + y_2)g}{2y_1 y_2}} \tag{19-20}$$

Also, from Eq. (19-18),

$$V = \frac{h}{c}\left(\frac{y_1 + y_2}{2y_1}\right)g \tag{19-21}$$

Thus, the height of the surge is

$$h = \frac{c}{g}\left(\frac{2y_1}{y_1 + y_2}\right)V \tag{19-22}$$

If the height of the surge is small relative to the depth of flow, Eqs. (19-21) and (19-22) may be approximated, respectively, by

$$V = \frac{h}{c}g \tag{19-23}$$

and

$$h = \frac{c}{g}V \tag{19-24}$$

B. *Meeting of Two Surges.* When two surges meet that are opposite in direction, the result is the generation of two new surges traveling in the reversed directions. This is illustrated in Fig. 19-5 with all notation indicated.

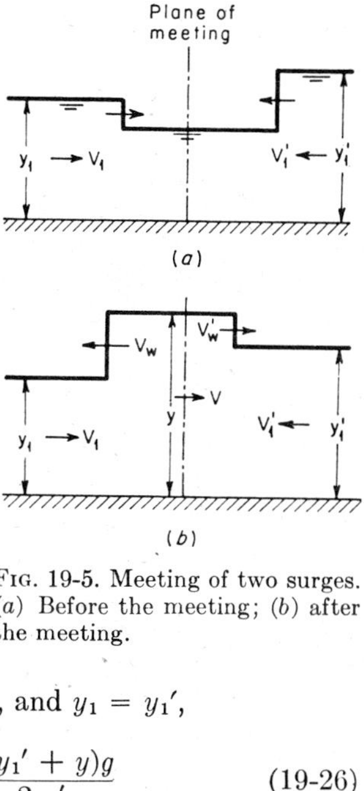

Applying Eq. (19-17) to the left-side new surge with $V_2 = -V$, $y_2 = y$, and $V_1$ replaced by $-V_1$,

$$(V_1 - V)^2 = (y_1 - y)^2\frac{(y_1 + y)g}{2y_1y} \tag{19-25}$$

Applying Eq. (19-17) to the right-side new surge with $V_2 = V$, $V_1 = -V_1'$, $y_2 = y$, and $y_1 = y_1'$,

$$(V_1' + V)^2 = (y_1' - y)^2\frac{(y_1' + y)g}{2y_1'y} \tag{19-26}$$

Fig. 19-5. Meeting of two surges. (a) Before the meeting; (b) after the meeting.

Solving the above two equations simultaneously, the unknowns $V$ and $y$ can be determined. The absolute wave velocities of the new surges can be determined from Eq. (19-16). Thus,

$$V_w = \frac{V_1y_1 - Vy}{y - y_1} \tag{19-27}$$

and

$$V_w' = \frac{V_1'y_1' + Vy}{y - y_1'} \tag{19-28}$$

When the height of the surges is small relative to the depth of flow,

Eq. (19-19) may be applied. Thus,

$$V_1 \pm V = \frac{h}{c} g \qquad (19\text{-}29)$$

The positive sign applies to the right-side surge and the negative sign to the left-side surge.

*C. Surge Crossing a Step.* In surge analysis a step on the channel floor may be real or fictitious. The fictitious step is usually assumed to simulate the effect of channel slope. The method of analysis, however, is the same in both cases.

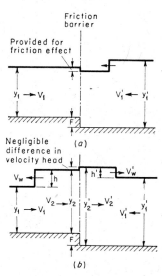

FIG. 19-6. Arrival of surge at a step and friction barrier. (a) Before the arrival; (b) after the arrival.

In previous discussions, the slope of channels has been assumed small. For channels of large slope, the analysis of surge movement will be illustrated by Example 19-2. In simplified calculations, the effect of slope may be treated by converting the slope into a series of steps. In this way the channel length is divided into a number of reaches. In each reach, the floor is considered horizontal, and the actual drop in floor elevation due to slope effect is represented by a step (Fig. 19-6) placed either in the middle or at one end of the reach. The height $F$ of the step is equal to the slope of the channel multiplied by the length of the reach. This simplified calculation is usually used in analyses in which the effect of channel friction is also considered (Art. 19-5).

When a surge arrives at a step, the result is to produce two new surges, one traveling upstream and the other downstream. Figure 19-6 illustrates the arrival of a surge at the step and the condition immediately after arrival. Applying Eq. (19-17) to the left-side new surge,

$$(V_1 - V_2)^2 = (y_1 - y_2)^2 \frac{(y_1 + y_2)g}{2y_1y_2} \qquad (19\text{-}30)$$

Applying Eq. (19-17) to the right-side new surge,

$$(V_1' + V_2')^2 = (y_1' - y_2')^2 \frac{(y_1' + y_2')g}{2y_1'y_2'} \qquad (19\text{-}31)$$

which is similar in form to Eq. (19-30). By geometric continuity,

$$y_2 + F = y_2'$$ (19-32)

By hydraulic continuity,

$$V_2 y_2 = V_2' y_2'$$ (19-33)

Solving the above four equations simultaneously, the unknowns $V_2$, $y_2$, $V_2'$, and $y_2'$ can be determined. The wave velocities can, therefore, be determined by Eq. (19-16).

When the height of surges is small relative to the depth of flow, Eq. (19-19) applies. Thus, Eqs. (19-30) and (19-31) may be written

$$V_1 - V_2 = \frac{h}{c} g$$ (19-34)

and

$$V_1' + V_2' = \frac{h'}{c'} g$$ (19-35)

where $c$ and $c'$ are the celerities of the right-side and left-side surges, respectively.

**Example 19-1.** A steady flow at 6.80 fps and 42.90 ft deep is suddenly stopped at the downstream end of the 9,700 ft reach of a frictionless rectangular channel. Determine the surge thus produced.

*Solution.* A reflected surge advancing upstream is produced. The velocity at the downstream end evidently changes from $V_1 = 6.80$ fps to $V_2 = 0$. By Eq. (19-17) or (19-20), with $y_1 = 42.90$ ft, the depth of the advancing surge $y_2$ can be computed as 51.09 ft.

Note that Eq. (19-17) or (19-20) must be solved by trial and error. A simplified procedure is to use Eq. (18-46) together with Eq. (19-24). Thus, Eq. (18-46) gives $c = \sqrt{32.2 \times 42.9} = 37.2$ fps, and then Eq. (19-24) gives $h = 37.2 \times 6.80/32.2 = 7.85$ ft, which makes $y_2 = 42.90 + 7.85 = 50.75$ ft. This value may be used as the best estimate for the trial-and-error solution of Eq. (19-17) or (19-20).

By Eq. (19-16), the wave velocity $V_w = 35.6$ fps. The time required for the wavefront to arrive at the upstream end of the reach is $9,700/35.6 = 272$ sec. The celerity is $35.6 + 6.8 = 42.4$ fps.

**Example 19-2.** A gradually varied steady flow is decreased at the lower end of an inclined rectangular channel by the sudden partial closing of a gate. Describe a method for determining the surge thus produced (also see Art. 19-5).

*Solution.* Referring to Fig. 19-7, the channel has a slope $S_0$ and carries a steady discharge $Q$. The depth $y$ and velocity $V$ of the steady flow at any section, say $nn$, can be computed.

For the determination of the surge due to sudden decrease of flow at section 00, a step computation may be employed. The channel is divided into a number of reaches, each having a length equal to $\Delta x$. The computation may start at section 00 and then proceed by steps from reach to reach. Consider the step computation from section $n'n'$ to section $nn$. The flow condition at section $n'n'$ is assumed to have been determined, and it is now required to determine the surge height $h$ and velocity $V_w$ at section $nn$

The discharge through the surge front is

$$\Delta Q_n = V_w b h \tag{19-36}$$

where $b$ is the width of the channel.

By Eq. (19-15), using Eq. (18-45) for $c$,

$$V_w = \sqrt{gy\left(1 + \tfrac{3}{2}\frac{h}{y}\right)} - V \tag{19-37}$$

where $y$ is the depth and $V$ is the velocity of flow at section $nn$. If the surge height is relatively small, say $h \leqq 0.1y$, the above equation may be replaced by

$$V_w = \sqrt{gy} - V \tag{19-38}$$

The time required for the surge to move from section $n'n'$ to $nn$ may be expressed as

$$\Delta t = \frac{\Delta x}{\bar{V}_w} \tag{19-39}$$

where
$$\bar{V}_w = \tfrac{1}{2}(V_w + V_w') \tag{19-40}$$

Let $W$ represent the shaded area (Fig. 19-7), which is a measure of the increase in

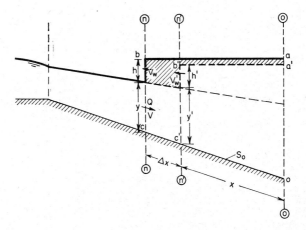

Fig. 19-7. Positive surge moving upstream in an inclined channel.

channel storage due to advance of the surge in time $\Delta t$. Thus,

$$W = \Delta Q \, \Delta t \tag{19-41}$$

where $\Delta Q$ is the reduction in discharge due to partial closing of the gate.

Eliminating $\bar{V}_w$ and $\Delta t$ from the above three equations, the velocity of surge may be written

$$V_w = \frac{2 \, \Delta Q \, \Delta x}{W} - V_w' \tag{19-42}$$

In the computation, first assume $h$. Thus, $W$ may be determined by geometry, assuming a horizontal water surface in the channel after the passing of the surge.

Then, compute the values of $V_w$ by Eqs. (19-37) and (19-42), respectively. If the two values of $V_w$ so computed do not agree, assume another $h$ and repeat the computation until the two values of $V_w$ agree and hence the correct values of $h$ and $V_w$ are obtained. To start the step computation at section 00, Eq. (19-36) may be used to replace Eq. (19-42), since in Eq. (19-36) the value of $\Delta Q_n$ at section 00 is equal to $\Delta Q$.

**Example 19-3.** A step with $F = 2.38$ ft is located at the upstream end of the reach considered in Example 19-1. Determine the flow condition immediately after the surge arrives at the barrier. The flow upstream from the reach under consideration has a steady velocity of 7.00 fps in the downstream direction and a depth of 41.65 ft.

*Solution.* At the step the surge produced in Example 19-1 is split into two component surges, one traveling farther upstream and the other, a reflected surge, traveling downstream. For the surge traveling upstream, Eq. (19-30) gives

$$(7.00 - V_2)^2 = (41.65 - y_2)^2 \frac{(41.65 + y_2)g}{83.30 y_2} \tag{19-43}$$

By Eq. (19-32), $y_2' = y_2 + 2.38$. Thus, for the surge traveling downstream, Eq. (19-31) gives

$$(0 - V_2')^2 = (48.71 - y_2)^2 \frac{(53.47 + y_2)g}{102.18(y_2 + 2.38)} \tag{19-44}$$

By continuity of flow, Eq. (19-33) gives

$$V_2 y_2 = V_2'(y_2 + 2.38) \tag{19-45}$$

Equations (19-43) to (19-45) may be solved simultaneously by trial and error. Assuming $V_2 = 0.52$ fps, Eq. (19-43) gives $y_2 = 49.34$ ft and Eq. (19-44) gives $V_2' = 0.50$ fps. Equation (19-45) serves as a check. Thus, $0.52 \times 49.34 \approx 0.50 \times 51.72$.

If Eq. (19-45) is not satisfied, other values of $V_2$ should be tried and the computation repeated until the condition of flow continuity at the step is well established.

It should be noted that, in this example, the water-surface elevations on the two sides of the step are not equal under steady-flow conditions; the difference is $41.65 + 2.38 - 42.90 = 1.13$ ft. This difference is due to the friction effect and can be treated in combination with the slope effect in surge analyses (see Art. 19-5).

The effect of friction in a reach may be assumed to be concentrated at a fictitious element known as the *friction barrier*. This element may be positioned conveniently at the section where a step is provided for the slope effect. On both sides of the barrier the water surfaces are kept horizontal, but the depths of flow are not equal; each represents the average depth of steady flow in its reach. The depth of steady flow may be determined by a flow-profile computation on the basis of a given channel roughness. When the surge arrives at the barrier, the faster water on one side of the barrier will bump into the slower water on the other side. The result is to shoot up a little water spout, which immediately separates the flow into two new surges, traveling in reversed directions. At the barrier there remains a little standing wave. This accounts for the difference between the two velocity heads that now exist on either side of the barrier. In general, this difference is so small that it can be neglected.

**Example 19-4.** Derive an expression showing the approximate amount of energy of a surge.

*Solution.* Consider an element of the surge having a length in the direction of the channel equal to unity; the potential energy of the surge is equal to the work done by lifting up the mass of water $whT$ to a height $h/2$, or

$$\text{P.E.} = \tfrac{1}{2} w h^2 T \tag{19-46}$$

where $w$ is the unit weight of water, $T$ is the top width, and $h$ is the surge height. The kinetic energy of the element is evidently equal to

$$\text{K.E.} = \frac{wV^2yT}{2g} \tag{19-47}$$

where $y$ is the depth of water and $V$ is the velocity of flow. By Eq. (19-23) or Eq. (19-19), as the case may be, the above equation may be reduced to

$$\text{K.E.} = \frac{wh^2gyT}{2c^2} \tag{19-48}$$

Assuming a surge of small height,

$$c = \sqrt{gy}$$

and the above equation becomes

$$\text{K.E.} = \tfrac{1}{2}wh^2T \tag{19-49}$$

The total energy of surge per unit length is, therefore,

$$E = \text{P.E.} + \text{K.E.} = wh^2T \tag{19-50}$$

**19-4. Negative Surges.** Negative surges are not stable in form, because the upper portions of the wave travel faster than the lower portions (Art. 19-1). If the initial profile of the surge is assumed to have a

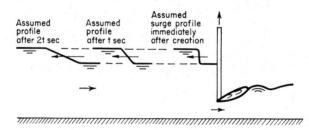

Fig. 19-8. Propagation of a negative surge due to sudden lift of a sluice gate.

steep front, it will soon flatten out as the surge moves through the channel (Fig. 19-8). If the height of the surge is moderate or small compared with the depth of flow, the equations derived for a positive surge can be applied to determine approximately the propagation of the negative surge. If the height of the surge is relatively large, a more elaborate analysis is necessary as follows:

Figure 19-9 shows a type D surge (Fig. 19-2) of relatively large height, retreating in an upstream direction. The surge is caused by the sudden lifting of a sluice gate. The wave velocity of the surge actually varies from point to point. For example, $V_w$ is the wave velocity at a point on the surface of the wave where the depth is $y$ and the velocity of flow through the section is $V$. During a time interval $dt$, the change in $y$ is $dy$. The value of $dy$ is positive for an increase of $y$ and negative for a decrease of $y$. By the momentum principle, the corresponding change in hydrostatic pressure should be equal to the force required to change the momentum of the vertical element between $y$ and $y + dy$. Considering a unit width of the channel and assuming $\beta_1 = \beta_2 = 1$,

$$\frac{w}{2} y^2 - \frac{w}{2} (y + dy)^2 = \frac{w}{g} (y + \tfrac{1}{2} dy)(V + V_w) \, dV \qquad (19\text{-}51)$$

Simplifying the above equation and neglecting the differential terms of higher order,

$$dy = -\frac{V + V_w}{g} \, dV \qquad (19\text{-}52)$$

As described previously (Art. 19-1), the whole wavefront can be assumed to be made up of a large number of very small waves placed

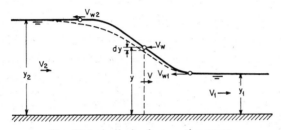

FIG. 19-9. Analysis of a negative surge.

one on top of the other. The velocity of the small wave at the point under consideration may be expressed according to Eq. (19-11) as

$$V_w = \sqrt{gy} - V \qquad (19\text{-}53)$$

Similarly, the velocity at the wave crest is

$$V_{w2} = \sqrt{gy_2} - V_2 \qquad (19\text{-}54)$$

and, at the wave trough,

$$V_{w1} = \sqrt{gy_1} - V_1 \qquad (19\text{-}55)$$

When the surge is not too high, a straight-line relation between $V_{w1}$ and $V_{w2}$ may be assumed. Thus, the mean velocity of the wave may be considered to be

$$V_m = \frac{V_{w1} + V_{w2}}{2} \qquad (19\text{-}56)$$

Now, eliminating $V_w$ between Eqs. (19-52) and (19-53),

$$\frac{dy}{\sqrt{y}} = -\frac{dV}{\sqrt{g}} \qquad (19\text{-}57)$$

Integrating this equation from $y_2$ to $y$ and from $V_2$ to $V$, and solving for $V$,

$$V = V_2 + 2\sqrt{gy_2} - 2\sqrt{gy} \tag{19-58}$$

From Eq. (19-53),

$$V_w = 3\sqrt{gy} - 2\sqrt{gy_2} - V_2 \tag{19-59}$$

Thus, the wave velocity at the trough of the wave is

$$V_{w1} = 3\sqrt{gy_1} - 2\sqrt{gy_2} - V_2 \tag{19-60}$$

Let $t$ be the time elapsed since the surge was created or, in this case, since the sluice gate was opened. At $t = 0$, the wavelength $\lambda = 0$. After $t$ sec, the wavelength is equal to

$$\lambda = (V_{w2} - V_{w1})t \tag{19-61}$$

The above analysis can be applied similarly to a negative surge of type C.

**Example 19-5.** Show that the equation of the wave profile, resulting from the failure of a dam is in the form of

$$x = 2t\sqrt{gy_2} - 3t\sqrt{gy} \tag{19-62}$$

where $x$ is the distance measured from the dam site, $y$ is the depth of the wave profile, $y_2$ is the depth of the impounding water, and $t$ is the time after the dam broke.

*Solution.* Since the impounding water has zero velocity, or $V_2 = 0$, the wave velocity by Eq. (19-59) is $V_w = 3\sqrt{gy} - 2\sqrt{gy_2}$. Since $V_w$ is in the negative direction of $x$, $x = -V_w t$, which gives Eq. (19-62).

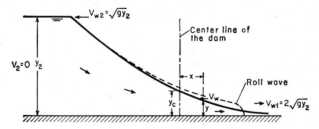

Fig. 19-10. Wave profile due to dam failure.

Equation (19-62) represents a parabola with vertical axis and vertex on the channel bottom, as shown in Fig. 19-10. At the site of the dam, $x = 0$ and the depth $y_c = 4y_2/9$. Owing to the channel friction, the actual profile takes the form indicated by the dashed line. This profile has a rounded front at the downstream end, forming a bore (see Example 18-1). At the upstream end, the theoretical profile thus developed has been checked satisfactorily with experiments by Schoklitsch [12].

**19-5. Surge in Power Canals.** Engineers are interested in the determination of the maximum stage of water that could be developed as a result of a sudden rejection of load in a power canal. This information is required in the design of the canal for establishing the height of wall necessary to prevent overflow.

Figure 19-11a shows the condition of steady flow in a power canal. The flow profile and the friction loss can be computed. When the load

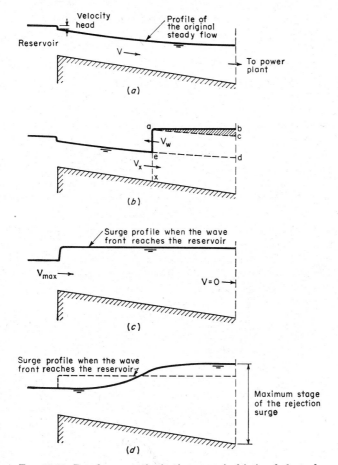

FIG. 19-11. Development of rejection surge in frictional channel.

is suddenly thrown off, a rejection surge advancing upstream is produced, as shown in Fig. 19-11b. According to usual observations, the water surface ab downstream from the wavefront is approximately level. Thus, when the wavefront reaches the reservoir, the water surface throughout the entire canal becomes level (Fig. 19-11c). However, a steadily increasing volume of water must pass through the wavefront to fill the space corresponding to *abc*. Because of this action and the effect of friction, the wavefront is being greatly reduced in height and velocity on its way to the reservoir. Furthermore, as the surge reaches the reservoir, the velocity of flow in the canal must show a progressive increase from a maximum at the reservoir to zero at the downstream end where there is no outlet for relief. As a result, water will be built up to a maximum stage at the downstream end, as shown in Fig. 19-11*d*, sometime soon after the arrival of the surge front at the reservoir.

For the determination of the maximum stage produced by the rejection surge,[1] Johnson [14,15] has applied an analytical method[2] to the design of the supply canal of the Queenston-Chippewa plant in the vicinity of Niagara Falls. In this example (Fig. 19-12*a*), the entire length of the canal is divided into four reaches each 9,700 ft long.

At the very beginning, $t = 0$, the flow is steady, and the flow profile can be computed. The drop in water-surface elevation in each reach is indicated at the division section between reaches, for example, 1.13 ft for reach 4 in Fig. 19-12*b* (see Example 19-3). The water surface in each reach is assumed level. Note that the friction in each reach at the steady-flow condition is considered in the computation of the flow profile. The slope effect of the channel is represented by a drop on the channel floor at the division section between the reaches, for example, 2.38 ft for reach 4 (Art. 19-3*C*). The water depths in feet are represented by the figures written vertically. The velocities in feet per second are represented by the figures written horizontally. In reach 4, for example, the depth is 42.90 ft and the velocity is 6.80 fps.

When the load is suddenly thrown off, a surge is developed at the downstream end of the canal (Fig. 19-12*c*). The computation of this initial surge has been shown in Example 19-1.

After 272 sec have passed since the surge was produced, the surge arrives at the barrier at the upstream end of reach 4 (Fig. 19-12*d*). The water depth throughout reach 4 is 51.09 ft, and the velocity of flow is zero. At the barrier, the surge is soon split into two component surges, one traveling upstream and the other downstream. The computation for these surges has been given in Example 19-3.

The component surge traveling downstream will soon reach the downstream end of the canal. After it reaches the end, it will be reflected. The reflected surge will travel upstream again.

The component surge traveling upstream will soon reach another friction barrier farther upstream. At the barrier it will split into two components, one traveling farther upstream and one traveling down-

---

[1] See [13] for another method.

[2] Johnson gave credit to P. Wahlman for this method.

stream. When one surge traveling upstream meets another surge traveling downstream, two new surges will emerge. The computation for the new surges has been described in Art. 19-3B.

The surges will continue to travel, split, and emerge. The computation

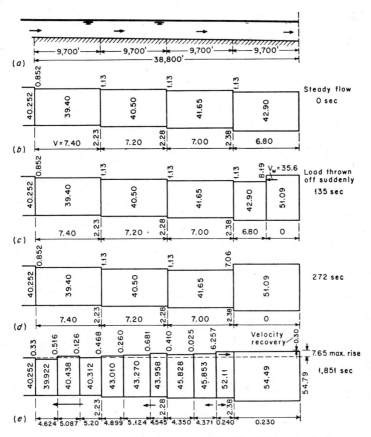

Fig. 19-12. Analysis of rejection surge by the Johnson method.

will follow accordingly until the maximum stage is obtained at the downstream end of the canal. In the example given by Johnson, the maximum stage is found to be 7.65 ft above the reservoir pool level (Fig. 19-12e). This will be reached 1,851 sec after the load is rejected.

It is apparent that the Johnson method is very laborious. The procedure becomes very involved as the computation continues, for numerous surges will be produced and propagated. The surge in a canal can also be studied by hydraulic models and electronic computers, which are sometimes found much easier though more expensive.

The analysis of surge is important also in the design of ventilated tailrace tunnels for underground hydropower stations. In such cases, demand surge is usually developed as a result of a sudden increase in the load output [16,17].

Rejection surges in power canals can be controlled by two commonly used devices: longitudinal side weirs along the canal and tilting gates on top of the spillway, either automatic or turbine-operated. The theory for longitudinal side weirs has been developed by Drioli [18], Schmidt [19], and Citrini [20,21]. Citrini's theory is based on the method of characteristics and has been verified satisfactorily by Gentilini [22], Penati [23], and De Marchi [24,25]. De Marchi has also reported experiments on the use of the tilting gate as a control device.

For a comprehensive discussion of unsteady flow, the reader should refer to the treatise by Frank [26].

**19-6. Surge in Navigation Canals.** Surges may occur in navigation canals as a result of lock operations, traffic disturbances, tidal actions, or other causes. Under severe conditions they will affect the canal traffic critically either by depressing the water level and thereby reducing the effective channel depth or by raising the water level and thus encroaching upon the freeboard. They will also impose sudden impact load upon vessels, canal structures, and machinery operating miter gates.[1]

In most navigation canals, however, surges are small and insignificant. Nevertheless, some consideration of the surge problem is desirable in canal design, particularly if the traffic is to be heavy and if the canal is long and controlled by high head gates. In this article, surges due to lock operations are mainly discussed. Surges due to traffic disturbances are excluded, for they are significant only for the consideration of vessel power requirements. Surges due to tidal actions are beyond the scope of this book, since they constitute an important topic in tidal hydraulics. Surges may also occur in lock chambers; this, however, is usually regarded as a special problem in lock design [15, pp. 190–213].

There are several methods of controlling surges in navigation canals, among them the following:

1. Increasing equalization time. The surge height is, in general, proportional to its discharge rate or inversely proportional to the time of lock equalization. Thus, the surge height can be reduced to any desired degree by appropriate increase in equalization time. In an existing canal, this can be done by throttling the inlet ports, and, in a new design,

---

[1] For an analysis of surges developed by partially or fully opening a miter gate, see [27].

by providing inlet ports of low capacity. This method is simple and inexpensive but has the disadvantage of delaying the traffic.

2. Increasing channel dimensions. An increase in channel depth will increase the celerity and reduce the surge height. An increase in channel width will decrease the surge height without change in celerity. In either case, the velocity of flow and hence the collision hazard are reduced.

3. Lateral reservoirs. These reservoirs are connected to the lock as well as to the canal with control valves, and are installed at the upstream as well as the downstream lateral sides of the lock. In filling the lock, water is taken in from the upstream reservoir, which is later to be filled up again to its original level by taking in water slowly from the upstream canal. In emptying the lock, water is released to the downstream reservoir, which is then to be emptied down to its original level by releasing water gradually to the downstream canal. In essence, the effect of the lateral reservoirs is to reduce the time of lock equalization without developing severe surges in the canal.

4. Channel expansions. Sudden expansions are provided in the canal on the upstream and downstream sides of the lock. Such expansions will produce negative reflections, which can cancel the traveling surges partially.

The method of analysis of surges in navigation canals can best be illustrated by a numerical example.[1] In navigation canals, surges of large height cannot be tolerated nor can the occurrence of high velocities. Thus the analysis can be greatly simplified in many problems by assuming possible surges of small height and flow of negligible velocity effects. Since the generation, propagation, and reflection of surges are essentially dynamic and gravitational phenomena, the surges can also be studied by model tests based on the Froude law.

**Example 19-6.** A surge is produced in a navigation canal by emptying the lock chamber. The discharge out of the chamber is shown as a function of time in Fig. 19-13$a$. The equalization time is 10 min. The canal has a rectangular section 200 ft wide and a mean water depth of 15 ft. The slope of the canal is assumed horizontal. Determine the surge profile.

*Solution.* The computation for the determination of the surge profile is shown in Table 19-1. In the analysis, the discharge is assumed to be released at intervals of time. In each interval a surge of small height is produced and will travel downstream at a speed computed by the formulas derived in the previous articles. Thus, the resulting surge configuration is formed by accumulating the fronts of the incremental surges. The columns in the table are explained as follows:

Col. 1. Time in sec since the discharge started. The interval of time is determined arbitrarily. For accurate determination, a small interval should be used.

Col. 2. Discharge in cfs per ft of channel width, equal to the total discharge shown by the hydrograph (Fig. 19-13$a$) at the corresponding time divided by 200 ft

[1] Similar methods with further approximations are used by the U.S. Army Corps of Engineers [28].

Col. 3.  Initial velocity of flow in fps before the incremental surge arrives, equal to $V_2$ (col. 4) of the previous step

Col. 4.  Final velocity of flow in fps after the incremental surge passes, equal to the discharge value in col. 2 divided by the nnal depth $y_2$ (col. 7) of the previous step. This is an approximation, because $y_2$ of the incremental surge under consideration is unknown as yet.

TABLE 19-1.  COMPUTATION OF SURGE PROFILE IN A NAVIGATION CANAL

| $T$ | $q$ | $V_1$ | $V_2$ | $y_1$ | $h$ | $y_2$ | $c$ | $V_w$ | $\Sigma h$ | $t$ | $L$ |
|-----|-----|-----|-----|-----|-----|-----|-----|-----|-----|-----|-----|
| (1) | (2) | (3) | (4) | (5) | (6) | (7) | (8) | (9) | (10) | (11) | (12) |
| 0 | 0 | 0 | 0 | 15.00 | 0 | 15.00 | 22.0 | 22.0 | 0 | 600 | 13,200 |
| 30 | 12.5 | 0 | 0.83 | 15.00 | 0.57 | 15.57 | 22.4 | 22.4 | 0.57 | 570 | 12,800 |
| 60 | 25.0 | 0.83 | 1.60 | 15.57 | 0.54 | 16.11 | 22.8 | 23.6 | 1.11 | 540 | 12,700 |
| 90 | 37.5 | 1.60 | 2.33 | 16.11 | 0.52 | 16.63 | 23.2 | 24.8 | 1.63 | 510 | 12,600 |
| 120 | 50.0 | 2.33 | 3.01 | 16.63 | 0.49 | 17.12 | 23.5 | 25.8 | 2.12 | 480 | 12,400 |
| 150 | 46.9 | 3.01 | 2.74 | 17.12 | −0.20 | 16.92 | 23.3 | 26.3 | 1.92 | 450 | 11,800 |
| 180 | 43.8 | 2.74 | 2.59 | 16.92 | −0.11 | 16.81 | 23.3 | 26.0 | 1.81 | 420 | 10,900 |
| 210 | 40.6 | 2.59 | 2.42 | 16.81 | −0.12 | 16.69 | 23.2 | 25.8 | 1.69 | 390 | 10,100 |
| 240 | 37.5 | 2.42 | 2.24 | 16.69 | −0.13 | 16.56 | 23.1 | 25.5 | 1.56 | 360 | 9,200 |
| 270 | 34.4 | 2.24 | 2.08 | 16.56 | −0.11 | 16.45 | 23.0 | 25.2 | 1.45 | 330 | 8,300 |
| 300 | 31.3 | 2.08 | 1.90 | 16.45 | −0.13 | 16.32 | 22.9 | 25.0 | 1.32 | 300 | 7,500 |
| 330 | 28.1 | 1.90 | 1.72 | 16.32 | −0.13 | 16.19 | 22.8 | 24.7 | 1.19 | 270 | 6,700 |
| 360 | 25.0 | 1.72 | 1.55 | 16.19 | −0.12 | 16.07 | 22.8 | 24.5 | 1.07 | 240 | 5,900 |
| 420 | 18.8 | 1.55 | 1.17 | 16.07 | −0.27 | 15.80 | 22.6 | 24.2 | 0.80 | 180 | 4,400 |
| 480 | 12.5 | 1.17 | 0.79 | 15.80 | −0.27 | 15.53 | 22.4 | 23.6 | 0.53 | 120 | 2,800 |
| 540 | 6.3 | 0.79 | 0.41 | 15.53 | −0.26 | 15.27 | 22.0 | 22.8 | 0.27 | 60 | 1,400 |
| 600 | 0 | 0.41 | 0 | 15.17 | −0.28 | 14.99 | 0 | 0 | −0.01 | 0 | 0 |

Col. 5.  Initial depth in ft, equal to the final depth $y_2$ of the previous step

Col. 6.  Height of the incremental surge in ft, computed by Eq. (19-19) or

$$h = \frac{c}{g}(V_2 - V_1) \qquad (19\text{-}63)$$

As an approximation, the value $c$ (col. 8) of the previous step is used in this equation. After $t = 150$ sec, $V_1$ becomes less than $V_2$; that is, the negative incremental surge occurs.  Thus, the computed $h$ is negative.

Col. 7.  Final depth of flow in ft, equal to the initial depth in col. 5 plus the height of the incremental surge in col. 6

Col. 8.  Celerity in fps, computed by Eq. (19-9)

Col. 9.  Absolute velocity of surge in fps, computed by Eq. (19-16)

Col. 10.  Cumulative value of the height of incremental surge (col. 6)

Col. 11.  Travel time in sec until the discharge stops, equal to the equalization time (600 sec) minus the time in col. 1 since the discharge started

Col. 12.  Travel distance in ft for each incremental surge until the discharge stops, equal to the product of the time in col. 11 and the absolute velocity in col. 9

Plotting the travel distance against the cumulative height of the incremental surges, the whole configuration of the surge is shown in Fig. 19-13b.  This is the surge profile in the downstream canal after a period equal to the equalization time is elapsed.  The maximum height of the surge is found to be about 2 ft, which is generally required in design for the determination of the freeboard and the water pressure against the channel walls. The surge height at the end of the equalization time should be zero. The value $-0.01$ as computed is due to the approximation of the slide-rule computation.

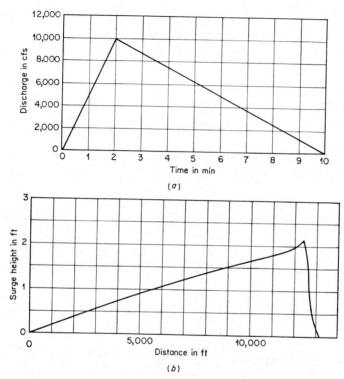

Fig. 19-13. Analysis of surge in a navigation canal. (a) Hydrograph; (b) surge profile.

**19-7. Surge through Channel Transitions.** When a surge arrives at a channel transition, it will usually split into two component surges, one traveling forward and the other backward. A typical case of a positive surge passing through a channel contraction has been described in Art. 19-3C. In this article, however, more general but simplified cases are presented.

Figure 19-14 shows four cases in which the positive and negative surges are passing through channel contractions and expansions. In each case, an incoming surge of height $h_1$ and celerity $c_1$ is split into a forward surge of height $h_2$ and celerity $c_2$ and a backward or reflected surge of height $h_3$ and celerity $c_3$. For simplicity, the surges are assumed of small height, so that simplified equations can be written. Furthermore, it is assumed that the water is initially at rest and that no energy losses occur at the transition.

By continuity of flow, the total amount of water passing through the transition should be constant. Therefore,

$$T_1 h_1 c_1 = T_2 h_2 c_2 + T_3 h_3 c_3 \tag{19-64}$$

where $T_1$, $T_2$, and $T_3$ are top widths of the surges.

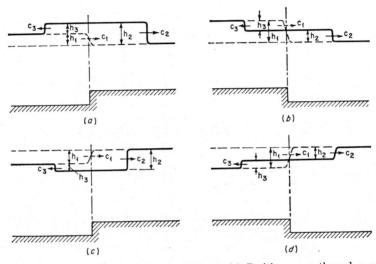

Fig. 19-14. Surge through channel transitions. (a) Positive surge through a contraction; (b) positive surge through an enlargement; (c) negative surge through a contraction; (d) negative surge through an enlargement.

By the principle of conservation of energy, the total amount of energy remains the same after the split of the incoming surge. With the aid of Eq. (19-50), the relationship of energy among the surges during a common time interval may be written as follows:

$$h_1{}^2 T_1 c_1 = h_2{}^2 T_2 c_2 + h_3{}^2 T_3 c_3 \tag{19-65}$$

For the case of a positive surge passing through a contraction (Fig. 19-14a), $c_1 \approx c_3$ and $T_1 = T_3$. Thus, Eqs. (19-64) and (19-65) become

$$T_1(h_1 - h_3)c_1 = T_2 h_2 c_2 \tag{19-66}$$
$$T_1(h_1{}^2 - h_3{}^2)c_1 = T_2 h_2{}^2 c_2 \tag{19-67}$$

From Eqs. (19-66) and (19-67) or by geometry,

$$h_1 + h_3 = h_2 \tag{19-68}$$

Solving Eqs. (19-66) and (19-68) for $h_2$ and $h_3$,

$$h_2 = \frac{2T_1c_1}{T_1c_1 + T_2c_2} h_1 \tag{19-69}$$

and

$$h_3 = \frac{T_1c_1 - T_2c_2}{T_1c_1 + T_2c_2} h_1 \tag{19-70}$$

The ratio of the reflected height to the initial height of a surge is known as the *reflection coefficient* $C_r$. Letting $T_2 = nT_1$ and using Eq. (19-70),

$$C_r = \frac{h_3}{h_1} = \frac{c_1 - nc_2}{c_1 + nc_2} \tag{19-71}$$

As a further approximation, $c_1 \approx c_2$; so

$$C_r = \frac{1 - n}{1 + n} \tag{19-72}$$

The relationship between $n$ and $C$ is shown below:

| Width ratio | Reflection coefficient | Reflection | Channel condition |
|---|---|---|---|
| $n = 0$ | $C_r = 1$ | Positive | A dead-end barrier |
| $n < 1$ | $C_r > 0$ | Partial positive | Contraction |
| $n = 1$ | $C_r = 0$ | None | No transition |
| $n > 1$ | $C_r < 0$ | Partial negative | Expansion |
| $n = \infty$ | $C_r = -1$ | Negative | Entrance to a lake or sea |

In the case of positive reflection, a positive surge is reflected as a positive surge and a negative surge as a negative surge. In the case of negative reflection, a positive surge is reflected as a negative surge, and vice versa.

**Example 19-7.** In a navigation canal, forebays are constructed between the lock and the canals in order to provide adequate accommodation for the traffic (Fig. 19-15). The depth of water in the downstream forebay and canal is 9 ft. The widths of the forebay and canal are 300 ft and 150 ft, respectively. Determine the approximate flow condition when a surge, produced by a sudden release of 1,800 cfs of water from the lock, arrives at the transition between the forebay and the canal.

*Solution.* The initial surge has a celerity approximately equal to $c_1 = \sqrt{9g} = 17.0$ fps and a height $h_1 = \Delta Q_1/c_1T_1 = 1,800/(17.0 \times 300) = 0.353$ ft. The celerity in the canal is approximately equal to $c_1$, since the depth is the same as it is in the forebay. By Eq. (19-69),

$$h_2 = \frac{2T_1c_1}{T_1c_1 + T_2c_2} h_1 = \frac{2 \times 300}{300 + 150} \times 0.353 = 0.471 \text{ ft}$$

Thus, $h_3 = h_2 - h_1 = 0.118$ ft. The reflection coefficient is $0.118/0.353 = 0.334$. By Eq. (19-71), $C_r = 0.333$.

The discharge entering the canal is $\Delta Q_2 = c_2 T_2 h_2 = 17.0 \times 150 \times 0.471 = 1,200$ cfs. The reflected discharge is $\Delta Q_3 = 1,800 - 1,200 = 600$ cfs.

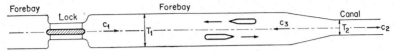

FIG. 19-15. Analysis of surge through the transition between forebay and canal.    (*After* J. Koženy [31].)

Now, if the transition between the canal and the lock is assumed gradual, as shown in Fig. 19-15, the computation can be made by letting $h_2 = h_1 + dh_1$ and $c_2 T_2 = c_1 T_1 + d(c_1 T_1)$. Accordingly, Eq. (19-69) may be written

$$\frac{dh_1}{h_1} = -\frac{d(c_1 T_1)}{2c_1 T_1 + d(c_1 T_1)} \approx -\frac{d(c_1 T_1)}{2c_1 T_1} \qquad (19\text{-}73)$$

Integrating and simplifying the above equation,

$$\log (h_1 \sqrt{c_1 T_1}) = \text{const} \qquad (19\text{-}74)$$

Similarly, it can be shown that

$$\log (h_2 \sqrt{c_2 T_2}) = \text{const} \qquad (19\text{-}75)$$

From the above two equations,

$$\frac{h_2}{h_1} = \sqrt{\frac{c_1 T_1}{c_2 T_2}} \approx \sqrt{\frac{T_1}{T_2}} \qquad (19\text{-}76)$$

With $T_1/T_2 = 2$, the above equation gives $h_2/h_1 = 1.414$. Thus, $h_2 = 1.414 h_1 = 0.499$ ft and $h_3 = 0.146$ ft. The corresponding $C_r = 0.413$, $\Delta Q_2 = 1,270$ cfs, and $\Delta Q_3 = 530$ cfs.

This example illustrates the application of the theory of surges to the hydraulic study of ship lock and forebay. Such applications have been described by many hydraulicians, among them Dantscher [29,30] and Koženy [31].

**19-8. Surge at Channel Junctions.**    When a surge arrives at a channel junction, it will split into several surges, each entering a connecting channel. A simple case, shown in Fig. 19-16, may be used to explain the phenomenon.

Figure 19-16a shows that a surge in channel I is approaching the junction of three rectangular channels. The surge has a height $h_1$ and celerity $c_1$. Channel I has a water area $A_1$ and depth of flow $y_1$. Since there are no surges in channels II and III, $h_2 = h_3 = 0$. The initial velocities in the channels are taken as zero merely for the sake of simplicity, although any velocities could be assumed.

When the incoming surge reaches the junction, its height is reduced because of the increased surface area presented to the surge by the two additional channels. Surges of reduced height $h$ will then travel through the two adjoining channels with celerities $c_2$ and $c_3$, respectively. Assuming that surge heights are small compared with the depth of water in the channels, the celerities can be computed by Eq. (18-46). In the meantime, a reflected surge will travel along channel I at a celerity approximately equal to $c_1$. Figure 19-16$b$ shows the condition at the junction immediately after the arrival of the incoming surge.

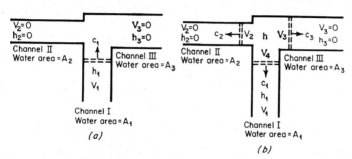

FIG. 19-16. Surge at channel junction. ($a$) Before arrival of surge; ($b$) after arrival of surge.

Since the surge heights are assumed small compared with the depths of flow in the channels, Eqs. (19-19) and (19-24) can be applied. Thus, the following equations can be written for channels I, II, and III, respectively:

$$\text{For channel I} \qquad h_1 - h = \frac{c_1}{g} (V_4 - V_1) \qquad (19\text{-}77)$$

$$\text{For channel I} \qquad h_1 = \frac{c_1}{g} V_1 \qquad (19\text{-}78)$$

$$\text{For channel II} \qquad h = \frac{c_2}{g} V_2 \qquad (19\text{-}79)$$

$$\text{For channel III} \qquad h = \frac{c_3}{g} V_3 \qquad (19\text{-}80)$$

By the law of continuity of flow, it is required that the quantity of water flowing into the junction be equal to that flowing out of the junction, or

$$A_1 V_4 = A_2 V_2 + A_3 V_3 \qquad (19\text{-}81)*$$

Solving the above equations simultaneously for $h$,

$$h = \frac{2h_1 A_1}{I c_1} \qquad (19\text{-}82)$$

$$\text{where} \qquad I = \frac{A_1}{c_1} + \frac{A_2}{c_2} + \frac{A_3}{c_3} \qquad (19\text{-}83)$$

* $V_4$ has a direction opposite to $c_1$.

If an incoming surge of height $h_2$ approaches the junction from channel II, then it can be shown that

$$h = \frac{2h_2 A_2}{I c_2} \qquad (19\text{-}84)$$

Similarly, if an incoming surge of height $h_3$ approaches the junction from channel III, then

$$h = \frac{2h_3 A_3}{I c_3} \qquad (19\text{-}85)$$

By the above principle, it is possible to analyze surges in a complicated channel network. Such a method has been developed by Swain [32,33] for an approximate determination of surge flows in an interconnected system of estuarine channels in response to tidal variations. In this method, the friction barrier is assumed to be located at the middle of a channel reach. The surges are assumed to have small heights compared with the depth of flow, so that simplified equations can be applied. To further expedite the computation, it is desirable to have coincidental arrival of surges at a barrier or junction at some given instant. This is made possible by the use of a procedure that involves a modification of the true length of the channel reaches. The analytic method developed by Swain was actually applied to a problem for the determination of flows in interconnected estuarine channels in the Delta area of California east of Suisun Bay. The same problem was studied by the U.S. Bureau of Reclamation using an elaborate hydraulic model [34–36] and an electronic analog model [37]. The results of the Swain method were checked satisfactorily.

**19-9. Pulsating Flow.** When the slope of a channel becomes very steep, supercritical flow of uniform depth in the channel will break into a train of traveling waves or pulses, known as *pulsating flow*. Such an unsteady flow occurs in various situations and in each situation it has specific significance. When it occurs in inclined flumes and spillways, the increased height of the flow requires additional freeboard to prevent spillage, and the concentrated mass of the wavefronts calls for additional structural safety factors against transient pressures and stresses. In hydraulic models, presence of the flow often interferes with similarity conditions. On farm lands and unstabilized roads, the high scouring capacity of the flow causes surface erosions. In chemical processes, the effect of the flow will increase the mass-transfer rate between gas and liquid diffusion reactions.

There have been numerous studies on the phenomenon of pulsating flow. Most of them, however, were made primarily in connection with the investigation of the mechanism of instability of flow (Art. 8-8). An analytical and experimental study of pulsating flow which has long interested hydraulic engineers was made by Thomas [38]. In this study pulsating flow was described as a flow consisting of two parts, a roughly tumbling head and a smooth tail section. The results of the study indicate that, for pulsating flow to occur in a wide rectangular channel, the channel slope must be more than 4 times the critical slope or the velocity more than twice the critical velocity. Another investigation was made by Mayer [39], who found that pulsating flow can be classified into two distinct types, namely, roll waves and slug flow.

According to Mayer, *roll waves* are characterized by transverse ridges of high vorticity. The regions between the crests are quiescent. The waves are initiated by finite as well as infinitesimal disturbances in the laminar boundary layer. The process can be enhanced by external causes, such as addition of water by rain, release of air bubbles in the upstream pool, roughening the channel entrance, or contact of the flow surface with disturbing air currents. For roll waves to form, however, the surface velocity of the undisturbed flow must be less than the wave velocity, and the channel slope must be supercritical. This requirement will ensure the breaking of waves at their downstream ends and thus allow a frontward steepening of wave configuration and subsequent increase of capillary effects. This process is primarily responsible for the formation of roll waves. In Mayer's experiment, no roll waves were observed on slopes of less than 3% and in no case was the Reynolds number in excess of 420.

*Slug flows* are characterized by surges of turbulent ridges with wave crests separated by highly agitated regions. In model channels, they are originated randomly at the side walls and in the channel as spotty bursts of turbulence, exhibiting characteristics similar to moving oblique hydraulic jumps. They are the result of transition from supercritical laminar to subcritical turbulent state of flow. For slug flows to form, the surface velocity must be greater than the wave velocity. This will ensure the steepening and breaking of waves at their upstream ends and thereby result in the development of moving hydraulic jumps. In Mayer's experiment, no slug waves were formed on slopes less than about 2%. The range of Reynolds number for slug flows was approximately 1,000 to 4,000. For Reynolds number greater than 4,000, the flow was thoroughly turbulent.

Considering a parabolic distribution of the velocity of a uniform flow in an inclined channel, the surface velocity given by Eq. (6-42) for $y = y_m$ is $gSy_m^2/2\nu$. The average velocity of the flow is given by Eq. (6-43) or $V = gSy_m^2/3\nu$. The surface velocity is, therefore, equal to 1.5 times the average velocity, or $1.5V$.

According to the previous description, a roll wave can be formed when the surface velocity is equal to or less than the absolute wave velocity, that is, when

$$1.5V \leqq V + c \tag{19-86}$$
or $$V/c \leqq 2 \tag{19-87}$$

Since $V/c$ is equal to the Froude number and since roll waves can be formed only on supercritical slopes, the range of Froude number for the formation of roll waves is $1 \leqq \mathbf{F} \leqq 2$. Solving Eq. (6-43) for $S$, it can be shown that $S = 3\mathbf{F}^2/\mathbf{R}$. Thus, the range of slope for the formation of roll waves is $3/\mathbf{R} \leqq S \leqq 12/\mathbf{R}$.

Slug flow can be formed when the surface velocity is greater than the wave velocity. Theoretically, therefore, the formation of slug flow will occur when $\mathbf{F} > 2$ and $S > 12/\mathbf{R}$.

## PROBLEMS

**19-1.** Prove Eq. (19-11).

**19-2.** Prove Eq. (19-15).

**19-3.** Assuming the energy loss in the moving hydraulic jump to be negligible, Koch and Carstanjen [27] have derived the following equation for the wave velocity of a surge:

$$V_w = \sqrt{\left(\frac{V_1 - V_2}{4}\right)^2 + gy_1} \pm \frac{V_1 + 3V_2}{4} \tag{19-88}$$

where the positive sign is for type $A$ and $C$ surges and the negative sign is for type $B$ and $D$ surges (Fig. 19-2). Verify this equation.

**19-4.** Assuming an initial depth of 20 ft, an initial velocity of 15 fps, and a rectangular channel cross section, compute the velocity and overrun of the bore shown in Fig. 19-3 and estimate the distance traveled by the bore in 7 min.

**19-5.** Compute the heights, depths, and wave velocities of the two component surges produced in Example 19-3.

**19-6.** A positive surge 0.63 ft high and 51.72 ft deep is moving in still water 51.09 ft deep with a wave velocity of 41.70 fps toward the dead end of a channel. Determine the height and wave velocity of the reflected surge after the original surge hits the dead end.

**19-7.** Solve Example 19-1 if the original steady flow has a velocity of 10 fps and a depth of 50 ft.

**19-8.** Solve Example 19-3, if the step has a height of $F = 3$ ft.

**19-9.** Two positive surges 3 and 2 ft in height, respectively, move in opposite directions toward each other in a frictionless horizontal channel where the water is initially stationary at a depth of 30 ft. The high surge has a wave velocity of 30 fps and the low surge a wave velocity of 20 fps. Determine the flow condition after the surges meet.

**19-10.** Solve Example 19-1 if the channel has a slope of 0.01. The initial steady flow is assumed uniform.

**19-11.** Show that the celerity formula in the form of Eq. (18-45) applies only to positive surges and that the corresponding celerity formula for negative surges is

$$c = \sqrt{gy\left(1 - \frac{3h}{2y}\right)} \tag{19-89}$$

**19-12.** Referring to Example 19-5, show that the crest velocity $V_{w2} = \sqrt{gy_2}$, that the trough velocity $V_{w1} = 2\sqrt{gy_2}$, that the velocity of flow through the dam site is $\frac{2}{3}\sqrt{gy_2}$, and that the discharge through the dam site is $\frac{8}{27}\sqrt{g}\,y_2^{3/2}$.

**19-13.** Continue the computation of the example illustrated in Fig. 19-12, and determine the flow conditions at 420, 504, 552, 743, and 767 sec, respectively, after the load was suddenly thrown off.

**19-14.** Solve Example 19-6 if the equalization time is (a) 8 min and (b) 12 min. The discharge from the lock increases linearly from 0 to 10,000 cfs for the first 20% of the time and then decreases linearly to 0 for the remaining part of the time. Study the effect due to change in equalization time.

**19-15.** Solve Example 19-7 if the discharge is 1,000 cfs.

**19-16.** Three horizontal frictionless channels 4, 6, and 8 ft wide meet at a junction. The water in the channels has an initial stationary depth of 10 ft. When an incoming surge 0.4 ft high approaches the junction from the narrowest channel, determine the flow condition after the surge enters the junction. Compute the reflection coefficient of the junction.

## REFERENCES

1. J. C. Schönfeld: Theoretical considerations on an experimental bore, *Proceedings of the 6th General Meeting, International Association for Hydraulic Research, The Hague 1955*, vol. 1, pp. A15–1 to A15–12, 1955.

2. T. B. Benjamin and M. J. Lighthill: On cnoidal waves and bores, *Proceedings, Royal Society of London*, vol. 224, no. 1159, pp. 448–460, July 22, 1954.

3. A. M. Binnie and J. C. Orkney: Experiments on flow of water from a reservoir through an open horizontal channel: II, The formation of hydraulic jump, *Proceedings, Royal Society of London*, ser. A, vol. 230, no. 1181, pp. 237–246, June 21, 1955.

4. J. A. Sandover and O. C. Zienkiewicz: Experiments on surge waves, *Water Power*, London, vol. 9, no. 11, pp. 418–424, November, 1957.

5. Robert E. Horton: Channel waves subject chiefly to momentum control, *U.S. Soil Conservation Service*, SCS-TP-16, May, 1938.

6. The Johnstown disaster, *Engineering News*, vol. 21, no. 23, pp. 517–518, June 8, 1889.

7. A. L. A. Himmelwright: The Johnstown flood, *Harper's Magazine*, vol. 167, pp. 443–455, September, 1933.

8. Richard O'Connor: "Johnstown: The Day the Dam Broke," J. B. Lippincott Company, Philadelphia, 1957.

9. The Heppner disaster, *Engineering News*, vol. 50, no. 3, pp. 53–54, July 16, 1903.

10. Commission finds failure of St. Francis Dam due to defective foundation, *Engineering News-Record*, vol. 100, no. 14, pp. 553–555, Apr. 5, 1928.

11. M. D. Chertousov: "Gidravlika: Spetsialnyĭ Kurs" ("Hydraulics: Special Course"), Gosenergoizdat, Moscow, 1957, pp. 437–453.

12. A. Schoklitsch: Über Dambruchwellen (On waves produced by broken dams), *Sitzungsberichte, Mathematisch-naturwissenschaftliche Klasse, Akademie der Wissenschaften in Wien*, vol. 126, pt. IIa, pp. 1489–1514, Vienna, 1917.

13. E. T. Haws: Surges and waves in open channels, *Water Power*, vol. 6, no. 11, pp. 419–422, November, 1954.

14. R. D. Johnson: The correlation of momentum and energy changes in steady flow with varying velocity and the application of the former to problems of unsteady

flow or surges in open channels, *Hydro-Electric Conference, 1922, Engineers and Engineering, The Engineers Club of Philadelphia*, pp. 234–240, July, 1922.

15. George R. Rich: "Hydraulic Transients," McGraw-Hill Book Company, Inc., New York, 1951, pp. 217–224.

16. Charles Jaeger: "Engineering Fluid Mechanics," translated from the German by P. O. Wolf, Blackie & Son, Ltd., London and Glasgow, 1956, pp. 381–392.

17. G. Bata: Utilisation des valeurs réduites dans le domaine des régimes transitoires des canaux ouverts et leur application dans le cas des galeries utilisées en reservoirs d'éclusées (Use of reduced values in the translatory regions of open channels and their application in the case of tunnels used as storage reservoirs), *Proceedings of the 6th General Meeting, International Association for Hydraulic Research, The Hague 1955*, pp. D8-1 to D8-10, 1955.

18. Carlo Drioli: Esperienze sul moto perturbato nei canali industriali (Experiment on surge in industrial canals), *L'Energia elettrica, Milano*, vol. 14, no. 4, pt. I, pp. 285–311, April; no. 5, pt. II, pp. 382–402, May, 1937.

19. Martin Schmidt: Zur Frage des Abflusses über Streichwehre (Discharge over side weir), *Technische Universität Berlin-Charlottenburg, Institut für Wasserbau, Mitteilung* 41, 1954.

20. Duilio Citrini: Sull'attenuazione di un'onda positiva ad opera di une sfioratore laterale (On the damping of a positive wave effected by a side weir), *L'Energia elettrica, Milano*, vol. 26, no. 10, pp. 589–599, October, 1949; reprinted as *Istituto di Idraulica e Costruzioni Idrauliche, Milano, Memorie e studi No. 76*, 1949.

21. Duilio Citrini: Sull'efficacia di uno sfioratore laterale nelle manovre di arresto completo (On the effectiveness of a side weir in the unsteady motion following full rejection of load), *L'Energia elettrica, Milano*, vol. 27, no. 2, pp. 77–80, February, 1950; reprinted as *Istituto di Idraulica e Costruzioni Idrauliche, Milano, Memorie e studi No. 79*, 1950.

22. B. Gentilini: L'azione di uno sfioratore laterale sull'onda positiva ascendente in un canale (The effect of a side weir on a positive ascending wave in a canal), *L'Energia elettrica, Milano*, vol. 27, no. 1, pp. 1–10, January, 1950; reprinted as *Istituto di Idraulica e Costruzioni Idrauliche, Milano, Memorie e studi No. 78*, 1950.

23. Savio Penati: Azione di uno sfioratore a ventola sull'onda positiva provocata dall'arresto delle macchine nel canale adduttore di un impiante idroelettrico (On the action of a side weir, controlled by a tilting gate, upon the positive translation wave generated in the canal of a power plant by the sudden closing of the turbines), *L'Energia elettrica, Milano*, vol. 31, no. 10, pp. 733–741, October, 1954; reprinted as *Istituto di Idraulica e Costruzioni Idrauliche, Milano, Memorie e studi No. 115*, 1954. On new model tests for the Tornavento Power Plant.

24. Giulio De Marchi: Action of side weirs and tilting gates on translation waves in canals, *Proceedings of the Minnesota International Hydraulics Conference, Joint Meeting of International Association for Hydraulic Research and Hydraulics Division of the American Society of Civil Engineers*, pp. 537–545, August, 1953; reprinted as *Istituto di Idraulica e Costruzioni Idrauliche, Milano, Memorie e studi No. 104*, 1953.

25. Giulio De Marchi: Azione di une sfioratore a ventola sull'onda positiva provocata dall'arresto delle macchine nel canale adduttore di un impianto idroelettrico (On the action of a side weir, controlled by a tilting gate, upon the positive translation wave generated in the canal of a power plant by the sudden closing of the turbines), *L'Energia elettrica, Milano*, vol. 30, no. 12, pp. 12–20, December, 1953; reprinted as *Istituto di Idraulica e Costruzioni Idrauliche, Milano, Memorie e studi No. 110*, 1953. On model tests for the Tornavento power plant.

26. Josef Frank: "Nichtstationäre Vorgänge in den Zuleitungs- und Ableitungs-kanälen von Wasserkraftwerken" ("Unsteady Flow in Headraces and Tailraces of Hydropower Plants"), Springer-Verlag, Berlin, June, 1957.

27. Alexander Koch and Max Carstanjen: "Von der Bewegung des Wassers und dabei auftretenden Kräften" ("Movement of Water and Associated Forces"), Springer-Verlag, Berlin, 1926, pp. 132–150.

28. U.S. Army Corps of Engineers: Hydraulic design: Surges in canals, *Civil Works Construction, Engineering Manual*, March, 1949, pt. CXVI, chap. 6, 13 pp.

29. Kasper Dantscher: Wanderwellen in Schiffahrtskanälen (Traveling waves in navigation canals), *Wasserkraft und Wasserwirtschaft*, Munich, vol. 35, no. 7, pp. 145–147, July 15, 1940.

30. Kasper Dantscher: Die Wanderwelle in Schiffahrtskanal (The traveling wave in a navigation canal), *Wasserkraft und Wasserwirtschaft*, Munich, vol. 35, no. 10, pp. 226–229, Oct. 15, 1940.

31. Josef Koženy, "Hydraulik" ("Hydraulics"), Springer-Verlag, Vienna, 1953, pp. 263–265.

32. Francis E. Swain: Determination of flows in interconnected estuarine channels, *U.S. Bureau of Reclamation, Technical Memorandum* 640, February, 1951.

33. Francis E. Swain: Determination of flows in interconnected estuarine channels produced by the combined effects of tidal fluctuations and gravity flows, *Transactions, American Geophysical Union*, vol. 32, no. 5, pp. 653–672, October, 1951.

34. D. J. Hebert and F. C. Lowe: Progress report on model studies of the Sacramento–San Joaquin Delta, Central Valley Project, California, *U.S. Bureau of Reclamation, Hydraulic Laboratory Report No. Hyd-142*, Apr. 10, 1944.

35. D. J. Hebert and J. E. Warnock: Skeleton outline of a plan for developing the Delta-Mendota Irrigation Water Supply and Salt-Water Repulsion in the Sacramento–San Joaquin Delta Region, Central Valley Project, *U.S. Bureau of Reclamation, Hydraulic Laboratory Report No. Hyd-145*, July 10, 1944.

36. Cherry Creek Dam and Reservoir: Report of model studies, spillway and stilling basin, *Hydraulic Laboratory Report No. Hyd-146*, prepared by U.S. Bureau of Reclamation for U.S. Army Corps of Engineers, July, 1944.

37. R. E. Glover, D. J. Hebert, and C. R. Daum: Application of an hydraulic problem, in Electrical analogies and electronic computers: A symposium, *Transactions, American Society of Civil Engineers*, vol. 118, pp. 1010–1016, 1953.

38. Harold A. Thomas: The propagation of waves in steep prismatic conduits, *Proceedings of Hydraulic Conference, State University of Iowa, Studies in Engineering, Bulletin* 20, March, 1940, pp. 214–229.

39. Paul G. H. Mayer: A study of roll waves and slug flows in inclined open channels, doctoral thesis, Cornell University, Ithaca, N.Y., September, 1957.

CHAPTER 20

# FLOOD ROUTING

**20-1. Routing of Flood.** It may be assumed that the configuration of a flood wave moving through a short regular channel reach where the channel resistance is relatively low will remain unchanged. The flood movement can be treated simply as a uniformly progressive flow, as discussed in Chap. 18. If, however, the channel is irregular and the resistance is high, the wave configuration will be modified appreciably as it moves through the reach. The determination of this modification of a flood flow is known as *flood routing*.

As described in Art. 18-7, Thomas has given two hydraulic methods for the solution of unsteady-flow equations. These methods can be used for the purpose of flood routing. However, they are too laborious for actual applications. More practical methods based on hydraulic principles will be described in the following two articles.[1]

In engineering hydrology, flood routing is an important technique necessary for the complete solution of a flood-control problem and for the satisfactory operation of a flood-prediction service. For such purposes, flood routing is recognized as a procedure required in order to determine the hydrograph at one point on a stream from the known hydrograph at an upstream point. Modern electronic machines can easily route a flood directly from its sources. Accordingly, the meaning of flood routing has been extended to include the routing of the movement of water from rainfall to runoff. The routing technique applies both to channel reaches and to reservoirs. In the latter case, it is called *reservoir routing*. When it is used to determine the combined flood at a downstream point due to floods in several upstream tributaries and in the main stream, the technique is known as *flood synthesis*.

The *hydraulic method* of flood routing is distinguished from the *hydrologic method* by the fact that the hydraulic method is based on the solution of the basic differential equations for unsteady flow in open channels whereas the hydrologic method makes no direct use of these equations but approximates in some sense to their solutions. The hydrologic method is in general simpler but fails to give entirely satisfactory results

[1] For other hydraulic methods of flood routing, see [1] to [3].

586

in problems other than that of determining the progress of a flood down a long river. For example, when a flood comes through a junction, backwater is usually produced. When a flood is regulated by a dam, surges are generally evolved. The backwater effect and the effect of surges in these problems can be accurately evaluated only by the basic hydraulic equations employed in the hydraulic method, but not by the hydrologic method.

**20-2. Method of Characteristics.** A strict hydraulic method of flood routing has been shown to be extremely complicated and difficult. However, various simplified methods have been developed for practical purposes. Many of these methods belong to the general *method of characteristics*, which is based on the solution of a set of characteristic equations of unsteady flow. Outstanding contributions to the development of such methods have been made by Massau [4,5], Henry [6], Bergeron [7,8], Khristianovich [9], Lévin [10], Craya [11], Arkhangelskiĭ [12], Holsters [13,14], Stoker [15–17], Putman [18], Lamoen [19], Dmitriev [20], Escoffier [21], Ransford [22], Lin [23], Uchida [24], Nougaro [25–28], Iwagaki and Sueishi [29–31], Isaacson, Stoker, and Troesch [32,33], and many others. The method developed by Lin will be described in this article.

According to Massau, the following equations for unsteady flow may be written:

$$\frac{\partial y}{\partial x} + \frac{V}{g}\frac{\partial V}{\partial x} + \frac{1}{g}\frac{\partial V}{\partial t} = S_0 - S_f \tag{20-1}$$

$$D\frac{\partial V}{\partial x} + V\frac{\partial y}{\partial x} + \frac{\partial y}{\partial t} = 0 \tag{20-2}$$

$$\frac{\partial y}{\partial x}\,dx + \frac{\partial y}{\partial t}\,dt = dy \tag{20-3}$$

$$\frac{\partial V}{\partial x}\,dx + \frac{\partial V}{\partial t}\,dt = dV \tag{20-4}$$

In the above equations, $\partial y/\partial x$ is the slope of water surface, $\partial y/\partial t$ is the change of depth of flow with respect to time, $\partial V/\partial x$ is the change of velocity with respect to distance, $\partial V/\partial t$ is the change of velocity with respect to time, $S_0$ is the channel slope, $S_f$ is the friction slope, $dy$ is the total change of depth, and $dV$ is the total change of velocity. Note that Eq. (20-1) is a dynamic equation representing Eq. (18-13) assuming $\alpha = 1$ and that Eq. (20-2) is the continuity equation identical with Eq. (18-5). Equation (20-3) indicates that the total change in depth is equal to the sum of the partial changes in depth due to distance and time, respectively. Similarly, Eq. (20-4) indicates that the total change in velocity is equal to the sum of the partial changes in velocity due to distance and time, respectively.

Solving the above four equations simultaneously for $\partial y/\partial x$,

$$\frac{\partial y}{\partial x} = \frac{-D(S_0 - S_f) + \dfrac{D}{g}\dfrac{dV}{dt} - \dfrac{V}{g}\dfrac{dy}{dt} + \dfrac{1}{g}\dfrac{dy}{dt}\dfrac{dx}{dt}}{\dfrac{1}{g}\left(\dfrac{dx}{dt}\right)^2 - \dfrac{2V}{g}\dfrac{dx}{dt} + \dfrac{V^2}{g} - D} \tag{20-5}$$

It may be assumed that a flood wave is composed of a great number of infinitesimal surges. The propagation of the flood wave may be treated as the propagation of the surges. These surges are formed as a result of disturbances caused by the flood, and each surge has a discontinuous surface profile. At the point of discontinuity, the water surface breaks and the slope $\partial y/\partial x$ has two values. Since the two surface slopes do not bear any definite relationship to each other, the value of $\partial y/\partial x$ must be indeterminate; or, mathematically, $\partial y/\partial x = \%$. When the denominator of Eq. (20-5) is set to zero,

$$dx = (V \pm c)\,dt \tag{20-6}$$

where $c = \sqrt{gD}$. For wide channels, $c = \sqrt{gy}$. When the numerator is set to zero and Eq. (20-6) is used,

$$d(V \pm 2c) = g(S_0 - S_f)\,dt \tag{20-7}$$

The above equations are known as the *equations of characteristics*. The method for deriving these equations was first given by Massau [4]. Later, Massau [5] developed a trial-and-error procedure for applying these equations to problems of unsteady flow. Owing to the laboriousness of the procedure, the method had not been very popular until later investigators, among them Lin, simplified the procedure through graphical and other approaches.

The equations of characteristics may be written:

$$\frac{dx}{dt} = V + c \tag{20-8}$$

$$d(V + 2c) = g(S_0 - S_f)\,dt \tag{20-9}$$

$$\frac{dx}{dt} = V - c \tag{20-10}$$

$$d(V - 2c) = g(S_0 - S_f)\,dt \tag{20-11}$$

It can be seen that Eqs. (20-8) and (20-10) are identical with Eq. (18-54), expressing the velocity of wave propagation. These equations can be represented graphically on an $xt$ plane, as shown in Fig. 20-1. For a finite time increment $\Delta t$, the point $p$ represents the position of the channel section under consideration at time $t + \Delta t$, and the points $u$ and $d$ represent, respectively, the positions of certain upstream and downstream sections at time $t$. The velocity of wave propagation can be represented by the slopes of lines constructed on the $xt$ plane. When the flow is subcritical,[1] as it is in most streams, that is, when $V < c$, the slope of the line $up$, a positive quantity, represents $V + c$ of Eq. (20-8), and the slope of the line $dp$, a negative quantity, represents $V - c$ of Eq. (20-10). These lines $up$ and $dp$ are hereafter referred to as *characteristics*. It is evident that point $u$ represents the position of the upstream section from which an infinitesimal surge, once developed, will arrive at

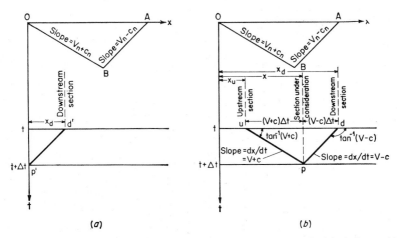

FIG. 20-1. Graphical representation of wave propagation for subcritical flow. (a) Flow condition at inflow; (b) flow condition in channel.

section $p$ after the time interval $\Delta t$. Similarly, point $d$ represents the position of the downstream section from which a surge once developed will arrive at section $p$ after $\Delta t$.

The flow conditions at the upstream and downstream sections are to be indicated by the subscripts $u$ and $d$, respectively. Integrating Eq. (20-9) from time $t$ to $t + \Delta t$, which interval is the time required for the wave to travel from the upstream section to the section under consideration,

$$V + 2c = V_u + 2c_u + gS_0 \Delta t - g \int_t^{t+\Delta t} S_f \, dt \qquad (20\text{-}12)$$

For a small value of $\Delta t$

$$\int_t^{t+\Delta t} S_f \, dt = \frac{(S_{fu} + S_f) \Delta t}{2}$$

[1] Theoretically, the method of characteristics is similarly applicable to supercritical flow. However, the possibility of disturbance due to formation of standing waves would have to be taken into account [23].

So Eq. (20-12) may be written

$$V + 2c = G_u + K \tag{20-13}$$

where

$$G_u = V_u + 2c_u + K_u \tag{20-14}$$

$$K_u = \frac{g(S_0 - S_{fu})\,\Delta t}{2} \tag{20-15}$$

and

$$K = \frac{g(S_0 - S_f)\,\Delta t}{2} \tag{20-16}$$

Similarly, the following equation may be obtained by integrating Eq. (20-11) over the interval required for the wave to travel from the downstream section to the section under consideration:

$$V - 2c = G_d + K \tag{20-17}$$

where

$$G_d = V_d - 2c_d + K_d \tag{20-18}$$

and

$$K_d = \frac{g(S_0 - S_{fd})\,\Delta t}{2} \tag{20-19}$$

Eliminating $K$ from Eqs. (20-13) and (20-17) and solving for $c$,

$$c = \frac{G_u - G_d}{4} \tag{20-20}$$

This equation can be used for computing $c$ at the time $t + \Delta t$ if the upstream and downstream flow conditions at the time $t$ are given.

Eliminating $c$ from Eqs. (20-13) and (20-17) and solving for $V - K$,

$$V - K = \frac{G_u + G_d}{2} \tag{20-21}$$

or, from Eq. (20-20),

$$V - K = G_d + 2c \tag{20-22}$$

Using the Manning formula, $S_f = n^2 V^2 / 2.22 R^{4/3}$. Substituting this expression for $S_f$ in Eq. (20-16) and solving for $V$,

$$V = \sqrt{\frac{16.1 S_0\,\Delta t - K}{7.25 n^2\,\Delta t}}\, R^{2/3} \tag{20-23}$$

From Eqs. (20-22) and (20-23), the values of $V$ and $K$ can be determined.

The solution for $c$ and $V$, however, can be simplified by a graphical procedure. Taking the wide channel as an example, $R = y = c^2/g$. Thus, Eq. (20-23) becomes

$$V = \sqrt{\frac{16.1 S_0\,\Delta t - K}{742 n^2\,\Delta t}}\, c^{4/3} \tag{20-24}$$

The units in this equation are expressed in terms of feet and seconds.

For units in miles and hours, the equation becomes

$$V = \sqrt{\frac{39{,}500 S_0 \, \Delta t - K}{1{,}410{,}000 n^2 \, \Delta t}} \, c^{\frac{2}{3}} \qquad (20\text{-}25)$$

Equation (20-24) or (20-25) contains three variables $c$, $V$, and $K$; $S_0$ and $\Delta t$ are known. For this equation, two auxiliary plots may be constructed: (1) a plot of $c$ against $V$ using $K$ as a parameter, which is called "the

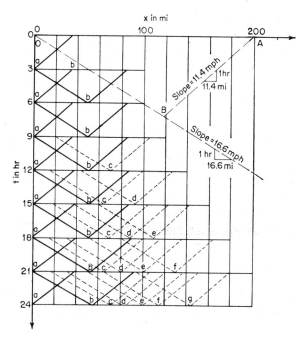

FIG 20-2a. Routing by the method of characteristics: the $xt$ plane.

plot of $c$ vs. $V$ for $K$" (Fig. 20-2e), and (2) a plot of $V - K$ against $V$ using $c$ as a parameter, which is called "the plot of $V - K$ vs. $V$ for $c$" (Fig. 20-2f). The use of these two plots will simplify the problem, which is to solve for $c$ and $V$ at time $t + \Delta t$ if the flow conditions $c$ and $V$ at the upstream and downstream sections at time $t$ are given.

In illustrating the application of the graphical procedure, it is assumed (1) that the channel is infinitely long and very wide, (2) that the initial flow is uniform and steady, and (3) that the time interval $\Delta t$ is constant. The data required for the solution include the initial flow condition, the inflow hydrograph[1] with the stage $y$ expressed as a function of time $t$, the channel roughness, the channel slope, and the length of the channel to be routed. The whole procedure is to be developed by steps at equal time

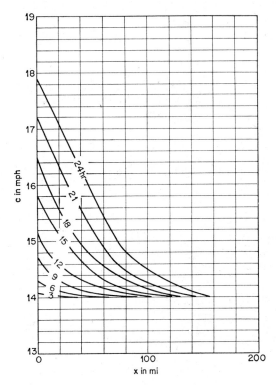

FIG. 20-2b. Routing by the method of characteristics: the $cx$ plane.

intervals. For any step, the procedure is as follows:

### A. Preliminary Computation

1. Compute the initial velocity $V_n$ and depth $y_n$ by the Manning formula, and the initial celerity by $c_n = \sqrt{gy_n}$.

2. Using Eq. (20-24) or (20-25) construct the plot of $c$ vs. $V$ for $K$ (Fig. 20-2e) and the plot of $V - K$ vs. $V$ for $c$ (Fig. 20-2f).

3. Construct the reference lines $OB$ and $AB$ (Fig. 20-1 and Fig. 20-2a).

---

[1] For other types of hydrograph, for example, in the form of the discharge $q = f(t)$, a modification of the procedure is necessary. For a detailed discussion, see [23].

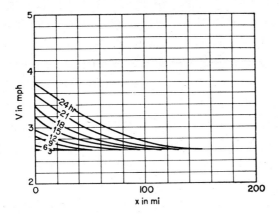

FIG. 20-2c. Routing by the method of characteristics: the $Vx$ plane.

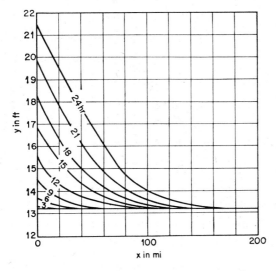

FIG. 20-2d. Routing by the method of characteristics: the $yx$ plane.

The slopes of these lines are equal to $V_n + c_n$ and $V_n - c_n$, respectively. Point $O$ may be placed at any position on the $x$ axis.

4. Construct the inflow hydrograph with $c$ plotted against $t$ (Fig. 20-2g). Since the given hydrograph is in the form of $y = f(t)$, it is necessary to convert $y$ to $c$ by the relation $c = \sqrt{gy}$.

5. Obtain the values of $c$ for various $t$ from the hydrograph constructed

in the preceding step, and plot them on the $cx$ plane at $x = 0$ (Fig. 20-2b). Also, plot the value of $V_n$ on the $Vx$ plane at $x = 0$ (Fig. 20-2c).

### B. Computation for Flow Condition at the Inflow

1. Draw a trial characteristic $p'd'$ (Fig. 20-1a) with a slope in the general direction of $AB$. From the inflow hydrograph (Fig. 20-2g), it can be

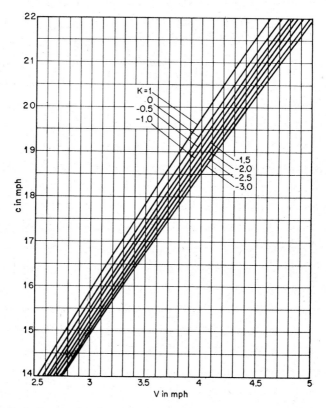

Fig. 20-2e. Routing by the method of characteristics: the $c$ vs. $V$ for $K$ plot.

seen whether the value of $c$ is increasing or decreasing at a given time. Accordingly, the slope of the trial characteristic should be either flatter or steeper than that of the previous step.

2. The values of $c$ and $V$ at time $t$ are assumed to have been determined and plotted against $x$, as shown in Fig. 20-2b and c. Accordingly, at the point where the trial characteristic intersects the horizontal line passing

through the time $t$ (Fig. 20-1$a$), the values of $c_d$ and $V_d$ are equal to the values of $c$ and $V$ at time $t$.

3. From the plot of $c$ vs. $V$ for $K$ (Fig. 20-2$e$), find the $K_d$ corresponding to $V_d$ and $c_d$, and then compute $G_d$ by Eq. (20-18).

4. Compute $V - K$ by Eq. (20-22) with the value of $c$ obtained from the inflow hydrograph (Fig. 20-2$g$).

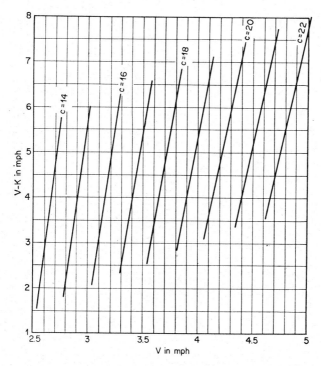

Fig. 20-2$f$. Routing by the method of characteristics: the $V - K$ vs. $V$ for $c$ plot.

5. Determine $V$ from the plot of $V - K$ vs. $V$ for $c$ (Fig. 20-2$f$).

6. Since the values of $c$ and $V$ are known, check the slope of the trial characteristic. The slope of this characteristic should be equal to the average of the slopes at its ends, or $[(V - c) + (V_d - c_d)]/2$. If necessary, repeat the procedure with a new trial characteristic until a satisfactory check is obtained.

*C. Computation of Flow Condition in the Channel*

1. Construct two trial characteristics $up$ and $pd$ at point $p$ and in the general directions of $OB$ and $AB$, respectively (Fig. 20-1$b$). To start

the computation, the point $p$ may be so located that the point $u$ is at $x = 0$ on the horizontal line passing through the time $t$.

2. From the $cx$ and $Vx$ planes of the previous computations (Figs. 20-2$b$ and 20-2$c$), determine $c_u$ and $V_u$ at $x_u$ and $c_d$ and $V_d$ at $x_d$ (Fig. 20-1$b$).

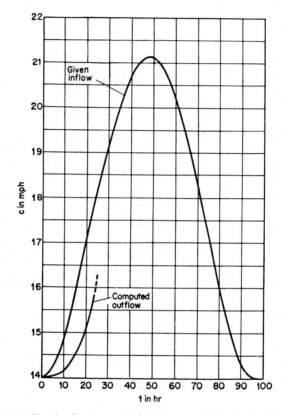

FIG. 20-2$g$. Routing by the method of characteristics: the hydrographs.

3. Determine $K_u$ and $K_d$ from the plot of $c$ vs. $V$ for $K$ (Figs. 20-2$e$).
4. Compute $G_u$ and $G_d$ by Eqs. (20-14) and (20-18), respectively.
5. Compute $c$ by Eq. (20-20).
6. Compute $V - K$ by Eq. (20-21).
7. Determine $V$ from the plot of $V - K$ vs. $V$ for $c$ (Fig. 20-2$f$).

8. With the flow conditions determined at a sufficient number of points along the channel, construct the plots of $V$ and $c$ vs. $x$ at the time $t + \Delta t$ on the $cx$ and $Vx$ planes (Figs. 20-2$b$ and 20-2$c$).

9. Extend the procedure step by step to the desired lengths of time and channel.

10. From the $cx$ plane, a hydrograph at any section of the channel can be constructed. Constructing a vertical line through the given $x$, the line will intersect the curves of the $cx$ plane, giving values of $c$ at different $t$. The value of $c$ may then be converted to $y$ by the relation $y = c^2/g$.

**Example 20-1.** An infinitely long and wide channel carries an initial uniform flow of 50 cfs per foot of width.[1] If a hydrograph represented by $y = 21.5 - 8.4 \cos (\pi t/48)$ ft is imposed on the upstream end of the channel, route the flood through the first 50 miles for a period of 24 hr. Given $n = 0.03$ and $S_0 = 1/5,280$.

*Solution.* The computation follows the procedure described above.

*A. Preliminary computation*

1. By the Manning formula, $y_n = 13.1$ ft. Thus, $V_n = 50/13.1 = 3.82$ fps $= 2.60$ mph, and $c_n = \sqrt{13.1g} = 20.6$ fps $= 14.0$ mph.

2. Using the mile-hour units, $\Delta t = 3$ hr, $n = 0.03$, and $S_0 = 1/5,280$. Equation (20-25) gives

$$V = \sqrt{\frac{22.4 - K}{3,810}} \, c^{\frac{5}{3}} \qquad (20\text{-}26)$$

By this equation, the auxiliary plots (Fig. 20-2e and $f$) are computed as shown in Table 20-1, p. 600.

3. On the $xt$ plane (Fig. 20-2a) construct the reference lines $OB$ and $AB$, the slopes of which are $2.60 + 14.0 = 16.6$ mph and $2.60 - 14.0 = -11.4$ mph, respectively.

4. Construct the inflow hydrograph (Fig. 20-2g) by the following equation:

$$c = \sqrt{gy} = \sqrt{g[21.5 - 8.4 \cos (\pi t/48)]} \text{ fps}$$
$$= 3.87 \sqrt{21.5 - 8.4 \cos (\pi t/48)} \text{ mph} \qquad (20\text{-}27)$$

5. By Eq. (20-27), compute the values of $c$ at the upstream end of the channel (at $x = 0$) for $t = 0, 3, \ldots, 24$ hr, and plot them in Fig. 20-2b. Also, plot the value of $V = 2.60$ mph for $x = 0$ and $t = 0$ in Fig. 20-2c.

*B. Computation for flow condition at inflow.* The step of computation from $t = 12$ to $t = 18$ hr will be taken for illustration, assuming that the values of $c$ and $V$ along the channel at $t = 12$ hr have been determined in a previous step. The following procedure describes the determination of $c$ and $V$ at the inflow at $t = 18$ hr.

1. Draw a trial characteristic at point $15a$ in the general direction of $AB$ (Fig. 20-2a). The slope of this characteristic should be somewhat flatter than that of the previous step, that is, flatter than the slope of the characteristic at $12a$, because the inflow hydrograph (Fig. 20-2g) indicates that $c$ is increasing during the interval from $t = 12$ to $15$ hr. The downstream end of this characteristic is at $t = 12$ hr and $x_d = 36$ miles.

2. With $x_d = 36$ miles and $t = 12$ hr, find $c_d = 14.38$ and $V_d = 2.72$ from Figs. 20-2b and c. These values are entered in cols. 9 and 8, respectively, of Table 20-2.

3. With $c_d = 14.38$ and $V_d = 2.72$, find $K_d = -0.64$ from Fig. 20-2e, and enter the value in col. 10 of Table 20-2. By Eq. (20-18), $G_d = 2.72 - 2 \times 14.38 - 0.64 = -26.68$, as shown in col. 12 of Table 20-2.

[1] This example is adapted from [23].

4. From the inflow hydrograph (Fig. 20-2$g$), $c = 15.84$ for $t = 15$. By Eq. (20-22), $V - K = -26.68 + 2 \times 15.84 = 5.00$, as shown in col. 13 of Table 20-2.

5. With $V - K = 5.00$ and $c = 15.84$, find $V = 3.19$ from Fig. 20-2$f$ and enter the value in col. 2 of Table 20-2.

6. The slope of the characteristic should be $(2.72 - 14.38 + 3.19 - 15.84)/2 = -12.16$, which gives $x_d = 12.16 \times 3 = 36.48$ miles. This value is close to $x_d = 36$ miles for the trial characteristic. If the agreement is not close, a new trial characteristic must be drawn and the computation repeated.

### C. Computation for flow condition in the channel

1. Draw two trial characteristics at 15$b$ in the general directions of $OB$ and $AB$. Note that the characteristic in the direction of $OB$ starts from the point 12$a$. Thus, $x_u = 0$, $x = 52$ miles, and $x_d = 86$ miles.

2. From Figs. 20-2$b$ and $c$, find $c_u = 15.22$ and $V_u = 2.96$ at $x_u = 0$, and $c_d = 14.02$ and $V_d = 2.59$ at $x_d = 86$ miles. Enter these values in cols. 5 to 8 of Table 20-2.

3. From Fig. 20-2$e$, find $K_u = -1.08$, as shown in col. 7 of Table 20-2, for $c_u = 15.22$ and $V_u = 2.96$; and also $K_d = 0$, as shown in col. 10, for $c_d = 14.02$ and $V_d = 2.59$.

4. By Eq. (20-14), $G_u = 2.96 + 2 \times 15.22 - 1.08 = 32.32$, as shown in col. 11 of Table 20-2. By Eq. (20-18), $G_d = 2.59 - 2 \times 14.02 - 0 = -25.45$, as shown in col. 12 of Table 20-2.

5. By Eq. (20-20), $c = (32.32 + 25.45)/4 = 14.44$, as shown in col. 3 of Table 20-2.

6. By Eq. (20-21), $V - K = (32.32 - 25.45)/2 = 3.44$, as shown in col. 13 of Table 20-2.

7. From Fig. 20-2$f$, find $V = 2.75$, as shown in col. 2 of Table 20-2, for $c = 14.44$ and $V - K = 3.44$.

8. Use the values of $c$ and $V$ to check the slopes of the trial characteristics. Thus, $x = (2.75 + 14.44) \times 3 = 51.57$ miles and $x_d = -(2.75 - 14.44) \times 3 + 51.57 = 86.64$ miles. The trial slopes are satisfactory. Otherwise, new characteristics should be drawn and the computation repeated.

9. Proceed with the computation step by step, as shown in Table 20-2.

10. Draw a vertical line at $x = 50$ miles on the $cx$ plane (Fig. 20-2$b$). The line intersects the curves, giving values of $c$ at various times. Plotting these values of $c$ against time, a hydrograph at $x = 50$ miles for a period of 24 hr is obtained, as shown in Fig. 20-2$g$. This hydrograph can be converted to $y = f(t)$ by means of the relation $y = c^2/g$.

It may be noted that, after the flow conditions at points $a$ and $b$ for each time interval are determined, part of the curves on the $cx$ plane and $Vx$ plane for the first 50 miles or so can be traced in approximately and then revised or refined by further determination of more points, such as $c$ and $d$, in the channel. It can be seen that the graphical procedure offers a practical solution of Massau's equations. Nevertheless, the computation involved is still complicated and requires practice for routine applications. For accurate solutions, the time interval $\Delta t$ should be reduced, all graphs should be prepared on large scales, and the computation should be carried out to sufficient significant figures. For Table 20-2, the computation was done on a slide rule, since the example was given only for illustrative purposes. The values in cols. 7 and 10 were roughly estimated from the curves; they are not accurate even to the decimal places shown. For accurate computation of $K$, Eqs. (20-15) and (20-19) should have been used.

In this particular example of a long uniform channel with initially uniform flow, it may be assumed that the values of $c$ and $V$ at a particular section of the wave profile do not change.   In other words, the flow may be considered uniformly progressive after the flow conditions at points $a$ and $b$ are determined.   This may be explained in Fig. 20-3 as below.

On the $cx$ plane, draw a horizontal line passing through the $t = 9$ hr curve at $x = 0$. This line intersects the $t = 12$ hr curve at $x = 13$ miles.   Similarly, a horizontal line

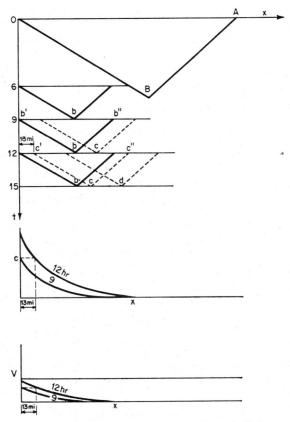

Fig. 20-3. Simplified procedure for Example 20-1.

on the $Vx$ plane is drawn through the $t = 9$ hr curve at $x = 0$.   This line intersects the $t = 12$ hr curve also at $x = 13$ miles.   It is, therefore, evident that values of $c$ and $V$ at the points ($t = 9$ hr, $x = 0$) and ($t = 12$ hr, $x = 13$ miles) are equal.   This evidence may simplify the further steps of the routing computation.   The dashed characteristics $cc'$ and $cc''$ at $15c$ may be drawn parallel to the characteristics $bb'$ and $bb''$, respectively, at $12b$.   The upstream point $c'$ of the characteristic $cc'$ is placed at $x = 13$ miles on the 12-hr line.   Thus, the values of $c$ and $V$ at $15c$ are equal to those at $12b$.   Similarly, the values of $c$ and $V$ at points $9b$, $12c$, and $15d$ are all equal and can be determined in the same way.   As a result, the computation of the values of $c$

and $V$ is needed only at point $a$ at the inflow and at point $b$ in the channel for each time interval. The values of $c$ and $V$ at other points in the channel can be determined by the simplified procedure shown by the dashed lines in Fig. 20-2a.

TABLE 20-1. COMPUTATION FOR THE AUXILIARY PLOTS IN EXAMPLE 20-1

| $K$ | $\sqrt{\dfrac{22.4 - K}{3,810}}$ | $c = 14,$ $c^{5/3} = 33.7$ | | $c = 16,$ $c^{5/3} = 40.3$ | | $c = 18,$ $c^{5/3} = 47.2$ | | $c = 20,$ $c^{5/3} = 54.3$ | | $c = 22,$ $c^{5/3} = 61.6$ | |
|---|---|---|---|---|---|---|---|---|---|---|---|
| | | $V$ | $V - K$ | $V$ | $V - K$ | $V$ | $V - K$ | $V$ | $V - K$ | $V$ | $V - K$ |
| 1.0 | 0.0750 | 2.53 | 1.53 | 3.03 | 2.03 | 3.54 | 2.54 | 4.07 | 3.07 | 4.63 | 3.63 |
| 0.0 | 0.0766 | 2.58 | 2.58 | 3.09 | 3.09 | 3.62 | 3.62 | 4.16 | 4.16 | 4.73 | 4.73 |
| −0.5 | 0.0776 | 2.62 | 3.12 | 3.13 | 3.63 | 3.66 | 4.16 | 4.22 | 4.72 | 4.78 | 5.28 |
| −1.0 | 0.0784 | 2.64 | 3.64 | 3.16 | 4.16 | 3.70 | 4.70 | 4.25 | 5.25 | 4.83 | 5.83 |
| −1.5 | 0.0792 | 2.67 | 4.17 | 3.20 | 4.70 | 3.74 | 5.24 | 4.30 | 5.80 | 4.88 | 6.38 |
| −2.0 | 0.0800 | 2.70 | 4.70 | 3.23 | 5.23 | 3.78 | 5.78 | 4.34 | 6.34 | 4.93 | 6.93 |
| −2.5 | 0.0809 | 2.73 | 5.23 | 3.26 | 5.76 | 3.82 | 6.32 | 4.39 | 6.89 | 4.99 | 7.49 |
| −3.0 | 0.0816 | 2.75 | 5.75 | 3.29 | 6.29 | 3.85 | 6.85 | 4.43 | 7.43 | 5.03 | 8.03 |

TABLE 20-2. STEP COMPUTATIONS OF FLOOD ROUTING BY THE METHOD OF CHARACTERISTICS

| Point | $V$ | $c$ | $K$ | $V_u$ | $c_u$ | $K_u$ | $V_d$ | $c_d$ | $K_d$ | $G_u$ | $G_d$ | $V - K$ |
|---|---|---|---|---|---|---|---|---|---|---|---|---|
| (1) | (2) | (3) | (4) | (5) | (6) | (7) | (8) | (9) | (10) | (11) | (12) | (13) |
| 3a | 2.61 | 14.07 | −0.11 | .... | ..... | ...... | 2.58 | 14.00 | 0 | ..... | −25.42 | 2.72 |
| 6a | 2.69 | 14.31 | −0.48 | .... | ..... | ...... | 2.59 | 14.02 | 0 | ..... | −25.45 | 3.17 |
| 6b | 2.60 | 14.02 | −0.01 | 2.61 | 14.07 | −0.11 | 2.58 | 14.00 | 0 | 30.64 | −24.42 | 2.61 |
| 9a | 2.86 | 14.71 | −0.69 | .... | ..... | ...... | 2.62 | 14.05 | −0.39 | ..... | −25.87 | 3.55 |
| 9b | 2.61 | 14.06 | −0.10 | 2.69 | 14.31 | −0.48 | 2.58 | 14.00 | 0 | 30.83 | −25.42 | 2.71 |
| 12a | 2.96 | 15.22 | −1.08 | .... | ..... | ...... | 2.67 | 14.16 | −0.75 | ..... | −26.40 | 4.04 |
| 12b | 2.68 | 14.25 | −0.40 | 2.86 | 14.71 | −0.69 | 2.58 | 14.00 | 0 | 31.59 | −25.42 | 3.08 |
| 15a | 3.19 | 15.84 | −1.81 | .... | ..... | ...... | 2.72 | 14.38 | −0.64 | ..... | −26.68 | 5.00 |
| 15b | 2.75 | 14.44 | −0.69 | 2.96 | 15.22 | −1.08 | 2.59 | 14.02 | 0 | 32.32 | −25.45 | 3.44 |
| 18a | 3.38 | 16.51 | −1.91 | .... | ..... | ...... | 2.83 | 14.68 | −1.20 | ..... | −27.73 | 5.29 |
| 18b | 2.82 | 14.72 | −0.83 | 3.19 | 15.85 | −1.81 | 2.62 | 14.08 | −0.24 | 33.08 | −25.78 | 3.65 |
| 21a | 3.59 | 17.21 | −2.34 | .... | ..... | ...... | 2.93 | 15.02 | −1.40 | ..... | −28.51 | 5.93 |
| 21b | 2.98 | 15.23 | −1.06 | 3.38 | 16.51 | −1.91 | 2.68 | 14.22 | −0.65 | 34.49 | −26.41 | 4.04 |
| 24a | 3.79 | 17.90 | −2.49 | .... | ..... | ...... | 3.08 | 15.55 | −1.50 | ..... | −29.52 | 6.28 |
| 24b | 3.08 | 15.55 | −1.49 | 3.59 | 17.21 | −2.34 | 2.70 | 14.32 | −0.60 | 35.67 | −26.54 | 4.57 |

Similar numerical methods for the solution of the differential equations of unsteady flow [Eqs. (20-1) to (20-4)] were developed by Stoker [16,17] and by Isaacson, Stoker, and Troesch [32,33]. The methods were applied with satisfactory results to three actual problems presented by the U.S. Army Corps of Engineers [34]: (1) movement of the 1945 flood in the 375-mile reach of the Ohio River from Wheeling, W.Va., to Cincinnati,

Ohio; (2) movement of the 1947 flood through the confluence of the Ohio and Mississippi rivers at Cairo, Ill.; and (3) movement of the 1948 and 1950 flood waves in the 184-mile long and narrow Kentucky Reservoir on the Lower Tennessee River. The second problem is the same as that described in Art. 11-10 and Fig. 11-15 except that the flow is treated as unsteady in the present problem. The computations for flow profiles were thus made for times $t = 0, 2.5, 4, 10$, and $\infty$ hr, after the beginning of the flood 50 miles up the Ohio River (see Fig. 11-15). The flow profiles for $t = \infty$ are identical with those computed for steady flow.

Solution of practical problems by the numerical method is generally very tedious. In order to speed up the computation work, the Corps has employed an electronic digital computer, such as the Remington-Rand UNIVAC I (Universal Automatic Computer I). For small quantities of work, however, the Corps has found that a part of the computation can be performed less expensively and more efficiently by a portable computer, such as the Burroughs E101 desk-size computer; the use of larger machines is justifiable only for very involved problems.

**20-3. Method of Diffusion Analogy.** An approximate hydraulic approach to the problem of flood routing in natural channels has been developed using the classical statistical theory of flow diffusion [35]. According to this theory, a differential equation may be written for the diffusion of an unsteady flow of particles as follows:

$$\frac{\partial N}{\partial t} = K \frac{\partial^2 N}{\partial x^2} \tag{20-28}$$

where $N$ is the number of particles, $t$ is the time, $x$ is the distance, and $K$ is a coefficient known as *diffusivity*. When the particles are flowing in a direction along the $x$ axis, this equation gives the particle distribution in the direction of flow as a function of time and position. This theory is commonly applied to problems of heat transfer [36]; there Eq. (20-28) represents *Fourier's general law of heat conduction*, in which $N$ designates temperature and $K$ is known as *thermal diffusivity* [37].

In natural streams, the disturbances of flow caused by local channel irregularities have definite magnitude at any time and position. They are mixed, dissipated, and diffused as the flow moves along the channel. In applying the theory of flow diffusion to the flow of water, it may be assumed that the diffusion of the disturbances is analogous to the diffusion of the particles. If the over-all effect of the disturbances on flow is represented by the variation in the flow depth $y$, Eq. (20-28) may be written

$$\frac{\partial y}{\partial t} = K \frac{\partial^2 y}{\partial x^2} \tag{20-29}$$

In natural streams the local irregularities provide irregular storage, and the above equation reflects the rate of change in channel storage due to irregularities. Including this item in Eq. (18-1) for continuity of flow in prismatic channels, the continuity equation for flow in natural channels may be written

$$\frac{\partial y}{\partial t} + \frac{\partial q}{\partial x} = K \frac{\partial^2 y}{\partial x^2} \tag{20-30}$$

It is assumed further that the channel is relatively wide and that the flow on the average is uniform and steady. Thus, the discharge per unit width of channel may be represented by the Chézy formula[1]

$$q = C \sqrt{S_0}\, y^{3/2} \tag{20-31}$$

Substituting this equation for $q$ in Eq. (20-30) and simplifying,

$$\frac{\partial y}{\partial t} + C \sqrt{S_0}\, \frac{\partial y^{3/2}}{\partial x} = K \frac{\partial^2 y}{\partial x^2} \tag{20-32}$$

This is the *basic differential equation for flood flow in natural streams*. It can be seen that the coefficient of $\partial y^{3/2}/\partial x$ in this equation depends on the channel resistance and slope and that the coefficient of $\partial^2 y/\partial x^2$ depends on the channel irregularities.

This equation was originally developed by Hayami [38] through an elaborate mathematical derivation. A similar method of routing based on diffusion analogy was also presented by Appleby [39]. The value of diffusivity $K$ in ordinary streams was estimated in the range from $10^6$ to $10^7$ cm²/sec. In large rivers, such as the Mississippi River in the United States and the Yangtse River in China, the value of $K$ would be of the order of $10^8$ cm²/sec.

A solution of Eq. (20-32) by Hayami results in the following equation for the propagation of a flood wave:

$$\frac{y - y_n}{y_0} = 1 - \frac{2}{\sqrt{\pi}} \int_0^{x/2\sqrt{Kt}} \exp\left[ \frac{V_w x}{2K} - X^2 - \left(\frac{V_w x}{4KX}\right)^2 \right] dX \tag{20-33}$$

where $y$ is the depth at a point a distance $x$ from the upstream end of the reach under consideration, $y_n$ is the normal depth of flow at the same point before the flood arrives, $y_0$ is the depth at the upstream end, $t$ is the time, $K$ is the diffusivity, $V_w = 1.5V$, $V$ is the mean velocity, and $X$ is the variable.

A fictitious wave having a constant depth and lasting a unit time interval $\Delta t$ may be assumed (Fig. 20-4). This wave is called a *unit flood*.

---

[1] The Manning formula may also be used. In this case, the second term on the left side of Eq. (20-32) would be written $(1.49 \sqrt{S_0}/n)\partial y^{5/3}/\partial x$.

The propagation of this unit flood may be determined by Eq. (20-33). As a numerical example, using $V_w = 70$ cm/sec; $K = 10^7$ cm²/sec; $\Delta t = 5$ hr; and $x = 2.2, 14, 21,$ and $32$ km, Hayami has computed the propagation of the unit flood, as shown in Fig. 20-4. It can be seen that,

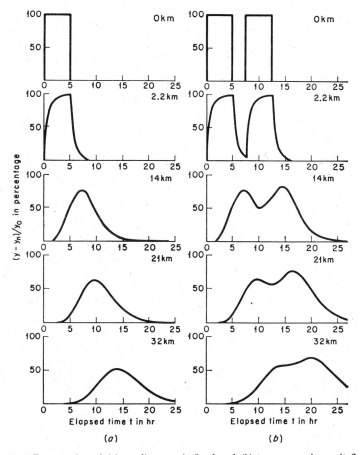

FIG. 20-4. Propagation of (a) a solitary unit flood and (b) two successive unit floods. (*After S. Hayami* [38].)

as the wave propagates downstream, its shape gradually becomes asymmetrical and flattens out.

In routing an actual flood, the hydrograph of the flood may be divided into a number of unit flood hydrographs (Fig. 20-5). All hydrographs are plotted with the time against the stage. The propagation of each unit flood can be computed by Eq. (20-33). By the principle of superposition, the propagated height of the given flood is equal to the sum of the propagated heights of all the unit floods. This method has been used to compute the propagation of a unit flood artificially produced in the Yedo River in Japan; the theoretical computations were found in good agreement with the observations. In order to simplify and expedite the routing procedure by this method, electronic analog computers have been developed on the basis of Eq. (20-32) and applied to several rivers in Japan with satisfactory results [40–44].

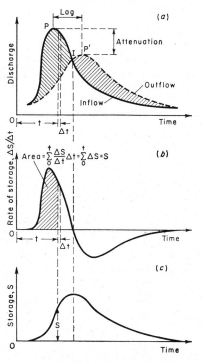

FIG. 20-6. Relationships among inflow, outflow, and storage in a channel reach due to a passing flood.

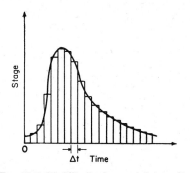

FIG. 20-5. Dividing hydrograph into unit-flood hydrographs.

**20-4. Principle of Hydrologic Routing.** When a flood wave passes through a channel reach, the inflow and outflow hydrographs at the upstream and downstream ends of the reach, respectively, are as shown in Fig. 20-6a. Assuming a negligible amount of loss or gain of water in the course of flow through the reach, the total areas under the hydrographs are equal, since the volume of the flood water is unchanged. In natural streams, the channel resistance and storage capacity are high; consequently the flood-wave characteristics will be considerably modified. As shown in Fig. 20-6a, the flood peak is attenuated and delayed. The difference between the ordinates of the inflow and outflow hydrographs, represented by the shaded areas in the figure, is equal to the rate of storage of water in the reach; that is,

$$\frac{\Delta S}{\Delta t} = I - O \qquad (20\text{-}34)$$

where $\Delta S / \Delta t$ is the change in storage during a period $\Delta t$, $I$ is the average inflow during $\Delta t$, and $O$ is the average outflow during $\Delta t$. The value of $\Delta S / \Delta t$ is positive when the storage is increasing and negative when the storage is decreasing. This equation constitutes the basis for a hydrologic procedure of routing in which $\Delta t$ is known as the *routing period*.

The rate of storage can be plotted against time, as shown in Fig. 20-6b, from which it can be seen that the storage is increasing before the time at which the inflow equals the outflow and decreasing after that time. The cumulative area below the storage-rate curve (shaded area in the figure) represents the volume of storage at a time $t$ after the beginning of the flood. By plotting this volume against the time, a storage-volume curve can be obtained, as shown in Fig. 20-6c. This curve has a peak representing the maximum volume of storage that occurs at the time when the inflow equals the outflow.

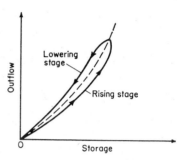

FIG. 20-7. The storage-outflow relationship.

If the storage is plotted against the outflow discharge, the resulting curve will generally take the form of a loop, such as that illustrated in Fig. 20-7. As shown in this figure, the storage for a given discharge on the rising (or falling) part of the flood wave will be greater than (or less than) the storage corresponding to the condition of steady flow. The storage-outflow relationship for the condition of steady flow is represented by the dashed curve, which is approximately at the average position of the two limbs of the loop.

The storage in a channel reach for unsteady flow depends primarily on the inflow and outflow discharges and on the geometric and hydraulic characteristics of the channel and its control features. It can be assumed that the upstream and downstream end sections of the reach have the same mean discharge and storage relationships with respect to the depth of flow $y$. Then the following equations may be written:

$$I = ay^n \tag{20-35}$$
$$O = ay^n \tag{20-36}$$
and
$$S_i = by^m \tag{20-37}$$
$$S_o = by^m \tag{20-38}$$

where $a$ and $n$ express the depth-discharge characteristics of the sections, $b$ and $m$ express the mean depth–storage characteristics of the reach, and $S_i$ and $S_o$ are the storages referring to the depths at the upstream and downstream end sections respectively. Eliminating $y$ from Eqs. (20-35) and (20-37) and from Eqs. (20-36) and (20-38),

$$S_i = b \left(\frac{I}{a}\right)^{m/n} \qquad (20\text{-}39)$$

and

$$S_o = b \left(\frac{O}{a}\right)^{m/n} \qquad (20\text{-}40)$$

Let $X$ be a dimensionless factor that defines the relative weights given to inflow and outflow in the determination of the storage volume within the reach. Then, the storage at any given time may be expressed as

$$S = XS_i + (1 - X)S_o \qquad (20\text{-}41)$$

When the stages in a reach are determined by the control at its down-stream end, for example, at the spillway of a level-pool reservoir, the storage is a sole function of the outflow; therefore, $X = 0$. If the storage due to backwater effect at the upstream end of the reservoir is significant, $X$ will be greater than zero. In uniform channels, equal weight is given to inflow and outflow, and $X = 0.5$.

Substituting Eqs. (20-39) and (20-40) for $S_i$ and $S_o$, respectively, in Eq. (20-41) and simplifying,

$$S = K[XI^x + (1 - X)O^x] \qquad (20\text{-}42)$$

where $K = b/a^{m/n}$ and $x = m/n$. In prismatic rectangular channels, discharge varies with the five-thirds power of the depth on the basis of the Manning formula, and storage varies with the first power. Since $n = \frac{5}{3}$ and $m = 1$, the exponent $x = 0.6$. In natural channels, $m$ may be considerably greater than unity and hence $x$ is larger than 0.6. Many hydrologic routing procedures have been developed on the general basis of Eq. (20-42). For simplicity and for practical purposes, $x$ is commonly assumed to be unity.

The hydrologic approach to the problem of flood routing is based on the storage-discharge relationship described above. It is assumed that dynamic effects of flow are negligible and that storage is a single-valued function of discharge. This assumption implies that the flow is changing slowly with time. Effects of abnormal surface slope in modifying discharge and in changing channel storage are, therefore, neglected.

This procedure is approximately correct for ordinary streams with small slopes. When storage is plotted against discharge, the resulting loop is usually narrow and an average curve may be fitted in to represent the storage as a single-valued function of the discharge. If the loop is wide, it can be reduced to a single-line relationship by an adjustment such as that employed in the Muskingum method [45]. In this method the adjustment is made possible by varying the values of $K$ and $X$ in Eq. (20-42).

In streams having steep slopes, the dynamic effects of flow are pronounced and cannot be neglected. Consequently, for such streams the hydrologic method of flood routing may be found unsatisfactory.

**20-5. Methods of Hydrologic Routing.** Numerous hydrologic methods of flood routing have been developed. Descriptions of these methods can be found in the literature on engineering hydrology [45–50]. In this article, therefore, the important methods will be mentioned only by name and references will be provided for further study. A simple hydrologic method, however, will be described in the next article.

In general, hydrologic methods of flood routing may be classified into two groups: the analytical and the instrumental.

There are many analytical methods of routing. For routing through reservoirs, the well-known Rippl mass curve [51] is widely used [52–54]. Other graphical methods of routing have also been developed, such as the method of Sorensen [55,56]. For routing through rivers, the storage-discharge relationship is simplified in the methods developed by Meyer [57], Puls [47,58,59], Wilson [60], Cheng [61], Johnstone and Cross [54], Knappen, Stratton, and Davis [56], and Chow [62]. Semigraphical procedures include the methods of Goodrich [63], Rutter, Graves, and Snyder [64], Wisler and Brater [65], and Steinberg [66]. Other simplified methods use a nomograph, as suggested by Linsley [67], a straight slide rule as suggested by Posey [68,69], and circular computers as suggested by Shepley and Walton [70]. A simplified method of successive average was developed by Tatum [48,71]. One rather popular and satisfactory method, known as *the Muskingum method* was developed by McCarthy [46,72]. In this method, Eq. (20-42) is used as the working equation, assuming $x = 1$; that is,

$$S = K[XI + (1 - X)O] \qquad (20\text{-}43)$$

where $K$ and $X$ are to be determined from the channel characteristics under study.

In flood forecasting or control and operation of multiple-purpose river projects, the stage of flood is a major concern and a procedure for *stage routing* is needed. For this purpose, a method involving the use of multiple-line charts was proposed by Lane [73]. An improved procedure was later developed by Kohler [74], which requires one chart for determining the normal relationship between gages in the main river and auxiliary charts, one for each tributary. These charts can be used to determine corrections to be applied to the predicted normal stage. The U.S. Mississippi River Commission [75] has used the Puls method of stage routing. For accurate prediction of stages on very flat rivers, a method of stage routing was suggested by Ray and Mondschein [76].

In connection with the design of levees for flood control, the routing

UNSTEADY FLOW

technique should be extended to solve the problem of so-called *flow-line computation*. This problem is to estimate the maximum elevation of the water surface at all points along the leveed channel during the passage of a design flood. Once this elevation is determined, the height of the levees is given by adding a suitable freeboard. For such purposes, a simple method of calculation was developed by W. M. Mulholland [46].

FIG. 20-8. Electronic flood-routing analog. (*Courtesy of M. A. Kohler, U.S. Weather Bureau.*)

In order to speed up routing operations, instrumental routing becomes necessary. For this purpose, two kinds of routing machines have been developed: the mechanical and the electronic.

Mechanical routing machines are usually designed for reservoir routing. The U.S. Army Corps of Engineers has constructed two types: an integrating machine designed by Tarpley [77] and a rolling-type flood router by Harkness [78; 45, pp. 674–676].

Electronic routing machines are electronic analog and digital computers. The principle of the electronic analog is to utilize the analogy between the flow of current in an electric circuit and the flow of water in a channel or river system. In other words, an electric circuit can be constructed with its circuit equation analogous to the routing equation.

The U.S. Weather Bureau [79–81,48] has developed an electronic analog, shown in Fig. 20-8. This machine automatically produces the outflow hydrograph while the operator traces the inflow hydrograph with a stylus. Resistances in the electric circuit can be adjusted to simulate the conditions for each reach of the river, as determined from past floods. The model illustrated in the figure has two inflow positions,

Fig. 20-9. GEDA flood computer. (*Courtesy of E. E. Abbott, U.S. Army Corps of Engineers.*)

allowing processing of two sources of inflow affecting the final outflow downstream. More positions can be added, if necessary. In other words, the machine also does flood synthesis. The use of such a machine has a decided advantage over analytical methods in that it solves the routing equation in differential rather than incremental form. Incremental form is often unavoidable in analytical methods. Furthermore, the entire hydrograph can be routed more rapidly. than by analytical computation.

Similarly, the U.S. Army Corps of Engineers uses a GEDA (Goodyear Electronic Differential Analyzer, Fig. 20-9) in preliminary studies of flood projects and in routing flood through reservoirs.

**20-6. A Simple Hydrologic Method of Routing.** The method to be described here is approximate but simple and suitable for practical purposes. Like most hydrologic methods of routing, this method is based on the following assumptions:

1. The channel is divided into a number of reaches. Each reach is relatively short and has practically constant physical characteristics. The flood is then routed successively from reach to reach. In general, the shortest practical reach is the section between the two nearest gaging stations.

2. The discharge data are given at equal time intervals or routing periods. Within this period the increase or decrease of inflow and outflow is assumed to vary linearly. A short routing period is preferable but will multiply the labor of computation.

3. The inflow and outflow are both taken as a measure of storage in the reach. This assumption is almost true if a flood is being routed through a level-pool reservoir where the variation in storage between the falling and rising stages of the flood wave is not appreciable. In the case of a stream, the length of a reach for routing must not be too long or these variations will be exaggerated. Theoretically, the length of the reach should not exceed the product of the routing period and the average velocity of the flow in the reach (why?), although it has been found in many cases that reaches considerably longer are permissible [54, pp. 173–175].

4. The flow in the reach, local accretions from ungaged tributary flows, ground water, rainfall or any form of precipitation, and local decrements due to evaporation or seepage are ignored if the amounts are small. If the amounts are large, they are either added to or deducted from the inflow as the case may be.

In routing a flood from the first routing period to the second routing period, let

$I_1$ and $O_1$ = instantaneous inflow and outflow, respectively, at the end of the first routing period or at the beginning of the second routing period

$S_1$ = storage in the reach at the beginning of the second routing period

$S_2$ = storage in the reach at the end of the first routing period or at the beginning of the second routing period

$\Delta t$ = routing period

Then

$$I = \frac{(I_1 + I_2)}{2} = \text{average inflow during } \Delta t$$

$$O = \frac{(O_1 + O_2)}{2} = \text{average outflow during } \Delta t$$

$$\Delta S = S_2 - S_1 = \text{change in storage during } \Delta t$$

Substituting these expressions in Eq. (20-34) and simplifying,

$$2\frac{S_1}{\Delta t} - O_1 + I_1 + I_2 = 2\frac{S_2}{\Delta t} + O_2 \tag{20-44}$$

If $I_1$, $I_2$, $O_1$, and $O_2$ are expressed in cfs, $S_1$ and $S_2$ in acre-ft, and $\Delta t$ in

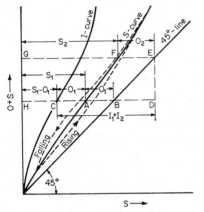

FIG. 20-10. Characteristic curves for flood routing.

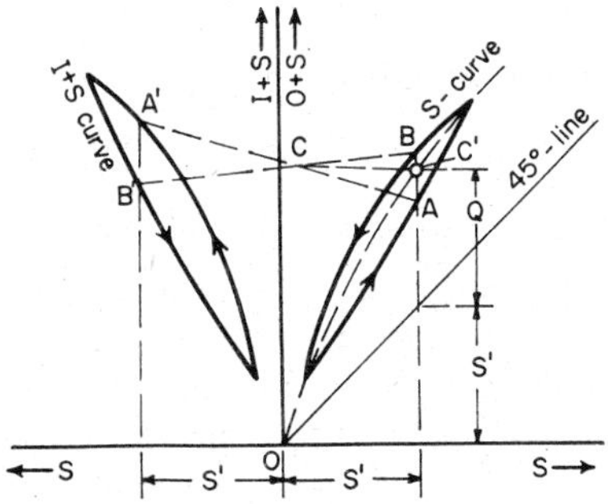

FIG. 20-11. Construction of the average $S$ curve from a wide $S$-curve loop.

days, noting that 1 cfs = 2 afd (acre-feet per day) approximately, then Eq. (20-44) becomes

$$\frac{S_1}{\Delta t} - O_1 + I_1 + I_2 = \frac{S_2}{\Delta t} + O_2 \tag{20-45}$$

When $\Delta t = 1$ day, as it is in most cases, the above equation becomes

$$S_1 - O_1 + I_1 + I_2 = S_2 + O_2 \tag{20-46}$$

This equation constitutes the basis of the present method. If $\Delta t$ is not equal to 1 day, then the values of $S_1/\Delta t$ and $S_2/\Delta t$ should be used in place of $S_1$ and $S_2$, respectively, for the computation and construction of the curves in the procedure to be described as follows:

A. *Construction of Characteristic Curves.* These curves are constructed on a plane of $S$ vs. $O + S$ (Fig. 20-10). The abscissa represents the storage in acre-ft, and the ordinate represents the sum of the outflow in cfs and the storage in acre-ft. The curves can be constructed given any two of these three items: information on inflow, information on outflow, and storage data of a historical flood in the reach under consideration. The third item can be calculated from the two given items by Eq. (20-34).

1. Draw the 45° *line*, starting at the origin at a slope of 45°.

2. Plot $S$ against $O + S$, obtaining the $S$ *curve*.

As described previously (Art. 20-4), the plot of storage against outflow will form a loop, and so will the plot of $S$ against $O + S$. If the loop of the $S$ curve is not wide, an eye-fitted average curve may be drawn to represent a linear relationship between $S$ and $O + S$. If the width of the loop is fairly wide, the average $S$ curve may be constructed as shown in Fig. 20-11. In this figure, a curve of $S$ against $I + S$ also in the form of a loop is plotted on the left side of the ordinate axis and the $S$ curve in loop form is plotted on the right side of the axis. On both sides of the ordinate axis, vertical lines are constructed at the equal abscissas corresponding to a certain storage $S'$. The lines intersect the loops at points $A$, $B$, $A'$, and $B'$. The points $A$ and $A'$ are on the limbs of the rising stage of the loops, and $B$ and $B'$ are on the limbs of falling stage. Draw straight lines $AA'$ and $BB'$, which intersect at $C$. Draw a horizontal line from $C$ to the right to meet the vertical intercept $AB$ at point $C'$. $C'$ is the required point on the average $S$ curve corresponding to the given storage $S'$. It can be shown that the ordinate of $C'$ represents the sum of $S'$ and a certain discharge $Q$ whose value is the average for the rising and falling of the flood stage.

3. Construct the *image curve* ($I$ curve in Fig. 20-10) whose abscissa is equal to $S_1 - O_1$. This is an image of the 45° line reflected horizontally on the left side of the curve. The curve may be constructed easily by making the horizontal intercept between the curve and the $S$ curve equal to the horizontal intercept between the $S$ curve and the 45° line.

*B. Determination of the Outflow.* This is based on the characteristic curves (Fig. 20-10) and the inflow hydrograph of the flood to be routed. The routing period is taken as 1 day.

1. The initial outflow at the beginning of the first routing period must be known or assumed. Note that, if the value is assumed, the error involved in assuming the value will not be magnified enough to produce appreciable effect on the result.

2. Locate a horizontal intercept $AB$ equal to the initial outflow between the 45° line and the $S$ curve.

3. Extend $AB$ toward the left to meet the $I$ curve at $C$.

4. Extend $AB$ toward the right to point $D$, making $CD = I_1 + I_2$.

5. Draw the vertical line $DE$ from $D$ upward to meet the 45° line at $E$.

6. Draw the horizontal line $EF$ from $E$ to the left to meet the $S$ curve at $F$.

7. Measure the length of $EF$, which is equal to the outflow at the end of the routing period, or $O_2$.

8. Continue the cycle of the above steps by starting from point $F$,

which corresponds to point $A$ in the previous cycle. Successive values of outflow can be obtained, and the outflow hydrograph can be constructed.

The above procedure for determining the outflow can be proved as follows: Extend $CD$ and $EF$ horizontally toward the left to meet the ordinate axis at $H$ and $G$, respectively. Then, from Fig. 20-10,

$$HD = HA - CA + CD = S_1 - O_1 + I_1 + I_2$$
$$GE = GF + FE = S_2 + FE$$
and
$$HD = GE$$
Therefore,
$$S_1 - O_1 + I_1 + I_2 = S_2 + FE \qquad (20\text{-}47)$$

Comparing this equation with Eq. (20-46), it is evident that $FE$ must be equal to $O_2$.

**Example 20-2.** The inflow and outflow data of a historical flood for a channel reach are given in cols. 1, 2, and 5 of Table 20-3. Determine the outflow hydrograph of a flood whose inflow data are given in cols. 1 and 2 of Table 20-4.

TABLE 20-3. COMPUTATION OF CHARACTERISTIC CURVES
(All quantities in thousands)

| (1) | (2) | (3) | (4) | (5) | (6) | (7) | (8) | (9) |
|---|---|---|---|---|---|---|---|---|
| | Inflow | | | Outflow | | Storage | | |
| Date | Given, cfs | Adj, cfs | Av, afd | Given, cfs | Av, afd | Change, afd | Accum, ac-ft | |
| | $I_1$ $I_2$ | $I_1 + I_2$ | | $O_1$ $O_2$ | $O_1 + O_2$ | $S_2 - S_1$ | $S_1$ $S_2$ | $O_1 + S_1$ $O_2 + S_2$ |
| March 23 | 23.6 | 22.8 | ..... | 18.5 | ..... | ...... | 27.5 | 46.0 |
| 24 | 59.5 | 57.4 | 80.2 | 29.5 | 48.0 | 32.2 | 59.7 | 89.2 |
| 25 | 164.1 | 158.5 | 215.9 | 94.5 | 124.0 | 91.9 | 151.6 | 246.1 |
| 26 | 279.2 | 269.6 | 428.1 | 211.2 | 305.7 | 122.4 | 274.0 | 485.2 |
| 27 | 277.7 | 268.2 | 537.8 | 270.8 | 482.0 | 55.8 | 329.8 | 600.6 |
| 28 | 195.9 | 189.2 | 457.4 | 229.3 | 500.1 | −42.7 | 287.1 | 516.4 |
| 29 | 133.9 | 129.4 | 318.6 | 168.5 | 397.8 | −79.2 | 207.9 | 376.4 |
| 30 | 96.1 | 92.8 | 222.2 | 119.7 | 288.2 | −66.0 | 141.9 | 261.6 |
| 31 | 74.5 | 71.9 | 164.7 | 96.8 | 216.5 | −51.8 | 90.1 | 186.9 |
| April 1 | 58.9 | 56.8 | 128.7 | 64.5 | 161.3 | −32.6 | 57.5 | 122.0 |
| 2 | 46.8 | 45.1 | 101.9 | 50.2 | 114.7 | −12.8 | 44.7 | 94.9 |
| 3 | 38.8 | 37.3 | 82.4 | 40.0 | 90.2 | −7.8 | 36.9 | 76.9 |
| 4 | 34.0 | 32.8 | 70.1 | 34.0 | 74.0 | −3.9 | 33.0 | 67.0 |
| 5 | 30.7 | 29.6 | 62.4 | 30.4 | 64.4 | −2.0 | 31.0 | 61.4 |
| 6 | 27.6 | 26.6 | 56.2 | 28.0 | 58.4 | −2.2 | 28.8 | 56.8 |
| 7 | 25.0 | 24.1 | 50.7 | 26.2 | 54.2 | −3.5 | 25.3 | 51.5 |
| Total... | 1,566.3 | 1,512.1 | ..... | 1,512.1 | | | | |

*Solution.* The computation for characteristic curves is shown in Table 20-3. In col. 2, the inflow data are made up of three parts: the daily inflow at the upstream end of the reach, either gaged or routed from the upstream reach; the daily inflow from gaged or routed tributaries entering the reach; and the local inflow contributed by ungaged tributaries and land areas draining directly into the stream. The local inflow may be evaluated directly from the distribution of rainfall of the storm over the area draining directly into the reach. As the total outflow of a flood is presumably equal to the total inflow, the sums of the values in cols. 2 and 5 should agree with

TABLE 20-4. COMPUTATION OF THE OUTFLOW HYDROGRAPH
(All quantities in thousands)

| (1) | (2) | (3) | (4) | (5) |
|---|---|---|---|---|
| | Inflow | | Outflow | |
| Date (day) | Given, cfs | Av, afd | Given, cfs | Adj, cfs |
| | $I_1$ $I_2$ | $I_1 + I_2$ | $O_1$ $O_2$ | $O_1$ $O_2$ |
| 1st | 20.0 | ..... | 20.3 | 20.3 |
| 2d | 113.2 | 133.2 | 65.0 | 64.8 |
| 3d | 180.0 | 293.2 | 129.0 | 128.8 |
| 4th | 71.0 | 251.0 | 126.0 | 125.8 |
| 5th | 40.5 | 111.5 | 70.0 | 69.8 |
| 6th | 32.0 | 72.5 | 40.0 | 39.8 |
| 7th | 25.0 | 57.0 | 29.0 | 28.8 |
| 8th | 22.5 | 47.5 | 24.0 | 23.8 |
| 9th | 20.0 | 42.5 | 21.0 | 20.8 |
| 10th | 19.0 | 39.0 | 19.5 | 19.3 |
| 11th | 17.5 | 36.5 | 18.9 | 18.7 |
| Total.... | 560.7 | ..... | 562.7 | 560.7 |

each other. As is usually the case, however, the sums here are not equal to each other. Assuming that the outflow values are closer to the true values than the inflow values, the inflow is adjusted by multiplying the values in col. 5 by the ratio 1,512.1/1,566.3 = 0.9654. The adjusted inflow values are listed in col. 3. The average inflow and outflow in afd are equal to $I_1 + I_2$ and $O_1 + O_2$, respectively, where $I_1$, $I_2$, $O_1$, and $O_2$ are in cfs. Values of $I_1 + I_2$ and $O_1 + O_2$ are given in cols. 4 and 6, respectively. The difference between the values in cols. 4 and 6 is equal to the change in storage listed in col. 7, since $(I_1 + I_2) - (O_1 + O_2) = S_2 - S_1 = \Delta S$. A positive value in col. 7 indicates that the storage is increasing; a negative value indicates that the storage is decreasing. Column 8 gives the cumulative storage computed from the values in col. 7. The first entry in col. 8, i.e., 27.5, represents the storage in the reach on March 23 just before the flood began, which should be given or estimated. The sum of the values in cols. 5 and 8, or $O_1 + S_1$, is entered in col. 9. From the values in cols. 8 and 9, the characteristic curves are constructed, as shown in Fig. 20-12.

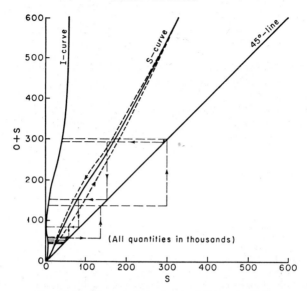

FIG. 20-12. Characteristic curves of Example 20-2.

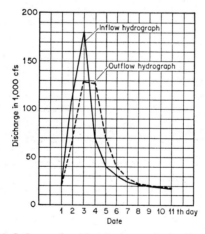

FIG. 20-13. Inflow and outflow hydrographs for Example 20-2.

The computation of the outflow from the inflow of a given flood is shown in Table 20-4. In cols. 1 and 2 are inflow data. Column 3 gives the average inflow in afd, or $I_1 + I_2$. In col. 4, the initial outflow is given as 20.3. Other values of outflow are obtained from the characteristic curves in accordance with the procedure described previously. The outflow values, except for the given initial outflow, are adjusted and entered in col. 5 so that the total inflow agrees with the total outflow. The inflow and outflow hydrographs of the given flood are constructed as shown in Fig. 20-13 from the values of cols. 1, 2, and 3.

## PROBLEMS

**20-1.** Extend the routing of the flood in Example 20-1 to a period of (*a*) 36 hr and (*b*) 120 hr.

**20-2.** Route the following hypothetical solitary flood through the channel reach described in Example 20-1:

| Time since flood began, hr | Celerity, cfs |
|:---:|:---:|
| 0 | 14.0 |
| 3 | 15.0 |
| 6 | 15.5 |
| 9 | 15.0 |
| 12 | 14.0 |

The flow conditions before and after the flood wave are uniform, having a celerity of 14.0 cfs.

**20-3.** Verify the unit-flood computation shown in Fig. 20-4.

**20-4.** In a level-pool reservoir in which discharge is not controlled, the peak outflow must occur where the outflow hydrograph intercepts the inflow hydrograph; that is, $P'$ in Fig. 20-6 must be at $I$. Why?

**20-5.** In the development of a flood-control project for a river basin, the largest flood on record is investigated. The discharges of this flood at an upstream station $A$ and a downstream station $B$ were observed, as shown in the accompanying table.

| Date | Inflow at Sta. A from | | | Outflow at Sta. B | | Discharges held out at Sta. A, due to proposed reservoirs, cfs |
|---|---|---|---|---|---|---|
| | Main, cfs | Tributaries, cfs | Local, cfs | Discharge, cfs | Gage ht, ft | |
| July 29 | 13,600 | 1,900 | 3,000 | 20,800 | 14.4 | 0 |
| 30 | 20,100 | 46,300 | 63,800 | 33,000 | 19.6 | 60,000 |
| 31 | 106,000 | 50,100 | 72,100 | 80,800 | 35.1 | 149,000 |
| Aug. 1 | 92,800 | 15,900 | 21,100 | 110,000 | 43.0 | 96,400 |
| 2 | 49,600 | 6,200 | 8,900 | 112,000 | 43.5 | 46,100 |
| 3 | 22,700 | 2,900 | 6,200 | 112,000 | 43.4 | 17,900 |
| 4 | 11,000 | 2,200 | 4,100 | 102,000 | 41.1 | 2,000 |
| 5 | 8,050 | 2,100 | 3,100 | 68,200 | 31.5 | 2,100 |
| 6 | 13,800 | 3,200 | 5,200 | 26,100 | 16.8 | 3,200 |
| 7 | 19,000 | 5,300 | 8,100 | 20,800 | 14.4 | 4,800 |
| 8 | 14,500 | 3,200 | 3,800 | 21,700 | 14.8 | 2,200 |

The total inflow at Sta. A is equal to the sum of discharges from main stream, tributaries, and local areas adjacent to the reach. The storage in the reach between Stas. A and B at the beginning of the flood is estimated at 50,000 acre-ft.

For the purpose of flood control, a system of reservoirs is proposed on the tributaries above Sta. A. It is found that the effect of the reservoirs is to hold out discharges from the flow at Sta. A, as shown in the last column of the table. Predict the

change in stage at Sta. B of the flood under investigation as a result of the proposed
plan, assuming that the discharge is a single-valued function of the stage.

## REFERENCES

1. N. J. Dahl: On non-permanent flow in open canals, *Proceedings of the 6th General
   Meeting, International Association for Hydraulic Research, The Hague 1955*, vol. 4,
   pp. D19-1 to D19-16, 1955.
2. Takeo Kinosita: Hydrodynamical study on the flood flow, in Floods, vol. III of
   *Symposia Darcy, International Association of Scientific Hydrology, Publication
   No. 42*, 1956, pp. 56–63.
3. D. N. Dietz: A new method for calculating the conduct of translation waves in
   prismatic canals, *Physica*, vol. 8, no. 2, pp. 177–195, February, 1941.
4. Junius Massau: Appendice au Mémoire sur l'intégration graphique (Appendix to
   Memoir on graphical integration), *Annales de l'Association des Ingénieurs sortis
   des Écoles Spéciales de Gand*, vol. 12, pp. 185–444, Ghent, Belgium, 1889.
5. Junius Massau: Mémoire sur l'intégration graphique des équations aux dérivées
   partielles (Graphical integration of partial differential equations with special
   applications to unsteady flow in open channels), *Annales de l'Association des
   Ingénieurs sortis des Écoles Spéciales de Gand*, vol. 23, pp. 95–214, Ghent, Belgium,
   1900.
6. Marc Henry: Propagation des intumescences dans un canal rectangulaire (Propagation of translatory waves in a rectangular channel), *Revue générale de l'hydraulique*, Paris, vol. 4, no. 19, pp. 17–24; no. 20, pp. 65-71, 1938.
7. Louis Bergeron: Méthode graphique générale de calcul des propagations d'ondes
   planes (General graphical method of computation of the propagations of plane
   waves), *Mémoires, Société des Ingénieurs Civils de la France*, pp. 407–497, July-
   August, 1937.
8. Louis Bergeron: Méthode graphique pour le calcul des ondes de translation
   (Graphical method for the computation of translatory waves), *Société Française
   des Mécaniciens, Bulletin No. 7*, Paris, 1953.
9. S. A. Khristianovich: Neustanovivsheiesia dvizhenie v kanalakh i rekakh (Unsteady motion in channels and rivers), in "Nekotoryie Voprosy Mekhaniki
   Sploshnoĭ Sredy" ("Several Questions on the Mechanics of Continuous Media"),
   Academy of Sciences, U.S.S.R., 1938, pp. 13–154.
10. Léon Lévin: Méthode graphique de calcul du mouvement non permanent dans
    les canaux à écoulement libre (Graphic method of computation of unsteady flow
    in open channels), *Le Génie civil*, vol. 119, no. 11-12, pp. 109–113, March 12–14,
    1942.
11. A. Craya: Calcul graphique des régimes variables dans les canaux (Graphical
    computation of variable regimes of flow in channels), *La Houille blanche*, Grenoble,
    new series, 1st yr., no. 1, pp. 19–38, November, 1945, and no. 2, pp. 117–130,
    March, 1946.
12. V. A. Arkhangelskiĭ: "Raschety Neustanovivshegosia Dvizheniia v Otkrytykh
    Vodotokakh" ("Calculation of Unsteady Flow in Open Channels"), Academy
    of Sciences, U.S.S.R., 1947.
13. H. Holsters: Le Calcul du mouvement non permanent dans les rivières par la
    méthode dite des "lignes d'influence" (The computation of unsteady flow in
    rivers by the so-called "influence-lines" method), *Revue générale de l'hydraulique*,
    Paris, vol. 13, no. 37, pp. 36–39, no. 38, pp. 93–94, no. 39, pp. 121–130, no. 40, pp.
    202–206, and no. 41, pp. 237–245, 1947.

14. H. Holsters: Le Calcul du mouvement non permanent dans les rivières par la méthode dite des "lignes d'influence" (Calculation of nonpermanent flow in rivers by the method known as "influence lines"), *La Houille blanche*, Grenoble, 8th yr., no. 4, pp. 495–509, August-September, 1953.

15. J. J. Stoker: The formation of breakers and bores, *New York University, Communications on Applied Mathematics*, vol. 1, no. 1, pp. 1–87, January, 1948.

16. J. J. Stoker: Numerical solution of flood prediction and river regulation problems, I: Derivation of basic theory and formulation of numerical methods of attack, *New York University, Institute of Mathematical Sciences, Report No. IMM-200*, 1953.

17. J. J. Stoker: "Water waves," vol. IV of "Pure and Applied Mathematics," Interscience Publishers, Inc., New York, 1957.

18. Henri J. Putman: Unsteady flow in open channels, *Transactions, American Geophysical Union*, vol. 29, no. 2, pp. 227–232, April, 1948. Discussion by Pin-Nam Lin, vol. 30, no. 2, pp. 302–306, April, 1949.

19. J. Lamoen: Tides and current velocities in a sea-level canal, *Engineering*, vol. 168, no. 4357, pp. 97–99, July 29, 1949.

20. G. J. Dmitriev: Vychislenie kharakteristik ustanovivshegosia plavno izmeniaiushchegosia dvizheniia v prizmaticheskikh ruslakh (Computation of characteristics of a steady gradually varying movement in prismatic channels), *Comptes rendus (Doklady) de l'Académie des Sciences de l'U.R.S.S., Akademiia Nauk S.S.S.R., Leningrad*, vol. 68, no. 5, pp. 825–827, 1949.

21. Francis F. Escoffier: A graphical method for investigating the stability of flow in open channels or in closed conduits flowing partly full, *Transactions, American Geophysical Union*, vol. 31, no. 4, pp. 583–586, August, 1950.

22. G. D. Ransford: Contribution to first order theory of translation waves, *La Houille blanche*, Grenoble, 6th yr., no. 6, pp. 761–763, September-October, 1951.

23. Pin-Nam Lin: Numerical analysis of continuous unsteady flow in open channels, *Transactions, American Geophysical Union*, vol. 33, no. 2, pp. 227–234, April, 1952. Discussions by J. C. Schönfeld and Pin-Nam Lin, vol. 34, no. 5, pp. 792–795, October, 1953.

24. Shigeo Uchida: On the analysis of flood wave in a reservoir by the method of characteristics, *Proceedings of the 2d Japan National Congress for Applied Mechanics*, pp. 271–276, 1952.

25. J. Nougaro: Recherches expérimentales sur les intumescences dans les canaux découverts (Experimental researches on translatory waves in open channels) *Société Française des Mécaniciens, Bulletin No. 9*, Paris, pp. 23–35, 1953.

26. J. Nougaro: Theoretical and experimental studies of the propagation of the translation waves in open channels, *Proceedings of the Minnesota International Hydraulics Convention, Joint Meeting of International Association for Hydraulic Research and Hydraulics Division of American Society of Civil Engineers*, pp. 555–559, August, 1953.

27. Jean Nougaro: Étude théorique et expérimentale de la propagation des intumescences dans les canaux découverts (Theoretical and experimental study of the propagation of translation waves in open channels), *Publications scientifiques et techniques du Ministère de l'Air, France, No. 284*, 1953.

28. J. Nougaro: Méthode graphique pour le calcul de la propagation des intumescences dans les canaux découverts (Graphical method for the computation of the propagation of translatory waves in open channels), *Proceedings of the 6th General Meeting, International Association for Hydraulic Research, The Hague 1955*, vol. 4, pp. D5–1 to D5–15, 1955.

29. Yuichi Iwagaki and Tomitaro Sueishi: On the unsteady flow in open channels with uniform lateral inflow (in Japanese), *Proceedings, Japan Society of Civil Engineers,* vol. 29, no. 11, Tokyo, November, 1954.

30. Yuichi Iwagaki: Fundamental studies on the runoff analysis by characteristics, *Kyoto University, Disaster Prevention Research Institute, Bulletin No.* 10, Kyoto, Japan, December, 1955.

31. Tomitaro Sueishi: On the run-off analysis by the method of characteristics (in Japanese), *Transactions, Japan Society of Civil Engineers,* no. 29, pp. 74–87, Tokyo, December, 1955.

32. E. J. Isaacson, J. J. Stoker, and B. A. Troesch: Numerical solution of flood prediction and river regulation problems: Report 2, Numerical solution of flood problems in simplified models of the Ohio River and the junction of the Ohio and Mississippi Rivers, *New York University, Institute of Mathematical Sciences, Report No. IMM*-205, 1954.

33. E. J. Isaacson, J. J. Stoker, and B. A. Troesch: Numerical solution of flood prediction and river regulation problems: Report 3, Results of the numerical prediction of the 1945 and 1948 floods in the Ohio River, of the 1947 flood through the junction of the Ohio and Mississippi Rivers, and of the floods of 1950 and 1948 through Kentucky Reservoir, *New York University, Institute of Mathematical Sciences, Report No. IMM-NYU-235,* 1956.

34. Edward A. Lawler and Frank V. Druml: Hydraulic problem solution on electronic computers, paper 1515, *Proceedings, American Society of Civil Engineers, Journal, Waterways and Harbors Division,* vol. 84, no. WW1, pp. 1–38, January, 1958.

35. Georg Joos: "Theoretical Physics," 2d ed., Hafner Publishing Company, New York, 1950, pp. 590–594.

36. Shih-I Pai: "Viscous Flow Theory," vol. II, "Turbulent Flow," D. Van Nostrand Company, Inc., Princeton, N.J., 1957, pp. 179–183 and 186–187.

37. Alfred Schack: "Industrial Heat Transfer," translated from the German by Hans Goldschmidt and Everett P. Partridge, John Wiley & Sons, Inc., New York, 1933, p. 29.

38. Shoitiro Hayami: On the propagation of flood waves, *Kyoto University, Disaster Prevention Research Institute, Bulletin* 1, Kyoto, Japan, December, 1951.

39. F. V. Appleby: Runoff dynamics: A heat conduction analogue of storage flow in channel networks, *Assemblée Générale de Rome,* 1954, *International Association of Scientific Hydrology, Publication No.* 38, vol. 3, pp. 338–348, 1954.

40. Tojiro Ishihara, Shoitiro Hayami, and Shigenori Hayami: On the electronic analog computer for flood routing, *Proceedings of the Japan Academy,* vol. 30, no. 9, pp. 891–895, Tokyo, 1954.

41. Tojiro Ishihara and Yasuo Ishihara: On the electronic analog computer for flood routing (in Japanese), *Transactions, Japan Society of Civil Engineers,* no. 24, pp. 44–57, Tokyo, April, 1955.

42. Tojiro Ishihara and Yasuo Ishihara: Electronic analog computer for flood flows in the Yodo River (in Japanese), *Proceedings, Japan Society of Civil Engineers,* vol. 41, no. 8, pp. 21–24, Tokyo, August, 1956.

43. Tojiro Ishihara: Application of electronic analog computer for flood routing to actual rivers (in Japanese), *Transactions, Japan Society of Civil Engineers,* no. 43, pp. 43–47, Tokyo, February, 1957.

44. Tojiro Ishihara, Shoitiro Hayami, and Shigenori Hayami: Electronic analog computer for flood flows, *Proceedings of the Regional Technical Conference on Water Resources Development in Asia and the Far East, United Nations Economic Commission for Asia and the Far East, Flood Control Series No.* 9, Bangkok, 1956, pp. 170–174.

45. B. R. Gilcrest: Flood routing, chap. X of "Engineering Hydraulics," edited by Hunter Rouse, John Wiley & Sons, Inc., New York, 1950, pp. 635–710.

46. Flood routing, chap. V of "Flood Control," The Engineer School, Fort Belvoir, Virginia, 1940, pp. 127–177.

47. Flood routing, chap. 6.10 of pt. 6, Flood Hydrology, vol. IV, Water Studies, *U.S. Bureau of Reclamation Manual*, Dec. 30, 1947.

48. Ray K. Linsley, Jr., Max A. Kohler, Joseph L. H. Paulhus: "Applied Hydrology," McGraw-Hill Book Company, Inc., New York, 1949, chap. 19, Stream routing, pp. 485–541.

49. Ven Te Chow: Hydrologic studies of floods in the United States, in Floods, vol. III of *Symposia Darcy, International Association of Scientific Hydrology, Publication No. 42*, 1956, pp. 134–170.

50. Flood routing, art. 3.17 of sec. 4, Hydrology, *U.S. Soil Conservation Service, Engineering Handbook, Supplement A*, 1957, pp. 1–28.

51. W. Rippl: The capacity of storage-reservoir for water-supply, *Minutes of Proceedings, Institution of Civil Engineers, London*, vol. 71, pp. 270–278, 1883.

52. Armin Schoklitsch: "Hydraulic Structures," translated from the German by Samuel Shulits, American Society of Mechanical Engineers, New York, 1937, vol. 1, pp. 65–67.

53. H. K. Barrows: "Water Power Engineering," 3d ed., McGraw-Hill Book Company, Inc., New York, 1943, pp. 199–201.

54. Don Johnstone and William P. Cross: "Elements of Applied Hydrology," The Ronald Press Company, New York, 1949, pp. 163–167.

55. Kenneth E. Sorensen: Graphical solution of hydraulic problems, *Transactions, American Society of Civil Engineers*, vol. 118, pp. 61–77, 1953.

56. Calvin Victor Davis (editor-in-chief): "Handbook of Applied Hydraulics," McGraw-Hill Book Company, Inc., New York, 2d ed., 1952. Sec. 1, River regulation by reservoirs, by Theodore T. Knappen, James H. Stratton, and Calvin V. Davis, pp. 1–21; and appendix B, Graphical aids to hydraulic computations, by Kenneth E. Sorensen, pp. 1229–1248.

57. Otto H. Meyer: Simplified flood routing, *Civil Engineering*, vol. 11, no. 5, pp. 306–307, May, 1941.

58. Louis G. Puls: Flood regulation of the Tennessee River, *House Document, No. 185*, 70th Congress, 1st Session, U.S. Government Printing Office, Washington, D.C., 1928, pt. 2, appendix B.

59. Stanley S. Butler: "Engineering Hydrology," Prentice-Hall Inc., Englewood Cliffs, N.J., 1957, pp. 208–212.

60. Walter T. Wilson: A graphical flood-routing method, *Transactions, American Geophysical Union*, vol. 22, pt. III, pp. 893–897, 1941.

61. H. M. Cheng: A graphical solution for flood routing problems, *Civil Engineering*, vol. 16, no. 3, pp. 126–128, March, 1946.

62. Ven Te Chow: A practical procedure of flood routing, *Civil Engineering and Public Works Review, London*, vol. 46, no. 542, pp. 586–588, August, 1951; reprinted as *University of Illinois, Civil Engineering Studies, Hydraulic Engineering Series No. 1*, Urbana, Ill., Nov. 1, 1951.

63. R. D. Goodrich: Rapid calculation of reservoir discharge, *Civil Engineering*, vol. 1, no. 5, pp. 417–418, February, 1931.

64. E. J. Rutter, Q. B. Graves, and F. F. Snyder: Flood routing, *Transactions, American Society of Civil Engineers*, vol. 104, pp. 275–294, 1939.

65. C. O. Wisler and E. F. Brater: A direct method of flood routing, *Transactions, American Society of Civil Engineers*, vol. 107, pp. 1519–1529, 1942.

66. I. H. Steinberg: A method of flood routing, *Civil Engineering*, vol. 8, no. 7, pp. 476–477, July, 1938.

67. R. K. Linsley: Use of nomographs in solving streamflow routing problems, *Civil Engineering*, vol. 14, no. 5, pp. 209–210, May, 1944.

68. C. J. Posey: Slide rule for routing floods through storage reservoirs or lakes, *Engineering News-Record*, vol. 114, pp. 580–581, Apr. 25, 1935.

69. Sherman M. Woodward and Chesley J. Posey: "Hydraulics of Steady Flow in Open Channels," John Wiley & Sons, Inc., New York, 1941, pp. 133–145.

70. J. M. Shepley and C. B. Walton: Solving reservoir problems with circular point-by-point computer, *Civil Engineering*, vol. 12, no. 3, pp. 154–155, March, 1942.

71. F. E. Tatum: A simplified method of routing flood flows through natural valley storage, unpublished memorandum, U.S. Engineer's Office, Rock Island, Ill., May 29, 1940.

72. G. T. McCarthy: The unit hydrograph and flood routing, unpublished manuscript, presented at a conference of the North Atlantic Division, U.S. Army, Corps of Engineers, June 24, 1938.

73. E. W. Lane: Predicting stages for the Lower Mississippi, *Civil Engineering*, vol. 7, no. 2, pp. 122–125, February, 1937.

74. Max A. Kohler: A forecasting technique for routing and combining flow in terms of stage, *Transactions, American Geophysical Union*, vol. 25, pt. VI, pp. 1030–1035, 1944.

75. Ralph E. King: Stage predictions for flood control operations, *Transactions, American Society of Civil Engineers*, vol. 117, pp. 690–698, 1952.

76. William E. Ray and Herman F. Mondschein: A method of forecasting stages on flat rivers, *Transactions, American Geophysical Union*, vol. 38, no. 5, pp. 698–707, October, 1957.

77. J. F. Tarpley, Jr.: A new integrating machine, *Military Engineer*, vol. 32, no. 181, pp. 39–43, 1939.

78. Frank B. Harkness: Harkness flood router: Specifications of construction and operation, *Patent File No.* 2,550,692, U.S. Patent Office, Washington, D.C., May 1, 1951.

79. R. K. Linsley, L. W. Foskett, and M. A. Kohler: Electronic device speeds flood forecasting, *Engineering News-Record*, vol. 141, no. 26, pp. 64–66, Dec. 23, 1948.

80. R. K. Linsley, L. W. Foskett, and M. A. Kohler: Use of electronical analogy in flood wave analysis, *Comptes rendus et rapports de l'Assemblée Générale d'Oslo,* 19–28 aôut 1948, *International Association of Scientific Hydrology, Publication No* 29, 1948, vol. I, pp. 221–227.

81. M. A. Kohler: Application of electronic flow routing analog, *Transactions, American Society of Civil Engineers*, vol. 118, pp. 1028–1045, 1953.

# APPENDIXES

$d_0$ = diameter      $R$ = hydraulic radius
$y$ = depth of flow      $T$ = top width
$A$ = water area      $D$ = hydraulic depth
$P$ = wetter perimeter      $Z$ = $A \sqrt{D}$ = section factor for critical-flow computation

| $\dfrac{y}{d_0}$ | $\dfrac{A}{d_0{}^2}$ | $\dfrac{P}{d_0}$ | $\dfrac{R}{d_0}$ | $\dfrac{T}{d_0}$ | $\dfrac{D}{d_0}$ | $\dfrac{Z}{d_0{}^{2.5}}$ | $\dfrac{AR^{2/3}}{d_0{}^{8/3}}$ |
|---|---|---|---|---|---|---|---|
| 0.01 | 0.0013 | 0.2003 | 0.0066 | 0.1990 | 0.0066 | 0.0001 | 0.0000 |
| 0.02 | 0.0037 | 0.2838 | 0.0132 | 0.2800 | 0.0134 | 0.0004 | 0.0002 |
| 0.03 | 0.0069 | 0.3482 | 0.0197 | 0.3412 | 0.0202 | 0.0010 | 0.0005 |
| 0.04 | 0.0105 | 0.4027 | 0.0262 | 0.3919 | 0.0268 | 0.0017 | 0.0009 |
| 0.05 | 0.0147 | 0.4510 | 0.0326 | 0.4359 | 0.0336 | 0.0027 | 0.0015 |
| 0.06 | 0.0192 | 0.4949 | 0.0389 | 0.4750 | 0.0406 | 0.0039 | 0.0022 |
| 0.07 | 0.0242 | 0.5355 | 0.0451 | 0.5103 | 0.0474 | 0.0053 | 0.0031 |
| 0.08 | 0.0294 | 0.5735 | 0.0513 | 0.5426 | 0.0542 | 0.0069 | 0.0040 |
| 0.09 | 0.0350 | 0.6094 | 0.0574 | 0.5724 | 0.0612 | 0.0087 | 0.0052 |
| 0.10 | 0.0409 | 0.6435 | 0.0635 | 0.6000 | 0.0682 | 0.0107 | 0.0065 |
| 0.11 | 0.0470 | 0.6761 | 0.0695 | 0.6258 | 0.0752 | 0.0129 | 0.0079 |
| 0.12 | 0.0534 | 0.7075 | 0.0754 | 0.6499 | 0.0822 | 0.0153 | 0.0095 |
| 0.13 | 0.0600 | 0.7377 | 0.0813 | 0.6726 | 0.0892 | 0.0179 | 0.0113 |
| 0.14 | 0.0668 | 0.7670 | 0.0871 | 0.6940 | 0.0964 | 0.0217 | 0.0131 |
| 0.15 | 0.0739 | 0.7954 | 0.0929 | 0.7141 | 0.1034 | 0.0238 | 0.0152 |
| 0.16 | 0.0811 | 0.8230 | 0.0986 | 0.7332 | 0.1106 | 0.0270 | 0.0173 |
| 0.17 | 0.0885 | 0.8500 | 0.1042 | 0.7513 | 0.1178 | 0.0304 | 0.0196 |
| 0.18 | 0.0961 | 0.8763 | 0.1097 | 0.7684 | 0.1252 | 0.0339 | 0.0220 |
| 0.19 | 0.1039 | 0.9020 | 0.1152 | 0.7846 | 0.1324 | 0.0378 | 0.0247 |
| 0.20 | 0.1118 | 0.9273 | 0.1206 | 0.8000 | 0.1398 | 0.0418 | 0.0273 |
| 0.21 | 0.1199 | 0.9521 | 0.1259 | 0.8146 | 0.1472 | 0.0460 | 0.0301 |
| 0.22 | 0.1281 | 0.9764 | 0.1312 | 0.8285 | 0.1546 | 0.0503 | 0.0333 |
| 0.23 | 0.1365 | 1.0003 | 0.1364 | 0.8417 | 0.1622 | 0.0549 | 0.0359 |
| 0.24 | 0.1449 | 1.0239 | 0.1416 | 0.8542 | 0.1696 | 0.0597 | 0.0394 |
| 0.25 | 0.1535 | 1.0472 | 0.1466 | 0.8660 | 0.1774 | 0.0646 | 0.0427 |
| 0.26 | 0.1623 | 1.0701 | 0.1516 | 0.8773 | 0.1850 | 0.0697 | 0.0464 |
| 0.27 | 0.1711 | 1.0928 | 0.1566 | 0.8879 | 0.1926 | 0.0751 | 0.0497 |
| 0.28 | 0.1800 | 1.1152 | 0.1614 | 0.8980 | 0.2004 | 0.0805 | 0.0536 |
| 0.29 | 0.1890 | 1.1373 | 0.1662 | 0.9075 | 0.2084 | 0.0862 | 0.0571 |
| 0.30 | 0.1982 | 1.1593 | 0.1709 | 0.9165 | 0.2162 | 0.0921 | 0.0610 |

Appendix A. Geometric Elements for Circular
Channel Sections (*continued*)

| $\dfrac{y}{d_0}$ | $\dfrac{A}{d_0{}^2}$ | $\dfrac{P}{d_0}$ | $\dfrac{R}{d_0}$ | $\dfrac{T}{d_0}$ | $\dfrac{D}{d_0}$ | $\dfrac{Z}{d_0{}^{2.5}}$ | $\dfrac{AR^{2/3}}{d_0{}^{8/3}}$ |
|---|---|---|---|---|---|---|---|
| 0.31 | 0.2074 | 1.1810 | 0.1755 | 0.9250 | 0.2242 | 0.0981 | 0.0650 |
| 0.32 | 0.2167 | 1.2025 | 0.1801 | 0.9330 | 0.2322 | 0.1044 | 0.0690 |
| 0.33 | 0.2260 | 1.2239 | 0.1848 | 0.9404 | 0.2404 | 0.1107 | 0.0736 |
| 0.34 | 0.2355 | 1.2451 | 0.1891 | 0.9474 | 0.2486 | 0.1172 | 0.0776 |
| 0.35 | 0.2450 | 1.2661 | 0.1935 | 0.9539 | 0.2568 | 0.1241 | 0.0820 |
| 0.36 | 0.2546 | 1.2870 | 0.1978 | 0.9600 | 0.2652 | 0.1310 | 0.0864 |
| 0.37 | 0.2642 | 1.3078 | 0.2020 | 0.9656 | 0.2736 | 0.1381 | 0.0909 |
| 0.38 | 0.2739 | 1.3284 | 0.2061 | 0.9708 | 0.2822 | 0.1453 | 0.0955 |
| 0.39 | 0.2836 | 1.3490 | 0.2102 | 0.9755 | 0.2908 | 0.1528 | 0.1020 |
| 0.40 | 0.2934 | 1.3694 | 0.2142 | 0.9798 | 0.2994 | 0.1603 | 0.1050 |
| 0.41 | 0.3032 | 1.3898 | 0.2181 | 0.9837 | 0.3082 | 0.1682 | 0.1100 |
| 0.42 | 0.3132 | 1.4101 | 0.2220 | 0.9871 | 0.3172 | 0.1761 | 0.1147 |
| 0.43 | 0.3229 | 1.4303 | 0.2257 | 0.9902 | 0.3262 | 0.1844 | 0.1196 |
| 0.44 | 0.3328 | 1.4505 | 0.2294 | 0.9928 | 0.3352 | 0.1927 | 0.1245 |
| 0.45 | 0.3428 | 1.4706 | 0.2331 | 0.9950 | 0.3446 | 0.2011 | 0.1298 |
| 0.46 | 0.3527 | 1.4907 | 0.2366 | 0.9968 | 0.3538 | 0.2098 | 0.1348 |
| 0.47 | 0.3627 | 1.5108 | 0.2400 | 0.9982 | 0.3634 | 0.2186 | 0.1401 |
| 0.48 | 0.3727 | 1.5308 | 0.2434 | 0.9992 | 0.3730 | 0.2275 | 0.1452 |
| 0.49 | 0.3827 | 1.5508 | 0.2467 | 0.9998 | 0.3828 | 0.2366 | 0.1505 |
| 0.50 | 0.3927 | 1.5708 | 0.2500 | 1.0000 | 0.3928 | 0.2459 | 0.1558 |
| 0.51 | 0.4027 | 1.5908 | 0.2531 | 0.9998 | 0.4028 | 0.2553 | 0.1610 |
| 0.52 | 0.4127 | 1.6108 | 0.2561 | 0.9992 | 0.4130 | 0.2650 | 0.1664 |
| 0.53 | 0.4227 | 1.6308 | 0.2591 | 0.9982 | 0.4234 | 0.2748 | 0.1715 |
| 0.54 | 0.4327 | 1.6509 | 0.2620 | 0.9968 | 0.4340 | 0.2848 | 0.1772 |
| 0.55 | 0.4426 | 1.6710 | 0.2649 | 0.9950 | 0.4448 | 0.2949 | 0.1825 |
| 0.56 | 0.4526 | 1.6911 | 0.2676 | 0.9928 | 0.4558 | 0.3051 | 0.1878 |
| 0.57 | 0.4625 | 1.7113 | 0.2703 | 0.9902 | 0.4670 | 0.3158 | 0.1933 |
| 0.58 | 0.4723 | 1.7315 | 0.2728 | 0.9871 | 0.4786 | 0.3263 | 0.1987 |
| 0.59 | 0.4822 | 1.7518 | 0.2753 | 0.9837 | 0.4902 | 0.3373 | 0.2041 |
| 0.60 | 0.4920 | 1.7722 | 0.2776 | 0.9798 | 0.5022 | 0.3484 | 0.2092 |
| 0.61 | 0.5018 | 1.7926 | 0.2797 | 0.9755 | 0.5144 | 0.3560 | 0.2146 |
| 0.62 | 0.5115 | 1.8132 | 0.2818 | 0.9708 | 0.5270 | 0.3710 | 0.2199 |
| 0.63 | 0.5212 | 1.8338 | 0.2839 | 0.9656 | 0.5398 | 0.3830 | 0.2252 |
| 0.64 | 0.5308 | 1.8546 | 0.2860 | 0.9600 | 0.5530 | 0.3945 | 0.2302 |
| 0.65 | 0.5404 | 1.8755 | 0.2881 | 0.9539 | 0.5666 | 0.4066 | 0.2358 |

Appendix A. Geometric Elements for Circular
Channel Sections (*continued*)

| $\dfrac{y}{d_0}$ | $\dfrac{A}{d_0{}^2}$ | $\dfrac{P}{d_0}$ | $\dfrac{R}{d_0}$ | $\dfrac{T}{d_0}$ | $\dfrac{D}{d_0}$ | $\dfrac{Z}{d_0{}^{2.5}}$ | $\dfrac{A R^{2/3}}{d_0{}^{8/3}}$ |
|---|---|---|---|---|---|---|---|
| 0.66 | 0.5499 | 1.8965 | 0.2899 | 0.9474 | 0.5804 | 0.4188 | 0.2407 |
| 0.67 | 0.5594 | 1.9177 | 0.2917 | 0.9404 | 0.5948 | 0.4309 | 0.2460 |
| 0.68 | 0.5687 | 1.9391 | 0.2935 | 0.9330 | 0.6096 | 0.4437 | 0.2510 |
| 0.69 | 0.5780 | 1.9606 | 0.2950 | 0.9250 | 0.6250 | 0.4566 | 0.2560 |
| 0.70 | 0.5872 | 1.9823 | 0.2962 | 0.9165 | 0.6408 | 0.4694 | 0.2608 |
| 0.71 | 0.5964 | 2.0042 | 0.2973 | 0.9075 | 0.6572 | 0.4831 | 0.2653 |
| 0.72 | 0.6054 | 2.0264 | 0.2984 | 0.8980 | 0.6742 | 0.4964 | 0.2702 |
| 0.73 | 0.6143 | 2.0488 | 0.2995 | 0.8879 | 0.6918 | 0.5100 | 0.2751 |
| 0.74 | 0.6231 | 2.0714 | 0.3006 | 0.8773 | 0.7104 | 0.5248 | 0.2794 |
| 0.75 | 0.6318 | 2.0944 | 0.3017 | 0.8660 | 0.7296 | 0.5392 | 0.2840 |
| 0.76 | 0.6404 | 2.1176 | 0.3025 | 0.8542 | 0.7498 | 0.5540 | 0.2888 |
| 0.77 | 0.6489 | 2.1412 | 0.3032 | 0.8417 | 0.7710 | 0.5695 | 0.2930 |
| 0.78 | 0.6573 | 2.1652 | 0.3037 | 0.8285 | 0.7934 | 0.5850 | 0.2969 |
| 0.79 | 0.6655 | 2.1895 | 0.3040 | 0.8146 | 0.8170 | 0.6011 | 0.3008 |
| 0.80 | 0.6736 | 2.2143 | 0.3042 | 0.8000 | 0.8420 | 0.6177 | 0.3045 |
| 0.81 | 0.6815 | 2.2395 | 0.3044 | 0.7846 | 0.8686 | 0.6347 | 0.3082 |
| 0.82 | 0.6893 | 2.2653 | 0.3043 | 0.7684 | 0.8970 | 0.6524 | 0.3118 |
| 0.83 | 0.6969 | 2.2916 | 0.3041 | 0.7513 | 0.9276 | 0.6707 | 0.3151 |
| 0.84 | 0.7043 | 2.3186 | 0.3038 | 0.7332 | 0.9606 | 0.6897 | 0.3182 |
| 0.85 | 0.7115 | 2.3462 | 0.3033 | 0.7141 | 0.9964 | 0.7098 | 0.3212 |
| 0.86 | 0.7186 | 2.3746 | 0.3026 | 0.6940 | 1.0354 | 0.7307 | 0.3240 |
| 0.87 | 0.7254 | 2.4038 | 0.3017 | 0.6726 | 1.0784 | 0.7528 | 0.3264 |
| 0.88 | 0.7320 | 2.4341 | 0.3008 | 0.6499 | 1.1264 | 0.7754 | 0.3286 |
| 0.89 | 0.7380 | 2.4655 | 0.2996 | 0.6258 | 1.1800 | 0.8016 | 0.3307 |
| 0.90 | 0.7445 | 2.4981 | 0.2980 | 0.6000 | 1.2408 | 0.8285 | 0.3324 |
| 0.91 | 0.7504 | 2.5322 | 0.2963 | 0.5724 | 1.3110 | 0.8586 | 0.3336 |
| 0.92 | 0.7560 | 2.5681 | 0.2944 | 0.5426 | 1.3932 | 0.8917 | 0.3345 |
| 0.93 | 0.7612 | 2.6061 | 0.2922 | 0.5103 | 1.4918 | 0.9292 | 0.3350 |
| 0.94 | 0.7662 | 2.6467 | 0.2896 | 0.4750 | 1.6130 | 0.9725 | 0.3353 |
| 0.95 | 0.7707 | 2.6906 | 0.2864 | 0.4359 | 1.7682 | 1.0242 | 0.3349 |
| 0.96 | 0.7749 | 2.7389 | 0.2830 | 0.3919 | 1.9770 | 1.0888 | 0.3340 |
| 0.97 | 0.7785 | 2.7934 | 0.2787 | 0.3412 | 2.2820 | 1.1752 | 0.3322 |
| 0.98 | 0.7816 | 2.8578 | 0.2735 | 0.2800 | 2.7916 | 1.3050 | 0.3291 |
| 0.99 | 0.7841 | 2.9412 | 0.2665 | 0.1990 | 3.9400 | 1.5554 | 0.3248 |
| 1.00 | 0.7854 | 3.1416 | 0.2500 | 0.0000 | $\infty$ | $\infty$ | 0.3117 |

(The use of the charts* requires no explanation.)


* Reproduced with the permission of the U.S. Agricultural Research Service, through the courtesy of Mr. W. O. Ree, from "Handbook of Channel Design for Soil and Water Conservation," prepared by Stillwater Outdoor Hydraulic Laboratory, U.S. Soil Conservation Service, SCS-TP-61, March, 1947, and revised June, 1954.

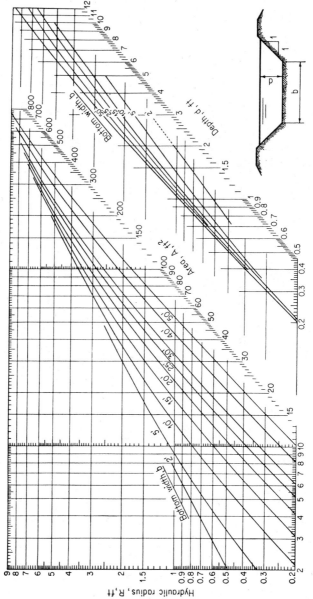

FIG. B-1. Geometric elements of trapezoidal channels with 1:1 side slopes.

630

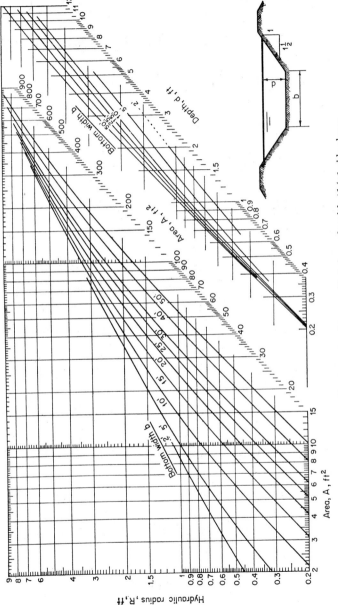

Fig. B-2. Hydraulic elements of trapezoidal channels with 1½:1 side slopes.

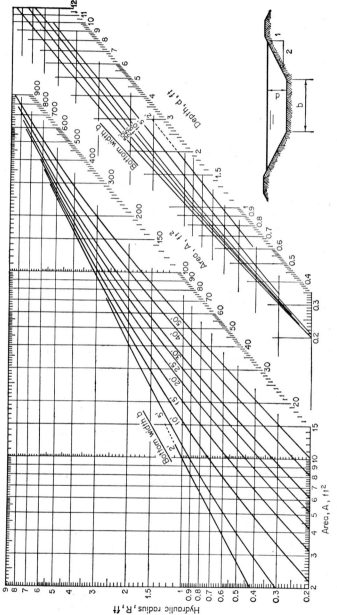

FIG. B-3. Hydraulic elements of trapezoidal channels with 2:1 side slopes.

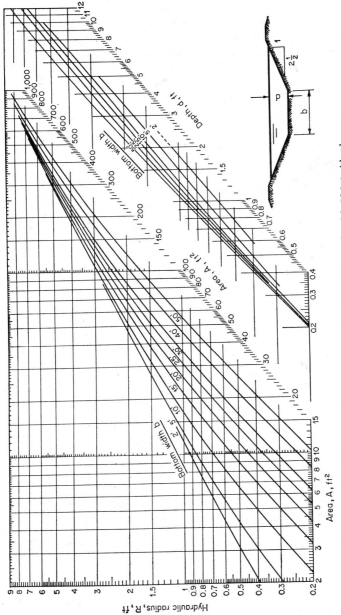

FIG. B-4. Hydraulic elements of trapezoidal channels with 2½:1 side slopes.

633

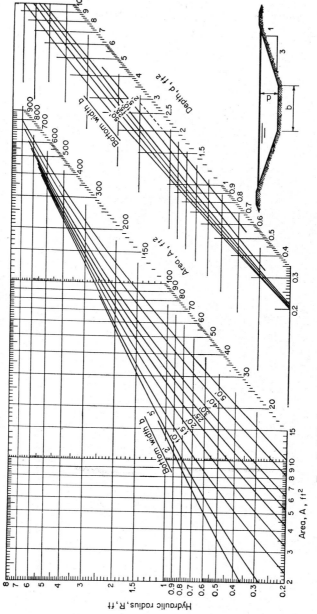

Fig. B-5. Hydraulic elements of trapezoidal channels with 3:1 side slopes.

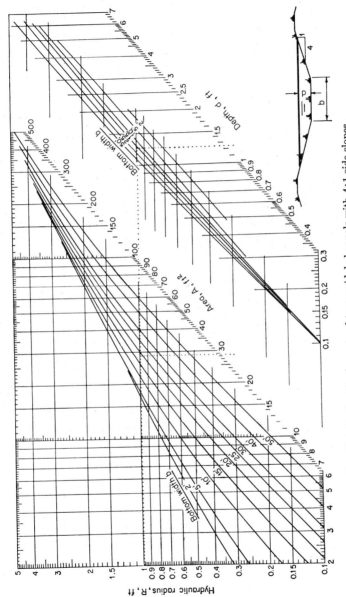

FIG. B-6. Hydraulic elements of trapezoidal channels with 4:1 side slopes.

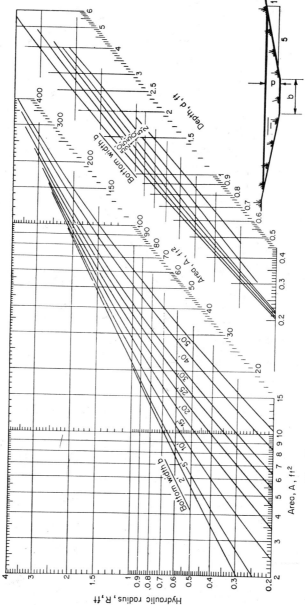

FIG. B-7. Hydraulic elements of trapezoidal channels with 5:1 side slopes.

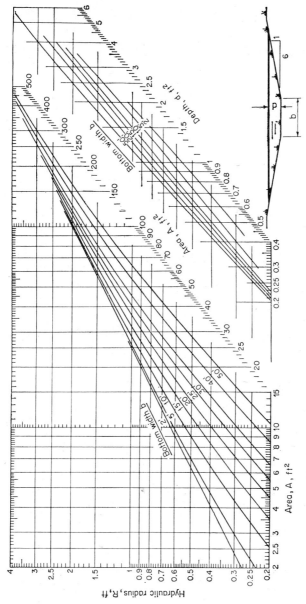

FIG. B-8. Hydraulic elements of trapezoidal channels with 6:1 side slopes.

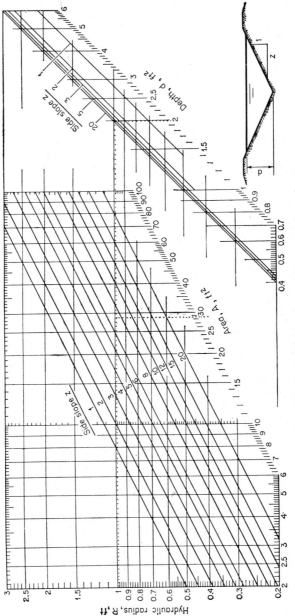

Fig. B-9. Hydraulic elements of triangular channels.

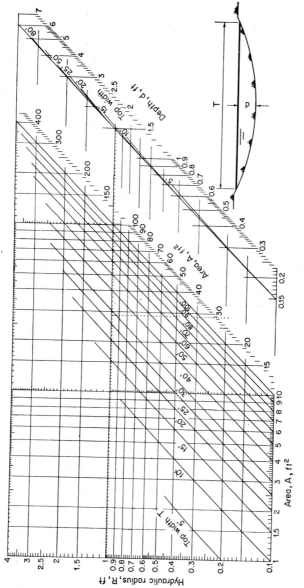

FIG. B-10. Hydraulic elements of parabolic channels.

APPENDIX C. NOMOGRAPHIC SOLUTION OF THE MANNING FORMULA*

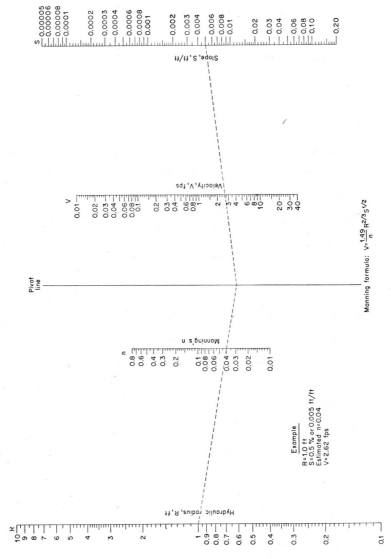

* Reproduced with the permission of the U.S. Agricultural Research Service, through the courtesy of Mr. W. O. Ree, from "Handbook of Channel Design for Soil and Water Conservation," prepared by Stillwater Outdoor Hydraulic Laboratory, U.S. Soil Conservation Service, SCS-TP-61, March, 1947, and revised June, 1954.

$$F(u,N) = \int_0^u \frac{du}{1 - u^N} \text{ and } F(u,N)_{-S_0} = \int_0^u \frac{du}{1 + u^N}$$

### Table D-1. The Varied-flow Function for Positive Slopes, $F(u,N)$

| N \ u | 2.2 | 2.4 | 2.6 | 2.8 | 3.0 | 3.2 | 3.4 | 3.6 | 3.8 | 4.0 |
|---|---|---|---|---|---|---|---|---|---|---|
| 0.00 | 0.000 | 0.000 | 0.000 | 0.000 | 0.000 | 0.000 | 0.000 | 0.000 | 0.000 | 0.000 |
| 0.02 | 0.020 | 0.020 | 0.020 | 0.020 | 0.020 | 0.020 | 0.020 | 0.020 | 0.020 | 0.020 |
| 0.04 | 0.040 | 0.040 | 0.040 | 0.040 | 0.040 | 0.040 | 0.040 | 0.040 | 0.040 | 0.040 |
| 0.06 | 0.060 | 0.060 | 0.060 | 0.060 | 0.060 | 0.060 | 0.060 | 0.060 | 0.060 | 0.060 |
| 0.08 | 0.080 | 0.080 | 0.080 | 0.080 | 0.080 | 0.080 | 0.080 | 0.080 | 0.080 | 0.080 |
| 0.10 | 0.100 | 0.100 | 0.100 | 0.100 | 0.100 | 0.100 | 0.100 | 0.100 | 0.100 | 0.100 |
| 0.12 | 0.120 | 0.120 | 0.120 | 0.120 | 0.120 | 0.120 | 0.120 | 0.120 | 0.120 | 0.120 |
| 0.14 | 0.140 | 0.140 | 0.140 | 0.140 | 0.140 | 0.140 | 0.140 | 0.140 | 0.140 | 0.140 |
| 0.16 | 0.161 | 0.161 | 0.160 | 0.160 | 0.160 | 0.160 | 0.160 | 0.160 | 0.160 | 0.160 |
| 0.18 | 0.181 | 0.181 | 0.181 | 0.180 | 0.180 | 0.180 | 0.180 | 0.180 | 0.180 | 0.180 |
| 0.20 | 0.202 | 0.201 | 0.201 | 0.201 | 0.200 | 0.200 | 0.200 | 0.200 | 0.200 | 0.200 |
| 0.22 | 0.223 | 0.222 | 0.221 | 0.221 | 0.221 | 0.220 | 0.220 | 0.220 | 0.220 | 0.220 |
| 0.24 | 0.244 | 0.243 | 0.242 | 0.241 | 0.241 | 0.241 | 0.240 | 0.240 | 0.240 | 0.240 |
| 0.26 | 0.265 | 0.263 | 0.262 | 0.262 | 0.261 | 0.261 | 0.261 | 0.260 | 0.260 | 0.260 |
| 0.28 | 0.286 | 0.284 | 0.283 | 0.282 | 0.282 | 0.281 | 0.281 | 0.281 | 0.280 | 0.280 |
| 0.30 | 0.307 | 0.305 | 0.304 | 0.303 | 0.302 | 0.302 | 0.301 | 0.301 | 0.301 | 0.300 |
| 0.32 | 0.329 | 0.326 | 0.325 | 0.324 | 0.323 | 0.322 | 0.322 | 0.321 | 0.321 | 0.321 |
| 0.34 | 0.351 | 0.348 | 0.346 | 0.344 | 0.343 | 0.343 | 0.342 | 0.342 | 0.341 | 0.341 |
| 0.36 | 0.372 | 0.369 | 0.367 | 0.366 | 0.364 | 0.363 | 0.363 | 0.362 | 0.362 | 0.361 |
| 0.38 | 0.395 | 0.392 | 0.389 | 0.387 | 0.385 | 0.384 | 0.383 | 0.383 | 0.382 | 0.382 |
| 0.40 | 0.418 | 0.414 | 0.411 | 0.408 | 0.407 | 0.405 | 0.404 | 0.403 | 0.403 | 0.402 |
| 0.42 | 0.442 | 0.437 | 0.433 | 0.430 | 0.428 | 0.426 | 0.425 | 0.424 | 0.423 | 0.423 |
| 0.44 | 0.465 | 0.460 | 0.456 | 0.452 | 0.450 | 0.448 | 0.446 | 0.445 | 0.444 | 0.443 |
| 0.46 | 0.489 | 0.483 | 0.479 | 0.475 | 0.472 | 0.470 | 0.468 | 0.466 | 0.465 | 0.464 |
| 0.48 | 0.514 | 0.507 | 0.502 | 0.497 | 0.494 | 0.492 | 0.489 | 0.488 | 0.486 | 0.485 |
| 0.50 | 0.539 | 0.531 | 0.525 | 0.521 | 0.517 | 0.514 | 0.511 | 0.509 | 0.508 | 0.506 |
| 0.52 | 0.565 | 0.557 | 0.550 | 0.544 | 0.540 | 0.536 | 0.534 | 0.531 | 0.529 | 0.528 |
| 0.54 | 0.592 | 0.582 | 0.574 | 0.568 | 0.563 | 0.559 | 0.556 | 0.554 | 0.551 | 0.550 |
| 0.56 | 0.619 | 0.608 | 0.599 | 0.593 | 0.587 | 0.583 | 0.579 | 0.576 | 0.574 | 0.572 |
| 0.58 | 0.648 | 0.635 | 0.626 | 0.618 | 0.612 | 0.607 | 0.603 | 0.599 | 0.596 | 0.594 |
| 0.60 | 0.676 | 0.663 | 0.653 | 0.644 | 0.637 | 0.631 | 0.627 | 0.623 | 0.620 | 0.617 |
| 0.61 | 0.691 | 0.678 | 0.667 | 0.657 | 0.650 | 0.644 | 0.639 | 0.635 | 0.631 | 0.628 |
| 0.62 | 0.706 | 0.692 | 0.680 | 0.671 | 0.663 | 0.657 | 0.651 | 0.647 | 0.643 | 0.640 |
| 0.63 | 0.722 | 0.707 | 0.694 | 0.684 | 0.676 | 0.669 | 0.664 | 0.659 | 0.655 | 0.652 |
| 0.64 | 0.738 | 0.722 | 0.709 | 0.698 | 0.690 | 0.683 | 0.677 | 0.672 | 0.667 | 0.664 |
| 0.65 | 0.754 | 0.737 | 0.724 | 0.712 | 0.703 | 0.696 | 0.689 | 0.684 | 0.680 | 0.676 |
| 0.66 | 0.771 | 0.753 | 0.738 | 0.727 | 0.717 | 0.709 | 0.703 | 0.697 | 0.692 | 0.688 |
| 0.67 | 0.787 | 0.769 | 0.754 | 0.742 | 0.731 | 0.723 | 0.716 | 0.710 | 0.705 | 0.701 |
| 0.68 | 0.804 | 0.785 | 0.769 | 0.757 | 0.746 | 0.737 | 0.729 | 0.723 | 0.718 | 0.713 |
| 0.69 | 0.822 | 0.804 | 0.785 | 0.772 | 0.761 | 0.751 | 0.743 | 0.737 | 0.731 | 0.726 |

\* The table of the varied-flow function for positive slopes $F(u,N)$ is reproduced from Ven Te Chow, Integrating the equation of gradually varied flow, *Proceedings, American Society of Civil Engineers*, vol. 81, paper no. 838, pp. 1–32, November, 1955. The table of the varied-flow function for negative slopes $F(u,N)_{-S_0}$ is reproduced from the author's closing discussion of this paper in *Proceedings*, vol. 83, *Journal of Hydraulics Division*, no. HY1, paper no. 1177, pp. 9–22, February, 1957.

TABLE D-1. THE VARIED-FLOW FUNCTION FOR POSITIVE SLOPES, $F(u,N)$ (*continued*)

| $\dfrac{N}{u}$ | 2.2 | 2.4 | 2.6 | 2.8 | 3.0 | 3.2 | 3.4 | 3.6 | 3.8 | 4.0 |
|---|---|---|---|---|---|---|---|---|---|---|
| 0.70 | 0.840 | 0.819 | 0.802 | 0.787 | 0.776 | 0.766 | 0.757 | 0.750 | 0.744 | 0.739 |
| 0.71 | 0.858 | 0.836 | 0.819 | 0.804 | 0.791 | 0.781 | 0.772 | 0.764 | 0.758 | 0.752 |
| 0.72 | 0.878 | 0.855 | 0.836 | 0.820 | 0.807 | 0.796 | 0.786 | 0.779 | 0.772 | 0.766 |
| 0.73 | 0.898 | 0.874 | 0.854 | 0.837 | 0.823 | 0.811 | 0.802 | 0.793 | 0.786 | 0.780 |
| 0.74 | 0.918 | 0.892 | 0.868 | 0.854 | 0.840 | 0.827 | 0.817 | 0.808 | 0.800 | 0.794 |
| 0.75 | 0.940 | 0.913 | 0.890 | 0.872 | 0.857 | 0.844 | 0.833 | 0.823 | 0.815 | 0.808 |
| 0.76 | 0.961 | 0.933 | 0.909 | 0.890 | 0.874 | 0.861 | 0.849 | 0.839 | 0.830 | 0.823 |
| 0.77 | 0.985 | 0.954 | 0.930 | 0.909 | 0.892 | 0.878 | 0.866 | 0.855 | 0.846 | 0.838 |
| 0.78 | 1.007 | 0.976 | 0.950 | 0.929 | 0.911 | 0.896 | 0.883 | 0.872 | 0.862 | 0.854 |
| 0.79 | 1.031 | 0.998 | 0.971 | 0.949 | 0.930 | 0.914 | 0.901 | 0.889 | 0.879 | 0.870 |
| 0.80 | 1.056 | 1.022 | 0.994 | 0.970 | 0.950 | 0.934 | 0.919 | 0.907 | 0.896 | 0.887 |
| 0.81 | 1.083 | 1.046 | 1.017 | 0.992 | 0.971 | 0.954 | 0.938 | 0.925 | 0.914 | 0.904 |
| 0.82 | 1.110 | 1.072 | 1.041 | 1.015 | 0.993 | 0.974 | 0.958 | 0.945 | 0.932 | 0.922 |
| 0.83 | 1.139 | 1.099 | 1.067 | 1.039 | 1.016 | 0.996 | 0.979 | 0.965 | 0.952 | 0.940 |
| 0.84 | 1.171 | 1.129 | 1.094 | 1.064 | 1.040 | 1.019 | 1.001 | 0.985 | 0.972 | 0.960 |
| 0.85 | 1.201 | 1.157 | 1.121 | 1.091 | 1.065 | 1.043 | 1.024 | 1.007 | 0.993 | 0.980 |
| 0.86 | 1.238 | 1.192 | 1.153 | 1.119 | 1.092 | 1.068 | 1.048 | 1.031 | 1.015 | 1.002 |
| 0.87 | 1.272 | 1.223 | 1.182 | 1.149 | 1.120 | 1.095 | 1.074 | 1.055 | 1.039 | 1.025 |
| 0.88 | 1.314 | 1.262 | 1.228 | 1.181 | 1.151 | 1.124 | 1.101 | 1.081 | 1.064 | 1.049 |
| 0.89 | 1.357 | 1.302 | 1.255 | 1.216 | 1.183 | 1.155 | 1.131 | 1.110 | 1.091 | 1.075 |
| 0.90 | 1.401 | 1.343 | 1.294 | 1.253 | 1.218 | 1.189 | 1.163 | 1.140 | 1.120 | 1.103 |
| 0.91 | 1.452 | 1.389 | 1.338 | 1.294 | 1.257 | 1.225 | 1.197 | 1.173 | 1.152 | 1.133 |
| 0.92 | 1.505 | 1.438 | 1.351 | 1.340 | 1.300 | 1.266 | 1.236 | 1.210 | 1.187 | 1.166 |
| 0.93 | 1.564 | 1.493 | 1.435 | 1.391 | 1.348 | 1.311 | 1.279 | 1.251 | 1.226 | 1.204 |
| 0.94 | 1.645 | 1.568 | 1.504 | 1.449 | 1.403 | 1.363 | 1.328 | 1.297 | 1.270 | 1.246 |
| 0.950 | 1.737 | 1.652 | 1.582 | 1.518 | 1.467 | 1.423 | 1.385 | 1.352 | 1.322 | 1.296 |
| 0.960 | 1.833 | 1.741 | 1.665 | 1.601 | 1.545 | 1.497 | 1.454 | 1.417 | 1.385 | 1.355 |
| 0.970 | 1.969 | 1.866 | 1.780 | 1.707 | 1.644 | 1.590 | 1.543 | 1.501 | 1.464 | 1.431 |
| 0.975 | 2.055 | 1.945 | 1.853 | 1.773 | 1.707 | 1.649 | 1.598 | 1.554 | 1.514 | 1.479 |
| 0.980 | 2.164 | 2.045 | 1.946 | 1.855 | 1.783 | 1.720 | 1.666 | 1.617 | 1.575 | 1.536 |
| 0.985 | 2.294 | 2.165 | 2.056 | 1.959 | 1.880 | 1.812 | 1.752 | 1.699 | 1.652 | 1.610 |
| 0.990 | 2.477 | 2.333 | 2.212 | 2.106 | 2.017 | 1.940 | 1.873 | 1.814 | 1.761 | 1.714 |
| 0.995 | 2.792 | 2.621 | 2.478 | 2.355 | 2.250 | 2.159 | 2.079 | 2.008 | 1.945 | 1.889 |
| 0.999 | 3.523 | 3.292 | 3.097 | 2.931 | 2.788 | 2.663 | 2.554 | 2.457 | 2.370 | 2.293 |
| 1.000 | ∞ | ∞ | ∞ | ∞ | ∞ | ∞ | ∞ | ∞ | ∞ | ∞ |
| 1.001 | 3.317 | 2.931 | 2.640 | 2.399 | 2.184 | 2.008 | 1.856 | 1.725 | 1.610 | 1.508 |
| 1.005 | 2.587 | 2.266 | 2.022 | 1.818 | 1.649 | 1.506 | 1.384 | 1.279 | 1.188 | 1.107 |
| 1.010 | 2.273 | 1.977 | 1.757 | 1.572 | 1.419 | 1.291 | 1.182 | 1.089 | 1.007 | 0.936 |
| 1.015 | 2.090 | 1.807 | 1.602 | 1.428 | 1.286 | 1.166 | 1.065 | 0.978 | 0.902 | 0.836 |
| 1.020 | 1.961 | 1.711 | 1.493 | 1.327 | 1.191 | 1.078 | 0.982 | 0.900 | 0.828 | 0.766 |
| 1.03 | 1.779 | 1.531 | 1.340 | 1.186 | 1.060 | 0.955 | 0.866 | 0.790 | 0.725 | 0.668 |
| 1.04 | 1.651 | 1.410 | 1.232 | 1.086 | 0.967 | 0.868 | 0.785 | 0.714 | 0.653 | 0.600 |
| 1.05 | 1.552 | 1.334 | 1.150 | 1.010 | 0.896 | 0.802 | 0.723 | 0.656 | 0.598 | 0.548 |
| 1.06 | 1.472 | 1.250 | 1.082 | 0.948 | 0.838 | 0.748 | 0.672 | 0.608 | 0.553 | 0.506 |
| 1.07 | 1.404 | 1.195 | 1.026 | 0.896 | 0.790 | 0.703 | 0.630 | 0.569 | 0.516 | 0.471 |
| 1.08 | 1.346 | 1.139 | 0.978 | 0.851 | 0.749 | 0.665 | 0.595 | 0.535 | 0.485 | 0.441 |
| 1.09 | 1.295 | 1.089 | 0.935 | 0.812 | 0.713 | 0.631 | 0.563 | 0.506 | 0.457 | 0.415 |
| 1.10 | 1.250 | 1.050 | 0.897 | 0.777 | 0.681 | 0.601 | 0.536 | 0.480 | 0.433 | 0.392 |
| 1.11 | 1.209 | 1.014 | 0.864 | 0.746 | 0.652 | 0.575 | 0.511 | 0.457 | 0.411 | 0.372 |
| 1.12 | 1.172 | 0.981 | 0.833 | 0.718 | 0.626 | 0.551 | 0.488 | 0.436 | 0.392 | 0.354 |

TABLE D-1. THE VARIED-FLOW FUNCTION FOR POSITIVE SLOPES, $F(u,N)$ (*continued*)

| N \ u | 2.2 | 2.4 | 2.6 | 2.8 | 3.0 | 3.2 | 3.4 | 3.6 | 3.8 | 4.0 |
|---|---|---|---|---|---|---|---|---|---|---|
| 1.13 | 1.138 | 0.950 | 0.805 | 0.692 | 0.602 | 0.529 | 0.468 | 0.417 | 0.374 | 0.337 |
| 1.14 | 1.107 | 0.921 | 0.780 | 0.669 | 0.581 | 0.509 | 0.450 | 0.400 | 0.358 | 0.322 |
| 1.15 | 1.078 | 0.892 | 0.756 | 0.647 | 0.561 | 0.490 | 0.432 | 0.384 | 0.343 | 0.308 |
| 1.16 | 1.052 | 0.870 | 0.734 | 0.627 | 0.542 | 0.473 | 0.417 | 0.369 | 0.329 | 0.295 |
| 1.17 | 1.027 | 0.850 | 0.713 | 0.608 | 0.525 | 0.458 | 0.402 | 0.356 | 0.317 | 0.283 |
| 1.18 | 1.003 | 0.825 | 0.694 | 0.591 | 0.509 | 0.443 | 0.388 | 0.343 | 0.305 | 0.272 |
| 1.19 | 0.981 | 0.810 | 0.676 | 0.574 | 0.494 | 0.429 | 0.375 | 0.331 | 0.294 | 0.262 |
| 1.20 | 0.960 | 0.787 | 0.659 | 0.559 | 0.480 | 0.416 | 0.363 | 0.320 | 0.283 | 0.252 |
| 1.22 | 0.922 | 0.755 | 0.628 | 0.531 | 0.454 | 0.392 | 0.341 | 0.299 | 0.264 | 0.235 |
| 1.24 | 0.887 | 0.725 | 0.600 | 0.505 | 0.431 | 0.371 | 0.322 | 0.281 | 0.248 | 0.219 |
| 1.26 | 0.855 | 0.692 | 0.574 | 0.482 | 0.410 | 0.351 | 0.304 | 0.265 | 0.233 | 0.205 |
| 1.28 | 0.827 | 0.666 | 0.551 | 0.461 | 0.391 | 0.334 | 0.288 | 0.250 | 0.219 | 0.193 |
| 1.30 | 0.800 | 0.644 | 0.530 | 0.442 | 0.373 | 0.318 | 0.274 | 0.237 | 0.207 | 0.181 |
| 1.32 | 0.775 | 0.625 | 0.510 | 0.424 | 0.357 | 0.304 | 0.260 | 0.225 | 0.196 | 0.171 |
| 1.34 | 0.752 | 0.605 | 0.492 | 0.408 | 0.342 | 0.290 | 0.248 | 0.214 | 0.185 | 0.162 |
| 1.36 | 0.731 | 0.588 | 0.475 | 0.393 | 0.329 | 0.278 | 0.237 | 0.204 | 0.176 | 0.153 |
| 1.38 | 0.711 | 0.567 | 0.459 | 0.378 | 0.316 | 0.266 | 0.226 | 0.194 | 0.167 | 0.145 |
| 1.40 | 0.692 | 0.548 | 0.444 | 0.365 | 0.304 | 0.256 | 0.217 | 0.185 | 0.159 | 0.138 |
| 1.42 | 0.674 | 0.533 | 0.431 | 0.353 | 0.293 | 0.246 | 0.208 | 0.177 | 0.152 | 0.131 |
| 1.44 | 0.658 | 0.517 | 0.417 | 0.341 | 0.282 | 0.236 | 0.199 | 0.169 | 0.145 | 0.125 |
| 1.46 | 0.642 | 0.505 | 0.405 | 0.330 | 0.273 | 0.227 | 0.191 | 0.162 | 0.139 | 0.119 |
| 1.48 | 0.627 | 0.493 | 0.394 | 0.320 | 0.263 | 0.219 | 0.184 | 0.156 | 0.133 | 0.113 |
| 1.50 | 0.613 | 0.480 | 0.383 | 0.310 | 0.255 | 0.211 | 0.177 | 0.149 | 0.127 | 0.108 |
| 1.55 | 0.580 | 0.451 | 0.358 | 0.288 | 0.235 | 0.194 | 0.161 | 0.135 | 0.114 | 0.097 |
| 1.60 | 0.551 | 0.425 | 0.335 | 0.269 | 0.218 | 0.179 | 0.148 | 0.123 | 0.103 | 0.087 |
| 1.65 | 0.525 | 0.402 | 0.316 | 0.251 | 0.203 | 0.165 | 0.136 | 0.113 | 0.094 | 0.079 |
| 1.70 | 0.501 | 0.381 | 0.298 | 0.236 | 0.189 | 0.153 | 0.125 | 0.103 | 0.086 | 0.072 |
| 1.75 | 0.480 | 0.362 | 0.282 | 0.222 | 0.177 | 0.143 | 0.116 | 0.095 | 0.079 | 0.065 |
| 1.80 | 0.460 | 0.349 | 0.267 | 0.209 | 0.166 | 0.133 | 0.108 | 0.088 | 0.072 | 0.060 |
| 1.85 | 0.442 | 0.332 | 0.254 | 0.198 | 0.156 | 0.125 | 0.100 | 0.082 | 0.067 | 0.055 |
| 1.90 | 0.425 | 0.315 | 0.242 | 0.188 | 0.147 | 0.117 | 0.094 | 0.076 | 0.062 | 0.050 |
| 1.95 | 0.409 | 0.304 | 0.231 | 0.178 | 0.139 | 0.110 | 0.088 | 0.070 | 0.057 | 0.046 |
| 2.00 | 0.395 | 0.292 | 0.221 | 0.169 | 0.132 | 0.104 | 0.082 | 0.066 | 0.053 | 0.043 |
| 2.10 | 0.369 | 0.273 | 0.202 | 0.154 | 0.119 | 0.092 | 0.073 | 0.058 | 0.046 | 0.037 |
| 2.20 | 0.346 | 0.253 | 0.186 | 0.141 | 0.107 | 0.083 | 0.065 | 0.051 | 0.040 | 0.032 |
| 2.3 | 0.326 | 0.235 | 0.173 | 0.129 | 0.098 | 0.075 | 0.058 | 0.045 | 0.035 | 0.028 |
| 2.4 | 0.308 | 0.220 | 0.160 | 0.119 | 0.089 | 0.068 | 0.052 | 0.040 | 0.031 | 0.024 |
| 2.5 | 0.292 | 0.207 | 0.150 | 0.110 | 0.082 | 0.062 | 0.047 | 0.036 | 0.028 | 0.022 |
| 2.6 | 0.277 | 0.197 | 0.140 | 0.102 | 0.076 | 0.057 | 0.043 | 0.033 | 0.025 | 0.019 |
| 2.7 | 0.264 | 0.188 | 0.131 | 0.095 | 0.070 | 0.052 | 0.039 | 0.029 | 0.022 | 0.017 |
| 2.8 | 0.252 | 0.176 | 0.124 | 0.089 | 0.065 | 0.048 | 0.036 | 0.027 | 0.020 | 0.015 |
| 2.9 | 0.241 | 0.166 | 0.117 | 0.083 | 0.060 | 0.044 | 0.033 | 0.024 | 0.018 | 0.014 |
| 3.0 | 0.230 | 0.159 | 0.110 | 0.078 | 0.056 | 0.041 | 0.030 | 0.022 | 0.017 | 0.012 |
| 3.5 | 0.190 | 0.126 | 0.085 | 0.059 | 0.041 | 0.029 | 0.021 | 0.015 | 0.011 | 0.008 |
| 4.0 | 0.161 | 0.104 | 0.069 | 0.046 | 0.031 | 0.022 | 0.015 | 0.010 | 0.007 | 0.005 |
| 4.5 | 0.139 | 0.087 | 0.057 | 0.037 | 0.025 | 0.017 | 0.011 | 0.008 | 0.005 | 0.004 |
| 5.0 | 0.122 | 0.076 | 0.048 | 0.031 | 0.020 | 0.013 | 0.009 | 0.006 | 0.004 | 0.003 |
| 6.0 | 0.098 | 0.060 | 0.036 | 0.022 | 0.014 | 0.009 | 0.006 | 0.004 | 0.002 | 0.002 |
| 7.0 | 0.081 | 0.048 | 0.028 | 0.017 | 0.010 | 0.006 | 0.004 | 0.002 | 0.002 | 0.001 |
| 8.0 | 0.069 | 0.040 | 0.022 | 0.013 | 0.008 | 0.005 | 0.003 | 0.002 | 0.001 | 0.001 |
| 9.0 | 0.060 | 0.034 | 0.019 | 0.011 | 0.006 | 0.004 | 0.002 | 0.001 | 0.001 | 0.000 |
| 10.0 | 0.053 | 0.028 | 0.016 | 0.009 | 0.005 | 0.003 | 0.002 | 0.001 | 0.001 | 0.000 |
| 20.0 | 0.023 | 0.018 | 0.011 | 0.006 | 0.002 | 0.001 | 0.001 | 0.000 | 0.000 | 0.000 |

TABLE D-1. THE VARIED-FLOW FUNCTION FOR POSITIVE SLOPES, $F(u,N)$ (*continued*)

| N / u | 4.2 | 4.6 | 5.0 | 5.4 | 5.8 | 6.2 | 6.6 | 7.0 | 7.4 | 7.8 |
|---|---|---|---|---|---|---|---|---|---|---|
| 0.00 | 0.000 | 0.000 | 0.000 | 0.000 | 0.000 | 0.000 | 0.000 | 0.000 | 0.000 | 0.000 |
| 0.02 | 0.020 | 0.020 | 0.020 | 0.020 | 0.020 | 0.020 | 0.020 | 0.020 | 0.020 | 0.020 |
| 0.04 | 0.040 | 0.040 | 0.040 | 0.040 | 0.040 | 0.040 | 0.040 | 0.040 | 0.040 | 0.040 |
| 0.06 | 0.060 | 0.060 | 0.060 | 0.060 | 0.060 | 0.060 | 0.060 | 0.060 | 0.060 | 0.060 |
| 0.08 | 0.080 | 0.080 | 0.080 | 0.080 | 0.080 | 0.080 | 0.080 | 0.080 | 0.080 | 0.080 |
| 0.10 | 0.100 | 0.100 | 0.100 | 0.100 | 0.100 | 0.100 | 0.100 | 0.100 | 0.100 | 0.100 |
| 0.12 | 0.120 | 0.120 | 0.120 | 0.120 | 0.120 | 0.120 | 0.120 | 0.120 | 0.120 | 0.120 |
| 0.14 | 0.140 | 0.140 | 0.140 | 0.140 | 0.140 | 0.140 | 0.140 | 0.140 | 0.140 | 0.140 |
| 0.16 | 0.160 | 0.160 | 0.160 | 0.160 | 0.160 | 0.160 | 0.160 | 0.160 | 0.160 | 0.160 |
| 0.18 | 0.180 | 0.180 | 0.180 | 0.180 | 0.180 | 0.180 | 0.180 | 0.180 | 0.180 | 0.180 |
| 0.20 | 0.200 | 0.200 | 0.200 | 0.200 | 0.200 | 0.200 | 0.200 | 0.200 | 0.200 | 0.200 |
| 0.22 | 0.220 | 0.220 | 0.220 | 0.220 | 0.220 | 0.220 | 0.220 | 0.220 | 0.220 | 0.220 |
| 0.24 | 0.240 | 0.240 | 0.240 | 0.240 | 0.240 | 0.240 | 0.240 | 0.240 | 0.240 | 0.240 |
| 0.26 | 0.260 | 0.260 | 0.260 | 0.260 | 0.260 | 0.260 | 0.260 | 0.260 | 0.260 | 0.260 |
| 0.28 | 0.280 | 0.280 | 0.280 | 0.280 | 0.280 | 0.280 | 0.280 | 0.280 | 0.280 | 0.280 |
| 0.30 | 0.300 | 0.300 | 0.300 | 0.300 | 0.300 | 0.300 | 0.300 | 0.300 | 0.300 | 0.300 |
| 0.32 | 0.321 | 0.320 | 0.320 | 0.320 | 0.320 | 0.320 | 0.320 | 0.320 | 0.320 | 0.320 |
| 0.34 | 0.341 | 0.340 | 0.340 | 0.340 | 0.340 | 0.340 | 0.340 | 0.340 | 0.340 | 0.340 |
| 0.36 | 0.361 | 0.361 | 0.360 | 0.360 | 0.360 | 0.360 | 0.360 | 0.360 | 0.360 | 0.360 |
| 0.38 | 0.381 | 0.381 | 0.381 | 0.380 | 0.380 | 0.380 | 0.380 | 0.380 | 0.380 | 0.380 |
| 0.40 | 0.402 | 0.401 | 0.401 | 0.400 | 0.400 | 0.400 | 0.400 | 0.400 | 0.400 | 0.400 |
| 0.42 | 0.422 | 0.421 | 0.421 | 0.421 | 0.420 | 0.420 | 0.420 | 0.420 | 0.420 | 0.420 |
| 0.44 | 0.443 | 0.442 | 0.441 | 0.441 | 0.441 | 0.441 | 0.440 | 0.440 | 0.440 | 0.440 |
| 0.46 | 0.463 | 0.462 | 0.462 | 0.461 | 0.461 | 0.461 | 0.460 | 0.460 | 0.460 | 0.460 |
| 0.48 | 0.484 | 0.483 | 0.482 | 0.481 | 0.481 | 0.481 | 0.480 | 0.480 | 0.480 | 0.480 |
| 0.50 | 0.505 | 0.504 | 0.503 | 0.502 | 0.501 | 0.501 | 0.501 | 0.500 | 0.500 | 0.500 |
| 0.52 | 0.527 | 0.525 | 0.523 | 0.522 | 0.522 | 0.521 | 0.521 | 0.521 | 0.520 | 0.520 |
| 0.54 | 0.548 | 0.546 | 0.544 | 0.543 | 0.542 | 0.542 | 0.541 | 0.541 | 0.541 | 0.541 |
| 0.56 | 0.570 | 0.567 | 0.565 | 0.564 | 0.563 | 0.562 | 0.562 | 0.561 | 0.561 | 0.561 |
| 0.58 | 0.592 | 0.589 | 0.587 | 0.585 | 0.583 | 0.583 | 0.582 | 0.582 | 0.581 | 0.581 |
| 0.60 | 0.614 | 0.611 | 0.608 | 0.606 | 0.605 | 0.604 | 0.603 | 0.602 | 0.602 | 0.601 |
| 0.61 | 0.626 | 0.622 | 0.619 | 0.617 | 0.615 | 0.614 | 0.613 | 0.612 | 0.612 | 0.611 |
| 0.62 | 0.637 | 0.633 | 0.630 | 0.628 | 0.626 | 0.625 | 0.624 | 0.623 | 0.622 | 0.622 |
| 0.63 | 0.649 | 0.644 | 0.641 | 0.638 | 0.636 | 0.635 | 0.634 | 0.633 | 0.632 | 0.632 |
| 0.64 | 0.661 | 0.656 | 0.652 | 0.649 | 0.647 | 0.646 | 0.645 | 0.644 | 0.643 | 0.642 |
| 0.65 | 0.673 | 0.667 | 0.663 | 0.660 | 0.658 | 0.656 | 0.655 | 0.654 | 0.653 | 0.653 |
| 0.66 | 0.685 | 0.679 | 0.675 | 0.672 | 0.669 | 0.667 | 0.666 | 0.665 | 0.664 | 0.663 |
| 0.67 | 0.697 | 0.691 | 0.686 | 0.683 | 0.680 | 0.678 | 0.676 | 0.675 | 0.674 | 0.673 |
| 0.68 | 0.709 | 0.703 | 0.698 | 0.694 | 0.691 | 0.689 | 0.687 | 0.686 | 0.685 | 0.684 |
| 0.69 | 0.722 | 0.715 | 0.710 | 0.706 | 0.703 | 0.700 | 0.698 | 0.696 | 0.695 | 0.694 |
| 0.70 | 0.735 | 0.727 | 0.722 | 0.717 | 0.714 | 0.712 | 0.710 | 0.708 | 0.706 | 0.705 |
| 0.71 | 0.748 | 0.740 | 0.734 | 0.729 | 0.726 | 0.723 | 0.721 | 0.719 | 0.717 | 0.716 |
| 0.72 | 0.761 | 0.752 | 0.746 | 0.741 | 0.737 | 0.734 | 0.732 | 0.730 | 0.728 | 0.727 |
| 0.73 | 0.774 | 0.765 | 0.759 | 0.753 | 0.749 | 0.746 | 0.743 | 0.741 | 0.739 | 0.737 |
| 0.74 | 0.788 | 0.779 | 0.771 | 0.766 | 0.761 | 0.757 | 0.754 | 0.752 | 0.750 | 0.748 |
| 0.75 | 0.802 | 0.792 | 0.784 | 0.778 | 0.773 | 0.769 | 0.766 | 0.763 | 0.761 | 0.759 |
| 0.76 | 0.817 | 0.806 | 0.798 | 0.791 | 0.786 | 0.782 | 0.778 | 0.775 | 0.773 | 0.771 |
| 0.77 | 0.831 | 0.820 | 0.811 | 0.804 | 0.798 | 0.794 | 0.790 | 0.787 | 0.784 | 0.782 |
| 0.78 | 0.847 | 0.834 | 0.825 | 0.817 | 0.811 | 0.806 | 0.802 | 0.799 | 0.796 | 0.794 |
| 0.79 | 0.862 | 0.849 | 0.839 | 0.831 | 0.824 | 0.819 | 0.815 | 0.811 | 0.808 | 0.805 |

TABLE D-1. THE VARIED-FLOW FUNCTION FOR POSITIVE SLOPES, $F(u,N)$ (continued)

| $N$ / $u$ | 4.2 | 4.6 | 5.0 | 5.4 | 5.8 | 6.2 | 6.6 | 7.0 | 7.4 | 7.8 |
|---|---|---|---|---|---|---|---|---|---|---|
| 0.80 | 0.878 | 0.865 | 0.854 | 0.845 | 0.838 | 0.832 | 0.828 | 0.823 | 0.820 | 0.818 |
| 0.81 | 0.895 | 0.881 | 0.869 | 0.860 | 0.852 | 0.846 | 0.841 | 0.836 | 0.833 | 0.830 |
| 0.82 | 0.913 | 0.897 | 0.885 | 0.875 | 0.866 | 0.860 | 0.854 | 0.850 | 0.846 | 0.842 |
| 0.83 | 0.931 | 0.914 | 0.901 | 0.890 | 0.881 | 0.874 | 0.868 | 0.863 | 0.859 | 0.855 |
| 0.84 | 0.949 | 0.932 | 0.918 | 0.906 | 0.897 | 0.889 | 0.882 | 0.877 | 0.872 | 0.868 |
| 0.85 | 0.969 | 0.950 | 0.935 | 0.923 | 0.912 | 0.905 | 0.898 | 0.891 | 0.887 | 0.882 |
| 0.86 | 0.990 | 0.970 | 0.954 | 0.940 | 0.930 | 0.921 | 0.913 | 0.906 | 0.901 | 0.896 |
| 0.87 | 1.012 | 0.990 | 0.973 | 0.959 | 0.947 | 0.937 | 0.929 | 0.922 | 0.916 | 0.911 |
| 0.88 | 1.035 | 1.012 | 0.994 | 0.978 | 0.966 | 0.955 | 0.946 | 0.938 | 0.932 | 0.927 |
| 0.89 | 1.060 | 1.035 | 1.015 | 0.999 | 0.986 | 0.974 | 0.964 | 0.956 | 0.949 | 0.943 |
| 0.90 | 1.087 | 1.060 | 1.039 | 1.021 | 1.007 | 0.994 | 0.984 | 0.974 | 0.967 | 0.960 |
| 0.91 | 1.116 | 1.088 | 1.064 | 1.045 | 1.029 | 1.016 | 1.003 | 0.995 | 0.986 | 0.979 |
| 0.92 | 1.148 | 1.117 | 1.092 | 1.072 | 1.054 | 1.039 | 1.027 | 1.016 | 1.006 | 0.999 |
| 0.93 | 1.184 | 1.151 | 1.123 | 1.101 | 1.081 | 1.065 | 1.050 | 1.040 | 1.029 | 1.021 |
| 0.94 | 1.225 | 1.188 | 1.158 | 1.134 | 1.113 | 1.095 | 1.080 | 1.066 | 1.054 | 1.044 |
| 0.950 | 1.272 | 1.232 | 1.199 | 1.172 | 1.148 | 1.128 | 1.111 | 1.097 | 1.084 | 1.073 |
| 0.960 | 1.329 | 1.285 | 1.248 | 1.217 | 1.188 | 1.167 | 1.149 | 1.133 | 1.119 | 1.106 |
| 0.970 | 1.402 | 1.351 | 1.310 | 1.275 | 1.246 | 1.319 | 1.197 | 1.179 | 1.162 | 1.148 |
| 0.975 | 1.447 | 1.393 | 1.348 | 1.311 | 1.280 | 1.250 | 1.227 | 1.207 | 1.190 | 1.173 |
| 0.980 | 1.502 | 1.443 | 1.395 | 1.354 | 1.339 | 1.288 | 1.262 | 1.241 | 1.221 | 1.204 |
| 0.985 | 1.573 | 1.508 | 1.454 | 1.409 | 1.372 | 1.337 | 1.309 | 1.284 | 1.263 | 1.243 |
| 0.990 | 1.671 | 1.598 | 1.537 | 1.487 | 1.444 | 1.404 | 1.373 | 1.344 | 1.319 | 1.297 |
| 0.995 | 1.838 | 1.751 | 1.678 | 1.617 | 1.565 | 1.519 | 1.479 | 1.451 | 1.416 | 1.388 |
| 0.999 | 2.223 | 2.102 | 2.002 | 1.917 | 1.845 | 1.780 | 1.725 | 1.678 | 1.635 | 1.596 |
| 1.000 | ∞ | ∞ | ∞ | ∞ | ∞ | ∞ | ∞ | ∞ | ∞ | ∞ |
| 1.001 | 1.417 | 1.264 | 1.138 | 1.033 | 0.951 | 0.870 | 0.803 | 0.746 | 0.697 | 0.651 |
| 1.005 | 1.036 | 0.915 | 0.817 | 0.737 | 0.669 | 0.612 | 0.553 | 0.526 | 0.481 | 0.447 |
| 1.010 | 0.873 | 0.766 | 0.681 | 0.610 | 0.551 | 0.502 | 0.459 | 0.422 | 0.389 | 0.360 |
| 1.015 | 0.778 | 0.680 | 0.602 | 0.537 | 0.483 | 0.440 | 0.399 | 0.366 | 0.336 | 0.310 |
| 1.02 | 0.711 | 0.620 | 0.546 | 0.486 | 0.436 | 0.394 | 0.358 | 0.327 | 0.300 | 0.276 |
| 1.03 | 0.618 | 0.535 | 0.469 | 0.415 | 0.370 | 0.333 | 0.300 | 0.272 | 0.249 | 0.228 |
| 1.04 | 0.554 | 0.477 | 0.415 | 0.365 | 0.324 | 0.290 | 0.262 | 0.236 | 0.214 | 0.195 |
| 1.05 | 0.504 | 0.432 | 0.374 | 0.328 | 0.289 | 0.259 | 0.231 | 0.208 | 0.189 | 0.174 |
| 1.06 | 0.464 | 0.396 | 0.342 | 0.298 | 0.262 | 0.233 | 0.209 | 0.187 | 0.170 | 0.154 |
| 1.07 | 0.431 | 0.366 | 0.315 | 0.273 | 0.239 | 0.212 | 0.191 | 0.168 | 0.151 | 0.136 |
| 1.08 | 0.403 | 0.341 | 0.292 | 0.252 | 0.220 | 0.194 | 0.172 | 0.153 | 0.137 | 0.123 |
| 1.09 | 0.379 | 0.319 | 0.272 | 0.234 | 0.204 | 0.179 | 0.158 | 0.140 | 0.125 | 0.112 |
| 1.10 | 0.357 | 0.299 | 0.254 | 0.218 | 0.189 | 0.165 | 0.146 | 0.129 | 0.114 | 0.102 |
| 1.11 | 0.338 | 0.282 | 0.239 | 0.204 | 0.176 | 0.154 | 0.135 | 0.119 | 0.105 | 0.094 |
| 1.12 | 0.321 | 0.267 | 0.225 | 0.192 | 0.165 | 0.143 | 0.125 | 0.110 | 0.097 | 0.086 |
| 1.13 | 0.305 | 0.253 | 0.212 | 0.181 | 0.155 | 0.135 | 0.117 | 0.102 | 0.090 | 0.080 |
| 1.14 | 0.291 | 0.240 | 0.201 | 0.170 | 0.146 | 0.126 | 0.109 | 0.095 | 0.084 | 0.074 |
| 1.15 | 0.278 | 0.229 | 0.191 | 0.161 | 0.137 | 0.118 | 0.102 | 0.089 | 0.078 | 0.068 |
| 1.16 | 0.266 | 0.218 | 0.181 | 0.153 | 0.130 | 0.111 | 0.096 | 0.084 | 0.072 | 0.064 |
| 1.17 | 0.255 | 0.208 | 0.173 | 0.145 | 0.123 | 0.105 | 0.090 | 0.078 | 0.068 | 0.060 |
| 1.18 | 0.244 | 0.199 | 0.165 | 0.138 | 0.116 | 0.099 | 0.085 | 0.073 | 0.063 | 0.055 |
| 1.19 | 0.235 | 0.191 | 0.157 | 0.131 | 0.110 | 0.094 | 0.080 | 0.068 | 0.059 | 0.051 |
| 1.20 | 0.226 | 0.183 | 0.150 | 0.215 | 0.105 | 0.088 | 0.076 | 0.064 | 0.056 | 0.048 |
| 1.22 | 0.209 | 0.168 | 0.138 | 0.114 | 0.095 | 0.080 | 0.068 | 0.057 | 0.049 | 0.042 |
| 1.24 | 0.195 | 0.156 | 0.127 | 0.104 | 0.086 | 0.072 | 0.060 | 0.051 | 0.044 | 0.038 |

TABLE D-1. THE VARIED-FLOW FUNCTION FOR POSITIVE SLOPES, $F(u,N)$ (continued)

| $u$ \ $N$ | 4.2 | 4.6 | 5.0 | 5.4 | 5.8 | 6.2 | 6.6 | 7.0 | 7.4 | 7.8 |
|---|---|---|---|---|---|---|---|---|---|---|
| 1.26 | 0.182 | 0.145 | 0.117 | 0.095 | 0.079 | 0.065 | 0.055 | 0.046 | 0.039 | 0.033 |
| 1.28 | 0.170 | 0.135 | 0.108 | 0.088 | 0.072 | 0.060 | 0.050 | 0.041 | 0.035 | 0.030 |
| 1.30 | 0.160 | 0.126 | 0.100 | 0.081 | 0.066 | 0.054 | 0.045 | 0.037 | 0.031 | 0.026 |
| 1.32 | 0.150 | 0.118 | 0.093 | 0.075 | 0.061 | 0.050 | 0.041 | 0.034 | 0.028 | 0.024 |
| 1.34 | 0.142 | 0.110 | 0.087 | 0.069 | 0.056 | 0.045 | 0.037 | 0.030 | 0.025 | 0.021 |
| 1.36 | 0.134 | 0.103 | 0.081 | 0.064 | 0.052 | 0.042 | 0.034 | 0.028 | 0.023 | 0.019 |
| 1.38 | 0.127 | 0.097 | 0.076 | 0.060 | 0.048 | 0.038 | 0.032 | 0.026 | 0.021 | 0.017 |
| 1.40 | 0.120 | 0.092 | 0.071 | 0.056 | 0.044 | 0.036 | 0.028 | 0.023 | 0.019 | 0.016 |
| 1.42 | 0.114 | 0.087 | 0.067 | 0.052 | 0.041 | 0.033 | 0.026 | 0.021 | 0.017 | 0.014 |
| 1.44 | 0.108 | 0.082 | 0.063 | 0.049 | 0.038 | 0.030 | 0.024 | 0.019 | 0.016 | 0.013 |
| 1.46 | 0.103 | 0.077 | 0.059 | 0.046 | 0.036 | 0.028 | 0.022 | 0.018 | 0.014 | 0.012 |
| 1.48 | 0.098 | 0.073 | 0.056 | 0.043 | 0.033 | 0.026 | 0.021 | 0.017 | 0.013 | 0.010 |
| 1.50 | 0.093 | 0.069 | 0.053 | 0.040 | 0.031 | 0.024 | 0.020 | 0.015 | 0.012 | 0.009 |
| 1.55 | 0.083 | 0.061 | 0.046 | 0.035 | 0.026 | 0.020 | 0.016 | 0.012 | 0.010 | 0.008 |
| 1.60 | 0.074 | 0.054 | 0.040 | 0.030 | 0.023 | 0.017 | 0.013 | 0.010 | 0.008 | 0.006 |
| 1.65 | 0.067 | 0.048 | 0.035 | 0.026 | 0.019 | 0.014 | 0.011 | 0.008 | 0.006 | 0.005 |
| 1.70 | 0.060 | 0.043 | 0.031 | 0.023 | 0.016 | 0.012 | 0.009 | 0.007 | 0.005 | 0.004 |
| 1.75 | 0.054 | 0.038 | 0.027 | 0.020 | 0.014 | 0.010 | 0.008 | 0.006 | 0.004 | 0.003 |
| 1.80 | 0.049 | 0.034 | 0.024 | 0.017 | 0.012 | 0.009 | 0.007 | 0.005 | 0.004 | 0.003 |
| 1.85 | 0.045 | 0.031 | 0.022 | 0.015 | 0.011 | 0.008 | 0.006 | 0.004 | 0.003 | 0.002 |
| 1.90 | 0.041 | 0.028 | 0.020 | 0.014 | 0.010 | 0.007 | 0.005 | 0.004 | 0.003 | 0.002 |
| 1.95 | 0.038 | 0.026 | 0.018 | 0.012 | 0.008 | 0.006 | 0.004 | 0.003 | 0.002 | 0.002 |
| 2.00 | 0.035 | 0.023 | 0.016 | 0.011 | 0.007 | 0.005 | 0.004 | 0.003 | 0.002 | 0.001 |
| 2.10 | 0.030 | 0.019 | 0.013 | 0.009 | 0.006 | 0.004 | 0.003 | 0.002 | 0.001 | 0.001 |
| 2.20 | 0.025 | 0.016 | 0.011 | 0.007 | 0.005 | 0.004 | 0.002 | 0.001 | 0.001 | 0.001 |
| 2.3 | 0.022 | 0.014 | 0.009 | 0.006 | 0.004 | 0.003 | 0.002 | 0.001 | 0.001 | 0.001 |
| 2.4 | 0.019 | 0.012 | 0.008 | 0.005 | 0.003 | 0.002 | 0.001 | 0.001 | 0.001 | 0.001 |
| 2.5 | 0.017 | 0.010 | 0.006 | 0.004 | 0.003 | 0.002 | 0.001 | 0.001 | 0.000 | 0.000 |
| 2.6 | 0.015 | 0.009 | 0.005 | 0.003 | 0.002 | 0.001 | 0.001 | 0.001 | 0.000 | 0.000 |
| 2.7 | 0.013 | 0.008 | 0.005 | 0.003 | 0.002 | 0.001 | 0.001 | 0.000 | 0.000 | 0.000 |
| 2.8 | 0.012 | 0.007 | 0.004 | 0.002 | 0.001 | 0.001 | 0.001 | 0.000 | 0.000 | 0.000 |
| 2.9 | 0.010 | 0.006 | 0.004 | 0.002 | 0.001 | 0.001 | 0.000 | 0.000 | 0.000 | 0.000 |
| 3.0 | 0.009 | 0.005 | 0.003 | 0.002 | 0.001 | 0.001 | 0.000 | 0.000 | 0.000 | 0.000 |
| 3.5 | 0.006 | 0.003 | 0.002 | 0.001 | 0.001 | 0.000 | 0.000 | 0.000 | 0.000 | 0.000 |
| 4.0 | 0.004 | 0.002 | 0.001 | 0.000 | 0.000 | 0.000 | 0.000 | 0.000 | 0.000 | 0.000 |
| 4.5 | 0.003 | 0.001 | 0.001 | 0.000 | 0.000 | 0.000 | 0.000 | 0.000 | 0.000 | 0.000 |
| 5.0 | 0.002 | 0.001 | 0.000 | 0.000 | 0.000 | 0.000 | 0.000 | 0.000 | 0.000 | 0.000 |
| 6.0 | 0.001 | 0.000 | 0.000 | 0.000 | 0.000 | 0.000 | 0.000 | 0.000 | 0.000 | 0.000 |
| 7.0 | 0.001 | 0.000 | 0.000 | 0.000 | 0.000 | 0.000 | 0.000 | 0.000 | 0.000 | 0.000 |
| 8.0 | 0.000 | 0.000 | 0.000 | 0.000 | 0.000 | 0.000 | 0.000 | 0.000 | 0.000 | 0.000 |
| 9.0 | 0.000 | 0.000 | 0.000 | 0.000 | 0.000 | 0.000 | 0.000 | 0.000 | 0.000 | 0.000 |
| 10.0 | 0.000 | 0.000 | 0.000 | 0.000 | 0.000 | 0.000 | 0.000 | 0.000 | 0.000 | 0.000 |
| 20.0 | 0.000 | 0.000 | 0.000 | 0.000 | 0.000 | 0.000 | 0.000 | 0.000 | 0.000 | 0.000 |

TABLE D-1. THE VARIED-FLOW FUNCTION FOR POSITIVE SLOPES, $F(u,N)$ (*continued*)

| N u | 8.2 | 8.6 | 9.0 | 9.4 | 9.8 |
|---|---|---|---|---|---|
| 0.00 | 0.000 | 0.000 | 0.000 | 0.000 | 0.000 |
| 0.02 | 0.020 | 0.020 | 0.020 | 0.020 | 0.020 |
| 0.04 | 0.040 | 0.040 | 0.040 | 0.040 | 0.040 |
| 0.06 | 0.060 | 0.060 | 0.060 | 0.060 | 0.060 |
| 0.08 | 0.080 | 0.080 | 0.080 | 0.080 | 0.080 |
| 0.10 | 0.100 | 0.100 | 0.100 | 0.100 | 0.100 |
| 0.12 | 0.120 | 0.120 | 0.120 | 0.120 | 0.120 |
| 0.14 | 0.140 | 0.140 | 0.140 | 0.140 | 0.140 |
| 0.16 | 0.160 | 0.160 | 0.160 | 0.160 | 0.160 |
| 0.18 | 0.180 | 0.180 | 0.180 | 0.180 | 0.180 |
| 0.20 | 0.200 | 0.200 | 0.200 | 0.200 | 0.200 |
| 0.22 | 0.220 | 0.220 | 0.220 | 0.220 | 0.220 |
| 0.24 | 0.240 | 0.240 | 0.240 | 0.240 | 0.240 |
| 0.26 | 0.260 | 0.260 | 0.260 | 0.260 | 0.260 |
| 0.28 | 0.280 | 0.280 | 0.280 | 0.280 | 0.280 |
| 0.30 | 0.300 | 0.300 | 0.300 | 0.300 | 0.300 |
| 0.32 | 0.320 | 0.320 | 0.320 | 0.320 | 0.320 |
| 0.34 | 0.340 | 0.340 | 0.340 | 0.340 | 0.340 |
| 0.36 | 0.360 | 0.360 | 0.360 | 0.360 | 0.360 |
| 0.38 | 0.380 | 0.380 | 0.380 | 0.380 | 0.380 |
| 0.40 | 0.400 | 0.400 | 0.400 | 0.400 | 0.400 |
| 0.42 | 0.420 | 0.420 | 0.420 | 0.420 | 0.420 |
| 0.44 | 0.440 | 0.440 | 0.440 | 0.440 | 0.440 |
| 0.46 | 0.460 | 0.460 | 0.460 | 0.460 | 0.460 |
| 0.48 | 0.480 | 0.480 | 0.480 | 0.480 | 0.480 |
| 0.50 | 0.500 | 0.500 | 0.500 | 0.500 | 0.500 |
| 0.52 | 0.520 | 0.520 | 0.520 | 0.520 | 0.520 |
| 0.54 | 0.540 | 0.540 | 0.540 | 0.540 | 0.540 |
| 0.56 | 0.561 | 0.560 | 0.560 | 0.560 | 0.560 |
| 0.58 | 0.581 | 0.581 | 0.580 | 0.580 | 0.580 |
| 0.60 | 0.601 | 0.601 | 0.601 | 0.600 | 0.600 |
| 0.61 | 0.611 | 0.611 | 0.611 | 0.611 | 0.610 |
| 0.62 | 0.621 | 0.621 | 0.621 | 0.621 | 0.621 |
| 0.63 | 0.632 | 0.631 | 0.631 | 0.631 | 0.631 |
| 0.64 | 0.642 | 0.641 | 0.641 | 0.641 | 0.641 |
| 0.65 | 0.652 | 0.652 | 0.651 | 0.651 | 0.651 |
| 0.66 | 0.662 | 0.662 | 0.662 | 0.661 | 0.661 |
| 0.67 | 0.673 | 0.672 | 0.672 | 0.672 | 0.671 |
| 0.68 | 0.683 | 0.683 | 0.682 | 0.682 | 0.681 |
| 0.69 | 0.694 | 0.693 | 0.692 | 0.692 | 0.692 |
| 0.70 | 0.704 | 0.704 | 0.703 | 0.702 | 0.702 |
| 0.71 | 0.715 | 0.714 | 0.713 | 0.713 | 0.712 |
| 0.72 | 0.726 | 0.725 | 0.724 | 0.723 | 0.723 |
| 0.73 | 0.736 | 0.735 | 0.734 | 0.734 | 0.733 |
| 0.74 | 0.747 | 0.746 | 0.745 | 0.744 | 0.744 |
| 0.75 | 0.758 | 0.757 | 0.756 | 0.755 | 0.754 |
| 0.76 | 0.769 | 0.768 | 0.767 | 0.766 | 0.765 |
| 0.77 | 0.780 | 0.779 | 0.778 | 0.777 | 0.776 |
| 0.78 | 0.792 | 0.790 | 0.789 | 0.788 | 0.787 |
| 0.79 | 0.804 | 0.802 | 0.800 | 0.799 | 0.798 |

TABLE D-1. THE VARIED-FLOW FUNCTION FOR POSITIVE SLOPES, $F(u,N)$ (continued)

| N / u | 8.2 | 8.6 | 9.0 | 9.4 | 9.8 |
|---|---|---|---|---|---|
| 0.80 | 0.815 | 0.813 | 0.811 | 0.810 | 0.809 |
| 0.81 | 0.827 | 0.825 | 0.823 | 0.822 | 0.820 |
| 0.82 | 0.839 | 0.837 | 0.835 | 0.833 | 0.831 |
| 0.83 | 0.852 | 0.849 | 0.847 | 0.845 | 0.844 |
| 0.84 | 0.865 | 0.862 | 0.860 | 0.858 | 0.856 |
| 0.85 | 0.878 | 0.875 | 0.873 | 0.870 | 0.868 |
| 0.86 | 0.892 | 0.889 | 0.886 | 0.883 | 0.881 |
| 0.87 | 0.907 | 0.903 | 0.900 | 0.897 | 0.894 |
| 0.88 | 0.921 | 0.918 | 0.914 | 0.911 | 0.908 |
| 0.89 | 0.937 | 0.933 | 0.929 | 0.925 | 0.922 |
| 0.90 | 0.954 | 0.949 | 0.944 | 0.940 | 0.937 |
| 0.91 | 0.972 | 0.967 | 0.961 | 0.957 | 0.953 |
| 0.92 | 0.991 | 0.986 | 0.980 | 0.975 | 0.970 |
| 0.93 | 1.012 | 1.006 | 0.999 | 0.994 | 0.989 |
| 0.94 | 1.036 | 1.029 | 1.022 | 1.016 | 1.010 |
| 0.950 | 1.062 | 1.055 | 1.047 | 1.040 | 1.033 |
| 0.960 | 1.097 | 1.085 | 1.074 | 1.063 | 1.053 |
| 0.970 | 1.136 | 1.124 | 1.112 | 1.100 | 1.087 |
| 0.975 | 1.157 | 1.147 | 1.134 | 1.122 | 1.108 |
| 0.980 | 1.187 | 1.175 | 1.160 | 1.150 | 1.132 |
| 0.985 | 1.224 | 1.210 | 1.196 | 1.183 | 1.165 |
| 0.990 | 1.275 | 1.260 | 1.243 | 1.228 | 1.208 |
| 0.995 | 1.363 | 1.342 | 1.320 | 1.302 | 1.280 |
| 0.999 | 1.560 | 1.530 | 1.500 | 1.476 | 1.447 |
| 1.000 | ∞ | ∞ | ∞ | ∞ | ∞ |
| 1.001 | 0.614 | 0.577 | 0.546 | 0.519 | 0.494 |
| 1.005 | 0.420 | 0.391 | 0.368 | 0.350 | 0.331 |
| 1.010 | 0.337 | 0.313 | 0.294 | 0.278 | 0.262 |
| 1.015 | 0.289 | 0.269 | 0.255 | 0.237 | 0.223 |
| 1.020 | 0.257 | 0.237 | 0.221 | 0.209 | 0.196 |
| 1.03 | 0.212 | 0.195 | 0.181 | 0.170 | 0.159 |
| 1.04 | 0.173 | 0.165 | 0.152 | 0.143 | 0.134 |
| 1.05 | 0.158 | 0.143 | 0.132 | 0.124 | 0.115 |
| 1.06 | 0.140 | 0.127 | 0.116 | 0.106 | 0.098 |
| 1.07 | 0.123 | 0.112 | 0.102 | 0.094 | 0.086 |
| 1.08 | 0.111 | 0.101 | 0.092 | 0.084 | 0.077 |
| 1.09 | 0.101 | 0.091 | 0.082 | 0.075 | 0.069 |
| 1.10 | 0.092 | 0.083 | 0.074 | 0.067 | 0.062 |
| 1.11 | 0.084 | 0.075 | 0.067 | 0.060 | 0.055 |
| 1.12 | 0.077 | 0.069 | 0.062 | 0.055 | 0.050 |
| 1.13 | 0.071 | 0.063 | 0.056 | 0.050 | 0.045 |
| 1.14 | 0.065 | 0.058 | 0.052 | 0.046 | 0.041 |
| 1.15 | 0.061 | 0.054 | 0.048 | 0.043 | 0.038 |
| 1.16 | 0.056 | 0.050 | 0.045 | 0.040 | 0.035 |
| 1.17 | 0.052 | 0.046 | 0.041 | 0.036 | 0.032 |
| 1.18 | 0.048 | 0.042 | 0.037 | 0.033 | 0.029 |
| 1.19 | 0.045 | 0.039 | 0.034 | 0.030 | 0.027 |
| 1.20 | 0.043 | 0.037 | 0.032 | 0.028 | 0.025 |
| 1.22 | 0.037 | 0.032 | 0.028 | 0.024 | 0.021 |
| 1.24 | 0.032 | 0.028 | 0.024 | 0.021 | 0.018 |

TABLE D-1. THE VARIED-FLOW FUNCTION FOR POSITIVE SLOPES, $F(u,N)$ (*continued*)

| N<br>u | 8.2 | 8.6 | 9.0 | 9.4 | 9.8 |
|---|---|---|---|---|---|
| 1.26 | 0.028 | 0.024 | 0.021 | 0.018 | 0.016 |
| 1.28 | 0.025 | 0.021 | 0.018 | 0.016 | 0.014 |
| 1.30 | 0.022 | 0.019 | 0.016 | 0.014 | 0.012 |
| 1.32 | 0.020 | 0.017 | 0.014 | 0.012 | 0.010 |
| 1.34 | 0.018 | 0.015 | 0.012 | 0.010 | 0.009 |
| 1.36 | 0.016 | 0.013 | 0.011 | 0.009 | 0.008 |
| 1.38 | 0.014 | 0.012 | 0.010 | 0.008 | 0.007 |
| 1.40 | 0.013 | 0.011 | 0.009 | 0.007 | 0.006 |
| 1.42 | 0.011 | 0.009 | 0.008 | 0.006 | 0.005 |
| 1.44 | 0.010 | 0.008 | 0.007 | 0.006 | 0.005 |
| 1.46 | 0.009 | 0.008 | 0.006 | 0.005 | 0.004 |
| 1.48 | 0.009 | 0.007 | 0.005 | 0.004 | 0.004 |
| 1.50 | 0.008 | 0.006 | 0.005 | 0.004 | 0.003 |
| 1.55 | 0.006 | 0.005 | 0.004 | 0.003 | 0.003 |
| 1.60 | 0.005 | 0.004 | 0.003 | 0.002 | 0.002 |
| 1.65 | 0.004 | 0.003 | 0.002 | 0.002 | 0.001 |
| 1.70 | 0.003 | 0.002 | 0.002 | 0.001 | 0.001 |
| 1.75 | 0.002 | 0.002 | 0.002 | 0.001 | 0.001 |
| 1.80 | 0.002 | 0.001 | 0.001 | 0.001 | 0.001 |
| 1.85 | 0.002 | 0.001 | 0.001 | 0.001 | 0.001 |
| 1.90 | 0.001 | 0.001 | 0.001 | 0.001 | 0.000 |
| 1.95 | 0.001 | 0.001 | 0.001 | 0.000 | 0.000 |
| 2.00 | 0.001 | 0.001 | 0.000 | 0.000 | 0.000 |
| 2.10 | 0.001 | 0.000 | 0.000 | 0.000 | 0.000 |
| 2.20 | 0.000 | 0.000 | 0.000 | 0.000 | 0.000 |
| 2.3 | 0.000 | 0.000 | 0.000 | 0.000 | 0.000 |
| 2.4 | 0.000 | 0.000 | 0.000 | 0.000 | 0.000 |
| 2.5 | 0.000 | 0.000 | 0.000 | 0.000 | 0.000 |
| 2.6 | 0.000 | 0.000 | 0.000 | 0.000 | 0.000 |
| 2.7 | 0.000 | 0.000 | 0.000 | 0.000 | 0.000 |
| 2.8 | 0.000 | 0.000 | 0.000 | 0.000 | 0.000 |
| 2.9 | 0.000 | 0.000 | 0.000 | 0.000 | 0.000 |
| 3.0 | 0.000 | 0.000 | 0.000 | 0.000 | 0.000 |
| 3.5 | 0.000 | 0.000 | 0.000 | 0.000 | 0.000 |
| 4.0 | 0.000 | 0.000 | 0.000 | 0.000 | 0.000 |
| 4.5 | 0.000 | 0.000 | 0.000 | 0.000 | 0.000 |
| 5.0 | 0.000 | 0.000 | 0.000 | 0.000 | 0.000 |
| 6.0 | 0.000 | 0.000 | 0.000 | 0.000 | 0.000 |
| 7.0 | 0.000 | 0.000 | 0.000 | 0.000 | 0.000 |
| 8.0 | 0.000 | 0.000 | 0.000 | 0.000 | 0.000 |
| 9.0 | 0.000 | 0.000 | 0.000 | 0.000 | 0.000 |
| 10.0 | 0.000 | 0.000 | 0.000 | 0.000 | 0.000 |
| 20.0 | 0.000 | 0.000 | 0.000 | 0.000 | 0.000 |

Table D-2. The Varied-flow Function for Negative Slopes, $F(u,N)_{-s_0}$

| u \ N | 2.0 | 2.2 | 2.4 | 2.6 | 2.8 | 3.0 | 3.2 | 3.4 | 3.6 | 3.8 |
|---|---|---|---|---|---|---|---|---|---|---|
| 0.00 | 0.000 | 0.000 | 0.000 | 0.000 | 0.000 | 0.000 | 0.000 | 0.000 | 0.000 | 0.000 |
| 0.02 | 0.020 | 0.020 | 0.020 | 0.020 | 0.020 | 0.020 | 0.020 | 0.020 | 0.020 | 0.020 |
| 0.04 | 0.040 | 0.040 | 0.040 | 0.040 | 0.040 | 0.040 | 0.040 | 0.040 | 0.040 | 0.040 |
| 0.06 | 0.060 | 0.060 | 0.060 | 0.060 | 0.060 | 0.060 | 0.060 | 0.060 | 0.060 | 0.060 |
| 0.08 | 0.080 | 0.080 | 0.080 | 0.080 | 0.080 | 0.080 | 0.080 | 0.080 | 0.080 | 0.080 |
| 0.10 | 0.099 | 0.100 | 0.100 | 0.100 | 0.100 | 0.100 | 0.100 | 0.100 | 0.100 | 0.100 |
| 0.12 | 0.119 | 0.119 | 0.120 | 0.120 | 0.120 | 0.120 | 0.120 | 0.120 | 0.120 | 0.120 |
| 0.14 | 0.139 | 0.139 | 0.140 | 0.140 | 0.140 | 0.140 | 0.140 | 0.140 | 0.140 | 0.140 |
| 0.16 | 0.158 | 0.159 | 0.159 | 0.160 | 0.160 | 0.160 | 0.160 | 0.160 | 0.160 | 0.160 |
| 0.18 | 0.178 | 0.179 | 0.179 | 0.180 | 0.180 | 0.180 | 0.180 | 0.180 | 0.180 | 0.180 |
| 0.20 | 0.197 | 0.198 | 0.199 | 0.199 | 0.200 | 0.200 | 0.200 | 0.200 | 0.200 | 0.200 |
| 0.22 | 0.216 | 0.217 | 0.218 | 0.219 | 0.219 | 0.220 | 0.220 | 0.220 | 0.220 | 0.220 |
| 0.24 | 0.234 | 0.236 | 0.237 | 0.238 | 0.239 | 0.240 | 0.240 | 0.240 | 0.240 | 0.240 |
| 0.26 | 0.253 | 0.255 | 0.256 | 0.257 | 0.258 | 0.259 | 0.259 | 0.260 | 0.260 | 0.260 |
| 0.28 | 0.272 | 0.274 | 0.275 | 0.276 | 0.277 | 0.278 | 0.278 | 0.279 | 0.280 | 0.280 |
| 0.30 | 0.291 | 0.293 | 0.294 | 0.295 | 0.296 | 0.297 | 0.298 | 0.298 | 0.299 | 0.299 |
| 0.32 | 0.308 | 0.311 | 0.313 | 0.314 | 0.316 | 0.317 | 0.318 | 0.318 | 0.319 | 0.319 |
| 0.34 | 0.326 | 0.329 | 0.331 | 0.333 | 0.335 | 0.337 | 0.338 | 0.338 | 0.339 | 0.339 |
| 0.36 | 0.344 | 0.347 | 0.350 | 0.352 | 0.354 | 0.356 | 0.357 | 0.357 | 0.358 | 0.358 |
| 0.38 | 0.362 | 0.355 | 0.368 | 0.371 | 0.373 | 0.374 | 0.375 | 0.376 | 0.377 | 0.377 |
| 0.40 | 0.380 | 0.384 | 0.387 | 0.390 | 0.392 | 0.393 | 0.394 | 0.395 | 0.396 | 0.396 |
| 0.42 | 0.397 | 0.401 | 0.405 | 0.407 | 0.409 | 0.411 | 0.412 | 0.413 | 0.414 | 0.41( |
| 0.44 | 0.414 | 0.419 | 0.423 | 0.426 | 0.429 | 0.430 | 0.432 | 0.433 | 0.434 | 0.435 |
| 0.46 | 0.431 | 0.437 | 0.440 | 0.444 | 0.447 | 0.449 | 0.451 | 0.452 | 0.453 | 0.454 |
| 0.48 | 0.447 | 0.453 | 0.458 | 0.461 | 0.464 | 0.467 | 0.469 | 0.471 | 0.472 | 0.473 |
| 0.50 | 0.463 | 0.470 | 0.475 | 0.479 | 0.482 | 0.485 | 0.487 | 0.489 | 0.491 | 0.492 |
| 0.52 | 0.479 | 0.485 | 0.491 | 0.494 | 0.499 | 0.502 | 0.505 | 0.507 | 0.509 | 0.511 |
| 0.54 | 0.494 | 0.501 | 0.507 | 0.512 | 0.516 | 0.520 | 0.522 | 0.525 | 0.527 | 0.529 |
| 0.56 | 0.509 | 0.517 | 0.523 | 0.528 | 0.533 | 0.537 | 0.540 | 0.543 | 0.545 | 0.547 |
| 0.58 | 0.524 | 0.533 | 0.539 | 0.545 | 0.550 | 0.554 | 0.558 | 0.561 | 0.563 | 0.567 |
| 0.60 | 0.540 | 0.548 | 0.555 | 0.561 | 0.566 | 0.571 | 0.575 | 0.578 | 0.581 | 0.583 |
| 0.61 | 0.547 | 0.556 | 0.563 | 0.569 | 0.575 | 0.579 | 0.583 | 0.587 | 0.589 | 0.592 |
| 0.62 | 0.554 | 0.563 | 0.571 | 0.578 | 0.583 | 0.578 | 0.591 | 0.595 | 0.598 | 0.600 |
| 0.63 | 0.562 | 0.571 | 0.579 | 0.585 | 0.590 | 0.595 | 0.599 | 0.603 | 0.607 | 0.609 |
| 0.64 | 0.569 | 0.579 | 0.586 | 0.592 | 0.598 | 0.602 | 0.607 | 0.611 | 0.615 | 0.618 |
| 0.65 | 0.576 | 0.585 | 0.592 | 0.599 | 0.606 | 0.610 | 0.615 | 0.619 | 0.623 | 0.626 |
| 0.66 | 0.583 | 0.593 | 0.600 | 0.607 | 0.613 | 0.618 | 0.622 | 0.626 | 0.630 | 0.634 |
| 0.67 | 0.590 | 0.599 | 0.607 | 0.614 | 0.621 | 0.626 | 0.631 | 0.635 | 0.639 | 0.643 |
| 0.68 | 0.597 | 0.607 | 0.615 | 0.622 | 0.628 | 0.634 | 0.639 | 0.643 | 0.647 | 0.651 |
| 0.69 | 0.603 | 0.613 | 0.621 | 0.629 | 0.635 | 0.641 | 0.646 | 0.651 | 0.655 | 0.659 |
| 0.70 | 0.610 | 0.620 | 0.629 | 0.637 | 0.644 | 0.649 | 0.654 | 0.659 | 0.663 | 0.667 |
| 0.71 | 0.617 | 0.627 | 0.636 | 0.644 | 0.651 | 0.657 | 0.661 | 0.666 | 0.671 | 0.674 |
| 0.72 | 0.624 | 0.634 | 0.643 | 0.651 | 0.658 | 0.664 | 0.669 | 0.674 | 0.679 | 0.682 |
| 0.73 | 0.630 | 0.641 | 0.650 | 0.659 | 0.665 | 0.672 | 0.677 | 0.682 | 0.687 | 0.691 |
| 0.74 | 0.637 | 0.648 | 0.657 | 0.665 | 0.672 | 0.679 | 0.684 | 0.689 | 0.694 | 0.698 |
| 0.75 | 0.643 | 0.655 | 0.664 | 0.671 | 0.679 | 0.686 | 0.691 | 0.696 | 0.701 | 0.705 |
| 0.76 | 0.649 | 0.661 | 0.670 | 0.679 | 0.687 | 0.693 | 0.699 | 0.704 | 0.709 | 0.713 |
| 0.77 | 0.656 | 0.667 | 0.677 | 0.685 | 0.693 | 0.700 | 0.705 | 0.711 | 0.715 | 0.719 |
| 0.78 | 0.662 | 0.673 | 0.683 | 0.692 | 0.700 | 0.707 | 0.713 | 0.718 | 0.723 | 0.727 |
| 0.79 | 0.668 | 0.680 | 0.689 | 0.698 | 0.705 | 0.713 | 0.719 | 0.724 | 0.729 | 0.733 |

TABLE D-2. THE VARIED-FLOW FUNCTION FOR NEGATIVE SLOPES, $F(u,N)_{-s_0}$ (*continued*)

| u \ N | 2.0 | 2.2 | 2.4 | 2.6 | 2.8 | 3.0 | 3.2 | 3.4 | 3.6 | 3.8 |
|---|---|---|---|---|---|---|---|---|---|---|
| 0.80 | 0.674 | 0.685 | 0.695 | 0.703 | 0.712 | 0.720 | 0.726 | 0.732 | 0.737 | 0.741 |
| 0.81 | 0.680 | 0.691 | 0.701 | 0.710 | 0.719 | 0.727 | 0.733 | 0.739 | 0.744 | 0.749 |
| 0.82 | 0.686 | 0.698 | 0.707 | 0.717 | 0.725 | 0.733 | 0.740 | 0.745 | 0.751 | 0.755 |
| 0.83 | 0.692 | 0.703 | 0.713 | 0.722 | 0.731 | 0.740 | 0.746 | 0.752 | 0.757 | 0.762 |
| 0.84 | 0.698 | 0.709 | 0.719 | 0.729 | 0.737 | 0.746 | 0.752 | 0.758 | 0.764 | 0.769 |
| 0.85 | 0.704 | 0.715 | 0.725 | 0.735 | 0.744 | 0.752 | 0.759 | 0.765 | 0.770 | 0.775 |
| 0.86 | 0.710 | 0.721 | 0.731 | 0.741 | 0.750 | 0.758 | 0.765 | 0.771 | 0.777 | 0.782 |
| 0.87 | 0.715 | 0.727 | 0.738 | 0.747 | 0.756 | 0.764 | 0.771 | 0.777 | 0.783 | 0.788 |
| 0.88 | 0.721 | 0.733 | 0.743 | 0.753 | 0.762 | 0.770 | 0.777 | 0.783 | 0.789 | 0.794 |
| 0.89 | 0.727 | 0.739 | 0.749 | 0.758 | 0.767 | 0.776 | 0.783 | 0.789 | 0.795 | 0.800 |
| 0.90 | 0.732 | 0.744 | 0.754 | 0.764 | 0.773 | 0.781 | 0.789 | 0.795 | 0.801 | 0.807 |
| 0.91 | 0.738 | 0.750 | 0.760 | 0.770 | 0.779 | 0.787 | 0.795 | 0.801 | 0.807 | 0.812 |
| 0.92 | 0.743 | 0.754 | 0.766 | 0.776 | 0.785 | 0.793 | 0.800 | 0.807 | 0.813 | 0.818 |
| 0.93 | 0.749 | 0.761 | 0.772 | 0.782 | 0.791 | 0.799 | 0.807 | 0.812 | 0.818 | 0.823 |
| 0.94 | 0.754 | 0.767 | 0.777 | 0.787 | 0.795 | 0.804 | 0.813 | 0.818 | 0.824 | 0.829 |
| 0.950 | 0.759 | 0.772 | 0.783 | 0.793 | 0.801 | 0.809 | 0.819 | 0.823 | 0.829 | 0.835 |
| 0.960 | 0.764 | 0.777 | 0.788 | 0.798 | 0.807 | 0.815 | 0.824 | 0.829 | 0.835 | 0.841 |
| 0.970 | 0.770 | 0.782 | 0.793 | 0.803 | 0.812 | 0.820 | 0.826 | 0.834 | 0.840 | 0.846 |
| 0.975 | 0.772 | 0.785 | 0.796 | 0.805 | 0.814 | 0.822 | 0.828 | 0.836 | 0.843 | 0.848 |
| 0.980 | 0.775 | 0.787 | 0.798 | 0.808 | 0.818 | 0.825 | 0.830 | 0.839 | 0.845 | 0.851 |
| 0.985 | 0.777 | 0.790 | 0.801 | 0.811 | 0.820 | 0.827 | 0.833 | 0.841 | 0.847 | 0.853 |
| 0.990 | 0.780 | 0.793 | 0.804 | 0.814 | 0.822 | 0.830 | 0.837 | 0.844 | 0.850 | 0.856 |
| 0.995 | 0.782 | 0.795 | 0.806 | 0.816 | 0.824 | 0.832 | 0.840 | 0.847 | 0.753 | 0.859 |
| 1.000 | 0.785 | 0.797 | 0.808 | 0.818 | 0.826 | 0.834 | 0.842 | 0.849 | 0.856 | 0.862 |
| 1.005 | 0.788 | 0.799 | 0.810 | 0.820 | 0.829 | 0.837 | 0.845 | 0.852 | 0.858 | 0.864 |
| 1.010 | 0.790 | 0.801 | 0.812 | 0.822 | 0.831 | 0.840 | 0.847 | 0.855 | 0.861 | 0.867 |
| 1.015 | 0.793 | 0.804 | 0.815 | 0.824 | 0.833 | 0.843 | 0.850 | 0.858 | 0.864 | 0.870 |
| 1.020 | 0.795 | 0.807 | 0.818 | 0.828 | 0.837 | 0.845 | 0.853 | 0.860 | 0.866 | 0.872 |
| 1.03 | 0.800 | 0.811 | 0.822 | 0.832 | 0.841 | 0.850 | 0.857 | 0.864 | 0.871 | 0.877 |
| 1.04 | 0.805 | 0.816 | 0.829 | 0.837 | 0.846 | 0.855 | 0.862 | 0.870 | 0.877 | 0.883 |
| 1.05 | 0.810 | 0.821 | 0.831 | 0.841 | 0.851 | 0.859 | 0.867 | 0.874 | 0.881 | 0.887 |
| 1.06 | 0.815 | 0.826 | 0.837 | 0.846 | 0.855 | 0.864 | 0.871 | 0.879 | 0.885 | 0.891 |
| 1.07 | 0.819 | 0.831 | 0.841 | 0.851 | 0.860 | 0.869 | 0.876 | 0.883 | 0.889 | 0.896 |
| 1.08 | 0.824 | 0.836 | 0.846 | 0.856 | 0.865 | 0.873 | 0.880 | 0.887 | 0.893 | 0.900 |
| 1.09 | 0.828 | 0.840 | 0.851 | 0.860 | 0.870 | 0.877 | 0.885 | 0.892 | 0.898 | 0.904 |
| 1.10 | 0.833 | 0.845 | 0.855 | 0.865 | 0.874 | 0.881 | 0.890 | 0.897 | 0.903 | 0.908 |
| 1.11 | 0.837 | 0.849 | 0.860 | 0.870 | 0.878 | 0.886 | 0.894 | 0.900 | 0.907 | 0.912 |
| 1.12 | 0.842 | 0.854 | 0.864 | 0.873 | 0.882 | 0.891 | 0.897 | 0.904 | 0.910 | 0.916 |
| 1.13 | 0.846 | 0.858 | 0.868 | 0.878 | 0.886 | 0.895 | 0.902 | 0.908 | 0.914 | 0.919 |
| 1.14 | 0.851 | 0.861 | 0.872 | 0.881 | 0.890 | 0.899 | 0.905 | 0.912 | 0.918 | 0.923 |
| 1.15 | 0.855 | 0.866 | 0.876 | 0.886 | 0.895 | 0.903 | 0.910 | 0.916 | 0.922 | 0.928 |
| 1.16 | 0.859 | 0.870 | 0.880 | 0.890 | 0.899 | 0.907 | 0.914 | 0.920 | 0.926 | 0.931 |
| 1.17 | 0.864 | 0.874 | 0.884 | 0.893 | 0.902 | 0.911 | 0.917 | 0.923 | 0.930 | 0.934 |
| 1.18 | 0.868 | 0.878 | 0.888 | 0.897 | 0.906 | 0.915 | 0.921 | 0.927 | 0.933 | 0.939 |
| 1.19 | 0.872 | 0.882 | 0.892 | 0.901 | 0.910 | 0.918 | 0.925 | 0.931 | 0.937 | 0.942 |
| 1.20 | 0.876 | 0.886 | 0.896 | 0.904 | 0.913 | 0.921 | 0.928 | 0.934 | 0.940 | 0.945 |
| 1.22 | 0.880 | 0.891 | 0.900 | 0.909 | 0.917 | 0.929 | 0.932 | 0.938 | 0.944 | 0.949 |
| 1.24 | 0.888 | 0.898 | 0.908 | 0.917 | 0.925 | 0.935 | 0.940 | 0.945 | 0.950 | 0.955 |
| 1.26 | 0.900 | 0.910 | 0.919 | 0.927 | 0.935 | 0.942 | 0.948 | 0.954 | 0.960 | 0.964 |
| 1.28 | 0.908 | 0.917 | 0.926 | 0.934 | 0.945 | 0.948 | 0.954 | 0.960 | 0.965 | 0.970 |

TABLE D-2. THE VARIED-FLOW FUNCTION FOR NEGATIVE SLOPES, $F(u,N)_{-s_0}$ (continued)

| $\dfrac{N}{u}$ | 2.0 | 2.2 | 2.4 | 2.6 | 2.8 | 3.0 | 3.2 | 3.4 | 3.6 | 3.8 |
|---|---|---|---|---|---|---|---|---|---|---|
| 1.30 | 0.915 | 0.925 | 0.933 | 0.941 | 0.948 | 0.955 | 0.961 | 0.966 | 0.981 | 0.975 |
| 1.32 | 0.922 | 0.931 | 0.940 | 0.948 | 0.955 | 0.961 | 0.967 | 0.972 | 0.976 | 0.980 |
| 1.34 | 0.930 | 0.939 | 0.948 | 0.955 | 0.962 | 0.967 | 0.973 | 0.978 | 0.982 | 0.986 |
| 1.36 | 0.937 | 0.946 | 0.954 | 0.961 | 0.968 | 0.973 | 0.979 | 0.983 | 0.987 | 0.991 |
| 1.38 | 0.944 | 0.952 | 0.960 | 0.967 | 0.974 | 0.979 | 0.985 | 0.989 | 0.993 | 0.996 |
| 1.40 | 0.951 | 0.959 | 0.966 | 0.973 | 0.979 | 0.984 | 0.989 | 0.993 | 0.997 | 1.000 |
| 1.42 | 0.957 | 0.965 | 0.972 | 0.979 | 0.984 | 0.989 | 0.995 | 0.998 | 1.001 | 1.004 |
| 1.44 | 0.964 | 0.972 | 0.979 | 0.984 | 0.990 | 0.995 | 1.000 | 1.003 | 1.006 | 1.009 |
| 1.46 | 0.970 | 0.977 | 0.983 | 0.989 | 0.995 | 1.000 | 1.004 | 1.007 | 1.010 | 1.012 |
| 1.48 | 0.977 | 0.983 | 0.989 | 0.994 | 0.999 | 1.005 | 1.008 | 1.011 | 1.014 | 1.016 |
| 1.50 | 0.983 | 0.990 | 0.996 | 1.001 | 1.005 | 1.009 | 1.012 | 1.015 | 1.017 | 1.019 |
| 1.55 | 0.997 | 1.002 | 1.007 | 1.012 | 1.016 | 1.020 | 1.022 | 1.024 | 1.026 | 1.028 |
| 1.60 | 1.012 | 1.017 | 1.020 | 1.024 | 1.027 | 1.030 | 1.032 | 1.034 | 1.035 | 1.035 |
| 1.65 | 1.026 | 1.029 | 1.032 | 1.035 | 1.037 | 1.039 | 1.041 | 1.041 | 1.042 | 1.042 |
| 1.70 | 1.039 | 1.042 | 1.044 | 1.045 | 1.047 | 1.048 | 1.049 | 1.049 | 1.049 | 1.048 |
| 1.75 | 1.052 | 1.053 | 1.054 | 1.055 | 1.056 | 1.057 | 1.056 | 1.056 | 1.055 | 1.053 |
| 1.80 | 1.064 | 1.064 | 1.064 | 1.064 | 1.065 | 1.065 | 1.064 | 1.062 | 1.060 | 1.058 |
| 1.85 | 1.075 | 1.074 | 1.074 | 1.073 | 1.072 | 1.071 | 1.069 | 1.067 | 1.066 | 1.063 |
| 1.90 | 1.086 | 1.085 | 1.084 | 1.082 | 1.081 | 1.079 | 1.077 | 1.074 | 1.071 | 1.066 |
| 1.95 | 1.097 | 1.095 | 1.092 | 1.090 | 1.087 | 1.085 | 1.081 | 1.079 | 1.075 | 1.071 |
| 2.00 | 1.107 | 1.103 | 1.100 | 1.096 | 1.093 | 1.090 | 1.085 | 1.082 | 1.078 | 1.075 |
| 2.10 | 1.126 | 1.120 | 1.115 | 1.110 | 1.104 | 1.100 | 1.094 | 1.089 | 1.085 | 1.080 |
| 2.20 | 1.144 | 1.136 | 1.129 | 1.122 | 1.115 | 1.109 | 1.102 | 1.096 | 1.090 | 1.085 |
| 2.3 | 1.161 | 1.150 | 1.141 | 1.133 | 1.124 | 1.117 | 1.110 | 1.103 | 1.097 | 1.090 |
| 2.4 | 1.176 | 1.163 | 1.152 | 1.142 | 1.133 | 1.124 | 1.116 | 1.109 | 1.101 | 1.094 |
| 2.5 | 1.190 | 1.175 | 1.162 | 1.150 | 1.140 | 1.131 | 1.121 | 1.113 | 1.105 | 1.098 |
| 2.6 | 1.204 | 1.187 | 1.172 | 1.159 | 1.147 | 1.137 | 1.126 | 1.117 | 1.106 | 1.000 |
| 2.7 | 1.216 | 1.196 | 1.180 | 1.166 | 1.153 | 1.142 | 1.130 | 1.120 | 1.110 | 1.102 |
| 2.8 | 1.228 | 1.208 | 1.189 | 1.173 | 1.158 | 1.146 | 1.132 | 1.122 | 1.112 | 1.103 |
| 2.9 | 1.239 | 1.216 | 1.196 | 1.178 | 1.162 | 1.150 | 1.137 | 1.125 | 1.115 | 1.106 |
| 3.0 | 1.249 | 1.224 | 1.203 | 1.184 | 1.168 | 1.154 | 1.140 | 1.128 | 1.117 | 1.107 |
| 3.5 | 1.292 | 1.260 | 1.232 | 1.206 | 1.185 | 1.167 | 1.151 | 1.138 | 1.125 | 1.113 |
| 4.0 | 1.326 | 1.286 | 1.251 | 1.223 | 1.198 | 1.176 | 1.158 | 1.142 | 1.129 | 1.117 |
| 4.5 | 1.352 | 1.308 | 1.270 | 1.235 | 1.205 | 1.183 | 1.162 | 1.146 | 1.131 | 1.119 |
| 5.0 | 1.374 | 1.325 | 1.283 | 1.245 | 1.212 | 1.188 | 1.166 | 1.149 | 1.134 | 1.121 |
| 6.0 | 1.406 | 1.342 | 1.292 | 1.252 | 1.221 | 1.195 | 1.171 | 1.152 | 1.136 | 1.122 |
| 7.0 | 1.430 | 1.360 | 1.303 | 1.260 | 1.225 | 1.199 | 1.174 | 1.153 | 1.136 | 1.122 |
| 8.0 | 1.447 | 1.373 | 1.313 | 1.266 | 1.229 | 1.201 | 1.175 | 1.154 | 1.137 | 1.122 |
| 9.0 | 1.461 | 1.384 | 1.319 | 1.269 | 1.231 | 1.203 | 1.176 | 1.156 | 1.137 | 1.122 |
| 10.0 | 1.471 | 1.394 | 1.324 | 1.272 | 1.233 | 1.203 | 1.176 | 1.156 | 1.137 | 1.122 |

TABLE D-2. THE VARIED-FLOW FUNCTION FOR NEGATIVE SLOPES, $F(u,N)_{-s_0}$ (continued)

| $u$ \ $N$ | 4.0 | 4.2 | 4.5 | 5.0 | 5.5 |
|---|---|---|---|---|---|
| 0.00 | 0.000 | 0.000 | 0.000 | 0.000 | 0.000 |
| 0.02 | 0.020 | 0.020 | 0.020 | 0.020 | 0.020 |
| 0.04 | 0.040 | 0.040 | 0.040 | 0.040 | 0.040 |
| 0.06 | 0.060 | 0.060 | 0.060 | 0.060 | 0.060 |
| 0.08 | 0.080 | 0.080 | 0.080 | 0.080 | 0.080 |
| 0.10 | 0.100 | 0.100 | 0.100 | 0.100 | 0.100 |
| 0.12 | 0.120 | 0.120 | 0.120 | 0.120 | 0.120 |
| 0.14 | 0.140 | 0.140 | 0.140 | 0.140 | 0.140 |
| 0.16 | 0.160 | 0.160 | 0.160 | 0.160 | 0.160 |
| 0.18 | 0.180 | 0.180 | 0.180 | 0.180 | 0.180 |
| 0.20 | 0.200 | 0.200 | 0.200 | 0.200 | 0.200 |
| 0.22 | 0.220 | 0.220 | 0.220 | 0.220 | 0.220 |
| 0.24 | 0.240 | 0.240 | 0.240 | 0.240 | 0.240 |
| 0.26 | 0.260 | 0.260 | 0.260 | 0.260 | 0.260 |
| 0.28 | 0.280 | 0.280 | 0.280 | 0.280 | 0.280 |
| 0.30 | 0.300 | 0.300 | 0.300 | 0.300 | 0.300 |
| 0.32 | 0.320 | 0.320 | 0.320 | 0.320 | 0.320 |
| 0.34 | 0.339 | 0.340 | 0.340 | 0.340 | 0.340 |
| 0.36 | 0.359 | 0.360 | 0.360 | 0.360 | 0.360 |
| 0.38 | 0.378 | 0.379 | 0.380 | 0.380 | 0.380 |
| 0.40 | 0.397 | 0.398 | 0.398 | 0.400 | 0.400 |
| 0.42 | 0.417 | 0.418 | 0.418 | 0.419 | 0.420 |
| 0.44 | 0.436 | 0.437 | 0.437 | 0.439 | 0.440 |
| 0.46 | 0.455 | 0.456 | 0.457 | 0.458 | 0.459 |
| 0.48 | 0.474 | 0.475 | 0.476 | 0.478 | 0.479 |
| 0.50 | 0.493 | 0.494 | 0.495 | 0.497 | 0.498 |
| 0.52 | 0.512 | 0.513 | 0.515 | 0.517 | 0.518 |
| 0.54 | 0.531 | 0.532 | 0.533 | 0.536 | 0.537 |
| 0.56 | 0.549 | 0.550 | 0.552 | 0.555 | 0.558 |
| 0.58 | 0.567 | 0.569 | 0.570 | 0.574 | 0.576 |
| 0.60 | 0.585 | 0.587 | 0.589 | 0.593 | 0.595 |
| 0.61 | 0.594 | 0.596 | 0.598 | 0.602 | 0.604 |
| 0.62 | 0.603 | 0.605 | 0.607 | 0.611 | 0.613 |
| 0.63 | 0.612 | 0.615 | 0.616 | 0.620 | 0.622 |
| 0.64 | 0.620 | 0.623 | 0.625 | 0.629 | 0.631 |
| 0.65 | 0.629 | 0.632 | 0.634 | 0.638 | 0.640 |
| 0.66 | 0.637 | 0.640 | 0.643 | 0.647 | 0.650 |
| 0.67 | 0.646 | 0.649 | 0.652 | 0.656 | 0.659 |
| 0.68 | 0.654 | 0.657 | 0.660 | 0.665 | 0.668 |
| 0.69 | 0.662 | 0.665 | 0.668 | 0.674 | 0.677 |
| 0.70 | 0.670 | 0.673 | 0.677 | 0.682 | 0.686 |
| 0.71 | 0.678 | 0.681 | 0.685 | 0.690 | 0.694 |
| 0.72 | 0.686 | 0.689 | 0.694 | 0.699 | 0.703 |
| 0.73 | 0.694 | 0.698 | 0.702 | 0.707 | 0.712 |
| 0.74 | 0.702 | 0.705 | 0.710 | 0.716 | 0.720 |
| 0.75 | 0.709 | 0.712 | 0.717 | 0.724 | 0.728 |
| 0.76 | 0.717 | 0.720 | 0.725 | 0.731 | 0.736 |
| 0.77 | 0.724 | 0.727 | 0.733 | 0.739 | 0.744 |
| 0.78 | 0.731 | 0.735 | 0.740 | 0.747 | 0.752 |
| 0.79 | 0.738 | 0.742 | 0.748 | 0.754 | 0.760 |

TABLE D-2. THE VARIED-FLOW FUNCTION FOR NEGATIVE SLOPES, $F(u,N)_{-S_0}$ (continued)

| $N$ \ $u$ | 4.0 | 4.2 | 4.5 | 5.0 | 5.5 |
|---|---|---|---|---|---|
| 0.80 | 0.746 | 0.750 | 0.755 | 0.762 | 0.768 |
| 0.81 | 0.753 | 0.757 | 0.762 | 0.770 | 0.776 |
| 0.82 | 0.760 | 0.764 | 0.769 | 0.777 | 0.783 |
| 0.83 | 0.766 | 0.771 | 0.776 | 0.784 | 0.790 |
| 0.84 | 0.773 | 0.778 | 0.783 | 0.791 | 0.798 |
| 0.85 | 0.780 | 0.784 | 0.790 | 0.798 | 0.805 |
| 0.86 | 0.786 | 0.791 | 0.797 | 0.804 | 0.812 |
| 0.87 | 0.793 | 0.797 | 0.803 | 0.811 | 0.819 |
| 0.88 | 0.799 | 0.803 | 0.810 | 0.818 | 0.826 |
| 0.89 | 0.805 | 0.810 | 0.816 | 0.825 | 0.832 |
| 0.90 | 0.811 | 0.816 | 0.822 | 0.831 | 0.839 |
| 0.91 | 0.817 | 0.821 | 0.828 | 0.837 | 0.845 |
| 0.92 | 0.823 | 0.828 | 0.834 | 0.844 | 0.851 |
| 0.93 | 0.829 | 0.833 | 0.840 | 0.850 | 0.857 |
| 0.94 | 0.835 | 0.840 | 0.846 | 0.856 | 0.864 |
| 0.950 | 0.840 | 0.845 | 0.852 | 0.861 | 0.869 |
| 0.960 | 0.846 | 0.861 | 0.857 | 0.867 | 0.875 |
| 0.970 | 0.851 | 0.866 | 0.863 | 0.972 | 0.881 |
| 0.975 | 0.854 | 0.859 | 0.866 | 0.875 | 0.883 |
| 0.980 | 0.857 | 0.861 | 0.868 | 0.878 | 0.886 |
| 0.985 | 0.859 | 0.863 | 0.870 | 0.880 | 0.889 |
| 0.990 | 0.861 | 0.867 | 0.873 | 0.883 | 0.891 |
| 0.995 | 0.864 | 0.869 | 0.876 | 0.885 | 0.894 |
| 1.000 | 0.867 | 0.873 | 0.879 | 0.887 | 0.897 |
| 1.005 | 0.870 | 0.874 | 0.881 | 0.890 | 0.899 |
| 1.010 | 0.873 | 0.878 | 0.884 | 0.893 | 0.902 |
| 1.015 | 0.875 | 0.880 | 0.886 | 0.896 | 0.904 |
| 1.020 | 0.877 | 0.883 | 0.889 | 0.898 | 0.907 |
| 1.03 | 0.882 | 0.887 | 0.893 | 0.902 | 0.911 |
| 1.04 | 0.888 | 0.893 | 0.898 | 0.907 | 0.916 |
| 1.05 | 0.892 | 0.897 | 0.903 | 0.911 | 0.920 |
| 1.06 | 0.896 | 0.901 | 0.907 | 0.915 | 0.924 |
| 1.07 | 0.901 | 0.906 | 0.911 | 0.919 | 0.928 |
| 1.08 | 0.905 | 0.910 | 0.916 | 0.923 | 0.932 |
| 1.09 | 0.909 | 0.914 | 0.920 | 0.927 | 0.936 |
| 1.10 | 0.913 | 0.918 | 0.923 | 0.931 | 0.940 |
| 1.11 | 0.917 | 0.921 | 0.927 | 0.935 | 0.944 |
| 1.12 | 0.921 | 0.926 | 0.931 | 0.939 | 0.948 |
| 1.13 | 0.925 | 0.929 | 0.935 | 0.943 | 0.951 |
| 1.14 | 0.928 | 0.933 | 0.938 | 0.947 | 0.954 |
| 1.15 | 0.932 | 0.936 | 0.942 | 0.950 | 0.957 |
| 1.16 | 0.936 | 0.941 | 0.945 | 0.953 | 0.960 |
| 1.17 | 0.939 | 0.944 | 0.948 | 0.957 | 0.963 |
| 1.18 | 0.943 | 0.947 | 0.951 | 0.960 | 0.965 |
| 1.19 | 0.947 | 0.950 | 0.954 | 0.963 | 0.968 |
| 1.20 | 0.950 | 0.953 | 0.958 | 0.966 | 0.970 |
| 1.22 | 0.956 | 0.957 | 0.964 | 0.972 | 0.976 |
| 1.24 | 0.962 | 0.962 | 0.970 | 0.977 | 0.981 |
| 1.26 | 0.968 | 0.971 | 0.975 | 0.982 | 0.986 |
| 1.28 | 0.974 | 0.977 | 0.981 | 0.987 | 0.990 |

TABLE D-2. THE VARIED-FLOW FUNCTION FOR NEGATIVE SLOPES, $F(u,N)_{-s_0}$ (*continued*)

| $\diagdown N$ $u \diagdown$ | 4.0 | 4.2 | 4.5 | 5.0 | 5.5 |
|---|---|---|---|---|---|
| 1.30 | 0.979 | 0.978 | 0.985 | 0.991 | 0.994 |
| 1.32 | 0.985 | 0.986 | 0.990 | 0.995 | 0.997 |
| 1.34 | 0.990 | 0.992 | 0.995 | 0.999 | 1.001 |
| 1.36 | 0.994 | 0.996 | 0.999 | 1.002 | 1.005 |
| 1.38 | 0.998 | 1.000 | 1.003 | 1.006 | 1.008 |
| 1.40 | 1.001 | 1.004 | 1.006 | 1.009 | 1.011 |
| 1.42 | 1.005 | 1.008 | 1.010 | 1.012 | 1.014 |
| 1.44 | 1.009 | 1.013 | 1.014 | 1.016 | 1.016 |
| 1.46 | 1.014 | 1.016 | 1.017 | 1.018 | 1.018 |
| 1.48 | 1.016 | 1.019 | 1.020 | 1.020 | 1.020 |
| 1.50 | 1.020 | 1.021 | 1.022 | 1.022 | 1.022 |
| 1.55 | 1.029 | 1.029 | 1.029 | 1.028 | 1.028 |
| 1.60 | 1.035 | 1.035 | 1.034 | 1.032 | 1.030 |
| 1.65 | 1.041 | 1.040 | 1.039 | 1.036 | 1.034 |
| 1.70 | 1.047 | 1.046 | 1.043 | 1.039 | 1.037 |
| 1.75 | 1.052 | 1.051 | 1.047 | 1.042 | 1.039 |
| 1.80 | 1.057 | 1.055 | 1.051 | 1.045 | 1.041 |
| 1.85 | 1.061 | 1.059 | 1.054 | 1.047 | 1.043 |
| 1.90 | 1.065 | 1.060 | 1.057 | 1.049 | 1.045 |
| 1.95 | 1.068 | 1.064 | 1.059 | 1.051 | 1.046 |
| 2.00 | 1.071 | 1.068 | 1.062 | 1.053 | 1.047 |
| 2.10 | 1.076 | 1.071 | 1.065 | 1.056 | 1.049 |
| 2.20 | 1.080 | 1.073 | 1.068 | 1.058 | 1.050 |
| 2.3 | 1.084 | 1.079 | 1.071 | 1.060 | 1.051 |
| 2.4 | 1.087 | 1.081 | 1.073 | 1.061 | 1.052 |
| 2.5 | 1.090 | 1.083 | 1.075 | 1.062 | 1.053 |
| 2.6 | 1.092 | 1.085 | 1.076 | 1.063 | 1.054 |
| 2.7 | 1.094 | 1.087 | 1.077 | 1.063 | 1.054 |
| 2.8 | 1.096 | 1.088 | 1.078 | 1.064 | 1.054 |
| 2.9 | 1.098 | 1.089 | 1.079 | 1.065 | 1.055 |
| 3.0 | 1.099 | 1.090 | 1.080 | 1.065 | 1.055 |
| 3.5 | 1.103 | 1.093 | 1.082 | 1.066 | 1.055 |
| 4.0 | 1.106 | 1.097 | 1.084 | 1.067 | 1.056 |
| 4.5 | 1.108 | 1.098 | 1.085 | 1.067 | 1.056 |
| 5.0 | 1.110 | 1.099 | 1.085 | 1.068 | 1.056 |
| 6.0 | 1.111 | 1.100 | 1.085 | 1.068 | 1.056 |
| 7.0 | 1.111 | 1.100 | 1.086 | 1.068 | 1.056 |
| 8.0 | 1.111 | 1.100 | 1.086 | 1.068 | 1.056 |
| 9.0 | 1.111 | 1.100 | 1.086 | 1.068 | 1.056 |
| 10.0 | 1.111 | 1.100 | 1.086 | 1.068 | 1.056 |

APPENDIX E.  TABLE OF THE VARIED-FLOW FUNCTIONS FOR
CIRCULAR SECTIONS*

* Prepared and supplied for publication through the courtesy of Mr. C. J. Keifer and Mr. H. H. Chu of the Department of Public Works, City of Chicago.  The step lines in the table show the location of normal depth.  They should not be crossed by interpolation.

| Q/Q₀ \ v/d₀ | 0.40 | 0.45 | 0.50 | 0.55 | 0.60 | 0.65 | 0.70 | 0.75 | 0.80 | 0.85 | 0.90 | 0.95 | 1.00 | 1.035 | 1.07 | 1.08 | 1.09 | 1.10 | 1.15 | 1.20 | 1.30 | 1.40 | 1.50 | 1.60 |
|---|---|---|---|---|---|---|---|---|---|---|---|---|---|---|---|---|---|---|---|---|---|---|---|---|
| 1.00 | 0 | 0 | 0 | 0 | 0 | 0 | 0 | 0 | 0 | 0 | 0 | 0 | 0 | 0 | 1.161 | 8.0250 | 3.9642 | 2.8582 | 1.3454 | 0.9166 | 0.5668 | 0.4075 | 0.3150 | 0.2543 |
| 0.99 | 0.0118 | 0.0124 | 0.0131 | 0.0140 | 0.0152 | 0.0167 | 0.0188 | 0.0216 | 0.0256 | 0.0322 | 0.0440 | 0.0721 | 0.1085 | 0.359 | 1.029 | 7.9478 | 3.8899 | 2.7897 | 1.3058 | 0.8894 | 0.5505 | 0.3959 | 0.3063 | 0.2472 |
| 0.98 | 0.0235 | 0.0246 | 0.0260 | 0.0278 | 0.0299 | 0.0330 | 0.0368 | 0.0420 | 0.0495 | 0.0613 | 0.0817 | 0.1276 | 0.1976 | 0.551 | 0.760 | 7.7504 | 3.7602 | 2.6859 | 1.2558 | 0.8567 | 0.5315 | 0.3830 | 0.2966 | 0.2397 |
| 0.97 | 0.0352 | 0.0368 | 0.0389 | 0.0416 | 0.0447 | 0.0489 | 0.0545 | 0.0620 | 0.0726 | 0.0891 | 0.1173 | 0.1776 | 0.2777 | 0.706 | 0 | 7.4791 | 3.5732 | 2.5499 | 1.1979 | 0.8207 | 0.5117 | 0.3695 | 0.2866 | 0.2318 |
| 0.96 | 0.0468 | 0.0490 | 0.0517 | 0.0551 | 0.0592 | 0.0648 | 0.0720 | 0.0817 | 0.0954 | 0.1164 | 0.1517 | 0.2255 | 0.3539 |  |  | 6.9735 | 3.3231 | 2.3801 | 1.1347 | 0.7822 | 0.4906 | 0.3555 | 0.2763 | 0.2238 |
| 0.95 | 0.0584 | 0.0611 | 0.0645 | 0.0686 | 0.0739 | 0.0806 | 0.0894 | 0.1012 | 0.1178 | 0.1431 | 0.1854 | 0.2716 | 0.3539 | 0.847 | 1.907 | 6.2042 | 3.0078 | 2.1832 | 1.0670 | 0.7424 | 0.4695 | 0.3412 | 0.2658 | 0.2156 |
| 0.94 | 0.0700 | 0.0732 | 0.0772 | 0.0822 | 0.0883 | 0.0964 | 0.1067 | 0.1207 | 0.1403 | 0.1699 | 0.2188 | 0.3173 | 0.4277 | 0.979 | 2.872 | 5.0418 | 2.6434 | 1.9675 | 0.9977 | 0.7016 | 0.4476 | 0.3269 | 0.2552 | 0.2074 |
| 0.93 | 0.0816 | 0.0854 | 0.0900 | 0.0957 | 0.1029 | 0.1121 | 0.1241 | 0.1402 | 0.1626 | 0.1964 | 0.2521 | 0.3625 | 0.5017 | 1.112 | 3.836 | 3.8403 | 2.2743 | 1.7504 | 0.9277 | 0.6608 | 0.4261 | 0.3125 | 0.2447 | 0.1991 |
| 0.92 | 0.0932 | 0.0975 | 0.1027 | 0.1093 | 0.1173 | 0.1279 | 0.1415 | 0.1597 | 0.1851 | 0.2232 | 0.2857 | 0.4086 | 0.5763 | 1.249 | 5.052 | 2.8740 | 1.9319 | 1.5427 | 0.8593 | 0.6203 | 0.4043 | 0.2982 | 0.2341 | 0.1909 |
| 0.91 | 0.1048 | 0.1096 | 0.1155 | 0.1228 | 0.1320 | 0.1437 | 0.1589 | 0.1793 | 0.2077 | 0.2501 | 0.3196 | 0.4549 | 0.6536 | 1.393 |  | 2.2140 | 1.6384 | 1.3347 | 0.7928 | 0.5809 | 0.3833 | 0.2840 | 0.2237 | 0.1827 |
| 0.90 | 0.1165 | 0.1218 | 0.1283 | 0.1365 | 0.1465 | 0.1596 | 0.1764 | 0.1990 | 0.2305 | 0.2775 | 0.3541 | 0.5031 | 0.7345 | 1.550 | 2.7491 | 1.7591 | 1.3963 | 1.1894 | 0.7303 | 0.5427 | 0.3623 | 0.2701 | 0.2134 | 0.1748 |
| 0.89 | 0.1281 | 0.1340 | 0.1412 | 0.1501 | 0.1613 | 0.1755 | 0.1941 | 0.2189 | 0.2535 | 0.3051 | 0.3893 | 0.5524 | 0.8214 | 1.735 | 1.9053 | 1.4460 | 1.1996 | 1.0472 | 0.6711 | 0.5062 | 0.3424 | 0.2564 | 0.2033 | 0.1668 |
| 0.88 | 0.1398 | 0.1462 | 0.1540 | 0.1639 | 0.1759 | 0.1916 | 0.2119 | 0.2390 | 0.2769 | 0.3334 | 0.4257 | 0.6046 | 0.9160 | 1.984 | 1.4754 | 1.2083 | 1.0391 | 0.9251 | 0.6167 | 0.4714 | 0.3226 | 0.2432 | 0.1934 | 0.1591 |
| 0.87 | 0.1515 | 0.1584 | 0.1670 | 0.1776 | 0.1909 | 0.2078 | 0.2299 | 0.2594 | 0.3007 | 0.3623 | 0.4632 | 0.6590 | 1.0224 | 2.330 | 1.0347 | 0.9067 | 0.8209 | 0.7312 | 0.5656 | 0.4386 | 0.3040 | 0.2302 | 0.1838 | 0.1515 |
| 0.86 | 0.1632 | 0.1707 | 0.1799 | 0.1915 | 0.2057 | 0.2242 | 0.2481 | 0.2801 | 0.3250 | 0.3921 | 0.5023 | 0.7180 | 1.1459 | 2.964 | 1.0082 | 0.8906 | 0.7981 | 0.7312 | 0.5189 | 0.4076 | 0.2856 | 0.2178 | 0.1744 | 0.1441 |
| 0.85 | 0.1750 | 0.1831 | 0.1930 | 0.2054 | 0.2209 | 0.2407 | 0.2665 | 0.3012 | 0.3498 | 0.4228 | 0.5433 | 0.7813 | 1.2979 | 2.9791 | 0.8635 | 0.7822 | 0.7066 | 0.6542 | 0.4764 | 0.3786 | 0.2686 | 0.2057 | 0.1654 | 0.1369 |
| 0.84 | 0.1868 | 0.1954 | 0.2061 | 0.2194 | 0.2360 | 0.2574 | 0.2852 | 0.3226 | 0.3754 | 0.4549 | 0.5868 | 0.8520 | 1.5020 | 1.9102 |  |  |  |  | 0.4373 | 0.3515 | 0.2518 | 0.1942 | 0.1566 | 0.1299 |
| 0.83 | 0.1986 | 0.2079 | 0.2193 | 0.2335 | 0.2515 | 0.2743 | 0.3043 | 0.3446 | 0.4016 | 0.4880 | 0.6332 | 0.9312 | 1.8352 |  |  |  |  |  | 0.4018 | 0.3261 | 0.2364 | 0.1830 | 0.1481 | 0.1231 |
| 0.82 | 0.2105 | 0.2205 | 0.2326 | 0.2478 | 0.2670 | 0.2915 | 0.3236 | 0.3671 | 0.4289 | 0.5231 | 0.6835 | 1.0245 | 2.5439 |  |  |  |  |  | 0.3692 | 0.3025 | 0.2212 | 0.1724 | 0.1399 | 0.1166 |
| 0.81 | 0.2224 | 0.2330 | 0.2460 | 0.2622 | 0.2827 | 0.3089 | 0.3435 | 0.3903 | 0.4571 | 0.5600 | 0.7386 | 1.1381 | 1.2046 |  |  |  |  |  | 0.3395 | 0.2805 | 0.2073 | 0.1621 | 0.1321 | 0.1103 |
| 0.80 | 0.2344 | 0.2456 | 0.2594 | 0.2768 | 0.2985 | 0.3267 | 0.3637 | 0.4142 | 0.4868 | 0.5997 | 0.8002 | 1.2900 |  |  |  |  |  |  | 0.3122 | 0.2600 | 0.1937 | 0.1524 | 0.1245 | 0.1043 |
| 0.79 | 0.2464 | 0.2583 | 0.2731 | 0.2915 | 0.3145 | 0.3448 | 0.3845 | 0.4390 | 0.5178 | 0.6423 | 0.8709 | 1.5271 |  |  |  |  |  |  | 0.2873 | 0.2410 | 0.1813 | 0.1431 | 0.1174 | 0.0984 |
| 0.78 | 0.2585 | 0.2712 | 0.2868 | 0.3064 | 0.3311 | 0.3633 | 0.4059 | 0.4647 | 0.5508 | 0.6891 | 0.9552 | 2.3868 |  |  |  |  |  |  | 0.2644 | 0.2233 | 0.1691 | 0.1343 | 0.1104 | 0.0928 |
| 0.77 | 0.2707 | 0.2841 | 0.3007 | 0.3215 | 0.3478 | 0.3822 | 0.4280 | 0.4917 | 0.5858 | 0.7409 | 1.0611 |  |  |  |  |  |  |  | 0.2435 | 0.2069 | 0.1581 | 0.1258 | 0.1038 | 0.0874 |
| 0.76 | 0.2830 | 0.2971 | 0.3147 | 0.3369 | 0.3649 | 0.4017 | 0.4509 | 0.5200 | 0.6237 | 0.8002 | 1.2090 |  |  |  |  |  |  |  | 0.2242 | 0.1916 | 0.1472 | 0.1179 | 0.0975 | 0.0823 |
| 0.75 | 0.2953 | 0.3103 | 0.3289 | 0.3524 | 0.3825 | 0.4217 | 0.4748 | 0.5499 | 0.6650 | 0.8696 | 1.4722 |  |  |  |  |  |  |  | 0.2066 | 0.1775 | 0.1375 | 0.1103 | 0.0915 | 0.0773 |
| 0.74 | 0.3077 | 0.3236 | 0.3433 | 0.3683 | 0.4002 | 0.4424 | 0.4997 | 0.5819 | 0.7110 | 0.9531 |  |  |  |  |  |  |  |  | 0.1912 | 0.1643 | 0.1279 | 0.1031 | 0.0857 | 0.0727 |
| 0.73 | 0.3203 | 0.3370 | 0.3579 | 0.3844 | 0.4186 | 0.4638 | 0.5259 | 0.6164 | 0.7630 | 1.0698 |  |  |  |  |  |  |  |  | 0.1754 | 0.1521 | 0.1193 | 0.0963 | 0.0803 | 0.0682 |
| 0.72 | 0.3329 | 0.3506 | 0.3727 | 0.4010 | 0.4374 | 0.4861 | 0.5536 | 0.6540 | 0.8239 | 1.2518 |  |  |  |  |  |  |  |  | 0.1616 | 0.1407 | 0.1107 | 0.0899 | 0.0751 | 0.0639 |
| 0.71 | 0.3456 | 0.3644 | 0.3879 | 0.4179 | 0.4570 | 0.5094 | 0.5832 | 0.6957 | 0.8980 | 1.5361 |  |  |  |  |  |  |  |  | 0.1489 | 0.1301 | 0.1032 | 0.0838 | 0.0702 | 0.0598 |
| 0.70 | 0.3585 | 0.3783 | 0.4032 | 0.4353 | 0.4770 | 0.5339 | 0.6151 | 0.7429 | 0.9955 |  |  |  |  |  |  |  |  |  | 0.1371 | 0.1202 | 0.0956 | 0.0781 | 0.0656 | 0.0560 |
| 0.69 | 0.3716 | 0.3925 | 0.4190 | 0.4531 | 0.4981 | 0.5598 | 0.6499 | 0.7979 | 1.1432 |  |  |  |  |  |  |  |  |  | 0.1263 | 0.1111 | 0.0890 | 0.0727 | 0.0612 | 0.0523 |
| 0.68 | 0.3848 | 0.4069 | 0.4350 | 0.4715 | 0.5199 | 0.5875 | 0.6885 | 0.8649 | 1.5361 |  |  |  |  |  |  |  |  |  | 0.1162 | 0.1026 | 0.0822 | 0.0676 | 0.0570 | 0.0488 |
| 0.67 | 0.3981 | 0.4216 | 0.4515 | 0.4906 | 0.5431 | 0.6173 | 0.7321 | 0.9524 |  |  |  |  |  |  |  |  |  |  | 0.1070 | 0.0948 | 0.0761 | 0.0628 | 0.0531 | 0.0455 |
| 0.66 | 0.4117 | 0.4365 | 0.4684 | 0.5104 | 0.5674 | 0.6499 | 0.7831 | 1.0841 |  |  |  |  |  |  |  |  |  |  | 0.0984 | 0.0873 | 0.0704 | 0.0583 | 0.0494 | 0.0424 |
| 0.65 | 0.4254 | 0.4518 | 0.4859 | 0.5311 | 0.5935 | 0.6859 | 0.8451 | 1.4102 |  |  |  |  |  |  |  |  |  |  | 0.0905 | 0.0805 | 0.0652 | 0.0540 | 0.0458 | 0.0394 |
| 0.64 | 0.4394 | 0.4675 | 0.5040 | 0.5529 | 0.6215 | 0.7268 | 0.9263 |  |  |  |  |  |  |  |  |  |  |  | 0.0831 | 0.0741 | 0.0602 | 0.0500 | 0.0425 | 0.0366 |
| 0.63 | 0.4537 | 0.4836 | 0.5228 | 0.5759 | 0.6522 | 0.7746 | 1.0492 |  |  |  |  |  |  |  |  |  |  |  | 0.0764 | 0.0682 | 0.0556 | 0.0462 | 0.0394 | 0.0339 |
| 0.62 | 0.4683 | 0.5002 | 0.5424 | 0.6005 | 0.6860 | 0.8329 | 1.3682 |  |  |  |  |  |  |  |  |  |  |  | 0.0701 | 0.0627 | 0.0513 | 0.0428 | 0.0365 | 0.0315 |
| 0.61 | 0.4832 | 0.5173 | 0.5630 | 0.6270 | 0.7248 | 0.9101 |  |  |  |  |  |  |  |  |  |  |  |  | 0.0643 | 0.0576 | 0.0472 | 0.0394 | 0.0337 | 0.0291 |
| 0.60 | 0.4985 | 0.5351 | 0.5847 | 0.6560 | 0.7699 | 1.0295 |  |  |  |  |  |  |  |  |  |  |  |  | 0.0589 | 0.0529 | 0.0435 | 0.0364 | 0.0311 | 0.0269 |

Statistical table (dense numerical two-way table). Column headers (top row, $x$-values) followed by rows labelled 0.59 down to 0.11.

| | 0.5142 | 0.5536 | 0.6079 | 0.6879 | 0.8252 | 1.3751 | .3181 | 0.2119 | 0.1604 | 0.1280 | 0.1077 | 0.0903 | 0.0779 | 0.0712 | 0.0654 | 0.0635 | 0.0618 | 0.0607 | 0.0539 | 0.0485 | 0.0399 | 0.0334 | 0.0287 | 0.0248 |
|---|---|---|---|---|---|---|---|---|---|---|---|---|---|---|---|---|---|---|---|---|---|---|---|---|
| 0.59 | 0.5304 | 0.5731 | 0.6328 | 0.7243 | 0.8996 | 1.0143 | 0.2596 | 0.1829 | 0.1416 | 0.1145 | 0.0970 | 0.0817 | 0.0708 | 0.0648 | 0.0593 | 0.0580 | 0.0564 | 0.0551 | 0.0492 | 0.0444 | 0.0367 | 0.0308 | 0.0264 | 0.0229 |
| 0.58 | 0.5472 | 0.5935 | 0.6600 | 0.7669 | | | 0.2176 | 0.1593 | 0.1254 | 0.1022 | 0.0875 | 0.0739 | 0.0642 | 0.0593 | 0.0542 | 0.0529 | 0.0514 | 0.0504 | 0.0450 | 0.0406 | 0.0336 | 0.0282 | 0.0243 | 0.0210 |
| 0.57 | 0.5647 | 0.6154 | 0.6902 | 0.8196 | | | 0.1851 | 0.1392 | 0.1113 | 0.0916 | 0.0789 | 0.0668 | 0.0583 | 0.0535 | 0.0492 | 0.0480 | 0.0468 | 0.0459 | 0.0410 | 0.0371 | 0.0308 | 0.0259 | 0.0223 | 0.0193 |
| 0.56 | 0.5830 | 0.6388 | 0.7246 | 0.8903 | | | | 0.1225 | 0.0990 | 0.0819 | 0.0711 | 0.0604 | 0.0528 | 0.0487 | 0.0447 | 0.0437 | 0.0426 | 0.0417 | 0.0374 | 0.0339 | 0.0281 | 0.0236 | 0.0204 | 0.0177 |
| 0.55 | 0.6022 | 0.6644 | 0.7649 | 1.0053 | | | | 0.1080 | 0.0882 | 0.0735 | 0.0640 | 0.0545 | 0.0478 | 0.0442 | 0.0406 | 0.0397 | 0.0387 | 0.0380 | 0.0340 | 0.0309 | 0.0257 | 0.0217 | 0.0187 | 0.0163 |
| 0.54 | 0.6227 | 0.6926 | 0.8146 | 1.8258 | | | | 0.1203 | 0.0786 | 0.0657 | 0.0572 | 0.0492 | 0.0433 | 0.0400 | 0.0369 | 0.0360 | 0.0351 | 0.0345 | 0.0309 | 0.0281 | 0.0234 | 0.0198 | 0.0171 | 0.0148 |
| 0.53 | 0.6446 | 0.7247 | 0.8817 | | | | | 0.1051 | 0.0844 | 0.0701 | 0.0589 | 0.0512 | 0.0444 | 0.0391 | 0.0361 | 0.0334 | 0.0327 | 0.0318 | 0.0313 | 0.0281 | 0.0255 | 0.0213 | 0.0180 | 0.0156 | 0.0136 |
| 0.52 | 0.6684 | 0.7623 | 0.9935 | | | | | 0.1187 | 0.0923 | 0.0748 | 0.0626 | 0.0526 | 0.0458 | 0.0400 | 0.0353 | 0.0327 | 0.0303 | 0.0295 | 0.0288 | 0.0283 | 0.0254 | 0.0231 | 0.0193 | 0.0163 | 0.0142 | 0.0123 |
| 0.51 | 0.6947 | 0.8089 | | | | | | 0.0811 | 0.0663 | 0.0557 | 0.0472 | 0.0410 | 0.0359 | 0.0318 | 0.0296 | 0.0274 | 0.0267 | 0.0260 | 0.0257 | 0.0255 | 0.0230 | 0.0210 | 0.0175 | 0.0149 | 0.0129 | 0.0112 |
| 0.50 | 0.7244 | 0.8717 | 0.3320 | | | | | 0.0714 | 0.0587 | 0.0496 | 0.0420 | 0.0370 | 0.0323 | 0.0286 | 0.0266 | 0.0247 | 0.0240 | 0.0235 | 0.0231 | 0.0208 | 0.0189 | 0.0159 | 0.0134 | 0.0117 | 0.0102 |
| 0.49 | 0.7591 | 0.9767 | 0.2360 | | | | | 0.0628 | 0.0521 | 0.0442 | 0.0377 | 0.0331 | 0.0290 | 0.0257 | 0.0239 | 0.0221 | 0.0217 | 0.0211 | 0.0208 | 0.0187 | 0.0171 | 0.0143 | 0.0122 | 0.0106 | 0.0092 |
| 0.48 | 0.8015 | 0.9564 | 0.1831 | | | | | 0.0554 | 0.0461 | 0.0391 | 0.0337 | 0.0296 | 0.0259 | 0.0230 | 0.0213 | 0.0200 | 0.0192 | 0.0190 | 0.0186 | 0.0168 | 0.0154 | 0.0129 | 0.0109 | 0.0095 | 0.0083 |
| 0.47 | 0.8585 | 0.2933 | 0.1475 | | | | | 0.0487 | 0.0408 | 0.0347 | 0.0300 | 0.0265 | 0.0232 | 0.0206 | 0.0192 | 0.0178 | 0.0173 | 0.0170 | 0.0167 | 0.0151 | 0.0138 | 0.0116 | 0.0099 | 0.0086 | 0.0075 |
| 0.46 | 0.9515 | 0.2069 | 0.1215 | | | | | 0.0429 | 0.0361 | 0.0308 | 0.0267 | 0.0235 | 0.0207 | 0.0186 | 0.0171 | 0.0160 | 0.0155 | 0.0152 | 0.0150 | 0.0135 | 0.0124 | 0.0104 | 0.0089 | 0.0077 | 0.0067 |
| 0.45 | 3.3677 | 0.1594 | 0.1014 | | | | | 0.0377 | 0.0319 | 0.0273 | 0.0237 | 0.0210 | 0.0184 | 0.0164 | 0.0152 | 0.0142 | 0.0139 | 0.0136 | 0.0138 | 0.0124 | 0.0110 | 0.0093 | 0.0080 | 0.0069 | 0.0061 |
| 0.44 | 0.2650 | 0.1275 | 0.0853 | | | | | 0.0332 | 0.0281 | 0.0240 | 0.0210 | 0.0186 | 0.0164 | 0.0146 | 0.0135 | 0.0127 | 0.0123 | 0.0121 | 0.0110 | 0.0099 | 0.0083 | 0.0071 | 0.0062 | 0.0054 |
| 0.43 | 0.1837 | 0.1042 | 0.0723 | | | | | 0.0291 | 0.0247 | 0.0212 | 0.0186 | 0.0164 | 0.0145 | 0.0130 | 0.0121 | 0.0113 | 0.0110 | 0.0108 | 0.0096 | 0.0088 | 0.0074 | 0.0063 | 0.0055 | 0.0048 |
| 0.42 | 0.1398 | 0.0862 | 0.0614 | | | | | 0.0255 | 0.0217 | 0.0187 | 0.0164 | 0.0144 | 0.0128 | 0.0115 | 0.0100 | 0.0098 | 0.0095 | 0.0094 | 0.0078 | 0.0066 | 0.0056 | 0.0049 | 0.0043 |
| 0.41 | 0.1107 | 0.0720 | 0.0524 | 0.0404 | | | | 0.0266 | 0.0223 | 0.0191 | 0.0165 | 0.0144 | 0.0127 | 0.0113 | 0.0101 | 0.0086 | 0.0084 | 0.0083 | 0.0075 | 0.0069 | 0.0058 | 0.0050 | 0.0043 | 0.0038 |
| 0.40 | 0.0895 | 0.0604 | 0.0447 | 0.0348 | | | | 0.0231 | 0.0195 | 0.0167 | 0.0143 | 0.0126 | 0.0111 | 0.0099 | 0.0089 | 0.0082 | 0.0076 | 0.0073 | 0.0067 | 0.0061 | 0.0051 | 0.0044 | 0.0039 | 0.0033 |
| 0.39 | 0.0733 | 0.0447 | 0.0382 | 0.0299 | | | | 0.0210 | 0.0170 | 0.0126 | 0.0110 | 0.0097 | 0.0087 | 0.0078 | 0.0072 | 0.0068 | 0.0067 | 0.0065 | 0.0064 | 0.0058 | 0.0053 | 0.0045 | 0.0039 | 0.0034 | 0.0029 |
| 0.38 | 0.0606 | 0.0430 | 0.0326 | 0.0257 | | | | 0.0174 | 0.0147 | 0.0126 | 0.0110 | 0.0096 | 0.0085 | 0.0076 | 0.0068 | 0.0060 | 0.0058 | 0.0057 | 0.0051 | 0.0047 | 0.0040 | 0.0034 | 0.0030 | 0.0026 |
| 0.37 | 0.0503 | 0.0363 | 0.0278 | 0.0221 | | | | 0.0150 | 0.0128 | 0.0110 | 0.0096 | 0.0085 | 0.0074 | 0.0066 | 0.0059 | 0.0052 | 0.0050 | 0.0050 | 0.0049 | 0.0044 | 0.0041 | 0.0033 | 0.0030 | 0.0026 | 0.0023 |
| 0.36 | 0.0419 | 0.0307 | 0.0237 | 0.0189 | 0.0155 | 0.0130 | | 0.0110 | 0.0094 | 0.0082 | 0.0071 | 0.0064 | 0.0057 | 0.0052 | 0.0047 | 0.0045 | 0.0044 | 0.0043 | 0.0038 | 0.0035 | 0.0030 | 0.0026 | 0.0022 | 0.0020 |
| 0.35 | 0.0350 | 0.0259 | 0.0201 | 0.0161 | 0.0137 | 0.0113 | | 0.0094 | 0.0082 | 0.0071 | 0.0062 | 0.0055 | 0.0050 | 0.0045 | 0.0039 | 0.0038 | 0.0037 | 0.0036 | 0.0032 | 0.0030 | 0.0026 | 0.0022 | 0.0019 | 0.0017 |
| 0.34 | 0.0292 | 0.0218 | 0.0170 | 0.0137 | 0.0113 | 0.0095 | | 0.0081 | 0.0069 | 0.0061 | 0.0054 | 0.0048 | 0.0043 | 0.0039 | 0.0036 | 0.0033 | 0.0032 | 0.0032 | 0.0030 | 0.0026 | 0.0022 | 0.0019 | 0.0017 | 0.0015 |
| 0.33 | 0.0244 | 0.0183 | 0.0144 | 0.0116 | 0.0098 | 0.0082 | | 0.0070 | 0.0060 | 0.0052 | 0.0046 | 0.0041 | 0.0038 | 0.0033 | 0.0029 | 0.0028 | 0.0027 | 0.0027 | 0.0026 | 0.0022 | 0.0019 | 0.0016 | 0.0014 | 0.0013 |
| 0.32 | 0.0203 | 0.0154 | 0.0121 | 0.0098 | 0.0082 | 0.0069 | | 0.0059 | 0.0051 | 0.0045 | 0.0039 | 0.0036 | 0.0031 | 0.0028 | 0.0025 | 0.0025 | 0.0025 | 0.0023 | 0.0022 | 0.0019 | 0.0016 | 0.0014 | 0.0013 | 0.0011 |
| 0.31 | 0.0169 | 0.0128 | 0.0102 | 0.0083 | 0.0069 | 0.0058 | | 0.0049 | 0.0043 | 0.0038 | 0.0033 | 0.0029 | 0.0026 | 0.0024 | 0.0022 | 0.0020 | 0.0019 | 0.0019 | 0.0018 | 0.0016 | 0.0014 | 0.0012 | 0.0010 | 0.0009 |
| 0.30 | 0.0139 | 0.0107 | 0.0085 | 0.0069 | 0.0057 | 0.0049 | | 0.0041 | 0.0036 | 0.0032 | 0.0029 | 0.0025 | 0.0022 | 0.0020 | 0.0018 | 0.0017 | 0.0017 | 0.0016 | 0.0015 | 0.0012 | 0.0010 | 0.0009 | 0.0008 |
| 0.29 | 0.0115 | 0.0089 | 0.0071 | 0.0057 | 0.0048 | 0.0041 | | 0.0035 | 0.0030 | 0.0026 | 0.0023 | 0.0021 | 0.0019 | 0.0017 | 0.0015 | 0.0014 | 0.0014 | 0.0014 | 0.0012 | 0.0010 | 0.0008 | 0.0007 | 0.0006 |
| 0.28 | 0.0094 | 0.0073 | 0.0058 | 0.0048 | 0.0040 | 0.0034 | | 0.0029 | 0.0025 | 0.0022 | 0.0019 | 0.0017 | 0.0016 | 0.0014 | 0.0013 | 0.0012 | 0.0012 | 0.0011 | 0.0010 | 0.0008 | 0.0007 | 0.0006 | 0.0005 |
| 0.27 | 0.0077 | 0.0060 | 0.0049 | 0.0039 | 0.0034 | 0.0028 | | 0.0024 | 0.0021 | 0.0018 | 0.0016 | 0.0014 | 0.0014 | 0.0013 | 0.0011 | 0.0010 | 0.0010 | 0.0010 | 0.0008 | 0.0007 | 0.0006 | 0.0005 | 0.0004 |
| 0.26 | 0.0062 | 0.0048 | 0.0039 | 0.0032 | 0.0027 | 0.0023 | | 0.0021 | 0.0018 | 0.0015 | 0.0013 | 0.0011 | 0.0010 | 0.0009 | 0.0009 | 0.0008 | 0.0008 | 0.0008 | 0.0007 | 0.0006 | 0.0005 | 0.0004 | 0.0004 |
| 0.25 | 0.0050 | 0.0039 | 0.0032 | 0.0026 | 0.0022 | 0.0019 | | 0.0017 | 0.0015 | 0.0012 | 0.0010 | 0.0009 | 0.0008 | 0.0008 | 0.0008 | 0.0007 | 0.0006 | 0.0006 | 0.0006 | 0.0005 | 0.0004 | 0.0003 | 0.0003 |
| 0.24 | 0.0040 | 0.0031 | 0.0025 | 0.0021 | 0.0018 | 0.0015 | | 0.0014 | 0.0012 | 0.0010 | 0.0008 | 0.0008 | 0.0007 | 0.0007 | 0.0006 | 0.0005 | 0.0005 | 0.0005 | 0.0005 | 0.0004 | 0.0003 | 0.0003 | 0.0002 |
| 0.23 | 0.0032 | 0.0025 | 0.0020 | 0.0017 | 0.0014 | 0.0012 | | 0.0011 | 0.0010 | 0.0008 | 0.0007 | 0.0006 | 0.0006 | 0.0005 | 0.0005 | 0.0004 | 0.0004 | 0.0004 | 0.0004 | 0.0003 | 0.0003 | 0.0002 | 0.0002 |
| 0.22 | 0.0025 | 0.0020 | 0.0016 | 0.0013 | 0.0011 | 0.0010 | | 0.0009 | 0.0008 | 0.0006 | 0.0005 | 0.0005 | 0.0004 | 0.0004 | 0.0004 | 0.0004 | 0.0003 | 0.0003 | 0.0003 | 0.0003 | 0.0002 | 0.0002 | 0.0002 |
| 0.21 | 0.0019 | 0.0016 | 0.0013 | 0.0010 | 0.0009 | 0.0008 | | 0.0007 | 0.0007 | 0.0005 | 0.0004 | 0.0004 | 0.0003 | 0.0003 | 0.0003 | 0.0003 | 0.0002 | 0.0002 | 0.0002 | 0.0002 | 0.0002 | 0.0001 | 0.0001 |
| 0.20 | 0.0015 | 0.0012 | 0.0010 | 0.0008 | 0.0007 | 0.0006 | | 0.0006 | 0.0005 | 0.0004 | 0.0004 | 0.0003 | 0.0003 | 0.0002 | 0.0002 | 0.0002 | 0.0002 | 0.0002 | 0.0002 | 0.0002 | 0.0001 | 0.0001 | 0.0001 |
| 0.19 | 0.0012 | 0.0009 | 0.0008 | 0.0007 | 0.0006 | 0.0005 | | 0.0004 | 0.0004 | 0.0003 | 0.0003 | 0.0002 | 0.0002 | 0.0002 | 0.0002 | 0.0002 | 0.0001 | 0.0001 | 0.0001 | 0.0001 | 0.0001 | 0.0001 | 0.0001 |
| 0.18 | 0.0009 | 0.0007 | 0.0006 | 0.0005 | 0.0004 | 0.0004 | | 0.0003 | 0.0003 | 0.0002 | 0.0002 | 0.0002 | 0.0002 | 0.0001 | 0.0001 | 0.0001 | 0.0001 | 0.0001 | 0.0001 | 0.0001 | 0.0001 | 0.0001 | 0.0001 |
| 0.17 | 0.0008 | 0.0006 | 0.0005 | 0.0004 | 0.0003 | 0.0003 | | 0.0002 | 0.0002 | 0.0002 | 0.0001 | 0.0001 | 0.0001 | 0.0001 | 0.0001 | 0.0001 | 0.0001 | 0.0001 | 0.0001 | 0.0001 | 0.0001 | 0.0001 | 0.0001 |
| 0.16 | 0.0006 | 0.0004 | 0.0004 | 0.0003 | 0.0003 | 0.0002 | | 0.0002 | 0.0002 | 0.0001 | 0.0001 | 0.0001 | 0.0001 | 0.0001 | 0.0001 | 0.0001 | 0.0001 | 0.0001 | 0.0001 | 0.0001 | 0.0001 | 0.0001 | 0.0001 |
| 0.15 | 0.0004 | 0.0003 | 0.0003 | 0.0002 | 0.0002 | 0.0002 | | 0.0001 | 0.0001 | 0.0001 | 0.0001 | 0.0001 | 0.0001 | 0.0001 | 0.0001 | 0.0001 | 0.0001 | 0.0001 | 0.0001 | | | | |
| 0.14 | 0.0003 | 0.0002 | 0.0002 | 0.0002 | 0.0001 | 0.0001 | | 0.0001 | 0.0001 | 0.0001 | 0.0001 | 0.0001 | 0.0001 | | 0.0001 | | | | | | | | |
| 0.13 | 0.0002 | 0.0002 | 0.0001 | 0.0001 | 0.0001 | 0.0001 | | 0.0001 | 0.0001 | 0.0001 | 0.0001 | | | | | | | | | | | | |
| 0.12 | 0.0001 | 0.0001 | 0.0001 | 0.0001 | 0.0001 | 0.0001 | | 0.0001 | | | | | | | | | | | | | | | |
| 0.11 | 0.0001 | 0.0001 | 0.0001 | 0.0001 | | | | | | | | | | | | | | | | | | | |

Last column: 0

## Table E-2. Varied-flow Function $Y$

| $v/d_c$ \ $Q/Q_c$ | 1.60 | 1.50 | 1.40 | 1.30 | 1.20 | 1.15 | 1.10 | 1.09 | 1.08 | 1.07 | 1.035 | 1.00 | 0.95 | 0.90 | 0.85 | 0.80 | 0.75 | 0.70 | 0.65 | 0.60 | 0.55 | 0.50 | 0.45 | 0.40 |
|---|---|---|---|---|---|---|---|---|---|---|---|---|---|---|---|---|---|---|---|---|---|---|---|---|
| 1.00 | 0.0482 | 0.0562 | 0.0680 | 0.0851 | 0.1128 | 0.1383 | 0.2102 | 0.3050 | 0.4660 | 0.0245 |  | 0.0016 | 0.0005 | 0.0004 | 0.0003 | 0.0002 | 0 | 0 | 0 | 0 | 0 | 0 | 0 | 0 |
| 0.99 | 0.0480 | 0.0560 | 0.0678 | 0.0849 | 0.1126 | 0.1380 | 0.2092 | 0.3034 | 0.4622 | 0.0234 | 0.0056 | 0.0034 | 0.0013 | 0.0009 | 0.0007 | 0.0006 | 0.0001 | 0.0001 | 0.0001 | 0.0001 | 0.0001 | 0.0001 | 0.0001 | 0.0001 |
| 0.98 | 0.0479 | 0.0558 | 0.0677 | 0.0846 | 0.1120 | 0.1374 | 0.2077 | 0.3008 | 0.4572 | 0.0186 | 0.0094 | 0.0053 | 0.0022 | 0.0016 | 0.0013 | 0.0010 | 0.0005 | 0.0004 | 0.0003 | 0.0003 | 0.0003 | 0.0003 | 0.0003 | 0.0003 |
| 0.97 | 0.0478 | 0.0556 | 0.0674 | 0.0841 | 0.1113 | 0.1366 | 0.2056 | 0.2974 | 0.4508 |  | 0.0132 | 0.0075 | 0.0033 | 0.0024 | 0.0019 | 0.0015 | 0.0009 | 0.0008 | 0.0007 | 0.0006 | 0.0005 | 0.0005 | 0.0005 | 0.0005 |
| 0.96 | 0.0477 | 0.0553 | 0.0671 | 0.0836 | 0.1105 | 0.1354 | 0.2025 | 0.2898 | 0.4428 | 0.0523 | 0.0171 | 0.0098 | 0.0045 | 0.0033 | 0.0026 | 0.0021 | 0.0014 | 0.0012 | 0.0011 | 0.0010 | 0.0009 | 0.0008 | 0.0008 | 0.0008 |
| 0.95 | 0.0474 | 0.0550 | 0.0668 | 0.0830 | 0.1093 | 0.1339 | 0.1985 | 0.2785 | 0.4296 | 0.0824 | 0.0213 | 0.0122 | 0.0060 | 0.0043 | 0.0034 | 0.0028 | 0.0019 | 0.0017 | 0.0016 | 0.0014 | 0.0013 | 0.0012 | 0.0012 | 0.0011 |
| 0.94 | 0.0470 | 0.0547 | 0.0663 | 0.0823 | 0.1079 | 0.1321 | 0.1919 | 0.2500 | 0.3563 | 0.1156 | 0.0258 | 0.0150 | 0.0075 | 0.0054 | 0.0043 | 0.0034 | 0.0025 | 0.0023 | 0.0021 | 0.0019 | 0.0017 | 0.0016 | 0.0015 | 0.0015 |
| 0.93 | 0.0468 | 0.0544 | 0.0658 | 0.0816 | 0.1065 | 0.1300 | 0.1838 | 0.2220 | 0.2932 | 0.1614 | 0.0310 | 0.0181 | 0.0093 | 0.0067 | 0.0053 | 0.0045 | 0.0032 | 0.0028 | 0.0026 | 0.0024 | 0.0022 | 0.0020 | 0.0019 | 0.0019 |
| 0.92 | 0.0466 | 0.0540 | 0.0652 | 0.0809 | 0.1051 | 0.1278 | 0.1736 | 0.2014 | 0.2465 | 0.2630 | 0.0368 | 0.0215 | 0.0112 | 0.0081 | 0.0064 | 0.0053 | 0.0040 | 0.0036 | 0.0032 | 0.0029 | 0.0027 | 0.0025 | 0.0024 | 0.0023 |
| 0.91 | 0.0462 | 0.0537 | 0.0648 | 0.0800 | 0.1034 | 0.1252 | 0.1656 | 0.1861 | 0.2164 | 0.2500 | 0.0436 | 0.0255 | 0.0132 | 0.0096 | 0.0076 | 0.0064 | 0.0047 | 0.0042 | 0.0039 | 0.0036 | 0.0033 | 0.0030 | 0.0029 | 0.0028 |
| 0.90 | 0.0458 | 0.0533 | 0.0641 | 0.0790 | 0.1028 | 0.1224 | 0.1577 | 0.1729 | 0.1940 | 0.2070 | 0.0522 | 0.0303 | 0.0157 | 0.0114 | 0.0076 | 0.0075 | 0.0057 | 0.0050 | 0.0045 | 0.0042 | 0.0042 | 0.0036 | 0.0035 | 0.0034 |
| 0.89 | 0.0456 | 0.0530 | 0.0634 | 0.0780 | 0.1000 | 0.1198 | 0.1512 | 0.1638 | 0.1793 | 0.1852 | 0.0648 | 0.0362 | 0.0181 | 0.0132 | 0.0088 | 0.0086 | 0.0065 | 0.0058 | 0.0053 | 0.0048 | 0.0045 | 0.0042 | 0.0040 | 0.0039 |
| 0.88 | 0.0452 | 0.0525 | 0.0627 | 0.0770 | 0.0983 | 0.1168 | 0.1447 | 0.1550 | 0.1665 | 0.1715 | 0.0833 | 0.0438 | 0.0212 | 0.0154 | 0.0103 | 0.0103 | 0.0075 | 0.0067 | 0.0061 | 0.0055 | 0.0052 | 0.0048 | 0.0046 | 0.0044 |
| 0.87 | 0.0448 | 0.0520 | 0.0619 | 0.0760 | 0.0966 | 0.1139 | 0.1394 | 0.1478 | 0.1573 | 0.1604 | 0.1193 | 0.0534 | 0.0244 | 0.0180 | 0.0118 | 0.0118 | 0.0086 | 0.0077 | 0.0070 | 0.0064 | 0.0059 | 0.0055 | 0.0053 | 0.0051 |
| 0.86 | 0.0444 | 0.0515 | 0.0613 | 0.0750 | 0.0950 | 0.1112 | 0.1344 | 0.1413 | 0.1492 | 0.1514 | 0.1577 | 0.0667 | 0.0282 | 0.0200 | 0.0135 | 0.0132 | 0.0097 | 0.0087 | 0.0079 | 0.0072 | 0.0067 | 0.0053 | 0.0060 | 0.0053 |
| 0.85 | 0.0439 | 0.0510 | 0.0607 | 0.0740 | 0.0931 | 0.1085 | 0.1297 | 0.1356 | 0.1422 | 0.1439 | 0.2360 | 0.0849 | 0.0325 | 0.0200 | 0.0153 | 0.0127 | 0.0110 | 0.0098 | 0.0088 | 0.0081 | 0.0074 | 0.0071 | 0.0067 | 0.0064 |
| 0.84 | 0.0435 | 0.0505 | 0.0598 | 0.0729 | 0.0913 | 0.1058 | 0.1251 | 0.1306 | 0.1365 | 0.1376 | 0.1919 | 0.1111 | 0.0377 | 0.0230 | 0.0173 | 0.0143 | 0.0123 | 0.0110 | 0.0099 | 0.0090 | 0.0081 | 0.0079 | 0.0075 | 0.0071 |
| 0.83 | 0.0430 | 0.0500 | 0.0590 | 0.0718 | 0.0898 | 0.1034 | 0.1213 | 0.1259 | 0.1313 | 0.1321 | 0.1735 | 0.1336 | 0.0445 | 0.0262 | 0.0196 | 0.0161 | 0.0138 | 0.0122 | 0.0110 | 0.0101 | 0.0090 | 0.0088 | 0.0083 | 0.0079 |
| 0.82 | 0.0426 | 0.0494 | 0.0583 | 0.0707 | 0.0879 | 0.1008 | 0.1178 | 0.1218 | 0.1266 | 0.1272 | 0.1594 | 2.182 | 0.0530 | 0.0299 | 0.0221 | 0.0180 | 0.0154 | 0.0136 | 0.0122 | 0.0112 | 0.0104 | 0.0097 | 0.0092 | 0.0087 |
| 0.81 | 0.0420 | 0.0488 | 0.0576 | 0.0696 | 0.0862 | 0.0986 | 0.1141 | 0.1178 | 0.1223 | 0.1230 | 0.1500 | 2.075 | 0.0649 | 0.0342 | 0.0250 | 0.0202 | 0.0171 | 0.0150 | 0.0136 | 0.0124 | 0.0115 | 0.0107 | 0.0101 | 0.0096 |
| 0.80 | 0.0416 | 0.0482 | 0.0568 | 0.0685 | 0.0847 | 0.0963 | 0.1110 | 0.1143 | 0.1185 | 0.1191 | 0.1427 | 0.1806 | 0.0880 | 0.0389 | 0.0284 | 0.0225 | 0.0190 | 0.0166 | 0.0148 | 0.0136 | 0.0126 | 0.0118 | 0.0112 | 0.0106 |
| 0.79 | 0.0410 | 0.0476 | 0.0559 | 0.0674 | 0.0830 | 0.0941 | 0.1080 | 0.1112 | 0.1150 | 0.1153 | 0.1363 | 0.1655 | 0.1603 | 0.0450 | 0.0319 | 0.0252 | 0.0202 | 0.0184 | 0.0164 | 0.0149 | 0.0139 | 0.0130 | 0.0123 | 0.0117 |
| 0.78 | 0.0405 | 0.0469 | 0.0552 | 0.0663 | 0.0816 | 0.0919 | 0.1052 | 0.1080 | 0.1115 | 0.1117 | 0.1310 | 0.1546 | 0.1710 | 0.0524 | 0.0358 | 0.0282 | 0.0236 | 0.0204 | 0.0179 | 0.0164 | 0.0153 | 0.0142 | 0.0134 | 0.0128 |
| 0.77 | 0.0399 | 0.0462 | 0.0544 | 0.0652 | 0.0799 | 0.0899 | 0.1024 | 0.1052 | 0.1084 | 0.1088 | 0.1260 | 0.1436 | 0.1596 | 0.0625 | 0.0408 | 0.0314 | 0.0260 | 0.0224 | 0.0198 | 0.0180 | 0.0166 | 0.0155 | 0.0147 | 0.0140 |
| 0.76 | 0.0396 | 0.0455 | 0.0537 | 0.0642 | 0.0784 | 0.0881 | 0.1008 | 0.1027 | 0.1056 | 0.1057 | 0.1217 | 0.1336 | 0.1504 | 0.0768 | 0.0463 | 0.0349 | 0.0288 | 0.0247 | 0.0216 | 0.0196 | 0.0181 | 0.0168 | 0.0159 | 0.0150 |
| 0.75 | 0.0389 | 0.0449 | 0.0528 | 0.0631 | 0.0768 | 0.0861 | 0.1000 | 0.1000 | 0.1026 | 0.1032 | 0.1177 | 0.1200 | 0.1437 | 0.1111 | 0.0543 | 0.0392 | 0.0318 | 0.0273 | 0.0238 | 0.0216 | 0.0197 | 0.0184 | 0.0172 | 0.0163 |
| 0.74 | 0.0384 | 0.0443 | 0.0521 | 0.0620 | 0.0755 | 0.0844 | 0.0978 | 0.0978 | 0.1002 | 0.1004 | 0.1143 | 0.1166 | 0.1378 | 0.8457 | 0.0638 | 0.0440 | 0.0352 | 0.0300 | 0.0260 | 0.0236 | 0.0214 | 0.0200 | 0.0188 | 0.0177 |
| 0.73 | 0.0379 | 0.0437 | 0.0513 | 0.0610 | 0.0740 | 0.0826 | 0.0954 | 0.0954 | 0.0976 | 0.0980 | 0.1110 | 0.1130 | 0.1325 | 0.2192 | 0.0788 | 0.0500 | 0.0388 | 0.0330 | 0.0288 | 0.0258 | 0.0233 | 0.0217 | 0.0203 | 0.0192 |
| 0.72 | 0.0375 | 0.0430 | 0.0505 | 0.0600 | 0.0727 | 0.0808 | 0.0932 | 0.0932 | 0.0954 | 0.0956 | 0.1078 | 0.1099 | 0.1280 | 0.1950 | 0.1044 | 0.0571 | 0.0429 | 0.0361 | 0.0313 | 0.0278 | 0.0252 | 0.0234 | 0.0218 | 0.0206 |
| 0.71 | 0.0369 | 0.0424 | 0.0498 | 0.0590 | 0.0713 | 0.0792 | 0.0909 | 0.0909 | 0.0932 | 0.0933 | 0.1049 | 0.1066 | 0.1235 | 0.1790 | 0.2047 | 0.0676 | 0.0485 | 0.0400 | 0.0347 | 0.0306 | 0.0274 | 0.0254 | 0.0237 | 0.0224 |
| 0.70 | 0.0363 | 0.0418 | 0.0489 | 0.0580 | 0.0699 | 0.0776 | 0.0888 | 0.0889 | 0.0909 | 0.0912 | 0.1022 | 0.1040 | 0.1197 | 0.1650 | 0.2500 | 0.0817 | 0.0548 | 0.0443 | 0.0379 | 0.0333 | 0.0300 | 0.0275 | 0.0254 | 0.0240 |
| 0.69 | 0.0358 | 0.0411 | 0.0481 | 0.0570 | 0.0687 | 0.0760 | 0.0870 | 0.0870 | 0.0890 | 0.0891 | 0.0995 | 0.1011 | 0.1161 | 0.1547 | 0.2105 | 0.1030 | 0.0631 | 0.0494 | 0.0418 | 0.0362 | 0.0326 | 0.0298 | 0.0274 | 0.0259 |
| 0.68 | 0.0354 | 0.0404 | 0.0473 | 0.0560 | 0.0673 | 0.0746 | 0.0851 | 0.0851 | 0.0867 | 0.0869 | 0.0969 | 0.0985 | 0.1127 | 0.1465 | 0.1920 | 0.1747 | 0.0744 | 0.0556 | 0.0458 | 0.0395 | 0.0352 | 0.0321 | 0.0298 | 0.0280 |
| 0.67 | 0.0348 | 0.0398 | 0.0464 | 0.0550 | 0.0660 | 0.0729 | 0.0831 | 0.0831 | 0.0848 | 0.0851 | 0.0945 | 0.0960 | 0.1094 | 0.1403 | 0.1796 | 0.3650 | 0.0880 | 0.0633 | 0.0506 | 0.0434 | 0.0384 | 0.0350 | 0.0324 | 0.0301 |
| 0.66 | 0.0343 | 0.0392 | 0.0458 | 0.0540 | 0.0648 | 0.0714 | 0.0813 | 0.0813 | 0.0830 | 0.0830 | 0.0923 | 0.0937 | 0.1062 | 0.1352 | 0.1690 | 0.1100 | 0.1100 | 0.0724 | 0.0563 | 0.0475 | 0.0418 | 0.0378 | 0.0349 | 0.0324 |
| 0.65 | 0.0338 | 0.0386 | 0.0449 | 0.0530 | 0.0635 | 0.0699 | 0.0796 | 0.0797 | 0.0812 | 0.0813 | 0.0902 | 0.0916 | 0.1036 | 0.1304 | 0.1595 | 0.2045 | 0.2250 | 0.0849 | 0.0636 | 0.0524 | 0.0458 | 0.0411 | 0.0379 | 0.0350 |
| 0.64 | 0.0332 | 0.0379 | 0.0442 | 0.0520 | 0.0622 | 0.0684 | 0.0778 | 0.0778 | 0.0794 | 0.0793 | 0.0881 | 0.0892 | 0.1009 | 0.1263 | 0.1519 | 0.1882 | 0.3250 | 0.0978 | 0.0716 | 0.0576 | 0.0498 | 0.0444 | 0.0408 | 0.0377 |
| 0.63 | 0.0328 | 0.0372 | 0.0432 | 0.0510 | 0.0609 | 0.0671 | 0.0759 | 0.0759 | 0.0775 | 0.0777 | 0.0857 | 0.0867 | 0.0982 | 0.1223 | 0.1450 | 0.1763 | 0.2590 | 0.1224 | 0.0824 | 0.0650 | 0.0552 | 0.0488 | 0.0446 | 0.0410 |
| 0.62 | 0.0322 | 0.0367 | 0.0426 | 0.0500 | 0.0599 | 0.0658 | 0.0746 | 0.0746 | 0.0759 | 0.0759 | 0.0840 | 0.0850 | 0.0959 | 0.1189 | 0.1400 | 0.1680 | 0.2314 | 0.2500 | 0.0935 | 0.0721 | 0.0600 | 0.0527 | 0.0478 | 0.0438 |
| 0.61 | 0.0317 | 0.0360 | 0.0418 | 0.0490 | 0.0586 | 0.0643 | 0.0728 | 0.0728 | 0.0742 | 0.0743 | 0.0820 | 0.0830 | 0.0936 | 0.1152 | 0.1348 | 0.1606 | 0.2120 | 0.3466 | 0.1109 | 0.0810 | 0.0658 | 0.0578 | 0.0519 | 0.0475 |
| 0.60 | 0.0310 | 0.0353 | 0.0411 | 0.0481 | 0.0575 | 0.0629 | 0.0713 | 0.0712 | 0.0727 | 0.0725 | 0.0801 | 0.0810 | 0.0913 | 0.1120 | 0.1308 | 0.1545 | 0.1976 | 0.2780 | 0.1376 | 0.0915 | 0.0736 | 0.0627 | 0.0559 | 0.0511 |
| 0.59 | 0.0304 | 0.0348 | 0.0402 | 0.0471 | 0.0562 | 0.0618 | 0.0682 | 0.0697 | 0.0710 | 0.0697 | 0.0782 | 0.0790 | 0.0890 | 0.1085 | 0.1267 | 0.1490 | 0.1866 | 0.2430 | 0.2776 | 0.1080 | 0.0822 | 0.0687 | 0.0608 | 0.0554 |

| | | | | | | | | | | | | | | | | | | | | | |
|---|---|---|---|---|---|---|---|---|---|---|---|---|---|---|---|---|---|---|---|---|---|---|
| 0.58 | 0.0600 | 0.0658 | 0.0756 | 0.0928 | 0.1290 | 0.3451 | 0.2265 | 0.1777 | 0.1437 | 0.1228 | 0.1054 | 0.0934 | 0.0830 | 0.0764 | 0.0710 | 0.0694 | 0.0682 | 0.0668 | 0.0604 | 0.0550 | 0.0461 | 0.0396 | 0.0341 | 0.0299 |
| 0.57 | 0.0653 | 0.0719 | 0.0838 | 0.1062 | 0.1650 | 0.2940 | 0.2133 | 0.1702 | 0.1390 | 0.1191 | 0.1024 | 0.0911 | 0.0810 | 0.0746 | 0.0693 | 0.0678 | 0.0653 | 0.0653 | 0.0591 | 0.0540 | 0.0452 | 0.0388 | 0.0336 | 0.0293 |
| 0.56 | 0.0705 | 0.0790 | 0.0939 | 0.1238 | 0.3909 | 0.2640 | 0.2006 | 0.1630 | 0.1343 | 0.1155 | 0.0997 | 0.0887 | 0.0790 | 0.0730 | 0.0678 | 0.0664 | 0.0651 | 0.0638 | 0.0579 | 0.0529 | 0.0442 | 0.0381 | 0.0330 | 0.0288 |
| 0.55 | 0.0772 | 0.0882 | 0.1060 | 0.1500 | 0.3596 | 0.2430 | 0.1909 | 0.1564 | 0.1299 | 0.1120 | 0.0968 | 0.0863 | 0.0770 | 0.0712 | 0.0662 | 0.0648 | 0.0636 | 0.0623 | 0.0564 | 0.0517 | 0.0432 | 0.0372 | 0.0323 | 0.0282 |
| 0.54 | 0.0840 | 0.0974 | 0.1200 | 0.1925 | 0.3080 | 0.2180 | 0.1828 | 0.1505 | 0.1260 | 0.1090 | 0.0944 | 0.0844 | 0.0753 | 0.0696 | 0.0647 | 0.0633 | 0.0622 | 0.0610 | 0.0553 | 0.0506 | 0.0422 | 0.0365 | 0.0317 | 0.0278 |
| 0.53 | 0.0923 | 0.1099 | 0.1406 | 0.9732 | 0.2803 | 0.2166 | 0.1755 | 0.1452 | 0.1220 | 0.1057 | 0.0919 | 0.0820 | 0.0734 | 0.0678 | 0.0632 | 0.0618 | 0.0608 | 0.0596 | 0.0540 | 0.0495 | 0.0414 | 0.0358 | 0.0310 | 0.0270 |
| 0.52 | 0.1014 | 0.1242 | 0.1703 | 3.3850 | 0.2580 | 0.2062 | 0.1686 | 0.1401 | 0.1186 | 0.1027 | 0.0895 | 0.0801 | 0.0717 | 0.0663 | 0.0618 | 0.0604 | 0.0594 | 0.0583 | 0.0528 | 0.0485 | 0.0405 | 0.0351 | 0.0303 | 0.0266 |
| 0.51 | 0.1127 | 0.1410 | 0.2267 | 3.3360 | 0.2425 | 0.1972 | 0.1623 | 0.1353 | 0.1150 | 0.0998 | 0.0872 | 0.0780 | 0.0700 | 0.0646 | 0.0603 | 0.0590 | 0.0579 | 0.0568 | 0.0517 | 0.0474 | 0.0396 | 0.0343 | 0.0297 | 0.0260 |
| 0.50 | 0.1253 | 0.1633 | | 0.3050 | 0.2293 | 0.1890 | 0.1562 | 0.1307 | 0.1117 | 0.0970 | 0.0850 | 0.0762 | 0.0682 | 0.0632 | 0.0590 | 0.0576 | 0.0568 | 0.0554 | 0.0503 | 0.0463 | 0.0387 | 0.0336 | 0.0291 | 0.0256 |
| 0.49 | 0.1418 | 0.1924 | 0.4503 | 0.2850 | 0.2183 | 0.1815 | 0.1502 | 0.1263 | 0.1083 | 0.0941 | 0.0825 | 0.0741 | 0.0663 | 0.0614 | 0.0574 | 0.0561 | 0.0551 | 0.0541 | 0.0493 | 0.0451 | 0.0378 | 0.0328 | 0.0285 | 0.0250 |
| 0.48 | 0.1609 | 0.2500 | 0.3751 | 0.2670 | 0.2085 | 0.1749 | 0.1452 | 0.1225 | 0.1054 | 0.0917 | 0.0803 | 0.0722 | 0.0648 | 0.0601 | 0.0561 | 0.0548 | 0.0540 | 0.0529 | 0.0480 | 0.0441 | 0.0369 | 0.0321 | 0.0279 | 0.0244 |
| 0.47 | 0.1870 | | 0.3419 | 0.2530 | 0.2000 | 0.1687 | 0.1400 | 0.1187 | 0.1023 | 0.0891 | 0.0782 | 0.0703 | 0.0632 | 0.0583 | 0.0546 | 0.0535 | 0.0527 | 0.0514 | 0.0468 | 0.0430 | 0.0360 | 0.0312 | 0.0272 | 0.0233 |
| 0.46 | 0.2235 | 5060 | 0.3152 | 0.2390 | 0.1912 | 0.1620 | 0.1350 | 0.1147 | 0.0993 | 0.0865 | 0.0761 | 0.0685 | 0.0616 | 0.0570 | 0.0533 | 0.0522 | 0.0512 | 0.0502 | 0.0458 | 0.0420 | 0.0351 | 0.0306 | 0.0267 | 0.0233 |
| 0.45 | 0.2980 | 0.4350 | 0.2960 | 0.2283 | 0.1838 | 0.1558 | 0.1300 | 0.1110 | 0.0962 | 0.0840 | 0.0739 | 0.0664 | 0.0598 | 0.0553 | 0.0517 | 0.0507 | 0.0499 | 0.0488 | 0.0444 | 0.0409 | 0.0342 | 0.0298 | 0.0259 | 0.0228 |
| 0.44 | 1.4143 | 0.3900 | 0.2790 | 0.2188 | 0.1770 | 0.1501 | 0.1256 | 0.1076 | 0.0935 | 0.0816 | 0.0718 | 0.0648 | 0.0582 | 0.0541 | 0.0505 | 0.0495 | 0.0488 | 0.0477 | 0.0434 | 0.0399 | 0.0335 | 0.0291 | 0.0252 | 0.0221 |
| 0.43 | 0.6000 | 0.3610 | 0.2658 | 0.2102 | 0.1708 | 0.1446 | 0.1212 | 0.1042 | 0.0908 | 0.0793 | 0.0698 | 0.0631 | 0.0568 | 0.0526 | 0.0492 | 0.0482 | 0.0473 | 0.0463 | 0.0423 | 0.0388 | 0.0326 | 0.0283 | 0.0247 | 0.0216 |
| 0.42 | 0.5000 | 0.3378 | 0.2525 | 0.2016 | 0.1643 | 0.1390 | 0.1170 | 0.1008 | 0.0880 | 0.0770 | 0.0680 | 0.0614 | 0.0552 | 0.0511 | 0.0478 | 0.0468 | 0.0459 | 0.0451 | 0.0409 | 0.0378 | 0.0317 | 0.0276 | 0.0241 | 0.0210 |
| 0.41 | 0.4530 | 0.3190 | 0.2410 | 0.1941 | 0.1585 | 0.1338 | 0.1128 | 0.0978 | 0.0853 | 0.0746 | 0.0660 | 0.0595 | 0.0536 | 0.0496 | 0.0463 | 0.0454 | 0.0447 | 0.0438 | 0.0398 | 0.0367 | 0.0308 | 0.0268 | 0.0234 | 0.0204 |
| 0.40 | 0.4116 | 0.3000 | 0.2307 | 0.1860 | 0.1528 | 0.1290 | 0.1090 | 0.0948 | 0.0823 | 0.0723 | 0.0641 | 0.0577 | 0.0519 | 0.0483 | 0.0451 | 0.0442 | 0.0434 | 0.0426 | 0.0388 | 0.0357 | 0.0299 | 0.0261 | 0.0228 | 0.0199 |
| 0.39 | 0.3873 | 0.2860 | 0.2216 | 0.1791 | 0.1475 | 0.1244 | 0.1055 | 0.0919 | 0.0801 | 0.0702 | 0.0621 | 0.0561 | 0.0506 | 0.0469 | 0.0438 | 0.0429 | 0.0423 | 0.0416 | 0.0376 | 0.0347 | 0.0290 | 0.0253 | 0.0222 | 0.0194 |
| 0.38 | 0.3644 | 0.2700 | 0.2118 | 0.1718 | 0.1418 | 0.1195 | 0.1018 | 0.0888 | 0.0775 | 0.0679 | 0.0602 | 0.0543 | 0.0490 | 0.0454 | 0.0425 | 0.0416 | 0.0409 | 0.0402 | 0.0364 | 0.0337 | 0.0281 | 0.0247 | 0.0215 | 0.0188 |
| 0.37 | 0.3450 | 0.2571 | 0.2037 | 0.1650 | 0.1369 | 0.1153 | 0.0985 | 0.0861 | 0.0750 | 0.0659 | 0.0584 | 0.0526 | 0.0475 | 0.0441 | 0.0412 | 0.0403 | 0.0397 | 0.0389 | 0.0353 | 0.0327 | 0.0272 | 0.0238 | 0.0208 | 0.0183 |
| 0.36 | 0.3248 | 0.2441 | 0.1950 | 0.1580 | 0.1316 | 0.1109 | 0.0950 | 0.0830 | 0.0724 | 0.0637 | 0.0564 | 0.0508 | 0.0458 | 0.0426 | 0.0398 | 0.0390 | 0.0383 | 0.0377 | 0.0342 | 0.0316 | 0.0264 | 0.0231 | 0.0201 | 0.0177 |
| 0.35 | 0.3090 | 0.2341 | 0.1872 | 0.1520 | 0.1271 | 0.1069 | 0.0917 | 0.0802 | 0.0700 | 0.0616 | 0.0546 | 0.0492 | 0.0444 | 0.0412 | 0.0386 | 0.0377 | 0.0372 | 0.0364 | 0.0331 | 0.0306 | 0.0256 | 0.0224 | 0.0195 | 0.0171 |
| 0.34 | 0.2940 | 0.2240 | 0.1794 | 0.1457 | 0.1222 | 0.1028 | 0.0882 | 0.0773 | 0.0676 | 0.0595 | 0.0527 | 0.0476 | 0.0429 | 0.0397 | 0.0373 | 0.0364 | 0.0359 | 0.0352 | 0.0319 | 0.0296 | 0.0246 | 0.0218 | 0.0189 | 0.0166 |
| 0.33 | 0.2804 | 0.2150 | 0.1722 | 0.1400 | 0.1176 | 0.0991 | 0.0851 | 0.0747 | 0.0652 | 0.0575 | 0.0509 | 0.0459 | 0.0414 | 0.0383 | 0.0359 | 0.0352 | 0.0347 | 0.0340 | 0.0308 | 0.0285 | 0.0238 | 0.0209 | 0.0182 | 0.0160 |
| 0.32 | 0.2667 | 0.2054 | 0.1650 | 0.1340 | 0.1128 | 0.0951 | 0.0819 | 0.0718 | 0.0627 | 0.0555 | 0.0490 | 0.0441 | 0.0398 | 0.0371 | 0.0347 | 0.0339 | 0.0335 | 0.0328 | 0.0298 | 0.0275 | 0.0230 | 0.0202 | 0.0176 | 0.0154 |
| 0.31 | 0.2552 | 0.1970 | 0.1581 | 0.1286 | 0.1084 | 0.0915 | 0.0788 | 0.0691 | 0.0603 | 0.0534 | 0.0472 | 0.0426 | 0.0384 | 0.0356 | 0.0333 | 0.0327 | 0.0322 | 0.0317 | 0.0286 | 0.0265 | 0.0221 | 0.0195 | 0.0170 | 0.0149 |
| 0.30 | 0.2432 | 0.1876 | 0.1513 | 0.1230 | 0.1038 | 0.0876 | 0.0755 | 0.0663 | 0.0580 | 0.0513 | 0.0454 | 0.0409 | 0.0370 | 0.0342 | 0.0321 | 0.0314 | 0.0309 | 0.0303 | 0.0274 | 0.0255 | 0.0213 | 0.0188 | 0.0163 | 0.0143 |
| 0.29 | 0.2320 | 0.1794 | 0.1449 | 0.1177 | 0.0994 | 0.0841 | 0.0725 | 0.0636 | 0.0556 | 0.0493 | 0.0436 | 0.0392 | 0.0351 | 0.0328 | 0.0308 | 0.0302 | 0.0297 | 0.0291 | 0.0264 | 0.0245 | 0.0205 | 0.0179 | 0.0157 | 0.0138 |
| 0.28 | 0.2203 | 0.1710 | 0.1383 | 0.1123 | 0.0951 | 0.0806 | 0.0695 | 0.0609 | 0.0533 | 0.0473 | 0.0419 | 0.0376 | 0.0340 | 0.0316 | 0.0296 | 0.0289 | 0.0284 | 0.0280 | 0.0253 | 0.0235 | 0.0197 | 0.0172 | 0.0150 | 0.0132 |
| 0.27 | 0.2109 | 0.1635 | 0.1320 | 0.1076 | 0.0910 | 0.0772 | 0.0665 | 0.0582 | 0.0511 | 0.0454 | 0.0401 | 0.0361 | 0.0326 | 0.0302 | 0.0283 | 0.0276 | 0.0273 | 0.0268 | 0.0244 | 0.0225 | 0.0189 | 0.0166 | 0.0144 | 0.0128 |
| 0.26 | 0.1998 | 0.1550 | 0.1258 | 0.1023 | 0.0865 | 0.0736 | 0.0636 | 0.0555 | 0.0487 | 0.0433 | 0.0384 | 0.0343 | 0.0311 | 0.0289 | 0.0271 | 0.0263 | 0.0261 | 0.0256 | 0.0233 | 0.0215 | 0.0181 | 0.0158 | 0.0138 | 0.0120 |
| 0.25 | 0.1903 | 0.1480 | 0.1197 | 0.0976 | 0.0825 | 0.0703 | 0.0607 | 0.0535 | 0.0466 | 0.0414 | 0.0366 | 0.0328 | 0.0297 | 0.0276 | 0.0258 | 0.0252 | 0.0249 | 0.0246 | 0.0222 | 0.0205 | 0.0173 | 0.0151 | 0.0132 | 0.0114 |
| 0.24 | 0.1795 | 0.1397 | 0.1137 | 0.0925 | 0.0783 | 0.0669 | 0.0577 | 0.0503 | 0.0443 | 0.0394 | 0.0349 | 0.0313 | 0.0284 | 0.0263 | 0.0246 | 0.0241 | 0.0238 | 0.0233 | 0.0212 | 0.0196 | 0.0165 | 0.0143 | 0.0126 | 0.0110 |
| 0.23 | 0.1707 | 0.1326 | 0.1080 | 0.0878 | 0.0747 | 0.0637 | 0.0549 | 0.0480 | 0.0423 | 0.0375 | 0.0332 | 0.0297 | 0.0270 | 0.0251 | 0.0234 | 0.0228 | 0.0226 | 0.0222 | 0.0201 | 0.0186 | 0.0157 | 0.0137 | 0.0120 | 0.0104 |
| 0.22 | 0.1603 | 0.1248 | 0.1020 | 0.0831 | 0.0704 | 0.0602 | 0.0518 | 0.0452 | 0.0401 | 0.0355 | 0.0314 | 0.0280 | 0.0254 | 0.0237 | 0.0221 | 0.0213 | 0.0213 | 0.0209 | 0.0192 | 0.0176 | 0.0150 | 0.0129 | 0.0114 | 0.0099 |
| 0.21 | 0.1530 | 0.1180 | 0.0962 | 0.0787 | 0.0670 | 0.0571 | 0.0493 | 0.0429 | 0.0381 | 0.0338 | 0.0299 | 0.0266 | 0.0242 | 0.0224 | 0.0210 | 0.0204 | 0.0201 | 0.0199 | 0.0181 | 0.0167 | 0.0142 | 0.0123 | 0.0107 | 0.0094 |
| 0.20 | 0.1425 | 0.1101 | 0.0905 | 0.0743 | 0.0627 | 0.0535 | 0.0464 | 0.0402 | 0.0356 | 0.0317 | 0.0281 | 0.0252 | 0.0227 | 0.0211 | 0.0197 | 0.0190 | 0.0190 | 0.0186 | 0.0168 | 0.0157 | 0.0133 | 0.0115 | 0.0100 | 0.0088 |
| 0.19 | 0.1343 | 0.1040 | 0.0850 | 0.0700 | 0.0591 | 0.0504 | 0.0436 | 0.0378 | 0.0335 | 0.0297 | 0.0263 | 0.0236 | 0.0210 | 0.0197 | 0.0185 | 0.0181 | 0.0178 | 0.0175 | 0.0159 | 0.0147 | 0.0126 | 0.0108 | 0.0094 | 0.0083 |
| 0.18 | 0.1250 | 0.0968 | 0.0794 | 0.0653 | 0.0551 | 0.0470 | 0.0407 | 0.0352 | 0.0313 | 0.0278 | 0.0246 | 0.0219 | 0.0197 | 0.0184 | 0.0173 | 0.0169 | 0.0167 | 0.0164 | 0.0150 | 0.0137 | 0.0118 | 0.0101 | 0.0088 | 0.0077 |
| 0.17 | 0.1167 | 0.0906 | 0.0739 | 0.0614 | 0.0515 | 0.0441 | 0.0382 | 0.0330 | 0.0292 | 0.0259 | 0.0229 | 0.0205 | 0.0184 | 0.0172 | 0.0162 | 0.0158 | 0.0156 | 0.0153 | 0.0140 | 0.0128 | 0.0109 | 0.0095 | 0.0082 | 0.0072 |
| 0.16 | 0.1077 | 0.0836 | 0.0685 | 0.0566 | 0.0476 | 0.0407 | 0.0353 | 0.0307 | 0.0271 | 0.0240 | 0.0213 | 0.0191 | 0.0173 | 0.0159 | 0.0146 | 0.0144 | 0.0142 | 0.0142 | 0.0129 | 0.0119 | 0.0101 | 0.0088 | 0.0076 | 0.0067 |
| 0.15 | 0.1000 | 0.0777 | 0.0631 | 0.0524 | 0.0442 | 0.0377 | 0.0327 | 0.0285 | 0.0250 | 0.0221 | 0.0197 | 0.0176 | 0.0158 | 0.0147 | 0.0138 | 0.0136 | 0.0133 | 0.0131 | 0.0120 | 0.0110 | 0.0094 | 0.0081 | 0.0070 | 0.0062 |
| 0.14 | 0.0913 | 0.0713 | 0.0579 | 0.0481 | 0.0403 | 0.0344 | 0.0300 | 0.0262 | 0.0230 | 0.0203 | 0.0181 | 0.0162 | 0.0145 | 0.0136 | 0.0127 | 0.0124 | 0.0122 | 0.0120 | 0.0110 | 0.0101 | 0.0086 | 0.0074 | 0.0064 | 0.0057 |
| 0.13 | 0.0837 | 0.0654 | 0.0529 | 0.0440 | 0.0370 | 0.0315 | 0.0274 | 0.0241 | 0.0210 | 0.0185 | 0.0165 | 0.0147 | 0.0132 | 0.0124 | 0.0116 | 0.0111 | 0.0109 | 0.0109 | 0.0102 | 0.0093 | 0.0078 | 0.0068 | 0.0059 | 0.0052 |
| 0.12 | 0.0752 | 0.0587 | 0.0478 | 0.0393 | 0.0333 | 0.0287 | 0.0249 | 0.0219 | 0.0190 | 0.0168 | 0.0149 | 0.0134 | 0.0120 | 0.0112 | 0.0103 | 0.0101 | 0.0101 | 0.0099 | 0.0092 | 0.0083 | 0.0071 | 0.0061 | 0.0053 | 0.0047 |
| 0.11 | 0.0679 | 0.0530 | 0.0429 | 0.0354 | 0.0300 | 0.0259 | 0.0225 | 0.0197 | 0.0171 | 0.0151 | 0.0134 | 0.0120 | 0.0107 | 0.0101 | 0.0094 | 0.0090 | 0.0089 | 0.0089 | 0.0083 | 0.0075 | 0.0064 | 0.0055 | 0.0048 | 0.0042 |
| 0.10 | 0.0598 | 0.0467 | 0.0380 | 0.0312 | 0.0266 | 0.0230 | 0.0200 | 0.0176 | 0.0152 | 0.0134 | 0.0119 | 0.0107 | 0.0095 | 0.0090 | 0.0084 | 0.0082 | 0.0081 | 0.0079 | 0.0073 | 0.0066 | 0.0057 | 0.0049 | 0.0042 | 0.0038 |
| 0.05 | 0.0245 | 0.0205 | 0.0161 | 0.0138 | 0.0114 | 0.0099 | 0.0086 | 0.0076 | 0.0067 | 0.0058 | 0.0052 | 0.0046 | 0.0041 | 0.0038 | 0.0036 | 0.0035 | 0.0035 | 0.0034 | 0.0031 | 0.0025 | 0.0021 | 0.0018 | 0.0016 |
| 0.00 | 0 | 0 | 0 | 0 | 0 | 0 | 0 | 0 | 0 | 0 | 0 | 0 | 0 | 0 | 0 | 0 | 0 | 0 | 0 | 0 | 0 | 0 | 0 |

# NAME INDEX

Abbot, H. L., 94n., 126
Ackers, P., 329, 352
Addison, H., 85
Agroskin, I. I., 401n., 436
Ahmad, N., 521
Airy, G. B., 553
Albertson, M. L., 204, 213, 521
Allen, J., 17, 217n., 246
Allen, J. W., 329, 352
Ambrose, H. H., 212
Anderson, A. G., 493, 518
Appleby, F. V., 602, 619
Aravin, V. I., 398n., 436
Arghyropoulos, P. A., 156
Arkhangelskiĭ, V. A., xn., 587, 617
Auroy, F., 391
Averianov, S. F., 36

Babbitt, H. E., 36, 295
Bakhmeteff, B. A., vii, x, 13n., 18, 37, 61, 206, 212–213, 246, 252–255, 294, 297, 306, 324–325, 393, 398–400, 409n., 423, 425, 427, 435, 437–438
Balloffet, A., 74n., 85
Banks, R. B., 136, 155
Barbarossa, H. L., 208, 213
Bardsley, C. E., 17, 459
Barillon, E. G., 358–359
Barker, C. L., 61
Barrows, H. K., 620
Bata, G., 584
Baticle, E., 253, 294
Bauer, W. J., 198–199, 212, 383, 391
Baumann, E. R., 295
Bazin, H. E., 17, 61, 94–95, 99, 126, 213, 363–364, 390, 393, 409, 434, 538, 552
Beebe, J. C., 393, 425, 434
Beij, K. H., 351
Bélanger, J. B., 30n., 37, 49n., 59n., 61–62, 217n., 246, 393, 434
Beloken, P. N., 138n., 156
Benjamin, T. B., 521, 583
Bennett, J., 16
Bergeron, L., 587, 617
Bermel, K. J., 85

Bernoulli, D., 40, 217n.
Berryhill, R. H., 437
Bettes, F., 17, 217n., 246
Bhoota, B. V., 460, 471–474, 517
Bidone, G., 393, 434
Binnie, A. M., 583
Biot, M. A., 248
Blaisdell, F. W., 361, 390, 393, 415, 435, 437–438, 517
Blasius, H., 17
Blench, T., xn., 126, 190
Blue, F. L., Jr., 459
Borland, W. M., 190
Böss, P., 42n., 61, 459, 519
Boudin, M., 227, 247
Boussinesq, J., 27, 37, 54n., 61, 217n., 358, 362n., 390, 455, 460, 537n., 552–553
Bovard, M., 352
Bowers, C. E., 493, 518, 522
Bowlus, F. D., 78, 85
Boyer, M. C., 207, 213
Bradley, J. N., 368–369, 381–382, 391–392, 436
Brahms, A., 94, 125, 168n.
Braine, C. D. C., 82, 85
Brater, E. F., 17, 37, 61, 85, 127, 156, 390, 607, 620
Bresse, J. A. C., 54n., 60n., 61, 217n., 246, 253, 258, 294, 357n., 393, 434
Bretting, A. E., 213
Brudenell, R. N., 369, 391
Bubendey, J. F., 501n., 519
Buehler, B., 369, 391
Busemann, A., 448n., 460
Butler, S. S., 620

Cagniard, L., 551
Camichel, C. M., 512, 521
Camichel, E., 521
Camp, T. R., 106, 127, 135, 327, 334n., 351
Campbell, F. B., 359
Cariño, I. D., 189
Carlson, E. J., 190–191

663

Carstanjen, M., 393, 434, 519, 582, 585
Carter, A. C., 191
Carter, R. W., 390, 476–477, 491–492, 494, 518
Chabert, J., 296
Chardonnet, E., 353
Charnomskiĭ, V. J., 263n., 295
Chatelain, P., 295
Cheng, H. M., 607, 620
Chertousov, M. D., viin., 295, 559, 583
Chézy, A., 93
Chien, N., 190
Chow, V. T., xn., xii, 83, 126–127, 155, 208, 213, 295, 352, 521n., 522, 607, 620, 641
Chu, H. H., 253, 261–262, 295, 657
Chugaev, R. R., xi, 66n., 83, 131n., 133, 155
Chun, Y. D., 295
Citrini, D., 74n., 84, 327, 351, 393, 435, 572, 584
Clayton, L. A., 493, 518
Coleman, G. S., 328, 351
Collinge, V. K., 329, 352
Conard, R. G., 191
Cone, V. M., 75n., 85
Contessini, F., 74n., 84
Corbett, D. M., 37
Coriolis, G., 27, 37
Cornish, V., 210, 213
Cotton, J. S., 85
Cowan, W. L., 106, 127
Cox, G. N., 392
Coyne, A., 384, 391
Crausse, É., viin., 62, 248, 520
Craya, A., 210, 214, 535n., 552, 587, 617
Creager, W. P., 361, 374, 389–390, 436
Cross, W. P., 607, 620
Crow, F. R., 85
Crump, E. S., 74n., 84
Cunningham, A. J. C., 99n., 126

Dahl, N. J., 550, 617
Dai, Y. B., 521
Dalrymple, T., 518
Danel, P., xi, 385
Dantscher, K., 578, 585
Darcy, H., 8n., 16, 95n., 126, 213, 393, 434
d'Aubuisson de Voisins, J. F., 8n., 16, 501, 519
Daugherty, R. L., 517
Daum, C. R., 585
Davis, A., 520
Davis, C. V., 390, 437, 607, 620
Dawson, J. H., 460, 468–469, 517
Delleur, J. W., 212

De Marchi, G., xi, 74n., 84, 237, 247, 327–328, 341, 351, 390, 519, 572, 584
De Mello Flôres, J. O., 435
de Prony, G., 93n.
Deymié, Ph., 551
Dietz, D. N., 551, 617
Dmitriev, G. T., 436, 587, 618
Doddiah, D., 521
Doeringsfeld, H. A., 61
Doland, J. J., 208, 213
Doll, E. H., 191
Donnelly, C. A., 437–438
Douma, J. H., 38, 391
Dressler, R. F., 214, 535n., 552
Drioli, C., 551, 572, 584
Druml, F. V., 619
du Boys, P., 168n., 190
Dupin, P., 521
Dupuit, A. J. E. J., 253, 294
Durand, W. F., 17

Eddy, H. P., 36
Ehrenberger, R., 38, 253
Einstein, H. A., 136, 155, 166n., 190, 208, 213
Einwachter, J., 393, 434–435
Eisenlohr, W. S., 37
Eisner, F., 11, 18
Elevatorski, E. A., 391, 404n.
Ellms, J. W., 351, 435
Ellms, R. W., 425, 438
Engel, F. V. A. E., 12n., 18, 74n., 84
Engels, H., 328, 351
Engelund, F., 452n., 460
Equiazaroff, I. B., 535n., 552
Escande, L., 390, 393, 435, 437, 510, 512, 519–521
Escoffier, F. F., 214, 237, 240, 242, 248, 295, 587, 618
Etcheverry, B. A., 166, 173, 189, 190
Euler, L., 40
Ezra, A. A., 272, 295

Fan, C. H., 170n.–171n., 191
Favre, H., 327, 329, 350, 352, 551
Fawer, C., 358
Fellenius, W., 507, 520
Feodoroff, N. V., 206, 213, 423, 437
Ferriday, R., 393, 434
Florey, Q. L., 169, 191
Forchheimer, Ph., 125, 170n., 191, 294, 327–328, 351, 358, 520, 534n., 550
Formica, G., 247, 464–468, 516–517
Forster, J. W., 393, 409–412, 435–436
Fortier, S., 166, 173, 190

Foskett, L. W., 621
Foster, H. A., 359
Frank, J., 295, 353, 551, 572, 585
Frazer, W., 329, 340, 352
Fredenhagen, V. B., 191
Freeman, J. R., 37, 437
French, J. L., 493, 518

Ganguillet, E., 94, 125
Ganguli, M. K., 391
Garot, F., 352
Gauckler, Ph., 99n., 126
Gentilini, B., 329, 351, 572, 584
Gherardelli, L., 247
Ghotankar, S. T., 437
Gibb, H. M., 36
Gibson, A. H., 37, 393, 434
Gilcrest, B. R., 550, 620
Glover, R. E., 191, 585
Goldschmidt, H., 619
Goodrich, R. D., 607, 620
Gotaas, H. B., 85
Grashof, F., 253, 294, 448
Graves, Q. B., 607, 620
Grimm, C. I., 296
Grover, N. C., 37
Grzywienski, A., 390
Guillou, J. C., 512n., 522
Gumensky, D. B., 391
Gunder, D. F., 225, 247

Hagen, G. H. L., 93n., 99n., 125
Hall, L. S., 38, 307n., 326
Hama, F. R., 204, 212
Harkness, F. B., 608, 621
Harleman, D. R. F., 438
Harms, F., 18
Harrington, A. W., 37
Harris, C. W., 379, 391
Harrison, A. S., 295
Harrold, J. C., 391
Hasumi, M., 32n.
Hathaway, G. A., 553
Haws, E. T., 583
Hayami, Shigenori, 619
Hayami, Shoitiro, 602–603, 619
Hebert, D. J., 585
Henry, H. R., 509, 521
Henry, M., 587, 617
Herbert, J. K., 459
Hering, R., 125
Herschel, C., 93n., 125
Hickenlooper, I. J., 512n., 522
Hickox, G. H., 37, 363, 390, 427, 435, 438
Higgins, G., 37

Himmelwright, A. L. A., 583
Hinderks, A., 459
Hinds, J., 312–314, 318, 326–327, 342, 350, 361, 389, 436
Holsters, H., 587, 617–618
Hom-ma, M., 16, 18, 237, 248, 295, 471, 517
Hopf, L., 150, 156
Horton, R. E., 53n., 61, 108, 127, 136, 150, 155–156, 392, 546, 553, 583
Houk, I. E., 125, 156, 189, 437, 476n., 501n., 518
Howe, J. W., 459
Hsing, P. S., 435
Hsu, E. Y., 359, 413–414, 436, 460, 471–474, 517
Humphreys, A. A., 94n., 126
Husted, A. G., 263n., 295

Ince, S., 61
Ingersoll, A. C., 517
Inglis, C. C., 74n., 84
Ippen, A. T., xi, 361, 390, 431, 438, 448n., 453, 460, 468–469, 517
Isaacson, E. J., 587, 600, 619
Ishihara, T., xi, 214, 248
Ishihara, Y., 214
Iwagaki, Y., 16–18, 204–205, 213, 347–348, 353, 553, 587, 619
Iwasa, Y., 210, 212, 214, 237, 248
Izzard, C. F., 347, 353, 543–544, 546, 553

Jaeger, C., xi, 55n., 61–62, 83, 237, 246–247, 358, 461, 517, 550, 584
Jameson, A. H., 74n., 84
Jansen, R. B., 246, 391
Jeffreys, H., 150, 156, 214
Jegorow, S. A., 16, 18
Jensen, R. A., 521
Johnson, C. F., 106n., 127
Johnson, J. W., 29, 37
Johnson, R. D., 570–571, 583
Johnstone, D., 607, 620
Jones, B. E., 533, 551
Jones, L. E., 296
Joos, G., 619
Justin, J. D., 361, 374, 389–390, 436

Kalinske, A. A., 435
Kandaswamy, P. K., 390
Karr, M. H., 436
Keifer, C. J., 253, 261–262, 295, 657
Kennedy, R. G., 166n., 190
Kennison, K. R., 393, 434

Kent, D. H., 520
Kestin, J., 212
Keulegan, G. H., 9, 17, 98, 202–205, 213–214, 347–348, 353, 550
Khafagi, A., 74n., 84
Kholodovsky, Professor, 255n.
Khristianovich, S. A., 587, 617
Kindsvater, C. E., 18, 390, 393, 425, 427, 435, 438, 476, 518
King, H. W., 17, 37, 53n., 61, 85, 108n., 127, 156, 390, 621
Kinosita, T., 550, 617
Kirpich, P. Z., 131n., 155
Kirschmer, O., xi, 10, 12, 17, 506, 520
Kleitz, M., 531, 551
Knapp, R. T., 448n., 453, 456–457, 460
Knappen, T. T., 607, 620
Koch, A., 393, 434, 582, 585
Koch, P., 247, 519
Kohler, M. A., 607–608, 620–621
Koloseus, H. J., 392
Kolupaila, S., xi–xii, 28, 37, 295
Koženy, J., 11, 18, 253, 294, 358, 507, 520, 578, 585
Krey, H. D., 519
Kuntzmann, J., 352
Kutter, W. R., 94, 125
Kviatkovskii, V. S., 28n.

Lacey, G., 166n., 190
Lagrange, J. L. de, 538, 552
Lamb, H., 537n., 539, 550
Lamoen, J., 587, 618
Lancefield, R. L., 459
Lane, E. W., 105, 127, 170n., 174, 190–191, 359, 390, 435, 476, 517, 607, 621
Langbein, W. B., 213
Lansford, W. M., 9, 17, 326
Lauffer, H., 38
Lawler, E. A., 619
Lazard, A., 238n., 248
Leach, H. R., 156, 271, 295
Lee, M., 253–254, 295
Leighly, J. B., 169, 191
Leliavsky, S., xn., 190, 406n., 436
Leopold, L. B., 166n., 190
Levi, I. I., 255n., 295
Lévin, L., 535n., 552, 587, 617
Levy, A. G., 435
Li, W. H., 327, 334–336, 351, 496, 518
Lighthill, M. J., 583
Lin, C. C., 214
Lin, P. N., 587–588, 618
Lindley, E. S., 190
Lindquist, E. G. W., 28n., 37, 100n., 125, 213, 393, 434

Linford, A., 74n., 84
Linsley, R. K., 607, 620–621
Lotter, G. K., 136–137, 155
Lowe, F. C., 585
Ludwig, J. H., 85
Ludwig, R. G., 85

McCarthy, G. T., 607, 621
McHenry, D., 191
McNown, J. S., 359
McPherson, M. B., 436
Maddock, T., Jr., 166n., 190
Maitre, R., 391
Manning, R., 98, 99n., 126
Marichal, A., 61, 390
Masoni, U., 253, 293
Massau, J., 587–588, 617
Massé, P., 237–238, 247, 551
Massé, R., 551
Matzke, A. E., 246, 259n., 295, 393, 398–400, 425, 427, 435, 438
Mavis, F. T., 80, 85, 493, 498, 518
Mayer, P. G. H., 581, 585
Merriman, M., 393, 434
Merten, A., 227, 237n., 247
Metcalf, L., 36
Metzler, D. E., 509
Meyer, O. H., 607, 620
Meyer-Peter, E., 350
Meyers, J. S., 105, 127
Meynardi, G., 353
Miller, C. N., 349, 351
Miller, C. R., 190
Mitchell, W. D., 326
Mockmore, C. E., 459
Molesworth, G. L., 189
Mondschein, H. F., 607, 621
Mononobe, N., 253, 295
Montagu, A. M. R., 437
Moore, W. L., 204, 398–399, 414n., 423, 436–437
Moots, E. E., 536n., 552
Morgan, C. W., 414n., 436
Morris, H. M., Jr., 12, 18, 196, 197n., 212, 493, 518
Mostkow, M. A., 61, 329, 337, 339n., 352
Mouret, G., 225, 227, 238n., 247
Mueller, O., 521
Mühlhofer, L., 136, 155
Mulholland, W. M., 608
Müller, R., 441, 459
Munch-Petersen, J., 452n., 460

Nagaratnam, S., 393, 435
Nagler, F. A., 493, 501, 518–520

Nebbia, G., 74n., 84, 393, 435
Nelidov, I. M., 246
Nelson, H. C., 17–18
Newman, A., 295
Newmark, N. M., xi
Nikuradse, J., 9, 17, 201n., 202, 212, 214
Nimmo, W. H. R., 329, 352
Noseda, G., 329, 339n., 352
Nougaro, J., 587, 618

Obolensky, S., 391
O'Brien, M. P., 29, 37, 213
O'Connor, R., 583
Olsen, O. J., 169, 191
Orkney, J. C., 583
Orth, J., 353
Owen, W. M., 17

Pager, G., 521
Pai, S. I., 619
Palmer, H. K., 78, 85
Palmer, V. J., 191
Pannell, J. R., 16
Parshall, R. L., 75, 85
Partridge, E. P., 619
Patterson, C. C., 496, 518
Patterson, G. W., 214
Paulhus, J. L. H., 620
Pavlovskiĭ, N. N., viin., 100n., 126, 131n., 136–138, 155, 156, 281
Penati, S., 572, 584
Perronet, J. R., 93n.
Pestrečov, Dr., 255n.
Peterka, A. J., 436
Pickels, G. W., 126
Pikalov, F. I., 436
Poggi, B., 433, 438, 459
Pohle, F. V., 535n., 552
Poincaré, H., 237, 247
Poncelet, J. V., 217n.
Posey, C. J., vii, 13n., 18, 246, 296, 435, 459, 607, 621
Powell, R. W., 95, 126, 204, 213–214
Prandtl, L., 9, 12, 17, 200–201, 212, 448n., 459
Prášil, F., 358–359
Preiswerk, E., 448n., 460
Price, W. H., 359
Puls, L. G., 521, 607, 620
Putman, H. J., 587, 618

Rafter, G. W., 53n., 390
Raju, S. P., 17, 459
Rakhmanoff, A. N., 131n., 155, 281n., 296

Ramser, C. E., 115, 127
Rand, W., 204, 212, 423, 437
Ransford, G. D., 587, 618
Ray, W. E., 607, 621
Rayleigh, Lord, 537n., 552
Raytchine, N., 295
Ré, R., 534n.–535n., 552
Ree, W. O., 85, 180, 191, 629, 640
Rehbock, Th., 13n., 18, 29n., 37, 362, 390, 414n., 501, 519
Reineke, H., 551
Reiss, S., 460
Riabouchinsky, 448n., 459
Rich, G. R., 584
Riegel, R. M., 393, 425, 434
Ripley, H. C., 455, 460
Rippl, W., 620
Ritter, A., 534n., 552
Robertson, J. M., xi, 14, 17–18, 435
Robinson, A. R., 204, 213
Rohwer, C., 85
Rouse, H., xi, 14–15, 18, 61, 246, 362, 390, 393, 429, 435, 438, 460, 471–474, 517, 521, 550
Roy, S. K., 391
Rühlman, M., 253, 294
Russell, J. S., 537–538, 552
Rutter, E. J., 607, 620

Sabathé, G., 519, 521
Safranez, K., 393, 398, 434, 436
Saint-Venant, A. J. C. Barré de, 210, 217n., 526, 528, 551–552
Sandover, J. A., 583
Sao, T. T., 393, 435
Saugey, 394n.
Schack, A., 619
Schaffernak, F., 253
Schlichting, H., 195, 212
Schmidt, M., viin., 329, 346, 352, 572, 584
Schneckenberg, E. C., 92, 125, 127
Schnepper, D., 127
Schoder, E. W., 28n., 37, 390
Schoklisch, A., 253, 295, 327, 351, 437, 459, 520–521, 535n., 552, 568, 583, 620
Schönfeld, J. C., 550, 583, 618
Schüller, J., 551
Schultz, E. A., 105, 127
Scimemi, E., 364n., 390, 507, 520
Scobey, F. C., 103, 115, 126–127, 166, 173, 190, 213, 326
Seddon, J. A., 531, 551
Serre, F., 358, 550
Shany, M. B., 392
Sharma, K. R., 437

Shchapov, N. M., 37
Shepley, J. M., 607, 621
Shima, S., 248, 471, 517
Shoemaker, R. H., Jr., 493, 518
Shukry, A., 25–26, 37, 437, 440–441, 443–447, 459
Shulits, Samuel, 295, 437, 459, 520, 620
Silber, R., viin., 247
Silberman, E., 17
Silvester, R., 295
Skrinde, R. A., 393, 409–412, 435–436
Smetana, J., 390, 393, 435
Smith, D., 328, 351
Snyder, F. F., 607, 620
Sorensen, K. E., 607, 620
Spangler, J., 507, 520
Stanley, C. M., 437
Stanton, T. E., 16
Stein, M. F., 351
Steinberg, I. H., 280n., 296, 607, 621
Stevens, J. C., 13n., 18, 78, 82–83, 85, 436, 438
Stoker, J. J., xn., 326, 535n., 550, 587, 600, 618–619
Stratton, J. H., 607, 620
Straub, L. G., 17, 493, 518
Streck, O., 520
Streeter, V. L., 189, 212
Strickler, A., 99n., 126, 206, 213
Sueishi, T., 587, 619
Supino, G., 550–551
Swain, F. E., 580, 585

Takasao, T., 553
Talwani, B. S., 437
Tarpley, J. F., Jr., 608, 621
Tatum, F. E., 607, 621
Taylor, E. H., 512–515, 522
Terrell, P. W., 190
Thomas, H. A., 214, 541, 551, 581, 585
Thomas, R., 521
Thompson, P. W., 459
Thomson, J., 439, 459
Tiffany, J. B., 436, 521
Tison, L. J., xi, 61, 247
Toch, A., 509–510, 521
Toebes, C., 92, 125
Tolkmitt, G., 253, 294
Tracy, H. J., 53n., 61, 476–477, 491–492, 518
Trautwine, J. C., Jr., 61, 126, 390

Troesch, B. A., 587, 600, 619
Tults, H., 352
Turner, K. B., 28n., 37

Uchida, S., 587, 618

Vanoni, V. A., 212
Van Vliet, R., 156
Vedernikov, V. V., 210, 214
Villemonte, J. R., 85
Vladislavljevitch, Z., 125
Vogel, H. D., 459
von Kármán, Th., 9, 17, 37, 201n., 212, 248, 448n., 452n., 459
Von Seggern, M. E., 253–254, 295

Wahlman, P., 570n.
Walton, C. B., 607, 621
Warnock, J. E., 437, 585
Weaver, R. M., 436
Weisbach, J., 8n., 16, 40, 401n., 436, 501, 519
Wells, E. A., Jr., 85
Werner, P. W., 346, 353
White, M. P., 246, 429
Whitham, G. B., 535n.
Wien, W., 18
Wilcox, E. R., 106n., 127
Wilkinson, J. H., 531, 551
Wilm, H. G., 85
Wilson, W. T., 607, 620
Wisler, C. O., 607, 620
Wittman, H., 459
Wolf, P. O., 61, 83, 246, 358, 517, 550, 584
Woodburn, J. G., 61
Woodward, S. M., vii, 106n., 127, 246, 296, 393, 434, 448, 459, 493, 518, 621
Wóycicki, K., 398n., 436

Yarnell, D. L., 106n., 127, 425, 493, 501–506, 518–519
Yassin, A. M., 155
Yen, C. H., 459
Yih, C. S., 214, 359

Zienkiewicz, O. C., 583

# SUBJECT INDEX

*A* profiles, 230
Abrupt drop for jump control, 412–414
Abrupt rise for jump control, 411–412
Acceleration line, 527
Adverse slope, 223, 259–260
Aeration of nappe, 362–363
Air entrainment, 33–36
Airy celerity equation, 539
All-American Canal, 188–189
Alluvial river bends, 455–456
Alternate depth, 41, 55n.
Angle of repose, 171–172
Artificial roughness, 202n.
Atterberg soil test, 173n.

Backwater, of bridge piers, 501–506
of constriction, 490–493
of dam, 319
effect of, 72
end point, 319
Backwater curve, 71, 222n.
Backwater envelope curve, 319
Backwater ratio, 491
Baffle piers, 415
Banking, 456
Bazin data, for broad-crested weir, 53n.
for channel roughness, 11, 95, 99n.
for overflow spillways, 363–364
for rough channels, 204
for sharp-crested weirs, 363, 382, 390
for wavy surfaces, 204
Bazin formula, 95
Bazin profile, 363
Bazin's *m*, 95
Bed load, 106
Bed-load function, 166n.
Bends in alluvial rivers, 455–456
Bernoulli energy equation, 40
Best hydraulic section, 160–162
Blasius equation, 8
Blasius-Prandtl-von Kármán curve, 10
Blue hole, 512n.
Bottom rack, flow through, 337–340
Boundary layer, computation, 198–200
development, 192–193

Boundary layer, laminar, 193
on overflow spillways, 199–200
roughness effect on, 200
turbulent, 193
of uniform flow, 89
Boussinesq coefficient, 27
Boussinesq number, 13n.
Boussinesq theory, 358
Box inlet drop spillway, 424
Bresse method, 258
Bresse theory, 357
Bridge piers, 482, 489, 501–506
Bridge piles, 482, 489
Bridges, submergence of, 482, 489
Broad-crested weirs, 52–53, 80
for jump control, 410–411
tests, Bazin, 53n.
Cornell, 53n.
Michigan, 53n.
Minnesota and Washington, 53n.

*C* profiles, 230
Canal drop, 415
Canal fall, 415, 432
Canals, 19
delivery of, 297–306
navigation, 572–575
outlet and entrance, 304–306
Capillary wave, 12
Cascades, ladder of, 433
Celerity, 13, 538–540, 582
Channel alignment, 103, 106–109
Channel contraction, 47–49, 258, 468–470, 479
Channel expansion, 57–59
Channel geometry, 20–24
principle of, 166n.
Channel irregularities, 103
Channel junctions, 321–323, 512–516
Channel sections, 20
best hydraulic, 160–162
circular (*see* Circular channels)
of constant critical flow, 82
of constant hydraulic radius, 152
geometric elements, 22–24

Channel sections, hydrostatic catenary, 22, 35, 161
  for irrigation canals, 175n.
  lintearia, 22
  parabolic (see Parabolic channels)
  rectangular (see Rectangular channels)
  semi-elliptical, of high order, 20n.
  trapezoidal (see Trapezoidal channels)
  triangular (see Triangular channels)
  velocity distribution in, 24–26
  vertical, 20
Channel size and shape, 104, 106–109
Channel slope (see Slope)
Channels, of adverse slope, 223, 259–260
  of compound sections, 138–140
  curved, energy loss in, 441
  erodible, 164–179
    types, ix
  with gradually closing crown, 67–68, 131–136, 230–231, 261–262
  grassed, 179–188
  horizontal (see Horizontal channels)
  ice-covered, 137–138, 153
  of large slope, 33
  lining, 157–158, 160
  mild, 223
  of negative slope (see adverse, above)
  open, 19, 26–27, 258
  prismatic and nonprismatic, 20
  steep, 223
  with variable hydraulic exponents, 260–261
  of variable slope, 238
  (See also Channel sections; Circular channels; Nonerodible channels; Nonprismatic channels; Parabolic channels; Rectangular channels; Rough channels; Slope; Trapezoidal channels; Triangular channels)
Characteristic depth, 238n.
Characteristic length, for Froude number, 13
  for Reynolds number, 7–8
  for turbulent mixing, 200
Characteristics, 589
Chézy formula, 93–94
Chézy's C, 93–98
  formulas for, Bazin, 95
    G. K., 94
    Manning, 100
    Pavlovskiĭ, 100
    Powell, 95
  for smooth and rough channels, 204
Chézy's resistance factor (see Chézy's C)
Chute, 19, 324
Chute blocks, 414

Circular channels, best hydraulic section, 161
  flow measurement in, 82–83
  geometric elements, 21, 23, 625–627
  hydraulic exponent $M$, 67
  hydraulic exponent $N$, 132
  Manning's $n$ in, 106, 134–135
  roughness variation in, 106, 135
  values, of $AR^{2/3}/d_0^{8/3}$, 130
    of $Z/d_0^{2.5}$, 65
  (See also Circular conduits)
Circular conduits, depth, of maximum discharge, 134–135, 152
  of maximum velocity, 134–135, 152
  flow characteristics in, 67–68, 129n., 132–136
  flow profiles in, 230–231
  roughness coefficient in, 106, 135
  varied-flow function, 262
Circulation constant, 446
Coefficient, Boussinesq, 27
  of contraction, 374–377
  Coriolis, 27
  of curve resistance, 444
  of discharge, for bottom racks, 339
    through constrictions, 478–492
    for overflow spillways, 366
    for sharp-crested weirs, 362, 368–369
    for submerged overflow spillways, 386
  of drag, 94n.
  of energy (see Energy coefficient)
  of energy loss, 468
  of friction, 171
  of pressure distribution, 32, 50
  of retardance, 179
  of roughness, 92
    Bazin's $m$, 95
    in circular conduits, 106, 135
    Horton table for, 108
    Kutter's $n$, 94
    Manning's $n$ (see Manning's $n$)
Cohesive material, permissible tractive force for, 165, 174
  permissible velocity for, 165
Complete method for unsteady flow, 541
Complete turbulence, 12
Composite roughness, 136–140
Concave flow, 30–31
Confluence of rivers, 321–323
Conjugate depth, 418
Conjugate normal depth, 231
Consolidated-shear test, 173n.
Constant critical flow, channel of, 82
Constant hydraulic radius channel, 152
Constrictions, 475–476
  backwater due to, 490–493

Continuity equation, 5
  of unsteady flow, 525–526
Continuous flow, 5
Contracted-opening method, 146, 476
Contraction, coefficient of, 374–377
Contraction distance, 258
Contraction ratio, 479
Contractions, 47–49, 468–470
Control, of flow, 70–74, 237
  of hydraulic jump, 408–414
Control section, 70, 234–237
  in lateral spillway channels, 342
Conversion loss, 310
Convex flow, 30–31
Conveyance, 128
Conveyance ratio, 479
Coriolis coefficient, 27
Cowan's method for Manning's $n$, 106–109
Creager profile, 364$n$.
  modified, 364$n$.
Critical depth, 41
  in circular section, 82
  curves for computation, 65
  overrun, 533
  in rectangular sections, 81–82
Critical discharge, 64
  through rectangular sections, 66
  through sections of various shapes, 81
Critical flow, application of energy principle, 42$n$.
  application of theorem of momentum, 54$n$.
  computation (see Critical-flow computation)
  criteria, 42–43, 55, 59–60, 63
  definition, 13, 43, 55
Critical-flow computation, 63–70
  hydraulic exponent for, 66–68
  section factor of, 64
Critical-flow flume, 74
  for closed conduits, 82–83
  San Dimas, 78
Critical-flow profiles, 238–241
Critical roughness, 195
Critical section, 63
Critical slope, 63
  at given normal depth, 142, 154
Critical-slope curve, 243
Critical state of flow, 13
Critical tractive force, 172
Critical velocity, 13
Cross waves, 448, 468
Culverts, 20
  flow through, 493–499
  flow profiles in, 265–266
  flow types in, 496–499

Culverts, hydraulically long, 494
  hydraulically short, 494
Curve resistance, coefficient of, 444
Curved vanes, 457
Curvilinear flow, 31–34

Dam-break problem, 534–536, 568
Darcy's friction factor, 211
Darcy-Weisbach formula, 8, 124
d'Aubuisson formula, 502
Delivery of canal, 297–306
  for constant discharge, 300–302
  for constant downstream depth, 299–300
  for constant upstream depth, 297–299
  for supercritical flow, 302–303
Delivery curve, 297
Demand surge, 559
De Marchi profile, 364$n$.
Denver tests, 364$n$.
Depth, alternate, 41, 55$n$.
  characteristic, 238$n$.
  conjugate, 418
  conjugate normal, 231
  critical (see Critical depth)
  of flow, 22
  of flow section, 22
  initial, 46
  normal, 91, 129
    in circular conduits, 230–231
    determination of, 140–142
  sequent, 46, 55$n$., 397
  transitional, 237$n$., 238, 242–244
Diffusivity, 601
Direct-integration method, 252–262
Direct jump, 45, 397
Direct step method, 262–265
Discharge, coefficient of (see Coefficient of discharge)
  through constrictions, 476–490
  critical, 64, 66, 81
  through culverts, 493–499
  through gates, 508
  in ice-covered channels, 137–138
  maximum, in canals, 299
  normal, 129
  for 1-ft fall, 281
  through piers, 501–506
  through pile trestles, 506
  service, 303
  transitional, 242
  through trash racks, 506–507
Discharge rating curve, 70
  for inflow to canals, 305
Discontinuous flow, 5
Displacement thickness, 193

Distribution (*see* Pressure distribution)
Disturbance lines, 449, 454–455
Douma formula, 36
Drag, coefficient of, 94n.
Drag force, 168n.
Drain tiles, roughness variation in, 135
Drawdown curve, 71
Drop, 20
Drop energy dissipator, 422n., 424–425
Drop number, 423
Drop spillways, 423–425
Drowned-out hydraulic jumps, 425
Drum gates, 380–382, 507n.
Dynamic equation, of gradually varied
  flow, 218–222
  for spatially varied flow, 332
  for uniformly progressive flow, 531
  for unsteady flow, 526–528
Dynamic viscosity, 8

Easement curve, 457
Eddy loss, 267
Efficiency of hydraulic jump, 396
Einstein's bed-load function, 166n.
End point of backwater, 319
Energy, minimum, theorem of, 42
  in nonprismatic channels, 46–49
  in open-channel flow, 39–40
  specific, 41
  in surges, 565–566
Energy coefficient, 27
  in spatially varied flow, 346
  at sudden transitions, 465–466
Energy dissipators, bucket-type, 408
  drop-type, 422n., 424–425
  hydraulic jump for, 404–408
  impact-type, 422n.
Energy equation, Bernoulli, 40
Energy grade line, 3
Energy gradient, slope of, 40
Energy line, 3
Energy loss, coefficient of, 468
  in hydraulic jump, 60
  (*See also* Losses)
Energy recovery through obstructions,
  500
Entrance to canals, 304–305
Equations of characteristics, 588
Equivalent n value, 136
Erodible channels, 164–179
  types, ix
Erosion below gates, 512
Escande profile, 364n.
Expansion in channel, 57–59
Expansion wave, oblique, 449, 454
Expansions, 470–474

Ezra method, 272–274
  for natural channels, 284–292

f-R relationship, 8–13
  for rough channels, 11–13
  for smooth channels, 9–10
Factor, of flow resistance, 91
  shape, 210
Fall increaser, 394n.
Fawer theory, 358
Fish skimmer, 337
Flip bucket, overflow spillways, 35–36
Flood discharge, computation, 146–148,
  476–490
Flood plain, roughness of, 104, 113
Flood routing, 586
Flood synthesis, 586
Flow, concave, 30–31
  continuous, 5
  convex, 30–31
  critical (*see* Critical flow)
  curvilinear, 31
  depth, 22
  discontinuous, 5
  gradually varied, 6–7
  gradually varied unsteady, 7
  instability of, 204
  isolated-roughness, 12n., 196
  laminar, 7
  open-channel (*see* Open-channel flow)
  overland, 544
  parallel, 30, 33
  passing islands, 320–321
  pipe, 4
  progressive, 540, 555–557
  pulsating, 580
  quasi-normal, 238n.
  quasi-smooth, 12n., 196
  rapid, 13
  rapidly varied, 6
  rapidly varied unsteady, 7
  regimes of, 14–16
  rough-surface, 196–198
  secondary, 12, 439
  shooting, 13
  skimming, 196
  slug, 581
  spatially varied (*see* Spatially varied
    flow)
  spiral, 25–26, 439–440
  state of, 7–14
  steady, 5
  steady uniform, 5
  streaming, 13
  subcritical, 13
  supercritical, 13

Flow, torrential, 13
  tranquil, 13
  turbulent (*see* Turbulent flow)
  uniform (*see* Uniform flow)
  unsteady (*see* Unsteady flow)
  unsteady varied, 6, 7, 523
  varied, 6
  wake-interference, 12$n$., 196
Flow control, 70–74, 237
Flow-line computation, 608
Flow measurement, 72–81
Flow-net analysis, 358, 374, 384
Flow profiles, analysis, 232–237
  in channels, of adverse slope, 259–260
    with gradually closing crown, 230–
      231, 261–262
    of variable hydraulic exponents, 261
    of variable slope, 238
  classification of, 226–232
  in closed conduits, 230–231
  critical, 238–241
  discontinuity in, 224
  in frictionless rectangular channels,
    292
  in horizontal channels, 259–260
  in nonprismatic channels, 235–237,
    306–309
  point of inflection in, 224–227, 292
  along side weir, 340–341
  of spatially varied flow, 235–237,
    333–337
  transitional, 238
  types, 225, 241
    nodal, 241
    saddle, 241
    spiral, 241
    vortex, 241
  typical examples, 229
  in wide horizontal channels, 292
Flow-resistance factor, 91
Flumed drop, 415
Flumes, 19
  Parshall, 72–81
Force, drag, 168$n$.
  plus momentum, 54$n$.
  shear, 168$n$.
  specific, 53–56
  of stream, 54$n$.
  tractive (*see* Tractive force)
Force coefficient, 50
Fort Collins tests, 364$n$.
Fortier-Scobey table of permissible
    velocities, 165–166
Fourier's law, 601
Free overfall, 44
Free surface, 3
Free vortex, 446

Freeboard, 159–160, 311
Friction, coefficient of, 171
Friction barrier, 562, 565
Friction factor, 8–13
Friction loss in transitions, 310
Friction velocity, 195, 201
Frictionless rectangular channels, 292
Froude number, 13, 43
Function, bed-load, 166$n$.
  varied-flow, 254

G. K. formula, 94
  graphical solution, 96
Ganguillet and Kutter formula (*see*
    G. K. formula)
Gates, drum, 380–382, 507$n$.
  overflow, 507$n$.
  radial (Tainter), 507–512
  rolling, 507–508
  sluice (*see* Sluice gates)
  Tainter (radial), 507–512
  underflow, 507–512
Gauckler formula, 99$n$.
GEDA flood computer, 609
Geometric elements, of channel section,
    22
  of circular section, 21, 23, 625–627
  curves of, 270–271
  of parabolic channels, 639
  of parabolic sections, 21
  of rectangular sections, 21
    rounded-cornered, 21
  of trapezoidal section, 21
  of triangular section, 21
    round-bottom, 21
Gradient, energy, 40
  velocity, 200
Gradual hydraulic jump, 45
Gradually varied flow, 6
  basic assumptions, 217–218
  dynamic equation of, 218–222
  for wide rectangular channels, 222
Gradually-varied-flow equation, 219–222
  in tapered channels, 246
Gradually varied unsteady flow, 7
Graphical-integration method, 249–252
Grassed channels, 179–188
  centipede, 180
  design, examples, 186–188
    for maximum capacity, 187–188
    for stability, 186–187
  design procedure, 184–188
  $n$-$VR$ curves, 182–183
  permissible velocity, 184–185
  retardance, classification, 181
    selection, 184

Grassed channels, selection of grass, 184
Gravity effect on flow, 13
Gravity wave, 13
Grimm method, 280n.

H profiles, 230
Hagen formula, 99n.
Hangchow bore, 558
Heppner flood, 558
High stage, 41
Highway gutter, flow in, 151
Horizontal channels, flow profiles in, 259–260
    spatially varied flow in, 333–337
Horizontal slope, 223
Horton equation, 546
Horton table for roughness coefficient, 108
Hydraulic bore, 534, 557–558
Hydraulic depth, 13, 23
Hydraulic drop, 43–44
    gradual, 45
Hydraulic exponent $M$, 66–68
    graphical determination, 68
Hydraulic exponent $N$, 131
    graphical determination, 133
    variation with depth, 132–134
Hydraulic exponents, of circular conduits, 67, 132
    for critical-flow computation (see Hydraulic exponent $M$)
    for uniform-flow computation (see Hydraulic exponent $N$)
Hydraulic grade line, 3
Hydraulic jump, 45–46
    applications, 393–394
    characteristics, 396–398
    control, 408–414
        abrupt drop for, 412–414
        abrupt rise for, 411–412
    direct, 45, 397
    drowned-out, 425
    efficiency, 396
    elimination of, in canals, 305–306
        at transitions, 57–59, 314
    as energy dissipator, 404–408
    energy loss in, 60
    gradual, 45
    height, 396
    initial depth, 46
    length, 398–399
    location, 399–404
    moving, 557
    oblique, 429–431
    oscillating, 395
    in parabolic channels, 432

Hydraulic jump, relative loss, 396
    sequent depth, 46
    in sloping channels, 425–429
    steady, 395–396
    strong, 395–396
    submerged below sluice, 60
    surface profiles, 399
    in trapezoidal channels, 431
    types, 395–396, 407–408
    undular, 45, 395
    weak, 395
Hydraulic radius, 23
Hydraulic routing, 586
Hydrograph, 543, 592
Hydrologic routing, 586, 604
Hydrostatic catenary, 22, 35, 161

Ice-covered channels, 137–138, 153
Impact-type energy dissipator, 422n.
Inflow-discharge-rating curve, 305
Initial depth, 46
    relative, 396
Inlet loss, 311
Instability of flow, 204, 210
Inverted siphon, 317–319
Irrigation canals, 175n.
Islands in rivers, 320–321
Isoclinal method, 346–347
Isolated-roughness flow, 12n., 196

Jaeger theorem, 55n.
Johnson method, 570–572
Johnstown flood, 558
Jones formula, 533
Junction problems, 321–323, 512–516
    for surges, 578–580

Kansas River, flow-profile computation, 276–292
    junction problem, 321
Kennedy formula, 166n.
Kinematic viscosity, 7–8
Kinetic-flow factor, 13n.
Kineticity, 13n.
Kirschmer data for rough channels, 11
Kleitz-Seddon principle, 529
Kutter's $n$, 94
    dimensions of, 98n.

Lacey's regime theory, 166n.
Ladder of cascades, 433
Lagrange celerity equation, 538
Laminar boundary layer, 193

Laminar flow, 7
  criterion, 7–8, 150
  unsteady, spatially varied, 543
Laminar sublayer, 194
Laminar surface flow, spatially varied,
    348–349, 543
  uniform, 149–150
Lane-Davis profile, 364n.
Lateral spillway channels, 342–346
  discharge in, 350
Lateral tractive force, 176
Leach diagram, 271–272
Length, characteristic, 7–8, 13
  mixing, 200
Limit, liquid, 173n.
  plastic, 173n.
Limit slope, 142, 243–244
Lining of channels, 157–158, 160
Lintearia, 22
Liquid limit, 173n.
Local phenomenon, 6, 43–46
Losses, energy, in channels, 218n.
  due, to conversion, 310
    to eddy, 267
  at inlet, 311
  at outlet, 311
  in pipes, 8
  at transitions, 310–311
Low stage, 41
Lower normal depth, 231
Lucite, 108n., 110


M profiles, 228
M value (see Hydraulic exponent M)
Maddock-Leopold's principle of channel
    geometry, 166n.
Manning formula, 98
  exponent for, 99n.–100n.
  for friction factor f, 124
  international adoption, 100n.
  nomographic solution, 640
Manning's n, 99
  in circular conduits, 106, 134–135
  composite roughness, 135–140
  determination of, 101–123, 206–210
    Cowan's method for, 106–109
  dimensions, 98n.–99n.
  of drain tiles, 135
  equivalent value, 136
  factors affecting, 101–108
  on flood plains, 104
  for friction factor f, 124
  for ice-covered channels, 137–138
  for Panama Canal, 105–106
  photographs of channels for, 114–123
  relation to roughness height, 206

Manning's n, for sewers, 106, 135
  table for, 108–114
  theoretical interpretation, 205
Maximum discharge, in canals, 299
  in circular conduits, 134–136
  theorem, 59n.
Maximum permissible velocity, 157, 165–
    167
Maximum velocity, 24–25
Meandering, 106–109
Method, of characteristics, 448n., 587
  of diffusion analogy, 601
  of direct integration, 252–262
  of finite increments, 541
  of numerical integration, 261–262, 341–
    346
  of permissible velocity, 164, 167–168
  of relaxation, 358, 374n., 384
  of singular point, 237–242
  of tractive force, 164, 175
  of trial and error for unsteady flow,
    541
Mild channels, 223
Mild slope, 63
Minimum-energy theorem, 42
Minimum permissible velocity, 158
Mississippi River, Bazin's m, 97
  Chézy's C, 97
  diffusivity, 602
  gagings, 94
  junction problem, 322–323
  Kutter's n, 97
  Manning's n, 105
  roughness data, 206–207
Missouri River, flow-profile computation,
    276–292
  junction problem, 321
Mixed progressive flow, 540
Mixing length, 200
Momentum of open-channel flow, 49–53
Momentum coefficient, 27
Momentum flux of stream, 54n.
Momentum principle, 49, 56–59
Monoclinal rising wave, 528
Moving hydraulic jump, 557
Muskingum method, 606–607


N value (see Hydraulic exponent N)
n-VR curves, 180, 182–183
Nagler formula, 501
Nappe, over spillways, 370–373, 387
  over weirs, 361
Nappe aeration, 362–363
Navigation canals, 572–575
Negative slope, 223
Negative surges, 566–568

Negatively progressive flow, 540
Neutralizing reach, 306
Nikuradse sand roughness, 202
Nikuradse's data for smooth and rough pipes, 201–204
Nodal flow profiles, 241
Noncohesive material, angle of repose, 171–172
  tractive force, 173–174
Nonerodible channels, 157
  design, by best hydraulic section, 161
  by width-depth ratio, 162–163
Nonerodible velocity, 165
Nonprismatic channels, 20
  application of momentum principle, 56–59
  energy in, 46–49
  flow profiles in, 235–237, 306–309
  gradually-varied-flow equation, 246
Nonsilting and noneroding velocity, 166
Nonsilting velocity, 158
Nonsustaining slope, 223, 259
Normal depth, 91, 129
  in circular conduits, 230–231
  conjugate, 231
  curves for computation, 130
  determination of, 140–142
  lower, 231
  upper, 231
Normal discharge, 129
Normal slope, 142
Number, Boussinesq, $13n.$
  Froude, 13, 43
  Reynolds, 7
  Vedernikov, 210
  Weber, ix

Oblique expansion wave, 449, 454
Oblique hydraulic jump, 429–431
Obstructions, 104, 106–109, 499–501
Ohio River junction problem, 322–323
Open channel, 19
  wide, 26–27
Open-channel flow, 3
  energy in, 39–40
  momentum in, 49–53
  state, 7–14
  types, 4–7
Open-flow tunnel, 20
Oscillating jump, 396
Oscillating wave, $523n.$
Outlet and entrance of canals, 304–306
Outlet loss, 311
Overflow gates, $507n.$
Overflow spillways (see Spillways)
Overland flow, 14, 149, 544

Overrun, 529
Overrun critical depth, 533

Panama Canal, roughness for, 105
Parabolic channels, 21, 188
  best hydraulic section, 161
  geometric elements, 639
  of high order, $20n.$
  hydraulic jump in, 432
Parallel flow, 30
  pressure distribution in, 33
Parshall flume, 72–81
Pavlovskiĭ formula, 100
Permissible maximum velocities, 165–166
Permissible tractive force, 165, 172–174
  (See also Tractive force)
Permissible velocities, for cohesive material, 165–167
  corrections for depth and sinuosity, 167
  in grassed channels, 184–185
  maximum, 157, 165–167
  method of, 167–168
  minimum, 158
  U.S.S.R. data, 166–167
Piers, baffle, 415
  bridge, 501–506
  in gated spillways, 370–380
Pile trestles, 506
Pipe flow, 3
Pitot sphere, 440
Plastic limit, $173n.$
Plasticity index, $173n.$
Positive slope, 223
Positive surge, 559–566
Positively progressive flow, 540
Powell formula, 95
Powell's $\epsilon$, 98
Power canals, 568–572
Prandtl-von Kármán curve, 12
Prandtl-von Kármán equation, 9
Prandtl-von Kármán universal-velocity-distribution law, 201
Pressure on gates, 510–512
Pressure coefficient, 32
Pressure distribution, 30–34
  coefficients, 32, 50
  in curvilinear flow, 34
  effect of slope on, 32–34
  hydrostatic law of, 30–32
  in parallel flow, 33
Pressure-distribution coefficients, 32, 50
Pressure-head correction, 31
Prismatic channel, 20
Progressive flow, 540, 554–557
Pulsating flow, 580

$Q$-constant curve, 300
Quasi-normal flow, 238n.
Quasi-smooth flow, 12n., 196

Radial (Tainter) gate, 507–512
Raft chute, 324
Rapid flow, 13
Rapidly varied flow, 6
    characteristics, 357
Rapidly varied unsteady flow, 7
Recovery of velocity head, 311
Rectangular channels, best hydraulic
    section, 61
    frictionless, flow profile in, 292
    geometric elements, 21
    hydraulic exponents, 66–67, 132
    round-cornered, 20–21
    values, of $AR^{2/3}/d_0^{5/3}$, 130
        of $Z/d_0^{2.5}$, 65
    wide, 26–27
Reflection coefficient, 577
Regime theory, 166n.
Regimes of flow, 14–16
Rehbock sill, 414n.
Rehbock weir formula, 362
Rejection surge, 559
Relative height of hydraulic jump, 396
Relative loss of hydraulic jump, 396
Relative roughness, 195
Reservoir routing, 586
Resistance modulus, 281n.
Retardance, coefficient of, 179
    degree of, 181
Reynolds number, 7
    critical, 8–9
Rippl mass curve, 607
River hydraulics, 19
Road surface, flow on, 348–349
Roll waves, 210, 535, 581
    discovery, 210
Rolling gates, 507–508
Rough channels, Bazin's data, 11, 204
    $f$-$\mathbf{R}$ relationship, 11
    Kirschmer's data, 11
    Varwick's data, 11–12
    velocity distribution in, 202
Rough pipes, Nikuradse's data, 202n.
Rough-surface flow, 196–198
Roughness, channel, artificial, 202n.
    Bazin data for, 11, 95, 99n.
    composite, 136–140
    critical, 195
    due, to alignment, 103, 106–109
        to bed load, 106
        to irregularities, 103
        to size and shape, 104, 106–109

Roughness, channel, of ice-covered
        channels, 137–138
    isolated, 196
    relative, 195
    size measure, 11
    surface (see Surface roughness)
    variation in sewers, 135
Roughness coefficient (see Coefficient, of
        roughness)
Roughness factor for overland flow, 545
Roughness height, 195–196
    related to Manning's $n$, 206
Routing, hydraulic, 586
    hydrologic, 586, 604
Routing period, 605
Rugosity coefficient, 92n.

$S$ profiles, 228–230
Saddle flow profiles, 241
SAF stilling basin, 415–417
Saint-Venant celerity equation, 538
San Dimas flume, 78
Scale ratio, model, 16
Scimemi profile, 364n.
Scouring, 103–104, 406–407, 512
Secondary flow, 12, 439
Section factor, for critical-flow computa-
        tion, 23, 64
    for uniform-flow computation, 23, 128
Separation of flow, 471
Sequent depth, 46, 55n.
    relative, 397
Service discharge in canals, 303
Sewers, roughness variation in, 135
Shape factor, 210
Sharp-crested weirs, 360–362
    Bazin data for, 363, 382, 390
    for jump control, 409–410
Shear force, 168n.
Shear velocity, 201
Sheet flow, 14, 148
Shock wave, 429n., 448n.
Shooting flow, 13
Side-channel spillways, 328
Side slopes of channel, 158–159
Side weirs, 340–341
Sills, in curved channels, 457
    for jump control, 408–409, 414
Silting, 103–104
Singular point, 238
Ski-jump spillways, 384–385
Skimming flow, 196
Slope, channel, adverse, 223
    change in, 232–234
    critical, 63, 142, 154
    definition, 40n., 94n.

Slope, channel, effect on pressure distribution, 32–34
  horizontal, 223
  large, 33
  limit, 142, 243–244
  mild, 63
  negative, 223
  nonsustaining, 223, 259
  normal, 142
  positive, 223
  side, 158–159
  small, 33
  subcritical, 63
  supercritical, 63
  sustaining, 223
  variable, 238
  zero, 223
 of channel bottom, 40
 for energy gradient, 40
 of energy line, 40
 in uniform flow, 40
 of water surface, 40
Slope-area method, 146–148
Slug flow, 581
Sluice gates, 507–510
  contraction distance after, 258
  flow profile after, 240, 257
  submerged jump after, 60
  vena contracta below, 401
Smetana profile, 364n.
Smooth pipes, Nikuradse data for, 201n., 204
Solitary wave, 537–538
Spatially varied flow, 5
  analysis of flow profiles, 235–237
  through bottom rack, 337–340
  with decreasing discharge, 328–329, 332–333, 346
  dynamic equation for, 332
  in horizontal channels, 333–337
  with increasing discharge, 327–332, 341–342
  method of numerical integration, 341–346
  through side weirs, 340–341
  surface flow, 347–349
  types of, 334
  unsteady surface, 543
Spatially-varied-flow equation, 332
Specific energy, 41
Specific-energy curve, 41–42
Specific force, 53–56
Specific-force curve, 54
Spillway channel, 306–309, 342–346
Spillways, drop, box inlet, 424
  straight, 423–425
 overflow, Bazin data for, 363–364

Spillways, overflow, boundary layer on, 199–200
  bucket at toe, 36, 384
  crest shapes, 363–365
  design of section, 367–368
  design head, 368–369
  discharge of, 365–370
  flip bucket, 35–36
  flow at toe, 382–384
  Fort Collins tests, 364n.
  gated, 370–374
  nappe profiles on, 370–373, 387
  pressure on, 374, 378–380, 387
  rating, 368–370
  submerged, 385–388
 side-channel, 328
 ski-jump, 384–385
Spiral flow, 25–26, 439
  strength, 440
Spiral flow profiles, 241
Stable hydraulic section, 176–179
Stage, 22
 high and low, 41
Stage-fall-discharge method, 280–284
Stage-versus-$Q/\sqrt{F}$ curve, 281
Stage routing, 607
Stand of grass, 180
Standard step method, 265–268
 for natural channels, 274–280
Standing swell, 402
Standing wave, 393n.
Stanton diagram, 8
State of flow, laminar, 7
  subcritical, 13
  supercritical, 13
  transitional, 7
  turbulent, 7
Steady flow, 5
Steady jump, 395–396
Steady uniform flow, 5
Steep channels, 223
Step method, direct, 262–265
 standard, 265–268, 274–280
Stilling basin, 404
 generalized design, 414–415
 SAF, 415–417
 with sloping apron, 427–429
 USBR, 415, 417–422, 427–429
Streaming flow, 13
Strength of spiral flow, 440
Strickler formula, 99n., 206
Strickler's constant, 206
Strong jump, 395–396
Subcritical slope, 63
Subcritical state of flow, 13
Sublayer, laminar, 194
Sudden transitions, 461–468

Supercritical slope, 63
Supercritical state of flow, 13
Superelevation, 439
Surface curve, 222
Surface flow, spatially varied, 347–349
  spatially varied unsteady, 543
  uniform, 148–150
Surface irregularities, 106–109
Surface roughness, 101–102
  concept, 194
  explanation, 194
  hydraulically rough, 195
  hydraulically smooth, 195
  wavy, 195
Surface tension, 7, 12
Surge, 557
  demand, 559
  energy in, 565–566
  at junctions, 578–580
  in navigation canals, 572–575
  negative, 566–568
  positive, 559–566
  in power canals, 568–572
  rejection, 559
  through transitions, 575–578
Suspended load, 106
Sustaining slope, 223

Tables, geometric elements of circular
    conduits, 625–627
  permissible velocities, 165, 185
  roughness coefficient $n$, 109–113
  varied-flow functions, 255, 259, 641–
    661
Tainter gate, 507–512
Theorem, of maximum discharge, $59n$.
  of minimum energy, 42
Thermal diffusivity, 601
Tidal hydraulics, xi, $523n$.
Top width, 22
Torrential flow, 13
Total force of stream, $54n$.
Tractive force, 168
  critical, 172
  distribution, 169
  lateral, 176
  method of design for, 175
  permissible, 165, 172–174
  unit, 168, 169, 173
Tractive-force ratio, 170–171
Tranquil flow, 13
Transition loss, 310–311
Transitional depth, $237n$., 238, 242–244
Transitional discharge, 242
Transitional profile, 238
Transitional state of flow, 7

Transitions, gradual, 47–49, 57–59, 310–
  319
  sudden, 461–468
  surges through, 575–578
Transitory zone of uniform flow, 90
Translatory wave, 523
Trapezoidal channels, best hydraulic
    section, 161–162
  geometric elements, 21, 629–637
  hydraulic exponent $M$, 66–67
  hydraulic exponent $N$, 131–132
  hydraulic jumps in, 431
  values, of $AR^{2/3}/d_0^{5/3}$, 130
    of $Z/d_0^{2.5}$, 65
Trash racks, 506–507
Triangular channels, 20
  best hydraulic section, 161
  geometric elements, 21, 639
  rounded-bottom, 20–21
Turbulence, complete, 12
Turbulent boundary layer, 193
Turbulent flow, 7
  criterion, 7–8, 150
  mean velocity, 204–205
  unsteady spatially varied, 546
  velocity distribution, 200–202
Turbulent surface flow, spatially varied,
  348
  uniform, 150

Ultrarapid velocity, 89
Underflow gates, 507–512
Undular jump, 45, 395
Uniform flow, 5
  computation, 128–150
  establishment, 88–91
  qualifications, 88
  instability, 210
  steady, 5
  theoretical equation for, 202–205
  transitory zone, 90
  unsteady, 5
Uniform-flow equations, theoretical,
  202–205
Uniform-flow formulas, 91
Uniform surface flow, 148–150
  criterion, 150
Uniformly progressive flow, 554–557
  dynamic equation, 531
  wave profile, 533–537
Uniformly progressive wave, 528
Unit flood, 602
Unit tractive force, 168
  distribution, 169
  maximum, 169
  permissible, 173

UNIVAC, 601
Universal-velocity-distribution law, 201
Unsteady flow, 5–6, 523
  continuity, 525–526
  dynamic equation, 526–528
  rapidly varied, 7
Unsteady uniform flow, 5
Unsteady varied flow, 6, 7, 523
Upper normal depth, 231
USBR stilling basins, 415, 417–422, 427–429

Varied flow, 6
  gradually, 6
  gradually unsteady, 7, 523
  rapidly, 6
  rapidly unsteady, 7, 523
  spatially, 5, 327
Varied-flow function, 254
  for adverse slopes, 259
  for circular conduits, 262
  tables, 255, 259, 641–661
Varwick's data for rough channels, 11–12
Vedernikov number, 210
Vegetal retardance, 179, 184
Vegetation roughness, 102–103, 106–109
Velocity, critical, 13
  friction, 195, 201
  measurement, 27
  nonerodible, 165
  nonsilting, 158
  and noneroding, 166
  shear, 201
  ultrarapid, 89
Velocity distribution, 24–26
  turbulent flow, 200–202
Velocity-distribution coefficients, 27–30
  for compound sections, 139–140
  equations for, 211
Velocity-distribution law, 201
Velocity gradient, 200
Velocity-head ratio, $13n$.
Velocity-head recovery, 311
Vena contracta below sluice, 401
Venturi flume, 74
Villemonte weir sill, 80

Viscosity, dynamic, 8
  effect on flow, 7
  kinematic, 7–8
  of water, 8
Vortex flow profiles, 241

Wake-interference flow, $12n$., 196
Wash-water troughs, 349
Water area, 22
Water seal, 317
Wave angle, 429
Wave profiles, uniformly progressive flow, 533–537
Wave suppressors, $422n$.
Waves, capillary, 12
  gravity, 13
  monoclinal rising, 528
  oblique expansion, 449, 454
  oscillatory, $523n$.
  propagation, 13, 537
  roll, 210, 535, 581
  shock, $429n$., $448n$.
  solitary, 537–538
  translatory, 523
  uniformly progressive, 528
Weak jump, 395
Weber number, ix
Weirs, broad-crested (see Broad-crested weirs)
  sharp-crested, 360–362
  Villemonte sill for, 80
Weisbach formula, 501
WES General Spillway Tests—CW 801, 364, $370n$., 374
WES standard spillway shapes, 364–365
Wetted perimeter, 22
Wide horizontal channels, 292
Wide open channel, 26–27
  critical and normal depths in, 258
Width-depth ratio, 162–163

Yangtze River, diffusivity, 602

Zero slope, 223